Lecture Notes in Artificial Intelligence   7002

Subseries of Lecture Notes in Computer Science

LNAI Series Editors

Randy Goebel
University of Alberta, Edmonton, Canada
Yuzuru Tanaka
Hokkaido University, Sapporo, Japan
Wolfgang Wahlster
DFKI and Saarland University, Saarbrücken, Germany

LNAI Founding Series Editor

Joerg Siekmann
DFKI and Saarland University, Saarbrücken, Germany

W0193315

Hepu Deng   Duoqian Miao   Jingsheng Lei
Fu Lee Wang (Eds.)

Artificial Intelligence and Computational Intelligence

Third International Conference, AICI 2011
Taiyuan, China, September 24-25, 2011
Proceedings, Part I

 Springer

Series Editors

Randy Goebel, University of Alberta, Edmonton, Canada
Jörg Siekmann, University of Saarland, Saarbrücken, Germany
Wolfgang Wahlster, DFKI and University of Saarland, Saarbrücken, Germany

Volume Editors

Hepu Deng
RMIT University, School of Business Information Technology
City Campus, 124 La Trobe Street, Melbourne, VIC 3000, Australia
E-mail: hepu.deng@rmit.edu.au

Duoqian Miao
Tongji University, School of Electronics and Information
Shanghai 201804, China
E-mail: miaoduoqian@163.com

Jingsheng Lei
Shanghai University of Electronic Power
School of Computer and Information Engineering
Shanghai 200090, China
E-mail: jshlei@126.com

Fu Lee Wang
Caritas Institute of Higher Education, Department of Business Administration
18 Chui Ling Road, Tseung Kwan O, Hong Kong, China
E-mail: pwang@cihe.edu.hk

ISSN 0302-9743   e-ISSN 1611-3349
ISBN 978-3-642-23880-2   ISBN 978-3-642-23881-9 (eBook)
DOI 10.1007/978-3-642-23881-9
Springer Heidelberg Dordrecht London New York

Library of Congress Control Number: 2011936133

CR Subject Classification (1998): I.2, H.3-4, F.1, I.4-5, J.3, K.4.4, D.2

LNCS Sublibrary: SL 7 – Artificial Intelligence

Typesetting: Camera-ready by author, data conversion by Scientific Publishing Services, Chennai, India

Printed on acid-free paper

Springer is part of Springer Science+Business Media (www.springer.com)

Preface

The 2011 International Conference on Artificial Intelligence and Computational Intelligence (AICI 2011) was held during September 24–25, 2011 in Taiyuan, China. AICI 2011 received 1,073 submissions from 20 countries and regions. After rigorous reviews, 265 high-quality papers were selected for publication in the AICI 2011 proceedings. The acceptance rate was 24%.

The aim of AICI 2011 was to bring together researchers working in many different areas of artificial intelligence and computational intelligence to foster the exchange of new ideas and promote international collaborations. In addition to the large number of submitted papers and invited sessions, there were several internationally well-known keynote speakers.

On behalf of the Organizing Committee, we thank Taiyuan University of Technology for its sponsorship and logistics support. We also thank the members of the Organizing Committee and the Program Committee for their hard work. We are very grateful to the keynote speakers, session chairs, reviewers, and student helpers. Last but not least, we thank all the authors and participants for their great contributions that made this conference possible.

September 2011

Hepu Deng
Duoqian Miao
Jingsheng Lei
Fu Lee Wang

Organization

Organizing Committee

General Co-chairs

Wendong Zhang   Taiyuan University of Technology, China
Qing Li   City University of Hong Kong, Hong Kong

Program Committee Co-chairs

Hepu Deng   RMIT University, Australia
Duoqian Miao   Tongji University, China

Steering Committee Chair

Jingsheng Lei   Shanghai University of Electric Power, China

Local Arrangements Co-chairs

Fu Duan   Taiyuan University of Technology, China
Dengao Li   Taiyuan University of Technology, China

Proceedings Co-chairs

Fu Lee Wang   Caritas Institute of Higher Education,
     Hong Kong
Ting Jin   Fudan University, China

Sponsorship Chair

Zhiyu Zhou   Zhejiang Sci-Tech University, China

Program Committee

Adi Prananto	Swinburne University of Technology, Australia
Adil Bagirov	University of Ballarat, Australia
Ahmad Abareshi	RMIT University, Australia
Alemayehu Molla	RMIT University, Australia
Andrew Stranier	University of Ballarat, Australia
Andy Song	RMIT University, Australia
An-Feng Liu	Central South University, China
Arthur Tatnall	Victoria University, Australia
Bae Hyeon	Pusan National University, Korea
Baoding Liu	Tsinghua University, China
Carmine Sellitto	Victoria University, Australia
Caroline Chan	Deakin University, Australia
CheolPark Soon	Chonbuk National University, Korea
Chowdhury Morshed	Deakin University, Australia
Chung-Hsing Yeh	Monash University, Australia
Chunqiao Tao	South China University, China
Costa Marly	Federal University of Amazonas, Brazil
Craig Parker	Deakin University, Australia
Daowen Qiu	Zhong Shan University, China
Dat Tran	University of Canberra, Australia
Dengsheng Zhang	Monash University, Australia
Edmonds Lau	Swinburne University of Technology, Australia
Elspeth McKay	RMIT University, Australia
Eng Chew	University of Technology Sydney, Australia
Feilong Cao	China Jiliang University, China
Ferry Jie	RMIT University, Australia
Furutani Hiroshi	University of Miyazaki, Japan
Gour Karmakar	Monash University, Australia
Guojun Lu	Monash University, Australia
Heping Pan	University of Ballarat, Australia
Hossein Zadeh	RMIT University, Australia
Ian Sadler	Victoria University, Australia
Irene Zhang	Victoria University, Australia
Jamie Mustard	Deakin University, Australia
Jeff Ang Charles	Darwin University, Australia
Jennie Carroll	RMIT University, Australia
Jenny Zhang	RMIT University, Australia
Jian Zhou T.	Tsinghua University, China
Jingqiang Wang	South China University, China
Jinjun Chen	Swinburne University of Technology, Australia
Joarder Kamruzzaman	Monash University, Australia
Kaile Su	Beijing University, China
Kankana Chakrabaty	University of New England, Australia

Table of Contents – Part I

Applications of Artificial Intelligence

Applications of Computational Intelligence

Automated Problem Solving

Biomedical Informatics and Computation

Brain Models/Cognitive Science

Data Mining and Knowledge Discovering

Distributed AI and Agents

Evolutionary Programming

Expert and Decision Support Systems

Fuzzy Computation

Fuzzy Logic and Soft Computing

Genetic Algorithms

Table of Contents – Part II

Heuristic Searching Methods

Immune Computation

Information Security

Information Theory

Intelligent Control

Intelligent Image Processing

Intelligent Information Fusion

Intelligent Information Retrieval

Intelligent Signal Processing

Knowledge Representation

Machine Learning

Table of Contents – Part III

Machine Vision

Natural Language Processing

Nature Computation

Neural Computation

Neural Networks

Particle Swarm Optimization

Pattern Recognition

Rough Set Theory

Support Vector Machine

QP Based Framework for Development and Formal Verification of Flight Control Software of UAV

Yuchao Zhang, Guoqi Li, and Juan Zhang

School of Reliability and System Engineering, Beihang University, Beijing, China
soarly_1915118@sina.com

Abstract. UAV is widely invested both in military and academic fields. The development and verification of UAV flight control software is an importance issues and hot topic. In this paper, a QP based method is present to develop and formally verify the UAV flight control software. The method combines the UML and OCL constraint language and output the UML file that constrained by OCL to XMI file. Then we input the XMI file to rule inference engine as facts. Aided by safety rules, the flight control software could be automatically verified. The method has many advantages and is hopeful to enhance the quality of UAV flight control software. It can also be used in similar scenarios.

Keywords: UML, OCL, Inference machine, Software Verification.

1 Introduction

UAV is a re-use aircraft that without the pilot and control the flight status, airline and other procedures by the wireless remote control or self-control program. It's widely used for aerial reconnaissance surveillance, communication-n, anti-submarine and electronic interference. UAVs have many advantages such as small taking-off site, can hovering in the air, low cost and so on [1]. It's a very potential research topics in the world, can be used for short-range military reconnaissance, urban search and rescue, low-level fire support missions etc. Recent studies and applications show that the UAV has great advantage in fire support, agricultural monitoring, marine exploration, traffic control and military.

The most crucial part is the automatic flight control system (Automatic Flight Control System) to small UAVs. The performances of small UAVs (including taking-off landing performance, operating flight performance, flight safety, reliability, and maintainability of automation systems, etc.) are largely depend on its flight control system design. The unmanned aerial vehicle flight control system is an important part for a variety of data collection, storage, processing, control output, data transmission and other functions, it cause great direct impact on the UAV flight performance[2].

Aircraft's control system is complex embedded real-time hybrid system; the core of the control software must be complex, reactive, discrete, real-time and high reliability. Fast and reliable flight control software must be based on the system function and behavior, the main ways to describe the system specifications is word or flow chart in the past. These methods of communication are difficult to make the entire designer

H. Deng et al. (Eds.): AICI 2011, Part I, LNAI 7002, pp. 1–8, 2011.

understand and implement, while the ambiguity and errors will be hidden until the late stages of integration testing.

Formal methods provides a executable verification standardized form for the function and behavior of complex systems modeling discrete, the state diagram is the most intuitive, practical one of the best modeling language.

In this paper, we research a flight control software prototype of unmanned aerial vehicles based on hierarchical state machine, and then establish a flight control software executable authentication function and behavior model while make formal verification, to detect and correct various errors in the early system design to make a great quality basis for test and design.

2   Presentations of QP

The quantum platform is an embedded systems programming concepts that made by Miro Samek(USA). It describe the transition between the description of the embedded software programming model use the describe ways of the transition between quantum energy states in the quantum mechanics, the quantum mechanics and quantum platform is not any real connection, just a concept borrowed it.

However, the quantum platform presents the state machine programming model of embedded system. Quantum platform divide different CPU resources into two levels: lightweight (or streamline level) NANO, and the. NANO is for the application of limited CPU resources, while the common full version for the abundant CPU resources. QP includes two parts: the level of event handlers (QEP) and real-time framework (QF). The real-time framework (QF) has great advantages in dealing with event-driven system and has been widely used in the embedded system. QP can provide clear logic of the system by using the hierarchical state machine. Then connect to the computer modeling system for active objects by QF and state machine combination [3].

The hierarchy state machines and event-driven framework have been rapid development and widely application in the last two decades, almost all of the current success commercial market are based on the hierarchy state machine (state diagram) and some tools similar to QF real-time driver framework. The state machine is the most famous formal approach used to describe real-time event-driven system, the most advanced way to describe status is the hierarchy state machine theory of UML.

Hierarchical state machine (Hierarchy State Machine) is the most intuitive method to model state behavioral and a good form method to achieve the event-driven system. It is mainly used to describe the object, subsystem, system lifecycle. Through the hierarchical state machine we can know the impact from all the state can reach and event objects can received of an object state and so on. Here are the related concepts of HSM.

1). Status: State is a stage such as to meet certain conditions, to perform some action or waiting for some event in the life cycle of an object.

2). Event: Event is an emerging phenomenon in specific time and space, which can trigger state transitions.

3). Conversion: Conversion is a one state node transfer to another state node.

The state and its transfer are the basic syntax elements of state chart. We assume the system state S, event E, the conditions C, the actions A, the reaction R, then the discrete model X is defined as behavior:

$$X = \{s_i(r_i) \xrightarrow{e[c]/a} s_j(r_j) \,|\, t\} \tag{1}$$

3 Model the Flying Control System

3.1 Top Model

The interactive part control of the flight control system includes rotation sensor, speed sensor, electronic compass, GPS, wireless communications components; engine throttle control, elevator, rudder, left aileron, right aileron, landing gear guide wheel. Using UML method to make Model and ensure system relations [4]. As the core of the flight control system, flight controllers include integrated flight data acquisition and control law generation, parameter adjustment, logic and timing judgments, equipment monitoring, autonomous navigation, remote communication and system self-test and so on[5][6]. At first, we definite the top-level module FC_program to describe the entrance and the process of entire software:

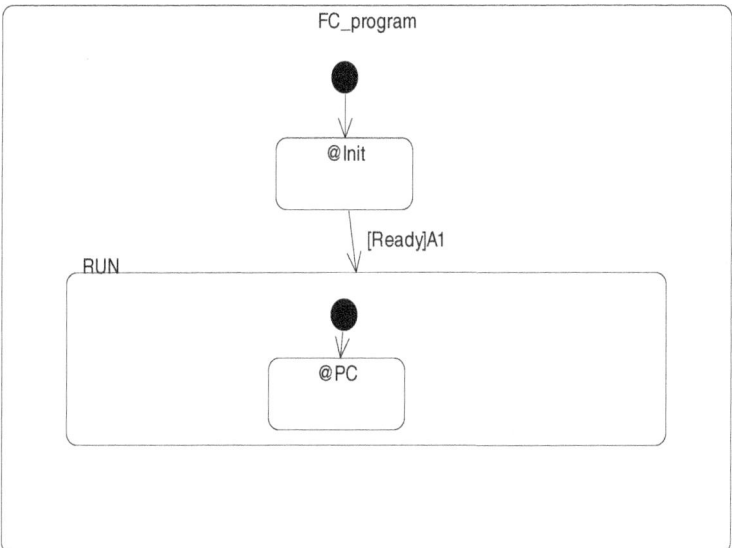

Fig. 1. State chart of top-level module FC_program

Run the system, and the status go into the initial state @ Init. The prefix @ indicates that the state can be broken down by a number of sub-state description, Init @ description acts include hardware initialization, power-down mode to determine, flight and navigation status and data clearing or recovery. At the end of initialization set conditions Ready to true, triggering the system transferred to the RUN state while into compound action A1 (set of hardware and software flag).

3.2   The PC Main Control Model

This module is the main part of the flight control system and describes the state of UAV flight changes and device state changes.

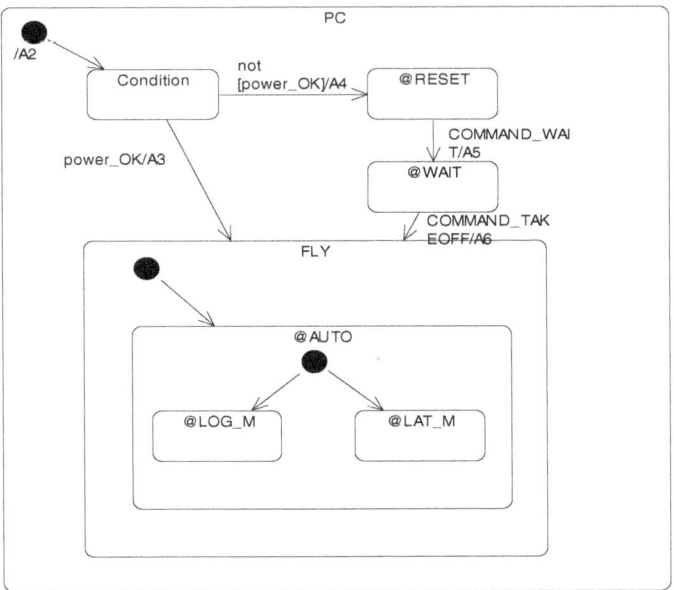

Fig. 2. State chart of main control module PC

After into the PC state, use the connector to select the transfer path way. If the power uncommon ,then directly return to flight state FLY, if normal, then transferred to the reset state RESET, and clear date in this state, when received the standby command (event COMMAND_WAIT occurred)in this state, the system transferred to the state @ WAIT. Similarly, when received command to take off (event COMMAND_TAKEOFF place) in the WAIT state, it will be transferred to state FLY and default trigged sub-state autonomous navigation activation AUTO to automatically complete the roll, climb and improve equality of action.

The AUTO state includes two states: horizontal and vertical control state control. Assume that the system is in direct state STRAIGHT now, when receiving the action instruction (deflection or down), the system shifted to the left (right) turn state LEFT (RIGHT), and achieve a given angle. After the completion of instruction, the system back to the command trigger-wait state, if receive the landing instructions in the flight, and then exit flight.

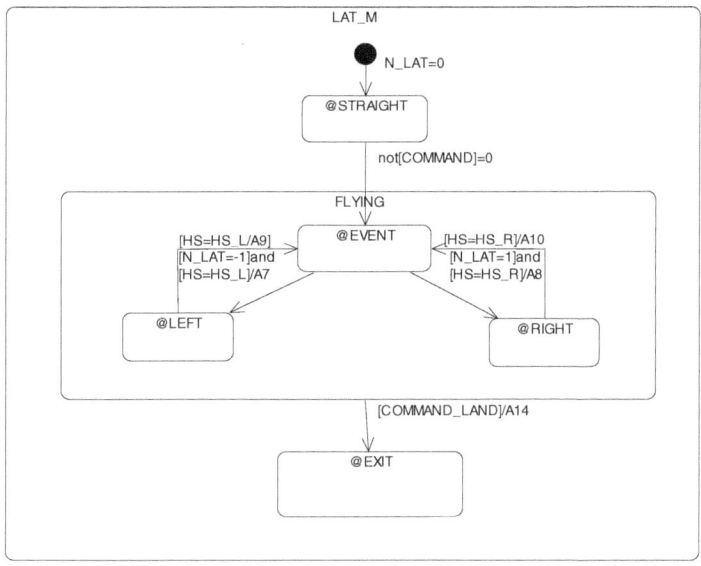

Fig. 3. State chart of turn control module LAT_M

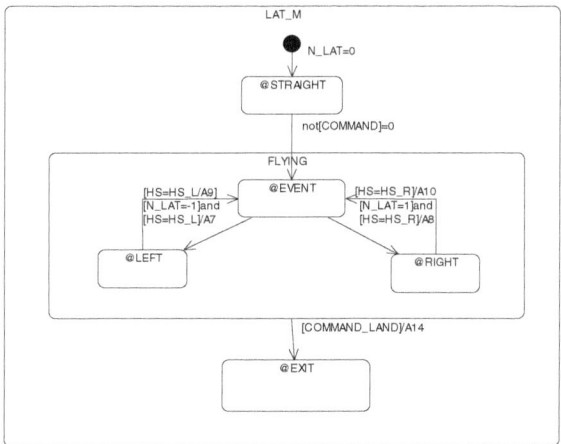

Fig. 4. State chart of rise control module LAT_M

4   Formalized on the State Chart by OCL

OCL (Object Constraint Language) is a limit way to direct the user model system [7]. It can be used to define the behavior of objects in the UML better, and specifies constraints to any class element. OCL has the following four characteristics [8]:

1). OCL is a query language and a constraint language;

2). OCL is based on mathematics, but did not use mathematical symbols;

3). OCL is a strongly typed language;

4). OCL is a declaratory (Declarative) language.

This article will use the OCL language to constraint the UML object, and to better represent the object that difficult to describe by simple graphical.

5   Verification and Validation

5.1   Convert UML by XMI Specification

UML is a visual modeling language, the graphical business models (such as a user instance diagram, class diagram, sequence diagram, state diagrams, etc.) contain the data structure and logical constraints, but the external manifestations of these business models are collection of graphics [9]. So they don't benefit in further development. To address this problem, we output the information of the model in the manifest file (XML) way to achieve the further treatment of the model and the information exchange between models.

5.2   Authentication by Inference Machine

Inference machine is a way that according to a certain and simulate the human thinking activity, to solve the problem based on reasoning provided by the user and give the user a satisfactory conclusion.

Inference structure is as follows:

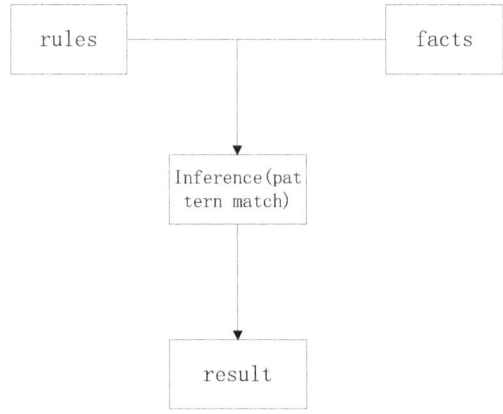

Fig. 5. Inference structure

The inference mechanism as shown below, at first the real-time obtain the initial facts from all the information that get from the sensor, then find all available rules by match facts to the left part of the rule (the premise) and constitute the conflict set to select a rule in conflict with certain conflict resolution strategies, thereby generating new facts in accordance. The new facts and the old facts cause a new round of matches, so continue to solution the problem, until no rule is activated. At last validate whether there is solution or not, if it is true the output all solutions (error messages), otherwise output no solution [10].

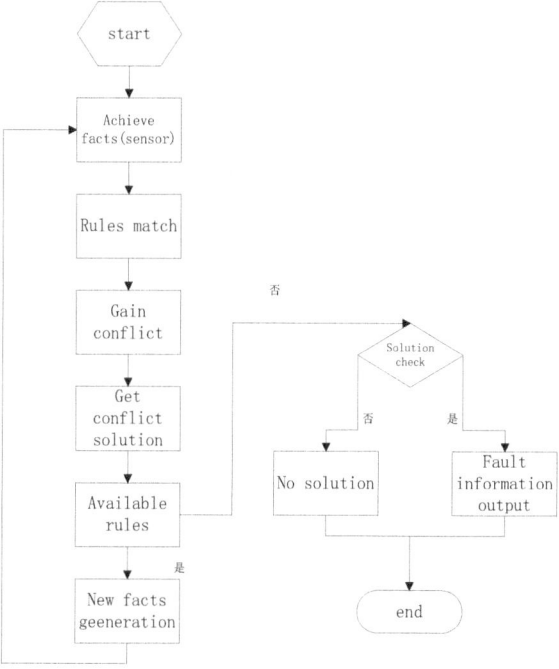

Fig. 6. Inference mechanism

We use the inference engine make pattern matching to determine if it is safe by the security rule set given from experts based safety-theory and the two chapters of the XMI + OCL. Through use of inference we match the collecting facts from the sensor and rule base to the safety rules, ensure the conclusions that the flight control software meets safety rules and confirmed the safety quality of the flight control software. Complete the security validation of flight control system software.

6   Conclusion

In this paper, we focus on the reality that increasing emphasis on UAV and the widely use of the newly popular QP Quantum platform, make the formal analysis of the flight control software safety by the hierarchical state machine method. We use UML to model the flight control software, and through to constraint language OCL to constrain the UML. As a formal constraint language, OCL made up the disadvantage of UML that as a semi-formal method. After the information in the UML model explicit output as XML file. It will work with OCL constraints as the fact that pattern matches in the inference engine with the safety rules given by experts, and finally makes judgment that the software system whether meets the safety rules. This formal verification method has some reference value to other similar safety critical embedded software system validation.

References

1. Quigley, M., Goodrich, M.A., Beard, R.W.: Semi-Autonomous Human-UAV Interfaces for Fixed- Wing Mini-UAVs. In: Proceedings of 2004 IEEE/RSJ International Conference on Intelligent Robots and Systems, pp. 2457–2462 (2004)
2. Fang, Z.: Output Feedback Control of a Quadrotor UAV Using Neural Networks. In: Proceedings of the 27th Chinese Control Conference, pp. 349–353 (2008)
3. Warmer, J., Kleppe, A.: The Object Constraint Language (2003)
4. Cai, G., Gu, T., Lam, C.P.: An approach for automatic test case generation from UML Statechart. In: Proceedings of the 9th Joint International Computer Conference (2003)
5. Koo, T.J., Sinopoli, B.: Aformal approach to reactive system design: a UAV flight management system design example. In: Proceedings of IEEE International Symposium on Computer-Aided Control System Design, Hawaii (1999)
6. Harei, D., Naamed, A.: The statement semantics of statecharts. In: Proceeding of the ACM Transactions on Software Engineering and Methodology, pp. 293–333 (1996)
7. Gunmath, P.: OCL exception handling. Texas A & M University, Texas (2004)
8. Nentwich, C., Emmerich, W., Finkelstein, A.: Flexible consistency checking. In: Proceedings of the ACM Transactions on Software Engineering and Methodology, pp. 28–63 (2003)
9. Muller, E., Zenker, A.: Business services as actors of knowledge transformation the role of KIBS in regional and innovation systems. Research Policy, 75–86 (1993)
10. Lauriente, M., Rolincik M.: An on-line expert system for diagnosing environmentally induced spacecraft anomalies using clips. N9332097 (1993)

A Matching Method between Music Scores and Performance Data in a Realtime Person-Computer Ensemble System

Tetsuya Mizutani[1], Keita Nishiyama[2], and Shigeru Igarashi[1]

[1] Department of Computer Science, University of Tsukuba, Tsukuba, Japan
{mizutani,igarashi}@cs.tsukuba.ac.jp
[2] College of Information Science, University of Tsukuba, Tsukuba, Japan

Abstract. A person-computer ensemble system is one of time-concerned cooperative systems, which performs *secondo* (the second part) in an ensemble played by a computer-controlled piano cooperating with *primo* (the leading part) played by a person performer.

In the realtime performance, to determine which key is touched, or played, by the person performer, the *matching* algorithm between the score and the realtime input from the person performer is essential. Especially, if there are some *mistouches* (playing incorrectly) or other mistake, error, etc., the program does not determine which note is performed just now and which note of the secondo will be done just after now. Therefore, the matching method that corrects these mistouches is very important.

In this paper, a simple and efficient matching algorithm is proposed.

Keywords: Artificial Intelligence, Musical Informatics, Ensemble System, Correction of the Mistouching keys.

1 Introduction

A *person-computer ensemble system* [9, 11–13, 15] is one of time concerned cooperative systems, which performs *secondo* (the second part) in an ensemble played by a computer-controlled piano cooperating with *primo* (the leading part) played by a person performer.

The ensemble system is an example of intelligent realtime programs appropriate for formal verification and analysis [1, 3]. $N\Sigma$-labeled calculus [6, 8, 10] is a formal system for verification for such *time-concerned* programs, which are meant intelligent programs of machines, or of persons, to treat matters not only mathematically time-dependent but also distinctively featured by subtle and sophisticated sensitivity, interest or person concern in exact time or timing, such as traffic control, ensemble in music, etc. The formal representation, verification and analysis of the system are in [11, 12].

For creating expressive performance by the ensemble system, we adopt the *rehearsal* program. By the rehearsal program, the system learns the tendency of the expression that the person performer thinks and/or plans. To do so, the

H. Deng et al. (Eds.): AICI 2011, Part I, LNAI 7002, pp. 9–17, 2011.

program records his/her performance of solo and calculates the tendency. The tendency of expression depends not only on the performer but also on the composition of music itself. Hence, it is necessary for the expressive performance to analyze the score of the composition and to experiment dependent on it. In [13], some experimental results of the various methods for creating more expressing the rehearsal data have been reported.

In the realtime performance, to determine which key is touched, or played, by the person performer, the *matching* algorithm between the score and the realtime input from the person performer is essential. When the matching is succeeded, the program recognizes which note is performed just now and which note of the secondo will be done just after now, and moreover, it calculates the local tempo of the performance and corrects the performance speed of the secondo. If there are some *mistouching*, i.e. playing an incorrect key, or other mistake, error, etc., the program does not determine which note is performed just now and which note of the secondo will be done just after now, and hence, it cannot correct the performance speed. Therefore, the matching method including correction of these mistouches is necessary. In this paper, a simple but efficient matching method is proposed, and also an experimental result is reported.

2   A Realtime Person-Computer Ensemble System

The ensemble system consists of two programs; the *rehearsal* and the *performance* ones.

The aim of the system is to perform secondo in an ensemble to drive a MIDI acoustic piano by the performance program cooperating with performing primo by a person pianist or other musician playing another MIDI instrument. Those two MIDI instruments are connected by a computer. MIDI (Musical Instrument Digital Interface) is a standard protocol for electronic musical instruments and computers to communicate, control, and synchronize with each other. A MIDI acoustic piano is an acoustic grand piano that can be played with MIDI codes. There is a 0.5[s] delay between the moment when each MIDI code as the input of the the piano and that when the corresponding key moves and actually sounds, since the actuator must adjust the timing of each group of notes which sound simultaneously. Hence, the program must output each MIDI code 0.5[s] before the moment when the actual performance is expected.

The program has the whole score data of ensemble. There are special notes called *reference notes* to measure the performance speed (or 'local tempo'), usually at the head of each or every other bar, depending on the structure and expected tempo of the score.

Before the cooperating performance, the rehearsal program records solo primo performed by the person performer. From this performance, the program calculates the *rehearsal data* which expresses the timing of performance of the whole reference notes, and *schedule* of performance of secondo. During the cooperating performance, the program modifies and updates the schedule in realtime from the actual performance of primo using the score data (including the reference notes), the rehearsal data and the schedule.

3   Formal Specification

The specification of the ensemble system is represented along with [11–13].

In these representations, at least six functions denoting below are important to design the system, where ω is the ordinal number of the natural numbers and $\omega + 1$ is ω with ∞.

- $\chi : \omega \to \omega$: each note of primo sent onto its key number,
- $\varphi : \omega \to \omega + 1$: each note of primo sent onto its "note-on" time actually played by a person performer, or ∞ if it is not played,
- $\pi : \omega \to \omega$: each note sent onto the *played* key number, possibly incorrect in case $\pi(l) \neq \chi(l)$,
- $\phi : \omega \to \omega + 1$: the time when a reference note of primo is predicted to perform, which is prepared as an element in the rehearsal data calculated by the rehearsal program.
- $\Psi : \omega \to (\omega + 1) \times 2$: sending each MIDI code onto a pair $\langle$the predicted time of issuing codes, "note-on"/"note-off"$\rangle$ of secondo, the former of which is expressed by $\Psi(m).\mathtt{time}$ and the latter $\Psi(m).\mathtt{play}$.
- $\psi : \omega \to (\omega + 1) \times 2$: the time of each note in secondo part sent onto $\langle$"note-on" time, "note-off" time$\rangle$, the former and the latter of which is expressed by $(\psi(x))_0$ and $(\psi(x))_1$, respectively, so as to issue MIDI codes either to depress or to release the key corresponding to the m-th note in secondo at these time, or never ($=\infty$).

It is essential to "predict" and "correct" for playing the secondo performance Ψ, or its actual output ψ, along with the that of primo φ, especially that of the reference notes ϕ. Hence, the correspondence between ϕ and ψ is very important for both design and verification of the system.

Additionally, the following variables and functions as indexes are used in the specification.

- $l \in \omega$ expresses the order of each primo note in the score.
- $j: \omega \to \omega$ is a function designating that n-th reference note is the $j(n)$-th note at the original order in the score.
- $x \in \omega$ denotes the order of each secondo note.
- u and $v: \omega \to \omega$ are functions that maps each second note onto the corresponding note-on and note-off MIDI codes, respectively.

A formal specification of the performance program of the system represented in $N\Sigma$-labeled calculus has been introduced in [11]. Table 1 is the specification represented by a *axiom tableau* [7, 8].

Explanation of variables and functions other than those described in the above are as follows.

- c_i and d_i ($1 \leq i \leq 6$) are the lower and upper bounds of computation and performance time of each program block, respectively. ε is also an upper bound that is only a few nanoseconds, i.e. a few steps of machine instruction.

Table 1. Axiom tableau for the performance program

index	condition	action	tense	label
1.1	$\Psi(\mathtt{m}).\mathtt{time} \leq \mathtt{Timer} + 500[\mathrm{ms}]$	$c_1 < \alpha = a_2 \leq d_1$	$1^{st} a_1, t$	*, **S**
1.2	**otherwise**	$c_1 < \alpha = GetState \leq d_1$		
2.1	$\mathtt{m} = u(x)$, $\Psi(\mathtt{m}).\mathtt{time} \leq \mathtt{Timer} + 400[\mathrm{ms}]$, $\Psi(\mathtt{m}).\mathtt{play} = \mathrm{on}$	$c_2 < \alpha = a_4 \leq d_2$, $(\psi(x))_0 = \infty[\mathrm{ms}]\ @\alpha$	$1^{st} a_2, t$	*, **S**
2.2	**otherwise**	$c_2 < \alpha = MIDIOut \leq d_2$		
3.1	$\mathtt{m} = u(x)$	$(\psi(x))_0 = \mathtt{Timer} + 500[\mathrm{ms}]@\alpha$	$1^{st} MIDIOut, t$	*, **S**, **P**, **L**
3.2	$\mathtt{m} = v(x)$	$(\psi(x))_1 = \mathtt{Timer} + 500[\mathrm{ms}]@\alpha$		
3.3	-	$c_3 < \alpha = a_4 \leq d_3$		
4	$\mathtt{m} = x$	$\alpha = GetState < \varepsilon, \mathtt{m} = x + 1\ @\alpha$	$1^{st} a_4, t$	*, **S**
5.1	$G(l,\ p)$,**global**	$c_5 < \alpha = a_6 < d_5$	$(p + 1)^{st} GetState$	*, **S**, **P**, **L**
5.2	**otherwise, global**	$\alpha = a_1 < \varepsilon$	$(p + 1)^{st} GetState$	
6.1	$Match(\mathtt{n},\ \varphi(l),\ \phi,\ j)$, $\mathtt{Gap} = x$	($\mathtt{Rate} = Rate(\mathtt{n} - 1,\ x)$, $\mathtt{Gap} = Gap(\mathtt{n})$, $l = j(\mathtt{n}))@\alpha$	$1^{st} a_6, t$	*, **S**
6.2	-	$c_6 < \alpha = a_1 \leq d_6$		
7.1		$\mathtt{Timer} = [\frac{U - \theta}{4 \times 10^6}]$	t	
7.2		$\alpha = a_1 = 1, (\mathtt{m} = 1, \mathtt{Gap} = 0, \mathtt{Rate} = 1)\ @\alpha$		*, **S**
7.3		$U = t + \theta$	t	
8		$\beta_{l\text{-}th} = \varphi(l)$		*, **P**, **L**

S: The performance program, **P**: The person pianist, **L**: Listeners.

- **n** is a program variable expressing the order in the score of the reference note just processing.
- **m** is a program variable denoting the order of predicted output of MIDI code "note-on"/"note-off".
- **Timer** is a program variable representing the timer counting up every 4 [ms], which is the resolution of the MIDI acoustic piano.
- **Rate** and **Gap** are program variables expressing the ratio of primo tempo and that of the rehearsal data, and the gap or difference between the performance time of a primo note and that of the corresponding rehearsal note, respectively.
- $Rate: \omega \to \omega \to \omega$ and $Gap: \omega \to \omega$ are functions expressing the ratio between the tempo of primo performance and that of the rehearsal data, and the gap or difference between the performance time of a primo note and that of the corresponding rehearsal note, respectively.
- α and β are *spurs*, served as the generalizations of schedulers [5], for the performance program and for the person performer.
- a_1, a_2, $MIDIOut$, a_4, $GetState$ and a_6 are *program labels*.

4   A Matching Method Dealt with Mistouches in a Realtime Performance

4.1   Matching Windows

To match the realtime input stream from the MIDI instruments played by the person performer and the corresponding score data, the *matching windows* method [11] is adopted.

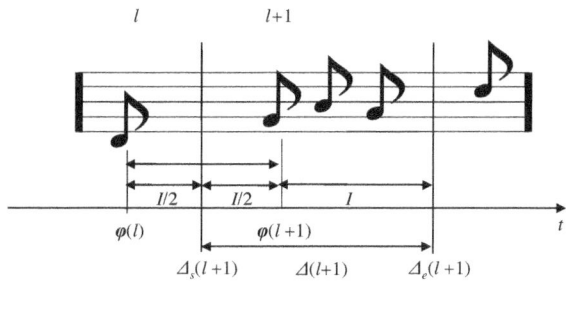

Fig. 1. The Matching Window

1. A matching window width for each l-th primo note is defined by an interval of integers $\Delta(l)$ such that $\varphi(l) \in \Delta(l)$. Δ_s and Δ_e are defined as the start and end endpoints, respectively, i.e. $\Delta(l) = [\Delta_s(l), \quad \Delta_e(l)]$. For each l-th primo note, the actual performance $\varphi(l)$ is predicted in $\Delta(l)$. In practice, it is prepared as $\Delta_s(l+1) = \varphi(l) + I/2$ and $\Delta_e(l+1) = \varphi(l) + I$, where $I = \varphi(l+1) - \varphi(l)$ (see Figure 1).

2. The prediction and correction of the performance are as follows. Let us consider the case that the performance program knows the actual values of φ up to $l = j(n)$ and is seeking the input of the $j(n+1)$-th reference note performed by the person pianist.

   The performance checks as frequently as possible whether or not the MIDI input port has received any MIDI signal. If the triple ⟨the input time z, the key number w, "note-on"⟩ coded in MIDI is recognized, then the program finds $i \geq n+1$ such that $z \in \Delta(j(i))$.

   (a) If $w = \chi(j(i))$, where $\chi(l)$ is the correct key number of l for primo, then the program updates the schedule ψ, treating the above z as $\varphi(j(i))$, as well as the tracking/expression parameters ϕ, n, etc. in accordance with certain strategies.

   (b) Otherwise, the matching is recognized as failure, i.e. the input MIDI signal is recognized as a *mistouch*.

4.2   Mistouches

For designing the matching program to correct the mistouches, the classification of the mistouches is necessary. In general, there are some trends of the mistouching as follows.

- The next keys to the correct one tends to be touched in the correct timing for the correct one, or at the same time.
- The computer program tends to sense a very weak stroke and recognize it as a mistouch. The person performer does not recognize the proper touch and

Fig. 2. Case 2: The input is too fast

Fig. 3. Case 3(a): The correct input

Fig. 4. Case 3(b): Some notes are skipped and matched

Fig. 5. Case 3(c): Some notes are skipped and not matched

the instrument (piano) does not sound actually. It is just a movement of the hand along with the musical expression, e.g. rhythm.

4.3   A Matching Strategy Dealt with Mistouches

Let ⟨the input time z, the key number w, the key strength v, "note-on"⟩ be the recognized MIDI signal. It is supposed that the program has been recognized up to the l-th primo note and is waiting the $(l + 1)$-th one.

A matching strategy with mistouches is as follows.

1. If the input strength v is too weak, then the input is not expected and the program ignores it.
2. If the input is faster than the beginning of the matching window, i.e., $z < \Delta_s(l + 1)$, then the input is treated as a mistouch and the program also ignores it (see Figure 2).
3. Let us consider the case that the input is in the matching window.
   Consider the case that $\Delta(l + 1), \Delta(l + 2), \ldots, \Delta(l + i)$ for some $i > 1$ are overlapped, i.e. $\Delta_e(l + 2) < \ldots < \Delta_e(l + i) < \Delta(l + 1)$, and the input is in the overlapped interval, i.e. $z \in [\Delta_s(l + i), \Delta_e(l + 1)]$.
   (a) If $\chi(l+1) = w$, then the input is recognized as the correct $(l+1)$-st note (see Figure 3).
   (b) If $\chi(l+1) \neq w$ but there is at least one note $l + j$ $(1 < j \leq i)$ such that key note is the same as that of w, i.e. $\chi(l + j) = w$, the input is treated as the $(l + j)$-th one and some notes between $l + 1$ and $l + j - 1$ are recognized as skipped (Figure 4).

(c) Otherwise, if there is no note of same key number, the program recognizes that the performer skips these notes.

In this case, the program is now waiting the $(l+i+1)$-th one (Figure 5).

This strategy is very simple and the computational complexity is linear to the number of key in the score, but obviously very effective to correct mistouches.

5   Experimental Result

Many experiments have been done for several scores and performances with mistouches and the successful results have been obtained.

Especially, the experiment with a professional pianist is introduced. The program has been inputted the score data of the first 4 bars (25 events) of the melody part of Humoreske Op. 101-7 by Dvořák (Figure 6) [2]. Two grace notes *are not included in the rehearsal data.* Then, the pianist performed the melody part *with these graces* but including some mistouches, and the program tried to match them in realtime. As shown in Table 2 of the result, this experiment has been done successfully.

6   Related Works

There are matching methods between input stream and score data. For example, the strategy proposed in [4] is used the dynamic programming technic. It is very strong but complex, i.e. the complexity is $O(n^2)$ where n is the number of keys to be investigated. Compared with it, the method proposed in this paper is very simple and effective (the complexity is $O(n)$).

And also, there are many related works for automatic ensemble systems. Most of them, e.g. [14, 16], etc. use HMM or other statistical methods to predict future rhythm and tempo of performance by person performer. Compared with them, this system uses *rehearsal* data created by the rehearsal of solo by a person performer to learn the expression pattern, while the cooperating program only calculates the tempo from the "history" of the performance.

Humoreske

Fig. 6. The first 4 bars of Humoreske Op. 101-7 by Dvořák

Table 2. Experiments

I	1	2	3	4	5	6	7	8	9	10	11	12	13	14
S	67	69	67	69	71	74	76	74	76 (grace)	79	78	81	79	78
P	67	69	67	69	**72**	74	76	74	**76**	79	78	81	(skipped)	78
M	S	S	S	S	S	S	S	S	F	S	S	S	F	S

I	15	16	17	18	19	20	21	22	23	24	25	26	27
S	81	79	76	71 (grace)	74	74	76	74	79	76	74	71	69
P	81	79	76	**71**	74	74	76	74	79	76	74	71	69
M	S	S	S	F	S	S	S	S	S	S	S	S	S

I: Index of notes.
S: Key number in the score.
P: Stroked key number by the pianist.
M: Matching; S: Success, F: Failure.
Boldfaced numbers and letters are indicated mistouches.

7   Conclusion

A simple and efficient matching algorithm for the realtime ensemble system that corrects mistouches, skips and other possible human errors is introduced and has been verified and analyzed experimentally.

Fundamentally, this method can be applied not only to music pieces whose primo part is monophonic but also polyphonic or harmonic ones. However, there are many difficulties practically. Especially, if there are many notes (of a chord) played simultaneously in a matching window, the matching strategy may not work properly. Moreover, this algorithm must be verified and analyzed in $N\Sigma$-labeled calculus. They are our future works.

References

1. Curzon, P., Ruksenas, R., Blandford, A.: An Approach to Formal Verification of Human-Computer Interaction. Formal Aspect of Computing 19, 513–550 (2007)
2. Eto, Y. (ed.): Flute Famous Collections, vol. 31, p. 112. Doremi Music Publishing (1986)
3. Damm, W., Hungar, H., Olderog, E.-R.: Verification of Cooperating Traffic Agents. International Journal of Control 79, 395–421 (2006)
4. Dannenberg, R.B.: An On-Line Algorithm for Real-Time Accompaniment. In: Proceedings of the 1984 International Computer Music Conference, pp. 193–198 (1985)
5. Igarashi, S.: The ν-Conversion and an Analytic Semantics. In: Information Processing, vol. 83, pp. 769–774. Elsevier Sci. Publ. B.V., Amsterdam (1983)
6. Ikeda, Y., Mizutani, T., Shio, M.: Formal System and Semantics of $N\Sigma$-labeled Calculus. In: The 2009 International Conference on Artificial Intelligence and Computational Intelligence, pp. 270–274. IEEE, Los Alamitos (2009)
7. Mizutani, T., Igarashi, S., Ikeda, Y., Shio, M.: Labeled @-Calculus: Formalism for Time-Concerned Human Factors. In: Calmet, J., Ida, T., Wang, D. (eds.) AISC 2006. LNCS (LNAI), vol. 4120, pp. 25–39. Springer, Heidelberg (2006)

8. Mizutani, T., Igarashi, S., Shio, M., Ikeda, Y.: Human Factors in Continuous Time-Concerned Cooperative Systems Represented by $N\Sigma$-labeled Calculus. Frontiers of Computer Science in China 2, 22–28 (2008)
9. Mizutani, T., Suzuki, T., Shio, M., Ikeda, Y.: Formal Specification and Experiments of an Expressive Human-Computer Ensemble System with Rehearsal. In: The 3rd IEEE International Symposium on Theoretical Aspects of Software Engineering, TASE 2009, pp. 303–304 (2009)
10. Mizutani, T., Igarashi, S., Ikeda, Y., Shio, M.: Formal Analysis of an Airplane Accident in $N\Sigma$-labeled Calculus. In: Deng, H., Wang, L., Wang, F.L., Lei, J. (eds.) AICI 2009. LNCS(LNAI), vol. 5855, pp. 469–478. Springer, Heidelberg (2009)
11. Mizutani, T., Igarashi, S., Shio, M., Ikeda, Y.: Labeled Calculi Applied to Verification and Analysis of Time-Concerned Programs I. Tensor, N.S. 71, 172–186 (2009)
12. Mizutani, T., Igarashi, S., Shio, M., Ikeda, Y.: Labeled Calculi Applied Verification and Analysis of Time-Concerned Programs II. Tensor, N.S. 71, 285–296 (2009)
13. Mizutani, T., Igarashi, S., Suzuki, T., Ikeda, Y., Shio, M.: A Realtime Human-Computer Ensemble System: Formal Representation and Experiments for Expressive Performance. In: Wang, F.L., Deng, H., Gao, Y., Lei, J. (eds.) AICI 2010. LNCS (LNAI), vol. 6319, pp. 256–265. Springer, Heidelberg (2010)
14. Raphael, C.: Automated Rhythm Transcription. In: ISMIR 2001: International Symposium on Music Information Retrieval, pp. 99–107 (2001)
15. Suzuki, T.: Creation and Analysis of Expression on an Ensemble System, Master's Thesis. Department of Computer Science, Graduate School of Systems and Information Engineering. University of Tsukuba (2009) (in Japanese)
16. Takeda, H., Nishimoto, T., Sagayama, S.: Joint Estimation of Rhythm and Tempo of Polyphonic MIDI Performance Using Tempo Curve and Hidden Markov Models. Journal of Information Processing 48, 237–247 (2007) (in Japanese)

Ship Water Fire-Fighting System Survivability Simulation Based on Intelligent Reconfiguration Arithmetic

Yue Hou, Jin-Yun Pu, and Xiao-Hong Chen

Naval Architecture and Power College
Naval University of Engineering
Wu-Han, 430033, China
Houyue1982@126.com

Abstract. The ship water fire-fighting system survivability is an important aspect of total ship survivability. But when the ship water fire-fighting system survivability is calculated, the crew active recoverability should be concerned. An intelligent reconfiguration arithmetic is founded to simulate the crew's recoverability in this paper. The graph theory and the virtual vertex are used to found the fire-fighting system logic model firstly. And then, the width first search is used to found intelligent water supply path generation arithmetic and intelligent reconfiguration arithmetic. At last, through examples test, we find that the intelligent reconfiguration arithmetic is feasible.

Keywords: Intelligent reconfiguration, Graph; Width first search, Virtual vertex, Water fire-fighting system.

1 Introduction

When the ship is attacked by the weapon in the war, the water fire-fighting system may be damaged and the ship fire-fighting ability will be decreased. So the water fire-fighting system survivability is very important in guaranteeing the ship fire-fighting ability and ship safety. The water fire-fighting system survivability must be calculated in the design stage[1,2]. A damage tree model is founded in reference 3[3]. But the damage tree model is a linear model and it is very complex in calculating survivability of water fire-fighting system which is a non-linear system[4].

When the water fire-fighting system is damaged, the crew will close or open valves to isolate the damaged pipes and open other pumps to recover the water pressure of the damaged pipes. The active intervening action of crew described above is called water fire-fighting system reconfiguration. So when the water fire-fighting system survivability is simulated, the crew reconfiguration should also be concerned. The crew reconfiguration ability is defined as recoverability which is an important aspect of survivability.

But the crew reconfiguration ability is often neglected in calculating the water fire-fighting system survivability, because the intelligent reconfiguration model which can simulate the crew reconfiguration action has not been founded. The water

H. Deng et al. (Eds.): AICI 2011, Part I, LNAI 7002, pp. 18–26, 2011.

fire-fighting system survivability simulation flow chart is given in part 2. The water fire-fighting system logic model based on graph theory is founded in part 3 and the intelligent reconfiguration model is found in part 4. Examples are calculated to compare the survivability index which concerns intelligent reconfiguration to survivability index which does not concerns in part 5. Conclusions are given in part 6.

2   Survivability Simulation Process

The average undamaged fire hydrants after weapon attack can be defined as the survivability index of water fire-fighting system. It can be calculated through Monte Carlo simulation. The Monte Carlo simulation process is founded as figure 1 as follows.

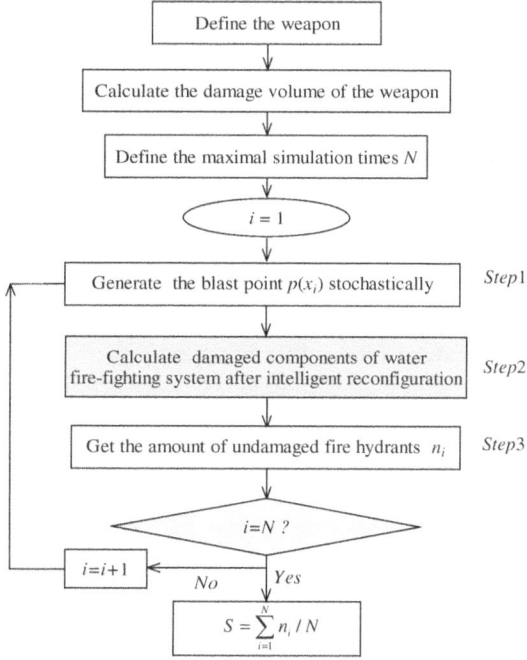

Fig. 1. Fire-fighting system survivability calculation process

In figure 1, S is the survivability index of water fire-fighting system, it indicates the average undamaged fire hydrants after weapon attack and intelligent reconfiguration. N is the maximal simulation times and n_i is the amount of the usable fire hydrants after Intelligent reconfiguration in ith simulation. The important model in figure1 is the intelligent reconfiguration model in step 2 which will be founded in part 3 and part 4.

3   Graph Model of Water Fire-Fighting System

The water fire-fighting system has a obvious character that it is composed of point and line. So the graph in math domain can be used to found water fire-fighting system function model.

3.1   Graph Theory

Graph is a mathematic tool which can be used in complex system description, arithmetic design and artificial intelligence.

Graph G is defined as follows:

$$G = (V, E)$$
$$V = \{V_1, V_2, ... V_n\}, \quad E = \{E_1, E_2, ... E_m\}$$

V is a set the graph vertex, E is a set of graph edges.

Because the water fire-fighting system physical model consists of different points and lines, the graph is a very useful method in modeling its physical model [5]. As an important description method of graph, the adjacent matrix is also used widely in this paper.

The vertex-vertex adjacent matrix $L(i, j)$ and edge- vertex adjacent matrix $J(i, j)$ are important concepts used to describe the graph structure [6]. They are also the basic of the intelligent reconfiguration.

3.2   Graph Model of Water Fire-Fighting System

The water fire-fighting system has a obvious character that it is composed of point and line. So the graph in math domain can be used to found water fire-fighting system function model.

The water fire-fighting system is composed of pump, pipe, pipe node, fire hydrant and valve. The pump, pipe node, fire hydrant and valve can be denoted as graph vertexes and pipe can be denoted as graph edge.

Considering the pump, pipe node, fire hydrant and valve has different function in the water fire-fighting system, so, the graph vertexes can be classified as four kinds.

1) The first kind is source vertex. The pump is used to pump water from sea, so it is the water source of the water fire-fighting system. The pump is defined as source vertex.

2) The second kind is virtual vertex. The pipe node has no actual function and it is the connective point of pipes only. The pipe node is defined as virtual vertex.

3) The third kind is switch vertex. When the pipes are damaged, the valve can be closed or opened to isolate or restore the seawater pressure. So the valve is defined as switch vertex.

4) The fourth kind is target vertex. The fire hydrant is used to spray seawater to put out the fire. The number of usable fire hydrant is the survivability index of water fire-fighting system. So the fire hydrant is defined as target vertex.

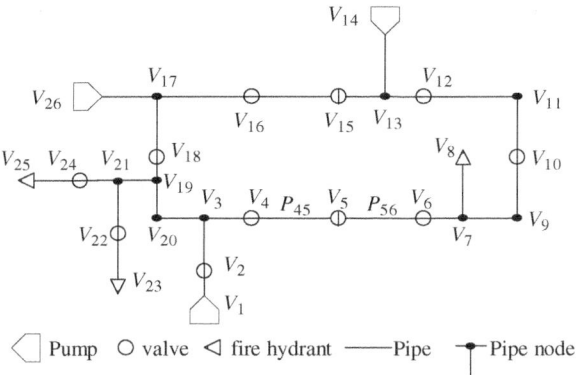

Fig. 2. Water fire-fighting system

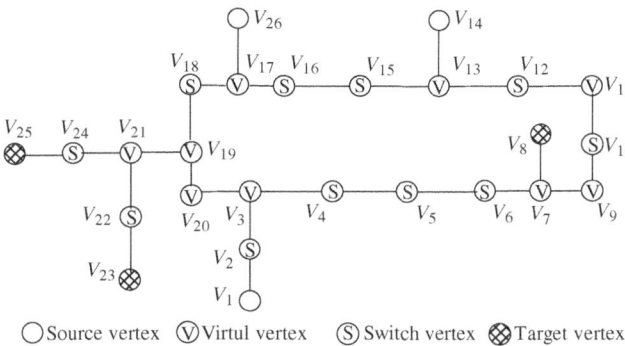

Fig. 3. Graph model of water fire-fighting system

Suppose a given water fire-fighting system is shown as figure 2. Its graph model is given as figure 3. The water fire-fighting system in figure 2 and figure 3 has three source vertexes, nine virtual vertexes, eleven switch vertexes and three target vertexes.

4   Intelligent Reconfiguration Arithmetic

When the water fire-fighting system is attacked by the weapon, the pump, pipe, fire hydrant and valve may be damaged. The intelligent reconfiguration arithmetic is used to simulate the crew's repair action. The intelligent reconfiguration arithmetic is founded based on the water fire-fighting system graph model and adjacent matrix. Intelligent reconfiguration consists of two steps.

1) Intelligent separation. When the pipes are damaged, the crew will close valves adjoining to the damaged pipes. So the Intelligent separation arithmetic is used to simulate crew's separation action.

2) Intelligent reconfiguration. The separation action may lead to the undamaged pipes lose water pressure, so, the crew will open special pumps or valves to create new water supply path [7].

4.1 Intelligent Separation Arithmetic

Let R be the set of distorted valves, T be the set of virtual vertex, K be the set of ruptured valves and E be the ruptured pipes set. Before the intelligent separation arithmetic foundation, three function definitions are given as follows.

1) Definition 1

Let F be the function of vertex V and T. If T consists of V, $F(T,V)=1$; else, $F(T,V)=0$.

2) Definition 2

Let G be the function of *vertex V and R. If R consists of V, $G(R,V)=1$; else,* $G(R,V)=0$.

3) Definition 3

Let H be the function of *vertex V and K. If K consists of V, $H(K,V)=1$; else,* $H(K,V)=0$.

Let S be the valves set need closing. The intelligent separation arithmetic is founded based on definitions given above.

*Step*1. Ruptured pipes set extension.

We have gotten that when the valve is ruptured, we suppose it is equivalent to the rupture of pipes that connective to the ruptured valves. So, we should add the pipes that connective to the ruptured valves to the ruptured pipes set E and get the new ruptured pipes set E^*.

*Step*2. Pop the first element $E^*(1)$ of E^* and find its connective vertexes in edge-vertex adjacent matrix J. Let the set of the vertexes found be V^*.

*Step*3. If $V^* = \Phi$, then go to step5,else Pop the first element $V^*(1)$ of V^*.

*Step*4. If $F(T,V^*(1))=1$ or $G(R,V^*(1))=1$, then find the vertexes connective to $V^*(1)$ and add the found vertexes to the bottom of V^*. Else if $H(K,V^*(1))=0$, add $V^*(1)$ to S. Go to step3.

*Step*5. Get the valves set need closing S.

Example1. In figure3, If $K=[V_{19}]$, $R=\Phi$ and $K=\Phi$ after attack, through the intelligent separation arithmetic reasoning, we can get,

$$S=[V_2,V_4,V_{24},V_{22},V_{16}]$$

From the two examples given above, we can get that different R corresponds to different separation results. When R is not empty, the valve need closing cannot be closed, So the arithmetic will expand search scope and search the new valves need closing.

4.2 Intelligent Reconfiguration Arithmetic

When the water fire-fighting system is damaged, the crew not only close the valves given in the intelligent separation arithmetic, but also open the pump or some valves to create new water supply path. The restoration action which will create new water supply path is called reconfiguration.

The intelligent reconfiguration arithmetic is founded to simulate the crew's reasoning in creating new water supply path. The water supply path search is the basis of the intelligent reconfiguration arithmetic and it will be founded firstly. Let V_y be the source vertex and V_t be the target vertex. The following arithmetic will create a water supply path $SP(V_y, V_t)$ from V_y to V_t using width first search method [8,9].

1) Definition 1

Let $C(V_i, V_j)$ be the connective set between V_i and V_j. $C(V_i, V_j)$ is composed of vertexes connective to V_i except V_j. For example, in figure3, $C(V_{21}, V_{19}) = [V_{22}, V_{24}]$.

2) Definition 2

Let $CreatTree(V_i | V_j)$ be the action of extension tree of V_i relative to V_j. $CreatTree(V_i | V_j)$ is a multi-offset tree in which parent vertex is V_i and offset vertexes are the elements of $C(V_i, V_j)$.

The intelligent water supply paths generation from V_y to V_t arithmetic is founded as follows.

*Step*1. Do $CreatTree(V_y | \phi)$ and get a multi-offset tree.

*Step*2. Suppose the parent node of a certain leaf node Le_i is Pe_i. Then, aiming at every leaf node Le_i, do $CreatTree(Le_i | Pe_i)$.

Step3. If the current leaves are all target vertex or source vertex, then go to step4, else, go to step2.

Step4. The trace from V_y to V_t in the multi-offset tree is the water path $SP(V_y, V_t)$.

For example, the intelligent generation tree of $SP(V_{26}, V_{23})$ is shown as figure 4.

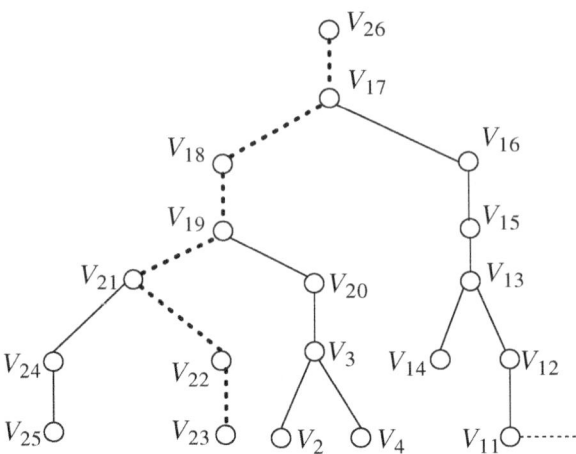

Fig. 4. Ruptured pipes

Through figure 4, we can get the water path $SP(V_{26}, V_{23})$.

$$SP(V_{26}, V_{23}) = [V_{26}, V_{17}, V_{18}, V_{19}, V_{21}, V_{22}, V_{23}] \text{, or}$$

$$SP(V_{26}, V_{23}) = [V_{26}, V_{17}, V_{16}, V_{15}, V_{13}, V_{12}, V_{11}, V_{10}, V_9,$$
$$V_7, V_6, V_5, V_4, V_3, V_{20}, V_{19}, V_{21}, V_{22}, V_{23}]$$

The intelligent reconfiguration arithmetic is founded based on the intelligent water supply paths generation arithmetic.

Let W be the set of source valves that do not loss function and V_t be the vertex that need supplying seawater.

Step1. Make intelligent separation decision and get valves set need closing S .

Step2. Pop the firstly element of W and Let it be $W(1)$.

Step3. Do $CreatTree(W(1)|V_t)$ and get $SP(W(1), V_t)$ .If $SP(W(1), V_t)$ contains any element of S , then go to step2, else, go to step4.

Step4. Get the water supply path $SP(W(1), V_t)$, exit arithmetic.

The switch valves and pump in $SP(W(1), V_t)$ should be opened to create a new water supply path to V_t . The number of $SP(W(1), V_t)$ may be more than one. The $SP(W(1), V_t)$ which contains the least amount of vertex is defined as the optimal water supply path.

For example, in figure 3, suppose V_{11} is damaged and V_1 losses function. Through intelligent separation arithmetic, we can get that $S = [V_{10}, V_{12}]$. V_{10} and V_{12} are closed to separate the damaged components. So, the fire hydrants V_8 will not get seawater.

Through the intelligent reconfiguration arithmetic, we can get that the new optimal water supply paths is

$$SP(V_{26}, V_8) = [V_{17}, V_{18}, V_{19}, V_{20}, V_3, V_4, V_5, V_6, V_7, V_8]$$

The switch valves in $SP(V_{26}, V_8)$ are $[V_{18}, V_4, V_5, V_6]$ and the closed of them should be opened to create new water supply path.

5 Simulation

From section 4, we can get that the usable fire hydrant will be increased under intelligent separation and intelligent reconfiguration. Suppose the number of usable fire hydrant and survivability index after damage is N_1 and S_1, the number of usable fire hydrant and survivability index after damage and intelligent separation is N_2 and S_2, the number of usable fire hydrant and survivability index after damage and intelligent reconfiguration is N_3 and S_3. Let α_1 be survivability recovery index after intelligent separation and α_2 be survivability recovery index after intelligent reconfiguration. Through section1, we can get,

$$\alpha_1 = \frac{N_2}{N_1} = \frac{S_2}{S_1}, \ \alpha_2 = \frac{N_3}{N_1} = \frac{S_3}{S_1}$$

According to survivability calculation process in figure1, the fire-fighting system survivability indexes are calculated under three different weapon and the survivability recovery indexes are given as table1.

Through table1, we can get that the crew's recovery ability is very important in increasing the water fire-fighting system survivability. The quantitative recovery ability can be calculated under the intelligent separation and intelligent reconfiguration arithmetic founded in this paper.

Table 1. Survivability recovery indexes under different weapon

weapon	α_1	α_2
1#	1.4	1.42
2#	1.1	1.25
3#	1.5	1.65

6 Conclusions

The water fire-fighting system is a network system and its survivability simulation is different from the linear system. Not only this difference, the crew's recovery ability should also be concerned in water fire-fighting system simulation.

To calculate the water fire-fighting system survivability, the graph model and intelligent reconfiguration arithmetic which is used to simulate the crew's reasoning in creating new water supply path are founded in this paper. Through simulation, we found that the intelligent reconfiguration arithmetic can simulate the crew's action well.

A new method which can calculate recovery ability quantitatively is founded in this paper. But, concerning the crew' recovery is a series of sequence actions, so, the dynamic survivability simulation should also be researched in deep in the future.

References

1. Pu, J.-y.: Ship Survivability. National Defense Industry Press, Beijing (2008)
2. Pu, J., Jin, t.: Ship damage control organization. National defense industry press, Beijing (2008)
3. Hou, y., Pu, j.-y., Cai, Y.-l.: Intelligent decision support system in damage control of damaged ship. In: Progress in Safety Science and Technology, vol. (4), Chang Sha, China, pp. 1908–1913 (2006)
4. Jia, j., Li, w., Zhang, f.-x.: Ship survivability assessment considering correlation. Ship Science and Technology 23(2), 109–113 (2010)
5. Shi, y.-w.: Utilizing graph theory in designing electricity distribution network management system. Guang Dong Power 16(5), 49–51 (2003)
6. Yang, H.: The reconfiguration paln after distribution network fault base on graph theory. Hu Bei Electricity 28(4), 7–9 (2004)
7. Li, j.-p.: The theory and application of the first-aid repair of equipment. Weapon industry press, Beijing (2000)
8. Wang, x.: Implement search techniques in artificial intelligence using C. Journal of Shannxi Normal University (Natural Science Edition) 27, 30–32 (1999)
9. Xu, x.-f., Gong, l.-n.: Fault diagnosis in transmission electricity network based on BFS and optimize algorithm. Proceedings of the CSU-EPSA 16(5), 5–8 (2004)

Maximum Likelihood Estimation of Double Alternative Step-Stress Accelerated Life Test for Electronics

Zhicao Zhao, Baowei Song, Xinping Wang, and Guozhen Zhang

College of Marine, Northwestern Polytechnical University,
Xi'an, Shaanxi, P.R. China
grass1114@163.com, songbaowei@nwpu.edu.cn,
wangxinping008@163.com, godskay@163.com

Abstract. For the application of double alternative step-stress accelerated life test in the life assessment of modern high reliable and long life electronic equipment, the maximum likelihood estimation (MLE) method is applied to make its life and reliability assessment in operating stress. With electronic product failure obeying exponential distribution, the likelihood equations of acceleration model parameters were established according to time convert. On the basis of acceleration model parameters and Fisher information matrix, the maximum likelihood estimation and approximate confidence interval of life expectancy in operating stress were acquired. In the end, random simulation method was used to prove the validity and advantages of the statistical method above compared with other method.

Keywords: Electronics, Exponential distribution, Maximum likelihood estimation (MLE), Double alternative step-stress accelerated life test, Fisher information matrix.

1 Introduction

With high reliability and long life being the characteristics of modern electronic equipments, the application of accelerated life tests in their life assessment becomes more widely. Single stress accelerated life test is the most commonly used present. But, there is always a limit to the stress rising, and product failure mechanism will change once above the limit. Thus the shorten testing time is restricted and acceleration effect is not significant. In order to reduce test time further, two stresses (such as temperature, voltage) can be choen as accelerating stresses together. The failure of modern electronic equipment alwayes obeyes exponential distribution and statistical analysis method of single stress accelerated life testing is quite advanced, as the reference [1-4] have described in detail. According to all these, the maximum likelihood estimation method of double alternative step-stress accelerated life test is discussed and the maximum likelihood estimation and approximate confidence interval of life expectancy in operating stress are acquired. In the end, results of

H. Deng et al. (Eds.): AICI 2011, Part I, LNAI 7002, pp. 27–34, 2011.
© Springer-Verlag Berlin Heidelberg 2011

simulation studies prove the validity and advantages of the statistical method above compared with other method.

2 Assumption and Description

Temperature and voltage play crucial roles in the electronic equipment life process. For the double alternative step-stress accelerated life test of temperature and voltage, the number of its stress combination is $k = a+b-1$, including a as number of temperature stresses and b as number of voltage stresses. The data processing of step-stress accelerated life test is based on the following assumptions [5].

Assumption 1: Both in operating stress combination S_0 and accelerating stress combinations $S_1, \cdots, S_k$, electronic equipment life distribution obeys exponential distribution, the distribution function respectively is:

$$F_i(t) = 1 - \exp(-t/\theta_i), t > 0, i = 0, 1, \cdots k \; . \tag{1}$$

Including θ_i as life expectancy in stress combination S_i.

Assumption 2: There is an acceleration model between Life expectancy θ_i and accelerating stress combination S_i as follows:

$$\ln \theta_i = \beta_0 + \beta_1 \varphi_1 \left(S_i^{(1)} \right) + \beta_2 \varphi_2 \left(S_i^{(2)} \right) + \beta_3 \left(\varphi_1 \left(S_i^{(1)} \right), \varphi_2 \left(S_i^{(2)} \right) \right) \; . \tag{2}$$

If there is no interaction between two stresses of stress combination S_i, the acceleration model can be simplified as

$$\ln \theta_i = \beta_0 + \beta_1 \varphi_1 \left(S_i^{(1)} \right) + \beta_2 \varphi_2 \left(S_i^{(2)} \right) \; . \tag{3}$$

The simplified model will be used below.

Assumption 3: The residual life of product relys only on its accumulated failure parts and stress combination, and has nothing to do with the cumulative way.

Specifically, the accumulated probability of failure $F(\tau_i)$ after operating time τ_i in stress combination S_i equals the accumulated probability of failure $F(\tau_{ij})$ after operating time τ_{ij} in stress combination S_j, as

$$F(\tau_i) = F(\tau_{ij}), \quad i \neq j \; . \tag{4}$$

It assumes that n electronic products of same kind go through failure terminated double alternative step-stress accelerated life test. A group of failure datas is acquired according to the method mentioned in reference [4]. These datas also mean that there are r_i failure time in stress combination S_i, just as following

$$t_{i1} \leq t_{i2} \leq \cdots \leq t_{ir_i}, \quad i = 1, 2, \cdots, k \ . \tag{5}$$

The failure time begins when the stress combination rises to S_i. There are differences between "Failure time" and "life data". In formula(5), only $t_{11}, t_{12}, \cdots, t_{1r_1}$ are life data and others are not. As these electronic products have been in $i-1$ stress combinations before S_i for a period of time. During this period, although no failure happens, there must be some damage to them. The key problem is how to convert the time in stress combination before S_i to the time in S_i, and make them compensation to t_{ij}, so as to acquire life data in S_i.

Lemma 1 [2]: In assumption, $t_{r,n}$ and $t_{s,n}$ $(r < s)$ are the r th and s th order statistics of sample A extracted from exponential distribution $F(t) = 1 - \exp(-t/\theta), t > 0$ and its capacity is n. Then $t_{s,n} - t_{r,n}$ is the $s-r$ th order statistic of sample B from the same exponential distribution and its capacity is $n - r$.

Then according to Lemma 1, failure time in formula(5) converts to life data of failure terminated constant-stress life test as follows:

$$\left. \begin{array}{cccc} S_1 & t_{11}, t_{12}, \cdots, t_{1r_1} & n & r_1 = R_1 \\ S_2 & t_{21}, t_{22}, \cdots, t_{2r_2} & n - R_1 & r_2 \\ \cdots & \cdots\cdots & \cdots & \cdots \\ S_k & t_{k1}, t_{k2}, \cdots, t_{kr_k} & n - R_{k-1} & r_k \end{array} \right\} . \tag{6}$$

Where R_i is the sum of failure number in former i stress combinations.

Lemma 2: For failure terminated constant-stress life test of k steps,

$$E(T_i) = r_i \theta_i, \quad i = 1, 2, \cdots, k \ . \tag{7}$$

where $T_i = \sum_{i=1}^{r_i} t_{ij} + (n_i - r_i)t_{r_i}$.

3 MLE of $\beta_0, \beta_1, \beta_2$

3.1 MLE

According to the likelihood function [6] of the life expectancy in various stress combinations and the acceleration model, the likelihood function of $\beta_0, \beta_1, \beta_2$ takes the form

$$L(\beta_0, \beta_1, \beta_2) = \prod_{i=1}^{k} \frac{n_i!}{(n_i - r_i)!} \frac{1}{\theta_i^{r_i}} \cdot \exp\left\{-\frac{1}{\theta_i}\left[\sum_{i=1}^{r_i} t_{ij} + (n_i - r_i)t_{ir_i}\right]\right\}. \tag{8}$$

Then let

$$\ln\theta_i = \beta_0 + \beta_1\varphi_i^{(1)} + \beta_2\varphi_i^{(2)}, \ln\theta_i = \beta_0 + \beta_1\varphi_i^{(1)} + \beta_2\varphi_i^{(2)},$$

$$\theta_i = \exp\left(\beta_0 + \beta_1\varphi_i^{(1)} + \beta_2\varphi_i^{(2)}\right), \frac{\partial\theta_i}{\partial\beta_0} = \theta_i, \quad \frac{\partial\theta_i}{\partial\beta_1} = \varphi_i^{(1)}\theta_i, \quad \frac{\partial\theta_i}{\partial\beta_2} = \varphi_i^{(2)}\theta_i,$$

$$i = 1, 2, \cdots k.$$

The likelihood equations of $\beta_0, \beta_1, \beta_2$ are obtained as follows

$$\begin{cases} \dfrac{\partial\ln L}{\partial\beta_0} = \displaystyle\sum_{i=1}^{k}(T_i/\theta_i - r_i) = 0 \\[2mm] \dfrac{\partial\ln L}{\partial\beta_1} = \displaystyle\sum_{i=1}^{k}\varphi_i^{(1)}(T_i/\theta_i - r_i) = 0 \\[2mm] \dfrac{\partial\ln L}{\partial\beta_2} = \displaystyle\sum_{i=1}^{k}\varphi_i^{(2)}(T_i/\theta_i - r_i) = 0 \end{cases} \tag{9}$$

Make $\theta_i = \exp\left(\beta_0 + \beta_1\varphi_i^{(1)} + \beta_2\varphi_i^{(2)}\right)$ and $T_i = \displaystyle\sum_{i=1}^{r_i} t_{ij} + (n_i - r_i)t_{r_i}$ applied in equations(9) and solve equations(9), then MLEs of $\beta_0, \beta_1, \beta_2$ are obtained as the form of $\hat{\beta}_0, \hat{\beta}_1, \hat{\beta}_2$.

$$\hat{\theta}_0 = \exp\left(\hat{\beta}_0 + \hat{\beta}_1\varphi_i^{(1)} + \hat{\beta}_2\varphi_i^{(2)}\right). \tag{10}$$

3.2 MLE of Life Expectancy θ_0 in Operating Stress Combination

Based on the acceleration model, MLE of life expectancy θ_0 in operating stress combination S_0 is as the form following

$$\hat{\theta}_0 = \exp\left(\hat{\beta}_0 + \hat{\beta}_1\varphi_i^{(1)} + \hat{\beta}_2\varphi_i^{(2)}\right). \tag{11}$$

4 Interval Estimation of Life Expectancy θ_0 in Operating Stress Combination

4.1 Fisher Information Matrix [7]

According to Logarithm likelihood function $\ln L$, there are

$$\frac{\partial^2 \ln L}{\partial \beta_0^2} = -\sum_{i=1}^{k} \frac{T_i}{\theta_i}, \frac{\partial^2 \ln L}{\partial \beta_0 \beta_1} = \frac{\partial^2 \ln L}{\partial \beta_1 \beta_0} - \sum_{i=1}^{k} \varphi_i^{(1)} \frac{T_i}{\theta_i}, \frac{\partial^2 \ln L}{\partial \beta_0 \beta_2} = \frac{\partial^2 \ln L}{\partial \beta_2 \beta_0} - \sum_{i=1}^{k} \varphi_i^{(2)} \frac{T_i}{\theta_i},$$

$$\frac{\partial^2 \ln L}{\partial \beta_1^2} = -\sum_{i=1}^{k} \left(\varphi_i^{(1)} \right)^2 \frac{T_i}{\theta_i}, \frac{\partial^2 \ln L}{\partial \beta_1 \beta_2} = \frac{\partial^2 \ln L}{\partial \beta_2 \beta_1} = -\sum_{i=1}^{k} \varphi_i^{(1)} \varphi_i^{(2)} \frac{T_i}{\theta_i},$$

$$\frac{\partial^2 \ln L}{\partial \beta_2^2} = -\sum_{i=1}^{k} \left(\varphi_i^{(2)} \right)^2 \frac{T_i}{\theta_i}.$$

where $\boldsymbol{\beta} = (\beta_0, \beta_1, \beta_2)'$. Then According to **Lemma 2**, the Fisher information matrix $\mathbf{I}(\boldsymbol{\beta})$ takes the form

$$\mathbf{I}(\boldsymbol{\beta}) = \begin{pmatrix} \sum_{i=1}^{k} r_i & \sum_{i=1}^{k} r_i \varphi_i^{(1)} & \sum_{i=1}^{k} r_i \varphi_i^{(2)} \\ \sum_{i=1}^{k} r_i \varphi_i^{(1)} & \sum_{i=1}^{k} \left(r_i \varphi_i^{(1)} \right)^2 & \sum_{i=1}^{k} r_i \varphi_i^{(1)} \varphi_i^{(2)} \\ \sum_{i=1}^{k} r_i \varphi_i^{(2)} & \sum_{i=1}^{k} r_i \varphi_i^{(1)} \varphi_i^{(2)} & \sum_{i=1}^{k} \left(r_i \varphi_i^{(2)} \right)^2 \end{pmatrix}. \tag{12}$$

4.2 Interval Estimation of Life Expectancy θ_0

Inverse matrix of $\mathbf{I}(\boldsymbol{\beta})$ is $\mathbf{H} = \mathbf{I}^{-1}(\boldsymbol{\beta})$.

According to references [8], $\ln \hat{\theta}_0$ obeys gradual normal distribution as follows

$$\ln \hat{\theta}_0 \sim N\left(\ln \theta_0, \sigma_0^2 \right). \tag{13}$$

where

$$\mathbf{Var}(\boldsymbol{\beta}) = \mathbf{H}. \tag{14}$$

$$\sigma_0^2 = Var(\hat{\beta}_0 + \hat{\beta}_1 \varphi_0^{(1)} + \hat{\beta}_2 \varphi_0^{(2)})$$
$$= H_{11} + H_{22} \left(\varphi_0^{(1)} \right)^2 + H_{33} (\varphi_0^{(2)})^2 + 2\varphi_0^{(1)} H_{01} + 2\varphi_0^{(2)} H_{02} + 2\varphi_0^{(1)} \varphi_0^{(2)} H_{12}. \tag{15}$$

Confidence interval of $\ln \theta_0$ in confidence level is

$$\left(\ln \hat{\theta}_0 - \sigma_0 u_{\alpha/2}, \ln \hat{\theta}_0 + \sigma_0 u_{\alpha/2} \right). \tag{16}$$

where $u_{\alpha/2}$ is $\alpha/2$ fractile quantile of $N(0,1)$ distribution.

Then confidence interval and sided confidence lower limit of θ_0 in confidence level $1-\alpha$ are

$$\left(\hat{\theta}_0 e^{-\sigma_0 u_{\alpha/2}}, \hat{\theta}_0 e^{\sigma_0 u_{\alpha/2}}\right) . \tag{17}$$

$$\hat{\theta}_{0L} = e^{-\sigma_0 u_\alpha} . \tag{18}$$

5 Simulation Studies

As known in its performance specification, some electronic devices keep the same failure mechanism and their life distributions obey exponential distribution in temperature range $40\,^{\circ}\text{C} \sim 150\,^{\circ}\text{C}$ and voltage range 100V~400V. Choose the temperature T (unit is absolute temperature K) and voltage V (unit is V) as two acceleration stress and arrange double alternative step-stress accelerated life test. Given the lack of real failure data, here we use computer simulation to generate test data instead. The steps sre as follows:

1) Establish the acceleration modle

$$\ln \theta_i = -20 + 2000\,0/T - 4.5\ln V . \tag{19}$$

2) Arrange the operating and acceleration T and V below:

$T_0=353K,T_1=373K,T_2=388K,T_3=403K:$
$V_0=100V,V_1=200V,V_2=300V,V_3=400V.$

Then the stress combination transforms as follows:$(1,1) \rightarrow (2,1) \rightarrow (2,2) \rightarrow (3,2) \rightarrow (3,3)$

3) Fix the sample size n=50 and the terminated failure number of each step are 4,5,6,7,8. Then cumulative number of total failure is 30.

4) Apply computer simulation to generate failure data.
The failure data are shown below in Table 1.

Table 1. Faliure Data of Simulation

Stress Combination	$T_i(K)$	$V(V)$	r_i	Failure Data
(1,1)	373	200	4	387.5 721.0 110 0.8 139 8.8
(2,1)	388	200	5	44.6886 92.0821 142.6949 190.6824 236.1525
(2,2)	388	300	6	9.2476 17.4023 27.2386 36.1064 44.7785 56.4964
(3,2)	403	300	7	1.3952 2.9558 4.6616 6.2531 8.0541 10.2029 11.8277
(3,3)	403	400	8	0.5409 1.1018 1.6042 2.2076 2.844 7 3.4356 3.9862 4.6464

After the hypothesis test of exponential distribution, we make the statistical analysis according to the method above and mentioned in reference [4]. The results are shown below in Table 2.

Table 2. Comparison of Acceleration Model Parameters

	Method 1	Method 2	Original Model
β_0	-20.184 9	-20.376 4	-20
β_1	199 45.058 8	201 36.239 1	200 00
β_2	-4.444 7	-4.481 7	-4.5
θ_0	7.633 5e+6	9.137 2e+6	8.318 2e+6

Then we test acceleration model parameters with method mentiond reference [4]. The result shows that temperature and voltage have phenomenal influences on logarithm of life expectancy.

The data comparison above shows that model parameters with the two methods above are both quite close to those in original model, but variance of method 1 is slightly smaller. On point estimation of life expectancy, the life expectancy of method 1(7.633 5e+6)is less than that in theory(8.318 2e+6), which means conservative in assessment and desirable in engineering practice. And the life expectancy of method 2(9.137 2e+6)is slightly higher than that in theory, which is slightly pushy. On estimation of confidence interval and confidence lower limit, life expectancy in theory falls in the confidence interval or above the confidence lower limit in both methods ((2.34e+6, 3.567 9e+7) and (3.155 6e+6,+∞) of Method 1 while (2.195 9e+6, 3.801 9e+7) and (3.002 9e+6, +∞) of method 2). But confidence interval of method 1 is smaller and the confidence lower limit is higher,which make method 1 slightly better than the way 2.

6 Conclusion

According to the simulation method above, we also generate many groups of simulated failure data, and make data analysis. The analysis results show that:

1) Life expectancy is close to that in theory in both methods. But life expectancy of method 1 is smaller than that in theory in the probability of more than 90%, while life expectancy of method 2 is bigger than that in theory in the probability of more than 90%.

2) True value coverage probability of 90% confidence interval and 90% confidence lower limit is almost 100% in both methods. But confidence interval of method 1 is smaller and the confidence lower limit is higher.

3) With the increase of failure terminated number of each stress combination and the number of total samples, variance of the logarithm of life expectancy obtained in both methods will gradually decrease and the confidence interval and the confidence lower limit will be more precise.

The results above show sufficiently the validity and advantages of the MLE method above compared with other method in the statistic analysis of double alternative step-stress accelerated life test data of electric equipments. And this method is also easy to achieve, easy for engineering staff to grasp, so suitable for application in engineering.

Acknowledgments. The authors are grateful to Associate Professor Qingwei Liang for her constructive suggestion. The authors also thank the sponsor for this opportunity to express viewpoint.

References

1. Fei, H.X., Zhang, X.X.: Maximum likelihood estimate of step-stress accelerated life testing under the exponential distribution. Mathematica Applicata 17(3), 398–404 (2004)
2. Wu, S.M., Peng, P.: Reliability evaluation of stepwise stress accelerated life testing under exponential distribution. Journal of Huaqiao University (Natural Science) 17(2), 111–117 (1996)
3. Jin, Y.F., Zhao, X.M.: Bayesian estimate of step-stress life-testing with random stress-change time. Journal of Northwestern Polytechnical University 22(2), 205–208 (2004)
4. Mao, S.S., Zhang, L.L.: Accelerated life tests. Science Press, Beijing (2000)
5. Nelson, W.: Accelerated life testing step-stress models and data analysis. IEEE Transactions of Reliability R-29 (1980)
6. Zhao, X.M., Xu, W., et al.: Mathematical statistics. Science Press, Beijing (2002)
7. Zhang, Z.H.: Accelerated life tests and statistical analysis. Beijing University of Technology Press, Beijing (2002)
8. Chen, X.R.: Introduction to mathematical statistics. Science Press, Beijing (1999)

Prediction of Grain Yield Using SIGA-BP Neural Network

Zhixian Niu and Wupeng Li

Computer Science and Technology College
Taiyuan University of Technology
Taiyuan, Shanxi, China
niuzx@163.com, 309615786@qq.com

Abstract. In order to improve the accuracy of forecasting grain yield, detailed analysis of the reason that the BP network is vulnerable to fall into local minimum was made, then the new method was adopted to solve the problem of BP network. This paper studies the self-adaptive immune genetic algorithm (SIGA), and then uses the SIGA to optimize the BP neural network weights and thresholds values, used the SIGA global search method to solve the local minimum values of BP network, and meanwhile established the SIGA-BP network prediction model about Henan province's grain yield. The simulation experiment results were that the average absolute error of grain yield predicted by the new model is 127.02ten thousand tons, the result shows that the SIGA-BP neural network model has higher prediction accuracy than the BP network model.

Keywords: BP neural network, Self-adaptive Immune Genetic Algorithm, Grain yield prediction.

1 Introduction

The grain yield of Henan province has called "China granary", there is common saying: "no grain instability, no food is riots", this region's grain yield changes will cause the economic fluctuations in Henan Province, and even lead to political unstable. Accurately predict grain yield is an important part for the Henan province and even the national grain security system, for the government to formulate rational grain purchase price and allocations plan, and arrange grain transporting have the extremely vital significance. At present, the researchers using some the main method to forecasting grain yield: regression predict method, GM (1, N) Grey forecasting method, neural network predict method, Genetic Algorithm neural network forecasting method etc[1]. Because the traditional modeling methods has many limiting factor, For example: Time series demand is normal distribution, Stability, independence, etc, so is not suitable for grain yield predict that is very complex. The BP neural network appear overcomes the above the constraints, and with its simple structure, convenient operation, received widespread application.

H. Deng et al. (Eds.): AICI 2011, Part I, LNAI 7002, pp. 35–42, 2011.

The BP neural network [3] has highly parallel structure and parallel processing ability, has the inherent nonlinear characteristics and self-study, organization, adaptive ability, etc. It is the one of the most widely of the neural network model, has independent object's mathematical model, Its performance advantage mainly reflects in pattern recognition, pattern classification, graphics processing, financial research and function approximation, etc. Although BP neural network has many advantages, but also has some flaws, such as: On the one hand BP algorithm is according to weights adjustment principle of the error's gradient descent is that every step is taken local optimal solution, the so-called "greed" algorithm[2]' and its searching essence is peer-to-peer search; On the other hand, because of BP network's weights and threshold is random generated that play a key influence to the BP network performance, distribution can be very uneven, may fall into saturated zone, this could leads to the network slow convergence speed and the local minimum values, etc[5]. Currently there are many books and papers to introduce the BP neural network theory, so in this papers will not to introduce. If you have interested in BP algorithm, you can read references [3][4], the two article have detailed instructions. According to the above shortages, this papers will use the Self-adaptive immune Genetic Algorithm (SIGA) in the references [6][7] to optimize the BP neural network weights and threshold, and solve the those disadvantages. The SIGA and the BP network together to form a new SIGA-BP grain predict model, and put the new prediction model applied into the Henan province's grain yield forecast. Through the MATLAB7.1 software simulation experiment, and results show that comparison with BP neural network forecasting method, This paper optimized network model predicted grain yield of Henan province achieved more accurate results and stability is better.

2   BP Neural Network Optimized by SIGA

2.1   Introduction of SIGA

Self-adaptive Immune Genetic Algorithms (Referred to SIGA)is a improved genetic algorithm that is based on Biological immune mechanism, its introducing the immune concentration regulation mechanism and adaptive strategies based on the standard genetic algorithm, thus suppresses the evolutionary process of individual degeneration phenomenon and assure diversity of species group, prevent "premature" happens . It is the same with immune algorithm, the problem to be solved look as antigen, Solution of the problem corresponding to antibody. With the antigen and antibody affinity describe the approximation degree of the feasible solution and the optimal solution[8]. The SIGA algorithm generally has six modules consists: Antigen recognition, the initial antibody yield, fitness calculation, memory cell update, antibody promotion and suppression, antibody produce, etc.

2.2   Optimization Process and Steps of BP Neural Network by SIGA

1)BP neural network adopt three layer structure, the parameters of BP network is introduced in the below application.

2) Antigen recognition, the problem to be solved look as the antigen, network optimize target function should make training sets Mean-square error (MSE) error is the smallest. Antigen as the algorithm is defined as follows:

$$E_i = \frac{1}{n} \sum_{i=1}^{n} (y_i - y_i')^2 \tag{1}$$

In the formula, n is the training sample total, y_i is the first of i antibody corresponding actual output values of neural network, y_i' is the expected output value of neural network.

3) Initial antibody yield, which produce BP network weights and threshold values. In this papers action random generate strategy, initial value between -1 and 1.

4) antibody code, adopt floating-point number to code the weights and threshold, so can effectively overcome the hamming cliff defects of binary code and gray code.

5) Calculate the fitness of antibody, corresponding to the affinity of immune theory concept, fitness function is defined as:

$$F_i = \frac{1}{\xi + E_i} \tag{2}$$

In the formula, ξ is a constant between 0 and 1.

6) Design of antibody concentration, the concentration of antibody is the ratio of t and N, that is, t is the number of similar fitness for antibody in group; N is the total number of antibody.

$$C_i = \frac{t}{N} \tag{3}$$

In the formula, t is the number between ξF_i and F_i, ξ is Similarity coefficient. According to experience, the general value is between 0.8 and 1.0.

7) ■ Select Operation P_s : Select method is based on the concentration of antibody produced adjustment mechanism, in the memory unit updating, if fitness high of antibody, then antibody concentration will continue to improve, but if the concentration reaches a certain value, then it will inhibit the yield of such antibodies; Otherwise, it will promote fitness low antibodies produce and be selected probability. This mechanism ensures the diversity of antibody. The probability of selection based on antibody concentration formula is:

$$p_s = \partial C_i (1 - F_i) + (1 - \partial) F_i \tag{4}$$

In the formula, $\partial \in [0,1]$ is adaptive parameters.

■ Crossover Operation P_c : In this paper, I improved the two point cross method of reference, design the parameters ξ that is adaptive crossover to ensure algorithm doesn't appear "precocious" phenomena in the later.

Set, $X_1^m = [x_1^1 x_2^1 \cdots x_n^1]$, $X_2^m = [x_1^2 x_2^2 \cdots x_n^2]$ are the two antibodies of the m generation. Between i point and j point to do two point arithmetic crossover, then produce the next generation of antibody. The formula is:

$$X_1^{m+1} = [x_1^1 \cdots x_i^{'} \cdots x_j^{'} x_{j+1}^1 \cdots x_n^1]$$
(5)

$$X_2^{m+1} = [x_1^2 \cdots x_i^{''} \cdots x_j^{''} x_{j+1}^2 \cdots x_n^2]$$
(6)

$$x_k^{'} = \xi_m x_k^1 + (1 - \xi_m) x_k^2$$
(7)

$$x_k^{''} = \xi_m x_k^2 + (1 - \xi_m) x_k^1$$
(8)

$$\xi_{m+1} = \begin{cases} \xi_m \dfrac{F_{Max} - F^{'}}{F_{Max} - F_{av}} & F^{'} > F_{av} \\ \xi_m & F^{'} < F_{av} \end{cases}$$
(9)

In the formula, F_{Max} is the biggest fitness value in the antibody group; F_{av} is the average of antibody fitness; $F^{'}$ is the bigger fitness values in the two crossover antibody, $\xi_1 \in [0,1]$.

■ Mutation Operation P_m: In this paper, I will using the reference [6] provide adaptive mutation rate formula for mutation operation, to ensure the diversity of species .the formula is:

$$p_m^i \square \begin{cases} p_m^{i-1} - \dfrac{(p_m^i - p_m^{i-1})*(F_{Max} - F)}{F_{Max} - F_{av}} & F > F_{av} \\ p_m^{i-1} & F < F_{av} \end{cases}$$
(10)

In the formula, P_m^i is mutation rate of the i generation variation individual; F is fitness function value of the variation individual.

8) Termination rules: Repeat the above operating until achieve maximum evolution generation Gen, or to meet network error conditions.

9) Executive BP algorithm operation, take weights and threshold of train completed as BP network final weights and threshold, then to prediction Henan province grain yield.

Designed in according with the above SIGA-BP network steps, this paper draw a corresponding grain yield prediction flow chart, following figure 1 and figure 2:

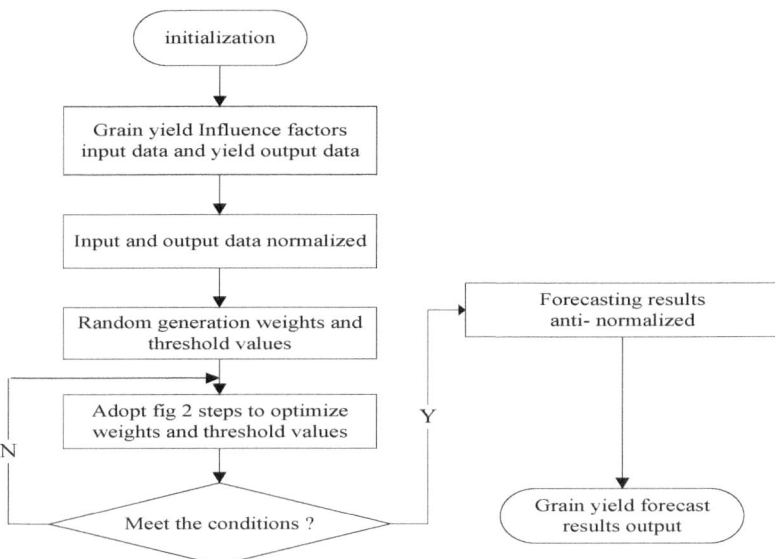

Fig. 1. SIGA-BP Neural network forecast grain yield flow chart

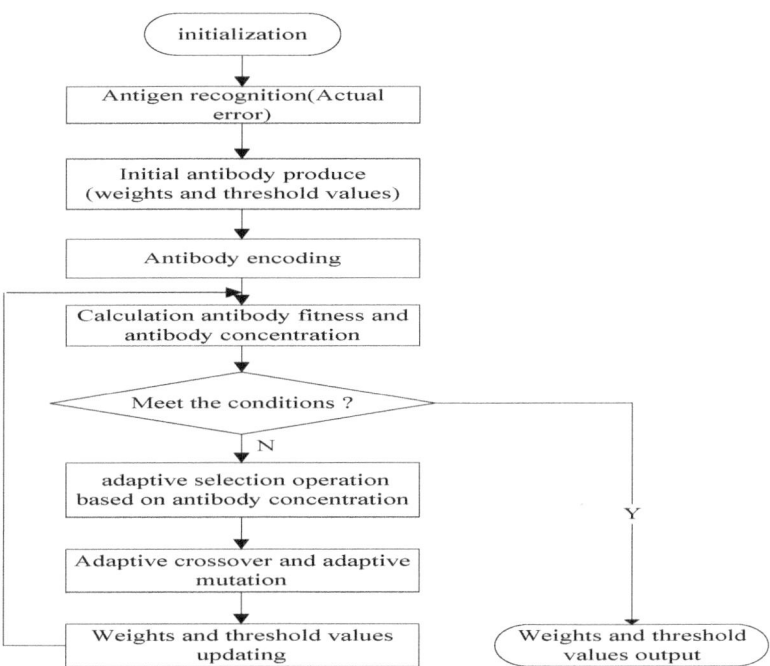

Fig. 2. SIGA optimize Weights and threshold values flow chart

3   Experimental Result Analysis

Grain yield is affected by much factors, it is a complex nonlinear system, some influencing factors is unknown. According to could measure and significance of agriculture. Through consult agricultural material and can be collected data. Finally, through SPSS17.0 software analysis, 12 kinds of major factors to be selected. Mainly as follows: grain grow area, Effective irrigation area, Fertilizer usage, The total power of agricultural machinery, Agricultural electricity consumption, Affected area, Damage area, Pesticides usage, Agricultural plastic mulch, The number of agricultural workers〗 Support agricultural funds devotion, Seed quality Etc 12 kinds of factors. Data from "Henan Statistical Yearbook" (2000-2010) and "Sixty years of new China Statistical Yearbook", take data of 1978-2002 as the training data of model, and 2002-2009 data as validation data.

3.1   Grain Data Normalized and Anti-normalized

Because of the different data units are not the same in the reality, in order to improve the training speed, we need to process the data. And in the BP neural network, data is normalized in general in order to input or output data access to a large area that is neurons activation function, improved the prediction accuracy and convergence speed. Usually input data is limited in between 0 and 1, but because of 0 and 1 are the neural network's upper and lower limits of response function, not to fit as input and output values, so in the experiment using formula(11) to conduct normalized, and forecast results using formula(12) to conduct anti-normalized.

$$Y = 0.1 + 0.8 * \frac{X - X_{min}}{X_{max} - X_{min}} \tag{11}$$

$$X = X_{min} + (Y - 0.1) * \frac{X_{max} - X_{min}}{0.8} \tag{12}$$

3.2   Establish SIGA-BP Grain Yield Prediction Model

In the simulation experiment, MATLAB 7.1 is used to realize SIGA-BP network model of grain yield prediction, and compared with the BP neural network grain yield prediction model.

In the paper, BP neural network use three layer structure. The number of input layer neurons is 12; The number of hidden layer is 18; The number of output layer is 1; The error of network training target is 0.0001; Transfer function of input layers using hyperbolic tangent s-type function; Transfer function of output layers using linear function; Learning rate is 0.01; The maximum training times is 1000; Species size is 120. In the same circumstances that input conditions and parameter setting, two different model to predict grain yield and contrast analysis results. As shown in figure 3 and table 1:

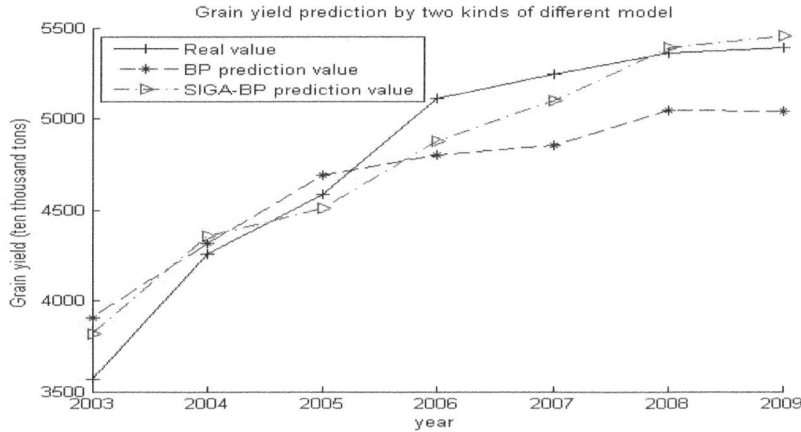

Fig. 3. Predict results comparison by two kinds of model

Table 1. Two kinds of model predict Grain yield of Henan province

Data \ year \ Method	2003	2004	2005	2006	2007	2008	2009	Mean Absolute error	Mean Relative error
Grain real value	3569.47	4260	4582	5112.3	5245.22	5365.48	5389.00		
B P	3908.44	4317.7	4690.61	4801.94	4854.89	5047.88	5042.61		
Absolute error	338.97	57.70	108.61	310.36	390.33	317.60	349.39	267.14	0.0558
Relative error	0.0949	0.0135	0.0237	0.0607	0.0744	0.0592	0.0643		
AIGA--BP	3820.07	4353.93	4509.03	4878.73	5097.55	5390.14	5454.50		
Absolute error	250.60	93.93	72.97	233.57	147.67	24.94	65.50	127.02	0.0284
Relative error	0.0702	0.0220	0.0159	0.0457	0.0282	0.0046	0.0121		

3.3   Experimental Results Contrast

In the paper, using the new built predict model SIGA-BP and BP neural network to predict the grain yield of Henan province, use the grain actual yield of 2003-2009 years as validation data, verify predict model of new construction. The above table 1 contains two different data results that use the different forecast mode. Through the table 1 draw: The mean absolute error of SIGA-BP is only 127.02 ten thousand of tons and the mean relative error is 2.84%. The mean absolute error of improved BP neural network is 267.14 ten thousand of tons and the mean relative error is 5.58%. We can clearly see the SIGA-BP model has a higher accuracy than the BP predict model through the above chart data, and through figure 3 and table 1 we can also see that SIGA-BP model predict result error is more stable, error results change range is smaller than BP model. We can draw the conclusion: the SIGA – BP prediction model can be applied to predict grain yield of Henan province.

4 Conclusion

In this paper, the main task is that together self-adaptive immune genetic algorithm with BP algorithm, present a new predict method of grain yield, namely is SIGA-BP neural network forecast model. The core of this model is that reference the characteristics of immunology and genetics, use the SIGA to optimize weights and threshold values of the BP neural network, then expand the weights search space of neural network, improve the learning efficiency and forecast accuracy of network system. The important is that in the same input conditions and the same parameter setting, through the simulation experiments show that the accuracy of new constructed model for predicting the grain yield is higher, and the stability is better.

References

1. Wang, Y., Li, T.: The research of grain yield prediction based on genetic neural network. Harbin Engineering University (2008)
2. Nikolaev, N.Y., Iba, H.: Learning polynomial feed – forward Neural Networks by genetic programming and back-propagation. IEEE Trans. Neural Networks 14(2), 337 (2003)
3. Zeng, X., Yu, B.: The research of image edge detection based on improved BP neural network. Microelectronics and Computer 26(8), 215–218 (2009)
4. Ji, L., Zhang, X.: Analysis and improvement of BP algorithm. Computer Science and Technology 16(10), 101–104 (2006)
5. Wang, Q., Lv, W., Ren, W.: Immune genetic algorithm and the application review in optimization problems. Computer Application and Research 26(12), 4428–4431 (2009)
6. Qiao, S., Tang, C., Dai, S.: SIAG: A new adaptive immune genetic algorithm. Zhongshan University Journals (Natural Science Edition) 47(3), 6–9 (2008)
7. Yan, X., An, W.: Adaptive immune genetic algorithm. Journal of Applied Mechanics 22(3), 445–448 (2005)
8. Itoh, H.: Genetic algorithm with immune adjustment mechanism. In: Proceeding of the Third IASTED International Conference on Computational Intelligence, pp. 79–84 (2007)

Identification of Friction Parameters Based on Genetic Algorithm in Servo Control System

Lifen Wu

Department of Computer Science and Technology,
JinZhong University, JinZhong, China
wulifenwlf@sina.com

Abstract. The friction is detrimental to the normal work of the servo system, but the friction mechanism is very complicated. In this paper, Tustin friction model is used as the friction parameter identification, reflecting the phenomenon of friction in the system, and laying the foundation for the friction compensation. Tustin model is a nonlinear friction one, and the friction properties can be reflected better with four friction parameters. In this paper, we use genetic algorithms for parameter identification of these parameters, and its search capabilities and more robust than traditional algorithms, to be more accurate recognition results.

Keywords: friction model, genetic algorithm, parameter identification.

1 Introduction

For a long time, the influence of friction in the servo system has always been a tricky problem for the vast number of machinery and control research scholars, and the friction plays a significant role in the position control and low velocity control of high precision servo system, which is the barrier of accelerated system performance[1]. Friction in low speed shows a strong nonlinear characteristics, which can not only make the system produce dead zone or limit cycle in the position servo, which led to steady-state error ,but also make the system produce crawling and oscillation in the speed servo, and even makes the system into chaos of disordered movement, greatly reducing system performance. In order to eliminate or reduce the impact of friction and further improve system performance, the considerable efforts in the mechanical structure have been made by people, but the cost of the way of mechanical structure reconstruction is high and difficult to achieve. It is necessary to identify the friction parameters of this system, compensate friction and reduce the influence on the system performance by the friction.

The model and the algorithm are two keys to determine the accuracy of the friction parameters. The appropriate friction model and the reasonable identification algorithm not only help to correctly understand the mechanism of friction and effectively predict the friction behavior, but also play an active and key role in the control and compensation of the friction servo system [2]. This paper uses Tustin friction model

H. Deng et al. (Eds.): AICI 2011, Part I, LNAI 7002, pp. 43–50, 2011.

and genetic algorithm respectively to do friction parameter identification in the motor servo system.

2 Tustin Friction Model

The nonlinear friction is mainly reflected in the static friction phase, the movement of objects in the vicinity of zero speed, and it will produce nonlinear friction. In 1982, Bo and Paveleseu proposed the index friction model [1]. Since the model can accurately estimate the friction force, and the parameters are few and easy to get, it still has a very wide range of applications. The mathematical description is as follows:

$$F(v) = F_c \, \text{sgn}(v) + (F_s - F_c) e^{-(v/v_s)^{\sigma}} + F_v v \,. \tag{1}$$

Of which: $F(v)$ is the friction; F_c is the Coulomb friction; F_v is the viscous friction coefficient; F_s is the maximum static friction; v_s is the Stribeck velocity, which determines the shape of the Stribeck curve.

Tustin model is a special case in the exponential models, and let $\delta = 1$, so Tustin model is obtained. The mathematical description of the Tustin friction model is as follows:

$$F(v) = F_c \, \text{sgn}(v) + (F_s - F_c) e^{-(v/v_s)} + F_v v \,. \tag{2}$$

The model can well describe the friction force near zero speed, and it contains a delayed exponential item, explains the phenomenon of micro-limit ring. In this paper, Tustin friction model is chosen for the system parameter identification.

3 Genetic Algorithm

Genetic algorithm draws on Darwin's theory of evolution and Mendel's genetics, and imitates natural evolution mechanism [3]. Its essence is an efficient, parallel, global search method. It can automatically acquire and accumulate knowledge about the search space in the search process, and adaptively control the search process to obtain the optimal solution [4]. The traditional optimization algorithm relies on the gradient information of a single evaluation function, and genetic algorithm is the process by simulating the natural evolution to search the optimal solution, which no longer adopts deterministic rules, but stressed that probability transition rules are used to guide the search process. Here we briefly outline the main flow of genetic algorithm.

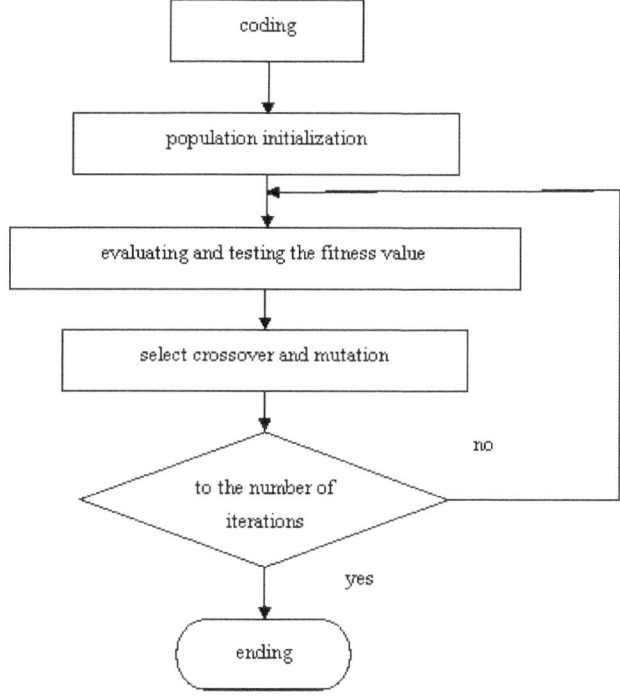

Fig. 1. The main flowchart of genetic algorithm

4   Algorithm Verification

In this paper, we adopt a set of ideal friction parameters as the actual value of the parameter, thus to verify the accuracy of the recognition result. Ideal parameter values in Table 1.

Table 1. Ideal parameter values of Tustin friction model

Parameters	Actual values	Units
F_s	1.5	$[N]$
F_c	1	$[N]$
v_s	0.001	$[m/s]$
F_v	0.4	$[N_s/m]$

Let the speed v = 0.005sin (12πt), and bring the ideal parameter values back to the model. Then a set of friction values F correspondent with the velocity v are obtained. Then v and F are used as known measured values, and four parameters of the model are identified by using the genetic algorithm in this paper. Compare the final results of identification and the actual values of the parameters to verify the rationality of the algorithm.

Set the population size M is 50; crossover probability is 0.75; mutation probability is 0.05; and G is the number of iterations. The initially search range of the parameters is: F_c is [0,10]; F_s is [0,10]; F_v is [0,1]; v_s is [0,10].

Table 2. Comparison of the ideal values and the recognition results

Parameters	Actual values	G=100	G=200	G=400
F_s	1.5	1.426	1.479	1.517
F_c	1	1.368	1.163	0.982
v_s	0.001	0.0016	0.0013	0.00094
F_v	0.4	0.453	0.435	0.408

Fig.2, Fig.3, Fig.4 respectively denotes the corresponding optimal objective function value convergence curves in the case of iteration 100, 200, 400.

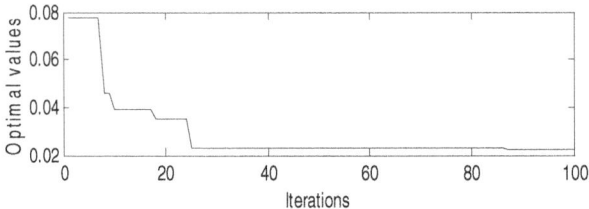

Fig. 2. The convergence curve of 100 iterations corresponding to the optimal objective function value

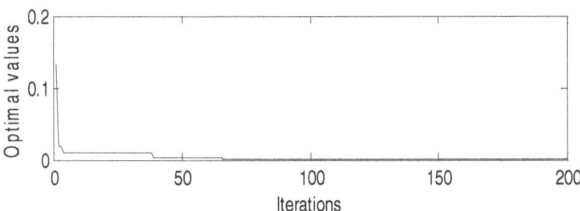

Fig. 3. The convergence curve of 200 iterations corresponding to the optimal objective function value

Seen from Fig.2, Fig.3, Fig.4, with the increase in the number of iterations, the optimal objective function values decrease, while four identified parameters are gradually approaching the true values, and in the case of infinite time, they are able to converge at the optimal solution.

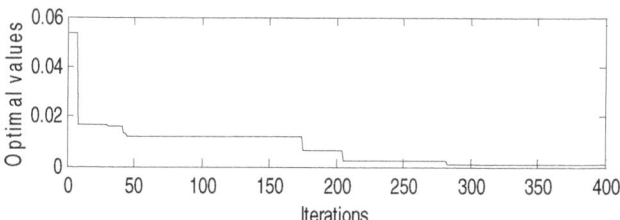

Fig. 4. The convergence curve of 400 iterations corresponding to the optimal objective function value

5 Parameter Identification

The rationality and accuracy of the parameter identification algorithm have been verified. In this paper, binary-coded is used as the encoding method of the genetic algorithm; the best retention strategies in selected operators are adopted, and the individual with the largest fitness value in current population is completely copied to the next generation, which ensure that the final result is the individual with the highest fitness seen for ages; the strategy of two cross is adopted in crossover operators; if the crossover operator is too large, then the fine model of the population will be damaged, while if it is too small, then a new individual will be led to produce slowly, and in this paper, the crossover probability is that Pc = 0.75; the strategy of dynamic mutation probability is adopted in mutation operators.

Fitness function F_i and objective function M are shown in the following Eq. 3 and Eq. 4, and the denominator(M+0.01) of the fitness function F_i is to prevent F_i appearing infinite when M is very small.

$$F_i = \frac{1}{M + 0.01}.$$ (3)

$$M = \frac{1}{n}(\sum_{i=1}^{n}(F - F^*)^2).$$ (4)

In this experiment, the servo system moves with the speed v as a sinusoidal movement pattern, and then the corresponding set of friction force F* is measured. The speed v brought into the Tustin model, the search range of F_c, F_s, F_v and v_s is respectively [0,1], [0,1], [0,0.5]and [0,1].In the process of gradual iteration, the error between F that calculated by the model and F* is getting smaller and smaller, so the number of iterations is ultimately gotten, and the more accurate identification results are achieved. The speed and friction data obtained from experimental tests are shown in Fig. 5.

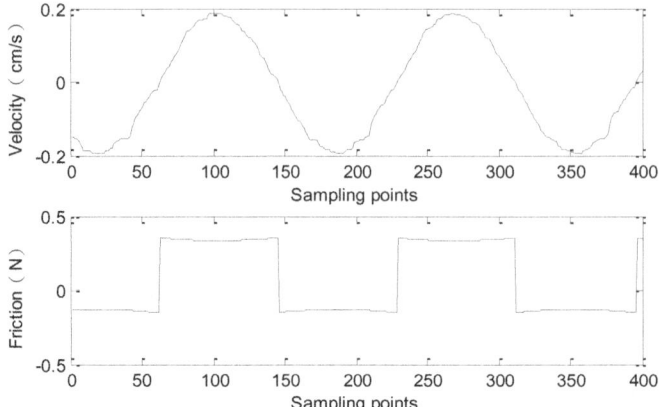

Fig. 5. Experimental data

With the experimental data, Tustin model and genetic algorithm, take the number of iterations G=200, G=500 and G=700 respectively as the friction parameter identification, and recognition results and associated identification diagrams are shown below.

Table 3. Friction parameter identification results of the servo system

Parameters	G=200	G=500	G=700
F_c	0.263	0.245	0.247
F_s	0.388	0.347	0.348
v_s	0.016	0.016	0.012
σ_2	0.037	0.019	0.026

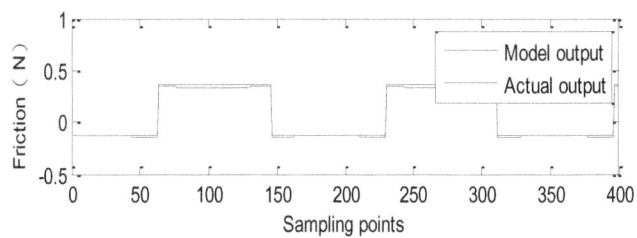

Fig. 6. Corresponding measured output friction and model output of 200 iterations

Comparing Fig. 6, Fig. 7 and Fig. 8, it is easy to know the friction parameter of 700 iterations is more precise.

Compared with the traditional algorithms (such as the exhaustive algorithm, the gradient algorithm, heuristic algorithm, etc), genetic algorithm is no longer a single point of search, but the parallel multi-point search, while the genetic algorithm does not require gradient information, and simply provide the objective function and adaptive function can, search capabilities and more robust than traditional algorithms, to be more accurate recognition results.

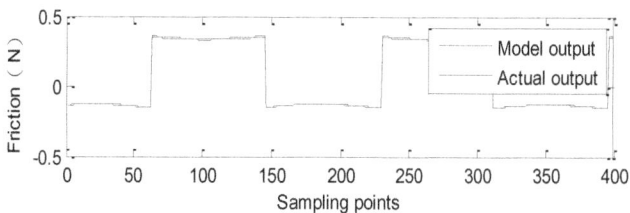

Fig. 7. Corresponding measured output friction and model output of 500 iterations

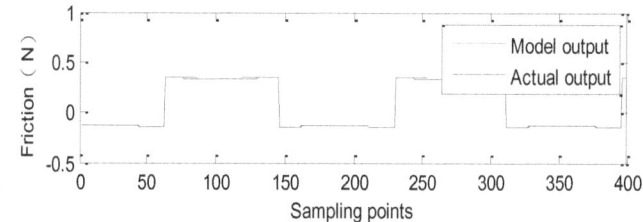

Fig. 8. Corresponding measured output friction and model output of 700 iterations

6 Conclusion

In this paper, friction parameters of the system are identified by genetic algorithm, and the mathematical model which describes the system friction phenomenon more accurately can be obtained. Furthermore the adverse effects of friction on the servo system can be reduced or even eliminated through the friction compensation. The genetic algorithm is applied to the identification, which has practical value in engineering applications.

References

1. Liu, H.: Parameter Identification of Friction Model with Generic Algorithms. Master thesis. Graduate School of Chinese Academy of Sciences (2007)
2. Jiao, Z., Qu, B., Xu, B.: Application of Genetic Algorithm to Friction Compensation in Direct Current Servo Systems. Journal of xi'an JiaoTong University 41(8), 944–948 (2007)
3. Zhang, W., Liang, Y.: Mathematical foundation of genetic algorithms. Southwest JiaoTong University Press, ChengDu (2000)
4. Lan, F., Wang, H.: Genetic Algorithm Programming Based on Matlab. GuangXi Physics 29(1), 32–34 (2008)

5. Yang, S., Zheng, M.: Simulation of Nonlinear Friction With Modeling Methodology. Journal of System Simulation 14(10), 1365–1368 (2002)
6. Wang, Y., He, L., Su, B.: Simulation of the friction model on Simulink. Electric Machines and Control 8(1), 60–62 (2004)
7. Kishore Kumar, R., Sandesh, S., Shankar, K.: Parametric Identification of Nonlinear Dynamic Systems Using Combined Levenberg–Marquardt and Genetic Algorithm. International Journal of Structural Stability and Dynamics 7(4), 715–725 (2007)
8. Altpeter, F.: Friction Modeling, Identification and Compensation. PhD thesis. Ecole Polytechnique Federale de Lausanne (1999)

Modeling of Water Dynamics on Soil in Water Storage Pit Irrigation

Jingling Li, Xihuan Sun, Juanjuan Ma, Jie Cui, Qiuli Liu, and Xing Shen

College of Water Resource Science and Engineering,
Taiyuan University of Technology, Taiyuan 030024 China
lijingling33@163.com

Abstract. In order to improve soil water use efficiency and under water storage pit irrigation condition, the soil water dynamics was evaluated by a two-dimensional model based on the finite volume method. The simulations of soil water content were compared with the water content measurements. The results showed: Good agreement was found between simulated and measured wetting front and water distribution during simulation period. It indicated that the two-dimensional mathematic model for water storage pit irrigation was correct and solving the model with finite volume method was feasible. The mathematical model can be satisfactorily used to describe the soil water properties under water storage pit irrigation.

Keywords: water storage pit irrigation, soil water movement, finite volume method, numerical simulation.

1 Introduction

Drought and soil erosions is one of the important environmental concerns, in the hill and mountain region, North of China, for this case, a water saving irrigation method is put forward—water storage pit irrigation. Water storage pit irrigation is a water saving irrigation and several pits are dug around the trunk of fruit tree in which water is stored for irrigation, through the sides of pits, water is transported to the roots of fruit tree [1], the most important feature of water storage pit irrigation is that it combined water saving irrigation with soil and water conservation, which can effectively solve the questions of drought and soil erosion, in the hill and mountain orchards region, North of China.

The dynamic of water movement in soil can be studied by mathematical modeling in water storage pit irrigation. The mathematical model improve the quantitative understanding of water distribution processes significantly and can be valuable tool in designing environmentally and economically sustainable water applications [2-5]. In this paper, a two-dimensional mathematical model based on the finite volume method that describes water movement is used to simulate the water movement on a sandy loam soil under water storage pit irrigation. The specific objective of the model simulation is to study the soil water content in water storage pit irrigation. The quantification is an important step towards a better management of water storage pit irrigation.

H. Deng et al. (Eds.): AICI 2011, Part I, LNAI 7002, pp. 51–58, 2011.
© Springer-Verlag Berlin Heidelberg 2011

2 Model Description

2.1 The Unsaturated Water Flow

The every layer soil is assumed homogeneous, isotropic porous media, the water infiltration under water storage pit irrigation condition can be considered as a uniform infiltration process which take the center of water storage pit as symmetry axis, then the soil water flow can be simplified the question of two-dimensional plane (Fig.1) according to the axial symmetry characteristics of water infiltration in water storage pit irrigation. The unsaturated water flow for water storage pit irrigation is described by the two-dimensional cylindrical coordinate form of the Richards' equation.

$$\frac{\partial \theta}{\partial t} = \frac{1}{r}\frac{\partial}{\partial r}\left(rK\left(h\right)\frac{\partial h}{\partial r}\right) + \frac{\partial}{\partial z}\left(K\left(h\right)\frac{\partial h}{\partial z}\right) - \frac{\partial K\left(h\right)}{\partial z} \tag{1}$$

where θ is the volumetric water content (cm³/cm³); h is the soil water pressure (cm); K is the soil unsaturated hydraulic conductivity (cm/min); z is the depth taken positive downward (cm); r is the horizon taken positive rightward (cm); and t is time (min).

The unsaturated soil hydraulic properties should be determined accurately, namely, the soil water retention curve, h, and the unsaturated hydraulic conductivity curve, K. these can be described by Van Genuchten equations. This model is represented as

$$\theta(h) = \theta_r + \left(\theta_s - \theta_r\right)\left[1 + |\alpha h|^n\right]^{-m} \tag{2}$$

$$K(h) = K_s S_e^l\left[1 - (1 - S_e^{1/m})^m\right]^2 \tag{3}$$

where

$$S_e = \left(\theta - \theta_r\right) / \left(\theta_s - \theta_r\right) \tag{4}$$

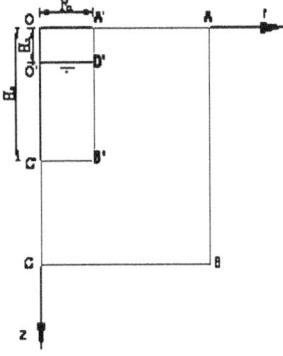

Fig. 1. Profile of water storage pits irrigation

where θ_r and θ_s are the residual and saturated water content (cm^3/cm^3), respectively; Ks is the saturated hydraulic conductivity (cm/min); Se is the effective water content; α is the inverse of the air-entry value; n is a pore-size distribution index; $m=1-1/n$ ($n>1$); and the pore-connectivity parameter l in the hydraulic conductivity function was estimated to be about 0.5 as an average for many soils.

2.2 Initial Conditions and Boundary Conditions

Equation (1) must be supplemented with appropriate initial and boundary conditions for calculating water flux and water content distributions.
1. Initial condition: The initial condition is given by

$$h(r,z,t) = h_0 \qquad t = 0 \tag{5}$$

where h_0 is the initial pressure head (cm)
2. Boundary conditions
   (1) Upper boundary (OA): the upper boundary condition in the model not account for the physical phenomena occurring at the soil surface: evaporation and precipitation. The second-type boundary condition is used

$$-K(h)\frac{\partial h}{\partial z} + K(h) = 0 \qquad t > 0 \tag{6}$$

   (2) Right boundary (AB) and lower boundary (CB):
Right boundary (AB):

$$h(r_{max}, z, t) = h_0 \tag{7}$$

Lower boundary (CB):

$$h(r, z_{max}, t) = h_0 \tag{8}$$

   (3) C'C boundary and A'D' boundary: considering the symmetry of water movement and not account for the pits evaporation, the second-type condition is used

$$-K(h)\frac{\partial h}{\partial r} = 0 \tag{9}$$

   (4) Infiltration boundary (D'B'): a water pressure potential boundary condition (third type) is used

$$h(r_0, z, t) = h_i \tag{10}$$

where r_0 is the radius of water storage pit (cm); hi is i-th position pressure potential of the infiltration side (cm)
   (5) Water storage pit bottom boundary (C'B'): the water storage pit is impermeable by water in order to reduce water deep leakage, a zero flux is assumed

$$-K(h)\frac{\partial h}{\partial z} + K(h) = 0 \tag{11}$$

3   Numerical Solutions by Finite Volume Method

3.1   Selection of Time Step

The time step can be adjusted automatically. Firstly the time step is adopted initially at $\Delta t=1$ min, then it shall be adjusted according to the solutions at time step numbered i for the next time step $i+1$ as follows:

$$\Delta t_{i+1} = \begin{cases} \alpha \Delta t_i, & \delta > 0.3 \\ \Delta t_i, & 0.08 < \delta < 0.3 \\ \beta \Delta t_i, & \delta < 0.08 \end{cases} \tag{12}$$

where δ is the relative variation ratio of the water head at time step i (h^i) , to that at previous time step i-$1(h^{i-1})$, α is a reduction factor valued as 0.75, β is an amplification factor with the value 1.5, the time step will increase till it reaches 5 min.

3.2   The Space and Time Discretization

The finite volume method is used to obtain a solution of (1) subject to the imposed initial and boundary conditions. The calculation region is divided into a series of rectangle grid system (control volume) and the variable is stored in the center of control volume. Applying the basic idea of the finite volume method [6], the discrete equation was deduced by control volume integral method, and realized by numerical method. The discrete equations are solved by using the Gaussian iteration algorithm, because of the nonlinearity, the solution cannot be calculated explicitly. Therefore, iteration is required within each time step to update the coefficient matrices. The values of pressure head, $h(r,z,t)$, are then used to compute $K(r,z,t)$. Applying the Basic Idea of the finite volume method to (1), only the most pertinent steps in the solution process are given here.

$$\int_t^{t+\Delta t} \int_{\Delta v} \frac{\partial \theta}{\partial t} dvdt = \int_t^{t+\Delta t} \int_{\Delta v} \frac{1}{r} \frac{\partial}{\partial r} \left(rK(h) \frac{\partial h}{\partial r} \right) dvdt + \int_t^{t+\Delta t} \int_{\Delta v} \frac{\partial}{\partial z} \left(K(h) \frac{\partial h}{\partial z} \right) dvdt - \int_t^{t+\Delta t} \int_{\Delta v} \frac{\partial K(h)}{\partial z} dvdt \tag{13}$$

Applying Gauss dimension reduction law first identity to (13), the final discrete format is given by

$$\left(C_p^{\ k} - a_P \right) h_P^{\ k+1} = a_W h_W^{\ k+1} + a_E h_E^{\ k+1} + a_N h_N^{\ k+1} + a_S h_S^{\ k+1} + b + C_p^{\ k} h_P^{\ k} - \left(\theta_P^{\ k} - \theta_P^{\ 0} \right) \tag{14}$$

where $k+1$ and k are current and last iteration number, respectively; $C_p^{\ k}$ is specific water capacity, 1/cm; $\theta_p^{\ k}$ and $\theta_p^{\ 0}$ are the soil water content of current time and that of last time, respectively, cm^3/cm^3.

4   Material and Methods

4.1   Material and Methods

The soil saturated hydraulic conductivity and the soil water characteristic curve were determined by using a constant-head parameter (TST-55A) and a centrifuge, respectively. All the experimental data were fitted by the RETC, namely, θr, θs, Ks, α and n were 0.022 cm^3/cm^3, 0.468 cm^3/cm^3, 0.007422 cm/min, 0.00687 and 1.424, respectively.

The soil sample was collected from apple orchards at Beiwang Village, Taigu County, Shanxi Province of China. A large volume of soil was obtained and air dried for the same time at the same temperature. The basic physical properties of the tested soil are presented in Table 1:

Table 1. The basic physical properties of the tested soil

Particle Sizes		
≤0.002mm	0.002~0.05mm	0.05~2mm
4.322	70.34	21.024
Field Capacity cm^3/cm^3	Initial Water Content cm^3/cm^3	Saturated Water Content cm^3/cm^3
0.22	0.024	0.486

The experimental setup consisted of a 300 wedge-shaped plexiglass containers, 120 cm high and with a 100-cm radius, the water storage pit was located at the corner of the soil container, the bottom of the water storage pit is impermeable by water (in order to reduce water deep leakage) (Fig. 2). The completely mixed air-dry soil was passed through a 2-mm sieve and packed in the container with 5-cm increments to obtain a constant bulk density of 1.4 g/cm^3.

The water was added to the soil through a Mariotte tube with a flexible hose. The outlet was located on the water storage pit at the corner of the soil container. To maintain zero evaporation at the soil surface, the soil was covered with a polyethylene sheet. The irrigation amount is 6L.

During the experiment, the positions of the moving wetting front on the soil surface and in the vertical plane were recorded visually at several times. After a predetermined volume of water had been applied, the soil was sampled with a metal tube (inside diameter 1 cm) after water applied. The sampling layout was radial intervals of 5 cm and vertical intervals of 10 cm, starting 20 cm from the center of water storage pit and moving outward to the edge of the wetted front.

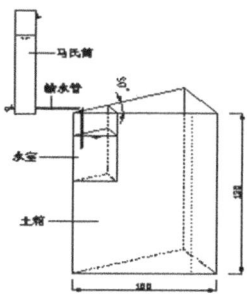

Fig. 2. Equipment for water storage pits infiltration

4.2 Statistical Evaluation of Simulated Results

The quantitative procedures of model evaluation consisted of the use of the statistical analysis to calculate the average error (E), the root mean square error (RMSE), the root mean square (RMS), the modelling efficiency (EF) and the coefficient of residual mass (CRM) between the measured and simulated water content values.

These relationships have the form.

$$E = \sum_{i=1}^{n} (S_i - M_i) / n \tag{15}$$

$$RMSE = 100 \left(\sum_{i=1}^{n} (S_i - M_i)^2 / n \right)^{1/2} \Big/ M \tag{16}$$

$$RMS = 100 \left(\sum_{i=1}^{n} (S_i - M_i)^2 / n \right)^{1/2} \tag{17}$$

$$EF = \left(\sum_{i=1}^{n} (M_i - M)^2 - \sum_{i=1}^{n} (S_i - M_i)^2 \right) \Big/ \sum_{i=1}^{n} (M_i - M)^2 \tag{18}$$

$$CRM = \left(\sum_{i=1}^{n} M_i - \sum_{i=1}^{n} S_i \right) \Big/ \sum_{i=1}^{n} M_i \tag{19}$$

where M_i and S_i are the simulated and measured value of water content, respectively and n is the number of water content values. The optimum values of E, RMSE, RMS, EF and CRM criteria are 0, 0, 0, 1, 0 respectively. Positive values of CRM indicate that the model underestimates the measurements and negative values for CRM indicate a tendency to overestimate.

5 Model Verification and Discussion

5.1 Wetting Front

Figure 3 shows the comparison of the observed and simulated positions of soil wetting front at different time. The results show that, although there were somewhat deviations for soil wetting front positions in the upper and bottom position of wetting soil, there was a good agreement between simulated and observed positions. A possible explanation for the deviations might be the possible effect of compensation accuracy of Mariotte tube. Alternatively the effect of soil macrospore flow might be underestimated.

5.2 Water Content in Soil

Comparison between measured and simulated soil water content are shown in Fig.4. The results in Fig.4 show that the soil water content was redistribution after water applied, the water content decreased gradually with increasing of radial distance from water storage pit, there was little water content on the soil surface, while there was a

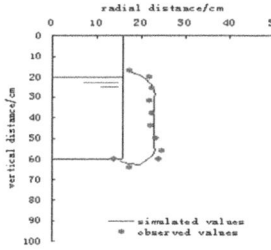 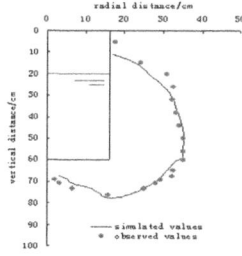

Fig. 3. Observed and computed positions of soil wetting front at different time (t=1h and t=12h)

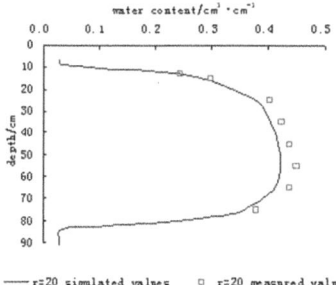 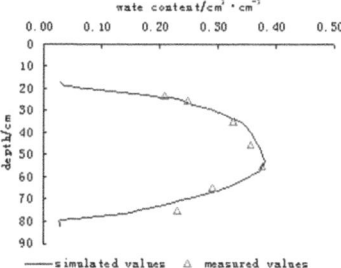

Fig. 4. Comparison between measured and simulated soil water content (r=20, r=30, t=24h)

maximum near the bottom of water storage pit. From this we can see, water content was distributed mainly in middle-deep layer of soil, which can prevent effectively water form evaporating.

Comparison between simulated and measured water content in Fig.4 show that, although there were somewhat deviations in several values, the statistical criteria of quantitative model evaluation were summarized as follows, E=-0.0138, RMSE=7.33%, RMS=2.497%, EF=0.903, CRM=0.00928, the numerical calculation error was small, there was a good agreement between simulated and measured water content.

6   Conclusion

A two-dimensional mathematical model on soil water movement for water storage pit irrigation is proposed and solved by finite volume method. The results showed: good agreement was obtained between simulated and measured wetting front and soil water content. The maximum relative error was less than 10%, the numerical calculation error was small that conforms to practical word needs. It indicated that the two-dimensional mathematic model was correct and solving the model with finite volume method was feasible. The accuracy of the simulation results was appropriate for decision-making purposes.

Acknowledgments. This study was financially supported by the National Natural Science Foundation of China and Key Project of Science and Technology Department of Shanxi Province of China.

References

1. Sun, X.H.: Water storage pit irrigation and its functions of soil and water conservation. Journal of Soil and Water Conservation 16, 130–131 (2002)
2. Guo, X.H., Sun, X.H., Ma, J.J.: Numerical simulation for root zone soil moisture movement of apple orchard under rainfall-irrigation-evaporation. Transactions of the Chinese Society for Agricultural Machine 40, 68–73 (2009)
3. Guo, W.H., Sun, X.H., Pan, J.F., Qiu, Y.Q.: Numerical simulation on soil moisture movement of non-homogeneous soil in single water storage pit. Journal of Taiyuan University of Technology 33, 214–218 (2002)
4. Ma, J.J., Sun, X.H., Li, Z.B.: Numerical simulation of homogenous soil moisture movement under varying-head infiltration of single water storage pit. Transactions of the CSAE 22, 205–207 (2006)
5. Ma, J.J., Sun, X.H., Guo, X.H., Li, Y.Y.: Numerical simulation on soil water movement under water storage pits irrigation. Transactions of the Chinese Society for Agricultural Machine 41, 46–51 (2010)
6. Lü, S.J., Qiao, Y., Liu, G.L.: Numerical simulation for one-dimensional unsaturated soil solute transport. Research of Soil and Water Conservation 19, 57–59 (2008)

Maneuvering Target Tracking Based on Swarm Intelligent Unscented Particle Filtering

Yue-Long Wang[1,2] and Fu-Chang Ma[1]

[1] Control Technology Research Institute, Taiyuan University of Technology,
Taiyuan 030024, China
[2] College of Electrical and Power Engineering, Taiyuan University of Technology,
Taiyuan 030024, China
wy_spring@163.com

Abstract. To improve the performance of maneuvering target tracking, a based on Swarm intelligent unscented particle filtering was proposed. In the new filter, application of the un-scented Kalman filter is used to generate the proposal distribution. Moreover, by introducing the thought of artificial fish school algorithm into particle filtering, the particle distribution and filtering accuracy can be improved. In simulation experiment, "Coordinated Turns" model is taken as dynamic model of maneuvering target. The simulation results show that unscented particle filtering optimized by the artificial fish swarm algorithm (AFSA-UPF) has quite higher tracking precision than the PF and UPF by analyzing the tracking performance and the root-mean-square error.

Keywords: Maneuver target tracking, Unscented particle filter, Artificial fish swarm algorithm.

1 Introduction

The primary aim of tracking a target is to exactly estimate state information of moving targets. In actual tracking system, however, when the target is under the condition of maneuvering state, such as change abruptly in movement or direction and occultation, etc and along with the enhancing of the targets maneuvering capability, one is faced with model uncertainties and a lock of statistical characteristics on the exogenous disturbance signals and noises. For reasons such as noted above, the system of maneuvering target tracking is described nonlinear. In order to solve the problem of nonlinear filtering, it is necessary to obtain a complete description of posteriori conditional probability density, which, however, is found almost impossible according to actual situation. As a result, in all practical applications, the nonlinear filtering is performed by using some form of approximation techniques such as the extended Kalman filter (EKF), the unscented Kalman filter (UKF) [1-2]. As EKF does not take cognizance of the amplitude of deviations during its computational cycle, errors may accumulate and the EKF loses track. The UKF uses a deterministic sampling approach to capture mean and covariance estimates, but cannot altogether avoid the problems of non-Gaussianity.

H. Deng et al. (Eds.): AICI 2011, Part I, LNAI 7002, pp. 59–65, 2011.
© Springer-Verlag Berlin Heidelberg 2011

The particle filtering (PF) [3], which is more capable of dealing with nonlinear and non-Gaussian system estimation problems, uses sequential Monte Carlo methods for on-line learning within a Bayesian framework. The conventional particle filtering approach is to use the state transition density as the proposal importance function, and draw particles from the above importance function. Because the state transition function does not take into account the most recent observation, the particles drawn from transition density may have very low likelihood, and their contributions to the posterior estimation become negligible. Therefore a standard PF suffers form degeneracy phenomenon as well as sample impoverishment. It may be noted that the use of appropriate importance function is significantly. In this paper, we propose swarm intelligent [4] unscented particle filtering [5] and apply this new approach to the problem of Maneuvering target tracking.

2 The Unscented Particle Filtering

2.1 The Unscented Kalman Filtering

The state and the measurement equations are

$$\begin{cases} x_k = f(k, x_{k-1}, v_{k-1}) \\ z_k = h(k, x_k, w_k) \end{cases} \tag{1}$$

where $x \in R^n$ denotes the state at time k and $z_k \in R^m$ is the corresponding measurement, $f(\cdot)$ and $h(\cdot)$ are system and measurement equations, respectively, v_k and w_k are system and measurement noises, respectively. The UKF algorithm is summarized in the following steps (For $k=1, 2..., N$):

- Selection of sigma points and weights for the states and covariance matrices

$$\begin{cases} x_{k-1}^0 = \hat{x}_{k-1}^0, \quad w_0 = \dfrac{\lambda}{n_s + \lambda} \\ x_{k1}^i = \hat{x}_{k-1}^i + (\sqrt{(n_s + \lambda)P_{k-1}})_i, \quad w_i = \dfrac{1}{2(n_s + \lambda)} \quad (i=1,2,\cdots n_s) \\ x_{k-1}^i = \hat{x}_{k-1}^i - (\sqrt{(n_s + \lambda)P_{k-1}})_i, \quad w_i = \dfrac{1}{2(n_s + \lambda)} \quad (i=n_s+1,\cdots,2n_s) \end{cases} \tag{2}$$

where n_s is the number of the states in the augmented state vector; $\lambda = \alpha^2(n_s + \kappa) - n_s$ is a scaling parameter with α determining how the sigma points are spread, typical value is 10-3, κ is a scaling parameter which can be used to incorporate up to fourth order precision in the transformation, usually set to zero. Where $(\sqrt{(n_s + \lambda)P_{k-1}})_i$ is the ith column of the matrix square root of $\sqrt{(n_s + \lambda)P_{k-1}}$.

- The predicted mean and covariance are computed as.

$$P_{k/k-1} = \sum_{i=0}^{2n_s} w_i \, (x_{k/k-1}^i - \sum_{i=0}^{2n_s} w_i x_{k/k-1}^i)(x_{k/k-1}^i - \sum_{i=0}^{2n_s} w_i x_{k/k-1}^i)^T + Q_{k/k-1} \tag{3}$$

$$P_{zz} = \sum_{i=0}^{2n_s} w_i \, (z_{k/k-1}^i - \sum_{i=0}^{2n_s} w_i z_{k/k-1}^i)(z_{k/k-1}^i - \sum_{i=0}^{2n_s} w_i z_{k/k-1}^i)^T + R_{k/k-1} \tag{4}$$

$$P_{xz} = \sum_{i=0}^{2n_s} w_i \, (x_{k/k-1}^i - \sum_{i=0}^{2n_s} w_i x_{k/k-1}^i)(z_{k/k-1}^i - \sum_{i=0}^{2n_s} w_i z_{k/k-1}^i)^T \tag{5}$$

- Update the state and covariance

$$\hat{x}_k = \hat{x}_{k/k-1} + P_{xz} P_z^{-1}(z_k - z_{k/k-1}) \tag{6}$$

$$P_k = P_X - (P_{xz} P_z^{-1}) P_Z (P_{xz} P_z^{-1})^T \tag{7}$$

2.2 Unscented Particle Filtering Algorithm

The distributions generated by the UKF generally have a broad overlap with the true posterior distribution which is partly due to the fact that the UKF computes the posterior covariance accurately to the third order (Gaussian prior) .All in all, the UKF is more likely to generate more accurate proposal distributions within the particle filtering framework. The unscented particle filtering algorithm is presented as follows

- Draws N samples equally from the initial density function ρ_0 and yields
  $\{ x_0^i, i=1,2,\ldots,N\}$,set $\hat{x}_0^i = E(x_0^i)$ and $P_0^i = E[(x_0^i - \hat{x}_0^i)(x_0^i - \hat{x}_0^i)^T]$ at time $k=0$.
- For k = 1, 2…, carry out the following steps:

Steps 1: For i=1: N, update the particles using the UKF algorithm.

Steps 2: Sampling: $x_k^i \sim q(x_k^i / x_{0:k}^i, z_{k/k-1}) = N(\hat{x}_k^i, P_k)$.

Steps3: Calculate importance weights for i=1: N, $w_k^i = w_{k-1}^i \dfrac{p(z_k / \hat{x}_k^i) p(\hat{x}_k^i / x_{k-1}^i)}{q(\hat{x}_k^i / \hat{x}_{0:k-1}^i, z_{1:k})}$.

Steps 4: For i=1: N, normalize the importance weights as $w_k^i = w_k^i / \sum_{i=1}^{N} w_k^i$.

- Estimate the mean state and covariance matrices of the set.

$$\hat{x}_k = \sum_{i=1}^{N} x_k^i w_k^i \tag{8}$$

$$P_k = \sum w_k^i (x_k^i - \hat{x}_k)(x_k^i - \hat{x}_k)^T \tag{9}$$

3   Unsccented Particle Filtering Optimized by the Artificial Fish Swarm Algorithm

Current implementations of the UPF for state estimation have considered the model error and measurement error covariances as constant and determined, but resulting in a large estimation error during sudden changes in state of the target. A solution to solve above problem can be possible using the unscented particle filtering optimized by the artificial fish swarm algorithm (AFSA-UPF).

3.1   Artificial Fish Swarm Algorithm

Artificial fish swarm algorithm (AFSA) [6-7] is an artificial intelligent algorithm based on the simulation of the fish swarm behaviors inside water.

Suppose there are N fishes in the colony. The current state of a AF is a vector $X_i = (x_1, x_2, \ldots, x_n)$, where X_i is the variable to be optimized. The food consistence of AF in the current position is represented by $Y = F(x)$, where Y is the objective function. The distance between the ith and jth individual AF can be expressed as $d_{ij} = ||X_j - X_i||$. A positive constant v represents the ray of a closed neighborhood of X_i. The AFSA is implemented by the following two main behaviors of artificial fish.

- Searching Behavior

If $Y_i < Y_j$, $X_{inext} = X_i + r \cdot s \cdot \dfrac{X_j - X_i}{\left\| X_j - X_i \right\|}$; Else $X_{inext} = X_i + r \cdot s$ .Where r $\in (0, 1)$ is a

random numbers, s is maximal moving step.

- Swarming behavior
- An AF at current state X_i seeks the companion's number N_f and their central position X_c in ``visual scope" of point x $(d_{ij} < v)$; if $Y_c/ N_f > \delta Y_i$, it means that at the center of the fish colony, there is enough food and it is not too crowded. Mathematical   expression   of   the   swarming   behavior:

If $\dfrac{Y_c}{N_f} > \delta \cdot Y_i$, $X_{inext} = X_i + r \cdot s \dfrac{X_c - X_i}{\left\| X_c - X_i \right\|}$; Else return searching behavior.

In the initial state of the algorithm, the variable of trial number should be defined according to the related facts

3.2   Unscented Particle Filtering Optimized by the Artificial Fish Swarm Algorithm

- Initialization: k=0, Draws N samples { $x_0^i, i=1,2,\ldots,N$} $\sim N(\hat{x}_0, P_0)$.
- For k = 1, 2..., carry out the following steps.

Steps 1: For i=1: N, update the particles using the UKF algorithm objective function is

chosen as $Y = [2\pi \hat{P}_k^i]^{-\frac{1}{2}} e^{-\frac{1}{2\hat{P}_k^i}(z_k - \hat{z}_k^i)^2}$.

Steps 2: Particles constantly update themselves towards a more realistic state by the artificial fish swarm algorithm.

Steps 4: Calculate importance weights and normalize the importance weights for $i = 1 : N$.

- Estimate the mean state and covariance matrices of the set by Eq. (8) and (9).

4 Simulation and Results

4.1 Simulation Model for Maneuvering Target Tracking

In order to verify the performance of AFSA-UPF in tracking a maneuvering target, computer simulations are conducted. Estimation performance is compared with UPF and standard particle filter in the following example:

Radar tracks objective performing coordinated turn. The system and measurement equations are given by

$$
X_k = \begin{bmatrix} 1 & \dfrac{\sin(\omega_k T)}{\omega_k} & 0 & -\dfrac{1-\cos(\omega_k T)}{\omega_k} & 0 \\ 0 & \cos(\omega_k T) & 0 & -\sin(\omega_k T) & 0 \\ 0 & \dfrac{1-\cos(\omega_k T)}{\omega_k} & 1 & \dfrac{\sin(\omega_k T)}{\omega_k} & 0 \\ 0 & \sin(\omega_k T) & 0 & \cos(\omega_k T) & 0 \\ 0 & 0 & 0 & 0 & 1 \end{bmatrix} X_{k-1} + \begin{bmatrix} 0.5T^2 & 0 & 0 \\ T & 0 & 0 \\ 0 & 0.5T^2 & 0 \\ 0 & T & 0 \\ 0 & 0 & T \end{bmatrix} W_{K-1} \tag{10}
$$

$$
Z_k = \begin{bmatrix} \sqrt{x_k^2 + y_k^2} \\ \text{artan} \dfrac{y_k}{x_k} \end{bmatrix} + V_k \tag{11}
$$

Where the State vector $X_K = [x_k, \dot{x}_k, y_k, \dot{y}_k, w_k]$; x and $\dot{x}$ are respectively the position and velocity of the moving object long the Cartesian frame X axis; and, y, $\dot{y}$ along the Y axis, ω denotes the turn rate, T are the data sampling time. We assume that the system noises W_k and measurement noises V_k are distributed by N (0, Q) and N (0, R), respectively.

Suppose the target's initial position and velocity are (x, y) = (100, 100) in meters and ($\dot{x}, \dot{y}$) = (10, −20) in m/s. The target's positions are sampled at every T=1s.The target normally moves with constant speed unless stated. It starts respectively at a 1° turn for 11≤k≥30 and at a -4° turn at for.

4.2 Simulation Results

To compare the performance of the three algorithms, Fig. 1 gives the two-dimensional target position and the tracking trajectory of each algorithm. Fig.2 depicts the RMS error in X directional axis and Y directional axis. Obviously, three filters all can keep good tracking performance in the initial stages of the tracking. However, when the

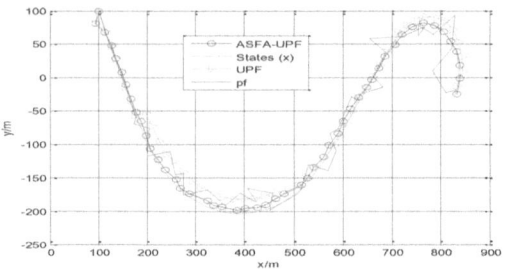

Fig. 1. Tracking trajectory of each algorithm

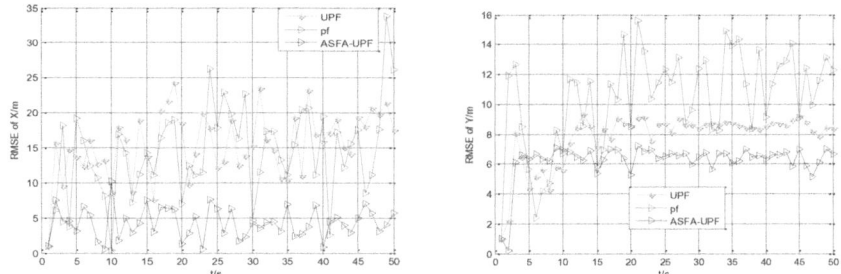

Fig. 2. RMSE of X direction and Y direction

target is under the condition of maneuvering state, the tracking trajectory of the AFSA-UPF gives a better performance compared with the UPF and PF. Simulation results shows that AFSA-UPF guarantees the estimation precision of target compared with PF and EKF in maneuvering target tracking.

5 Conclusion

In this paper, an algorithm based on the swarm intelligent unscented particle filtering has been suggested and applied for the maneuvering target tracking. The experimental results show that the filter is less sensitive to uncertainty in the exogenous signals statistics and dynamical model, can achieve higher prediction precision compared with the PF and the UPF. It indicates that the proposed method is effective and practicable in maneuvering targets state prediction of the tracking system. Next steps of our works should consider finding a better method to save computation time and further improve the robust of the estimation.

References

1. Bar-Shalom, Y., Li, X.R., Kirubarajan, T.: Estimation with applications to tracking and na-vigation: theory, algorithm and software. Wiley, New York (2001)
2. Huerta, J.M., Vidal, J.: Mobile tracking using UKF, time measures and LOS-NLOS expert knowledge. In: IEEE. Dept. of Signal Theory and Communications, University Polytechnic de Catalunya Jordigirona (2005)

3. Haug, A.J.: A tutorial on Bayesian estimation and tracking techniques applicable to nonlinear and non-Gaussian processes. MITRE Technical Report (2005)
4. Park, C.S., Tahk, M.J., Bang, H.: Multiple Aerial Vehicle Formation Using Swarm Intelligence. In: AIAA Guidance, Navigation, and Conference and Exhibit, pp. 5729–5737. AIAA, Austin (2003)
5. van der Merwe, R., Doucet, A., de Freitas, N., et al.: The unscented particle filte. Cambridge University Engineering Department (2000)
6. Li, X.L., Ma, H., Zhang, C.J.: Embedded Bionic Intelligence Optimization Scheme for Complex Systems. In: IEEE Int. Conf. Information Acquisition, pp. 1359–1363. IEEE, Weihai (2006)
7. Li, X.: A New Intelligence Optimization Method: Artificial Fish School Algorithm. Zhejiang University, Hangzhou (2003)

The Bounded Rationality Model-Based Game Intelligent Decision-Making Method

Qiang Zhou[1], Chunming Gao[1], and Zhigang Meng[2]

[1] Engineering Laboratory Building 454, Hunan University, Changsha, 410082, China
[2] Computer Building 411, Central South University, Changsha, 410083, China
{zhon7491456,gcm211}@163.com, mzg541@126.com

Abstract. Based on humanity, efficiency and maintainability of the intelligent design requirement, this article presents a novel game intelligent decision-making method through comparing with the other intelligent decision-making methods. The NPCs perception and decision-making process were respectively illustrated from two aspects-bounded rationality and satisfactory criterion, which are the core characteristics of the bounded rationality model. And the introduced criterions overcome the drawback concerning the 'perceived blind spot' by the perception sensitivity and enhance the intelligence by the utility function. Finally, it verifies the advantages of this method by the intelligent football battle platform.

Keywords: Game, intelligent decision-making method, bounded rationality model, bounded rationality, satisfactory criterion.

1 Introduction

In the past 10 years, many game AI researchers and developers have often regarded the AI technology as a 'smart' code driving the video game's NPCs (Non-Player Characters). And this 'smart' mainly represents that the NPCs can complete path planning, collision avoidance or the other external behaviors, which can be looked as a lower-level intelligence. Nowadays, by introducing neural networks, genetic algorithms, artificial life, cognitive models, and the other theories concerning the human behavior, they can let the NPCs learn and simulate strategies and behavioral pattern which the players use in the video game to improve NPCs' intelligence, therefore, the NPCs would be able to autonomously and really make intelligent decision and interact with the environment in the complex game scene. Therefore it would greatly enhance the gameplay and immersion in playing games.

The major design criterions of the game artificial intelligence include humanity, efficiency and maintainability, etc. Comparing the common intelligent decision-making method, this article will use model-based intelligent decision-making method to enhance the control of decision-making models. And in order to make more intelligent NPCs, this article introduces the bounded rationality model of the behavioural decision theory to model-based decision -making method. So the new

H. Deng et al. (Eds.): AICI 2011, Part I, LNAI 7002, pp. 66–73, 2011.

method not only reserves the efficiency and maintainability of the model-based method, but also contains the humanity of the bounded rationality model.

2 Related Work

According to the different needs of video games, the AI researchers design different game intelligent decision-making systems to solve the game intelligent problems.

Since the 1970s, the rule-based intelligent decision making method [1], as the games leading technology of artificial intelligence, has began to be widely used in many games, such as Pong, Pac-Man, Joust and other simple games or Warcraft Ⅲ, Quake, Simbionic and other massive multiplayer games. This method based on a set of established facts and man's knowledge of specific problem areas, simulates the pattern of human inertial thinking and reasoning, so as to make the decision-making system more coherent and understandable. However, the fragile and instable rules largely influenced by the developer intelligence lead to the decrease of the NPCs' intelligence, moreover, they will increase the cost of development and maintenance.

In order to solve these problems rules system facing, Jeff Orkin is the first to propose the method of goal-based intelligent decision-making method [2] in 2003, and then he successfully has used this method in the F.E.A.R [3]. This method constructs planners to simulate the planning process when people have the explicit goal, and output a set of behaviors which meets the goal or the pre-conditions. Consequently, it breaks the restrict of the rules to make the NPCs' behaviors more natural and various, at the same time, improve the reusability of the module. But in the dynamic real-time scenes, if the NPCs face the multi-goals and the complicated problem about the execution behaviors, this method cannot solve all of these problems.

Game AI researchers seek a breakthrough in many ways, such as the strategy, need, model, etc, to meet the NPCs' demand for intelligent decision-making in a dynamic real-time scene. Among these ways, the model-based intelligent decision-making method [4] has successfully been transplanted into the SOAR intelligent engine to strengthen the intelligence of the Quake Ⅲ. This method contains many decision-making models, and system solves the decision-making problems through managing, manipulating and modifying these model's parameters and dates. Hence, it improves the system's efficiency and flexibility, and also lets the modification and maintenance more convenient. If using this method to design an effective intelligent decision-making system, the basic architecture of decision-making model is considered key point in system design.

3 The Design of Decision-Making Model

People generally implement strategies and behaviors by collecting the world information, assessing their own knowledge and ability, and adding some individual emotion and personality factors. The above process is also called behavioural decision theory. So the bounded rationality model, as the classical model of behavioural decision theory, is applied to the model-based intelligent decision-making method. It not only retain the original advantages of decision method, for instance flexibility, efficiency, convenience, etc, but also can make the NPCs possess human characteristics.

3.1 Bounded Rationality Model

Bounded Rationality Model [5], known as Simmon's Model or Bounded Rationality Model, develops on the two basic propositions, completely rational and optimization principle of the rational decision model facing problems in the theoretical description and practical application. Simon aiming at these two respects puts forward consequential amendments.

Therefore, bounded rationality and satisfactory criterion as the core propositions of the bounded rationality model, could correct the rational decision-making model of radical past and fit man's choices in the real world. Hence, we also consider the above two basic aspects in the design and implementation of intelligent decision – making models.

3.2 Bounded Rationality

In order to make the NPCs independently control their own behaviors and internal states in the absence of human intervention, the system requires them to continually detect scene changes and collect information, so as to make a final decision pursuant to the information changes. The principle of bounded rationality makes the NPCs obtain the information in the perceptible scope. In the past games, the scope of game NPCs perception including auditory sense, visual sense, olfactory sense, as well as other aspects perception, is initialized as the discrete set of variables, and the area outside of the scope for game NPCs was 'perceived blind spot'. However, in reality, this area is not entirely non-perception, but is a declining model.

In the case of visual perception system, people have two eyes, a total visual range 200 °, and 120 ° of the visual overlap (binocular) [6]. People focus the light behind the eyes, and detect light and color with the rod cells and cone cells. Visual sensitivity in the center of fixation is the strongest area, and rapidly weakens as the distance to the center. Based on the human visual perception theory, there are two major problems while games use cone and visual range to ascertain the visual perception scope:

Overestimate the distant edges of the visual scope, and overlook near visual scope.
Set outside the visual scope as a non-visual scope.

In order to solve the above problems, and to let the NPCs maximize the simulation of human visual perception, this article creates a new visual model(Figure 1):

Assumption 1: The maximum ascertainable angle is ω;
Assumption 2: Within the ascertainable visual angle the range of visibility is from a to b;
Assumption 3: Outside of the visual scope the visual susceptibility showed exponent;
Assumption 4: If the visual susceptibility is less than 50%, these data are automatically ignored by the NPCs;
Based on the above assumptions, the boundary line equations of the ascertainable visual scope is:

$$f(x) = \begin{cases} x \cdot \cot(\omega/2) \\ -x \cdot \cot(\omega/2) \\ -(e^{kx} + e^{-kx})/2 + a + 1 \end{cases} \quad (\theta = \frac{180 - \omega}{2}, |x| < b \cdot \cos\theta, d = a + 1 - 2b \cdot \sin\theta, k = \frac{\ln\frac{d + \sqrt{d-4}}{2}}{b \cdot \cos\theta}). \quad (1)$$

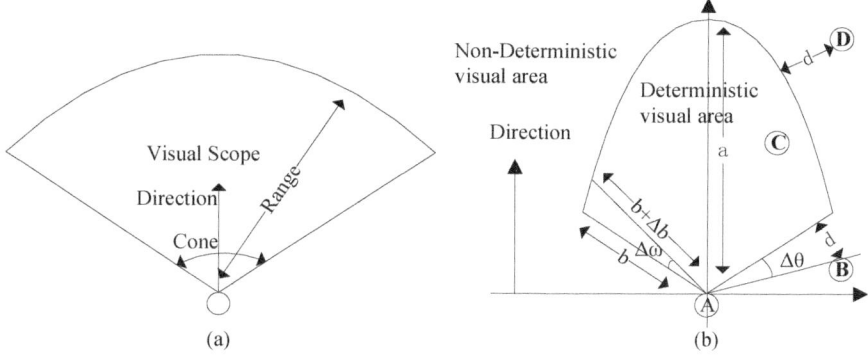

Fig. 1. Two kinds of visual perception model: (a) A past visual model built up by the cone and range; (b) A new visual model based on the theories of the uncertainties and probability distribution

Set the visual sensitivity in the visual scope(Visual Point P(x1,y1)):

If the visual point P in the ascertainable visual scope, then the sensitivity is 100%;

If the visual point P outside the enclosed area, the shortest distance by calculating the visual point to the boundary lines is d.

If P is close to two curves, we will use susceptibility formula: $P = e^{-kd}$. Otherwise, we will choose susceptibility formula: $P = e^{-k(\theta - \text{lactan}(y1/x1)|)}$. (k is the constant coefficient used to control the speed of decline)

According to the above description of visual perception sensitivity, it can make us have a basic understanding of sensitivity design. The other perception system can be reconstructed through the similar method.

Except the influence of own natural abilities, their emotional, cognitive, personality and other subjective factors also play a very important role in the perception system. In a dynamic environment, person and other creatures cannot address all perceptible information in the perceptible scope, they are often influenced by individual subjective preferences, and select partial information from all as the follow-up decision-making input.

Definition: If X is a finite-element set{x1, x2, x3, ..., xn}, preference relation R is the ordered pairs which contains two elements x1、 x2∈X, and satisfies R ∈ X × X.

If there is a preference relation R between two elements x1, x2, it can be expressed as (x1、 x2) ∈R or x1Rx2.

In a game, if the preference relation set is A{aRb, bRc, dRf}, at the time t, intelligent role gets the scene information set SI(t){a, b, c, d, e, f}, and finally obtains SI'(t){a, d, e} through the preference relation set A.

3.3 Satisfactory Criterion

Through the preceding bounded perception, the NPCs can get the preference information set SI′(t). Under the effect of its own perceptron models, SI′(t) can be transformed into the property description information set I(t) which can be understood by game NPCs. The size and change of the individual property set I(t) will trigger the appropriate response, to accordingly deal with these changes, achieve the transformation between the NPCs states, and complete the final decision, which can be expressed as:

$$S(t) = f(S(t-1), b(t), I(t)).$$ (2)

In formula (2), S(t) represents the game NPC state at the time t. b(t) indicates a behavior queue to achieve the transformation of states under the influence of the I(t).

In the actual game scene, there is not only a single set of behaviors to complete the transformation of states, but is an alternative behavior set B(t), which contains more than one behavior queue $b_i(t)$ meeting the above criterion. How to select a behavior queue as the final output which enables game NPC more intelligent, involves satisfactory decision theory. Theoretical study on various aspects of the satisfactory decision can be divided into the following two aspects [7]: the 'membership' function and the utility function.

However, because the 'membership' function lacks an objective standard, practical measures, and the results tend to vary and is difficult to evaluate, this decision - making model takes the utility function as a satisfactory evaluation criterion to solve decision-making problems.

Supposing that game NPCs in a situation generate alternative behavior set B(t), there is such a function u(b(t)) that reflects executive effects on intelligent role of behavior queue b(t)□B, so in the behaviors set B(t) the utility function [8] is defined as u(b(t)). In fact, utility function can be seen as decision makers' preference value function. For example, there are two behavior queues b1(t) and b2(t) in the alternative behavior set B(t), and if u(b1) > u(b2), it can be viewed as decision makers more preference to b1(t).

The above description of the utility function is behavior execution results under certain circumstances, but in many dynamic real-time scenes, game NPCs cannot gain complete information, and the target is changing, so the results of interference by various factors become uncertain. Game NPCs can expect the final behavior execution results according to the existing behavior data, and generate the behavior execution probability distribution, for this reason, the utility function is changed into:

$$U\left(b_i(t)\right) = \sum_{S_i \in S} P\left(S_i | b_i(t)\right) u\left(b_i(t)\right).$$ (3)

In formula (3), P(Si|bi(t)) represents the probability while the state is Si after executing the behavior queue bi(t).

According to the optimized utility function, we can calculate the NPCs each behavior queues' utility, based on satisfactory criterion, and choose the corresponding behavior queue that the utility value is maximum (or minimum) as NPCs decision-making output. Hence, game NPCs decision -making function is described as:

$$b(t) = \{b_k(t) | \max(\text{or min})(U(b_i(t)))\} (0 \le i \le n).$$ (4)

4 Realization and Application

By the previous description about the bounded rationality model-based intelligent decision -making method, we know that this method will improve the game NPCs' intelligence from the previous two aspects. In order to verify the advantages of this method, this article uses this method to respectively confront the rule-based method and the goal-based method on a simple intelligent football battle platform [9].

Judging from the overall process of the two sides battle, the advantages of this method show in the following two aspects:

1)   The optimization of perception scope

Through the comparison and analysis of Figure 1, based on the bounded rationality principle, the decision-making model resets game NPCs perception scope in accordance with the principles of human perception. And it uses the probability distribution to set the perceptive sensitivity outside of the ascertainable perception scope, which can address the 'perceived blind spot' of the past perception model and make NPCs' information more accurate.

Nevertheless, it will expand the perception scope, and increase the amount of information processing, thus the system will have a huge burden. But preference rational factors, which are used in the decision model, will reduce the amount of data processing in the decision-making process. From the analysises, the bounded rationality perception model will process more information, but the increase between two methods is not large, so that it will not increase the burden of subsequent decision-making.

2)   The optimization of decision-making

In the following condition as shown in figure 2, as players' view to decide which behavior the goalkeeper will take, most of them may choose to defend the opponent B. If using three different intelligent decision-making methods, the result will be different.

The goalkeeper's rule transformation chart shows that the goalkeeper will take the 'Defence' behaviors, and set the defensive goal as the opponent A because the player with ball is the opponent A. If using the goal-based intelligent decision-making method, the goalkeeper's goal is also to defend. In that case, the goalkeeper focuses on the ball, so the ultimate goal as the previous method is also the opponent A. In the face of such a situation, using the bounded rationality model-based intelligent decision -making method, the goalkeeper will no longer be the sole target. The goalkeeper obtains and processes information including the ball, player A, player B, player C, player E, player F through bounded perception. According to the outside perception information, the goalkeeper confirms the next goal which is to prevent the opponent from shooting, and behavior alternative set B(t){Defending A, Defending B, Defending C}. Based on the threat by the opponent and the teammate defensive

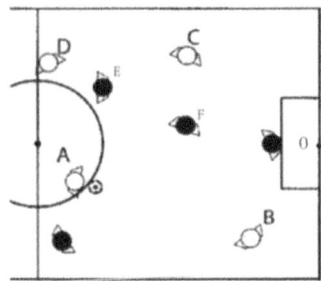

Fig. 2. A fight scene in the battle platform

Table 1. The Opponent Behaviors Effect And The Probability Of Goalkeeper Behavior

Opponent	The opponent behavior	Threat	Prevent shooting	Prevent passing
Opponent A	Holding the ball	0.3	0.9	0.4
Opponent B	Into the best collusion Area	0.75	0.4	0
Opponent C	Into the collusion Area	0.7	0.6	0

strength, the goalkeeper combining with the perceptive information set the probability distribution of behavioral outcomes(Table1).

According to the probability distribution of behavioral outcomes and the goalkeeper decision function, the system will be based on the current war situation between the two sides, establish corresponding utility function table(Table 2). After that, it will combine with the utility function table and the probability distribution to output the final satisfactory behavior. An example of the opponent C, the expected utility is U=-0.7*2+0.6*10+0.5*0=4.6, and the expected utility of the other two can be calculated using the similar method (Table 3). Because the goalkeeper defending goal is to not let the opponent shoot, the system will choose the smallest utility value: Defending B as the behavior output, so as to let the opponents in own team's defensive scope.

Table 2. The Goalkeeper'S Utility Function

The opponent behavior	Negative utility value	Our team behavior	Positive utility value
Holding the ball	10	Prevent passing	0.5
Into the best collusion Area	4	Prevent shooting	10
Into the collusion Area	2		

Table 3. The Goalkeeper expected utility

Next behavior	Defending A	Defending B	Defending C
Expected utility	8	1	4.6

By comparing these two aspects, we can clearly find that the method more realistically simulates human perception and decision-making process. For this reason, the behaviors of NPCs are more credible and humanized. Based on assessing the utility, the criteria makes NPCs' behaviors break the rules of conduct restrictions and be more autonomous.

5 Conclusion

For the video games, the application of the bounded rationality model can make up the defects on the perception scope setting and decision-making process, and game NPCs' performance will be more natural, and real to improve the gameplay and immersion. At the same time this method will modularize the NPCs' decision-making, which not only facilitates the control of each character, but also avoids interference between multi-role decision-making, so it is able to enhance the efficiency of the game intelligent decision-making process and reduce consumption of the system update and maintain. However, the costs of the whole intelligent computing process will increase, and how to decrease the calculation costs also becomes the next optimized target.

Acknowledgments. This work is partially supported by the national high-tech program (863) (2007AA010404) and the National Science & Technology Pillar Program (2007BAH14B00, 2007BAH14B03) of China. Thanks go to the members of the Institute of Digital Media of Hunan University for encouragement and discussions.

References

1. Millington, I., Funge, J.: Artificial Intelligence for Games, 2nd edn., pp. 427–459. Morgan Kaufmann Publishers, San Francisco (2009)
2. Orkin, J.: Applying Goal-Oriented Action Planning to Games. Charles River Media. AI Game Programming Wisdom, 2217–2229 (2003)
3. Orkin, J.: Three states and a plan: the AI of FEAR. In: Proceeding of the 2006 Game Developers Conference (GDC 2006), pp. 41–46 (2006)
4. Prieditis, A., Dalal, M.: Applying Model-Based Decision-Making Methods to Games: Applying the Locust AI Engine to Quake III. Course Technology, 211–222 (2006)
5. Harbert, S.: Administrative Behavior: A Study Of Decision Making Processes In Administrative Organization. Macmillan Publishing Co. Inc., New York (1971)
6. Wandell, B.: Foundations of Version. Sinauer Associates (1995)
7. Wang, Q.: Modeling a class of bounded rationality and decision analysis method. Huazhong University Doctoral Dissertation (2009)
8. Russell, S., Norvig, P.: Artificial Intelligence.: A Modern Approach, 3rd edn., pp. 610–626. Prentice Hall, Englewood Cliffs (2010)
9. Buckland, M.: Programming Game AI by Example. Wordware Publishing (2005)

Fault Diagnosis of Turbine Unit Equipment Based on Data Fusion and RBF Neural Network

Fei Xia[1,2], Hao Zhang[1,2], Jianqiao Long[1], Conghua Huang[1],
Daogang Peng[1], and Hui Li[1]

[1] School of Electric & Automatic Engineering, Shanghai University of Electric Power,
Shanghai, China
[2] CIMS Research Center, Tongji University, Shanghai, China
`xiafei@shiep.edu.cn`

Abstract. The monitoring of turbine in operation condition and fault diagnosis system in power plant is the key to guarantee the units long-term security and economic operation. The turbine faults were determined by a variety of factors, which brought many difficulties to the fault diagnosis. In general condition, using the RBF neural network can make the turbine fault diagnosis right. However, in some time, as the judging value of the method for multiple fault types were close, it was difficult to determine the fault type accurately. A fault diagnosis method for turbine based on data fusion and RBF neural network was proposed in the paper. Combined with the advantages of data fusion, the method can be used to avoid the situations when the fault types were unable to be determined. The algorithm has been demonstrated by the experimental results. Therefore, the application of fault diagnosis, using the method proposed in the paper can determine the fault type accurately, which played an important role in detecting and eliminating faults in time.

Keywords: fault diagnosis, turbine unit equipment, data fusion, RBF neural network.

1 Introduction

Electric power industry is the foundation of the national economy [1-4]. The running status of power system is directly related to the normal operation and stable development of the national economy. Mechanical equipment in modern industrial process is being developed in the direction of maximization, complication, high speed and automation. With constant increment of the capacity of generators, the demand for its reliable operation in high-speed, full-load and continuous condition is getting higher and higher. Condition monitoring and effective fault diagnosis is the important measures to ensure normal and safe operation of turbine generator unit. The monitoring data is obtained by sensors surrounding equipment. However, these sensors in the operation of the complex environment will bring the uncertain factors, directly affecting the accuracy of the fault diagnosis. In order to improve the accuracy of fault diagnosis, various information of the equipment need to be obtained.

H. Deng et al. (Eds.): AICI 2011, Part I, LNAI 7002, pp. 74–81, 2011.

Data fusion technology is a kind of intelligent diagnosis technology, which develops rapidly at present. It has the advantages of using redundancy and complementary information contained among the data sources, which can improve the accuracy and robustness of the decision-making system, thus providing an effective approach to improve fault diagnostic rate of turbine [5-6]. Data fusion technology has developed rapidly since it was proposed. It applied in military, meteorology robot and penetrated into industrial automation field and succeeded. Definition of data fusion can be summarized as follows. It is a data processing process which automatically completes the comprehensive analysis of some measured data of sensors gained by computer technology according to time sequences and completes the required task of decision-making and estimate. Data fusion technology provides a theoretical support for the safety assessment of equipment. D-S (Dempster-Shafer) evidence theory has been successfully applied in fault diagnosis field [7-11]. Its biggest advantage lies in the comprehensive utilization of information of each sensor, which provides the probability of various fault of the present moment. So it improves the accuracy and reliability. This course of data fusion belongs to decision-level fusion. Its input is real time value and change trend of on-site signals after calibrated, alarm protection statistics and typical samples. Its output is the possible fault state of equipment and credibility.

Besides information fusion technology, the technique of artificial neural network is one of the important tools in the mechanical fault diagnosis field. Its abilities of self-learning, nonlinear mapping, the function approximation, parallel computing and fault tolerance and so on provide a powerful method for a new fault diagnosis system. With the credibility of its fault symptoms as input, fault diagnosis system based on artificial neural network outputs the credibility of the corresponding fault through the artificial neural network of parallel numerical calculation, thus completing the recognition of the fault mode. Although BP neural network has very good nonlinear mapping capability and flexible network structure etc, it has shortcomings of slow convergence speed. Radial basis function (RBF) network is a nuclear classifier, and the transfer function of the neurons can form a series of reception areas partly covered which constitute a complicated decision domain. And then comprehensive classification is made through output layer. It is better than the BP neural network whether in approximation ability, ability and learning speed etc.

Above-mentioned analysis, in order to improve the accuracy of fault diagnosis, this paper puts forward the following fault diagnosis method for turbine generator unit: first, carry out monitoring on possible signs of fault using multi-sensor, and then apply different RBF neural networks to diagnose the fault symptoms category to get preliminary credibility on fault of each network, finally use a data fusion method based on D-S evidence theory to make fusion on preliminary credibility of each sensor network to obtain the final result of fault diagnosis. This method has not only used the stronger nonlinear mapping ability of the neural network, but also realized the effective fusion on multi-sensor data, which improves correctness and stability of the fault diagnosis system. In the next part of this paper, data fusion, the related concept of RBF neural network and the fault diagnosis algorithm put forward in this paper are introduced successively. The algorithm is applied to the simulation experiment of turbine generator unit. Through the fault diagnosis experiment contrast with BP neural network and the RBF neural network, this algorithm can effectively improve the fault diagnosis accuracy of turbine generator unit.

2   Frame of Algorithm

Powell. M.J.D proposed a multi-variable interpolation radial basis function (RBF) in 1985, Broomhead. D-S and Lowe applied RBF to the design of artificial neural network and constructed radial basis function artificial neural network for the first time in 1988, namely RBF neural network. From then on, people launched a series of RBF neural network research, and also made a lot of encouraging results. Theorem has been proved that RBF network can approximate the nonlinear function and the approximation is unique. RBF network not only has the full power of the comprehensive general network characteristics such as nonlinear mapping, fault tolerance, adaptability, parallel processing and information processing capability etc., which the BP network has, but greater than the BP network capacity of local approximation, not easy to fall into local minimum points, fast training speed and so on.

The RBF network is a three-layer feed forward network with instructors and its structure is similar to BP network: the first layer is input layer, which consists of source nodes; the second layer is hidden layer and the number of elements is selected automatically within the given framework according to the accuracy requirements; the third layer is output layer, which responds to the role of input mode. Network can be generally described using the following formula:

$$f(x) = W_0 + \sum_{j-1}^{M} W_j G(\|x - c_j\| / 2\sigma_j^{-2}), i = 1, \ldots \ldots M \tag{1}$$

$G = (\|x - c_j\| / 2\sigma_j^{-2}), i = 1, \cdots \cdots M$ is called the basis function. It is RBF function, a local distribution, and attenuation of non-negative non-linear function for the center radial pairs. The most commonly used basis function $G(\bullet)$ is Gaussian kernel function. Its expression is described as follows:

$$G_j = \exp(-\|x - c_j\|^2 / 2\sigma_j^2), j = 1, 2 \ldots \ldots M \tag{2}$$

Where G_j is the output of hidden layer of the unit j, σ_j is normalized parameters of the hidden nodes function of number J (or broadband parameters), which determines the scope of the center corresponding basis function. Where $X = (x_1, x_2, \cdots\cdots, x_n)^T$ is the input vector of input layer. c_j is j-unit basis hidden layer function cluster center vector (central vector of center of each hidden layer is stored in connection centers between the vector and the input of all kinds neurons), general obtained through various clustering methods. While $\|\bullet\|$ means the distance between vectors in N-dimensional space, usually call Euclidean space.

Network's output for each input layer node is a weighted sum of it and the output G_j of each hidden layer neurons. According to the definition of Gaussian distribution function, the relationship of output G of hidden layer neurons and input vector X should obey normal distribution. That is, when the distance between X and the central vector c_j in close proximity, G_j close to the maximum; contrary G_j decreases. If X and c_j at a distance exceeding the width σ_j (that is, far from the center), the output can be approximately zero, which means there is no contribution to the output layer. This realizes the local perception and makes the RBF network has more capacity of local approximation than the BP network has.

For the turbine generator unit, this paper presents a fault diagnosis method based on multi-sensor data fusion and neural networks. First, according to fault feature of the turbine generator unit, different types of sensors are used to obtain the corresponding fault characteristic. Because these different fault symptoms are the same type of fault, so the neural network is applied to build a diagnostic network for each type of sensor in order to get preliminary credibility for the fault type. Although the BP neural network has very good nonlinear mapping ability and flexible network architecture, etc, there is shortcoming of slow convergence speed. The RBF neural network in terms of approximation capability, classification ability and learning speed are better than BP neural network, so the RBF neural network is used here. Judgments made by these networks are got independently based on different types of sensors. In order to reduce the uncertainty of fault diagnosis, the results of the diagnosis network of each independent sensor need to be fused. In this paper, using D-S evidence theory method, the preliminary credibility got from the diagnosis of each independent sensor network will be synthesized on the diagnosis results according to fusion rules. Here, the identification framework corresponds to the type of fault. Besides the failure category, the "not sure" category is increased. This is more in line with the real judgment of the situation. The credibility after fused is the judgments to the possibilities of various faults by diagnosis system. Based on these judgments, the final fault type can be obtained by the corresponding rules. The flow chart of the algorithm is shown in Figure 1.

It needs advanced technology that conducting condition monitoring and analysis on the steam turbine to determine whether there is abnormality or fault of equipment. The monitoring data is obtained by sensors surrounding equipment. However, these sensors in the operation of the complex environment will bring the uncertain factors, directly affecting the accuracy of the fault diagnosis. In order to improve the accuracy of fault diagnosis, various information of the equipment need to be got. With the proposed multi-sensor fusion method, uncertainty of the fault diagnosis of the turbine generator unit can be solved. The data processed by the system accurately reflects the extent of the different fault types. These fusion results as a basis for diagnosis improve the fault diagnosis rate and play an important role in the turbine's safety production.

3   Stimulation

The condenser is one of the important auxiliary equipment to turbine in power plant, and the good or bad operating condition of condenser is directly related to the safe and economic operation of the turbine, so condenser fault diagnosis has been concentrated so much attention. To validate the algorithm proposed in the paper, the corresponding simulation has been done. In this section, firstly, the set of fault symptoms and fault types was introduced. Next, for what proposed above, the RBF neural network was used to do fault diagnosis test. After that, using the proposed data fusion based on RBF neural network was tested on the same fault symptoms and fault types. At last, the diagnostic results obtained by using different methods were discussed.

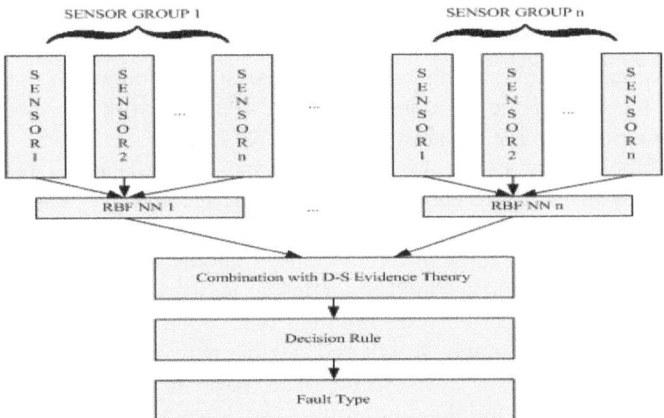

Fig. 1. Schema of Fault Diagnosis Algorithm

3.1 Symptom Set and Fault Set

The type of condenser fault is quiet many. According to the summary of the literature [7], 14 typical condenser faults were as the fault set, represented with Yj, such as circulating water pump failure, condenser with water, ejector failure, vacuum pump failure and so on. Meanwhile, 16 parameters obtained from the SIS, DCS, or MIS in the power plant directly can be chosen as the fault symptoms of condenser, denoted by Xi, which can reflect the fault performances of the condensing equipment of turbine in power plant basically. The main symptom parameters were the change rate of vacuum decline, the current of circulating pump motor, the outlet pressure of circulating pump, temperature rise of cooling water and so on.

After the fault set and fault symptoms were confirmed, fault symptoms were transformed into the value between 0 and 1 according to the rules in literature [12]:

$$X_i = \begin{cases} 1.00 & shutdown upper \lim t \\ 0.75 & Alarm upper \lim it \\ 0.50 & Normal operation t \qquad i = 1,2,\cdots,16 \\ 0.25 & Alarm lower \lim it \\ 0.0 & shutdown lower \lim it \end{cases} \qquad (3)$$

The some typical fault training samples can be set up on the basis of the rules above and have been shown in Table 1.

In order to test the algorithm proposed in the paper, the following three sets of test data were used. Data 1 was *(0.75, 0.50, 0.50, 0.50, 0.50, 0.50, 0.55, 0.75, 0.75, 0.50, 0.75. 0.45, 0.50, 0.50, 0.50, 0.50)*, whose corresponding fault was Y13; and data 2 was *(0.75, 0.56, 0.50, 0.75, 0.50, 0.50, 0.55, 0.75, 0.75, 0.50, 0.70. 0.50, 0.50, 0.50, 0.50, 0.50)*, whose corresponding fault was Y9; and data 3 was *(1.00, 0.50, 0.45, 0.50, 0.50, 0.55, 0.50, 0.25, 0.75, 0.70, 0.50. 0.48, 0.50, 0.50, 0.53, 0.55)*, whose corresponding fault was Y4.

Table 1. Fault set and fault symptoms

Fault	Fault symptoms							
type	X1	X2	X3	X4	X5	X6	X7	X8
Y1	1.00	0.0	0.25	0.25	0.50	0.50	0.50	0.75
Y2	1.00	0.50	0.50	0.50	0.50	0.50	0.50	0.25
Y3	1.00	0.50	0.50	0.50	0.75	0.75	0.75	0.75
Y4	1.00	0.50	0.50	0.50	0.50	0.50	0.50	0.25
Y5	0.75	0.50	0.25	0.50	0.50	0.50	0.50	0.75
Y6	0.75	0.50	0.50	0.50	0.25	0.25	0.50	0.50
Y7	0.75	0.50	0.50	0.50	0.75	0.75	0.50	0.50
Y8	0.75	0.50	0.50	0.50	0.75	0.75	0.75	0.50
Y9	0.75	0.50	0.50	0.75	0.50	0.50	0.50	0.75
Y10	0.75	0.50	0.50	0.50	0.50	0.50	0.50	0.25

3.2 Diagnosis Based on RBF NN

Firstly, 16 fault symptom data above were diagnosed by using the RBF neural network. Using k-means clustering algorithm in MATLAB 2008 to construct the RBF neural network, the training samples in Table 1 were used to train the network. The RBF network was with 3-layer structure, having a total of 16 input nodes (corresponding to 16 kinds of fault symptoms), 14 output nodes (corresponding to 14 kinds of fault type). The diagnostic results have been shown in Table 2.

The diagnostic results showed that the maximal fault probability of Test Data 1 was 0.923, corresponding to the fault type Y13. The ultimate fault probability of Test Data 2 was 0.8714, whose corresponding fault type was Y9. The supreme fault probability of Test Data 3 was 0.7495, in accordance with fault type Y4. The fault types of three groups of test data were consistent with the known fault types, indicating that using RBF neural networks can export the corresponding fault type accurately, with higher accuracy.

3.3 Diagnosis Based on Data Fusion

According to the algorithm of fault diagnosis in Figure 1, three RBF sub-networks were formed on the types of fault symptoms, after all of their diagnostic results were obtained, each output of the sub-networks was fused by using DS evidence theory method. For the Test Data 2, the diagnostic result was that the output value of Y9 was 0.8617 after fusion, though it decreased comparing with it obtained by using RBF directly, the outputs of corresponding faults Y2, Y4 and Y8 reduced greatly, lower than 0.35. Therefore, It was clear that the corresponding fault of Test Data 2 was Y9, in accordance with known fault type. For the Test Data 3, the output value of Y4 was 0.7023 after fusion, which decreased little comparing with it obtained by using RBF directly, the outputs of Y2 and Y13 were less than 0.30. In this way, the case of misdiagnosis or unable diagnosis caused by the too close faults Y4 and Y13 was avoided when the single RBF neural network was used to diagnose.

Table 2. The diagnostic results

Fault type	Test Data 1	Test Data 2	Test Data 3
Y1	0.0101	0.0354	0.0181
Y2	0.0381	0.5257	0.3313
Y3	0.0090	0.0026	0.0026
Y4	0.0240	0.6374	0.7495
Y5	0.0000	0.0000	0.0002
Y6	0.0058	0.0120	0.0235
Y7	0.0077	0.0026	0.0271
Y8	0.0228	0.5830	0.0007
Y9	0.0000	0.8714	0.0000
Y10	0.0051	0.0025	0.0522
Y11	0.0229	0.0761	0.0683
Y12	0.0329	0.1955	0.0317
Y13	0.9230	0.0000	0.6269
Y14	0.1020	0.0264	0.0207

3.4 Discussion

For diagnosing the typical faults of condenser by using the single RBF neural network and the method based on data fusion separately, from the diagnostic results, we can see that single RBF neural network can determine the fault type of the test data properly, but can't avoid the case the output values of the multiple fault types were close. In this case, it is difficult to determine the fault type that the condenser encountered exactly, the situation of unable determine appearing. In response to this situation, the method of combining RBF neural network with D-S evidence theory was proposed in the paper, which improved the accuracy of fault diagnosis.

4 Conclusions

The method of fault diagnosis for turbine was proposed based on data fusion and the RBF neural network in the paper. The experimental results have shown that the method can improve the accuracy of diagnosis effectively. In identifying the fault, it avoided the case of unable determine appeared when multiple faults were close and the condition of misdiagnosis. The method played an important role in the diagnosing the fault type accurately for the turbine operation. In the follow-up work, the method can be improved by testing more data and integrated in the corresponding fault diagnosis system.

Acknowledgments. This work is supported by "Chen Guang" project supported by Shanghai Municipal Education Commission and Shanghai Education Development Foundation, supported by Shanghai Rising-Star Program (No. 10QA1402900), supported by Leading Academic Discipline Project of Shanghai Municipal education Commission, supported by Project Supported by the State Key Program of National Natural Science Foundation of China.

References

1. He, Y., Lu, W., Chu, F.: Research on Condition Running Inspection and Fault Diagnosis System for Power Set. Journal of Vibration, Measurement & Diagnosis 26(8), 269–273 (2006)
2. Ye, Q., Wu, X.-p., Song, Y.-x.: Fault diagnosis method based on D-S theory of evidence and AHP. Journal of Naval Universit of Engineering 18(4), 12–17 (2006)
3. Wen, X.-q., Xu, Z.-m., Sun, Y.-y., Sun, L.-f.: A Model for Condenser Fault Diagnosis Based on Least Squares-support Vector Machine and Simulation Application. Turbine Technology 30(2), 204–206 (2010)
4. Jiang, J.-g.: Fault Diagnosis of Condenser Based on Wavelet Neural Network. Industrial Engineering Journal 16(4), 40–43 (2010)
5. Ma, J., Zhang, Y.-s.: Condensation Sets Fault Diagnosis Based on Data Fusio. Turbine Technology 51(2), 141–143 (2009)
6. Qi, Z.-w., Gu, C.-l.: Application of fault diagnosis to equipment based on modified D-S evidential theory. Journal of Naval University of Engineering 20(1), 11–14 (2008)
7. Ma, J., Zhang, Y.-s.: Condensation Sets Fault Diagnosis Based on Data Fusion. Turbine Technology 51(2), 141–143 (2009)
8. Liu, B.-j., Xiao, B., Fu, H.: Discussion of Data Fusion Algorithm Based on D-S Evidential Theory and Fuzzy Mathematics. Microprocessors (3), 70–72 (2007)
9. Xiong, X., Wang, J., Niu, T., Song, Y.: A Hybrid Model for Fault Diagnosis of Complex Systems. Electronics Optics & Control 16(2), 56–59 (2009)
10. Niu, G., Han, T., Yang, B.S.: Multi-agent decision fusion for motor fault diagnosis. Mechanical Systems and Signal Processing 21, 1285–1299 (2007)
11. Yang, B.S., Kim, K.J.: Application of Dempster-Shafer theory in fault diagnosis of induction motors using vibration and current signals. Mechanical Systems and Signal Processing 20, 403–420 (2006)
12. Wang, W., Zhang, R., Sheng, W., Xu, Z.: Condenser Fault Diagnosis Based on Fuzzy Rule and SVM. Journal of Engineering for Thermal Energy and Power 24(4), 476–480 (2009)

Design of Taxi Vehicle Monitoring System Based on GPS/GPRS

Tiemei Yang, Wei Xiao, and Jianling Guo

School of Electronics and Information Engineering, Taiyuan University of
Science and Technology, Taiyuan 030024, China
yangtie01@sina.com, xw8002@163.com, gjl922@126.com

Abstract. According to the needs of the security operation taxi, a kind of vehicle
monitoring terminal device which takes C8051F040 microcontroller as the core,
combining GPS, GPRS and LCD was proposed. This device will show the
superiority of C8051F040 microcontroller, which is high-speed, low-power, and
has rich interface. Through the application of GPS, LCD, and the GPRS module
which communicate with the monitor center, the device may realize functions
such as vehicles localization, vehicles monitoring and dispatching etc. This paper
describes hardware design and flow process of related procedure in detail.

Keywords: Global Positioning System (GPS), General Packet Radio Service
(GPRS), Liquid Crystal Display(LCD), Vehicle Monitor Terminal, Single-chip
Microcontroller.

1 Introduction

As one of urban public transportation modes, the transportation department requests the
taxi on the standardization of the management, and the need to ensure the security of
vehicles and drivers has been more and more concentrated by Taxi Company. Using
information technology, vehicles localization technology, sensor technology, control
technology and other high-new technologies to reform the traditional transportation
modes has became the main method to develop the public transportation.

The vehicle monitor terminal device, which is used for data acquisition, information
display, connection with in-vehicle equipment and communication with the monitoring
center, it is installed in the monitored taxi to help the monitoring center and the driver
understand the current real-time information, such as latitude and longitude, speed,
direction and situation of the road...etc, and it can also record the travel route of a recent
period of time to guarantee the security of taxi and driver. It not only can send the
real-time information to monitoring center, but also receive the orders issued by
monitoring center. It is very convenient for the monitoring center to implement
real-time distance supervision and scheduling.

The system is composed of two parts: The superior machine (i.e. monitoring
center) realizes the monitor and the vehicles dispatch management, the lower position
machine (i.e. vehicle carries supervisory device) realizes the information acquisition

H. Deng et al. (Eds.): AICI 2011, Part I, LNAI 7002, pp. 82–88, 2011.

and the data processing. The superior machine can receive PC machine instruction; simultaneously through the serial port transmit data to PC machine, and through GPRS/Internet network connect to the lower position machine. The control software of monitoring center is compiled by C++. This vehicle monitor system is possible to be used as other vehicle monitor system (for example intelligent public transportation dispatching system [1], engineering machinery long-distance vehicle monitor system etc.) through corresponding hardware and software improvement.Fig.1 is the vehicle monitor system's total frame diagram.

Fig. 1. System total frame diagram

2   System Function Module

This article only shows the lower position machine part, which can be divided into the following several main modules: The single-chip microcontroller nucleus module, GPS signal gathering module, GPRS communication module, LCD display module, keyboard module, indicator module, external memory module and power source module.

The C805lF040 has 100 pins, MC55I has 50 pins. Considering the complexity of circuit diagram, the following article has only given the partial electric circuit schematic diagram when describing each function module.

2.1   Core Control Module

The vehicle monitor terminal device choose Silicon Laboratories Corporation's C8051F040 [2] single-chip microcontroller as the core control unit, it has the completely compatible instruction essence with the MCS-51; This single-chip microcontroller uses assembly line processing technology, thus improving the instruction executing efficiency; It has integrated JTAG, supports online programming; And it uses low voltage power supply (2.7~3.6 V); It has a 64KB Flash ROM, 256 byte internal memory and 4KB exterior memory that can satisfy the application memory function of the whole system; Simultaneously it has 64 I/O ports which can be independently set for input/output pattern; It also integrates 5 timer/counters to meet the need of fixing time and counting; It has many kinds of bus interfaces, including UART, SMBUS (compatible with IIC) ,SPI bus and CAN bus, the two UART ports may realize the full-duplex correspondence, the correspondence baudrate can be set separately. Considering the continuity and extension of the system, we have already expanded CAN bus interface while designing. Fig.2 shows one commonly used simple reliable and can automatic reset RC reset circuit.

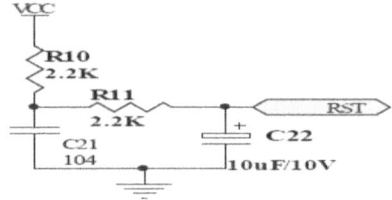

Fig. 2. System reset circuit diagram

2.2 GPS Satellite Positioning Module

The vehicle monitor terminal device adopts GS-87 as a GPS module, it is a high-performance and low-power intelligence satellite receive module. The working voltage of GS-87 is 3.3V, it can connected with the single-chip microcontroller directly to realize serial communication, the communication protocol may use the baudrate which oneself defines(4800-system defaults, 9600, 19200, 38400); GS-87 follows NMEA_0183 standard, the localization accuracy reach to 10m, which can satisfy the localization request of vehicles, and receive 6 kinds of sentence forms, the RMC form adopted by this system is the most suitable to the practical requirement for the vehicle localization. The single-chip microcontroller connects with GS-87 through the UART0, and use software programming controlling to process the information received from GPS and extract information which the user needs.

2.3 GPRS Wireless Transmission Module

The vehicle monitor terminal device selects MC55I as the GPRS module; it is the important part to establish correspondence between the vehicles carries equipment and monitoring center. The superiority of MC55I module lies in permanent online, fast data storage and faster data downloading speed, its GPRS charge is reasonable which is based on the current capacity cost; this module support's voltage range is 3.3 to 4.8V.

The MC55I module inlays the TCP/IP agreement stack; it does not need to implement software operations again such as dialing, TCP/IP agreement analysis while connecting to Internet network. The single-chip microcontroller connects with MC55I through the UART1, and uses AT command to control the GPRS module connecting with monitoring center server, their correspondence baudrate can be selected according to the need. It can send the vehicles real-time information to the monitoring center and receive command information from the monitoring center through the terminal GPRS module of vehicle. Obviously, AT command is the instruction that controls MC55I module, it is also the software interface of single-chip microcontroller and GPRS module [3].

2.4 Display Module

Through the programming can send contents that need (for example vehicles and driver's serial number, latitude and longitude degree value, speed, direction, time, date...etc.) to LCD module to be displayed. The LCD module will simultaneously display the information that received from the monitoring center (such as passenger rent a car site, front situation on road...etc.).

The vehicle monitor device chooses the TSINGTEK Company's HG1286412-B-LWH-LV LCD module whose working voltage is 3.3V. The display module connects with single-chip microcontroller that can select both serial and parallel. In order to ensure that programming is convenient and the single-chip microcontroller I/O mouth is sufficient, we set the PSB pin high directly while hardware designing, which causes system adopting parallel mode. The LCD module maximum can control 4 lines each of 16 Chinese characters display that cannot satisfy the request of system's all contents display. Therefore we choose paging display which uses different keys to control the display of different page's content. This function can realized through programming the keyboard module.

The indicator module is composed of LED, and is used for indicating each mold of system various running statuses, such as GPS and GPRS...etc., and fault warning...etc.

2.5 Memory Module

It needs to expand the external memory when the single-chip microcontroller internal data memory cannot meet the requirement of data storage. The received GPS data of this system is massive, so there is an expanded memory chip which is ATMEL Corporation's AT24C64 whose working voltage is 3.3V to store the real-time data that received from GPS. This chip provides storage space with 64 KB and supports the IIC bus agreement. It only needs two bus lines to connect with the single-chip microcontroller, one is serial data line SDA, the other is serial clock line SCL, and it can improve the hardware efficiency and simplify circuit design. The memory can be implemented the read-write operation through the programming, thus storing the data which received from GPS into the chip temporarily, and extracting the data from the external memory when execute data processing. Through serial port multiplying (transmit AT command to close GPRS while vehicle terminal has stopping, UART1 can used to communicate with computer), the computer can extract data from memory to backup directly. Shown in Fig.3 is AT24C64 circuit connection diagram.

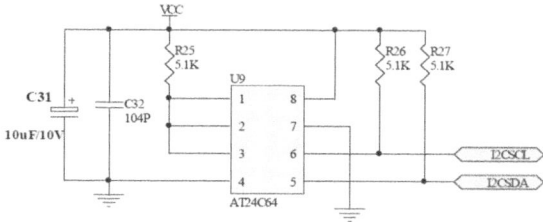

Fig. 3. AT24C64 circuit diagram

2.6 Power Source Module

The module supply the power for the entire vehicle terminal movement needed, the accumulator cell of a car is 12V generally; it must pass through the voltage convert module to convert into working voltage of the terminal various modules firstly before application. The convert module use LM2576 which produced by the American Country Semiconductor Company as the core transform chip, its input voltage rang from 5V to 40V, and output voltage can be fixed voltage such as 3.3V or 5V, it can also output adjustable voltage, the current maximum value of output is 3A that can satisfy the request of the GPRS summit—2A. Fig.4 is the power circuit's schematic diagram.

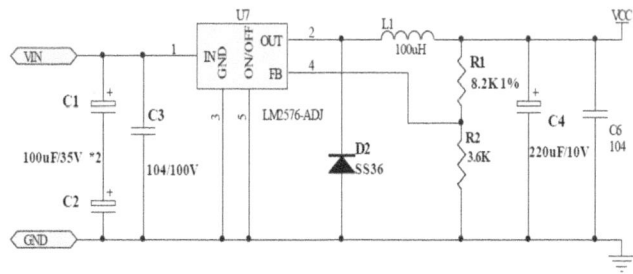

Fig. 4. Power source circuit diagram

3   System Project Design

The data that GS-87 gathered is sent to the single-chip microcontroller through the UART0 transmissions, and real-time saved to external memory by IIC bus, then programming processing data that receive from GPS transmits to the UART1, and transmits to monitoring center to execute bidirectional communication through MC55I ,simultaneously sends in LCD to display. The UART1 can communicate with the PC machine when GPRS is locking, which can take out the date from external memory promptly and realize upgrading of software function. JTAG is used to online programming when the system is developing. The LCD part uses the keyboard to control; it can use page display to display contents respectively such as latitude and longitude, velocity, direction, time, date, the vehicle and the driver's serial number. The indicator is used for indicating terminal switch, whether there is GPS signal, whether data is effective [4], GPRS link make-and-break and other various modules' active

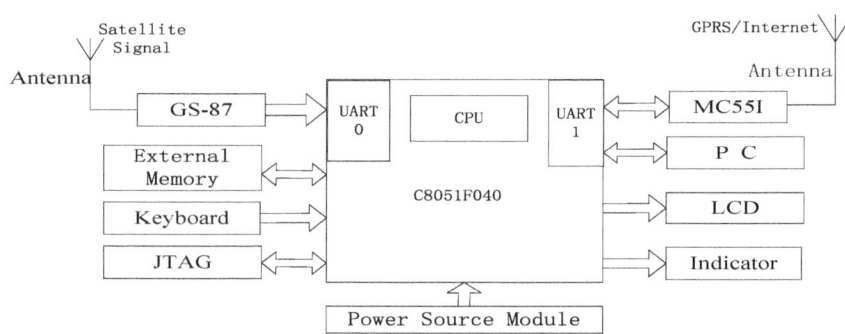

Fig. 5. System project diagram

status, reminding and warning the driver by LED lamp twinkle at the same time. The power source module supply power for each module of system. Fig.5 is the project frame diagram for the vehicle monitor system.

4 System Software Design

The vehicle terminal software uses the single-chip microcontroller C language to compile. The whole process is as follows: Supply power for the terminal, complete each module initialization and open interrupt, then GPS start working; The single-chip microcontroller receive GPS data through UART0, and analysis the data at the same time, judging whether the gathering data is accurate and effective. If the data is valid, store it to external memory, simultaneously extract the programmed localization information to UART1; if the date is invalid, and then return to interrupt entrance. The single-chip microcontroller synchronization control GPRS module to link GPRS network and register monitoring center, after registering successfully, the procedure enters main loop. The vehicle terminal real-time transmits data to the monitoring center as well as receives disposition order from center, and displays the related information on LCD. The single-chip microcontroller can also monitor the network connection situation automatically according to the feedback information from GPRS module, and realize automatic link when the line is broken [5]. Because the procedure is quite complex and huge, underneath has only given the UART0 interrupts and the master routine software flow charts, respectively for Fig.6, Fig.7 shows.

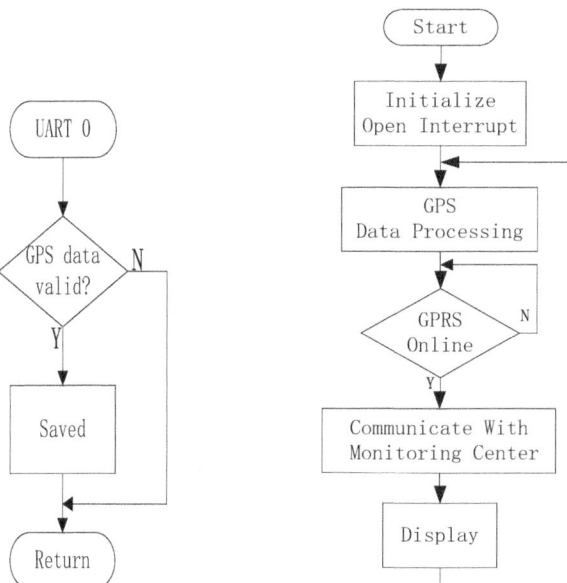

Fig. 6. UART0 interrupt flow chart   **Fig. 7.** Main routine flow chart

5   Conclusions

This vehicle monitor system has stable and reliable performance after trial operation. The vehicle monitor system based on GPS and GPRS is a system engineering which utilizes the multi-technologies, hardware and software unify. The development of electron, correspondence and computer realm is extremely rapid. Simultaneously, people's request of intellectualized degree is also improving. In brief, with the increasing progress of technology, we must make full use of advanced communication method, perfect geography information, powerful database, and other methods to consummate and improve our system continuously, and make the system easy to operation and maintenance.

Acknowledgment. This work is supported by:

1) Training Program on Taiyuan University of Science and Technology College Students Innovation Experiment

2) Doctor Initial Foundation of the Taiyuan University of Science and Technology, No: 20092009.

References

1. Gao, A.-l., Wang, H.-g., Bi, Y.: Design of the Intelligent Public Bus Vehicle Equipment Based on C8051F040. Measurement & Control Technology (2010)
2. Silabs: Perliminary C8051F040/1/2/3, http://www.silabs.com
3. Ma, T., Yang, H.-y.: The Design and Implementation of Vehicle Carried Terminal Based on GPS/GPRS. Electronic Measurement Technology (2009)
4. Tian, R.-c., Huang, J.: Design and Implementation of Vehicle Supervision Terminal Based on GPS/GPRS. Modern Electronisc Technology (2008)
5. Li, P.-j.: Single-chip Microcomputer Switched in Internet Based on GPRS Network. Microelectronics and Computer (2006)

Initial-Boundary Value Existing Problem in Nonlinear Elastic Beam Equations

Run-Fang Li and Hu-Xiao Luo

Department of Mathematics, Taiyuan University of Technology
030024 Taiyuan, China
lirunfang@tyut.edu.cn, wshrm7@126.com

Abstract. It's often ignored that in nonlinear partial differential equations, there has the unique solutions in the process of seeking numerical solutions for the system solutions. So the rationality of simplifying an finite-dimensional system cannot be ensured, or even worse, the incorrect conclusions may be resulted in. In this paper, the Sobolev space is used as a tool to improve the existence and uniqueness for the weak solution of a class of nonlinear elastic beam equations, for FPU problem by the way of Galerkin's method and local extension method.

Keywords: Galerkin's method, Sobolev space, existence of weak solution.

1 Introduction

In this paper, we first study some simple equations, Fermi, Pasta, Ulam [1] puts forward a famous (FPU) problem in 1974: Why solid has limited heat conductivity? They use one-dimensional grid to describe the solid, the motion law of the grid is revealed by below equations:

$$\begin{cases} m\dfrac{\partial^2 u_i}{\partial x^2} = k(u_{i+1} - 2u_i + u_{i-1})(1 + \alpha(u_{i+1} - u_{i-1})) \\ u_0 = u_N = 0 \\ i = 1, 2, \cdots, N-1 \end{cases} \tag{1}$$

Where k is the linear elastic constants, α is the non-linear strength and $\alpha > 0$, u_i is the i the replace seat starting from balance position. Ktuskal and Zabusky [2] consider FPU problem from a continuous view in 1983, get the following equation by using a series of transformations :

$$\frac{\partial^2 u}{\partial t^2} - \varepsilon^2 \delta^2 \frac{\partial^4 u}{\partial x^4} - \varepsilon c^2 \frac{\partial u}{\partial x} \cdot \frac{\partial^2 u}{\partial x^2} - c^2 \frac{\partial^2 u}{\partial x^2} = 0 \tag{2}$$

Here $\varepsilon < 0$, c, δ are arbitrary constants. Solitary wave solutions of equation (2) have been discussed. The following nonlinear beam equation is studied in Literature [3]:

H. Deng et al. (Eds.): AICI 2011, Part I, LNAI 7002, pp. 89–94, 2011.
© Springer-Verlag Berlin Heidelberg 2011

$$\frac{\partial^2 u}{\partial t^2}+\frac{\partial^4 u}{\partial x^4}-(\alpha+\int_0^l(\frac{\partial u}{\partial x})^2\,dx)\frac{\partial^2 u}{\partial x^2}=0$$

Where α is a constant, l is the length of the beam, $u(x,t)$ is the displacement of the beam at the point x while at the time t .This is a beam equation with an axial force. The following nonlinear beam equation is studied in Literature [4]:

$$\frac{\partial^2 u}{\partial x^2}+\frac{\partial^4 u}{\partial x^4}-[\beta+k\int_0^l u_\xi(\xi,t)^2\,d\xi]\frac{\partial^2 u}{\partial x^2}=0$$

The author has proved the existence, uniqueness and regularity of the global solution of the Initial-boundary value problem under certain homogeneous boundary conditions by using Galerkin method.

In this paper, we consider a beam equation which is more general than equation (3):

$$\frac{\partial^2 u}{\partial t^2}+\alpha\frac{\partial^4 u}{\partial x^4}-\beta\left|\frac{\partial u}{\partial x}\right|^2\frac{\partial^2 u}{\partial x^2}+\gamma\frac{\partial^2 u}{\partial x^2}=f(u)$$

$$\tag{3}$$

$$u(x,0)=u_0(x),\qquad \dot{u}(x,0)=u_1(x)$$

$$\tag{4}$$

$$u(0,t)=u(l,t)=u^{(2)}(0,t)=u^{(2)}(l,t)=0$$

$$\tag{5}$$

Where, $\alpha>0$, $\beta>0$, $\gamma<0$, α, β and γ are constants, l is the length of the beam, $u(x,t)$ is the displacement of the beam at the point α while at the time .We will show the existence of the weak solution of the system (3)~(5) by using Galerkin method and Local extension method.

In this paper, for convenience, we denote

$$u^{(k)}=\frac{\partial^k u}{\partial x^k},\qquad \dot{u}=\frac{\partial u}{\partial t},\qquad \ddot{u}=\frac{\partial^2 u}{\partial t^2}$$

and so on. Thus, the equation (3) transfers to the following equation (6):

$$\ddot{u}+\alpha u^{(4)}-\beta\left|u^{(1)}\right|^2 u^{(2)}+\gamma\cdot u^{(2)}=f(u)$$

$$\tag{6}$$

2 Definition and Lemma

Definition: If $f\in L^2(\Omega),u\in L^2(\Omega)$, A^* is the adjoint operator of A and u satisfy:

$$(u,A^*\varphi)=(f,\varphi)\qquad \forall\varphi\in C_0^\infty(\Omega)$$

$$\tag{2.1}$$

Say u is the weak solution of the boundary value problem

$$\begin{cases}Au=f & (x,t)\in\Omega\times(0,T)\\ Bu=f & (x,t)\in\partial\Omega\times(0,T)\end{cases}$$

Lemma 1: [2] (^{Poincare}) let $f\in L^1(\Omega)$ and suppose $f(\xi)$ for some $\xi\in\overline{\Omega}$. Then

$$|f|\le\frac{l}{\sqrt{2}}|f^{(1)}|$$

$$\tag{2.2}$$

Where, $|\cdot|$ is the norm of $L^2(\Omega)$, $f^{(1)}$ is the first derivative of f with respect to x .

Lemma 2: [3] Set $\omega_j = \sin\dfrac{j\pi x}{l}, j=1,2,\cdots,$, then $\{\omega_j\}$ is a basis of space X_1, X_2 and $L^2(\Omega)$.

3 The Existence of Weak Solution

Theorem: Set 1)$f(s) \in C^1, f'(s)$ is bounded above, so there exists a constant C, such that 1)$f'(s) \leq C, \forall s \in R, f(0) = 0$;

2)$u_0(x) \in X_2, u_1(x) \in L^2(\Omega)$ then there exists $u = u(x,t)$ satisfy the equation

$$(\ddot{u}, \varphi) + \alpha(u^{(2)}, \varphi^{(2)}) - \beta(|u^{(1)}|^2 u^{(2)}, \varphi) + \gamma(u^{(2)}, \varphi) = (f(u), \varphi)$$

$$\alpha > 0, \ \beta > 0, \ \gamma > 0, \ \forall \varphi \in X_2$$

$$(3.1)$$

under initial conditions $u(x,0) = u_0, \dot{u}(x,0) = u_1$ (3.2)

and

$$u \in L^\infty(0,T;X_2)_, \quad \dot{u} \in L^\infty(0,T;L^2(\Omega))$$

Such u is the weak solution of equation (4).
The proof of Theorem as following.

3.1 The Existence of Approximate Solution $u_m(t)$

Suppose the orthogonal basis of X_2 is $\{\omega_j\}(j=1,2,\cdots)$. For any fixed natural number m , denote V_m is a subspace of limited dimension which is spanned by $\omega_1, \omega_2, \cdots \omega_m$ Thus $V_m \subset X_2$, so the Galerkin approximate solution in subspace V_m in the problem (3)~(5) can be denoted by

$$u_m(t) = \sum_{i=1}^m g_{im}(t)w_i(x)$$

$$(3.3)$$

then the Galerkin equation of (6) as follow:

$$(\ddot{u}_m, w_j) + \alpha(u_m^{(2)}, w_j^{(2)}) - \beta(|u_m^{(1)}|^2 u_m^{(2)}, w_j) + \gamma(u_m^{(2)}, w_j) = (f(u_m), w_j) \ (1 \leq j \leq m)$$

Under initial conditions:

$$u_m(0) = u_{0m} = \sum_{i=1}^m \alpha_{jm} w_j, \quad u(0) = u_{1m} = \sum_{i=1}^m \beta_{jm} w_j$$

$$(3.4)$$

Denote: $u_{0m} \to u_0$ in X_2 strong

$$u_{1m} \to u_1 \text{ in } L^2(\Omega) \text{ strong}$$

$$(3.5)$$

And α_{jm} is Fourier coefficients of $u_0(x)$ spread out into
Fourier series in X_2 .

It shows that (3.4), (3.5) is an initial problem of the nonlinear differential equations by $g_{jm}(t)$. By the Peano theorem in ordinary differential equations, there exists $t_m > 0$, such that there exists a unique solution

$g_{jm}(t)(j=1,2,\cdots m)$ in $[0,t_m]$, then we know there exists a unique approximate solution :

$$u_m(0 < t < t_m)$$

3.2 Prior Estimate of Approximate Solution

Multiply (3.4) by $\dot{g}_{jm}(t)$, sum for $j = 1,2,\cdots,m$. This gives:

$$(\ddot{u}_m,\sum_{j=1}^{m}\dot{g}_{jm}w_j)+\alpha(u_m^{(2)},\sum_{j=1}^{m}\dot{g}_{jm}w_j^{(2)})+\beta(u_m^{(1)}u_m^{(2)},\sum_{j=1}^{m}\dot{g}_{jm}w_j)+\gamma(u_m^{(2)},\sum_{j=1}^{m}\dot{g}_{jm}w_j)=(f(u_m),\sum_{j=1}^{m}\dot{g}_{jm}w_j)$$

$$(\ddot{u}_m,\dot{u}_m)+\alpha(u_m^{(2)},\dot{u}_m^{(2)})+\beta(u_m^{(1)}u_m^{(2)},\dot{u}_m)+\gamma(u_m^{(2)},\dot{u}_m)=(f(u_m),\dot{u}_m) \qquad (3.6)$$

$$(|u_m^{(1)}|^2 u_m^{(2)},\dot{u}_m)=-(|u_m^{(1)}|^2 u_m^{(1)},\dot{u}_m^{(1)})=-\frac{1}{2}|u_m^{(1)}|^2\frac{d}{dt}|u_m^{(1)}|^2=-\frac{1}{4}\frac{d}{dt}|u_m^{(1)}|^4$$

$$\sum_{j=1}^{m}\dot{g}_{jm}(t)(\ddot{u}_m,w_j)+\alpha\sum_{j=1}^{m}\dot{g}_{jm}(t)(u_m^{(2)},w_j^{(2)})+$$

$$\beta\sum_{j=1}^{m}\dot{g}_{jm}(t)(u_m^{(1)}u_m^{(2)},w_j)+\gamma\sum_{j=1}^{m}\dot{g}_{jm}(t)(u_m^{(2)},w_j)=\sum_{j=1}^{m}\dot{g}_{jm}(t)(f(u_m),w_j)$$

Substituting into (3.6), we have:

$$\frac{d}{dt}(|\dot{u}_m|^2+\alpha|u_m^{(2)}|+\frac{\beta}{2}|u_m^{(1)}|^4-\gamma|u_m^{(1)}|^2)\leq 2C|u_m||\dot{u}_m|\leq C(|u_m|^2+|\dot{u}_m|^2)$$

Integrate the above inequality with respect to t from 0 to $t(0 < t < T)$ then

$$|\dot{u}_m|^2+\alpha|u_m^{(2)}|+\frac{\beta}{2}|u_m^{(1)}|^4-\gamma|u_m^{(1)}|^2\leq|\dot{u}_m(0)|^2+\alpha|u_m^{(2)}(0)|+\frac{\beta}{2}|u_m^{(1)}(0)|^4-\gamma|u_m^{(1)}(0)|^2+C\int_0^t(|u_m|^2+|\dot{u}_m|^2)dt \quad (3.7)$$

By boundary conditions, $u_m(0,t)$, so by lemma1,
we have

$$|u_m|\leq\frac{l}{\sqrt{2}}|u_m^{(1)}| \qquad (*)$$

And by boundary conditions, $u_m(0,t)=u_m(l,t)=0$, and so by Mid-value theorem there exist $\xi\in(0,l)$ such that $u_m^{(1)}(\xi,t)=0$, then lemma1 now implies that

$$|u_m^{(1)}|\leq\frac{l}{\sqrt{2}}|u_m^{(2)}|$$

The above inequality and inequality (*) imply:

$$|u_m|\leq\frac{l^2}{2}|u_m^{(2)}|$$

So inequality (3.7) get into

$$\left|\ddot{u}_m\right|^2 + \alpha\left|u_m^{(2)}\right| + \frac{\beta}{2}\left|u_m^{(1)}\right|^4 - \gamma\left|u_m^{(1)}\right|^2 \le \left|\ddot{u}_m(0)\right|^2 + \alpha\left|u_m^{(2)}(0)\right| + \frac{\beta}{2}\left|u_m^{(1)}(0)\right|^4 - \gamma\left|u_m^{(1)}(0)\right|^2 + C\int_0^t (\left|u_m^{(2)}\right|^2 + \left|\ddot{u}_m\right|^2)dt \quad (3.8)$$

As suppose (2) follow:

$$\left|\ddot{u}_m(0)\right|^2 + \alpha\left|u_m^{(2)}(0)\right| + \frac{\beta}{2}\left|u_m^{(1)}(0)\right|^4 - \gamma\left|u_m^{(1)}(0)\right|^2 \to \left|u_1\right|^2 + \alpha\left|u_0^{(2)}\right|^2 + \frac{\beta}{2}\left|u_m^{(1)}(0)\right|^4 - \gamma\left|u_0^{(1)}\right|^2$$

Then by Gronwall inequality, we know the right side of (3.8) is uniform boundedness about m, so the left side is also bounded. It is said that

$$\dot{u} < C , \left|u_m^{(2)}\right| < C , \left|u_m^{(1)}\right| < c \quad (3.9)$$

From the boundedness above, we know $u_m(t)$ is meaningful in $[0,T]$ for all the natural number m and all $t_m = T$, there $T > 0$ and T is fixed.

Since

$$\left|u_m\right|_{X_2}^2 = \left|u_m\right|^2 + \left|u_m^{(1)}\right|^2 + \left|u_m^{(2)}\right|^2$$

From (3.9) we have: $\left|u_m\right|_{X_2} < C$

3.3 The Convergence of $u_m(t)$

Form the boundedness above, we know there exists a subsequence $\{u_\mu\}$ of $\{u_m\}$, when $\mu \to \infty$,

$$u_\mu \to u \text{ in } L^\infty(0,T;X_2) \qquad \text{weak*,}$$
$$\dot{u}_\mu \to \gamma \text{ in } L^\infty(0,T;L^2(\Omega) \qquad \text{weak*,}$$
$$u_\mu^{(1)} \to u^{(1)} \text{ in } L^\infty(0,T;L^2(\Omega)) \qquad \text{weak*}$$
$$u_\mu^{(2)} \to u^{(2)} \text{ in } L^\infty(0,T;L^2(\Omega)) \qquad \text{weak*}$$
$$\left|u_m^{(1)}\right|u_m^{(2)} \to \left|u^{(1)}\right|^2 u^{(2)} \text{ in } L^\infty(0,T;L^2(\Omega)) \text{ weak*}$$

Take the limit of (3.6), we yield

$$(\ddot{u},\varphi + \alpha(u^{(2)},\varphi) - \beta(\left|u^{(1)}\right|^2 u^{(2)},\varphi) + \gamma(u^{(2)},\varphi) = (f(u),\varphi)$$

Thus, the existence of the weak solution in $[0,T]$ of system (3)~(5) is proofed.

Acknowledgement. This paper is founded by National Natural Science Foundation (60772101), Shanxi Youth Science Foundation (2007021016), Shanxi University Technology research and development project (20090011), Shanxi Youth Science Foundation (2010021017-1) and Taiyuan 2010 University Students innovation and entrepreneurship projects (100115107).

References

1. Fermi, E., Pasta, J., Ulam, S.: Studies of Nonlinear Problems. In: Newell (ed.) LNAM, vol. 15, pp. 143–196. American Math. Society, Providence (1974)
2. Kruskai, M.D., Zabusky, K.J.: Progress on the FPU nonlinear string problem. In: Kruskai, M.D. (ed.) Princeton Plama Physics Laboratory Annual Rept. MATT-Q-21, Princeton, NJ (1983)
3. Kriiegers, W.: The effect of axial force on the vibration of hinged bars. Journal of Applied Mechanics 17, 35–36 (1950)
4. Ball, J.M.: Initial-boundary value problems for an extensible beam. J. Mathe. Anal. 42, 61–88 (1973)

Modeling for Heat-Exchangers of Heat-Setting Machine*

Yibo Zhang and Ren Jia

Institute of Automation, Zhejiang Sci-Tech University
Hangzhou, China
zhangy41@yeah.net

Abstract. A model for heat-exchangers of heat-setting machine is proposed. First, techniques of heat exchangers in heat-setting machines is introduced. Then on basis of Newton cooling law, heat transfer formula is proposed. Third, three heat damps between oil, tube body and air are introduced respectively. According to basic heat transfer theory, equation for temperatures of heated air is obtained. Practice data and simulating data are compared and mean and variance are calculated. Result shows that error is less than 2%, which means high precision of the proposed model.

Keywords: modeling for heat-exchangers, heat-setting machines, Newton cooling law.

1 Introduction

Heat-setting machine is a kind of equipment for ironing wet fabric that has dyed and rinsed. Its main function is to reduce crumpled of fabric by ironing with hot air, whose temperature is between 140℃ and 300℃.

Normally, a heat-setting machine consists of 9 or 10 ironing oven continuously connected. Normal temperature air, which is heated by hot oil through heat-transformer, is blown to wet fabric in ironing oven. Each ironing oven shares the same techniques while functions and parameters are different [1].

Heat exchangers are first process in ironing oven of heat-setting machine. Heat transfer oil is heated to 280℃-340℃ in boiler and sent to heat exchanger through pipes, by through which air with normal temperature absorbs heat energy and rises to a higher temperature. Because there is one heat exchanger in each ironing oven, there are ten heat exchangers in a single heat-setting machine. Temperatures of hot air in each ironing oven are different.

There are three main controlled parameters in each heat exchanger: flux of air, flux and temperature of oil. In order to achieve temperature needed, three parameters should be well controlled, which means high precision model of heat exchanger should be obtained first.

Some researches are concerned on heat-setting machine, such as [2], which is mainly discussing a kind of heat-setting machine with electric and magnetic energy. Most

---

* This work is supported by National 863 High Technology Development Program (2009AA04Z139) & Zhejiang Natural Science Foundation (Y1110686).

H. Deng et al. (Eds.): AICI 2011, Part I, LNAI 7002, pp. 95–100, 2011.

researches, such as [3] and [4], introduces control method for some parameters (temperature, speed or tensile force) of heat-setting machine. No researches concerned on energy consumption modeling and control technology. With development of printing and dyeing industry, energy consumption saving is playing more and more important role, so modeling and control technology for energy consumption is essential.

In this paper, modeling for energy consumption of heat-setting machine is proposed. On basis of techniques of ironing ovens in heat-setting machine, fabric temperature-raising formula aiming at each workshop section is deduced. And then heat transfer expression of heat-setting machine is proposed. So energy consumption are calculated and tested in practice.

Organization of this work is shown as following: The second part introduces ironing oven in heat-setting machine, and how temperature of fabric raised. By considering different conditions, modeling for ironing ovens are illuminated for three kinds of processes. Then modeling for energy consumption is considered in part 3. In part 4, practice data and modeling data are compared and analyzed. At last, conclusion is drawn in part 5.

2   Energy Modeling for Heat-Setting Machine

There are two heat transfer process in heat-setting machine. First, hot heat-transfer oil is send to heat exchangers, where cold air is heating up. Second, wet fabric is dried by heated air. Two processes of modeling are illuminated as following.

Simplified sketch map of heat exchanger is shown in Fig. 1.

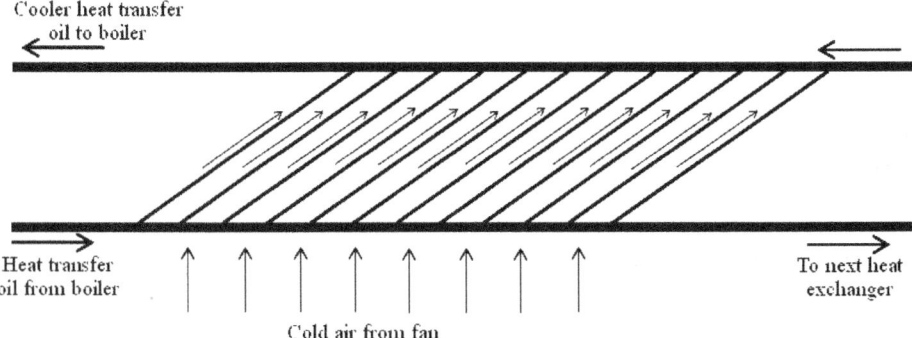

Fig. 1. A single heat exchanger in heat-setting machine

In this work, T and t denote Temperature and Time respectively, with subscript f (fabric) or s (surroundings). Heat transfer oil is send to heat exchangers through metal tubes. Electric fans blow cold air to get across and absorb heat to a high temperature. Heat transfer oil, with flux m and initial temperature t_i, exchanges heat in inner surface by convection. Considering a tiny columniation with length dx and diameter equal to tubes, then heat exchange can be obtained by energy balance equation: $dq = q'Pdx$, where q' denotes special heat (W/m^2), and P denotes circle length of tube, which equal to πD for roundness tube.

According to Newton cooling law:

$$\frac{dT}{dx} = \frac{q'P}{\dot{m}c} h(T_b - T) \tag{1}$$

where c, h, T_b and T denote specific heat of heat transfer oil, coefficient of convection heat exchange, temperature of inner tube and average temperature of oil respectively.

Total heat damp can be separated as following heat damps in series:

(1) Heat damp between oil and inner surface of tube (R_1)

$$R_1 = \frac{1}{\pi D h_1} \tag{2}$$

where D denotes inner diameter, and h_1 denotes coefficient between oil and inner tube surface:

$$h_1 = \frac{Nu\lambda}{D} \tag{3}$$

where λ denotes heat conducting coefficient, Nu denotes Nu-Number equals to 3.66 when laminar flow. When turbulence exists in velvet tube, if difference in temperature is less, Nu can be calculated by formula of Dittus-boelter:

$$Nu = 0.023 \, \mathrm{Re}_f^{0.8} \, \mathrm{Pr}_f^{0.4} \text{ (Heating Oil)} \tag{4}$$

$$Nu = 0.023 \, \mathrm{Re}_f^{0.8} \, \mathrm{Pr}_f^{0.3} \text{ (Cooling Oil)} \tag{5}$$

where Re_f and Pr_f denote Renault-Number and Puandtl-Number with average temperature of oil respectively.

If difference in temperature is more than $100°C$, Sieder-Tate associate formula is adopted:

$$Nu = 0.027 \, \mathrm{Re}_f^{0.8} \, \mathrm{Pr}_f^{1/3} (\mu_f / \mu_w)^{0.14} \tag{6}$$

where μ_f and μ_w denote oil viscosity with average temperature of oil and inner tube separately.

(2) Heat damp of tube body (R_2)

$$R_2 = \frac{1}{2\pi\lambda} \ln \frac{D_w}{D} \tag{7}$$

where D_w denote external diameter of tube

(3) Heat damp between external wall of tube and air (R_3)

$$R_3 = \frac{1}{\pi D_w h_3 v_s^{0.8}} \tag{8}$$

where h_3 denotes heat transfer coefficient between external wall of tube and air.

According to basic heat transfer theory,

$$q' = \frac{T_b - T}{R_1} = \frac{T_s - T_b}{R_1 + R_2 + R_3} \tag{9}$$

where T_s denotes average temperature of air. Because distribution of tubes is dense, temperature of air close to external wall of tube are considered equal to average temperature.

Eliminate T_b by (1) and (9):

$$\frac{\dot{m}c \sum\limits_{j=1}^{3} R_j}{Ph(T_s - T)} dT = dx \tag{10}$$

Integrate length of tube:

$$\int_{T_{in}}^{T_o} \frac{\dot{m}c \sum\limits_{j=1}^{3} R_j}{Ph(T_s - T)} dT = \int_0^l dx \tag{11}$$

where T_i and T_o denote oil temperatures of inlet and outlet.

Then

$$l = \frac{\dot{m}c}{Ph} \sum\limits_{j=1}^{3} R_j \ln \frac{T_s - T_{in}}{T_s - T_o} \tag{12}$$

Resolving (12), it turns into:

$$T_s = T_o + (T_{in} + T_o) / \left(1 - e^{\frac{lPh}{\dot{m}c \sum\limits_{j=1}^{3} R_j}} \right) \tag{13}$$

Considering there are ten ironing ovens in a single heat-setting machine, and flux can be controlled, (13) can be rewritten as:

$$T_s^{(j)} = T_O + (T_{in} + T_O) / \left(1 - e^{\frac{lPh}{\dot{m}_j c \sum_{i=1}^{3} R_i}} \right) \quad j = 1, 2, ..., 10 \tag{14}$$

where j denotes the j th ironing oven.

3 Modeling Analyses

The model is verified by experiments in different conditions, which are list in Table 1.

Table 1. Data for Temperature Difference

	Temperature in each Ironing Oven (℃)												
	1#	2#	3#	4#	5#	6#	7#	8#	9#	10#	T_{in}	T_O	V_s
Environment Temperature	170	175	185	190	200	200	200	195	20	20	280	276	1.5
Model Temperature	171	178	186	189	199	199	199	193	0	0			
Environment Temperature	180	190	195	210	210	210	205	200	20	20	285	280	1.1
Model Temperature	180	189	195	211	211	211	206	211	0	0			
Environment Temperature	150	155	160	170	170	170	170	165	160	20	259	256	1.1
Model Temperature	151	153	160	169	169	169	169	166	159	0			
Environment Temperature	145	150	155	160	160	160	160	155	150	20	251	247	1.5
Model Temperature	145	151	155	159	159	159	159	153	153	0			

Means of errors between environment temperatures and model temperatures are 1.07, 1.05, 1.11 and 1.125 in different speed, while standard deviations are 0.064, 0.081, 0.083 and 0.14 respectively. All errors are no more than 2%. These static data denote temperatures of model are closed to these of real system. These errors of energy consumptions and temperatures are mainly produced by heat wasting between heat-setting machine and nature environment.

It can be also seen from Table 1 that errors reduce gradually, which means speed of temperature raising reduced when environment temperature change less.

Temperatures and energy consumptions are shown in Fig. 4.

It can be seen from Fig. 4 that temperatures obviously reduced in the tenth ironing oven, and energy consumptions contain stable simultaneity because of cooling processes do not absorb heat energy.

4 Conclusion

Energy consumption modeling is proposed in this work. With fabric temperature-raising formula, energy consumption modeling is obtained. The further research is concerted on optimal energy consumption under precondition of technics, which means setting temperatures quantity of ironing ovens in each workshop section can be calculated by algorithms.

References

1. Chen, Y.F.: Practical process technology for printing and dyeing of weave. Chemical Engineering Publishing Company (2008)
2. Li, G.E.: Development and Application of Electric and Magnetic Heat-Setting Machine. Zhejiang University (2010)
3. Qu, W.T., Zhang, S.L.: Multivariable fuzzy control technology of heat setting machine. Journal of Textile Research 26(4), 111–114 (2005)
4. Hu, L.F.: Design for control system of stretching heat-setting machine based on PLC and Converter. Tianjing Industry University (2007)
5. Hu, H.P.: Theory of Heat Exchange. Chinese Science and Technology University Publishing (2004)

Models and Algorithm of Maximum Flow Problem in Uncertain Network

Chen Zhou[1] and Jin Peng[2]

[1] College of Mathematics & Science, Shanghai Normal University, Shanghai 200234, China
[2] Institute of Uncertain Systems, Huanggang Normal University, Hubei 438000, China
pengjin01@tsinghua.org.cn

Abstract. Network flow problem covers a wide range of engineering and management applications. The maximum flow problem is to find the maximum amount of flow from the source to the sink within a network. Different from the existing works, this paper investigates maximum flow problem in which all arc capacities of the network are uncertain variables. Some models of maximum flow problem with uncertain arc capacities are exhibited. And then, the algorithm for solving maximum flow problem is introduced. As an illustration, an example is provided to show the effectiveness of the algorithm.

Keywords: uncertainty theory, uncertain variable, uncertainty distribution, uncertain network, maximum flow problem.

1 Introduction

The maximum flow problem's predecessors can be shown as early as the 1930s. Tolstŏi [14] studied the transportation problem and described a number of solution approaches. The transportation issue, which later evolved into the maximum flow problem, became more complex [12].

Somers [13] proposed a new approach to the problem of computing its distribution and expected value via a corollary of the max-flow min-cut theorem. In [1], Grimmett and Welsh studied the problem of finding the maximum flow through a capacitated network in which the set of capacities is a collection of independent random variables, drawn from some known distributions. Winston [15] introduced LINGO to solve maximum flow problem.

Liu and Kao [10] investigated the network flow problems in which the arc lengths of the network were fuzzy numbers. Ji, Yang and Shao [3] considered a generalized fuzzy version of maximum flow problem in which arc capacities were fuzzy variables. The problem discussed in [3] was to find a maximum flow under some chance constraints with respect to credibility measure of arc flow of network. A genetic algorithm is introduced to solve the problem. Kumar and Kaur [4] presented the fuzzy linear programming formulation of fuzzy maximal flow problems and a method for finding the fuzzy optimal solution. Moreover, Kumar and Kaur [5] proposed a new algorithm to find the fuzzy maximal flow by representing the flow as normal triangular fuzzy numbers.

H. Deng et al. (Eds.): AICI 2011, Part I, LNAI 7002, pp. 101–109, 2011.
© Springer-Verlag Berlin Heidelberg 2011

In order to deal with some uncertain phenomena, uncertainty theory was founded by Liu [6] in 2007, refined by Liu [7] in 2010, and became a branch of mathematics based on the normality, self-duality, countable subadditivity, and product measure axioms. Product measure axiom was proposed by Liu [8], and then it produced the operational law for uncertain variables. In uncertainty theory, uncertain measure is used to measure the belief degree of an uncertain event. Based on uncertainty theory, Liu [9] established uncertain programming. Peng and Li [11] considered a spanning tree problem of uncertain network and proposed three types of minimum spanning tree models for uncertain network. Han and Peng [2] studied the maximum flow problem of uncertain network on some cases by means of inverse uncertainty distribution. Different from the existing works, in this paper we will present some uncertain programming models for maximum flow problem with uncertain arc capacities. An algorithm and an illustrative example are provided.

The rest of this paper is organized as follows: Section 2 presents some preliminary concepts and results selected from uncertainty theory. In Section 3, we show the model of maximum flow problem with uncertain arc capacities. The algorithm for solving maximum flow problem is introduced in section 4. In Section 5, we present a numerical example to illustrate the effectiveness of the model and algorithm. The last section contains some concluding remarks.

2 Preliminaries

In this section, we present some definitions and results in uncertainty theory.

Let Γ be a nonempty set and L be a σ-algebra over Γ. Each element Λ in the σ-algebra is called an event.

The set function M over L is called an uncertain measure if it satisfies the normality, self-duality, and countable subadditivity axioms. The triplet (Γ, L, M) is called an uncertainty space and an uncertain variable is defined as a function from this space to the set of real numbers ([6]).

An uncertain variable ξ can be characterized by its uncertainty distribution $\Phi : \rightarrow [0, 1]$, which is defined by Liu [6] as follows

$$\Phi(x) = M\left\{\gamma \in \Gamma \mid \xi(\gamma) \leq x\right\}. \tag{1}$$

An uncertain distribution Φ is called regular if its inverse function $\Phi^{-1}(\alpha)$ exists and is unique for each $\alpha \in (0,1)$.

Liu [6] introduced the independence concept of uncertain variables. For any Borel sets $B_1, B_2, \cdots, B_m$ of R, the uncertain variables $\xi_1, \xi_2, \cdots, \xi_m$ are independent if and only if

$$M\left\{\bigcap_{i=1}^{m}\{\xi_i \in B_i\}\right\} = \min_{1 \le i \le m} M\{\xi_i \in B_i\}. \tag{2}$$

A real-valued function $f(x_1, x_2, \cdots x_n)$ is said to be strictly increasing (Liu [7]) if $f(x_1, x_2, \cdots x_n) \le f(y_1, y_2, \cdots y_n)$ whenever $x_i \le y_i$ for $i = 1, 2, \cdots, n$, and $f(x_1, x_2, \cdots x_n) < f(y_1, y_2, \cdots y_n)$ whenever $x_i < y_i$ for $i = 1, 2, \cdots, n$.

We assume that the constraint function $g_j(x, \xi_1, \xi_2, \cdots, \xi_n)$ is strictly increasing with respect to $\xi_1, \xi_2, \cdots, \xi_k$ and strictly decreasing with respect to $\xi_{k+1}, \xi_{k+2}, \cdots, \xi_n$. According to Liu [7], if $\xi_1, \xi_2, \cdots, \xi_n$ are independent uncertain variables with uncertainty distribution $\Phi_1, \Phi_2, \cdots \Phi_n$, respectively, then the chance constraint $M\{g_j(x, \xi_1, \xi_2, \cdots, \xi_n) \le 0\} \ge \alpha_j$ holds if and only if

$$g_j(x, \Phi_1^{-1}(\alpha_j), \cdots, \Phi_k^{-1}(\alpha_j), \Phi_{k+1}^{-1}(1-\alpha_j), \cdots, \Phi_n^{-1}(1-\alpha_j)) \le 0.$$

In the following, we list several types of inverse uncertainty distributions in [7].

The inverse uncertainty distribution of linear uncertain variable L(a, b) is

$$\Phi^{-1}(\alpha) = (1-\alpha)a + \alpha b. \tag{3}$$

The inverse uncertainty distribution of zigzag uncertain variable Z(a, b, c) is

$$\Phi^{-1}(\alpha) = \begin{cases} (1-2\alpha)a + 2\alpha b, & if \ \alpha \le 0.5, \\ (2-2\alpha)b + (2\alpha-1)c, & if \ \alpha \ge 0.5. \end{cases} \tag{4}$$

The inverse uncertainty distribution of normal uncertain variable N(e, σ) is

$$\Phi^{-1}(\alpha) = e + \frac{\sigma\sqrt{3}}{\pi}\ln\frac{\alpha}{1-\alpha}. \tag{5}$$

The inverse uncertainty distribution of lognormal uncertain variable LOGN(e, σ) is

$$\Phi^{-1}(\alpha) = \exp(e)(\frac{\alpha}{1-\alpha})^{\frac{\sigma\sqrt{3}}{\pi}}. \tag{6}$$

Let ξ is an uncertain variable with uncertainty distribution Φ, then the inverse uncertainty distribution of $-\xi$ is

$$\Psi^{-1}(\alpha) = -\Phi^{-1}(1-\alpha). \tag{7}$$

3 The Model of Maximum Flow Problem

Let $D = (V, A, W)$ be a directed network consisting of n nodes, where $V = \{1, 2, \cdots, n\}$, $A = \{(i, j) \mid i, j \in V\}$ and $W = \{w_{ij} \mid (i, j) \in A\}$. The classical maximum flow problem is to send the maximum possible flow from a specified source node (node 1) to a specified sink node (node n), where there is no upper bound on that flows. At each node, the total supply equal total demand. In other words, $b_i = 0$ for all $i \in V$. Let ω_{ij} represent the upper bound of the flow through arc (i, j) and x_{ij} the flow through arc (i, j). In this case, we can show the following model

$$\begin{cases} \max \quad z = x_{n1} \\ s.t. \\ \sum_{j=1}^{n} x_{ij} - \sum_{j=1}^{n} x_{ji} = 0 \ \ for \ all \ i \in V \\ 0 \leq x_{ij} \leq \omega_{ij} \qquad for \ all \ (i, j) \in A. \end{cases}$$

In many situations, however, we do not know the capacities of arcs. In these cases, the capacities of arcs are approximately estimated by the expert. We can obtain expert's experimental data by means of uncertain statistic and give the uncertainty distributions of uncertain capacities. Here we assume that the capacity of arc (i, j) is an uncertain variable ξ_{ij}. After giving a confidence level α_{ij} for the uncertain capacity of each arc (i, j), we can establish the following uncertain programming model for the maximum flow problem

$$\begin{cases} \max \quad z = x_{n1} \\ s.t. \\ \sum_{j=1}^{n} x_{ij} - \sum_{j=1}^{n} x_{ji} = 0 \qquad for \ all \ i \in V \\ M\{x_{ij} - \xi_{ij} \leq 0\} \geq \alpha_{ij} \ \ for \ all \ (i, j) \in A \\ x_{ij} \geq 0 \qquad for \ all \ (i, j) \in A. \end{cases}$$

Furthermore, if all ξ_{ij} are assumed to be independent uncertain variables with uncertainty distributions Φ_{ij} respectively, then we can transform the above model into corresponding deterministic form

$$
\begin{cases}
\max \quad z = x_{n1} \\
s.t. \\
\displaystyle\sum_{j=1}^{n} x_{ij} - \sum_{j=1}^{n} x_{ji} = 0 \quad for \ all \ i \in V \\
0 \le x_{ij} \le \Phi_{ij}^{-1}(1 - \alpha_{ij}) \ for \ all \ (i, j) \in A.
\end{cases}
$$

Example 1. Assume that decision variables x_{ij} are nonnegative amount of flow on arc (i, j) of a network, and ξ_{ij} are independent linear uncertain variables $L(a_{ij}, b_{ij})$ on arc (i, j) of the network. Then for any given confidence level $\alpha_{ij} \in (0,1)$, the model of maximum flow problem of uncertain network can be represented as

$$
\begin{cases}
\max \quad z = x_{n1} \\
s.t. \\
\displaystyle\sum_{j=1}^{n} x_{ij} - \sum_{j=1}^{n} x_{ji} = 0 \quad for \ all \ i \in V \\
0 \le x_{ij} \le \alpha_{ij} a_{ij} + (1 - \alpha_{ij}) b_{ij} \ for \ all \ (i, j) \in A.
\end{cases}
$$

Example 2. Assume that decision variables x_{ij} are nonnegative amount of flow on arc (i, j) of a network, and ξ_{ij} are independent zigzag uncertain variables $Z(a_{ij}, b_{ij}, c_{ij})$ on arc (i, j) of the network. Then for any given confidence level $\alpha_{ij} \in (0.5, 1)$, the model of maximum flow problem of uncertain network can be represented as

$$
\begin{cases}
\max \quad z = x_{n1} \\
s.t. \\
\displaystyle\sum_{j=1}^{n} x_{ij} - \sum_{j=1}^{n} x_{ji} = 0 \quad for \ all \ i \in V \\
0 \le x_{ij} \le 2\alpha_{ij} b_{ij} + (1 - 2\alpha_{ij}) c_{ij} \ for \ all \ (i, j) \in A.
\end{cases}
$$

Example 3. Assume that decision variables x_{ij} are nonnegative amount of flow on arc (i, j) of a network, and ξ_{ij} are independent normal uncertain variables $N(e_{ij}, \sigma_{ij})$ on arc (i, j) of the network. Then for any given confidence level

$\alpha_{ij} \in (0,1)$, the model of maximum flow problem of uncertain network can be represented as

$$
\begin{cases}
\max \quad z = x_{n1} \\
s.t. \\
\displaystyle\sum_{j=1}^{n} x_{ij} - \sum_{j=1}^{n} x_{ji} = 0 \qquad\qquad for\ all\ i \in V \\
0 \leq x_{ij} \leq e_{ij} + \dfrac{\sigma_{ij}\sqrt{3}}{\pi} \ln \dfrac{1-\alpha_{ij}}{\alpha_{ij}} \quad for\ all\ (i,j) \in A.
\end{cases}
$$

Example 4. Assume that decision variables x_{ij} are nonnegative amount of flow on arc (i,j) of a network, and ξ_{ij} are independent lognormal uncertain variables LOGN(e_{ij}, σ_{ij}) on arc (i,j) of the network. Then for any given confidence level $\alpha_{ij} \in (0,1)$, the model of maximum flow problem of uncertain network can be represented as

$$
\begin{cases}
\max \quad z = x_{n1} \\
s.t. \\
\displaystyle\sum_{j=1}^{n} x_{ij} - \sum_{j=1}^{n} x_{ji} = 0 \qquad\qquad for\ all\ i \in V \\
0 \leq x_{ij} \leq \exp(e_{ij})(\dfrac{1-\alpha_{ij}}{\alpha_{ij}})^{\frac{\sqrt{3}\sigma_{ij}}{\pi}} \quad for\ all\ (i,j) \in A.
\end{cases}
$$

4   Algorithm for Solving Maximum Flow Problem

The maximum flow problem is finding a legal flow through a flow network that is maximal. Sometimes it is defined as finding the value of such a flow. The maximum flow problem can be seen as special case of more complex network flow problems. The maximal flow is related to the cuts in a network by the max-flow min-cut theorem. The Ford-Fulkerson algorithm computes the maximum flow in a flow network. There exist several specialized algorithms, such as Ford-Fulkerson algorithm, to solve maximum flow problems. LINDO and LINGO, or MATLab are used to realize the algorithms. In the following, we will introduce the LINGO program to find the maximum flow of uncertain network.

```
MODEL:
1]SETS:
2]NODES/1..n/;
3]ARCS(NODES, NODES)/All arc (I, J)∈A/
4]:CAP, FLOW;
5]ENDSETS
6]MAX=FLOW(n, 1);
7]@FOR(ARCS(I,J): FLOW(I, J)≤CAP(I, J));
8]@FOR(NODES(I): @SUM(ARCS(J, I): FLOW(J,
I))=@SUM(ARCS(I,J): FLOW(I, J)));
9]DATA;
10]CAP=The capacities of arcs in line 3;
11]ENDDATA
END
```

Now we explain the program in more detail. Line 2 and 3 define the nodes and arcs of the flow network respectively. Line 4 indicates that an arc capacity and a flow are associated with each arc. Line 5 ends the definition of the relevant sets. We represent that our objective is to maximize the flow through the artificial arc (which equals the flow into the sink) in line 6. Line 7 specifies the arc capacity constraints that the flow through each arc cannot exceed the arc's capacity. Line 8 creates the conservation of flow constraints. In this way, it is ensured that the flow into node i equals the flow out of node i for each node i. Line 9 begins the DATA section. We input the arc capacities in line 10. Line 11 ends the DATA section and the END statement ends the program. Typing GO yields the solution.

5 Example

Assume that there is a street network of a city. Managers want to count the maximum flow of traffic from node 1 to node 5 in Figure 1. On the way from node 1 to node 5, vehicles must pass through some or all the intersections 2, 3 and 4. The maximum flow of traffic that can pass through each arc is shown in Table 1. We assume that arc capacities are independent zigzag uncertain variables.

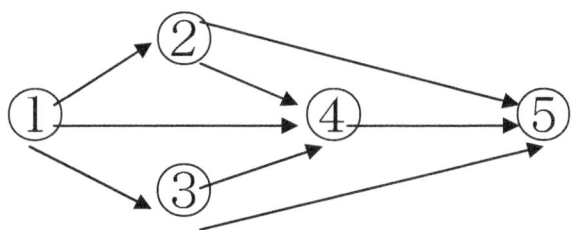

Fig. 1.

Table 1.

Arc	(1, 2)	(1, 3)	(1, 4)	(2, 3)
Capacity	$\xi_{12}{\sim}Z(10,20,30)$	$\xi_{13}{\sim}Z(20,30,40)$	$\xi_{14}{\sim}Z(5,10,15)$	$\xi_{23}{\sim}Z(4,5,6)$
Arc	(2, 5)	(3, 5)	(4, 3)	(4, 5)
Capacity	$\xi_{25}{\sim}Z(26,27,28)$	$\xi_{35}{\sim}Z(10,15,20)$	$\xi_{43}{\sim}Z(13,14,15)$	$\xi_{45}{\sim}Z(18,19,20)$

For simplicity, we assume that all the pre-determined confidence levels α_{ij} are equal to 0.7. Now we can express the following model for the uncertain maximum flow problem

$$
\begin{cases}
\max \quad z = x_{n1} \\
s.t. \\
\sum_{j=1}^{5} x_{ij} - \sum_{j=1}^{5} x_{ji} = 0 \qquad for \ \ all \ \ i \in V \\
0 \le x_{ij} \le 1.4b_{ij} - 0.4c_{ij} \ \ for \ \ all \ \ (i, j) \in A,
\end{cases}
$$

where b_{ij}, c_{ij} are the components of zigzag uncertainty distribution $Z(a_{ij}, b_{ij}, c_{ij})$. By applying the approach proposed in above section, we obtain the optimal solution $x_{12} = 16.0000$, $x_{13} = 13.0000$, $x_{14} = 8.0000$, $x_{23} = 0.0000$, $x_{25} = 16.0000$, $x_{35} = 13.0000$, $x_{43} = 0.0000$, $x_{45} = 8.0000$ with optimal objective value z = 37.0000, which is the maximum flow of traffic from node 1 to node 5 in the uncertain flow network.

6   Conclusion

In this paper, we establish some models of maximum flow problem with uncertain arc capacities. With the help of uncertainty theory, these models can be transformed into the corresponding deterministic models. In order to find the optimal solution of the proposed mathematical programming models, we can use LINGO or other mathematical softwares. At last, we presented a numerical example to illustrate the effectiveness of the model and algorithm.

Acknowledgments. This work is supported by the National Natural Science Foundation (No.60874067), the Hubei Provincial Natural Science Foundation (No.2010CDB02801), and the Scientific and Technological Innovation Team Project (No.T201110) of Hubei Provincial Department of Education, China.

References

1. Grimmett, G.R., Welsh, D.J.A.: Flow in Networks with Random Capacities. Stochastics An International Journal of Probability and Stochastic Processes 7, 205–229 (1982)
2. Han, S., Peng, Z.: The maximum Flow Problem of Uncertain Network, http://orsc.edu.cn/online/101228.pdf
3. Ji, X., Yang, L., Shao, Z.: Chance Constrained Maximum Flow Problem with Fuzzy Arc Capacities. In: Huang, D.-S., Li, K., Irwin, G.W. (eds.) ICIC 2006. LNCS(LNAI), vol. 4114, pp. 11–19. Springer, Heidelberg (2006)
4. Kumar, A., Kaur, M.: Solution of Fuzzy Maximal Flow Problems Using Fuzzy Linear Programming. International Journal of Computational and Mathematical Sciences 5, 62–67 (2011)
5. Kumar, A., Kaur, M.: An Algorithm for Solving Fuzzy Maximal Flow Problems Using Generalized Trapezoidal Fuzzy Numbers. International Journal of Applied Science and Engineering 8, 109–118 (2010)
6. Liu, B.: Uncertainty Theory, 2nd edn. Springer, Berlin (2007)
7. Liu, B.: Uncertainty Theory: A Branch of Mathematics for Modeling Human Uncertain. Springer, Berlin (2010)
8. Liu, B.: Some Research Problems in Uncertainty Theory. Journal of Uncertain Systems 3, 3–10 (2009)
9. Liu, B.: Theory and Practice of Uncertain Programming. Springer, Berlin (2009)
10. Liu, S.T., Kao, C.: Network Flow Problems With Fuzzy Arc Lengths. IEEE Transactions on Systems, Man, and Cybernetics—Part B: Cybernetics 34, 765–769 (2004)
11. Peng, J., Li, S.: Spanning Tree Problem of Uncertain Network. In: Proceedings of the 3rd International Conference on Computer Design and Applications (ICCDA 2011), Xi'an, Shaanxi, China, May 27-29 (2011)
12. Schrijver, A.: On the History of the Transportation And Maximum Flow Problems. Mathematical Programming 91, 437–445 (2002)
13. Somers, J.E.: Maximum Flow in Networks with A Small Number of Random Arc Capacities. Networks 12, 241–253 (1982)
14. Tolstŏi, A.N.: Metody Nakhozhdeniya Naimen'shego Summovogo Kilometrazha Pri Planirovanii Perevozok v Prostranstve. In: Planirovanie Perevozok, Sbornik pervyi, Transpechat' NKPS, Moscow, pp. 23–55 (1930)
15. Winston, W.L.: Operations Research: Applications and Algorithms, 3rd edn. Wadsworth, Belmont (1994)

A Tracking Method of Formation Satellites Cluster for Single-Beam and Multi-target TT&C Equipments

Jian-Ping Liu, Jing Li, Jian Bai, and Pei-Jun Yu

State Key Laboratory of Astronautic Dynamics
Xi'an Satellite Control Center
Xi'an, China
ljpnudt@sina.com

Abstract. In order to slowing current tensional status of tracking, telemetry and command (TT&C) resources and developing farthest capabilities of multi-target TT&C equipments, the problem about single-beam and multi-target TT&C Equipments tracking synchronously formation satellites cluster is researched in this paper. Based on smooth and reliable multi-target tracking principle and characteristic of single-beam antenna axis pointing to main target, confirming methods of main tracking target for single-beam and multi-target TT&C Equipments based on two tracking modes are proposed, Simulation results show that this tracking method is feasible and valid.

Keywords: TT&C, single-beam multi-target tracking problem, formation satellites cluster.

1 Introduction

Now multi-target TT&C system [1,2] utilizes CDMA based on spread spectrum and call-response cooperative TT&C mode, so it must require frequency consistency of each spacecraft TT&C transponder tracked. When single-beam and multi-target (SBMT for short) TT&C equipment tracks, firstly moving directions of this multi-target need keep consistency which means that targets move toward the same direction relative to antenna pointing of TT&C equipment, then each target must be seen from this equipment which means that each target is covered by antenna beam. Formation satellites cluster [3, 4] has received much attention in recent years because of the possible advantages of replacing a single, complex satellite with a cluster of smaller ones. Characteristics of formation satellites cluster include: each satellite uses the same spread spectrum transponder, and relative range is close from several hundred meters to several kilometers generally among satellites, and all satellites form a certain geometrical formation Configuration such as line, circle, triangle etc. these characteristics provide possibility for SBMT TT&C equipment tracking synchronously formation satellites cluster, which develops farthest capabilities of multi-target TT&C equipments and slow current tensional status of TT&C resources.

   In engineering, SBMT TT&C equipment applies first capturing and first tracking method [5,6], which means that which target firstly enters covering area of antenna

H. Deng et al. (Eds.): AICI 2011, Part I, LNAI 7002, pp. 110–118, 2011.

beam is the main target that antenna axis pointing to, but this method may lose other target during tracking multi-targets because tracking other targets depend on single-beam antenna axis pointing direction. The key of SBMT TT&C equipment tracking problem is the choice of main target. Good choice means that targets are tracked smoothly and reliably, and poor choice means that some target may be lost. So a determination method of main tracking target for SBMT TT&C equipments based on two tracking modes is proposed in this paper.

2 SBMT TT&C Equipment

Performance index for SBMT TT&C equipment includes 3dB beamwidth, antenna gain, G/T, baseband processing capacity etc, the parameters determining tracking capability of multi-target TT&C equipments is 3dB beamwidth and baseband processing capacity. In order to ensuring that SBMT TT&C equipment can track synchronously formation satellites cluster, two conditions need at lest be met: One is that antenna angle of each satellite covered by antenna beam of the equipment is less than half of 3dB beamwidth, the other is the number of satellites is less than baseband processing capacity.

Tracking modes of SBMT TT&C equipment include auto-tracking mode and digital-leading mode. For auto-tracking mode, the angles driving antenna running depend on the main target tracked, which means that main target drives auto-tracking mode, so main target and others need be distinguished during tracking multi targets, which ensures that antenna beam can cover multi targets, and at the same time antenna axis points to main target . For digital-leading mode, the angles driving antenna running depend on real-time calculating values, so main target and others need not be distinguished, which only needs that antenna beam droved by real-time calculating angles can cover all along multi targets. Real-time calculating angles is actually derived from some target track, and this target may be real, or may be virtual, in this paper this target is still thought of as main target. In the following, the confirming methods of main tracking target based on above two tracking modes are discussed.

3 Determination of Main Target

Fig1 shows SBMT TT&C equipment tracking formation satellite cluster view, where SBMT TT&C equipment is ground-based or space borne, its 3dB beamwidth is β, baseband processing capacity is n, and formation satellite cluster is made up of n satellites. Tracking prediction for each satellite are denoted generally vector R which includes range ρ, azimuth angle A and elevation angle E. According to the above hypothesizes, the determination method of main target is shown as follows.

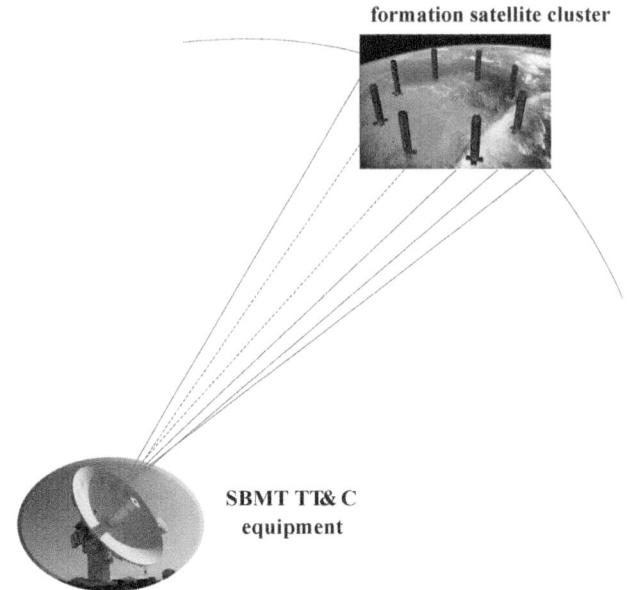

Fig. 1. SBMT TT&C equipment tracking formation satellite cluster view

3.1 Auto-Tracking Mode

The determination method of main target based on auto-tracking mode is to resolve how to choose a satellite s from formation satellite cluster S and make antenna beam tracking this satellite till it is lost. This method is as follows:

1. Determine common period of time

According to tracking prediction of all n satellites, common period of time $(t_1, t_2, ..., t_m)$ is calculated which is the period of time when antenna beam covers synchronously all satellites too.

$$(t_1, t_2, ..., t_m)=T_1 \cap T_2 \cap .... \cap T_n \tag{1}$$

Where T_i $(i=1, 2, ..., n)$ indicates the period of time of satellite s_i tracking prediction.

2. Calculate span angle set B

The span angle is the angle relative to SBMT antenna between two satellites. Based on the common period of time $(t_1, t_2, ..., t_m)$, span angle $\beta_{i,j}^k$ is calculated between satellite s_i and s_j at time t_k, where i indicates that s_i is main target, $i=1, 2, ..., n$; j indicates that s_j is the other target, $j=1, 2, ..., i-1, i+1, ..., n$; k indictes time t_k, $k=1, 2, 3, ..., m$, all these span angles form set B.

$$\beta_{i,j}^k = \arccos(\frac{R_{i,k} \bullet R_{j,k}}{\rho_{i,k}\rho_{j,k}}) \tag{2}$$

$$B = \left\{\beta_{1,2}^1, \beta_{1,2}^2, ..., \beta_{1,2}^m, \beta_{1,3}^1, ..., \beta_{1,3}^m, ... \beta_{1,n}^m, \beta_{2,1}^1, ..., \beta_{2,n}^m, ..., \beta_{n,1}^1, ..., \beta_{n,n-1}^m\right\} \tag{3}$$

Where $R_{i,k}$ and $R_{j,k}$ are tracking prediction vectors of satellite s_i and s_j at time t_k.

3. Calculate span angle improved set B'

According to span angle set B, compare $\beta_{i,j}^k$ with 3dB beamwidth β. If $\beta_{i,j}^k \leq \beta$, then when target s_i is main target, target s_j is covered by antenna beam at time t_k. If $\beta_{i,j}^k > \beta$, then when target s_i is main target, target s_j is not covered by antenna beam at time t_k, it may be lost, so target s_i can not be thought of as main target, all the span angle which is the angle relative to SBMT antenna when target s_i is main target need be deleted from B. So span angle improved set B' is denoted:

$$B' = \left\{\beta_{i,j}^k \mid i = i_1, i_2, ..., i_{n'}; j = 1,2,...,i-1,i+1,...,n; k = 1,2,...,m\right\} \tag{4}$$

Where $i_1, i_2, ..., i_{n'}$ are residual feasible main targets.

4. Determinate statistical matrix Q

Seen from antenna tracking target, user needs a little smaller span angle and smooth tracking, so statistics q based on period of time is established, which not only considers mean value e, but also considers standard deviation σ. Namely, $q = \omega_1 e + \omega_2 \sigma$, where ω_1 and ω_2 are weights, and $0 \leq (\omega_1, \omega_2) \leq 1$, which value is due to user requirement. According to span angle improved set B', $q_{i,j}$ is determinated by subset { $\beta_{i,j}^k$ / $k=1,2,...,m$ } from B', so statistical matrix Q is denoted

$$Q = \begin{bmatrix} q_{i_1,1} & q_{i_1,2} & \cdots & q_{i_1,i_1-1} & q_{i_1,i_1+1} & \cdots & q_{i_1,n} \\ q_{i_2,1} & q_{i_2,2} & \cdots & q_{i_2,i_2-1} & q_{i_2,i_2+1} & \cdots & q_{i_2,n} \\ \vdots & \vdots & \vdots & \vdots & \vdots & \vdots & \vdots \\ q_{i_{n'},1} & q_{i_{n'},2} & \cdots & q_{i_{n'},i_{n'}-1} & q_{i_{n'},i_{n'}+1} & \cdots & q_{i_{n'},n} \end{bmatrix} \tag{5}$$

3.2 Determinate Main Target

Seen from single antenna beam covering multi targets, span angles between main target and all the others are much smaller and much better, so main target determinated is the target which has minimum mean value of all the span angles. According to statistical matrix Q, main target is determined as follows:

$$\min_{i \in (i_1, i_2, \ldots, i_n)} \frac{\sum\limits_{j \in (1,2,\ldots,i-1,i+1,\ldots,n)} q_{i,j}}{n-1} \tag{6}$$

3.3 Digital-Leading Mode

The determination method of main target based on digital-leading mode is to resolve how to choose a virtual satellite s' and make antenna beam tracking s' till tracking time finished, and apply the tracking prediction angles of s' to drive antenna axis for tracking formation satellites cluster. So the key of determination of main target is to how to determinate the location of s'. In this paper, considering the characteristic of formation flying satellites which is that all satellites form a certain geometrical formation configuration, the geometrical center of formation configuration can be thought of as s'. Now the determination method of this geometrical center is shown as follows.

At arbitrary time $t_k \in (t_1, t_2, \ldots, t_m)$, all the tracking predictions $(R_1^k, R_2^k, \ldots, R_n^k)$ of formation satellites cluster are known, and it is knows that each prediction is denoted by (ρ, A, E) which is in sphere coordinate system, so firstly sphere coordinate system is transformed to Cartesian coordinate system as follow:

$$\begin{cases} x_i^k = \rho_i^k \cos E_i^k \cos A_i^k \\ y_i^k = \rho_i^k \cos E_i^k \sin A_i^k \quad i = 1,2,\ldots,n \\ z_i^k = \rho_i^k \sin E_i^k \end{cases} \tag{7}$$

And this geometrical center R_c^k in Cartesian coordinate system is denoted by

$$\begin{cases} x_c^k = \dfrac{\sum\limits_{i=1,\ldots,n} \rho_i^k \cos E_i^k \cos A_i^k}{n} \\[3mm] y_c^k = \dfrac{\sum\limits_{i=1,\ldots,n} \rho_i^k \cos E_i^k \sin A_i^k}{n} \\[3mm] z_c^k = \dfrac{\sum\limits_{i=1,\ldots,n} \rho_i^k \sin E_i^k}{n} \end{cases} \tag{8}$$

Then R_c^k in Cartesian coordinate system is transformed to (ρ_c^k, A_c^k, E_c^k) in sphere coordinate system. Repeating each time $k = 1,2,...,m$, finally the trajectory of this geometrical center of formation satellites cluster is produced like ($R_c^1, R_c^2,..., R_c^m$).

Obviously, the determination method of main target based on digital-leading mode is simple, but it needs more precise tracking predictions of all satellites.

According to a determination method of main tracking target for SBMT TT&C equipments based on two tracking modes in previous section, Figure 2 shows the tracking method process of formation satellites cluster for single-beam and multi-target TT&C Equipments.

4 Simulations

Assume formation satellites cluster which is made up of 4 satellites, orbital elements are shown in table 1, parameters of a SBMT TT&C equipment is shown in table 2, simulation time is from 2010-7-1 12:00 to 2010-7-2 12:00.

Table 1. Orbital elements of this 4 satellites

	s_1	s_2	s_3	s_4
$a(m)$	7166.444098	7166.444158	7166.409122	7166.373146
$e(°)$	0.001544179	0.000938533	0.001149309	0.002124435
$i(°)$	97.8851480	97.8851480	97.8851637	97.8851797
$\omega(°)$	209.6810508	282.6002451	16.5538836	118.3254771
$\Omega(°)$	279.9967370	279.9967313	279.9967519	279.9967838
$M(°)$	350.3466306	277.4272843	183.4738143	81.7027467

According to the tracking method in this paper, it is assumed that the first common period of time is considered. For auto-tracking mode, its statistical matrix Q is $\begin{bmatrix} 0.2828° & 0.6556° & 0.6570° \\ 0.2828° & 0.4113° & 0.5504° \\ 0.6556° & 0.4113° & 0.3163° \end{bmatrix}$, where both weight ω_1 and ω_2 are 0.5, then based on the principle of minimum mean value, the main target is s_2. Figure3 (a)-(d) shows the simulation results, (a)-(d) represent span angle curves when s_1、 s_2、 s_3、 s_4 is main target respectively. Each curve looks like hill shape, it is because the range of each target changes from close to far, and then changes close. Seen from Fig4, when s_2 is main target, other three span angles are all less than 1°, and variation scope is much little too. For digital-leading mode, Figure5 shows span angle curves of 4 satellites relative to geometrical center of this formation configuration, all the span angles are less than 0.9°, and variation scope is much little too.

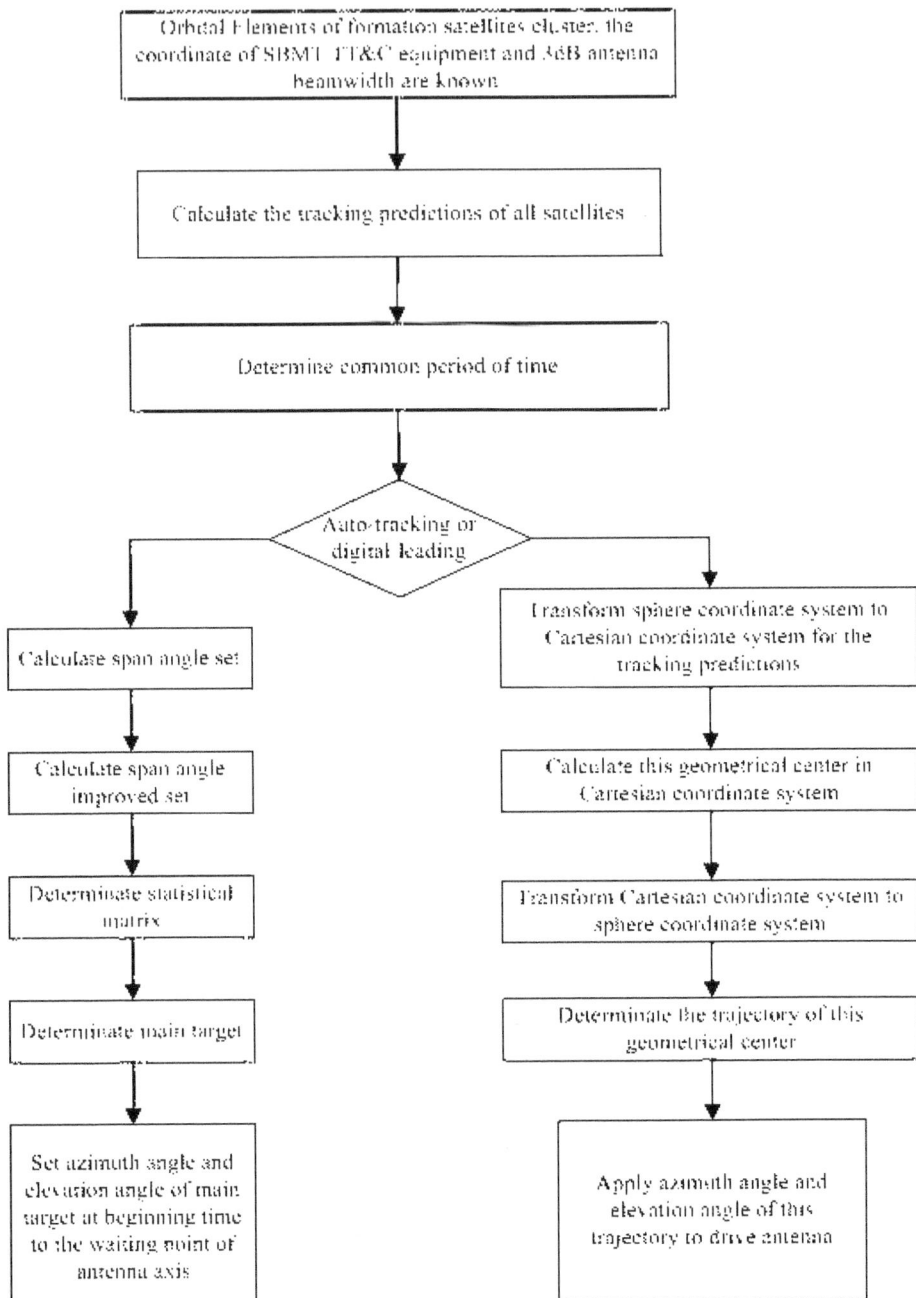

Fig. 2. The tracking method process

Table 2. Parameters of a SBMT TT&C equipment

Coordinates	(40.04°N, 75.595°W)
3dB beamwidth	±2°
Baseband processing capacity	4

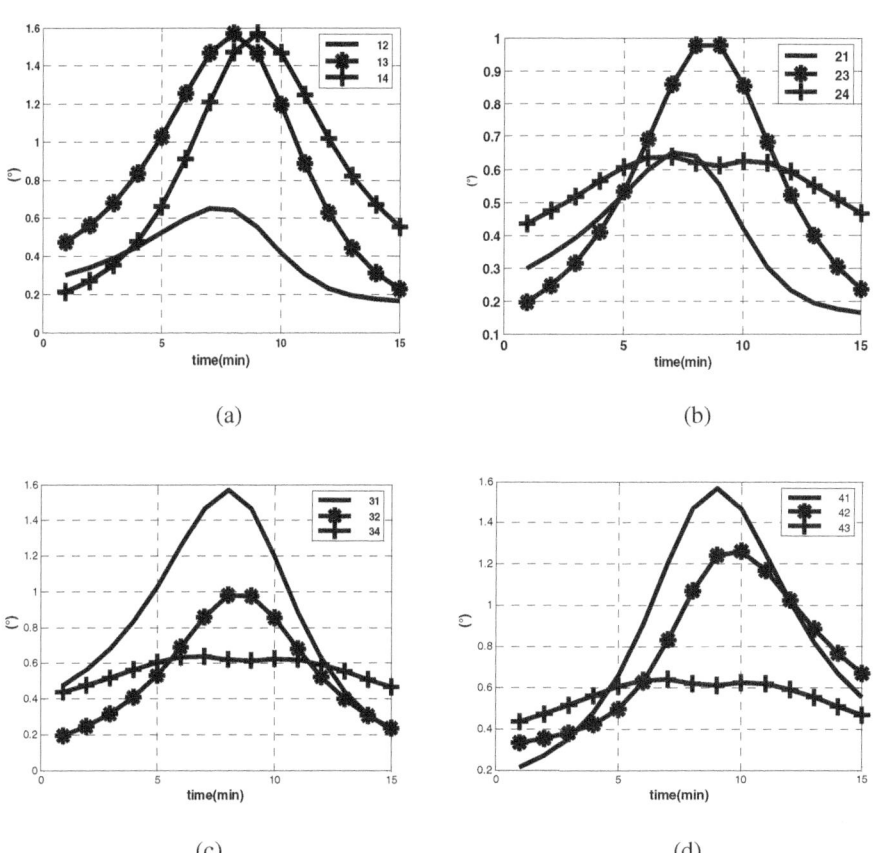

(a)   (b)

(c)   (d)

Fig. 3. Span angle curves when s_1、 s_2、 s_3、 s_4 is main target respectively(a) s_1, (b) s_2, (c) s_3, (d) s_4

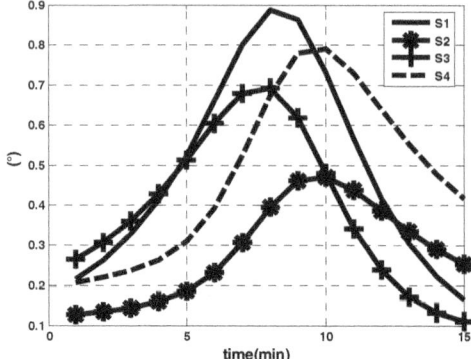

Fig. 4. Span angle curves of 4 satellites relative to geometrical center of this formation configuration

5 Conclusion

In order to slowing current tensional status of TT&C resources and developing farthest capabilities of multi-target TT&C equipments, the problem about single-beam and multi-target TT&C Equipments tracking synchronously formation satellites cluster is researched in this paper. Based on smooth and reliable multi-target tracking principle and characteristic of single-beam antenna axis pointing to main target, confirming methods of main tracking target for single-beam and multi-target TT&C Equipments based on two tracking modes are proposed, Simulation results show that this tracking method is feasible and valid. Furthermore, this method is adapted to spaceborne SBMT TT&C Equipments and other SBMT radar.

References

1. Consultative Committee for Space Data Systems (CCSDS), Radio Frequency and Modulation Systems, Part 1 Earth Stations, CCSDS 411.0 G-2, pp. 5.9–1,2. NASA, Washington, DC
2. Wei, B., Luo, W.: Multi-target TT&C System Research of Spacecraft. Radio Engineering 35(7), 26–30 (2005)
3. Massonnet, D.: The interferometric cartwheel, a constellation of passive satellites to produce radar images that can be coherently combined. Int J. of Remote Sensing 22(12), 2413–2431 (2001)
4. Goodman, N.A.: Processing of Multiple-Receiver Spaceborne Arrays for Wide-Area SAR. IEEE Trans. On Geosci. and Remote Sensing. 40(4), 841–852 (2002)
5. Qiu, Z.Y., Peng, Z., Ping, L.Y.: A novel multi-beam array antenna for tracking formation satellites. In: Eleventh International Space Conference of Pacific-basin Societies, pp. 211–221. Chinese Society of Astronautics, Beijing (2007)
6. Li, J., Liu, J., Bai, J.: Synchronous TT&C Research for Non-formation satellites. In: STTC 2010, pp. 143–147 (2010)

Synchronization of the Fractional Order Finance Systems with Activation Feedback Control

Yanzhi Wang[*] and Chunrui Zhang

Department of Mathematics, Northeast Forestry University,
Harbin, 150040, P.R. China
wangyanzhi_6728@163.com

Abstract. Synchronization of fractional order chaotic dynamical systems is receiving increasing attention in recent decades. In this article, a fractional-order financial system is proposed and we utilize active control technique to synchronize this fractional order chaotic dynamical system based on the stability theory of fractional order systems. It is observed that synchronization is faster as the order tends to one. Finally, the numerical simulations are given to verify the feasibility of the results.

Keywords: Synchronization, Fractional order, Control, Chaos, Finance systems.

1 Introduction

Fractional calculus is a 300-year-old mathematical topic. It has been proved to be useful in physics, engineering and even financial analysis in the last few decades. And fractional models have been shown by many researchers to adequately describe the operation of a variety of physical and biological processes and systems. Nowadays, synchronization of these chaotic systems has been given much concern and study. Synchronization of chaotic systems has been focus of attention in recent literature owing to its applications in secure communications of analog and digital signals [1] and for developing safe and reliable cryptographic systems [2]. A variety of approaches which include nonlinear feed-back control [3], adaptive control [4], back-stepping design [5] and active control/feedback linearization [6] have been proposed for synchronization of chaotic systems.

In author's pervious work, the dynamics for fractional-order finance chaotic systems has been extensively investigated. The rigorous proof of existence and uniqueness of solutions for the fractional-order finance chaotic system has been provided. We also show that chaos exists in fractional-order finance system with orders less than 3. A minimum effective dimension is calculated for the

[*] Corresponding author.
The author's research was supported by the Northeast Forestry University Graduate thesis funded projects gram 09. E-mail address: wangyanzhi_6728@163.com.
The author's research was supported by the National Natural Science Foundations of China (No 10771045, No 10871056). Tel.: 86-0451-82190543; E-mail address: math@nefu.edu.cn.

H. Deng et al. (Eds.): AICI 2011, Part I, LNAI 7002, pp. 119–127, 2011.

commensurate order 2.53 and incommensurate order system 2.35. On the other hand, our aim is to synchronize two finance fractional order systems, which can be identical or nonidentical. To achieve this goal, the active control method was constructed to synchronize the finance fractional-order systems. This approach, based on stability theory of fractional-order systems, is simple, theoretically rigorous and convenient to realize synchronization. We found that synchronization is faster as the order tends to one and also proof that phenomenon.

This paper is organized as follows. In Section 2, the definition of fractional-order derivative and fractional-order system's synchronization theory are introduced. In Section 3, the active control technique is applied to synchronize the fractional-order finance system. Numerical simulations have performed the effectiveness and feasibility of the presented synchronization techniques.

2 Fractional Differential and Fractional-Order System's Synchronization Theory

2.1 Introduction to Fractional Calculus and Numerical Method

The operator $_aD_t^q$, called differ-integral operator, is commonly used in fractional calculus as notation for taking both the fractional derivative and the fractional integral in a single expression. This operator is defined as follows [7]

$$_aD_t^q = \begin{cases} \dfrac{d^q}{dt^q} & \text{Re}[q] > 0, \\ 1 & \text{Re}[q] = 0, \\ \int_a^t (d\tau)^{-q} & \text{Re}[q] < 0. \end{cases} \tag{2.1}$$

The Caputo definition of the fractional derivative, which sometimes is called smooth fractional derivative, is described as

$$_0D_t^q f(t) = \begin{cases} \dfrac{1}{\Gamma(m-q)} \displaystyle\int_0^t \dfrac{f^{(m)}(\tau)}{(t-\tau)^{q+1-m}} d\tau, & m-1 < q < m, \\ \dfrac{d^m}{dt^m} f(t), & q = m. \end{cases} \tag{2.2}$$

where m is the first integer which is not less than q.

Numerical methods used for solving ODE have to be modified for solving FODE. A modification of Adams–Bashforth–Moulton algorithm is proposed by Diethelm et al. in [8-10] to solve FODE. To explain the method we consider the following differential equation

$$\begin{cases} D_t^{\,q} x(t) = f(t, x(t)), & 0 \le t \le T \\ x^{(k)}(t)\,|_{t=0} = x_0, & k = 0, 1, \cdots, m-1 \end{cases} \tag{2.3}$$

This differential equation is equivalent to the Volterra integral equation.

$$x(t) = \sum_{k=0}^{\lceil q \rceil -1} x_0^{(k)} \frac{t^k}{k!} + \frac{1}{\Gamma(q)} \int_0^t (t-s)^{q-1} f(s, y(s)) ds \tag{2.4}$$

By setting $h = T / N$ and $t_n = nh (n = 0, 1, \cdots, N)$, (2.4) is determined as follows

$$x_h(t_n + 1) = \sum_{k=0}^{\lceil q \rceil -1} x_0^{(k)} \frac{t^k}{k!} + \frac{h^q}{\Gamma(q+2)} f(t_{n+1}, x_h^p(t_n + 1)) + \frac{h^q}{\Gamma(q+2)} \sum_{j=0}^{n} a_{j,n+1} f(t_j, x_h(t_j))$$

where

$$x_h^p(t_n + 1) = \sum_{k=0}^{\lceil q \rceil -1} x_0^{(k)} \frac{t^k}{k!} + \frac{1}{\Gamma(q)} \sum_{j=0}^{n} b_{j,n+1} f(t_j, x_h(t_j))$$

and

$$a_{j,n+1} = \begin{cases} n^{q+1} - (n-q)(n+1)^q, & j = 0 \\ (n-j+2)^{q+1} + (n-j)^{q+1} - 2(n-j+1)^{q+1} & 1 \le j \le n \\ 1 & j = n+1 \end{cases}$$

$$b_{j,n+1} = \frac{h^q}{q}((n+1-j)^q - (n-j)^q).$$

The approximation error is determined as follows $\max_{j=0,1,\cdots,N} |x(t_j) - x_h(t_j)| = O(h^p)$, where $p = \min(2, 1+q)$. The numerical solution of a fractional order system can be obtained by applying the method mentioned.

2.2 Fractional-Order System's Asymptotic Stability Theory

For n dimensional fractional system, if all the eigenvalues $(\lambda_1, \lambda_2, \cdots, \lambda_n)$ of the Jacobian matrix of some equilibrium point satisfy $|\arg(\lambda_i)| > q\pi / 2$, $q = \max\{q_1, q_2, \cdots, q_n\}$ (see Fig.1), then the fractional-order system is asymptotically steady at the equilibrium [11,12]. On the previous article has done a detailed analysis of the commensurate and incommensurate fractional system. Not repeat it here. A necessary condition for fractional system to remain chaotic is keeping the eigenvalue λ in the unstable region. This means

$$\tan(q\frac{\pi}{2}) > \frac{|\operatorname{Im}(\lambda)|}{\operatorname{Re}(\lambda)} \Rightarrow q > \frac{2}{\pi}\tan^{-1}(\frac{|\operatorname{Im}(\lambda)|}{\operatorname{Re}(\lambda)}) \qquad (2.5)$$

Define: $\Delta = \det(diag([\lambda^{Mq_1} \ \lambda^{Mq_2} \ \cdots \ \lambda^{Mq_n}]) - J)$ This condition is equivalent to the following inequality $\frac{\pi}{2M} - \min_i |\arg(\lambda_i)| < 0$. The

term $\frac{\pi}{2M} - \min_i |\arg(\lambda_i)|$ is called the instability measure for equilibrium points in

fractional order systems (IMFOS). Hence, a necessary condition for fractional order system to exhibit a chaotic attractor is

$$IMFOS \geq 0$$

In the subsequent section we demonstrate that the condition (2.11) is not sufficient for chaos to exist.

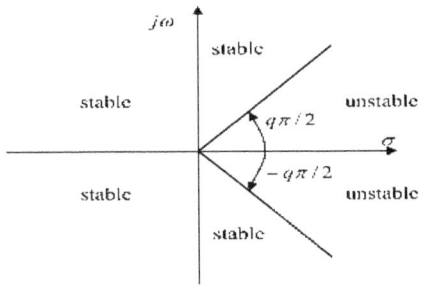

Fig. 1. Stability region of the FODE system with order $0 < q \leq 1$

2.3 Fractional-Order System's Synchronization Theory [13]

Given the fractional order chaotic system, i.e., the drive system is

$$D^q X(t) = AX(t) + BF(CX) + D$$

Here, $X \in R^{n \times 1}, A \in R^{n \times n}, B \in R^{n \times n}, C \in R^{n \times n}, D \in R^{n \times n}$ are continuous matrixes, and $CX \in R^1$, $0 < q \leq 1$. Let the corresponding response system be

$$D^q X^*(t) = AX^*(t) + BF(CX^*) + D + u(t)$$

where $X^* \in R^{n \times 1}$, $u(t)$ is the active control function. Define the error of the systems is $e(t) = X(t) - X^*(t)$. The fractional error equation can be described as

$$D^q e(t) = Ae(t) + BE(X, X^*) + u(t)$$

$E(X, X^*)$ is determined directly from Eq. (2) and (3). Here, let the control function be

$$u(t) = M(X, X^*) + Ne(t)$$

where $M(X, X^*)$ is determined by $BE(X, X^*)$, and N is the control parameter matrix.

3 Fractional-Order Finance Model and Activation Feedback Control

The fractional-order finance system [14] can be written in the form as below:

$$
\begin{cases}
\dfrac{d^{q_1} x^*}{dt^{q_1}} = z^* + (y^* - a)x^* \\[2mm]
\dfrac{d^{q_2} y^*}{dt^{q_2}} = 1 - by^* - x^{*2} \\[2mm]
\dfrac{d^{q_3} z^*}{dt^{q_3}} = -x^* - cz^*
\end{cases}
\tag{3.1}
$$

where a is the saving amount, b is the cost per investment, and c is the elasticity of demand of commercial markets, $0 < q_i < 1, i = 1,2,3$. It is obvious that all three constants a, b, c are nonnegative.

Consider the system (3.1) with parameter $(a, b, c) = (3.0, 0.1, 1.0)$ and $q_1 = q_2 = q_3 = q$. In this case a system shows regular behavior if it satisfies

$$q < \frac{2}{\pi} \min_i |\arg(\lambda_i)| \approx 0.8437$$

Supposed system (3.1) is the drive system, the response system can be described as follows

$$
\begin{cases}
\dfrac{d^{q_1} x^*}{dt^{q_1}} = z^* + (y^* - a)x^* + u_a \\[2mm]
\dfrac{d^{q_2} y^*}{dt^{q_2}} = 1 - by^* - x^{*2} + u_b \\[2mm]
\dfrac{d^{q_3} z^*}{dt^{q_3}} = -x^* - cz^* + u_c
\end{cases}
\tag{3.2}
$$

u_a, u_b, u_c are the control functions. Define the error variables are $e_x = x^* - x, e_y = y^* - y, e_z = z^* - z$, then the error system can be obtained as

$$
\begin{cases}
\dfrac{d^{q_1} e_x}{dt^{q_1}} = e_z - ae_x + x^* y^* - xy + u_a \\[2mm]
\dfrac{d^{q_2} e_y}{dt^{q_2}} = -be_y - x^{*2} + x^2 + u_b \\[2mm]
\dfrac{d^{q_3} e_z}{dt^{q_3}} = -e_x - ce_z + u_c
\end{cases}
\tag{3.3}
$$

Let the activation feedback control function be

$$
\begin{cases}
u_a = -x^* y^* + xy + v_a \\[2mm]
u_b = x^{*2} - x^2 + v_b \\[2mm]
u_c = v_c
\end{cases}
\tag{3.4}
$$

and v_a, v_b, v_c are the control inputs. Select

$$
\begin{pmatrix} v_a \\ v_b \\ v_c \end{pmatrix} = N \begin{pmatrix} e_x \\ e_y \\ e_z \end{pmatrix}
$$

where

$$
N = \begin{pmatrix} a-1 & 0 & -1 \\ 0 & b-1 & 0 \\ 1 & c & -1 \end{pmatrix}
$$

Obviously, the value of N can satisfy all latent root of Jacobi matrix of Eq. (3.2) at the zero are -1. Based on the stability theory of fractional-order systems, the drive system (3.1) and the response system (3.2) can achieve chaotic synchronization.

4   Numerical Simulation

In the following numerical simulation, the parameters are chosen as $(a,b,c) = (3.0, 0.1, 1.0)$. The fractional order q and the time step are chosen as $q = 0.96$ and $s = 0.01$ s, respectively. Fig.2 shows that the finance fractional-order system is chaotic. The initial conditions for drive system are $x(0) = 2, y(0) = 3, z(0) = 2$. where as the initial conditions for response system are $x^*(0) = 3$, $y^*(0) = 4$, $z^*(0) = 1$. We perform the numerical simulations for the two cases of fractional order q from 0.98 to 0.84 of the drive system (3.1) and response system (3.2). Figs. 3-8 show synchronization between fractional systems and error system.

It is clear that the error in synchronization decreases as the order is increased. In other words, for larger value of the synchronization starts earlier.

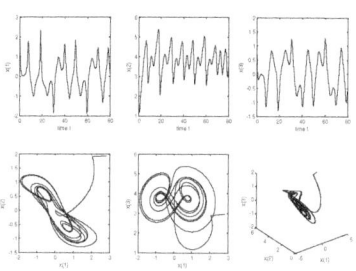

Fig. 2. Figure of system (3.2) for $q = 0.96$

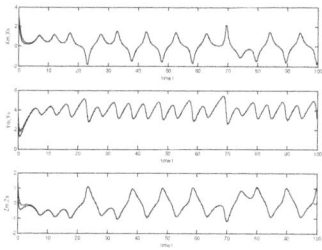

Fig. 3. The states of the dynamical system (3.2) and the response system (3.3) with $q = 0.89$

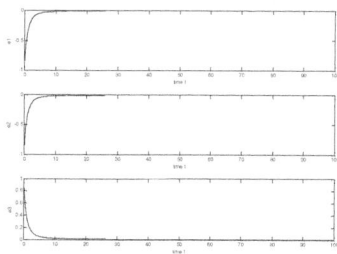

Fig. 4. Error state of the driving system (3.2) and the response system (3.3) with $q = 0.89$

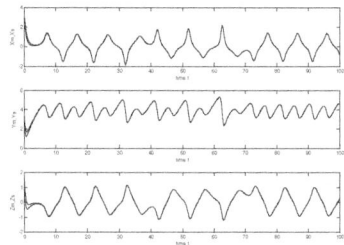

Fig. 5. The states of the dynamical system (3.2) and the response system (3.3) with $q = 0.93$

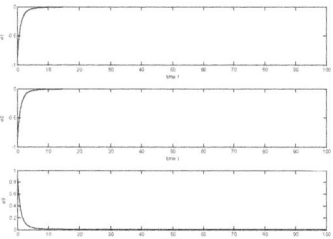

Fig. 6. Error state of the driving system (3.2) and the response system (3.3) with $q = 0.93$

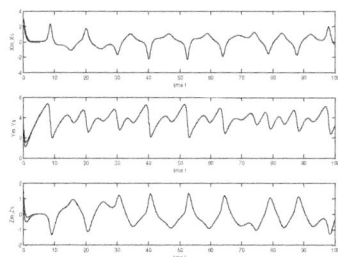

Fig. 7. The states of the dynamical system (3.2) and the response system (3.3) with $q = 0.98$

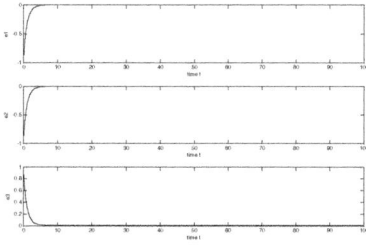

Fig. 8. Error state of the driving system (3.2) and the response system (3.3) with $q = 0.98$

5 Conclusions

Based on the stability theory of fractional-order systems, this paper analyses the synchronization conditions of a class of fractional order chaotic systems with activation feedback method. The method is always effective in the fractional order chaotic systems theoretically. Numerical simulations show the activation feedback method can be applied in chaos synchronization, hyperchaos synchronization and limit cycle synchronization of fractional systems.

References

1. Hilfer, R.: Applications of fractional calculus in physics. World Scientific, USA (2001)
2. He, R., Vaidya, P.G.: Implementation of chaotic cryptography with chaotic synchronization. Phys. Rev. E 57(2), 1532 (1998)
3. Huang, L., Feng, R., Wang, M.: Synchronization of chaotic systems via nonlinear control. Phys. Lett. A 320, 271 (2004)
4. Park, J.H.: Adaptive synchronization of Rossler system with uncertain parameters. Chaos Solitons Fractals 25, 333–338 (2005)
5. Bowong, S., Moukam Kakmeni, F.: Synchronization of uncertain chaotic systems via backstepping approach. Chaos Solitons Fractals 21, 999–1011 (2004)
6. Shahiri, M., Ghaderi, R., Ranjbar, A., Hosseinnia, S.H., Momani, S.: Chaotic fractional-order Coullet system: synchronization and control approach. Commun. Nonlinear Sci. Numer. Simulat. 15, 665–674 (2010)
7. Tavazoei, M.S., Haeri, M.: A necessary condition for double scroll attractor existence in fractional-order systems. Ameria: Physics Letters A 367, 102–113 (2007)
8. Diethelm, K., Ford, N.J., Freed, A.D.: A predictor–corrector approach for the numerical solution of fractional differential equations. Nonlinear Dynam. 29, 3–22 (2002)
9. Diethelm, K.: An algorithm for the numerical solution of differential equations of fractional order. Electron. Trans. Numer. Anal. 5, 1–6 (1997)
10. Diethelm, K., Ford, N.J.: Analysis of fractional differential equations. J. Math. Anal. Appl. 265, 229–248 (2002)
11. Matignon, D.: Stability results for fractional differential equations with application to control processing. Computational Engineering System Application 2, 963–968 (1996)
12. Mohammad, S.T., Mohammad, H.: A note on the stability of fractional order systems. Math. Comput. Simulat. (2007)
13. Wang, X.Y., Song, J.M.: Synchronization of the fractional order hyperchaos Lorenz systems with activation feedback control. Commun. Nonlinear Sci. Numer. Simulat. 14, 3351–3357 (2009)
14. Chen, W.C.: Nonlinear dynamics and chaos in a fractional-order financial system. Chaos Solitons and Fractals 36, 1305–1314 (2008)

Differential Evolution Algorithm with Fine Evaluation Strategy for Multi-dimensional Function Optimization Problems

Xiaoyu Lin[1], Lijin Wang[1], Yiwen Zhong[1,*], and Hui Zhang[2]

[1] College of Computer and Information Science,
Fujian Agriculture and Forestry University, Fuzhou, China
linxiaoyu@foxmail.com, style_wang@sina.com,
yiwenzhong@fjau.edu.cn
[2] Pervasive Technology Institute, Indiana University, Indianapolis, USA
huizhang@indiana.edu

Abstract. For multi-dimensional function optimization problems, classical differential evolution (DE) algorithm may deteriorate its intensification ability because different dimensions may interfere with each other. To deal with this intrinsic shortage, this paper presents a DE algorithm framework with fine evaluation strategy. In the process of search, solution is updated and evaluated dimension by dimension. In each dimension, the updated value will be accepted only if it can improve the solution. In case that there is no improvement found in any dimension, the new solution, which is calculated using classical mutation operator only, will be accepted in low probability. This strategy can improve diversification and keep DE algorithm from premature convergence. Simulation experiments were carried on typical benchmark functions, and the results show that fine evaluation strategy can improve the performance of DE algorithm remarkably.

Keywords: Differential Evolution, Fine Evaluation Strategy, Multi-dimensional Function Optimization, Interference Phenomena.

1 Introduction

Differential evolution (DE) [1] algorithm is a popular population based intelligent optimization algorithm. Due to its several attractive features, such as simplicity, ease of implementation, reliability and high performance, it is one of the intelligent techniques most favored by engineers for solving continuous optimization problems [2]. Despite having those striking features and successful applications to various fields, DE is sometimes criticized for its slow convergence rate for computationally expensive problems [3]. It is clear that although DE is undoubtedly a good algorithm, there are considerable margins of improvement, especially in solving difficult problems. To improve DE's performance, researchers proposed many different modified DEs. In [2], F. Neri and V. Tirronen divide those modified versions of DE into two classes:

---

* Corresponding author.

H. Deng et al. (Eds.): AICI 2011, Part I, LNAI 7002, pp. 128–136, 2011.

1. DE integrating an extra component. This class includes those algorithms which use DE as an evolutionary framework which is assisted by additional algorithmic components. The algorithms belonging to this class can be clearly decomposed as a DE framework and additional components. Typical algorithms of this class include DE with Trigonometric Mutation [4-7], DE with Simplex Crossover Local Search [8, 9], DE with Population Size Reduction [10, 11] and DE with Scale Factor Local Search [12-14].

2. Modified structures of DE. This class includes those algorithms which make a substantial modification within the DE structure, in the search logic and the selection etc., in the hope to enhance the performance of the original DE. Typical algorithms of this class include Self Adaptive Control Parameters [15-18], Opposition Based DE [19-21], Global-Local Search DE [22, 23] and Self Adaptive Coordination of Multiple Mutation Rules [24].

From those above studies which aim to improve DE, it can be concluded that DE is sensitive to control parameters. Both class of modified DE show that appropriate parameters may improve its performance remarkably. But even with cunningly set parameters, the DE's convergence speed is still very slow compared to iterative improvement local search algorithms. Like particle swarm optimization, DE can locate the area of the optimum quickly, but once in the region of the optimum, it could not continue the search at a finer grain for a multi-dimensional function problem. One of the reasons is that different dimensions may interfere with each other, this phenomenon deteriorates the intensification ability of population based intelligent optimization algorithms like DE. In order to tackle the dimensions interference problem and to improve DE's intensification ability, this paper presents a DE algorithm framework with fine evaluation strategy. In the proposed algorithm, solution will be processed dimension by dimension. In each dimension, if the updated value can improve the solution, it will be accepted. Otherwise, the original value is retained. In order to keep algorithm from premature convergence, the solution calculated by classical mutation operator will be accepted in low probability if there is no improved solution found in any dimension.

2 Differential Evolution Algorithm

2.1 Standard Differential Evolution

Suppose there is a minimization problem of an objective function $f(\mathbf{X})$, where $\mathbf{X}$ is a vector of N design variables in a decision space $\mathbf{D}$. DE starts with a population of NP candidate solutions which may be represented as $\mathbf{X}_{i,g}$, $i = 1, \ldots, NP$, where i denotes the index of individual in population and g denotes the generation to which the population belongs. The working of DE depends on the manipulation and efficiency of three main operators; mutation, crossover and selection which briefly described as following [3].

Mutation: Mutation operator is the prime operator of DE and it is the implementation of this operation that makes DE different from other Evolutionary algorithms. The mutation operation of DE applies the vector differentials between the existing population members for determining both the degree and direction of perturbation applied to the individual subject of the mutation operation. In each generation, DE randomly selects two, three, four or five individuals in the population; the concrete number of individuals selected is depended on the mutation strategy used. Then DE produces a new individual using corresponding mutation strategy. The most often used mutation strategies implemented in the DE are listed below.

DE/rand/1: $V_{i,g+1} = X_{r_1,g} + F * (X_{r_2,g} - X_{r_3,g})$ (1)

DE/rand/2: $V_{i,g+1} = X_{r_1,g} + F * (X_{r_2,g} - X_{r_3,g}) + F * (X_{r_4,g} - X_{r_5,g})$ (2)

DE/best/1: $V_{i,g+1} = X_{best,g} + F * (X_{r_1,g} - X_{r_2,g})$ (3)

DE/best/2: $V_{i,g+1} = X_{best,g} + F * (X_{r_1,g} - X_{r_2,g}) + F * (X_{r_3,g} - X_{r_4,g})$ (4)

DE/rand-to-best/1: $V_{i,g+1} = X_{r_1,g} + F * (X_{best,g} - X_{r_2,g}) + F * (X_{r_3,g} - X_{r_4,g})$ (5)

where, $i = 1, \ldots, NP$, $r_1, r_2, r_3, r_4, r_5 \in \{1, \ldots, NP\}$ are randomly selected and satisfy: $r_1 \neq r_2 \neq r_3 \neq r_4 \neq r_5$, $F \in [0, 1]$, F is a real constant factor which controls the amplification of differential variation [1], and $X_{best,g}$ is the best solution found so far by the total population.

Crossover: once the mutation phase is complete, the crossover process is activated. The perturbed individual $V_{i,g}$ and the current population member $X_{i,g}$ are subject to the crossover operation, that finally generates the candidates $U_{i,g}$ as follows:

$$u_{j,i,g+1} = \begin{cases} v_{j,i,g+1} & if\ rand_j \leq CR\ OR\ j = k \\ x_{j,i,g} & otherwise \end{cases}$$ (6)

where $j = 1 \ldots n$, $k \in \{1, \ldots, n\}$ is a random parameter, chosen once for each i, and the crossover rate, $CR \in [0, 1]$, another control parameter of DE, is set by the user.

Selection: Each candidate $U_{i,g}$ is compared with its counterpart $X_{i,g}$ in the current population, it replaces $X_{i,g}$ if and only if $f(U_{i,g}) \leq f(X_{i,g})$; otherwise no replacement occurs. As a result, all the individuals of the next generation are as good as or better than their counterparts in the current generation.

Equation (1) to (5) indicates that DE generates offspring by perturbing the solutions with a scaled difference of two or more randomly selected individual vectors or best solution found so far. The success of DE is due to an implicit self-adaptation contained within the algorithmic structure. Step size in the mutation is progressively reduced and the search is performed in the neighborhood of the solutions. During the early stages of the optimization process, the solutions tend to be spread out within the decision space, so the step size of mutation is relatively big. As the optimization process, solutions of the population tend to concentrate in promising parts of the decision space, so the step size of mutation becomes relatively small. In other words, due to its structure, a DE scheme is highly explorative at the beginning and then becomes more and more exploitative as the search goes on. Although this mechanism seems, at first glance very efficient, it hides a limitation. If for some reason the algorithm does not succeed at generating offspring solutions which outperform the corresponding parent, the search is repeated again with similar step size and will likely fail by falling into an undesired stagnation condition [25]. In other words, the main drawback of DE is that the scheme has, for each stage of the optimization process, a limited amount of exploratory moves and if these moves are not enough to generate new promising solutions, the search can be heavily compromised. It is clear that successful functioning of a DE depends on the parameter setting of the three control parameters mentioned above. Too small a population size can contain too limited an amount of moves, while too large a population size may contain a high number of ineffective moves which can likely mislead the search. If too small it could cause premature convergence and if too large it could cause stagnation. Regarding the scale factor F and the crossover rate CR, these settings may be a difficult task. The setting of these two parameters is neither an intuitive nor a straightforward task but is unfortunately crucial for guaranteeing the algorithmic functioning.

2.2 Self-Adapting Control Parameters in Differential Evolution

As stated above, the setting of F and CR is neither an intuitive nor a straightforward task. In order to avoid the manual parameter setting of F and CR, a simple and effective strategy has been proposed in [15]. This strategy is called Self-Adapting Control Parameters in Differential Evolution. The DE algorithm employing this strategy, namely jDE, consists of the following. When the initial population is generated, two extra values between 0 and 1 are also generated for each individual. These values represent f and cr related to the individual under analysis. Each individual is composed of a solution and its control parameters:

$$\mathbf{X}_i = (x_{1,i}, x_{2,i}, ..., x_{j,i}, ..., x_{n,i}, f_i, cr_i) \tag{7}$$

At each generation, the ith individual's parameters f_i and cr_i are updated according to the following schemes:

$$f_i = \begin{cases} F_l + F_u * rand1, & if\ rand2 < \tau_1 \\ f_i, & otherwise \end{cases} \tag{8}$$

$$cr_i = \begin{cases} rand3, & if\ rand4 < \tau_2 \\ cr_i, & otherwise \end{cases} \tag{9}$$

where r and j, $j \in \{1, 2, 3, 4\}$, are uniform pseudo-random values between 0 and 1; τ_1 and τ_2 are constant values which represent the probabilities that parameters are updated, F_l and F_u are constant values which represent the minimum value that f_i could take and the maximum variable contribution to f_i respectively. The newly calculated values of f_i and cr_i are then used for generating the offspring. The mutation, crossover and selection operators are identical to that of a standard DE. This self-adaptation seems to greatly enhance the robustness properties of a standard DE and has also shown a good performance.

3 DE Algorithm Framework with Fine Evaluation Strategy

3.1 Interference Phenomena

Here we use an example to describe the interference phenomena of multi-dimensional function optimization problems. Suppose there is a 2-dimensional function $f(\mathbf{X}) = x_1^2 + x_2^2$. In t-th iteration, the solution $\mathbf{X}^t = (0.5, 0.5)$, and function value $f(\mathbf{X}^t) = 0.5$. Suppose after mutation and crossover operator, we have candidate solution $\mathbf{U}^{t+1} = (0, 1)$ and $f(\mathbf{U}^{t+1}) = 1$. We can see that $f(\mathbf{U}^{t+1}) > f(\mathbf{X}^t)$. But if we update the first dimension only, we can get a new candidate solution $\mathbf{U} = (0, 0.5)$ and $f(\mathbf{U}) = 0.25$. We have $f(\mathbf{U}) < f(\mathbf{X}^t)$.

So, if we can update and evaluate the solution dimension by dimension, and accept only those that can improve the solution, then DE can search the solution space more finely. This strategy can evaluate the produced solution more finely, so we call it as fine evaluation strategy.

3.2   DE Algorithm Framework with Fince Evaluation Strategy

Algorithm 1. DEwithFineEvaluationStrategy

```
Initialize parameter f and p;
For each from 1 to NP
  Produce solution x[i] randomly;
End For
g = FindBest( x );
While ( End condition is not met )
  For each i from 1 to NP
    Improved =false;
    For each dimension j from 1 to N
      Calculate new j-dimensional solution newX[j];
      delta = Difference(x[i], newX[j], j);
      If ( delta < 0 ) Then
        x[i][j] = newX[j];
        Improved = true;
      End if
    End for
    If ( not Improved AND random(0,1)<p ) Then x[i]=newX;
    If ( x[i] is better than g ) then g = x[i];
  End for
End while
Return g.
```

Algorithm 1 is the DE algorithm framework using fine evaluation strategy. Where x is a 2-dimensional array which represents solutions, $x[i]$ represents the i-th solution, and $x[i][j]$ represents the j-th dimensional value of i-th solution. The $newX$ is a 1-dimensional array which is used to store the updated solution in each iteration. Function Difference is used to calculate the difference of function value between the first parameter $x[i]$ and the new solution, which is get through replacing $x[i][j]$ with the second parameter $newX[j]$. Parameter p is used to control the probability to accept unimproved solutions, without it, DE will fall into local minimum easily.

4 Simulation Results

4.1 Experimental Approach

For comparison, the experiments use four non-linear benchmark functions which are used in many literatures. Those functions are listed as following:

(1) Sphere Function

$$f_1(\mathbf{x}) = \sum_{i=1}^{n} x_i^2, \quad |x_i| \leq 100$$

(2) Generalized Rosenbrock's Function

$$f_2(\mathbf{x}) = \sum_{i=1}^{n-1} (100(x_{i+1} - x_i^2)^2 + (x_i - 1)^2), \quad |x_i| \leq 30$$

(3) Generalized Rastrigrin's Function

$$f_3(\mathbf{x}) = \sum_{i=1}^{n} (x_i^2 - 10\cos(2\pi x_i) + 10), \quad |x_i| \leq 5.12$$

(4) Generalized Griewank's Function

$$f_4(\mathbf{x}) = \frac{1}{4000} \sum_{i=1}^{n} x_i^2 - \prod_{i=1}^{n} \cos(\frac{x_i}{\sqrt{i}}) + 1, \quad |x_i| \leq 600$$

In order to observe the performance of DE algorithms with and without fine evaluation strategy, we will use 30-dimensional (referred as 30-D hereafter) and 100-dimensional (referred as 100-D hereafter) test function. Each experiment was run 20 times with random initial values of $\mathbf{x}$ in the range indicated in corresponding equation. Population sizes were set to $3*N$. The DE, which uses the DE/rand/1 mutator, has been run with $F = 0.7$ and $CR = 0.3$ in accordance with the suggestions given in [26]. The jDE has been run with $F_1 = 0.1$, $F_u = 0.9$, and$\tau_1 = \tau_2 = 0.1$, as suggested in [15]. Parameter p is set to 0.01 in fine evaluation strategy.

4.2 Experiment Results

Tables 1 to table 4 are the results for fixed iteration number. Those tables list the algorithm name, average fitness and standard error (SD) for 20 runs of the four test functions respectively. The iteration number of DE+FES and jDE+FES is fixed to 1000, and the iteration number of DE and jDE is set to those values, so its run time is not less than DE+FES and jDE+FES. In case algorithm can reach the global optima all the time, we give the average iteration number and run time in parentheses in Average column. In case algorithm can reach the global optima partly, we give the success rate in parentheses in Average column.

Table 1 is the results on Sphere function. It shows that DE+FES is far better than DE and jDE+FES is far better than jDE both on 30-D and 100-D cases. DE+FES is better than jDE+FES both on 30-D and 100-D cases, and jDE is better than DE both on 30-D and 100-D cases.

Table 2 is the results on Rosenbrock function. It shows that DE+FES is better than DE and jDE+FES is better than jDE both on 30-D and 100-D cases. jDE+FES is a little better than DE+FES on 30-D case, but DE+FES is better than jDE+FES on 100-D case. DE is a little better than jDE on 30-D case, but jDE is far better than DE on 100-D case.

Table 3 is the results on Rastrigin function. It shows that DE+FES is far better than DE and jDE+FES is far better than jDE both on 30-D and 100-D cases. Both DE+FES and jDE+FES can reach the global optima quicly, but DE and jDE never.

Table 4 is the results on Griewank function. It shows that DE+FES and jDE+FES can reach the global optima quickly always both on 30-D and 100-D cases. jDE can reach the global optima always on 30-D case, but never on 100-D case. DE can never reach the global optima in all cases.

Table 1. Performances for Fixed Iteration Times on Sphere Functions

Algorithm	D	Average	SD
DE	30	8.9461E-13	6.404E-13
DE+FES	30	3.561E-54(.10)	1.583E-53
jDE	30	5.465E-27	6.731E-27
jDE+FES	30	9.096E-51	2.291E-50
DE	100	53.1794	10.3301
DE+FES	100	1.979E-52(.25)	8.854E-52
jDE	100	1.0506E-5	2.6148E-6
jDE+FES	100	3.439E-49	8.663E-49

Table 2. Performances for Fixed Iteration Times on Rosenbrock Functions

Algorithm	D	Average	SD
DE	30	15.7861	0.6114
DE+FES	30	0.1921	0.1210
jDE	30	19.5760	13.1422
jDE+FES	30	0.1199	0.1116
DE	100	2142.35	440.912
DE+FES	100	22.707	23.0842
jDE	100	95.7096	0.7182
jDE+FES	100	36.1659	29.0180

Table 3. Performances for Fixed Iteration Times on Rastrigin Functions

Algorithm	D	Average	SD
DE	30	22.131	5.6687
DE+FES	30	0 (57, 0.115)	0
jDE	30	4.527E-5	1.693E-4
jDE+FES	30	0 (51, 0.110)	0
DE	100	676.30	28.56
DE+FES	100	0 (57, 1.183)	0
jDE	100	400.48	13.97
jDE+FES	100	0 (52, 1.125)	0

Table 4. Performances for Fixed Iteration Times on Griewank Functions

Algorithm	D	Average	SD
DE	30	4.9284E-4	2.2041E-3
DE+FES	30	0 (133, 0.175)	0
jDE	30	0 (661, 1.163)	0
jDE+FES	30	0 (94, 0.102)	0
DE	100	1.5760	0.1527
DE+FES	100	0 (72, 1.070)	0
jDE	100	6.7442E-6	1.6438E-6
jDE+FES	100	0 (62, 0.743)	0

5 Conclusion

In order to deal with interference phenomena of multi-dimensional function optimization problems, this paper presents a DE algorithm framework with fine evaluation strategy. In the proposed framework, DE updates and evaluates solution dimension by dimension, and greedy strategy is used to decide whether accept the updated solution or not. This strategy combines the idea of iterative improvement algorithm into DE seamlessly. The experiment simulations, which were carried on typical benchmark functions, indicate that fine evaluation strategy can improve the intensification ability of DE algorithm remarkably.

Acknowledgment. This work was supported by Nature Science Foundation of Fujian Province of P. R. China (No. 2008J0316).

References

1. Storn, R., Price, K.: Differential Evolution – A Simple and Efficient Heuristic for global Optimization over Continuous Spaces. Journal of Global Optimization 11, 341–359 (2028), doi:10.1023/A:1008202821328
2. Neri, F., Tirronen, V.: Recent advances in differential evolution: a survey and experimental analysis. Artificial Intelligence Review 33, 61–106 (2010), doi:10.1007/s10462-009-9137-2
3. Ali1, M., Pant1, M., Abraham, A.: Simplex Differential Evolution. Acta Polytechnica Hungarica 6(5), 95–115 (2009)
4. Fan, H.Y., Lampinen, J.: A trigonometric mutation operation to differential evolution. Journal of Global Optimization 27, 105–129 (2003), doi:10.1023/A:1024653025686
5. Hu, S., Huang, H., Czarkowski, D.: Hybrid trigonometric differential evolution for optimizing harmonic distribution. In: IEEE International Symposium on Circuits and Systems, vol. 2, pp. 1306–1309 (May 2005), doi:10.1109/ISCAS.2005.1464835
6. Angira, R., Santosha, A.: Optimization of dynamic systems: a trigonometric differential evolution approach. Computer & Chemical Engneering 31, 1055–1063 (2007), doi:10.1016/j.compchemeng.2006.09.015
7. Angira, R., Santosh, A.: A modified trigonometric differential evolution algorithm for optimization of dynamic systems. In: Proceedings of the IEEE Congress on Evolutionary Computation, pp. 1463–1468 (June 2008), doi:10.1109/CEC.2008.4630986
8. Noman, N., Iba, H.: Enhancing differential evolution performance with local search for high dimensional function optimization. In: Proceedings of the 2005 Conference on Genetic and Evolutionary Computation, pp. 967–974 (June 2005), doi:10.1145/1068009.1068174
9. Noman, N., Iba, H.: Accelerating differential evolution using an adaptive local search. IEEE Transaction on Evolutionary Computation 12, 107–125 (2008), doi:10.1109/TEVC.2007.895272
10. Brest, J., Maŭcec, M.S.: Population size reduction for the differential evolution algorithm. Appllied Intelligence 29, 228–247 (2008), doi:10.1007/s10489-007-0091-x
11. Brest, J., Zamuda, A., Bošković, B., Maucec, M.S., Žumer, V.: High-dimensional real-parameter optimization using self-adaptive differential evolution algorithm with population size reduction. In: IEEE World Congress on Computational Intelligence, pp. 2032–2039 (June 2008), doi:10.1109/CEC.2008.4631067
12. Neri, F., Tirrone, V.: Scale factor local search in differential evolution. Memetic Computing 1, 153–171 (2009), doi:10.1007/s12293-009-0008-9
13. Tirronen, V., Neri, F., Rossi, T.: Enhancing differential evolution frameworks by scale factor local search—part I. In: IEEE Congress on Evolutionary Computation, pp. 94–101 (May 2009), doi:10.1109/CEC.2009.4982935
14. Neri, F., Tirronen, V., Kärkkäinen, T.: Enhancing differential evolution frameworks by scale factor local search—part II. In: Proceedings of the IEEE Congress on Evolutionary Computation, pp. 118–125 (May 2009), doi:10.1109/CEC.2009.4982938
15. Brest, J., Žumer, V., Maucec, M.: Self-adaptive differential evolution algorithm in constrained real-parameter optimization. In: IEEE Congress on Evolutionary Computation, pp. 215–222 (December 2006), doi:10.1109/CEC.2006.1688311
16. Brest, J., Greiner, S., Bošković, B., Mernik, M., Žumer, V.: Self-adapting control parameters in differential evolution: a comparative study on numerical benchmark problems. IEEE Trans. Evol. Comput. 10, 646–657 (2006), doi:10.1109/TEVC.2006.872133
17. Zamuda, A., Brest, J., Bošković, B., Žumer, V.: Differential evolution for multiobjective optimization with self adaptation. In: Proceedings of the IEEE Congress on Evolutionary Computation, pp. 3617–3624 (September 2007), doi:10.1109/CEC.2007.4424941

18. Brest, J., Zamuda, A., Žumer, V.: An analysis of the control parameters'adaptation in DE. In: Chakraborty, U.K. (ed.) Advances In Differential Evolution, vol. 143, pp. 89–110 (July 2008), doi:10.1007/978-3-540-68830-3_3

19. Rahnamayan, S., Tizhoosh, H., Salama, M.M.A.: Opposition-based differential evolution for optimization of noisy problems. In: Proceedings of the IEEE Congress on Evolutionary Computation, pp. 1865–1872 (September 2006), doi:10.1109/CEC.2006.1688534

20. Rahnamayan, S., Tizhoosh, H., Salama, M.M.A.: Quasi-oppositional differential evolution. In: Proceedings of the IEEE Congress On Evolutionary Computation, pp. 2229–2236 (September 2007), doi:10.1109/CEC.2007.4424748

21. Rahnamayan, S., Tizhoosh, H., Salama, M.M.A.: Opposition-based differential evolution. In: IEEE Transaction on Evolutinary Computation, vol. 12, pp. 64–79 (February 12, 2008), doi:10.1109/TEVC.2007.894200

22. Chakraborty, U.K., Das, S., Konar, A.: Differential evolution with local neighborhood. In: Proceedings of the IEEE Congress on Evolutionary Computation, pp. 2042–2049 (September 2006), doi:10.1109/CEC.2006.1688558

23. Das, S., Abraham, A., Chakraborty, U.K., Konar, A.: Differential evolution with a neighborhood-based mutation operator. IEEE Transaction on Evolutionay Computation 13, 526–553 (2009), doi:10.1109/TEVC.2008.2009457

24. Qin, A.K., Suganthan, P.N.: Self-adaptive differential evolution algorithm for numerical optimization. In: Proceedings of the IEEE Congress on Evolutionary Computation, vol. 2, pp. 1785–1791 (September 2005), doi:10.1109/CEC.2005.1554904

25. Lampinen, J., Zelinka, I.: On stagnation of the differential evolution algorithm. In: Proceedings of 6th International Mendel Conference on Soft Computing, pp. 76–83 (June 2000), doi: 10.1.1.35.7932

26. Zielinski, K., Wang, X., Laur, R.: Comparison of adaptive approaches for differential evolution. In: Rudolph, G., Jansen, T., Lucas, S., Poloni, C., Beume, N. (eds.) PPSN 2008. LNCS, vol. 5199, pp. 641–650. Springer, Heidelberg (2008), doi:10.1007/978-3-540-87700-4-64

Test Case Automatic Generation Research Based on AADL Behavior Annex

Yu-Lan Yang[1,*], Hong-Bing Qian[1,**], and Yang-Zhao Li[2,***]

[1] G313, Software Engineering Institute, New Main Building, Beihang University
No. 37, College Road, Haidian District, Beijing, China
[2] Information Center, China Three Gorges Corporation, Beijing China
powerdesler@gmail.com, qhb@buaa.edu.cn,
li_yangzhao@ctgpc.com.cn

Abstract. Test case generation is essential to software test. Software test efficiency can be greatly improved through test case automatic generation. AADL Behavior Annex is an extension of AADL which can describe detailed behavior of AADL component. In this paper, we discuss a test case automatic generation method based on the AADL Behavior Annex. This method contains two parts: automatic generation of test sequences and automatic generation of test data. The former generates test sequences through dominator analysis; the later uses subsection gradient descent algorithm to generate test data.

Keywords: software test, AADL Behavior Annex, automatic test case generation, subsection gradient descent algorithm.

1 Introduction

With the development and evolution of Model Driven Architecture, model driven ideas and methods are changing the traditional software development which considers code development as most important. Platform-independent application established by MDA and associated OMG modeling Standards can be realized through any open or proprietary platform, including Web Services, .NET, CORBA, J2EE and others. Object Management Group (OMG) developed a series of standards, including UML which was used to describe the various models. Although it is not born for the MDA, but as one of the most influential modeling language, UML has become the de facto standard modeling language. However, for safety-critical embedded systems, UML does not fully meet its requirements of performance attributes and hardware-related properties. Characteristics for embedded systems, Society of Automotive Engineers (SAE) Architecture Description Language Sub-Committee, Embedded Computing Systems Committee, Avionics Company in October 2004 jointly promulgated the aviation standards AS5506, proposed Architecture Analysis and Design Language (AADL). AADL is a language for specifying, analyzing and automatic integrating the

---

[*] Research area: software test and measurement.
[**] Research area: software test, software measurement.
[***] Research area: business intelligence.

H. Deng et al. (Eds.): AICI 2011, Part I, LNAI 7002, pp. 137–145, 2011.

critical real-time performance of distributed computer systems [3]. It provides a new way to analyze model-based and model-driven approach system design.

In order to support the system architecture modeling and analysis, and meet the different requirements, AADL provides a language extension mechanism. The behavior annex is an extension of AADL with annex form. It can describe detailed behavior of AADL software component, etc. thread and subprogram, and it provides more fully and more detailed basis for code automatic generation.

2   AADL Behavior Annex

AADL Behavior Annex is a sublanguage of AADL; it can be attached to AADL component, such as subprogram, thread. It describes component behavior. The behavior annex describes a transition system with six optional sections: annex behavior _specification {**<state variables>?<initialization>?<states>?<transitions>?<connections>?<composite_declaration>* **}. The <state variables> section declares typed identifiers; the state variables must be initialized in the <initialization> section; the <state> section declares automaton states; the <transitions> section defines transitions from a source state to a destination state; the <connections> section extends the one which is already presented in AADL and allows the specification of links between entry points and their corresponding implementations; the <composite_declaration> section declares composite states. In the <states> section, states can be qualified as *initial, complete, return, urgent* or *composite*. Subprograms and threads start from *initial* state, subprograms terminate in *return* state; threads end in *complete* state and resume from that state at next dispatch. The *Urgent* states are intended mainly for model checking purposes. A sub state-machine can be attached to a *composite* state.

The states transition in behavior annex is based on Extend Finite State Machine (EFSM). EFSM is an extension of Finite State Machine (FSM). Based on FSM, EFSM increases variable, transition guard and transition action. These features enrich EFSM semantic. An EFSM is a six tuple $<S, S_0, I, O, T, V>$. S is non-empty states set; S_0 is initial state; I is non-empty input event set; O is non-empty output event set; T is non-empty states transition set; V is variable set. Element t of T is a six tuple $<Head(t), Tail(t), I(t), P(t), Action, O(t)>$. $Head(t)$ is source state of transition t; $Tail(t)$ is destination state of transition t; $I(t)$ is input event of set EFSM, it can be empty; $P(t)$ is guard of transition t, it can be empty; $Action$ is action of transition t, It consists of variable assignment, branch selection, loop and send the message composition, it can be empty; $O(t)$ is output event set of EFSM, it can be empty. When EFSM receives the event input $I(t)$, if the guard $P(t)$ is satisfied, EFSM transits from initial state or current state $Head(t)$ to the next state and trigger transition actions.

Behavior annex introduced transition priority rules. If there are many satisfied guards in the current state's transitions, current state transits to the next state from the highest priority transition; if there are many highest priority transitions, current state transits to the next state from a highest priority transition which is randomly chosen.

3   Background and Related Work

Research of EFSM-based test case automatic generation focuses on the test sequence generation, test data generation and sequence feasibility. [9] proposes a test sequence generation approach based on EFSM transition feasibility analysis. The approach expands EFSM into Transition Executability Analysis (TEA) tree and generates executable test sequences. [10] resolves test sequences feasibility problem by removing relevant edges of EFSM. This approach departs EFSM edges whose predicates in action conflicted with others into independent sub-graphs, and then generates test cases by using existed FSM test sequence generation methods. But this method requires that the predicate and action in EFSM must be linear expression, and recursion, pointer can't exist in EFSM. [4] uses dominator analysis and backtrack to generate executable test sequences. By dominator analysis, each state node of the EFSM is given a corresponding weight and identifies hot spots. Then a path from hot spot state node to initial state node is generated. Backtrack is applied to find other paths if the path is infeasible. Approaches mentioned above have a defect: not consider the case that input variables exist in predicates when conducting feasibility analysis. Only certain values are assigned to input variables can test sequence feasibility analysis be performed. This problem can be solved by automatically generating data which satisfy predicate. Usually used methods of test data automatic generation include simulated annealing [2], scatter search [5], genetic algorithm, tabu search and so on. [6] uses subsection gradient descent algorithm to generate test data. If no test data which fully meets the feasibility requirements of test sequence, the algorithm can restrict variables in a smaller range, so the burden of artificial selection is reduced. [8] introduces different cost function of string data and uses genetic algorithm to automatically generate string data satisfying predicate requirements.

4   Test Case Generation

Since AADL behavior annex can describe detailed behavior of AADL components, not only for automatic code generation process it provides a sufficient and detailed basis, but also the foundation for test cases automatic generation is established. By analyzing the EFSM described in AADL behavior annex, this paper generates test cases to meet branch coverage criterion. A test case set contains two parts: (1) test sequence set that input event sequence starts from the initial state or the current state; (2) the determined value set of input variables which in each test sequence of test set triggered by state transition. This requires the value of the input variables must satisfy all guards on the state transition in a test sequence. So the test case generation algorithm is divided into two parts: test sequence generation and test data generation.

4.1   Test Sequence Generation

Behavior annex allows branches to exist in action of transition. For the convenience of automatic test data generation, firstly a process called normalization [9] of behavior annex EFSM is performed, that ensures no branch exists in action of transition. Extract branches in transition action and transform it into sub-states.

1. "if" expression, with the form $if(P)\{E_1\}E_2$. P is logical expression, E_1, E_2 are *NULL* or expression without branch. Create two sub-states S_1, S_2 and two transitions t_1, t_2. $Head(t_1)$, $Head(t_2)=S_1$, $Tail(t_1)$, $Tail(t_2)=S_2$, $P(t_1)=P$, $P(t_2)$ is *NULL*, $Action(t_1)=E_1$, $Action(t_2)=E_2$.

2. "if else" expression, with the form $if(P_1)\{E_1\}else$ or $if(P_2)\{E_2\}...else\{E_n\}$, the meanings of $P_1...P_{n-1}$, $E_1...E_n$ are the same mentioned above. Create two sub-states

S_1, S_2 and n transitions $t_1...t_n$. $Head(t_1)...Head(t_n)=S_1$, $Tail(t_1)...Tail(t_n)=S_2$, $P(t_1)=P_1$, $P(t_2)=(\ \neg P_1 \wedge P_2 \ )...P(t_n)=(\ \neg P_1 \wedge \neg P_2 \ ... \ \neg P_{n-1} \ )$, $Action(t_1)=E_1$, $Action(t_2)=E_2...Action(t_n)=E_n$.

3. "for" expression, with the form $for(P)\{E_1\}E_2$. Create one sub-states S_1 and two transitions t_1, t_2. $Tail(t_1)=S_1$, $P(t_1)=P$, $P(t_2)= \ \neg P$; $Head(t_i)=S_1$, $Action(t_i)=E_i$, i=1,2. An *if else* expression transformation example is given in Fig 1.

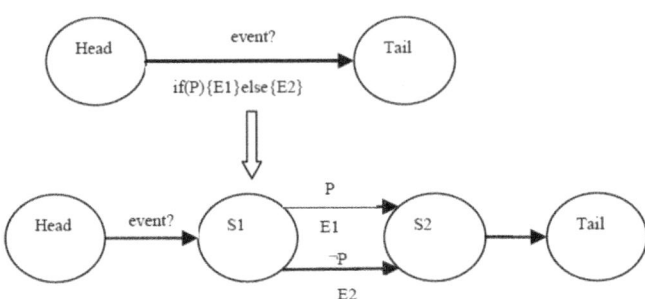

Fig. 1. Example of "if else" expression transformation

After completion of normalization, dominator analysis [4] is applied on EFSM for calculating the weight of each state node. Weight will be used later in sequence generation. A node a is said to dominate node b if covering b implies that a has also been covered. As shown in Figure 2, nodes S0, S1dominate nodes S2...S5, S2 dominates S4. Let two nodes a, b weights Wa, Wb respectively and a dominates b, then $Wb=Wa+1$. If node S does not dominate other nodes, its weight is 0. In figure 2, weights of S0, S1...S5 are 0, 1, 2, 2, 3, and 2.

Test sequence is composed of a series of orderly state nodes and transition edges. Transitions include guards and actions which do not contain a branch. To generate test sequences under branch coverage criterion, the following algorithm is proposed.

1. Exit if there no uncovered edges in EFSM. Or choose a uncovered edge t_i which satisfies (a)tail node has maximum weight, (b) if more than one edge to meet the condition a, the highest priority edge is chosen; if such an edge is still more than one then choose one randomly from those edges. Point pointer p to t_i. Call the edge pointed by p current edge; call the head node of edge pointed by p current node.

2. Mark the current edge and the current node as selected edge and selected node. If current node is initial node, then record sequence from initial node to head node of t_i as Seq_1: $S_{initial}$, t_{k0}, ...S_{ki}, t_i and go to step 4; else go to step 3.

3. For the in edges of current node, select an edge t' whose head node's weight is no greater than current node's weight within following decreasing priority: (a) uncovered, (b) its head node's weight is smallest, (c) priority is highest. If all in edges of current node are covered, select edge t' with rules (b), (c). Make p point to t', then go to step 2.

4. Find a sequence Seq_2: $S_{k(i+1)}$, $t_{k(i+1)}$...S_{end} which $S_{k(i+1)}$ is the tail node of t_i and S_{end} is the end state node(such as *return* state node) of EFSM. If the sequence contains

loop path, then the loop path only appears once in the sequence. Mark Seq_2 as selected post sequence. Combine Seq_1, Seq_2 into one sequence Seq_i which starts from the initial state node and terminates at the end state node. Go to step 5.

5. Verify the feasibility of Seq_i. If Seq_i is feasible, mark transition edges in Seq_i as covered and reset all uncovered transition edges, stat nodes and sequence; go to step 1. Or go to step 6.

6. If exist unselected post sequence Seq_2', combine $Seq1$ and Seq_2' into new Seq_i, go to step 5 ; or choose a new Seq_1 according to rules in step 2, 3; if a new Seq_1 exists, reset selected post sequences and go to step 6. If no new Seq_1 exists, mark t_i as covered and redundant, then reset uncovered transition edges, state nodes and sequences; go to step 1.

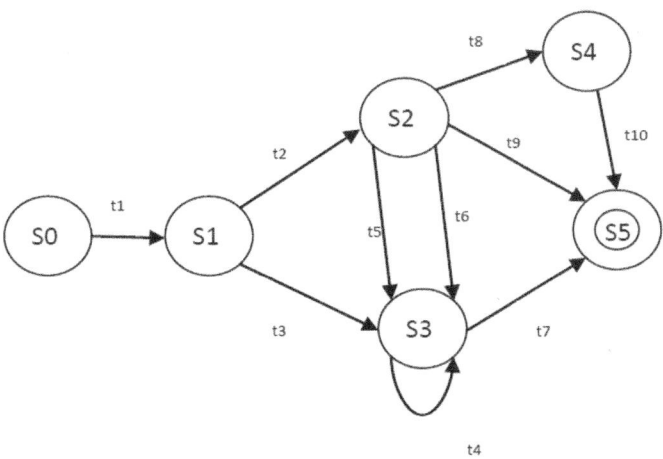

Fig. 2. An EFSM example

In the above process a feasibility analysis of the test sequence needed to be conducted for checking whether all guards are satisfied. In the feasibility analysis we should determine whether there are input variables to satisfy all transition guards within their limited values range. If there are such input variables, generate the data through the automatic test data generation algorithm to meet these requirements.

4.2 Test Data Generation

Among many test data generation algorithm, subsection gradient descent algorithm is characterized as faster converging, less iterating. It is adopted in this paper. With interval reduction, subsection gradient descent algorithm mainly consists of three phases [6]:

1. Initialization: convert state transition expression of test sequences into regular expression. That means right part of assignment expression, left and right part of guard expression only contain input variables and (or) constant expression.

2. Interval reduction: utilize guard on state transitions to reduce the value range of input variables. This process can accelerate the convergence of subsection gradient descent algorithm.
3. Determine the value of the input variable: select feasible test data by using subsection gradient descent algorithm.

Establish a variable-expression table in the initialization process which is given as table 1

Table 1. Variable-Expression Table

variable	expression
identifier	regular expression

Fill the identifiers and corresponding expressions of variables in definition part of behavior annex in the table, and then start the analysis of test sequence from the first transition. If current expression is assignment expression and there are variables in right part of it, replace the variable in right part of assignment expression with its regular expression found in variable-expression table. Then add or replace the identifier which is the left part of assignment expression and its altered expression in variable-expression table. Similar replacement is applied on left and right part of guard expression

The purpose of interval reduction is to reduce the range of input variables, so the determination value of input variables could be quicker. Since interval reduction goes very complex when guard expression contains three or more different input variables, expression which only contains no more than two input variables will be analyzed. The general relational expression is $aX\ op1\ bY\ op2\ c\ cond\ 0$. a, b, c are constant and a, b are not all zero; X, Y are variables, $op1$, $op2$ are arithmetic operators(+, -, *, /), $cond$ is condition operator(>, >=, <, <=, =, !=). Limited space, no specific methods are given in this paper. Note that when $op1$ is multiplication or division, the situation, one of X, Y's upper or lower bound is positive and other is negative, should be respectively discussed.

After the two former phases, the value of input variables can be determined using subsection gradient descent algorithm. Main steps of the algorithm are: (1) Divide the interval of variables into subintervals and determine the objective function. (2) Generate initial values of variables randomly from unused subintervals. (3) Output variables values and stop if the values satisfy all the guards on transitions, else go to step 3. (4) Determine the direction of the object function gradient which descend most quickly and calculate the optimal step length; adjust the value of the input variables. If little adjustment room is left, go to step 2, else go to step 3.

The approach is shown specifically as follows:

1. Object function determination. Using branch function [7] to map the branch predicate to a real value function which is shown in table 2:

Table 2. Branch Function. Note that $E1$ and $E2$ are arithmetic expressions, $RE1$ and $RE2$ are relation expression

branch predicate	branch function
$E1\ (x) > E2\ (x)$, $E1\ (x) >= E2\ (x)$	$f(x) = E2\ (x) - E1\ (x)$
$E1\ (x) < E2\ (x)$, $E1\ (x) <= E2\ (x)$	$f(x) = E1\ (x) - E2\ (x)$
$E1\ (x) \neq E2\ (x)$	$f(x) = - abs\ (E1\ (x) - E2\ (x))$
$R\,E1\ (x)$ and $R\,E2\ (x)$	$f(x) = \max(f1\ (RE1\ (x)), f2\ (RE2\ (x)))$
$R\,E1\ (x)$ or $R\,E2\ (x)$	$f(x) = \min(f1\ (RE1\ (x)), f2\ (RE2\ (x)))$
$not\ (R\,E1\ (x))$	$f(x) = -f1\ (R\,E1\ (x))$

Object function $F(X) = \sum_{i=1}^{n} f_i(X)$; where X is input variable, n is number of constrains. When all constraints are satisfied the objective function should be equal to or less than zero, generally less than zero.

2. Gradient descent direction determination. The goal is making function less than zero. Function has maximum change rate in the gradient direction of the function at one point, so make the negative gradient direction as the search direction. Gradient of a function is a n-dimensional vector which can be defined as $\nabla F(X) = \dfrac{\partial F}{\partial X} = [\dfrac{\partial F}{\partial x_1}, \dfrac{\partial F}{\partial x_2}, ..., \dfrac{\partial F}{\partial x_n}]^T$. Negative gradient unit vector is

$$g = -\frac{\nabla F(X)}{\|\nabla F(X)\|} \tag{1}$$

where $\|\nabla F(X)\|$ is gradient vector modulus.

3. Optimal step length determination. For the $k+1$ iterations there are

$$X^{(k+1)} = X^{(k)} - h\nabla F(X^{(k)}) \tag{2}$$

where h is step length parameter. According to (1) rewrite (2) as

$$X^{(k+1)} = X^{(k)} + h\|\nabla F(X^{(k)})\| g^{(k)} = X^{(k)} + \lambda g^{(k)}, \ \lambda = h\|\nabla F(X^{(k)})\| \tag{3}$$

So

$$F(X^{(k+1)}) = F(X^{(k)} + \lambda g^{(k)}) \tag{4}$$

Let the step $\lambda^{(k)} \geq 0$ which makes $F(X^{(k+1)})$ the smallest along the negative gradient direction. Select the optimal step length $\lambda^{(k)}$ is actually to find the minimum value of $F(X^{(k+1)})$. Derivate formula (4) and make it equal to zero

$$\frac{dF(X^{(k+1)})}{d\lambda^{(k)}} = \frac{dF(X^{(k)} + \lambda^{(k)} g^{(k)})}{d\lambda^{(k)}} = 0 \tag{5}$$

Expand $F(X^{(k+1)})$ in the quadratic approximate Taylor progression

$$F(X^{(k+1)}) = F(X^{(k)}) + \nabla^T F(X^{(k)})\Delta X + \frac{1}{2}(\Delta X)^T A\Delta X \tag{6}$$

$\Delta X = X^{(k+1)} - X^{(k)}$, $A = \nabla^2 F(X^{(k)})$ that is Hessian matrix. Substitute formula (4) into formula (6) and make it equal to zero after the derivation

$$\frac{dF(X^{(k)} + \lambda^{(k)} g^{(k)})}{d\lambda^{(k)}} = \nabla^T F(X^{(k)}) g^{(k)} + (g^{(k)})^T A g^{(k)} \lambda^{(k)} = 0 \tag{7}$$

According to formula (7) we can get optimal step length at a certain point. Replace solution with its absolute value if solution is negative. If a variable value outside its range, then limit the value in its value interval. A small real number ε should be defined in the iteration process. Stop iteration when $\| X^{(k+1)} - X^{(k)} \| < \varepsilon$. This indicates that little room is left to adjustment; other unused subintervals should be tried.

5   Test Data Generation Experiment

An experiment of test data generation algorithm is performed based on matlab platform. Matlab symbolic computation is used to process the derivatives and the Hessian matrix. We selected 120 input sequences. Experiment platform: CPU is Inter Core2 Duo, memory space is 2G. The experiment result is shown in table 3:

Table 3. Experiment Result

input sequences amount	average sequence predicate amount	average nonlinear sequence predicate amount
20	6	2
80	6	3
20	6	4
feasible input sequences amount	average execution time when no solution (s)	average execution time when find solution (s)
20	0	0.997
74	4.51	1.04
18	10.8	2.79

The experiment showed that the higher the order of the branch function, the more nonlinear constraints, no solution possibility of input sequence may be greater, and execution time may be longer. Experiment also found that for the same configuration performance the results may be different; for the same branch function, different interval length will affect the final execution results. How to generate feasible test data quickly needs further study.

6   Conclusion

This paper discusses a test case automatic generation method by analyzing threads and subprogram behavioral model described by AADL behavior annex and identifying transitions relationship between model components states, in accordance with the test case generation algorithm to generate test cases, under the goal that achieve the automatic generation of test cases from the AADL model. Not only the quality and development process specifications of software are ensured, but also the workload of the testing process is reduced and the efficiency of software development is improved. For how to automatic generate test case with non-numeric input variables and algorithm optimization, more research will be performed in the future.

Acknowledgements. This work is supported by One Eleventh Five-Year Project of The General Reserve Department of PLA, one Basic Software Project of COSTIND). and Major National Science and Technology Programs of Core Electronics Components, High-end General Chips and Basic Software (CHB) of China under grant NO. 2009ZX01045-005-002.

References

1. Liu, Y.-J., Kang, J.-C., Lu, W.-F.: Overview of Model-Driven Architecture. Computer Science 33(3) (2006) (in Chinese)
2. Tracey, N., Clark, J., Mander, K.: Automated flaw finding using simulated annealing. In: International Symposium on Software Testing and Analysis, vol. 30(1), pp. 73–81 (1998)
3. Yang, Z.-B., Pi, L., Hu, K., Gu, Z.-H., Ma, D.-F.: AADL: An Architecture Design and Analysis Language for Complex Embedded Real-Time Systems. Journal of Software 21(5), 899–915 (2010)
4. Eric Wong, W., Restrepo, A., Qi, Y., Choi, B.: An EFSM-based Test Generation for Validation of SDL Specifications. In: AST 2008 (May 11, 2008)
5. Blanco, R., Tuya, J., Adenso-Díaz, B.: Automated test data generation using a scatter search approach. Information and Software Technology 51, 708–720 (2009)
6. Zhang, Y., Qian, L.-Q., Wang, Y.-F.: Automatic Testing Data Generation in the Testing Based on EFSM. Chinese Journal of Computers (2004) (in Chinese)
7. Korel, B.: Automated software test data generation. IEEE Transactions on Software Engineering 16(8), 870–879 (1990)
8. Alshraideh, M., Bottaci, L.: Automatic Software Test Data Generation For String Data Using Heuristic Search with Domain Specific Search Operators. UK Software Testing Research III, 137–148 (2005)
9. Huang, C.-M., Chiang, M.-S., Jang, M.-Y.: UIOE: a protocol test sequence generation method using the transition executability analysis (TEA). Computer Communications 21, 1462–1475 (1998)
10. Duale, A.Y., Umit Uyar, M.: A Method Enabling Feasible Conformance Test Sequence Generation for EFSM Models. IEEE Transactions On Computers 53(5) (May 2004)

Distributed Train-Group Modeling and Simulation Based on Cellular Automaton and Multi-agent

Zifeng Wang[1,2], Li Ruan[1,2], Limin Xiao[1], Yao Zheng[1], and Yunfan Dong[1]

[1] School of Computer Science and Engineering,
Beihang University, Beijing 100191, China
[2] State Key Laboratory of Rail Traffic Control and Safety,
Beijing Jiaotong University, Beijing 100044, China
{wangzifeng0324,zyshren}@163.com, {ruanli,xiaolm}@buaa.edu.cn,
dongyunfan@yahoo.com.cn

Abstract. Based on cellular automaton and multi-agent model, we propose a novel hybrid model for distributed simulation of train-group in the railway traffic. An improved cellular automaton model is designed for simulating the underlying structure of the railroad and a multi-agent model is used for dynamic scheduling of the train-group. The combination of both models answers for the distributed simulation of train-group on the railroad. Simulation and scheduling strategies are proposed to analyze and solve the problems about safety operation and dynamic scheduling. In the end, we analyze the characteristics of train flows and dealing with the emergencies of the railroad net. Experimental results show that the hybrid model is proper and efficient for distributed simulation of train-group of the railroad net.

Keywords: cellular automaton, multi-agent, train group, distributed simulation.

1 Introduction

With the rapid development of rail transportations, the speed of trains get further enhanced and the scale of rail net get further expanded, the challenges of safety issues of train operation and dynamic scheduling are growing. If there is a fault or emergency in the infrastructure, which can't be solved in a short term, trains will be delayed, which will cause great economic losses. Although the artificial rechanneling can reduce the detaining and delay of trains to some extent, the efficiency is relatively low, and the rechanneling may result into a consecutive influence and affect the operation of trains on other lanes.

Designing a reasonable scheduling strategy by real-time simulation can effectively figure out the above-mentioned issues. Take into account greater data processing aroused by larger scale of rail net and greater number of trains, and effectiveness required by simulation, we decide to use a distributed modeling method to improve simulation efficiency. Recently, in the railroad transportation field, the modeling methods mainly include modeling based on cellular automaton [1], modeling based on Petri Nets [3], train-group operation modeling based multi-agent system [4][5], and multi-dimensional space-temporal model of rail security [6][7]. We will analyze

H. Deng et al. (Eds.): AICI 2011, Part I, LNAI 7002, pp. 146–154, 2011.

the characteristics of cellular automaton and multi-agent and explore the combination of both for distributed simulation of train-group on the rail net.

The rest of paper is organized as follows: In section 2, we introduce the related work on multi-agent and cellular automaton applied into rail transportation, analyze the characteristics of both models, and explore the possibility to combine the two models. Section 3 presents how to combine the two models and model for rail transportation. Section 4 demonstrates the possibility of the hybrid model to achieve the simulation of railway transportation and solve the problems of dynamic scheduling by analyzing the characteristics of train flows and dealing with the emergencies in the rail net.

2   Related Work and Analysis of Models

Cellular automaton is a classic model for traffic flow simulation. Nagel and Schreckenberg [1] developed a one-dimensional cellular automaton model for traffic flows on a single lane. This was the first time cellular automaton which was used in transportation simulation. In 2005, Keping Li [2] developed a new cellular automaton model based on the above-mentioned NaSch model, and took the model into modeling moving block system and fixed block system to analyze the characteristics of train flow in rail transportation.

Modeling based agent is mainly used to solve the complex problems of train dispatching and dynamic scheduling. K. Fischer [9] proposed an MAS system that modeled a society of transportation companies whose goal was to deliver a set of dynamically given orders satisfying the given cost and time constraint. A decentralized agent system was designed using agent approach to solve the dynamic scheduling problem in [10].

Multi-agent can be used to solve the dynamic scheduling problem. Take vehicles as agents, and realize dynamic scheduling through the communication of agents [8]. But the agent-oriented programming is complex, and great communications between agents will decrease the efficiency of the system, while it is easy to realize the railroad simulation using cellular automaton with simple rules, but cellular automaton lacks the capacity to deal with dynamic scheduling problems and with same characteristics of cells. Thus, combination of the two models will be a great choice.

3   Train-group Modeling Based on Multi-agent and Cellular Automaton

3.1   Train-Group Simulation Model

The simulation model is a hybrid model based on multi-agent and cellular automaton. Since the control rules of cellular automaton are simple, so the modeling underlying infrastructure is designed based on improved cellular automaton model; In order to implement the distributed simulation and solve dynamic scheduling problem, the modeling upper structure is based on multi-agent. The whole structure of the hybrid model is shown in Fig. 1.

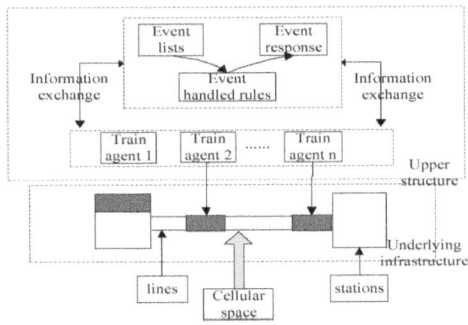

Fig. 1. The structure of hybrid model

3.2 Underlying Infrastructure of Hybrid Model

The underlying infrastructure is consisted of rail tracks and trains, stations on them. The model is implemented by combining cellular automaton with multi-agent, and train agents are added into cellular space.

The improved NaSch cellular automaton model is used for underlying infrastructure modeling. According to the characteristics of Chinese railway, we study and analyze the operation of trains by considering only one direction. We divide the lane into L cells, the scale of every one equals, and we tag them $i=1, 2... L$. And we assume that the time is discrete. Every cell has two states: empty or occupied by a train, the speeds of trains are $v_n=0, 1... v_{max}$.

According to kinematical theory, the minimum security distance between two trains S_n is determined by the following formula:

$$S_n = v_{max}^2 / (2d) + SMD,$$

v_{max} is the maximum speed of trains, d represents the acceleration/deceleration of train n, SMD is the safety margin distance. In order to get S_n, every train must know its position and the position of leading train.

Model the moving block system of rail transportation: Every train agent on the lane sends information of its position to the following train agent, then every train agent can calculate its distance to the leading one -- the number of cells gap between train n and the leading train $n-1$, in addition with its position. If the leading one of first train who enters the lane is a station, it can calculate the distance gap_s between itself and the station. Moreover, the train agent also can get the distance x_c when it decelerates into the station according to its current velocity v_n.

Based on NaSch cellular automaton model [1] and the one for railroad simulation designed by Keping Li [2], we design the operating rules of an improved cellular automaton for railroad transportation. Compared with urban traffic flows, the accidental changes rarely happen in railroad transportation, so we do not take into account the probabilistic changes of velocity. In addition, every station is able to contain more than one train at the same time.

The first case: train n runs behind train $n-1$:

The pseudo code of operation strategy is as follows in Fig. 2.

Step 1 acceleration/deceleration:
If gap > S_n
  $v_n = \min(v_n + a, v_{max})$;
else if gap < S_n
  $v_n = \max(v_n - d, 0)$;
else
  $v_n = v_n$;

Step 2 movement:
  $x_n = x_n + v_n$;

While (N > 0)
  Allow a train to step into the station;
  Step 1 acceleration/deceleration:
    if gap_s > x_c
      $v_n = \min(v_n + a, v_{max})$;
    else if gap_s < x_c
      $v_n = \max(v_n - d, 0)$;
    else
      $v_n = v_n$;

  Step 2 movement
    $x_n = x_n + v_n$;
    N--;
If N=0
  The same with the algorithm in Case 1;

Fig. 2. The train n is behind train n-1 **Fig. 3.** The train n is behind a station

The second case: The train n is behind a station. (Assume that maximum trains in a station are N). The pseudo code of operation strategy is as follows in Fig. 3.

If there's an unoccupied track in the station, then train n is permitted into the station. If N equals to 0, no trains will be allowed to enter the station. We can regard the station as a static train agent, so the operation strategy is same with case one.

3.3   Upper Structure of Hybrid Model

The Structure of Multi-agent System. The modeling of upper Structure is based on multi-agent model. It mainly uses its advantages in solving complex dynamic problems and its distributed structure to solve the safe operation and dynamic scheduling problem.

We choose appropriate entitative and functional agent: train as entitative agent and regional decision-making agent as functional agent.

The Fig. 4 as follows is a figure of upper structure based on multi-agent model.

Train Agent. Every train agent has some attributes, including train name, maximum v_{max}, acceleration/deceleration a/d and timetable.

Train agents will operate according to the settled timetable, and keep the communication with the heading train agent: receive the position, calculate the distance headway *gap*. If the heading one is a station, *gap_s* will be calculated instead.

When emergencies arise on the railroad, the train agent will send a dynamic scheduling request to the regional decision-making agent in the region. Then regional agent answers for the request and updates the latest timetable.

Regional Decision-making Agent. Every regional decision-making agent manages a certain part of railroad network. It locates on a distributed physical node.

Regional decision-making agent responds for train agent's requests, and communicates with other regional decision-making agents to corporate to handle dynamic scheduling together when required. Then, it will evaluate the results and update the new train timetable. It also has to manage the train agents in its region.

The evaluation criteria are consisted of two items: First, the smaller time expenses of dynamic scheduling T; Second, the higher degree of compliance with the original timetable. To avoid the situation that the changeable timetable affects other trains' operation, we set the second condition prior to the first one.

The time expense of dynamic scheduling T mainly is the time spent on the updated tracks for the train. Here it can be considered into solving two problems: Get the K_{th} shortest path problem; The time expenses for the competition of trains on the same track.

The K_{th} shortest path problem can be realized using A* heuristic algorithm; as to the second problem, we can use history data to calculate out the time we need.

Following Table 1 is the variables we define, which are used in the schedule algorithm.

Agent Communication. We use messaging mechanism for agent communication. The structure is as follows:

> Message {   Station point_boundary,   Station src_bug;
>   Station des_bug,   Timetable *pTimetable; };

Regional decision-making agent sends request message for communication and corporation to other agents, including *point_boundary*, the start and destination point of faulty lane, and timetable. And the other regional decision-making agents return the timetable from *point_boundary* to *des_bug*.

Table 1. The variable list

Variable name	Definition
Region Agent	The Regional decision-making agent in one region;
point_boundary	The boundary stations between the regional decision-making agent and another one;
src_station	The heading station of the faulty lane;
key_stations	The stations that the train have to arrive and stop at some time;
src_bug	The source point of faulty lane;
des_bug	The destination point of faulty lane;
src_dispatch	The source point of dynamic scheduling;
des_dispatch	The destination point of dynamic scheduling;
des_station	The destination station of train operation;
kth_path	The kth shortest path;
t1_kpath	The time expenses without considering the competition of rail resources;
t2_origin	The time expenses with considering the competition of rail resources;
T(k)_kpath	The whole time expenses of train operation on the kth shortest path;
T_kpath	The minimum T(k)_kpath among the k shortest paths;
X_k	The degree of compliance with the original timetable;

And the pseudo code of dynamic scheduling is as follows in Fig. 5.

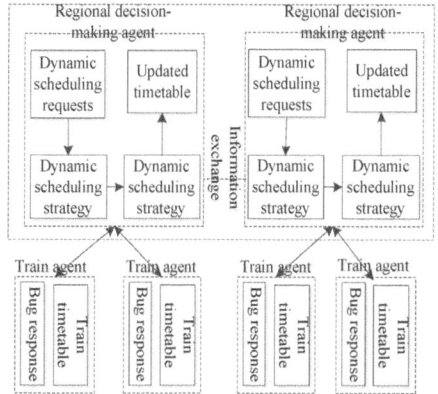

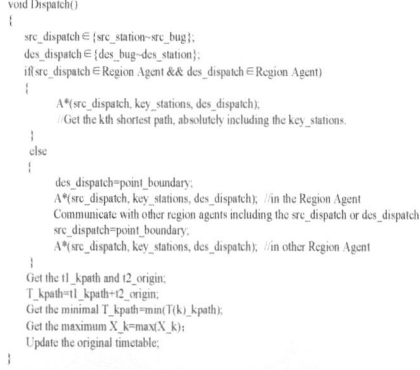

Fig. 4. The upper structure based on multi-agent model

Fig. 5. The pseudo code of dynamic scheduling

4   The Train-Group Simulation Based on Hybrid Model

When the train-group operates normally on the railroad, not involved into unexpected situations, we simulate and analyze the operation of the train groups. Set $L=800$, and the time span of simulation $T=1000$, the parameters a and d to 1, the station is located in 500, the length of the block area Ls to 50, v_{max} to 5, the number of tracks in the stations N to 1. We conform to the operation strategy of the above-mentioned cellular automaton on the lane. During the initial analysis, SMD is set to 10. We reproduce the move-stop wave of the railway traffic flow in the space-time graph. Black dots represent the location of trains in the Fig. 6 as follows.

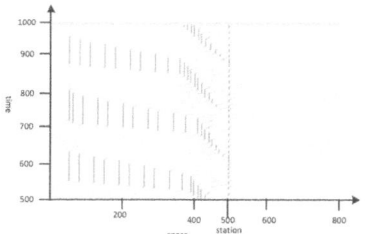

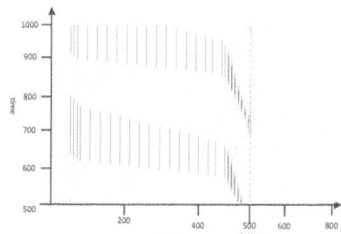

Fig. 6. The space-time graph of train-group, $L=800$, $T=1000$, $v_{max}=10$, $Ls=50$, $SMD=10$, The station is located in 500; black dots represent the location of trains at some time.

Fig. 7. The space-time graph of train-group operation when the value of SMD is 4

When the density of trains reaches to a certain limit, the stop-wait waves arise on the lane. That is mainly because the train-group is mixed, the high-speed trains and ordinary trains will be involved into the competition of railroad resources, and the slow trains or the ones behind others have to stop and wait.

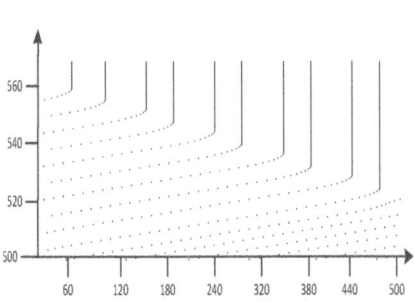

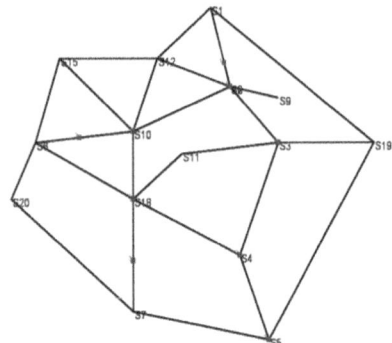

Fig. 8. The space-time graph when the fault arises on the lane

Fig. 9. The railroad net of trains operation, the red rectangles represent train, the number in the left corner is train ID

In order to improve the throughput of the lane, we reduce the value of *SMD*. In our study, when the value is reduced to 4, the lanes overlap, and the collisions arise. As shown in Fig. 7. *SMD* is relevant to the density of trains and speeds of mixed train-group. Due to the cycle of communication between trains is designed to 1s, and in more than 1 second distance, theoretically the trains will have enough time to react to special situations, so it is safe when $SMD > v_{max}$. In this study, the value of *SMD* is at least the half of v_{max}, which will get the maximal throughput of the lane with the trains operating safely.

If a lane suffers from a fault and shortage of any scheduling measures at some time, the trains will have to delay, and the delays will occupy great lots of track resources and influent the operation of other trains on the lane. As shown in Fig. 8, there is a fault on the front lane, take no actions, and finally when the railroad resources are depleted, a large area stops arise.

In this study, we achieve a preliminary research of the hybrid model. We design the train agents based on objects, the communications between agents based on socket in Windows System, and the underlying communication platform is based on BH RTI distributed simulation run-time infrastructure. The hardware environment is constituted by three Window xp computers, three trains operate on each computer, and the operations of nine trains are shown in the whole railroad net. As shown in Figure 9, the red rectangles represent the trains, the left corner of train is the ID of the train. RDA(Regional decision-making agent) is partitioned by simple rules, as shown in Table 2.

Table 2. The table of regional decision-making agent

Name of RDA	Stations included	Boundary Stations	Trains included
RDA 1	S15/S6/S20/S10/S18/S7	S10/S18/S7	T1/T4
RDA 2	S1/S12/S10/S8/S9	S10/S12/S8	T2/T5/T3/T6/T7
RDA 3	S11/S18/S3/S19/S4/S7/S5	S18/S7/S3/S19	T8,T9

Using the mechanism of state synchronization in BH RTI, each node will display the operation of nine trains synchronously, the initial timetable is shown in Table 3. (In order to deal with simply, the time is stored as float type, the arrival time and departure time is put in each bracket, and the bold station is the ones that the train have to stop at some time)

Table 3. The initial timetable of trains

Train name	The timetable of the train
T1	**S1**(1,00;1,15)->S8(2,00;2,10)->**S3**(3,00;3,15)->S4(4,00;4,20)->**S5**(5,00;5,05)
T2	**S6**(1,10;1,15)->S10(2,30;2,35)->S8(3,20;3,25)->**S9**(4,00;4,06)
T3	**S7**(1,00;1,10)->S18(2,00;2,20)->S11(3,30;3,40)->**S3**(5,00;5,10)->**S19**(6,00;6,10)
T4	**S1**(0,50;0,55)->S8(1,30;1,35)->**S3**(2,10;2,15)->S4(3,10;3,20)->**S5**(4,00;4,05)
T5	**S6**(1,00;1,04)->S10(1,30;1,35)->S8(3,20;3,25)->**S9**(4,00;4,06)
T6	**S7**(0,30;0,35)->S18(1,30;1,35)->S11(5,30;5,40)->**S3**(6,00;6,10)->**S19**(7,00;7,10)
T7	**S7**(-10,00;-10.10)->S18(-11,00;-11,20)->S11(0,30;0,40)->**S3**(1,30;1,35)->**S19**(3,00;3,10)
T8	**S5**(0,00;0,10)->S4(1,30;1,35)->S18->**S6**
T9	**S5**(1,30;1,35)->S4(2,30;2,35)->S18(3,00;3,15)->**S6**(4,00;4,20)

Assuming that, there is a fault between *S6-S10,* and the time to overtime the fault is 10,00. *T5* and *T2* which will pass the lane at some time need to reschedule. According to the results of the above-mentioned dynamic scheduling algorithm, two lanes available, *S6->S15->S10* and *S6->S18->S10,* but the former one takes a shorter time, because *T8* and *T9* will get through the latter one at some time. According to the evaluating criteria, when both lanes get the same similarity to the original timetable, so the former lane *S6->S15->S10* is chosen.

In this study, we achieve the pre-research of hybrid model to simulate the operation of train-group in a distributed infrastructure, so we just get a few trains and partition several regional decision-making agents to study. At the meantime, we just get three computers to constitute our hardware environment. Although these tasks can be achieved on only one computer, when the scale of railroad net is larger and larger and deal with thousands of trains, there will be great significance to study in the distributed infrastructure.

5   Conclusion

We proposed a new hybrid model to achieve the distributed simulation modeling of the train-group based on improved cellular automaton and multi-agent, to deal with dynamic schedule of train-group on the railroad net.

In the paper, we mainly focus on the design and analysis of the distributed simulation model. In our future work, we will design a new parallel dynamic scheduling algorithm to get a better efficiency on a distributed infrastructure. And optimize the partition strategy of regional decision-making agent, to reduce the communication between train agents and improve the efficiency of operation. Finally, we didn't fully consider the actual details in real railway system, so there are some gaps between the simulation results and those in the real environment. We will focus a lot on them in the future.

Acknowledgement. This paper is supported by the fund of the State key Laboratory of Rail Traffic Control and Safety (Contract No. RCS2008K001), Beijing Jiaotong University，the National Natural Science Foundation of China under Grant No. 60973007, the Doctoral Fund of Ministry of Education of China under Grant No. 20101102110018 and the Fundamental Research Funds for the Central Universities under Grant No. YWF-10-02-058.

References

1. Nagel, K., Schreckenberg, M.J.: Cellular automaton model for freeway traffic. Phys. I 2, 2221 (1992)
2. Li, K.P., Gao, Z.Y., Ning, B.: Cellular automaton model for railway traffic. Journal of Computational Physics 209, 179–192 (2005)
3. Li, H., et al.: A New Type of Timed Petri Nets with Hard Real-Time Deadlanes. In: Proc. of the 2nd Asian Control Conf., Seoul Korea (1997)
4. Ye, Y., Zhang, Z., Jia, L.: Train Group Operation Multi-agent Model. RITS 26(4), 109–113 (2005)
5. Bocker, J., Lind, J., Zirkler, B.: Using a Multi-agent Approach to Optimize the Train Coupling and Sharing System. European Journal of Operational Research 134, 242–252 (2001)
6. Qin, Y., Qiu, N., Jia, L., Guo, M.: Study on the Unified Framework of Traffic modeling and Simulation based on the Multi-dimensional Spatio-temporal Model. In: Chinese Control and Decision Conference, pp. 3773–3778 (2008)
7. Koncz, N.A., Adams, T.M.: A Data Model for Multi-dimensional Transportation Applications. International Journal of Geographical Information Science 16(6), 551–569 (2002)
8. Chen, B., Cheng, H.H.: A Review of the Applications of Agent Technology in Traffic and Transportation Systems. IEEE Transactions Intelligent Transportation Systems 11(2) (June 2010)
9. Fischer, K., Kuhn, N., Muller, H.J., Muller, J.P., Pischel, M.: Distributed, knowledge-based,reactive scheduling of transportation tasks. In: Proc.10th Conf. Artif. Intell. Appl., Los Alamitos, CA, pp. 47–53 (1994)
10. Kohout, R., Erol, K.: In-time agent-based vehicle routing with a stochastic improvement heuristic. In: Proc. 16th Nat. Conf. AAI, 11th IAAI Conf., Menlo Park, CA, pp. 864–869 (1999)

Analyzing of Mean-Shift Algorithm in Gray Target Tracking Technology

Shuang Zhang[1,2], Yu-Ping Qin[2], and Gang Jin[1]

[1] The Engineering & Technical College,
Chengdu University of Technology, Leshan, 614000, China
[2] The Institute of Optics and Electronics,
Chinese Academy of Sciences, Chengdu, 610209, China
zhangshuanghua1@126.com

Abstract. Target tracking technology is an extreme important project in computer vision technology area. Its development can directly force the development of the automatic steer technique. According to target tracking, scientists research out many important tracking algorithms. Mean-shift algorithm is an important computational method in various of target tracking algorithms, which adopts the features of anti-size change, anti-rotation change, and few manual intervention showing the extremely vital role in modern target tracking area. While not all tracking techniques can achieve good effects to it. Therefore, the article analyzed the algorithm from the aspect of practical engineering. And use local difference algorithm to make further improvement to it. Finally through three groups of tracking examples to point out the advantages and disadvantages of this algorithm and the advantages of improved algorithm, and expanded the algorithm using sides.

Keywords: target tracking, mean-shift, automatic steer, local difference.

1 Introduction

With the development of the computer technology and big improvement of computing power, computer vision technology becomes the hottest and most important project in computer area. Computer vision technology is designed to realize computer's simulation of mankind, to realize computer's perception, understanding and explanation of sceneries and environment. Moving target tracking technology is an important project in target tracking area, which consists of various advanced technology in different areas, such as image processing, pattern recognition, artificial intelligence, auto control etc. Moving target tracking technology can real-time collect the location of the target and track the target automatic. Its task can be summarized as: obtaining the numbers of the targets and the state of each target, including location, speed, acceleration and other movement parameters, further obtaining to learn the characteristic parameters of the target after confirmation of the final motion trail of the moving target. The key point of this technology is divide the targets completely, extract the characters reasonable, identify the target accurately, meanwhile, the time need to realize this algorithm and ensure the real time are also needed to be considered.

H. Deng et al. (Eds.): AICI 2011, Part I, LNAI 7002, pp. 155–162, 2011.

But the extended target tracking technology is an extremely important and difficult project in moving target tracking technology. Due to it adopts the features of intricate background interference, easy blocked by other objects, various changes of the target size etc, almost all the current algorithms cannot track the target in a good way and quite often lost the target. So find a universality extended target tracking algorithm become the urgent problem need to be solved in extended target tracking field. Mean shift algorithm is a good way to solve this problem because its specific features of anti-size change, anti-rotation change, and few manual intervention coefficients.

2 Mean-Shift Algorithm

Mean shift algorithm is a practical algorithm proposed by Fukunag and Hostetler, which adopts the characters of less calculation and high velocity, Dorin Comaniciu applies it into target division [2] and target tracking [3] effectively.

Take the binary image for example, the iterative process of the mean shift algorithm as follows:

The objective function is the density of "1" as shown in the image, its estimation formula as below:

$$\hat{f}(y) = C \sum_{i=1}^{n} k \left(\left\| \frac{y - x_i}{h} \right\|^2 \right) \tag{1}$$

In the formula, the physical significance of each symbol is the same as before. If the order is $\nabla \hat{f}(x) = 0$, the iterative formula of the window center (tracking point) as below:

$$y_{j+1} = \frac{\sum_{i=1}^{n} x_i k' \left(\left\| \frac{y_j - x_i}{h} \right\| \right)}{\sum_{i=1}^{n} k' \left(\left\| \frac{y_j - x_i}{h} \right\| \right)} \qquad j = 1, 2 \cdots \tag{2}$$

When $\left\| y_{j+1} - y_j \right\| < \varepsilon$ (ε is the convergence domain), that is the center distance of the window is small enough, the iterative will stop, this distance is obtained by twice calculation. As shown in figure 1, mean-shift process essentially is the process of maximizing the objective function convergence.

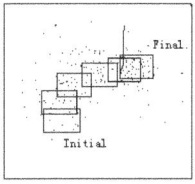

Fig. 1. Scheme of mean-shift iteration process

3 Extended Target Tracking Technology

3.1 Target Model

Target histogram model is the corresponding probability density of each imaging grey level bases on targets in detection area. Grey level probability density is obtained by non-parametric estimation technology. Suppose the target trace point is y, the detection area is rectangle center on y and the width of the window is h, the location of the pixel in the area is shown as $\{\mathbf{x}_i\}_{i=1\cdots n}$, features of the pixel location, such as grey level, vein, edge or wavelet filter response and so on is shown as $b(\mathbf{x}_i)$, $b(\mathbf{x}_i)$ can be a scalar formed by one character, also can be a scalar formed by several characters. In this article, we just consider using grey level feature and quantizing it to m value, well then the function $b: R^2 \rightarrow \{1 \cdots m\}$ is the grey level index mapping of x_i pixel. Due to the target may be affected by background and shelter, the reliability of periphery pixel is very low, therefore, the pixel far away from center, the smaller of the distributive weight, the grey level probability density id the function of the pixel location:

$$\hat{p}_u(\mathbf{y}) = C_1 \sum_{i=1}^{n} k_1 \left(\left\| \frac{\mathbf{y}-\mathbf{x}_i}{\mathbf{h}} \right\|^2 \right) \delta \left[b(\mathbf{x}_i) - u \right] \qquad u = 1 \cdots m \qquad (3)$$

Among which C_1 is the normalization constant, which can be obtained from condition of $\sum_{u=1}^{m} \hat{p}_u = 1$; $k_1(\mathbf{x})$ is the distribution function of the pixel location weight, the definition as follows:

$$k_1(\mathbf{x}) = \begin{cases} \dfrac{2}{\pi}\left(1 - \|\mathbf{x}\|^2\right) & \|\mathbf{x}\| \le 1 \\ 0 & otherwise \end{cases} \qquad (4)$$

3.2 Based on Local Difference Grey Target Tracking Improved Algorithm

Only using the original grayscale feature of image to describe gray target is not reliable, we must make the improvement. Here we extracted target local gray probability characteristics, local contrast mean difference characteristics, local average gradient strength characteristics, and take these features space mapping to grayscale image space. Combined with the original grayscale image, constitute gray target image joint feature space. Each feature defined as follows:

(1) Local contrast mean difference (LCMD)

$$LCMD(i,j) = \frac{1}{n_{in}} \sum_{(k,l) \in N_{in}(i,j)} f(k,l) - \frac{1}{n_{out}} \sum_{(k,l) \in N_{out}(i,j)} f(k,l) \qquad (5)$$

(i, j) for local window center, (k, l) for pixel position in the window. Defined in local window local contrast mean difference also included windows n_{in} and outside windows n_{out}, mainly to differentiate image prospect and background information.

(2) Local average gradient strength(LAGS)

$$LAGS(i, j) = \frac{1}{n_{in}} \sum_{(k,l)\in N_{in}(i,j)} G_{in}(k,l) - \frac{1}{n_{out}} \sum_{(k,l)\in N_{out}(i,j)} G_{out}(k,l) \qquad (6)$$

Among

$G_{in}(k,l) = G_{in}^h + G_{in}^v, \quad G_{in}^h = \left| f(k,l) - f(k,l+1) \right|, \quad G_{in}^v = \left| f(k,l) - f(k+1,l) \right|$.

LAGS can effectively accumulate within the local window of the target area and background region for strength, and the intensity differences gradient of low gray target, has strong characterization ability.

(3) Local gray level probability(LGLP)

Suppose $f(i, j)$ for infrared image sequence a frame arbitrary point (i, j) pixel grayscale value. The window for (i, j) the center for $(2r+1) \times (2r+1)$ any point $f(i+m, j+n)$ within the set of grey value within the total grayscale value window ratio, namely:

$$p_{ij}(m,n) = f(i+m, j+n) / \sum_{\lambda_x=-r}^{r} \sum_{\lambda_y=-r}^{r} f(i+\lambda_x, j+\lambda_y) \qquad (7)$$

Among $(m, n = -r, -r+1, \cdots, 0 \cdots, r-1, r)$, and point (i, j) all neighborhood $p_{ij}(m,n)$ sum of all points for 1.

Considering the system real time, respectively quantize LGLP, LAGS, LCMD, and GREY feature space, calculate weighted histograms p_u^{LCMD} , p_u^{LGLP} , p_u^{GRAY} , and the space for fusion processing, can histogram of the target after improved histogram mode:

$$P_u^{fusion} = \alpha \cdot p_u^{LCMD} + \beta \cdot p_u^{LCGS} + \gamma \cdot p_u^{LGLP} + \xi \cdot p_u^{GRAY} \qquad (8)$$

Among them $\alpha = 0.2 \times C_u \times \rho_y^{LCMD}$ $\beta = 0.2 \times C_u \times \rho_y^{LCGS}$, $\gamma = 0.2 \times C_u \times \rho_y^{LGLP}$, $\xi = 0.4 \times C_u \times \rho_y^{GRAY}$, used to balance each character space in general fusion weighted histogram, ρ_y for similarity coefficient, C_u for normalization coefficient, obtained by $\alpha + \beta + \gamma + \xi = 1$.

3.3 Similarity Measurement

Generality, mark the target center with 0, candidate target with y, from the target model defined by the formula, we can confirm the histogram model of the target and the candidate target as follows:

$$\text{Target}: \hat{\mathbf{P}}_0 = \left\{ \hat{p}_u \right\}_{u=1\cdots m} \tag{9}$$

$$\text{Candidate target}: \hat{\mathbf{P}}_y = \left\{ \hat{p}_u(\mathbf{y}) \right\}_{u=1\cdots m} \tag{10}$$

Similar function defines the tolerance measurement of target and candidate target, in order to adjust the differences between different targets, a distance measurement need to be defined, we define the distance between two discrete distribution as follows:

$$d = \sqrt{1 - \rho\left[\hat{\mathbf{P}}_0, \hat{\mathbf{P}}_y\right]} \tag{11}$$

where,

$$\hat{\rho}(\mathbf{y}) \equiv \rho\left[\hat{\mathbf{P}}_0, \hat{\mathbf{P}}_y\right] = \sum_{u=1}^{m} \sqrt{\hat{p}_u(\mathbf{y})\, \hat{p}_u} \tag{12}$$

is the sample estimation value of Bhattacharyya parameter. M is the COS of the included angle between $\left(\sqrt{\hat{p}_1}, \cdots, \hat{p}_m\right)^{\mathrm{T}}$ and $\left(\sqrt{\hat{p}_1(\mathbf{y})}, \cdots, \hat{p}_m(\mathbf{y})\right)^{\mathrm{T}}$.

3.4 Mean-Shift

Mean-shift is a practical algorithm to calculate the optimal solution. Dorin Comaniciu etc effectively use it to target division and target tracking. Adopts Bhattacharyya ratio ρy, at point $\hat{p}_u(\mathbf{y}_0)$ (y for searching point) for Taylor expansion and collates to:

$$\rho\left[\mathbf{P}_0, \mathbf{P}_y\right] \approx \frac{1}{2}\sum_{u=1}^{m}\sqrt{\hat{p}_u(\mathbf{y}_0)\,\hat{p}_u} + \frac{C_1}{2}\sum_{i=1}^{n} w_i k_1\left(\left\|\frac{\mathbf{y}-\mathbf{x}_i}{\mathbf{h}}\right\|^2\right) \tag{13}$$

Among,

$$w_i = \sum_{u=1}^{m}\sqrt{\frac{\hat{p}_0}{\hat{p}_u(\mathbf{y}_0)}}\,\delta[b(\mathbf{x}_i)-u] \tag{14}$$

The corresponding window center iterative type:

$$\mathbf{y}_{j+1} = \sum_{i=1}^{n}\mathbf{x}_i w_i k_1'\left(\left\|\frac{\mathbf{y}_j-\mathbf{x}_i}{\mathbf{h}}\right\|\right) \Bigg/ \sum_{i=1}^{n} w_i k_1'\left(\left\|\frac{\mathbf{y}_j-\mathbf{x}_i}{\mathbf{h}}\right\|\right) \qquad j=1,2\cdots \tag{15}$$

4   Application of the Mean-Shift Extended Target Tracking

Mean-shift plays an important role in image tracking area due to its specific features. We did some tests to the color and grey level targets below to find its advantage and disadvantage in tracking area.

4.1   Example of the Color Target

Color target tracking technology is a normal technology in modern video monitoring technology. It is very common in supermarket video monitor, street monitor and police system. Therefore, color target tracking technology is also a practical technology in daily life.

Fig. 2. Frame 1

Fig. 3. Frame 8

Fig. 4. Frame 25

Fig. 5. Frame 50

After the text, we get 50 frame images within 150ms so the handling time of each single frame is 3ms. The offset of 50 frames is between 0 to 4 pixels. The results show that the color targets supply a lot of information when build the color histogram because of its abundant color features. So in the image tracking process, the result shown in the images is fast and accurate, which can meet the requirements of the real-time tracking.

4.2   Real Tracking Example of the Grey Level Target

Grey level imaging tracking is one of important projects in modern military field, especially the infrared target tracking technology. Grey level imaging tracking is an important technology in night vision tracking field due to its anti-interference of light and shade.

Fig. 6. Frame 1

Fig. 7. Frame 8

Fig. 8. Frame 25

Fig. 9. Frame 50

After the text, we get 50 frame images within 145ms so the handling time of each single frame is 3ms. But most offset of 50 frames is between 0 to 4 pixels, when the object exists ghosting, the offset exceeds the window width, the target lose directly. The result shows that, the information of the grey level target is not abundant and the background interference is very strong, as a result, simple mean-shift algorithm has difficulty in tracking grey level target.

Therefore, some methods must be used to increase the information quantity of the grey level target, in this way the mean-shift algorithm can get the color target tracking result in grey level target tracking process and heighten the target tracking precision.

4.3   Based on the Local Difference Mean Shift Algorithm Gray Target Tracking

Using local difference to extract the local gray image gray-scale probability, local contrast mean difference, local average gradient strength features, and mapping it to gray image, and with original grayscale image space together constitute extended gray image feature space, and adopt special based on nuclear function of reduced-order weighted histogram to describe.

Fig. 10. Frame 1

Fig. 11. Frame 8

Fig. 12. Frame 25   **Fig. 13.** Frame 50

Accidentally have drifted through test get 50 frame image amount to 165ms, single frame processing time about 3.3 ms. Most of the track point in the chosen target center, the move also in 1-3 pixels, when object exists virtual shadow, target can also accurate tracking. All is to say, using the improved the stability of migration arithmetic average better than using directly stability.

5 Conclusion

Mean shift is an important algorithm in target tracking area because of its unique semi-automatic tracking feature. This algorithm is already widely used in color target tracking area. But due to the facts that the image color information of the grey level imaging is not enough, the imaging character difference between the target and background is small, the conventional histogram easily trapped into local similarity, and cause the problem of tracking point drift or shake. Therefore, simple mean-shift algorithm tracking grey level image is not advisable. This paper puts forward based on local difference mean-shift algorithm. After experiments prove, the improved algorithm has strong stability.

References

1. Fukunaga, K., Hostetler, L.D.: The Estimation of the Gradient of a Density Function with Applications in Pattern Recognition. IEEE Trans. Information Theory 21(5), 32–40 (1975)
2. Comaniciu, D., Meer, P.: Mean Shift: a Robust Approach toward Feature Space Analysis. IEEE Trans. Pattern Anal. Mach. Intell. 24(5), 603–619 (2002)
3. Comaniciu, D., Ramesh, V., Meer, P.: Kernel-based Object Tracking. IEEE Trans. Pattern Anal. Mach. Intell. 24(5), 564–577 (2003)
4. Kailath, T.: The Divergence and Bhattacharyya Distance Measures in Signal Selection. IEEE Trans. Comm. Technology 15(2), 253–259 (1999)
5. Lowe, D.G.: Distinctive image features from scale-invariant keypoints. International Journal Computer Vision 60(2), 91–110 (2004)

Emergency Logistics Routing Optimization Algorithm Based on FSACO

Li-Yi Zhang[1], Teng Fei[1], Ting Liu[1], Jin Zhang[2], and Yi Li[1]

[1] Information Engineering College,
Tianjin University of Commerce, Tianjin, China
[2] Office of Equipment,
First Hospital of Shanxi University of Medicine, Taiyuan, China
{zhangliyi,feiteng,liuting}@tjcu.edu.cn

Abstract. Emergency logistics routing problem, which is premise with the time requirements for emergency logistics and aims at maximum saving delivery time for relief supplies, is a reasonable arrangement of vehicles to run routes. According to the characteristics of time which emergency logistics emphasis on, the delivery route optimization model which the number of delivery vehicles less than demand areas is been established, besides, it has been solved by the Fish-Swarm Ant Colony Optimization (FSACO). Simulation results show that the algorithm compared with ant colony algorithm has better optimization quality.

Keywords: Emergency logistics, Routing Optimization, Fish-Swarm Ant Colony Optimization.

1 Introduction

In recent years, major disasters and public health events occur frequently, it is caused heavy casualties and huge economic losses, and emergency logistics is born out in this cause. Emergency logistics is a narrow concept, mainly refers to emergency logistics activities that conducted in country or region in response to various natural disasters, major accidents or unexpected dangers. It is relatively late to research emergency logistics in home, and mainly the macro research, less research micro issues of emergency logistics path optimization. Emergency logistics routing problem, which is premise with the time requirements for emergency logistics and aims at maximum saving delivery time for relief supplies, is a reasonable arrangement of vehicles to run routes. FSACO is the use of crowding factor of Fish-Swarm Algorithm to improve the optimization ability of Ant colony Optimization, in this paper, FSACO is applied to solve the model in the emergency logistics path optimization, Simulation results demonstrate its effectiveness and superiority to solve the problem.

H. Deng et al. (Eds.): AICI 2011, Part I, LNAI 7002, pp. 163–170, 2011.

2 Model of Emergency Logistics Routing Optimization Type Style and Fonts

2.1 Modeling of the Basic Ideas

After the cataclysm happening, because of the increasing requirements of each demand points, the lack of the vehicles at emergency delivery centre is revealed to be serious, therefore this issue concentrates on the model to optimize the circumstance when the number of the vehicles at the emergency delivery centre is less then the number of the emergency accesses to demand points. In emergency logistics, time is highly valued considering to each demand point, therefore emergency supplies must be delivered within the prescribed time, and otherwise, they will not be send to the destination in time because of road conditions. The number of emergency distribution accesses should be determined by the quantity of vehicles at emergency delivery centre. The demand points passed by should be formulated by the maximum loading capacity of the vehicles and the prescribed distribution time. Most of the vehicles at emergency delivery centre are raised from another place, thus each car will not return to the centre after the distribution of emergency supplies. The optimization of emergency logistics accesses could be actually converted to VRP problems with a hard time window.

2.2 Modeling

(1) Rescue vehicles belong to the same kinds of models, not consider of the maximum distance in the distribution and whether a fault has.

(2) When the vehicle load has been considered, material volume is not considered.

(3) There is a straight connecting line between the affected point and rescue center or in all affected points.

(4) All road conditions are ideal, without consideration of vehicle speed influence for them.

On this assumption, the mathematical model in the shortest delivery time has been established:

$$\min t = \sum_{i=1}^{n}\sum_{j=1}^{n}\sum_{k=1}^{l} t_{ij} w_{ijk} + \sum_{i=1}^{n}\sum_{k=1}^{l} \tau_i \pi_{ij} \tag{1}$$

S.T

$$t_{ij} = d_{ij} / v \tag{2}$$

$$\sum_{i=1}^{n} q_i \varphi_{ik} \leq Q \tag{3}$$

$$\sum_{k=1}^{l} \varphi_{ik} = 1 \tag{4}$$

$$\sum_{i=1}^{n} w_{ijk} = \varphi_{jk} \tag{5}$$

$$\sum_{j=1}^{n} w_{ijk} = \varphi_{ik} \tag{6}$$

$$t_j = t_i + t_{ij} w_{ijk} + \tau_i \pi_{ik} \tag{7}$$

$$t_i \leq T_i \tag{8}$$

$$w_{ijk} = \begin{cases} 1 & \text{kth vehicle drives i to j} \\ 0 & otherwise \end{cases} \tag{9}$$

$$\varphi_{ik} = \begin{cases} 1 & \text{The task of i point is compeleted by kth vehicle} \\ 0 & otherwise \end{cases} \tag{10}$$

$$\pi_{ik} = \begin{cases} 1 & \text{i is final point of kth vehicle} \\ 0 & otherwise \end{cases} \tag{11}$$

Where, (x_0, y_0) is the coordinates for the rescue center, l is the number of vehicles, Q is load-carrying capacity, q_i is the needing number of every needing spot, n is needing points, (x_i, y_i) is needing point coordinates, T_i is specified delivery time of needing points, d_{ij} is distance between needing point i and point j, t_{ij} is traveling time.

Formula (1) is the objective function for the model, including the delivery time and unloading time; Formula (2) defined the affected point traveling time of vehicles, v is the average speed in no road barrier influence; Formula(3) ensure that each car of the load is not more than payload; Formula(4) has formulated that every affected point can be dispatched only by one car; the relationship between formula (5) and (6) is the relationship between variable w_{ijk} and variable φ_{ik}; formula (7) is the time cars taking to reach the affected point j, t_i is the time arriving at affected point i, τ_i is the unloading time; formula (8) is the finish time cars arriving at the affected point i, which is can not lag the time T_i; formula (9) and (10) are the definitional formulas of variables w_{ijk} and φ_{ik}; formula (11) is the judgment whether the unloading time of affected point i should be calculated into the total time.

3 Emergency Logistics Routing Optimization Algorithm

3.1 Ant Colony Optimization

Suppose, there are n cities, m is the number of ants in ant colony, $d_{ij}(i, j = 1, 2..n)$ shows the distance between city i and j.

$$d_{ij} = \sqrt{(x_i - x_j)^2 + (y_i - y_j)^2} \tag{12}$$

Let τ_{ij} be residual pheromone of branch i, j at time t. when $t = 0$, the strength of pheromone on the path is equal. $\tau(0) = C$ (C is constant). As time goes on, new pheromone has been added, the old pheromone will volatile, $1-\rho$ indicates the essential level of pheromone. When all ants complete a tour, each side of the pheromone is adjusted by the-following equation.

$$\tau_{ij}(t+n) = (1-\rho) \cdot \tau_{ij}(t) + \Delta\tau_{ij}(t) \tag{13}$$

$$\Delta\tau_{ij}(t) = \sum_{k=1}^{m} \Delta\tau_{ij}^{k}(t) \tag{14}$$

Where, $\Delta\tau_{ij}(t)$ is pheromone increment on the traveled path ij , initial time, $\Delta\tau_{ij}(t)=0$. $\Delta\tau_{ij}^{k}(t)$ is section k of ants release pheromones on the edge of ij in the course of travel.

$$\Delta\tau_{ij}^{k}(t) = \begin{cases} Q/L_k & \text{section k of ants pass edge ij in the course of this tour} \\ 0 & \text{else} \end{cases} \tag{15}$$

Where, Q is constant, L_k is the length of the loop formed by section k of ants n the course of travel. Where the ant transfer is determine by p_{ij}^k in the tour.

$$P_{ij}^{k} = \begin{cases} \dfrac{[\tau_{ij}(t)]^{\alpha} \cdot [\eta_{ik}(t)]^{\beta}}{\sum\limits_{s \in allowed_k} [\tau_{is}(t)]^{\alpha} \cdot [\eta_{is}(t)]^{\beta}} & if \ j \in allowed_k \\ \\ 0 & other \end{cases} \tag{16}$$

Where, $allowed_k = \{C - tabu_k\}$ is city collection that ant can be selected. $tabu_k$ is taboo table, it records the city which ant k has been passed, used to describe the memory of artificial ants. $\eta_{ij}(t)$ is some heuristic information, $\eta_{ij}(t) = 1/d_{ij}$. α , β reflects the importance of pheromone and heuristic pheromone.

3.2 Construction of Crowding Factor

Fish-Swarm Algorithm has the characteristics of global search capability, combined by Fish-Swarm Algorithm and Ant Colony Optimization.Crowding factor is introduced to Ant Colony Optimization, in order to enhance optimize quality of Ant Colony Optimization in emergency logistics routing optimization. Crowding factor of Fish-Swarm Algorithm describes the degree of colony aggregation, it is controlled the number of ants gathering by crowding factor in Ant Colony Optimization. When looking for the path,it is hoped that the number of aggregation ants around the optimum solution is more, moreover, the number of ants gathered around in the second-best solution have few or no have. Because of the introduction of crowding factor, ants are not too early to gather in the high pheromone path, in this way, Fish-Swarm Algorithm improve the global search ability.Crowding factor is constructed by formula (17).

$$h_{ij}(t) = 1 - \tau_{ij}(t) / \sum_{i \neq j} \tau_{ij} \tag{17}$$

$$\delta(t) = \gamma e^{-bt} \tag{18}$$

Where, $\delta(t)$ is congestion threshold, γ is extremely near level, b is threshold variation coefficient.

Suppose, the ant finds a path through the formula (16), and $h_{ij}(t) > \delta(t)$, it is said that the path to the low level of crowding, then choose this path. Otherwise, it will re-select the other path according to formula (16).

3.3 Solved the Model by Fish-Swarm Ant Colony Algorithm

Emergency logistics optimization model for solving flow path is shown in Figure 1.

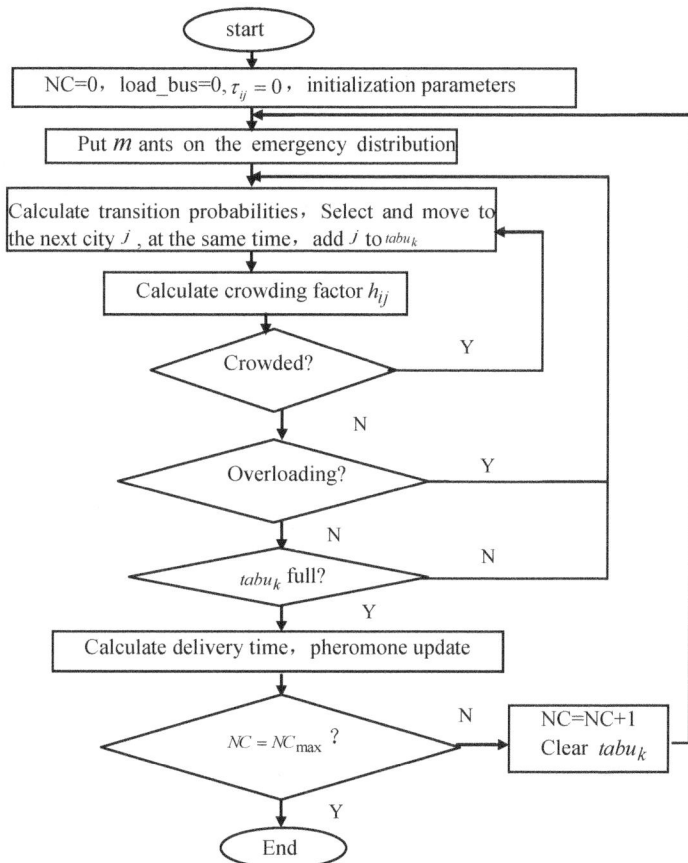

Fig. 1. Flow chart of emergency logistics routing optimization based on FSACO

4 Computer Simulation

Suppose, emergency distribution center(number is 0) has 3 vehicles with a capacity of 8 tons, which distribute materials to 20 hit point, the average speed is $v = 15km/h$ .Known to emergency distribution center coordinate is (3.2, 14.1), the coordinates of each point, requirements (units are tons), end time and unloading time, such as shown in Table 1. Extremely near level, $\gamma = 0.9$ threshold variation coefficient $b = 0.0002$, reference [5] gives the basis for parameter settings of α、β、ρ, obtained after repeated testing, when $\alpha = 1$、$\beta = 5$、$\rho = 0.6$, computing results is best distance between emergency distribution center and demand points or among the various demand points uses formula (12).

Table 1. The coordinates of each point, requirements, end time and unloading time

No.	coordinate (km)	end time (h)	unloading time (h)	Requirements (t)
1	(3.8, 5.5)	14.6	0.1	0.8
2	(15.2, 10.9)	13.8	0.2	0.6
3	(18.6, 12.9)	12.3	0.2	0.4
4	(11.9, 8.2)	5.0	0.3	1.6
5	(10.2, 9.5)	6.3	0.1	0.8
6	(5.3, 9.6)	10.4	0.1	0.6
7	(0.6, 9.9)	12.6	0.1	1.9
8	(6.1, 15.0)	8.5	0.1	1.3
9	(7.6, 19.2)	10.3	0.1	1.8
10	(16.0, 15.7)	12.0	0.2	1.8
11	(15.3, 15.2)	11.8	0.1	0.4
12	(1.6, 14.7)	9.8	0.1	1.6
13	(9.0, 9.2)	7.1	0.1	1.1
14	(5.4, 13.3)	9.8	0.1	1.6
15	(7.8, 10.0)	13.9	0.1	1.0
16	(18.6, 7.8)	11.6	0.2	0.8
17	(14.5, 5.3)	9.4	0.1	1.4
18	(15.0, 18.7)	5.8	0.2	1.2
19	(9.8, 5.0)	6.1	0.3	0.4
20	(1.4, 6.9)	10.0	0.1	1.4

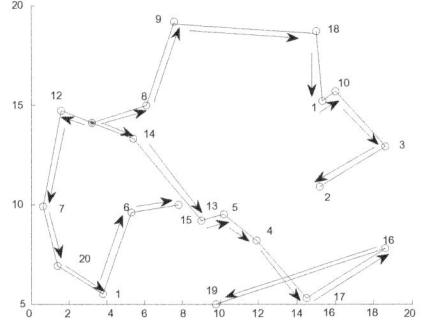

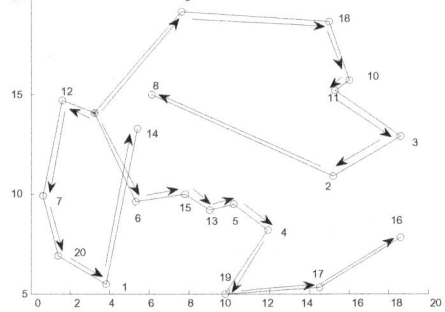

Fig. 2. A curve of Ant Colony Optimization

Fig. 3. A curve of Fish-Swarm Ant Colony Optimization

Figure 2 shows the curve of Ant Colony Optimization , three routes are:

0→8→9→18→11→10→3→2,0→12→7→20→1→6→15,0→14→13→5→4→17→16→19.

Figure 3 shows the curve of Fish-Swarm Ant Colony Optimization, three routes are:

0→9→18→10→11→3→2→8,0→12→7→20→1→14,0→6→15→13→5→4→19→17→16.

Figure 4 is comparison of convergence with Ant Colony Optimization and Fish-Swarm Ant Colony Optimization. Figure 4 shows that, in solving emergency logistics distribution routing problem, Fish-Swarm Ant Colony Optimization can find a shorter delivery time, and its convergence rate is better than Ant Colony Optimization.

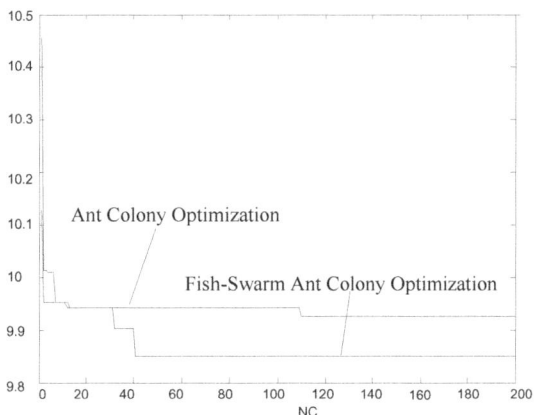

Fig. 4. Comparison of convergence with Ant Colony Optimization and Fish-Swarm Ant Colony Optimization

5   Conclusion

In this paper, model of emergency logistics path optimization has been established, and, the model is solved by Fish-Swarm Ant Colony Optimization.Simulation shows that the optimal results are better than Ant Colony Optimization. This is because of the introduction of the crowding factor in the early stages of Fish-Swarm Ant Colony Optimization, the ant's ergodicity can be increased, and the optimization quality is improved. The study of emergency logistics path optimization model is still in the exploratory stage, constraints and modeling should be improved in the future, in order to closer to the actual needs.

Acknowledgment. This work is supported by Funding Issues of Soft Science Research Projects in Shanxi Province (2010041077-3).

References

1. Gao, L.: Emergency Logistics and Military Logistics. China Logistics and Purchasing 36(3), 21–23 (2003)
2. Dorigo, M.: Ant colony system: A cooperative learning approach to the traveling salesman problem. IEEE Transactions on Evolutionary Computation 1(1), 53–66 (1997)
3. Yang, L., Pan, C.: Transportation Path Design of Emergency Medical Supply. Logistics Technology 27(11), 84–86 (2004)
4. Gu, H.: Applications in Emergency Logistics Vehicle Scheduling based on Immune Algorithm. Logistics Technology (11), 24–27 (2003)
5. Ye, Z., Zheng, Z.: Study on the parameters in Ant colony algorithm——An example to TSP. Wuhan University (Information Science) 29(7), 597–601 (2004)

Efficient Solutions for a Problem in Currency Systems

Xiaodong Wang[*] and Daxin Zhu

School of Mathematics and Computer Science,
Quanzhou Normal University,
362000 Quanzhou, P.R. China

Abstract. In this paper, an efficient recursive construction algorithm based on the backtracking search algorithm is presented for the construction of accurate implication sets. The new techniques suggested improve the time and space complexities of the backtracking search algorithm dramatically.

1   Introduction

In this paper, we consider the following combinatorial problem encountered in monetary systems.

Suppose $C(k)$ is a monetary system that divides the currency denomination into $k+1$ decimal levels:

$$\{1,2,5\}; \{10,20,50\}; \cdots; \{10^i, 2 \times 10^i, 5 \times 10^i\}; \cdots; \{10^k\}.$$

For example, China's currency system (RMB) can be classified as $C(4)$.

Notation: $c(i,j), 0 \le i \le k, 0 \le j \le 2$ denote the levels of monetary values. The monetary value of level i can be written as $c_i = (c(i,0), c(i,1), c(i,2))^\top, 0 \le i \le k$. In particular, when $i = k$, $c_k = (10^k, 0, 0)^\top$.

For any integer $n \in I^+$ we can obviously express n by the above currency system as follows

$$n = \sum_{i=0}^{k} \sum_{j=0}^{2} a(i,j)c(i,j) \tag{1}$$

where $a(i,j) \in I^+, 0 \le i \le k, 0 \le j \le 2$.

Denote $a_i = (a(i,0), a(i,1), a(i,2))^\top, g(a_i, c_i) = a_i^\top c_i, 0 \le i \le k$ and $a = (a_0, a_1, \cdots, a_k)^\top$.

Then, the integer n can be expressed by

$$n = \sum_{i=0}^{k} a_i^\top c_i = \sum_{i=0}^{k} g(a_i, c_i) \triangleq f(k,a) \tag{2}$$

[*] This work is partially supported by NSF of Fujian Grant #2009J01295 and the Haixi Project #A099 to X. Wang.

H. Deng et al. (Eds.): AICI 2011, Part I, LNAI 7002, pp. 171–178, 2011.

For a given $n \in I^+$, the above representation is obviously not unique in general. The different values of a satisfying (1) will give different representations of the positive integer n. Set $A(k,n) = \{a \mid f(k,a) = n\}$ constitutes all representations of a positive integer n in the given currency system. For example, when $k = 4, n = 3$ we have

$$
A(4,3) = \left\{ \begin{pmatrix} 1\;1\;0 \\ 0\;0\;0 \\ 0\;0\;0 \\ 0\;0\;0 \\ 0\;0\;0 \end{pmatrix}, \begin{pmatrix} 3\;0\;0 \\ 0\;0\;0 \\ 0\;0\;0 \\ 0\;0\;0 \\ 0\;0\;0 \end{pmatrix} \right\}
$$

Let a and b be two-dimensional arrays. $b \leq a$ if and only if $b(i,j) \leq a(i,j)$, $0 \leq i \leq k$, and $0 \leq j \leq 2$; $b < a$ if and only if both $b \leq a$ and $b \neq a$.

Let

$$
s(k,a) = \{f(k,b) \mid f(k,a) = n, 0 < b \leq a\} \tag{3}
$$

Set $s(k,a)$ is defined as an implication set of the positive integer n, which is the collection of all the money under the representation a.

For example, when

$$
a = \begin{pmatrix} 1\;1\;0 \\ 0\;0\;0 \\ 0\;0\;0 \\ 0\;0\;0 \\ 0\;0\;0 \end{pmatrix} \in A(4,3)
$$

we have $s(4,a) = \{1,2,3\}$.

Set

$$
R(k,n) = \bigcap_{a \in A(k,n)} s(k,a) \tag{4}
$$

is defined to be an accurate implication set of the positive integer n in the given currency system.

For any $x \in R(k,n)$, regardless of the kind of par value of the currency that composes the positive integer n, it certainly contains x.

For example, suppose the currency system is in RMB. A person has money \$5.27 ($n = 527$). If his money is composed of one \$5 piece ($c(2,2) = 500$), one 2 angle piece ($c(1,1) = 20$) , one 5 cent coin ($c(0,2) = 5$), and one 2 cent coin ($c(0,1) = 2$). In our definition, $k = 4$ and

$$
a = \begin{pmatrix} 0\;1\;1 \\ 0\;1\;0 \\ 0\;0\;1 \\ 0\;0\;0 \\ 0\;0\;0 \end{pmatrix} \in A(4,527).
$$

In this case, he cannot come up with \$0.17. That is, $17 \notin s(4,a)$.

However, regardless of the kind of par value of the currency, he can certainly take out \$0.02 because without one 2 cent coin or two 1 cent coins he cannot scrape together \$5.27. In other words, $2 \in R(4, 527)$.

In addition to \$0.02, he can certainly take out \$5.00, \$0.2, \$0.07, \$5.2, \$0.27, and so on. These amounts of money, as they are called, are certainly taken out of the \$5.27.

The main problem concerned in this paper is for the given positive integers k and n, how to find the corresponding accurate implication set $R(k, n)$ efficiently.

2   Backtracking Algorithm

2.1   A Simple Backtracking Algorithm

According to Definition 3, the accurate implication set of the given positive integers k and n in the currency system $C(k)$ can be formulated as (4). Based on this formula we can design a simple backtracking algorithm [1,2,3] to find $R(k, n)$ as follows.

Algorithm 1: Backtrack($t, index$)

---

1 if $t = 0$ then
2   for $i \leftarrow 1$ to n do
3   if $test[i] = 0$ then $s[i] \leftarrow 0$;
4   return;
5   end
6 else
7   for $i \leftarrow index$ downto 1 do
8   if $base[i] \leq t$ then
9   Add($base[i]$);
10   Backtrack($t - base[i], i$);
11   Del($base[i]$);
12   end
13   end
14 end

A recursive function call Backtrack($n, baselen$) will compute the set

$$R(k, n) = \{t \mid s[t] \neq 0\}.$$

2.2   Backtrack Pruning

If par value 1, 2, and 5 are used to compose the money, then positive integer 10 can be one of the following 10 different representations.

Let $E = \{e_i, i = 1, \cdots, 10\}$.

Table 1. Representations of 10

$e_1 = (10,0,0)$	$e_2 = (8,1,0)$
$e_3 = (6,2,0)$	$e_4 = (4,3,0)$
$e_5 = (2,4,0)$	$e_6 = (0,5,0)$
$e_7 = (5,0,1)$	$e_8 = (3,1,1)$
$e_9 = (1,2,1)$	$e_{10} = (0,0,2)$

Lemma 1. For the positive integers $m = 10$, $m = 12$ and $m \geq 14$, if $m = g(a_0, c_0) = \sum_{j=0}^{2} a(0,j)c(0,j)$, then there must be an integer $d \in E$ such that $d \leq a_0$.

When $m < 10$, there must be no $d \in E$ such that

$$m = g(a_0, c_0) = \sum_{j=0}^{2} a(0,j)c(0,j) \text{ and } d \leq a_0.$$

Otherwise, we have $10 = g(d, c_0) \leq g(a_0, c_0) = m < 10$, which is a contradiction.

When $m = 11$, we can take $a_0 = (0,3,1)$, then there is no $d \in E$ such that $11 = g(a_0, c_0)$ and $d \leq a_0$. The value for a_0 is unique.

When $m = 13$, we can take $a_0 = (0,4,1)$, then there is no $d \in E$ such that $13 = g(a_0, c_0)$ and $d \leq a_0$. The value for a_0 is also unique.

Let

$$n = f(k, a) = \sum_{i=0}^{k} a_i^\top c_i = \sum_{i=0}^{k} g(a_i, c_i);$$

$$D(a, i) = \{d \leq a_i \mid d \in E\}, 0 \leq i \leq k.$$

The integer transformation $\sigma(a, i)$ can be defined as follows.

(1) If $D(a, i)$ is not empty, then for any $d \in D(a, i)$,

$$\sigma(a, i) = (a_0, \cdots, a_i - d, a_{i+1} + (1,0,0), \cdots, a_k).$$

(2) If $D(a, i)$ is empty, then $\sigma(a, i) = a$.

Lemma 2. For any $a \in A(k, n)$ we have,

(1) $\sigma(a, i) \in A(k, n), 0 \leq i \leq k$.

(2) $s(k, \sigma(a, i)) \subseteq s(k, a), 0 \leq i \leq k$.

Theorem 3

$$R(k, n) = \bigcap_{a \in A(k,n)} s(k, a) = \bigcap_{a \in B(k,n)} s(k, a) \bigcap_{a \in F(k,n)} s(k, a)$$

where

$$B(k, n) = \{a \in A(k, n) \mid \sigma(a, i) = a, 0 \leq i \leq k\};$$

$$F(k, n) = \{a \in B(k, n) \mid a_i^\top c_0 \in \{1, 2, 3, 4, 5, 6, 7, 8, 9, 11, 13\}\}$$

By making use of the constraints of $F(k, n)$ in Theorem 3, we can add pruning condition in the backtracking algorithm to improve the searching speed as follows [4].

Algorithm 2: Backtrack($t, index$)

---
1 **if** $t = 0$ **then**
2   **for** $i \leftarrow 1$ **to** n **do**
3   **if** $test[i] = 0$ **then** $s[i] \leftarrow 0$;
4   **return**;
5   **end**
6 **else**
7   **for** $i \leftarrow index$ **downto** 1 **do**
8   **if** $base[i] \leq t$ **then**
9              $k \leftarrow \mathrm{div}(i - 1, 3) + 1$;
10             $m[k] \leftarrow m[k] + base[\mathrm{mod}(i - 1, 3) + 1]$;
11   **if** $i = baselen$ **or** $m[k] < 14$ **and** $m[k] \neq 12$ **and** $m[k] \neq 10$ **then**
12   Add($base[i]$);
13   Backtrack($t - base[i],i$);
14   Del($base[i]$);
15   **end**
16             $m[k] \leftarrow m[k] - base[\mathrm{mod}(i - 1, 3) + 1]$;
17   **end**
18   **end**
19 **end**

2.3 Recursive Constructing Algorithm

$$\mathrm{div}(x, y) = \left\lfloor \frac{x}{y} \right\rfloor ; \mathrm{mod}(x, y) = x - y \left\lfloor \frac{x}{y} \right\rfloor .$$

Lemma 4. Let

$$G_1(k, n) = \{a \in F(k, n) \mid a_0^T c_0 = \mathrm{mod}(n, 10)\}$$

$$G_2(k, n) = \{a \in F(k, n) \mid a_0^T c_0 = 10 + \mathrm{mod}(n, 10)\}$$

(1) If $\mathrm{mod}(n, 10) \notin \{1, 3\}$, then $F(k, n) = G_1(k, n)$.
(2) If $\mathrm{mod}(n, 10) \in \{1, 3\}$, then $F(k, n) = G_1(k, n) \bigcup G_2(k, n)$.

Theorem 5
(1) If $\mathrm{mod}(n, 10) \notin \{1, 3\}$, then

$$R(k, n) = \bigcap_{a \in G1(k,n)} s(k, a).$$

(2) If $\mathrm{mod}(n, 10) \in \{1, 3\}$, then

$$R(k, n) = \left(\bigcap_{a \in G1(k,n)} s(k, a) \right) \bigcap \left(\bigcap_{a \in G2(k,n)} s(k, a) \right).$$

Lemma 6. Let

$$s_0(k,a) = \{f(k,b) \mid 0 < b \le a, b_i = 0, 0 \le i \le k\},$$

$$s_1(k,a) = \{f(k,b) \mid 0 < b \le a, b_0 = 0\},$$

$$s_2(k,a) = s(k,a) - s_0(k,a) - s_1(k,a).$$

Then, for any $a \in G_1(k,n) \bigcup G_2(k,n)$, we have

$$s(k,a) = s_0(k,a) \bigcup s_1(k,a) \bigcup s_2(k,a).$$

Let A and B be two sets of integer. The circle plus operation for sets A and B is defined as

$$A \oplus B = \{x + y \mid x \in A, y \in B\}.$$

The multiplication of a set A by an integer m is defined as

$$m \times A = \{mx \mid x \in A\}.$$

Lemma 7. Let

$$T_0 = R(k, \mathrm{mod}(n,10));$$

$$T_1 = 10 \times R(k-1, \mathrm{div}(n,10));$$

$$T_2 = \bigcap_{a \in G_2(k,n)} s_0(k,a);$$

$$T_3 = 10 \times R(k-1, \mathrm{div}(n,10) - 1).$$

Then

$$\bigcap_{a \in G_1(k,n)} s_0(k,a) = T_0 \tag{5}$$

$$\bigcap_{a \in G_1(k,n)} s_1(k,a) = T_1 \tag{6}$$

$$\bigcap_{a \in G_1(k,n)} s_2(k,a) = T_0 \oplus T_1 \tag{7}$$

$$\bigcap_{a \in G_2(k,n)} s_1(k,a) = T_3 \tag{8}$$

$$\bigcap_{a \in G_2(k,n)} s_2(k,a) = T_2 \oplus T_3 \tag{9}$$

Lemma 8. Let $k > 1$, $x \in R(k,n)$ and $\mod(x, 10) > 0$, then

$$\mod(x, 10) \in R(k, \mod(n, 10)).$$

Theorem 9 Let

$$T_0 = R(k, \mod(n, 10));$$

$$T_1 = 10 \times R(k - 1, \div(n, 10));$$

$$T_2 = \bigcap_{a \in G_2(k,n)} s_0(k,a);$$

$$T_3 = 10 \times R(k - 1, \div(n, 10) - 1);$$

$$T_4 = R(k, 10 + \mod(n, 10)).$$

(1) If $\mod(n, 10) \notin \{1, 3\}$, then $R(k, n) = T_0 \bigcup T_1 \bigcup (T_0 \oplus T_1)$.
(2) If $\mod(n, 10) \in \{1, 3\}$, then

$$R(k, n) = (T_0 \bigcup T_1 \bigcup (T_0 \oplus T_1)) \bigcap (T_3 \bigcup T_4 \bigcup (T_3 \oplus T_4)).$$

(3) $R(0, n) = \{1, 2, \cdots, n\}$.

According to Theorem 9, we can design a recursive constructing algorithm for computing $R(k, n)$ as follows.

Algorithm 3: RecuConstruct(k, n, s)

---

1 **if** $k = 0$ **or** $n < 14$ **then** Direct(k, n, s);
2 Direct$(k, \mod(n, 10), a)$;
3 RecuConstruct$(k - 1, \div(n, 10), s)$;
4 Combine(a, s) ;
5 **if** $\mod(n, 10) \in (1, 3)$ **then**
6   Direct$(k, 10 + \mod(n, 10), a)$;
7   RecuConstruct$(k - 1, \div(n, 10) - 1, s0)$;
8   Combine$(a, s0)$;
9   Intersection$(s0, s)$;
10 **end**

---

3   Maximal Elements

Let
$$g(k,n) = \max_{1 \leq i \leq n} \{|R(k,i)|\};$$
$h(k,n)$ satisfying $g(k,n) = |R(k,h(k,n))|$.

Lemma 10. $g(0,n) = n$; $h(0,n) = n$.
Proof. It follows from $R(0,n) = \{1,2,\cdots,n\}$.

Lemma 11. If $\mathrm{div}(n,10^k) \leq 1$ and $m \geq k$, then $R(k,n) = R(m,n)$.
Proof. It follows from $\mathrm{div}(n,10^k) \leq 1$ that for any $a \in A(k,n)$, we have $n =$
$$f(k,a) = \sum_{i=0}^{k} a_i^\top c_i;\ \mathrm{div}(n,10^k) = \mathrm{div}(a_k^\top c_k,10^k) = a_k^\top c_0 \leq 1, \text{ and thus, } A(k,1) =$$
$A(k,2) = 0$.

If $m \geq k$, then for any $a \in A(m,n)$, we have $n = f(m,a) = \sum_{i=0}^{m} a_i^\top c_i$;
$\mathrm{div}(n,10^k) = \mathrm{div}(a_k^\top c_k,10^k) \leq 1$, and thus, $a_i = 0$ for all $i > k$; $A(k,1) = A(k,2) = 0$.

Therefore, $R(k,n) = R(m,n)$.

Theorem 12 If $\mathrm{div}(n,10^k) \leq 1$, then
   (1) If $n \geq 40$, then

$$g(k,n) = 6g(k,div(n+1,10)-1)+5 \tag{10}$$

   (2) If $n > 3$, then

$$g(k,n) \leq \frac{3}{2}g(k,n-1)+\frac{1}{2} \tag{11}$$

4   Conclusions

We have suggested efficient techniques for constructing the accurate implication sets of a given monetary system. We also give exact solutions for computing the maximal elements of e accurate implication set. The proposed combinatorial problem was solved completely.

References

1. Bird, R.: Pearls of Functional Algorithm Design, pp. 125–133. Cambridge University Press, Cambridge (2010)
2. Bitner, J.R., Reingold, E.M.: Backtrack programming techniques. Communications of the ACM 18, 651–656 (1975)
3. Cormen, T.H., Leiserson, C.E., Rivest, R.L.: Introduction to Algorithms. MIT Press, Cambridge (2001)
4. Kleinberg, J., Tardos, E.: Algorithm Design. Addison Wesley, Reading (2005)

Improved Gaussian Mixture Model for Moving Object Detection

Gang Chen, Zhezhou Yu[*], Qing Wen, and Yangquan Yu

College of Computer Science and Technology,
Jilin University, Changchun, Jilin, China
chengang09@mails.jlu.edu.cn, yuzz@jlu.edu.cn,
wenqing2213@163.com, yyq224444@yahoo.com.cn

Abstract. Detection of moving objects in image sequence is a fundamental step of information extraction in many vision applications such as visual surveillance, people tracking, traffic monitoring. Many background models have been introduced to deal with different problems. Gaussian mixture model is considered to be one of the most successful solutions. It is a robust and stable method for background subtraction. It can efficiently deal with multimodal distributions caused by shadows, swaying trees and other knotty problems of the real world. However, the method suffers from foreground objects bending into the background too fast. In addition, it can not deal with the problem of slow-moving objects. In this paper, an efficient method is presented to deal with the problem through improvement on the background updating period using different learning rates for the estimated background and foreground pixels. The experiment result shows the method works better than the typical Gaussian mixture model.

Keywords: Background model, moving object detection, Gaussian mixture model.

1 Introduction

A static camera observing a scene is a common case in a video surveillance application. Detecting moving objects is an essential step toward high-level image processing. The most typical method for this problem is background subtraction. Then how to efficiently model and update the background model becomes the challenging aspect of such approaches.

In [7], the kalman-filtering is used for adaptive background estimation in order to separate the foreground from the background. Subpixel edge map is used to model the background of the images in a video sequence [8]. The single Gaussian model was used in [1] to model the background. In this paper [1], each pixel is considered to have a probability density function, and a pixel from a new image is considered to be a background pixel if its value meets its density function. But pixel values often have

---

[*] Corresponding author.

H. Deng et al. (Eds.): AICI 2011, Part I, LNAI 7002, pp. 179–186, 2011.
© Springer-Verlag Berlin Heidelberg 2011

more complex distributions, and more appropriate models are needed. Stauffer and Grimson use an adaptive Gaussian mixture model to describe the background [3]. The model can lessen the effect of small repetitive motion caused by shadows, swaying trees and computer monitors. Much work has been done to improve the model. In [5], an L-recent window is introduced to improve the accuracy of the estimate and the performance of the tracker allowing fast convergence on a stable background model. In [6], recursive equations are used to update the parameters and but also to simultaneously select the appropriate number of components for each pixel.

The paper is organized as follows. In the next section, we will have a review of Gaussian mixture model proposed by Stauffer and Grimson [2,3,4]. In section 3, we present how our method updates the background model. In section 4, we present some experiments.

2 Adaptive Gaussian Mixture Model

In the approach of adaptive Gaussian mixture model, each pixel in the scene is modeled by a mixture of K Gaussian distributions. Taking into account lighting changes, scene changes, and moving objects, the model using Gaussian mixture is more reliable and adaptive than single Gaussian model and other background models.

2.1 Construction of Gaussian Mixture Model

At any time, t, what is known about a pixel, $\{x_0, y_0\}$, Equation (1) shows its history, where I is the image sequence.

$$\{X_1, ..., X_t\} = \{I(x_0, y_0, i) : 1 \le i \le t\} \tag{1}$$

$$P(X_t) = \sum_{i=1}^{K} \omega_{i,t} * \eta(X_t, \mu_{i,t}, \Sigma_{i,t}) \tag{2}$$

$$\eta(X_t, \mu, \Sigma) = \frac{1}{(2\pi)^{\frac{n}{2}} |\Sigma|^{\frac{1}{2}}} e^{-\frac{1}{2}(x-\mu_i)^T \Sigma_k^{-1}(x-\mu_k)} \tag{3}$$

The recent history of each pixel, $\{X_1, ..., X_t\}$, is modeled by a mixture of K Gaussian distributions. The probability observing a certain pixel value X_t at time t can be written as Equation (2) where K is the number of distributions, $\omega_{i,t}$ is the weight parameter of the ith Gaussian component, $\mu_{i,t}$ is the mean parameter of the Gaussian component. $\eta(X_t, \mu, \Sigma)$ is the normal distribution of ith component where μ is the mean and $\Sigma_i = \sigma_i^2 I$. is the covariance of the ith component. A new pixel will be presented by one of the Gaussian distributions and used to update the model.

2.2 Parameters Update

Every new pixel value is checked against the existing K Gaussian distributions, until a match is found. A match is defined as a pixel value within 2.5 standard deviations of a distribution.

The first Gaussian component that matches the test value will be updated by the following update equations,

$$\omega_{k,t} = (1-\alpha)\omega_{k,t-1} + \alpha(M_{k,t}) \tag{4}$$

$$\mu_t = (1-\rho)\mu_{t-1} + \rho X_t \tag{5}$$

$$\sigma_t^2 = (1-\rho)\sigma_{t-1}^2 + \rho(X_t - \mu_t)^T (X_t - \mu_t) \tag{6}$$

$$\rho = \alpha\eta(X_t \mid \mu_k, \sigma_k) \tag{7}$$

Where α is the learning rate, $M_{k,t}$ is 1 for the model which matched and 0 for the remaining Gaussian distributions. If none of the K Gaussian distributions match the current pixel value, then the least probable distribution is replace with a new distribution using the current value as its mean and initialized with a high variance, low prior weight. $1/\alpha$ defines a time constant which determines the speed of the parameters changing.

The μ and σ parameters are updated only when the current pixel value match one of the distributions. The second learning rate ρ is defined using the parameter α.

2.3 Background Estimation

The K distributions are ordered by the fitness value ω_k/σ_k , the most likely background distributions remain on top and the less probable background distributions gravitate towards the bottom, and finally replaced by a new distribution. This fitness value increases both a distribution gains more weight and as the variance deceases.

The first B distributions are used for modeling the background, where T is a threshold measuring of the minimum portion of the data that should be accounted for by the background. It is described as follows.

$$B = \arg\min_b (\sum_{k=1}^{b} \omega_k > T) \tag{8}$$

The variance of the moving object is expected to remain larger than the background pixel, and the particular pixel of moving object gains less supporting evidence than the background pixel.

3   Our Method

The typical Gaussian mixture model takes a strategy as follows: For each pixel in new image, if the pixel is well described by any of the K Gaussian distributions, we update the background model by the learning rate α, otherwise we replace the least probable distribution with a new distribution with the current value as its mean value, an initially high variance and low priority weight.

The Gaussian mixture model is an on-line learning method; it can adjust the background model according to the environment around, such as lighting changes.

When we update the background model, the learning of background objects is what we expected. In this paper, we present a method to employ different updating strategy for background and foreground regions. In this way, we can lessen the effect of foreground to the background, especially slow-moving objects, avoid over learning problem. In the same time, we can keep the foreground objects in view for a longer time.

3.1   Outline of the Method

Define f_t as the tth frame in the video image sequence, b_t as the background image after updating the Gaussian mixture model using the tth frame, and $X_t(i, j)$ represents the value of the pixel at (i, j) in a frame.

(1)   Initialization: The L-recent window method [6] is used here during the initialization stage. We employ the first k frames to construct the Gaussian mixture model. Define t=k.

(2)   Foreground and background pixel estimation: We get the tth background image and get the foreground pixel using the way we defined in part 2.

(3)   Background updating: The $(t+1)^{th}$ frame is obtained from video image sequence and we have got the foreground and background pixel from the tth frame at step 2. Employ the updating method introduced in part 3 to update the Gaussian Mixture background method.

(4)   End condition: If the video image sequence is not over, define t = t+1. Process the next video image as the way we describe in step 2 and 3; else, the processing procedure is over.

3.2   Foreground and Background Pixel Estimation

Equation (8) shows how we define the background model using Gaussian mixture. Pixels may present a single background color or multiple background colors resulting from repetitive motions or shadows. So we select the first B distribution for the model.

In common, we select the most probable distribution forming the background image even a pixel presents multiple colors, here we define a pixel as a foreground pixel if a pixel doesn't fit Equation (8) and define a pixel as a background pixel if the pixel fits Equation (8). A foreground image is formed using the foreground and background pixels in the way we define. This will lead to a phenomenon that one object may not be presented in the background image and not presented in the foreground image during a certain time until the distribution of the color of the object becomes the dominant distribution of the pixel.

Due to the temporal correlation of image sequences, we use the tth foreground image for an estimation of the $(t+1)^{th}$ foreground image approximately. Gaussian mixture model is a statistical method, so the temporary foreground regions will not impact the model and the estimation is effective.

$$\begin{cases} X_{t+1}(i, j) \in \mathit{fre} & \mathit{if}\,(f_t(i, j) = Max) \\ X_{t+1}(i, j) \in bg & \mathit{if}\,(f_t(i, j) = Min) \end{cases} \tag{9}$$

Equation (9) shows our approximations and assumptions where $f_t(i, j)$ represents the pixel value of foreground image at position (i, j) after updating the background model using the first t frames and $X_{t+1}(i, j)$ represents the pixel of the $(t+1)^{th}$ frame at the position (i, j). $X_{t+1}(i, j)$ is estimated as a foreground pixel only if $X_t(i, j)$ is a foreground pixel, and vice versa. Max and Min are symbols used for differentiating between foreground and background pixels.

3.3 Background Updating Method

The pixels in the $(t+1)^{th}$ frame are classified as foreground pixels and background pixels approximately using the first t frames through the method described in part 2. In [3, 6], the foreground pixels share the same learning rate as the background pixels in the process of updating the background model, this is not what we expected. The foreground pixels bend into the background too fast. To handle this problem, we employ two different learning rates, define γ_1 as the learning rate of background pixel, γ_2 as the learning rate of foreground pixel and $\gamma_1 > \gamma_2$. For each pixel $X_{t+1}(i, j)$, the learning rate is defined as Equation (10).

$$\begin{cases} \alpha = \gamma_1 & X_{t+1}(i, j) \in bg \\ \alpha = \gamma_2 & X_{t+1}(i, j) \in \mathit{fre} \end{cases} \tag{10}$$

The process of employing the improved updating method is described as follows.

(1) The pixel $X_{t+1}(i, j)$ is checked against the existing K Gaussian distributions modeled by the history of the pixel, if a match is found, go to step 2; else if none of the distributions match the pixel, go to step 3.

(2) We can get it from the foreground image if the pixel $X_{t+1}(i, j)$ is an estimated foreground pixel according to our assumptions in part 2. If the estimated pixel $X_{t+1}(i, j)$ is a foreground pixel, update the Gaussian mixture background model

using the learning rate γ_2 and the learning rate for μ and σ is adjusted according to γ_2. The parameters of the Gaussian mixture model are described as follows using the method described in [3].

$$\omega_{k,t+1} = (1-\gamma_2)\omega_{k,t} + \gamma_2(M_{k,t+1}) \tag{11}$$

$$\mu_{t+1} = (1-\rho)\mu_t + \rho X_{t+1} \tag{12}$$

$$\sigma_{t+1}^2 = (1-\rho)\sigma_t^2 + \rho(X_{t+1} - \mu_{t+1})^T (X_{t+1} - \mu_{t+1}) \tag{13}$$

$$\rho = \gamma_2\eta(X_{t+1} \mid \mu_k, \sigma_k) \tag{14}$$

If the pixel is an estimated background pixel, update the Gaussian mixture background model using the learning rate γ_1 and the learning rate for μ and σ is adjusted according to γ_1. When this step is over, go to step 4. The parameters of the Gaussian mixture model for back ground pixels are adjusted as the foreground pixels.
(3) Replace the least probable distribution with a new distribution using the current value as its mean and an initially high variance, and a low weight parameter.
(4) Process the next pixel in the $(t+1)^{th}$ frame, until all the pixels are done.

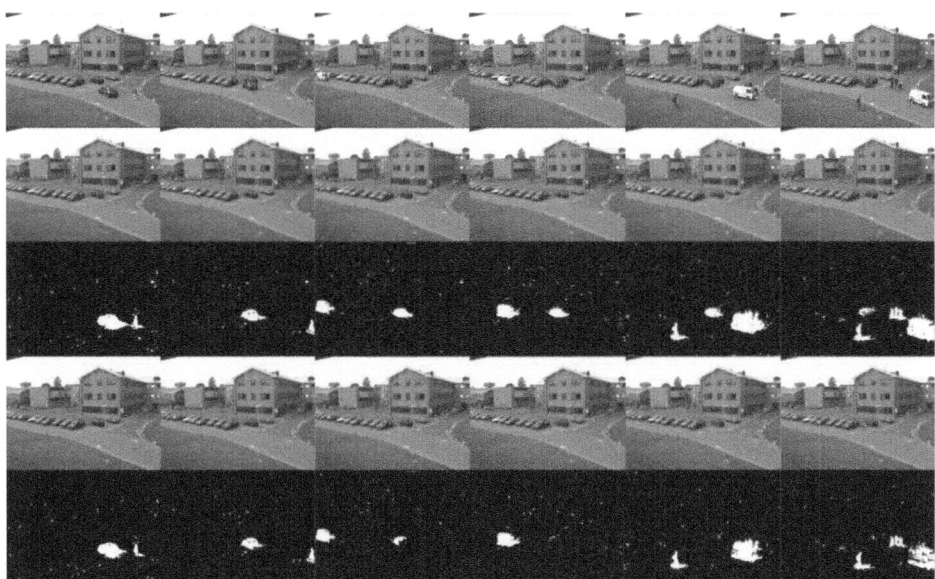

Fig. 1. The figure shows the experiment of our improved method comparing with the traditional Gaussion mixture model. The top row displays the original sequence at frames 600, 650, 700, 750, 900 and 950 respectively. The second and third rows show the background and foreground images adopting our improved method. The last two rows are the results of typical Gaussion mixture model for background and freground images.

The updating method can lessen the effect of moving object to the background modeling, especially the effect of slow-moving object. In addition, it can keep the foreground object keep in view for a longer time, and this is beneficial to object detection.

4   Experiment Results and Conclusion

This section demonstrates the comparative experiment results of the traditional Gaussian mixture model and our proposed method. We used an adaptive mixture of five Gaussian components. The threshold T for the traditional Gaussian mixture model and our improved method was both set at 0.70. The learning rate for the traditional GMM is set at 0.005; the learning rates γ_1 and γ_2 for our improved method were set at 0.005 and 0.001.

Figure.1 shows a sequence of video image from the Internet containing people and cars in it. We can see a car coming into view at the 600th frame, and stop in one place at 650th frame. At the 700th frame, the car begins to blend into the background model using the traditional Gaussian mixture model. Apparently, the foreground objects blend into the background too quickly. We can get it that the car begins blending into the background model at the 950th frame using our proposed method. Better segmentation can be seen from our method so that the moving object we may be interested in stays in view for a longer time.

The 950th frame shows the situation when a slow-moving object is in view. At the 950th frame, some small holes are formed inside the van in the foreground of Gaussian mixture model and the rear of the van is not so clear because of the van is painted one color and slow-moving so that the foreground pixels bend into background quickly. We can see the foreground image adopted our proposed method; it is clearer and provides a better segmentation of the moving object.

In this paper, an efficient method is presented to deal with the problem of foreground objects bending into the background too fast and the impact of slow-moving objects. The experiment shows the method works better than the typical Gaussian mixture model.

References

1. Wren, C.R., Azarbayejani, A., Darrell, T., Pentland, A.P.: Real-time tracking of the human body. IEEE Transaction on Pattern Analysis and Machine Intelligence, PAMI 19(7), 780–785 (1997)
2. Grimson, W.E.L., Stauffer, C., Romano, R., Lee, L.: Using adaptive tracking to classify and monitor activities in a site. In: IEEE Computer Society Conference on Computer Vision and Pattern Recognition, CVPR, pp. 22–29 (1998)
3. Stauffer, C., Grimson, W.E.L.: Adaptive background mixture models for real-time tracking. In: IEEE Computer Society Conference on Computer Vision and Pattern Recognition, CVPR, vol. 2 (1999)
4. Stauffer, C., Grimson, W.E.L.: Learning patterns of activity using real-time tracking. IEEE Transactions on Pattern Analysis and Machine Intelligence 22(8), 747–757 (2000)

5. KaewTraKulPong, P., Bowden, R.: An improved adaptive background mixture model for real-time tracking with shadow detection. In: AVBS (2004)
6. Zivkovic, Z.: Improved Adaptive Gaussian Mixture Model for Background Subtraction. In: International Conference on Pattern Recognition, ICPR, vol. 2, pp. 28–31 (2004)
7. Ridder, C., Munkelt, O., Kirchner, H.: Adaptive Background Estimation and Foreground Detection using Kalman-Filtering. In: Proceedings of International Conference on Recent Advances in Mechatronics, ICRAM 1995, pp. 193–199 (1995)
8. Jain, V., Kimia, B.B., Mudy, J.L.: Background Modeling Based on Subpixel Edges. In: IEEE International Conference on Image Processing, vol. (4), pp. 321–324 (2007)

A Clustering Algorithm of Wireless Sensor Networks Based on PSO

Yubin Xu and Yun Ji

School of Computer Science and Technology,
Taiyuan University of Science and Technology, Taiyuan, China
xyub@sohu.com, jiyun8906@163.com

Abstract. The routing protocol of WSN based on clustering hierarchy has been one of the important research topics. An improved strategy based on LEACH (Low Energy Adaptive Clustering Hierarchy) is proposed in this paper, which uses the PSO algorithm to optimize clustering process by considering the energy, the communication costs, the load balance and other factors to determine the cluster-head node. The simulation results show that the improved algorithm can solve the problems in LEACH, such as uneven clustering, uneven load of the cluster-head node and other disadvantages, and it can prolong the WSN lifetime.

Keywords: PSO, wireless sensor network, cluster-based routing protocol, lifetime.

1   Introduction

A wireless sensor network consisting of a large number of cheap micro-sensor nodes can be deployed in the monitoring area and can form a self-organizing network through wireless communication mode. The sensor nodes can collaborate to perceiving, collecting and processing data from the network and transmit the information to the observer. The sensor nodes are very limited by energy, and the battery can not be replaced, and the node's abilities of computing, communication and memory are all limited. So the wireless sensor network route protocol must achieve the goal of reducing the energy consumption and prolonging the network lifetime. Among all the protocols, the cluster routing protocol is a important point in research because of it's excellent energy saving property and adaptability. LEACH is the earliest cluster protocol of the proposed protocols. LEACH incorporates randomized rotation of the high-energy cluster-head position such that it rotates among the sensors in order to avoid draining the battery of any one sensor in the network. The cluster-head node must receive data from all the cluster members, perform signal processing functions on the data, and transmit data to the base station. The randomized rotation method can average the energy dissipation of the entire network and the energy dissipation can be evenly distributed to each sensor node. But because of the election of cluster head is randomized, it may cause some problems such as uneven distribution of the cluster head, uneven energy loading and so on. So LEACH can not effectively prolong the lifetime of the network.

H. Deng et al. (Eds.): AICI 2011, Part I, LNAI 7002, pp. 187–194, 2011.

This paper propose a clustering algorithm of wireless sensor network based on PSO, which use the PSO algorithm to optimize clustering process by considering the energy, the communication costs, the node's load balance and other factors to determine the cluster-head node, it can effectively balance the network's energy dissipation and prolong the network's lifetime.

2   Question Description

Divides and rules is a very ancient but practical strategy. In wireless sensor networks, stemming from the needs of management convenient, frugal energy consumption, extension network lifetime, we usually use the cluster routing protocol. This algorithm divides the entire network into the connected regions, each region has two kinds of nodes, one is cluster head nodes the other is ordinary nodes. Among them, the cluster head nodes need to coordinate the work of cluster nodes, responsible for data integration and forward, therefore, how to determine the cluster head nodes seems particularly important.

LEACH protocol is the first cluster routing protocol proposed in wireless sensor networks. It is based on cluster class structure and hierarchical technology protocol. Compared with the traditional protocol, it can conserve the energy of high degree. Subsequent cluster routing protocol (HEED[2], TEEN[3], PEGASIS[4], etc.) mostly developed from its foundation.

LEACH is operated by round. At the initial set up phase, each node generates a (0, 1) random number between, and compares it with a threshold, less than the threshold is the cluster head node.

Cluster head broadcast the information that it is become a cluster head to the other nodes, other nodes in accordance with received radio signal information's strength decide to join the cluster. Since then enter a stable phase. Cluster head node creates a TDMA schedule for the cluster and broadcast it to the cluster node. Cluster nodes transmit data to cluster head at the specified time schedule. Cluster head carry out data integration and then sent to the base station.

Through the research discovery, LEACH election method of the head cluster is random, so the head cluster in terms of quantity and distribution on the location are unstable. This will cause some problem: a). the problem of the number of head cluster. When the head cluster number is too little, it will lose the meaning of stratification, when the head cluster number is too much, because the head cluster communicates directly with the base station, would lead to excessive energy consumption across the network. b). the head cluster location problem. Head cluster's partial location would result in some communication radius too large, uneven energy consumption, thus affecting the network lifetime. c). head cluster energy problem. LEACH algorithm's randomness may cause some low energy nodes become head cluster, while the head node's energy consumption is the largest in network, thus assume such a mission will run out of energy and cause these nodes premature deaths.

In this paper, take the equalizing network consumption as a starting point, proposed a cluster routing protocol based on PSO algorithm, by optimizing the choice of the head cluster to avoid the occurrence of the above questions, thus prolonging the survival period of the entire network.

3   PSO Algorithm Summary

The PSO algorithm regards as community's in individual in the multi-dimensional space does not have the quality and the size particles. Assuming that at a D-dimensional search space, there are n particles, at each iteration i, the particles' location is expressed as $X_i = (x_{i1}, x_{i2}, \cdots, x_{iD})$, the corresponding flying velocity expression is $V_i = (v_{i1}, v_{i2}, \cdots, v_{iD})$. At each iteration, the particles track two extremums to update its own velocity and location. An extremal particles themselves are so far to search the optimal solution is called individual extremum, expressed as $P_i = (P_{i1}, P_{i2}, \cdots, P_{iD})$, another extreme is all particles to the current search for the optimal solution, known as global extremum, expressed as $P_g = (p_{g1}, p_{g2}, \cdots, p_{gD})$. The particle velocity and position are iterated by (1) and (2):

$$V_i^{t+1} = \omega V_i^t + c1 rand()(P_i - X_i^t) + c2 rand()(p_g - X_i^t) \tag{1}$$

$$X_i^{t+1} = X_i^t + V_i^{t+1} \tag{2}$$

where i=1, 2,…, N, N expresses the individual number in the group; ω is the inertia coefficient; t is the iteration number; c1 is the weight given to the attraction to the previous best location of the current particle and c2is the weight given to the attraction to the previous best location of the particle neighborhood; rand() is a sampling of a uniformly-distributed random variable in [0,1].

4   Description of PSO-Based Clustering Algorithm

PSO-based clustering algorithm needs the entire network node location information. This information can be obtained by GPS or related positioning algorithm. We assume that each node's location information is known.

4.1   Initializing

Nodes in the network and network environment are initialized.

4.2   Getting the Information of Location and Energy

Each node in the network transmits it's location and energy information to the base station. Now the base station record each node's location information P{p_1, p_2,…,p_n}, and energy information E{e_1, e_2,…,e_n}. Parameter n is the numbers of sensor nodes, parameter p_i is the location at node i, parameter e_i is the energy at node i.

4.3   Determining the Cluster Head Based PSO

In order to adapt to the discrete characteristics of wireless sensor networks, we definite a location mapping equation:

$$Q(X_i)=\{Xn \mid min(\parallel X_n \text{-} X_i \parallel ,1 \leq i \leq n) \tag{3}$$

Equation (3) means that if the particles location can't corresponds to the nodes location, we can find a nearest node to replace.

We form the fitness function just consider the main disadvantage of LEACH. Literature [1] provides the method of optimum number of clusters.

Because we expect the higher energy node has the priority to become a cluster head, so we definite equation:

$$f1(i)= \sqrt[Head\_num]{\prod_{i=1}^{Head\_num}(E_i - \bar{E})} \tag{4}$$

Head_num is the optimum number of clusters, E_i is the energy of the randomly selected node i, $\bar{E}$ is the average energy of the entire network nodes. From the formula (4), we can find that the greater the f1(i)'s value is, the higher selected node's energy is.

We expect the cluster-head's position is good (the communication cost is minimum in the cluster), so we definite a equation:

$$f2(i)= \sum_{i=1}^{Head\_num} \frac{Num_i}{Dis\tan ce_i}. \tag{5}$$

the Num_i is number of nodes at the i clusters, the $Distance_i$ is the sum of distance from cluster nodes to the cluster-head node. From the formula (5), we can find that the greater the f2(i)'s value is , the smaller the communication costs is, when the selected node as the cluster head node.

If the number of nodes included in the cluster is not equal, it can cause the amount of data which cluster process is not equal. So the load-balancing of the cluster head is also a important performance of the cluster.

We expect the number of nodes belonged to each cluster-head is equal, we definite a equation:

$$f3(i)= \frac{Head\_num}{\sum_{i=1}^{Head\_num}(Num_i - \bar{N})^2} \tag{6}$$

the $\bar{N}$ is the average number of nodes of the entire network. We can find that the greater the f3(i)'s value is, the more balance the number of cluster's nodes is.

So we have a fitness function equation:

$$f(i)=\alpha \times \sqrt[Head\_num]{\prod_{i=1}^{Head\_num}(E_i - \bar{E})} + \beta \times \sum_{i=1}^{Head\_num} \frac{Num_i}{Dis\tan ce_i} + \gamma \times \frac{Head\_num}{\sum_{i=1}^{Head\_num}(Num_i - \bar{N})^2} \tag{7}$$

where $\alpha + \beta + \gamma = 1$ and $\alpha, \beta, \gamma \in [0,1]$.

The detailed algorithm is explained as:

Step1: initializing particle swarm scale to m (m<n), for each particle i, initializing its position and velocity, using (3) to adjust the location of particles.

Step 2: using the fitness function (3) computes the fitness, so the optimal value of individual (pbest) and the optimal value of swarm (gbest) can be obtained.

Step 3: using (1) and (2) to iterate, a new position and velocity is obtained, then using (3) adjusts particle location.

Step 4: determining whether the condition meets the end, if not, go to step 2, otherwise, selecting the node which has the gbest value as a cluster head node.

Step 5: the cluster head node collects all the data from the nodes and transmits the information to the base station after integration.

5   Simulation Experiment

5.1   Energy Model and Network Environment Parameter Setting

In order to compare the improved algorithm performance, this paper uses the wireless channel model and the energy formula in literature [1] to calculate the energy loss of the routing protocol. This model is composed by transmits the electric circuit, the power amplifier and accepts the electric circuit. When the sender send k bit data to the distance of d receiver, the sender and the receiver both loss the energy as follows:

$$E_{Tx}(k, d) = E_{Tx\text{-}elec}(k) + E_{Tx\text{-}amp}(k, d) = E_{elec}*k + \varepsilon_{amp}*k*d^2 \tag{8}$$

$$E_{Rx}(k) = E_{Rx\text{-}elec}(k) = E_{elec}*k \tag{9}$$

This paper uses Matlab software to simulate the improved algorithm performance. At an ideal channel conditions, neglect the interference and signal conflict etc. impacts of random factors, examining 100 nodes randomly distributed in the 100m×100m area of sensor networks. Node's energy loss primary considers the send and the receive energy loss of the data packets and the control packets, and packet data fusion energy.

Assume nodes' coordinate from (0,0) to (100m, 100m). The base station is located at x = 50m, y = 175m. Each node is set to the initial energy 0.5 J, nodes send and receive data for energy consumption 50nJ/b, data fusion energy consumption for 5nJ/b, $\varepsilon_{two\text{-}ray\text{-}amp}=0.0013pJ$, $\varepsilon_{friss\text{-}amp}=10pJ$.

The literature [1] gives the optimal number of cluster head calculation formula for calculating the optimal number of cluster head is 5, that is Head_num=5; the parameter of the fitness function is α sets 0.4, β sets 0.4, γ sets 0.2.

5.2   Simulation Results and Analysis

Figure 1 is the use of PSO algorithm to optimize cluster. Among them, the asterisk indicates elected cluster head. We can see that the cluster head distribution is uniform.

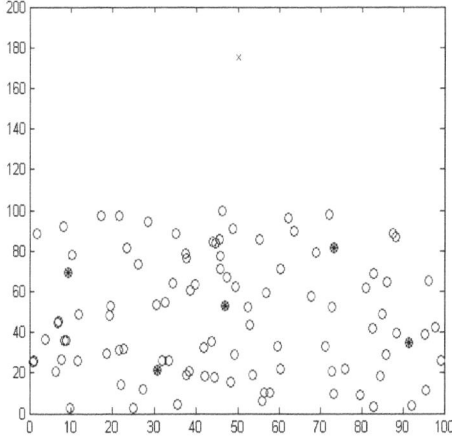

Fig. 1. The effect of the clustering using PSO

Figure 2 compares the two algorithms of network survival time. Can be seen that the proposed PSO-based clustering algorithm better than LEACH clustering algorithm has a longer survival time of the network. Compared with LEACH, the improved algorithm to make the first node of the extended time of death expanded 246%.

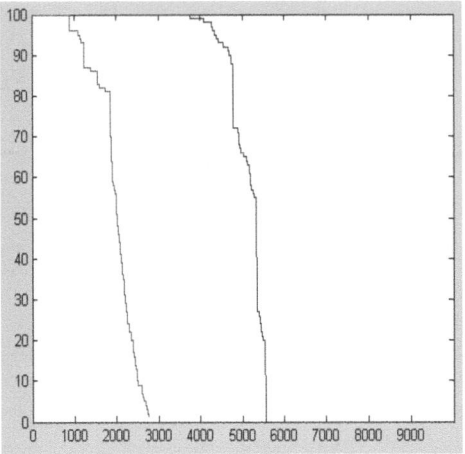

Fig. 2. The comparison of the network survival time

Figure 3 compares the two algorithms of load balancing degree. The load balancing degree reflects in each cluster round the average node degree of coverage. We can see that the improved algorithm having a better load balancing degree.

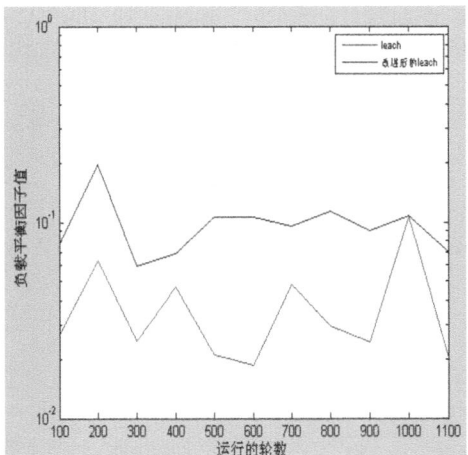

Fig. 3. the comparison of the LBF

Figure 4 compares the two algorithms at each round of the average energy consumption. Chart shows that the improved algorithm at each round has basic balance average energy consumption, made up of LEACH algorithm deficiencies of uneven energy consumption. Over all at the same time the improved algorithm at each round of the average energy consumption less than the LEACH algorithm.

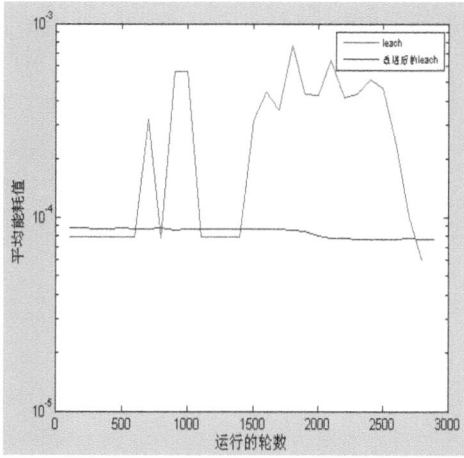

Fig. 4. The comparison of the average energy consumption

6 Conclusion

In this paper, we propose a cluster algorithm of wireless sensor network based on PSO. The algorithm improves and optimizes LEACH. The simulation results show that this algorithm can effectively avoid the disadvantages such as the cluster-head is not evenly deployed, the cluster-head's load is not balance and so on, so the improved strategy prolongs the whole network's lifetime. The future work is how to choose the parameters of the fitness function.

References

1. Heinzelman, W.: Application-Specific protocol architectures for wireless networks. Ph.D. Thesis. Massachusetts Institute of Technology, Boston (2000)
2. Younis, O., Heed, F.S.: A hybrid energy-efficient, distributed clustering approach for ad-hoc sensor networks. IEEE Trans. On Mobile Computing 3(4), 660–669 (2004)
3. Manjeshwar, A., Sgrawal, D.P.: TEEN: A Routing Protocol for Enhanced Efficiency in Wireless Sensor Networks. In: Proc. of the 15th Parallel and Distributed Processing Symp. in San Francisco, pp. 2009–2015. IEEE Computer Society, Los Alamitos (2001)
4. Lindsey, S., Raghavendra, C.S.: PEGASIS: Power-Efficient gathering in sensor information systems. In: Proc. of the IEEE Aerospace Conf., pp. 1125–1130. IEEE Aerospace and Electronic Systems Society, Montana (2002)

5. Kennedy, J., Eberhart, R.C., Shi, Y.: Swarm Intelligence. Morgan Kaufmann, San Francisco (2001)
6. Zeng, J., Jie, J., Cui, Z.: Particle swarm algorithm. Science Press, Beijing (2004)
7. Ying, L., Haibin, Y., Peng, C.: Application of PSO optimization based on clustering of wireless sensor network routing protocols. Journal of Control and Decision 21(4), 453–456 (2006)
8. Zou, X., Cao, Y., Liu, X., Gao, X.: Based on discrete particle swarm of WSN clustering routing algorithm. Journal of Wuhan University 54(1), 099–103 (2008)

Simulation Analysis of Heat Transfer of Power Battery[*]

Maode Li and Feng Wang

College of Mechanical Engineering, Tongji University,
4800 Cao-an Road, Shanghai 201804, China
limaode@tongji.edu.cn

Abstract. Based on the model of battery temperature rising established, several kinds of temperature rising processes are analyzed by means of numerical simulation including heat dissipation by natural convection without fin or with fin and forced convection with fin. The comparison and analysis are made for temperature rising process about their temperatures of center and across section plane. It shows that from the results, with the increasing of discharging ratio, the temperature rising and temperature difference of power batter will increase obviously. It is effective to reduce temperature rising by means of forced air convection, but the temperature difference will still keep a big value and with a poor effect. Here it is proposed to decrease the temperature difference both with fin and forced air convection.

Keywords: battery, temperature rising, heat dissipation, simulation.

1 Basic Radiation form of Battery and Simulation Model

The power battery gives out more heat when it discharges with a higher ratio. And this will causes a temperature rising and capacity decaying if heat transfer with environment is not enough. It is unprofitable for battery application. So it is necessary to use heat-removal system to keep the battery under a proper temperature range. At present, there are six basic forms of heat-removal system commonly used[1,2,3,4,5], which are shown as fig.1 to fig.6.

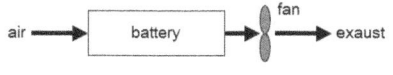

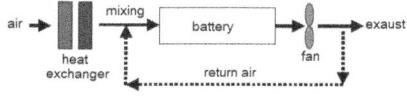

Fig. 1. Passive form of air cooling system

Fig. 2. Passive form of air cooling systemwith recovering waste heat

---

[*] Foundation Program: Natural Science Foundation of Shanghai-08ZR1419900.

H. Deng et al. (Eds.): AICI 2011, Part I, LNAI 7002, pp. 195–203, 2011.

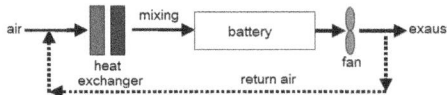
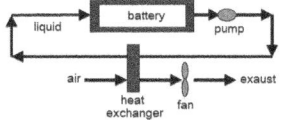

Fig. 3. Active form of air cooling systemwith recovering waste heat

Fig. 4. Active form of liquid cooling system

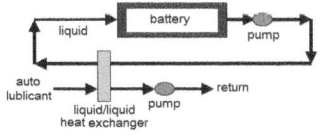
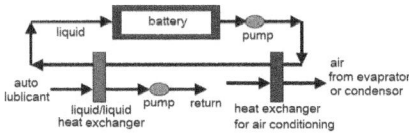

Fig. 5. Active convertible form of preheating or cooling with liquid

Fig. 6. Active form preheating or cooling with liquid

2   Numerical Simulation of Heat Dissipation with Fin Under Natural Convection

In general, a power battery source will consists of many elemental cells, which is often called battery pack. Here a power battery of polymer lithium ion phosphate with capacity of 36V/10A is split to 12 cells, based on each cell, the simulation model is applied, and the battery composed of 12 cells. Each polymer cell consists of out-film (plastic material with aluminum) and the interior, the out film will not produce heat but to affect the heat transfer process. The interior part is made of several kinds of electric chemical materials, which is supposed to be uniform and isotropic, some geometric and physical properties are listed as in table 1.

Table 1. Basic parameters of elemental cell of polymer lithium ion phosphate

Cell type	Mass (g)	Size (mm×mm×mm)
LiFePO$_4$ (3.2V/10Ah)	236.38	130×110×10
Density (kg/m3)	Special heat (J/kg·K)	Conductivity (W/m·K)
1653	1350	0.60

During charging and discharging, the temperature rising is directly related with its internal heat source, geometric type and heat transfer situation at boundary. It is useful to arrange some extending surface as fin to increase heat dissipation, so as to enhance the heat transfer from the inner to border.

For an elemental cell, its heat conduction model of three dimensions can be described as following.

$$\rho c_p \frac{\partial t}{\partial \tau} = \lambda(\frac{\partial^2 t}{\partial x^2} + \frac{\partial^2 t}{\partial y^2} + \frac{\partial^2 t}{\partial z^2}) + \frac{I^2 R_i}{V} \qquad (1)$$

$$\frac{\partial t}{\partial x}\Big|_{x=\pm a} = 0. \frac{\partial t}{\partial x}\Big|_{x=0} = 0. \frac{\partial t}{\partial y}\Big|_{y=0} = 0. \frac{\partial t}{\partial z}\Big|_{z=0} = 0. \qquad (2)$$

$$x \in [-a,a], \quad y \in [-b,b], \quad z \in [-c,c]$$

$$t_{\tau=0} = t_0$$

In the process of discharging of battery, some important parameters are discharging ratio as 1.0C and 2.0C, fin height 10mm, width 5mm , initial temperature 290K and boundary condition as natural convection.

Simulation of Temperature Rising of Battery Discharging at 1.0C

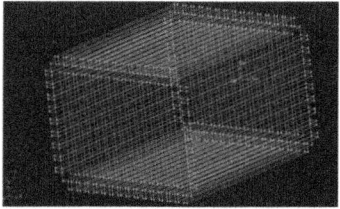

Fig. 7. Geometric model of battery with fin

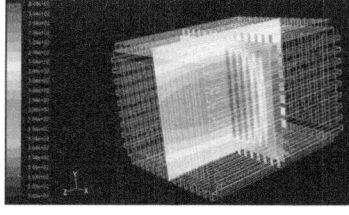

Fig. 8. Battery temperature cloud at center plane

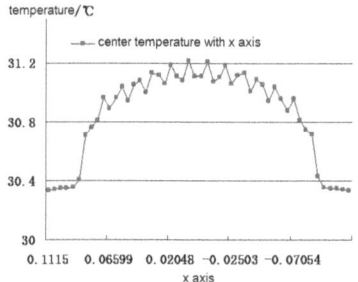

Fig. 9. Battery temperature distribution at center line at time 1800s

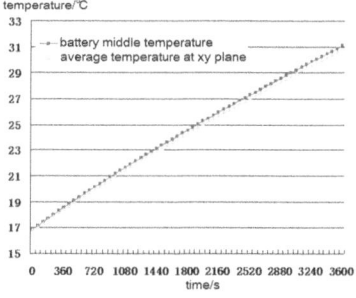

Fig. 10. Temperature comparison of different sites

From fig.8 to 10 it shows that, when battery discharges at 1.0C and with a natural convection heat transfer at border, the battery produces less inter heat and the temperature rising speed at center across section is lower. Heat dissipation of natural convection is enough to make the temperature at center to about 30℃, which is under the condition of safe range.

Simulation of Temperature Rising of Battery Discharging at 2.0C

Fig. 11. Battery temperature cloud

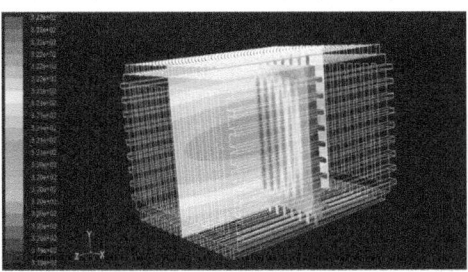

Fig. 12. Battery temperature cloud at center plane

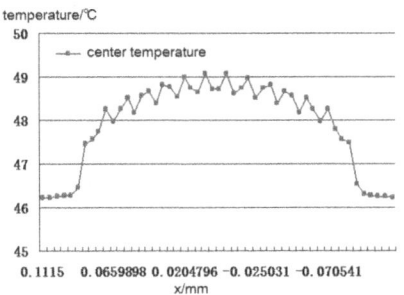

Fig. 13. Temperature distribution at center line

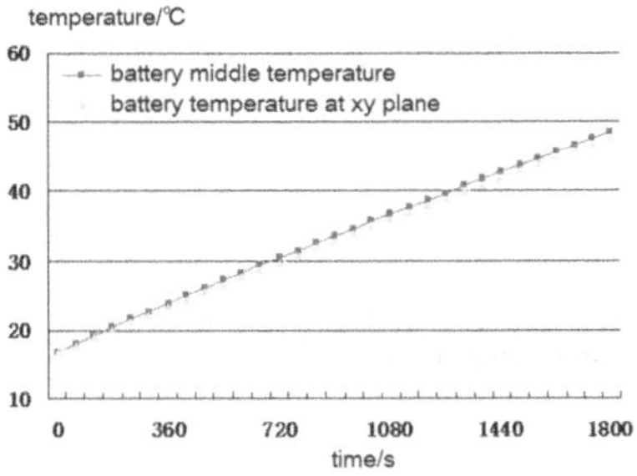

Fig. 14. Temperature comparison at different sites

From fig.12 to 14 it shows that, when battery discharges at 2.oC and with a natural convection heat transfer at border, the battery produces more inter heat which $q_{2.0C}$ is about to $4q_{1.0C}$, so the temperature rising at center across section obviously than that of under condition of discharging at 1.0C, in time interval 1800s, temperature rises from 17℃ to about 50℃ and even more higher than 65℃ if continue to discharge, which goes beyond the safe range. The ability of heat dissipation by natural convection is not enough.

3   Numerical Simulation of Heat Dissipation with Fin under Forced Convection

Based on the analysis of heat dissipation with natural convection, the battery with fin is put in a channel space with air flow of initial parameters of 4m/s and 290K, discharging at 1.0C and 2.0C, fin height and width is 10mm and 5mm respectively. Then under this kind of condition, the numerical simulation is made by means of Fluent Program, and the results are shown as in fig.16 to 24.

Numerical simulation of discharging at 1.0C

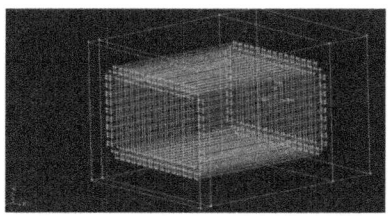

Fig. 15. geometric model of battery with fin

Fig. 16. Battery center temperature cloud

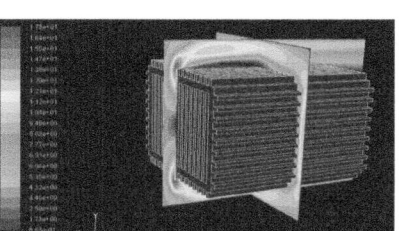

Fig. 17. Side flow velocity distribution

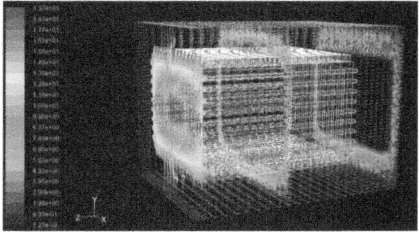

Fig. 18. Flow velocity at top and across section

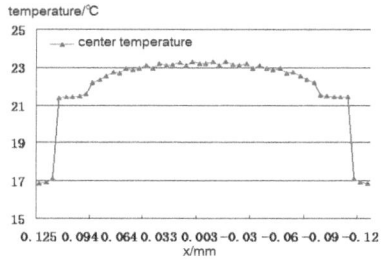

Fig. 19. Battery temperature at central line(3600s)

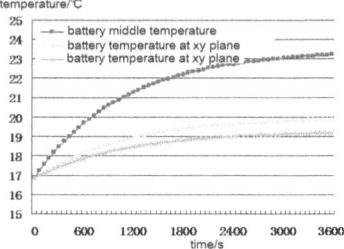

Fig. 20. Temperature comparison

Numerical Simulation of Discharging at 2.0C

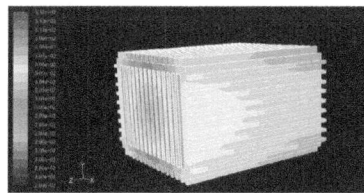

Fig. 21. Whole block temperature cloud

Fig. 22. Central plane temperature cloud

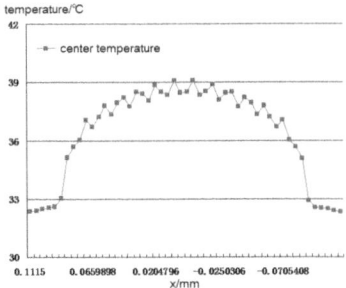

Fig. 23. Battery temperature at central line

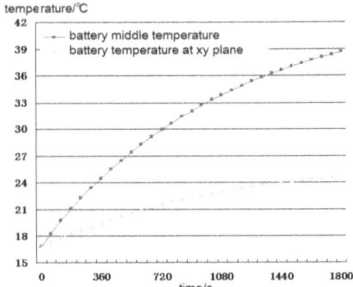

Fig. 24. Temperature comparison

The relationship of central temperature versus time is shown as in fig.16 to 20, which is under condition of discharging at 1.0C, with forced convection at border. Because of less heat produced discharging at 1.0C but with better heat dissipation fact of forced convection, the central temperature rising speed is lower than that of natural convection, in time interval of 1800s the central temperature reaches to about 25°C, the temperature difference is only increased to 8°C,which is tended to a constant of 25°C. So heat dissipation of forced convection is effective.

From fig 21 to 24 it shows that, under condition of discharging at 2.0C and with forced convection at border, the relationship of central temperature versus time is shown as in Fig.21 to 24. Because the more internal heat is produced discharging at 2.0C, which is about fore times of the heat at 1.0C, so with same air flow velocity of 4/s, the speed of temperature rising at center is much faster than that of the above, but the central temperature rising tends to be a constant, and it tends to 39°C and temperature difference to 22°C in 1800s.

4   Comparison of Temperature Rising under Three Conditions

According to the above simulation model as in equation (1) and (2), here a series of comparison under different condition of natural convection without fin, natural convection with fin and forced convection with fin are arranged and plotted as in fig.25 to 31.

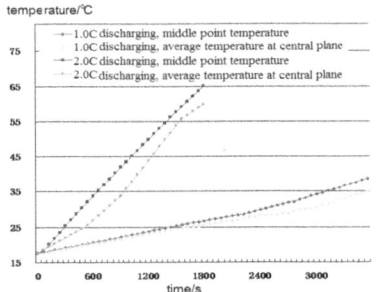

Fig. 25. Comparison of temperature rising without fin

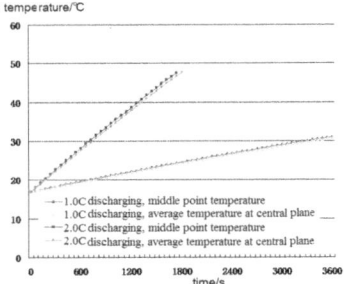

Fig. 26. Comparison of temperature rising with fin

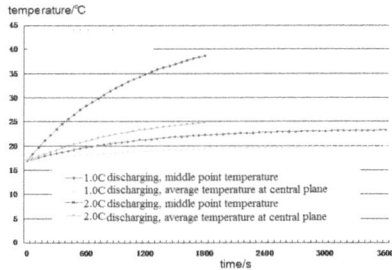

Fig. 27. Comparison of temperature rising with fin and forced convection

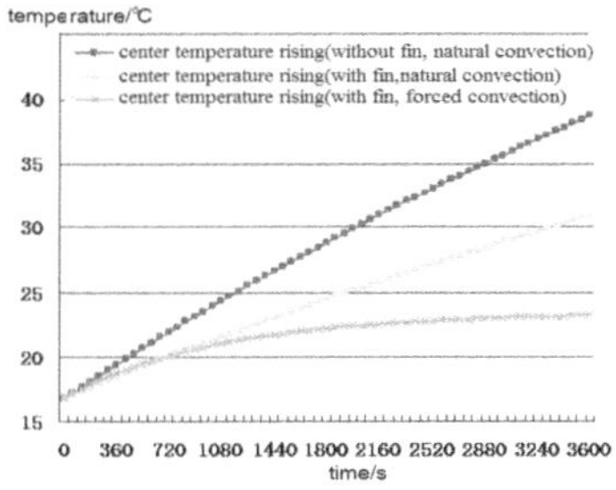

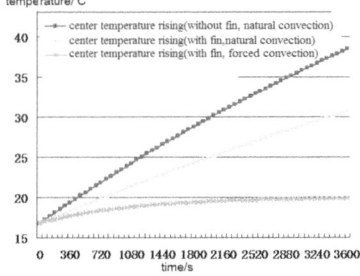

Fig. 28. Center temperature, 1.0C discharging

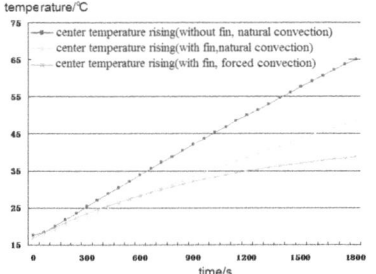

Fig. 29. Average temperature at central plane, 1.0C discharging

Fig. 30. Center temperature, 2.0C discharging

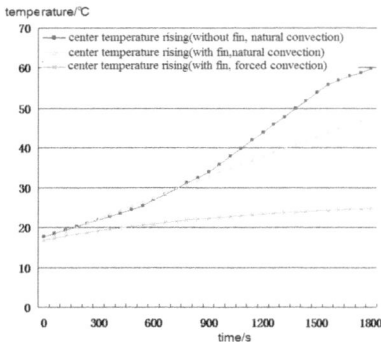

Fig. 31. Average temperature at central plane, 2.0C discharging

From fig.28, for one without fin, natural convection and discharging at 1.0C, center temperature of battery reaches to 40°C in time interval of 3600s. But when discharging at 2.0C and the others are same with that in fig.28, the center temperature is obviously higher because of the more internal heat produced, and the center temperature reaches to 65°Cin time interval of 3600s. From fig.25 to 31, it shows that, when at a higher discharging ratio, internal heat produced will be increased and to cause a more temperature rising, so thermal control or management is needed. When only the fin for heat dissipation is arranged, the temperature rising could be decreased to some extent, although the effect is inferior to that with forced convection, but the consistence of temperature distribution of each cell will be better which is good for battery circulation. When to use forced convection, the internal heat produced can be transferred effectively and to keep a lower temperature rising in a safe range, and the consistence of temperature distribution of each cell of battery will be better if to install fin properly.

5   Conclusions

From the above discussion under different conditions such as fin, convection forms and discharging ratio based on simulation results, some preliminary conclusions could be sum up as following.

In the process of discharging at 1.0C, heat dissipation with fin and natural convection, the internal heat could be removed effectively and center temperature could be less than 32°C. But when discharging at 2.0C with same conditions, the internal heat will not be easy to remove by means of natural convection and the center temperature will reach more than 50°C.

When with forced convection, even if the discharging ratio to 2.0C, the internal heat could be transferred to out and the maximum temperature only reaches to about 40°C which is in a safe range.

From all of these kinds of conditions, a comparison table about temperature rising, temperature difference and some others facts is concluded as in Table 2.

Table 2. A comparison of battery properties under different conditions

Heat dissipation	Average temperature	Consistence of cells	Invest	complexity
Natural convection, Without fin	high	poor	lower	lower
Natural convection, With fin	middle	good	middle	middle
Forced convection, With fin	lower	better	high	high
Forced convection, Without fin	lower	poor	middle	middle

References

1. Khateeb, S.A., Farid, M.M., Selman, J.R., et al.: Design and simulation of a lithium-ion battery with a phase change material thermal management system for an electric cooler. Journal of Power Sources 128(2), 292–307 (2004)
2. Pals, C.R., Newman, J.: Thermal modeling of the lithium/polymer battery. Journal of the Electrochemical Society 142, 3274 (1995)
3. Al Hallaj, S., Maleki, H., Hong, J., et al.: Thermal modeling and design considerations of lithium-ion batteries. Journal of Power Sources 83(1-2), 1–8 (1999)
4. Chen, S., Wan, C., Wang, Y.: Thermal analysis of lithium-ion batteries. Journal of Power Sources 140(1), 111–124 (2005)

5. Chen, Y., Evans, J.W.: Thermal analysis of lithium polymer electrolyte batteries by a two dimensional model-thermal behavior and design optimization. Electro-chemical Acta 39(4), 517–526 (1994)
6. Hatchard, T., MacNeil, D., Basu, A.: Thermal model of cylindrical and prismatic lithium-ion cells. Journal of the Electrochemical Society 148, A755 (2001)
7. Verbrugge, M.W., Conell, R.S.: Electro chemical and thermal characterization of battery modules commensurate with electric vehicle integration. Journal of the Electrochemical Society 149, A45 (2002)
8. Wang, C., Srinivasan, V.: Computational battery dynamics (CBD)–electrochemical/thermal coupled modeling and multi-scale modeling. Journal of Power Sources 110(2), 364–376 (2002)
9. Rahman, M., Shuttleworth, R.: Thermoelectric power generation for battery charging, pp. 186–191. IEEE, Los Alamitos (2002)

Adaptive Combination of Subband Adaptive Filters with Selective Partial Updates

Chang Liu, Miao He, and Wei Xia

Department of Electronic Engineering,
University of Electronic Science and Technology of China, Xiyuan Road, 2006,
611731 Chengdu, China
chaneaaa@163.com

Abstract. Combining the concepts of adaptive combination and selective partial updates (SPU) in the normalized subband adaptive filter (NSAF), an adaptive combination of two NSAFs with SPU (SPU-CNSAF) is presented. The proposed scheme not only reduces the computational complexity but also provides a good convergence performance. Simulation results show the efficiency of the proposed scheme. In addition, the SPU concept can also be extended to some other combination schemes such as the combination of normalized least mean square (NLMS) filters, recursive least squares (RLS) filters and affine projection (AP) filters.

Keywords: adaptive filters, normalized subband adaptive filter (NSAF), adaptive combination, selective partial update (SPU).

1 Introduction

Adaptive filtering is an important technique in a wide range of applications such as adaptive equalization, echo cancellation, system identification and adaptive beamforming [1-3]. Among all the adaptive algorithms, the least-mean-square (LMS) algorithm is the most popular and widely adopted one due to its simplicity and robustness. However, correlated input signals tend to deteriorate its convergence performance [1]. To overcome this problem, the normalized subband adaptive filtering (NSAF) [4] has been proposed. It is derived from the principle of minimum disturbance, with its improved convergence rate and close steady-sate error compared to the normalized LMS (NLMS)-based adaptive filter. However, similar to the NLMS-based adaptive filter, a tradeoff between fast convergence rate and small steady-state error is a requirement of the NSAF. To meet this conflicting requirement, an adaptive combination of two normalized subband filters (CNSAF) with large and small step sizes has been proposed in [5, 6]. Both component filters of the CNSAF are adapted independently by their own design rules, and the mixing parameter that controls the combination is adapted by means of a gradient descent method to minimize the quadratic error of the overall filter. The advantage of this method is that it can obtain both fast convergence rate and small steady-state misadjustment. In addition, this combination approach can be extended to other kinds of filers such as recursive-least-square (RLS) filters [7], LMS filters [7-10] and affine projection (AP) filters [11].

H. Deng et al. (Eds.): AICI 2011, Part I, LNAI 7002, pp. 204–211, 2011.

Another main problem of the adaptive algorithms is the computational complexity. In some applications such as acoustic echo cancellation (AEC), a large number of filter coefficients are needed. The computational complexity is proportional to the number of filter coefficients. In order to reduce the computational complexity, the adaptive filter algorithms with selective partial updates (SPU) have been proposed [12]. The SPU adaptive algorithms update only the selected blocks of filter coefficients at every iteration by using a selection criterion. The SPU-NLMS [13], SPU transform domain LMS (SPU-TD-LMS) [14] and SPU normalized subband adaptive filter (SPU- NSAF) [15] are several variants of this SPU scheme.

In this paper, the adaptive combination and SPU concepts in the NSAF are combined and an adaptive combination of two SPU-NSAF filters (C-SPU-NSAF) is established. Unlike the conventional CNSAF scheme, the filter coefficients of each component NSAF are partially updated in each subband rather than the entire filter at every iteration. Compared to the conventional CNSAF, it reduces substantially the computational complexity due to the partial update of the filter coefficients while obtaining the close convergence rate.

2   NSAF and CNSAF

2.1   NSAF

The NSAF model is shown in Fig. 1. The desired signal arises from the model $d(n) = \mathbf{w}_o^T \mathbf{u}(n) + v(n)$, where $\mathbf{w}_o = [w_{o,0}, w_{o,1}, \cdots, w_{o,M-1}]^T$ is the tap-weight vector of the unknown system of length M, $\mathbf{u}(n) = [u(n), u(n-1), \cdots, u(n-M+1)]$ is the input signal vector and $v(n)$ is the background noise, assumed to be zero mean ,and independent of $u(n)$, its variance is σ_v^2.

The input signal $u(n)$ and desired signal $d(n)$ are partitioned into N subband signals $u_i(n)$ and $d_i(n)$ via the analysis filters $H_i(z)$, $i = 0, 1, \cdots N-1$. The subband signals, $d_i(n)$ and $u_i(n)$ are critically decimated to a lower sampling rate commensurate with their bandwidth. We use the variable n to index the original sequences, and k to index the decimated sequence for all signals. The decimated subband signals can be defined as $y_{i,D}(k) = y_i(kN) = \mathbf{w}^T(k)\mathbf{u}_i(k)$ and $d_{i,D}(k) = d(kN)$, where $\mathbf{u}_i(k) = [u_i(kN), u_i(kN-1), \cdots, u_i(kN-M+1)]^T$ is the input data vector for the ith subband and the vector $\mathbf{w}(k) = [w_0(k), w_1(k), \cdots, w_{M-1}(k)]^T$ represents the coefficients of the adaptive filter. Hence, we define the desired signal vector as

$$\mathbf{d}_D(k) = \mathbf{U}^T(k)\mathbf{w}_o + \mathbf{v}(k), \tag{1}$$

where $\mathbf{U}(k) = [\mathbf{u}_0(k), \mathbf{u}_1(k), \cdots, \mathbf{u}_{N-1}(k)]$ is the input matrix, $\mathbf{v}(k) = [v_0(k), v_1(k), \cdots, v_{M-1}(k)]^T$ is the noise vector and $v_i(k)$ is the ith subband noise which is identically and independently of the input data. Assuming that it is zero mean and its variance is $\sigma_{v,i}^2$. The update equation of the NSAF can be written as

$$\mathbf{w}(k+1) = \mathbf{w}(k) + \mu \sum_{i=0}^{N-1} \frac{\mathbf{u}_i^T(k)}{\left\| \mathbf{u}_i(k) \right\|^2} e_{i,D}(k), \tag{2}$$

where μ is the step-size and $e_{i,D}(k)$ is the decimated subband error signal and can be obtained by

$$e_{i,D}(k) = d_{i,D}(k) - y_{i,D}(k) = d_{i,D}(k) - \mathbf{w}^T(k)\mathbf{u}_i(k). \tag{3}$$

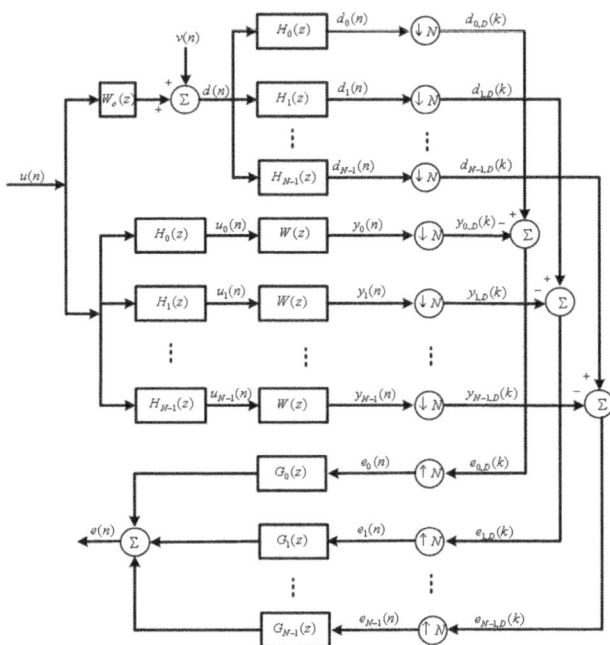

Fig. 1. NSAF structure

2.2 CNSAF

The CNSAF [6] is described in Fig. 2, where we just illustrate one subband structure. As shown in Fig. 2, the filter outputs of component filters $y_{i,p}(n)$ are critically decimated to generate $y_{i,D,p}(k) = \mathbf{u}_i^T(k)\mathbf{w}_p(k)$ for $i = 0, 1, \cdots, N-1$ and $p = 0, 1$, where $\mathbf{w}_p(k)$ is the tap-weight vector. The subband error signals of component filters are defined as $e_{i,D,p}(k) = d_{i,D}(k) - y_{i,D,p}(k)$. Then the update equation of the component NSAFs can be expressed as

$$\mathbf{w}_p(k+1) = \mathbf{w}_p(k) + \mu_p \sum_{i=0}^{N-1} \frac{\mathbf{u}_i(k)}{\left\| \mathbf{u}_i(k) \right\|^2 + \varepsilon} e_{i,D,p}(k), \tag{4}$$

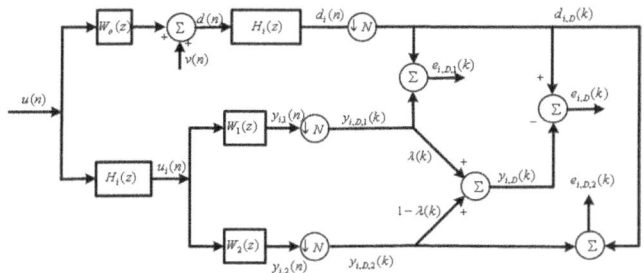

Fig. 2. NSAF structure CNSAF structure for one subband

where μ_p for $p = 0,1$ are the step-sizes of the component NSAFs. Assuming that $\mu_1 > \mu_2$, then $\mathbf{w}_1(k)$ has a faster convergence rate but a larger steady-state misadjustment than $\mathbf{w}_2(k)$ does. ε is the regularization parameter.

By applying the convex combination idea, the subband outputs and tap-weight vector of the overall filter are defined respectively as

$$y_{i,D}(k) = \lambda(k)y_{i,D,1}(k) + [1 - \lambda(k)]y_{i,D,2}(k), \tag{5}$$

$$\mathbf{w}(k) = \lambda(k)\mathbf{w}_1(k) + [1 - \lambda(k)]\mathbf{w}_2(k), \tag{6}$$

where $\lambda(k)$ is a mixing parameter that lies between zero and one.

Hence, the overall subband errors can be given as

$$e_{i,D}(k) = d_{i,D}(k) - y_{i,D}(k). \tag{7}$$

$\lambda(k)$ is adjusted by means of a gradient descent method, which minimizes the sum of the subband error powers of the overall filter, i.e., $\sum_{i=0}^{N-1} e_{i,D}^2(k)$. However, instead of directly adjusting $\lambda(k)$, we can adapt a variable $a(k)$ which defines $\lambda(k)$ via a sigmoidal function as $\lambda(k) = [1 + e^{-a(k)}]^{-1}$. The update of $a(k)$ can be given

$$a(k+1) = a(k) - \frac{1}{2}\frac{\partial \sum_{i=0}^{N-1} e_{i,D}^2(k)}{\partial a(k)}$$

$$= a(k) + \mu_a \eta(k)[1 - \eta(k)]\sum_{i=0}^{N-1} e_{i,D}(k)[y_{i,D,1}(k) - y_{i,D,2}(k)], \tag{8}$$

where μ_a is the step-size for updating $a(k)$ and must be set to a high value. In or to avoid the halt of the update for $a(k)$ whenever $\lambda(k)$ is too close to zero or one, [6] limit $a(k)$ in a symmetric interval [-4, 4].

3 Proposed SPU-CNSAF

In this section, for each component filter $\mathbf{w}_p(k)$, we consider that updating S blocks out of B blocks in each subband at every iteration. By partitioning $\mathbf{u}_i(k)$ and $\mathbf{w}_p(k)$ into B blocks each of length L which are defined as (Note that $B = M/L$ is an integer)

$$\mathbf{u}_i(k) = [\mathbf{u}_{i,1}^T(k), \mathbf{u}_{i,2}^T(k), \cdots, \mathbf{u}_{i,B}^T(k)]^T, \tag{9}$$

$$\mathbf{w}_p(k) = [\mathbf{w}_{p,1}^T(k), \mathbf{w}_{p,2}^T(k), \cdots, \mathbf{w}_{p,B}^T(k)]^T. \tag{10}$$

Let $\mathbf{F} = \{j_1, \ j_2, \ \cdots, \ j_S\}$ denote the indices of the updating S blocks out of B blocks. In this case, the SPU-CNSAF solves the following optimization problem

$$\min_{\mathbf{w}_{p,\mathbf{F}}(k+1)} \left\| \mathbf{w}_{p,\mathbf{F}}(k+1) - \mathbf{w}_{p,\mathbf{F}}(k) \right\|^2, \tag{11}$$

which is subjected to the set of S constraints imposed by the decimated filter output

$$d_{i,D}(k) = \mathbf{w}^T(k+1)\mathbf{u}_i(k), \tag{12}$$

Where

$$\mathbf{w}_{p,\mathbf{F}}(k) = [\mathbf{w}_{p,j_1}^T(k), \mathbf{w}_{p,j_2}^T(k), \cdots, \mathbf{w}_{p,j_s}^T(k)]^T. \tag{13}$$

By using the Lagrange multipliers approach, the component filter update equation is given as

$$\mathbf{w}_{p,\mathbf{F}}(k+1) = \mathbf{w}_{p,\mathbf{F}}(k) + \mu_p \mathbf{U}_{\mathbf{F}}(k)[\boldsymbol{\Lambda}_{\mathbf{F}}(k)]^{-1}\mathbf{e}_{D,p}(k), \tag{14}$$

Where

$$\mathbf{U}_{\mathbf{F}}(k) = [\mathbf{U}_{j_1}^T(k), \mathbf{U}_{j_2}^T(k), \cdots, \mathbf{U}_{j_s}^T(k)]^T, \tag{15}$$

is the $SL \times N$ matrix

$$\mathbf{U}_{j_m}(k) = [\mathbf{u}_{0,j_m}^T(k), \mathbf{u}_{1,j_m}^T(k), \cdots, \mathbf{u}_{N,j_m}^T(k)]^T \quad (m = 0, \cdots, S) \tag{16}$$

$$\mathbf{e}_{D,p}(k) = [e_{0,D,p}(k), e_{1,D,p}(k), \cdots, e_{N-1,D,p}(k)]^T, \tag{17}$$

and $\boldsymbol{\Lambda}_{\mathbf{F}}(k) = \mathrm{diag}(\mathbf{U}_{\mathbf{F}}^T(k)\mathbf{U}_{\mathbf{F}}(k))$ is the diagonal matrix [4]. (14) can also be written as

$$\mathbf{w}_{p,\mathbf{F}}(k+1) = \mathbf{w}_{p,\mathbf{F}}(k) + \mu_p \sum_{i=0}^{N-1} \frac{\mathbf{u}_{i,\mathbf{F}}(k)}{\left\| \mathbf{u}_{i,\mathbf{F}}(k) \right\|^2 + \varepsilon} e_{i,D,p}(k), \tag{18}$$

where

$$\mathbf{u}_{i,\mathbf{F}}(k) = [\mathbf{u}_{i,j_1}^T(k), \mathbf{u}_{i,j_2}^T(k), \cdots, \mathbf{u}_{i,j_s}^T(k)]^T. \tag{19}$$

To determine which blocks to be updated, we assume that ε is sufficiently small and apply the smallest squared-Euclidean-norm criterion to find S blocks as

$$\begin{aligned}
\mathbf{F} &= \arg\min_{\mathbf{F}} \left\| \mathbf{w}_{p,\mathbf{F}}(k+1) - \mathbf{w}_{p,\mathbf{F}}(k) \right\|^2 \\
&= \arg\min_{\mathbf{F}} \left\| \mu_p \sum_{i=0}^{N-1} \frac{\mathbf{u}_{i,\mathbf{F}}(k)}{\left\| \mathbf{u}_{i,\mathbf{F}}(k) \right\|^2 + \varepsilon} e_{i,D,p}(k) \right\|^2 \\
&= \arg\min_{\mathbf{F}} \left\{ \sum_{i=0}^{N-1} \frac{\left| e_{i,D,p}(k) \right|^2}{\left\| \mathbf{u}_{i,\mathbf{F}}(k) \right\|^2} \right\}.
\end{aligned} \tag{20}$$

The computational complexity of the selection of the blocks according to (20) is very high. Hence, we may derive a simplified criterion.

To reduce the computational complexity, we use a simplified criterion for the selection of the blocks to update. According to [15], we compute the values $\sum_{i=0}^{N-1} \left\| \mathbf{u}_{i,j}(k) \right\|^2$ for $j = 1, \cdots, B$ and the indices of the set $\mathbf{F}$ correspond to the indices of S largest values of $\sum_{i=0}^{N-1} \left\| \mathbf{u}_{i,j}(k) \right\|^2$ for $j = 1, \cdots, B$.

The computational complexity of the combination of NLMS filters (CNLMS), CNSAF and proposed SPU-CNSAF has been presented in Table 1. It is well-known that NLMS operation needs $2M + 2$ multiplications. For CNLMS with two NLMS filters, it requires $4M + 4$ multiplications per iteration. The CNSAF requires $4M + 3NK + 4N + 5/N + 3$ multiplications per iteration [6], where K is the length of channel filters of the analysis filter bank, while the SPU-CNSAF needs $2M + 2SL + 3NK + 4N + 5/N + 3$ multiplications per iteration. It saves $2M - 2SL$ multiplications compared to the CNSAF due to the partial update of filter coefficients. In addition, $O(B) + B \log_2 S$ comparisons are needed for the SPU-CNSAF while using the heapsort algorithm [16].

4 Simulation Results

The proposed scheme is evaluated in a system identification context. The input signal, $u(n)$, is an AR(1) signal generated by

$$G(z) = \frac{1}{1 - 0.8z^{-1}}. \tag{21}$$

The length of unknown system, $\mathbf{w}_0$, and adaptive filter is 256. A cosine-modulated filter banks with number of subbands $N = 8$ are used, whose prototype filter has $K = 128$ taps. The white Gaussian noise with 20dB signal to noise ratio (SNR) is added to the system. The symmetric interval for $a(k)$ is [-4, 4], The default values of $\mu_a = 100$, $\varepsilon = 0.001$, $L = 4$ and $B = 64$ are used.

Normalized mean square deviation (NMSD) which is defined as

$$20 \log_{10} \left\| \mathbf{w}(k) - \mathbf{w}_0 \right\| / \left\| \mathbf{w}_0 \right\|. \tag{22}$$

is used to show the performance. All the NMSD learning curves are obtained by averaging over 50 independent trials.

Fig. 3 shows the NMSD learning curves of the SPU-SAF [15] and the proposed SPU-CNSAF. The large step size $\mu_1 = 0.7$ and small step size $\mu_2 = 0.05$ are used. At

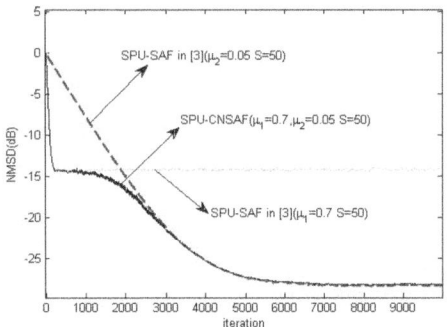

Fig. 3. NMSD curves of two SPU-SAF filters with step-sizesμ₁=0.7 and μ₂=0.03, as well as that of their adaptive combination (SPU-CNSAF)

every iteration, 50 blocks out of 64 in each subband are selected to update. It is clear to see that the proposed SPU-CNSAF obtains both fast convergence rate and small steady-state MSD compared with the SPU-SAF.

In Fig. 4, the NMSD learning curves of the conventional CNSAF and the proposed SPU-CNSAF are compared. For the CNSAF, the large and small step sizes are selected to be 1 and 0.08, respectively. The step-sizes of the proposed SPU-CNSAF are selected to get approximately the same NMSD for all algorithms after convergence. In order to observe the convergence performance of the proposed SPU-CNSAF, different updating blocks are being used. It can be seen in Fig. 4 that the convergence rate of the proposed scheme is close to that of the conventional CNSAF with the increase of the parameter S.

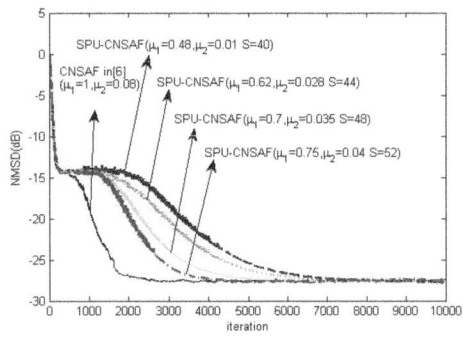

Fig. 4. NMSD curves of the CNSAF and SPU-CNSAF

5   Conclusion

The SPU-CNSAF is proposed to obtain both fast convergence rate and small steady-state MSD. Compared to the conventional CNSAF, the proposed scheme not only reduces the computational complexity but also provides a comparable performance.

Furthermore, the SPU concept can also be extended to some other combination schemes such as the combination of NLMS, RLS and AP.

Acknowledgments. This work was supported by 2009 Guangdong-Hongkong major breakthrough in key fields project(200920523300005), Sichuan key technology support program (2010GZ0149) and Basic research university funding from special operations (ZYGX2010J020).

References

1. Widrow, B., Stearns, S.D.: Adaptive Signal Processing. Prentice-Hall, Englewood Cliffs (1985)
2. Haykin, S.: Adaptive Filter Theory, 4th edn. Prentice-Hall, Upper Saddle River (2002)
3. Sayed, A.H.: Adaptive Filters. Wiley, New York (2008)
4. Lee, K.A., Gan, W.S.: Improving convergence of the NLMS algorithm using constrained subband updates. IEEE Signal Process. Lett. 11(9), 736–739 (2004)
5. Azplicueta, L.A., Figueiras-Vidal, A.R., Arenas-Garcia, J.: Acoustic echo cancellation in frequency domain using combination of filters. In: 19th Int. Congress on Acoustic, ICA (2007)
6. Ni, J., Li, F.: Adaptive combination of subband adaptive filters for acoustic echo cancellation. IEEE Trans. Consumer Electronics 56(3), 1549–1555 (2010)
7. Arenas-Garcia, J., Martinez-Ramon, M., Navia-Vazquez, A., F-Vidal, A.R.: Plant identification via adaptive combination of transversal filters. Signal Processing 86, 2430–2438 (2006)
8. Arenas-Garcia, J., Gomez-Verdejo, V., F-Vidal, A.R.: New algorithms for improved adaptive convex combination of LMS transversal filters. IEEE Trans. Instrumentation and Measurement 54(6), 1078–1090 (2005)
9. Arenas-Garcia, J., F-Vidal, A.R., Sayed, A.H.: Mean-square performance of a convex combination of two adaptive filters. IEEE Trans. Signal Processing 54(3), 1078–1090 (2006)
10. Candido, R., Silva, M.T.M., Nascimento, V.H.: Transient and steady-state analysis of affine combination of two adaptive filters. IEEE Trans. Signal Processing 58(8), 4064–4078 (2010)
11. Dogancay, K.: Partial-update adaptive signal processing-design. In: Analysis and Implementation. Elsevier, Amsterdam (2008)
12. Dogancay, K., Tannkulu, O.: Adaptive filtering algorithms with selective partial updates. IEEE Trans. Circuits and Systems II: Analog and Digital Signal Processing 48(8), 762–769 (2001)
13. Dogancay, K.: Complexity considerations for transform-domain adaptive filters. Signal Processing 83, 1177–1192 (2003)
14. Abida, M.S.E., Husoy, J.H.: Selective partial update and set-member subband adaptive filters. Signal Processing 88, 2463–2471 (2008)
15. Knuth, D.E.: Sorting and searching, the art of computer programming, 2nd edn., vol. 3. Addison-Wesley, Reading (1973)
16. Ni, J., Li, F.: A variable step-size matrix normalized subband adaptive filter. IEEE Trans. Audio, Speech and Language Processing 18(6), 1290–1299 (2010)

Application of Shortest Path Search Algorithm in Disaster Decision Support System

Huijuan Zhao[1,2] and Dongmei Huang[2]

[1] Glorious Sun School of Business and Management
Donghua University, Shanghai, China
[2] Information College, Shanghai Ocean University
Shanghai, China
hjzhao@shou.edu.cn

Abstract. Core setting region could facilitate disaster relief and strength communication among setting regions when emergent disaster happens. Shortest path search algorithms could be applied. Dijkstra algorithm is discussed and is improved to solve the confirmation of core setting region. It ensures that the core setting region is the nearest to the farthest region. The improved algorithm turns out to be practical.

Keywords: Shortest Path Search Algorithm, Dijkstra Algorithm, Core setting region, Disaster Decision Support System.

1 Introduction

People in disaster region will be evacuated to the safe setting region chosen in advance when emergent disaster happened. Some research work [1] focused on evacuating path has been carried out. Setting regions are confirmed according to their location, safety, economic factors and so on. It will be better if one or more setting regions are selected as the core setting ones and other regions for auxiliary ones for that it will be helpful to facilitate transport urgent commodity and medical resources among the regions to help mutually. The selection of core setting regions turns out to be the problem which region or regions are the nearest one to the farthest setting region.

Shortest path problem [2-3] is the classical one in graph theory. The problem is divided into 2 types. They are single source shortest path problem and shortest path problem between all vertexes. Single source shortest path problem is the basis. Solutions to the problem are dynamic programming, heuristic algorithm A* algorithm, Dijkstra algorithm and etc. There are some research work on serial and some on parallel algorithm [4-5]. And Dijkstra is the most classical one among them.

H. Deng et al. (Eds.): AICI 2011, Part I, LNAI 7002, pp. 212–218, 2011.

2 Dijkstra Algorithm and Improvement

2.1 Dijkstra Algorithm

Establish directed graph G=(V,E).
V is the set of vertexes.
E is the set of edges.

Each edge has a non-negative value, that is, each edge<u, v>∈E and w(u, v)≥0. Support s is the source vertex and D[i] is the shortest path length from vertex s to vertex i.

The shortest path d_j, (i∈{V-s}) from the chosen source vertex s to the other vertexes(V-s) will be calculated according to the shortest path length in descending order.

The algorithm [6] is as followings:

- Directed Graph G(V,E).

V is divided into 2 sets: S and T. S is the set of vertexes to which the shortest path has be calculated from the source; T is the set of vertexes to which the shortest path is still unknown, which means the shortest path has not be calculated. So T=V-S.

At the beginning, S={s}, T=V-{s}; w[i][j] stands for the value from vertex i to vertex j.

$$D[i] = \begin{cases} w(s,i), <s,i>\in E \\ \infty, <s,i> \notin E \end{cases}$$

- Choose V_j ∈ {V-s} to meet the condition : D[j]=Min{D[i] }, V_j is the destination of the shortest path from V_s. And then update S=S ∪ {V_j};
- Modify the shortest path length from V_s to V_k∈{V- V_s }.
  The method is:

      IF (D[j]+Edges[j][k]<D[k]) THEN
          D[k]=D[j]+Edges[j][k]
      ELSE
            D[k]=D[k]
  Edges[j][k] is the weight value from V_j to V_k;

- If S=V, the shortest paths from the source Vs to the other vertexes are totally calculated, the algorithm is completed. If S≠V, go to step 2.

2.2 Improvement of Dijkstra Algorithm

Dijkstra algorithm mainly aims at calculating the shortest path from one point to the others. Each setting region is chosen as source to calculate the shortest paths to the other regions. Dijkstra algorithm is improved to solve the problem to confirm the core setting region.

The details of the improved algorithm are as followings:

- Support a directed graphic G (V, E), V is the set of setting regions, n stands for the number of setting regions, E is the set of edges among regions. Each edged could be with weight value, which stands for the distance between 2 regions or crowdedness or something else;

- Choose each region in G (V, E) as source in turn and then calculate the shortest path length Dsi from the source s (s ∈ V) to the other regions j (i ∈ V and i≠s) with the improved algorithm. n-1 shortest path could be got and they are combined to form a row in a table. The n-1 values stand for the shortest path length from s to the other regions. The shortest path length from source to itself is 0. All regions in G are selected as source and n rows of the shortest path could be calculated;

  Compare and find the max value of column in every row of the table created in step 2 and a new column Ds (s∈V) is added to the table. The value in column Ds is known as the shortest path length from source to the farthest setting region. Sum up the shortest path values in every row and another new column $T_S = \sum_{i=1}^{n} Dsi$ (i∈V and i≠s) is added in the table; the value in the columns stands for the total of the shortest path length from source s to the other regions;

- Compare and find the minimum value Dij in column Ds.

  During the procedure to find minimum value, some sorting algorithm could be applied, such as heap sort algorithm. With the help of sort algorithm, efficiency of improved algorithm could be improved.

  The value in column Ds means it takes the minimum time to get the farthest setting region j from source i. If there are more than 1 same values in Column Ds, choose the minimum value from column Ts. The value stands for that it takes the minimum time to get the farthest region and the other region from the source. Thus, region i is chosen as the core setting region. It could facilitate rescue allocation, efficiency and communication.

According to the confirmed core setting region s and the shortest paths Dsi to the other setting regions, the second, the third and other core setting region could be made certain. The confirmation of core setting regions could be give a outline to the construction of the regions and is helpful in disaster decision support system.

3 Case Study

To illustrate the improved Dijkstra algorithm, a case is given below.

In Fig.1, 5 setting regions are selected after analysis according to some conditions. Some roads exist among the 5 regions. Directed graphic G (V, E) is abstracted from the actual situation. The 5 regions are abstracted 5 vertexes, which are P, Q, R, S and T. The vertex set is V. Roads between 2 setting regions are abstracted edges in graphic G. The road could be one way or two and the limitation could be canceled or added in emergency. 2 directed edges are drawn in graphic if two ways are allowed between 2 regions. The weight value on the directed edge may stand for distance, crowdedness, fee etc. The 2 weight values on the directed roads between 2 setting regions could be different because of direction and crowdedness, e.g. The two directed edges have 2 different weight values between P and Q.

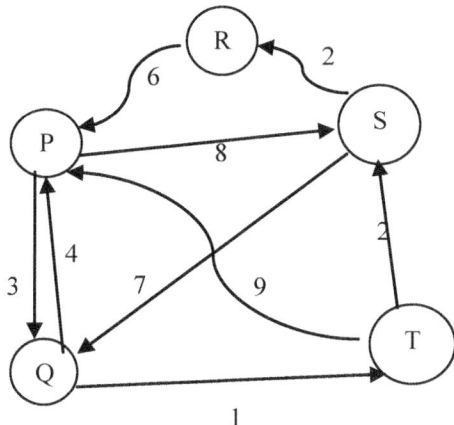

Fig. 1. Directed Graphic G (V, E)

Analyze and calculate with the improved Dijkstra algorithm as followings:
Calculate the shortest paths and their length from every vertex as source region to the other ones with the original Dijkstra algorithm, 5 Tables will be achieved.

Table 1. Shortest Path from P to the other regions

Destination	Shortest Path	Length of Shortest Path
Q	P->Q	3
R	P->Q->T->S->R	8
S	P->Q->T->S	6
T	P->Q->T	4

Table 2. Shortest Path from Q to the other regions

Destination	Shortest Path	Length of Shortest Path
P	Q->P	4
R	Q->T->S->R	5
S	Q->T->S	3
T	Q->T	1

Table 3. Shortest Path from R to the other regions

Destination	Shortest Path	Length of Shortest Path
P	R->P	6
Q	R->P->Q	9
S	R->P->S	14
T	R->P->Q->T->S	12

Table 4. Shortest Path from S to the other regions

Destination	Shortest Path	Length of Shortest Path
P	S->R->P	8
Q	S->Q	7
R	S->R	2
T	S->Q->T	8

Table 5. Shortest Path from T to the other regions

Destination	Shortest Path	Length of Shortest Path
P	T>P	9
Q	T->S->Q	10
R	T->S->R	4
S	T->S	2

- Gather shortest paths of each setting region to the others, the max value in the shortest paths and the total of the shortest paths from source to the other setting regions and Table 6 is formed, which is shown as followings.

Table 6. Shortest Path from each region to the others

Destination / Source	P	Q	R	S	T	Ds	Ts
P	0	3	8	6	4	8	21
Q	4	0	5	3	1	5	13
R	6	9	0	14	12	14	41
S	8	7	2	0	8	8	25
T	9	10	4	2	0	10	25

- Analyze Table 6.
  The shortest path length from P to the farthest setting region is 8.
  The shortest path length from Q to the farthest setting region is 5.
  The shortest path length from R to the farthest setting region is 14.
  The shortest path length from S to the farthest setting region is 8.
  The shortest path length from T to the farthest setting region is 10.
From the above, it takes the minimum time to get the farthest region from setting region Q. Region Q is chosen as the core setting region. Rescue resource, medical

treatment rescue personnel and equipment etc. could be sent to the farthest region as soon as possible among the regions when emergent disaster happens.

If there are 2 or more same minimum values of shortest path length, which is in Column Ds of Table 6, the extra step is to choose the minimum value of Column Ts and then the core setting region is confirmed.

According to the shortest paths from the confirmed core setting region to the others, the second core region could be made certain after the core region is confirmed.

In table 6 the second max value in column Ds is 8 and two cells have the value. According to the improved algorithm, compare the value in Column Ts of the two rows and choose the smaller value in Ts. So setting region P is confirmed as the second core setting region.

In addition, other core regions could be confirmed by the calculated shortest path. In the case, when region Q is selected as core setting region:

The shortest path to region P is Q->P;

The shortest path to R is Q->T->S->R;

The shortest path to S is Q->T->S;

The shortest path to T is Q->T;

Region T is covered the most times in the paths and then region T is selected as the second setting region. Region S is selected as the third core region; Region R and Q are selected as the fourth and the fifth one.

4   Simulation

Improved Dijkstra algorithm is programmed and run in Matlab.

The input of the program is the setting regions and the weight values among the regions. The output is the core setting region in turn and the shortest path.

In Fig. 2, the outstanding Q is the confirmed core setting region and the outstanding edges are the shortest paths to the other regions from the core region. The result shows the improved algorithm could solve the problem how to confirm the core setting region in disaster decision support system.

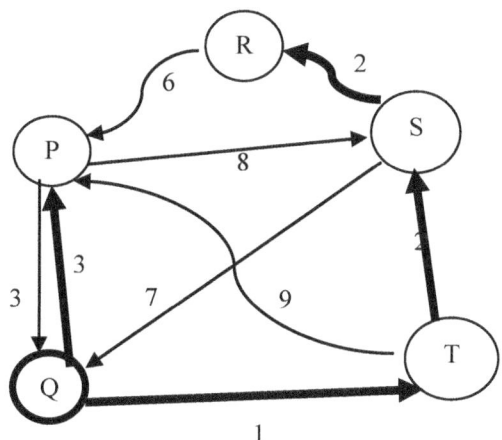

Fig. 2. Simulation of the Improved Algorithm

5 Conclusion

Dijkstra algorithm of the shortest path search problem is been improved. A practical solution is provided for confirming and building core setting region in disaster decision support system.

Confirmation of core setting region could facilitate resources allocation and setting region construction in disaster rescue and decision support system. It is practical to disaster rescue. How to value the weight of edges among setting regions and how to improve efficiency in large scale is the next research field.

Acknowledgment. This work was supported by "Demonstrating application of Bohai sea environment information integration and dynamic management technology". The project ID is 200905030.

References

1. Huang, D.-m., Fang, Q.: Application of Improved Dijkstra Algorithm in Storm Surge System. Computer Engineering (October 2010)
2. Cherkassky, B.V., Goldberg, A.V., Radzik, T.: Shortest paths algorithms: Theory and experimental evaluation. Mathematical Programming 73(2) (1996)
3. Li, X.-f., Zhang, H.-l., Liu, Z.-j., Wang, R.-b.: Problem for shortest path problem based on heuristic algorithm. Journal of Jilin University (Engineering and Technology Edition) (January 2011)
4. Lu, Z., Shi, J.: Design and implementation of parallel shortest path search algorithm. Computer Engineering and Applications (March 2010)
5. Hribar, M.R., Taylor, V.E.: Temination detection for parallel shortst path algorithms. Technical Report CSE-97-004 Computer Science-Engineering, EECS Department. Northwestern University, Chicago (1997)
6. Dijkstra, E.W.: A note on two problems in connexion with graphs. Numerische Mathematik 1(1) (1959)

Opposition-Based Learning Estimation of Distribution Algorithm with Gaussian Copulas and Its Application to Placement of RFID Readers

Ying Gao, Xiao Hu, Huiliang Liu, Fufang Li, and Lingxi Peng

Department of Computer Science and Technology,
Guangzhou University, Guangzhou, 510006, P.R. of China
falcongao@sina.com.cn

Abstract. Estimation of distribution algorithms are a class of optimization algorithms based on probability distribution model. In this paper, we propose an improved estimation of distribution algorithm using opposition-based learning and Gaussian copulas. The improved algorithm employs multivariate Gaussian copulas to construct probability distribution model and uses opposition-based learning for population initialization and new population generation. By estimating Kendall's tau and using the relationship of Kendall's tau and correlation matrix, Gaussian copula parameters are firstly estimated, thus, joint distribution is estimated. Afterwards, the Monte Carte simulation is used to generate new individuals. Then, the opposite numbers have also been utilized to improve the convergence performances. The improved algorithm is applied to some benchmark functions and optimal placement of readers in RFID networks. The relative experimental results show that the improved algorithm has better performance than original version of estimation of distribution algorithm and is effective in the optimal placement of readers in RFID networks.

Keywords: Estimation of distribution algorithm, Opposition-based learning, Gaussian copulas, RFID networks.

1   Introduction

Optimization problems are widely encountered in various fields of science and technology. In recent years, there has been an increasing interest in evolutionary algorithm using probabilistic models, i.e., estimation of distribution algorithms[1] (EDA). Instead of using conventional crossover and mutation operations, EDAs use probabilistic models to sample the genetic information in the next population. The performance of an EDA highly depends on how well it estimates and samples the probability distribution. According to the type of interaction between variables in individuals that is allowed in the model of the probability distribution, EDAs are classified as univariate, bivariate or multivariate. The univariate EDAs do not consider any interactions among variables in the solution. The univariate EDAs are computationally inexpensive, and perform well on problems with no significant interaction among variables. However, these algorithms tend to fail on the problems, where higher order interactions among variables exist. The bivariate EDAs consider

H. Deng et al. (Eds.): AICI 2011, Part I, LNAI 7002, pp. 219–227, 2011.

pair-wise interactions among variables in the solution. This class of algorithms performs better in problems, where pair-wise interaction among variable exists. However, it fails in problems with multiple variable interactions.

The multivariate EDAs consider interaction between variables of order more than two. The model of probability distribution obviously becomes more complex than the one used by univariate and bivariate EDAs. The complexity of constructing such model increases exponentially to the order of interaction making it infeasible to search through all possible models. Many multivariate EDAs use probabilistic graphical modelling techniques for this purpose. In particular, directed graphical models (Bayesian networks)[2] and undirected graphical model (Markov Random Field)[3] have been widely studied and are established as a useful approach to estimate and sample the distribution in multivariate EDAs. In recent, copulas is also used in multivariate EDAs[4]. Copulas encompass the entire dependence structure of multivariate distributions, and not only the corrections. Together with the marginal distribution of the vector elements, they define a multivariate distribution which can be used to generate random vectors with this distribution.

Radio Frequency Identification (RFID) systems have become very popular in recent years. The goal of RFID systems is to establish a wireless network. How to reasonable implement this network is a difficult issue in current RFID application system[5-6]. Since the radio range of the readers is limited to a few meters, typically many readers are required to monitor these items (possibly huge). Hence, for a cost effective implementation of the system, an important issue is to find out the minimal number of readers (along with their positions) that are sufficient enough to cover all the items. The placement of the RFID readers in a RFID network and to find minimal number of readers to cover the entire region is a NP hard problem. Hence suitable optimization algorithm may be applied to solve this problem, which can result in first convergence with minimum resource requirement.

This paper introduces an improved EDA using opposition-based learning and Gaussian copulas. The proposed algorithm employs multivariate Gaussian copulas to construct probability distribution model and uses opposition-based learning for population initialization and new population generation. By estimating Kendall's tau and using the relationship of Kendall's tau and correlation matrix, Gaussian copula parameters are firstly estimated, thus, joint distribution is estimated. Afterwards, the Monte Carte simulation is used to generate new individuals. Then, the opposite numbers have been utilized to improve the convergence performances. The proposed algorithm is applied to some benchmark functions and optimal placement of readers in RFID network. The relative experimental results show that the algorithm has better performance than original version of EDA and is effective in the optimal placement of readers in RFID networks.

2   Gaussian Copula

A copula[7] is a distribution function with known marginals. Any continuous Multivariate joint distribution of n random variables x_1, x_2,..., x_n

$F(x_1,x_2,...,x_n)=\text{Prob}\{X_1 \leq x_1, X_2 \leq x_2,...,X_n \leq x_n\}$, can be represented by a copula C as a function of the marginal distribution $F_{X_i}(x_i)=\text{Prob}\{X_i \leq x_i\}, i=1,2,\cdots,n$;   i.e.

$$F(x_1, x_2, ..., x_n) = C(F_1(x_1), F_2(x_2), ..., F_n(x_n)) \overset{\Delta}{=} C(u_1, u_2, ..., u_n) \tag{1}$$

Where $u_i = F_{X_i}(x_i), i = 1, 2, \cdots, n$ and $C(u_1, u_2, ..., u_n)$ is the associated copula function. Furthermore, application of the chain rule shows that the corresponding density function $f(x_1, x_2, ..., x_n)$ can be decomposed as

$$f(x_1, x_2, ..., x_n) = \frac{\partial^n C(u_1, u_2, ..., u_n)}{\partial u_1 \partial u_2 ... \partial u_n} \overset{\Delta}{=} c(u_1, u_2, ..., u_n) \cdot f_1(x_1) \cdot f_2(x_2) \cdot ... \cdot f_n(x_n) \tag{2}$$

From the above it may be seen that the joint density function is the product of the marginals $f_i(x_i), i = 1, 2, \cdots, n$ and copula densities function $c(u_1, u_2, ..., u_n)$.

Let $\mathbf{R} = (r_{i,j}), i = 1, 2, \cdots, n, j = 1, 2, \cdots, n$ be a symmetric, positive definite matrix with unit diagonal entries. The *multivariate Gaussian copula* is defined as

$$C(u_1, u_2, ..., u_n; \mathbf{R}) = \Phi_{\mathbf{R}}(\varphi^{-1}(u_1), \varphi^{-1}(u_2), \cdots, \varphi^{-1}(u_n)) \tag{3}$$

Where $\Phi_{\mathbf{R}}$ denotes the standardized multivariate normal distribution with correlation matrix $\mathbf{R} = (r_{i,j}), i = 1, 2, \cdots, n, j = 1, 2, \cdots, n$. $\varphi^{-1}(x)$ denotes the inverse of the univariate standard normal distribution $\varphi(x)$.

The corresponding density is

$$c(u_1, u_2, ..., u_n; \mathbf{R}) = \frac{1}{|\mathbf{R}|^{1/2}} \exp\left(-\frac{1}{2}\omega^T(\mathbf{R}^{-1} - \mathbf{I})\omega\right) \tag{4}$$

with $\omega = (\varphi^{-1}(u_1), \varphi^{-1}(u_2), \cdots, \varphi^{-1}(u_n))^T$

A simple method [8] based on Kendall's tau for estimating the correlation matrix $\mathbf{R}$. The method consists of constructing an empirical estimate of Kendall's tau for each bivariate margin of the copula and then using relationship (5)

$$\tau(\mathbf{X}_k, \mathbf{X}_m) = \frac{2}{\pi} \arcsin(r_{k,m}) \tag{5}$$

To infer an estimate of the relevant element of $\mathbf{R}$. More specifically we estimate $\tau(\mathbf{X}_k, \mathbf{X}_m)$ by calculating the standard sample c coefficient

$$\hat{\tau}(\mathbf{X}_k, \mathbf{X}_m) = \frac{2}{n(n-1)} \sum_{1 \leq i < j \leq n} sign\left[(X_{i,k} - X_{j,k})(X_{i,m} - X_{j,m})\right] \tag{6}$$

From the original data vectors $\mathbf{X}_1, \mathbf{X}_2, ..., \mathbf{X}_N$, and write the jth component of the ith vector as $X_{i,j}$; this yields an unbiased and consistent. An estimator of $r_{k,m}$ is then given by $\hat{r}_{k,m} = \sin(\frac{\pi}{2}\hat{\tau}(\mathbf{X}_k, \mathbf{X}_m))$. In order to obtain an estimator of the entire matrix $\mathbf{R}$ we can collect all pairwise estimates $\hat{r}_{k,m}$ and then construct the estimator

$$\hat{\mathbf{R}} = \left(\sin(\frac{\pi}{2} \hat{\tau}(\mathbf{X}_k, \mathbf{X}_m)) \right), k = 1, \cdots N, m = 1, \cdots, N \tag{7}$$

A multivariate random numbers $\mathbf{X} = (X_1, X_2, \ldots, X_n)$ with distribution function $F_{\mathbf{X}}$ defined by assigning marginals $F_{X_1}, F_{X_2}, \cdots, F_{X_n}$ and a Gaussian copula function $\Phi_{\mathbf{R}}$ can be generated as follows [8].

Algorithm 1.

(1) Find the Cholesky decomposition of $\mathbf{R}$, so that $\mathbf{A}\mathbf{A}^T = \mathbf{R}$, with $\mathbf{A}$ lower triangular;

(2) Generate a sample of n independent random variables $(Z_1, Z_2, \ldots Z_n)$ from $N(0, 1)$;

(3) Set $\mathbf{Y} = \mathbf{A}\mathbf{Z}$ with $\mathbf{Z} = (Z_1, Z_2, \ldots, Z_n)^T$ and $\mathbf{Y} = (Y_1, Y_2, \ldots, Y_n)^T$;

(4) Return $\mathbf{X} = (X_1, X_2, \ldots, X_n) = (F_1^{-1}(\varphi(Y_1)), F_2^{-1}(\varphi(Y_2)), \ldots, F_n^{-1}(\varphi(Y_n)))$.

3   Opposition-Based Learning

The scheme of opposition-based learning was first introduced by H.R. Tizhoosh[9-10]. The opposition-based learning is general enough and can be utilized in a wide range of learning and optimization fields to make algorithms faster. Opposite numbers are defined as follows:

Let $\mathbf{x} = (x_1, x_2, \ldots, x_n)$ be an n-dimensional vector, where $x_i \in [a_i, b_i], i = 1, 2, \ldots, n$. The opposite vector of $\mathbf{x} = (x_1, x_2, \ldots, x_n)$ is defined by $\mathbf{x}' = (x_1', x_2', \ldots, x_n')$ where $x_i' = a_i + b_i - x_i$.

Assume $f(\mathbf{x})$ is a fitness function which is used to measure candidate's optimality. According to the opposite point definition, $\mathbf{x}' = (x_1', x_2', \ldots, x_n')$ is the opposite of $\mathbf{x} = (x_1, x_2, \ldots, x_n)$. Now, if $f(\mathbf{x}') \geq f(\mathbf{x})$, then point $\mathbf{x}$ can be replaced with $\mathbf{x}'$; otherwise we continue with $\mathbf{x}$. Hence, the point and its opposite point are evaluated simultaneously to continue with the fitter one [9-10].

4   An Estimation of Distribution Algorithm Using Opposition-Based Learning and Gaussian copulas

EDAs differ from traditional evolutionary algorithms. Instead of applying genetic operators, EDAs estimate a probability distribution over the search space based on how the parent individuals are distributed in the search space, and then sample the offspring individuals from this distribution. Let $P(t)$ be the population of solutions at generation t. A pseudocode for EDAs is shown as follows:

1) $t \leftarrow 0$, generate the initial population P(t) with M individuals at random;
2) Select a collection of N solutions S (t), with $N < M$, from P (t);
3) Estimate a probabilistic distribution from S (t);
4) Generate the new population by sampling from the distribution of S (t);
5) $t \leftarrow t+1$,if stopping criterion is not reached go to step 2);

We incorporate the opposition-based learning mechanism into EDAs in order to improve the convergence performances of EDAs. The opposite numbers are used in population initialization and also for generating new populations during the evolutionary process. Copulas have attracted significant attention in the recent literature for modeling multivariate observations. An important feature of copulas is that they enable us to specify the univariate marginal distributions and their joint behavior separately. Therefore, copulas can be used in multivariate EDAs. The implementation of EDAs using multivariate Gaussian copula is described as follows:

Step1 Initialize a population Q(0) randomly and calculate opposite population $Q'(0)$ by the opposite vector;

Step2 $t \leftarrow 0$, Select M the fittest individuals from the initial population Q(0) and the opposite population $Q'(0)$ as the initial population P(0);

Step3 Select a collection of N solutions S (t), with $N < M$, from P(t), and estimate marginals distribution $\hat{F}_{X_1}, \hat{F}_{X_2}, \cdots, \hat{F}_{X_n}$ from S (t);

Step4 Estimate the parameters $\hat{R}$ by using (6) and (7);

Step5 Generate new individuals by using Algorithm 1 to form population Q(t);

Step6 Calculate opposite population $Q'(t)$ by the opposite vector;

Step7 Select M the fittest individuals from the set $Q(t) \cup Q'(t)$ as the next generation population P($t+1$);

Step8 If the given stopping condition is not met, goto Step3;.

5   Placement of Readers in RFID Network

The key components of an RFID system[5-6] are the tags and the RFID readers. The RFID readers communicate with the tags by reading/writing the information stored on them. The reader has a limit on its interrogation range, within which the tags can be read by the reader. The placement of readers in RFID network is modeled in the following way. Assume we have a X×Y room with obstacle(walls or large metal objects that can block signal) in it. A number of RFID tags are evenly distributed in the area that needs signal coverage. For a RFID reader i, its detection range $R_\square$ is a function proportional to its emitting power $P_\square$. That is $R_i = f(P_\square)$. We simplify the model by claiming that if the distance between a tag and a reader i is smaller than R_i and there is no obstacle between them, then the tag can receive the signal sent by the reader. If a tag can receive the signal sent by exactly one reader, we say that the tag is detected by the reader. However, if a tag can receive the signal sent by more than one reader, it usually cannot respond to either of the readers because of the nature of passive RFID tags. We say that the tag is interfered. For each of the readers to be deployed in a placement, we need to consider following parameters:

(x, y): The position of the reader in the room, where $x \in [0;X]$ and $y \in [0; Y]$.
P: The emitting power of the reader which directly affect the detection range R of the reader. Depends on the model of the reader, the emitting power could be adjusted but limited in a range.

Fitness Function: The fitness function is for measuring the goodness of a plan. Usually, the cost, the ratio of covered area and the ratio of the interfered area are the major factors need to be considered.

The cost function can be expressed as:

$$f_1 = C - \text{number} \times \text{unit\_price} \qquad (8)$$

Where C is the maximum cost or the budget. This function measures how much we can gain by deploying fewer readers.

The cover rate function and the interference rate function are:

$$f_2 = \frac{\# \text{DetectedTa\ gs}}{\# \text{TotalTags}} \qquad (9)$$

$$f_3 = \frac{\# \text{Interfered\ Tags}}{\# \text{TotalTags}} \qquad (10)$$

The fitness function of the placement of readers is a weighted sum of these factors:

$$f = w_1 f_1 + w_2 f_2 + w_3 f_3 \qquad (11)$$

Where w_1, w_2, w_3 are corresponding rate of the functions.

Encoding: A placement of readers needs to be encoded so that it can be used in the proposed algorithm. A placement of readers Z with n readers can be expressed as a vector $Z = (x_0 \dots x_n, y_0 \dots y_n, P_0 \dots P_n)$ where x_0, y_0 and P_0 are the x-coordinate,

y-coordinate, emitting power.

6   Results from Simulations

In order to test efficiency of the improved EDA using opposition-based learning and Gaussian copula (IEDA). The performance of the proposed algorithm is compared with that of the original EDA. The following some well-known benchmark functions have been used to test.

1) $f_1(\mathbf{x}) = \sum_{i=1}^{n} x_i^2$

2) $f_2(\mathbf{x}) = \sum_{i=1}^{n} (x_i^2 - 10\cos(2\pi x_i) + 10)$

3) $f_3(\mathbf{x}) = \frac{1}{4000} \sum_{i=1}^{n} x_i^2 - \prod_{i=1}^{n} \cos\left(\frac{x_i}{\sqrt{i}}\right) + 1$

4) $f_4(\mathbf{x}) = \sum_{i=1}^{n} \left(\sum_{j=1}^{i} x_j \right)^2$

5) $f_5(\mathbf{x}) = \sum_{i=1}^{n} |x_i| + \prod_{i=1}^{n} |x_i|$

6) $f_6(\mathbf{x}) = \dfrac{\sin^2 \sqrt{x_1^2 + x_2^2} - 0.5}{[1 + 0.001 (x_1^2 + x_2^2)]^2} + 0.5,$

7) $f_7(\mathbf{x}) = \max_{i=1}^{n} \{|x_i|\},$

8) $f_8(\mathbf{x}) = -20 \exp\left(-0.2 \sqrt{\dfrac{1}{30} \sum_{i=1}^{n} x_i^2} \right) - \exp\left(\dfrac{1}{30} \sum_{i=1}^{n} \cos(2\pi x_i) \right) + 20 + e,$

9) $f_9(\mathbf{x}) = \sum_{i=1}^{n-1} \left(100 \left(x_i - x_{i-1}^2 \right)^2 + \left(x_{i-1} - 1 \right)^2 \right),$

All test functions have a global minimum with a fitness value of 0. Population size N=50. All functions were implemented in 10 dimensions except for the two-dimensional f_6. The maximum number of iterations is set to 500 in each running. Tables 1 listed the mean fitness value and standard deviation of the best solutions averaged over 20 trails on $f_1 \sim f_9$ functions. According to Table1, IEDA outperforms the standard EDA for the benchmark functions. A simplified 25m×25m square working area with 60 tags is used for the simulation. 15 RFID readers, whose radiated power is adjustable in the range from 0 to 30 dBm, are considered to serve this area. An optimal placement of readers in the area is listed in Tables2.

Table 1. The best fitness values with the standard deviation for $f_1 \sim f_9$ function

	Algorithm	Dim	Average	Standard Deviation
f_1	EDA	10	2.4946e-9	7.8879e-9
	IEDA	10	1.6984e-39	5.1775e-39
f_2	EDA	10	27.2191	81.1401
	IEDA	10	23.2034	70.3898
f_3	EDA	10	0.0934	0.1520
	IEDA	10	0.0870	0.3907
f_4	EDA	10	39.0811	105.9316
	IEDA	10	9.7705e-12	3.4890e-11
f_5	EDA	10	1.2780e-16	4.0387e-16
	IEDA	10	1.3211e-17	3.2496e-17
f_6	EDA	2	0.0024	0.0078
	IEDA	2	6.4485e-4	0.0024
f_7	EDA	10	0.1334	0.3602
	IEDA	10	2.0757e-16	6.4604e-16
f_8	EDA	10	16.1978	53.1960
	IEDA	10	14.2594	38.6077
f_9	EDA	10	25.2022	96.8900
	IEDA	10	8.2975	25.1218

Table 2. An optimal placement of readers

Reader	x	y	Radiated Powers
1	2.5489	3.0304	21.3514
2	7.2371	3.7563	16.6279
3	10.2967	4.6238	23.1172
4	18.0451	3.9602	21.7136
5	2.2561	9.0510	24.3267
6	8.3967	11.8251	23.1827
7	17.2134	11.6923	20. 1287
8	3.8712	16. 2198	22. 4982
9	8.5346	15.6257	26.1281
10	16.8234	15.2781	18.6438
11	22.5639	3.8712	20.6724
12	5.78436	23.0005	19.7342
13	4.38645	22.6123	20.4326
14	21.9965	3.8721	21.7651
15	23.1132	3.0065	23.7612

7   Conclusions

We proposed an improved EDA using opposition-based learning and Gaussian copulas. The proposed algorithm employs opposition-based learning for population initialization and new population generation. The multivariate Gaussian copulas is used to construct probability distribution model. The algorithm is applied to some well-known benchmarks and optimal placement of readers in RFID Network. The results show that the algorithm has better performance than original version of estimation of distribution algorithm and is effective in the placement of readers in RFID networks.

References

1. Larranaga, P., Lozano, J.A.: Estimation of Distribution Algorithms: A New Tool for Evolutionary Computation. Kluwer Academic Publishers, Dordrecht (2002)
2. Pelikan, M.: Hierarchical Bayesian Optimization Algorithm: Toward a New Generation of Evolutionary Algorithms. Springer, New York (2005)
3. Shakya, S.: DEUM: A Framework for an Estimation of Distribution Algorithm based on Markov Random Fields. PhD thesis. The Robert Gordon University, Aberdeen, UK (April 2006)
4. Gao, Y.: Multivariate Estimation of Distribution Algorithm with Laplace Transform Archimedean Copula. In: IEEE International Conference on Information Engineering and Computer Science, vol. 1, pp. 273–277 (December 2009)
5. Yang, Y., Wu, Y., Xia, M., Qin, Z.: A RFID Network Planning Method Based on Genetic Algorithm. In: 2009 International Conference on Networks Security, Wireless Communications and Trusted Computing, pp. 534–537 (2009)

6. Chen, H., Zhu, Y.: RFID Networks Planning Using Evolutionary Algorithms and Swarm Intelligence. In: 4th International Conference on Wireless Communications, Networking and Mobile Computing, pp. 1–4 (October 2008)
7. Nelsen, R.B.: An Introduction to copula. Springer, New York (1998)
8. Luciano, U.C.E., Vecchiato, W.: Copula Methods in Finance. John Wiley & Sons Ltd., England (2004)
9. Tizhoosh, H.R.: Opposition-Based Reinforcement Learning, J. Adv. Comput. Intell. Inf. 10(3), 578–585 (2006)
10. Shokri, M., Tizhoosh, H.R., Kamel, M.: Opposition-based Q (l) algorithm. In: 2006 IEEE World Congress on Computational Intelligence, Vancouver, BC, Canada, pp. 646–653 (2006)

Memristive Multilevel Memory with Applications in Audio Signal Storage

Xiaofang Hu, Shukai Duan[*], and Lidan Wang

School of Electronics and Information Engineering,
Southwest University, Chongqing 400715, China
{yuefang,duansk,ldwang}@swu.edu.cn

Abstract. Memristor, a two-terminal device with dynamic conductance depending on the charge or the flux flowing it was predicted by Leon Chua about four decades ago and named the fourth fundamental circuit element. In 2008, Hewlett Packard (HP) laboratory announced they have found the missing memristor in nano-scale physical device. Since that memristor has garnered extensive interests among numerous researchers and proposed in many applications. In this paper, an implement scheme of a memristive multilevel memory with a single unit storing a bit multilevel information (several bits of binary data) is presented. A record/play system with the memristive multilevel memory is designed as an application in audio signal storage. Due to the multilevel memory ability and nano-scale size of the memristor, this design possesses simpler, smaller circuit structure, greater data density and nonvolatile. A series of computer simulations verify the effectiveness of the memristive memory and provide a new solution for audio signal storage and processing.

Keywords: Memristor, Multilevel memory, Record/Play system, Audio signal storage.

1 Introduction

In 1971, Leon Chua theoretically formulated and defined a simple electronic element based on the symmetry arguments of circuit theory, named it memristor [1]. Similar to resistor defined by voltage v and current i, capacitor defined by charge q and voltage v, and inductor defined by flux φ and current i, the memristor is defined by the flux φ and charge q. For about four decades, memristor had not draw much attention since the physical device did not emerged until the recent TiO_2-based nano-scale practical memristor was developed by the HP Labs in 2008[2,3]. Since the startling existence of the memristor in the sandwiched oxide film was reported as a discovery of the missing circuit element, it immediately garnered extensive interests among numerous researchers throughout the world. Due to the superior properties, memristors have prospective promising applications in nonvolatile memory [4], artificial neural networks [5], chaotic circuits [6], logic operation [7], and signal processing [8].

---

[*] Corresponding author.

H. Deng et al. (Eds.): AICI 2011, Part I, LNAI 7002, pp. 228–235, 2011.

Nano-scale memristor with memory capability, low energy (~1pJ/operation), fast switching (<10ns), high write endurance (10^{10}), multiple-state operation, stack-ability, scalability and CMOS compatibility, brings new hope for the further development of nonvolatile memory technology [9]. Vontobel et al. from HP labs proposed a nano-scale binary crossbar memory system with memristors as memory elements [4]. Sung Hyun et al. suggested building a high-density Boolean logic crossbar array based on a Si memristive system without using of active transistors [10]. Qiang fei et al. presented a memristor-CMOS hybrid integrated circuit for reconfigurable logic, demonstrating the compact integration of nano memristor with the CMOS circuit [11]. H. Kim et al. proposed a method that enables the memristor to be used as multilevel memory using a reference resistance array by forcing the memristor to stick at a set of predetermined fixed reference resistance values [12].

In this paper, we present a memristive multilevel memory with application in audio signal storage, which may provide theoretical and experimental evidences for the realization of memristive multilevel and analog memory and provide a new solution for audio signal processing.

2 HP Memristor Model and Characteristics Analysis

HP memristor model (Fig.1(a)) consists of two TiO_2 layers sandwiched between two platinum electrodes. Where, one TiO_2 layer missing some oxygen is called doped region TiO_{2-x} (x is about 0.05). The oxygen vacancies (called dopant) make this region inhabit metallic and conductive. The other layer is pure TiO_2 called undoped region. A positive voltage on the device repels the oxygen deficiencies (positive) in the metallic TiO_{2-x} layer, sending them into the undoped TiO_2 region below. That causes the boundary between the two regions to move, increasing the percentage of conducting TiO_{2-x} and thus the conductivity of the entire device. The more positive voltage is applied, the more conductive the device becomes [3]. Oppositely, a negative voltage decreases the conductivity of the device. Fig.1 (b) shows the simplified equivalent circuit illustrating the total resistance of the memristor (memristance) is the sum of the two TiO_2 layer's resistance. Fig.1(c) is the memristor circuit symbol.

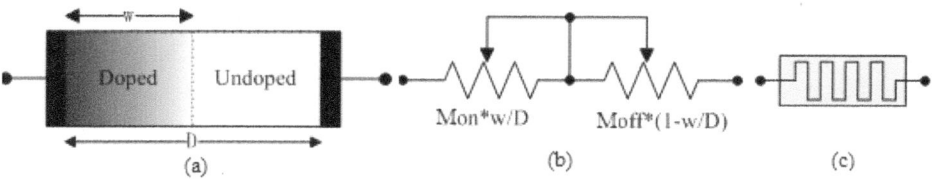

Fig. 1. HP memristor model. (a) Schematic of physical model; (b) equivalent circuit; (c) circuit symbol.

A typical mathematical model of the memristor can be described by [8],

$$M(t) = M_{on} x(t) + M_{off} (1 - x(t)),$$ (1)

where
$$x(t) = \frac{w(t)}{D} \in [0,1].$$
(2)

where $x(t)$ is called the internal state variable; D and $w(t)$ are the thickness of the TiO_2 layers and the doped region, respectively. M_{off} and M_{on} are the limit memristances for $x(t)=0$ and $x(t)=1$, respectively.

The memristor also obeys the Ohm'Law except that the memristance is variable.

$$v(t) = M(t)i(t).$$
(3)

The motion speed of the boundary between the doped and undoped regions is

$$\frac{dx}{dt} = \frac{\mu_v M_{ON}}{D^2} i(t) f(x),$$
(4)

where $\mu_v \approx 10^{-14} m^2 s^{-1} V^{-1}$ is average drift mobility. $f(x)$ is a window function (Biolek window function) to simulate the nonlinear dopant drift at boundaries.

$$f(x) = 1 - (x - \mathrm{sgn}(-i))^{2p},$$
(5)

where p is a positive integer called the control parameter and $sgn(.)$ is a sign function.

Characteristics of the memristor have been analyzed by simulations. The parameters of memristor model are set as: $M_{off}=38K\Omega$, $M_{on}=100\Omega$, $M_{int}=34210\Omega$, $D=10nm$, $p=10$. By applying a unbalance voltage $\pm v_0 \sin(\omega_0 t)^2$ with $v_0=1.5V$, $f_0=1.0Hz$ (Fig.2(a)), we can observe the symbolic pinched hysteresis loop (in Fig.2(b)) of memristor, in which for six segments of voltages, there are six loops

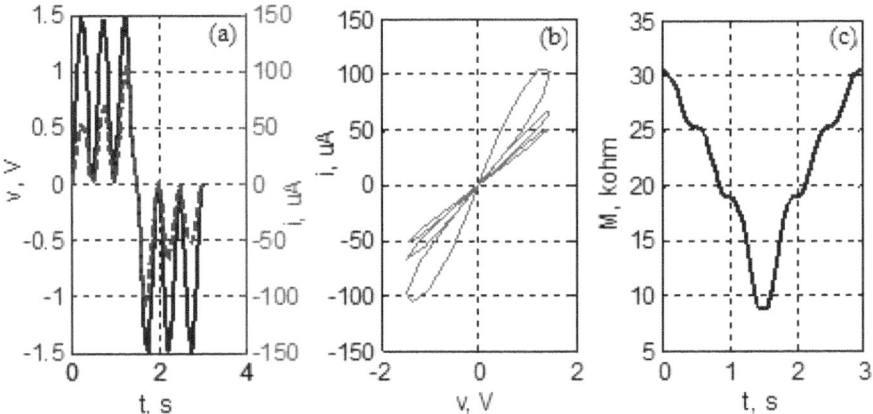

Fig. 2. For bias voltage $\pm v_0 \sin^2(w_0 t)$ (a) v-t plot (blue real) and i-t plot (red dashed); (b) i-v plot and (c) M-t plot

confined to the first and the third quadrants of the *i-v* plain corresponding to the positive and negative voltages, respectively. All of the loops pass through the origin, which implies the memory ability of memristor. When the bias is zero (means the power goes off), the current also comes to zero so the charge passing through the device does not change and the memristance remain the last state until a voltage is applied again. Oppositely, if the current is not zero, the memristance would change after the power cuts off then this device is not a memristor anymore. The first three *i-v* loops tend to expand with the time increasing in the first quadrant and the last three ones shrink in the third quadrant. That is because the change of the memristance is faster with a bigger current based on the equation (4) also with more obvious hysteresis, and vice versa. Fig.2(c) shows the memristance decreasing and increasing continuously with the input voltages changing.

3   Memristive Multilevel Memory and Audio Signal Storage

The combination of memristor and nano-wire crossbar interconnects technology absorbed great interests of researchers. A memristive crossbar array memory using for multilevel information storage contains a m×n crossbar array with cross points placed with memristors, column and row switch mux used for addressing the target memristor in the control of the address encoder output, voltage converter, read/write circuit, and read circuit.

When information is send to the voltage converter (including amplifiers and a fixed power source), if the write signal is active, the amplifier amplifies the input information to a voltage (greater than write-threshold) that is applied to the target memristor to put it in a required resistance state. If the read signal is active, a sub-threshold read voltage in the voltage converter is applied to the selected memristor. The current flowing through the memristor is read out by the read circuit which contains comparator and amplifier, where the comparator can compare the read current with some thresholds to get an output current corresponding to the multilevel information stored in the memristor. And then the current is converted to an appropriate voltage signal to output.

An audio record/play system with memristive multilevel memory is proposed and its diagram is shown in Fig.3. Analog audio signal is input to the system through amplifier, low pass filter, sample/hold circuit and quantize circuit as a general digital record/play system. The quantized signal is input to the voltage converter directly without coding and then stored in the memristive crossbar array in the control of the read/write control circuit and the address encoder as described above. It should be noted that based on the multilevel resistance states of memristor, a quantized signal (multilevel information) is stored in a single memory unit in the form of memristance instead of occupying 8 or16 binary memory units as in general digital system. when the audio signal is played, the read circuit reads out the current passing through the target unit, compares the current with thresholds and converts it to the corresponding voltage (quantized signal) also as explained in the last sub-section. Then the voltage signal is smoothed and filtered by low pass filter and amplified by op-amp recovering the input analog audio signal. The speaker change the audio signal to sound that can be hear.

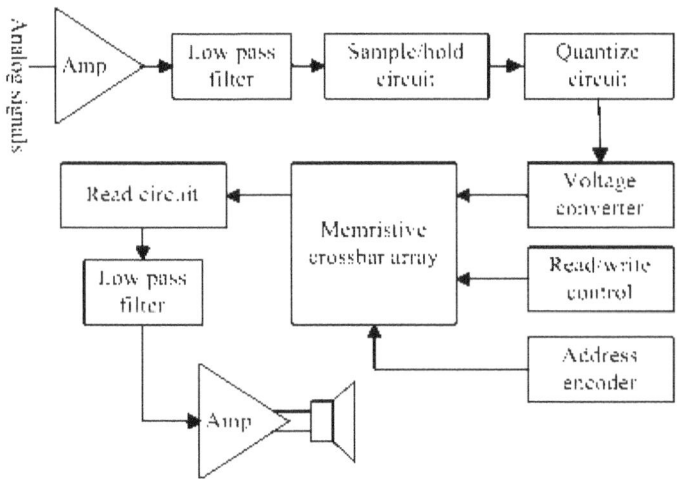

Fig. 3. Diagram of audio record/play system with memristive memory

By using of the variable resistance, nano-scale size and   memory ability of memristor, this system exhibits greater memory capacity and smaller, simper circuit saving the coding, encoding and D/A circuit in general digital audio record/play system. In the next section we will verify the effectiveness of the system by computer simulations.

4   Computer Simulations and Analysis

The audio record/play system with memristive memory has been simulated using software MATLAB in this section. The simulations aim to check if the audio signal is stored in the memristive memory in multilevel information correctly, and if the stored signal is recovered accurately.

As all known audio can be divided into regular and irregular audio according to the characteristics of sound wave. Where, regular audio is continuously varying analog signal that can be represented by a continuous curve called sound wave. Sound has three factors tone, intensity and timbre which depend on the three parameters frequency, amplitude and phase of a sound wave or sine wave. Here, we use an analog audio signal $X_{in} = \sin(\omega_1 t) + \sin(\omega_2 t) + \sin(\omega_3 t)$ for 0.1s, where f_1, f_2 and f_3 are 20Hz, 50Hz and 100Hz, respectively, shown in Fig.4 (a). Based on the Nyquest sampling laws, $f_s \geq 2f_{\max}$, where f_s is the sampling frequency and f_{max} is the largest frequency of an input analog signal, we set the sampling frequency in this experiment as 500Hz and there are 51 sample points in 0.1s shown in Fig.4(b). The number of the quantization level is set to 256 (2^8=256). The quantized signal is presented in Fig.4(c) in which the vertical axis is not in unit of volt (V) but represents the quantization level that used for selecting the writing voltages to put memristors in corresponding

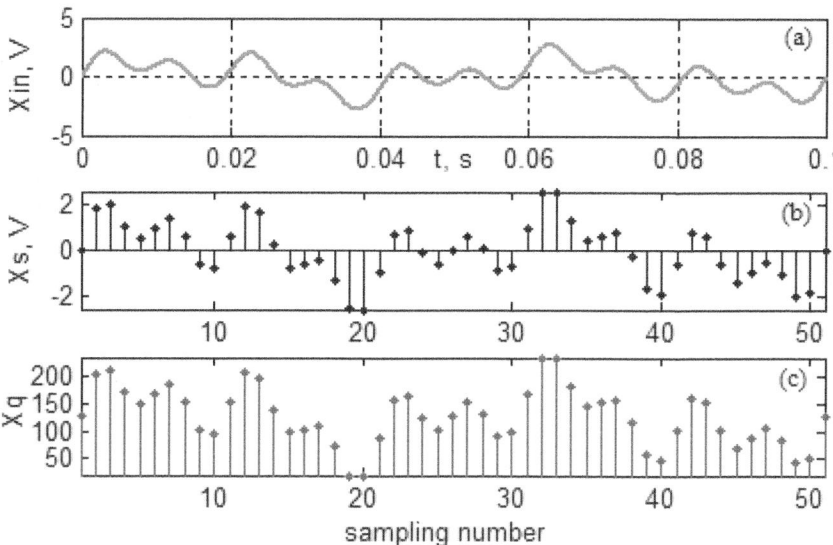

Fig. 4. An input audio signal. (a) Input audio signal; (b) sampled signal; (c) quantized signal levels.

resistance states.The memristance is also divided into 256 levels to store 256 kinds of multilevel information. The audio signal are stored in 51 memristive memory units. The writing and reading steps are given as follows:

Step1: Impose a 1V DC voltage (write voltage) on a memristor, realize 256 voltage pulses with different durations by controlling the running time and record these durations as write voltage standards for getting different memristances corresponding to 256 multilevel information values.

Step2: Suppose that the 256 different memristances are fixed resistors, a 0.1V read voltage is applied to these resistors respectively and get 256 different comparing currents (threshold currents) which are also corresponding to 256 multilevel information values.

Step3: Read in the 51 quantized signal values to the memristive crossbar array sequentially.

Step4: According to the quantized signal levels, apply the write voltage pulse (1V) with some certain duration set in step 1 to the memristor in the crossbar array and put it in the corresponding memristance state.

Step5: Apply a 0.1 V read voltage to the memristors and get the read currents. Since the read voltage is smaller than the write threshold voltage so it cannot change the stored memristance.

Step6: By comparing the read currents with the threshold currents got in step 2, the stored quantized signals are determined and read out.

Step7: Recover the input analog audio signal from the read signal through low pass filter, and the result is shown in Fig.5.

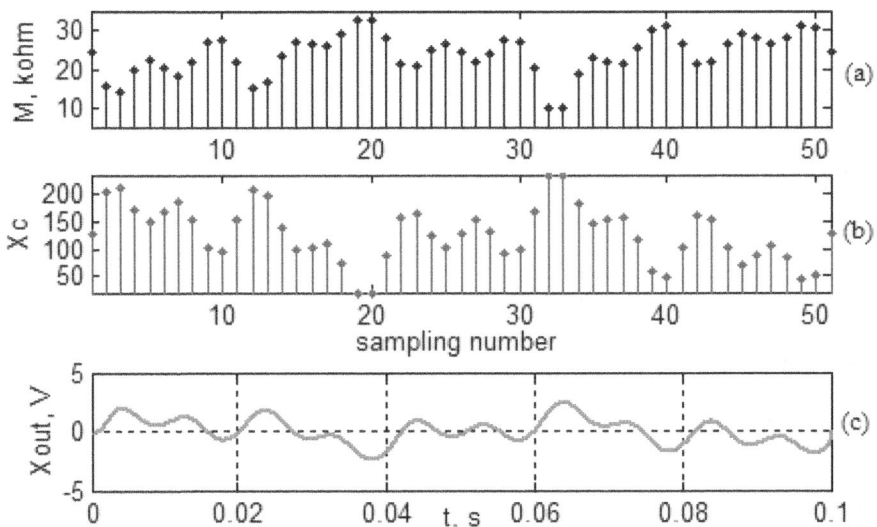

Fig. 5. Audio signal recovering. (a) The stored memristance corresponding to the quantized signal; (b) the recovered quantized signal; (c) the recovered audio analog signal.

Fig.5(a) shows the memristance stored in the memory units corresponding to the 51 quantized signal values. Appling a read voltage, we can get the read currents passing through the memory units. By comparing the read currents with the thresholds and converting them to the corresponding levels, the quantized signal can be recovered accurately presented in Fig.5(b), which verifies the effectiveness of the storage and recover of the memristive memory. Then, the quantized signal are converted into proper voltages and smoothed by low pass filter. The output is shown in Fig.5(c) indicating the input audio signal is recovered successfully.

5   Conclusions and Discussions

A memristive multilevel memory that uses nano-scale memristors as memory elements based on the crossbar array is proposed in this paper. The HP TiO$_2$-based memristor is reviewed and studied including the mathematical model and the simulations for the typical characteristics. A record/play system with memristive crossbar array memory is proposed. Different from the general digital record/play system, this design saves the coding, encoding and D/A circuit with simpler structure, smaller area and greater data density. Reported simulation results verify the effectiveness of the multilevel memory scheme and may bring new hope for the record/play system's further development.

Acknowledgments. The work was supported by the National Natural Science Foundation of China under Grant 60972155, the Natural Science Foundation of Chongqing under Grant CSTC2009BB2305, the Fundamental Research Funds for the Central Universities under Grant XDJK2010C023, the National Science Foundation for Post-doctoral Scientists of China under Grant CPSF20100470116, the Doctoral Foundation of the Southwest University under Grant SWUB2008074, the Teaching Reform Studying Foundation of Higher Education of Chongqing under Grant 09-2-011 and the Teaching Reform Studying Foundation (2009JY053 and 2010JY070).

References

1. Chua, L.O.: Memristor - the Missing Circuit Element. IEEE Trans. Circuit Theory 18, 507–519 (1971)
2. Strukov, D.B., Snider, G.S., Stewart, D.R., Williams, R.S.: The Missing Memristor Found. Nature 453, 80–83 (2008)
3. Williams, R.S.: How We Found the Missing Memristor. IEEE Spectrum 45, 507–519 (2008)
4. Vontobel, P.O., Robinett, W., et al.: Writing to and Reading from A Nano-scale Crossbar Memory Based on Memristors. Nanotechnology 20, 425204_1–425204_21 (2009)
5. Jo, S.H., Chang, T., Ebong, I., et al.: Nanoscale Memristor Device as Synapse in Neuromorphic Systems. Nano. Lett. 10, 1297–1301 (2010)
6. Muthuswamy, B.: Memristor Based Chaotic Circuits. IETE Technical Review 26, 417–429 (2009)
7. Borghetti, J., Snider, G.S., Kuekes, P.J., et al.: 'Memristive' Switches Enable 'Stateful' Logic Operations via Material Implication. Nature 464, 873–876 (2010)
8. Hu, X.F., Duan, S.K., Wang, L.D., Liao, X.F.: Memristive Crossbar Array with Applications in Image Processing. Sci. China Inf. Sci. 41, 500–512 (2011) (in Chinese)
9. Yang, J.J., Zhang, M.-X., Strachan, J.P., et al.: High Switching Endurance in TaOx Memristive Devices. Appl. Phys. Lett. 3, 232102_1–232102_3 (2010)
10. Jo, S.H., Kim, K.-H., Lu, W.: High-density Crossbar Arrays Based on a Si Memristive System. Nano. Lett. 9, 870–874 (2009)
11. Xia, Q., Robinett, W., Cumbie, M.W., et al.: Memristor -CMOS Hybrid Integrated Circuits for Reconfigurable Logic. Nano. Lett. 9, 3640–3645 (2009)
12. Kim, H., Sah, M.P., Yang, C., Chua, L.O.: Memristor-based Multilevel Memory. In: 12th International Workshop on Cellular Nanoscale Neworks and their Applications, Berkeley, CA, USA, pp. 1–6 (2010)

A Heuristic Test Data Generation Approach for Program Fault Localization

Saeed Parsa, Hamid Rafati PorShokooh, Saman Teymouri,
and Mojtaba Vahidi-Asl

Department of Software Engineering,
Iran University of Science and Technology, Tehran, Iran
{parsa,m_vahidi_asl}@iust.ac.ir,
{h_rafati,steymouri}@comp.iust.ac.ir

Abstract. The aim of this paper is to improve the reliability of programs by generating test cases considering different execution paths of the program. The method introduced in this paper assumes that only a single failing run is available for the program and applies a genetic algorithm which searches for the most similar failing and passing runs in terms of their executed predicates. By contrasting the similar passing and failing runs, the predicates that are different in two executions could be reported as fault relevant ones. We have also applied the *k-means* clustering technique to partition test cases according to their corresponding execution paths in order to ensure about the quality of software and locate the existing faults of the program. To evaluate the accuracy of the proposed method, we have conducted some case studies on a number of Siemens programs including different faulty versions. The results show the capability of the proposed method in generating a wide variety of test cases which could cover different program execution paths. The results also show the effectiveness of the approach in localizing faults according to detected fault relevant predicates.

Keywords: Software Testing, Fault Localization, Test Case Generation, Genetic Algorithm.

1   Introduction

The major goal of software companies is to produce reliable bug free products. To ensure the reliability and quality of software, a comprehensive testing process should be done before the deployment phase. Software testing is the process of examining software product in pre-defined ways to check whether the behavior is according to the expected behavior. Typically, one objective of software testing is designing minimal number of test cases such that they manifest as many faults as possible [15][16].

In this paper, we attempt to integrate the process of software testing with fault localization. Two well-known fault localization techniques are statistical debugging [2] and program slicing [3]. Statistical debugging techniques rely on a huge number of failing and passing test cases which are often collected from end users as error

H. Deng et al. (Eds.): AICI 2011, Part I, LNAI 7002, pp. 236–243, 2011.

reports. These reports are analyzed using statistical methods to construct statistical model of program behavior that is used to pinpoint the location of faults [1].However, for many applications we have no access to user reports (i.e., a collection of failing and passing test cases) and we only have got one failing test case. In these situations, program slicing techniques could be applied. Among different variations of program slicing techniques, backward dynamic slicing computes all executed statements having influence on a specific execution point [4]. However, dynamic slices could be large and hence considerable human effort might be needed to find the faulty code.

For many applications, we merely have a single failing run and we have two important concerns. Firstly, how we could generate test cases in order to ensure the reliability of the software. Secondly, how we could generate a passing test case for which the dynamic behavior of the program is the most similar with its behavior for the existing failing test case. By finding the most similar passing to the failing test case and contrast their corresponding dynamic behaviors, we could report the differences as the fault suspicious code that is responsible for the program failure [6]. This paper attempts to address the mentioned problems. Assuming that there is only one failing test case available, namely the starting test case, we slightly alter the existing test case by considering m-combinations of input parameters ($m=1..n$, n is the number of input parameters) to generate new test cases. To be more precisely, we first select a one parameter subset and change the corresponding values (i.e. $\binom{n}{1}$), then subsets of two parameters (i.e. $\binom{n}{2}$), until all the n elements are changed (i.e. $\binom{n}{n}$).During the process of test case generation, we may also find other failing test cases and hence the proposed approach could detect more than a single bug in the program. this process could be known as heuristic test data generation.

The proposed approach has two significant consequences: (1) Testing different paths of program (2) Program bug localization. The problem of generating the most similar passing to failing test cases in terms of their corresponding execution paths is known to be NP-complete [9] and there is no effective way to find the solution. Thus, we try to solve the problem by formulating it as a search problem and applying genetic algorithms to find the best solution.

The remaining part of this paper is organized as follows. In section two, related works in the context of test case generation is presented. Section three describes the proposed method in detail. The experimental results are shown in section four. Finally, conclusions and future works are mentioned in section five.

2   Related Work

Different approaches have been proposed for test case generation [18]. They could be roughly categorized to random, intelligent (i.e. heuristic), path based and goal based techniques. The random techniques generate a huge amount of test data in a blind manner. However, in these techniques the testing requirements are not considered in generating test data and a big proportion of data might be redundant and useless.

Intelligent techniques on the other side perform some analysis during generation of test data which makes the technique more expensive when a huge amount of analysis is required for specific applications. The path based techniques generate test cases which could traverse particular paths of a given program. In goal based techniques the aim is to generate inputs which could traverse paths among two specific points of the program [10].

Recently, different approaches for test case generation using genetic algorithms have been introduced [7][11]. Due to the complexity of software testing problems, genetic algorithms could be best applied to search for optimal (or near-optimal) solutions. The approach presented by Pargaset. al. [11] uses genetic algorithm to automate the process of goal based test data generation. Given particular goals like specific statements, branches, paths or definition-use pair in a program under test, it seeks for a test data which could cover the desired goals.

Girgiset. al. [12] has proposed a technique that uses GA guided by the data flow dependencies in the program to search for test data which fulfills data flow path selection criteria, namely the all-uses criterion. Singla's and Rai presented anautomatic test-data generation technique that uses a particle swarm optimization (PSO) to generate test data that satisfy data-flow coverage criteria[13].

The idea of comparing similar failing and passing runs to find the differences as the cause of failure was first purposed by [6]. However, the method assumes that a large number of failing and passing test cases are available and among these test cases it finds the most similar ones to contrast. Therefore, it does not attempt to minimize the difference between failing and passing runs. For some programs, the difference might be too large which confuses the programmer to locate the origin of failure. In contrast, our purposed method assumes that only single faulty path is available and tries to find a test case corresponding to the most similar passing one.

3   An Overview of the Method

The proposed method has three main stages: 1) Test case generation 2) clustering the execution traces 3) Narrowing down the passing and failing traces using genetic algorithm. Each main phase is described in detail in the following sub-sections.

3.1   Test Data Generation

Before describing the process of test case generation, we first define the failing and passing test cases.

Definition 1. Given program P and a set of test cases, Tc_P: each test case, tc_j consists of input parameters, I_j, and the corresponding desired output, O_j. After executing P on tc_j, $Exp_P(tc_j)$, the output result would be $\acute{O}_j$: $Exp_P(tc_j) = \acute{O}_j$. Test case tc_j is called failing test case, tc_j^{fail}, if: $\acute{O}_j \neq O_j$ and otherwise it is named passing test case, tc_j^{pass}. Therefore, the set of test cases in Tc_P is split into two disjoint categories: Tc_P^{Pass} for passing test cases and Tc_P^{fail} for failing test cases.

In this paper, we assume that there is only one failing test case which is considered as our initial point to generate other test cases. We name this significant test case, tc_{start}^{fail}.

To generate test cases, we first study the data structure of the available failure inducing input. Then we decompose tc_{start}^{fail} to its parameters. In next step, in each iteration of the proposed algorithm, a subset of input parameters, (i.e. m-combinations of the input) and their corresponding values are changed in order to generate new test cases. With this slight variation, we try not to deviate too much from the existing faulty path corresponding to tc_{start}^{fail}.

To record the execution path that is generated by running the program with a particular test data, it is required to insert some probes before specific points of the program. These specific points, namely predicates, could be the decision making statements (e.g. conditions, loops, function calls, etc.) where the execution path of the given program is determined.   The process is known as instrumentation.

Definition 2. Running the instrumented program P with test case tc_j generates an execution path, $Epath_P^j$, which is a sequence of executed predicates (i.e. predicates that are evaluated as TRUE). The execution vector is a binary vector $Evec_P^j = (X_1, X_2, \dots, X_n)$ in program execution pace, where X_i is the value of predicate x_i in that run (i.e. '1' if the predicate is evaluated as True and '0', otherwise).

In remaining parts of the paper when we talk about the distance between two execution paths A and B we actually address the difference in their corresponding execution vectors, $Evec_P^A$ and $Evec_P^B$. It is also important to label each execution vector as fail/pass according to the program termination status in that particular run.

3.2   Clustering the Execution Vectors

By mapping each particular run to an adequate vector, now we can use Euclidean distance to measure the similarity of executions in terms of their execution vectors. It is clear that execution vectors with more common features (i.e. executed predicates) may share the more execution sub-paths and vice versa.

Definition 3. Given program P, The similarity of two test cases tc_m and tc_n , $\Delta(tc_m, tc_n)$, is defined in terms of the Euclidean distance between their corresponding execution vectors, $Evec_P^m$ and $Evec_P^n$.

To identify different execution paths, we use the K-means clustering technique [14] on our failing and passing execution vectors. This strategy helps us to make our test data richer by considering the clusters (i.e. execution paths) in isolation.

Definition 4. Given a set of test cases for program $P(tc_1, tc_2, tc_3, \dots, tc_m)$, without regarding the fail/pass label of the test cases, where each test case is represented as n-dimensional vector, $Evec^i$, k-means clustering aims to partition the m test cases into k sets ($k \leq m$) CL = $\{cl_1, cl_2, \dots, cl_k\}$ according to the following within-cluster function which minimizes the sum of squared Euclidean distances:

$$\underset{CL}{arg\,min} \sum_{i=1}^{k} \sum_{tc_j \in cl_i} \|tc_j - c_i\|^2 \qquad (1)$$

Where c_i is the center of execution vectors in the cluster cl_i.

3.3   Applying a Genetic Algorithm to Generate Similar Paths

A typical Genetic algorithm starts with an initial population including a set of solutions so called individuals. Each individual, also known as a chromosome, is conventionally a string of bits associated with a fitness value that determines the probability of survival of an individual chromosome in the next generation [7][17]. In our application each chromosome is the string of input parameters. To evolve the initial population into a new generation there are four significant mechanisms: 1) initialization 2) selection 3) crossover and mutation 4) termination. Each mentioned stage is described in detail in the following sub-sections.

Initialization and Selection. The set of input test parameters corresponding to execution vectors in each cluster is considered as the initial population for the genetic algorithm. For each cluster, at first place, the corresponding population is explored to find the most proper failing test case. The adequacy is determined according to the distance of the corresponding execution failing vector with the corresponding passing vectors in the neighborhood. The corresponding test case is considered as the pattern of our genetic algorithm. The fitness function computes the Euclidean distance between the execution vector of the pattern and the execution vector of the generated test case.

Mutation and Cross over operations. To generate a new population of test cases, two major operators are used, cross over and mutation. The crossover operation involves two chromosomes (i.e. parents) exchanges substring information at random position in the string to produce two new strings (i.e. children). A predefined percentage of population is selected as parents in each iteration to form the new population. In this paper we have used one point cross over technique. To be more precise, the population individuals are sorted according to their corresponding fitness values. Then, for 30% of individuals from the bottom of the population (i.e. the solutions with the least fitness values) we have applied the cross over operation. The reason for choosing the test cases with large Euclidean distance from the candidate failing test case is to evolve the solutions as much as possible. At this point, the chosen test cases are paired to form parents and for each pair we do as follows. Assuming that each solution (i.e. parent) consists of n parameters, a number, namely i, is randomly selected in the range of $[0,n]$ and parameters from i to n are swapped in two given parents. The new children are evaluated by the fitness function and replaced by their corresponding parents.

To perform mutation, a predefined amount of the population (i.e. 20% in our application) is randomly selected. After that, in each selected individual an input parameter (i.e. gene) is chosen randomly and the corresponding value is replaced with some other value in the range of the parameter. The new individual is evaluated by the fitness function and being replaced by its parent if the corresponding fitness value is improved after the modification of the parameter.

Termination. The termination condition is if the successive iterations no longer produce better results. This is controlled by a time threshold in order to avoid the infinite loop problem. The final population contains test cases which are sorted according to the distance to the candidate test case. Therefore, the passing test case with the highest priority is our desired solution. Now, it is only required to contrast both paths to find the differences. The differences are predicates which could be suspicious for the failure of the program.

The genetic algorithm is applied on all clusters which specify different execution paths. With this strategy, we try not to miss the faults which appear in different paths of the program. Furthermore, it is possible that the genetic algorithm in one cluster could generate better results in comparison with other clusters.

4   Experimental Results

In this section we show the effectiveness of applying genetic algorithm on generating a passing test case which has the least distance with the starting failing test case. Fig. 2 shows the results of applying genetic algorithm to reduce the distance in the first version of Print-Tokens program. In the Figure, the trend of genetic algorithm in different clusters for reducing the distance between starting failing test case and the generated passing one in version 1 of the program is presented. Fig. 2 compares the genetic and the heuristic method (i.e. *m*-combination changes of the parameters to generate new test cases) in reducing the distance in version 3 of the same program. Fig. 3 shows that in some situations, the heuristic test case generation method has generated the passing test case with the least distance and therefore there is no need for applying the genetic algorithm. This shows that for some cases, the heuristic method is adequate by itself to find the cause of failure. The overall evaluation of the method on some versions of Tcas, schedule and Print-Tokens programs is presented in table 1.

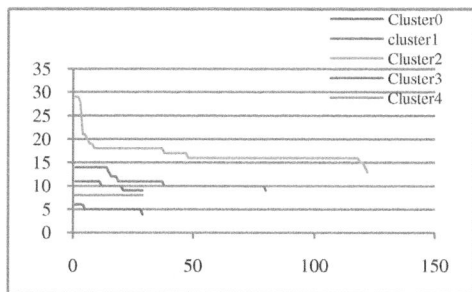
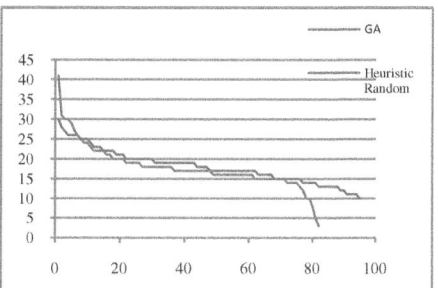

Fig. 1. The Trend of Genetic algorithm in reducing the distance between faulty and passing execution in different clusters in version 1 of Print-Tokens

Fig. 2. The comparison of Genetic and heuristic method in reducing the distance in version 3 of Print-Tokens

5   Concluding Remarks

In this paper, a new method has been introduced for testing and bug localization in programs. We start from one single failing run to generate new passing and failing test cases in a heuristic manner. Using a genetic algorithm, we try to generate passing test cases for which their corresponding execution vectors have the least difference with the available failing test case. The results show the capability of our proposed method in both generating test cases for testing different paths of a program and finding fault relevant predicates to locate the origin of failure. For many versions, the exact location of failure is included in the difference set of predicates resulted from comparing similar passing and failing runs. For other versions, by a little examination of code we could find the origin of failure according to the reported fault relevant predicates. By applying the genetic algorithm on different test cases without regarding its failing or passing state, we could considerably increase the path coverage of the test cases.

However, some issues should be considered for our future work. We may introduce a ranking model to prioritize predicates according to their fault relevance. We will attempt to evaluate the method on larger programs with more complex structure. We would like to evaluate the method in circumstances that instead of a failing test case, there is only single passing one. Improving the genetic algorithm by considering the probability distributions of the predicates may also be studied for our future work.

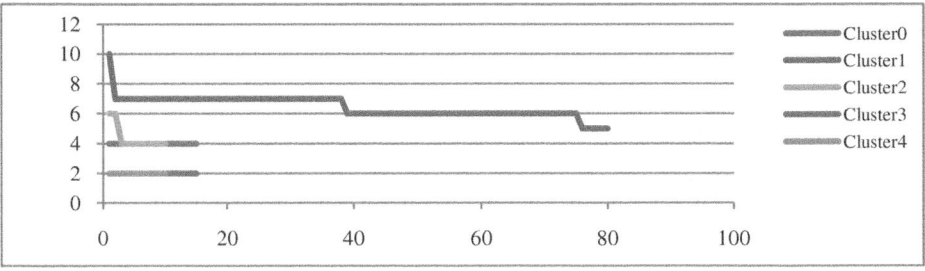

Fig. 3. The capability of the heuristic method in finding very similar passing and failing test cases without the need for applying the genetic algorithm

Table 1. The overall evaluation of the proposed method on some versions of tcas, schedule and Print-Tokens programs

program	Cluster	Optimum cluster	Best Initial distance	Final distance	Distance between failure origin And reported predicates (LOC)
Print-Tokens (V1)	5	0	6	4	0
Print-Tokens (V2)	5	3	12	10	1
Print-Tokens (V3)	5	3,4	2	2	0
Print-Tokens (V5)	5	0	1	1	0
Print-Tokens (V7)	6	3	7	2	0
Schedule (V1)	5	0	7	3	2
Schedule (V4)	2	0	4	2	2
Schedule (V8)	5	0	3	1	3
Tcas (V1)	2	1	3	2	0
Tcas (V3)	2	1	3	3	0
Tcas (v4)	2	0	3	3	0
Tcas (V5)	2	0	3	2	0
Tcas (V6)	2	1	2	2	0

References

1. Liu, C., Yan, X., Fei, L., Han, J., Midkiff, S.: SOBER: Statistical model-based bug localization. In: Proceedings of the 10th European Software Engineering Conference and 13th ACMSIGSOFT International Symposium on Foundations of Software Engineering, pp. 286–295. ACM Press, New York (2005)
2. Liblit, B., Aiken, A., Zheng, A.X., Jordan, M.I.: Bug isolation via remote program sampling. In: Proceedings of the ACM SIGPLAN Conference on Programming Language Design and Implementation, pp. 141–154. ACM Press, New York (2003)
3. Zhang, X., Gupta, R., Zhang, Y.: Precise dynamic slicing algorithms. In: IEEE/ACM International Conference on Software Engineering (ICSE), Portland, pp. 319–329 (2003)
4. Agrawal, H., De Millo, R., Spafford, E.: Debugging with dynamic slicing and backtracking. Software Practice and Experience (SP&E) 23(6), 589–616 (1993)
5. Zeller, A.: Why Programs Fail: A Guide to Systematic Debugging. Morgan Kaufmann, San Francisco (2006)
6. Renieris, M., Reiss, S.: Fault localization with nearest neighbor queries. In: Proceedings of the 18th IEEE International Conference on Automated Software Engineering, pp. 30–39 (2003)
7. Mantere, T., Alander, J.T.: Evolutionary software engineering, a review. Journal of Applied Soft Computing Archive 5(3), 315–331 (2005)
8. Software Infrastructure Repository, http://www.cse.unl.edu/_galileo/sir
9. Lei, Y., Tai, K.: In-parameter-order: a test generation strategy for pairwise testing. In: Proceedings of the Third IEEE International High-Assurance Systems Engineering Symposium, Washington DC, pp. 254–261 (1998)
10. Korel, B.: Automated software test data generation. IEEE Transactions on Software Engineering (1990)
11. Pargas, R.P., Harrold, M.J., Robert, R.P.: Test-data generation using genetic algorithms. In: Software Testing, Verification and Reliability (1999)
12. Girgis, M.R.: Automatic test data generation for dataflow testing using genetic algorithm. Journal of Universal Computer Science 11(6), 898–915 (2005)
13. Singla, S., Singla, P., Rai, H.M.: An Automatic Test Data Generation for Data Flow Coverage Using Soft Computing Approach. International Journal of Research and Reviews in Computer Science (IJRRCS) 2 (2011)
14. Tan, P., Steinbach, M., Kumar, V.: Introduction to data mining. Pearson, Addison Wesley (2006)
15. Desikan, S., Ramesh, G.: Software testing Principles & Practices. Pearson Education, London (2007)
16. Ammann, P., Offutt, J.: Introduction to software testing. Cambridge University Press, Cambridge (2008)
17. Sivanandam, S.N., Deepa, S.N.: Introduction to Genetic Algorithms. Springer, Heidelberg (2010)
18. Edvardsson, J.: A survey on automatic test data generation. In: Proceedings of the Second Conference on Computer Science and Engineering in Link, pp. 21–28 (1999)

Weak Economic Emergency Medical Devices Routing Optimization Based on Uniform Mutation Ant Colony Algorithm

Jin Zhang[1], Teng Fei[2], Ting Liu[2], Li-yi Zhang[2,*], and Xinyi Zhao[2]

[1] Office of Equipment, First Hospital of Shanxi University of Medicine, Taiyuan, China
[2] Information Engineering College, Tianjin University of Commerce, Tianjin, China
Zhangjin_taiyuan@126.com,
{zhangliyi,liuting,feiteng}@tjcu.edu.cn

Abstract. According to the principle of the weak economy, mathematical model of emergency logistics routing optimization has been established in this paper, and the model is solved by the uniform mutation ant colony algorithm, simulation shows that the optimal results of uniform mutation ant colony algorithm are better than ant colony algorithm. At the same time, compared with the mathematical model of the smallest time, mathematical model of emergency logistics routing optimization reduce the distribution costs on the basis of time requirements which should be satisfied.

Keywords: emergency logistic, weak economy, routing optimization, uniform mutation, ant colony algorithm.

1 Introduction

Emergency medical devices logistics distribution means space leap that medical equipment is from supplied principal to requirements principal, its research is how to schedule transportation reasonably in the sudden public incidents, in order to achieve balance between time and transportation costs, that makes medical devices required by affected point can be transported as soon as possible to the affected point. Therefore, the main goal of emergency logistics is to pursue maximize time efficiency and minimize disaster losses, it has obvious weak economy. Of course, the weak economy can not show that the emergency logistics should not consider the cost, or it will inevitably lead enormous waste and loss. Such as, sudden public emergency events like swin flu occurred in 2009, emergency medical devices distribution has strong preventive characteristics, requirement on time is not so urgent like the earthquake emergency logistics. This requires balanced economic on the premise of timeliness goals which should be ensured, through co-ordination arrangements, with the purpose to implement Minimal transportation costs and the shortest transit time by overall arrangement of resources, mode of the most economical transport, selecting transport routes. Waste can be maximally reduced, emergency logistics aim at lowest cost and maximum efficiency is brought to completion.

H. Deng et al. (Eds.): AICI 2011, Part I, LNAI 7002, pp. 244–250, 2011.

2   Model of Weak Economic Emergency Logistic Routing

Based on analysis we can see above, under the weak economy, the mathematical model of emergency logistics is to minimize transportation costs based on time requirements. To simplify operation, easy to model, make the following assumptions:

(1) Each affected point corresponding to the medical devices reserve center and demand for each affected point are known.

(2) Transport distance of the medical devices reserve center together with affected points and among affected points is known, as average speed of vehicles running is given, it is equivalent to know the running time.

(3) Vehicles service for each affected points by going the rounds, only have situation of discharge without loading.

(4) Each affected points service from one vehicle and only once.

(5) Average speed of vehicles is known and is certain, traveling distance is proportionate to traffic time.

(6) The needs of all affected points can be satisfied in terms of volume and transit time.

(7) Demand of single affected point is less than the maximum load of single vehicle.

On this assumption, the mathematical model of the total cost of distribution is:

$$\min Z = \sum_{k=1}^{m} \left(\sum_{j=0}^{L} \sum_{i=0}^{L} c_{ijk} x_{ijk} + c_k \right) \tag{1}$$

Where, Z is the total cost of distribution; parameter c_{ijk} is the cost of the vehicle k from i towards j ; c_k is fixed fee of vehicle k ; x_{ijk} is whether vehicle k is from i towards j ,if yes, $x_{ijk} = 1$,otherwise to be zero.

S.T.

$$\sum_{i=0}^{L} g_i y_{ki} \leq Q \quad k \in [1, m] \tag{2}$$

Where, Q is vehicle load; g_i is demand of affected point i , $g_i \leq Q$, y_{ki} is task of point i is whether completed by the vehicle k ,if yes, $y_{ki} = 1$, otherwise to be zero.

$$\sum_{k=1}^{L} y_{ki} = 1 \quad i = 1, 2, \cdots, L \tag{3}$$

$$\sum_{j=1}^{L} \sum_{i=1}^{L} x_{ijk} = 1 \quad i = 1, 2, \cdots, L , i \neq j , k \in [1, m] \tag{4}$$

$$t_{kj} = t_{ki} + s_i + t_{kij} \quad k \in [1, m] \tag{5}$$

Where, t_{ki} is time to reach i of vehicle k, s_i is unloading time of affected point i, t_{kij} is the time of the vehicle k from i towards j.

$$\sum_{k=1}^{m}\sum_{i=1}^{L} x_{0ik} - \sum_{k=1}^{m}\sum_{j=1}^{L} x_{j0k} = 0 \tag{6}$$

$$\sum_{k=1}^{m}\sum_{i=1}^{L} x_{0ik} - \sum_{k=1}^{m}\sum_{j=1}^{L} x_{j0k} = 0 \tag{7}$$

Where, t_i^e is allow time for the latest that medical devices delivery to affected point i. If the arrival time later than this time, that this solution is invalid.

$$t_{kij} = \delta_{ij} \frac{d_{ij}}{v_k} \tag{8}$$

Where, v_k is average speed of vehicle k; δ_{ij} is traffic factor, in this paper, two conditions of normal and peak is considered, values are 1 and 1.5.

$$c_{ijk} = d_{ij} U_k \tag{9}$$

Where, U_k is per unit distance travel cost of vehicle k.

Objective functional expression(1) means that in the emergency vehicle routing problem the minimum cost generated in weak economic conditions of emergency logistics, constraint items; formula(2) means total demand of affected point that vehicle k service for don't allow more than vehicle load; formula(3) means each affected point only allows one vehicle to access one time; formula(4) means any of affected points discharge in only one vehicle; formula(5) means affected point i, j is distributed by vehicle k, in addition, i is predecessor of j; formula(6) means the number of vehicles dispatched is equal to the number of vehicles returned; formula(7) means the time that relief supplies is conveyed to the affected point must be within the single sideband time window; formula(8) means the time of the vehicle k from i towards j, and consider the traffic situation; formula(9) means the cost of the vehicle k from i towards

3   Emergency Logistics Routing Optimization Algorithm

In the ant colony algorithm, the mutation is an important operator. Uniform mutation means a random number accord with uniform distribution within a certain range is used to replace the original gene value on each locus in individual encoded string by a smaller probability. The specific operation is:

(1) Specify each gene mutation point of individual encoded string in due order;
(2) For each variation point a random number which is taken in the range from the corresponding gene with probability p_m replaces the original gene value.

Figure 1 shows the flows chart that weak economic emergency medical devices vehicle routing optimization is solved by uniform mutation ant colony algorithm.

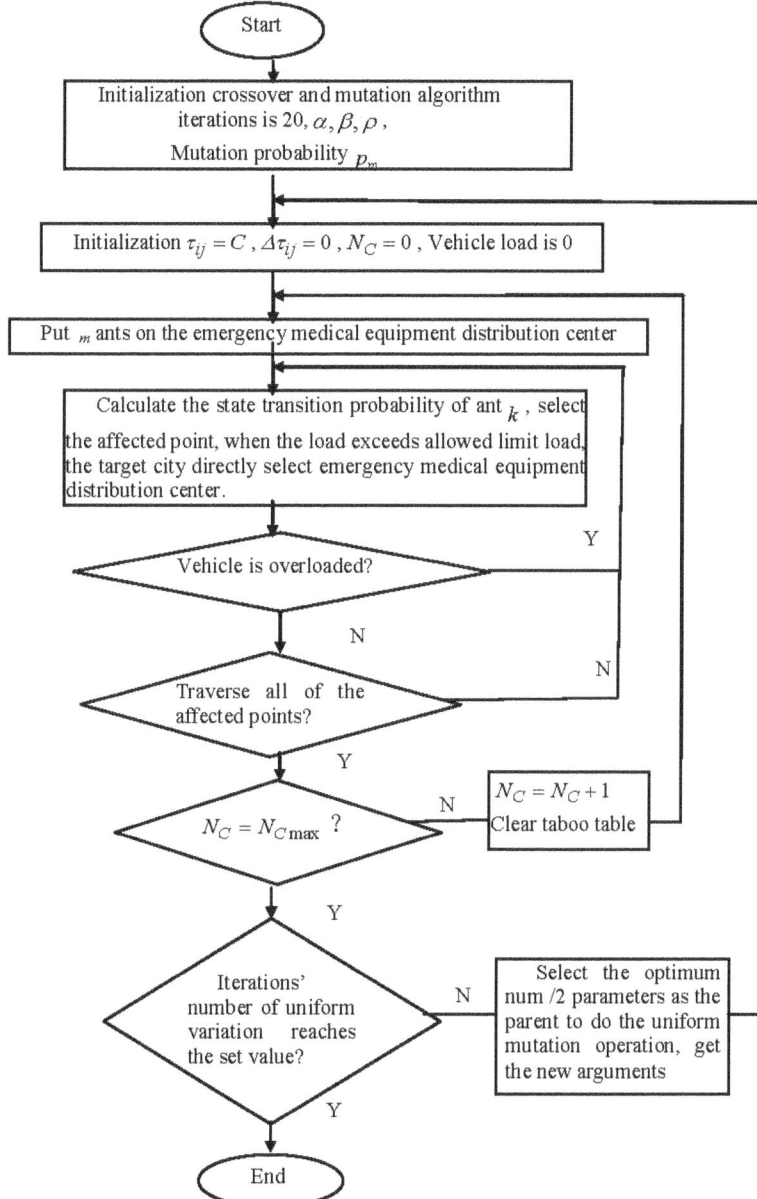

Fig. 1. The flows chart that weak economic emergency medical devices vehicle routing optimization is solved by uniform mutation ant colony algorithm.

4   Computer Simulation

Suppose reference coordinates of medical devices emergency logistics distribution companies is (2012, 1767), Table 1 shows the coordinates of affected points together with emergency medical agencies and related data. Unit of demands q_i of affected points together with emergency medical agencies is ton, unit of start time of each task and discharge time is hour, the capacity of the vehicle is limited to 8 tons, average speed is 65 unit reference distance per hour, the company has 5 delivery vehicles. Suppose the cost of vehicle travel is high, that is, if the cost of a vehicle increased is much higher than the operating costs of other vehicles, therefore, emergency medical devices distribution which vehicles is participated in is requested as little as possible. Mutation probability $p_m = 0.05$, crossover and mutation algorithm iterations Generation_num=20.

Table 1. Experimental basis for data

Affected points number	Coordinates	Demand	Start time	Unloading time
1	(404, 912)	2	1	0.4
2	(639, 1315)	1.5	4	0.6
3	(1477, 1244)	3	1.5	0.2
4	(3012, 1199)	3	2	0.1
5	(2488, 1535)	1.5	3	0.3
6	(1326, 1056)	2	2	0.5
7	(638, 929)	2.5	3.5	0.4
8	(2196, 1004)	3	1.5	0.3
9	(2012, 1879)	3.5	2	0.4
10	(3286, 1970)	2	1.5	0.5
11	(2507, 770)	3	1	0.2
12	(538, 1229)	2.5	5	0.3
13	(1196, 2004)	3	1.5	0.2
14	(912, 790)	2.5	2	0.5
15	(686, 1708)	2	1.5	0.3
16	(1007, 2270)	3.5	1	0.2
17	(2007, 970)	3	3	0.3
18	(2562, 1756)	3.5	1	0.2

Figure 2 is a comparison curve of optimal solution in 100 ants, in the circumstances that other operating environments of ant colony algorithm and uniform mutation ant colony algorithm is same. Figure 3 is the average which the generations of ants solve. Figures 4 and 5 are Optimum operating line curve which is solved by uniform mutation ant colony algorithm based on the weak economy and Minimum time (see [2]).

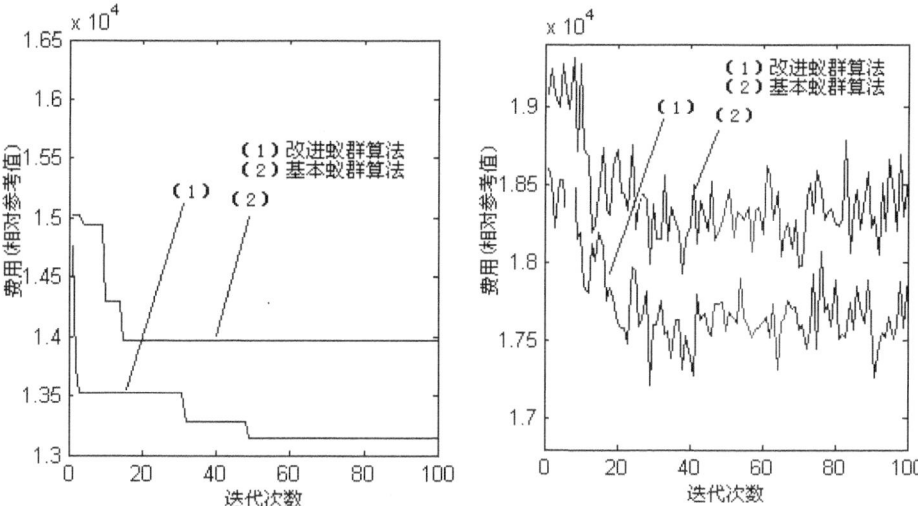

Fig. 2. Optimal solution curves of two algorithms

Fig. 3. Average optimal solution curves of two algorithms

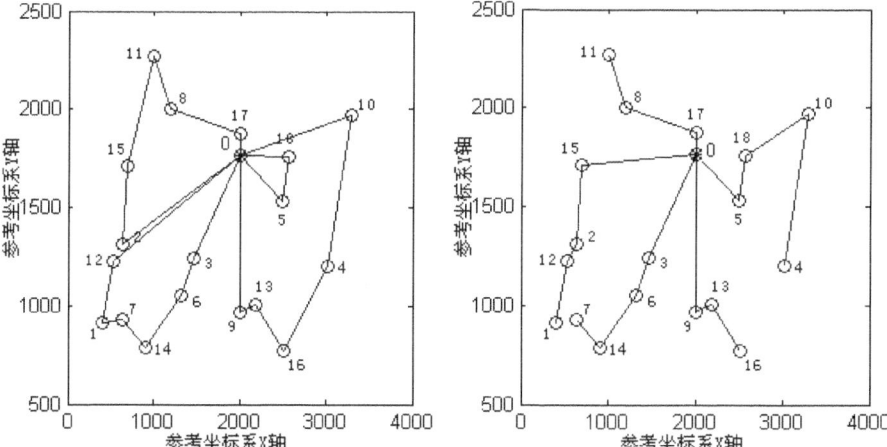

Fig. 4. An optimal solution roadmap of uniform mutation ant colony algorithm under weak economy

Fig. 5. An optimal solution roadmap of uniform mutation ant colony algorithm under minimum time

Four paths figure 4 received are: (0-5-18-0)、(0-10-4-11-8-17-0)、(0-3-6-14-7-1-12-0)、(0-2-15-16-13-9-0), five paths figure 5 acquired are: (0-5-18-10-4)、(0-17-8-11)、(0-3-6-14-7)、(0-15-2-12-1)、(0-9-13-16).

The figure shows optimum solution of distribution of emergency medical devices under weak economy, which uniform mutation ant colony algorithm solves, can be obtained. Performance of convergence rate and convergence characteristics is improved.

Compared with the minimum cost function based on time, weak economic conditions is not only meet the medical devices can be arrived to the affected point within the specified time, but also consider the economic benefits, in order to save cost.

5   Conclusion

Mathematical model of emergency logistics routing optimization has been established in this paper, and the model is solved by the uniform mutation ant colony algorithm, simulation shows that the optimal results of uniform mutation ant colony algorithm are better than ant colony algorithm. At the same time, compared with the mathematical model of the smallest time, mathematical model of emergency logistics routing optimization reduce the distribution costs on the basis of time requirements which should be satisfied.

Acknowledgment. This work is partially supported by Funding Issues of Soft Science Research Projects in Shanxi Province (2010041077-3).

References

1. Liu, Z.: Features of the Regional Emergency Logistics. Statistics and Decision 1, 186–188 (2009)
2. Zhang, J.: Research of Medical Devices Vehicle Routing Problem. Taiyuan University of Ph.D. thesis, Taiyuan (2010)
3. Zhang, L., Liu, T., Sun, Y., Li, Q.: Research of genetic algorithm optimization neural network weights blind equalization algorithm based on real number coding. Computer Engineering and Applications 45(11), 162–164 (2009)
4. Tian, G., Li, M., Wei, X.: Several Solution of Traveling Salesman Problem (TSP). Computer Simulation 23(8), 153–158 (2006)

Statistical Debugging Using a Hierarchical Model of Correlated Predicates

Saeed Parsa, Maryam Asadi-Aghbolaghi, and Mojtaba Vahidi-Asl

Department of Software Engineering,
Iran University of Science and Technology, Tehran, Iran
{parsa,m_vahidi_asl}@iust.ac.ir, m_asadi@comp.iust.ac.ir

Abstract. The aim of statistical debugging is to identify faulty predicates that have strong effect on program failure. In this paper predicates are fitted into a linear regression model to consider the vertical effect of predicates on each other and on program termination status. Prior approaches have merely considered predicates in isolation. The proposed approach in this paper is a two-step procedure which includes hierarchical clustering and the Lasso regression method. Hierarchical clustering builds a tree structure of correlated predicates. The Lasso method is applied on the clusters in some specified levels of the tree. This makes the method scalable in terms of the size of a program. Unlike other statistical methods which do not provide any context of the failure, the predicates contained in the group that is provided by this method can be used as the bug signature. The method has been evaluated on two well-known test suites, Space and Siemens. The experimental results reveal the accuracy and precision of the approach comparing with similar techniques.

Keywords: Automatic Bug Finding, Statistical Debugging, Hierarchical Clustering, Lasso Method, Fault Relevant Predicates.

1 Introduction

Although great efforts are made by software companies to remove software faults during in-house testing process, they cannot confidently claim that their deployed software is free of bugs [6]. Generally, a number of latent faults manifest themselves during operations in the hands of end users [1]. This has motivated many researchers during past few years to seek for techniques which automate the process of bug finding [8][12]. Among fault localization techniques, statistical debugging methods have achieved great success [2][3][4][5]. Statistical debugging approaches apply program logs representing the value of the predicates at failing and passing runs to find the fault relevant ones [5].

The majority of statistical debugging techniques cannot detect specific bugs caused by undesired interactions between predicates because they only consider predicates in isolation [4][5]. The situation becomes worse when bug(s) is located in multiple and probably far apart statements. Furthermore, many of these techniques merely provide the debugger with a single line of code or predicate while assuming that he/she has

H. Deng et al. (Eds.): AICI 2011, Part I, LNAI 7002, pp. 251–256, 2011.
© Springer-Verlag Berlin Heidelberg 2011

"perfect bug understanding " [21]. However, if the programmers are provided with a group of highly fault relevant predicates, they can find the origin of the bug and correct it, easier. To consider the simultaneous impact of predicates on each other and on the program termination status a logistic regression model [9] could be best applied [13]. To this end, ridge regression method [19] and a combination of ridge and lasso regression methods are applied [20]. For large programs with huge number of predicates ridge regression cannot provide interpretable models [10] while lasso models do. However, lasso does not identify correlated predicates. To resolve the difficulty, the predicates could be clustered according to their correlation.

In this paper, inspired from [22], a combination of a hierarchical clustering technique [24] and lasso method is presented. The hierarchical clustering provides a nested structure of correlated predicates. A distinct lasso model is then built for each level of the hierarchy to detect the fault relevant predicates. Finally we apply the majority voting technique on selected predicates of all involving levels to find out which predicate has got the highest suspiciousness score in the majority of levels. With this strategy, we improve the accuracy and precision of the method in finding and ranking fault relevant predicates. The clustering technique also helps us to identify correlated faulty predicates as the bug signature.

The remaining part of this paper is organized as follows. In section two, an overview of the method is described. The experiments and results are shown in section three. Finally concluding remarks and future works are depicted in section four.

2   The Method Overview

In this section, the main idea of the proposed technique is described in detail. The main phase of the technique is done in four stages: 1) preprocessing stage 2) constructing the hierarchical tree 3) building the lasso model and 4) identifying the fault relevant predicates.

2.1   The Preprocessing Phase

In order to construct statistical model from runtime behavior of a program, we should execute it several times with different test cases to collect the value of predicates in each run. To achieve this, it is required to insert some extra code before each predicate which is called instrumentation [6]. In this work, we have considered both function calls and branch statements to design the predicates [12].

2.2   Building the Nested Structure of Correlated Predicates

In order to construct the nested correlated structure of predicates, some initial steps should be performed [23]. First instrumented program is run by different test cases and the number of times each predicate has been evaluated as *True* in a particular run is collected and logged into a database. Then the data is normalized for clustering. The clustering is made according to the *Pearson* correlation coefficient [24] between two predicate values: $P_m=\{p_{m1}, p_{m2}, \ldots, p_{mN},\}$ and $P_n=\{p_{n1}, p_{n2}, \ldots, p_{nN},\}$ where p_{ij} depicts the number of times that predicate p_i is evaluated as *True* in the execution j and N is the number of executions. The Pearson coefficient is computed as follows:

$$\gamma_{m,n} = \frac{1}{N} \sum_{i=1..N} \left(\frac{p_{mi} - \overline{P_m}}{\sigma_{P_m}} \right) \left(\frac{p_{ni} - \overline{P_n}}{\sigma_{P_n}} \right) \tag{1}$$

The $\overline{P_m}$ and $\overline{P_n}$ in (1) are the average of values in P_m and P_n, respectively. σ_{P_m} and σ_{P_n} are the standard deviation of the corresponding predicates. The result would be a correlation matrix which represents the correlation between predicates. To achieve this, the *Average Linkage Clustering* [10] could be applied on the matrix. The algorithm for constructing the hierarchy is iterative: At first stage, for each actual predicate of the program, as the leaf of the tree, a predicate vector is assigned. Using these vectors, the correlation matrix is built according to the *Pearson* coefficient in (1). At this point, the highly correlated predicates are identified and clustered to form pseudo-predicates as the parents of leaves. Again a vector is allocated to each pseudo-predicate which contains the average value of all predicate vectors which are included in it. In a similar manner, we compute the *Pearson* correlation coefficient between this pseudo-predicate and all other predicates or pseudo-predicates. In this stage, the second level of the hierarchy from the bottom is constructed. The process continues until all pseudo-predicates and the remaining actual predicates are clustered to form the root of the hierarchy. The final result is a tree structure of correlated predicates.

2.3 Fitting Predicates to Lasso Model

The least absolute shrinkage and selection operator (lasso), first proposed by Tibshirani [11], shrinks some coefficients and tends to give zero to the remaining coefficients. The aim is to choose the coefficients, $\hat{\beta}_j$, $j=1, 2,... n$, that minimize the following equation, over all β_j, $j=1, 2, ... n$:

$$. \ \beta^{lasso} = \arg \min_\beta \sum_{i=1}^{N} (y_i - \beta_0 - \sum_{j=1}^{n} p_{ij}\beta_j)^2 \quad \text{subject to} \quad \sum_{j=1}^{n} |\beta_j| \le s \tag{2}$$

The parameter s in (2) behaves as a constraint and if it is chosen adequately small, some of the coefficients may become zero. Therefore, lasso could be considered as a continuous subset selection technique which makes it appropriate for identifying bug relevant predicates. The loss function in (2) could be also converted to:

$$\|y - P\beta\|_2^2 + \lambda\|\beta\|_1 \tag{3}$$

Where y is the vector of program termination status in different runs, β is predicate coefficient matrix, P is the predicate (or pseudo-predicate) matrix and λ is the shrinkage tuning parameter. Finding an appropriate value for λ is a challenging problem, because with inadequate value we may lose fault relevant predicates. Lasso combines good features of naïve subset selection and ridge regression techniques and eliminates their drawbacks. It improves prediction accuracy that naïve subset selection suffers from and gives an interpretable model which is the main drawback of ridge regression.

As shown in previous section, the nested structure of predicates could be viewed as a tree. For each program, according to its size and complexity, a predefined number of levels of the tree are specified for which the lasso model should be constructed. At each specified level, the program runs are split into two categories of train and test sets. In order to find an appropriate shrinkage parameter for level x, first the lasso model is built with different values for λ. An appropriate shrinkage parameter is the one for which the corresponding lasso model constructed from the test set has the best prediction power.

2.4   Ranking Predicates

As mentioned in the previous section, for each specified level an individual lasso model is constructed. The predicates with non-zero coefficients are scored according to their weights. Using a majority voting technique, the predicates are ranked based on their score in different models (i.e. levels). Since the bug is not necessarily included in the predicate, we should scrutinize the code manually to find the cause of failure. Typically, the statistical debugging technique evaluates their effectiveness on the amount of manual code inspection by the user.

3   Experimental Results

In this section, the evaluation results of our approach on Siemens test suite and Space program are compared with some well known proposed techniques for software debugging. Siemens suite is available at [16]. The hierarchical clustering is performed using [23][24] and the lasso model is constructed using [14][15]. Among all built levels for a program, one third of levels in the middle are chosen to construct the lasso model. The cross validation involves almost 10% of a given program runs as the test set and 90% of it is the train set. In table 1, the number of localized bugs in terms of manually code inspection for each program in Siemens suite is presented. As shown in the table, the results are very interesting and manifest the high effectiveness of the proposed approach. Some versions have not been included in the experiments due to the segmentation faults, lack of failing test cases, and existence of a fault in the header file and none convergence of the lasso model. The proposed approach is compared with some other techniques in table 2. In overall the proposed technique has outperformed all other debugging techniques in terms of manual code inspection to locate the origin of failure.

In order to show the scalability of our approach, the proposed method is applied to Space [2]. Among 19 versions that we have evaluated the method, 16 faults were located by less than 0.5% of code examination and overall less than 10% lines of code examination is required for all 19 faults of this program. Tarantula [2] could locate 12 faults of Space by less than 1% of code examination.

Table 1. The result of proposed technique on Siemens programs

Code inspection	Schedule	Schedule2	Print_tokens	PrintTokens2	Replace	Totinfo	Tcas	Total
< 1 %	2	2	3	5	13	10	5	40
< 10 %	5	7	4	7	18	16	32	89
< 20 %	5	8	5	9	23	21	38	109
used versions	5	8	5	9	23	21	38	109
All versions	9	10	7	10	32	23	41	127

Table 2. A complete comparison with some outstanding debugging techniques

Percentage of Examined Code	Proposed Method	Tarantula [2]	SOBER [3]	Liblit05 [7]	Context Aware[4]	CT [17]	Argus [8]	NN (perm)[18]
< 1 %	40	17	10	11	38	6	0	0
< 10 %	89	68	52	68	67	34	74	18
< 20 %	109	75	85	96	73	49	98	28
< 30 %	109	87	91	102	-	67	107	41

4   Concluding Remarks and Future Work

In this paper a new statistical approach for software debugging has been proposed. Two important issues are considered in this paper: 1) eliminating all irrelevant and redundant predicates to obtain a small subset of faulty predicates and 2) finding a group of fault relevant predicates as the context of bug for better understanding the origin of failure and fixing the bug. The approach constructs a tree view structure according to the correlation among predicates. Then, an average linkage clustering technique is applied on correlation matrix of predicates. The lasso model is constructed for some specified levels and high ranked predicates are identified and reported as faulty predicates. Since the clustering method groups correlated predicates, the result of applying lasso on generated predicates is more accurate and efficient. The grouping effect of the method helps the programmer to identify groups of fault relevant predicates as bug signatures.

Our experiments has been done on Siemens test suite and Space program. The results are promising and show the effectiveness of the proposed techniques in comparison with other debugging techniques. For future work, we aim to extend the work on larger and more complex programs with multiple bugs. We may also consider the static structure of the program in identifying correlated predicates.

References

1. Liblit, B.: Cooperative Bug Isolation. PhD thesis. University of California, Berkeley (2004)
2. Jones, J.A., Harrold, M.J.: Empirical evaluation of the tarantula automatic fault localization technique. In: 20th IEEE/ACM International Conference on Automated Software Engineering, pp. 273–282. ACM Press, Long Beach (2005)
3. Liu, C., Yan, X., Fei, L., Han, J., Midkiff, S.P.: Sober: Statistical model-based bug localization. In: 10th European Software Eng. Conf./13th ACM SIGSOFT Int'l Symposium Foundations of Software Engineering, pp. 286–295. ACM Press, Lisbon (2005)
4. Jiang, L., Su, Z.: Context-aware statistical debugging: from bug predictors to faulty control flow paths. In: Twenty-Second IEEE/ACM International Conference on Automated Software Engineering, pp. 184–193. ACM Press, Atlanta (2007)
5. Arumuga Nainar, P., Chen, T., Rosin, J., Liblit, B.: Statistical debugging using compound Boolean predicates. In: International Symposium on Software Testing and Analysis, pp. 5–15. ACM Press, London (2007)
6. Zeller, A.: Why Programs Fail: A Guide to Systematic Debugging. Morgan Kaufmann, San Francisco (2006)

7. Liblit, B., Naik, M., Zheng, A., Aiken, A., Jordan, M.: Scalable Statistical Bug Isolation. In: Int'l Conference Programming Language Design and Implementation, Chicago, pp. 15–26 (2005)
8. Fei, L., Lee, K., Li, F., Midkiff, S.P.: Argus: Online statistical bug detection. In: Baresi, L., Heckel, R. (eds.) FASE 2006. LNCS, vol. 3922, pp. 308–323. Springer, Heidelberg (2006)
9. Chatterjee, S., Hadi, A., Price, B.: Regression Analysis by Example, 4th edn. Wiley Series in Probability and Statistics, New York (2006)
10. Hastie, T.J., Tibshirani, R.J., Friedman, J.: The Elements of Statistical Learning: Data Mining Inference and Prediction. Springer, New York (2001)
11. Tibshirani, R.: Optimal Reinsertion: Regression shrinkage and selection via the lasso. J. R. Statist. Soc. 58, 267–288 (1996)
12. Zheng, A.X., Jordan, M.I., Liblit, B., Naik, M., Aiken, A.: Statistical debugging: simultaneous identification of multiple bugs. In: 23rd International Conference on Machine Learning, pp. 1105–1112. ACM Press, NY (2006)
13. Liblit, B., Aiken, A., Zheng, X., Jordan, M.I.: Bug isolation via remote program sampling. In: ACM SIGPLAN 2003 Conference on Programming Language Design and Implementation, pp. 141–154. ACM Press, San Diego (2003)
14. Friedman, J., Hastie, T., Tibshirani, R.: Lasso: Glmnet for Matlab - Lasso (L1) and elastic-net regularized generalized linear models
15. Friedman, J., Hastie, T., Tibshirani, R.: Lasso: Glmnet for R (2011), http://cran.r-project.org/web/packages/glmnet/index.html
16. Software-artifact infrastructure repository, http://sir.unl.edu/portal
17. Cleve, H., Zeller, A.: Locating causes of program failures. In: 27th International Conf. on Software Engineering, St. Louis Missouri, pp. 342–351 (2005)
18. Renieris, M., Reiss, S.: Fault localization with nearest neighbor queries. In: 18th IEEE International Conference on Automated Software Engineering, Montreal, pp. 30–39 (2003)
19. Parsa, S., Vahidi-Asl, M., Arabi, S.: Finding Causes of Software Failure Using Ridge Regression and Association Rule Generation Methods. In: Ninth ACIS International Conference on Parallel/Distributed Computing, Phuket, pp. 873–878 (2008)
20. Parsa, S., Arabi, S., Vahidi-Asl, M.: Statistical Software Debugging: From Bug Predictors to the Main Causes of Failure. In: Software Metrics and Measurement: SMM 2009 in Conjunction with the Second International Conference on Application of Digital Information and Web Technologies, London, pp. 802–807 (2009)
21. Cheng, H., Lo, D., Zhou, Y., Wang, X.: Identifying Bug Signatures Using Discriminative Graph Mining. In: International Symptoms on Software Testing and Analysis, pp. 141–151. ACM Press, Chicago (2009)
22. Park, M., Hastie, T., Tibshirani, R.: Averaged gene expressions for regression. Biostatistics Journal, 212–227 (2007)
23. Eisen, M.: Hierarchical Clustering: Cluster and TreeView are an integrated pair of programs for analyzing and visualizing the results of complex microarray experiments, http://rana.lbl.gov/EisenSoftware.htm
24. Eisen, M., Spellman, P., Brown, P., Botstein, D.: Cluster analysis and display of genomewide expression patterns. Proceedings of the National Academy of Sciences of the United States of America 95, 14863–14868 (1998)

Analysis of Permanent-Magnet Synchronous Motor Chaos System

Guo-Qing Huang[1,2] and Xin Wu[2]

[1] School of Civil Engineering and Architecture,
Nanchang University, Nanchang, China
[2] Department of Physics, Nanchang University, Nanchang, China
huanggq@ncu.edu.cn

Abstract. This paper proposed the dynamic properties of permanent-magnet synchronous motors (PMSM).Nonlinear characteristic and basic dynamic properties of PMSM chaotic system are studied by the ways of nonlinear dynamic theory such as Lyapunov exponents, bifurcation diagram, phase diagram. In addition, the system is also analyzed by the Smaller Alignment Index (SALI) method and the fast Lyapunov indictor (FLI) method in order to trace a control parameter which is threshold between ordered and chaotic orbits. Finally, the chaotic behaviors in the fractional order unified system are numerically investigated.

Keywords: Fractional order, PMSM, Fast Lyapunov indicator, Small alignment index.

1 Introduction

The study of chaotic behavior in nonlinear systems has attracted more and more attention because of a broad variety of applications in various fields of science and technology. Its importance for applications began to be widely used only within past several decades. Since several pioneering works, Lorenz found chaos in a simple system of three autonomous ordinary differential equations[1].many papers and monographs well studied the nonlinear characteristics and basic dynamic properties of the Lorenz system [2.3].The use of computer is very helpful for the development of chaotic dynamics. Now, chaotic dynamics is a rising interdisciplinary field which combines nonlinear dynamics and other sciences.

The nonlinear dynamic properties of motors are widely studied, which deals with speed controlling and oscillating of motors since 1970s. The mathematical models of PMSM are multi-variable, nonlinear, and strongly coupled, therefore the system show complex behavior. The PMSM displays behaviors in the special condition.[4-6].

Although fractional calculus has a long history, the applications of fractional calculus to physics and engineering are just last decades [7]. Various systems show fractional order dynamics, such as iscoelastic system [8], dielectric polarization [9], electrode–electrolyte polarization [10] and electromagnetic wave [11]. In this paper,fractional calculus applied to the dissipative PMSM system. Meanwhile, the

H. Deng et al. (Eds.): AICI 2011, Part I, LNAI 7002, pp. 257–263, 2011.

fast Lyapunov indicators [12] and the smaller alignment index [13] are firstly used to treat the dissipative PMSM system so that a universal rule of the transitivity to chaos on a certain control parameter is easily uncovered.

2 The System Model and Numerical Investigations

The transformed model of PMSM with the smooth air gap which based on d-q axis, is described [6]:

$$\frac{d\tilde{i}_d}{dt} = -\tilde{i}_d + \tilde{\omega}\tilde{i}_q + \tilde{u}_d$$
$$\frac{d\tilde{i}_q}{dt} = -\tilde{i}_q - \tilde{\omega}\tilde{i}_d + \gamma\tilde{\omega} + \tilde{u}_q \tag{1}$$
$$\frac{d\tilde{i}_d}{dt} = \sigma(\tilde{i}_q - \tilde{\omega})_q - \tilde{T}_L$$

where $\tilde{i}_d, \tilde{i}_q$ and $\tilde{\omega}$ are the state variables, which represent currents and motor angular frequency, respectively, $\tilde{u}_d$ and $\tilde{u}_q$ the direct- and quadrature-axis stator voltage components, respectively, $\tilde{T}_L$ the external load torque, $\tilde{\omega}$ is motor angle frequency, σ and γ are system parameters.

The chaotic behaviors of Eq.(1) with different parameter set are displayed in Fig.5. When Runge-Kutta-Fehlberg integrator of variable time steps, is used to integrate the system (1), we obtain the chaotic attractor in Fig .1, where initial condition $(\tilde{i}_d, \tilde{i}_q, \tilde{\omega})$=(20.0.01,-5) and (σ ,γ)=(5.46,20).

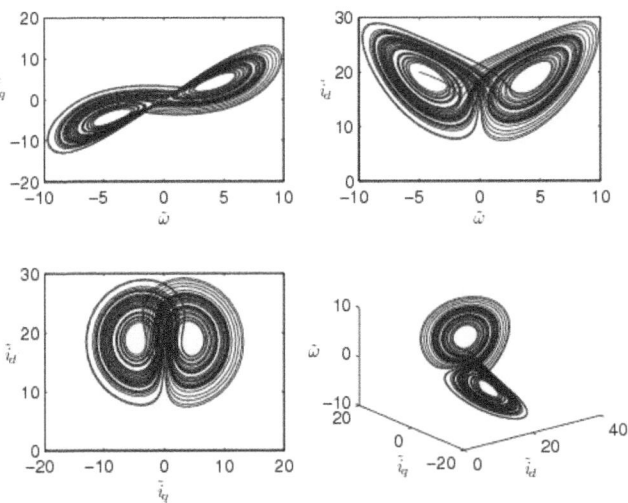

Fig. 1. Phase portraits of the system with γ=20

3   Chaotic Indicators

There are various methods to separate between chaotic and ordered orbits. Now we propose some of the methods to deal with our problems.

3.1   Lyapunov Exponents

Lyapunov exponents have become one of the most popular, useful methods to distinguish whether a system is chaotic or not. The largest one of them is defined as:

$$\lambda_1 = \lim_{t \to \infty} \frac{1}{t} \log \frac{|\xi(t)|}{|\xi(0)|} \tag{2}$$

where $\xi(0)$ and $\xi(t)$ stand for tangent vectors at times 0 and t, respectively. Abounded system is said to be chaotic if $\lambda_1 > 0$, but regular as $\lambda_1 < 0$. To avoid all Lyapunov directions converging to the same tangent vector the Gram-Schmidt orthogonalization must be used in every step. The 1st, 2nd, 3rd, .., and k^{th} Lyapunov exponents $(\lambda_1, \lambda_2, \lambda_3, .. \lambda_k)$ are charge from large to small.

All Lyapunov exponents of the three-dimensional system (1) can be attained, where initial conditions are $(\tilde{i}_d, \tilde{i}_q, \tilde{\omega})$=(20.0.01,-5), the cases of parameter γ=10,and γ=20 are independently considered, and the integration of each case does not stop until t=20000.three Lyapunov exponents, i.e., $(\lambda_1, \lambda_2, \lambda_3)$=(-0.25, -0.44, -24.8), are enough to show that the system for the case γ=10 is Lyapunov stable and its attractor is a stable fixed point and the system is ordered orbits. For γ=20, there are one positive and two negative Lyapunov exponents $(\lambda_1, \lambda_2, \lambda_3)$=(1.55, -1.05, -27.4) . The onset of such a positive Lyapunov exponent determines that the system is dynamically unstable and chaotic.

3.2   Fast Lyapunov Indicator

Fast Lyapunov indicator comes from a variant of the maximum Lyapunov exponent. in FLI, the renormalization is not needed use, so overflow of the lengths of tangential vectors of a chaotic orbit can be avoided. It was firstly introduced by Froeschlé et al., and then followed as [12]:

$$FLI(t) = \log_{10}|\xi(t)| \tag{3}$$

This indicator grows with $\log_{10}(t)$ in entirely different laws for ordered and chaotic motions. In other words, an exponential increase of the FLI indicates the chaoticity of the orbit, while an algebraical growth means the regularity of the orbit. In addition, this indicator was further developed as the two-particle method [17]. Several papers [14, 15, 16] have reported that the method of FLI is a faster, more sensitive tool to distinguish between the ordered and chaotic cases than the method of Lyapunov exponents, especially for weak chaotic systems

3.3   Small Alignment Index

The construction of small alignment index is still come from the idea of the computation of two Lyapunov exponents in some degree. The small alignment index (SALI) method was introduced in [13] and has already been proved to be an efficient method to diagnose between chaotic and regular motion in conservative dynamical systems. Named as the small alignment index of the form from [13]

$$SALI(t) = \log_{10}(\min\{|\hat{\xi}_1(t) + \hat{\xi}_2(t)|, |\hat{\xi}_1(t) - \hat{\xi}_2(t)|\}) \qquad (4)$$

However, the method has never been used to analyze PMSM system. In our opinion, it is still suitable for a this system because the speed of the SALI converging to zero is strongly connected to the characteristic of orbits but does not at all depend on the conservative or dissipative natures of the system. Precisely speaking, the SALI converges exponentially to zero for chaotic orbits in dissipative systems, but does algebraically (or tends to a certain non-vanishing constant) for ordered motions.

Numerical analysis of individual orbits is concerned, Lyapunov exponents, FLI and SALI are successfully confirmed to be efficient tools to discriminate between chaotic and regular motions in the PMSM system. In the following, we shall mainly use them to research the effect of the variation of the parameter on chaos.

3.4   Various Orbits with a Transition to Chaos on the Parameter

As some control parameter is smoothly changed, a bifurcation is highly convenient to find a sudden change of a qualitatively different result for a nonlinear system. A period doubling, quadrupling, etc., and chaotic behavior can be surveyed clearly with the help of the bifurcation. As shown in Fig.4, there is an abrupt changing from one attractor to two attractors as the parameter γ spans 14.93. Since then, the chaos has become stronger and stronger as the parameter increases.

In addition, the SALI method in Fig. 3 is good to illustrate the transition to chaos on the parameter γ. When γ vibrates around 14.5, all the SALIs arrive quickly at the value -16 before $t=10^4$. This is an apparent marker of the appearance of chaos. Here the integration time for each parameter is not more than 10^4. If the SALI equates -16 before this time, let the integration stop and give the parameter γ another value so that the next integration begins. The same result is also obtained in Fig. 2 by means of the FLI method. A more interesting method is attributed to the entire set of Lyapunov exponents, namely, Lyapunov spectra in Fig.5, which offer enough dynamical information that γ=14.93 is a threshold value from order to chaos.

In brief, all the methods of bifurcation, SALI, FLI and Lyapunov exponents exhibit almost the same rules of the varying to chaos on the same parameter. That is to say, γ=14.93 is a threshold value from order to chaos, and the chaos gets stronger and stronger as the parameter γ is smoothly changed from small to large.

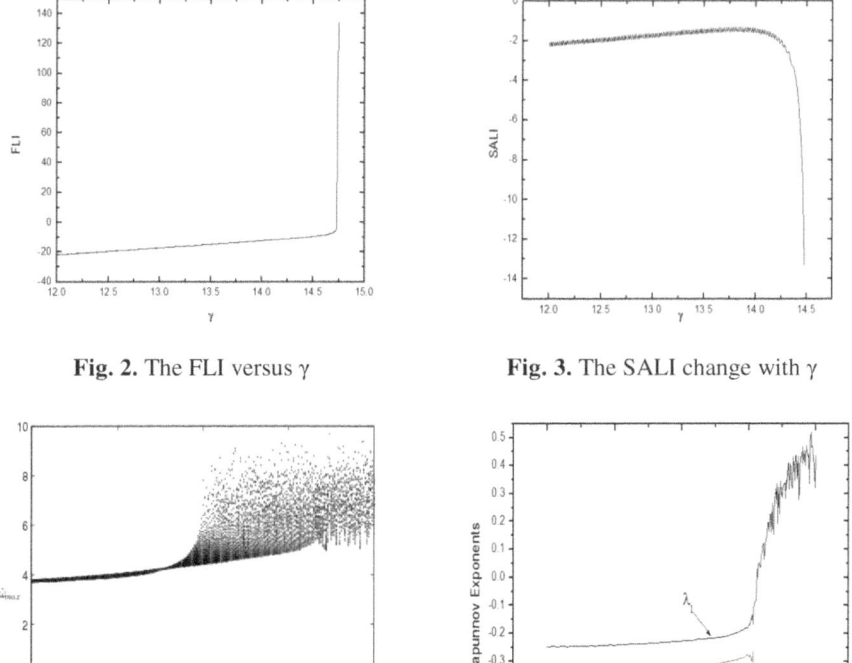

Fig. 2. The FLI versus γ

Fig. 3. The SALI change with γ

Fig. 4. Bifurcation diagrams of ω_{max} versus γ

Fig. 5. Laypunov exponents versus γ

4   The Fractional Order PMSM System

There are several definitions of fractional derivatives [7]. Perhaps the best known is the Riemann–Liouville definition, which is given by:

$$\frac{d^{\alpha} f(t)}{d^{\alpha} t} = \frac{1}{\Gamma(n - \alpha)} \frac{d^{n}}{dt^{n}} \int_{\alpha}^{t} \frac{\tau}{t - \tau} d\tau \tag{5}$$

where n-1<<α<n and $\Gamma(\cdot)$ is Gamma function. To solve engineering problem, the Laplace transform method is often used. Here, we consider the fractional order PMSM system which is replaced by a fractional derivative as follows [4, 5, 6]:

$$\frac{d^{\alpha} \tilde{i}_{d}}{dt^{\alpha}} = -\tilde{i}_{d} + \tilde{\omega} \tilde{i}_{q} + \tilde{u}_{d}$$

$$\frac{d^{\alpha} \tilde{i}_{q}}{dt^{\alpha}} = -\tilde{i}_{q} - \tilde{\omega} \tilde{i}_{d} + \gamma \tilde{\omega} + \tilde{u}_{q} \tag{6}$$

$$\frac{d^{\alpha} \tilde{i}_{d}}{dt^{\alpha}} = \sigma (\tilde{i}_{q} - \tilde{\omega})_{q} - \tilde{T}_{L}$$

Where α is the fractional order, 0<α≤1.Numerical simulations are performed for α=0.95. The simulation results display that chaos indeed exist in the fractional order PMSM system with order less than 3. With α=0.95, chaotic behavior are found and the phase portraits are shown in Figs.6, respectively. We can also see that the chaotic attractors with α=0.95 in the fractional order PMSM system are similar and look like the Chen attractor.

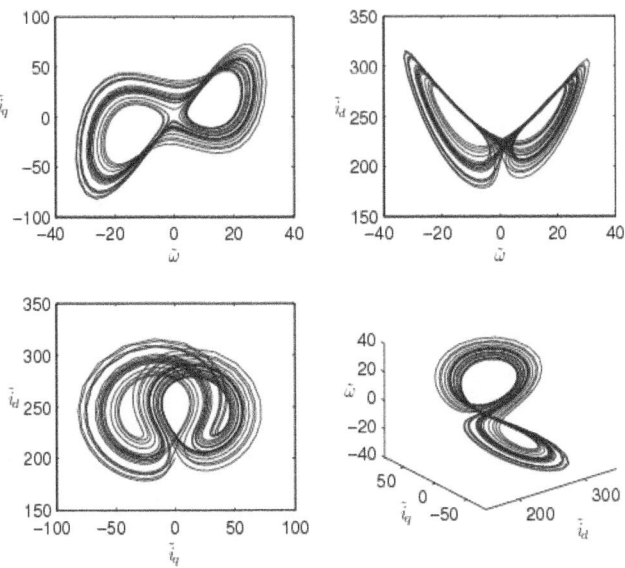

Fig. 6. Attractors of the fractional order unified system

5   Conclusion

The methods of bifurcation, Lyapunnov spectra, fast Lyapunov indicators and small alignment indexes are independently applied to search for the dependence of the transitivity to chaos on the variation of the parameter γ. As a result, they do attained the same results that γ=14.93 is a threshold value from order to chaos, and the strength of chaos increases with parameter γ. The PMSM system with the fractional order exists in chaotic behavior.

References

1. Lorenz, E.N.: Deterministic nonperiodic flow. Atmos. Sci. 20, 130–141 (1963)
2. Ueta, T., Chen, G.: Bifurcation analysis of Chen's attractor. Int. J. Bifurcat. Chaos 10, 1917–1931 (2000)
3. Chen, G., Ueta, T.: Yet another chaotic attractor. Int. J. Bifurcat. Chaos 9, 1465–1466 (1999)

4. Bifurcations and Chaos in a Permanent-Magnet Synchronous Motor. Fundamental Theory And Applications 49(3), 383 (March 2002)
5. Hemati, N.: Stange attractors in brushless DC motors. IEEE Trans. Circuits Syst. I 41, 40–45 (1994)
6. Liu, D., Ren, H.P., Liu, X.Y.: Chaos control in permanent magnet synchronous motors. In: IEEE Circuits and Systems, ISCAS 2004, vol. 4, pp. 732–735 (May 2004)
7. Podlubny, I.: Fractional Differential Equations. Academic Press, New York (1999)
8. Koeller, R.C.: Application of fractional calculus to the theory of viscoelasticity. Appl. Mech. 51(2), 299–307 (1984)
9. Sun, H.H., Abdelwahad, A.A., Onaral, B.: Linear approximation of transfer function with a pole of fractional order. IEEE Trans. Automat. Control 29(5), 441–444 (1984)
10. Ichise, M., Nagayanagi, Y., Kojima, T.: An analog simulation of noninteger order transfer functions for analysis of electrode process. Electroanal. Chem. 33, 253–265 (1971)
11. Heaviside, O.: Electromagnetic Theory, Chelsea, New York (1971)
12. Froeschlé, C., Lega, E.: n the Structure of Symplectic Mappings. The Fast Lyapunov Indicator: a Very Sensitive Tool. Celest. Mech. Dyn. Astron. 78, 167 (2000)
13. Skokos, C.: Alignment indices: A new, simple method for determining the ordered or chaotic nature of orbits. Phys. A 34, 10029–10043 (2001)
14. Wu, X.: Is the Hamiltonian geometrical criterion for chaos always reliable? Journal of Geometry and Physics 59, 1357–1362 (2009)
15. Wu, X.: A new interpretation of zero Lyapunov exponents in BKL time for Mixmaster cosmology. Research in Astronomy and Astrophysics 10, 211–219 (2010)
16. Wu, X., Huang, T.Y.: Computation of Lyapunov exponents in general relativity. Phys. Lett. A 313, 77 (2003)
17. Wu, X., Huang, T.Y., Zhang, H.: Lyapunov indices with two nearby trajectories in a curved spacetime. Phys. Rev. D 74, 083001 (2006)

A Pulse Design Method Based on Cognitive UWB

RunFang Hao and JuMin Zhao

College of Information Engineering
TaiYuan University of Technology
Taiyuan, China
txlhrf@126.com
.

Abstract. The impulse response of the pulse shaper affects the spectral properties of radiated signals, so tuning spectra by pulse shaping is feasible in Impulse Radio UWB system. This paper analyzes the problem of tuning radiated UWB signals to meet spectral restriction taking orthogonal Hermite pulses for instance. A simple work model of cognitive UWB system presented in this paper may adapt its spectrum to environment need automatically. The simulation results indicate that shaping the spectrum by tuning the pulse waveform is effective. The UWB systems coexist with other wireless systems without interference each other according to the work model.

Keywords: Cognitive Radio, Pulse Design, Ultra Wideband.

1 Introduction

Ultra-wideband (UWB) radio has attracted increasing interests for its potential applications in short-range high-data-rate wireless communications. Unlike the conventional carrier-based wireless communication systems, UWB radio technologies encode large amounts of information over a series of impulsive pulse using extremely low power of radio energy. For this reason, it has been widely believed that UWB radio has emerged as a tempting solution for next generation wireless communication requiring high data rates. However, the transmitted signal occupies very large bandwidths of up to a few gigahartz so that they overlap with the existing narrowband systems unavoidably, therefore an UWB radio will face/cause severe interference from/to the narrowband systems nearby [1]. The coexistence and compatibility become a critical issue. On February 14, 2002 Federal Communications Commission (FCC) in the United States released spectrum mask and paved a way for achieving coexistence with traditional and protected radio services.

Cognitive Radio (CR) has introduced as a technology to solve the coexistence, interferences avoidance and matching with any regulatory spectral mask problem. CR can ascertain the local environments and adapt to real-time conditions of its operating wireless environment, including the ability to sense spectrum usage by neighboring devices, change operating frequency, adjust output power and modify transmission parameters.[2] On the other hand, UWB radio technology inherently is suitable for a versatile PHY layer and adaptable to various wireless channel conditions. Starting from

H. Deng et al. (Eds.): AICI 2011, Part I, LNAI 7002, pp. 264–269, 2011.
© Springer-Verlag Berlin Heidelberg 2011

these considerations, some researchers proposed a new strategy to exploit the advantages and unique features of integrating the cognitive radio with UWB technologies, namely "Cognitive UWB Radio" [3].The final goal remains to form wireless networks that cooperatively coexist with other wireless networks and devices

Because the impulse response of pulse shaper affects the Power Spectral Density (PSD) of transmitted signals in UWB system, shaping the spectrum by modifying the pulse waveform is effective [4]. If we can design and develop smart UWB devices able to adapt to the environment by changing the spectral shape and features of the radiated signals, UWB radio signals cooperatively coexist with other wireless networks and devices. Consequently researchers have investigated various design methods of UWB signal wave optimization in order to dynamically generate a set of adaptive UWB pulse waveform based upon need in a real time manner for cooperative spectrum sharing. The adaptive pulse provides us the physical basis and can change its waveform to meet the FCC spectrum mask and mitigate interference.

The pulse design method based on the linear combination of orthogonal prolate spheroidal wave functions and Gassian functions has been investigated in [1] and [4] respectively. The widely adopted Gaussian monocycle is not flexible enough to meet spectral mask. The pulse design method based on the prolate spheroidal wave functions is implemented diffcultly.We focus on the design method of Hermite pulse based on CR. In this paper. The Hermit series expansion is useful because of the following properties and advantages[5]: (i) The modified hermite basis functions are orthogonal, (ii) The modified hermite polynomials can easily be computed.

The paper presents a simple work model by combining Cognitive Radio (CR) and UWB efficiently to modify pulse waveform by tuning transmission factors adaptively. For this purpose the properties of orthogonal Hermite pulses is introduced in section 2. Section 3 discusses a new cognitive UWB system model and section 4 simulates taking orthogonal Hermite pulses for instance. Section 5 draws conclusions.

2   Transmit Spectrum and Pulse Shaper

A typical modulation in UWB radios is binary pulse position modulation (PPM), in conjunction with time hopping (TH) codes that are used to enable multiple access (MA) and smooth the transmit-spectra [4]. With p(t) denoting the pulse shaper with $\varepsilon_p := \int p^2(t)dt$, the emitted waveform from a single UWB transmitter is

$$u(t) = \sum_{k=-\infty}^{+\infty} \sqrt{\frac{\varepsilon}{\varepsilon_p}} p(t - kT_f - c_k T_c - s(\lfloor k / N_f \rfloor)\Delta) \tag{1}$$

Where ε is the transmitted energy per pulse, T_f is the frame duration consisting of N_c chips, $c_k \in [0, N_c - 1]$ is the N_f-periodic TH sequence, T_c is the chip period, $s(n)$ represents the information symbol, and Δ is the PPM modulation index. With k indexing frames in (1), each information symbol is transmitted over N_f frames, which explains the floor operation $\lfloor k / N_f \rfloor$, and implies that the effective symbol duration is $T_s := N_f T_f$. To implement TH, each frame is divided into N_c chips, each of duration T_c, i.e., $T_f = N_c T_c$. Upon defining the symbol level pulse shaper as

$$p_s(t) = \sum_{k=0}^{N_f-1} \frac{1}{\sqrt{\varepsilon_p}} p(t - kT_f - c_k T_c) \tag{2}$$

The transmitted signal can be rewritten as $u(t) = \sum_n \sqrt{\varepsilon} p_s(t - nT_s - s(n)\Delta)$. The power spectrum density (PSD) of the latter can be calculated as follows:

$$\phi_{uu}(f) = \varepsilon \frac{1}{T_s} |P_s(f)|^2 \times \left[\frac{1 - \cos(2\pi\Delta f)}{2} + \frac{1 + \cos(2\pi\Delta f)}{2T_s} \sum_{k=-\infty}^{\infty} \delta\left(f - \frac{k}{T_s}\right) \right] \tag{3}$$

Where $p_s(f)$ is the Fourier Transform (FT) of $p_s(t)$, whose nonzero frequency support is determined by the pulse shaper $p(t)$, and its shape depends on the specific TH code c_k.

3 Orthogonal Hermite Pulse

The Hermite function defined as follows:

$$he_0(t) = 1$$

$$he_n(t) = (-1)^n e^{\frac{t^2}{2}} \frac{d^n}{dt^n}\left(e^{-\frac{t^2}{2}}\right) \tag{4}$$

Obviously, above Hermite function is not orthogonal. The modified orthogonal Hermite polynomials $h_n(t)$ are descried by [5]:

$$h_n(t) = (-1)^n e^{\left(\frac{t}{2t_p}\right)^2} \frac{d^n}{dt^n}\left(e^{-\frac{t^2}{2t_p^2}}\right) \tag{5}$$

Where n is the pulse orders, and n = 0, 1, …, $-\infty < t < \infty$, t_p is the pulse width regular element.

The orthogonal Hermite Pulse having advantageous properties as follows:

(1)   The pulses duration does not change with pulse order. But the complexity of the waveform increase with increasing pulse order n.

(2)   The number of zero crossing equals the pulse order.

(3)   The differentiating operation of the transmitter and receiver antennas has no effect on the orthogonality of the pulses.

(4)   The pulse has zero dc components when pulse order n is larger than zero.

The spectrum of Orthogonal Hermite Pulses mainly contains low frequency components and does not match with FCC spectrum mask. In order to gain more flexibility the orthogonal Hermite polynomials $h_n(t)$ is modified as follows:

$$p_n(t) = h_n(t)\sin(2\pi f_c t) \qquad (6)$$

4   A Simple Cognitive UWB System Model

Cognitive Radio may sense its work environment and dynamically adjust transmitter parameters such as frequency, modulation, and power and so on to change pulse waveform based upon need [6]. The UWB system Model with CR shown in Fig.1 introduces queuing mechanism, which includes parameters queue and different UWB systems queue for the first time. Therefore we acquire the most appropriate spectrum and problem of interference can be solved effectively.

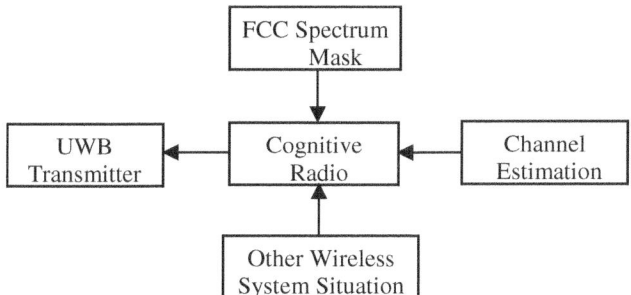

Fig. 1. UWB System Model with Cognitive Radio

5   Computer Simulation

The modulated Hermite pulses of order $n=1{\sim}8$ meet FCC emission mask. The spectrum of Hermit pulse varies with transmitter parameters. According to the work model we change the pulse waveforms by tuning three transmitter factors t_p, n and f_c.

(1) Adjusting pulse width regular element t_p to meet FCC spectrum Mask.

If the tp increases, which is a parameter that controls pulse width, the bandwidth of the pulse becomes narrower. Consequently, the bandwidth can be fitted into the bounds of the spectrum mask if the hermite pulses of higher order are used. Figure 2 shows the pulse width and the limit of the enabled orders when the bandwidth fits into 3.1 GHz to 10.6 GHz when t_p changes from 0.7 to 1.3 and pulse order $n=1$. However the orthogonality of the pulse is not maintained if the width regular element is different.

(2) Selecting different pulse order n to control Multiuser Interference.

Because Hermite pulses are orthogonal mutually the adoption of different waveforms in the two networks reduces Bit Error Rate (BER). As shown in Fig.3 two cases are studied when reference system adopts second order Hermite pulse but interference system adopt second and third order Hermite pulse respectively when the value of t_p is 1.08.

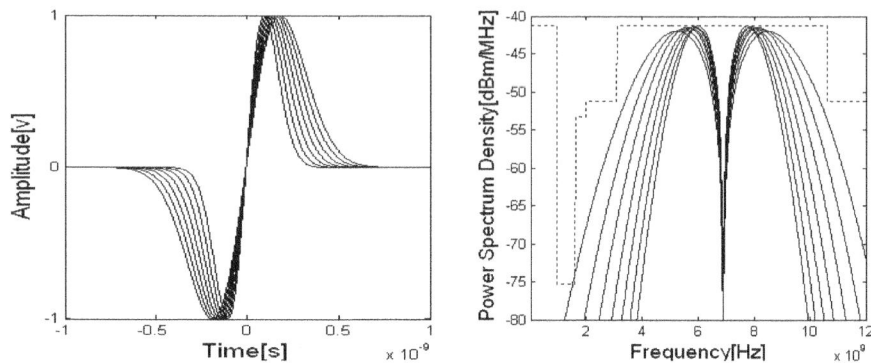

Fig. 2. Pulse shape and PSD of HR pulse with t_p =0.7-1.3,n=1

(3) Shifting central frequency f_c to mitigate single or multi Narrow Band Interference (NBI).

The single and multi-NBI can be mitigated by Selecting appropriate central frequency f_c and pulse order. Suppose that two narrow band systems are working at 5.85GHz and 7.8GHz we adopt second order Hermite pulse with two zero crossings at above two frequency points and let f_c = 6.85GHz. Fig.4 show NBI at 5.85GHz and 7.8GHz is counteracted successfully.

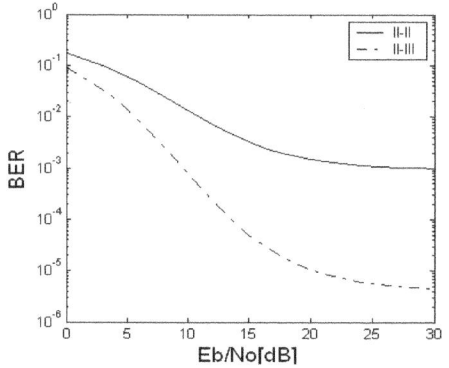

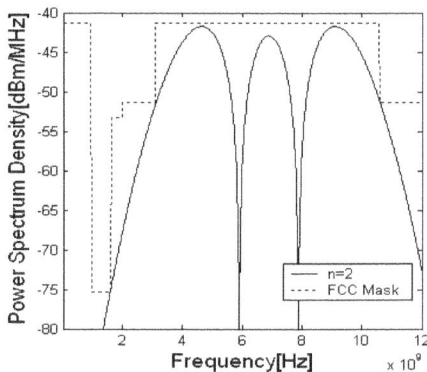

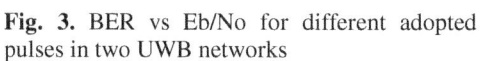

Fig. 3. BER vs Eb/No for different adopted pulses in two UWB networks

Fig. 4. Multi-NBI Mitigation

6   Conclusion

The paper presents a simple cognitive UWB system model with queuing mechanism. In accordance with this model a good spectrum was obtained by tuning transmitter parameters adaptively. It can support dynamic avoidance of narrow-band interference. Implementing a true cognitive UWB radio is still quite challenging today because the limitations of current digital processing technologies, intelligent spectrum-sensing capabilities and dynamic waveform generation algorithms. So our next-step work is to find better pulse design methods and algorithms for acquiring a perfect cognitive UWB system.

Acknowledgments. This paper is funded by: National Natural Science Foundation (60772101); Shanxi Youth Science Foundation (2007021016); Shanxi University Technology research and development project (20090011); Shanxi Youth Science Foundation   (2010021017-1); Taiyuan 2010 University Students innovation and entrepreneurship projects   (100115107).

References

1. Zhang, H.: Multiple Signal Waveforms Aadaption in Cognitive Ultra-Wideband Raido Evolution. IEEE Journal on Selected Areas in Communications 24, 878–884 (2006)
2. Zhou, X.: Cognospectrum: Spectrum Adaptation and Evolution in Cognitive Ultra-Wideband Raido. In: Proc. 2005 IEEE International Conference on Ultra-Wideband (ICU 2005), Zurich, Switzerland, September 5-8, pp. 713–718 (2005)
3. Lansford, J.: UWB Coexistence and Cognitive Radio,
   http://www.alereon.com/images/whitepapers/
   Lansford_UWB_&_Cognitive_Radio_5-04.pdf.2004
4. Benedetto, M.-G.D., De Nardis, L.: Tuning UWB Signals by Pulse Shaping: towards Context-Aware Wireless Networks,
   http://www.cttc.es/spjournal-uwb.2005
5. Yusoff, M.A.: Application of Hermite-Rodriguez functions to pulse shaping analog filter design. World Academy of Science, Engineering and Technology 36, 180–183 (2007)
6. Chiani, M., Giorgetti, A., Liva, G.: Ultra Wide Bandwidth communications towards cognitive Radio (June 02, 2004),
   http://www-csite.deis.unibo.it/Staff/giorgetti/
   pubblicazioni/Conferences/emc05_mcaggl.pdf

SysML Aided Safety Analysis for Safety-Critical Systems

Guoqi Li and Boxuan Wang

School of Reliability and System Engineering, Beihang University,
Beijing, China
gqli@buaa.edu.cn

Abstract. Traditionally safety analysis on hardware and software are carried out separately, so the analysis on the interface of hardware and software is a difficult problem and a week point of the kind of analysis. To meet the challenge, this paper present a SysML aided method for safety analysis by providing heuristic rules of transforming diagrams of SysML to FMEA and FTA. A case study on a typical control system is given for illustration.

Keywords: SysML, safety analysis, safety-critical system.

1   Introduction

Safety analysis is an important issue in safety engineering. It could be carried out at design or integration stages of life cycle of a safety-critical system. At design stage, it could provide criterion for determine safety level of components and could discover week points of the design. On the other hand, at integration stage, it provides evidence for system quality and produces test cases. There are many methods for safety analysis. Among them, FMEA (Failure Mode and Effect Analysis) and FTA (Fault Tree Analysis) are classic ones [1].

Traditionally, safety analysis on hardware and software are carried out separately with different method. However, with the development of microelectronics technology, more and more functions are implemented by software. It's difficult to draw a clear line between hardware and software. So, the analysis on the interface of hardware and software is a difficult problem. To meet the challenge, many efforts are provided, such as SystemC [2] and model checking [3]. However, the methods are too theoretical and difficult to be used in practical engineering. Recently, SysML is introduced to safety engineering and preliminary hazard analysis is adopted and applied to a SysML based requirements specification [4]. SysML is a general purpose modeling language for systems engineering applications. It supports the specification, analysis, design, verification and validation of a broad range of systems and systems-of-systems. These systems may include hardware, software, information, processes, personnel, and facilities [5]. SysML is a specified as a profile (dialect) of the UML (Unified Modeling Language), which is widely used in software engineering and has proved it's practical and sophisticated.

In this paper, a SysML aided method for safety analysis is presented for safety analysis. We provide the heuristic rules of transforming diagrams of SysML to FMEA and FTA based on our similar researches on UML [6]. What's more, a case study on a typical intelligent control system is given for illustration.

H. Deng et al. (Eds.): AICI 2011, Part I, LNAI 7002, pp. 270–275, 2011.

2   From Diagrams of SysML to FMEA or FTA

In the paper "SFTA based safety analysis for bridge pattern" [6], two rules of transforming from UML to FTA are presented.

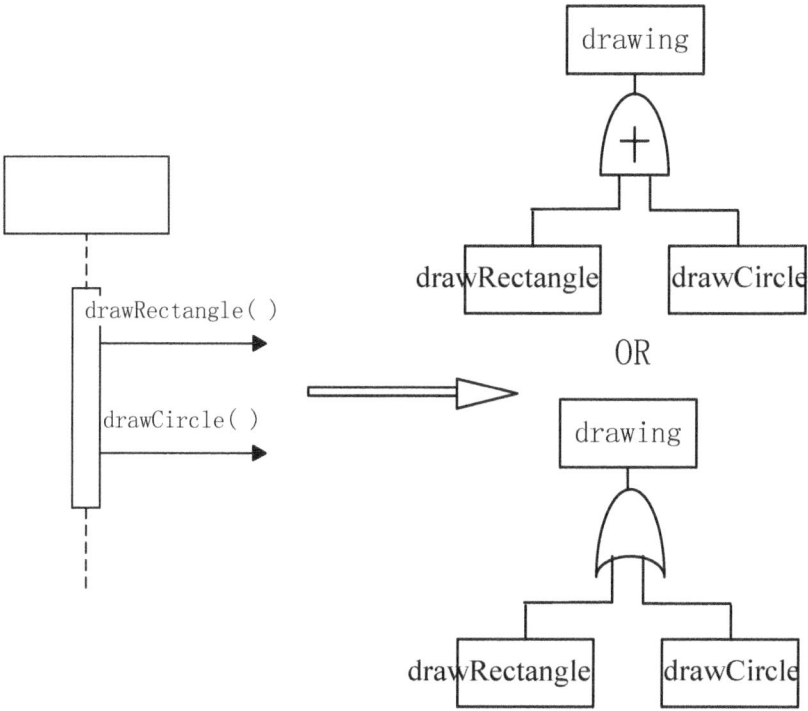

Fig. 1. Transforming rule 1 of from sequence diagram to FTA. The gate is OR gate or AND gate should be selected according to specific conditions.

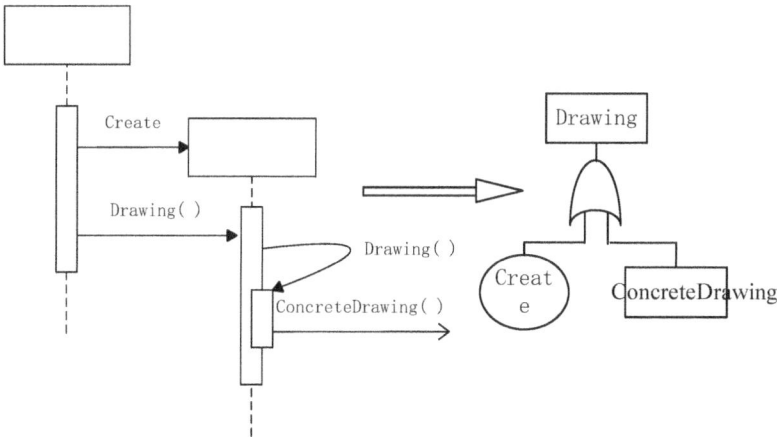

Fig. 2. Transforming rule 2 of from sequence diagram to FTA

Practically, the heuristic rules are derived from sequence diagrams and statecharts diagrams. Statecharts diagrams also called hierarchy definite states machine diagrams.

3   Case Study

3.1   Description of the System

The example is also used in the famous paper on Software FMEA [7]. The operational objective of the system is to maintain the ball at a predefined height in the tube. The software in the microprocessor provides the control mechanism; it implements a proportional controller (P-controller)-that is, the output signal is proportional to the amount of error in the ball's position relative to the set-point. The software is written in assembly language, which is assembled and downloaded into the system EEPROM. This ensures that the program stays in the EEPROM when the system power is out. A schematic diagram of the system is shown in Figure 3.

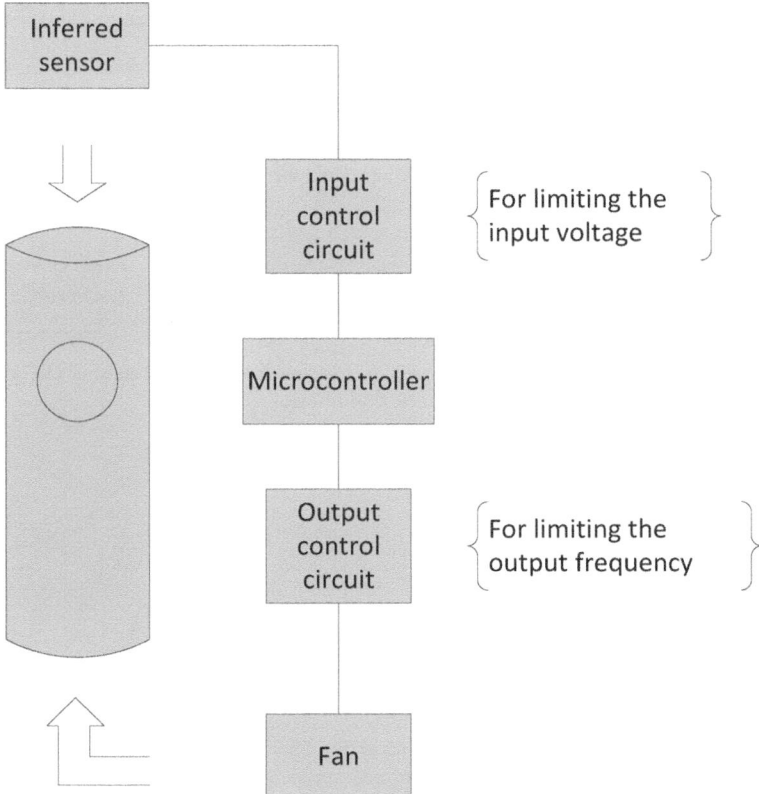

Fig. 3. Blocking diagram of the closed loop control system [7]

In the closed-loop control system, a sensor monitors the system output (the position of the ball) and feeds the data to a controller which adjusts the control (the ball position) as necessary to maintain the desired system output. Feedback from measuring the ball's position allowed the controller to dynamically compensate for changes to the ball's position. It is from this feedback that the paradigm of the control loop arises: the control affects the system output, which in turn is measured and looped back to alter the control.

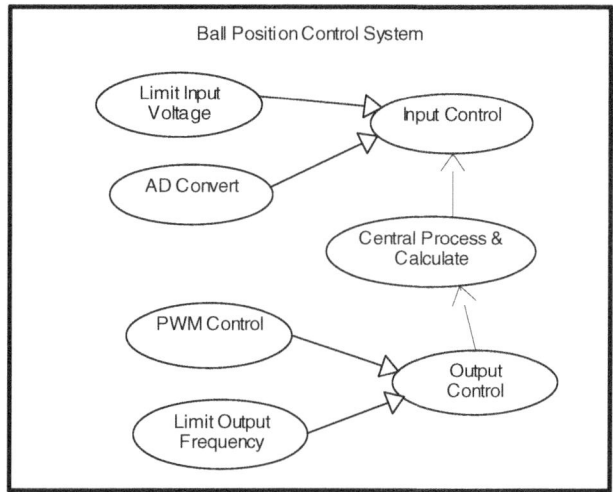

Fig. 4. Use case diagram of the system

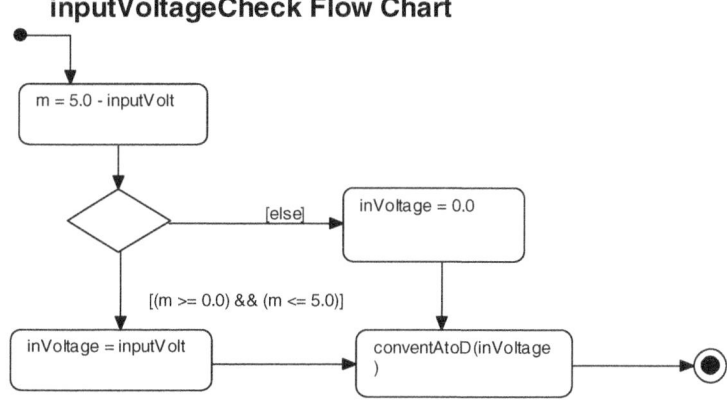

Fig. 5. Flow chart diagram of the system

3.2   SysML for the System

A use case diagram in the SysML is a type of behavioral diagram defined by and created from a Use-case analysis. Its purpose is to present a graphical overview of the functionality provided by a system in terms of actors, their goals (represented as use cases), and any dependencies between those use cases.

A flowchart is a type of diagram that represents an algorithm or process, showing the steps as boxes of various kinds, and their order by connecting these with arrows. This diagrammatic representation can give a step-by-step solution to a given problem. Process operations are represented in these boxes, and arrows connecting them represent flow of control. Data flows are not typically represented in a flowchart, in contrast with data flow diagrams; rather, they are implied by the sequencing of operations. Flowcharts are used in analyzing, designing, documenting or managing a process or program in various fields.[8]

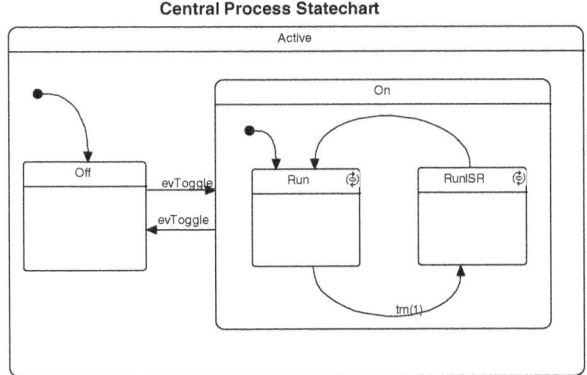

Fig. 6. Statecharts diagram of the system

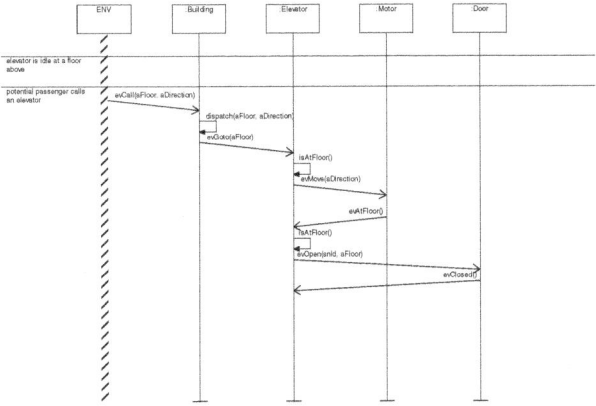

Fig. 7. Sequence diagram of the system

A statecharts diagram is a type of diagram used in computer science and related fields to describe the behavior of systems. Statecharts diagrams require that the system described is composed of a finite number of states; sometimes, this is indeed the case, while at other times this is a reasonable abstraction. There are many forms of state diagrams, which differ slightly and have different semantics.

A sequence diagram in SysML is a kind of interaction diagram that shows how processes operate with one another and in what order. It is a construct of a Message Sequence Chart.

4   Conclusion and Future Works

The main contribution of the paper is to present a SysML aided method for safety analysis by providing heuristic rules of transforming diagrams of SysML to FMEA and FTA. A case study on a typical control system is given for illustration.

In our future works, more practical works are plan to be conducted and more deep exploration will be carried out on the topic

References

1. Tribble, A.C., Miller, S.P.: Software intensive systems safety analysis. IEEE Aerospace and Electronic Systems Magazine 19(10), 21–26 (2004)
2. Zarandi, H.R., Miremadi, S.G.: Fault tree analysis of embedded systems using SystemC. In: Proceedings of Reliability and Maintainability Symposium, pp. 77–81 (2005)
3. Hsiung, P.-A., Chen, Y.-R., Lin, Y.-H.: Model Checking Safety-Critical Systems Using Safecharts. IEEE Transactions on Computers 56(5) (2007)
4. Thramboulidis, K., Scholz, S.: Integrating the 3+1 SysML view model with safety engineering. In: 2010 IEEE Conference on Emerging Technologies and Factory Automation (ETFA), pp. 1–8 (2010)
5. SysML Open Source Specification Project, http://www.sysml.org
6. Li, G., Lu, M., Liu, B.: SFTA based saftey analysis for bridge pattern. In: Proceedings of 2009 8th International Conference on Reliability, Maintainability and Safety, ICRMS 2009, pp. 522–525. IEEE Computer Society, Los Alamitos (2009)
7. Bowles, J.B., Wan, C.: Software failure modes and effects analysis for a small embedded control system. In: Proceedings of Reliability and Maintainability Symposium, pp. 1–6 (2001)
8. ISO, Information processing – Documentation symbols and conventions for data, program and system flowcharts, program network charts and system resources charts. International Organization for Standardization (1985)

Research on Low Delay 11.2kbps Speech Coding Algorithm*

Zhefeng Zhao, Gang Zhang, and Yiping Wang

College of Information Engineering, Taiyuan University of Technology,
030024 Taiyuan, China
zhaozhefeng@163.com

Abstract. This paper presented a 11.2kbps speech coding algorithm, whose delay is 2.5ms and sampling rate is 8kHz. A 20 dimensional CELP is used in this algorithm, while self-adaptive codebook search cascaded with algebra codebook search are adopted in vector quantization. The PC simulation shows the synthetic speech quality after PESQ test is close to that of G.728 at 16kbps.

Keywords: speech coding, low delay, LD-CELP; PESQ, codebook search.

1 Introduction

The ideal speech coding algorithm requires not only high synthetic speech quality, but also low delay, small memory capacity of program and data, and low complexity etc. The size of excited codebook should be decreased in order to further reduce coding rate of traditional LD-CELP algorithm, which will always lead to the synthetic speech quality sharply declines. While in the sake of improving synthetic quality, frame length needs to be largely disposed. But it will prolong coding delay.[1]

Based on LD-CELP, this paper put forward a dual codebook (self-adaptive codebook and algebra codebook) excited linear predictive algorithm with lower delay. Simulation experiment result shows that this algorithm has the equivalent synthetic effect with LD-CELP, but coding rate of 11.2kbps is lower than 16kbps of LD-CELP.

2 Outline of Encoders

The delay of 2.5ms is obtained at sampling rate of 8k and a frame includes 20 sampling points in this algorithm. 20 dimensional coding excited linear predictive technology is adopted in order to reduce the energy of error signal between actual speech and synthetic speech in coding.[2] For the analysis of synthetic linear predictive error signal, two-stage codebook is used in vector quantization, that is, self-adaptive codebook and algebra codebook are separately adopted, and quantization parameters are transmitted. At the end of decoder, decoding synthetic speech is

---

* This work was partially funded by Shanxi Province Foundation for Returness(2009-31), International Scientific and Technological Cooperation Projects in Shanxi Province(2008-081026).

H. Deng et al. (Eds.): AICI 2011, Part I, LNAI 7002, pp. 276–281, 2011.

obtained by addition of decoding self-adaption codebook and decoding algebra codebook as excited signal to excite linear predictive synthetic filter.

PCM signal $s(n)$ after mean quantization firstly passes perceptual weighting filter W1, then become weighting speech vector $v(n)$, and then minus zero-input response $r(n)$, so objective vector $x(n)$ of codebook search is obtained, that is, $x(n)=v(n)-r(n)$. $x(n)$ passes codebook search module VQ which is made up of self-adaptive codebook and algebra codebook, in the one hand, code vector index and gain index transmitted in signal channel are obtained; in the other hand, synthetic filter S1 is excited by excited signal $e(n)$,so synthetic speech $s_q(n)$ is achieved. Synthetic filter adjuster periodically adjusts the filter coefficients of synthetic filters S1 and S2, the input of which was synthetic speech $s_q(n)$. Similarly, perceptual weighting filter adjuster periodically adjusts perceptual weighting filter W1 and W2, the input of which is $s(n)$.

Codebook search module VQ is made up of five parts, which are self-adaptive codebook search, the second stage objective vector calculation, algebra codebook search, algebra code vector calculation and gain predictive filter. Excited vector $e(n)$ is achieved by two-stage codebook search of objective vector $x(n)$. The diagram is showed as Fig.1.

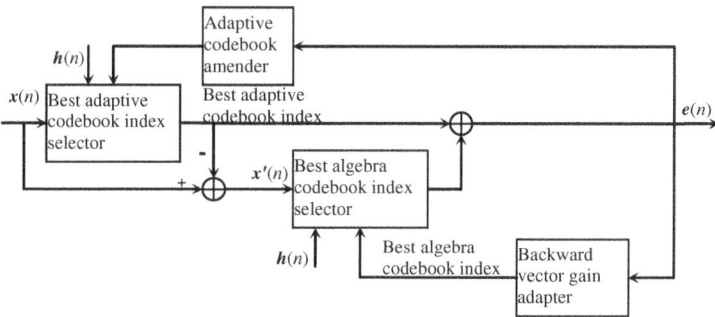

Fig. 1. Diagram of codebook search module

2.1   The Structure of Self-Adaptive Codebook

Self-adaptive codebook is composed of a first-in and first-out memory whose length is 275, which is referred to as $BC(n)$, $n=0,...,274$. This memory with length of 275 consists 256 codebook vectors y_j, $j=0,...,255$. The relationship between both is denoted as (1)

$$y_j = \{BC(j),BC(j+1),...,BC(j+19)\}^T, j=0,...,255 \qquad (1)$$

The optimal self-adaptive code vector y_j of current frame is achieved by evaluating the least mean square error between $x(n)$ and y_j ,that is

$$D = \| x(n)- G_pHy_j \|^2 \qquad (2)$$

Where, G_p is gain actual value of self-adaptive codebook correspondingly.

The optimal self-adaptive code vector is y_j whose error D is the least, and the gain is[3]

$$G_p = x(n)^T H y_j \big/ \left\| H y_j \right\|^2 \qquad (3)$$

$\hat{G}_p$ is obtained by scalar quantization of G_p according to Fig.1, consequently, the optimal quantization vector y_j is achieved by self-adaptive codebook search, which is used to calculate objective vector $x'(n)$ of the second stage codebook search

$$x'(n) = x(n) - \hat{G}_p y_j \qquad (4)$$

In the other hand, the optimal excited vector $e(n)$ is achieved by adding it to the optimal quantization vector of the second stage.

Self-adaptive codebook gain quantization is a scalar quantization, whose quantization intervals and quantization values are showed as Tab.1.

2.2   The Structure of Algebra Codebook

Algebra codebook adopts the similar algebra structure form as that of G.729[4], and the difference is that 4 non-zero pulses are included in 40 dimensional vectors in G.729, but 5 non-zero pulses are included in 20 dimensional vectors here. The structure is showed as Tab.1.

Table 1. Structure of algebra codebook

Pulse	Sign	Position
i0	±1	0, 5, 10, 15
i1	±1	1, 6, 11, 16
i2	±1	2, 7, 12, 17
i3	±1	3, 4, 8, 9, 13, 14, 18, 19

Because non-zero pulses in algebra codebook have already included sign information, their values adopt positive values quantization, and quantization proposal is showed as Tab.2.

Table 2. Gain quantization of algebra codebook

Ordinal No.	The quantity turns zone	The quantity turns value
0	$[2.7732, +\infty)$	3.4836
1	$[1.6758, 2.7732)$	2.0627
2	$[1.0276, 1.6858)$	1.3090
3	$[0, 1.0276)$	0.7462

Through the similar algebra codebook search algorithm to that of G.729, positions, signs and gain G_c of 5 non-zero pulses could be obtained.

The filters in this algorithm are back-forward regenerative, so end information does not need transmitting in signal channel, and only the optimal excited code vector indexes are transmitted. Self-adaptive codebook is made up of 256 20 dimensional vectors, which can be represented by 8 bit, and self-adaptive codebook gain is quantized by 3 bit. Thus, self-adaptive codebook totally needs 11 bit quantization.

The position information in algebra codebook is presented by 2+2+2+2+2bit=10bit, and sign information occupies 5 bit, so the total is 15 bit. Its gain is quantized by 4 positive values, that is to say, the gain of algebra codebook is quantized by 2 bit. The frame length in this algorithm is 20, and each frame is quantized by 28 bit, so the total coding rate is 11.2 kbps.

3 The Implementation of Encoder and the Evaluation of Performance

In order to evaluate the performance of this algorithm, PESQ of ITU-T P.862[5] is used. Tab.3 shows the comparison of encoder of this algorithm with PESQ of G.728. PESQ value of this algorithm is decreased by 0.16 with comparison to that of G.728. Fig.2 shows the wave comparison diagram of original speech of one sentence of female and male, quantized speech of G.728 and quantized speech of this algorithm. From the figure, we can see that encoding effect in this algorithm is close to that of G.728. There is also no obvious difference between them in audio effect.

Table 3. Pesq comparison between g.728 and this algorithm

Ordinal No.	G728	The calculate way
1	3.66	3.53
2	3.86	3.32
3	3.66	3.12
4	3.97	3.34
5	3.74	3.47
6	3.78	3.29
7	3.90	3.38
8	3.91	3.67
9	4.02	3.29
10	4.00	3.44
11	3.31	3.43
12	3.22	3.61
13	3.38	3.48
14	3.40	3.42
15	3.61	3.41
16	3.49	3.34
17	3.54	3.44
18	3.56	3.19
19	3.52	3.48
20	3.47	3.77
21	3.57	3.67
22	3.45	3.56
23	3.61	3.57
24	3.71	3.39
25	3.59	3.50
26	3.41	3.38
27	3.48	3.45
28	3.64	3.42
29	3.67	3.44
30	3.43	3.40
Average	3.62	3.44

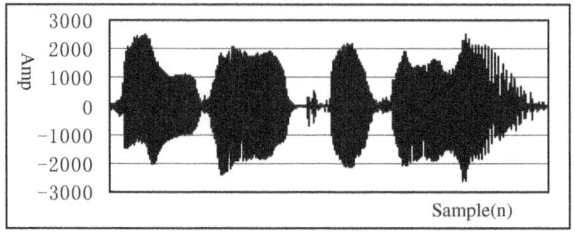

(a1) original speech of female voice 1

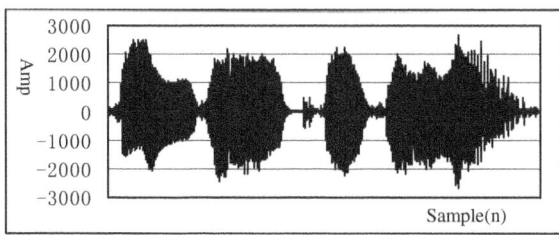

(a2) synthetic speech of female voice 1 of G.728

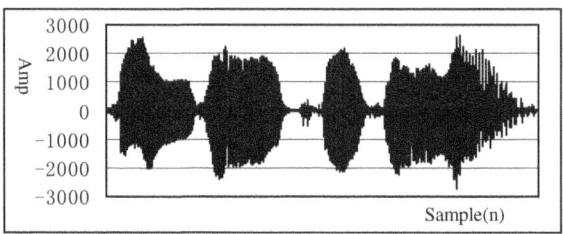

(a3) synthetic speech of female voice 1 of this algorithm

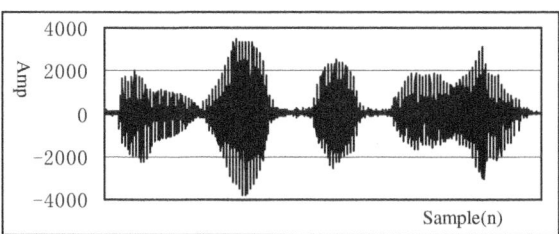

(b1) original speech of male voice 1

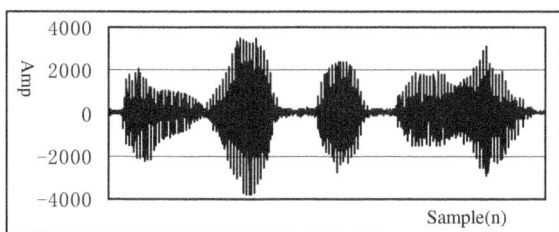

(b2) synthetic speech of male voice 1 of G.728

Fig. 2. Comparison diagram of quantization wave

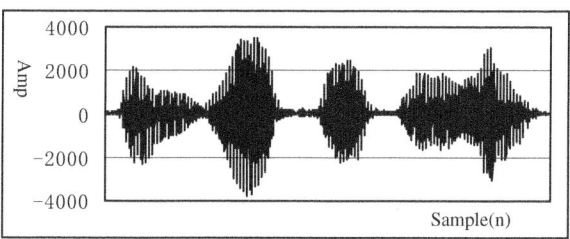

(b3) synthetic speech of male voice 1 of this algorithm

Fig. 2. (*continued*)

4   Conclusion

The main purpose of this paper is to present a speech encoding algorithm with low delay and low coding rate, whose algorithm delay is 2.5 ms and coding rate is 11.2 kbps, and its encoding quality is close to that of G.728. In order to achieve this goal, two-stage codebook search method is used instead of codebook search method in G.728, and frame length is 20 sampling points. Through these measures, a better balance point is found between coding rate and delay.

References

1. CCITT: Recommendation G.728, Coding of speech at 16kb/s using low-delay code excited linear prediction, Geneva (1992)
2. Wu, S., Zhang, G.: 8Kbit/s LD-aCELP Speech Coding with Backward Pitch Detection. In: Asia-Pacific Conference on Information Processing, Shenzhen, pp. 434–437 (2009)
3. Zhang, G., Xie, K., Zhang, X., Huangfu, L.: Improving G.728's hybrid window and excitation gain. In: IEEE Asia-Pacific Conference on Circuits and Systems, Tainan, Taiwan, pp. 185–188 (2004)
4. ITU-T: Recommendation of G729, Coding of speech at 8 kbs using conjugate-structure algebraic-code-excited linear prediction, CS-ACELP (1996)
5. ITU-T: Recommendation P.862, Perceptual evaluation of speech quality (PESQ): An objective method for end-to-end speech quality assessment of narrow-band telephone networks and speech codecs (2001)

Further Remarks on $(\alpha\lambda, \lambda')$-Continuity in Generalized Topological Spaces*

Zhang Chun-Yan and Bai Shi-Zhong

School of Mathematics and Computational Science
Wuyi University, Guangdong 529020, P.R. China
shizhongbai@yahoo.com.cn, zhangqingwell@163.com

Abstract. The concept of $(\alpha\lambda, \lambda')$-continuity was introduced by Min [7], based on the concept of (λ, λ')-continuity by Császár [3]. Now, we introduce the concept of $(\alpha\lambda, \lambda')$-continuity at a point and investigate some properties of $(\alpha\lambda, \lambda')$-continuity, and study some properties of $(\alpha\lambda, \lambda')$-continuous image.

Keywords: generalized topology, (λ, λ')-continuity, $(\alpha\lambda, \lambda')$ -continuity.

1   Introduction

Császár introduced the theory of generalized topological spaces, in which he studied the notions of continuous functions, interior and closure operators, neighborhood systems, compactness and connectedness in generalized topological spaces [1-6]. This theory is one of the most important developments in general topology in recent years. Then, Min introduced generalized continuous functions defined by $\lambda - \alpha$-open sets, λ-semiopen sets, λ-preopen, and $\lambda - \beta$-semiopen sets in generalized topological spaces [7].

The purpose of this paper is to introduce the concept of $(\alpha\lambda, \lambda')$-continuity at a point and investigate some properties of $(\alpha\lambda, \lambda')$-continuity, and study some properties of $(\alpha\lambda, \lambda')$-continuous image as well.

2   Preliminaries

We recall the definitions of the most essential concepts needed in the following. Let X be a set, $expX$ denotes the power set of X. We call a class $\lambda \subset expX$ a generalized topology [3] (briefly GT) if $\emptyset \in \lambda$ and any union of elements of λ belongs to λ. We call the pair (X, λ) a generalized topological space (briefly GTS). For a GTS (X, λ), the elements of λ are called λ-open sets and the complements of λ-open sets are called λ-closed sets. For $A \subset X$, the λ-interior of A denoted by $i(A)$(or iA) is the union of all λ-open sets contained in A, and the λ-closure of A denoted by $c(A)$(or cA) is the intersection of all λ-closed sets containing A. Then

---

* This work is supported by the NSFCs of China (No. 10971125 and No. 61070150).

H. Deng et al. (Eds.): AICI 2011, Part I, LNAI 7002, pp. 282–287, 2011.
© Springer-Verlag Berlin Heidelberg 2011

we have $ii(A) = i(A)$, $cc(A) = c(A)$, $i(A) = X - c(X - A)$, $c(A) = X - i(X - A)$, $icic(A) = ic(A)$ and $cici(A) = ci(A)$ [3]. A set $A \subset X$ is said to be $\lambda - \alpha$-open (resp. λ-semiopen, λ-preopen, $\lambda - \beta$-open) [5] if $A \subset ici(A)$ (resp. $A \subset ci(A)$, $A \subset ic(A)$, $A \subset cic(A)$). The complement of a $\lambda - \alpha$-open (resp. λ-semiopen, λ-preopen, $\lambda - \beta$-open) set is called $\lambda - \alpha$-closed (resp. λ-semiclosed, λ-preclosed, $\lambda - \beta$-closed). We denote by $\alpha(\lambda)$ the collection of all $\lambda - \alpha$-open set of the space (X, λ).

Let (X, λ) and (Y, λ') be GTS's. Then a function $f : X \to Y$ is said to be (λ, λ')-continuous [3] if $B \in \lambda'$ implies that $f^{-1}(B) \in \lambda$. f is said to be $(\alpha\lambda, \lambda')$-continuous if $B \in \lambda'$ implies that $f^{-1}(B) \in \alpha(\lambda)$ [7].

3 $(\alpha\lambda, \lambda')$-Continuous Function

Definition 3.1. Let (X, λ) and (Y, λ') be GTS's. Then a function $f : X \to Y$ is said to be $(\alpha\lambda, \lambda')$-continuous at $x \in X$ if for each λ'-open set V containing $f(x)$, there exists a $\lambda - \alpha$-open set U containing x, such that $f(U) \subset V$.

Theorem 3.2. Let $f : X \to Y$ be a function between the GTS's (X, λ) and (Y, λ'). If f is $(\alpha\lambda, \lambda')$-continuous at $x \in X$, then the following holds.

(1) For any $\lambda' - \alpha$-open set V containing $f(x)$, there exists a $\lambda - \alpha$-open set U containing x such that $f(U) \subset ici(V)$.

(2) For any λ'-preopen set V containing $f(x)$, there exists a $\lambda - \alpha$-open set U containing x such that $f(U) \subset ic(V)$.

(3) $x \in ici(f^{-1}(V))$ for each λ'-open set V containing $f(x)$.

(4) $x \in f^{-1}(ici(V))$ for each $\lambda' - \alpha$-open set V containing $f(x)$.

(5) $x \in ici(f^{-1}(ici(V)))$ for each $\lambda' - \alpha$-open set V containing $f(x)$.

(6) $x \in f^{-1}(ic(V))$ for each λ'-preopen set V containing $f(x)$.

(7) $x \in ici(f^{-1}(ic(V)))$ for each λ'-preopen set V containing $f(x)$.

Proof. (1). Let V be a $\lambda' - \alpha$-open set of containing $f(x)$. Then $f(x) \in V \subset ici(V)$. Since $ici(V)$ is λ'-open, from the definition of $(\alpha\lambda, \lambda')$-continuous at $x \in X$, there exists a $\lambda - \alpha$-open set U containing x such that $f(U) \subset ici(V)$.

(2). This is analogous to proof of (1).

(3). Let V be any λ'-open set containing $f(x)$. From the definition of $(\alpha\lambda, \lambda')$-continuous at $x \in X$, there exists a $\lambda - \alpha$-open set U containing x, such that $f(U) \subset V$. Then $U \subset f^{-1}f(U) \subset f^{-1}(V)$. Thus $x \in U \subset ici(U) \subset ici(f^{-1}(V))$.

(4). This follows directly from (1).

(5). Let V be a $\lambda' - \alpha$-open set of containing $f(x)$. Then $f(x) \in V \subset ici(V)$. Since $ici(V)$ is λ'-open, from the definition of $(\alpha\lambda, \lambda')$-continuous at $x \in X$, there exists a $\lambda - \alpha$-open set U containing x such that $f(U) \subset ici(V)$. This implies $x \in U \subset f^{-1}f(U) \subset f^{-1}(ici(V))$. Thus $x \in U \subset ici(U) \subset ici(f^{-1}(ici(V)))$.

(6). This follows directly from (2).

(7). This is analogous to proof of (3).

Theorem 3.3. Let $f : X \to Y$ be a function between the GTS's (X, λ) and (Y, λ'). Then the following are equivalent:

(1) f is $(\alpha\lambda, \lambda^{'})$-continuous.
(2) $f^{-1}(B)$ is a $\lambda - \alpha$-closed set in X for each $\lambda^{'}$-closed set B in Y [7].
(3) $f(cic(A)) \subset c(f(A))$ for each set A in X [7].
(4) $cic(f^{-1}(B)) \subset f^{-1}(c(B))$ for each set B in Y [7].
(5) $f^{-1}(i(B)) \subset ici(f^{-1}(B))$ for each set B in Y [7].
(6) f is $(\alpha\lambda, \lambda^{'})$-continuous at every point $x \in X$.

Proof. We prove only $(1) \Leftrightarrow (6)$.

$(1) \Rightarrow (6)$. Let f be $(\alpha\lambda, \lambda^{'})$-continuous, $x \in X$ and B be $\lambda^{'}$-open set of Y containing $f(x)$. Then $x \in f^{-1}(B) \subset ici(f^{-1}(B))$. Let $A = f^{-1}(B)$, then A is $\lambda - \alpha$-open set containing x and $f(A) = ff^{-1}(B) \subset B$. Thus, f is $(\alpha\lambda, \lambda^{'})$-continuous at every point $x \in X$.

$(6) \Rightarrow (1)$. Let B be a $\lambda^{'}$-open set of Y and $x \in f^{-1}(B)$. Then $f(x) \in B$. By hypothesis there exists a $\lambda - \alpha$-open set A containing x such that $f(A) \subset B$. Then

$x \in A \subset f^{-1}f(A) \subset f^{-1}(B)$ and $x \in A \subset ici(A) \subset ici(f^{-1}(B))$.

Hence $f^{-1}(B) \subset ici(f^{-1}(B))$, i.e. $f^{-1}(B)$ is $\lambda - \alpha$-open. Thus f is $(\alpha\lambda, \lambda^{'})$-continuous.

Theorem 3.4. Let (X, λ) and $(Y, \lambda^{'})$ be GTS's, and $f : X \to Y$ be a one-to-one and onto function. Then f is $(\alpha\lambda, \lambda^{'})$-continuous iff $i(f(A)) \subset f(ici(A))$ for each set A in X.

Proof. Let f be $(\alpha\lambda, \lambda^{'})$-continuous and A be any set in X. Then $f^{-1}(i(f(A)))$ is a $\lambda - \alpha$-open set in X. By the Theorem 3.3(5) and the fact that f is one-to-one, we have

$f^{-1}(i(f(A))) \subset ici(f^{-1}f(A)) = ici(A)$.

Again, since f is onto, we have

$i(f(A)) = ff^{-1}(i(f(A))) \subset f(ici(A))$.

Conversely, let B be a $\lambda^{'}$-open set in Y. By hypothesis,

$f(ici(f^{-1}(B))) \supset i(ff^{-1}(B)) = i(B) = B$.

Since f is one-to-one, we have

$ici(f^{-1}(B)) = f^{-1}f(ici(f^{-1}(B))) \supset f^{-1}(B)$.

Hence $f^{-1}(B)$ is a $\lambda - \alpha$-open set in X. Thus f is $(\alpha\lambda, \lambda^{'})$-continuous.

Theorem 3.5. Let $f : X \to Y$ be a function between the GTS's (X, λ) and $(Y, \lambda^{'})$. If f is $(\alpha\lambda, \lambda^{'})$-continuous, then the following holds.

(1) $c(f^{-1}(B)) = ci(f^{-1}(B))$ for each $\lambda^{'}$-open set B in Y.
(2) $ic(f^{-1}(B)) = i(f^{-1}(B))$ for each $\lambda^{'}$-closed set B in Y.
(3) $ic(f^{-1}(c(B))) = i(f^{-1}(c(B)))$ for each set B in Y.
(4) $c(f^{-1}(i(B))) = ci(f^{-1}(i(B)))$ for each set B in Y.
(5) $cic(f^{-1}(B)) \subset f^{-1}(cic(B))$ for each $\lambda^{'} - \beta$-open set B in Y.
(6) $ici(f^{-1}(B)) \supset f^{-1}(ici(B))$ for each $\lambda^{'} - \beta$-closed set B in Y.
(7) $cic(f^{-1}(B)) \subset f^{-1}(ci(B))$ for each $\lambda^{'}$-semiopen set B in Y.
(8) $ici(f^{-1}(B)) \supset f^{-1}(ic(B))$ for each $\lambda^{'}$-semiclosed set B in Y.
(9) $c(f^{-1}(B)) \subset ic(f^{-1}(ic(B)))$ for each $\lambda^{'}$-preopen set B in Y.
(10) $i(f^{-1}(B)) \supset ci(f^{-1}(ci(B)))$ for each $\lambda^{'}$-preclosed set B in Y.

(11) $c(f^{-1}(B)) \subset ic(f^{-1}(ici(B)))$ for each $\lambda' - \alpha$-open set B in Y.
(12) $i(f^{-1}(B)) \supset ci(f^{-1}(cic(B)))$ for each $\lambda' - \alpha$-closed set B in Y.

Proof. (1). Let B be a λ'-open set in Y. By definition of the $(\alpha\lambda, \lambda')$-continuous function, we have $f^{-1}(B) \subset ici(f^{-1}(B))$. Thus
$c(f^{-1}(B)) \subset cici(f^{-1}(B)) = ci(f^{-1}(B)) \subset c(f^{-1}(B))$.
(3). Let B be a set in Y. Since $c(B)$ is λ'-closed in Y, from (2), we have
$ic(f^{-1}(c(B))) = i(f^{-1}(c(B)))$.
(5). Let B be a $\lambda' - \beta$-open set in Y. Then $B \subset cic(B)$. From the Theorem 3.3(4), we have $cic(f^{-1}(B)) \subset f^{-1}(c(B)) \subset f^{-1}(cic(B))$.
(7). Let B be a λ'-semiopen set in Y. Then $B \subset ci(B)$. Since every λ'-semiopen set is $\lambda' - \beta$-open, by (5), we have
$cic(f^{-1}(B)) \subset f^{-1}(cic(B)) \subset f^{-1}(cic(ci(B))) = f^{-1}(ci(B))$.
(9). Let B be a λ'-preopen set in Y. Then $B \subset ic(B)$. Since $ic(B)$ is λ'-open, by definition of the $(\alpha\lambda, \lambda')$-continuous function, we have
$f^{-1}(B) \subset f^{-1}(ic(B)) \subset ici(f^{-1}(ic(B)))$.
Thus $c(f^{-1}(B)) \subset cici(f^{-1}(ic(B)) = ci(f^{-1}(ic(B)))$.
(11). This is analogous to proof of (9).
(2).(4).(6).(8).(10).(12). Obvious.

Remark 3.6. None of the converses of the Theorem 3.5 (1-12) does hold. Next, we only need to prove that none of the converses of the Theorem 3.5 (1,3,5,7,9,11) does hold.

Example 3.7. Let $X = \{a, b, c\}$. Consider two generalized topologies $\lambda = \{\emptyset, \{a\}, \{b\}, \{a, b\}\}$ and $\lambda' = \{\emptyset, \{b, c\}\}$ on X, and the identity function $f : (X, \lambda) \to (X, \lambda')$. Obviously, the Theorem 3.5 (1) holds. For the Theorem 3.5 (3), by computing we obtain
$ic(f^{-1}(c(\{a\}))) = ic(f^{-1}(\{a\})) = ic(\{a\}) = i(\{a, c\}) = \{a\}$,
$i(f^{-1}(c(\{a\}))) = i(f^{-1}(\{a\})) = i(\{a\}) = \{a\}$,
and
$f^{-1}(c(\{b\})) = f^{-1}(c(\{c\})) = f^{-1}(c(\{a, b\})) = f^{-1}(c(\{a, c\})) = f^{-1}(c(\{b, c\}))$
$= f^{-1}(c(X)) = f^{-1}(X)$,
$ic(f^{-1}(X)) = i(f^{-1}(X)) = \{a, b\}$.
Thus the Theorem 3.5 (3) holds. But f is not $(\alpha\lambda, \lambda')$-continuous.

Example 3.8. Let $X = \{a, b, c\}$. Consider two generalized topologies $\lambda = \{\emptyset, \{a\}, \{b, c\}, X\}$ and $\lambda' = \{\emptyset, \{a, b\}, X\}$ on X, and the identity function $f : (X, \lambda) \to (X, \lambda')$. By easy computations we get that the Theorem 3.5 (5) and (7) all hold. But f is not $(\alpha\lambda, \lambda')$-continuous.

Example 3.9. Let $X = \{a, b, c\}$. Consider two generalized topologies $\lambda = \{\emptyset, \{a, b\}, X\}$ and $\lambda' = \{\emptyset, \{b, c\}\}$ on X, and the identity function $f : (X, \lambda) \to (X, \lambda')$. By easy computations it follows that the Theorem 3.5(9) and (11) all hold. But f is not $(\alpha\lambda, \lambda')$-continuous.

4 Properties of $(\alpha\lambda, \lambda')$-Continuous Image

Proposition 4.1. Let (X, λ_1), (Y, λ_2) and (Z, λ_3) be GTS's, and $f : X \to Y$ and $g : Y \to Z$ be functions. If f is (λ_1, λ_2)-continuous and g is $(\alpha\lambda_2, \lambda_3)$-continuous, then $g \circ f$ is $(\alpha\lambda_1, \lambda_3)$-continuous.

Now let $K \neq \emptyset$ be an index set, $X_k \neq \emptyset$ for $k \in K$, $X = \prod_{k \in K} X_k$ the Cartesian Product of sets X_k, and λ_k is a topology of X_k and λ the product topology of the factors λ_k. We denote by p_k the projection $p_k : X \to X_k$.

Theorem 4.2. Let (X_k, λ_k) and (Y_k, μ_k) be GTS's and K a finite set. If $f_k : X_k \to Y_k$ are $(\alpha\lambda_k, \mu_k)$-continuous, then the product $\prod_{k \in K} f_k : \prod_{k \in K} X_k \to \prod_{k \in K} Y_k$ is $(\alpha\lambda, \mu)$-continuous.

Proof. We prove only $k = 2$. Let $B = \bigcup(A_i \times B_j)$, where the A_i's and B_j's are generalized open sets of Y_1 and Y_2, respectively. B is a generalized open set of $Y_1 \times Y_2$. Hence we have
$$(f_1 \times f_2)^{-1}(B) = (f_1 \times f_2)^{-1}(\bigcup(A_i \times B_j)) = \bigcup(f_1 \times f_2)^{-1}(A_i \times B_j)$$
$$= \bigcup(f_1^{-1}(A_i) \times f_2^{-1}(B_j)).$$
That $(f_1 \times f_2)^{-1}(B)$ is a generalized α-open set of $X_1 \times X_2$ follows from the Theorem 4.3 in [6]. Thus $f_1 \times f_2$ is $(\alpha\lambda, \mu)$-continuous.

Theorem 4.3. Let K be a finite set, (Y, μ) and (X_k, λ_k) be GTS's and λ_k strong for every $k \in K$. If $f : Y \to \prod_{k \in K} X_k$ is $(\alpha\mu, \lambda)$-continuous, then $p_k \circ f$ is $(\alpha\mu, \lambda_k)$-continuous.

Proof. This follows directly from the Proposition 2.7 in [6] and the Proposition 4.2.

Theorem 4.4. Let (X_k, λ_k) be GTS's and λ_k strong for $k = 1, 2$, and $f : X_1 \to X_2$ a function. If the graph $g : X_1 \to X_1 \times X_2$ of f is $(\alpha\lambda_1, \lambda)$-continuous, then f is $(\alpha\lambda_1, \lambda_2)$-continuous.

Proof. This follows directly from the Theorem 4.3.

A space X is called $\lambda - \alpha$-compact iff it is λ-compact for $\lambda = ici$, i.e. each $\lambda - \alpha$-open cover of X has a finite subcover [2].

Theorem 4.5. Let (X, λ_1) and (Y, λ_2) be GTS's, and $f : X \to Y$ be $(\alpha\lambda_1, \lambda_2)$-continuous. If A is $\lambda_1 - \alpha$-compact in (X, λ_1), then $f(A)$ is λ_2-compact.

Proof. Let φ be a λ_2-open cover of $f(A)$. Since f is $(\alpha\lambda_1, \lambda_2)$-continuous, $f^{-1}(\varphi) = \{f^{-1}(B) : B \in \varphi\} \subset \alpha\lambda_1$. Let $x \in A$, then $f(x) \in f(A)$ and by φ is a λ_2-open cover of $f(A)$, there exists $B \in \varphi$ with $f(x) \in B$. Hence $f^{-1}(\varphi)$ is a $\lambda_1 - \alpha$-open cover of A. Since A is $\lambda_1 - \alpha$-compact, there exists a finite subfamily ψ of φ such that $f^{-1}(\psi)$ is $\lambda_1 - \alpha$-open subcover of A. Obvious, ψ is a λ_2-open subcover of $f(A)$. Thus $f(A)$ is λ_2-compact.

Corollary 4.6. Let (X, λ_1) and (Y, λ_2) be GTS's, and $f : X \to Y$ be $(\alpha\lambda_1, \lambda_2)$-continuous and onto. If X is $\lambda_1 - \alpha$-compact, then Y is λ_2-compact.

Let (X, λ) be a GTS and $A \subset X$, the $\lambda - \alpha$-interior of A denoted by $i_\alpha(A)$ is the union of all $\lambda - \alpha$-open sets contained in A, and the $\lambda - \alpha$-closure of A denoted by $c_\alpha(A)$ is the intersection of all $\lambda - \alpha$-closed sets containing A[4].

Let $A, B \subset X$, the A and B are called $\alpha(\lambda)$-separated if $c_\alpha(A) \cap B = A \cap c_\alpha(B) = \emptyset$. A GTS (X, λ) is called α-connected if $(X, \alpha(\lambda))$ is connected [4].

Theorem 4.7. Let (X, λ_1) and (Y, λ_2) be GTS's, and $f : X \to Y$ be $(\alpha\lambda_1, \lambda_2)$-continuous. If A is $\lambda_1 - \alpha$-connected in (X, λ_1), then $f(A)$ is λ_2-connected.

Proof. Let $f(A) = U \cup V$, $c(U) \cap V = U \cap c(V) = \emptyset$ and $P = f^{-1}(U)$, $Q = f^{-1}(V)$. Then
$$A \subset f^{-1}f(A) = f^{-1}(U) \cup f^{-1}(V) = P \cup Q.$$
From the Theorem 3.13 in [7] we have
$$c_\alpha(P) = c_\alpha(f^{-1}(U)) \subset f^{-1}(c(U)), \ c_\alpha(Q) = c_\alpha(f^{-1}(V)) \subset f^{-1}(c(V)).$$
It follows that
$$c_\alpha(P) \cap Q \subset f^{-1}(c(U)) \cap f^{-1}(V) = f^{-1}(c(U) \cap V) = f^{-1}(\emptyset) = \emptyset,$$
$$P \cap c_\alpha(Q) \subset f^{-1}(U) \cap f^{-1}(c(V)) = f^{-1}(U \cap c(V)) = f^{-1}(\emptyset) = \emptyset.$$
Let $G = A \cap P$ and $H = A \cap Q$, then $A = G \cup H$ and $c_\alpha(G) \cap H = G \cap c_\alpha(H) = \emptyset$. Since A is $\lambda_1 - \alpha$-connected, $G = \emptyset$ or $H = \emptyset$. We may assume that $G = \emptyset$. Then $A = H \subset Q$, and so $f(A) \subset f(Q) = ff^{-1}(V) \subset V$. It follows that $U = U \cap f(A) \subset U \cap V = \emptyset$. This show that $f(A)$ is λ_2-connected.

Corollary 4.8. Let (X, λ_1) and (Y, λ_2) be GTS's, and $f : X \to Y$ be $(\alpha\lambda_1, \lambda_2)$-continuous and onto. If X is $\lambda_1 - \alpha$-connected, then Y is λ_2-connected.

References

1. Császár, Á.: Generalized open sets. Acta Math. Hungar. 75, 65–87 (1997)
2. Császár, Á.: γ-compact spaces. Acta Math. Hungar. 87, 99–107 (2000)
3. Császár, Á.: Generalized topology, generalized continuity. Acta Math. Hungar. 96, 351–357 (2002)
4. Császár, Á.: γ-connected sets. Acta Math. Hungar. 101, 273–279 (2003)
5. Császár, Á.: Generalized open sets in generalized topologies. Acta Math. Hungar. 106, 53–66 (2005)
6. Császár, Á.: Product of generalized topologies. Acta Math. Hungar. 123, 127–132 (2009)
7. Min, W.K.: Generalized continuous functions defined by generalized open sets on generalize topological spaces. Acta Math. Hungar. 125 (2009)

The Selection of the Step-Size Factor in the Variable Step-Size CMA

Jia Liu[1] and Baofeng Zhao[2,*]

[1] Department of Electronic Information Engineering,
Shanxi Polytechnic College, Taiyuan 030006, China
[2] College of Mining Engineering, Taiyuan University of Technology,
Taiyuan 030024, China
zhaobaofeng@tyut.edu.cn

Abstract. This paper analyses the selection of the step-size factor in a new variable step-size constant modulus algorithm (CMA) based on mean square error (MSE) and determines the value range of the step-size factor by computer simulation, which establishes the solid foundation to the convergence superiority of the new algorithm by computer simulation.

Keywords: Blind equalization, Variable step-size, CMA.

1 Introduction

Blind equalization is a kind of self-adaptive equalization technology without sending a training signal which only utilizes the statistical information of the received signal to equalize the dispersive characteristic of the channel. The equal model of the blind equalizer is shown in Figure.1 [1]

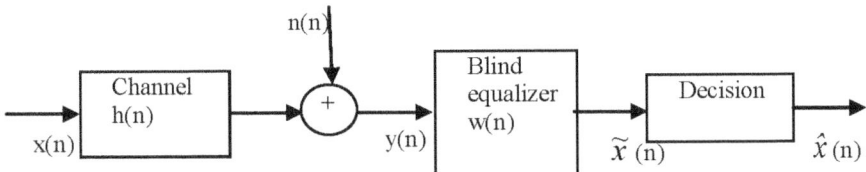

Fig. 1. Structure of blind equalization

In Figure.1, $x(n)$ is the original input signal sent by transmitter, $h(n)$ is the impulse response of the transmission channel, $n(n)$ is noise, $y(n)$ is the undeceived sequence and also the input signal of the equalizer, its input vector is

$$\mathbf{Y}(n) = [y(n), y(n-1), \cdots, y(n-N+1)]^T$$

---

[*] Corresponding author.

H. Deng et al. (Eds.): AICI 2011, Part I, LNAI 7002, pp. 288–291, 2011.
© Springer-Verlag Berlin Heidelberg 2011

$\tilde{x}(n)$ is the recovered signal outputted by the equalizer, $\hat{x}(n)$ is the decision output signal, $e(n)$ is the error signal $e(n) = \hat{x}(n) - \tilde{x}(n)$, the equalizer is a transversal filter its length is N, its tap coefficient vector is

$$\mathbf{W}(n) = [w_1(n), w_2(n), \cdots, w_N(n)]^T$$

According to the signal transmission theory get

$$y(n) = h(n) * x(n) + n(n) = \sum_i h(i) x(n-i) + n(n) \tag{1}$$

The output of the equalizer is

$$\tilde{x}(n) = \sum_{i=1}^{N} w_i(n) y(n-i+1) = \mathbf{W}^T(n) \mathbf{Y}(n) \tag{2}$$

Among the several kinds of equalization algorithms, CMA (Constant Modulus Algorithm) introduced by Goard[2] and Triechiar[3] is widely used many communication systems, for it has less mount of computing and better convergence performance and it is easy to realize. But the fixed step-size of the conventional CMA makes the convergence rate and the convergence precise become a contradiction, which makes the development and the application of CMA limited.

In CMA the iteration formula of the tap coefficient is

$$\mathbf{W}(n+1) = \mathbf{W}(n) + \mu \tilde{x}(n) \left[R_2 - |\tilde{x}(n)|^2 \right] \mathbf{Y}^*(n) \tag{3}$$

Where, μ is the step-size, ordinarily a little positive constant.

$$R_2 = E\left\{ |x(n)|^4 \right\} \Big/ E\left\{ |x(n)|^2 \right\} \tag{4}$$

2   Variable Step-Size CMA

The application to variable step-size in CMA is that at the beginning of the convergence enlarge the step-size value to improve the convergence rate, near to the convergence reduce the step-size value to improve the convergence precise. Among many variable step-size constant modulus algorithms, a common method is using MSE to control the step-size's variation. The following formulas show a variable step-size constant modulus algorithm based on MSE [4].

$$\mathbf{W}(n+1) = \mathbf{W}(n) + \mu(n) \tilde{x}(n) \left[R_2 - |\tilde{x}(n)|^2 \right] \mathbf{Y}^*(n) \tag{5}$$

$$\mu(n+1) = \mu(n) + \beta [MSE(n+1) - MSE(n)] \tag{6}$$

Where $\mu(n)$ is a variable step-size. The $MSE(n)$ is defined as

$$MSE(n) = E\{[e(n)]^2\} = E\{[\hat{x}(n) - \tilde{x}(n)]^2\} \tag{7}$$

Where β is the step-size factor.

3   The Selection of the Step-Size Factor

To guarantee convergence the value of β must make the maximum of $\mu(n)$ is smaller than μ_{max}, μ_{max} is decided by the following formula [5]

$$\mu_{max} = 2/3\,tr\,(R)\tag{8}$$

Where R is the self-correlation matrix of the input signal, $tr(R)$ is the trace of the matrix R.

The specific value of β should be determined by computer simulation on the above condition. For example, from figure.2 to figure.5 show respectively the variable curves of the step-size $\mu(n)$, when the step-size factor β are 0.001, 0.01, 0.1 and 0.5. The input signal is 4PAM, SNR is 20dB, the filter order is 11, and the simulation channel is a typical telephone channel [6].

$$H_i(z) = 0.005 + 0.009z^{-1} - 0.024z^{-2} + 0.854z^{-3} - 0.218z^{-4} + 0.049z^{-5} - 0.016z^{-6}\tag{9}$$

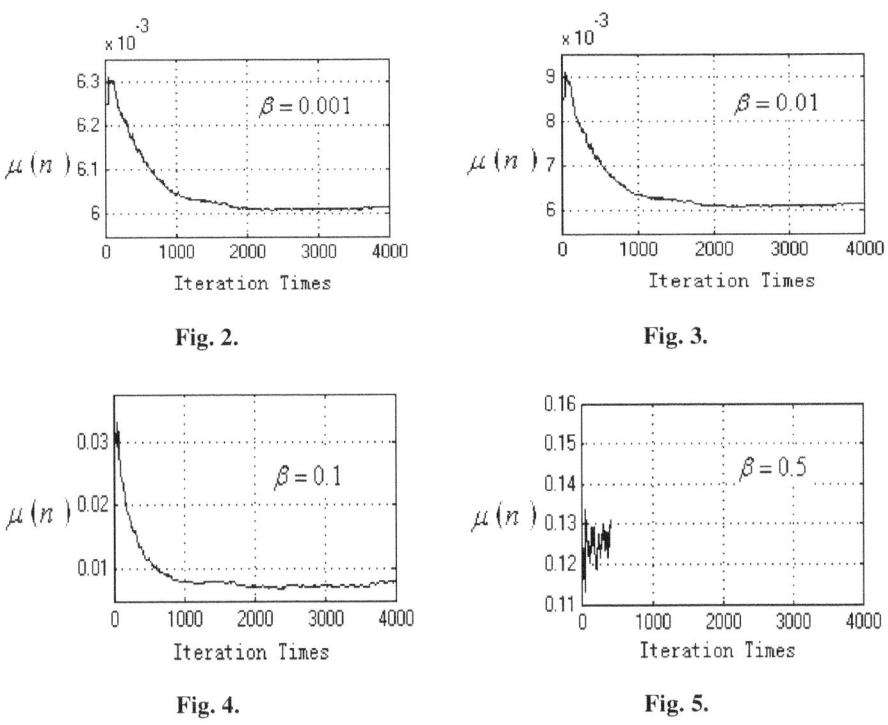

Fig. 2.   Fig. 3.

Fig. 4.   Fig. 5.

According to the figures, when $\beta \geq 0.5$ the algorithm can not convergence, when $\beta = 0.001$ or when $\beta = 0.01$, the value of $\mu(n)$ is very small and steady, it shows the steady-state residual error of the algorithm is small, but the convergence rate is slow. When $\beta = 0.1$, the initial step-size of the algorithm is large, the algorithm converges quickly, the value of $\mu(n)$ after convergence is equal to the value when $\beta = 0.001$ and $\beta = 0.01$, there will be the very small steady-state residual error. To sum up, on the above simulation conditions, the value of the step-size factor β should be about 0.1.

4   Conclusion

In this paper, according to a variable step-size Constant Modulus Blind Equalization Algorithm based on MSE how to determine the value of the step-size factor is proposed. Combing the selection principle of the step-size factor with computer simulation we illustrate the selection process of the step-size factor in 4PAM system. The determination of the value of the step-size factor is very important for a new improved algorithm to prove its convergence superiority.

References

1. Zhang, L., Zhang, X., Wang, H., Sha, D.: Blind Equalization Technology and Development. Journal of Taiyuan University of Technology 27(6) (2002)
2. Godard, D.N.: Self-recovering equalization and carrier tracking in two-dimensional data communication systems. IEEE Trans. on Communication 28, 1867–1875 (1980)
3. Treichter, J.R.: A new approach to multi-path correction of constant modulus signals. IEEE Trans. ASSP 31, 459–471 (1983)
4. Zhao, B., Zhao, J., Zhang, L.: A Variable Step-Size Constant Modulus Blind Equalization Algorithm based on the variation of MSE. Journal of Taiyuan University of Technology 36(4) (2005)
5. Raymond, H.: A Variable Step Size LMS Algorithm. IEEE Trans. on Signal Processing 40, 1633–1642 (1992)
6. Zhao, Y., Liu, D., Zhang, N.: A Blind Equalization Algorithm for FPGA Realization. Journal of China Institute of Communications 22(8) (2001)

Towards Autonomic Computing:
A New Self-Management Method

Fu Duan, Xiaoli Li, Yi Liu, and Yun Fang

Taiyuan University of Technology, TYUT
Taiyuan, China
fyun63@126.com

Abstract. Autonomic computing is a new technology which aims to hide the software complexity by means of "technologies managing technologies". The paper concludes and analysis the related concept of autonomic computing, the architecture and the working mechanisms of autonomic elements based on the relevant specialist work. Then the architecture and implementation method of automatic computing system are presented. Finally, the research problems and future directions of autonomic computing are discussed.

Keywords: autonomic computing, autonomic computing system, adaptive control theory, agent theory.

1 Introduction

The complexity of computer software's architecture and organizations is increasing with the evolution of networks. It has changed the systematic architecture and makes the system manager gradually lose the effective management to it. In this context, the automatic computing is born.

The core idea of autonomic computing is that it can hide system software complexity by means of "technologies managing technologies". It is to say that the system manager conveys the management ideas to computer system, and then it can automatically choose the corresponding solutions when they meet different problems. It needn't the IT manager intervention during the operation of the system. So the self-management is the representative character of the autonomic computing systems.

2 Automatic Computing

2.1 The Characteristics of Autonomic Computing

The essence of autonomic computing is that it can free system manager from the details of system operation. It includes four characteristics, self-configuration, self-healing, self-optimization and self-protecting. In the following paper, we will describe the four properties in details:

H. Deng et al. (Eds.): AICI 2011, Part I, LNAI 7002, pp. 292–299, 2011.

a)   Self-configuration: It refers to the system can automatically configure their components correctly and adapt the changes of the environment according to the strategies provided by IT manager among the system operation processes [13].

b)   Self-optimization: It means the system can automatically achieve the resources configuration properly and get the high efficiency and meet the customer's or business' demands.

c)   Self-healing: It refers to the system can automatically detect, diagnosis errors and repair the problems resulting from bugs as soon as possible and provide the continuous possibility of business application.

d)   Self-protection: Autonomic systems with the self-protection have the function in predicting, inspecting, identifying and protecting attractions from external environment and malicious attacks.

2.2 Autonomic Elements

The autonomic element consists of five components, including monitor component, analysis component, plan component, execution component and knowledge. The autonomic manager forms a monitoring-analysis-planning-execution control loop. The function of each module of independent elements is shown in the following paper:

a)   Sensor: The autonomic manager perceives the external environment and gets the managed resources' characters and corresponding state by sensors.

b)   Effector: The autonomic manager informs the managed resources to send requirement by the effectors component.

Autonomic managers can manage internal resources and provide standard interfaces to receive external management by sensor/effector group. The autonomic managers working mechanisms will be concrete elaborated in section 2.3.

The components connect each other by common message bus instead of rigid control flow. They can achieve cooperation by asynchronous communication technology.

c)   Monitor component mainly provides mechanisms to search, synthesis, and filtration, manage and report the state details about the managed resources.

d)   Analysis component makes the concrete analysis according to the different situations and decides the strategies which are adopted by the autonomic manager.

e)   Plan component provides the mechanisms and applies the policy information to guild plan work.

f)   Execute component controls the execution according to the target strategies.

Of course, the components also coordinate each other. The monitor component and analysis component provide the ability in self-awareness and external awareness laid a foundation for autonomic deciding. They also can decide the system self-adapting goals. The plan component and execute component can achieve the adaptive ability when the system deviates from the expected goals. The four components depend on the support of the knowledge.

The knowledge which is the core component in autonomic manager deposits the sharing knowledge of data (including some system logs, strategies and some measures, etc.) used for the four components. The knowledge stored in the knowledge can divide into three categories: state determining knowledge, policy knowledge and solving problem knowledge.

a)   State determining knowledge: It is used to be ware of the state of managed resources and external environment including monitoring data and symptoms.

b)   Policy knowledge: It refers to the strategies which are appointed by IT manager and acquired through machine learning.

c)   Solving problem knowledge: It includes system installing, configuration and planning knowledge.

The managed resources are either hardware resources or software resources which they need have the character of self-management. It is known that the hardware and software about distributed systems are from different supporters. So if we want to solve the character of heterogeneous, we should build sensor and effector by standard and ontology technologies. The conceptual architecture of autonomic element is shown in Fig1.

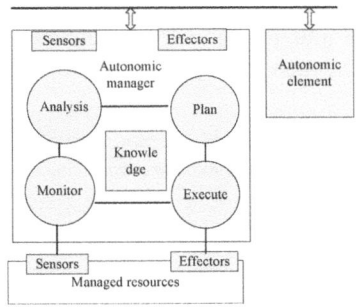

Fig. 1. The conceptual architecture of autonomic element

2.3   The Working Mechanism of Autonomic Computing

The working mechanism of autonomic computing mainly includes four steps [1]:

①   Self-awareness/context awareness: This is the basic of the achievement of autonomic management and maps the system's symptom on the special time to related state. Self-awareness is aware of managed resources and context-awareness is aware of external environment.

②   The decision based on special policy: This is the core in the autonomic manger. Autonomic manager takes different decisions according to PA, PG and PU (PA stands for action strategy, PG stands for goal strategy and PU stands for utility function).

③   The plans executing of goal: If the result is abstract in step②, the planning component of autonomic manager Start a planning progress based on the current state and seek the steps of actions which meet for correlated planning problems' goals.

④   The execution of action planning: It monitors the execution of the action by effectors, then inspect that whether the action's conditions is met. If operation is failures, we need restart or re-planning a new path.

Every controlling has a different working mechanism according to different problems domain and the goal of autonomic management.

2.4   The Life Cycle of Autonomic Elements

It is well known that software product has a software life cycle according to the concept of software engineering. Autonomic element is the same to it but it has different by its "autonomic" role. It can provide the support to the self-management since the birth of the cycle of autonomic elements. The cycle of autonomic element starts with designing and implementation [10]. Then the autonomic elements enter into the testing phase and pass a variety of related testing phases, verify whether they meet for the requirements. If they pass the testing and verification, they enter to the configuration and running state. At last, the autonomic elements will die by uninstall. During the operation, the autonomic elements will enter into different process under the driven of different events. The operation states include ready state, wait state, migration state and invoke state, etc. How does the each state convert?

The autonomic elements do some initial works when the ready state starts. They don't come to the active state until the former state is over. They can optimize, protect, upgrade, repair and self-configure under the condition of active state. If the conditions are changed to be unsatisfied during the progress of the active state, they will become wait state. They can enter into the active state until the conditions meeting them. If the manager or the autonomic computing system needs to suspend its work, the autonomic elements will enter into hanging state instead of active state. It doesn't become active state until invoked. It will become migration sate when the autonomic elements need move to other nodes. The migration state is over when the goal node starts execution. The autonomic elements will enter into the ready state again when they terminate and exit. If the work need, they will start a new life cycle until the function realizes.

3   The Autonomic Computing System

The combination of self-adaptive software theory and the control theory promotes the generation of the autonomic computing system. It is composed of the automatic elements which need meet the following requirements [15]:

(1)   They must have the character of self-management which is the core idea of the autonomic computing. So if the autonomic computing system has the character of autonomic, the basic component unit need has the self-management characteristics.

(2)   They need have good cooperative management each other so that the services and functions of themselves is easily understand and easily accessed by other autonomic elements under the circumstances of ensuring themselves normally to operate. Let the whole autonomic computing system achieve integral optimal on the basis of guaranteeing the local optimal.

(3)   They can management itself action according to the external environment and are able to accept the top level correct strategies and refuse to the new strategies which are conflict with the original strategies.

The relationships among them can be P2P (Peer-to-Peer) or hierarchy because the autonomic computing system is composed by multiple automatic elements.

Definition: An autonomic computing system can be defined as S=<A, F>, A= {a_1, a_2, a_3…} stands for all the autonomic elements in the autonomic computing system. The "F" is said to have autonomic elements mapped to a set of elements as a function which is called dependent function. For example, when "a" depends on "b" stands that "a" is able to provide services provided that "b" is able to provide service to "a". F(a) means the set of all the autonomic elements units which are depended by "a".

Constructing an autonomic computing system is not overnight, it is divided into five levels according to the maturity model of autonomic computing [12]: basic level, management level, predicting level, adaptation level and full autonomic level.

3.1   The Architecture of the Autonomic Computing System

The autonomic element is the basic unit of the automatic computing system. If we want to achieve the "autonomic" nature, it requires the autonomic elements and autonomic computing platforms have the character of interoperability. The common services can make them have the ability of high awareness and fully understand the environment [10]. The architecture of the automatic computing system is shown in the following paper:

DSC: Development Solution Center can effectively capture the information about the autonomic elements installation and configuration. It can eliminate the complexity aroused by eliminating format and tools. Ensuring the system have the character of self-configuration is one function of it. An autonomic computing system can have one or more DSC.

ADF: The main function of Autonomic Directory Facilitator is to provide yellow services to other autonomic elements. If the autonomic element need provide services, they must register in the ADF at first. They also can query the needed services at the same time. An automatic computing system can have multiple ADF.

AMF: Address Mapping Facilitator is the necessary component in the autonomic computing system. It can provide the white page services to the other autonomic elements so that they can get an effective identifier from the AMF which maintains the identifier directory of all the registered autonomic elements.

SF: Security Facilitator is mainly responsible for proving security services to autonomic computing.

MTS: The main function of Message Transport System is to provide telecommunications services between the two different autonomic computing systems. MTS shielding the communication details and the physical address of the autonomic element and make the communications between the autonomic elements present transparent.

Behavior library and component library are used to composing the templates.

In the architecture of the autonomic computing system, it becomes possible to achieve the dynamic configuration by DSC. It can undertake the self-configuration and self-optimization which are based on the services through ADF. Among the autonomic elements can communicate through their names and eliminate the complexity brought by different address by AMF. So MTS makes the autonomic computing system have the self-management feature in the macro.

3.2   The Realization Method of the Autonomic Computing System

How to make the thought use to the real system becoming an important research area since the idea of the autonomic computing presented. Many experts have the further exploration. We know the building of the autonomic computing system need a series of existing theories supporting, such as agent theory, adaptive control theory, services oriented technology, machine learning and optimization theory, etc. In the following paper, we'll discuss some technologies in details.

1)   Agent theory:

Agent theory provides a new way for distribution open system analysis, designing and implementation. Agent can refer to the hardware which has the characteristics of autonomic, initiative, social skills and response ability or computing system based on the software. Web services is a new web application model, distributed computing model and the effective mechanism for the data and information integration. The semantic web services discovery's goal is the retrieval efficiency and the degree of automation of improvement.

To make full use of the advantage of them, experts combine them   and present two different theory methods to build autonomic computing system. One is the combination of web services and action strategy and reaction agent, the other is based on the combination of semantic web services and goal strategy and deliberative Agent.

2)   Adaptive control theory

The adaptive control system can timely obtain the dynamic characteristics of the managed object and the system errors through measuring the input/output information. According to the change and a certain design method, it makes decisions and modifies the controller parameters autonomously to adapt control signal to meet the changes of object and disturbance, to maintain optimal control performance of system. Feedback control is the principle of "detecting the deviation and correcting the deviation".   Therefore, through the appropriate expansion, adaptive control theory and feedback control theory can be used to establish autonomic computing system, especially the optimization system.

3)   *Learning and optimization theory*

How can we transfer the management system knowledge form human experts to the autonomic computing system? The main idea is to present a learning theory according to the theory how the experts solve a problem when they meet different systems and build a solving model which can automatically perform the same task on a new system. Although facilitating acquisition from the human experts and producing system can promote the autonomic character, it is a challenge. Autonomic element which interacts with each other need learn to solve problems based on their experiences in a complex autonomic computing system. Self-optimization also can be a challenge because adaption changes behavior of agent to reach optimization. The optimization is examined at full autonomic level.

4   Conclusions and Future Works

Autonomic computing as a new field has some mature theories which are presented by the related experts from the core idea presented to now. This paper mainly make a conclusions and analysis the basic concept of the autonomic computing, the architecture and working mechanisms of autonomic computing system, the development of autonomic computing system and the realization method of the autonomic computing system based on the basis of the existing work.

Although there is a deep exploration in the autonomic computing field, the software life cycle of autonomic computing has not developed a unified, structured development model so far, there isn't an optimal method which can dynamically adjust according to external changes and accept the static strategy receiving from knowledge in the autonomic computing application methods.

Key research problems and future directions are presented as follows.

(1)   The realization method of the autonomic computing system

Although the method basic on the agent and strategy can provide some autonomic characters from different angles, they have their own characteristic. If we can take their advantages and effectively combined them using in constructing the autonomic computing system, it will be a research hot spot.

(2)   The life cycle of autonomic elements

Although the life cycle of autonomic elements is presented like software at present, it lacks of the unified describe language, tools to it. For example, UML can realize the visualized modeling of software system, but there isn't unified language used to describe the life cycle of autonomic elements.

(3)   The application of the autonomic computing

With the increasing of software complexity, using the idea of autonomic computing to other areas becomes a new hot point, such as database, Computer graphics, etc. Using the core idea of autonomic computing which refers to self-management realizing the autonomy can reduce manager's burden and achieve the effective management.

Acknowledgments. This paper is sponsored by .Natural Science Foundation of Shanxi Province (2008011039), Key Technologies R&D Program of Shanxi Province (2007031129, 20080322008).

References

1. Liao, B., Yao, Y., Gao, J.: Conceptual Model and Realization Methods of Autonomic Computing. Journal of Software 19, 779–802 (2008)
2. Dearle, A., Kirby, G.N.C., McCarthy, A.J.: A Framework for Constraint-Based Deployment and Autonomic Management of Distributed Applications. In: Proceedings of the International Conference on Autonomic Computing, ICAC 2004 (2004)
3. Diaconescu, A., Mos, A., Murphy, J.: Automatic Performance Management in Component Based Software Systems. In: Proceedings of the International Conference on Autonomic Computing, ICAC 2004 (2004)

4. Huang, A.C., Fox, A.: Cheap Recovery: A Key to Self-Managing State. ACM Transactions on Storage 1(1), 38–70 (2004)
5. Demsky, B., Rinard, M.: Automatic Data Structure Repair for Self-Healing Systems. In: First Workshop on Algorithms and Architectures for Self-Managing Systems (2003)
6. Zhang, H., Shi, Z.: The software engineering method of autonomic computing. Small Miniature Computer System (2006)
7. Zhang, H., Shi, Z.: Research on agent-based autonomic computing. Institute of Computing Technology Chinese Academy of Science (2005)
8. Nami, M.R., Bertels, K.: A Survey of Autonomic Computing Systems
9. Kephart Ditches, D.: The vision of autonomic computing. IEEE Computer Society, Los Alamitos (2003)
10. Wang, f., Li, f.: A kind of optimization model of autonomic computing system. Computer Technology And Development (June 2006)
11. Kephart, J., Chess, D.: The Vision of Autonomic Computing, vol. 36, pp. 41–50. IEEE Computer Society, Los Alamitos (2003), doi:10.1109/ MC.2003.1160055
12. Loeser, C., Ditze, M., Altenbernd, P., Rammig, F.: GRUSEL-A self optimizing, bandwidth aware Video on Demand P2P Application. In: Proceedings of the International Conference on Autonomic Computing, ICAC 2004 (2004)
13. Kandasamy, N., Abdelwahed, S., Hayes, J.P.: Self-Optimization in Computer Systems via Online Control: Application to Power Management. In: Proceedings of the International Conference on Autonomic Computing, ICAC 2004 (2004)
14. Appavoo, J., et al.: Enabling Autonomic Behavior in Systems Software with Hot Swapping. IBM Systems Journal 42(1), 60–76 (2003)
15. Qu, G., Hariri, S., Jangiti, S.: Et lanoline Monitoring and Analysis for Self-Protection against Network Attacks. In: Proceedings of the International Conference on Autonomic Computing, ICAC 2004 (2004)

Automatic Image Tagging Based on Regions of Interest

Sheng-Hui Li, Chun-Ming Gao, and Hua-Wei Pan

College of Information Science and Engineering,
Hunan University, Changsha, China
{sbdht6,gcm211,hw_pan}@163.com

Abstract. Automatic image tagging seeks to assign relevant words to images that describe the actual content found in the images without intermediate manual annotation. One common problem shared by most previous learning approaches for automatic image tagging is that the segmented regions in the image were considered as equally important and were processed equally. The goal of this paper is to develop a novel annotation approach based on regions of interest to take into account the users' real experience and fix a visual weight for each region according to the degree of interest. To do this, we firstly segmented the image into several regions. And then it calculated the degree of interest for each region according to the experiments of human visual attention and cognitive psychology. Each region will be assigned a visual weight at the third step. We can obtain the prior probability of the region given the concept. At the stage of the automatic annotation, we can calculate posterior probability with the Bayesian Theorem to get the most likely concept to tag the unseen image. The proposed methodology is examined in a well-known benchmark image collection and the results demonstrated its competitiveness.

Keywords: Automatic image tagging, Bayesian Theorem, visual weight, regions of interest.

1   Introduction

Content-based image retrieval has experienced considerable research activity since the early 1990s. Success of such systems was limited mainly due to the semantic gap between the low-level features and the high-level semantic concepts in the image. To overcome this difficulty, researchers proposed image retrieval based on semantic then, which bridged this gap between visual similarity and semantic similarity according to directly associate images to semantic features such as words or concepts. Due to an exponential growth of digital images in everyday, manually tagging the image brings a huge burden to users and is not convenient at all. The automatic image tagging has become a key issue in image retrieval based on semantic. Several algorithms in this direction have been proposed. These methods generally can be divided into two groups: statistical models and image classification. Traditionally, scholars have tended to use region-based image descriptors for automatic image annotation as the features extracted from the whole image may not properly represent the characteristics of the objects in image. The goal of image segmentation is to

H. Deng et al. (Eds.): AICI 2011, Part I, LNAI 7002, pp. 300–307, 2011.

extract the object existed in image and the descriptors based on the region in image are more in line with the users' experience. Previously, the model of automatic image annotation treated the segmented region equally important. However, the regions are not equally important in the cognitive process as the information contained in different regions is different. This paper proposes a novel method of automatic image tagging in which we assigned a visual weigh to each region in the process of training.

This paper is structured as follows. Section 2 reviews related work in the direction of automatic image tagging. Section 3 presents the process of calculating degree of interest and the visual weights for all segmented regions. Section 4 introduces the annotation approach we proposed using the visual weight for each region. Experimental results on a well-known benchmark image collection are shown in Section 5. Finally, Section 6 contains concluding remarks and directions for future work.

2   Related Work

There has been some work on statistical model and image classification. Most of the statistical models are unsupervised learning methods that attempt to learn the association between visual features and keywords by estimating the probability of keywords given regional image features [1, 2, 3, 4, 5]. The first automatic image annotation model, called the co-occurrence model, was deployed by Mori et al. [1], who exploited the co-occurrence information of low level image features and words. Duygulu et al. [2] used a machine translation model that is applied in order to translate words into blobs by recasting the problem as cross-lingual information. Jeon et al. [3] improved on the results of retrieval and applied the cross-media relevance model (CMRM) to the annotation work. Lavrenko et al. [4] developed the continuous-space relevance model (CRM) to build continuous probability density functions that describe the process of generating blob features. Feng et al. [5] used a multiple Bernoulli relevance model (MBRM), which outperforms CRM. There are also some image classification approaches. Li et al. [14] implemented ALIP system using the two-dimensional multi-resolution hidden Markov models (2D MHMMs). Edward et al. [13] construct a classifier using Support Vector Machines (SVMs) and Bayes Point Machines (BPMs) to annotate the images. More recently, Stathopoulos and Jose et al. [6] proposed a novel Bayesian hierarchical method for estimating mixture models of Gaussian components, which was called Bayesian mixture hierarchies model (BHGMM).

3   Degree of Interest and Visual Weights

To measure the importance of each region in the cognitive process, we refer the concepts including regions of interest and degree of interest. Region of interest (region of interest referred to as ROI) is the region which most likely attract users, and most likely express the content of the image [7]. Ideally, the ROI should be selected by users and extraction ROI should be based on the user's evaluation criteria. The personality existing in the cognitive process in image leads to ROI is a concept that is difficult to define [9]. We use the degree of interest to measure how we are interested in region. The Itti-Koch et al. [10] model of visual attention considers the task of attention selection from a bottom-up perspective. The model generates map of the most salient points in an image. The Stentiford et al. [11] model of visual attention is also biologically inspired. The most salient points can be extracted and individually inspected and the most salient regions can be segmented using region-growing techniques but it may be the part of the ROI. These two models are both that calculated the difference between its low-feature and low-feature of its surrounding regions to select the ROI. We use the concept of degree of interest of the region to measure the importance of the region. Experiments of eye movements in cognitive psychology show that the human vision system will always have more choice to choose the area which contains more information [12]. The region which has max value of degree of interest should be considered as ROI. Here we consider that the other regions are also important in the image whereas these regions have smaller values of degree of interest. We assign a visual weight to each region according to the degree of interest.

3.1 Calculate the Degree of Interest for Each Region

We calculate the degree of interest for each region inspired by the experiments of human visual attention and cognitive psychology. In the process, we consider the two factors which affect the value of the degree: variety of color value between the two neighbored regions and the area ratio. Image I which is r rows and s columns is composed of N segmented regions: $I=(R_1,\cdots,R_N)$. We ignored the regions which were smaller than a threshold size in our approach, RC is the region collection we calculated. We can calculate average value of color $g(i)$ for the ith segmented region R_i by (Eq. (1))

$$g(i)=\frac{1}{|R_i|}\sum_{(i,j)\in 1_i} I[i,j], i\in[1,N], i\in Z \tag{1}$$

The number $|R_i|$ is the sum of the number of the pixel in the ith segmented region. The value $I[i,j]$ is the color value of the pixel (i,j) .

The process of calculating the degree of interest for each region is explained as follows:

Step 1: the variety of color value $Dis(i)$ for each region with immediate neighborhood regions can be calculated by (Eq. (2)). In the experiment of the visual attention model [10] people are more likely to be attracted by the region which is much variation with the neighbored regions. The color feature is the most important feature in our cognitive process, especially in the first sight. The greater variety the region has, the more attention will be paid.

$$Dis(i)=\sum_{i=1, i\neq j, L(i,j)}^{N} |g(i)-g(j)| \tag{2}$$

$L(i,j)$ represents that the ith region is immediate neighbored by the jth region.

Step 2: the area ratio $S(i)$ for each region is calculated by (Eq. (3)). From the experiment of eye movement in cognitive psychology [12], the more information the region contains, the region has more choice to be gazed.

$$S(i) = \frac{|R_i|}{\sum_{R_i \in RC} |R_i|} \tag{3}$$

Step 3: the degree of interest for each region will be calculated by (Eq. (4))

$$I(i) = \frac{Dis(i)}{\sum_{i=1}^{N} Dis(i)} \times w_1 + S(i) \times w_2 \tag{4}$$

The weight w_1 and w_2 are the powers for variety of color value and the area ratio.

3.2 Calculate the Visual Weight for Each Region

Visual weight for each region can be set by (Eq. (5))

$$w_{R_i} = n \times \frac{I(i)^\alpha}{\sum_{I_i \in I} I(i)^\alpha} \tag{5}$$

The symbol weight w_{R_i} is the weight for the ith region and α is a smoothing parameter. The visual weight increases as the increase of the parameter α. The factor $n \times \dfrac{1}{\sum_{I_i \in I} I(i)^\alpha}$ is normalization factor which ensures the equation $\sum_{i=1}^{N} w_{I_i} = 1$.

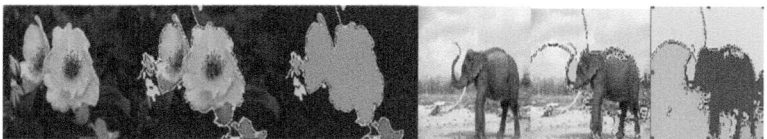

Fig. 1. Examples of extraction of regions of interest

4 Automatic Image Tagging

The process of automatic image tagging will be introduced briefly by the following sentences. Firstly, set of regions were segmented by the image segmentation algorithm. And then we calculated the degree of interest for each region and calculate the visual weight for each region. In the third step, we can obtain the prior probability of the region given concept. We use the visual weight for each region rather than treat each region as the same important in the training process. At the stage of the automatic annotation, we can calculate posterior probability given region with the Bayesian Theorem and combine all the concepts obtained to describe the unlabelled image.

4.1   Low-Level Feature Extracting and Similarity Calculation

The low-level feature of each region will be extracted to express the content of the region. We ignored the regions which were smaller than a threshold size in the training and test process. The symbol F_{R_i} is the low-level feature vector of the ith region after normalization. The total dimensions include the follow feature: RGB, area, location of the region(x, y), convexity, mean oriented energy, 30 degree increment, energy covariance and mean entropy. We use Euclidean Distance to measure the distance of between two features vectors. The distance $dis(R_i,R_k)$ is the Euclidean distance between the feature vector between region R_i and region R_k, which is calculated by (Eq. (6)).

$$dis(R_i,R_k)=\|F_{R_i}-F_{R_k}\| \tag{6}$$

Then the similarity can be calculated by the standardization of $dis(R_i,R_k)$ by (Eq. (7)).

$$sim(R_i,R_k)=1-norm(dis(R_i,R_k)) \tag{7}$$

4.2   Calculate the Prior Probability

Suppose $IMG=(T,D)$ is the image dataset, T is the training set, and D is the test image set, and we want to automatically select a set of concepts $K=(K_1,K_2,\cdots,K_m)$ to describe the content of the image. For the m images in set T, we can segment them into lots of regions which are represented by $I_T=(I_1,I_2\cdots,I_n)$, it also can be expressed by $I_T=((R_{11},R_{12},\cdots,R_{1l_1}),\cdots,(R_{n1},R_{n2},R_{nl_n}))$, where l_i is the number of segmentation for the ith image in the training set. We can use $K_{R_{ij}}=(k_1,k_2,\cdots,k_{l_{R_{ij}}})$ to annotate region R_{ij}, where $l_{R_{ij}}$ is the number of describing the region R_{ij} and $k_i \in K$.

In the classic probability model, we clustered the regions and annotated each region once as that we consider all the segmented regions in the same image are equally important. Here we cancel the process of clustering regions as clustering-based schemes is often limited and assigned a visual weight that calculated in the previous section to each region in the statistical process. The number of the regions in I_i appear in the training set will change from left to right.

$$\begin{pmatrix} R_{i1} & R_{i2} & \cdots R_{il_i} \\ \updownarrow & \updownarrow & \updownarrow \\ K_{R_{i1}} & K_{R_{i2}} & \cdots K_{R_{il_i}} \end{pmatrix} \rightarrow \begin{pmatrix} w_{i1}R_{i1} & w_{i2}R_{i2} & \cdots & w_{il_i}R_{il_i} \\ \updownarrow & \updownarrow & \updownarrow \\ w_{i1}K_{R_{i1}} & w_{i2}K_{R_{i2}} & \cdots & w_{il_i}K_{R_{il_i}} \end{pmatrix}$$

That is the regions in the same image are treated unequally as the regions are not important is the process of cognitive processes. Easily we can obtain the prior probability $P(R_i|K_j)$, which is the conditional probability for region R_i given concept K_j.

4.3   Calculate the Posterior Probability

We will assume that each region is generated by one or more classes in a pre-determined set of classes in the event that we treat each concept as a class. The probability that region R_i categorizing into concept K_j is $P(K_j|R_i)$, that is the probability for class K_j given that the region R_i was observed. It means that the probability that we use K_j to annotate the region R_i is $P(K_j|R_i)$. Here we assume that the events of observing K_j and R_i are mutually independent. $P(K_j|R_i)$ can be calculated with Bayesian theorem by (Eq.(8)). The Bayesian framework has been shown in articles [6][8] that can provide a numerically stable and computationally efficient algorithm, while the complexity of the solution. Here we briefly introduce the Bayesian framework.

$$P(K_j|R_i) = \frac{P(R_i|K_j)P(K_j)}{P(R_i)} = \frac{P(R_i|K_j)P(K_j)}{\sum_{K_m \in K} P(R_i|K_m)P(K_m)} \tag{8}$$

The priors $P(K_j) = \frac{|K_j|}{|K|}$ are set to the relative frequency of occurrence of concept K_j in the training set. The number $|K_j|$ denotes the actual number of times the concept occurred in the training. $|K| = \sum_{K_i \in K} |K_i|$. The probability $P(R_i)$ is a constant in the event that the training set is fixed. We can predict that $k = \mathrm{argmax}(P(R_i|K_j)P(K_j))$ is the most likely concept to be used to tag the region R_i.

For each segmented region R_i' in a unlabeled image, we can calculate the probability $P(K_j|R_i')$ by (Eq.(9)) according to comparing all the training regions.

$$P(K_j|R_i') = \sum_{k=1}^{n} (sim(R_i',R_k) \times P(K_j|R_k)) \tag{9}$$

The similarity $sim(R_i',R_k)$ between R_i' and R_k is calculated previously and the posterior probability $P(K_j|R_k)$ is calculated by the (Eq.(8)). We select those concepts that make the probability $P(K_j|R_i')$ greater than a threshold to describe the region. And finally we combine all the concepts obtained through all the segmented regions to tag the image.

5   Experiment and Discuss

We use the dataset in Duygulu et al. [2] model. The dataset consists of 5000 images from 50 Corel Stock Photo cds. The dataset has 100 topics and each topic is composed of 100 images. Overall, the dataset is formed by 374 words. We divided the dataset randomly into 2 parts, with 40% as the training set and 60% as the test set.

Figure 1 shows some steps in the process of calculating the degrees of interest for regions in 2 example images.

Figure 2 shows the precision for our proposed method (BROI), as well as CMRM [3] model and CRM [4] for 15 frequent words.

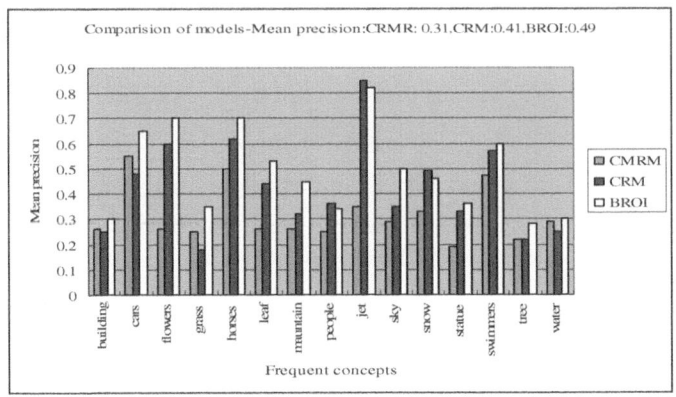

Fig. 2. Mean precision comparision of three methods

As is vividly showed in Figure 2, the proposed method works better for most concepts in precisions of annotation, especially for those concepts which describe the image in which the region segmented more validate and more salient. Average precision of the proposed method is improved by 19% compared with CRM. However, the precision of annotation some concepts are smaller than CRM. The reason may be the dataset contains similar images, which have almost the same set of tagging results but is categorized in different title or the objects are dispersing from the aspect of the low-feature in those images.

6   Conclusions and Future Work

The experimental results show that the proposed method is a good choice for automatic image tagging. This approach is more in line with the users' experience. Based on this work, better segmentation algorithm will probably be introduced and also we can take account into the semantic relatedness between concepts to improve the annotation results. And more comprehensive comparisons between this approach and other techniques using different datasets need to be addressed in the future work. We believe that the proposed approach is a good choice for related direction.

References

1. Mori, Y., Takahashi, H., Oka, R.: Image-to-word transformation based on dividing and vector quantizing images with words. In: International Workshop on Multimedia Intelligent Storage and Retrieval Management (1999)
2. Duygulu, P., Barnard, K., de Freitas, J.F.G., Forsyth, D.A.: Object recognition as machine translation: Learning a lexicon for a fixed image vocabulary. In: Heyden, A., Sparr, G., Nielsen, M., Johansen, P. (eds.) ECCV 2002. LNCS, vol. 2353, pp. 97–112. Springer, Heidelberg (2002)

3. Jeon, J., Lavrenko, V., Manmatha, R.: Automatic Image Annotation and Retrieval using Cross-Media Relevance Models. In: Proceedings of International ACM Conference on Research and Development in Information Retrieval, pp. 119–126 (2003)
4. Lavrenko, V., Manmatha, R., Jeon, J.: A Model for Learning the Semantics of Pictures. In: Proceedings of the 16th Conference on Advances in Neural Information Processing Systems (2003)
5. Feng, S., Manmatha, R., Lavrenko, V.: Multiple Bernoulli Relevance Models for Image and Video Annotation. In: IEEE Conference on Computer Vision and Pattern Recognition, vol. 2, pp. 1002–1009 (2004)
6. Stathopoulos, V., Jose, J.: Bayesian mixture hierarchies for automatic image annotation. In: Boughanem, M., Berrut, C., Mothe, J., Soule-Dupuy, C. (eds.) ECIR 2009. LNCS, vol. 5478, pp. 138–149. Springer, Heidelberg (2009)
7. Schmid, C., Mohr, R.: IEEE Local grayvalue invariants for image retrieval. Transactions on Pattern Analysis and Machine Intelligence 19(5), 530 (2009)
8. Ghahramani, Z., Beal, M.J.: Propagation algorithms for variational Bayesian learning. In: Advances in Neural Information Processing Systems, vol. 13. MIT Press, Cambridge (2001)
9. Tian, Q., Sebe, N., Lew, M.S., et al.: Image retrieval using wavelet-based salient points. Journal of Electronic Imaging 10(4), 835–849 (2001)
10. Itti, L., Koch, C., Niebur, E.: A model of saliency-based visual attention for rapid scene analysis. IEEE Transactions on Pattern Analysis and Machine Intelligence 20(11), 1254–1259 (1998)
11. Bamidele, A., Stentiford, et al.: An attention-based approach to content based image retrieval. British Telecommunications Advanced Research Technology Journal on Intelligent Spaces 22(3) (2004)
12. Ying, Z.: Experimental Psychology, vol. 580. Peking University Press, Beijing (2000)
13. Chang, E., Kingshy, G., Sychay, G., Wu, G.: Cbsa: Content-Based soft annotation for multimodal image retrieval using Bayes point machines. IEEE Trans. on CSVT 13(1), 26–38 (2003)
14. Li, J., Wang, J.: Automatic linguistic indexing of pictures by a statistical modeling approach. IEEE Trans. on Pattern Analysis and Machine Intelligence 25(19), 1075–1108 (2003)

A Multigroup Parallel Genetic Algorithm for Multiple Sequence Alignment

Jiawei Luo, Li Zhang, and Cheng Liang

School of Information Science and Engineering,
Hunan University Changsha, 410082, China
luojiawei@gmail.com, {zhang177li,alcs417}@163.com

Abstract. In view of the problem that the genetic algorithm is easy to fall into local optimization and converge slowly at the later stage of multiple sequence alignment, we propose a multigroup parallel genetic algorithm. We utilize the methods of multigroup parallel and migration strategy, and design a new mutation operator, which enhance its ability to achieve good quality solutions. Then some sequences are chosen from the BALIBASE database 1.0 as test data and the experiment results show the effectiveness of our method.

Keywords: Protein sequences, Multiple sequence alignment, Multigroup parallel, Genetic algorithm.

1 Introduction

Multiple Sequence Alignment (MSA) of Biological information is a basic problem which has great significance. A best alignment of multiple sequence alignment is used for predicting protein structures, getting the effect of protein family conserved motifs for maintaining the three-dimensional structure of protein, also is used to analyze phylogenetic relation implied in the protein [1]. As a combinatorial optimization problem of NP-completeness, many of researchers devote themselves to research the approximate solutions and made meaningful results.

Multiple sequence alignment algorithms may be classified into three classes: exact methods, progressive method and iterative method. The classical algorithm of exact methods is Needlman-Wunsch[2] algorithm which is based on dynamic programming, but limited to 3 number of sequences, and is not fit for long sequences. The progressive method was first brought forward by Hogeweg[3], then was perfected by Feng[4] and Taylor[5]. The best-known algorithms based on progressive multiple alignment include MULTALIGN [7] and CLUSTALW [6] software system which has come into wide use. The main advantages of progressive alignment methods are speed and simplicity, while the main disadvantage of which is that mistakes in the initial alignments of the most closely related sequences are propagated to the multiple alignments of a late date. Furthermore, the iterative-based approach which use various strategies like simulated annealing, genetic algorithm, Hidden Markov Model strategies (HMMS), is applied to the multiple sequence alignment. SAGA[7] is based on genetic algorithm(GA), which was put forward by Notredame

H. Deng et al. (Eds.): AICI 2011, Part I, LNAI 7002, pp. 308–316, 2011.
© Springer-Verlag Berlin Heidelberg 2011

and Higglns; Eddy.s proposed an algorithm called HMMT[8] that is based on HMMS; and DIALIGN[9] posed by Motredama is based on segment-to-segment comparisons attempting to use local information. Based on the idea of parallel computing and multigroup evolution game, some researchers separated the whole population of genetic algorithm into sub-group, and increased genotypic models by exchanging the information between the sub-group, which is proposed to overcome premature convergence and slow convergent speed in the later evolution process of genetic algorithm. Now, multigroup parallel genetic algorithm has been used in Many-Valued Function, PID control and so on, which has obtained better results.

To deal with the shortcoming of GA mentioned above, this paper proposes a multigroup parallel genetic algorithm which uses one way ring as topological structure and stochastic migration strategy to increase population species, designs a new kind of mutation operator by making use of the features that gap would rarely occurred alone in MSA. A set of test cases from BAliBASE1.0 are used as reference to evaluate the efficiency of the algorithm and the experiment results show the effectiveness of our method.

2   Problem Description

2.1   Multiple Sequence Alignment

A sequence with length n is a string composed of n characters from a finite alphabet set $\sum$, $\sum$ ={A, C, G, T}, which denote four different nucleotide respectively, for DNA; as for Protein sequences, $\sum$ consists of 20 characters of amino acids. Let $S = (s_1, s_2, \ldots, s_n)$, $s_i = s_{i1}s_{i2} \ldots s_{il_i}$ $(1 \leq i \leq n), s_{ij} \in \sum (1 \leq j \leq l_i)$, l_i represents the length of s_i. A multiple alignment of S is specified by a matrix

$$A = (a_{ij}), 1 \leq i \leq n, 1 \leq j \leq l, \max(l_i) \leq l \leq \sum_{i=1}^{n} l_i \text{ , where: (1) } a_{ij} \in \sum \cup \{-\}, \text{"-"}$$

denotes the gap letter;(2) each row $a_{i1}a_{i2} \ldots a_{il}$ of A is exactly the corresponding sequence s_i, if we remove all gap letters;(3) there is no column contains only gaps in matrix A.

2.2   Objective Function

Although different objective functions are designed for MSA, there are mainly two common objective function: SP[3](weighted Sums-of-Pairs with affine gap penalties) function and COFFEE[10](Consistency based Objective Function For alignment Evaluation) function. SP function depends on the substitution matrix, gap penalty, gap extension penalty and parameters. COFFEE function depends on the multiple sequence alignment and a library of all pairwise alignment of the sequences in the alignment. Here we use SP function with affine gap as our objective function. Let N be the number of sequences; L is the length of sequences, aij is the character for position j in sequences i. The score of the j column which have N sequences is:

$$SP(j) = \sum_{i=1}^{N-1} \sum_{k=i+1}^{N} p(a_{ij}, a_{kj}) \tag{1}$$

Let Sum_open(i) be the number of gap opening in sequences i, Sum_extend(i) be the number of gap extension in sequences i, GOP is a standard of gap opening penalty, GEP is a standard of gap extension penalty. The penalty score of i sequence is defined as:

$$Penalty(i) = GOP \times Sum\_open(i) + GEP \times Sum\_entend(i) \tag{2}$$

So, the final score for an alignment A which have N sequences can be expressed as follows:

$$SUM(A) = \sum_{j=1}^{L} SP(j) - \sum_{i=1}^{N} Penalty(i) \tag{3}$$

3   A Multiple Parallel Genetic Algorithm for Multiple Sequence Alignment

3.1   Coding Method

GA used particular gene representations which are composed of binary code, decimal code and alphabetic code and so on. For the purpose of convenience of operation and investigation, binary coding [7] is adopted as our coding method to create a binary matrix BMatrix(Fig. 1), where '0' denotes the presence of a gap, '1' denotes a letter at the relative position of the original sequence. As we know, the sequence lengths are different, and the length of the aligned sequences does not exceed 1.2 times of maximum sequence size according to reference [13], we use 1.2 times of maximum sequence size as the length of the aligned sequences. For the short sequences, we randomly inserted gaps in the initial population.

3.2   Genetic Operators

Consider the complexity of MSA, several genetic operators are designed to avoid local optimum, which could enhance the capabilities to find the global optimal solutions.

3.2.1   Local Adjustment Mutation Operators

The better evolutionary strategies are needed in order to speed up the convergence. Inserting a gap to the left or to the right of the same position in each of the selected sequences often generates a better arrangement. Three local adjustment operators are designed: the BlockShuffle operator and the LocalShuffle operator are from the reference [12]; the mutation operator was designed by making use of the feature that gap would rarely occurred alone in MSA, the basic idea of which is to select a sequence of the multiple alignment randomly, firstly find a character position where its both sides are gaps, and then find a gap position where its both sides are characters, after that mutate the character position to '0' and the gap position to '1', as Fig. 1 exemplifies.

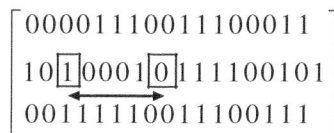

Fig. 1. Local mutation operator example: mutate

3.2.2 Global Adjustment Mutation Operators

The initialization of GA have a large amount of information which was distant from the optimal solution, choosing, crossing and variation operation can remove these individuals distanced from the optimal solution extremely. We use global mutation operators, which contain GapBlocMove[11] operator, MergeSpace[13] operator, SingleCrossover operator and UniformCrossover[7] operator. Global mutations operators have better effect on avoid local optima.

3.2.3 The Selection Operator

In GA, the intent of the selection operator is to select the superior and eliminate the inferior. The better individual evaluated by fitness has a high probability to access into the next generation while the inferior individual has a low probability. This paper adopts elite selection. The mechanisms of which are: sorting the individuals based on their fitness measured by objective function, selecting several good individuals first, and randomly choosing individuals in the remaining to consist the next generation jointly.

3.2.4 The Migration Operator

We apply the so-called coarse-grained parallel model. One way ring is used as topological structure that not only insures the diffusion of the good individuals between groups, but also isolates subgroups the better to protect the diversity, convergence rate is slow but the quality of solutions is higher [14]. Migration strategy is from one subgroup to another, the random selected individuals from one subgroup can only migrate to an adjacent one, and the individuals in the adjacent subpopulation were displaced randomly.

4   Algorithm Description

The Multigroup parallel genetic algorithm can be presented in pseudo code as follows:
   Input: the N number of original sequences
   Output: a group of the optimal aligned sequences.

```
   Begin
       1.  Initial population alignment sequences Roats and
           binary matrix BMatrixs of N chromosomes;
       2.  Evaluate fitness according to Roats, save the best
           one to Best;
       3.  While(not termination-condition)
       4.    if(i%20==0)  Apply migrate operation;   //i is
             iterations
       5.    for un=1 to Pop-Number do
       6.       Apply BlockShuffle operation to BMatrixs with a
             probability;
```

```
7.        Apply LocalShuffle operation to BMatrixs with a
          probability;
8.        Apply Mutate operation to BMatrixs with a
          probability;
9.        Apply GapBlockMove operation to BMatrixs with a
          probability;
10.       Apply MergeSpace operation to BMatrixs with a
          probability;
11.       Apply OneCrossover operation to BMatrixs with a
          probability;
12.       Apply UniformCrossover operation to BMatrixs
          with a probability;
13.       Calculate Roats and fitness according to
          BMtrixs, save the best one to
              initialBest;
14.       Elite selection;
15.    End for
16.    if (fitness of Best < fitness of initialBest)
       Best = initialBest;
17. End while
End
```

Line 1 inputs initial sequence, inserts gaps into the sequences randomly, produces N number of alignment sequence and BMatrix matrix. Line 2 uses the formula 3 to evaluate the alignment and saves the current best alignment to Best. Line 4, migrate operation specific process is: selecting 25 percent individuals in current subgroup randomly, migrating these individuals to an adjacent one and the individuals in the adjacent subgroup were displaced randomly. Lines 6-12 refine an alignment through a serious of genetic operators with a probability within subgroups, Pop-Number is the number of subgroups. Line 13 obtains Roats and fitness according to BMatrixs, and saves the best one of every generation to initialBest. Line 14 is the selection operation, sorting the individuals based on their fitness, selecting 50 percent good individuals and 50 percent of the remaining was selected in a random fashion. Line 16 compares fitness of Best with fitness of initialBest, the big one was saves to Best.

The algorithm terminates when the current best alignment is not improved after 3000 times iterations, which show that various operators were unable to optimize the alignment result. The top limit of iterations is Tmax, the threshold method gives consideration to both the optimization performance and the time performance of the algorithm.

5   The Experimental Results

The parameters have been set as follows: population size N = 60; Pop-Number = 3; Tmax = 30000; the probabilities for various operators BlockShuffle, LocalShuffle, GapBlocMove, MergeSpace, Mutate and Crossover are: Pb = 0.36, Pl = 0.36, Pg = 0.25, Pme = 0.15, Pmu = 0.36, Pc=0.15 respectively; the migration interval is 20. The experimental sequences comes from benchmark BAliBASE1.0[15]. The BLOSUM62 matrix is chosen as the substitute matrix for protein sequences. GOP = 11, GEP = 1, the gap string at the beginning or end of sequences is not penalized. SPS(Sum-of-Pairs Score) that is calculated by BaliScore algorithm is used to evaluate the final alignment[7]. BAliBASE1.0 and BaliScore[15] can be downloaded from ftp://ftp-igbmc.u-strasbg.fr/pub/BAliBASE, the test result of other reference algorithms is downloaded from http://bips.u-strasbg.fr/en/Products/Databases/BAliBASE/prog scores.html.

Table 1. The resulting of test for Ref1

name	length	identity	CLUS TALX	SAGA	DIAL IGN	MULTA LIGN	HMMT	Our method
1idy	5*65	14%	0.705	0.342	0.018	0.566	0.138	0.502
1havA	5*200	15%	0.446	0.411	0.130	0.419	0.133	0.141
1dox	4*105	46%	0.919	0.879	0.859	0.799	0.806	0.830
1fmb	4*105	49%	0.981	0.979	0.959	0.995	0.863	0.964
2fxb	5*65	51%	0.945	0.951	0.945	0.945	0.930	0.946
9rnt	5*105	57%	0.974	0.965	0.864	0.965	0.832	0.919
1led	4*250	43%	0.946	0.923	0.516	0.940	0.761	0.840
1ppn	5*230	46%	0.989	0.983	0.648	0.973	0.856	0.903

Table 2. The resulting of test for Ref2

name	length	identity	CLUS TALX	SAGA	DIAL IGN	MULTA LIGN	HMMT	Our method
1aboA	16*80	26%	0.650	0.489	0.384	0.528	0.724	0.603
1idy	22*60	28%	0.515	0.548	0.000	0.401	0.353	0.733
1csy	19*100	29%	0.154	0.154	0.000	0.154	0.000	0.701
1r69	20*80	26%	0.675	0.475	0.675	0.675	0.000	0.552
1tvxA	16*70	34%	0.552	0.448	0.000	0.138	0.276	0.552
1tgxA	19*80	35%	0.727	0.773	0.630	0.696	0.622	0.594
1ubi	17*97	32%	0.482	0.492	0.000	0.000	0.053	0.640

Table 3. The resulting of test for Ref3

name	length	identity	CLUS TALX	SAGA	DIAL IGN	MULTA LIGN	HMMT	Our method
1idy	27*70	20%	0.273	0.364	0.000	0.045	0.227	0.524
1r69	23*85	19%	0.524	0.524	0.524	0.000	0.000	0.288
1ubi	22*105	20%	0.146	0.585	0.000	0.000	0.366	0.254
1wit	19*110	22%	0.565	0.484	0.500	0.242	0.323	0.555
4enl	19*480	41%	0.547	0.672	0.050	0.652	0.050	0.410

Table 4. The resulting of test for Ref4

name	length	identity	CLUS TALX	SAGA	DIAL IGN	MULTA LIGN	Our method
1pysA	4*790	29%	0.000	0.250	0.750	0.000	0.427
1ckaA	10*820	26%	0.000	0.375	1.000	0.000	0.237
1lkl	8*830	28%	1.000	0.000	1.000	0.000	0.190
1ycc	9*210	36%	0.485	0.485	0.727	0.485	0.437
2abk	7*520	30%	0.000	0.000	1.000	0.000	0.153
Kinase1	7*490	28%	0.000	0.000	1.000	0.000	0.184

Table 5. The resulting of test for Ref5

name	length	identity	CLUS TALX	SAGA	DIAL IGN	MULTA LIGN	Our method
1pysA	10*320	25%	0.429	0.429	0.762	0.429	0.216
1qpg	5*510	35%	1.000	0.521	1.000	1.000	0.525
1thm1	15*310	32%	0.412	0.765	0.765	0.412	0.360
1thm2	7*240	38%	0.774	0.774	1.000	0.774	0.508
1eft	8*320	19%	0.000	0.000	0.579	0.000	0.059
S52	5*340	29%	1.000	1.000	1.000	1.000	0.506
Kinase1	5*380	26%	0.806	0.806	0.806	1.000	0.238

Ref1 consists of a small number of equidistant sequences with similar lengths, observing table1, our method is inferior to CLUSTALX, SAGE and MULTALIN and superior to DIALIGN and HMMT markedly; Ref2 contains alignments of a family, plus up to three'orphan'sequences, observing table2, our method and CLUSTALX are comparable, and better than other algorithms; Ref3 consists of up to four families, with <25% ID between any two sequences from different families, observing table3, the test result is inferior to CLUSTALX and SAGA, but is superior to other two algorithms. Ref4 and Ref5 contain sequences with large N/C-terminal extensions or internal insertions, respectively, observing table4, the test result is inferior to DIGLIGN, superior to other three algorithms for Ref4, observing table5, our method is worse than other algorithms as a whole for Ref5. The analysis shows that our method obtained a better alignment with advantages on global optimization, when there is a family but more sequences.

Since MSA itself is not a single optimization problem and solution of the problem has no uniqueness, we must remain both the developmental direction of optimal solution of groups and the whole group diversity in the process of each iteration for the problem. In that case, increasing population diversity and maintaining the optimality is indispensable. Our method can solve the problem well. The results in Fig.2 and Fig.3 show that the change of the algorithm performance with and without the migration operation. It can be seen from the figure that the algorithm with genetic operators converges faster to the better solution and the quality of the alignment is improved significantly.

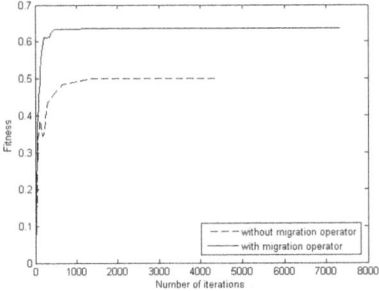

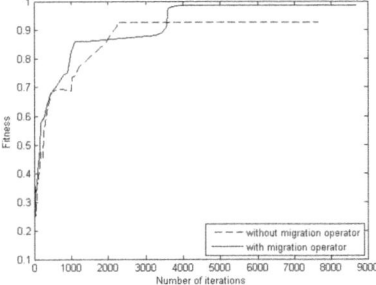

Fig. 2. The convergent for 1idy_ref1   **Fig. 3.** The convergent for 2fxb_ref1

6 Conclusion

This paper presents multigroup parallel genetic algorithm for multiple sequences alignment. In view of the slowly converge at the later stage of the genetic algorithm, we introduced a migration operator with the guidance of population diversity, and designed a new mutation operator based on the characteristic of MSA, made the whole search capability and the ability of local search improve greatly. Then some sequences are chosen from the standard BALIBASE database 1.0 to test the algorithm and the results show that our method can effectively solve the problems caused by GA for MSA, and supplies a new way for settling MSA problem.

Acknowledgments. This paper was supported by the National Natural Science Foundation of China, Grant No.60873184 and the Natural Science Foundation of Hunan Province, Grant No.07JJ5086.

References

1. Guan, W.H., Xu, Z.Y., Zhu, P.: Nonlinear prediction analysis of properties in protein sequences. Journal of Food Science and Biotechnology 27, 71–75 (2008)
2. Needleman, S.B., Wunsch, C.D.: A general method applicable to the search for similarities in the amino acid sequence of two proteins. Journal of Molecular Biology 48, 443–453 (1970)
3. Hogeweg P. Hesper B. The alignment of sets of sequences and the construction of phylogenetic trees: An integrated method. Journal of Molecular Evolution. 20, 175–18 (1984)
4. Feng, D.F., Doolittle, R.F.: Progressive sequence alignment as a prerequisite to correct phylogenetic trees. Journal of Molecular Evolution 25, 351–360 (1987)
5. Taylor, W.R.: A flexible method to align large numbers of biological sequences. Journal of Molecular Evolution 28, 161–169 (1988)
6. Thompson, J.D., Higgins, D.G., Gibson, T.J.: CLUSTALX: improving the sensitivity of progressive multiple sequence alignment through sequence weighting position-specific gap penalties and weight matrix choice. Nucleic Acids Research 22, 4468–4673 (1944)
7. Notredame, C., Higgins, D.G.: SAGA: sequence alignment by genetic alignment. Nucleic Acids Research 24, 1515–1524 (1996)
8. Krogh, A., Brown, M., Mian, I.S., Sjolander, K., Haussler, D.: Hidden Markov models in computational biology. Applications to protein modeling. J. Mol. Biol. 235, 1501–1531 (1994)
9. Motredama, B.: DIALIGN2: improvement of the segment to segment approach to multiple sequence alignment. Bioinformatics 15, 211–218 (1999)
10. Notredame, C., Holm, L., Higgins, D.G.: COFFEE: An objective function for multiple sequence alignment. Bioinformatics 14, 407–422 (1998)
11. Huo, H., Stojkovic, V., Xie, Q.: A quantum-inspired genetic algorithm based on probabilistic coding for multiple sequence alignment. Journal of Bioinformatics and Computational Biology 1, 59–75 (2010)
12. Thomsen, R., Fogel, G.B., Krink, T.: A Clustal Alignment Improver using Evolutionary Algorithms. In: Proceedings of the Fourth Congress on Evolutionary Computation, vol. 1, pp. 121–126 (2002)

13. Huo, H., Stojkovic, V.: Two-Phase Quantum Based Evolutionary Algorithm for Multiple Sequence Alignment. In: Wang, Y., Cheung, Y.-m., Liu, H. (eds.) CIS 2006. LNCS (LNAI), vol. 4456, pp. 11–21. Springer, Heidelberg (2007)
14. Matsumura, T., Nakamura, M., Okech, J., et al.: A parallel and distributed genetic algorithm on loosely-coupled multiprocessor system. IEICE Trans Fundam. Electron. Commun. Comput. Sci. E81A(4), 540–546 (1998)
15. Notredame, C., Higgins, D.G., Heringa, J.: T-Coffee: A novel method for fast and accurate multiple sequence alignment. J. Mol. Biol. 302, 205–217 (2000)

Research on the Protein Secondary Prediction Using a Symmetric Binding Form of Organization[*,**]

Sheng Xu, Shanshan Xu, and Ning Ye

School of Information technology
Nanjing Forestry University, Nanjing, China
{286331417,529031585}@qq.com, ye.ning@yahoo.com.cn

Abstract. Protein structure prediction plays an important role in the expression and analysis of the protein sequences. As the high performance analytical instruments will need a high cost, so the way through the algorithm to get the secondary structure information has become a very important method. The traditional secondary prediction is directly based on comparing the sequences, which relied solely on the Hamming distance to classify them. Analyzing this data organization method, it not only inconsistent with the practical problems, but also throws away a lot of information. In the end the accuracy is often too low. Research shows that each amino acid can be seen as a force with its own size and direction. With the effect of all amino acids force, they form the spatial structure of the protein sequence. And then we can describe the distortions in the way similar to the description of the force diagram. It is difficult to determine whether the amino acid sequence in a forward or a reverse order, so the symmetrical position of amino acids will have a similar effect to the middle area. Based on the above analysis, we use a symmetrical binding form of organization to construct a new input sample. When testing the accuracy we use the neural network method. Because the force in different positions is different, so we add a property factor to the neural network model. Then the power of amino acids in different positions can be adjusted by the property factor. In the end we can not only get the most suitable parameters to get a high accuracy, but also reveal the relations between the different amino acids.

Keywords: protein secondary prediction, amino acid interaction, symmetry constraints.

1 Introduction

Protein structure plays an important role in life science and the spatial structure of secondary structure prediction is one of the most crucial steps. Currently, experimental determination of protein secondary structure is far behind the rate of the primary structure (amino acid sequence) determination of the speed [1]. So in theory, begin to analyze the protein sequences from the primary structure of the information brought to predict protein secondary structure is extremely important.

---

[*] Natural Science Foundation of Jiangsu Province Project (BK2009393).
[**] Natural Science Foundation of China (30671639).

H. Deng et al. (Eds.): AICI 2011, Part I, LNAI 7002, pp. 317–324, 2011.
© Springer-Verlag Berlin Heidelberg 2011

Proteins are composed by amino acids, and they are expressed by strings. As the Fig. 1 shows, the amino acid sequence is just the protein primary structure only. Protein sequence in the organism actually has its own spatial space. Usually there are three forms: H (α-helix), E (β-sheet) and C (coil). Then the secondary prediction is to predict the spatial structure based on the amino acid level shown in Fig. 1 **Structure** [2].

Protein sequence= ASTPD GDNVITVPDDEYILDVA
Structure   = CC C CEEEEEEECCCCCHHHHH

Fig. 1. Amino acid sequence and its corresponding state

When predict the protein secondary, each protein has a specific structure. However many different sequences may have a basic form. In other words, proteins with similar sequences tend to fold into a similar spatial structure. If their sequences have the same amino acid about 25%~30% or more, then these two proteins can fold into a similar spatial structure. Thus, if an unknown protein has an enough similarity to an already known protein, you can believe that they have a similar secondary structure. The most reliable method to predict is to base on the above ideas called the sequence alignment method. By comparing the protein sequence, we can find the evolution between the proteins and then get the secondary structure. The accuracy was generally above 85% [3]-[5].

But if their similarities are less than 25%., then the above methods will encounter difficulties. The alignment method in predicting must search the entire database, so it will also spend too much time. Also the size of building a database will be another complex place.

This time is to consider other methods of non-alignment, and the forecast accuracy is usually only about 65% [6]. These algorithms are usually only used the Hamming distance in the sequence to identify the classification. It is not only inconsistent with the practical problems, but also loses a lot of information. For these problems, this paper conducted in-depth study, and gives the relevant solution.

2   Symmetric Binding Forms of Organzation

Here describe the way to process the forecast data set. First select a sliding window, and the current under test amino acid **T** is in the center of the window as shown in Fig.1 **Protein_Sequence.** Then we consider all the amino acids in the window (the width of the window is **W**) to determine the state of **T.**

Divide the input sequence into **m×num** sequences. That is each amino acid has **m** samples, and there are total **num** groups, for example, sequences corresponding to Fig.1 are:

Traindata=(ASTPD, STPDA, TPDGD, PDGDN, DGDNV, GDNVI, NVITV)

Then train the input samples, while the distance between samples is the Hamming distance (1)

$$dis = \begin{cases} 1 & X_{ki} = X_{k'i} \\ 0 & X_{ki} \neq X_{k'i} \end{cases} \tag{1}$$

Here X_{ki} represents the **ith** amino acid in **kth** sample. At this time the **dis** in the corresponding position is 1 if the string is the same otherwise **dis** is 0. Using the cluster method we will get the hidden layer nodes [7], and then put them into the neural network, and the output layer will give the classification. Now analyze the shortcomings of the above data organization method.

2.1 Reverse

Consider a protein sequence:

Protein_Sequence'=(VDLIYEDDPVTIVNDGDPTSA).
The Hamming distance between the two sequences (**Protein_Sequence** and **Protein_Sequence'**) is great. Because the **Protein_Sequence'** is happen to be in a reverse order. According to the Hamming distance, the two sequences will have a very different state in each position. However, the **Protein_Sequence'** may be just measured from the back, and the fact is that these two sequences have the same state. Traditional organization methods, **OldData**, will lose much information. Here we suppose that the impact on the amino acid structure is symmetric constraint. The anterior and posterior segment of amino acids is not related in the **OldData** set. The **NewData**, as described below, constrain the current state by the same intervals before and after the current amino acid. Shown in Fig. 2, and now we enhance the constraint, at this point, an analysis of selected **G** in **Protein_Sequence** will has a form like this:

$$X = ((G,G),(D,D),(P,N),(T,V),(S,I),(A,T)) \tag{2}$$

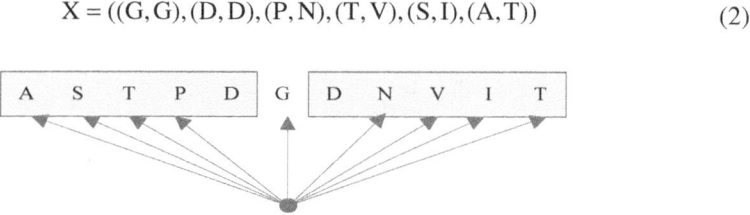

Fig. 2. Amino acid sequence of symmetry constraints

2.2 Statistical Information

The traditional method is equivalent to compare two strings. Only consider whether they are the same, and they use the Hamming distance to describe the distance whose definition is too simple. Also ignore the overall messages. Now add the statistical information [8], for instance, the input sample, such as (2) shows. The ith position X_i=(**X_left,X_right**) means the amino acid which is i position away from the center amino acid in the sequence is (**X_left,X_right**) or (**X_right, X_left**). Now we have X_1=(**G,G**),and that is mean the **G** is the middle of the window ,then the value of the X_1 is the probability of each state (**H,E,C**) for this amino acid **G** at this position. Similarity, the X_3=(**P,N**) means the probability of each state for the third position is (P,N) or (N,P). At this point the input sample of each dimension is further transformed into a **W×3** matrix: $\mathbf{X_i'}=(\mathbf{X_i\_H,X_i\_E,X_i\_C})$. Here $\mathbf{X_i\_H}$ represents the probability that the state is H when the ith position from the center amino acid is $\mathbf{X_i}$, $\mathbf{X_i\_E}$ and $\mathbf{X_i\_C}$ are similar. This structure not only adds more constraints, but also adds probability information and more metrics to use and not limited to the Hamming distance. So the first drawback to **OldData** will be resolved. This sample will have a better separability than the **OldData**. For example, when there is just a small number of hidden nodes in the neural network. For example when the **Hidden** is 2, using **OldData** and the effect of the hidden layer output shown in Fig 3 on the left. Actually two different types of samples are coincidence after the operation and so it is difficult to separate them. When using the **NewData**, the result shown in Fig. 3 on the right side. So it can be distinguished easily at the above situation with the **NewData**.

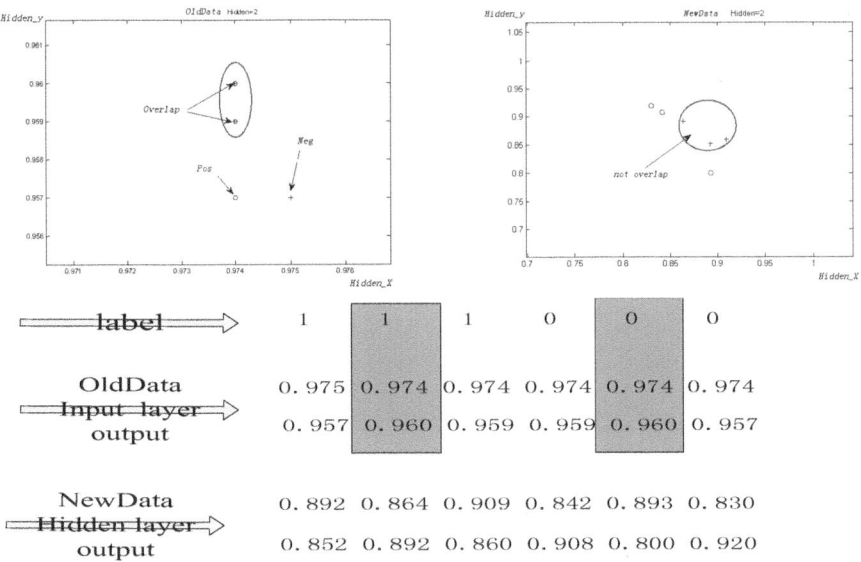

Fig. 3. The output of the hidden layer nodes from **OldData** sets and **NewData** collection

Now summary of the data set, in fact, the difference in structure state is due to a force around the current amino acid. Just like the force applied to the object, we can draw the force diagram to the amino acids. Consider a protein sequence: **Protein_Sequence=ASTPDGDNVIT**. That is **W** is 11, then the total force will be divided to 6 pairs. Now analyze the state of **G**. Currently when test the **Protein_Sequence**, to convenience we often convert the string to a digital form, and the corresponding transformation is:

A R N D C Q E G H I L K M F P S T W Y V B Z X
1 2 3 4 5 6 7 8 9 10 11 12 13 14 15 16 17 18 19 20 21 22 23

At this point, in accordance with the above analysis. We get a new organization of form called Symmetry constraints:

X=((G,G),(D,D),(P,N),(T,V),(S,I),(A,T))

and the digital form is:

X=((8,8),(4,4),(15,3),(17,20),(16,10),(1,17))

Now shown in Fig. 4, totally 6 pairs force on the current amino acids **G**, and the forms are **F(left, right, k)**, and the **totalF** is (3).

$$totalF = \sum_{i=1}^{6} \lambda_i \cdot F_i \, (left, right, k) \tag{3}$$

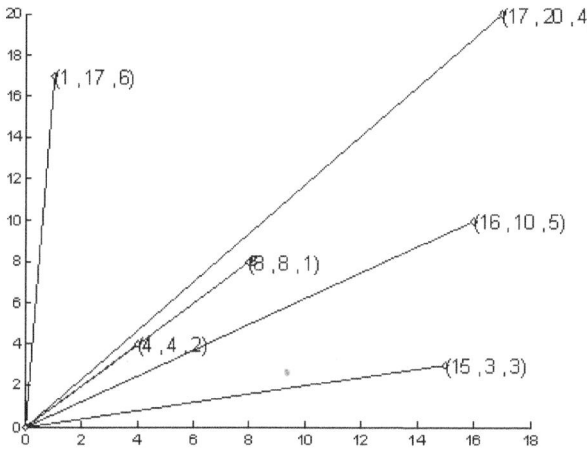

Fig. 4. A similar force to the protein sequence

As shown in Figure 4, when the current amino acid numbered is 8. Considering the surrounding amino acids, the structure to become an H state is 0.6, the E is 0.20 and the C is 0.20. So the force in the way mentioned above is :F(8,8,1)=(0.60,0.20,0.20) At this time, we can get the totalF from (4).

$$\begin{aligned} totalF &= \lambda_1 \times F_1(8,8,1) + \lambda_2 \times F_2(4,4,2) + \lambda_3 \times F_3(15,3,3) \\ &+ \lambda_4 \times F_4(17,20,4) + \lambda_5 \times F_5(16,10,5) + \lambda_6 \times F_6(1,7,6) \end{aligned} \tag{4}$$

At this point the **totalF** is the sample as input into the trained neural network. When statistical the probability of various states of **F**, we definition:

$$F(right, left, k) = (F(right, left, k) + F(left, right, k))/2 \tag{5}$$

This improves the traditional problem in the **OldData** set, we can get a good result even in a reserve order. Together with the back and forth amino acids makes more structural information be preserved. Instead of separately consider the adjacent amino acids; we consider the global information to solve the second question. Using of the statistical information and adding the Euclidean distance, so the third problem will also be solved.

There are different methods to test the **NewData**, like [9],[10]. Here we use the neural network to do the test. Instead of the traditional method [10], we discuss a new neural network model. After the preprocess, for example the normalization operation, for each input samples, we multiplied each of them by a factor λ_i like (6) and the (7) describes the factors in input samples. Base on the above analysis, we know that the αX is the **totalF**. The $\mathbf{Y_i}$ is the output of the net and the $\mathbf{H}$ is a function in the hidden layer. The ω is the weight matrix between the hidden layer and the output layer. Here we suppose there are $\mathbf{n}$ nodes in the hidden layer and $\mathbf{m}$ properties for each sample.

$$Y_i = \sum_{c=1}^{n} \omega_{ic} H_c(\alpha X) \tag{6}$$

$$\alpha = (\lambda_1, \lambda_2, \lambda_3, ..., \lambda_m)^T \tag{7}$$

Then deal with the new network by genetic algorithm optimization to get α, that is the contribution of each property for the classification. Corresponds to the prediction of protein secondary is just the role of different amino acids on the structure states. Using of the optimized α can get the highest classification accuracy.

3   Experiment and Discussion

Make the new organization as the input to the neural network to test the **NewData** set. Experimental data is from the Rost and Sander dataset (RS121) data collection. Now choose 60 sequences and use the cross-validation method to do the experiment. The data collection is divided into the traditional Hamming distance (**OldData**), and improved data collection (**NewData**). Each of them has six elements and each element has a train set (50 protein sequences) and a different test set (10 protein sequences):

OldData = (OldData1, OldData2, OldData3, OldData4, OldData5, OldData6)

NewData = (NewData1, NewData2, NewData3, NewData4, NewData5, NewData6)

RBF neural network is a good method to do the protein classification. Experiments show that the number of nodes in the hidden layer should not too much [11]. Here we find when there are 20 hidden nodes we will get a good result; and the length of the training samples in each element are chosen 100,500 1000 5000 and all. Respectively Center Method (use K-means to get the center nodes) and Optimization Method algorithm (use gradient descent to get the weight matrix) are tested on **OldData.** Then we choose the Center Method to the traditional RBFNN and the improved RBFNN which has been added the property factor on **NewData**. Here the dimension of the input sample **W** is 17, and the accuracy is shown in Fig. 5. Corresponding to the different elements in the **OldData** and **NewData,** we give the corresponding experimental.

After the improvements in the selection of the data set, the Center Method is significantly improved and higher than the data based on **OldData** [12] about 6% ~ 10% ,and also better than the Optimization Method based on **OldData** about 3% to 7%. The **NewData** is able to save more structural information to improve the classification accuracy and further confirmed the previously described **OldData** deficiencies. When use the **NewData** the sample size is 1000, we will achieve the highest prediction rate which is about 71.05% by add the property factor to the RBFNN.

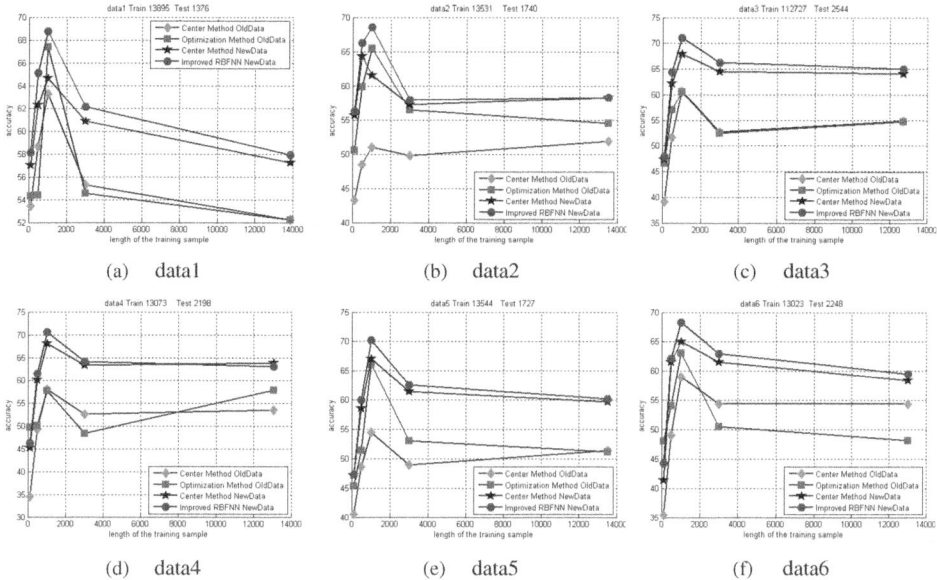

Fig. 5. Comparing the accuracy of various algorithms

4 Conclusion

Currently, prediction of protein secondary is often considering the Hamming distance and losing a large number of sequences structural information. Consider that there are pairs of symmetry force to the amino acid. Design a new data organization, which is not only overcome the various defects in the traditional organizational form, but also save the sequence internal useful information, and use a new neural network model which is added a property factor to further improve the accuracy.

Acknowledgment. Natural Science Foundation of Jiangsu Province Project (BK2009393), National Natural Science Foundation (30671639).

References

1. Li, W., Chen, Y., Zhao, Y.: Multi-layer ensemble classifiers on protein secondary structure prediction. In: Huang, D.-S., Wunsch II, D.C., Levine, D.S., Jo, K.-H. (eds.) ICIC 2008. LNCS, vol. 5226, pp. 79–85. Springer, Heidelberg (2008)
2. Chou, K.C., Shen, H.B.: Recent progress in protein subcellular location prediction. Analytical Biochemistry 370, 1–16 (2007)
3. Li, F.M., Li, Q.Z.: Using pseudo amino acid composition to predict protein subnuclear location with improved hybrid approach. Amino Acids 34, 119–125 (2008)
4. Stolorz, P., Lapedes, A., Xia, Y.: Predicting protein secondary structure using neural net and statistical methods. Journal of Molecular Biology 225(2), 363–377 (1992)

5. Shen, H.B., Chou, K.C.: Predicting protein subnuclear location with optimized evidence-theoretic K-nearest classifier and pseudo amino acid composition. Biochemical and Biophysical Research Communications 337, 752–756 (2005)
6. Lin, Z., Pan, X.M.: Accurate prediction of protein secondary structural content. Journal of Protein Chemistry 20, 217–220 (2001)
7. Sun, J., Shen, R., Han, P.: An Original RBF Network Learning Algorithm. Chinese Journal Of Computers Â 26(11) (2003)
8. Chou, K.C., Shen, H.B.: Protident: A web server for identifying proteases and their types by fusing functional domain and sequential evolution information. Biochemical and Biophysical Research Communications 376, 321–325 (2008)
9. Gao, Q.B., Wang, Z.Z., Yan, C., Du, Y.H.: Prediction of protein subcellular location using a combined feature of sequence. Febs Letters 579, 3444–3448 (2005)
10. Cai, Y.D., Liu, X.J., Chou, K.C.: Artificial neural network model for predicting protein subcellular location. Computers and Chemistry 26, 179–182 (2002)
11. Bianchini, M., Frasconi, P., Gori, M.: Learning without local minima in radial basis function networks. IEEE Transactions on Neural NetWorks 6(3), 749–756 (1995)
12. Whitehead, B.A.: Cooperative competitive genetic evolution of radial basis function centers and widths fortime series prediction. IEEE Transactions on Neural Networks 7(4), 869–880 (1996)

Exploring Brain Activation Patterns during Heuristic Problem Solving Using Clustering Approach

Dazhong Liu

International WIC Institute, Beijing University of Technology, Beijing, 100124, China
School of Mathematics and Computer Science, Hebei University, Baoding, 071002, China
liudazhong@hbu.edu.cn

Abstract. In the present study, brain activation patterns of heuristic problem solving were investigated in the context of the puzzle Sudoku experiment by using a two-stage clustering approach. The cognitive experiment was composed of easy tasks and difficult tasks. In the two-stage clustering approach, K-means served as the data selection role in the first stage and the affinity propagation (AP) served as partition role in the second stage. Functional magnetic resonance imaging (fMRI) was used to collect the slow event related paradigm data. Simulated fMRI datasets were used to evaluate the validity of the clustering method and compare the performance of fuzzy c-means (FCM) as an alternate method in the first stage. Test results illustrated that the performance of K-means in this role was better than that of FCM. Further, the proposed method was applied to the heuristic problem solving fMRI data and the results showed that the brain activation patterns observed in the experiment exhibited compact and coherent activity mode in dealing with different cognitive tasks.

Keywords: heuristics problem solving, clustering, functional magnetic resonance imaging (fMRI).

1 Introduction

In recent years, human heuristics problem solving has been studied in a number of investigations by using the functional magnetic resonance imaging (fMRI) techniques. To explore the brain neural mechanisms of cognitive process in problem solving, different cognitive tasks such as Tower of Hanoi, the savage and the missionary puzzle etc., have been used [1-3]. However, these tasks are time consuming in the experiment. Therefore, a simplified 4*4 Sudoku task was used in our research. The puzzle Sudoku is to fill a 4×4 grid with the digits from 1 to 4, and each digit in each column, each row, and each of the four 2×2 boxes appears only one time [4,5]. Fig 1 (a) is a right answer. To further simplify the task, we divided it into two kinds, one is the easy task and the other is the difficult task. The easy task (Fig 1 (b)) is asked to fill one grid marked by '?' given heuristic context in one row or column, and the difficult task (Fig. 1 (c)) will fill the grid marked by '?' given heuristic context in one row and column. When participant is finding the answers in the two kinds of tasks, the brain is scanned by the fMRI equipment, and the brain images are collected, yielding a huge of observations. In the experiment, a slow

H. Deng et al. (Eds.): AICI 2011, Part I, LNAI 7002, pp. 325–331, 2011.

event-related methodology was used, and the separate trials were randomly presented. After that, the dataset will be analyzed by some kinds of methods, which roughly are divided into two main categories: model-driven methods and data-driven methods. In this study, we applied our proposed two- stage clustering method, a kind of data-driven methods to analyze the dataset. The goal of the present study was to investigate the brain activation patterns on heuristic problem solving using our proposed clustering approach.

The remainder of this paper is organized as follows. In Section 2, we introduce the dataset used in our experiment and describe our method. In Section 3, experimental results are analyzed by the proposed approach. Finally, Section 4 gives concluding remarks.

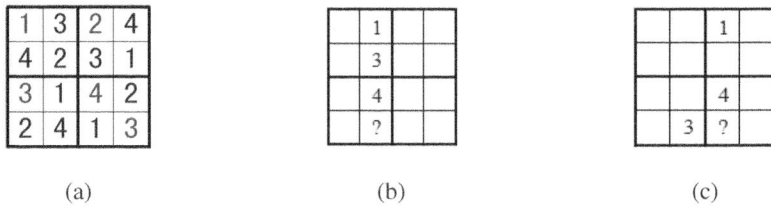

(a)	(b)	(c)

Fig. 1. The answers of 4*4 Sudoku and two types of heuristics

2 Analysis Clustering Method and Materials

2.1 Analysis Clustering Method

The aim of this work was to discover functional brain activity patterns in the cognitive experimental. To explore blood oxygen level-dependent (BOLD) effect signals, a kind of two-stage clustering analysis was applied. It consists of two clustering algorithms K-means and AP [8], and each clustering algorithm employs specific similarity measure. Every clustering method is appropriate for its corresponding situations. This two-stage clustering method has already been applied in the exploring the functional brain connectivity networks (BI 2011. http://wi-consortium.org/conferences/amtbi11/index.html). The entire program was implemented using Matlab and SPM5 toolbox (http://www.fil.ion.ucl.ac.uk/spm/ext/). In this work, we used SPM5 to preprocess (realignment, normalization/registration and smoothing) the fMRI sequences. After that, a new 4-D dataset were obtained by calculating the autocovariance value series (AVS) of each voxel. K-means just used the Euclidean-based distance of AVS of each voxel to partition the dataset into some groups. K-means was used to pick up the signal response regions. For the next stage, AP was used to further partition the group with the fewest voxels, and to explore the details of the phases or amplitude of the signal. After the clustering, the groups will be overlapped on the structure brain map. We first use K-means to perform data reduction for reducing the sensitivity to noise, and then AP is used to explore the details of the brain activity. As a data reduction role, FCM can be used instead of K-means in the first stage. At last, we select K-means, and the reason will be discussed in the session 3.1.

2.2   Sudoku Task Experiment

As session I introduced, the experiment tasks included two types of tasks, easy heuristic tasks and difficult heuristic tasks, and presented randomly. The slow event related fMRI data were recorded, allowing the BOLD response to go back to baseline after each trial. Each trial of the experiment started with a red star shown for 2 seconds as warning, and then the participant would see the task stimulus as shown in fig.1 (b) or (c), and he/she would solve the puzzle in the following period of 20 seconds. When participants found out the solution of '?', they would press a button immediately and spoke out the answer.

A MR scanner equipment was used to acquire the fMRI images. A SS-EPI (single shot echo planar imaging) sequence sensitive to BOLD signals was used. The functional images parameters were TR = 2000 ms, axial slices with AC-PC from the bottom of brain.

3   Results

3.1   Results with Synthetic Data Set

In our proposed method, two clustering methods were combined, in which one clustering performed data reduction task and the other carried out grouping task from the reduced dataset. We compared the performance of FCM as the first stage cluster with that of K-means. To test our analysis method on the synthetic fMRI data, fully artificially fMRI phantom was constructed similar to the one described in [9]. The simulated dataset was constructed with three small activation foci of 21 voxels each. Three kinds of slow event-related pattern signals with different period and amplitude were generated and added on each location. To simulate the actual situation, all the three kinds of signals convolved with the hemodynamic response function (HRF) of SPM sampled at TP = 2 s. Gaussian noise with standard deviation varying from 0.2 to 3.5 was added to the signal. The data was smoothed spatially as commonly done for fMRI (FWHM=4.5mm=1.5 voxel) at the preprocessing step, and then a cluster number was set for the first clustering stage.

Receiver operating characteristic (ROC) curve can be used to assess performance of method and determine the criterion for different conditions according to true-positive ratio versus false-positive ratio (i.e. sensitivity versus 1-specificity) at each point of the curve [10]. An ideal algorithm would detect signals with 100% sensitivity and 100% specificity, and therefore its ROC curve would be closest to upper left corner of the plot. In the same way as [10], we chose the cluster number varied from 3 to 8 as the threshold in the first stage of our method.

First, the error rates were computed at different cluster number with two noise levels, and then ROC was performed in the same situation. The results are shown in Fig. 2. It can be seen that the ROC curve all pass near the upper left corner of the plot. The plot illustrates that the difference of the performance for the two cluster methods is not significant. However, FCM has a parameter m (the fuzzy index that determines the degree of fuzziness of the membership function) to be chosen. We computed the ROC and the error rate at three different fuzzy index values m=1.02, 1.12 and 1.22, respectively. The different fuzzy index value will result in different performance as depicted in Fig. 3. Therefore, K-means was selected as the first stage cluster method from the perspective of performance and complexity. After the algorithm determined, we need to choose the K-means cluster numbers. Although the error rate declined as the cluster number increases, the true-positive ratio remains unchanged. However, a bigger cluster number means much more work for the second stage. Therefore, we can choose the small number, say, four as the K-means cluster number.

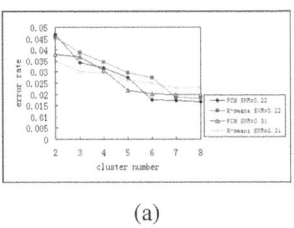
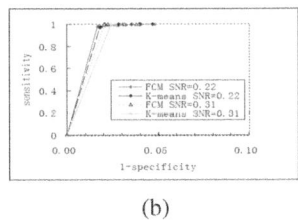

(a)   (b)

Fig. 2. Performance comparing for the K-means and FCM. (a) Error rate against the cluster number at the two noise levels. (b) Roc curve at the two noise levels.

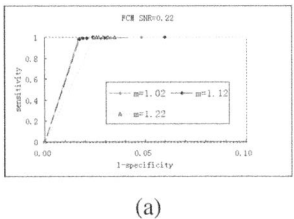
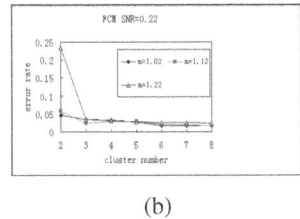

(a)   (b)

Fig. 3. FCM performance plot given the three fuzzy index values. (a) Roc curve at the three m values. (b) Error rate against the cluster number at the three m values.

3.2 Results with Human Data Set

For the human heuristics problem solving fMRI data, initially, the real data sets were preprocessed. SPM5 was used as a preprocessing tool. After the pre-processing steps, the two-stage clustering analysis was carried out. To investigate the brain activity patterns in the situation of easy task and difficult task, we divided the whole response time series into two parts, one is easy task time series, and the other is difficult task time series. Each part was clustered by the proposed two-stage method. From the easy part, three groups (named as ge1, ge2 and ge3) were obtained with 3985, 826, and 94 voxels in each, and the overlay map is shown in Fig. 4. From the difficult part, two groups (named as gd1 and gd2) were acquired with 4829 and 444 voxels in each, and the overlay map depicted in Fig. 5. The above two overlay maps rendered by using xjView (http://www.alivelearn.net/xjview/). For each voxel in each pair of group, an analysis of variance (ANOVA) was performed on the mean positive amplitude of original BOLD time series. The F statistic and p-value are [F $(1, 86596)$ = 4026.54, P< 0.001], [F $(1, 73420)$ = 4026.54, P< 0.001], [F $(1, 16558)$ = 1435, P< 0.001], [F $(1, 79093)$ = 115.57, P< 0.001], for the pairs (ge1, ge2), (ge1, ge3), (ge2, ge3), and (gd1, gd2), respectively. Therefore, each group is significant different from the others. To confirm that the groups are BOLD response signals to the tasks stimuli, the time series of the difficult task response groups are shown in Fig. 6.

Group ge1 mainly includes occipital, parietal, cerebelum, lingual, fusiform, cuneus, precuneus, angular, temporal and vermis cortical regions. Ge2 mainly includes parietal, precuneus, postcentral, supplementary motor area (SMA), and postcentral cortical regions. Ge3 mainly includes postcentral, and precentral cortical regions. Gd1 mainly includes occipital, cerebelum, parietal, fusiform, precuneus, lingual, cuneus, angular, temporal, SMA, and middle frontal cortical regions. Gd2 mainly includes superior parietal, precuneus and precentral cortical regions. These five groups of cortical regions exhibit compact and coherent activity patterns and illustrate a dynamic combination brain mode in dealing with different cognitive tasks.

4 Discussions and Conclusions

In this paper, a completely data-driven combining method was applied in exploratory fMRI analysis. Of course the combining strategy can be usually found in the area of data mining and fMRI analysis [10-14]. To our best knowledge, K-means and AP unified method has not been employed. In the proposed method, the initial cluster number for K-means was decided by domain knowledge, and we need not denote a cluster number for AP. The similarities used in AP do not necessarily satisfy the triangle inequality, however the similarity matrix will consume the memory for the 4-D fMRI dataset. Hence, data reduction should be adopted. FCM can be used as the reduction stage; however, more parameter should be decided in advance. K-means can be used solely in cascaded manner with two distance measures and two initial cluster number must be considered.

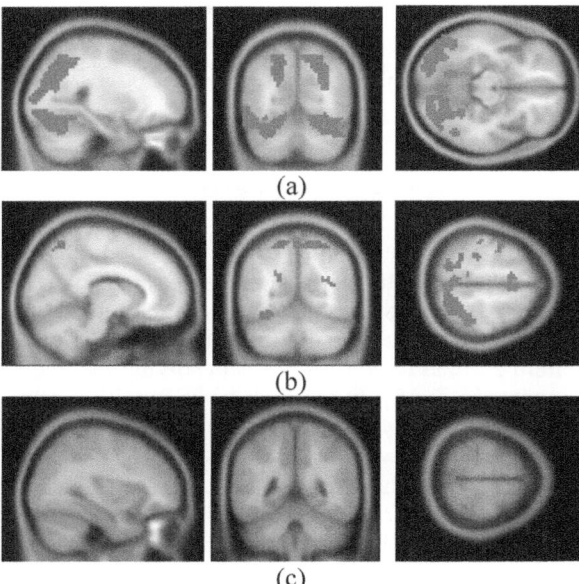

(a)

(b)

(c)

Fig. 4. Overlap maps of easy task clustering result. (a)   group one ge1(b) group two ge2 (c) group three ge3.

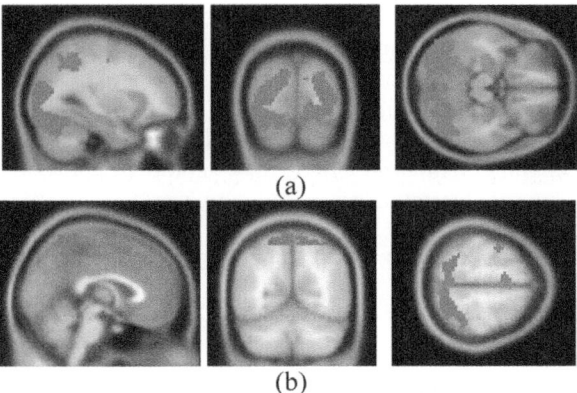

Fig. 5. Overlap maps of difficult task clustering result. (a)   group one gd1(b) group two g2.

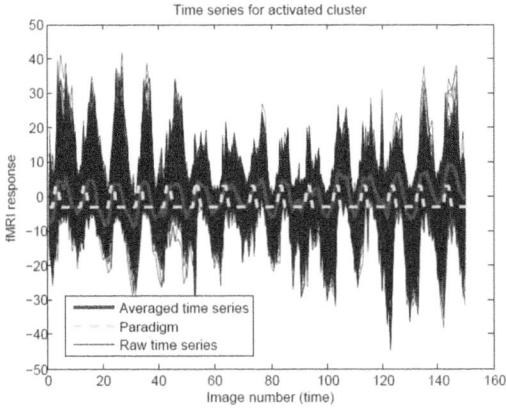

Fig. 6. Time series of group one gd1

It is reported that the precuneus might play an important role in retrieval of heuristic information, the occipital gyrus might engage in rearrangement of visual stimulus and the cerebellum might be involved in attentional resources deployment [3]. The involvement of the brain activity areas including occipital, parietal, cuneus, precuneus, cerebellum cortical regions in problem solving that we found is consistent with many other studies [1-5, 15]. In the high-level cognition, some regions such as prefrontal and parietal are strongly interconnected. Using the proposed method, the dynamic group working mode was discovered under task-specific condition. This working mode can be seen as the exhibition of functional brain connectivity [16]. Because clustering method uses distance measure to group the time series, and this implies that the degree of temporal correlation in the same group is higher than in different groups. Contrast to the traditional model base methods, model free methods need not to choose HRF. The model free methods are always considered as complementary role of the model base statistical inferential methods.

There are several works to do, including seeking the new data reduction strategy, confirming the method using many more real datasets in future.

References

1. Anderson, J.R., Albert, M.V., Fincham, J.M.: Tracing Problem Solving in Real Time: fMRI Analysis of the Subject-paced Tower of Hanoi. Journal of Cognitive Neuroscience 17(8), 1261–1274 (2005)
2. Danker, J.F., Anderson, J.R.: The roles of prefrontal and posterior parietal cortex in algebra problem solving: A case of using cognitive modeling to inform neuroimaging data. NeuroImage 35, 1365–1377 (2007)
3. Qiu, J., Li, H., Jou, J., Liu, J., Luo, Y., Feng, T.: Neural correlates of the "Aha" experiences: Evidence from an fMRI study of insight problem solving. CORTEX 46, 397–403 (2010)
4. Wang, R., Xiang, J., Zhou, H., Qin, Y., Zhong, N.: Simulating Human Heuristic Problem Solving: A Study by Combining ACT-R and fMRI Brain Image. In: Zhong, N., Li, K., Lu, S., Chen, L. (eds.) BI 2009. LNCS(LNAI), vol. 5819, pp. 53–62. Springer, Heidelberg (2009)
5. Xiang, J., Chen, J., Zhou, H., Qin, Y., Li, K., Zhong, N.: Using SVM to Predict High-Level Cognition from fMRI Data: A Case Study of 4*4 Sudoku Solving. In: Zhong, N., Li, K., Lu, S., Chen, L. (eds.) BI 2009. LNCS(LNAI), vol. 5819, pp. 171–181. Springer, Heidelberg (2009)
6. Duda, R.O., Hart, P.E.: Pattern Classification and Scene Analysis, pp. 189–225. John Wiley & Sons, New York (1973)
7. Bezdek, J.C.: Pattern Recognition with Fuzzy Objective Function Algorithms. Plenum, NY (1981)
8. Frey, B.J., Dueck, D.: Clustering by Passing Messages between Data Points. Science 315(5814), 972–976 (2007)
9. Yang, J., Zhong, N., Liang, P.P., Wang, J., Yao, Y.Y., Lu, S.F.: Brain Activation Detection by Neighborhood One-class SVM. In: Proceedings of the 2007 IEEE/WIC/ACM International Conferences on Web Intelligence and Intelligent Agent Technology – Workshops, pp. 47–51 (2007)
10. Chuang, K., Chiu, M., Lin, C.C., Chen, J.: Model-free Functional MRI Analysis Using Kohonen Clustering Neural Network and Fuzzy C-means. IEEE Transactions on Medical Imaging 18, 1117–1128 (1999)
11. Dimitriadou, E., Barth, M., Windischberger, C., Hornik, K., Moser, E.: A Quantitative Comparison of Functional MRI Cluster Analysis. Artificial Intelligence in Medicine 31, 57–71 (2004)
12. Fadili, M.J., Ruan, S., Bloyet, D., Mazoyer, B.: A Multistep Unsupervised Fuzzy Clustering Analysis of fMRI Time Series. Human Brain Mapping 10, 160–178 (2000)
13. Formisano, E., Martino, F.D., Valente, G.: Multivariate analysis of fMRI time series: classification and regression of brain responses using machine learning. Magnetic Resonance Imaging 26, 921–934 (2008)
14. Ye, J., Lazar, N.A., Li, Y.: Geostatistical Analysis in Clustering fMRI Time Series. Statistics in Medicine 28(19), 2490–2508 (2009)
15. Sohn, M.-h., Goode, A., Stenger, V.A., Carter, C.S., Anderson, J.R.: Competition and representation during memory retrieval: Roles of the prefrontal cortex and the posterior parietal cortex. PNAS 100, 7412–7417 (2003)
16. Friston, K.J., Frith, C.D., Liddle, P.F., Frackowiak, R.S.J.: Functional connectivity.: The Principal Component Analysis of Large (PET) Data sets. J. Cereb. Blood Flow Metab. 13, 5–14 (1993)

Auditory Feature Binding and Its Hierarchical Computational Model

Guangping Zhuo and Xueli Yu

College of Computer and Software in Taiyuan University of Technology,
79 Yingze West Street, Taiyuan City, Shanxi Province, PRC
Zhgp72@gmail.com, Xuli3287@263.net

Abstract. When we intend to grasp a sound target, perhaps its signal is in the presence of competing signals. An effective solution is to concentrate on the target's sound features selected and extracted from the various mixed auditory features. This is so-called auditory feature binding. It plays an important role in the cognitive and neuroscience. In this paper, we will describe the conceptual frame named "auditory feature binding" and then put forward its hierarchical computational model. We think that it may be used in machine auditory perception which will over-fly from the primary audition sense to the senior audition perception and cognition. Besides, we will later combine it with visual feature binding to realize cooperation of vision-audition cross-modal perception which is emphasized in the National Science Fund of China Project "Research on Synergic Learning Algorithm of vision-audition Cross-modal Coherence".

Keywords: auditory feature binding, hierarchical computational model, vision-audition cross-modal.

1 Introduction

As is known in the field of cognition, the "Feature Binding Problem" is always playing an important role across many disciplines, including psychology, cognitive and neuroscience. Yet, as was said by Kandel[1], the Nobelist, "It is surprised and disappointed that although feature binding problem is so important to both the functional and mechanistic understanding of cognition, although increasing attention and enormous research resources are devoted, we still cannot achieve consensus towards binding mechanisms." For example, how visual feature binding is processed, how auditory feature binding is realized, and what is the probability and cooperative mechanism in the process of audition –vision cross-model feature binding.[2] We are not very clear about them so far.

The problem of extracting acoustic signal of interest from background is called sound source separation and this will contribute to the further perception and cognitive task on the target. In psychoacoustics, we know as the "cocktail party problem".

The problem of auditory feature binding indicates that various auditory information such as pitch, intensity, timbre, location, and target's identity are processed in

H. Deng et al. (Eds.): AICI 2011, Part I, LNAI 7002, pp. 332–338, 2011.

separate brain regions and the brain must combine them from several different sensory modalities and then generate a complete and accurate internal representation. Numerous researches in neuro-anatomy and neuro-physiology have testified it.

We have so far come to the following agreements in our research:

1. Since information is processed in different portion of brain or subsystem neurons, the neurons participating in the same information process should be consistent via neural synchronization, which requires a particular mechanism within the neurons. That is to say when external stimuli come into the brain, neurons corresponding to the features of the same object will form a dynamic neural assembly by temporal and spatial synchronous neural oscillation, and the dynamic neural assembly, as an internal representation in the brain, codes the object.

2. The complicated perception and actions usually require parallel processing of different targets and events. The information must be processed in different locations and must be separated or differentiated in order to properly accomplish the relevant corresponding reaction.

3. Most auditory perceptual and cognitive functions require making corresponding choices from numerous backup information databases. Auditory feature binding systems usually emphasize one portion of information, and then integrate the information with the relevant contents as prerequisite condition.

4. We are trying to answer the question that when given input stimuli, which neurons will and how to form dynamic synchronization.

5. Our auditory feature binding and its hierarchical computational model should be formed according to the cognitive neuroscience.

2 Analysis about Physiological Mechanism of Auditory Feature Binding

Human ears provide us a complex mechanism for transducing pressure variations in the air to neural impulses in auditory nerve fibers. The process of audition includes mechanics, electricity, chemistry, nerve impulse, nerve centre information processing and other steps. The collection of sound wave from the outer ear to inner ear's basilar membrane is a mechanical movement. The stirred hair cells will cause the changing in electric charges, which further causes the release of chemical media, and causes excited neurons variations and impulses, etc. The excitation will propagate to the central nervous system and causes a series of complicated information processes, and eventually result in auditory perception. It is worth the whistle that the cochlea performs a frequency analysis and the spire ganglion cells is the first stage of nerve mechanism that sends out impulse. The frequency scope of human audition is 20Hz—20000Hz. And different auditory nerves have optimal response to different frequencies.

The auditory system is complex with four relay stations(Cochlear nucleus, Superior olive, Inferior colliculus, Medial geniculate body) between periphery and cortex rather than one in the visual system(Lateral geniculate nucleus). In comparison to the auditory periphery, central parts of the auditory system are less understood. It is noteworthiness that number of neurons in the primary auditory cortex is comparable to that in the primary visual cortex despite the fact that the number of fibers in the auditory nerve is far fewer than that of the optic nerve (thirty thousands vs. hundred millions).

3   Cognitive Model of Auditory Feature Binding

Our cognitive model of auditory feature binding (AFB) is assumed as follows: [2]

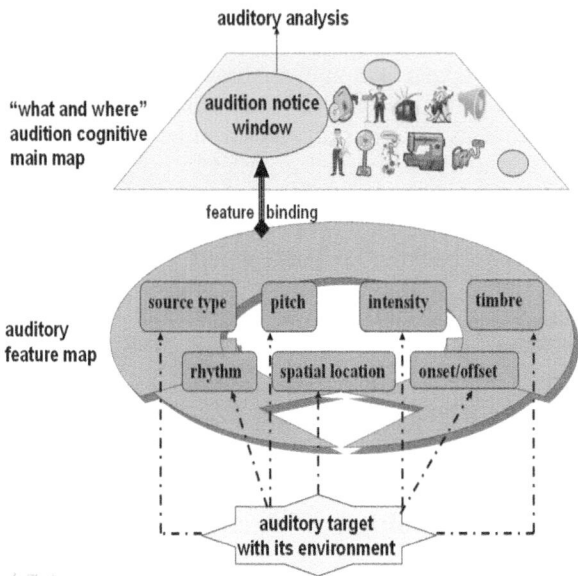

Fig. 1. Cognitive Model of Auditory Feature Binding

This model includes a "what and where" audition cognitive main map and a set of relatively independent feature map. The "what and where" main map is used to identify auditory targets. The feature map includes two kinds of information: one is used to label whether the feature is within the auditory region, the other one is about the specific spacial and temporal arrangement of some hidden information. The "audition notice window" is moving in "what and where" cognitive main map to select the relevant features from specific map. At the same time, it robustly excludes other auditory target features from the level of recognition or cognition. After binding the features, we can match them with the pre-saved templates, semantic database, emotional database to get the relevant recognition and cognition. So the corresponding action can also be fulfilled. Therefore, "what and where" uses the auditory featuring binding system to realize the perception and cognition about the auditory targets.

Based on the cognitive model of auditory feature binding in Fig.1, we can further realize the cognitive model of vision-audition cross-model coherence as follows:

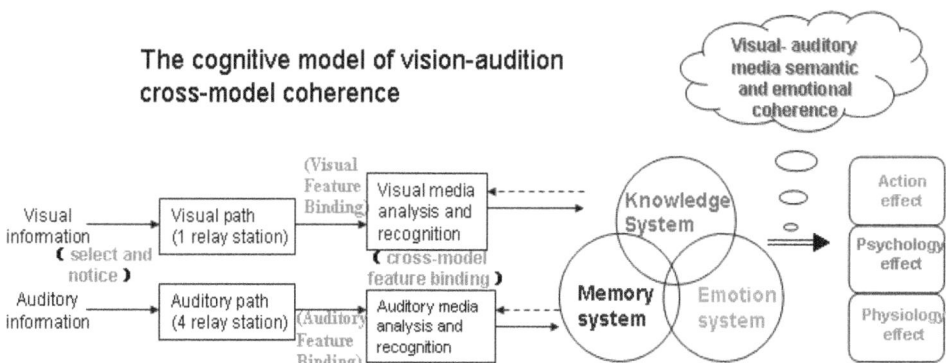

Fig. 2. cognitive model of vision-audition cross-model coherence

This model is funded by National Scientific Fundation Project ""Research on Synergic Learning Algorithm of vision-audition Cross-modal Coherence"" (#60873139).

4   Hierarchical Computational Model for AFB

Our model is a network model composed of interconnected neurons. The network can synchronize stimuli-evoked oscillations in different regions of the auditory cortex if the regions have similar or related local coding properties. Neurons in our model contain two types of inputs, namely "feature-access" inputs and "correlating" inputs, and they are coupled via multiplication as well.[3] In this model we also introduced noisy neural idea, Bayesian method and competition mechanism to be tackled. It is the fact that neural activity is characterized by a high degree of irregularity, which is caused by various noises in neural system. But On the other hand, the existence of noises makes the modeling of neurons more complicated and robust. In our model, firing of neurons is not controlled by a conventional threshold, but is described by a firing probability. That is to say different input will change the firing probability of a neuron. In our model, we adopt the noisy firing strategy. So, as a result, the outputs of neurons in our model are probabilities but not pulse.

In our auditory perceptual and cognitive research, we use a neuron to represent a corresponding perceptual object. Its "feature-access" pre-synaptic neurons usually denote its composing features or compartments and its "correlating" pre-synaptic neurons indicate other objects, which have more or less relations with this neuron. Thus, if X is the neuron we concern, fi is its "feature-access" presynaptic neuron, and wi is weight for synaptic connection, which indicates the importance of fi as a part in the whole entity X, we can accordingly get the following formula :

$$P(X) = \sum_i w_i P(f_i) \qquad (1)$$

based on the relationship of parts and whole. If all the correlating inputs are conditionally independent, furthermore, if we consider the influence from correlating inputs, we can get the next formula as follows based on Bayesian theorem.

$$P(X|r_1, r_2, \ldots) = P(X) \prod_j w'_j P(r_j) = \sum_i w_i P(f_i) \prod_j w^1_j P(r_j) \tag{2}$$

Here, rj is its correlating pre-synaptic neuron, and w'j = P(rj|X)/P(rj) is weight for synaptic connection, which represents the importance of rj to X. P(X) is the prior probability calculated from feature-accessing information. P(X|r1,r2,rl3,…) is the post probability after getting information from correlating inputs. P(rj) is the firing probability of rj). And wi and w'j are determined by the statistical correlation of the pre- and post-synaptic neurons. So it makes the model adaptive and has learning ability.

Sufficient biological evidence shows that there are numerous competition phenomena in the neural activities of brain. Accordingly, we import formula (3) about competitive mechanism into our model:

$$P_{compete}(X_i) = \frac{P_{pre-compete}(X_i)}{\sum_{j=1}^{n} P_{pre-compete}(X_j)} \tag{3}$$

(let X1, X2, …, Xn be n neurons that are competitive each other; P pre-compete(Xi) is the firing probability of Xi before competition; P compete(Xi) is the firing probability of Xi after competition). The outputs of neurons are determined by their own inputs, the outputs of their neighbors and the competition among correlated neurons.

Finally, we design the following hierarchical computational model for AFB:

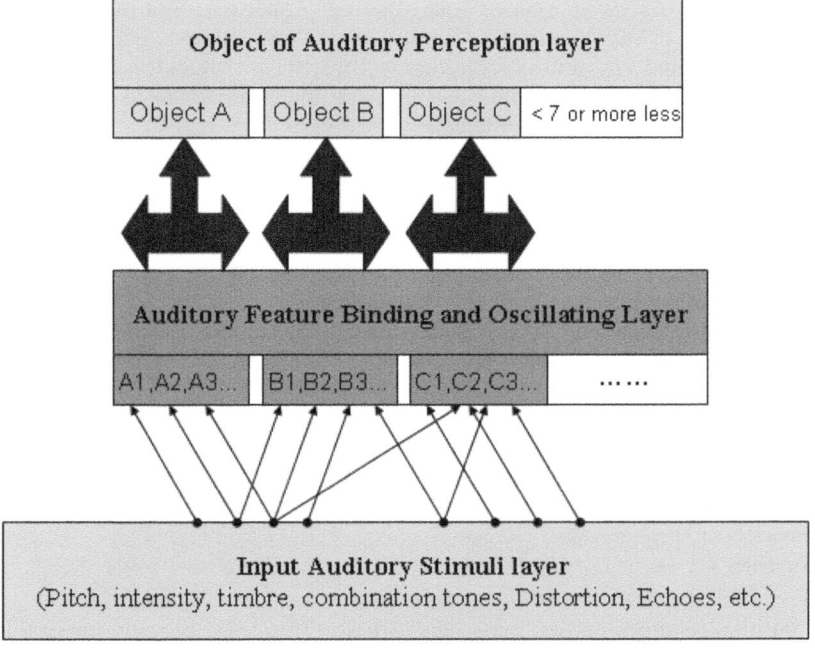

Fig. 3. Hierarchical computational model for AFB

Notes:

1. The entire model is a 3-layer network. The bottom layer is the acoustic input layer. Neurons in this layer correspond to pure auditory stimuli.

2. The middle layer is composed of the features of the different perceptual objects. In this layer, the "feature-access" and correlating" is processed.

3. Neurons except owned by the bottom layer will integrate their feature-access and correlating inputs based on Formula (1) and (2) above to update their firing probabilities at each time step. If a neuron has competitors, formula (3) will adjust its firing probability after each updating.

4. As time goes by, the firing probabilities of neurons will change continually. When this process converges, viz. all firing probabilities fix disregarding time changing, the winner neuron in the top layer indicates the auditory perceptual result.

5. We built 50 random Hierarchical Computational Models for AFB and performed simulations. During the 50 simulations, all the models converge fast. The average round of oscillation is 3.4. Mostly a simulation will converge after 3 or 4 recursions. We will describe and test the results through a group of experiments in the next paper.

6. From the simulation experiment results, we found it can accomplish the recognition and cognition task including some sound types: music from different musical instruments (two types each experiment), voices from different two speaker (including different age, gender, linguistic origin, mood, etc), two natural sounds (mainly including various animals).[4]

5   Conclusion

This thesis described the auditory feature binding and its hierarchical computational model. The linchpin is hierarchical computational model. It can accomplish feature binding by simulation. We have found that feature binding and perception gaining are performed simultaneously, and they facilitate each other. Auditory feature binding is fulfilled via convergent oscillation. Specially, the model has firm neurobiological support, for it is proposed based on the fact that coupling of inputs on a dendrite is a combination of addition and multiplication.

In the task of cognition, the auditory and visual mutual enhancement perception binding will later be deeply researched. Considering the memory, skills, problem solving, fortitude character, and other process in perceptual binding mechanism, we will further set up a generalized multi-model binding theory.

Acknowledgment. This paper was supported by the National Natural Science Foundation of China under Grant No.60873139, which title is the Research on Synergic Learning Algorithm of Audio-vision Cross-modal Coherence. It is also partially supported by the Provincial Natural Science Foundation of China under Grant No.2008011040. Acknowledges all persons supported this work, especially thanks to professor YU for taking time to review the details of the paper and giving her insightful comments.

References

1. Albright, T.D., Kandel, E.R., Posner, M.I.: Cognitive neuroscience. Curr. Opin. Neurobiol. 10(5), 612–624 (2000)
2. Zhuo, G., Yu, X.: Real-world Auditory Perception Based on Auditory Feature Binding. In: 2010 International Conference on Computational Aspects of Social Networks (2010)
3. Eckhorn, R., Reitboeck, H.J., Arndt, M., et al.: Feature linking via synchronization among distributed assemblies: Simulation of results from
4. Yu, X., Li, Z., Zhou, C., Zhuo, G., Liu, Z.: A Design Proposal of Game-Based Professional Training System for Highly Dangerous Professions. College of Computer and Software in Taiyuan University of Technology (2009)
5. http://www.cse.ohio-state.edu/pnl
6. http://www.casabook.org/

Hierarchical K-Means Clustering Algorithm Based on Silhouette and Entropy

Wuzhou Dong[1], JiaDong Ren[1], and Dongmei Zhang[2]

[1] College of Information Science and Engineering, Yanshan University,
Qinhuangdao, China
[2] Qinhuangdao Port CO., LTD Qinhuangdao, China
dongwz@hebeea.edu.cn, jdren@ysu.edu.cn, zhangdongdongmei@126.com

Abstract. Hierarchical K-means clustering is one of important clustering task in data mining. In order to address the problem that the time complexity of the existing HK algorithms is high and most of algorithms are sensitive to noise, a hierarchical K-means clustering algorithm based on silhouette and entropy(HKSE) is put forward. In HKSE, the optimal cluster number is obtained through calculating the improved silhouette of the dataset to be clustered, so that time complexity can be reduced from $O(n2)$ to $O(k \times n)$. Entropy is introduced in the hierarchical clustering phase as the similarity measurement avoiding distance calculation in order to reduce outlier effect on the cluster quality. In the post processing phase, the outlier cluster is identified by computing the weighted distance between clusters. Experiment results show that HKSE is efficient in reducing time complexity and sensitivity to noise.

Keywords: Hierarchical clustering, Silhouette, Entropy.

1 Introduction

Clustering is one of the analyzing method [1] in data mining and pattern recognition field. Up to now, researchers have proposed many clustering algorithms, among which the partition and hierarchical clustering methods [2] are most common.

K-means [3] is a representative classic partition algorithm. In this algorithm, K is obtained through minimizing objective function. K-means has higher efficiency compared with hierarchical method. However, the number of clusters K needs to be fixed iteratively. Common method trial-and-error depends on specific clustering algorithm. In addition, computation efficiency of trial-and-error is not high when determining the number of clusters. In order to address these problems, L.F. Chen proposed a method named COPS [4] based on hierarchical method to determine the optical number in large dataset clustering. In COPS, the optical number of clusters was obtained by constructing cluster quality curve. However, the parameter would affect the clustering results.

C.R. Lin pointed that K-Means had linear time complexity, but the clustering quality was not good. In order to improve the clustering efficiency, C.R. Lin presented a new algorithm CSM [5, 6], which combined K-Means with hierarchical

H. Deng et al. (Eds.): AICI 2011, Part I, LNAI 7002, pp. 339–347, 2011.

clustering method. Although CSM had better efficiency, K had to be fixed in advance. Sid LAMROUS introduced silhouette [7] as a measurement into the proposed divided hierarchical clustering algorithm, which was based on non-binary tree. Each node of the tree had m(m∈ [2,5]) sub-clusters. The node was divided by using K-means algorithm. For each node, the number of sub-cluster was determined through using silhouette. J.F. Lu proposed a K-means initialization method, which reduced and sampled dataset with weighted hierarchy structure. This method could find cluster centroid better, and it also extended clustering into high dimensional data space. However, the number of clusters K should be selected before clustering [8]. In order to address the problem that the cluster centroid and the number of clusters K should be selected before clustering, Chen proposed HK (Hierarchical K-means) algorithm [9]. In HK, the number of initial clusters and the centroid of cluster were firstly fixed by using agglomerative hierarchical clustering algorithm. Then the clustering was improved with K-means. HK had high time complexity in hierarchical clustering phase. In order to improve algorithm efficiency, W.C. Li proposed a method, in which cluster number was determined by using silhouette. This proposed method was superior compared with HK, but its time cost reached to $O(n2)$. In addition, the proposed method was sensitive to noise [10].

In this paper, we propose HKSE, a new method for Hierarchical K-means Clustering algorithm based on silhouette and entropy. In HKSE, IS (Improved Silhouette), WDMC (Weighted Distance Matrix between Clusters) are defined. Optimal number of clusters is determined through computing the average Improved Silhouette of the dataset, so time complexity can be reduced. Entropy is introduced to HKSE as a similarity measurement to reduce sensitivity to noise. Clusters are weighted according to the size of clusters to improve the clustering quality.

This paper is organized as follows: In section II, we give the basic concepts and definitions. In section III, we present our hierarchical clustering algorithm called HKSE. Section IV shows the experimental results of the clustering algorithm. Finally we conclude the paper in section V.

2   Basic Concepts and Definitions

Definition 1. IS (Improved Silhouette).

Let S be a dataset consisting of clusters C1, C2...Ct. The distance between each object oi(oi∈ Cj, j∈ [1,t]) and the centroid of its own cluster is denoted as ai. bi is the minimum distance between oi and each centroid of the other t-1 clusters. The IS(oi) is defined as formula(1).

$$IS(o_i) = \frac{b_i - a_i}{\max(a_i, b_i)} \tag{1}$$

In formula(1), the meanings of ai and bi have changed compared with the traditional silhouette computation. Both ai and bi denote the distance to the cluster centroid.

The average IS of dataset corresponding to different partition is calculated. The maximal IS of the dataset corresponds to the optimal partition of the dataset.

We take point A in Fig. 1 as an example to show the IS computation of a data point.

(1)   Obtain   the   centroids   of   clusters   C1,   C2,   C3   respectively:
Centroid1= $\left(\dfrac{1+1+1+2+2}{5},\dfrac{0+1+1+2+2}{5}\right)$ = (1.4, 1.2), Centroid2=(4.4, 4.8),
Centroid3=(6.5, 0.8333);

(2)   Calculate aA, the distance between A and the centroid of its own cluster:
$a_A=\sqrt{(1-1.4)^2+(0-1.2)^2}$ =1.2649. The distances between A and each centroid of C2 and C3 can be obtained similarly, and they are 5.8822 and 5.5628 respectively. Since bA denotes the minimum distance according to the definition of IS, thus let bA=5.8822.

(3)   The IS of A can be obtained based on formula

(4)   IS(A)=(bA-aA)/max(aA, bA)=0.7850.

The IS values of other points can be calculated similarly.

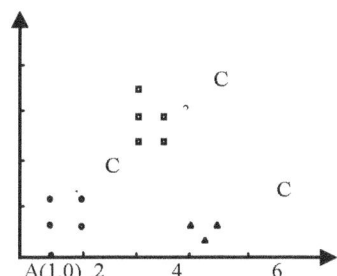

Fig. 1. Silhouette calculation process

Definition 2. WDMC(Weighted Distance Matrix between Clusters)

Let C1,C2,...,Ck be clusters of data set S. |Ci| is the number of data points in Ci. wi is assigned according to the data points number of Ci. wi is defined as formula(2).

$$wi=\frac{|C_i|}{|C_1|+|C_2|+...+|C_k|} \quad (i=1,2,...,k) \tag{2}$$

Weighted distance between Ci and Cj is defined as formula(3).

$$wdij=\frac{1}{w_i}\sum_{j=1}^{k}\left|centroid_i-centroid_j\right| \tag{3}$$

Where wi=min(wi, wj), and $\left|centroid_i-centroid_j\right|$ is Euclidean distance between centroids of Ci and Cj.

For Ci(i=1,2,...,k), the weighted Euclidean distance between Ci and other k-1 cluster centroids is calculated. WDMC Mc can be obtained as formula(4).

$$Mc= \begin{bmatrix} wd_{11} & wd_{12} & ... & wd_{1n} \\ wd_{21} & wd_{22} & ... & wd_{2n} \\ ... & ... & ... & ... \\ wd_{n1} & ... & ... & wd_{nn} \end{bmatrix}_{(wdij \neq wdji)} \tag{4}$$

WDMC reflects different importance of cluster through assigning different weight according to cluster size. For Ci, suppose its weight is small and distance between Ci and most clusters is large, the probability that Ci is outlier cluster become high. Thus, outlier cluster can be recognized through comparing weighted distance between clusters and distance threshold. wdij is not equal to wdji, for different cluster size has different effect to weighted distance.

3   Hierarchical K-Means Clustering Algorithm Based on Silhouette and Entropy

3.1   Find-K Algorithm

In HKSE, we plot the curve about the average IS of dataset to be clustered and the number of partitions. The optimal number of clusters is determined by the maximum of the curve, since the average IS of a dataset not only reflects the density of clusters, but also the dissimilarity between clusters.

Algorithm Find-K
Input: S
Output: K
  begin
  1: partition S into t clusters: C1, C2...Ct, according to the geometry distribution of S
  2: repeat
  3: {
  4:   for (i=1; i<=t; i++)
  5:     {for (each object x in Ci)
  6:       {calculate ISi(x), the improved silhouette of x;
  7:       calculate $\overline{IS_i}$, the average Improved Silhouette of S, and $\overline{IS_i} = \frac{1}{n}\sum_{i=1}^{t}\sum_{x \in c_i} IS_i(x)$;
  8:       plot the curve about t and $\overline{IS_i}$ in the 2-dimensional coordinate system;
  9:       }
  10:     t:=t+1;
  11:     }
  12: } until (the curve reaches the maximum)
  13: K: =t;
  end

In algorithm Find-K, dataset S is firstly partitioned into t clusters: C1, C2...Ct, according to the geometry distribution of S. IS is introduced into the algorithm

Find-K. In Find-K, The closer the improved silhouette of a cluster to 1, the more likely the objects belong to the same cluster. The curve, which is about cluster number t and the average IS, is plotted. The number of clusters corresponding to the maximum of the curve is the optimal number of clusters.

3.2   Outlier-C Algorithm

Cluster effect is positive to the number of data points that the cluster contains. In other words, the more data points the cluster contains, the bigger weight of the cluster will be. Outlier clusters always contain a small quantity of data points. In this paper, $K+\mu$ clusters are weighted. Outlier cluster can be recognized by comparing weighted distance between clusters with weighted distance threshold. Thus, clustering sensitivity to the outliers can be reduced.

Algorithm Outlier-C
Input: $K+\mu$ clusters
Output: K clusters

   begin
   1: While number of clusters is not equal to k do
   2: Calculate weighted Eucliden distance between centroids of $K+\mu$ clusters respectively
   3: Construct Mc for $k+\mu$ clusters /*Mc is weighted distance matrix for $k+\mu$ cluster */
   4: Array the data of Mc in ascending sequence;
   5: Put the arrayed data in a sequence list Q;
   6: Take f as distance threshold between $k+\mu$ clusters.

$$f = \frac{\sum\limits_{i=1}^{k+\mu}\sum\limits_{j=1}^{k+\mu} wd(C_i, C_j)}{(k+\mu)^2}$$

   7: Find cluster Ci that has farthest distance to f.
   8: Take Ci as critical cluster.
   9: Dispose the clusters behind Ci in Q.
   10: EndWhile
   11: Return(k clusters)
   end

θ, hierarchical clustering extent parameter, is introduced to Algorithm Outlier-C in order to dispose outlier clusters. Thus, the sensitivity to noise can be reduced. The value of μ is determined by θ.

In algorithm Outlier-C, the average weighted distance between clusters is taken as similarity degree threshold. Thus, these clusters, which are far more than threshold and have fewer data points compared with most of clusters, can be considered as outlier clusters. Each element value in Mc is arrayed. The problem of searching and comparing in matrix is converted into binary searching problem. The time efficiency of algorithm is improved.

3.3   HKSE Algorithm

Traditional clustering algorithms always adopt distance as similarity measurement. However, clustering quality of traditional clustering algorithm is not good, for distance is sensitive to outlier. Entropy, one of a measurement, can reflect the degree that the cluster is composed by data points of same category. The closer the entropy of a cluster is to 0, the bigger the purity of cluster belonging to same cluster will be. In HKSE, entropy is considered as similarity measurement. Agglomerative hierarchical clustering is instructed by the entropy change after combined with new data point. The parameters of HKSE are as follows: S is the dataset to be clustered; n is the number of data object; μ is a parameter; K is the number of clusters.

Algorithm HKSE
Input: S, n, μ
Output: K
    begin
    1: Call Find-K
    2: label each data object in S as a single cluster
    3: repeat
    4: for each cluster C, Put C in other clusters
    5: Calculate the incremental entropy of each cluster supposing the data object is joined
    6: Assign the data object to the cluster whose incremental entropy is least
    7: re-label the clusters obtained from step 6
    6: n=n-1
    7: until n=K+μ
    8: Call Outlier-C
    end

In HKSE, the cluster combination is directed by the entropy calculation. Supposed O is a data point. Let Δi and Δj denote entropy increment after O is put in Ci and Cj respectively. If $\Delta i < \Delta j$, O is assigned to Ci, otherwise to Cj. Compared with algorithm HK, HKSE takes entropy as similarity measurement instead of distance. Our proposed algorithm considers data point density of cluster in order to reduce the sensitivity to noise.

4   Experimental Results

Our experiments are conducted on a computer with 2.4Ghz Intel CPU and 512M main memory. The operating system of the computer is Microsoft Windows XP.

    HKSE is compared with HK to evaluate the performance of HKSE. All the algorithms are implemented in Visual C++.

    We perform our experiments on UCI data sets iris, breast-cancer, credit-g and letter. The efficiency and performance of HKSE and NHK have been compared in our experiment. Parameter θ denotes the fulfillment extent of hierarchical clustering. The value of θ in traditional HK algorithm is in the range of [0.4,0.6] according to literature[11]. In this paper, our experiments are conducted under the premise that the value of θ is 0.5. Parameters of four data sets are shown in Table 1.

Table 1. Parameters of the testing sequence data sets

1. Dataset	1. name	1. Size	1. clusters
1. D1	2. Iris	2. 150	2. 3
1. D2	3. breast-cancer	3. 277	3. 2
1. D3	4. credit-g	4. 900	4. 2
1. D4	5. letter	5. 20000	5. 26

4.1 The Efficiency Analysis

We perform our experiments on UCI data sets D1, D2, D3 and D4. NHK and HKSE are carried out on the data sets respectively in order to compare algorithm performance. Running time result is shown in figure 2.

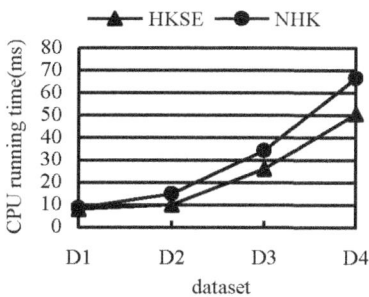

Fig. 2. HKSE and NHK comparison in terms of running time

In NHK, distance between each data point needs to be calculated in order to obtain the optimal cluster number. Thus, the time complexity of HK reaches to $O(n2)$. In HKSE, silhouette is introduced to simplify the calculation of cluster number. We only need to calculate distance between each cluster centroid. The CPU running time is reduced largely. For k clusters, time complexity can be reduced to $O(k \times n)$. The time performance superiority is especially obvious when the data set scale is large.

4.2 The Accuracy Analysis

2%、4%、6%、8% and 10% noise are inserted into D3 respectively. After algorithms NHK and HKSE are ran with D3, the experiment results are shown in figure 3. Clustering quality is measurement of clustering algorithm. In the agglomerative hierarchical clustering phase of HKSE, entropy is adopted as similarity measurement instead of distance. Data object is combined according to entropy increment. Thus, distance calculation is avoided. Sensitivity to noise can be reduced. Thus, clustering result is improved.

From figure 3, we can draw the conclusion that both NHK and HKSE can obtain the correct clustering result when the cluster distribution is clear and noise is few in data set to be clustered. The misclassification percentages of both algorithms are low,. However, when noises in the data set to be clustered become more, clustering with HKSE can obtain better result, for entropy is used to direct the combination of clusters without calculation of distance. Thus, the misclassification rate of HKSE is lower than that of NHK.

From 1% to 5% outlier data points are added in data set D1 respectively. HKSE and NHK are run in D1 respectively. The clustering result is shown in figure 4.

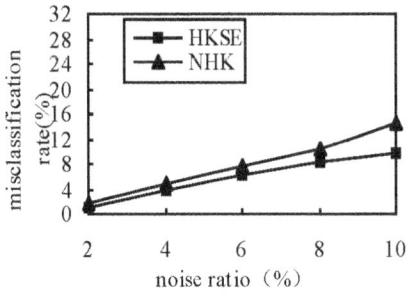
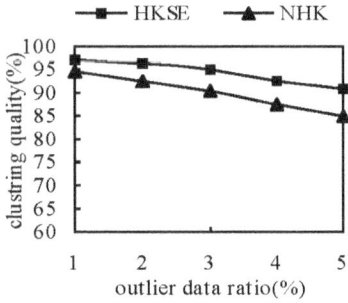

Fig. 3. Misclassification rate graph with the varing noise ratio

Fig. 4. The cluster quality graph with the varing outlier ratio

In post process of HKSE, clusters are weighted according to cluster size. Outlier cluster is recognized by comparing weighed distance between clusters and distance threshold. Thus, sensitivity to outlier data point of clustering is reduced. From figure 4, conclusion can be draw that HKSE is better than NHK in the ability of dealing with outlier data points.

5   Conclusions

Existing HK clustering algorithm has problem that time complexity is high and is sensitive to noise. In order to address the problem, HKSE is proposed in this paper. In HKSE, the IS curve is draw incrementally. The optimal cluster number is determined by maximum in IS curve. The time complexity can be reduced from $O(n2)$ to $O(k \times n)$. In the hierarchical clustering process, entropy is introduced as the similarity measurement in order to avoid distance calculation. Thus, the sensitivity to noise is reduced. In the post phase of HKSE, clusters are weighted according to cluster size. Experiments result shows that HKSE is efficient in reducing time complexity and sensitivity to noise.

Acknowledgments. This work is supported by the Natural Science Foundation of Hebei Province P. R. China under Grant No.F2010001298. The authors also gratefully acknowledge the valuable comments and suggestions of the reviewers, which have improved the presentation.

References

1. Dong, F.Y., Liu, J.j., Liu, B.: Study on improved grey integrated clustering method and its application. In: IEEE International Conference on Grey Systems and Intelligent Services, pp. 702–707 (2009)
2. Liu, L., Huang, L.H., Lai, M.Y.: Projective ART with buffers for the high dimensional space clustering and an application to discover stock. Associations Neurocomputing 72, 1283–1295 (2009)
3. Li, M.J., Ng, M.K., Cheung, Y.M.: Agglomerative fuzzy K-Means clustering algorithm with selection of number of clusters. IEEE Transactions on Knowledge and Data Engineering 20, 1519–1534 (2008)
4. Chen, L.F., Jiang, Q.S., Wang, S.R.: A Hierarchical Method for Determining the Number of Clusters. Journal of Software 19, 62–72 (2008)
5. Lin, C.R., Chen, M.S.: A Robust and Efficient Clustering Algorithm based on Cohesion Self-Merging. In: Inf. Conf. 8th ACM SIGKDD on Knowledge Discovery and Data Mining, pp. 582–587 (2002)
6. Lin, C.R., Chen, M.S.: Combining Partitional and Hierarchical Algorithms for Robust and Efficient Data Clustering with Cohesion Self-Merging. IEEE Transaction On Knowledge and Data Engineering 17, 145–159 (2005)
7. Lamrous, S., Taileb, M.: Divisive Hierarchical K-Means. In: International Conference on Computional Intelligence for Modeling Control and Automation, and International Conference on Intelligent Agent, Web Technologies and Internet Commerce, pp. 18–23 (2006)
8. Lu, J.F., Tang, J.B., Tang, Z.M.: Hierarchical initialization approach for K-Means clustering. Pattern Recognition Letters, 787–795 (2008)
9. Chen, T.S., Tsai, T.H., Chen, Y.T.: A Combined K-means and Hierarchical Clustering Method for Improving the Clustering Efficiency of Microarray. In: Proceeding of 2005 International Symposition on Intelligence Signal Processing and Communication System, pp. 405–408 (2005)
10. Li, W.C., Zhou, Y., Xia, S.X.: A Novel Clustering Algorithm Based on Hierarchical and K-means Clustering. In: Proceedings of the 26th Chinese Control Conference, pp. 605–609 (2007)
11. Chen, B., Tai, P.C., Harrison, R.: Novel Hybrid Hierarchical-K-means Clustering Method (H-K-means) for Microarray Analysis. In: Proceedings of the 2005 IEEE Computational Systems Bioinformatics Conference, pp. 105–108 (2005)

Simultaneous Multicomponent Spectrophotometric Kinetic Determination by a Hybrid Intelligent Computing Method

Ling Gao and Shouxin Ren

Department of Chemistry, Inner Mongolia University, Huhhot, Inner Mongolia, China
lingyuxi@hotmail.com, cersx@mail.imu.edu.cn

Abstract. The improved PLS regression algorithm was developed by adding a preprocessor based on DOSC and WPT for enhancing the ability in the extraction of characteristic information and the quality of regression. The kinetic intelligent computing approach that combines kinetic-catalytic method with DOSC-WPT-PLS does not require a detailed kinetic model of the chemical system to obtain the order of reaction and rate constants. No reference to this method has been found. A program (PDOSCWPTPLS) was designed to perform the simultaneous spectrophotometric kinetic determination of Mn (II), Ag (I) and Fe (III). The relative standard errors of prediction (RSEP) obtained for all components using DOSC-WPT-PLS, WPTPLS and PLS were compared for evaluating their predictive capability. Experimental results demonstrated that the DOSC-WPT-PLS method had the best performance among the three methods and the results delivered by DOSC-WPT-PLS were significantly better.

Keywords: Intelligent computing method, Direct orthogonal signal correction; Wavelet packet transforms; Partial least squares, Kinetic simultaneous determination of Mn (II), Ag (I) and Fe (III).

1   Introduction

Spectral methods based on thermodynamic equilibrium would fail on components with quite similar spectra and overlapping spectra. Thus, the methods based on differences among the kinetic behaviors of different components can be used as an effective alternative. The so-called kinetic-catalytic methods are much more sensitive, which are based on the catalytic role of transition metal ions such as Mn (II), Ag (I) and Fe (III) on the redox indicator reaction between various organic compounds such as rhodamine B and some inorganic oxidants in presence of certain ligand as an activator. These kinetic-catalytic methods have high sensitivity and sufficient accuracy without expensive and special equipments. A method for the simultaneous determination of three kinds of metal ions is applied here, based on the kinetic difference of the metal ions. In the past few years, kinetic intelligent computing methods have received growing attention. Analytical chemists have realized the potential of kinetic intelligent computing methods and regarded them as highly effective tools. Such kinetic intelligent computing methods do not require a detailed kinetic model of the chemical system to obtain the order of reaction and rate constants.

H. Deng et al. (Eds.): AICI 2011, Part I, LNAI 7002, pp. 348–355, 2011.

Nowadays, due to the easy and fast acquisition of data, researchers seek to maximize the information obtained from raw data by using intelligent computing techniques [1]. In order to enhance the predictive ability of multivariate calibration models, raw data are often pre-processed for the elimination of irrelevant information prior to calibration. In order to avoid removing relevant information for prediction, Wold and coworkers developed a novel pre-processing technique for raw data called orthogonal signal correction (OSC) [2]. The goal of this algorithm is to remove information in the response matrix D, which is mathematically orthogonal and unrelated to concentration matrix C. The information to be taken out is the so-called structured noise, which can come from different sources such as baseline, instrument variation and measurement conditions, interfering physical and chemical process and other interferences. Westerhuis and coworkers introduced an appealing OSC method named direct orthogonal signal correction (DOSC) [3]. DOSC is a direct method that allows its components to be obtained by using only the simple least squares without the work of iteration procedure. Hence, like OSC, DOSC is also applied to remove structured noise that is extraneous to the concentration variables. The noise and irrelevant information and quality of regression model may be enhanced by combining DOSC with wavelet transform (WT) and wavelet packet transform (WPT). The DOSCWPT pre-process method is a hybrid technique that combines the best properties of the two techniques and could dramatically increase the problem-solving capacity. WT represents relatively recent mathematical developments, and can offer a successful time-frequency signal for enhanced information localization [4, 5]. WT and WPT [6-9] have the ability to provide information in the time and frequency domain thus can be used for the purpose of converting data from its original domain into wavelet domain, in which the representation of a signal is sparse and the signal denoising is easier to be carried out. These characteristics of WT and WPT make it possible to perform data compression, relevant information extraction and denoising. The aim of this work is to propose a method named direct orthogonal signal correction and wavelet packet transform with partial least squares (DOSC-WPT-PLS), which is based on partial least squares regression combined with DOSC and WPT as pre-processed tools, for simultaneous multicomponent kinetic determination. This method combines the concepts of DOSC and WPT with PLS regression for enhancing the ability in extraction of characteristic information and the quality of regression. The approach of DOSC combined with WPT and PLS seems to be the first application to the simultaneous kinetic determination of Mn (II), Ag (I) and Fe (III). The three kinds of metal elements are common elements and appear in a variety of environmental, industrial and geological samples, making the simultaneous determination of the three kinds of metals a very important significance.

2   Theory

2.1   Direct Orthogonal Signal Correction

The DOSC algorithm is based on least squares steps to pick up components that are orthogonal to matrix C and account for the largest variation of D. The first step of DOSC is to decompose C into two orthogonal parts. The first part is the projection of C onto D, called $\hat{C}$. The second part is the residual part F that is orthogonal to D.

$$C = P_D C + A_D C = \hat{C} + F \qquad (1)$$

where $P_D = D(D^T D)^{-1} D^T = DD^+$, $A_D = I - P_D = I - DD^+$, I is the identity matrix and D^+ is the Moore-Penrose inverse of D. The second step decomposes D into two parts:

$$D = \hat{D} + E = P_{\hat{c}} D + A_{\hat{c}} D \qquad (2)$$

One part $\hat{D}$ has the same range as $\hat{C}$ and another part E is orthogonal to D. Therefore, the columns of $A_{\hat{c}} D$ span a subspace of D that is orthogonal to both $\hat{C}$ and $C = \hat{C} + F$, since F is also orthogonal to D. For kinetic data, since the number of time scale (J) is usually much greater than the number of samples (I), it can be found that $C = \hat{C}$, so D can be directly orthogonalized by making the projection onto C rather than onto $\hat{C}$:

$$D = \hat{D} + E = P_c D + A_{\hat{c}} D \qquad (3)$$

Having found this orthogonal subspace $A_{\hat{c}} D$, principal component analysis (PCA) is now applied to find the principal component T corresponding to the largest singular value. If more DOSC components are necessary, more principal components can be obtained in this step. The T is finally expressed as a linear combination of D:

$$T = DW \qquad (4)$$

where W is the weight matrix for the determination of DOSC components and equals to $D^+ T$, where D^+ is the Moore-Penrose generalized inverse of the original matrix D. The DOSC-corrected absorbance-time curves of the calibration data can now be written as:

$$D_{dosc} = D - T P^T \qquad (5)$$

where TP^T is the orthogonal part removed from the original absorbance-time curves. P is the loading matrix and can be expressed as:

$$P = D^T T (T^T T)^{-1} \qquad (6)$$

Once the weight W and the loading P have been computed for absorbance-time curves in the test set D_u, the correction can be performed as follow:

$$D_{u\,dosc} = D_u - D_u W P^T. \qquad (7)$$

2.2   WPT Denoising

A wavelet packet $W_{j\,n\,k}$ is generated from the base function:

$$W_{j\,n\,k}(x) = 2^{-j/2} W_n (2^{-j} x - k) \qquad (8)$$

where indices j, n, k are the scale, the oscillation and the localization parameter respectively, $j, k \in Z$, $n = 0, 1, 2, \cdots 2^j - 1$, where Z means the set of integers. In wavelet packet analysis, a signal $f(x)$ represents the sum of orthogonal wavelet packet function $W_{jnk}(x)$ at different scales, oscillations and localizations:

$$f(x) = \sum_j \sum_n \sum_k C_{jnk} W_{jnk}(x) \tag{9}$$

where C_{jnk} are the wavelet packet coefficients. The coefficients C_{jnk} can be obtained from:

$$C_{jnk} = \int_{-\infty}^{\infty} f(x) W_{jnk}(x) dx \tag{10}$$

The discrete wavelet transform (DWT) can be implemented by means of Mallat's pyramid algorithm [9]. DWT can be characterized as a recursive application of the high-pass and low-pass filters that form a quadrature mirror filter (QMF) pair. The theoretical background about DWT has been described in details [1]. In WPT, the QMF is not only applied to the approximations but also to the details. The recursion is simply to filter and downsample all outputs of the previous level. An algorithm of fast wavelet packet transform (FWPT) is expressed as:

$$W_{j+1\,2n} = HW_{jn} \tag{11}$$

$$W_{j+1\,2n+1} = GW_{jn} \tag{12}$$

where $W_{0,0}$ indicates the measured signal f, $H = \{h_l\}_{l \in Z}$ and $G = \{g_l\}_{l \in Z}$ are the low-pass and high-pass matrix filters. The first and second indices of W indicate the level of decomposition and its position at that level. The reconstruction can be implemented by:

$$W_{jn} = H^* W_{j+1\,2n} + G^* W_{j+1\,2n+1} \tag{13}$$

where H^* and G^* represent the conjugate matrix of H and G.
Decomposition and reconstruction are easily implemented using this algorithm.

The wavelet packet denoising procedures include four steps: (1) WPT; (2) the estimation of the best basis; (3) the thresholding of wavelet packet coefficients; (4) reconstruction. The best basis was selected according to entropy-based criterion proposed by Coifman and Wickerhauser [6]. Shannon entropy was applied in this case. The thresholding operation was implemented by the SURE method proposed by Donoho [10] based on Stein's unbiased risk estimation.

2.3   DOSC-WPT-PLS

The DOSC-WPT-PLS algorithm can be summarized as follows:
(1). The whole set of absorbance-time curves obtained from standard mixtures is used to build the experimental data matrix D. Before starting the DOSC-WPT-PLS calculation, mean centering and data standardization are performed.

(2). The DOSC method is one of most promising signal correction tools. With DOSC, the D matrix is corrected by subtracting the structured noise that is orthogonal to the concentration matrix C. The structured noise belongs to system variation unrelated to predictive components.

(3). The DOSC-corrected data matrix is transformed to WP domain by the FWPT algorithm. Different wavelet packet functions and decomposition levels are selected by trial and error. The best basis can be defined as the basis giving the minimum entropy or maximum information of the signal energy distribution. Signal reconstructions can be converted back into original domain using only selected WP coefficients by the inverse FWPT algorithm.

(4). The DOSC-WPT corrected data from matrix D and D_u are obtained for further PLS operation.

Three programs (PPLS, PWPTPLS and PDOSCWPTPLS) were designed to perform the simultaneous kinetic multicomponent determination.

3   Experiment

A Shimadzu UV-240 spectrophotometer with an optional program unit named optional model OPI-2 and TU-double beam of light UV-Vis spectrophotometer were used for all experiments. A series of mixed standard solutions containing various ratios of Mn (II), Ag (I), and Fe (III) ions was prepared by adding 2.00 mL 100.00 μg mL^{-1} solution of rhodamine B, 3.00 mL 1.00 mol L^{-1} sodium formate and formic acid buffer solution (pH = 3.10), 6.00 mL 2.00 ×10^{-3} g L^{-1} solution of 1,10-phenanthroline, 5.00 mL 8.00 ×10^{-4} mol L^{-1} solution of KIO$_4$ to 25 mL standard flasks, and diluted to volume with distilled water. A blank solution was prepared by distilled water. Kinetic data were recorded by TU-double beam of light UV-Vis spectrophotometer. Four parameters were selected: Lag time (5s), data sampling interval (0.1s), scan time (40s) and the record wavelength (556 nm). Absorbance was measured at a 0.1 second time interval for different standard mixtures. All the operations were performed at room temperature (19-20°C). An absorption matrix for calibration, D, was built up from these data. A kinetic absorption matrix for prediction, D_u, was also built up using the same procedures.

4   Results and Discussion

4.1   Wavelet Packet Transform Based Denoising

Here, we selected mean value of matrix D as original signal f. WPT of the signal f was carried out using the FWPT algorithm. Each level consists of 2^j blocks. Thus, level 0 consists of a single block (2^0); level 1 consists of two blocks (2^1); level 2 four blocks (2^2). Blocks for subsequent levels were derived in a similar manner. Some of the WP coefficients obtained by FWPT are shown in Fig. 1. Each coefficient is identified by a couple of indices (j, n), where j is the level of decomposition and n is the position of the block at that level. It is obvious that the w $(j, 0)$ only has a positive part and is similar to the approximation parts of wavelet transform. The others are composed of both positive and negative parts.

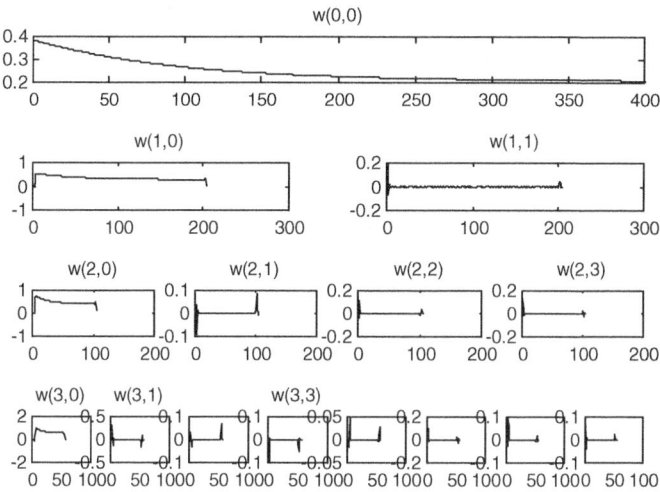

Fig. 1. Some of WP coefficients obtained by wavelet packet transform

Each block of the coefficients describes the components of signal f related to a certain frequency band. The features of signal f can be extracted from different WP blocks of coefficients. The information in WP is redundant. WPT allows the original signal f to be represented by various combinations of low and high frequency components, one of these combinations is w (3, 0) + w (3, 1) + w (2, 1) + w (1, 1). Thus, WP decomposition gives a lot of bases from which one can look for the best representation of original signal f. The best basis is preferably selected from full binary tree to ensure that no redundant information is included. The best basis only covers the complete horizontal block and did not include the overlapping vertical block. Thus, the best basis can be composed from a single decomposition level or a combination of levels to achieve the optimum time-frequency representation of original signals. After finding the best basis, a threshold was applied to WP coefficients. Only the WP coefficients of which absolute values were higher than a predefined threshold value were retained. In the absorbance-time profiles measurements, the analytical signals usually center in low frequency part, whereas the noise in high frequency part. In the WP domain, the denoising was implemented by the best basis selection and thresholding operation. Finally, by utilizing inverse FWPT, denoised WP coefficients were converted into the original domain. This time-frequency resolution gives WP the flexibility to represent different types of signals. The aim of WP denoising is to extract desired information from a complex instrument output.

4.2   DOSC-WPT-PLS

The success of obtaining a reliable result by the DOSC-WPT-PLS method depends strongly on the judicious choice of relative parameters. Five parameters were optimized in the DOSC-WPT-PLS method: wavelet function, decomposition level (L), the number of DOSC factors, tolerance factor and the number of PLS factors. Through investigations, Db 4, L = 4, the number of DOSC components = 3, tolerance factor = 0.001 and number of PLS factors = 3 were selected as optimal parameters in this case.

A training set of 16 samples formed by the mixture of Mn (II), Ag (I) and Fe (III) was designed according to four-level orthogonal array design with the L_{16} (4^5) matrix. The absorbance–time curves measured between 0 s and 40 s at 0.1 s intervals after Lag time 5 s were extracted from the training set as matrix D. The experimental data obtained from the training set were arranged in matrix D, where each row corresponds to the absorbance of different mixture at a given time and each column represents the kinetic curve obtained at a given mixture. A set of 9 synthetic unknown samples was measured in the same way as the training set, and then test matrix D_u was built.

With DOSC-WPT-PLS, one can treat each absorbance–time curves for a given mixture. Therefore, using the same method, each row vector of matrix D and D_u was corrected by DOSC to remove structured noise, denoised by WPT with best basis selection and thresholding operation, and then calibrated by applying the PLS model. Using program PDOSCWPTPLS, the concentrations of Mn (II), Ag (I) and Fe (III) for a test set was calculated. Actual concentrations and recoveries of Mn (II), Ag (I) and Fe (III) are calculated. The experimental results showed that the RSEP for all components were 7.16%.

4.3   A Comparison of DOSC-WPT-PLS, WPT-PLS and PLS Methods

In order to evaluate the DOSC-WPT-PLS method, three methods (DOSC-WPT-PLS, WPT-PLS and PLS) were tested in the study with a set of synthetic unknown samples. Actual concentrations and recoveries of each component with the DOSC-WPT-PLS, WPT-PLS and PLS methods are calculated. The SEP and RSEP for the three methods are given in Table 1. The RSEP for all components with DOSC-WPT-PLS, WPT-PLS and PLS were 7.16%, 11.7% and 12.7%, respectively. These results indicate that DOSC-WPT-PLS performs better than WPT-PLS and PLS. From Table 1.

Table 1. SEP and RSEP values for Mn (II), Ag (I) and Fe (III) system by the three methods

Method	SEP (μg mL^{-1})				RSEP (%)			
	Mn (II)	Ag (I)	Fe (III)	Total elements	Mn (II)	Ag (I)	Fe (III)	Total elements
DOSC-WPT-PLS	0.006	0.021	0.045	0.029	3.43	4.30	9.63	7.16
WPT-PLS	0.023	0.067	0.041	0.047	12.3	13.9	8.72	11.7
PLS	0.023	0.071	0.049	0.051	12.3	14.6	10.4	12.7

It can be seen that DOSC-WPT-PLS is successful at the simultaneous kinetic determination of Mn (II), Ag (I) and Fe (III) and is expected to be applied to other similar research fields.

5   Conclusion

A method named DOSC-WPT-PLS was developed and employed to perform the automatic calculations for the simultaneous kinetic determination of Mn (II), Ag (I) and Fe (III). The combination of DOSC and WPT as a pre-processing tool prior to calibration can efficiently remove both the systematic structured variation that is independent of concentration and the random variation in raw data. The DOSC-WPT-PLS method has been shown to be a successful approach to the simultaneous kinetic determination of Mn(II), Ag (I) and Fe (III) and gives improved performance of determination comparing with PLS and WPT-PLS.

Acknowledgment. The authors would like to thank National Natural Science Foundation of China (21067006 and 60762003) for the financial support of this project.

References

[1] Dieterle, F., Busche, S., Gauglitz, G.: Difference approaches to multivariate calibration of nonlinear sensor data. Anal. Bioanal. Chem. 380, 383–396 (2004)

[2] Wold, S., Antti, H., Lindgren, F., Ohman, J.: Orthogonal signal correction of near-infrared spectra. Chemometr. Intell. Lab. Syst. 44, 175–185 (1998)

[3] Westerhuis, J.A., de Jong, S., Smilde, A.G.: Direct orthogonal signal correction. Chemometr. Intell. Lab. Syst. 56, 13–25 (2001)

[4] Mallat, S., Hwang, W.L.: Singularity detection and processing with wavelets. IEEE Trans. Inform. Theory 38(2), 617–643 (1992)

[5] Daubechies, I.: Orthogonal bases of compactly supported wavelets. Commun. Pure Appl. Math. 41, 909–996 (1988)

[6] Coifman, R.R., Wickerhauser, M.V.: Entropy-based algorithms for best basis selection. IEEE Trans. Inform. Theory 38(2), 713–718 (1992)

[7] Jawerth, B., Sweldens, W.: An overview of wavelet based multiresolution analyses. SIAM Review 36(3), 377–412 (1994)

[8] Walczak, B., Bogaert, B.V.D., Massart, D.L.: Application of wavelet packet transform in pattern recognition of near-IR data. Analytical Chemistry 68(10), 1742–1747 (1996)

[9] Donald, D., Everingham, Y., Coomans, D.: Integrated wavelet principal component mapping for unsupervised clustering on near infra-red spectra. Chemometrics and Intelligent Laboratory Systems 77(1-2), 32–42 (2005)

[10] Donoho, D.L.: De-noising by soft-thresholding. IEEE Trans. Inform. Theory 41(3), 613–627 (1995)

A Classification Rule Acquisition Algorithm Based on Constrained Concept Lattice

Xujun Zhao

School of Computer Science and Technology,
TaiYuan University of Science and Technology,
TaiYuan, People's Republic of China
zxj0226@126.com

Abstract. Concept lattice is an effective tool for data analysis. Constrained concept lattice, with the characteristics of higher constructing efficiency, practicability and pertinence, is a new concept lattice structure. For classification rule acquisition, a classification rule acquisition algorithm based on the constrained concept lattice is presented by using the concept of partition support according to the relationship between node's extent of constrained concept lattice and equivalence partition of data set. The experiment results validate the higher classification efficiency and correctness of the algorithm by taking UCI (University of California Irvine) data sets as the formal contexts.

Keywords: Constrained Concept Lattice, Classification Rule, Partition Support, Background Knowledge, Consistent Node.

1 Introduction

Classification is one of the main research fields in data mining. By analyzing the data, the relationship between the conditions attributes and the classification attributes can be expressed as a particular form which will provide users with the interested knowledge. At present, the typical classification rule extraction methods include rough set, neural network and concept lattice, etc[1-4].

Concept lattice is an effective tool for classification knowledge extraction and embodies the generalized and specialized relation between nodes. Nowadays, there are two main categories, the first category is that to use constructing algorithm of concept lattice, a fully lattice is established, and then the rules are extracted from the lattice. The typical constructing algorithms include: improving the rule learner algorithm about discovering classification rule is proposed in [5]. By using the relationship between parent node and child node, the integrating method of classification rules based on concept lattice is proposed in [6]. The second category is that a corresponding half-concept lattice based on the data sets is constructed under the certain parameters in [7], but to set the appropriate parameters is very difficult.

Constrained concept lattice is a new concept lattice structure, which describes interest background knowledge to users using predicate logic, and the background knowledge is used during the concept lattice constructing in [8]. Thus, the time-space

H. Deng et al. (Eds.): AICI 2011, Part I, LNAI 7002, pp. 356–363, 2011.
© Springer-Verlag Berlin Heidelberg 2011

complexity can be effectively reduced, the practicability and pertinence of the extracted knowledge is further enhanced. In this paper, a classification rule extraction algorithm based on constrained concept is presented by using partition support and extension support. Firstly, extension support and partition support are computed in the algorithm, which scares the distribution of the classification properties on nodes extension. Secondly, according to the extent support and partition support, classification rules are extracted by using node intension. Finally, the experimental results validate that the algorithm has higher constructing efficiency and classification accuracy by using the UCI standard data set as formal contexts.

2   General Concept Lattice and Constrained Concept Lattice

A formal context is a triple $K = (G, M, I)$, the elements in G are called objects, and the elements in M are called attributes. I is a binary relation between G and M. And this binary relationship can form a concept lattice structure L.

Let $K = (G, M, I)$ be a formal context, L is a concept lattice that is constructed by the K. Each node is an ordered pair called concept, namely $C(A, B)$, where $A \in \rho(G)$ is called the extent of nodes, $B \in \rho(M)$ is the intent of nodes.

During the process of constructing concept lattice, users are not interested in all attributes that contained in the concept intent. We can construct the concept lattice by the guide of the user's interest and understanding for data sets, thus make the structure of the concept lattice more pertinent and practical. While adopting the predicate logic to express knowledge, we define the predicates which describe the background knowledge at first, and point out the precise meaning of each predicate, then join relevant predicates with the conjunction, form a predicate formula P to express complete background knowledge.

Every nodes in concept lattice is described as $C((A, B), P)$, where P is constrained condition, and $P((A, B))=$True, $A \subseteq G$ is the extent of concept, $B \subseteq M$ is the intent of concept, and A and B satisfy two following conditions:

$$A = B' = \{g \in G \mid \forall m \in B, gIm\} \tag{1}$$

$$B = A' = \{m \in M \mid \forall g \in A, gIm\} \tag{2}$$

The concept lattice with this structure is called constrained concept lattice, namely, $<L(G, M, I, P), \leq, P>$, where $L(G,M,I,P)$ is the concept(node) sets that satisfy the constrained condition P. Let $C_1((A_1, B_1), P)$ and $C_2((A_2, B_2), P)$ be the any two different nodes, where C_1 is the sub concept of C_2 (C_2 is the super concept of C_1). We define $h_1 \leq h_2 \Leftrightarrow B_2 \subseteq B_1 \Leftrightarrow A_1 \subseteq A_2$ ($h_2 \leq h_1 \Leftrightarrow B_1 \subseteq B_2 \Leftrightarrow A_2 \subseteq A_1$). If there is not $C_3((A_3,B_3), P)$, satisfy $h_1 \leq h_3 \leq h_2$, then define C_2 is the father node of C_1, C_1 is the son node of C_2.

3   Classification Rule Extraction

Classification rule extraction is one of the main research fields in data mining, which gets the information of the classification properties by analyzing the training data set, and then applies to the given data set. Its purpose is to classify or predict. Extraction of classification rules is to find the dependent relationship between the conditions attributes and the classification attributes, and to get the rules of cond→cl, where cond is the conjunctive form of condition attribute values, cl is a certain classification attribute value.

For classification tasks, attributes in training sample data set $DB=(G,M_c \cup \{t\},I)$ can be divided into the condition attributes and the classification attributes, where M_c is condition attribute set, t is the classification attribute. According to different values of classification attribute t, namely t_1,t_2,t_3..... t_m, G can be divided into m-equivalent classifications, denoted by G_1,G_2.....G_m. In the equivalent division G_i, $t_i(1 \le i \le m)$ is the classification attribute value of data object.

Classification rule reflects a dependent relationship between the condition attribute and the classification attribute. It is one of the key problems of extracting rules how to describe the condition attribute and classification attribute, and to set up their dependence relation. For a given the training sample data set DB, the classification attribute is depicted by the equivalent division G_i, the condition attribute is depicted by the intention of constrained concept lattice, and the dependence relation between condition attribute and classification attribute is established by the nodes extension and the equivalent division G_i, so the constrained concept lattice is a kind of effective method of extract classification rules and constrained concept lattice is used as a classification rule extraction tool. Let $DB=(G,M_c \cup \{t\}$ be the training sample data set, where G is a object set, M_c is a conditional attribute set. $K=(G,M_c,I)$ is a formal context of the constrained concept lattice. Constrained concept lattice is constructed by P and CCLA in [8], where P is the background knowledge and CCLA is the constrained concept lattice construction algorithm. For any constrained concept lattice node C ((A, B), P), G_i is the i-equivalent division. If $A \subseteq G_i$, classification rule $B \to t_i$ can be extracted. If $A \not\subseteq G_i$, $A \cap G_i \ne \phi$ and classification attribute value t_i has the maximum probability, classification rule $B \to t_i$ can be extracted.

Lattice node extension number is the number of records which meet its intension in the training sample data set DB. If the node extension number is too small, it is indicated that the corresponding intension probability in the DB is very small, and its importance is greatly weak, so these nodes are considered as meaningless or noise. Whether the objects in the extension are noise data by defining extension support degree ES. When ES> ES_{min}, classification rules are extracted from the nodes, where ES_{min} is the extension support degree threshold. In addition, the introduction of the partition support is used to measure the different categories probability and then determines the classification attribute value of the classification rules.

Definition 1. For any node C ((A, B), P) in constrained concept lattice, A's extension support ES and partition support PS are defined as follows:

$$ES=|A|/|U| \tag{3}$$

$$PS=|A \cap m(t_i)|/|A| \quad (i=1,...m) \tag{4}$$

Where | A | is the number of objects included the node extension, | U | is the total number of records, $|A \cap m(t_i)|$ is the number of objects which not only satisfy the intention B but also belong to t_i, t_i is a classification attribute value, and ES, PS satisfy following conditions:$0 < ES \le 1, 0 \le PS \le 1$.

By ES definition, when the ES value is higher, the data objects described by B are more and the classification rules from B are more important. When the ES value is lower, the data objects described by B are less and the B's ability to describe data objects is lower. So we should set ES threshold ES_{min} and extract the rules using larger value nodes. At the same time, by PS definition, PS is used to measure the distribution of the classification attribute value in A.

Let ES_{min} be the threshold of the extension support, C((A, B), P) be any node in the constrained concept lattice, ES be the extension support of A. When $ES \geq ES_{min}$, the partition support PS is counted. If $A \subseteq G_i$ and PS=1, the rule $B \rightarrow t_i$ is correct. If $A \cap G_i \neq A \neq \Phi, |M_i|$ and t_i can be recorded where $|M_i|$ is the number of the intersection and t_i is a classification attribute value, $PS=|M_i| /|A|$ can be computed, the largest PS value and its t_i can be selected, then classification rules $B \rightarrow t_i$ can be extracted.

Definition 2. For any classification rule $B \rightarrow t_i$, the rule is called the compatible rule if PS = 1, and the rule is called the incompatible rule if $0 \leq PS \square 1$. For any node C((A, B), P)$\in$L, the node C is called compatible node if $A \subseteq G_i$, the node C is called incompatible node if $A \not\subset G_i$.

Let DB = (G, Mc $\cup$ {t}, I) be the training sample data set. the data object in G are plotted into m-equivalent division according to classification attribute value $t_1, t_2, t_3 \ldots$ t_m, namely $G_1, G_2 \ldots G_m$. K=(G,M_c,I) is formal context and P is background knowledge, L is constrained concept lattice and ES_{min} is the threshold of the extension support. Then has the following theorems established:

Theorem 1. Let C ((A, B), P) be any node in L, ES is the extension support of A and ES $\geq ES_{min}$. if $\forall g \in A = B', g \in G_i (1 \leq i \leq m)$, the classification rules $B \rightarrow t_i$ can be extracted, and it is compatible rule.

Proof: For any node C((A, B) ,P) in L, owing to $\forall g \in A$ and $g \in G_i$, $g \in A \subseteq G_i$, and t_i is the classification attribute value corresponding G_i, so PS value corresponding t_i is $|A \cap m(t_i)|/| A | =| A |/| A |=1$. According to the definition 2, node C is the compatible node, the compatible classification rules $B \rightarrow t_i$ can be extracted.

Theorem 1 shows that when ES $\geq ES_{min}$ and $A \subseteq G_i$, PS value corresponding t_i is 1, the corresponding lattice node is compatible node, the compatible classification rule $B \rightarrow t_i$ can be directly extracted.

Theorem 2 Let node C((A, B) , P) be any node in L, if $\exists g$, k$\in$ A,$g \in G_i, k \in G_j (1 \leq i \leq m, 1 \leq j \leq m),| M | > | N|$,where $M=A \cap G_i, N =A \cap G_j$,then the probability of t_i is greater than t_j .

Proof: According to the definition of the partition support PS, $PS(t_i)= | M |/| A |$, $PS(t_j)= | N |/| A |$, where $PS(t_i)$ is the PS value corresponding t_i, $PS(t_j)$ is the PS value corresponding t_j. When $| M |>| N |, | M |/| A |>| N |/| A |$, so $PS(t_i)> PS(t_j)$, namely the probability of t_i is greater than t_j

In theorem 2, for any node C ((A, B), P) in the lattice, A and t_i corresponding PS value is determined, namely the classification attribute values distribution in A remains the same. When the classification attributes t_i and its PS value is higher, the probability of t_i is greater; the accuracy of the classification rules $B \rightarrow t_i$ is higher.

For the classification rules $b_1 \wedge c_2 \rightarrow t_i$ and $b_1 \rightarrow t_i$, $b_1 \rightarrow t_i$ is a generalization rule of $b_1 \wedge c_2 \rightarrow t_i$. Clearly, if some data can be correctly classified by the rule $b_1 \wedge c_2 \rightarrow t_i$, then these data must be correctly classified by the rule $b_1 \rightarrow t_i$ too. But if some data can be correctly classified by the rule $b_1 \rightarrow t_i$, these data can not necessarily be correctly classified by the rule $b_1 \wedge c_2 \rightarrow t_i$. Thus, $b_1 \wedge c_2 \rightarrow t_i$ is a redundant classification rule of $b_1 \rightarrow t_i$.

The classification rules are extracted from constrained concept lattice where the constrained concept lattice nodes are scanned from top-down. When the extension nodes are completely contained by an equivalence division, the classification rules are directly extracted. When the relationship is not fully contained, the maximum PS value becomes the classification attribute of the classification rule.

4   CRACCL Algorithm and Analysis

Based on above-mentioned analysis and discussing, according to theorem 1and theorem 2, we can directly extract the classification. We find the maximum PS value as the classification attribute. The algorithm is described as follows:

Algorithm CRACCL(Classification rule acquisition algorithm based on Constrained Concept Lattice)

Input: constrained concept lattice L, the threshold of the extension support ES_{min};
Output: Classification rule set

```
1) For any lattice node C( (A, B), P )∈L   Do
2)     If  |A|>N×ES_min Then
3)        For Each C ancestor nodes C′   Do
4)            If  PS ≠ 1 Then
5)               For i=1 to m   Do
6)                   If  A∩G_j=A Then ruleset=ruleset∪{B→t_j }
7)                   Else For k=1 to m Do
8)                          If  A∩G_k≠A≠∅   then   PS_k=| A∩m(t_k) |
/|A|   Else   PS_k=0;
9)                          End For
10)                       select the classification attribute
value t_r corresponding the maximum PS value, ruleset=
ruleset∪{B→t_r};
11)             End If
12)           End For
13)        End If
14)     End For
15)   End If
16) End For
17) End CRACCL
```

The algorithm provides a classification rule extraction method, line 2 is how to choose nodes satisfied ES_{min}; line 3-4 line is that the ancestor nodes are scanned and processed to avoid extraction of redundant rules; line 6 determines whether the extension of node is G_i subset; line 7-10 is how to extract classification rules according to judge the partition support size. According to the algorithm, the time complexity of computing intersection between node extension and its G_i is $O(m)$, the time complexity of computing the partition support is $O(m)$ too, the time complexity of scanning and processing the ancestor nodes is $O(n)$ (n is the number of the ancestor nodes),the time complexity of extracting classification rule by each node is $O(m^2 \times n)$. So if the classification rules are extracted from |E| nodes, the time complexity of CRACCL is $O(|E| \times m^2 \times n)$.

5   Experimental Analysis

The experimental environment is: PentiumVI-3.0G CPU, 512M memory, Windows XP operating system, ORACLE9i DBMS. Three UCI data sets (namely monk3, tic-tac-toe and car data set) are used to analyze and validate CRACCL algorithm. In monk3, tic - tac - toe and car data sets, the different constrained condition and ES_{min} are provided in the first experiment. Then the experimental results of the extract classification rule number and classification accuracy are given in table 1 to 3. Using tic-tac-toe and car data, the determinate constrained condition P and different ES_{min} are provided in the second experiment. Then the experimental results of the extract classification rule number and classification accuracy are given in table 4 and 5.

Table 1 to table 2 shows that, in the process of constrained concept lattice construction, with the restrained degree of P weaker, the nodes satisfied P gradually increase, the time-consuming of constrained concept lattice construction also gradually increase, the extract classification rule number also gradually increase, therefore the constrained condition P has great influence on the constrained concept lattice construction, the classification rule extraction and classification efficiency, namely the restrained degree of P is higher, the efficiency is higher. In the process of constrained concept lattice construction, these nodes satisfied the constrained conditions P are generated only, some nodes unsatisfied P and contained classification information can not be generated. So the P has certain influence on classification accuracy, namely the restrained degree of P is weaker, the classification accuracy is higher. In summary, the P has great impact on the constrained concept lattice construction, the classification rules extraction, classification efficiency, and classification accuracy. So according to the experience and knowledge on the classification task and the data interpretation, the user can select the constrained conditions P which contains classification information, and avoid selecting constrained conditions P which lost classified information. Thus, it can not only ensure the classification accuracy, but also effectively improve the classification efficiency.

Table 1. The experiment result of monk3 data set

constrained condition P	accuracy rate	error rate	classification rule number	structure time	node number
a203 $\wedge$ a302	91.667%	8.333%	5	1s	86
a203	95.833%	4.167%	53	1s	246
a302	100%	0%	126	1s	336
a203 $\vee$ a302	100%	0%	174	2s	496
Φ	100%	0%	558	3s	1183

Table 2. The experiment result of tic-tac-toe data set

constrained condition P	accuracy rate	error rate	classification rule number	structur e time	node number
righter upper is x ∧ middle right is blank	95.833%	4.167%	8	6s	529
middle right is blank	98.449%	1.551%	80	13s	2782
righter upper is x	100%	0%	153	20s	4347
righter upper is x ∨ middle right is blank	99.19%	0.81%	225	31s	6600
Φ	100%	0%	1259	179s	21581

In table 3 and table 4, as the ES_{min} increase gradually, the concept lattice nodes whose extension support degree is more than ES_{min}, will gradually decrease, the number of concept lattice nodes extracting classification rules also will gradually decrease. As its extension support degree less than ES_{min}, some nodes containing classification information cannot extract classification rules, so the classification accuracy reduced. Therefore, the ES_{min} has great influence on the number of classification rules, classification efficiency and classification accuracy, namely the ES_{min} is larger, the number of classification rules is less, the classification efficiency is higher, and the classification accuracy is lower. Thus, for the given training sample data sets DB, it is requisite that the users select appropriate ES_{min}, try to retain the concept lattice nodes containing classification information, and extract classification rules from these nodes, thereby ensure the classification accuracy, and effectively improve the classification efficiency.

Table 3. The experiment result of tic-tac-toe data set

ESmin	accuracy rate	error rate	classification rule number
0.01	100%	0%	1103
0.02	100%	0%	350
0.03	100%	0%	140
0.04	98.449%	1.551%	80
0.05	98.449%	1.551%	53

Table 4. The experiment result of car data set

ESmin	accuracy rate	error rate	classification rule number
0.01	89.815%	10.185%	216
0.02	89.815%	10.185%	164
0.03	85.185%	14.815%	52
0.04	85.185%	14.815%	36
0.05	85.185%	14.815%	36

6 Conclusions

In this article, a classification rule acquisition algorithm CRACCL based on the constrained concept lattice is presented by using the concept of extension support and partition support. The extension support is calculated by using the extension of lattice node, and the partition support is calculated according to the relationship between node's extent of constrained concept lattice and equivalence partition of data set, then the classification rules are extracted from the constrained concept lattice. The experiment results show that the classification rules extracted by CRACCL algorithm can effectively improve the classification efficiency and correctness of the algorithm.

References

1. Ma, J., Chen, Y.: A Data Mining Algorithm Based on Rough Set Theory. Computer Science 35(6), 213–216 (2008)
2. Zhang, D., Wang, Y., Huang, H.: Fuzzy Rough Model Based Rough Neural Network Modeling. Acta Automatica Sinica 34(8), 1016–1023 (2008)
3. Hu, K., Lu, Y., Shi, C.: An Integrated Mining Approach for Classification and Association Rule Based on Concept Lattice. Journal of Software 11(11), 1479–1484 (2000)
4. Wang, H., Hu, X., Zhao, W.: The Discovery of Classification Rules Based on Quantitative Relatively Reduced Concept Lattice. Journal of Fudan University 43(5), 761–765 (2004)
5. Xie, K., Zhao, J., Zhang, D., et al.: A Fast Multi-Dimensional Packet Classification Algorithm Using Counting Bloom Filter. Acta Electronica Sinica 38(5), 1046–1052 (2010)
6. Sahami, M.: Learning classification rules using lattices. In: Proceeding of the ECML 1995, pp. 343–346 (1995)
7. Wang, Y., Li, M.: Classification Rule Acquisition Based on Extended Concept Lattice. Journal of Computer Applications 27(10), 2376–2378 (2007)
8. Zhang, J., Zhang, S., Hu, L.: Constrained Concept Lattice and Its Construction Method. CAAI Transactions on Intelligent Systems 2(1), 31–38 (2006)

An Efficient Continuous Attributes Handling Method for Mining Concept-Drifting Data Streams Based on Skip List

Zhenzheng Ouyang[1], Yuhai Gao[1], Mingjun Li[2], and Jianshu Luo[1]

[1] School of Science, National University of Defense Technology, Changsha, China
[2] Army Unit 63961, Beijing, China
oyz21@163.com, gyh927@sina.com
Limj9803@163.com, ljsh3115@sina.com

Abstract. This paper focuses on continuous attributes handling for mining data stream with concept drift. CVFDT is one of the most successful methods for handling concept drift efficiently. In this paper, we revisit this problem and present an algorithm named SL_CVFDT on top of CVFDT. It is fast as hash table when inserting, seeking or deleting attribute value, and it also can sort the attribute value. The average time cost of search, insertion and deletion is $O(\log_2 n)$, and average memory cost of point is $O(n)$. At the same time, it can get best split point just traverse the skip list once.

Keywords: Data Streams, Concept Drift, Continuous Attribute, Skip List, SL_CVFDT.

1   Introduction

Actually a difficult problem in on-line learning such as data mining is that the target concept to be learned is not clearly given by the pre-given characteristic attributes but depends on some hidden context. For examples, Spam e-mail sender may be removed from the black list to the white list because of the changes of the recipient's knowledge and interests. The reasons for these changes are usually hidden and unpredictable in advance. The changes of hidden context may lead to changes in target concept and result in concept drift [1]. A good learning algorithm should be able to track these changes as soon as possible and modify its own model in accordance with these changes.

Classification technique is an important subject in data stream mining, but most data stream mining algorithms make the assumption that training data is a random sample drawn from an independent, identical and stationary distribution. Unfortunately, most of the data streams available violate this assumption. The distribution mostly changes over time. That is, there is concept drift in data streams. How to effectively handle concept drift arising in data stream is an important research topic in the fields of data mining and machine learning. CVFDT [2] can effectively solve concept drift, but still there are some other important problems which need to be solved, such as reuse of the historical old concept, continuous attributes handling and so on.

H. Deng et al. (Eds.): AICI 2011, Part I, LNAI 7002, pp. 364–371, 2011.

Based on CVFDT, this paper focus on handling continuous attributes of data stream with concept drift and we proposes a concept drift processing algorithm called SL_CVFDT which is based on skip list. On searching and inserting and deleting the continuous attribute values in this algorithm, the average time complexity is $O(\log 2n)$ and the average pointer space complexity is $O(2n)$. At the same time, the best divided node of the continuous attributes can be calculated by one traverse using the attribute being ordered of the skip list.

The rest of this paper is organized as follows: in section 2 we describe some related work; in section 3 we introduce some technical details of SL_CVFDT; in section 4 we present a series of experiments. Section 5 is conclusion and gives future research plan.

2   Related Work

2.1   Concept Drift

Let t be a time stamp, data stream can be represented as an infinite sequence $d_t = (x_t, y_t)$, in which x_t identifies the data's feature vector in data stream and y_t is class label. Concept drift describes a changing target concept. We consider two concepts A and B. Concept drift algorithm handles the examples $\{d_1, d_2, ..., d_n\}$ in order. The target concept is stably A before the example d_t. After examples flows, the target concept will be stably B again. The concept drifts from A to B between i_d and $i_{d+\Delta_x}$.

Studying the classification of data streams with concept drift is one of the important tasks in the field of data stream mining and it is also a challenging research focus now. The most ideal method is to recognize when the concept drift occurs in order to handle concept drift. And then it would be timely to re-train and update the classification model. However, this problem is not that simple as it looks like. So far, the problem about how to design a reliable and sensitive method for detecting the concept drift is far from being resolved [3].

2.2   Skip List Structure

Skip list is an expand list which is like balanced binary tree in performance. There are more than one pointer on each node in order to search quickly. Skip list is constituted of layers. The bottom layer is a normal and orderly list. Each higher layer is a subset of the layer under it. The elements in ith layer will appear in the $i+1$th layer with the probability of p. On average, each element appears in $1 / (1-p)$ lists and the element in the top layer appears in $O(\log 1/p \ n)$ lists.

2.3   CVFDT

The existing method for handling concept drift can be divided into three which are example selection, example weights and integrated learning algorithm.

The purpose of example selection is selecting examples related to current model. Example selection is the most common method for handling concept drift. It maintains a sliding window as the new example arrives. Algorithms based on sliding window include FLORA Series [1], FRANN [4], TMF[5] and so on. Many methods by deleting noise and irrelevant and needless examples are also contained in example selection. Example weights method weights the examples by some learning algorithms (such as SVM) [6]. Mostly examples are weighted according to the arrival time or the relevance to current model. Integrated learning algorithm contains STAGGER [7], Harries and Sammut's Concept Cluster [8], Wang and so on [10-14].

CVFDT is an efficient algorithm which is an extension of VFDT to handle concept drift [2, 15]. The specific construction process of CVFDT is as follows, it starts from a leaf node to collect examples from data stream. With the increasing of examples, when it is time for determining the best split attribute with a high degree of confidence, we turn the leaf node into a test node and repeat the learning process for the new leaf node. CVFDT maintains a window of training examples. It keeps its window consistent by updating the learned decision tree when examples come in and out of the window. Specially, when a new example arrives, it will be added to all the decision tree nodes which it passed by. And when an example is removed from decision tree, it also needs to be removed from all the affected nodes and all the statistical test need to be restarted. When concept drift occurs, it generates an alternative sub tree in parallel on the node. When the precision of alternative sub tree is much larger than the original sub tree, the original sub tree will be replaced and released.

CVFDT is an extension to VFDT which maintains VFDT's speed and accuracy but adds the ability to detect and respond to concept drift in the example-generating process. Like other systems with this capability, CVFDT works by keeping its model consistent with a sliding window of examples. However, It does not need to learn a new model from scratch every time a new example arrives; instead, it updates the sufficient statistics at its nodes by incrementing the counts corresponding to the new example, and decrementing the counts corresponding to the oldest example in the window. CVFDT and VFDT have a similar process of HT tree generating. CVFDT maintains the statistics on all the nodes, but VFDT maintains the statistics only on leaf nodes.

3   SL_CVFDT Algorithm

Based on CVFDT and using the technique of skip list, we designed and implemented an algorithm named SL_CVFDT which effectively handled continuous attributes in data streams with concept drift.

In our previous work, we used binary sort tree and threaded binary sort tree to handle continuous attribute problem in data stream mining. But the binary sort tree is prone to degradation so as to affect the efficiency of the algorithm. Skip list average has a better efficiency in search, insertion and deletion while its implementation is easier.

3.1   Skip List Structure

SL_CVFDT maintains a skip list for each continuous attribute. Skip list is an ordered linked list. Each node contains variable chains (pointers). The ith list which skips these nodes only containing lower layers forms a single linked list. There is a i-level pointer every $2i$ elements. One element is called i-chain element when it is on the $0 \sim i$-level chains and it is not on the $i+1$-chian.

Every skip List Node has the attributes such as *keyValue*, *classTotals[k]*, *nextNode* and so on. *keyvalue* is used to record the attribute *i* of arriving examples. The vector *classTotals[k]* records the count of examples whose attribute *i* takes the value of *keyValue* and the class label is *k*. *NextNode* is used to record the node successor. Besides, in order to maintain the skip list and select the best split point, SL_CVFDT set a head pointer which points to all the element domain and the internal pointers for every continuous attribute and set a tail pointer array *last[maxLevel]* which points to all the internal pointers.

The node structure of skip list is shown in Fig. 1.

```
Typedef struct TSLNodeStruct{
    real keyValue;          /*value of continuous attribute*/
    int classTotals[k];       /*the count of each class examples *
    struct TSLNodeStruct *next; /*next node pointer*/
}TSLNode
```

Fig. 1. Node structure of skip list

```
Procedure  SLbestSplit(SLtreePtr ptr,int *belowPrev[])
Begin
    if ( ptr->next == NULL) then  break;
    for ( k = 0 ; k < count ; k++)
        *belowPrev[k] += ptr->classTotals[k];
    Calculates the  information gain using *belowPrev[];
    SLbestSplit(ptr->next,int *belowPrev[]);
End
```

Fig. 2. The Best split point selecting process of SL_CVFDT

3.2   Attribute Value Inserting Process

For newly arrived example, SL_CVFDT need to maintain every skip list attribute and the maintaining process is composed of searching and inserting. It searches along the pointers from the pointer head and start from the highest layer. When one of the attribute values is larger than the values to be inserted or they are equal, the searching goes to the next layer. Searching along the pointers of the lower layer, it gradually approaches the attribute values to be inserted and it will not stop until all the attributes of pointers on the o-layer is lager or equal to the attribute values to be inserted. If there is not the same attribute value, one new node should be set. The layer's number of the new generated node is calculated by special function. The new node is inserted after the element pointed by *last[0]* and it is the same situation on the other layers.

3.3   Deletion Process of Skip List While Example Outflows the Sliding Window

In order to handle concept drift, SL_CVFDT keeps a window of training examples. When the examples come in and out of the window, we update the learned decision tree so as to make it consistent with the window. We need abandon old examples when the training examples come out of the current window of training examples and make an operation of deletion for the skip list of attribute. Removal process is made up with search and deletion. Firstly, we search the attribute to be deleted, so we can delete this attribute from 0-th list to k-th list. Otherwise, deleting this attribute will lead to the deletion of higher list, so we need to modify the number of lists.

Because skip list is an ordered linked list, while selecting the best split point, through the linked list we can start from the head pointer to traverse the entire attribute tree in order to calculate the information gain of all candidate nodes. In order to know the information gain of one attribute, we need to calculate the information gain of all the alternative division of this attribute. For every alternative division node, tow parts of information gain are calculated as formula (1).

$$\text{info}(A_j(i)) = P(A_j \leq i) * iLow(A_j(i)) + P(A_j > i) * iHigh(A_j(i)) \tag{1}$$

In the formula above i is a split point. $iLow(A_j(i))$ is the information of $A_j \leq i$ and $iHigh(A_j(i))$ is information of $A_j > i$. They are calculated as follow:

$$iLow(A_j(i)) = -\sum_K P(K = k \mid A_j \leq i) * \log(P(K = k \mid A_j \leq i)) \tag{2}$$

$$iHigh(A_j(i)) = -\sum_K P(K = k \mid A_j > i) * \log(P(K = k \mid A_j > i)) \tag{3}$$

The process of getting best split point is shown in fig. 2 which starts from the head node.

For a skip list with n attributes, the worst time complexity of search, insertion and deletion operation is $O(n+maxLevel)$. The average time complexity is $O(\log_2 n)$. For the space complexity, the worst case is that all attribute values are likely located in layer $maxLevel$. Each node has $maxLevel+1$ pointer, so the space complexity is $O(n \cdot maxLevel)$. Usually, n attribute values are located in layer 0. $n/2$ Attribute values are located in layer 1 and $n(1/2)^i$ nodes are located in layer i. Therefore, the total pointers number of n nodes count is $2n$ and the average number is 2.

4   Experimental Results

In order to verify the effectiveness of our continuous attributes handling method (based on skip list) for mining data stream with concept drift, referring to [7], we designed several sets of experiments to respectively verify the scalability, effectiveness, efficiency of SL_CVFDT to handle the continuous attributes classification problem in concept drifting data stream with noise. The experimental environment is Core 2 Duo 2.0G CPU, 2G memory and the operation is Windows XP. We use the data streams generated by TreeData [16]. The parameters are set as follow: $\delta = 10^{-7}, \tau = 5\%, n_{min} = 300$.

4.1   Algorithm Efficiency for Handling Continuous Attributes

Table 1 show the experimental results of SL_CVFDT when continuous attribute is 20, discrete attribute is 0, the noise data is 0%. Experimental results show that SL_CVFDT algorithm can effectively handle continuous attributes problem in concept drifting data streams.

Table 1. SL_CVFDT'S Efficiency on Dealing with Continuous Attributes

Example Count	Error Rate	Tree Size	Time	Memory （M）
10000	8.3534	9	2	13.24
15300	4.4458	11	2	29.34
20800	4.4600	11	3	45.15
35000	1.6540	16	5	79.39
43000	0.7650	18	8	127.11
63000	0.7312	22	29	210.13

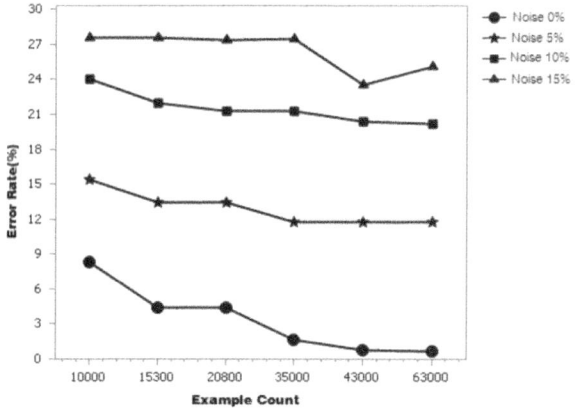

Fig. 3. The impact of noise data on SL_CVFDT's precision

4.2   The Impact of Noise Data on the Algorithm

The first set of experiments show the algorithm effectiveness of handling continuous attributes when concept drift occurs. But how is the algorithm's noise resisting ability? The second set of experiments is used to verify the algorithm's anti-noise ability. We respectively got the performance of SL_CVFDT when the noise ratio is 0%, 5%, 10%, 15%. The set of experiments set that the continuous attribute is 20, discrete attribute is 0, and data adopt the way of flowing through. The impact of noise data on the algorithm mainly reflected on precision. The impact is not obvious in tree size, learning time and memory usage. The impact of noise data on the algorithm precision is shown as fig. 3 which shows that the algorithm has a very good convergence under a variety of noise ratios.

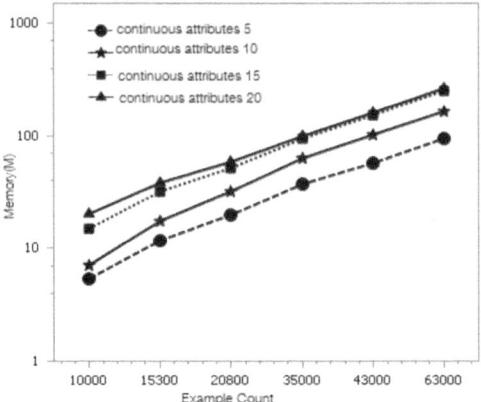

Fig. 4. The impact of continuous attribute number on SL_CVFDT's precision

4.3   The Impact of Continuous Attribute Number on Algorithm

The number of continuous attributes more or less directly affects the performance of the algorithm. How is the performance of algorithm under different continuous attribute numbers? The third set of experiments is used to verify the performance of algorithm under different continuous attribute number. Experimental results show that the impact mainly reflects on storage usage. Figure 4 shows the comparison under different continuous attribute numbers. CVFDT is based on Hoeffding inequality. It can ensure the accuracy of processing a large number of data. The experimental results show that the memory usage of this algorithm is stable under different continuous attribute numbers.

5   Conclusion

For dealing with continuous attribute in mining concept drifting data streams, this paper propose an algorithm SL_CVFDT which combined skip list technique with CVFDT system. The average time complexity of SL_CVFDT is example search, example insertion and example deletion operation in handling continuous attributes, while the total skip list pointer space complexity is . Based on Entropy theory and Fayyad's results, the best split point of the continuous attributes can be calculated by one traverse using the ordered attributes of the skip list. Experiments show that SL_CVFDT boasts good scalabilities, efficiency and stabilities in handling continuous attribute problems of concept drifting data streams. 2 (log) On(2) On

In future, we would like to improve SL_CVFDT in some direction. Firstly, even though SL_CVFDT can effectively handle continuous attributes, the memory increased and the space complexity is large in the worst situation, the space complexity of SL_CVFDT needs to study theoretically. Secondly, current experiment just uses simulation data, the performance of this algorithm in the real data streams needs to be verified.

References

1. Widmer, G., Kubat, M.: Learning in the presence of concept drift and hidden contexts. Machine Learning 23(1), 69–101 (1996)
2. Hulten, G., Spencer, L., Domingos, P.: Mining time-changing data streams. In: Proceedings of the Seventh ACM SIGKDD International Conference on Knowledge Discovery and Data Mining, pp. 97–106. ACM Press, New York (2001)
3. Kuncheva, L.I.: Classifier Ensembles for detecting concept change in streaming data: overview and perspectives. In: Proceedings of the Second Workshop SUEMA, ECAI 2008, Partas, Greece, pp. 5–9 (2008)
4. Kubat, M., Widmer, G.: Adapting to drift in continuous domains, in Technique Report ÖFAI-TR-94-27. Austrian Research Institute for Artificial Intelligence, Vienna (1994)
5. Salganicoff, M.: Tolerating concept and sampling shift in lazy learning using prediction error context switchingg. AI Review, Special Issue on Lazy Learning 11, 133–155 (1997)
6. Klinkenberg, R.: Learning drifting concepts: Example selection vs. Example weighting. Intelligent Data Analysis, Special Issue on Incremental Learning Systems Capable of Dealing with Concept Drift (2004)
7. Cunningham, P., Nowlan, N.: A case-based approach to spam filtering that can track concept drift. In: ICCBR-2003 Workshop on Long-Lived CBR Systems (2003)
8. Schlimmer, J.C., Granger, R.H.: Incremental learning from noisy data. Machine Learning 1(3), 317–354 (1986)
9. Harries, M.B., Sammut, C.: Extracting hidden context. Machine Learning 32, 101–126 (1998)
10. Wang, H., Fan, W., Yu, P., Han, J.: Mining concept-drifting data streams using ensemble classifiers. In: The 9th ACM International Conference on Knowledge Discovery and Data Mining, SIGKDD 2003 (2003)
11. Freund, Y., Hsu, D.: A new Hedging algorithm and its application to inferring latent random variables. In: The Computing Research Repository (CoRR), vol. 6 (2008)
12. Kolter, J.Z., Maloof, M.A.: Dynamic weighted majority: An ensemble method for drifting concepts. Journal of Machine Learning Research 8, 2755–2790 (2007)
13. Ouyang, Z., Zhao, Z., Li, M.: An ensemble classifier framework for mining noisy data streams. Journal of Computational Information Systems 6(3) (2010)
14. Ouyang, Z., Luo, J., Hu, D.: An ensemble classifier framework for mining imbalanced data streams. Journal of ACTA Electronica Sinica 38(1) (2010)
15. Hulten, G., Domingos, P., Spencer, L.: Laurie Spencer. Mining massive data streams. Journal of Machine Learning Research 1 (2005)
16. Domingos, P., Hulten, G.: Mining High-Speed Data Streams. In: Proceedings of the Association for Computing Machinery Sixth International Conference on Knowledge Discovery and Data Mining, pp. 71–80 (2000)

The Decision Tree Application in Agricultural Development

JingGui Lu, Yi Liu, and Xiaoli Li

College of Computer and Software,
Taiyuan University of Technology, TYUT
Taiyuan, China
lujg58@163.com, liuyi0066@126.com, liyh2004_2005@sina.com.cn

Abstract. In the agricultural production, There are many factors play a Decisive role in agricultural output through a comprehensive way , to explore the key factors, this paper introduce the ID3 algorithms to analyze the various factors affecting trying to identify the core factors of production control. In the article, firstly, introduces the basic concept of decision tree and the ID3 algorithm, then analyze Lin Xian's agricultural output value data of 20 years and formed the preliminary decision tree, then combined with actual situation to generate the decision tree clip; Finally, through the experience of agricultural experts, formed the final decision tree to produces more actual set of rules that in agricultural investment decisions, which has the corresponding reference value to improve agricultural output, and has been proved has very good effect.

Keywords: Decision tree, ID3 algorithm, Agricultural output.

1 Introduction

The applications of the information industry spread in society life with the its rapid development in the progress of the times, among the application of the computer technology, the network technology and the communication technology can do help to the development of national economy, thus it accelerates the pace of the times. Further and more important, it has much significance to apply the information technology to the agricultural output in Linxian because of the low per capita income and slow growth.

As we can see from the statistics of Linxian's economic conditions that although the proportion of Linxian' agricultural output in its gross output is declining with years going, it still has a 60 percent, so that it has been always very important for Linxian's development to work on an analysis of kinds of the agricultural data to find out its development rule and how the factors influence the agricultural output. Lots of data which are full of valuable information have been collected during the county's development, but today's database management system is not able to find out the rules and relationships among the data. Therefore, this paper aims to use decision tree to do preliminary data mining attempts basing on the data about the county's agriculture, try to discover some

H. Deng et al. (Eds.): AICI 2011, Part I, LNAI 7002, pp. 372–379, 2011.

valuable information hidden behind the data and test the classified forecast decision tree, which formed by ID3 algorithm, and generate the rule set, in order to give a hand to the deciding of agricultural policy.

1.1   Concept of the Decision Tree

Data Mining is a progress that through analyzing and handling massive data sets or large, incomplete and noisy raw data from the database, people can draw potentially useful knowledge, information, models and trends which are unknown ,to have a deep understanding of data and more effective use of data[1],[2].

At the same time, the process of data mining can be viewed as a process of drawing models from the data, which can be classified as association model, classification model, regression model, clustering model, outlier analysis model and time series models according to the models' practical applications. Among the models, the classification model is mainly used to analyze the supervised data, which can summarize a model that is able to distinguish the data object ID by analyzing the training data sets. In the classification model, the most famous method is the decision tree method, decision tree for classification and similar to a flow chart. A root node of the decision tree often contains the most attributes, and its internal nodes represent a test of every attribute. The branches of the decision tree represent test results and the tree leaf is often the representative of the class. The highest level of the tree is the root node, which is the beginning of the decision tree. What's more, the number of child nodes of every node has something to do with the algorithm used by the decision tree. For example, every decision tree node has two branches if CART algorithm is used with the decision tree called double-tree, and the decision tree is named multi-tree when its node contains more than two child nodes or branches. Each branch of the tree is either a new decision node, or the end of the tree, which is called the leaves.

The process of using the decision tree classify the records in the practice is actually a traversal process from the top to the end along the decision tree. Different answers to every question encountering on every node will lead to different branches, till the leaf node. This can be called the decision tree's process of analysis.

Using the decision tree method for data classification, it normally takes two steps. First, an initial decision tree should be generated from the training sets. Secondly, the above decision tree will be modified and adjusted, which is against a case that some branches of the initial decision tree are constructed according to the abnormal data of training sample sets.

Usually the pruning method is to use the statistical methods to remove the most unreliable branches or child trees, so that to improve the speed of forecast and classified identification and the ability of correctly classify new data.

2   Algorithm ID3

2.1   The Concept of ID3[3]-[7]

ID3 algorithm is the most influence algorithm in Decision-Tree algorithm, it first proposed by Quinlan, ID3 is developed from CLS algorithm, in which algorithm, attribute chose through the information gain value. The size of the acquired information gain is bigger, the less the uncertainty is. So that classification efficiency and quality are greatly raised, and very extensive in reality .It is by far the most popular algorithm in decision tree area.

ID3 algorithm is a greedy algorithm. It uses a top-down, divide and rule strategy, through continuous cycle processing, gradually refinement, find a relatively accurate until the decision tree. It's tectonic decision tree is the top-down similar to IF - Then rules tree. Using this method the constitutive can be simpler, tectonic tree structure in tectonic process calculation is lesser, and especially suitable for large-scale data set's use to solve problems.

The basic idea of the ID3 algorithms is as follows:

(1)Select the whole training examples' scale of integrating PN random subset of PN as at present.

(2)Based on the information entropy drop speed for the standard, the selection of every test attributes, forming the current subsets of decision tree.

(3)Order to scan all training examples; find out the current decision tree exception, if no exceptions, then training ended.

(4)Combining the current subsets of some training with some examples in (3) the exception found in forming new subsets, turn (2).

The learning strategies of ID3 algorithm could be described as the following several aspects:

(1) When began to establish decision-making tree, root node contain all the training samples.

(2) If a node samples are part of the same category, the node becomes leaf nodes, and tags for this category; otherwise, will the information entropy as inspiration knowledge to choose appropriate to the branch attribute, divided into several small subset samples, this property will become the corresponding node testing attributes. In the ID3 algorithm, all the attribute values are discrete values, so if existing in the original data for value, it needs to its discrimination.

(3) A test attribute values are each of the corresponding a will be creating branch, also corresponds to a classified subset.

(4) Recursively apply the above (1) - (3) processing of data processing. So if a property in a node to appear, so it won't appear on the node tree produced son after the node. ID3 algorithm produces not contained the decision tree has repeated decision son tree.

(5) stop condition is a node of the samples of all belong to the same category; Or is without attributes can apply to partition the current samples, if appear this kind of circumstance, then according to the principle of the minority is subordinate to the majority will be compulsory for the current node leaf nodes.

2.2   ID3 Algorithm Concrete Operation Process Description

In the decision tree algorithm, the structure of the use of the information gain typically methods to help determine which generated when each node is the right properties should choose, so that they can select the highest information gain, namely entropy reduce degree maximum attributes as test attributes of the current node, in order to make its obtained after the division of the training samples required minimum amount of information subset. That is, using the attributes of the current node samples contained divides, will make all samples produced the different categories of mixed subset to minimize the information theory, so using this decision tree is constructed to object can be effectively reduced the number of classification, thus ensuring a decision tree generated practical and simple.

ID3 algorithm generated by decision tree of the specific steps as follows: we assumed known PN, then for training subset.

If all the examples PN training subset is an example, are all produced a Yes node and termination; If trained in all instances are PN son for counterexample, then generate a No node and termination; Otherwise the strategy choice according to the algorithm one attribute set A value type A, for A1, A2,... An, and generate new node.

Will the instance training subset according to its property PN A value division, generation n A subset PN1, respectively, for PN2 remember... PNn.

Will this algorithm in each subset recursively on application.

Because in the ID3 algorithm, the information entropy drops speed is one of the key to select the test attributes of standard (the information entropy is the decline of certainty down). Information based on entropy of attribute the selection process is as follows:

Assume a PN contains P training subset of examples and N a positive example of a negative, then we put PZ and PF is training subset of 2 training PN PZ called the subsets, which is the positive example sets, and is called the PF counterexample set of training subset. Is an example of positive example sets belonging to probability for PZ $p/(p+n)$, belong to the example set PF probability for an$n/(p+n)$, then the information entropy can be expressed as:

$$I(p,n) = -\frac{p}{p+n} \cdot \log_2\left(\frac{p}{p+n}\right) - \frac{n}{p+n}\log_2\left(\frac{n}{p+n}\right) \tag{1}$$

We choose an attribute A as decision tree roots test attributes with m a different,

A discrete values, A1, A2... Am, they will train PN into m a subset PN2 subsets, PN1... PNi PNm, assuming that have A positive examples and PI ni A negative example, PNi information entropy for subset I (PI, ni), criterion with attribute A test attributes expectations for the information entropy for:

$$E(A) = \sum_{i}^{m} \frac{pi + ni}{p+n} I(pi, ni) \tag{2}$$

So, the information gain is

$$gain(A) = I(p,n) - E(A) \tag{3}$$

From equation (3), which can be seen when the equation (2) the value of (A) the hours, the information gain greater gain (A), i.e. attribute A classified information to provide, the greater the option A after which the smaller the uncertainty. In the ID3 algorithm, we will select information gain maximum gain (A) the biggest attributes as the root, and then A decision tree to new division recursively subset of the operation of similar, can generate need decision tree.

3   The ID3 Algorithm in Application and the Conclusion

3.1   Data Pretreatment

Many factors affect agricultural output, the light from the data itself we can't clear what factors are the main factors, and how it affects the agricultural output value. Therefore, we are concerned with the development of agricultural production value may think the centralized structure factors are analyzed, and then a decision tree to cut by decision tree will affect the relatively small out factors, the main factors identified, generating rules. In this paper, we chose the site, agricultural population, sowing area, agriculture livestock number, average temperature, sunshine time, the frost-free period, such as decision rainfall in agricultural output value of input attribute, because agricultural output value is according to the whole county agricultural output value of to compute, it is not very important location factor, the removal of the original data[8] obtained in table 1 shows:

Table 1. Original Data

ID	Pop.	Area	Ani.	Temp.	Sun	Free	Rain
1	400599	144.31	18341	9.2	2862.9	184	639.2
2	403508	143.28	18928	9.1	2796.3	199	440.3
3	...	...	...	...	...	...	...

Then data form is generalized processing, the low levels of original data into a high level of concept to handle data mining. In this example, to agricultural population if population in calendar year above average is recorded as 1, in average is recorded as 0; a For sowing area, if seeding area accounts for the years that the total area of arable land statistics shows will remember 98% for 1, otherwise notes for 0; For animal husbandry, broken down by 60% of the division will be expanding, than as the notes for 1, less than the notes for 0; The temperature threshold, according to data, will remember the above 9 degrees for 1, said for good temperature condition, 9 degrees below zero; remember Each year to sunshine time, because the sunshine time relatively close to, also yielding around, with 28 hours to as rules, think on the basis of sunlight for good in its case, under the light is a bit poor thinks; The frost-free period criterion with half a year as a border, namely, greater than this world 182 days will remember for 1, less than the world record for 0; According to the average rainfall 60% of the whole value to the world than divider, written for 1, less than the world record for 0. Thus gain data table as shown table 2:

Table 2. Experimental Data

ID	Pop.	Area	Ani.	Temp.	Sun	Free	Rain	Output
1	0	1	1	1	1	1	1	0
2	0	1	1	1	0	1	0	0
3	...	...	...	...	...	...	...	...

3.2 Data Mining Processing

Because to investigate all other factors on the influence of GDP, so as the training subset selection GDP, then $p = 8, n = 13$, its information entropy can be expressed as:

$$I(p, n) = -\frac{8}{21} \log_2 \frac{8}{21} - \frac{13}{21} \log_2 \frac{13}{21} \qquad (4)$$

With each attribute for test attributes of information entropy as expectations shows in table 3:

Table 3. Experimental Data

$E(Pop.)$	0.551	$E(Area)$	0.309
$E(Ani.)$	0.483	$E(Temp.)$	0.976
$E(Sun)$	0.915	$E(Free)$	0.925
$E(Rain)$	0.758		

For each attribute calculated the information gain results such as shown in table 4:

Table 4. Experimental Data

$gain(Pop.)$	0.408	$gain(Area)$	0.650
$gain(Ani.)$	0.476	$gain(Temp.)$	-0.107
$gain(Sun)$	0.044	$gain(Free)$	0.034
$gain(Rain)$	0.201		

From the table 4 knowable, obtain information gain the biggest attribute is sowing area, namely sowing area for agricultural production value influence is the largest, so choose sowing area as classification decisions prediction model the roots of a tree. Similar to calculate, then can get classification rule decision tree figure 1:

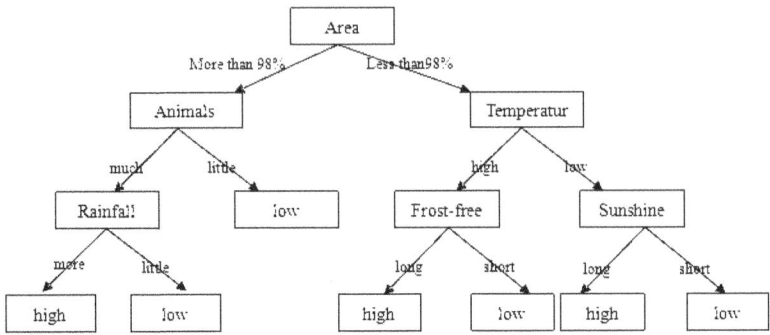

Fig. 1. The Decision Tree

3.3   Results and Analysis

Applying the above model and the decision tree algorithm for extracting from database to generate recording as test set of rules affect agricultural GDP, joined the rules the repository. Below is a list of several of the main rules:

1) IF area more than 98% and Animals have much and rainfall more THEN output is high

2) IF area more than 98% and Animals have much and rainfall little THEN output is low

3) IF area more than 98% and Animals litter THEN output is low

4) IF area less than 98% and Average is high and Frost-free is long THEN output is high

5) IF area less than 98% and Average is high and Frost-free is short THEN output is low

6) IF area less than 98% and Average is high and Sunshine is long THEN output is high

7) IF area less than 98% and Average is high and frost-free is short THEN output is low

Can see planting area of agricultural output value influence is the biggest, this is consistent with the reality. Because if no sowing area as a guarantee, so no matter how much influence other factors, agricultural output value is inevitably will be at a lower level. And we think in advance, what is different in which demographic factors is not too big effect. This also from another side said surface, with the development of The Times, LinXian of agricultural mechanization degree in raising, is gradually get rid of the past depend entirely on the manpower to production so that although investment in agricultural production in reducing the number of the labor force, but output but is instead ascension, this has caused some labor into other industries to development, promote the development of the overall economy.

4   Conclusion

In this articlethe ID3 algorithm is applicant to analysis various factors, which affect the Linxian County agriculture output. Using the decision tree theory, we analysis the primary data, and than the quite reasonable and effective data warehouse has built, the decision tree has been generate and trim by ID3 algorithm, we obtain the decision tree classification forecast model. It will provide suggestions for the government to arrange agricultural production.

Acknowledgments. This paper is supported by Natural Science Foundation of Shanxi Province (2008011039),Key Technologies *R&D* Programme of Shanxi Province (2007031129, 20080322008).

References

1. Han, J.: Micheline Data Mining and Technology. Machinery industry press, Beijing (2006)
2. Mao, G.: Data Mining Principles and Algorithms. Tsinghua university press, Beijing (2005)
3. Liu, S.: Data Mining Technology and Application. Tsinghua university press, Beijing (2005)
4. Lu, S., Wilhelm, R.: Automating tolerance synthesis: a framework and tools. J. Manuf. Syst. 10(4), 279–296 (1991)
5. Cheng, B., Maghsoodloo, S.: Optimization of mechanical assembly tolerances by incorporating Taguchi's quality loss function. J. Manuf. Syst. 14(4), 264–276 (1995)
6. Fisher, R.A.: The use of multiple measurements in taxonomic problems. Ann. Eugen. 7, 179–188 (1936)
7. Bhattacharjee, A.: Some aspects of mango (Mangifora Indica L) leaf growth features in varietal recognition. M.S. Thesis. Calcutta University, Calcutta, India (1986)
8. Editorial LinXian. LinXian fifty years (1999)

A Survey of Outlier Detection Methodologies and Their Applications

Zhixian Niu, Shuping Shi, Jingyu Sun, and Xiu He

College of Computer Science and Technology, Taiyuan University of Technology,
Taiyuan, Shanxi, China 030024
{niuzx,shiping201}@163.com, sunjingyu@tyut.edu.cn

Abstract. Outlier detection is a data analysis method and has been used to detect and remove anomalous observations from data. In this paper, we firstly introduced some current mainstream outlier detection methodologies, i.e. statistical-based, distance-based, and density-based. Especially, we analyzed distance-based approach and reviewed several kinds of peculiarity factors in detail. Then, we introduced sampled peculiarity factor (SPF) and a SPF-based outlier detection algorithm in order to explore a lower-computational complexity approach to compute peculiarity factor for real world needs in our future work.

Keywords: Outlier Detection, k^{th} nearest neighbor, SPF, SPF-Outlier Detection.

1 Introduction

Outlier detection refers to the problem of finding patterns in data that do not conform to expected behavior. These non-conforming patterns are often referred to as anomalies, discordant observations, exceptions, aberrations, surprises, peculiarities or contaminants in different application domains. Anomaly detection finds extensive use in a wide variety of applications such as fraud detection for credit cards, insurance or health care, intrusion detection for cyber-security, fault detection in safety critical systems, and military surveillance for enemy activities [1].

Many anomaly detection techniques have been specifically developed for certain application domains, while others are more generic. In this paper, we reviewed some outlier detection techniques and analyzed their computational complexity. Due to their higher computational complexity, we introduced sampled peculiarity factor (SPF) and SPF-Outlier detection algorithm.

2 Some Common Outlier Detection Methodologies

2.1 Statistical Based Outlier Detection

The underlying principle of any statistical anomaly detection technique is: "An outlier is an observation which is suspected of being partially or wholly irrelevant because it

H. Deng et al. (Eds.): AICI 2011, Part I, LNAI 7002, pp. 380–387, 2011.

is not generated by the stochastic model assumed" [1]. In literature [1], the author applied parametric and non-parametric techniques to fit a statistical model which was built for normal data to test the unseen instances. Parametric techniques assumed the knowledge of underlying distribution and estimated the parameters from the given data, for example, such techniques assume that the data is generated from a Gaussian distribution. The parameters are estimated using Maximum Likelihood Estimates (MLE). A simple outlier detection technique, often used in process quality control domain, is to declare all data instances that are more than 3δ distance away from the distribution mean μ, where δ is the standard deviation for the distribution. The $\mu\pm3\delta$ region contains 99.7% of the data instances [1, 8]. Of course, the normal data are belonged to different distribution, because of the trait of data, we should model diverse distribution.

Non-parametric techniques do not generally assume knowledge of underlying distribution, such that the model structure is not defined a prior, but is instead determined from given data.

The statistical outlier detection technique depends on the nature of statistical model that is required to be fitted on the data. The main problem with these approaches is that in a number of situations, the user might simply not have enough knowledge about the underlying data distribution [8].

2.2   Distance Based Outlier Detection

In order to overcome the disadvantage of statistical based, Knorr and Ng proposed the following distance-based definition for outliers that is both simple and intuitive as well as being computationally feasible for large sets of data points. This basic technique has been applied to detect land mines from satellite ground images and to detect shorted turns (anomalies) in the DC field windings of large synchronous turbine-generators [3,5].

Given a distance measure on a feature space, there are many different definitions of distance-based outliers. Four popular definitions are as follows:

1. Outliers are the examples for which are fewer than p other examples within distanced [5].

2. Outliers are the top n examples whose distance to the kth nearest neighbor is greatest [6].

3. Outliers are the top n examples whose average distance to the k nearest neighbors is greatest.

4. Outliers are the top n examples whose sum distance to the k nearest neighbors is greatest.

The first definition is the same to Knorr and Ng's which had some shortcomings, for example , it required a important parameter about distance d which would be hard to determine, in literature [6],the author modified the definition by neglecting d, and got the second definition. It was based on the distance of the kth nearest neighbor $D^k(p)$, with the maximum D^k as outliers. The definition of outlier was that given a k and n, a point p is an outlier if no more than n-1 other points in the data set have a higher value for D^k than p. At the same time, three different algorithms were introduced. The nested-loop algorithm scans the database for each point. For each point which maintains a list of the nearest points and was considered, a check is made to see if dist (p, q) is smaller than the distance of the k nearest neighbor found so far. If the check succeeds, q is included in the list of the k nearest neighbors for p (if the list has more than k neighbors, the point must be not outlier, so deleted it from the list). By computing for a block of points together the algorithm can be made I/O efficient. Even with the I/O optimization, computational complexity of nested-loop approach still requires $O(N^2)$. If the dimensionality of points is high, this is very expensive. So experts illustrated new way by using a spatial index like an R*-tree to substantially reduced distance computations. Supposing that we have calculated $D^k(p)$ for p by looking at a subset of the input points, the value that we have is clearly an upper bound for the actual $D^k(p)$. If the minimum distance between and the MBR of a node in the R*-tree exceeds the value that we have currently, none of the points in sub-tree rooted under the node will be among the nearest neighbors of p. This optimization lets us prune entire sub-trees containing points irrelevant to the k nearest neighbor search for p, then distance computations were decreased. But the cost of building was also very high. In order to improve the performance, partition-based algorithm was proposed to prune out points whose distances from their k nearest neighbors are so small that they cannot possibly make it to be outlier. Furthermore, by partitioning the data set, it is able to make this determination for a point without actually computing the precise value of $D^k(p)$. The results from a real-life NBA and synthetic data sets were shown that partition based algorithm scales well with respect to both data set size and data set dimensionality. Furthermore, it outperforms the nested-loop and index-based algorithms by more than an order of magnitude for a wide range of parameter settings.

In literature [10], a simple nested loop algorithm that in the worst case is quadratic which was shown can give near linear time performance when the data is in random order and a simple pruning rule is used. Calculating outlier score was using the third definition. But this algorithm depends on a random order, if the data is not in random order and is sorted then the performance can be poor.

2.3   Density Based Outlier Detection

Density based anomaly detection techniques are used to estimate the density of the neighborhood of each data instance. An instance which lies in a neighborhood with low density is declared to be anomalous while an instance that lies in a dense neighborhood is declared to be normal.

Breunig et al [1999, 2000] assign an anomaly score to a given data instance, known as Local Outlier Factor (LOF) which is widely used. For any given data instance, the LOF score is equal to ratio of average local density of the kth nearest neighbors of the instance and the local density of the data instance itself. For a normal instance lying in a dense region, its local density will be similar to that of its neighbors, while for an anomalous instance, its local density will be lower than that of its nearest neighbors. Hence the anomalous instance will get a higher LOF score [3].

Tang et al. [2002] discuss a variation of the LOF, which they call Connectivity-based Outlier Factor (COF). COF identifies outliers as points whose neighborhoods is sparser than the neighborhoods of their neighbors. The difference between LOF and COF is the manner that the k neighborhoods for an instance is computed. In COF, the neighborhood for an instance is computed in an incremental mode. The distance between an instance and a set of instances is defined as the minimum distance between the given instance and any instance belonging to the given set. The neighborhood is grown in this manner until it reaches size k. Once the neighborhood is computed, the anomaly score (COF) is computed in the same manner as LOF. In fact, COF is more complex than LOF.

In literature [2, 3] it was called LPF (local peculiarity factor).In order to comprehend the notion of LPF, we discussed Peculiarity Factor first, and then analyzed LPF in details.

A central notion of peculiarity oriented mining (POM) is the peculiarity factor (PF) introduced by Zhong et al [6, 7]. In particular, two levels of peculiarity can be identified, representing attribute peculiarity and record peculiarity. When compared with applications of POM, there is still a lack of theoretical and quantitative analysis of the sensitivity, reasonability, and applicability of the PF [4]. In literature [2] presented a theoretical analysis of the PF, and advanced the notion of Local Peculiarity Factor (LPF) and its application in outlier detection. Later, literature [3] further developed this notion to solve classification problem. For convenience, we reviewed two notions of peculiarity factor and analyzed computational complexity.

1) Peculiarity Factor(PF)

Two levels of PF can be identified, representing attribute PF (denoted by PFa) for one-dimensional data and record PF (denoted by PFr) for multi-dimensional data.

Definition 1. Suppose that $\{C_1, C_2, \cdots, C_n\}$ is a sample set with n points and each point $C_i = (C_{i1}, C_{i2}, \cdots, C_{im})$ is described by attributes $A_1, A_2, \cdots, A_m$. Then for the dataset, the attribute PF of the attribute value C_{ij} is defined by:

$$PF(C_{ij}) = \sum_{l=1}^{n} D(C_{ij}, C_{lj}) = \sum_{l=1}^{n} \left| C_{ij} - C_{lj} \right|^{\alpha} \tag{1}$$

where α is a parameter, $D(x_1, x_2)$ are such conceptual distances.

And for the dataset, the record PF of the point C_i is defined by:

$$PF(C_i) = \sum_{l=1}^{n} \sqrt{\sum_{j=1}^{m} \beta_j \times \left(PF(C_{ij}) - PF(C_{lj}) \right)^2} \tag{2}$$

The peculiarity factor is determined by the parameter α, which may be adjusted by users and $\alpha = 0.5$ is used as default. For the record PF, we also need the weights β_j's for attributes, which are given by users and $\beta_j = 1$ is used as default [2].

This is more consistent with the attribute PF. But if the attribute PF can accurately describe the peculiarity of the data on each attribute, we can simply define the record PF of a point by the weighted sum of the attribute PF values on all attributes, that is,

$$PF(Z_i) = \sum_{j=1}^{m} \beta_j \times PF(Z_{ij}) \tag{3}$$

But the PF value of a point with conceptual distances to all the other sample data cannot describe its location in the distribution accurately. A bit modification by defining the PF locally it can have more good properties, that is Local Peculiarity Factor.

2)   Local Peculiarity Factor(LPF)

Definition 2. Suppose that $\{C_1, C_2, \cdots, C_n\}$ is a sample set with n points and each point $C_i = (C_{i1}, C_{i2}, \cdots, C_{im})$ is described by attributes $A_1, A_2, \cdots, A_m$. Then for the dataset, the attribute LPF of the attribute value C_{ij} is defined by:

$$LPF(C_{ij}) = \sum_{C_{lj} \in N_k(C_{ij})} D(C_{ij}, C_{lj}) \tag{4}$$

Where α is a parameter and $N_k(C_{ij})$ is the set of k near neighbors of C_{ij} in the set $\{C_{1j}, C_{2j}, \cdots, C_{nj}\}$, that is, $N_k(C_{ij})$ consists of k near neighbors of C_i on attribute A_j. And the record LPF of the point C_i is defined by:

$$LPF(C_i) = \sum_{j=1}^{m} \beta_j LPF(C_{ij}) \tag{5}$$

where β_j is the weight of attribute A_j.

It is known from the above definition, computing the LPF and PF were time-consuming, because of repetitiveness computation. The computational complexity of all attributes' PF was O(m*n*n), while all attributes' LPF was O(m*n*(k+klogn)). It is obvious that the computational complexity is not fit for some application which requires higher real-time, so we introduced sample peculiarity factor to reduce computational complexity.

3   Sampled Peculiarity Factor(SPF) and SPF-Outlier Algorithm

From the view of statistic, because of fewer peculiarity data in the dataset, we can computer the LPF for every data point from a subset which contains many normal data. On the one hand, it can save computational complexity, on the other hand, the precision of identifying peculiarity data does not reduce so much. So we advanced the method of sampling to ameliorate the efficiency.

3.1   Sampled Peculiarity Factor(SPF)

Definition 3. Suppose that $T=\{C_1, C_2, \cdots, C_n\}$ is a sample set with n points and $S=\{S_1, S_2, \ldots, S_t\}$ is a sample subset from T, each point $S_i = (S_{i1}, S_{i2}, \cdots, S_{im})$ is described by attributes $A_1, A_2, \cdots, A_m$. Then for the dataset, the attribute SPF of the attribute value S_{ij} is defined by:

$$SPF(S_{ij}) = \sum_{S_l \in S} D(S_{ij}, S_{lj}) = \sum_{C_l \in S} |S_{ij} - S_{lj}|^{\alpha} \tag{6}$$

And for the dataset, the record SPF of the point S_i is defined by:

$$SPF(S_i) = \sum_{S_i \in S} \sqrt{\sum_{j=1}^{m} \beta_j (SPF(S_{ij}) - SPF(S_{lj}))^2} \qquad (7)$$

Eq7 can be predigested as follow:

$$SPF(S_i) = \sum_{j=1}^{m} \beta_j SPF(S_{ij}) \qquad (8)$$

Where parameter α, β_j, $D(x_1, x_2)$ are the same to equations which we mentioned before.

Due to the traits of peculiarity data which are a relatively small number of objects and very different from other objects in the dataset, in general, it is reasonable to use well-proportioned sampling method that the balance of selected subsets are better.

3.2 SPF-Outlier Detection Algorithm

Due to relative low computational complexity, we illustrated anomaly detection algorithm based SPF which was more suitable for identifying online outlier. Computational complexity of this algorithm is O (mnt+nlogn); mnt is the part for computering SPF while nlogn is the part for sorting. We give the anomaly detection algorithm based on SPF as follow.

INPUT dataset $T = \{C_1, C_2, \ldots C_n\}$, $S = \{S_1, S_2, \ldots S_n\}$, the parameter q determining the number of outliers.

OUTPUT   q Outliers

PROCEDURE

(1) for   i = 1 to n.

(2) calculate the SPF value of S_i, SPF(S_i) according to Eq6 and Eq8.

(3) end for.

(4) Sort SPF(S_i)s in descending order, and mark data points corresponding to the former q ones as outliers.

For the application which has high demand for real-time, it is much better to choose Linear Sampling which can save CPU time for sampling.

3.3 Experiment

In order to evaluate the effectiveness of SPF and SPF-Outlier detection algorithm, we compare these detection algorithm based on PF, LPF and SPF by experiment. We use UCI datasets which provides real dataset as experiment dataset.

We introduce the concept of receive operating characteristic curve (ROC) and area under the curve (AUC), which have been used to evaluate the performance of outlier detection algorithms [8,9]. The AUC is the area under the ROC curve. The ideal ROC curve has 0% false alarm rate and 100% detection rate. However, the ideal ROC curve can only be approximated in practice and AUC quantitatively evaluate the approximation. Outlier detection algorithms with AUC closer to 1 have ROC closer to the ideal ROC, and are better algorithms [2].

We implemented UCI dataset-the Shuttle dataset which consists of 14500 instances with label 1, 2, 3, 4, 5, 6 or 7, and each record has 9 numerical attributes. We created five data sets by selecting classes 2, 3, 5, 6 and 7 to be detected as outliers compared to the biggest remaining class 1.

From the experiment, we know that AUC acquired from LPF-Outlier algorithm is highest, while occupancy CPU time in different ratio of sample from SPF-Outlier are relative low. When the ratio of sample exceed 0.4, its AUC surpass the AUC acquired from PF-Outlier. When the ratio of sample is 0.05, their AUC are mainly the same, but occupancy CPU time of the SPF-Outlier algorithm only has 1/20 and 1/30 of other two algorithm.

Based on previous analysis, the definition of SPF and the results of experiment, all of these showed that SPF-Outlier is effective in reducing the computational complexity, and enhancing the performance.

4   Conclusion

In this paper, we tried to provide a structured and comprehensive overview of the research on outlier detection technology. Several outlier detection technologies were reviewed which are based on statistics, distance, and density. We analyzed distance based and density based in details, especially for the kth nearest neighbor which was used in lots of literatures combining with top n approach to calculate the outlier score and LPF or LOF. Local peculiarity factor (LPF) are important concepts employed to describe the peculiarity of points in POM, but it had higher computational complexity. In order to overcome this problem, we introduced a sampled approach and a SPF-Outlier detection algorithm which were proved efficient in reducing the computational complexity, and enhancing the performance with losing a few precisions both theory and experiment. Furthermore, some right sampling methods could be used to computer SPFs in order to meet real-time requirement.

References

1. Chandola, V., Banerjee, A., Kumar, V.: Anomaly detection: a survey. ACM Computing Survey 41(3), 1–54 (2009)
2. Yang, J., Zhong, N., Yao, Y.Y., et al.: Local peculiarity factor and its application in outlier detection. In: Proceedings of the 14th ACM SIGKDD International Conference on Knowledge Discovery and Data Mining, pp. 776–784. The ACM, Nevada (2008)
3. Yang, J., Zhong, N., Yao, Y.Y., et al.: Peculiarity analysis for classifications. In: Proceedings of the 2009 IEEE International Conference on Data Mining, pp. 607–616. IEEE Computer Society, Washington, DC, USA (2009)
4. Zhong, N., Yao, Y.Y., Ohshima, M., Ohsuga, S.: Interestingness peculiarity, and multi-database mining. In: Proceedings of the 2001 IEEE International Conference on Data Mining, pp. 566–573 (2001)
5. Knorr, E., Ng, R.: Algorithms for mining distance-based outliers in large datasets. In: Proceedings of the 12th International Conference on Very Large Data Bases, pp. 392–403 (1998)

6. Ramaswamy, S., Rastogi, R., Kyuseok, S.: Efficient algorithms for mining outliers from large data sets. In: Proceedings of the 2000 ACM SIGMOD International Conference on Management of Data, pp. 427–438 (2000)
7. Zhong, N., Ohshima, M., Ohsuga, S.: Peculiarity oriented mining and its application for knowledge discovery in amino-acid data. In: Cheung, D., Williams, G.J., Li, Q. (eds.) PAKDD 2001. LNCS (LNAI), vol. 2035, pp. 260–269. Springer, Heidelberg (2001)
8. Xue, A.: Study on Spatial Outlier Mining. Zhen Jiang, Jiang Su University (2008)
9. Chen, B., Chen, S., Pan, Z., et al.: Survey of outlier detection technologies. Journal of Shandong University, Engineering Science 39(6), 13–23 (2009)
10. Bay, S.D., Mark, S.: Mining distance-based outliers in near linear time with randomization and a simple Pruning rule. In: Proc. of the ACM SIGMOD Int'1 Conf. on Knowledge Discovery and Data Mining, pp. 29–38 (2003)

Discovering Association Rules Change from Large Databases

Feiyue Ye[1], Jixue Liu[2], Jin Qian[1], and Yuxi Shi[1]

[1] Jiangsu Teachers University of Technology
Changzhou, China
{yfy,qj}@jstu.edu.cn
[2] School of Computer and Information Science University of South Australia
Adelaide, Australia
Jixue.liu@unisa.edu.au

Abstract. Discovering association rules and association rules change (ARC) from existing large databases is an important problem. This paper presents an approach based on multi-hash chain structures to mine association rules change from large database with shorter transactions. In most existing algorithms of association rules change, the mining procedure is divided into two phases, first, association rules sets are discovered using existing algorithm for mining association rules, and then the association rules sets are mined to obtain the association rules change. Those algorithms do not deal with the integration effect to mine association rules and association rules change. In addition, most existing algorithms relate only to the single trend of association rules change. This paper presents an approach which mines both association rules and association rules change and can mine the various trends of association rules change from a multi-hash chain structure. The approach needs only to scan the database twice in the whole mining procedure, so it has lower I/O spending. Experiment results show that the approach is effective to mine association rules using the multi-hash chain structure. The approach has advantages over the Fp-growth and Apriori algorithm in mining frequent pattern or association rules from large databases with shorter transaction. Besides, the experiment results also show that the approach is effective for mining association rules change and it has better flexibility. The application study indicates the approach can mine and obtain the practicable association rules change.

Keywords: Data mining, Association rules, Association rules change.

1 Introduction

The rapid advancement of the computer technology has driven the applications of computer information management system in every walk of life. A large amount of data has been accumulated in databases. These data is a gold mine of knowledge, which has proved invaluable in helping various decision-making processes. So how to discover the knowledge and how to discover the knowledge effectively became an important research area in computer science. Mining association rules is an important

H. Deng et al. (Eds.): AICI 2011, Part I, LNAI 7002, pp. 388–395, 2011.
© Springer-Verlag Berlin Heidelberg 2011

task of data mining. Existing research work for association rules mining focuses mainly on the efficiency of the mining methods [4-6], whereas the quality of the mined association rules has received little attention. An example of the importance of data mining quality is time-series databases. In these databases, the intensity of the association rules may change with time. This leads to the problem that the association rules derived from existing algorithms may not be applicable in future situations. Therefore, the application of association rules can be difficult. On the other hand, existing association rule mining algorithms cannot identify the trends of association rules so that some useful rules might be overlooked. So how mining association rules change has become an important issue. Researchers have put forwards some effective methods for mining association rules or frequent pattern change [1-3], but many problems still need to study. For example, how can association rules and association rules change be mined synthetically? How can all trends of association rules change be mined once? Aiming at solving these problems, this paper proposes an approach based on the multi-hash chain structures and the techniques of the artificial neural networks to mine association rules changes synthetically. With this algorithm, both the association rules and various trends of the association rules can be mined.

In [7], the framework of method for integrated mining association rules and association rules change is given. This article improves partially the method and provides much more details about the method for association rules and association rules change mining, and complements experiment results is showed. In addition, the application where the proposed method will be used is detailed.

2 Constructing Multi-Hash Chain

2.1 Hash Function

The hash function of the item i_{k_j} (where k_j is item number) in 1-frequent itemsets is given below:

$$h(k_j)=k_j \tag{1}$$

Let the item number of n-itemsets $X=i_1 i_2 \ldots i_n$ be $B=\{1,2,\ldots,n\}$, again let $X'=i_{k1} i_{k2} \ldots i_{km}$ be one of the subset of item X, the set of item number of X' be $B'=\{k_1,k_2,\ldots,k_m\}$, then $X' \subseteq X$ and $B' \subseteq B$, then The hash function of multi-item itemsets of X' is given below:

$$h(k_1,k_2,\cdots,k_m) = (\sum_{i=1}^{m} \alpha(k_i)) \bmod p \tag{2}$$

Where $\alpha(k_i)$ may be select from 2^{k_i-1} and $2k_i-1$ and 10^{k_i-1}, P is a prime number.

2.2 The Hash Chain Structure

Definition 1. Let $I=\{i_1, i_2, \cdots, i_m\}$ be a set of all items in a transaction database $D=<T_1,T_2,\cdots,T_n>$, where $T_i (i \in [1 \cdots n])$ is a transaction which contains a set of items in I. Let B be a sub itemset of I. The *support* to B, denoted by *sup(B)*, by D is the number of transactions in D containing B. B is frequent if *sup(B)* is no less than a predefined minimum support threshold [4]. If the number of items in B is n, n is called the *cardinality* of B and B is called a n-frequent itemset.

Definition 2. Let $I' = \{i_{p_1}, i_{p_2}, \cdots, i_{p_m}\}$ be the set of items in all 1-frequent itemsets. Let X_k be k^{th} transaction of the database. The projection of X_k to I' is $A_k = I' \cap X_k = \{i_{q_1}^k, i_{q_2}^k, \cdots, i_{q_{n_1}}^k\}$. Then the projection of D to I' is $A = \{A_1, A_2, \cdots, A_N\}$, called the 1-frequent database A.

Chain address	pointer

Fig. 1. The node structure of head table

$Count_1$	...	$Count_n$	pointer

Fig. 2. The node structure of chain table 1-item hash chain

Countset	Gcountset	$X_{(m)}$	pointer

Fig. 3. The node structure of chain table of multi-item hash chain

The hash chain structure consists of a head table of a multi-hash chain, the head table of the chain table and chain table nodes. The head table of multi-hash chain is used to save the cardinality of an itemset and the pointer to corresponding hash chain. Figure 1 shows the head table of chain table. Figure 2 shows the chain table node of the 1-item hash chain, where the "$count_i$" (i=1, 2, $\cdots$,n) stands for the support in the ith partition of 1-frequent item. The figure 4 shows the chain table node of the multi-item hash chain, in figure 3, where the *Countset* equals {count$_1$, count$_2$, $\cdots$,count$_n$}, it stands for the set of the direct count of itemset $X_{(m)}$ from the 1-frequent itemset projection in the each partition, the G*count$_i$* equals {Gcount$_1$, Gcount$_2$, $\cdots$, Gcount$_n$} stands for the count of itemset $X_{(m)}$ generating from the all 1-frequent itemset projection in each partition.

2.3 The Algorithm of Constructing Multi-Hash Chain

Definition 3. Let X be an itemset and k be a positive integer. All subsets of X with cardinality k are denoted by $X'=Subsets$ (X, k).

The algorithm for constructing multi-hash chain (CMHashChain) consists of two step. Firstly, the 1-item hash chain of the 1-frequent itemset and the multi-hash chain of the projection transaction of 1-frequent itemsets is constructed, and then the projection transaction of 1-frequent itemsets is recursively processed for forming multi-item hash chain structure. It is simple to construct the 1-item hash chain of frequent itemset according to formula (1), it is omitted. The algorithm to construct multi-item hash chain is as follow:

Algorithm 1. CMHashChain1

```
Input: the transaction database D, min_support
Output: multi-hash chain structure of the projection transaction
of 1-frequent itemsets
1)   Partitioning the projected database D into D₁, D₂, ···, Dₙ
according to time period t₁, t₂, ···, tₙ;
2)   Scanning D₁, D₂, ···, Dₙ and obtain the 1-frequent itemsets
I'₁, I'₂, ···, I'ₙ respectively;
3)   For (n'=1, to n, n'++) do begin;
4)     Forall transaction in D do begin;
5)         Aₙ' = I'ₙ' ∪ Xₙ' = {i_{q₁}, i_{q₂}, ···, i_{q_{n1}}} ;
6)         hash(h(Aₙ') , |Aₙ'|, n', 1);
7)     End
8)   End
```

Fig. 4. The algorithm of CMHashChain1

Algorithm 2. CMHashChain2

```
Input: multi-hash chain structure of the projection transaction
of 1-frequent itemsets
Output: multi-hash chain structure
1)   M=max(cardinality of itemset in the hash chain)
2)   For (m=M, to 3, m--) do begin;
3)     Forall nodes in n-item hash chain do begin
4)         read Countset, X_{(m)};
5)         If ∃j (1≤j≤n) count_j≥1 then
6)           GenerateMulti-itemHashchain (X_{(m)}, m, Countset);
7)         Endif
8)     End
9)   End
```

Fig. 5. The algorithm of CMHashChain2

GenerateMulti-itemHashchain ($A_{n'}$, $|A_{n'}|$, *Countset*)

```
1)   h(Aₙ') = (∑_{j=1}^{|Aₙ'|} α(i_{qⱼ})) mod p ;
2)   Hash(h(Aₙ'), |Aₙ'|, Countset);
3)   RecursionCalculate(Aₙ' , |Aₙ'|, Countset);
4)   Return
```

Fig. 6. The algorithm of generate multi-hash chain

RecursionCalculate($A_{n'}$, $/A_{n'}/$, Countset))

```
1) For (i =/Aₙ·/, to 3, i --) do begin
2)      forall X=Subset(Aₙ·, i) do begin//definition 4
3)         GenerateMulti-itemHashchain ( X, i ,Countset);
4)      End
5)   End
6) Return
```

Fig. 7. The algorithm to generate subset recursively

The main algorithm to construct the multi-hash chain structure is shown in figure 4. The algorithm for generating multi-item hash structure and generating subset recursively are showed figure 6 and figure 7 respectively. The *Hash* ($h(A_{n'})$, $/A_{n'}/$, n', 1) stands for constructing the hash chain table at address $h(A_{n'})$ in $/A_{n'}/$-item hash chain and the count is add 1 in n'^{th} time period. The Hash($h(A_{n'})$, $/A_{n'}/$, Countset) stands for constructing the hash chain table at address $h(A_{n'})$ in $/A_{n'}/$-item hash chain and the count contained in *Gcountset* is add by corresponding partition count in the *Countset*.

3   Mining Association Rules Change

Lemma 1. if itemsets X is global frequent, then it is frequent at least in one segment $D_i (1 \leq i \leq n)$.

Definition 4. Let the support and confidence of rule $X_1 \rightarrow X_2$ from $D_1, D_2, \cdots, D_n$ be sup_1, sup_2, $\cdots$, sup_n and $conf_1$, $conf_2$, $\cdots$, $conf_n$ respectively. If $\exists i$ ($1 \leq i \leq n$)   make $sup_i \geq min\_sup$ and $conf_i \geq min\_conf$, then the support association rules change m_s from $D_1, D_2, \cdots, D_n$ is given below:

$X_1 \rightarrow X_2$:{ $sup_0, sup_1, \cdots, sup_n$}

And the confidence association rule change m_c from $D_1, D_2, \cdots, D_n$ is given below:

$X_1 \rightarrow X_2$:{ $conf_0, conf_1, \cdots, conf_n$}

Apriori property. All nonempty subsets of a frequent itemset must also be frequent.

Lemma 2. By the Apriori property, if the multi-hash chain has be constructed, then all subsets of the frequent itemsets that appear in n-itemsets hash chain must also appear in corresponding 1-itemsets to (n-1)-itemsets hash chain.

According to above definition, lemma and property, the algorithm for mining association rules change is given in the following:

Algorithm 2. The algorithm for mining ARC (ARC algorithm)

Input: Multi-hash chain structure; support threshold min_sup and confidence threshold min_conf.

Output: the set of ARC

```
1)  Ms= ∅ ; Mc= ∅  //Support and confidence change set
2)  For (i =2, to n, i++) do begin
3)    Forall i-items hash chain do begin
4)      Forall hash chain node do begin
5)        Read itemset X and each part support (sup₁, sup₂ ···, supₖ )
6)        If ∃ j (1≤j≤k) make supⱼ≥ min_sup then
7)          Forall subset of X do begin
8)            forming support change rule mₛ
9)            If ∃ j (1≤j≤k) make confⱼ≥ min_conf then
10)             forming confidence change rule mᴄ
11)           endif
12)           Ms=Ms∪mₛ; Mc= Mc∪mᴄ;
13)       Endif
14)     End
15)   End
16) End
17) Return Ms, Mc
```

Fig. 8. The algorithm for mining ARC

The algorithm for mining ARC is showed in figure 8, all the itemsets and the each part support are read and the association rules support change and association rules confidence change are formed by definition 4.

4   Performance Study for Mining Frequent Pattern and Association Rules Based on Multi-hash Chain Structure

To evaluate the efficiency of the algorithm for mining frequent pattern and association rules, we conducted some experiments. All experiments are conducted on a 2.0 GHz AMD HP machine with 2.0G of main memory, running Microsoft Windows XP. The algorithm is implemented in Visual C++6.0. While the version of Apriori and FP-growth that we used is available at http://fuzzy.cs.uni-magdeburg.de/~borgelt/. All reports of the runtime of these algorithms include both the time of constructing corresponding structure and mining frequent itemsets or association rules or association rules change. They also include both CPU time and I/O time. We use two kind datasets in the experiments, that is, the datasets generated by data generator and a real word dataset. The parameter D, P and I stands for total transaction number, total pattern number and total item number respectively. For example, the D100kP10000I10 stands for 100K transactions, 10000 patterns and 10K items. The average length of the all transaction which is generated by data generator is five.

We do comparatively some experiments to analysis the performance of the algorithm based on multi-hash chain structure. For convenience we call the algorithm for mining frequent pattern based on multi-hash chain structure as MHC. Figure 9 shows the runtime of the three algorithms on data set D100P10000I10. When the

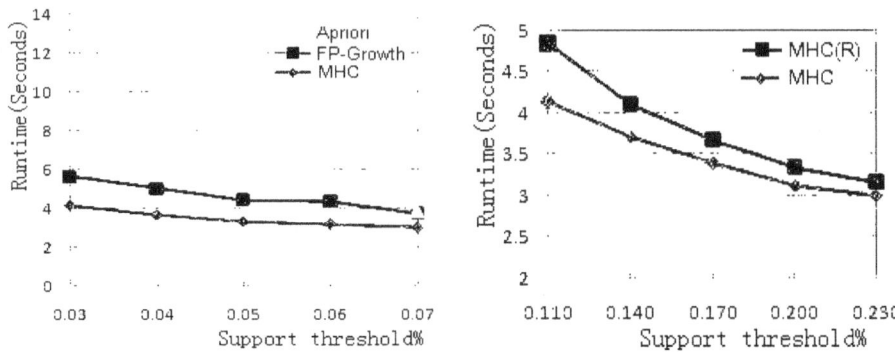

Fig. 9. Runtime on data set D100kP10000I10   **Fig. 10.** Experiment on data set D100kP2000I2

support threshold is high, Apriori and FP-growth and MHC have similar performance. When the support threshold becomes low, FP-growth and MHC is much faster than Apriori. In all cases, MHC is the fastest one.

Figure 10 shows the runtime of mining the frequent pattern and association rules using multi-hash chain structure respectively. The MHC stands for algorithm for mining frequent pattern and the MHC(R) stands for algorithm for mining association rules, the experiment result shows MHC(R) is effective, that is, the time spending for forming association rules from the multi-hash chain structure is not excessive on the given dataset.

Table 1. The result for mining ARC and classing

Rule	Support and confidence (%)	Part 1	Part 2	Part 3	Part 4	Type of rule
22799=>	Support	0.54	0.54	0.51	0.32	2
52499	confidence	12	14	23	13	5
52406=>	Support	0.23	0.25	0.37	0.61	1
52407	confidence	14	17	21	29	1
52407=>	Support	0.23	0.25	0.37	0.61	1
52406	confidence	19	27	28	32	1
52406=>	Support	0.18	0.12	0.25	0.36	1
52499	confidence	15	13	19	18	4
52407=>	Support	0.28	0.22	0.45	0.77	5
52499	confidence	17	15	26	20	3

5   Application Study

We made application study on a dataset of the chain supermarket (from Oct. 1996 to April 1997) to verify the practicability of the approach for mining ARC. Firstly, dataset is divided into four parts by the transaction time. And then we use the ARC algorithm to mine the ARC and use the artificial neural networks to classify the ARC and obtain the classified rules. The artificial neural networks are trained according to five classes including ascend, decline, stabilization, basic stabilization, randomization and it is used to classify ARC into five classes. The table 1 shows partial result. The support threshold and confidence threshold is 0.30% and 15% respectively. In Table 1, we can see that is ascending for the ARC between 52407 (Coca Cola) and 52406 (Sprite). Thus it can be seen that our approach can mine and obtained the practicable rules from the real world dataset. In Table 1, the 1, 2, 3, 4, 5 stand for ascend, decline, stabilization, basic stabilization and randomization respectively.

6 Conclusion

This paper presents the approach for mining association rules change from large transaction databases with shorter transactions, Experiment results show that our approach is effective for mining association rule change. The application study shows our approach can obtain some different change tend association rules by mining once, so our approach has advantages over existing approaches for mining association rule change from large transaction database with shorter transaction.

Acknowledgment. This work was supported in part by the Jiangsu Science Foundation of University (No. 08KJD520006).

References

1. Bing, L., Wynne, H., Ming, Y.: Discovering the Set of Fundamental Rule Changes. In: Proceedings of the ACM SIGKDD International Conference on Knowledge Discovery & Data Mining, pp. 335–340 (2001)
2. Tanbeer, S.K., Ahmed, C.F., Jeong, B.-S., Lee, Y.-K.: Discovering Periodic-Frequent Patterns in Transactional Databases. In: Theeramunkong, T., Kijsirikul, B., Cercone, N., Ho, T.-B. (eds.) PAKDD 2009. LNCS(LNAI), vol. 5476, pp. 242–253. Springer, Heidelberg (2009)
3. Wai, H.A., Keith, C.C.: Mining changes in association rules: a fuzzy approach. Fuzzy Sets and Systems 149, 87–140 (2005)
4. Agrawal, R., Srikant, R.: Fast algorithms for mining association rules. In: Proc. VLDB 1994, pp. 487–499 (1994)
5. Han, J., Pei, J., Yin, Y., et al.: Mining frequent patterns without candidate generation: a frequent-pattern tree approach. Data Mining and Knowledge Discovery 8, 53–87 (2004)
6. Yen, S.-J., Lee, Y.-S., Wang, C.-K., Wu, J.-W., Ouyang, L.-Y.: The Studies of Mining Frequent Patterns Based on Frequent Pattern Tree. In: Theeramunkong, T., Kijsirikul, B., Cercone, N., Ho, T.-B. (eds.) PAKDD 2009. LNCS (LNAI), vol. 5476, pp. 232–241. Springer, Heidelberg (2009)
7. Ye, F., Wang, J., Wu, S., Chen, H., Huang, T., Tao, L.: An Integrated Approach for Mining Meta-rules. In: Perner, P., Imiya, A. (eds.) MLDM 2005. LNCS (LNAI), vol. 3587, pp. 549–557. Springer, Heidelberg (2005)

Discovery of Direct and Indirect Sequential Patterns with Multiple Minimum Supports in Large Transaction Databases

Weimin Ouyang and Qinhua Huang

Modern Education Technology Center,
Shanghai University of Political Science and Law
201701 Shanghai, China
{oywm,hqh}@shupl.edu.cn

Abstract. Sequential patterns mining is an important research topic in data mining and knowledge discovery. The objective of mining sequential patterns is to find out frequent sequences based on the user-specified minimum support threshold, which implicitly assumes that all items in the data have similar probability distribution. This is often not the case in real-life applications. If the frequencies of items vary a great deal, we will suffer the dilemma called the rare item problem. In order to resolve the dilemma, an algorithm to discover sequential patterns with multiple minimum supports model is proposed, which can specify a different minimum item support for different item. The algorithm can not only discover sequential patterns formed between frequent sequences, but also discover sequential patterns formed either between frequent sequence and rare sequence or among rare sequences only. Moreover, an algorithm for mining direct and indirect sequential patterns with multiple minimum supports is designed simultaneously.

Keywords: multiple supports, data mining, sequential patterns.

1 Introduction

Sequential patterns mining is an important research topic in data mining and knowledge discovery, which is firstly proposed by R. Agrawal [1]. While association rules mining is to find the intra-transaction relations, sequential patterns mining is to find the inter-transactions relations. A sequential pattern is formed as ⟨AB⟩ , where A and B are disjoint item sets, and its support is no less than a user-specified minimum support.

Inspired by the idea of indirect association rules [2], we set forth the concept of indirect sequential patterns. Consider a pair of item x and y, which are rarely present together in a transaction sequences. If both items are highly dependent on the presence of another itemsets M, then the pair of x and y is said to be indirectly associated by M, called as mediator.

H. Deng et al. (Eds.): AICI 2011, Part I, LNAI 7002, pp. 396–403, 2011.
© Springer-Verlag Berlin Heidelberg 2011

Since the indirect sequential patterns discovery problem has been proposed, we call traditional sequential patterns as direct sequential patterns for convenience in this paper.

The user-specified minimum support threshold is a key element of mining sequential patterns, which is used to prune the search space and to limit the number of rules generated. Using only a single minimum support implicitly assumes that all items in the database have similar frequencies in the database. This is often not true in real-life applications. In many applications, some items appear frequently, while others appear rarely. If the frequencies of items vary a great deal, we will suffer the dilemma of rare item problem. If minsup is too high, we will not discover those sequential patterns that involve rare items in the data. If minsup is too low, in order to discover sequential patterns that involve both frequent and rare items, it will cause combinatorial explosion because those frequent items will be associated with one another in all possible ways and many of them are meaningless.

In order to conquer the rare item problem, Liu [3] expanded the existing association rule model to allow user to specify a different minimum item support for each item, which is calculated for each item based on the percentage of its support. Although this percentage-based approach can improve the performance over single minsup based approaches, it still suffers from both "rule missing" and "rule explosion" problems, because the minimum item support for each item is calculated by its support multiplied with a uniform percentage.

In order to improve the method proposed by Liu [3], we calculate the minimum item support for each item by a monotonous decreasing power function such as $\dfrac{1}{\sqrt{x}}$ instead of the uniform percentage.

Consequently, the difference between the minimum item support for each item and its support will vary in an expected way. For the frequent items, the difference is small; while for the rare items, the difference is large. Thus, the minimum item support for frequent item is slightly less than its support, and the minimum item support for rare item is much lower than its support.

In this paper, we combine these two extensions to propose a novel approach to mining both direct and indirect sequential patterns with multiple minimum supports.

The rest of the paper is organized as follows. The definitions for direct and indirect sequential patterns with multiple minimum supports are given in Section 2. In Section 3, we describe the discovery algorithm for mining direct and indirect sequential patterns with multiple minimum supports. Section 4 presents our primary experimental results. The conclusions are made in the last section.

2 Problem Definition

2.1 Sequential Patterns

Let $I = \{i_1, i_2, \ldots, i_m\}$ be a set of literals called items. Let the database $D = \{ t_1, t_2, \ldots, t_n \}$ be a set of transactions, where each transaction is a subset of I. A non-empty subset of I is called itemset. An itemset containing k items is called k-itemste. The support of an itemset X, denoted as sup(X), is defined as the number of transactions containing X in D. An itemset is frequent if its support is greater than a user-specified threshold of minsup.

A sequence is an ordered list of itemsets such as s = $\langle s_1\ s_2\ ...s_u \rangle$, where each itemset s_i is an element of the sequence. An item can appear only once in an itemset, but can occur multiple times in different itemsets of a sequence. Items in an itemset are assumed to be sorted in lexicographical order. A sequence with k items, where $k = \sum_j | s_j |$, is called a k-sequence, where $| s_j |$ denotes the number of items in itemset s_j.

A sequence t = $\langle t_1 t_2\ ...\ t_v \rangle$ is called a subsequence of s = $\langle s_1 s_2\ ...\ s_u \rangle$ if there exist integer $1 \le j_1 < j_2 < ... < j_v \le u$, such that $t_1 \subseteq s_{j_1}$, $t_2 \subseteq s_{j2}$, $\cdots$, $t_v \subseteq s_{j_v}$. A sequence database SD is a set of tuple (sid,t), where sid is the sequence identifier and t is a sequence. A tuple (sid,t) is said to contain a sequence s if s is a subsequence of t. The support of a sequence s, sup(s), is defined as the number of tuples in the sequence database SD containing sequence s. A sequence is frequent if the support of the sequence is no less than the predefined minimum support threshold minsup. The maximally large sequences are called sequential patterns.

The algorithm proposed by Agrawal and Srikant to mine sequential patterns from large transaction databases is divided into five phases [1]: (1) Sort phase. The transaction database is sorted by customer ID as the major key and transaction time as the minor key. The phase converts the original transaction database into a database of customer sequences; (2) Large itemset phase. The set of all the large itemsets are found from the customer sequences database by the similar method with the process of mining association rules. Note that the counting of itemset is for customer sequence not for transaction. When an itemset occurs more than one time in a customer sequence, it is counted just once for this customer sequence. (3) Transformation phase. In this phase, each large itemset is mapped to a contiguous integer and the original customer sequences are transformed into the mapped integer sequences. (4) Sequence phase. The set of transformed integer sequences are used to find large sequences among them. (5) Maximum phase. The maximally large sequences are derived and output to users.

2.2 Indirect Sequential Patterns

Inspired by the idea of indirect associations, we put forward the concept of indirect sequential patterns. As a result, traditional sequential pattern is called as direct sequential pattern.

Let sequence s_1 be $\langle a_1 a_2\ ...\ a_k \rangle$, and sequence s_2 be $\langle b_1 b_2...b_k \rangle$. The indirect sequential pattern is defined as follows:

Definition 1. The pair of sequences s_1 and s_2 is said to be joinable if one of the following conditions is hold:

(1) $a_i = b_i$ for i = 1,2, ... ,k-1;
(2) $a_i = b_i$ for i = 2,3, ... ,k;
(3) $a_i = b_{i-1}$ for i = 2, 3... ,k;

In the context of indirect sequential patterns, we set $a_k = x$, $b_k = y$, $\langle a_1 a_2 \ldots a_{k-1} \rangle$ = M if condition (1) is satisfied; or set $a_1 = x$, $b_1 = y$, $\langle a_2 a_3 \ldots a_k \rangle$ = M, $s_1 = Mx$, $s_2 = My$, if condition (2) is satisfied; or set $a_1 = x$, $b_k = y$, $\langle a_1 a_2 \ldots a_{k-1} \rangle$ = M, $s_1 = xM$, $s_2 = yM$, if condition (3) is satisfied, and $s_1 = xM$, $s_2 = My$.

Definition 2. A pair of itemsets x and y is said to be a indirect sequential pattern via a mediator sequence M, if $s_1 = Mx$(or $s_1 = xM$), $s_2 = My$(or $s_2 = yM$) and the following conditions are satisfied:

(1) sup($\langle xy \rangle$)$<t_s$;
(2) There exists a non-empty set M such that:
  (a) sup(s_1)$>=t_f$, sup(s_2)$>=t_f$,
  (b) dep(x, M)$>=t_d$, dep(y, M)$>=t_d$, where dep(A, B) is a measure of the dependence between itemsets A and B.

The thresholds t_s, t_f and t_d are called sequencepair support threshold, mediator support threshold, and dependence threshold, respectively. We usually set $t_f >= t_s$ in practice.

In this paper, we use the denotation $\langle xyM \rangle$ to represent the indirect sequential pattern between itemsets x and y via mediator M, and use the IS measure [4] as the dependence measure for condition 2(b). Given a pair of itemsets A and B, its IS measure can be computed as the following equation:

$$IS(A,B) = \frac{P(A,B)}{\sqrt{P(A) \times P(B)}}$$

where P represents the probability that the given itemsets appears in the transaction database.

2.3 Multiple Minimum Supports

In multiple minimum supports model, every item i_j of the itemset $I = \{i_1, i_2, \ldots, i_m\}$ has been assigned a minimum item support based on its support value sup(i_j), denoted as mis(i_j), and LS is denoted as predefined least minimum support.

Definition 3: the minimum item support of an item i_j is defined as

$$mis(i_j) = \begin{cases} m(i_j) & \text{if } m(i_j) > LS \\ LS & \text{otherwise} \end{cases}$$

$$m(i_j) = \sup(i_j) - \frac{1}{\sqrt{\sup(i_j)}}$$

Definition 4: The minimum support for a sequence X is the minimum of minimum supports of the items contained in the sequence, denoted as mis(X).

Definition 5: A sequence X is said to be frequent if $\sup(X) \geq mis(X)$.

3   Discovery Algorithm for Mining DIRECT and INDIRECT Sequential Patterns with Multiple Minimum Supports

By extensions of the indirect and the multiple minimum supports, we proposed an algorithm for mining direct and indirect sequential patterns with multiple minimum supports. The algorithm generates frequent sequences by making multiple passes over the data set. However, in contrary to single minsup approaches which follow "downward closure property" (all the subsets of a frequent sequence are frequent), multiple minimum support approaches follow "sorted closure property". Note that the items in an sequence are arranged in increasing order of their MIS values from left to right. Notations used in this algorithm are described as Table 1.

Algorithm. MDISP(Mining Both Direct and indirect Sequential Patterns with Multiple Minimum Supports)
Input: Database D, Least minimum support LS;
Output: Set of direct sequential patterns SDSP, set of indirect sequential patterns SISP;
Begin

(1) SDSP = $\varnothing$; SISP = $\varnothing$;
(2) C_1 = {candidate 1-sequence};

(3) For each sequence $c \in C_1$ do $m(c) = \sup(c) - \dfrac{1}{\sqrt{\sup(c)}}$;

(4) If m(c)<LS mis(c) = LS Else mis(c) = m(c);
(5) F_1={ c| c $\in$ C_1 $\wedge$ sup(c)>=mis(c)};
(6) F_1 = sort(F_1, MIS);
(7) SDSP = SDSP $\cup$ F_1; S_1= $\varnothing$;
(8) For (k=2;F_{k-1} $\neq \varnothing$;k++) {
(9) C_k = Candiate_Gen(F_{k-1});
(10)   For each transaction sequence t in D do {
(11)   Temp$_t$ = k-sequence in both t and C_k;
(12)   For each itemset i in Temp$_t$ do i.count++;
(13)   }
(14) F_k = {c| c $\in$ C_k $\wedge$ sup(c)>=mis(c)};
(15) S_k = C_k − F_k;
(16)   for each S $\in$ S_k {
(17)   x = last_itemset(S);
(18)   y = secondlast_itemset(S);
(19)   M = S − {x,y};
(20)   if (sup(x, y)<t_s AND dep({x},M)>=t_d AND dep({x},M)>=t_d)
(21)   SISP = SISP $\cup$ {<x, y, M>};
(22)   }
(23)   SDSP = SDSP $\cup$ F_k;
(24) }
End.

Table 1. Notations

Notation	meaning
tn	The total number of transactions in database
tm	The total number of items
tc	The total number of customers
C_k	the set of candidate itemsets with k items
L_k	the set of large itemsets with k items
S_k	the set of candidate sequences with k itemsets
SDSP	the set of all direct sequential patterns
SISP	the set of all indirect sequential patterns
LS	The predefined Least minimum support
t_s	The predefined sequencepair support threshold
t_f	The predefined mediator support threshold
t_d	The predefined dependence threshold

4 Experiment

To test the performance of our proposed algorithms we have done some experiments. The computation environments are Pentium 3.0GHz, memory of 2G, operating system of Windows XP. The algorithm is implemented with C++. The synthetic experiment data are generated by Assocgen [1] program of IBM Almaden research center. The meanings of parameters are showed in Table 2.

We set parameters C=10, T=5, S=4, I=2.5, NS =500, NI =2500, N =10000, total number of customers D=100000, and the generated dataset is named as C10T5S4I25. Figure 1 shows the algorithm executing time variance with least minimum support decreasing from 1% to 0.2%, where the mininterest is set to 70%. It demonstrates that the algorithm increases with the declining of least minimum support LS.

Table 2. Parameters

Symbol	Meaning
D	Number of customers(=size of database)
C	Average number of transactions per Customer
T	Average number of items per Transaction
S	Average length of maximal potentially large Sequences
I	Average size of Items in maximal potentially large sequences
NS	Number of maximal potentially large Sequences
NI	Number of maximal potentially large Sequence
N	Number of items

To examine the scalability of algorithm we increased the numbers of customer D from 50,000 to 150000, with LS=1%, mininterest=70%. The results are shown in Figure 2. The executing time is increased almost linearly with the increasing of dataset size. It can be concluded our algorithm has a good scalable performance.

C10T5S4I25

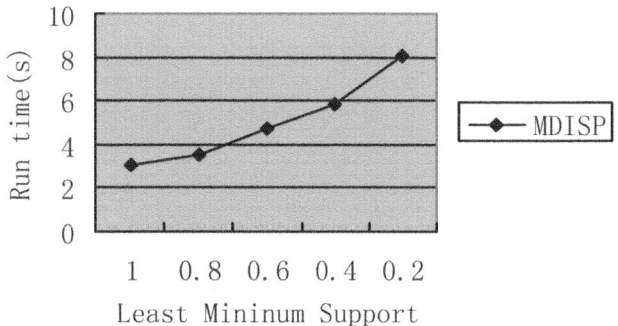

Fig. 1. Execution times

C10T5S4I15

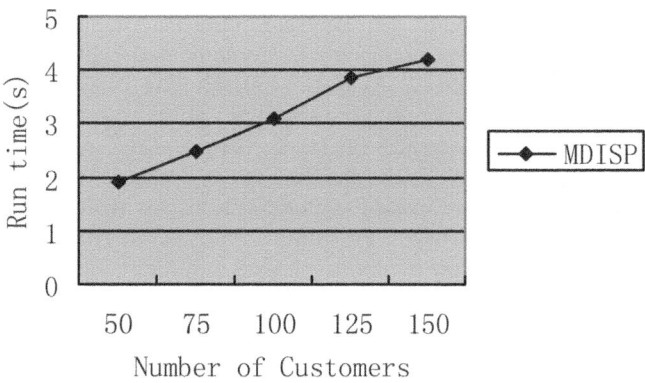

Fig. 2. Scale-up: Number of customers

5   Conclusion and Future Work

In order to resolve the rare item problem, we propose an algorithm to discover sequential patterns with multiple minimum supports model which can specify a different minimum item support for different item. The algorithm can discover both of direct and indirect sequential patterns with multiple minimum supports. The experiments demonstrated that the algorithm is efficient and scalable.

As a future work, we will address fuzzy indirect sequential patterns with multiple minimum supports from large transaction database with quantitative items.

References

1. Agrawal, R., Srikant, R.: Mining sequential patterns. In: The Proc. 1995 Int. Conf. on Data Engineering, Taibei, Taiwan (March 1995)
2. Tan, P.N., Kumar, V.: Indirect Association: Mining Higher Order Dependences in Data. In: Proc. Of the 4th European Conference on Principles and Practice of Knowledge Discovery in Databases, Lyon, France, pp. 632–737 (2000)
3. Liu, B., Hsu, W., Ma, Y.: Mining Association Rules with Multiple Minimum Supports. SIGKDD Explorations, 337–341 (1999)
4. Piatetsky-Shapiro, G.: Discovery, Analysis and Presentation os Strong Rules. In: Knowledge Discovery in Databases, pp. 229–248. AAAI/MIT, Menlo Park, CA (1991)

Application of Data Mining in Relationship between Water Quantity and Water Quality

Dingsheng Wan[1,*], Haoyun Wu[2], Shijin Li[1], and Fang Cheng[2]

1 School of Computer & Information, HoHai University, Naning, 210098, China
[2] Taihu Basin Authority, Shanghai, 200434, China
Dshwan@hhu.edu.cn

Abstract. From the angle of data mining, we adopt association rules, clustering and other technologies to obtain the association between the water quality under WangTing gate with the sub-flow on both sides of WangYu River. In order to have a comprehensive analysis about the impact that diverting water from ChangShu hub and sub-flow on both sides of WangYu river making on the water quality, this article introduces a new conception: the efficiency of diverting water from ChangShu hub to Taihu lake, and obtain the association between the efficiency and water quality of inflow, providing technical support of further analysis on diverting water from the Yangtze's role in improving water quality, water environment of the Taihu Lake and the basin.

Keywords: Association Rules, Clustering, Hypothesis Testing, Sub-flow, Water Quality of inflow.

1 Introduction

Since the implementation of Yangtze River-Taihu Lake Water Diversion Project in 2002, through the scientific schedule of water resource, a total of 4 billion cubic meters water was diverted from the Yangtze river, of which 2 billion cubic meters was diverter into Taihu Lake, and 2 billion cubic meters was diverter into river network areas of both sides of the WangYu River.

Diverting 3.1 billion m^3 water into the upper reaches of HuangPu River from TaiPu Gate, and it plays an important role in increasing volume of water, improving water quality and water environment, which was also an effective attempt of 'restrict the quietness with activity, discharge sewage with purified water, make up for drying up with abundance, improve water quality' in the Taihu Lake basin [1]. From the angle of data mining, we adopt association rules, clustering and other technologies to obtain the association between the water quality under WangTing gate with the sub-flow on both sides of WangYu River, providing technical support of further analysis on the role of diverting water from the Yangtze in improving water quality, water environment of the Taihu Lake and the river network basin.

---

* This work is supported by National Natural Science Foundation of China (No.51079040), '948 Projects' of MWR (Ministry of Water Resources P. R. China) (No.201016).

H. Deng et al. (Eds.): AICI 2011, Part I, LNAI 7002, pp. 404–412, 2011.

Classical association rules mining focuses predominantly on databases containing Boolean data only. However in the real world, there are quantitative attributes like age, salary, output, and categorical attributes like nation, profession. To process data with such attributes, Yonatan Aumann proposed a definition of quantitative association rules [2]. Ramakrishoan Srikant proposed that adopting classic association rules mining method mine the Boolean-type data that mapping from quantitative and categorical attributes [3]. Takeshi Fukuda proposed that optimize association rules for numerical attributes, including oprimized support rules and optimized confidence rules [4]. Chan Man Kuok proposed that mine quantitative association rules with fuzzy logical method, which design algorithm on the basis of given fuzzy set [5]. To solve the problem, Ada Wai-chee FU proposed a method of obtains fuzzy sets with clustering [6]. While this paper according to the special nature of water quality data, introduces a method of mining quantitative association rules on the basis of discretizing continuous water quality data.

2 Correlation Theory

Association Rule Mining is mining useful information about the association between data items. Association rule is a rule of the form $X=>Y$, in which X and Y are disjoint itemsets, thus $X\cap Y=\varphi$. Support and confidence threshold values are used in mining to eliminate useless rules. Support expresses the frequency of rules, and confidence shows the reliability of rules. The specific description is as follows: $support(X=>Y)=P(X \cup Y); Confidence(X=>Y) =P(Y \mid X)$.

Basing on the relation of objects discovered in data, clustering divides objects into groups, aiming at the objects are similar (related) within the same group while dissimilar (unrelated) between groups. Greater similarity within a group leads to greater difference between groups, thus a better clustering. In certain meanings, cluster analysis is just the beginning of other targets (such as data aggregation). Data mining is one of the domains that clustering plays an important role in.

In statistics, if the difference is caused by sampling error, it is called no statistical significance, if not, it is statically significant difference. Hypothesis testing is the way to distinguish them; it tests the probability (P) of the event that difference is caused by sampling, which is called null hypothesis. Thus P is as small as possible on condition that it satisfies the boundary. In statistics, using **$P=a$** as the boundary, in which **a** is called significance level, and **a** is often set to 0.1 for medium significance, 0.05 for significance, and 0.01 for high significance [7].

When dealing with different measurement data, sample means are often distinct even with the same population means because of the sampling error. So we cannot take it for granted that population means are different for the sample means are different, but should adopt hypothesis testing to test the difference.

3 Relationship between Water Quantity and Water Quality

3.1 Data Preparation

The data we used in this paper is the hydrological data gathering from the Taihu Lake Basin between 1/1/2002 to 12/31/2008, including water inflow of ChangShu hub and WangTing, the sub-flow of WangYu River and water quality of WangTing Gate. Considering the primary problem of the water environment of Taihu, we chose DOX, COD_{Mn}, TN, NH_3-N and TP as indicators evaluating water quality of WangTing Gate. In this paper, we concerned with COD_{Mn} and NH_3-N to analyze the influence of sub-flow of WangYu River on them. We can get the sub-flow of WangYu River by making the inflow of ChangShu hub minus the inflow of WangYu River. As it takes 3 to 4 days for diverting water from ChangShu hub to WangTing Gate, so today's sub-flow of WangYu River is equal to the inflow of ChangShu hub four days ago minus today's inflow of WangYu River. Finally, we sift the data that the inflow of WangTing is greater than 0 and the tendency of sub-flow of WangYu River is increasing as the final data for analysis.

3.2 Association Rules Mining

Since sub-flow (data denotes by dafl, 10 thousand m^3/day) of WangYu River is continuous data, we discretize it to get association rules with high confidence.

$$(dafl \in [v1,v2]) => (COD_{Mn} \text{ increased, water quality worsen}) \qquad (1)$$

$$(dafl \in [v3,v4]) => (NH_3\text{-N increased, water quality worsen}) \qquad (2)$$

$$(dafl \in [v5,v6]) => (COD_{Mn} \text{ decreased, water quality improved}) \qquad (3)$$

$$(dafl \in [v7,v8]) => (NH_3\text{-N decreased, water quality improved}) \qquad (4)$$

Continuous attributes discretization is the key of quantitative rules mining; it concerns the process of transferring continuous attribute into different intervals. In this paper we adopt k-means clustering algorithm to transfer the sub-flow data into four discrete intervals, and denote each interval by Cluster. The discretization fully considers the similarity of the interval data and the relative distance between the values. As shown in Table 1, *Mean* is the mean value of *dafl* in each Cluster, while *stdDev* represents the variance, *Minimum* and *Maximum* denote minimum and maximum value within Cluster, thus [Minimum, Maximum] represents the discrete interval, and *N* is the number of data in each Cluster.

To mine association rules with the form shown in (1) and (2), we use COD_{Mn}_class to represent the trend of the COD_{Mn} content, $COD_{Mn}\_class = increase$ represents the content increased(comparing to the day before), $COD_{Mn}\_class = nochange$ represents no change of the content, and $COD_{Mn}\_class = decrease$ represents decreased. NH_3-N is dealt in the same way.

We notice that dafl increases continuously sometimes (data is identified by date, while increase continuously means the data is continuous on date), while sometimes it only increases in a single day. We wish to mine comprehensive association rules with high confidence level to represent the reason of COD_{Mn}'s increasing, so we use *dafl_class* to show the way dafl increases, if it increases continuously, *dafl_class=more*, otherwise, *dafl_class=one*. Next we'll analyze whether *dafl_class* is related to COD_{Mn}*_class* and NH_3-*N _class*.

Table 1. Discrete interval of dafl

Cluster	Mean	StdDev	Minimum	Maximum	N
	746.2648	326.9289	-488	1743	252
1	-175.25	213.0374	-488	-28	4
2	474.6875	153.1967	93	678	96
3	876.7667	148.2216	682	1220	134
4	1427.944	156.4599	1238	1743	18

Therefore, cluster, *dafl_class*, COD_{Mn}*_class* and NH_3-*N_class* are used in the mining. Data is identified by date, with corresponding cluster value, *dafl_class*, COD_{Mn}*_class* and NH_3-*N_class*.

In this paper, we use SAS EM (SAS Enterprise Miner) to mine association rules, support threshold is set to 5%, and confidence threshold is 50%. Thus we obtain association rules with high support and confidence level as bellow:

cluster 4 => COD_{Mn} increase(support=4.37%, confidence=61%)

Meaning: When the sub-flow of WangYu River is on the interval [1238, 1743], it is most likely to lead COD_{Mn} increase.

more &cluster 2 => COD_{Mn} decrease(support=15.87%, confidence=56%)

Meaning: when the sub-flow of WangYu River is on the interval [93,678], and remains on this interval for several days, it is most likely to lead COD_{Mn} decrease.

one & cluster 2=> NH_3-N increase(support=6.75%,confidence=70.83%)

Meaning: when the sub-flow of WangYu River is on the interval [93,678] discontinuously, it is most likely to lead NH_3-N increase.

more & cluster 2=> NH_3-N decrease(support=18.25%, confidence=63.8%)

Meaning: when the sub-flow of WangYu River is on the interval [93,678] discontinuously, it is most likely to lead NH_3-N decrease.

3.3 Mean Test

From the association rules listed above, we can notice that when dafl is on the interval with great number (dafl∈[1238,1743]), it is most likely to lead to the COD_{Mn} increase, when dafl is on the interval with small number(dafl∈[93,678]), it is most likely to lead the COD_{Mn} decrease. This is the association rule with high confidence level we mined from existing data, to prove this; we compare the mean value of dafl when COD_{Mn} increasing (COD_{Mn}*_class=increase*) with that when COD_{Mn} decreasing (COD_{Mn}*_class = decrease*), if the former is significantly greater, it proves the association rules we obtained above.

Because of the unknown distribution of dafl, we adopt nonparametric test to get the mean value of dafl when COD_{Mn}_class equals to increase and decrease separately. We use the SAS procedure *proc npar1way* to do the test.

Table 2. The mean statistics of dafl

Variable	COD_{Mn} class	N	Mean	StdDev	Minimum	Maximum
dafl	decrease	110	715.01	316.87	-131	1662
daf	increase	106	790.01	341.77	-488	1743

In Table 2, *N* represents number of observation of each group, thus the group with COD_{Mn} *class* = *decrease* has 110 data, while the other has 106. *Mean* is the mean value; *stdDev* denotes standard deviation; *Minimum* and *Maximum* represent the minimum and maximum number of each group.

Table 3. Non-parametric mean test statistics of the association between sub-flow of WangYu River and COD_{Mn}

Wilcoxon Scores (Rank Sums) for Variable dafl Classified by Variable $COD_{Mn}\_$class				
$COD_{Mn}\_$class	N	Sum of score	Expected under H_0	Stddev under H_0	Mean score
decrease	110	11091.0	11935.0	459.183687	100.827273
increase	106	12345.0	11501.0	459.183687	116.462264

Data in this table was obtained through Wilcoxon rank-sum test to get the difference between the sample data of each group. *Sum of score* is the rank sum of each group; *Expected under H_0* and *Std dev under H_0* are the rank sum and rank criterion of each group on condition that hypothesis stands; *Mean score* denotes the mean rank of each group.

Table 4. Non-parametric mean test result of the association between sub-flow of WangYu River and COD_{Mn}

Wilcoxon Two-Sample Test			
Statistic		12345.0000	
Normal Approximation			
Z	1.8370	One-Sided Pr>Z	0.0331
Two-Sided Pr>|Z|		0.0662	
t Approximation			
One-Sided Pr>Z	0.0338	Two-Sided Pr>|Z|	0.0676
Kruskal-Wallis Test			
Chi-Square	3.3784	DF	1
Pr > Chi-Square		0.0661	

From Table 4 we can see that Statistic = 12345.0, it treats dafl as the test statistics on condition that $COD_{Mn}\_class=increase$ (Wilcoxon rank-sum treats the sample with minimum number as test statistics), the *P* value is 0.0331<0.05 in One-Sided test

(Pr>Z) of the Normal Approximation test, which indicates that the mean values of dafl are significantly different in two situations, the value on condition that $COD_{Mn}\_class =increase$ is significantly greater than it when $COD_{Mn}\_class=decrease$. In One-Sided test of t Approximation test, the P value is 0.0338<0.05, denotes the same result.

4   Efficiency of Diverting Water from ChangShu Sub to Taihu

To analyze the influence of diverting water from ChangShu hub and sub-flow of WangYu River on water quality of Taihu, we introduce a new concept that is the efficiency of diverting water from ChangShu hub to Taihu lake (the inflow of WangTing/the flow diverting from ChangShu hub), and expect to get the association between the efficiency of diverting water to Taihu with the inflow's water quality.

4.1   Mining Association Rules between the Efficiency of Diverting Water to Taihu and Water Quality of Inflow

The test gets association rules between the efficiency and water quality with high support and confidence level adopting association rules mining.

(Efficiency $\in [0.026, 0.253])$=>COD_{Mn} increase (support = 4.44%, confidence = 64.7%)

Meaning: When the efficiency of diverting water to Taihu is on the interval [0.026, 0.253]; it is most likely to lead COD_{Mn} increase.

(Efficiency $\in [0.547, 0.951])$=>NH_3-N decrease (support = 34.68%, confidence = 61.43%)

Meaning: when the efficiency is on the interval [0.026, 0.543]; it is most likely lead NH_3-N decrease.

(Efficiency$\in [0.026, 0.543])$=>NH_3-N increase (support = 24.19%, confidence = 55.56%)

Meaning: when the efficiency is on the interval [0.547, 0.951]; it is most likely to lead NH_3-N decrease.

4.2   Mean Tests on the Efficiency

Adopting hypothetic test method to compare the mean value of efficiency when COD_{Mn} increases ($COD_{Mn}\_class=increase$) and decreases ($COD_{Mn}\_class\square decrease$). If the mean value are different, indicating that the efficiency do have influence on the change of COD_{Mn}. Likewise, it applies to NH_3-N.

Table 5. Non-parametric mean test statistics of the association between the efficiency of diverting water to Taihu and COD_{Mn}

Wilcoxon Scores (Rank Sums) for Variable dafl Classified by Variable COD_{Mn} _class					
COD_{Mn}_class	N	Sum of score	Expected under H_0	Stddev under H_0	Mean score
decrease	110	12980.0	11935.0	459.185737	118.00000
increase	106	10456.0	11501.0	459.185737	98.641509

From Table 5 and Table 6, *Statistic* = 10456.0000, it treats efficiency as the test statistics on condition that $COD_{Mn}\_class=increase$ (Wilcoxon rank-sum treat the sample with minimum number as test statistics), the P value is 0.0115< 0.5 in One-Sided test (*Pr>Z*) of the Normal Approximation test, which indicates that the mean value of efficiency are significantly different in two situations, the value on condition that $COD_{Mn}\_class=decrease$ is significantly greater than it when $COD_{Mn}\_class=increase$. In One-Sided test of t Approximation test, the P value is 0.0120<0.05, denotes the same result. Thus, greater efficiency leads to reduced COD_{Mn} more likely.

Table 6. Non-parametric mean test result of the association between the efficiency of diverting water to Taihu and COD_{Mn}

Wilcoxon Two-Sample Test			
Statistic		10456.0000	
Normal Approximation			
Z	-2.2747	One-Sided Pr>Z	0.0115
Two-Sided Pr>|Z|		0.0229	
t Approximation			
One-Sided Pr>Z	0.0120	Two-Sided Pr>|Z|	0.0239
Kruskal-Wallis Test			
Chi-Square	5.1791	DF	1
Pr > Chi-Square		0.0229	

Table 7. Non-parametric mean test statistics of the association between the efficiency of diverting water to Taihu and NH_3-N

Wilcoxon Scores (Rank Sums) for Variable dafl Classified by Variable NH_3-N _class					
NH_3-N class	N	Sum of score	Expected under H_0	Stddev under H_0	Mean score
decrease	133	18149.50	16492.0	559.774843	136.462406
increase	114	12478.50	14136.0	559.774843	109.460526

Table 8. Non-parametric mean test result of the association between the efficiency of diverting water to Taihu and NH_3-N

Wilcoxon Two-Sample Test			
Statistic		12478.5000	
Normal Approximation			
Z	-2.9601	One-Sided Pr>Z	0.0015
Two-Sided Pr>|Z|		0.0031	
t Approximation			
One-Sided Pr>Z	0.0017	Two-Sided Pr>|Z|	0.0034
Kruskal-Wallis Test			
Chi-Square	8.7676	DF	1
Pr > Chi-Square		0.0031	

From Table7 and Table 8, *Statistic*□12478.5000, it treats efficiency as the test statistics on condition that *NH₃-N _class=increase* (Wilcoxon rank-sum treats the sample with minimum number as test statistics), the *P* value is 0.0015< 0.5 in One-Sided test(Pr>Z) of the Normal Approximation test, which indicates that the mean value of efficiency are significantly different in two situations, the value on condition that *NH₃-N_class=decrease* is significantly greater than it when *NH₃-N_class=increase*. In One-Sided test of t Approximation test, the *P* value is 0.0017<0.05, denotes the same result. Thus, greater efficiency leads to reduced NH₃-N more likely.

5 Conclusion

Adopting association rules mining, we get the result that when the sub-flow of WangYu River is on the interval [1238, 1743](10 thousand cubic meters/day), it is most likely to lead COD$_{Mn}$ increase; when it remains on the interval [93,678] for several days, it is most likely to lead COD$_{Mn}$ decrease. When the sub_flow of WangYu River is on the interval [93,678], but not continuously, it is most likely to lead NH₃-N increase; When the sub_flow of WangYu River is on the interval [93,678] and remains on it for several days,it is most likely to lead NH₃-N decrease. Through nonparametric tests, we get that the mean value of sub-flow of WangYu River on condition that COD$_{Mn}$_class=increase is significantly greater than the value on condition that COD$_{Mn}$_class=decrease, indicating that the sub-flow of WangYu River do have influence on water quality of WangTing hub, the sub-flow of WangYu River when COD$_{Mn}$ increases is greater than that when COD$_{Mn}$ decreases generally, it further proves that the association rules we get correspond with objective facts [8].

In order to have a comprehensive analysis about the impact that diverting water from ChangShu hub and sub-flow on both sides of WangYu River making on the water quality, this article introduces a new conception: the efficiency of diverting water from ChangShu hub to Taihu lake (the inflow of WangTing / the flow diverting from ChangShu hub). Through association rules mining, we obtain that when the efficiency is on the interval [0.026,0.253], it is most likely to lead COD$_{Mn}$ increase; when it is on the interval [0.026,0.543], it is most likely to lead NH₃-N increase and when it is on the interval [0.547,0.951], it is most likely to lead NH₃-N decrease. Adopting nonparametric tests, we get that the greater efficiency of diverting water to Taihu leads to improved water quality of inflow.

References

1. Liu, N.: A Preliminary Exploitation of Experiment Project of Water Diversion from the Yangtze River to Taihu Lake. China Water Kesources (2004)
2. Aumann, Y., Lindell, Y.: A Statistical Theory for Quantitative Association Rules. Intelligent Information Systems 20(3), 255–283 (2003)
3. Srikant, R., Agrawal, R.: Mining Quantitative Association Rules in Large Relational Tables. In: Proc. SIGMOD, pp. 1–12 (1996)

4. Fukuda, T., Morimoto, Y., Morishita, S., et al.: Mining Optimized Association Rules for Numeric Attributes. In: Proceedings of the 15th ACMSIGACT-SIGMOD-SIGART Symposium on Principles of Databases Systems (PODS 1996), pp. 182–191 (1996)
5. Kuok, C.M., Fu, A., Wong, M.H.: Mining Fuzzy Association Rules in Database. ACM SIGMOD Record 27(1), 41–46 (1998)
6. Fu, A.W.-C., Wong, M.H., Sze, S.C., et al.: Finding Fuzzy Sets for the Mining of Fuzzy Association Rules for Numerical Attributes. In: Proceedings of the 1st International Symposium on Intelligent Data Engineering and learning (IDEAL 1998), pp. 263–268 (1998)
7. Zhu, X.: Application of nonparametric statistic in market research. Statistical Education (2004)
8. Study on key technologies of Yangtze-Taihu Water Diversion, pp. 182–183 (2010)

Multi-relational Data Semi-supervised K-Means Clustering Algorithm

Zhanguo Xia, Wentao Zhang, Shiyu Cai, and Shixiong Xia

School of Computer Science and Technology, China University of Mining and Technology,
Xuzhou, Jiangsu, China
{xiazg,xiasx}@cumt.edu.cn, baihe04@126.com, caishy@tom.com

Abstract. Based on the traditional K-means clustering algorithm, a new semi-supervised K-means clustering algorithm (MMK-means) is proposed in this paper, in which use semi-supervised learning method to solve the problem of clustering on multi-relational data set. In order to improve the quality of clustering results, the algorithm making full use of the various relationships between objects and attributes to guide the choice of the marked data, and use these relationships to the initial center of clusters. Experimental results on Financial Data database verify the accuracy and effectiveness of the algorithm.

Keywords: K-means clustering, semi-supervised learning, multi- relational data; data mining.

1 Introduction

The information technology swept the world since the 80th of the last century, and it quickly permeated in all areas of the society, human society has entered into an information age. With the exponential growth of information presentation, data mining (also known as knowledge discovery) came into being, and it becomes a hot topic in the study of artificial intelligence in recent years.

People often assume that the data is constituted of the same type, independent and unrelated with others entities [1] in the traditional Data Mining, and is committed to find a meaningful pattern in a single data table, which is described in a single data source of information for data analysis. But the real world is most of the data have relationship with each others, and the data is constituted of a variety of different types of entities, and the data attributes maybe not the same kinds of type, and the entities have relation- ship with each other through a variety of interrelated [2] . When the data mining environments from the traditional single table extends to a multi-table state, on the accurate description of an object may contain many tables. If extracts the data knowledge only from one of simply table and ignore the multi-relational features, the results obtained by the inevitable one-sided. In order to improve the accuracy of mining results, the multi-relational features between the data must be appropriate.

In many practical applications of data mining field, the actual data are often constituted by the large number of unmarked data and a small amount of marked data [3]. As getting a large number of unmarked data is very easy, but the small amount of

H. Deng et al. (Eds.): AICI 2011, Part I, LNAI 7002, pp. 413–420, 2011.

marked data often requires access to the cost of expensive and sometimes impossible to get all the marked data. The semi-supervised learning is a learning process that is to use a small amount of marked data[4] to guide the clustering of unmarked data, and it is attended by many researchers in recent years [5].

Currently, the researchers have proposed many semi-supervised learning methods[6]. In general, the semi-supervised learning problem can be divided into two categories: semi-supervised classification problems and semi-supervised clustering problem [7]. The former is based on supervised classification, through the unmarked data to guide the clustering process, to improve the classification accuracy; the latter is based on unsupervised clustering, through the marked data to guide the clustering process to improve the clustering quality.

In this paper, the semi-supervised clustering algorithm is improved by the traditional K-means clustering algorithm which is mainly used to process multi-relational data set, extracted the various kinds of relationships from the multi-relational data, and added the semi-supervised information during in the algorithm execution, and proposed a multi-relational data semi-supervised K-means clustering algorithm. The algorithm has the following characteristics:

(1) In-depth analysis of various kinds of relationships in the multi-relational data set. For example, the relationship information between their own attribute, the relationship information between those attributes, the information object itself, the relationship information between those objects;

(2) Through analysis the multi-relational data, and extract relevant semi-supervised information to guide K-means clustering algorithm, the traditional K-means clustering algorithm is improved to obtain high-quality clustering results;

(3) In the improved multi-relational data K-means clustering algorithm, through comprehensive analysis of the relationship between various kinds of attributes and objects, build the corresponding semi-supervised information, together guide the clustering process to improve the clustering results.

This paper first introduces the relevant issues and corresponding symbols of the multi-relational data semi-supervised K-means clustering, and then given the description of the improved K-means clustering algorithm in a multi-relational data sets, and added the semi-supervised information. Finally, given the experimental results of the algorithm in the multi-relational data sets bank, and the results were analyzed and summarized to discover useful knowledge.

2 Definitions of Multi-relational Data Semi-supervised Clustering

2.1 Related Definitions

In this paper, based on the research of semi-supervised learning and the problems of multi-relations data clustering, it gives the definitions of the problems which is related to the multi-relational data semi-supervised clustering algorithm.

In the study of the research of multi-relational data in semi-supervised clustering, there are many types of objects and various kinds of relationships between these objects exist in the multi-relations data sets. We can mark a small part of them as marked objects; the remaining object is unmarked objects. Let T denote a multi-relational data set and let T^k denote the marked objects in the multi-relational data set T, and R denote the relationships between these objects exist in the multi-relations data set T, and then: $T=\{T_1,T_2,\ldots,T_m\}$, $T1=\{t_{11},t_{12},\ldots t_{1n}\}$, $\ldots$ $Tm=\{t_{m1},t_{m2},\ldots t_{mn}\}$, there exists m different types of marked objects, and the number of each type of object is $n_i(1<=i<=m)$; and each marked object T_i has its own property [8], defined as $T_i.P$.

There is some marked objects in the multi-relations data set T, which is defined as $T_k=\{T_{1k},T_{2k},\ldots,T_{mk}\}$, and $T_{ik}=\{(t_{i1},r_{i1}),(t_{i2},r_{i2}),\ldots,(t_{in},r_{in})\}$ is the marked objects in T_i, n denote the number of the marked objects in T_i.

In the multi-relational data semi-supervised K-means clustering algorithm, for each cluster C_i in the clustering result, the relationship between their own properties can be expressed as the radius of such clusters. The largest distance between the data objects in the cluster to the center of the cluster is defined as the radius of the cluster[9]. Let $C_r[i]$ denote the radius of the cluster C_i, and then: $C_r[i]=\max distance(t_i,c_ic)$, $distance(t_i,c_ic)$ denote the value of the distance between one data object t_i of the cluster C_i and the center c_ic of the cluster C_i.

For the cluster C_i and cluster C_j of the clustering result, the relationships between these objects in the cluster C_i and C_j can be expressed as $£(i , j)$, then:

$$£ (i, j) = \frac{dis (i, j)}{| Ci |}, \quad dis (i, j) =|t|distance(t,c_ic)\leq C_r[max],t\in C_j$$

$distance(t,c_ic)$ is the distance between the data object t and the center c_ic of the cluster C_i, $C_r[max]$ is the maximum value of the radius of all the cluster.

For the given two cluster C_i and C_j, the distance between those two clusters can be expressed as dis(C_i, C_j), then:dis(C_i, C_j) = min dis(c_ic,t), and the minimum distance between all of the objects in the cluster C_j and the center c_ic of the cluster C_i.

2.2 Instances of Multi-relational Data Set

In this paper it use a multi-relational financial data set instance of a bank, the instance is the data set on PKDD'99 Financial Data[10]. It contains a total of 8 types of objects, ie T = {{account}, {loan}, {order}, {transactions}, {card}, {disp}, {client}, {district}}; and each types of objects have their own properties and their own part of the marked objects. The multi-relational database contains the multiple relationships between objects and attributes, such as object account and transactions relations is the relationship between objects and objects, and the property account_id and account of object transactions is the relationship between the attributes and properties, and each type of objects and their properties is naturally exist the relationships between objects and attributes. All kinds of relationships exists in the multi-relational database will have a great effect on the choice of the marked data and the final results of multi-relational data clustering.

3   Multi-relational Data Semi-supervised Clustering Algorithm

3.1   K-Means Clustering Algorithm

K-means algorithm is a clustering algorithm based on Euclidean distance, it use Euclidean Distance as the evaluation criteria of the data similarity, and use criterion function of the error sum of squares as clustering criterion function.

The implementation of the algorithm is as follows:

(1) It is randomly selected k objects from the data set T as initial cluster centers, and initialized to a cluster;

(2) It measured the Euclidean distance of the remaining objects in the data set to each initial center, and classified to the nearest cluster center of the class cluster;

(3) Recalculate the cluster mean assigned to each object of class, updating the cluster centers of the clusters;

(4) Repeat (2) - (3) steps until convergence or reaching a fixed number of iterations, the algorithm terminates, and returns the results by clustering.

The multi-relational data semi-supervised K-means clustering algorithm in this article is based on the traditional K-means algorithm, through the new selection method of the initial cluster (cluster center) and the object similarity measure to improve the clustering result of the multi-relational data semi-supervised clustering. The new algorithm after improved is called multi-relational data semi-supervised K-means clustering algorithm (MMK-means).

3.2   MMK-Means Algorithm

MMK-means algorithm can make full use of the various relationships between objects and attributes to guide the choice of marked data, and through these relationships between objects and attributes to divide the initial cluster, and using the result as the semi-supervised information to guide the clustering process. At the same time by using the characteristics of the data and practical significance to evaluate and analyze the clustering results, and verify the validity of the algorithm, thus making it for multi-relational data semi-supervised learning. The code description of the algorithm is as follows:

```
Algorithm: MMK-means(T,Tk,R,N).
Input: Multi-relational dataset S,Marked dataset Tk,data relational R, Cluster
number N
Output: Clustering result ClusterSet C
Matrix m = buildMatrix(T);              (1)
ArrayList a = buildClassData(Tk,R);     (2)
ClusterSet c = initClusterCenter(m,N);  (3)
MMKmeansClustering(c,m,a);              (4)
return C;
```

Fig. 1. The code description of the MMK-means algorithm

Algorithm (1): buildMatrix(T).
Input: Multi-relational dataset T
Output: Matrix m
ArrayList<DataItem> rows = m.rows;
m.setWidth(items.length);
foreach DataItem t in DataSet S do
    foreach Point p in DataItem t do
        p = t.rowdata;
    rows.add(t);
m.setHeight();
return m;
	Algorithm (3): initClusterCenter(m,N).
	Input: Matrix m, Cluster number N
	Output: ClusterSet c
	ClusterSet c = null;
	foreach int i to num do
	    foreach Point p in Matrix m do
	        Point center =
	        randomInitPointCenter(p,m);
	c.add(new Cluster(center));
	return c;

Algorithm (2): buildClassData(Tk,R).
Input: Marked dataset Tk,data relational R Output: ArrayList a
ArrayList a = null; int label,oldLabel; int labelCount = 0; String relation = null;
foreach DataItem t in DataSet T do
    foreach Point p in DataItem t do
        if(label != oldLabel&& pi.hasRelation(pj))
            labelCount++; relation = iRj;
a.add(labelCount ,relation);
return a;

Algorithm (4): MMKmeansClustering(c,m,a).
Input: ClusterSet c, Matrix m, ArrayList a Output: ClusterSet c
foreach Cluster clu in ClusterSet c do
    clustering(clu,m);
    while(clu.centerNoChange())
        foreach Point p in Matrix m do
        if(p.relation(a).hasNoRelationWith(clu)) break;
    checkEnd(m);
Output c;

Fig. 2. The code description of algorithm(1)- algorithm(4)

MMK-means algorithm have a total of four input parameters, followed by multi-relational data set T, the marked objects data set T^k in the data set T, the multi-relational relationships R exists in the marked objects data set T^k, the number of clusters N that the clustering results is divided. The algorithm output is the number of the data that each cluster contains, the number of clustering, classification accuracy and other relevant information.

Algorithm (1) obtain all of the data in the multi-relational data set T in first, the number of the ranks of the data set corresponding into a multi-dimensional matrix m, the matrix of each data item corresponds to a data of the data set. Algorithm (2) obtain all of the marked data in the data set T^k in first, It is stored the identifies in each label, when obtain the next identity label determined whether the same with the oldLabel, if not the same and the data point has relationship with another data point in the data set, increment the counter labelCount 1, and record the relationship between the two data point, and store the information in a list for later use in the algorithm. Algorithm (3) use the input multi-dimensional matrix m and the number of clusters N, and then randomly select N data items as cluster center of cluster in the multi-dimensional matrix m and ensure that the N randomly generated data items not the same, then use the selected N data items to generate N clusters, and put those clusters into clusters c to return. Algorithm (4) use the output result m, a, c of the algorithm (1) - (3) as input parameters, and input MMKmeansClustering(c,m,a) to cluster. First, begin the first cluster, and update the cluster center of cluster, if the cluster centers do not change, the cluster number of the counter increase by 1, and then update the average of the cluster, when the average of all the clusters no longer change then cluster end. Finally, output results of the clustering algorithm, such as cluster number, and correct classification rate and other information.

4   Experimental Results and Analysis

The experiment in this article is on the data set on PKDD'99 Financial Data, the instance is a multi-relational financial data set instance of a bank.

In the experiment we mainly use the {tansactions}, the annual transactions in 1993 in the transactions table , a total of 28205 records; and {account} 4500 records of account information in the account table, and by {disp} 5369 records in the disp table associated with {client} 5369 records of the customer information in the client table.

The experiments in this article is running on Windows 7 operating system, use the Java programming language to develop, Java development environment is JDK 1.6 and Netbeans 6.9.1. The experiment hardware environment is: CPU is Intel Core2 2.93GHz, and memory 2G.

First, let F, B, A, P denote the number of transactions (frequency), the balance of the amount (balance), the amount of the account in each transaction (amount), using percentage of funds (percentage), then according to the combined effect of four factors make the two comparing experiments, one is as important as these four factors, denote as 0.25F+0.25B+0.25A+0.25P, and Another with the actual situation (the higher the transaction amount, the higher transaction frequency for the bank to create the greater profit) to set the value, and denote as 0.3F+0.2B+0.4A+0.1P. Of course, these weights can also be set to other values according to the actual situation in the experiments.

All of the accounts can be divided into five categories according to the maximum and minimum value of these four factors. At the same time to meet the weight of the four factors 0.25F+0.25B+0.25A+0.25P and 0.3F+0.2B+0.4A+0.1P. The statistics of the accounts number distribution, the results shown in Figure 3.

The results of clustering divided into five categories clusters in the two clustering algorithms, each cluster contains the information of the cluster that the accounts belong to, the number of accounts in each cluster will be ascending order, and then sort the results for the analysis, the analysis process is as follows:

From Figure 4 the K-means algorithm experimental result, the figure of the accounts number, we can analysis the following conclusions: (1) The Brown curve in the Figure 4 is the experimental results in the K-means algorithm, which is the overlay of the red, blue, green three color line charts, and the three line charts denote the number of accounts of the balance of the account, the amount of the account, the account number those three factors experimental results in the K-means algorithm after sorting, through the figure we can get that the three factors experimental results are the same. (2) The yellow line represent the using percentage of funds which is the ratio of the amount of the account and the balance of the account, and the blue line represent the 0.3F +0.2 B +0.4 A +0.1 P which is combined to the actual situation of the various factors to set the weights, so that the result of them are both in keeping with the actual situation. However, those two curves are very different, it is much smaller of the accounts number in the minimum cluster the using percentage of funds and the 0.3F +0.2 B +0.4 A +0.1 P obtain than the other two curve line which denote the other two factors in the K-means algorithm experimental, But it is much larger of the accounts number in the maximum cluster, while the other two curves are relatively smooth, making the results are both not accurate than that two.

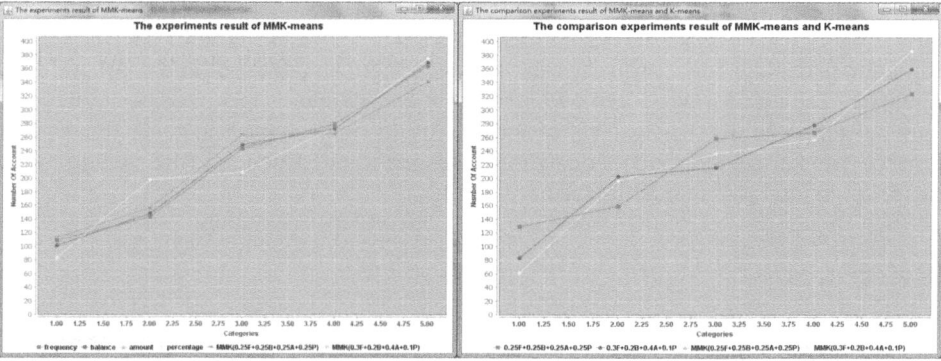

Fig. 3. Distribution of each factor accounts statistics   **Fig. 4.** The experiments result of K-means

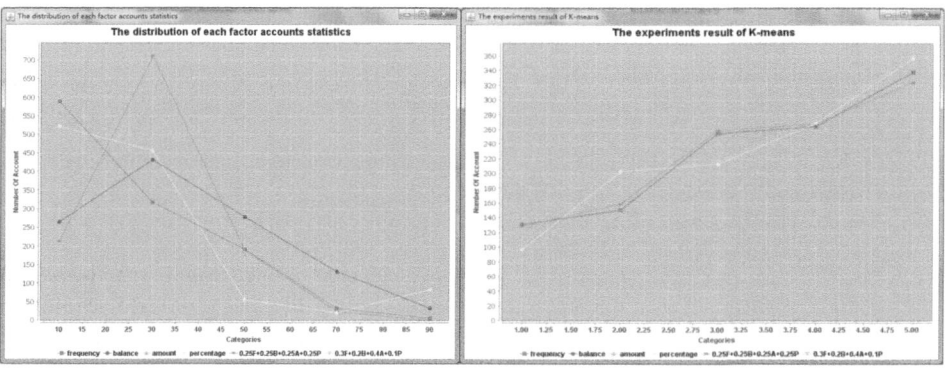

Fig. 5. The experiments result of MMK-means   **Fig. 6.** Comparison of MMK-means and K-means

5 Conclusions

The traditional K-means clustering algorithm cannot effectively solve the problem of clustering on the multi-relational data set, in order to use semi-supervised learning method to solve the problem of clustering on multi-relational data set. So a new semi-supervised K-means clustering algorithm (MMK-means) is proposed in this paper which is based on the traditional K-means clustering algorithm. The MMK-means algorithm based on the K-means clustering algorithm, through making full use of the various relationships between objects and attributes to guide the choice of the marked data, and use these relationships between objects and attributes to the initial center of clusters, and use the results of the classified information to guide the semi-supervised clustering process to improve the quality of clustering results. Finally, the experimental results on the multi-relational data sets Financial Data verify the accuracy and effectiveness of the algorithm.

The operating efficiency of the current algorithm requires further improvement in the actual operation, especially needs relatively large amount of the work in pre-processing of data, the data requirements are relatively high; how to add the actual situation to deal with text property analysis and selection on the multiple relational data Financial Data, and how to deal with those text data to semi-supervised clustering and how to comprehensive analysis the clustering results of the numerical data and text data to access to knowledge, and so many questions yet to be resolved, which should focus on resolving the problem in the further work.

References

1. Zhang, M., Yu, J.: Fuzzy partitional clustering algorithms. Journal of Software 15(6), 858–869 (2004)
2. Alfred, R.: Summarizing Relational Data Using Semi-Supervised Genetic Algorithm-Based Clustering Techniques. Journal of Computer Science 6(7), 775–784 (2010)
3. Anthony, A.P.: Ph.D. Stochastic and iterative techniques for relational data clustering, 175 pages, 3359070. University Of Maryland, Baltimore County (2009)
4. Yin, X., Han, J., Yu, P.S.: CrossClus: User-Guided Multi-Relational Clustering. In: Data Mining and Knowledge Discovery (DAMI), vol. 15(3), pp. 321–348 (2007)
5. Sun, J.G., Liu, J., Zhao, L.Y.: Clustering algorithms research. Journal of Software 19(1), 48–61 (2008)
6. Li, K.L., Cao, Z., Cao, L.P., Zhang, C., Liu, M.: Some Developments on Semi-Supervised Clustering. PR & AI 22(5), 735–742 (2009)
7. Yin, X., Hu, E., Chen, S.: Discriminative Semi-Supervised Clustering Analysis with Pair wise Constraints. Journal of Software 19(11), 2791–2802 (2008)
8. Gao, Y., Liu, D.Y., Qi, H., Liu, H.: Semi-Supervised K-means clustering algorithm for multi-type relational data. Journal of Software 19(11), 2814–2821 (2008)
9. Xiao, Y., Yu, J.: Semi-Supervised Clustering Based on Affinity Propagation Algorithm. Journal of Software 19(11), 2803–2813 (2008)
10. PKDD 1999, Discovery Challenge Guide to the Financial Data Set (1999),
    http://lisp.vse.cz/pkdd99/Challenge/berka.htm

A Clustering-Ensemble Approach Based on Voting

Fanrong Meng, Xuejiao Tong, and Zhixiao Wang

School of Computer Science and Technology
China University of Mining and Technology
221116, Xuzhou, Jiangsu, China
{mengfr62,tong-xuejiao,softstone416}@163.com

Abstract. Clustering-ensemble can protect private information, process distributed data and reuse of knowledge, besides, noise and outliers have little effect on clustering results. This paper proposes a new clustering ensemble algorithm, based on voting, introduce correlation to represent the similarity of clusters. The correspondence between labeled vectors can be established because clusters with lager correlation share the same cluster labels. After reunification, the labeled vectors will be used to decide the final cluster result. Analysis and experiments show that the proposed algorithm could be used to clustering-ensemble and effectively improve the clustering results.

Keywords: clustering-ensemble, consensus function, lable matching, voting.

1   Introduction

Kleinberg proposed and proved cluster is inherently an ill-posed problem whose solution violates at least one of the common assumptions about scale-invariance, richness and consistency. Any kind of clustering algorithms may be better than others in a particular model. Selecting appropriate clustering algorithm for any data set needs to understand specific technology and prior knowledge, which even hard to experts. Clustering-ensemble was developed under the circumstance that lacking of background knowledge of the field. It combines the results of the multiple basic clustering to obtain better result. Clustering-ensemble issues can be defined as combining multiple cluster members to obtain a better clustering result.

Clustering-ensemble became a hotspot of machine learning research in the mid-90s, early ensemble learning research focused on supervised learning, clustering-ensemble start until recent years. Compared with single clustering algorithm, clustering-ensemble has the following advantages: robustness, novelty, stability and confidence estimation, and parallelization and scalability [1]. Clustering-ensemble major needs to solve two problems: first, how to produce different clustering members, and second, how to get a unified clustering result.

At present, clustering-ensemble is focused on the second issue, combining cluster members also known as consensus function problem. TANG Wei and ZHOU Zhi-hua in [2] proposed a Bagging-based selective cluster ensemble algorithm, which through aligning different clustering results and selecting component learners with the help of mutual information weight. WANG Hong-jun et al in [3] had found that the algorithm

H. Deng et al. (Eds.): AICI 2011, Part I, LNAI 7002, pp. 421–427, 2011.

by regarding every base clustering as one attribute of the original data is more extendable and flexible. They designed a latent variable cluster ensemble (LVCE) model in this way. Reference [4] proposed a new clustering ensemble method, which generated a new feature space from initial clustering outputs. Reference [5] Used voting to determine the final clustering results. Reference [6] proposed an efficient way to reset cluster labels, and used SDEM algorithm for spatial database.

This paper studies clustering-ensemble technology and proposes a consensus function RELABEL, first using k-means to produce cluster members, then introduces correlation to unify cluster labels, at last vote on this basic to produce the final clustering results.

2   Cluster Ensemble

Assume that $X=(x1, x2, x3, x4,\ldots\ldots xn)$ Represents the data set of N samples, run M times cluster algorithm on X will produce M cluster members $C=(C1,C2,C3,\ldots\ldots Cm)$, C_j represents cluster result generated by jth cluster algorithm. $xi\text{->}\{C1(xi), C2(xi),C3(xi),\ldots\ldots Cm(xi)\}$ represents the result of ith sample, given by all the cluster members, $Cj(xi)$ represents the label of ith sample which is given by the jth cluster member. Basic clustering results can be expressed as shown in Fig. 1. Then, set up consensus function F to fuse each vector C_i, and get the labeled vector $C*$ in the end, cluster ensemble can be described as follows $F:\{C1,C2,C3,\ldots\ldots Cm\}\text{->}C*$.

	C_1	C_2	C_3	C_4		C_m
X_1	2	1	2	3	...	2
X_2	2	1	4	3	...	1
X_3	1	2	5	1	...	3
X_4	1	2	2	1	...	3
⋮	⋮	⋮	⋮	⋮	⋮	⋮
X_n	2	3	4	2	...	2

Fig. 1. Basic clustering

Consensus function is designed to obtain better average performance clustering result by fusing multiple clustering results. Consensus function is the key of clustering-ensemble, Common consensus function methods include voting, co-association matrix, mutual information, hypergraph and so on [7-9]. Matching labels must be resolved before voting, also known as re-labeling. Supervised classification already contains label information, so there is no problem of inconsistent labels. Different from supervised classification, unsupervised clustering-ensemble cannot directly be used to decide the final labels due to lacking of prior knowledge of the samples. For example, for the cluster labeled vector(1, 1, 1, 2, 2, 3) and (2, 2, 2, 3, 3, 1), the label of these two cluster vectors is inconsistent, but in fact represent the same result. Labeled vectors must be matched to establish the corresponding relation of each other before voting step. Voting method as a consensus function is effective.

3 Relabel Algorithm

Labels of a sample given by different cluster members are not necessarily the same, cannot be directly used for voting, the labels must be matched before determining the final label.

3.1 Basic Matching Method

Basic cluster can partition X into K parts. The clustering result can be labeled by a vector $\lambda = [\lambda 1, \lambda 2, \lambda 3, \lambda 4 \ldots \lambda n]$, $\lambda i \in \{1,2,3 \ldots K\}$ is cluster label.

In different cluster members, the same class labels are often different and cannot be directly used for voting. In order to combine the cluster members, the labeled vectors must first establish the correspondence between each other. In general, the corresponding clustering labels must hold maximum number of the same objects. Therefore, we can match the labeled vectors according to the heuristics. Assume that there are two labeled vectors C(a) ={C1(a), C2(a), C3(a),…,Ck(a)} and C(b)= {C1(b), C2(b), C3(b),…,Ck(b)}, every vector divides the data set into K classes. First , calculate the number of the same objects which label are Ci(a) and Cj(b) into a K*K matrix named REL. Secondly, select the maximum of REL to get the corresponding relation, then remove the relevant row and column from matrix REL. Thirdly, repeat the former steps until all vectors have established the corresponding relation.

When there are H (H>2) labeled vectors, select one of these as a standard and match other vectors with the standard. Matching algorithm needs a scan of H-1 vectors and (H-1)*K2 space to store the matrix REL. The matching process is efficient and rapid.

3.2 Information Distortion Problem and Improvement

Through experiments and analysis, we find that there exists information distortion problem in the matching process. Assume that there are a labeled vector A and a standard vector B, A= { $C_1^{(A)}$, $C_2^{(A)}$} and B={ $C_1^{(B)}$, $C_2^{(B)}$ }. In vector A, the number of objects which are labeled $C_1^{(A)}$ is 20, and the number of objects which are labeled $C_2^{(A)}$ is 15. In vector B, the number of objects which are labeled $C_1^{(B)}$ is 17, and the number of objects which are labeled $C_2^{(B)}$ is 18. If you follow the basic matching method you can obtain a correlation matrix as follows: $\begin{bmatrix} 9 & 11 \\ 5 & 10 \end{bmatrix}$, So the corresponding relation is that $C_1^{(A)}=C_2^{(B)}$ and $C_2^{(A)}=C_1^{(B)}$. In this process, the amount of information used is 16(11+5). If the correspondence is that $C_1^{(A)}=C_1^{(B)}$ and $C_2^{(A)}=C_2^{(B)}$, the amount of information used is 19(10+9). In fact, the second corresponding relation is better, and it uses more information, and more in line with the actual situation. From the above analysis, we know that it is inappropriate to determine the correlation just by the number of the same objects. Correlation between clusters is relevant to not only the number of the same objects but also the sizes of the clusters themselves.

In fact, there are 15 objects are labeled with $C_2^{(A)}$, in which 10 also being labeled with $C_2^{(B)}$, 20 objects are labeled with $C_1^{(A)}$, while in which only 11 also being labeled with $C_2^{(B)}$. Although the number of objects which are labeled with $C_1^{(A)}$ and $C_2^{(B)}$ is large than the number of objects which are labeled with $C_2^{(A)}$ and $C_2^{(B)}$, the latter accounts for the number of objects labeled with $C_2^{(A)}$ of 2/3. The similarity of $C_2^{(A)}$ and $C_2^{(B)}$ is large.

From the above analysis, we can know, it is not enough to determine the correlation between clusters alone with the number of same objects. So we introduce mutual information to represent correlation. The correlation of $C_i(a)$ and $C_j(b)$ is defined as:

$$\text{Re}lation(C_i^{(a)}, C_j^{(b)}) = \log \frac{n_{i,j}}{n_i^{(a)} + n_j^{(b)} - n_{i,j}} \tag{1}$$

$n_{i,j}$ means the number of objects which are labeled with $C_i^{(a)}$ in vector $C(a)$, meanwhile are labeled with $C_j^{(b)}$ in vector $C(b)$. $n_i^{(a)}$ means the number of objects which are labeled with $C_i^{(a)}$ in vector $C(a)$, $n_j^{(b)}$ means the number of objects which are labeled with $C_j^{(b)}$ in vector $C(b)$. The correlation between the vectors with the corresponding relations is the largest.

3.3 Algorithm Description of Relabel

Using correlation to represent the similarity between clusters, and then establish corresponding relation of each others. Algorithm is described as follows:

Input: dataset X, number of clusters K

Output: cluster label C*(x) for data object x

```
For h=1 to H Do

  λ(h)=k-means(K,X)

  /*λ(h)={C₁(h), C₂(h), C₃(h),...,Ck(h)} */

End of for

λ(base)=randomly selected from{λ(h)}, h=1,2, …H

Delete λ(base) from {λ(h)},h=1,2, …H

For each λ(h) in {λ(h)} do

  For i=1 to K, j=1 to K do

      REL(i, j)=Relation(Ci(h),Cj(base))

      End of for

/*REL is a k*k matrix, Relation(A, B) is computed using (1)*/

      Γ={}

      While Γ≠{C₁(base),C₂(base),...,Ck(base)}  Do

      (u,v)=argmax(REL(i,j))

      /*REL(u,v)is the biggest element*/
```

```
C_v^(h)=C_u^(base)

/*align C_v(h) to C_u^(base)*/

Delete  REL(u,*)

Delete  REL(*,v)

Γ=Γ∪{C_v^(h)}

      End  of  While

End  of  For
```

This method using k-means produces cluster members, the time complexity of generating H cluster members is $H*O(nKt)$, and the time complexity of label matching process is $H*O(K^2)$, and RELABEL algorithm's time complexity is $H*O(nkt+K^2)$. Where, n is the number of objects, K is the number of clusters, t is iteration number of k-means, H is the number of cluster members.

4 Experimental Analysis

This paper uses three data sets in UCI study (http://archive.ics.uci.edu/ml/datasets.html) the specific chosen data sets are shown in table 1.

Table 1. Description of Data Sets

Data set	size	Number of attributes	Number of classes
iris	150	4	3
wine	178	13	3
bupa	345	6	2

Category information contained in the data, which reflects the internal distribution of the data, can be used to evaluate the clustering result.

Suppose that there are a known category vector C, expressed by $\{C_1,C_2,....C_k\}$, and a labeled vector λ which can be expressed as $\{\lambda_1,\lambda_2,...\lambda_k\}$. after the label matching algorithm, each λ_i in the labeled vector shall correspond to a C_j in the category vector. Suppose S_i is the number of λ_i in C_j then the result of clustering labeled vector can be measured by Micro-p, the specific definition is as following:

$$\text{Micro-p}=\frac{1}{n}\sum_{i=1}^{K}S_i \qquad (2)$$

The lager the value of Micro-p is, the higher the accuracy of the cluster result is. This evaluation applies only to measure the clusters producing fixed number of clustering. Therefore, in this experiment, the category number of each cluster in clustering is fixed.

Generating cluster members by k-means using the inherent randomness of it, cluster results of the basic cluster and clustering-ensemble are displayed in table 2. The performance of proposed clustering-ensemble algorithm is better than the average performance of basic clustering, close to or higher than the highest accuracy of basic clustering.

Table 2. Accuracy of Basic Clustering and Relabel

Algorithm Data set	Result of k-means		RELABLE
	Max	Average	
Iris	0.89333	0.87333	0.90133
Wine	0.70225	0.66573	0.72476
Bupa	0.55362	0.55101	0.55362

Table 3. Error Rates of Different Algorithms on Iris

H	K	CSPA	HGPA	MCLA	Re-label
5	3	0.12267	0.38000	0.10667	0.11333
10	3	0.13067	0.46667	0.10667	0.11600
15	3	0.12400	0.38200	0.10667	0.11200
20	3	0.12867	0.40267	0.10667	0.09867
30	3	0.13133	0.40867	0.10667	0.10733

The effect of relabeling is similar to MCLA, HGPA is relatively worse. Accuracy of clustering-ensemble does not increase with the cluster members increased.

The proposed algorithm is compared with the CSPA, GPA and CLA, which have proved to be effective. Table 3 lists several experimental results of clustering ensemble algorithm, with different size of cluster members, and each result is the average of ten operations.

Experiment on Iris data set shows that the accuracy is highest when the size of cluster members is 20.

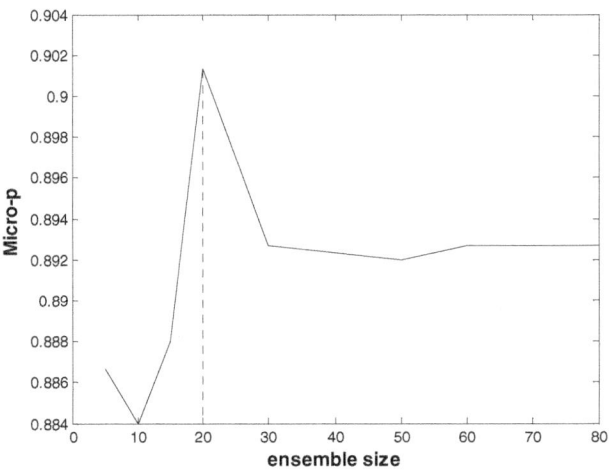

Fig. 2. Size of cluster members effects on clustering-ensemble performance

In order to research the relationship between the size of cluster members and clustering performance, we draw the curve which reflects the size of cluster members effecting on the performance of clustering-ensemble. It can be seen from Fig 2, cluster performance is not improved with the cluster members increased. In the proposed algorithm, clustering-ensemble performance decreased when the size of cluster members to a certain extent. The reason may be that cluster members whose error rates relatively high are also increasing with the cluster members increasing, and these members affect the final clustering result.

The performance of clustering-ensemble is based on basic clustering results, generally speaking, clustering-ensemble performance is better if the results of basic clustering are better. Clustering-ensemble performance also can be better if the basic clustering is diverse. Better results do exist on these data sets, but this paper focuses on the effectiveness of clustering-ensemble algorithm.

5   Conclusion and Future Work

This paper proposes a label matching algorithm, which takes into account the information distortion problem, using correlation to represent the similarity between clusters. Unified labels are used for voting to determine the final clustering results .Clustering-ensemble as an effective method, there are many problems to be solved the next step will focus on the size of cluster members effect on the performance of the clustering-ensemble.

References

1. Topchy, A., Jain, A.K., Punch, W.: Clustering Ensembles: Models of Consensus and Weak Partitions. IEEE Transactions on Pattern Analysis and Machine Intelligence 27, 1866–1881 (2005)
2. Tang, W., Zhou, Z.-H.: Bagging-Based Selective Cluster Ensemble. Journal of Software 16, 496–502 (2005)
3. Wang, H.-J., Li, Z.-S., Cheng, Y.: A Latent Variable Model for Cluster Ensemble. Journal of Software 20, 825–833 (2009)
4. Azimi, J., Abdoos, M., Analoui, M.: A New Efficient Approach in Clustering Ensembles. In: Yin, H., Tino, P., Corchado, E., Byrne, W., Yao, X. (eds.) IDEAL 2007. LNCS, vol. 4881, pp. 395–405. Springer, Heidelberg (2007)
5. Fern, X.Z., Brodley, C.E.: Random projection for high dimensional data clustering: a cluster ensemble approach. In: Proc. 20th International Conference on Machine Learning, ICML, Washington, DC, pp. 186–193 (2003)
6. Dudoit, S., Fridlyand, J.: Bagging to improve the accuracy of a clustering procedure. Bioinformatics 19, 1090–1099 (2003)
7. Anandhi, R.J., Subramanyam, N.: Efficient Fusion of Cluster Ensembles Using Inherent Voting. In: Intelligent Agent & Multi-Agent System, pp. 1–5 (2009)
8. Fred, A.L.N.: Finding consistent clusters in data partitions. In: Kittler, J., Roli, F. (eds.) MCS 2001. LNCS, vol. 2096, pp. 309–318. Springer, Heidelberg (2001)
9. Strehl, A., Ghosh, J.: Cluster ensembles-a knowledge reuse framework for combining multiple partitions. Journal of Machine Learning Research 3, 583–617 (2002)

Spatio-temporal Outlier Detection Based on Context:
A Summary of Results

Zhanquan Wang, Chao Duan, and Defeng Chen

Department of Computer Science and Engineering,
East China University of Science and Technology, Shanghai, China
zhqwang@ecust.edu.cn, duanchaoaaa@126.com, chendefeng918@163.com

Abstract. Spatio-temporal outlier detection plays an important role in some applications fields such as geological disaster monitoring, geophysical exploration, public safety and health etc. For the current lack of contextual outlier detection for spatio-temporal dataset, spatio-temporal outlier detection based on context is proposed. The pattern is to discover anomalous behavior without contextual information in space and time, and produced by using a graph based random walk model and composite interest measures. Our approach has many advantages including producing contextual spatio-temporal outlier, and fast algorithms. The algorithms of context-based spatio-temporal outlier detection and improved method are proposed. The effectiveness of our methods is justified by empirical results on real data sets. It shows that the algorithms are effective and validate.

Keywords: Spatio-Temporal outliers, Context, Composite Interest Measures.

1 Introduction

Spatio-temporal outlier detection, also called anomaly detection in space and time, is an important branch of the data mining research [1][2][3]. Most of the existing approaches identify outliers from a global point view for spatio-temporal datasets. However, sometimes an instance may not be an outlier when compared to the rest of the spatio-temporal dataset but may be a spatio-temporal outlier in the context of a subset of dataset from point view of space and time. This type of outlier detection is called contextual spatio-temporal outlier detection. There are many applications in the real world, for example. In the Masai Mara national reserve (MMNR) in Kenya [10], there are many species, such as wildebeest and zebra, they are gregarious species, but two groups often lives nearby. It is important for us to find that some wildebeets often live in other group, it is a anomalous behavior, the reverse is also true. The existing methods can't find the pattern. We propose one new method to detect spatio-temporal outlier based context using a graph rand and define composite interest measures. Firstly a transition matrix can be generated from data set according to the relation, Then contexts and contextual outlier at each timeslot are defined using a graph based random walk model. The spatio-temporal contextual outlier can be produced by

H. Deng et al. (Eds.): AICI 2011, Part I, LNAI 7002, pp. 428–436, 2011.

defining composite interest measures which are suitable to the real application. Our contributions are: discover spatio-temporal contextual outliers detection (STCOD) without a prior contextual information is proposed; It includes the definition and interpretation for composite interest measures which are applicable to the real applications; A new and computationally efficient STCOD mining method is presented; It includes comparisons of approaches and experimental designs. The rest of the paper is organized as follows. Section 2 reviews some background and related works in outlier detection data mining. Section 3 proposes basic concepts to provide a formal model of STCOD. STCOD mining algorithms are presented in section 4. The experimental results are proposed in section 5 and section 6 presents conclusions and future work.

2   Related Work

The quality of identified contextual outliers heavily relies on the meaningfulness of the specified context [9], many existing approaches require a priori contextual information, for example, S.Salvador[7] can get states and rules for time series anomaly detection which needs priori contextual information. S. Shekhar[2] proposes many outlier methods, but don't deal with time series anomaly and can't deal with it under unknown contextual information. X. Song[3] proposes conditional anomaly detection, it can deal with the specified context, but need contextual information. Tan[19] introduces random walk model for global outlier detection and used the principal eigenvector of the transition matrix as global outlier score, but it don't process contextual outliers and spatio-temporal dataset. Skillicorn[8] uses spectral graph analysis to explore anomalous structure in a graph. The methods are focused on outlier detection in a global point of view, and don't address contextual outliers and spatio-temporal dataset. X. Wang[6] can deal with the patterns without priori contextual information by proposing a probabilistic approach based on random walk, but it can't process spatio-temporal dataset. Our works explore meaningful contexts and contextual outlier for spatio-temporal applications using a random walk graph and spectral analysis[2][11] which is a powerful tool to study the structure of a graph at each timeslot, where we use transition matrix to study how to get unknown contextual information for spatio-temporal data and how to define composite interest measures which are applicable to real applications.

3   Statement and Algorithm Modeling

For spatio-temporal data, we proposed a spatio-temporal framework to deal with context-based spatio-temporal outlier detection. The spatio-temporal framework is as follow: a framework of spatio-temporal framework STF, an object(node) set: $O=\{o_0,...,o_1,...,o_{n-1}\}(0 \leqslant i \leqslant n-1)$, n is number of nodes at each timeslot. $T=\{t_0,...,t_1,...,t_{n-1}\}(0 \leqslant i \leqslant m-1)$, m is the number of timeslot. So we can define $STF=\{O_0,...O_{m-1}\}$, $STF=OXT$, O_i is the object set at the timeslot t_i.

3.1   Spatio-temporal Contextual Outlier Detection

The random walk graph and contextual outliers is omitted due to space limit[7]. A method that can detect the contextual outlier for spatio-temporal dataset with the non-main eigenvector is proposed. In the model, a unique graph of 2-labeling/2-coloring is defined in every non-main eigenvector of the transitional matrix. Intuitively, given a 2-coloring graph, each sub-graph could be regard as a context. Assume S^+ is a sub-graph and S^- is another, we can get the probability of a node be visited from the beginning of S^+ or S^-. There are some nodes called contextual outliers if the probability of nodes visited by S^+ or S^- is equal. Fig.1 shows an example of spatio-temporal contextual outlier.

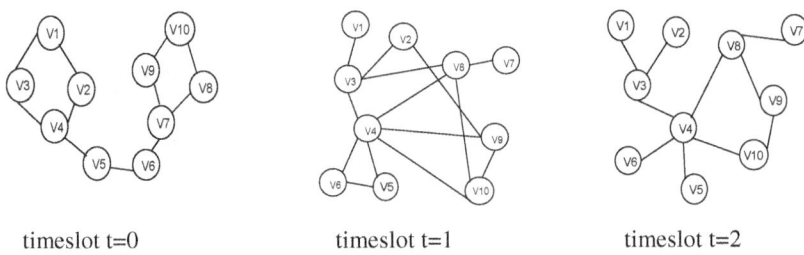

timeslot t=0   timeslot t=1   timeslot t=2

Fig. 1. An example for STCODs

Definition 1: Assume (S^+, S^-) is a 2-coloring of G, S^+ is a index set of the nodes marked +, and S^- is a index set of the nodes marked -. They are satisfied the follow condition: $S^+ \neq \varphi, S^- \neq \varphi, S^+ \cup S^- = \{1,...,n\}$. Then we can call (S^+, S^-) a pair of contexts of G. And the random walk in G can be called a contextual random graph.

Definition 2 (fixed expectation): Assuming G is a random walk graph, W a transitional matrix, μ_i is the expectation of random variable[8], if μ_i satisfies the follow condition: $\mu_i = c \sum_{j=1}^{n} \mu_j w_{ij}, \forall i, 0 \leqslant i \leqslant n\ 1$, where c is a constant of time-independent, then we call $\mu = (\mu_0, \mathsf{L}, \mu_{n\ 1})^T$ is the fixed expectation for the contextual random walk of S^+ and S^-.

If W is a positive transitional matrix, then every non-main eigenvector of W can uniquely determine a pair of contexts and the corresponding fixed expectation. Particularly, assume v is an eigenvector which corresponds to the eigenvalue $\lambda < 1$ of W. So we can regard v as a non-main eigenvector of W and get the follow lemma:

Lemma 1: Given a non-main eigenvector v of a positive transitional matrix, then $\sum_{i=1}^{n} v(i) = 0$, where $v(i)$ is an item of v.

According to lemma 1, we can define a 2-coloring of G with v, it can provide a pair of contexts: $S^+ = \{i : \mathbf{v}(i) > 0\}, S = \{i : \mathbf{v}(i) < 0\}$.

Now consider the contextual random walk with (S^+, S^-) in G, we can get follow theorems:

Theorem 1 (the fixed expectation of a contextual random walk): If assume $\mu = (\mu_0, \ldots, \mu_{n-1})^T$, $\mu_i = \dfrac{\mathbf{v}(i)}{\sum_{j=1}^{n} |\mathbf{v}(j)|}, \forall i, 0 \leqslant i \leqslant n-1$, where v is non-main

eigenvector corresponding to the eigenvalue λ of W, so definition 2 is satisfied. Therefore, μ is a fixed expectation of contextual random walk graph. Theorem 1 indicates that every non-main eigenvector uniquely determines a 2-coloring graph(S^+, S^-) and its fixed expectation μ. According to the theorem 1, we can define the contextual outlier with fixed expectation.

Definition 3 (contextual outlier value): Assume G is a random walk graph, W a positive transitional matrix, then the contextual outlier value of node i is $|\mu_i|$, and μ_i is the fixed expectation which defined according to Theorem 1.

According to the definition above, we can know that the contextual outlier value of any node is between 0 to 1. A small value indicates that the node is a contextual outlier.

We compute its contextual outlier value for all nodes in time slot t=0,1,2. The detailed part is shown in [9]

$\mu =$	$\mu =$	$\mu =$
0.1168	0.0652	−0.1307
0.1096	0.0845	−0.0452
0.1096	0.1664	−0.2766
0.1332	−0.1467	−0.0956
0.0309	−0.1766	−0.0271
−0.0309	−0.1766	−0.0271
−0.1332	0.0364	0.0749
−0.1096	0.0931	0.1585
−0.1096	0.0370	0.1120
−0.1168	0.0175	0.0523
timeslot t=0	timeslot t=1	timeslot t=2

Definition 4: Given a spatio-temporal dataset, a spatial contextual outlier measure is value to judge if the node is contextual outlier. We know v5,v6 in time slot t=0, v7,v9,v10 in time slot t=1, v5,v6 in time slots t=2 are the contextual outlier if spatial contextual outlier threshold is 0.04.

Definition 5: Given a spatio-temporal pattern and a set T of timeslots, such that $T = \{t_1,...,t_j,...,t_m\}(0 \leqslant j \leqslant m-1)$. The time contextual outlier measure of the pattern is the fraction of timeslots where the patterns occur the total number of timeslots.

Given a spatio-temporal dataset of STF, and spatial contextual outlier threshold θ_c, the composite measure of pattern P_i is a composition of the spatial contextual outlier and the time prevalence measures as shown below.

$$\Pr ob_{t_i \in T}(c\_outlier(P_i, timeslot \ t_i) \leqslant \theta_c) \tag{3}$$

Where $\Pr ob$ stands for probability of overall prevalence time slots, and $c\_outlier$ stands for spatial contextual outliers.

Consider a spatio-temporal dataset of STF and a threshold pair (θ_c, θ_t), where θ_t is time prevalence threshold. $STCOD$ is a prevalent pattern if it's composite measures satisfy the following.

$$\Pr ob_{t_i \in T}(c\_outlier(P_i, timeslot \ t_i) \leqslant \theta_c) \geqslant \theta_t \tag{4}$$

Where $\Pr ob$ stands for probability of overall prevalence time slots, $c\_outlier$ stands for spatial contextual outliers. θ_c is the spatial contextual threshold and θ_t is the time prevalence threshold. We can know v5, v6 are spatio-temporal contextual outlier if $\theta_t = 0.6$.

3.2   Analysis for Model

Spatio-temporal contextual outliers produced from our methods are correct because the patterns satisfy threshold pairs. The patterns are complete because our algorithms can find any STCODs as long as it satisfies our definitions and rules. The model average time complexity is $O(n^2 m)$.We omit the detail analysis due to space limit.

4   Mining STCODs

In the section, we discuss the implementation of our spatio-temporal contextual outlier score in practice. We propose a novel hierarchical algorithm which iteratively partitions the data set for each time slots until the size of the sub graph is smaller than a user specified threshold pairs. In every time slots, we acquire the contextual outlier value of spatial object with the method of contextual outlier detection mentioned above. Set a threshold θ_c, our method can judge if the node is a spatial contextual outlier, then we get spatio-temporal outlier based on context according to θ_t. The naïve algorithm1 of context-based spatio-temporal outlier detection is omitted due to space limit. We only describe the fast algorithm for spatio-temporal contextual outlier which is more efficient than naïve method.

Algorithm2: fast spatial-temporal contextual outlier detection

---

Inputs: spatio-temporal data set STF, G,W, θ_c, θ_t ;

Output: spatial-temporal contextual outliers(STCOD)

```
 1: STCOD← φ , TOS(i) ←0,Lt← φ , Sum(i) ←0;i←0
 2: for each  t_i ∈ T   do
 3:    for each i∈ STF do
 4:        Tr(t_i ,i)=0;
 5:    end;
 6:    creat random walk graph G and transition matrix W;
 7:    STCOD (G, W,α,θ_c ) ;
 8:        Add L to Lt;
 9:        for each i∈ L do
10:            if   TOS(i) > θ_t  then
11:                    STCOD=STCOD ∪ {i};
12:                    Delete i item from L and Lt;
13:            else    Tr(t_i ,i)=1;
14:            end;
15:        end;
16:        for each i∈ L do
17:          Sum(i)= Sum(i)+ Tr(t_i ,i);
18:          TOS(i)= Sum(i) /m ;
19:        end;
20:        i++;
21: end;
22: for each i∈ Lt do
23:        if   TOS(i) > θ_t   then
24:                STCOD=STCOD ∪ {i};
25:        end
26: end
27: return STCOD;
```

The time complexity of algorithm is a time polynomial. The algorithm involves calculating the first and second largest eigenvalue and eigenvector of an n × n matrix, where n is the number of nodes. So its complexity is mainly determined by the complexity of eigen-decomposition. Second time cost is sorting data by outlier value. Therefore, we would adopt an efficient method to calculate eigenvalue and eigenvector. As a trick of outliers is that they are composed by minority objects, so the first modified part is: we don't necessarily consider all the objects in the process of calculation. When making spatio-temporal contextual outlier detection, we can set a threshold β, only put the objects whose outlier value is smaller than threshold β into the sort list L. It can keep the most normal data without any unnecessary operation in order to improve algorithm. When calculate outlier in the time series, we don't need to deal with all objects, but only a minority objects, so the size of the sort list will be greatly reduced. When judging spatial contextual outlier, we can set a threshold θ_c, the objects whose outlier value is smaller than θ_c will regard as outlier. In our algorithm, we adopt the latter approach. We can put the judging work into algorithm1, just need set $\beta = \theta_c$; When judging outlier in the time slots, some nodes have already satisfied the judging condition before dealing with all the time slots and not be judged as spatio-temporal contextual outliers, so the second modified part is: it is unnecessary to continue to deal with these nodes at the rest timeslots. The improved algorithm is described as the fast algorithm.

5   Experimental Evaluation

In this section, we present our experimental evaluations of several design decisions and workload parameters on our STCOD mining algorithms. We used two real-world training dataset, (mail log for users and vehicle data set). We evaluated the behavior of two algorithms. Fig.2 shows the experimental setup to evaluate the impact of design decisions on the performance on these methods. Experiments were conducted on a Windows XP, 2.0GHz Inter Pentium 4 with 1.5GB of RAM.

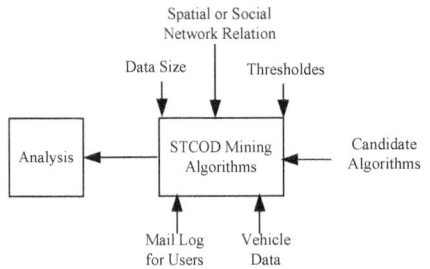

Fig. 2. Experimental setup

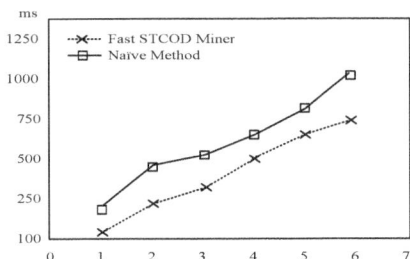

Fig. 3. The relationship between the number of timeslots and time

According to the location information of the vehicle we establish transition matrix with spatial relation R(R=100). Experiment analysis would be done according to number of time slots and threshold θ_c, θ_t. The solid line represent the naïve algorithm, and dotted line represent the improved algorithm (fast algorithm). From the Fig.3, we can find that the running time of the improved algorithm is shorter than the original algorithm, and the gap is increasing along as the number of time slots increasing. Because the improved algorithm has exclude the most normal data with the thresholds, which reduces a lot of operate time.

On the Fig.4, it shows the relationship between threshold θ_c and running time. The number of time slots and the other threshold θ_t are 6 and 0.7, we can see that with the increase of the threshold θ_c, running time of the fast algorithm is increasing, but the overall running time is less than the naïve algorithm.

On the Fig.5, it shows the relationship between threshold θ_t and running time. Assume the times m and the other threshold θ_c are both fixed value, we can see that with the increase of the threshold θ_t, the overall running time of the fast method is less than the naive algorithm.

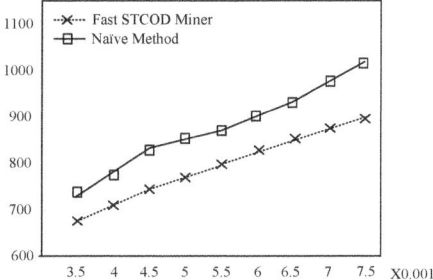

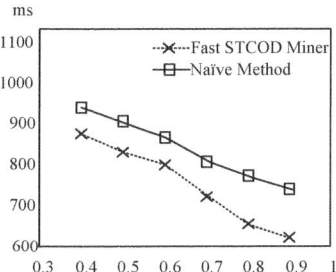

Fig. 4. The relationship between threshold θ_c and running time

Fig. 5. The relationship between threshold θ_t and running time

From the experiment analysis above, we can draw a conclusion that the improved algorithm is more efficient than the original algorithm. The experimental evaluations were presented for mail log for users from our department. It also shows our methods can deal with STCOD patterns and effective and validate. We don't show the detailed results for mail log data for users due space limits.

6   Conclusion

We defined spatio-temporal contextual outlier detection and its mining problem, and proposed a new monotonic composite interest measure. We presented a novel and computationally efficient algorithm for mining patterns and its improved method, and proved that the model is correct and complete in finding spatio-temporal contextual outliers. Our experimental results using the vehicle dataset from the real world provide further evidence of the viability of our approach. For future work, we would like to explore the relationship between the proposed composite interest measures and spatio-temporal statistical measures of interaction[2]. We plan to develop other new computationally efficient algorithms for mining STCODs. So further study variation of transition matrix due to multi-scale of space or time, and space and time.

Acknowledgement. The authors are very grateful to the financial support from the National Natural Science Foundation of China under Grant No. 60703026

References

1. Han, J.W., Kamber, M.: Data mining concepts and techniques. Morgan Kaufmann Publishers, San Francisco (2001)
2. Shekhar, S., Chawla, S.: Spatial databases: a tour. Prentice Hall, Englewood Cliffs (2003)
3. Song, X., Wu, M., Jermaine, C.M., Ranka, S.: Conditional anomaly detection. IEEE Trans. Knowl. Data Eng. 19(5) (2007)
4. Moonesinghe, H.D.K., Tan, P.N.: Outlier detection using random walks. In: ICTAI (2006)
5. Kou, Y., Lu, C.T., Chen, D.: Spatial weighted outlier detection. In: SDM (2006)

6. Wang, X., Davidson, I.: Discovering contexts and contextual outliers using random walks in graphs. In: ICDM (2009)
7. Salvador, S., Chan, P., Brodie, J.: Learning states and rules for time series anomaly detection. In: Proc.17th Intl. FLAIRS Conf. (2004)
8. Skillicorn, D.B.: Detecting anomalies in graphs. In: ISI (2007)
9. Liu, F.T., Ting, K.M., Zhou, Z.H.: Isolation forest. In: ICDM, pp. 413–422 (2008)
10. Barnet, V., Lewis, T.: Outlier in statistical data. John Wiley & Sons, New York (1994)
11. Chung, F.: Spectral graph theory. American Mathematical Society, Providence (1997)

Mining Interesting Infrequent and Frequent Itemsets Based on Minimum Correlation Strength

Xiangjun Dong

School of Information, Shandong Polytechnic University
Jinan 250353, China
dongxiangjun@gmail.com

Abstract. IMLMS (interesting MLMS (Multiple Level Minimum Supports)) model, which was proposed in our previous works, is designed for pruning uninteresting infrequent and frequent itemsets discovered by MLMS model. One of the pruning measures used in IMLMS model, *interest*, can be described as follows: to two disjoint itemsets A,B, if $interest(A,B)=|s(A\cup B) - s(A)s(B)|<mi$, then $A\cup B$ is recognized as uninteresting itemset and is pruned, where $s(\cdot)$ is the support and mi a minimum interestingness threshold. This measure, however, is a bit difficult for users to set the value mi because $interest$ (A,B) highly depends on the values of $s(\cdot)$. So in this paper, we propose a new measure, *MCS* (minimum correlation strength) as a substitute. *MCS*, which is based on correlation coefficient, has better performance than *interest* and it is very easy for users to set its value. The theoretical analysis and experimental results show the validity of the new measure.

Keywords: infrequent itemset, frequent itemset, negative association rule, multiple minimum supports, prune, correlation coefficient.

1 Introduction

As we have known, the traditional association rule is the form $A\Rightarrow B$, whose support (s) and confidence (c) meet a minimum support (ms) threshold and a minimum confidence (mc) respectively. This is the famous support-confidence framework [1]. Recently, how to mine negative association rules (NARs) at the forms $A\Rightarrow\neg B$, $\neg A\Rightarrow B$ and $\neg A\Rightarrow\neg B$ has been attracted attention and how to mine infrequent itemsets has also been attracted much attention because many valued NARs can be discovered from infrequent itemsets [2, 3, 4, 5, 6]. In ref. [5], a MLMS (Multiple Level Minimum Supports) model, which assigns different minimum supports to itemsets with different lengths, was proposed to discover infrequent itemsets and frequent itemsets simultaneously. In order to prune those uninteresting itemsets discovered by the MLMS model, in ref. [6], an IMLMS (Interesting MLMS) model was proposed later by using the similar pruning measures as that in [2].

One of the pruning measures used in IMLMS model, *interest*, can be described as follows: to two disjoint itemsets A,B, if $interest(A,B)=|s(A\cup B) - s(A)s(B)|<mi$, then $A\cup B$ is recognized as uninteresting itemset and is pruned, where $s(\cdot)$ is the support

H. Deng et al. (Eds.): AICI 2011, Part I, LNAI 7002, pp. 437–443, 2011.

and *mi* a minimum interestingness threshold. This measure, however, is a bit difficult for users to set the value of *mi* because *interest* (A, B) highly depends on the values of $s(\cdot)$. In fact, many interesting measures have been proposed in association rules mining, such as interestingness, chi-squared test, correlation coefficient, Laplace, Gini-index, Piatetsky-Shapiro, Conviction and so on, and many researches have discussed how to select the right measure [7, 8, 9, 10, 11]. Among these measures, correlation coefficient is a good one and the authors in [11] used it to mine negative association rules. In this paper, we also use correlation coefficient to replace the measure *interest* which was used in IMLMS model to improve performance, and we call the new measure as minimum correlation strength (*MCS*), denoted as ρ_{MCS}. That is, to two disjoint itemsets A, B, if the correlation coefficient of A, B, $\rho(A, B)$, is less than a given minimum correlation strength ρ_{MCS}, then $A \cup B$ is recognized as uninteresting itemset and is pruned. Later discussion will show that the measure *MCS* has better performance and is easier to be set than *interest*.

The main contributions of this paper are as follows:

1. We propose a new pruning measure named *MCS* to improve the performance of IMLMS model.
2. We demonstrate the validity of the measure *MCS* by theoretical analysis and experiments.

The rest of the paper is organized as follows: Section 2 discusses the *MCS* pruning method. Section 3 is the experiments and section 4 is conclusions.

2   MCS Pruning Method

2.1   Review of the IMLMS Model

Let $I=\{i_1, i_2,\ldots, i_n\}$ be a set of n distinct literals called items, and TD a transaction database of variable-length transactions over I, and the number of transactions in TD is denoted as $|TD|$. Each transaction contains a set of item $i_1, i_2,\ldots,i_m \in I$ and each transaction is associated with a unique identifier TID. A set of distinct items from I is called an itemset. The number of items in an itemset A is the length of the itemset, denoted by $len(A)$. An itemset of length k are referred to as k-itemset. Each itemset has an associated statistical measure called support, denoted by s. For an itemset $A \subseteq I$, $s(A)=A.count / |TD|$, where $A.count$ is the number of transactions containing itemsets A in TD. The support of a rule $A \Rightarrow B$ is denoted as $s(A \cup B)$ or $s(A \Rightarrow B)$, where $A, B \subseteq I$,and $A \cap B =\Phi$. The confidence of the rule $A \Rightarrow B$ is defined as the ratio of $s(A \cup B)$ over $s(A)$, i.e., $c(A \Rightarrow B) = s(A \cup B) / s(A)$.

In MLMS model, different minimum supports are assigned to itemsets with different lengths. Let $ms(k)$ be the minimum support of k-itemsets ($k=1,2,\ldots,n$), $ms(0)$ be a threshold for infrequent itemsets, $ms(1) \geq ms(2) \geq,\ldots, \geq ms(n) \geq ms(0)>0$, for any itemset A,

if $s(A) \geq ms(len(A))$, then A is a frequent itemset; and

if $s(A) < ms(len(A))$ and $s(A) \geq ms(0)$, then A is an infrequent itemset.

The IMLMS model use the modified pruning method used in [2] to prune uninteresting frequent itemsets by the equation 1-3, and to prune uninteresting infrequent itemsets by the equation 4-6.

M is a *frequent itemset of potential interest* in the MLMS model if

$$fipi(M) = s(M) \geq ms(len(M)) \wedge (\exists A, B: A \cup B = M) \wedge fipis(A, B), \tag{1}$$

where $fipis(A, B)=(A \cap B = \Phi) \wedge (f(A,B, ms(len(A \cup B)), mi) = 1), \tag{2}$

$$f(A, B, ms(len(A \cup B)), mi) = \frac{s(A \cup B) + interest(A, B) - (ms(len(A \cup B)) + mi) + 1}{|s(A \cup B) - ms(len(A \cup B))| + |interest(A,B) - mi| + 1}. \tag{3}$$

N is an *infrequent itemset of potential interest* if

$$iipi(N) = s(N) < ms(len(N)) \wedge s(N) \geq ms(0) \wedge \tag{4}$$

$$(\exists A, B: A \cup B = N) \wedge iipis(A, B) ,$$

where $iipis(A, B) = (A \cap B = \Phi) \wedge (f(A,B, ms(0), mi) = 1), \tag{5}$

$$f(A, B, ms(0), mi) = \frac{s(A \cup B) + interest(A, B) - (ms(0) + mi) + 1}{|s(A \cup B) - ms(0)| + |interest(A,B) - mi| + 1}. \tag{6}$$

2.2 MCS Pruning Method

In equation 1-6, *interest(A,B)* is an interestingness measure and *interest(A,B)*=|s(A∪B) - s(A)s(B)|, *mi* is a minimum interestingness threshold given by users or experts. This measure is first proposed by Piatetsky-Shapiro [12]. It's a good measure to prune uninteresting itemsets in some cases, but it is a bit difficult for users to set the value of *mi* because *interest (A,B)* changes with the values of s(·) . Take the data in table 1 for example, the maximum value of *interest(A,B)* is 0.0099 when s(A), s(B)=0.01, while the maximum value of *interest(A,B)* is 0.09 when s(A), s(B)=0.1, how to give the value of *mi*? In a database, with the length of an itemset increasing, the support of the itemset decreases. So using a single minimum *interest* is unfair to all itemsets with different supports. Perhaps you may say "use a changeable *mi* to itemsets with different supports", maybe this approach works, but now the problem becomes "how to change the value of *mi* is fair"?

In fact, the essence of the Piatetsky-Shapiro measure *interest(A,B)*=|s(A∪B) - s(A)s(B)| is that the itemsets *A,B* is uninteresting if |s(A∪B) - s(A)s(B)| ≈0, i.e., if the correlation of itemsets *A,B* is not strong enough, itemsets *A,B* is not interesting and can be pruned. So we can use the measure *Correlation coefficient* as a substitute.

Correlation coefficient measures the degree of linear dependency between a pair of random variables. The correlation coefficient between *A* and *B* can be written as

$$\rho(A, B) = \frac{s(A \cup B) - s(A)s(B)}{\sqrt{s(A)(1 - s(A))s(B)(1 - s(B))}}, \tag{7}$$

where s(*)≠0, 1 [3, 11] .

The range of $\rho(A, B)$ is between −1 and +1.The correlation coefficient and its strength are discussed in [13]. According to this book, a variable α ($0 \leq \alpha \leq 1$) is used to express the correlation strength. α=0.5, the strength is large, 0.3, moderate, and 0.1, small. This means that the itemsets whose correlation is less than 0.1 is unvalued. In real application, the value of α can be given by users or experts.

Table 1. Data for comparison between *interest(A,B)* and |ρ(A, B)|

(a)					(b)				
s(A)	s(B)	s(A∪B)	interest(A,B)	|ρ(A,B)|	s(A)	s(B)	s(A∪B)	interest(A,B)	|ρ(A, B)|
0.01	0.01	0.001	0.0009	0.091	0.1	0.1	0.01	0.0000	0.000
0.01	0.01	0.002	0.0019	0.192	0.1	0.1	0.02	0.0100	0.111
0.01	0.01	0.003	0.0029	0.293	0.1	0.1	0.03	0.0200	0.222
0.01	0.01	0.004	0.0039	0.394	0.1	0.1	0.04	0.0300	0.333
0.01	0.01	0.005	0.0049	0.495	0.1	0.1	0.05	0.0400	0.444
0.01	0.01	0.006	0.0059	0.596	0.1	0.1	0.06	0.0500	0.556
0.01	0.01	0.007	0.0069	0.697	0.1	0.1	0.07	0.0600	0.667
0.01	0.01	0.008	0.0079	0.798	0.1	0.1	0.08	0.0700	0.778
0.01	0.01	0.009	0.0089	0.899	0.1	0.1	0.09	0.0800	0.889
0.01	0.01	0.01	0.0099	1.000	0.1	0.1	0.1	0.0900	1.000

Now let's compare *interest(A,B)* and |ρ(A, B)|. The data in table 1 demonstrate the cases that the value of s(A), s(B) is 0.01 and 0.1. The range of *interest(A,B)* is [0.0001,0.0099] in table 1 (a) when s(A), s(B) is 0.01, [0,0.09] in table 1 (b) when s(A), s(B) is 0.1. This means the range of *interest(A,B)* is greatly influenced by the value of s(A) and s(B). While the range of |ρ(A,B)| is [0,1] either in table 1 (a) or in table 1 (b). This means the range of |ρ(A,B)| is only influenced by the correlation strength of A and B, not by the value of s(A) and s(B). Fig. 1 (a), (b) shows the changes of the data in table 1 (a), (b) respectively. From figure 1 we can see the changes of the range of *interest(A,B)* and |ρ(A, B)| more clearly. Although the data in table 1 only show the case when s(A), s(B) is small, we will get the same result when s(A), s(B) is large or when one is small, the other is large.

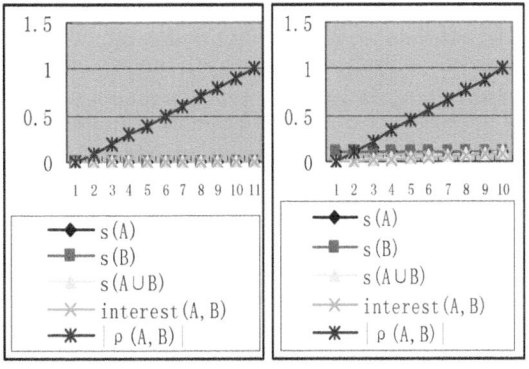

Fig. 1. The changes of the data in table 1 (a), (b)

So we can set a minimum correlation strength $ρ_{MCS}$ ($0 \leq ρ_{MCS} \leq 1$) as a constraint to prune less correlative itemsets. In details, for itemsets $A, B \subseteq I$, $A \cap B = \Phi$, if |ρ(A, B)| $< ρ_{MCS}$, then $A \cup B$ is uninteresting and is pruned. This is the MCS pruning method.

We don't need to modify the equation 1-6, the only things we do are: 1) to replace *interest(A,B)*=|s(A∪B) - s(A)s(B)| with *interest(A,B)*= |ρ(A,B)|; and 2) to replace *mi* with $ρ_{MCS}$.

We don't need to modify the algorithm *Apriori_IMLMS* either, but we change the algorithm name to *Apriori_IMLMS_MCS* to distinguish the algorithm name.

2.3 Algorithm

```
Algorithm Apriori_IMLMS_MCS
Input: TD: Transaction Database;
  ms(k)(k=0,1,…,n): minimum support threshold;
Output: FIS: set of interesting frequent itemsets;
  inFIS: set of interesting infrequent itemsets;
(1) FIS=Φ; inFIS=Φ;
(2) temp₁ = {A|A∈1-itemsets,s(A)≥ms(0)};
    FIS₁ = {A|A∈temp₁ .s(A)≥ms(1)};
    inFIS₁ = temp₁-FIS₁;
(3) for (k=2;tempₖ₋₁≠Φ;k++) do
    begin
    (3.1) Cₖ = apriori_gen(tempₖ₋₁, ms(0));
    (3.2) for each transaction t∈TD do
            begin
            /*scan transaction database TD*/
            Cₜ=subset(Cₖ, t);
            for each candidate c ∈ Cₜ
                    c.count++;
            end
    (3.3) tempₖ = {c|c∈Cₖ (c.count/|TD|)≥ms(0)};
          FISₖ = {A|A∈tempₖ .A.count/|TD|≥ms(k)};
          inFISₖ = tempₖ - FISₖ;
    (3.4) /*prune all uninteresting itemsets in FISₖ */
            for each itemset  M in FISₖ do
                    if NOT (fipi(M)) then
            FISₖ =FISₖ - { M }
    (3.5)/*prune all uninteresting itemsets in inFISₖ */
            for each itemset N in inFISₖ do
            if NOT (iipi(N)) then
                inFISₖ =inFISₖ - { N }
    end
(4) FIS = ∪FISₖ; inFIS = ∪inFISₖ;
(5) return FIS and inFIS;
```

The explanation of the algorithm *Apriori_IMLMS_MCS* can be referred to [6].

3 Experiments

The real dataset records areas of www.microsoft.com that each user visited in a one-week timeframe in February 1998. Summary statistical information of the dataset is: 32711 training instances, 5000 testing instances, 294 attributes and the mean area visits per case is 3.0 (http://www.cse.ohio-state.edu/~yanghu /CIS788_dm_proj.htm# datasets).

Table 2. The number of the interesting inFIS and the interesting FIS with different mi. ($ms(1)$=0.025, $ms(2)$=0.02, $ms(3)$=0.017, $ms(4)$=0.013, $ms(0)$=0.01)

ρ_{MCS}		k=1	k=2	k=3	k=4	Total	
0	FIS	-	37	24	3	64	150
	inFIS	-	43	40	3	86	
0.05	FIS	-	30	24	3	57	121
	inFIS	-	22	39	3	64	
0.1	FIS	-	19	24	3	46	95
	inFIS	-	14	32	3	49	
0.2	FIS	-	12	25	3	30	53
	inFIS	-	7	14	2	23	
0.25	FIS	-	12	10	3	25	39
	inFIS	-	4	9	1	14	
0.3	FIS	-	9	8	2	19	25
	inFIS	-	3	2	1	6	

Table 2 shows the number of the interesting infrequent itemsets and the interesting frequent itemsets with different ρ_{MCS} when $ms(1)$=0.025, $ms(2)$=0.02, $ms(3)$=0.017, $ms(4)$=0.013, and $ms(0)$=0.01. From table 4 we can see that the total number of *FIS* and *inFIS* is 150, 121, 95, 53, 39, 25 when ρ_{MCS} =0, 0.05, 0.1, 0.2, 0.25, 0.3 respectively. With ρ_{MCS} increasing, the total number decreases obviously. Table 4 also gives the number of *FIS* and *inFIS* in different k. These data show that the MCS pruning method can efficiently prune the uninteresting itemsets as the IMLMS model.

4 Conclusions

In order to prune the uninteresting itemsets discovered by MLMS model, IMLMS model was proposed by using a pruning measure $interest(A,B)$=|$s(A\cup B)$ - $s(A)s(B)$|<mi. This measure, however, is not easy enough for users to set the value of mi because $interest$ (A,B) highly depends on the values of s(·), as discussed in section 2.2. So in this paper, a new measure, minimum correlation strength *MCS*, has been proposed as a substitute. If |$\rho(A, B)$| <ρ_{MCS}, then $A\cup B$ is uninteresting and is pruned. The theoretical analysis and experimental results show that *MCS* has better performance than *interest* and its value is very easy to be set.

Acknowledgements. This work was partly supported by Excellent Young Scientist Foundation of Shandong Province of China under Grant No. 2006BS01017.

References

1. Agrawal, R., Imielinski, T., Swami, A.: Mining Association Rules between Sets of Items in Large Database. In: Proceedings of the 1993 ACM SIGMOD International Conference on Management of Data, pp. 207–216. ACM Press, New York (1993)

2. Wu, X., Zhang, C., Zhang, S.: Efficient Mining of both Positive and Negative Association Rules. ACM Transactions on Information Systems, 381–405 (2004)
3. Dong, X., Niu, Z., Shi, X., Zhang, X., Zhu, D.: Mining Both Positive and Negative Association Rules from Frequent and Infrequent Itemsets. In: Alhajj, R., Gao, H., Li, X., Li, J., Zaïane, O.R. (eds.) ADMA 2007. LNCS (LNAI), vol. 4632, pp. 122–133. Springer, Heidelberg (2007)
4. Dong, X., Wang, S., Song, H.: 2-level Support based Approach for Mining Positive & Negative Association Rules. Computer Engineering, 16–18 (2005)
5. Dong, X., Zheng, Z., Niu, Z., Jia, Q.: Mining Infrequent Itemsets based on Multiple Level Minimum Supports. In: Proceedings of the Second International Conference on Innovative Computing, Information and Control (ICICIC 2007), Kumamoto (2007)
6. Dong, X., Niu, Z., Zhu, D., Zheng, Z., Jia, Q.: Mining Interesting Infrequent and frequent Itemsets based on MLMS Model. In: Tang, C., Ling, C.X., Zhou, X., Cercone, N.J., Li, X. (eds.) ADMA 2008. LNCS (LNAI), vol. 5139, pp. 444–451. Springer, Heidelberg (2008)
7. Tan, P.-N., Kumar, V., Srivastava, J.: Selecting the Right Interestingness Measure for Association Patterns. In: Proceedings of the 8th ACM SIGKDD International Conference on Knowledge Discovery and Data Mining, Edmonton (CA), pp. 32–41 (2002)
8. Tan, P.-N., Kumar, V., Srivastava, J.: Selecting the right objective measure for association analysis. Information Systems 29, 293–313 (2004)
9. Hilderman, R.J., Hamilton, H.J.: Applying Objective Interestingness Measures in Data Mining Systems. In: Zighed, D.A., Komorowski, J., Żytkow, J.M. (eds.) PKDD 2000. LNCS (LNAI), vol. 1910, pp. 432–439. Springer, Heidelberg (2000)
10. Geng, L., Hamilton, H.J.: Interestingness Measures for Data Mining: A Survey. ACM Computing Surveys 38(3), Article 9 (2006)
11. Antonie, M.-L., Zaïane, O.: Mining Positive and Negative Association Rules: An Approach for Confined Rules. In: Boulicaut, J.-F., Esposito, F., Giannotti, F., Pedreschi, D. (eds.) PKDD 2004. LNCS (LNAI), vol. 3202, pp. 27–38. Springer, Heidelberg (2004)
12. Piatetsky-Shapiro, G.: Discovery, analysis, and presentation of strong rules. In: Knowledge Discovery in Databases, pp. 229–248. AAAI Press/MIT Press (1991)
13. Cohen, J.: Statistical Power Analysis for the Behavioral Sciences, 2nd edn. Lawrence Erlbaum, New Jersey (1988)

An Improved Sequential Clustering Algorithm

Yingxia Liu[1], Bo Gao[2], and Xingming Zhang[1]

[1] School of Computer Science & Engineering South China University of Technology,
Guangzhou, P.R. China
[2] Information Center of the Economic & Information Commission of Guangdong Province
hbapril@foxmail.com, cszxm@scut.edu.cn

Abstract. In this paper, it designs an improved sequential clustering approach, which compensates for shortcomings in existing algorithms. This method uses bisecting k-means clustering framework and reduces the computing time through adding the cosine similarity comparison when sequences can not satisfy the pruning condition, while the accuracy is still in an acceptable range.

Keywords: sequential clustering, bisecting k-means, cosine similarity comparison.

1 Introduction

Advances in sensing and storage technology and dramatic growth in applications such as internet search, digital imaging, and video surveillance have created many high-volume, high-dimensional datasets[1]. To understand and learn, the first thing is to organization them into sensible groups. In pattern recognition, basically, there are two methods on data analysis. One is the supervised learning, to separate one class from the others, it uses a training dataset to get a classifier to predict the correct output for any valid input, and classification is an example. The other is unsupervised learning, such as clustering, which involves data without any known labels. It is a common methodology and a more challenging problem than classification.

The main problem in clustering is how to define the similarity function. For sequential clustering, sequence similarity requires considering about both elements and order relations. Popular sequence similarity measure functions are edit distance, affine weighted distance[2], Hamming distance, Frequency distance[3], Frequency transformation distance and q-gram distance[4]. In addition, cosine similarity[5] and Jaccard similarity are also used in sequence similarity[6]. Edit distance is often used because of its full consideration of elements and order relations, while its computation complexity is O(m*n).

2 Definitions and Properties Related

We use the definitions and properties in the paper abut GSClu[7] , simply described as follows:

Sequence $S = s_1 s_2 ... s_n, s_k \in \Sigma (1 \leq k \leq n)$ is the element of S, $\Sigma = (a_1, a_1 ... a_T)$ is the alphabet, $T = |\Sigma|$ is cardinal number of it and $n = |S|$ is the length of sequence S.

H. Deng et al. (Eds.): AICI 2011, Part I, LNAI 7002, pp. 444–449, 2011.

$SN(S) = (n_1, n_2, ..., n_T)$ is the sign of S, a_i occurs ($1 \le i \le T$) times in S. Suppose two sequences S1, S2, and the signs of them $SN(S_1) = (n_1^1, n_2^1, ..., n_T^1)$ $SN(S_2) = (n_1^2, n_2^2, ..., n_T^2)$

then sign distance is $SD(S_1, S_2) = \max\left(\sum_{i=1}^{T} I_i^P (n_i^1 - n_i^2), \sum_{j=1}^{T} I_j^N (n_j^2 - n_j^1)\right)$.

If $n_i^1 > n_i^2$, $I^r = 1$, else $I^r = 0$; if $n_j^2 > n_j^1$, $I_j^N = 1$ else $I_j^N = 0$.

$V_S = \{n_1, n_2, ..., n_T, d_1, d_2, ..., d_T\}$ is the profile vector of S $n_i (1 \le i \le T)$, is the element of SN(S), $d_i (1 \le i \le T)$ is the sum distance between letter a_i and the first letter in S. Profile vector represents the basic information about the letters and their positions. After scanning all sequences once, we get a profile vector for each sequence.

It has been proved that edit distance $ED(S_1, S_2)$, its lower bound is $SD(S_1, S_2)$ and upper bound is $|S_1| + |S_2|$ in GSClu. The first pruning condition to avoid computing edit distances is:

If $\max\left(SD(P, S_2), ED(S_1, S_2)/2\right) \ge |P| + |S_1|$
then $ED(P, S_2) \ge ED(P, S_1)$. (1)

The second condition is based on detecting subsequence edit distances. P_k, S_{1k} are subsequences of P and S1. $|P| = m$, $|S_1| = n$ known the edit distance $ED(P, S_1)$, $ED(P, S_2) \ge 0$ generally;

If $ED(P, S_{1t}) - (m - n) \ge ED(P, S_2)$,
then $ED(P, S_1) \ge ED(P, S_2)$. (2)

Indeed, it can reduce time complexity to some extent. However, when the lengths of sequences are close to each other and edit distances are smaller than their length differences. That is, the conditions: $\max\left(SD(P, S_2), ED(S_1, S_2)/2\right) \ge |P| + |S_1|$, $ED(P, S_{1t}) - (m - n) \ge ED(P, S_2)$ neither of them can be satisfied. More computations about subsequence edit distances $ED(P, S_{1t})$ will be executed. Here, we change this strategy, use an example to explain. If P and S1 have a common sequence $CS(P, S_1)$. L is the length of $CS(P, S_1)$; to detect subsequence similarity, we compute from length 0 to k ($k = \min(m, n)$).

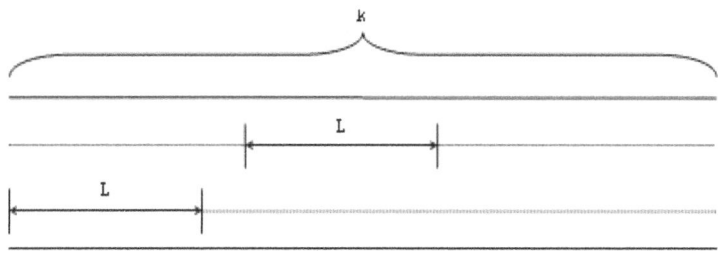

$$ED(P_k, S_{1k}) = ED(P_{k-L}, S_{1k-L}) + ED(P_L, S_{1L}) = ED(P_{k-L}, S_{1k-L})$$

Fig. 1. Subsequences edit distance,k is the length of pattern string and l is the length of their common string

If $k > L$, then $ED(P_i, S_{1k}) = ED(P_{i-L}, S_{1k-L}) + ED(P_L, S_{1L}) = ED(P_{i-L}, S_{1k-L})$.
If $k > L$ and $ED(P_{i-L}, S_{1k-L}) < (m - n)$,

then $ED(P, S_{1k}) - (m - n) < 0 \leq ED(P, S_2)$.   (3)

So there is no need to compute all the subsequences. If we know the cosine similarity (described later) $\cos \theta$, we can estimate $CS(P, S_1)$ through the length and, then $\cos \theta$ stop when it meets (3).

Let V_{S1} and V_{S2} are profile vectors of sequence S_1 and S_2, then cosine similarity,

$\cos \theta = \cos(V_{S1}, V_{S2}) = V_{S1} \cdot V_{S2} / (|V_{S1}| \cdot |V_{S2}|)$, $V_{S1} \cdot V_{S2} = \sum_{i=1}^{2T} V_{S1i} V_{S2i}$ is inner product.

$|V_{S1}| = \sqrt{V_{S1} \cdot V_{S1}}$ Smaller $\cos \theta$ indicates S_1 and S_2 are closer. Instead of computing a optimal alignment table, which needs an extra space to keep alignment results for each sequence, we use this cosine similarity to measure the whole similarity of a cluster C, record as csim. For each loop, we choose the cluster with max csim which represents for lowest similarity to decompose.

3 Flow of Algorithm

We also use bisecting k-means[8] clustering algorithm. Bisecting k-means is from document clustering[5], its time complexity is linear with the number of sequences. Suppose our algorithm is called IGSClu, and then its flow is:

Input: Dataset SS contains all sequences, k;
Output: k clusters of the sequences;
Scanning dataset, compute the sign $SN(S)$ and profile vector V_S for each sequence;
Construct a cluster contains all sequences for the first time, and push into the cluster stack ST; cluster number CN=1; set id of the cluster with max csim, max_csim_id=0;

While (CN < k)
{
    Pop from ST; get a cluster P with max csim.
    Find two center points in P, CO1 and CO2, the longest and the shortest sequence;Compute edit distance between them. Let new clusters are P1, P2;
    While (sequence number in P1 and P2 is smaller than in P)
    {
        For (each sequence S in P)
        {
        Compute $SD(S, CO1)$, $LD(S, CO1)$, $SD(S, CO2)$, $LD(S, CO2)$;
            If $\max\left(SD(P, S_2), ED(S_1, S_2)/2\right) \geq |P| + |S_1|$ push S into P1;
            else if $\max\left(SD(P, S_1), ED(S_1, S_2)/2\right) \geq |P| + |S_2|$ push S into P2;
            else if $LD(S, CO1) \geq LD(S, CO2)$
                Compute $ED(S, CO2)$, $\cos(V_s, V_{co1})$, estimate CS length,
                $l = CS(S, CO1)$ then detect subsequence $ED(S_k, CO1_k)$,
                if it meets (3), stop and push S into P1;
                else compute $ED(S, CO1)$ and decide where to put S.
        else

Compute $ED(S,CO1)$ and $\cos(V_s, V_{co2})$, estimate CS length ,
    $l = CS(S, CO2)$, then detect subsequence $ED(S_i, CO2_i)$,
    if it meets (3), stop and push S into P2;
    else compute $ED(S, CO2)$ and decide where to put S.
  }//end for
}//end while1
CN=CN+1;
Compute csim of P1 and P2, push them into ST;
}//end while2

4 Experiment Result

IGSClu is implemented in C++, run on a computer with 2GHz. We run on simulate data produced as follows[7]: Given alphabet (cardinal number is 10). First, generate k sequences with different lengths; represent k clusters, called seed sequences. Then generate other sequences through changing lengths and elements on seed sequences. Simulate data are described as $K5C5000L100\Delta50VL5VP10$, K represents for K clusters, C is the number of sequences, L is the reference length, $\Delta50$ represents 50 bases length changes, so the lengths of five seed sequences are 100,150,200,250,300. Each cluster produced by inserting or deleting any element in S with a probability no more than 5% and substitute any element with a probability no more than 10%. We use simulate datasets ds1~ ds6 and real data Retail sales dataset[9] refer in the paper. Then compare running time and WCS with GSClu.

Given cluster C_j with n_j sequences, $CS_j = \sum_{S \in C_j, S' \in C_j} ED(S, S') / (n_j(n_j - 1))$ is the

compactness of, C_j and $WCS = \sum_{j=1}^{k} n_j \times CS_j$ stands for the affection of the algorithm.

Fig.2 shows that IGSClu spends less time than GSClu because of the improved pruning condition. In ds6, each seed sequence is produced dependently, close to natural classification, sequences are more close to each other, but it will not detecting all k-subsequences, which cuts the running time. WCS (Fig.3) fall slightly because vector comparison is a rough estimate.

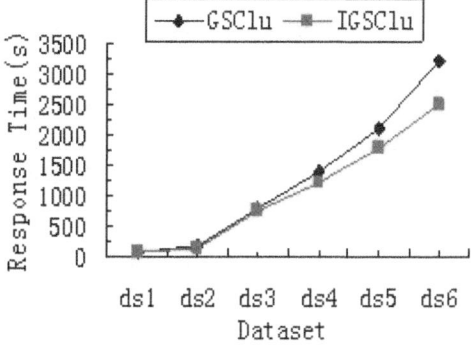

Fig. 2. Time vs. number of sequences

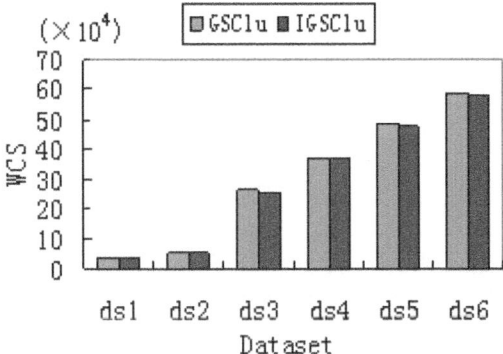

Fig. 3. WCS comparison on datasets

Running on Retail dataset, we found that most sequences follow the first pruning condition: $\max\left(SD(P, S_2), ED(S_1, S_2)/2\right) \geq |P| + |S_1|$, Fig.4 shows WCS a decline with about 10% because of Retail data is more discrete.

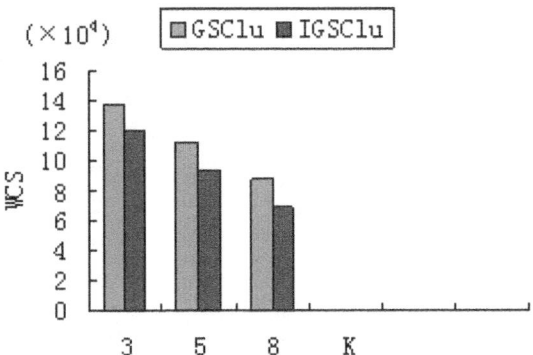

Fig. 4. WCS comparison on Retail dataset

5   Conclusion

In this paper, an improved algorithm for sequential clustering was proposed. According to experiments, the method can be appropriate for sequential clustering with a faster speed. The future work is to perform this method on biology in discovering sequence indels (insertions and deletions). Clustering can reduce dimensionality on sequencing data then discovering indels can be partitioned into small-scale problems.

References

1. Jain, A.K.: Data Clustering: 50 Years beyond K-Means. Pattern Recognition Letters (2009)
2. Gesfield, D.: Algorithms on strings, trees, and sequences. Cambridge University Press, Cambridge (1997)

3. Kahveci, T., Singh, A.K.: An efficient index structure for string databases. In: Proc.Of the 27th Int'l Conf. On Vear Large Data Bases, VLDB, pp. 351–360 (2001)
4. Ukkonen, E.: Approximate string matching with q-gram and maximal matching. Theory Computer Science 1, 191–211 (1992)
5. Steinbach, M., Karypis, G., Kumar, V. : A Comparison of Document Clustering Techniques. In: KDD Workshop on Text Mining (2000)
6. Dai, D.-B., Tang, S.-L., Xiong, Y.: Research on sequence data similarity query. PhD thesis. Fudan University (2009)
7. Dai, D.-B., Tang, S.-L., Xiong, Y.: Clustering Algorithms Based on Global and Local Similarity. Journal of Software Sequence 21(4) (2010)
8. Kashef, R., Kamel, M.S.: Enhanced bisecting k-means clustering using intermediate cooperation. Pattern Recognition 42(11), 2557–2569 (2009)
9. Datasets: `http://fimi.ua.ac.be/data/`

An Effective Feature Selection Method Using Dynamic Information Criterion

Huawen Liu[1,2], Minshuo Li[1], Jianmin Zhao[1], and Yuchang Mo[1,3]

[1] Department of Computer Science, Zhejiang Normal University,
Jinhua 321004, China
[2] Key Laboratory of Symbol Computation and Knowledge Engineering of
Ministry of Education, Changchun 130012, China
[3] School of Computer Science and Engineering, Southeast University,
Nanjing 211189, China
{hwliu,lmshappy,zjm,myc}@zjnu.cn

Abstract. With rapid development of information technology, dimensionality of data in many applications is getting higher and higher. However, many features in the high-dimensional data are redundant. Their presence may pose a great number of challenges to traditional learning algorithms. Thus, it is necessary to develop an effective technique to remove irrelevant features from data. Currently, many endeavors have been attempted in this field. In this paper, we propose a new feature selection method by using conditional mutual information estimated dynamically. Its advantage is that it can exactly represent the correlation between features along with the selection procedure. Our performance evaluations on eight benchmark datasets show that our proposed method achieves comparable performance to other well-established feature selection algorithms in most cases.

Keywords: Feature selection, classification, mutual information, data mining, learning algorithm.

1 Introduction

With rapid development of information technology, dimensionality of data in many application scenarios is often characterized by hundreds or even thousands of features. The high dimensionality of data may bring many adverse situations to pattern classification. Many of features are correlated with each other and useless to classification. Moreover, the high dimensionality will also lead to over-fitting situation and even raise the so-called problem of 'curse of dimensionality' [1].

Feature selection aims at removing useless or insignificant features for class discrimination and retaining as many salient features as possible, so as to characterize the main property of data. Since it can bring lots of potential benefits to learning algorithms [2], such as reducing computational cost, improving prediction performance and avoiding over-fitting, feature selection has been extensively studied and many outstanding feature selection algorithms have been addressed [3, 4]. Generally, feature selection methods can be roughly categorized into embedded,

H. Deng et al. (Eds.): AICI 2011, Part I, LNAI 7002, pp. 450–455, 2011.

wrapper, filter and hybrid models [3, 4]. Since the embedded and wrapper models are tightly coupled with specified learning algorithms, their computational costs are relatively expensive.

The filter model evaluates the goodness of feature with pre-specified criteria, which is independent of learning algorithms. Due to its computational efficiency, it is very popular in reality. Liu and Yu [3] summarized the evaluation criteria into four major groups, i.e., distance (e.g., Euclidean distance), information (e.g., entropy and information gain), dependency (e.g., Pearson's correlation coefficient and t-test) and consistency measures [5], where the information ones exploit information entropy to evaluate features.

Since information entropy is capable of measuring non-linear correlation and quantifying the uncertainty of feature, the information criteria have been widely adopted in feature selection [4]. As a typical example, MIFS [9] and mRMR [6] measures the relevance between features by mutual information. Further, Kwak and Choi [10] developed a revised MIFS, called MIFS-U, by adding $I(C; S)$ into the penalized operator. Recently, Novovicova et al. [11] replaced the sum operation with a maximum one in mMIFS-U to further improve performance.

Apart from mutual information, other information metrics have also been adopted in feature selection. As a typical example, Yu and Liu in FCBF [12] focused on symmetrical uncertainty (shortly, SU) to represent the information correlation between features and classes. Bell and Wang [13] adopt unconditional variable relevance as their criterion function in evaluating features. Levi and Ullman [14] employed conditional mutual information as their evaluation criterion. Recently, Liu et al. [7] employed a normalized mutual information to choose salient genes for cancer classification. Several extensive experiments have also demonstrated that the information criteria work well in most cases [8].

Since information criteria in traditional selection algorithms are estimated on the whole sampling space, this may raise a problem, that is, once the training data has been given, the values of information criteria are also fixed and will not be changed throughout the whole selection process. This is unreasonable because the quantity of unrecognized instances in the training data is getting smaller and smaller during the training procedure of classifiers, and the rest unrecognized instances are more important than those recognized ones in evaluating the interestingness of features. To tackle with this issue, in this paper, a new feature selection algorithm, called FSDIC, is proposed. The evaluation criterion used here of FSDIC is a dynamic one, which can exactly represent the correlation between features.

The structure of the rest is organized as follows. Section 2 presents some basic concepts about information entropy. In Section 3, a new feature selection algorithm using dynamic information criterion is proposed. Experimental results conducted on UCI data sets to evaluate the performance of our approach are provided in Section 4. Finally, conclusions and future works are given in the end.

2   Information Entropy

Information entropy is one of fundamental concepts in information theory. Let X be a discrete random variable and $p(x)$ be its marginal probability density distribution. The uncertainty of X can be measured by information entropy $H(X)$, which is defined as $H(X) = -\sum p(x)\log p(x)$.

Given two variables X and Y, their joint entropy $H(X, Y)$ is represented as $H(X,Y) = -\sum\sum p(x,y)\log p(x,y)$. To further measure how much information is shared between two features (variables), a concept, called mutual information, is introduced and denoted as

$$I(X;Y) = \sum\sum p(x,y)\log\frac{p(x,y)}{p(x)p(y)}.$$

Note that the more relevant two variables are, the higher their mutual information is, and $I(X; Y) = 0$ means that these two variables are totally irrelevant to each other. According to its definition, we can rewrite mutual information as $I(X; Y) = H(X) + H(Y) - H(X, Y)$.

3   An Effective Feature Selection Method

Let $T=(D, F, C)$ be a dataset, where C and D denote the class labels and instances represented by features $F=\{f_1, ..., f_m\}$, respectively. Generally speaking, the task of feature selection is to choose a minimum optimal subset S of F such that the representative power of S is as strong as possible. From the view of information theory, the learning process of classifier is to minimize the uncertainty of the known observations S regarding to the class labels C. This is inherently consistent with $I(C; S)$, which contains important dependence information between the selected subset S and the labels C. If $I(C; S)$ of features S with C is very small, S are irrelevant to C and they contribute nothing to the distribution of the classes.

In traditional methods, the probability distributions of features on sampling space will not be altered any more after the training dataset has been given. This may raise a problem that the information criteria estimated on the given data cannot exactly represent the information provided by features along with the feature selection procedure.

Assume S is the selected subset of features, instances in a dataset D can be exclusively classified into two disjoint partitions: recognized D_l and unrecognized ones D_u, where $D=D_u\cup D_l$ and $D_u\cap D_l =\varnothing$. During the learning process of a classifier, Du will be continuously identified in the light of available knowledge embodied by S. Usually, the feature with the largest information criterion estimated on D will be selected, where each instance has the same weight. However, if the classifier has more powerful discrimination ability, it should select a good feature f embodying most information of D_u in the next step. This implies that D_u should be placed more emphasis than D_l.

From the classification perspective, the information contained within D_l is useless and D_u is more important than D_l during the rest learning procedure. Therefore, $I(C; f)$ or its conditional one, which estimated on the whole instances D in the traditional selection methods, can not exactly represent the relevance between f and C.

Based on above analysis, we propose a new feature selection algorithm called FSDIC, where the conditional mutual information is dynamically re-estimated on D_u, not the whole space D. The details of our algorithm (FSDIC) are given as Alg. 1. The distinctness of FSDIC with others lies in that our evaluation criterion is conditional mutual information and its value is dynamically estimated on unrecognized instances.

Algorithm 1. Feature selection with dynamic information criterion

1) Initialize relative parameters, e.g., $S = \varnothing$, $D_l = \varnothing$, and $D_u = D$;
2) For each candidate feature, calculate its $I(S; f|C)$ on D_u;
3) Select the feature with the largest value of criterion, and add it into S;
4) Remove the instances recognized by the selected feature from D_u;
5) If D_u or F is empty, return S as the final result; Otherwise, go back to Step 2 to select the next feature.

---

4   Performance Evaluation

To evaluation the performance of FSDIC, several experiments have been carried out on eight UCI datasets [15] with different types and sizes. Table 1 provides their general information.

Table 1. The brief descriptions of datasets

No	Datasets	instances	features	classes
1	Internet advertisers	3279	1558	2
2	KDD synthetic control	600	60	6
3	Kr-vs-kp	3196	36	2
4	Lymph	148	18	4
5	Mushroom	8124	22	2
6	Musk clean1	476	166	2
7	Musk clean2	6598	166	2
8	Sponge	76	44	3

In our experiments, MIFS [9], FCBF [12], MIFS-U [10] and mMIFS-U [11] were taken as the baseline. The reason of choosing them is that they represent four different types of MIFSA. Moreover, a popular learning algorithm, i.e., C4.5, was employed to to validate the classification performances. All experiments were conducted under the platform of Weka toolkit [16]. In order to achieve impartial results, three ten-fold cross validations had been adopted in verifying classification capability and its average values were the final results.

The results of classification performance of individual classifier induced by five feature selectors on the datasets are presented in Table 2, where the Original column in each table denotes the performance of the corresponding classifier over the original datasets without using selectors. The bold value refers to the largest one among five feature selection methods in the same classifier.

Table 2. A comparison of performances of five feature selectors in the C4.5 classifier

No	Original	FSDIC	mMIFS-U	MIFS-U	MIFS	FCBF
1	96.83	97.20	97.20	96.98	96.14	96.98
2	93.00	92.54	77.19*	78.02*	87.15	77.30*
3	99.44	99.16	97.95	96.98*	96.57	96.98*
4	78.59	79.35	73.51	73.51	73.29	72.59*
5	100.00	100.00	99.41	99.41	98.62	99.90
6	87.76	85.12	84.91	81.12*	78.38	84.70
7	96.63	95.51	94.84	95.03	93.62	94.85
8	92.50	92.32*	92.32*	92.32*	92.32	92.32*

In the C4.5 classifier (Table 2), the predominance of FSDIC is still distinct, because the classification performance of selected features induced by FSDIC are the highest ones among five selectors over all of these datasets. For the Sponge dataset (i.e., No. 8), FSDIC significantly degraded the performance of the classifier. However, its performance is the same with other selection algorithms, and slightly lower than the original one. For the rest selectors, the significantly worse cases are range from two to four.

5   Conclusions

Feature selection plays a unique role in pattern analysis and data mining. In this paper, we developed a new feature selection algorithm, whose evaluation criterion is conditional mutual information. Unlike other feature selection methods using information criterion, our method estimates conditional mutual information dynamically on unrecognized instances, not the whole sampling space. Its advantage is that candidate features are irrelevant or redundant for classification regarding to recognized instances. Simulation experimental results on eight UCI benchmark datasets show that the proposed method works well and outperforms other classical feature selectors in most cases.

Acknowledgments. This work is supported by the National NSF of China (60903011), Doctor Point Founds of Educational Department of China (20090092120030), the NSF of Zhejiang Province (Y1100689), Opening Fund of Key Discipline of Computer Software and Theory of Zhejiang Province at ZJNU (ZSDZZZZXK05) and Opening Fund of Key Laboratory of Symbol Computation and Knowledge Engineering of Ministry of Education (93K-17-2010-K02).

References

1. Duda, R.O., Hart, P.E., Stork, D.G.: Pattern Classification, 2nd edn. John Wiley & Sons, New York (2001)
2. Hilario, M., Kalousis, A.: Approaches to dimensionality reduction in proteomic biomarker studies. Briefings in Bioinformatics 9(2), 102–118 (2008)

3. Liu, H., Yu, L.: Toward Integrating Feature Selection Algorithms for Classification and Clustering. IEEE Transactions on Knowledge and Data Engineering 17(4), 491–502 (2005)
4. Liu, H., Sun, J., Liu, L., Zhang, H.: Feature selection with dynamic mutual information. Pattern Recognition 42(7), 1330–1339 (2009)
5. Arauzo-Azofra, A., Benitez, J.M., Castro, J.L.: Consistency measures for feature selection. Journal of Intelligence Information System 30, 273–292 (2008)
6. Peng, H., Long, F., Ding, C.: Feature Selection Based on Mutual Information: Criteria of Max–Dependency, Max–Relevance, and Min–Redundancy. IEEE Transactions on Pattern Analysis and Machine Intelligence 27(8), 1226–1238 (2005)
7. Liu, H., Liu, L., Zhang, H.: Ensemble Gene Selection by Grouping for Microarray Data Classification. Journal of Biomedical Informatics 43(1), 81–87 (2010)
8. Liu, H., Liu, L., Zhang, H.: Feature Selection using Mutual Information: An Experimental Study. In: Ho, T.-B., Zhou, Z.-H. (eds.) PRICAI 2008. LNCS (LNAI), vol. 5351, pp. 235–246. Springer, Heidelberg (2008)
9. Battiti, R.: Using Mutual Information for Selecting Features in Supervised Neural Net Learning. IEEE Transactions on Neural Networks 5(4), 537–550 (1994)
10. Kwak, N., Choi, C.H.: Input feature selection by mutual information based on Parzen window. IEEE Transactions on Pattern Analysis and Machine Intelligence 24(12), 1667–1671 (2002)
11. Novovičová, J., Somol, P., Haindl, M., Pudil, P.: Conditional Mutual Information Based Feature Selection for Classification Task. In: Rueda, L., Mery, D., Kittler, J. (eds.) CIARP 2007. LNCS, vol. 4756, pp. 417–426. Springer, Heidelberg (2007)
12. Yu, L., Liu, H.: Efficient Feature Selection via Analysis of Relevance and Redundancy. Journal of Machine Learning Research 5, 1205–1224 (2004)
13. Bell, D.A., Wang, H.: A Formalism for Relevance and Its Application in Feature Subset Selection. Machine Learning 41, 175–195 (2000)
14. Levi, D., Ullman, S.: Learning to classify by ongoing feature selection. Image and Vision Computing 28(4), 715–723 (2010)
15. Asuncion, A., Newman, D.J.: UCI Repository of machine learning databases. Department of Information and Computer Science. University of California, Irvine (2007), http://www.ics.uci.edu/~mlearn/MLRepository.html
16. Witten, I.H., Frank, E.: Data Mining-Pracitcal Machine Learning Tools and Techniques with JAVA Implementations, 2nd edn. Morgan Kaufmann Publishers, San Francisco (2005)

Service Cooperation-Based Trusted and Autonomic Virtual Organizations

Ji Gao[1,2] and Hexin Lv[1]

[1] College of Information Science & Technology
Zhejiang Shureng University, Hangzhou, China, 310015
[2] College of Computer Science & Technology
Zhejiang University, Hangzhou, China, 310027
gaoji1@zju.edu.cn, hexin10241024@sina.com

Abstract. This paper proposes a multi-agent model for achieving service cooperation-based trusted and autonomic VOs (Virtual organizations), called IGTASC, which depends on three technologies to make service cooperation both trusted and autonomic: institution-governed autonomic cooperation, policy-driven self-management, and community facilitation management. It is the close coupling of those technologies that supports effectively not only the resolution of the so-called "trust" crisis which occurs due to business services across different management domains but also the realization of autonomic service cooperation and hence the large-scale deployment of VOs.

Keywords: service cooperation, institution-governed, trusted, policy-driven, virtual organization.

1 Introduction

Along with the development of Service-Oriented Computing (SOC)[1] and Service-Oriented Architecture (SOA)[2], constructing Virtual Organizations (VOs) by creating Service cooperation (i.e. service-oriented cooperation) has become the mainstream approach for reforming the development of application software systems in Internet computing environment. While the service cooperation can be created dynamically, on requirement, and in low cost by composing business services distributed on Internet, the inherent non-controllability of business services across different management domains has brought on the so-called "trust" crisis that the success and benefit of cooperation cannot be ensured, and thereby seriously prevented VOs from being deployed and applied in a large scale.

In order to conquer the crisis, this paper proposes a multi-agent model for Institution-Governed Trusted and Autonomic Service Cooperation, called IGTASC, which also can eliminate the dilemma that the requirements of "Autonomy" and "Trust" conflict with each other, which has worried the research of autonomic computing and multi-agent systems for a long time.

IGTASC depends on three technologies to make service cooperation both trusted and autonomic: institution-governed autonomic cooperation, policy-driven

H. Deng et al. (Eds.): AICI 2011, Part I, LNAI 7002, pp. 456–466, 2011.

self-management, and community facilitation management. The technology of institution-governed autonomic cooperation formulates domain e-institutions (electronic institu- tions) as service cooperation regulations to govern agents' cooperation behaviors in macro level so that it can be trusted that service cooperation created dynamically by agents will achieve required objectives as long as those agents all conform to relevant regulations respectively. However, how to ensure that all of individuals (agents) conform to those regulations is confronted with a real challenge because of the inherent non-controllability of agents across different management domains.

The technologies of policy-driven self-management and community facilitation management can just be used to overcome this challenge. The former aims at using management policies to drive agents to make their own micro behaviors comply rationally with relevant regulations while the latter deploys the agents enacting cooperation facilitation-oriented roles formulated in the agent community in order to provide cooperation assistance and to maintain cooperation order (i.e. force the agents in application domains to conform to the regulations). Thereby, the macro-level government can be exerted reliably to the agents participating in cooperation. It is the close coupling of the three technologies that supports effectively both the resolution of "trust" crisis and the realization of autonomic service cooperation.

From the point of view for achieving autonomic service cooperation, the mechanisms of "Institution-Governed"[3,4] and "Policy-Driven"[5,6] are oriented to collectivity cooperation and individual behaviors respectively, but can complement each other well. Therefore, they should be integrated closely in order to facilitate effectively the development of autonomic service cooperation. of course, business services should be encapsulated into the skills of individuals (i.e. agents).

However, at present, the research on "Institution-Governed" focuses only on how to use Multi-Agent technology to develop the theories and methods of intelligent application, and is not yet transformed into meeting service-oriented concepts. It is this status that makes the research be isolated from the practice of mainstream service-oriented Internet computing and lack the theory and application results oriented to Operationalisation. By adopting service-oriented approach, the mechanisms of "Institution-Governed" and "Policy-Driven" will be reconstructed in order to enable them to be integrated closely into the real applications.

This paper is organized as follows. Section 2 proposes the Trusted and Autonomic VOs (TAVOs) and supporting environment. Section 3 shows how the institution-governed autonomic cooperation, policy-driven self-management, and community facilitation management are modeled. Section 4 describes the support of IGTASC to developing TAVOs. Finally, the conclusions are given in Section 5.

2   Three-Level Virtual Society for TAVOs to Live

IGTASC restricts the organizational form of a TAVO to the mode explained below in order to make this form of VOs still possesses wide application extents while enabling IGTASC to exhibit better performance.

In human society, the most familiar cooperation form is an alliance based on service providing-requiring relations, which is sponsored and created by some physical organization to satisfy certain business requirements (such as making new products, solving complex problems, searching for knowledge, purchasing merchandise, etc.). Such an alliance often concerns multiple binary collaborations which are all sponsored and managed by the same party (as service consumer). Also, service providers themselves may complete their service provision by creating the cooperation alliances which, but, are in the next level and are not controlled by the upper-level alliance manager.

Although there may be the requirement for direct interactions between the providers of different services, these interactions can be removed by partitioning business activities reasonably and arranging the appropriate messages sent by the alliance manager. Also, although there are other cooperation modes in human society, the cooperation in the mode of alliance is still the mainstream and can suit to the requirement of complex cooperation by creating nested alliances. Therefore, not losing generality, IGTASC proposes to implement a TAVO by creating the alliance which is managed centrally by the sponsor and in which there is no interaction between other members. Of course, every member of a VO should set up an agent as its broker.

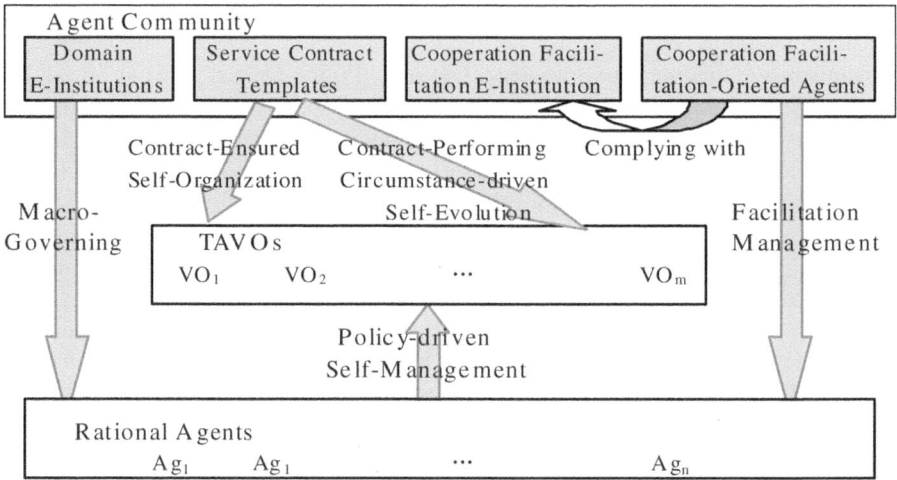

Fig. 1. Three-level virtual society supported by three technologies constituting model IGTASC

In order to support effectively the autonomic construction, running, and evolution of VOs, IGTASC proposes a three-level Virtual Society (VS) as the environment where VOs live and work (Figure 1). VS is defined as a 3-tuple:

VS = (AC, TV, RA)

• AC: the Agent Community for VOs and agents to live. As the first level of VS, AC accommodate a variety of e-institutions in order to provide the regulations for constraining the cooperation behaviors of community members (agents), and manages and maintains community order depending on the cooperation facilitation-oriented agents which will be described in section 3.3.

• TV: the set of TAVOs. As the second level of VS, TV promises community members to freely constitute VOs for achieving the business objectives of VO sponsors by conforming to domain e-institutions. Because of the rationality and autonomy of VO members (which are rational agents in the bottom level of VS) and the cooperation facilitation management provided by the agent community, those VOs become both trusted and autonomic.

• RA: the set of rational agents registering in the agent community. As the bottom level of VS, RA accommodates a variety of heterogeneous business operation-oriented agents providing and / or consuming business services as long as the interaction between these agents conforms to relevant domain e-institutions. Here, by implementing policy-driven self-management, these agents make their own cooperation behaviors conform to the regulations formulated in relevant e-institutions, and thus become trusted and further result in trusted VOs.

3 Model IGTASC and Its Supporting Technologies

In such a three-level virtual society, achieving the service cooperation-based TAVOs is a systematic engineering under the support of three technologies relatively independent but supplementing each other: domain e-institutions, policy-driven self-management, and community facilitation management (see Figure 1). Thus, IGTASC is defined as a 3-tuple:

IGTASC = (IGAC, PDSM, CFM)

• IGAC: the institution-governed autonomic cooperation, which aims at formulating domain e-institutions as the regulations to govern agents' service cooperation behaviors in macro level.

• PDSM: the policy-driven self-management, which models agents as the rational individuals which provide and / or consume business services in the mode defined by relevant e-institutions, are driven by management policies, and make their own behaviors accept the macro government of outer constraints (see section 3.2).

• CFM: the community facilitation management, which deploys a team of agents which provide facilitation services on the regulations formulated in the e-institution for cooperation facilitation. It is the joint work of those management-oriented agents that provide cooperation assistance and maintain cooperation order.

3.1 Domain E-Institution

Human societies have already established a great variety of institutions, from the big ones like the strategic collaboration between nations to the small ones like city traffic and market trade. By borrowing their structure modes, the model IGTASC partitions the regulations formulated in an e-institution into two parts: social structure standards and coupling cooperation behavior norms. The former, as the hard constraints cooperation participants can not violate, aims at determining completely the mode and context for realizing service providing-requiring cooperation in the macro level so that the non-determinability of cooperation can be reduced largely. In contrast, the latter is the soft constraints imposed on run-time behaviors of agents, and therefore their violation (e.g. the norm of service quality) can not be forbidden forcedly.

However, setting up coupling sanction means can facilitate greatly norms to be complied with.

Accordingly, the E-Institution of application domain D is represented as a 3-tuple:

E-Institution^D = (S-Structure^D, B-Norm^D, Ontology^D), where

- S-Structure^D: the social structure standards of application domain D, which is also represented as a 3-tuple:
  S-Structure^D = (B-Service^D, B-O-Role^D, DBP^D), where
  - B-Service^D: the set of business services provided or consumed in domain D;
  - B-O-Role^D: the set of business operation-oriented roles which agents in domain D can enact in service cooperation;
  - DBP^D: the Distributed Business Process in domain D, which aims at describing the process for multiple agents to cooperatively complete business activities in D;

- B-Norm^D: the set of cooperation behavior norms in domain D, which specify the obligations, forbiddances, and rights (promises) which agents, while enacting business operation-oriented roles and participating in service providing-requiring cooperation, should conform to or possess.

- Ontology^D: the ontology of domain D, which is the conceptual description of domain D and used to support the formulation of social structure standards and cooperation behavior norms.

Each business service is defined as a set of business transactions (i.e., operators) provided by it, and it is those transactions that can be invoked to complete the relevant activities required by consumers. Each role ($\in$ B-O-Role^D) specifies a set of business transaction roles, which are relevant to different services, enacted by this role, the rights for the role to invoke some services, the obligations for providing some business services, and the possible service state transition (from one service to another) in cooperation.

DBP^D is defined as a partial-order set composed of a number of binary collaborations. There may be nested binary collaborations and bottom-layer ones correspond to business services. A binary collaboration specifies the business transaction roles enacted by two participants, the cooperation activities included, and the obligations for those roles.

A norm is represented, with extended Deontic Logic [7], as OB$_{bor}^D$($\rho \leq \delta \mid \sigma$), FB$_{bor}^D$($\rho \leq \delta \mid \sigma$), or PB$_{bor}^D$($\rho \leq \delta \mid \sigma$), indicating respectively that, when σ holds true, the role *bor* ($\in$ B-O-Role^D) is obligated to, forbidden to, or authorized to make ρ true before deadline δ (here ρ, δ, and σ are all the propositions describing service cooperation status). It is the norms that become the constituents for defining obligations and rights of *bor* and in *bc* ($\in$ DBP^D). Embedding norms into *bor* and *bc* enables norms to be disposed and installed soundly in structural and systematical mode, hence facilitates completeness, consistence, and maintenance of norms.

3.2 Policy-Driven Self-Management

The policy-driven self-management models agents as the rational individuals which provide and / or consume business services according to the social structures in domain e-institutions, has their autonomic behaviors accept the macro-government of the outer constraints, and are driven by management policies. Here, the outer constraints include cooperation behavior norms formulated in domain e-institutions and the business instructions (high-level business goals and transaction principles) sent over by agents' owners; and management policies are used as the principles or rules for agents to decide cooperation behaviors according to these outer constraints and cooperation status.

In order to supporting service cooperation, the Policy-Driven Self-Management (PDSM) is defined as a multi-tuple:

$$PDSM = (\text{A-Role, O-Instruction, A-State, A-Service, A-Goal, A-Activity, LBP,}$$
$$\text{P-T-Event, A-Policy, triggering, planning),}$$

where 'A-Role' denotes the set of the business operation-oriented roles (which may pertain to different e-institutions) enacted by an agent ag, 'O-Instruction' the set of business instructions sent over by the owner of ag, 'A-State' the set of service cooperation states perceived by ag, 'A-Service' the set of business services relative to ag.

'A-Goal' denotes the set of business goals of ag, which are partitioned into two types: service-providing (G_p) and service-acquiring (G_a), that is A-Goal = $G_p \cup G_a$, while 'A-Activity' is the set of local business activities for supporting service cooperation, which are partitioned into three types: norm-conforming(Ac_{nc}), service-providing(Ac_{sp}), and service-acquiring (Ac_{sa}), that is A-Activity =$Ac_{nc} \cup Ac_{sp} \cup Ac_{sa}$.

'LBP' denotes the set of lbps (local business processes). A lbp ($\in$LBP) is composed of activities (Ac_{sa}) complying with a certain execution order. While an atomic activity a_i ($\in Ac_{sp}$) is performed by invoking a single operator (e.g., a business transaction provided by a internal or outside business service), the composed activity a_j ($\in Ac_{sp}$) is performed by starting a lbp.

'P-T-Event' is the set of policy trigger events while 'A-Policy' denotes the set of internal policies for managing ag' cooperation behaviors. Each po ($\in$ A-Policy), designed as a group of behavior rules, can be activated by some e ($\in$P-T-Event) in order to decide and drive a proper business activity according to current states and relevant local business instructions. The policies are partitioned into three types: service-request-response (P_{srr}), service-providing (P_{sp}), and service-acquiring (P_{sa}), that is, A-Policy = $P_{srr} \cup P_{sp} \cup P_{sa}$.

The mapping functions of triggering and planning are defined as follows:

- triggering: P-T-Event $\rightarrow$ A-Policy, which indicates to trigger a relevant policy;

- planning: $Ac_{sp} \nrightarrow$ LBP $\rightarrow \mathbb{P}Ac_{sa}$ (here, $\mathbb{P}$ denotes power set and $\nrightarrow$ denotes partial function); when a composed activity a ($\in Ac_{sp}$) is performed, a starts the lbp ($\in$LBP) relevant to a, as a plan, to perform next-layer service-acquiring activities.

The policy-driven self-management of an agent ag is illustrated in Figure 2. The backbone process is partitioned into three stages: generating trigger events, activating relevant management policies, and driving (deciding) proper business activities. First, the event e_1 ($\in$P-T-Event) generated by an outer service request activates the service request response policy po_1 ($\in P_{srr}$), which drives the service norm-conforming activity a_1 ($\in Ac_{nc}$) relevant to the requested business service bs_1 ($\in$ A-Service).

Then, *ag* checks the right of service request party and its own condition for providing bs_1, and thus creates the trigger event e_2 ($\in$P-T-Event). Again, e_2 or some internal service request event e_3 activates the service-providing policy po_2 ($\in P_{sp}$), which drives the activity a_2 ($\in Ac_{sp}$) to be performed by invoking the requested business transaction bt_1 provided by bs_1.

If a_2 needs to be performed by executing a local business process *lbp* ($\in$LBP) and some business activities in *lbp* should be executed by invoking outer business services, *ag* generates event set E (P-T-Event) (see the double lines and arrows in Figure 2), which activates policy set P (P_{sa}) and further drives activity set Ac (Ac_{sa}). Then *ag* creates, by negotiation and optimized selection, the cooperation relationships for acquiring these next-layer services. Thereby, *ag* and the agents selected to provide these services together compose dynamically the VO aiming at completing a_2, and *ag* becomes the sponsor and manager of this VO.

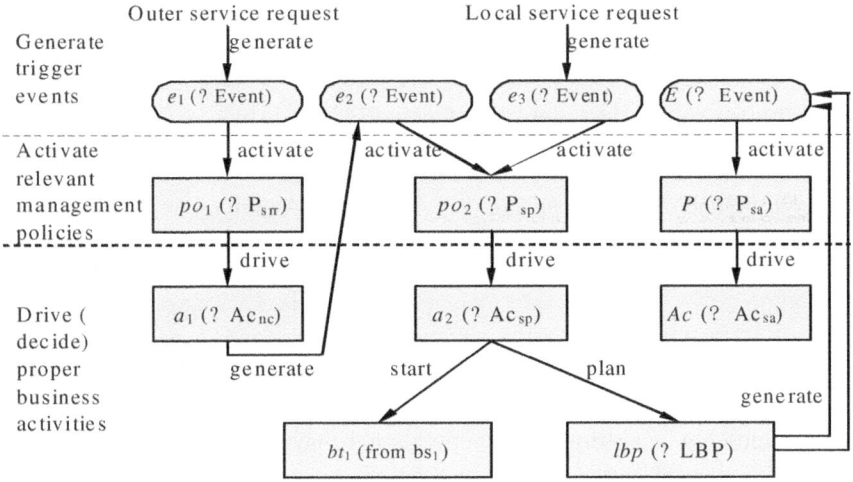

Fig. 2. The policy-driven self-management of agent behaviors when creating service cooperation and VO

Because management policies include the knowledge about how to select local business activities according to social structure standards and cooperation behavior norms in e-institutions, such agent behavior self-management can achieve effectively the policy-driven mapping from macro-government to micro-behaviors. Therefore, agents enable their own social behaviors to accept always the macro-government of behavior norms (and local business instructions), becoming trusted rational individuals.

3.3 Community Facilitation Management

Because of the lack of effective means for providing cooperation assistance and maintaining the cooperation order, depending only on domain e-institutions and rational agents can not yet ensure that all cooperation participants conform to relevant regulations. By formulating a cooperation facilitation e-institution and deploying a team of agents which provide facilitation services on cooperation facilitation-oriented roles in this e-institution, the community facilitation management can assist the creation of cooperation relationships and force agents to conform to cooperation behavior norms and service contracts dynamically created.

The Community Facilitation Management (CFM) is defined as a 5-tuple:

CFM = (E-Institution^F, CFA, Mi-Info, Ma-Info, S-C-Template)

Here, E-Institution^F indicates the cooperation facilitation e-institution, which formulates the regulation for governing cooperation facilitation management. Similar to E-Institution^D,

E-Institution^F = (S-Structure^F, B-Norm^F, Ontology^F)

S-Structure^F = (F-Service, C-F-Role, DBP^F)

S-Structure^F possesses the definition Similar to S-Structure^D, and formulates four cooperation facilitation-oriented roles in a community: S-F-Role = {Community-authority, Service-matchmaker, Arbitrator, Monitor}. Therein, Community-authority is configured with the facilitation services of role registration for business operation-oriented agents, reputation query, role registration query, reputation updating, etc., Service-matchmaker capability advertisement, partner recommendation, etc., Arbitrator notarization for business service cooperation contracts, contract violation arbitration, etc., and Monitors the services for receiving reports of executing contract-performing protocols, monitoring contracts, analyzing contract violation, etc.

Three types of facilitation services are formulated: F-Service = Information-Archiving ∪ Assisting ∪ Regulating. Therein, Information-Archiving = {agent-role-registration, capability-advertisement, contract-notarization, contract-performing-report-receiving}, which aims at receiving the shared information archived in the community in order to use the information as the bases for the other two types to work; Assisting = {partner-recommendation, reputation-query, role-registration-query}, which aims at assisting the creation and optimization of service cooperation; and Regulating = {contract-monitoring, contract-violation-analyzing, contract-violation-arbitration, reputation-updating}, which forms the forced-mode regulation mechanism.

CFA denotes the set of agents enacting the above roles. By providing the Information-Archiving services, these agents receive micro-level information items (pertaining to Mi-Info) sent by business operation-oriented agents, and then transform them into macro-level items (pertaining to Ma-Info) as the bases for supporting service cooperation. Because micro-level items have accepted checkups, agents registered in the community strengthen their creditability.

While the Assisting services redound to optimizing the search and choice of cooperation partner, the Regulating services form the regulating mechanism composed of five phases: indicting (requesting arbitration), analyzing (and verifying), arbitrating, monitoring (by receiving contract-performing reports), and reputation-updating (as sanction means) in order to drive and force agents to rationally conform to behavior norms and service contracts (see Figure 3).

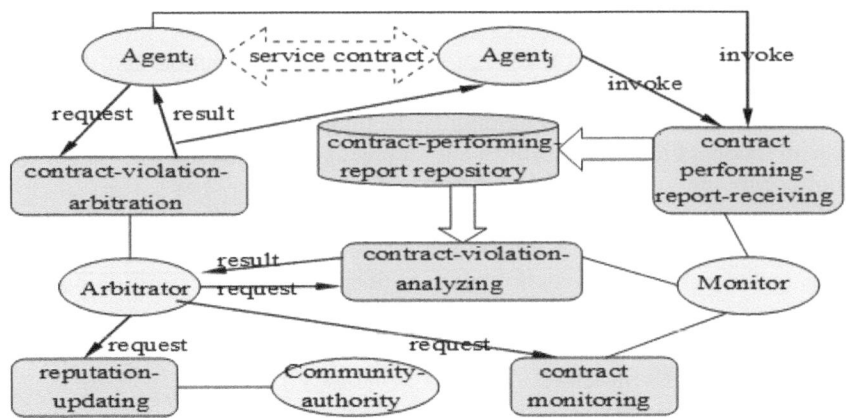

Fig. 3. Contract-based regulating mechanism (the dotted arrow indicates that agents i and j cooperate on contract)

S-C-Template denotes the set of service contract templates used to instantiate business service contracts. Through the detailed partition of application domains, providing and instantiating the parameterized and domain-shared contract templates are both feasible and not very difficult.

A service contract is composed of two parts: the basic information and a contract-performing protocol. The former specifies the business transaction roles enacted by both parties, period of validity for this contract, service content (e.g. the operation or product items, price, number, and deadline), service quality, etc. while the latter is designed as a partial-order set composed of protocol entries represented as contract-performing norms. By making contract notarization, the above regulating mechanism can drive and force agents to conform to service contract-performing protocols.

4   Two-Stage Development of TAVOs

Based on the model IGTASC, a TAVO can be created to overcome the limitation resulting from the non-autonomy of service cooperation and to obtain the excellent quality difficult to be acquired by non-autonomic VOs, specially the self-organization and self-evolution of service cooperation. We have created the IGTASC-based Development Framework for TAVO (DFTAVO), which supports the development of a TAVO in two stages: VO creation and VO running. DFTAVO has completed its prototype design (including an agent modeling and running platform) and been used to establish several experimental TAVOs, such as small meeting arrangement, knowledge provision, multi-part device cooperation production, and multi-department crisis cooperation transaction.

VO Creation. According to section 2, the self-organization process of a TAVO is sponsored by some agent. For example, in order to arrange a small meeting, the agent ag receiving the task from its owner will firstly determine, based on a lbp ($\in$LBP), the services which should be provided from the outer and accept the instructions of service applicability constraints from its owner. Then *ag* requests the matchmaker agent in the community to recommend the service providers satisfying those constraints and makes optimized selection from these providers (and relative acquaintances if exist). Note, *ag* is also the organizer, which invokes the negotiation services formulated in the cooperation facilitation e-institution to carry through the policy-driven providing-requiring negotiation, and creates signed two-party service contracts with chosen service providers. Thus, the TAVO completes its self-organization and *ag* becomes the manager of this TAVO. Besides, the agents as service providers may also complete the provision of these services by creating next-level TAVOs.

VO running. Since the VOs created by self-organization use service contracts as the assurance of service providing-requiring cooperation, the running of VOs becomes the process in which members perform cooperation activities alternately according to contract-performing protocols. Because service contract-performing protocols are represented as the partial-order sets of contract-performing norms (see section 3.3) which have the features of soft-constraints, the abnormal change of the service cooperation circumstance may occur when some contract is violated (e.g. some contract-performing norm is violated). Thus, whether VOs can self-evolve flexibly along with the change of contract-performing circumstance becomes the key for VOs to be used as the feasible pattern of service cooperation. Thereby, DFTAVO has been designed to support circumstance-driven self-adaptation and self-evolution of cooperation.

5 Conclusions

By developing and closely coupling the three technologies: institution-governed autonomic cooperation, policy-driven self-management, and community facilitation management, the model IGTASC proposed in this paper can resolve the "trust" crisis encountered by service cooperation-based VOs.

Along with solving this "trust" crisis, IGTASC can eliminate the limitation resulting from non-autonomic service cooperation, therefore makes the autonomy and change-response ability of service cooperation exhibit the advantage of robustness and intelligence. Furthermore, IGTASC also establishes the solid foundation for the institution-governed and contract-ensured hierarchical-cooperation self-organization of VOs and the contract-performing circumstance-driven cooperation self-adaptation and self-evolution of VOs, and thus makes the service cooperation-based VOs possess high performance of self-organization and self-evolution.

Contrasting with the popular e-institutions, IGTASC also exhibits prominent properties. Typical e-institutions use scenes composed of landmarks (objectives) sequences as basic units[8]. Due to the lack of enough structures, there is no way to use these units to describe the complicated structure of dbp ($\in$DBP) effectively, and also no way to describe the cooperation ability and requirement relevant to landmarks. As a comparison, IGTASC uses services and business transactions contained in them as the basic units for achieving cooperation, and therefore can eliminate the above limitation effectively.

Further research work will be the formal semantics of model IGTASC and the support system for finding and providing business services. The former aims at creating the semantic foundation for the automatic verification of domain e-institutions and TAVOs while the latter aims at providing sound and trusted cooperation facilitation services for agents providing and / or consuming business services on domain e-institutions.

Acknowledgements. We gratefully acknowledge the support of the Priority Theme Emphases Project of Zhejiang Province, China (Grant 2010C11045), the National Science Foundation of China (Grant 60775029), and the National High-Technology research and Development Program (863) of China (Grant 2007AA01Z187).

References

1. Papazoglou, M.P., et al.: Service-oriented computing: state of the art and research challenges. IEEE Computer 40(11), 38–45 (2007)
2. Stal, M.: Using architectural patterns and blueprints for service-oriented architecture. IEEE Softw. 23(2), 54–61 (2006)
3. Boella, G., van der Torre, L., Verhagen, H.: Introduction to the special issue on normative multiagent systems. Auton. Agent Multi-Agent Syst. 17, 1–10 (2008)
4. Aldewereld, H., Dignum, F., Meyer, J.-J.C.: Designing protocols for agent institutions. In: Proceedings of AAMAS 2007, Honolulu, Hawaii, US, pp. 138–140 (May 2007)
5. Kaiser, M.: Toward the realization of policy-oriented enterprise management. IEEE Computer 40(11), 57–63 (2007)
6. Strassner, J., Raymer, D.: Implementing next generation services using policy-based management and autonomic computing principles. In: 10th IEEE/IFIP on Network Operations and Management Symposium, NOMS 2006, pp. 1–15 (2006)
7. Van der Torre, L.: Contextual deontic logic: Normative agents, violations and independence. Special Issue on Computational Logic in Multi-Agent Systems, Annals of Mathematics and Artificial Intelligence 37(1-2), 33–63 (2003)
8. Dignum, V.: A model for organizational interaction: Based on agents, founded in logic. Ph.D. Thesis Dissertation, Utrecht University (2003) ISBN 90-393-3568-0

TD-Trust: A Time Domain Based P2P Trust Model

Dong Li, Zhengtao Zhu, Chunling Cheng, and Fei Du

Dept. of Computer Science, Nanjing University of Posts and Telecommunications
Nanjing, China
dong1028@gmail.com

Abstract. This paper proposes a time domain based trust model (TD-Trust) in P2P networks. In this model, time domain analysis is built on the processes of calculating direct and recommendation trust respectively on the basis of DHT mechanism. By tracing the behavior trend of peers, this model enables system to monitor the states of peers in the view of oscillation and malice continuity so that unsteady and aggressive peers get suppressed in time by reducing their trust values. The paper also proposes architecture based on DHT mechanism to store and manage the trust values of peers. Simulation results show that TD-Trust model is highly efficient to identify malicious peers and improve the success rate of transactions in P2P networks.

Keywords: P2P, trust model, time domain, DHT.

1 Introduction

A peer-to-peer(P2P) is any distributed network architecture composed of peers that make a portion of their resources directly available to other peers, without the need for central coordination instances [1].

Due to the decentralized and anonymous natures, current P2P networks suffer many malicious actions such as collusion and fraud. Since there is no third-party certification, traditional security mechanism has no longer sufficed for the wants of the P2P networks.

This paper presents an effective trust model based on time domain (TD-Trust). The model adopts two main kinds of factors together to help service requester evaluate peers that provide service. One is direct trust and the other is recommendation trust. On the basis of DHT(Distributed Hash Table), peers acting as service requester "push" the direct trust to corresponding peers that store recommendation information about evaluated peers after a transaction. That is, the trust of an evaluated peer is stored on another peer by DHT algorithm, and a service requester need to calculate direct trust from local records and recommendation trust from remote records. Time domain analysis is built on the processes of calculating direct and recommendation trust respectively. TD-Trust divides time shaft into units and put trust data into right unit according to the time of transaction so that a behavior trend curve of a peer gets to be sketched. Hence, the model is easy to have a well prophylactic effect on

H. Deng et al. (Eds.): AICI 2011, Part I, LNAI 7002, pp. 467–474, 2011.
© Springer-Verlag Berlin Heidelberg 2011

peer's characteristics of oscillation and malicious continuity. Some widely recognized vulnerabilities, such as collusion and malicious fraud, can be suppressed effectively in this trust model. The paper is organized as follow. Section 2 introduces the related works. Section 3 presents the proposed trust model based on time domain. In section 4, implementation strategies about TD-Trust model are introduced. The simulations and results are shown in section 5. In the last section, we draw conclusions.

2   Related Works

There are a lot of researches on trust mechanism based on reputation. In this section, we mention some works that are most related to our research.

Chen proposes an aggregation-based reputation evaluation algorithm for P2P networks [2]. And in paper [3], strategy is drawn up to cope with several different kinds of collusion. In paper [4], CommuTrust is proposed. Its implementation is over community-based P2P structures, where data transaction is performed based on intra- and inter-community credentials. But all works mentioned above can not be applied to more P2P networks owing to the dependence on central peers.

Hughes D points out the phenomenon of "Free Riding" [5] and many related researches have been done [6, 7]. Currently a most effective method to cope with "Free Riding" is to adopt the incentive measure.

Jia Fan et al. [8] and Yong Zhang et al. [9] both propose trust models based on the concept of time domain in their respective research. Their point of emphasis is to depict the protracted and procedural character of trust building. By assigning weight factors to time-units, trust values at different time will have different reference values. This paper is exactly inspired by the method for studying the peer trust.

3   Trust Model Based on Time Domain

In order to reflect the concept of timeliness, TD-Trust takes the time of transaction into account. Hence, trust turns to be a cumulative process in time domain. Trust at different time-unit is to be assigned different attenuation quotient.

3.1   The Time-Decay Factor in Time Domain

Traditional linear or decay functions [8,10] hava difficulties in depicting the attenuation of trust accurately. Hence, TD-Trust takes the attenuation standard derived from Sigmoidal Richards function. The time-decay factor δ is defined as

$$\delta = f(t) = [a^{1-d} + e^{-k(t-t_c/2)}]^{-1/(1-d)} \, , d > 1 \tag{1}$$

where t_c is current time, t is the time of transaction, a is maximum function value, d and k denote the gradient of function.

3.2 Direct Trust in TD-Trust Model

Suppose a transaction which peer i requests to peer j is completed. Peer i rates the service that peer j has offered. The trust value of the single transaction, which peer i has in peer j, S_{ij} is defined as

$$S_{ij} = \begin{cases} +1, & \textit{satisfied} \\ 0, & \textit{neutral} \\ -1, & \textit{dissatisfied} \end{cases} \tag{2}$$

Divide a period of time ending with current time into N time-units. In time-unit m ($1 \leq m \leq N$), the direct trust value $DT_{ij}^{(m)}$ between peer i and peer j is defined as

$$DT_{ij}^{(m)} = \frac{\sum_{k=1}^{I_{ij}^m} S_{ij}^{(m)}}{I_{ij}^m} \tag{3}$$

where I_{ij}^m denotes the number of transactions between peer i and peer j during time-unit m.

The direct trust value DT_{ij}^{t} between peer i and peer j before current time t is

$$DT_{ij}^{t} = \frac{\sum_{m=1}^{N} DT_{ij}^{(m)} \times \delta_{(m)}}{N} \tag{4}$$

where $\delta_{(m)}$ denotes the time-decay quotiety in time-unit m.

3.3 Recommendation Trust in TD-Trust Model

Let Ω_j^m denotes a set of recommenders of peer j, peer r is a recommender. $r \in \Omega_j^m$. The recommendation trust value $RT_{ij}^{(m)}$, which peer i has in peer j in time-unit m, is

$$RT_{ij}^{(m)} = \frac{\sum_{k=1}^{|\Omega_j^m|} DT_{r_kj}^{t_k} \times DT_{ir_k}^{t}}{|\Omega_j^m|} \tag{5}$$

where $|\Omega_j^m|$ is the number of recommenders of peer j, $DT_{r_kj}^{t_k}$ is the direct trust value that recommender r_k has in peer j before time t_k. While $DT_{ir_k}^{t}$ denotes the direct trust value that peer i has in recommender r_k before current time t.

The recommendation trust RT_{ij}^{t} between peer i and peer j before current time t is

$$RT_{ij}^{t} = \frac{\sum_{m=1}^{N} RT_{ij}^{(m)} \times \delta_{(m)}}{N} \tag{6}$$

where $\delta_{(m)}$ denotes the time-decay quotiety in time-unit m.

3.4 Global Trust in TD-Trust Model

The global trust value G_{ij} is defined as

$$G_{ij} = w_{ij} \times DT_{ij}^{t} + (1 - w_{ij}) \times RT_{ij}^{t} \tag{7}$$

where w_{ij} is the confidence factor that peer i has in peer j.

3.5 Oscillation and Malice Continuity from Peer

In P2P networks, people always tend to have transactions with the peers that own higher trust values and perform steadily.

For example, if a peer suddenly offers malicious services continuously, it may be thought to perform badly in the next transaction. Similarly, a peer being unsteady and subject to fluctuation will not be trustworthy. TD-Model analyzes the trust values of a peer's recent transactions to monitor the state of peer opportunely.

Let α denote the oscillation factor. The algorithm calculating α is as follows:

Algorithm. ComputeOscillationFactor()

```
//Suppose there are N time-units before current time t
for each time-unit m before current time t
    if (b_oscillated(m,m-1) == true)  then
    //trust values of adjacent time-units differ greatly
        count_o++;//count of oscillated performance
    end if
    if(b_maliciousContinuity(m)==true)  then
    //perform badly from time-unit m to t continuously
        count_c++;//count of malicious continuity
    end if
end for
return (1-count_o/N)*(1-count_c/N)
```

4 Implementation Strategies

How to store and manage the trust values of peers is an important topic in P2P networks. Currently, many trust models use DHT (Distributed Hash Table) mode to solve the problem. In this mode, each peer has a unique ID. The trust value about peer j is stored on the peer u whose ID meets the condition that ID_u equals h(ID_j) where h() is the hash function. DHT mode improves security and balances the bandwidth consumption in P2P networks.

Fig.1 shows a basic procedure of a transaction between peer i (service requester) and peer j (service provider). Peer r is the peer that stores the trust values about peer j.

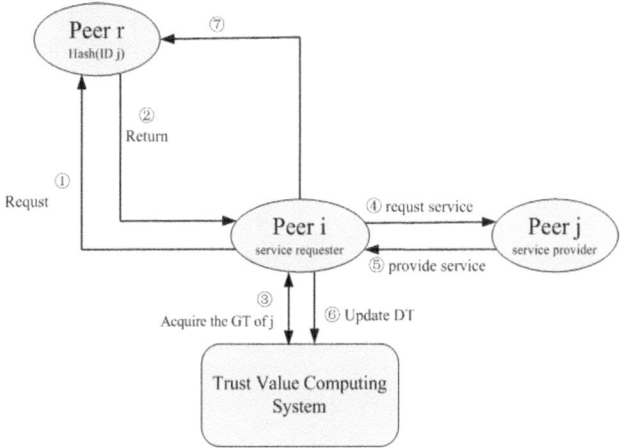

Fig. 1. The basic procedure of a transaction

As we can see from Fig.1, the procedure is as follows:

1. Peer i requests to peer r for the trust values of peer j;
2. Peer r returns a set of direct trust values that all peers have on peer j in the network (Ω_j^m); The direct trust value is defined in the formula(4);
3. After peer i gets the set, it calculates the current global trust of peer j and decides whether to transact with peer j;
4. If peer i trusts peer j, then requests service from peer j;
5. Peer j provides service to peer i;
6. After the transaction, peer i makes a judgment of peer j(satisfied, neutral or dissatisfied). Then, peer i updates the local records;
7. Peer i updates its direct trust value about peer j and sends the new direct trust value to peer u.

5 Simulations and Results

In this section, we conduct a series of experiments in a P2P network to evaluate the proposed trust mechanism. The simulation is based on java programming. In the experimental environments, we involve 1000 peers to simulate the network with TD-Model. The proportion of good peer, normal peer and malicious peer changes flexibly in accordance with the purpose of research. We make three types of experiments, focusing on the success transaction rate, collusion and oscillation monitoring, respectively.

5.1 Success Transaction Rate

An effective trust model in P2P networks should guarantee and improve the success rate of transaction while suppressing malicious peers. The experimental result indicates that TD-Trust can realize this purpose. We set the proportion of malicious peers as 20%, 40% and 60% respectively. The result is as follows:

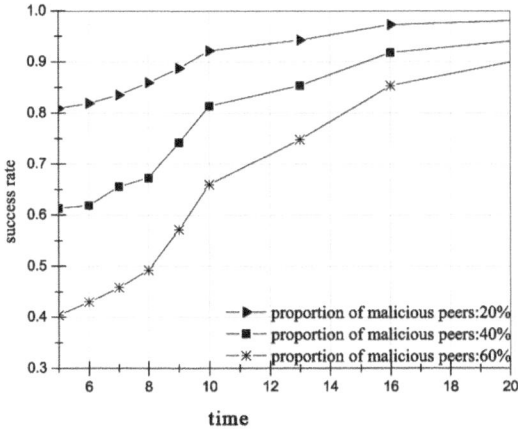

Fig. 2. The curve of success rate increasing

As we can see from Fig.2, with the system running, the success transaction rate increases. The system keeps operating correctly and safely under the environment that the proportion of malicious peers in the system reaches 60% in height.

5.2 Collusions

Malicious peers form collectives working together to introduce maliciousness into the network. We conduct an experiment with TD-Model to examine its resistance to collusion. At the same time, we simulate a traditional trust model which is lack of analysis in time domain to make a contrast with TD-Model. The result is as follows:

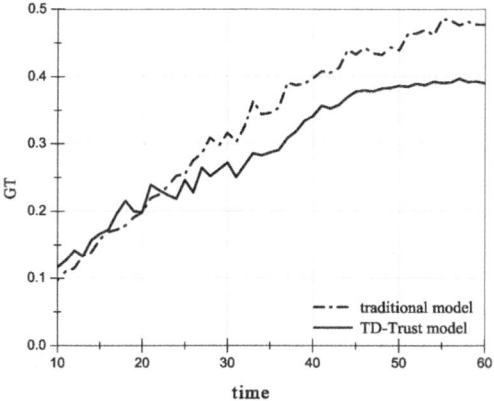

Fig. 3. Resistance to collusion

As we can see from Fig.3, with the system running, the trust value of malicious peer increases because of those false evaluations from its collusion collective. TD-Trust, relying on two-time trust attenuation in time domain of direct trust and recommendation trust respectively, is better able to resist collusion than traditional trust model.

5.3 Oscillation Monitoring

We first select some normal peers and monitor their trust values. After a period of time, these peers start to exhibit the characteristic of oscillation. Similarly, we simulate a traditional trust model which is unable to monitor the oscillation of peers:

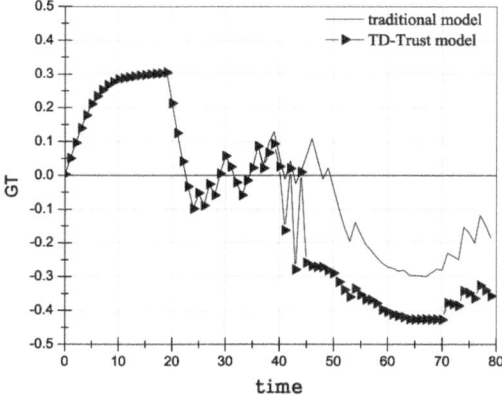

Fig. 4. Oscillation monitoring

From Fig.4, we can see that the unsteady peers get to be monitored by TD-Trust in time and be suppressed soon, while traditional model lags in response.

6 Conclusions

Trust between peers is a key issue for security guarantee in P2P networks. In this paper, a trust model based on time domain is proposed. This model takes full advantage of the time property of transactions. Each record of evaluation is to be attenuated in the calculation of direct trust and of recommendation trust respectively. The monitoring program prevents customers from being injured by unsteady peers. In summary, TD-Trust combines the historical analysis with last-period forecast to provide reliable safety guarantees for P2P networks.

References

1. Schollmeier, R.: A definition of peer-to-peer networking for the classification of peer-to-peer architectures and applications. In: IEEE International Conference on Peer-to-Peer Computing (P2P 2001), pp. 101–102. IEEE Press, Linkoping Sweden (2001)
2. Chen, J.-y., Sun, J.-z., Zhang, Y.-p.: Aggregation-based Reputation Evaluation Algorithm for P2P E-commerce. Computer Engineering 35(1), 138–139 (2009)
3. Lian, Q., Zhang, Z., Yang, M., Zhao, B.Y., Dai, Y., Li, X.: An Empirical Study of Collusion Behavior in the Maze P2P File-Sharing System. In: 27th International Conference on Distributed Computing Systems, pp. 56–56. IEEE Press, Toronto (2007)
4. Xue, F., Feng, G., Zhang, Y.: CommuTrust: A Trust and Secure Architecture in Community-based P2P Overlay Networks. In: 2nd International Conference on Future Computer and Communication (ICFCC), pp. V3-811–V3-816. IEEE Press, Wuhan (2010)
5. Hughes, D., Coulson, G., Walkerdine, J.: Free Riding on Gnutella Revisited: The Bell Tolls? IEEE Distributed System Online 6(6), 1 (2005)
6. Adar, E., Huberman, B.A.: Free riding on Gnutella. First Monday 5(10), 2 (2000)
7. Ham, M.J., Agha, G.: ARA: a robust audit to prevent free-riding in P2P networks. In: Fifth IEEE International Conference on Peer-to-Peer Computing, P2P 2005, pp. 125–132. IEEE Press, Los Alamitos (2005)
8. Jia, F., Xie, D., Yang, Y.-x.: Trust model in time-domain for P2P networks. Computer Engineering and Applications 43(19), 115–117 (2007)
9. Zhang, Y., Wang, K.W., Li, K., Qu, W.Y., Xiang, Y.: Time-decay based P2P Trust Model. In: Networks Security, Wireless Communications and Trusted Computing (NSWCTC 2009), pp. 235–238. IEEE Press, Wuhan (2009)
10. Yu, H.-t., Zhang, J.-h., Zhong, Z.: Trust model in P2P network based on time factor and punitive measures. Computer Engineering and Applications 45(20), 115–117 (2009)

Research on Pressure Loss for the Reverse-Flow Extended-Tube Muffler*

Jie Yao[1], Zhao-Xiang Deng[1,2], Pei-Ran Li[1], and Liang Yang[2]

[1] State Key Laboratory of Mechanical Transmission, Chongqing University,
Chongqing 400044, China
[2] State Key Laboratory of Vehicle NVH and Safety Technology, Chongqing 401120, China
yaojie5@gmail.com

Abstract. This paper presents a CFD model of reverse-flow extended-tube muffler which is analyzed by a set of experimental tests, in order to acquire the relations between the structure and its corresponding pressure loss; a lot of research have been done through the numeric simulation. For the specific model, the distance from inlet pipe's rear to the end cap has a large impact on the pressure loss, furthermore, a critical value about the distance has been found: If the distance is less than the critical value, the pressure loss will sharply rise; If the distance is larger than it, the pressure loss will change little. In the end, to calculate the critical value about the distance, evaluation formulary is displayed, which possesses great importance to the design of muffler and its pressure loss prediction.

Keywords: reverse-flow extended-tube, pressure loss, the critical distance, CFD.

1 Introduction

Pressure loss is a key factor to evaluate the aerodynamic performance of vehicle muffler. Pressure loss could badly affect the engine efficiency. High pressure loss can lead to increase of back-pressure which is corresponding to the power loss of the internal combustion engines, so with high pressure loss, the engine will consume more fuel[1] .Therefore, during the process of muffler design, the consideration of structure effect on the pressure loss has become a hot topic nowadays [2][3].Semi-empirical formula method is generally applied to reactive muffler design, and the fact is this method can't promise necessary precision, while the application of high-precision experimental method always require a large amount of investment, which is not suitable for the beginning of product design. Taking these factors into account, m¹any scholars turn to the CFD technology for help.

Many researchers have used the CFD technology to carry out the simulation of pressure loss. Middelberg.JM [4] The earliest user of CFD technology to study the internal pressure loss for muffler; Hu Xiaodong [5][6] has done lots of pressure loss

---

* Key Research Program of Chongqing :CSTC2008AB6108.

H. Deng et al. (Eds.): AICI 2011, Part I, LNAI 7002, pp. 475–483, 2011.

study on a single and dual-chamber resistance muffler via this method. Liu Cheng, Ji Zhenlin [7] also calculated the three kinds of mufflers' pressure loss with the help of GT-POWER software. Shao [8] used CFD methods to calculate the accuracy of HVAC piping pressure loss problems. Kim [9] using the finite element software on a expansion chamber muffler complex flow field simulation. Fang Jianhua [10] used CFD to calculate the structure of the excavator muffler with complex flow field simulation, analysis of the causes of pressure loss. But now research on pressure loss of the muffler is for most of the situation downstream. (the significance of reflux into the tube) this paper, computational fluid dynamics (CFD) method was used to study pressure loss of the reverse-flow extended-tube muffler. We had analyzed the situation in the upstream uniform flow into the muffler pressure loss variation. The reverse-flow extended-tube muffler pressure loss prediction method was got.

2 Basic Theory of Fluid Dynamics for Muffler

Many fluid mechanics research and numerical simulation results show that can be used in engineering on realistic turbulent simulation method is still based on solving Reynolds time-averaged equation and associated transport equation turbulent quantity simulation method, i.e. turbulent orthodoxy simulation method. In orthodoxy model, using the longest, accumulate the most experienced is mixed length model and the $k-\varepsilon$ model. $k-\varepsilon$ model was established by Spalding and Launder in 1972 proposed two equation turbulent model, from the experimental phenomena of a half empirical formulas [11]. Two equations model in lower computational cost is based on guarantee good calculation accuracy, and therefore the most widely was used in engineering. This paper also adopts the model for calculating model. $k-\varepsilon$ model is mainly by solving two additional equation, the k equation and the ε equation (k equation is expressed as turbulent kinetic equation, ε equation is expressed as turbulent dissipative equation) to determine turbulence viscosity coefficient, thus solving turbulent stress. The model of the control equations for:

Turbulent kinetic energy (k) equations:

$$\frac{\partial(\overline{\rho}k)}{\partial t}+\frac{\partial(\overline{\rho}\,\overline{u}_j k)}{\partial x_i}=-\frac{\partial}{\partial x_j}\left[(\mu+\frac{\mu_t}{\sigma_k})\frac{\partial k}{\partial x_j}\right]+\mu_t\frac{\partial \overline{u}_j}{\partial x_i}\left(\frac{\partial \overline{u}_i}{\partial x_j}+\frac{\partial \overline{u}_j}{\partial x_i}\right)-\overline{\rho}\varepsilon \qquad (1)$$

Turbulent kinetic energy dissipation rate (ε) equations:

$$\frac{\partial(\overline{\rho}\varepsilon)}{\partial t}+\frac{\partial(\overline{\rho}\,\overline{u}_j\,\varepsilon)}{\partial x_i}=-\frac{\partial}{\partial x_j}\left[(\mu+\frac{\mu_t}{\sigma_\varepsilon})\frac{\partial \varepsilon}{\partial x_j}\right]+C_1\frac{\varepsilon}{k}\mu_t\left(\frac{\partial \overline{u}_i}{\partial x_j}+\frac{\partial \overline{u}_j}{\partial x_i}\right)-C_2\frac{\varepsilon^2}{k} \qquad (2)$$

Turbulence viscosity coefficient:

$$\mu_t=\overline{\rho}C_\mu\frac{k^2}{\varepsilon} \qquad (3)$$

Type: μ for turbulence viscosity, $\overline{\rho}$ For fluid average density ; x_i , x_j for coordinates component , $\overline{u_i}$, $\overline{u_j}$ For fluid along x_i and x_j direction of velocity component average; i= 1, 2, 3, representing the three coordinate direction; C_1 , C_2 , σ_k , σ_ε , C_μ is the experience constant, the current widespread use of launder and Spalding recommended values for 1.11, 1.92, 1.00, 1.30, 0.09.

3 Model and Boundary Conditions

3.1 Physical Model

As a classical resistance unit, mufflers with extended pipes possess well acoustic performance, and among these mufflers, reverse-flow ones could not only allow the diversion of flow, but also prolong the effective extended length, so they have been widely used. This kind of muffler is displayed as Fig. 1.a, based on this structure, this paper provides much research on the potential rules between the structure feature and its pressure loss.

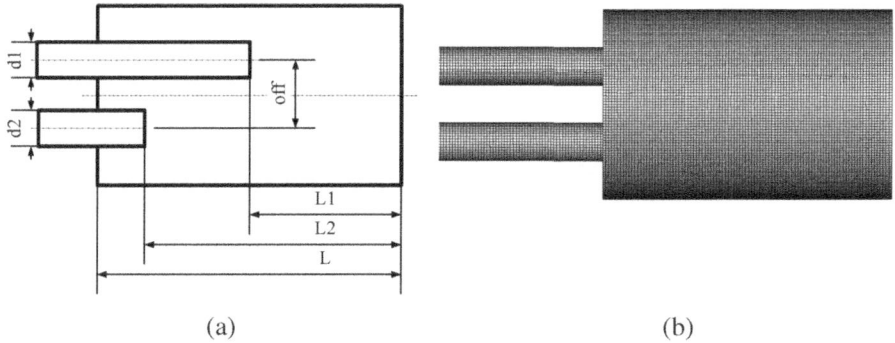

(a)	(b)

Fig. 1. a Reverse-flow extended tube muffler   **b**. Reverse-flow extended tube muffler meshedrawing

This article utilizes CATIA to establish the 3-D model, and then the model is meshed by hexahedron elements under the ANSA background. Besides, for model's inlet, outlet and shell surface, we set different element Id. After all the work above, the finite element models are then attained as Fig.1.b shows.

In order to simplify the issues, the following assumptions are listed: (1) performance parameters for the muffler and the flow field are constants, (2) the flow is turbulent among the steady flows; (3) ignore the influence of gravity (4) inlet velocity of flow is stable and without pulse influence.

3.2 Boundary Condition Settings

Setting boundary conditions is a crucial step for numerical analysis, for it is directly related to the accuracy of the calculated results. This paper chooses ANSYS-CFX to calculate the $k - \varepsilon$ model. In order to assure the same comparisons standards, the field status of the entry surface is simplified to be stable. The CFD model's internal fluid flow field is turbulence and consists of incompressible air. The velocity near the wall is regarded as 0. The average velocity of floe in the entry is between 10~60 m/s, and at the end of outlet the average static pressure is 0Pa. For the abstract calculation, the time pace is adaptive type and the convergence value is the difference of two neighboring results' root mean square, which is below 1×10^{-4}.

4   Verify the Accuracy of Calculation

In order to ensure the validity of the numerical results, in this paper, a test model was used to measure the pressure loss. Fig. 2. shows the test device by the fan, motor, inverter, pitot tube, pressure meter, muffler test pieces, taking pressure tube and other accessories.

Test cases are the inlet and outlet total pressure value, the difference between the inlet and outlet is the pressure loss is the test pieces, and compared with calculation results of ANSYS CFX software, the results shown in Fig. 3.

Comparative results show that ANSYS CFX software to calculate high agreement with the experimental results, due to the loss and partial loss along the way and the

Fig. 2. Reverse-flow extended tube muffler pressure loss test sets physical map

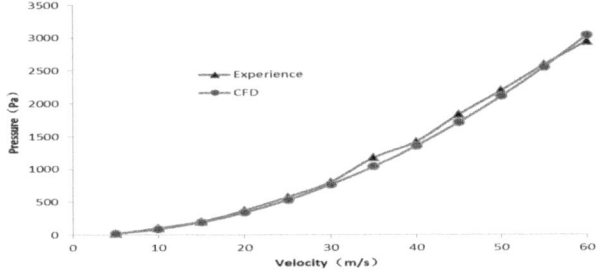

Fig. 3. Reverse-flow extended tube muffler comparison of pressure loss

flow measurement error caused in an acceptable range, so can use the CFD software can be used for muffler Calculation of pressure loss.

5   Analysis on Computation Results

ANSYS CFX was used to every model in two-equation turbulence model equations, change L1 and L2 of the distance from 10mm to 300mm. A series of data was made of three-dimensional map diagram, as shown in Fig. 4.

Fig. 4 shows that the L1 of the distance within a certain range when the pressure loss while the effect of the outlet control within the relatively large impact on pressure loss. Keep L2 distance constant, change L1, when L1 less than some length, reverse-flow extended tube muffler pressure loss with a sharp increase and decrease of L1, When L1 greater than this range, with the increase of L1, the pressure loss will keep constant. When is less than this distance range, the length of inlet tube increase ,pressure loss will be amplified, at the same time, when is more than this distance range, the length of outlet tube increase, pressure loss will be amplified.

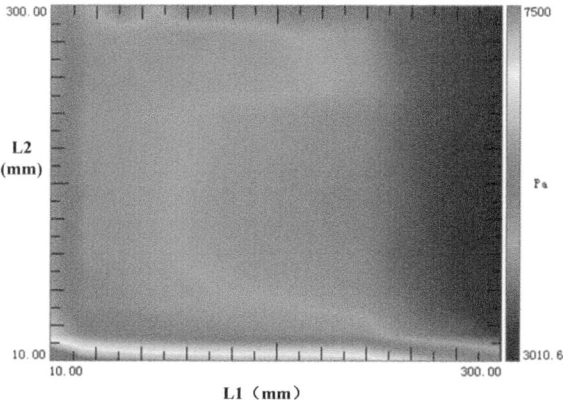

Fig. 4. Three-dimensional graph of the reverse-flow extended-tube muffler pressure loss

5.1   Reverse-Flow Extended-Tube Muffler Various Parameters on the Impact of Pressure Loss

Earlier in reverse-flow extended tube muffler pressure loss into the rule is in a particular state of the inlet and outlet diameter and gaseous state, the following discussion of inlet and outlet of pipe diameter, temperature, and air speed parameters on the pressure loss.

Fig. 5. a can be seen that the main factors of influence critical distance is the inlets pipe diameters, in order to consider outlet tube of influence to this distance, change the outlet of pipe diameter 40mm, 60mm and 80mm, calculation of different L1; the influence of pressure loss from Fig. 5. a, we can see that the outlet tube diameter of that distance of the impact is not big, but with the increases of outlet tube , the muffler pressure loss greatly reduces.

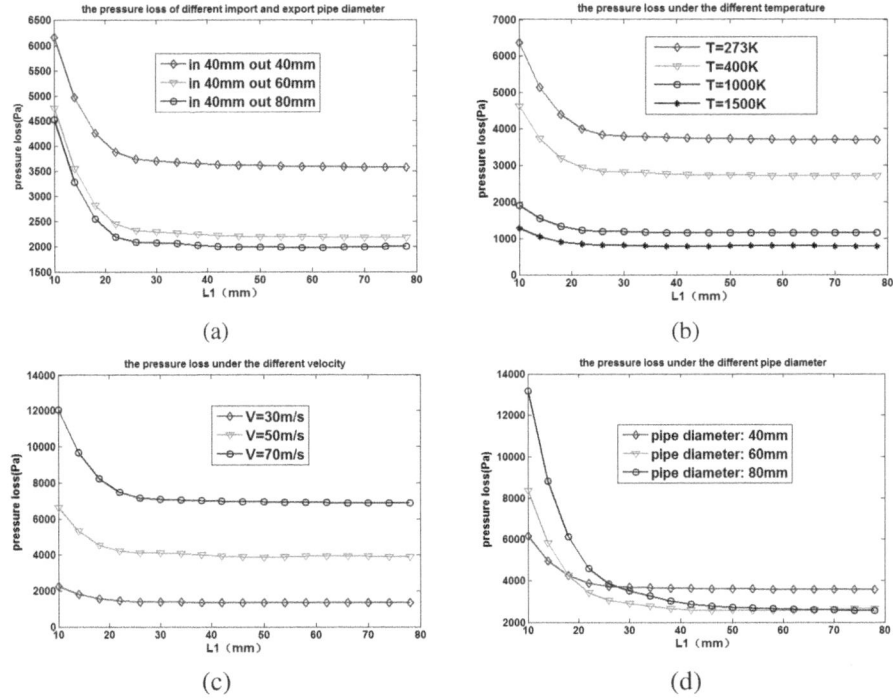

Fig. 5. a. different inlet and outlet pipe diameter (**b.** different temperature,**c.** different velocity,**d.** different pipe diameter)reverse-flow extended-tube muffler pressure loss with L1 changes

When the inlet tube from the end after a certain distance to the range, the pressure loss is essentially the same, mainly due to the air inlet tube at this time can be fully expanded greatly reduced by the resistance, and in the outlet tube from the end unchanged Under the inlet tube at this time the pressure loss along the main loss of this part of the losses are small, so the critical distance, the pressure loss is expressed as a horizontal line. Description After more than critical distance, the length of the inlet tube on the pressure loss was less affected.

The pressure loss of the resistance muffler was concerned by the internal air density and viscosity of air, and the physical properties of air was affected by the environment temperature. In the calculation of the pressure loss process should be considered in gas temperature. The CFD method to calculate the pressure loss, research reverse-flow extended tube muffler under different temperature conditions, pressure loss of changing trends for L1 changing.

Fig. 5. b can see as L1 increases, the pressure loss gradually decrease, when L1 reach a certain value, then the pressure loss basically unchanged. And with the increase of temperature, pressure loss gradually decrease, but as L1 increased, pressure loss variation trend is changeless, just change the amplitude decreases. The distance that L1 scope is not related to temperature, and under the same boundary conditions, with the increase of temperature, pressure loss will decrease.

Fig. 5. c shows that the curve, with different speed for inlet pipe, that as L1 changed, how pressure loss changed; it can be seen from the graph with figure 4 the same trend that this distance is not related to velocity, in the same boundary conditions, the higher the velocity, the higher pressure loss.

From the above analysis, we can see, apparently L1 that reverse-flow extended tube muffler inlet pipes the distance from the rear wall exists a critical range, and the scope for reverse-flow extended tube muffler is the inherent parameters. For this distance range, through the statistics obtained a estimate formula, such as type (4). This estimate formula can be used to estimate and analyze the pressure loss of reverse-flow extended tube muffler.

$$L_C = S/d \tag{4}$$

Type (4) : S for inlet pipes circulation area; d for inlet pipes circulation diameter; L_C for the critical distance.

5.2 Prediction and Verification of Critical Distance

From estimating formula observation, the key factor that influences critical distance is the inlet tube diameter. We changed the inlet of pipe diameter for different diameter. It is calculated to verify the correctness of the estimation formulae. Table 1 for through the formulas for calculating the muffler critical distance.

Table 1. Extended tube muffler critical distance prediction

tube diameter	40mm	60mm	80mm
thickness	2mm	2mm	2mm
L_C	28.27433mm	43.9823mm	59.69026mm

Fig. 5. shows that the curve that pressure loss with the L1 changing under different diameters for inlet and outlet. We can see from the graph, as distance of L1 increases, the pressure loss gradually decrease, when L1 get to the critical distance, pressure loss will basically unchanged. Moreover, the critical distance and forecast is consistent, illustration, critical distance estimation formulae are effectively. It can be used to predict pressure loss of reverse-flow extended tube muffler.

6   Engineering Application Example

Fig. 6. for a project with internal combustion engine exhaust three Chambers muffler of geometric model, expansion chamber of cross-sectional is circular. Between one cavity and other cavity it connected through extended tube. Based on the CFD, the muffler is optimized.it get the table 3 simulation data.

According to the above conclusions, not changing the muffler acoustics characteristics, we made two kinds of projects, project one for the third cavity exchange inlet pipes 2 and 3 of outlet tube length, project two for second cavity exchange inlet pipes 3 and 4 outlet tube length. By critical distance estimation formulae (4) we can know, critical distance estimation for 36.1 mm. According the above conclusions, Improvement of the third cavity can cause pressure loss increases.

In table 3, it displayed on the inlet speed 100m/s pressure loss of different structures. Pressure loss of project one, for 44171.91 Pa, and the original model in the same boundary conditions, the pressure loss for 41516.22 Pa, improved the pressure loss increases, and the predictions expected. Improvement of the second cavity can cause pressure loss reduce. In the table 2, pressure loss of project two for 41161.24 Pa, and the original model in the same boundary conditions, the pressure loss for 41516.22 Pa, the pressure loss is reduced, and the predictions corresponding. So we can get the conclusion, critical distance for the reverse-flow extended-tube muffler in pressure loss of prediction and design is credible, has a great practical value.

Table 2. Pressure loss simulation data of the muffler

	original model	Project1	Project2
Velocity(m/s)	PL(Pa)	PL(Pa)	PL(Pa)
30	3772.816	4003.544	3738.253
40	6690.2	7104.27	6629.517
50	10432.73	11088.14	10341.22
60	15000.63	15936.47	14868.61
70	20392.9	21672.81	20214.41
80	26612.44	28309.63	26380.07
90	33653.93	35802.59	33358.93
100	41516.22	44171.91	41161.24

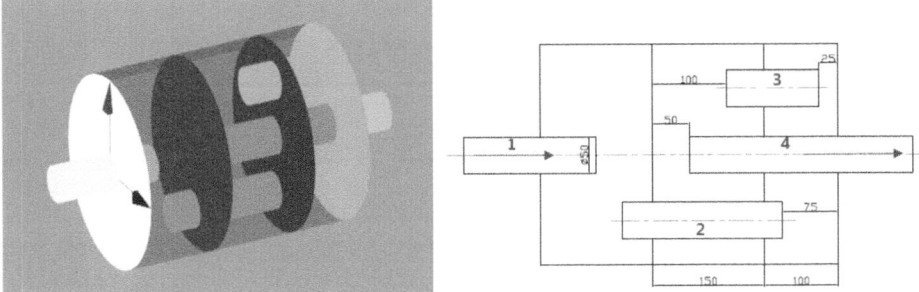

Fig. 6. A muffler geometric model and its three cavity size

7 Conclusion

Through computing and simulating the reverse-flow extended-tube muffler, the muffler pressure loss at a certain boundary condition is analyzed .The pressure loss law of the reverse-flow extended-tube muffler is got. So some specific conclusions are obtained, as follows:

(1) Critical distance of the inlet pipe plays an important role in the pressure loss for the reverse-flow extended-tube muffler. If distance that inlet pipe end to the posterior wall is less than the critical distance, the pressure loss will cause a sharp rise. On the contrary, the distance more than the critical distance, the pressure loss will be little change. Critical distance is closely related with the inlet tube diameter, with temperature, flow rate, outlet pipe diameter changes, it is not changes. Critical distance is the intrinsic parameters of the reverse-flow extended-tube muffler.

(2) Distance in the inlet and outlet of pipe to the posterior wall greater than the critical distance, the inlet tube extended   length has little effect to the muffler of pressure loss, the extended length of exit pipe has great impact on the pressure loss;

(3) A critical distance of estimation formulae was got in Research, and the formula was verified validity;

(4) Through design an application example to illustrate the critical distance on reverse-flow extended-tube muffler design and the pressure loss of prediction is credible, and it has a great practical value ;

(5) The more temperature increases, the less the pressure loss of the reverse-flow extended-tube muffler changes. With the increase of flow rate, the pressure loss of the reverse-flow extended-tube muffler will increase. The diameter of outlet-pipe has little effect on the critical distance, but the increase of the diameter can greatly reduce the pressure Loss of muffler;

References

1. He, Y., Deng, Z.: Noise Control In Automobile. China Machine Press, Bengjing (1999)
2. Jiang, P., Fu, X., Wu, B.: Optimization Design and Overall Evaluation Indices of Automotive Exhaust Muffler. Automotive Engineering 30(3), 230–247 (2008)
3. Hu, X.D., Zhou, Y.Q., Fang, J.H., et al.: Computational Fluid Dynamics Research on Pressure Loss of Cross-Flow Perforated Muffler. Chinese Journal of Mechanical Engineering 20(2), 88–93 (2007)
4. Middelberg, J.M., Barber, T.J.: CFD analysis of the acoustic and mean flow performance of simple expansion chamber mufflers. In: 2004 ASME International Mechanical Engineering Congress and Exposition (Conference code: 64903), pp. 151–156. ASME, Anaheim (2004)
5. Hu, X.-d., Zhou, Y.-q., Fang, J.-h.: CFD computation of pressure loss of single and dual-chamber resistance mufflers. China Mechanical Engineering 17(24), 567–572 (2006)
6. Hu, X.-d., Zhou, Y.-q., Fang, J.-h., et al.: Muffler structure optimization research of digging machine based on CFD. Journal of System Simulation 19 (2007)
7. Liu, C., Ji, Z.-l., Guo, X.-l., Xu, H.-s.: Effects of Configurations on Pressure Losses in Automotive Exhaust Muffler. Automotive Engineering 30(12), 1113–1116 (2008)
8. Shao, L., Riffat, S.B.: Accuracy of CFD for predicting pressure loss in HVAC duct fittings. Applied Energy 51(3), 233–248 (1995)
9. Kim, M.H.: Three 2 dimensional numerical study on the pulsating flow inside automotive muffler with complicated flow path. In: SAE 2001 World Congress. SAE Paper, M.I (2001)
10. Fang, J.-h., Zhou, Y.-q., Hu, X.-d., et al.: CFD simulation of exhaust muffler with complicated structures for an excavator. Transactions of CSICE 27(1), 6873 (2009)
11. Launder, B.E., Spalding, D.B.: Lectures in mathematical models of turbulence. Academic Press, London (1972)

Lateral Jet Interaction Model Identification Based on Genetic Programming

Shi-Ming Chen[1], Yun-Feng Dong[1], and Xiao-Lei Wang[2]

[1] School of Astronautics, Beijing University of Aeronautics and Astronautics,
Beijing, P.R. China
[2] Science and Technology on Space System Simulation Laboratory,
Beijing Simulation Center, Beijing, P.R. China
csm7531@sa.buaa.edu.cn, sinosat@buaa.edu.cn,
wangxiaolei_2345@126.com

Abstract. Precise lateral jet interaction models are required for missiles' blending control strategies. Because of the complicated flow field, the interaction models are multivariable, complex and coupled. Traditional aerodynamics coefficients model identification used Maximum-likelihood estimation to adjust the parameters of the postulation model, but it is not good at dealing with complex nonlinear models. A genetic programming (GP) method is proposed to identify the interaction model, which not only can optimize the parameters, but also can identify the model structure. The interaction model's inputs are altitude, mach number, attack angle and fire number of jets in wind channel experiment results, and its output is interaction force coefficient. The fitness function is root mean square error. Select suitable function set and terminal set for GP, then use GP to evolve model automatically. The identify process with different reproduced probability; crossover probability and mutation probability are compared. Results shows that GP's result error is decrease 30% than multi-variable regression method.

Keywords: genetic programming, lateral jet, model, identification, missile.

1 Introduction

Requirement for the improvement of homing guidance performance against highly maneuverable targets, the lateral jet control system was used to improve the response of the guided missiles [1, 2]. Existing aero-fin controlled missiles have delayed response time and limitations on maneuvering at low velocity or high altitude. The lateral jet control system is one of the possible and effective approaches for the vehicle maneuvering because it can be applied to overall speed and altitude range, with quick respond and high effectiveness. Therefore, the lateral jet attitude control has been a preferred concept as a new guided missile. But it also has drawbacks like operating time restriction because of the space limitation for jet propellant [3]. The control system blending the conventional aero-fin control and lateral jet control can reach the high response and the high agility [1, 2].

The interaction models are very important to the blending control system. The aerodynamic characteristics of a lateral jet [4] are the local shock-shock interaction,

H. Deng et al. (Eds.): AICI 2011, Part I, LNAI 7002, pp. 484–491, 2011.

which consists of separation shock, bow shock, barrel shock and mach disk around jet nozzle, and the downstream interaction by the counter rotating vortices. So the interference induced by the jet is extremely complicated.

Maximum-likelihood estimation (MLE) is the most commonly used technique for identify aerodynamics coefficients [2]. The MLE technique postulates a parametric model (usually linear, more recently nonlinear) and adjusts the parameters to minimize the negative logarithm of the likelihood that the model output fits a given measurement error. When the model is too complicated, the polynomial model may be disagree with real model.

Genetic programming was first explored in depth in 1992 by John R. Koza [5]. In his famous book "Genetic Programming: On the Programming of Computers by Mean of Natural Selection" he pointed out that virtually all problem in artificial intelligence, machine learning, adaptive systems, and automated learning can be recast as a search for a computer program, and that genetic programming provides a way to successfully conduct the search for a computer program in the space of computer programs.

Unlike the other optimization method such as Genetic Algorithm (GA) and Ant Colony Algorithm (ACA) only can optimize parameters, GP can not only optimize the parameters of expression, but also can optimize the structure of models [6-8]. So GP is suitable for multivariate complicated model identification without a priori knowledge [9-12].

The paper is organized as follows. Section II discusses the model identification problem. Detailed GP representation, operators, fitness function and optimize procedure are given in Section III. The application of the method is studied in Section IV. The final section is devoted to conclusions.

2 Model Identification

Suppose that there are 10 lateral jets uniform distributed in missile XY plane, the symmetry plane is XZ plane.

Interaction force coefficient K_f is association with altitude H, Mach number Ma, attack angle α and fire number of jets N.

$$K_f=f(H, Ma, \alpha, N) . \tag{1}$$

The model identification objective is to find function f to represent the K_f, as described in Eqn. (1).

Table 1. Interaction Force Coefficients when H=10km, Ma=2

α(deg) N	2	3	5	7	9
-30	0.1080	0.3172	0.4689	0.5708	0.6458
-20	0.2744	0.4435	0.6309	0.7359	0.7952
-10	0.7595	0.8325	0.9090	0.9393	0.9472
0	0.9417	0.9627	0.9609	0.9627	0.9508
10	0.8983	0.8879	0.9048	0.9191	0.9323
20	0.9178	0.9302	0.9626	0.9753	0.9828

There are 270 results with different altitude, Mach number, attack angle and fire number of jets from wind channel experiment. Table 1 shows partial point under condition of H=10km and Ma=2.

3   Genetic Programming

Genetic programming is a symbolic optimization technique, developed by John Koza [5]. It is based on so called "tree representation". This representation is extremely flexible, since trees can represent computer programs, mathematical equations or complete models of process systems. This scheme has been already used for circuit design in electronics, algorithm development for quantum computers, and it is suitable for generating model structures.

3.1   Model Representation in GP

Opposite to the common optimization methods, in which potential solutions are represented as numbers (vectors), in symbolic optimization algorithms, the potential solutions are represented by a structure of several symbols [13]. One of the most popular methods for representing structures is the binary tree; for example Fig. 1 shows the tree representation of the expression $0.3x_0+2.3x_1+0.01x_2$.

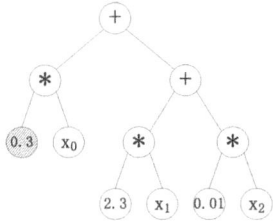

Fig. 1. GP syntax tree representing $0.3x_0+2.3x_1+0.01x_2$

A population member in GP is a hierarchically structured tree consisting of functions and terminals. The functions and terminals are selected from a set of functions (operators) and a set of terminals. For example, the set of operators F can contain the basic arithmetic operators: {+, −, ×, /, sin, cos, IFLTE}. "IFLTE" is the "if less than equal" function. If the first argument is less than the second argument IFLTE returns the third argument, otherwise it return the fourth argument. It may also include other mathematical functions, Boolean operators, conditional operators or any user-defined operators. The set of terminals T contains the arguments for the functions. For example T={x0, x1, x2, n} with x0, x1 and x2 being three independent variables, and n represents the random parameters. Now, a potential solution (program) may be depicted as a rooted, labeled tree with ordered branches, using operations (internal nodes of the tree) from the function set and arguments (terminal nodes of the tree) from the terminal set.

On top of all, GP can be used with polynomial models. To achieve it, one has to restrict the set of operators and introduce some simple syntactic rules. For example, if the set of operators is defined as F = {+,×} and there is a syntactic rule that exchange the internal nodes that are below a '×'-type internal node to '×'-type nodes, the algorithm will generate only polynomial models.

3.2 Genetic Operators

Genetic Programming is an Evolutionary Algorithm. It works with a set of individuals (potential solutions), and these individuals form a generation. In every generation, the algorithm evaluates the individuals, selects individuals for reproduction, generates new individuals by mutation, crossover and direct reproduction, and finally creates the new generation.

The initial step is the creation of an initial population. Generally it means generating individuals randomly to achieve high diversity. The first step is fitness evaluation, i.e. calculation of fitness values of individuals. Usually, the fitness value is calculated based on a cost function. After that, in the selection step, the algorithm selects the parents of the next generation and determines which individuals survive from the current generation. The most widely used selection strategy is the roulette-wheel selection, every individual has a probability to be selected as parent, and this probability is proportional to fitness value.

When an individual is selected for reproduction, three operations can be applied: direct reproduction, mutation and crossover (recombination). The probability of mutation is pm, the probability of crossover is pc, and the probability of direct reproduction is pr.

The direct reproduction puts the selected individual into the new generation without any change.

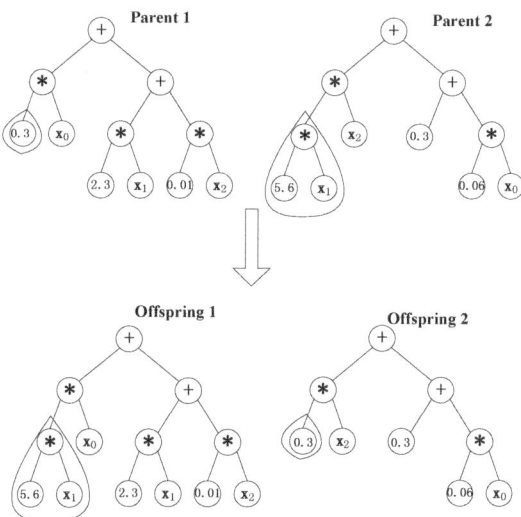

Fig. 2. GP one-point crossover

In crossover two individuals are selected, and their tree structures are divided at a randomly selected crossover point, and the resulting sub-trees are exchanged to form two new individuals. There are two types of crossover, one-point and two-point crossover. In one-point crossover, the same crossover point selected for the two parent-trees, in two-point crossover, the two parent-trees are divided at different points. Fig. 2 shows the one-point crossover.

In mutation a random change is performed on the selected tree structure by a random substitution. If an internal element (an operator) is changed to a leaf element (an argument), the structure of the tree will change too. In this case, one has to pay attention to the structure of the tree to avoid bad-formed binary trees. Fig. 3 shows the mutation operator.

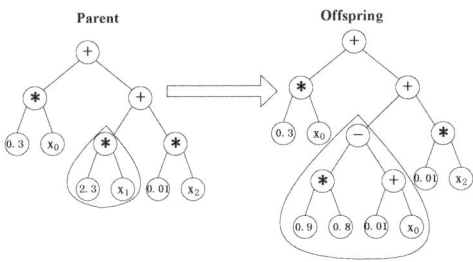

Fig. 3. GP mutation

3.3 Fitness Function

The fitness function has two aspects, in the first hand it reflects the goodness of a potential solution from the viewpoint of the cost function, and on the other hand, it reflects a selection probability. Usually, the fitness function is based on the square error (SE) between estimated and measured output. However, during symbolic optimization, it is worth using correlation coefficient instead of square error, as [13] suggests it, in Eqn. (2).

$$\text{Fitness} = 1/(1+\text{RMSE}) , \tag{2}$$

Where RMSE is the root mean square of error.

3.4 Evolve Procedure

A computational flow chart for the application of the GP technique for model identification is given in Fig. 4. The procedure begins with the specification of an initial population, and a desired number of generations. The fitness of each individual in the population is next evaluated. Genetic operators are next carried out on a few chosen members of the population. A mix of reproduce, crossover and the mutation operations was used in every generation. The finesses of the new members are next evaluated, and if these are as good as or better than the existing fitness, the corresponding members are retained. New members with fitness magnitudes worse than the lowest fitness in the

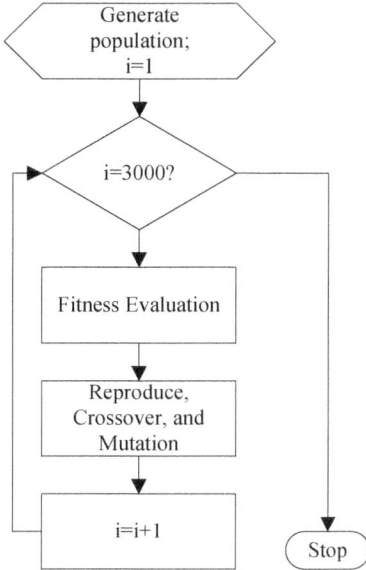

Fig. 4. Flowchart for GP

population are deleted, and the process is repeated. The GP process is terminated when the generation number reaches the initially specified number.

4 Identification Result

Base on experiments we found that with the parameters given in Table 2 the GP is able to find good solutions.

Table 2. Parameters of GP in the Application Examples

Terminal Set	x0,x1,x2,x3,n	Population size	200
Function Set	+,−,×,sin, cos, IFLTE	Maximum Generation	3000
Type of selection	roulette-wheel	Max depth of individual	8
Type of crossover	one-point	Probability of reproduce	0.3
Type of mutation	sub-tree-mutation	Probability of crossover	0.2
		Probability of mutation	0.3

The best fitness is 0.799, and the best individual is

```
(s(((0.017090)*((((x3)+(((x3)-(x1))+(I(0.622864)L(x2)T
(3.394165)F(x0))))-((I((x0)-(x2))L(x0)T((-1.381226)
-(x1))  F((x1)-(4.824524)))+(c((x2)*
(-1.599121)))))+(x2)))  *(3.118591))))
```

Traditional Maximum-likelihood estimation method postulates a linear or polynomial parametric model and adjusts the parameters with regression methods.

Then we get the model error of polynomial model and best model from GP methods, as shown in Table 3. It shows that, increasing the orders from 4 to 10, the error only decrease less than 2%, but GP's model error is decrease 30% than the 4 orders polynomial model.

Table 3. Error of Different Models

Model	RMSE
4 orders polynomial model	0.3592
10 orders polynomial model	0.3526
Best model from GP method	0.2468

5 Conclusion

Comparing conventional identification methods against GP method, the former do not guarantee that the model can be an acceptable representation.

In the search for the lateral jet interaction model, the GP identification method has been demonstrated to perform effectively. The GP identification method is suitable for identify the multivariable and nonlinear model.

Acknowledgment. The authors thank Beijing Simulation Center for their support and for providing data used in this work. The author also thanks the financial support of science and technology on space system simulation laboratory fund item of china.

References

1. Liu, Z., Liang, X., Cao, B., et al.: An Optimal Backstepping Design for Blended Aero and Reaction-Jet Missile Autopilot. J. Appl. Sci. 6(12), 2623–2628 (2006)
2. Hirokawa, R., Sato, K., Manabe, S.: Autopilot Design for a Missile with Reaction-Jet using Coefficient Diagram Method. In: AIAA-2001, vol. 4162 (2001)
3. Min, B., Lee, J., Byun, Y.: Investigation of the Shock Interaction Effect on the Lateral Jet Controlled Missile. In: AIAA-2003, vol. 3932 (2003)
4. Burchett, B., Costello, M.: Model Predictive Lateral Pulse Jet Control of an Atmospheric Rocket. Guid. Control Dynam. 25(5), 860–867 (2002)
5. Koza, J.: Genetic Programming: on the Programming of Computers by Means of Natural Selection. The MIT Press, Cambridge (1992)
6. Winkler, S., Affenzeller, M., Wagner, S.: New Methods for the Identification of Nonlinear Model Structures based upon Genetic Programming Techniques. In: 15th International Conference on Systems Science, pp. 386–393 (2004)
7. Madar, J., Abonyi, J., Szeifert, F.: Genetic Programming for the Identification of Nonlinear Input-Output Models. Ind. Eng. Chem. Res. 44(9), 3178–3186 (2005)
8. Rodriguez-Vazquez, K., Fonseca, C.M., Fleming, P.J.: Identifying the Structure of Nonlinear Dynamic Systems using Multiobjective Genetic Programming. IEEE, Trans. On Systems, Man, and Cybernetics-Part A: Systems and Humans 34(4), 531–545 (2004)

9. Han, P., Zhou, S., Wang, D.: A Multiobjective Genetic Programming/ NARMAX Approach to Chaotic Systems Identification. In: 6th World Congress on Intelligent Control and Automation, pp. 1735–1739 (2006)
10. Yuan, X., Bai, Y.: Stochastic Nonlinear System Identification using Multiobjective Multipopulation Parallel Genetic Programming. In: Chinese Control and Decision Conference, pp. 1148–1153 (2009)
11. Madar, J., Abonyi, J., Szeifert, F.: Genetic Programming for System Identification. Intell. Sys. Des. and Appl. (2004)
12. Polynkin, A., Toropov, V.: Multidisciplinary Optimization of Turbomachinary based on Metamodel built by Genetic Programming. In: AIAA-2010, vol. 9397 (2010)
13. Banzhaf, W., Nordin, P., Keller, R.E., et al.: Genetic Programming: An Introduction on the Automatic Evolution of Computer Programs and its Applications. Morgan Kaufmann, San Francisco (1998)

Three-Dimensional Localization Algorithm Based on LIE

Weihua Xiang*, Zhaoyan Qu, Huakui Wang, and Jing Li

College of Information Engineering, Taiyuan University of Technology,
Taiyuan 030024, China
13700518880@139.com, 512818501@qq.com,
huakuiw@sohu.com, 155242526@qq.com

Abstract. The localization technique is an important requirement in wireless sensor networks (WSNs). Many localization algorithms in WSNS have been proposed. This paper presents a novel three-dimensional localization algorithms LIE-3D in WSNs. This approach is about that the target sensor performed LIE-3D test to judge the grid of the vote, which narrowed down the possible location areas, and finally calculate the intersection of these areas part of the mass center, as the location of the node to be positioning. As a result, theoretical analysis and experimental results show that LIE-3 D depends on no ranging measures or global infrastructure, it presents a low-cost solution for self-localization of densely deployed and large scale WSNs in 3D spaces.

Keywords: wireless sensor networks, Three-dimensional localization, Localization accuracy, grid.

1 Introduction

Wireless sensor network (WSN)is a network which consists of a large amount of simple structure, low cost miniature sensors .WSNs have an endless array of potential applications in both military and civilian applications, including robotic land-mine detection, battlefield surveillance, target tracking, environmental monitoring, wildfire detection, and traffic regulation, to name just a few. In these applications, node location information is crucial for sensor network monitoring activities. Event location is important information for node monitoring news. Meanwhile, some of the wireless sensor network protocol such as based on geographic information routing also need to locate information for support [1 ~ 3] .Therefore, node localization technology is one of the important research content in wireless sensor networks, it has very important theoretical significance and practical application value.

So far, in view of the different problems and application, we have been put forward various WSN localization algorithm. such as DV - HOP algorithm, centroid localization algorithm[3,4], The above researches are limited in two-dimensional space node localization, While deployed in three-dimensional space have more rich location information in wireless sensor networks compared to the wireless sensor network in two-dimensional space, and have more network size and distribution density, So it is

H. Deng et al. (Eds.): AICI 2011, Part I, LNAI 7002, pp. 492–499, 2011.

difficult to promotion to the actual application of three-dimensional space because of the existing two-dimensional positioning system limited to power and cost. And the representative of the two-dimensional localization method for LIE is based on the theory of planar, and cannot be directly applied to three-dimensional space. Therefore it is necessary to use a kind of energy saving and cheap method to solve three-dimensional space positioning in wireless sensor network. This paper presents a positioning algorithm- LIE - 3D, which is suitable for three-dimensional space in wireless sensor network, it can effectively estimate the position of sensor nodes in three-dimensional space, and have relatively low communication cost.

1.1 LIE-3D Localization Algorithm

First of all, According to the application of wireless sensor network environment , as the assumptions: The area deployed in Wireless sensor networks is three-dimensional; Node location in Wireless sensor network is fixed, and do not have mobility; Node in Wireless sensor networks is random deployed in the application area; Unknown nodes in Wireless sensor networks have the same processing ability; Unknown node itself in Wireless sensor networks can maintain data structure which storage the relevant information, including node ID, position, transmission power, and its transmit scope [6]. The basic idea of LIE-3D Localization algorithm is as followings: The surrounding space of unknown nodes is divided into many cube small grids [7], If the anchor node judge that a small grid is in its coverage area ,so it will take a vote to the small grid. After the vote, the most votes grid is the largest possible area, we take the centroid position of the largest possible area as estimate area of unknown nodes, So, first of all we need a way to divide and judge the surrounding area of unknown nodes, this paper provides LIE-3D algorithm to solve the problem.

1.2 Two Dimensional LIE Algorithm and Performance Analysis

A square area randomly distributes N nodes, including K anchor nodes. Assuming all the node location is a rectangular range, if the round communication range approximate for its constraint box of Inner concatenated square, it will constraint node location which is called linear constraints. And considering more constraint of the anchor node, it could reduce the uncertainty of the node location. Pending a node S has m neighbors anchor node S_{k_1},...., S_{k_n}, coordinates are(x_1, y_1),...(x_m, y_m).In order to facilitate research, the above area is discrete [8], A_s express the all possible location area, random variables $X = |A_s|$ shows grid number of A_s , n shows cell density. Among them, $1 \le X \le (n+1-2\rho)^2$, $\rho = \left[\dfrac{rn}{\sqrt{2}s} \right]$ 。 By using coordinate transformation, S is

Located in （0,0）,and if p = $\dfrac{(2\rho+1)^2}{(n+1)^2}$ and so $q = 1 - p = 1 - \dfrac{(2\rho+1)^2}{(n+1)^2}$.

The core of the algorithm is :if m is not 0, in that way , A_s is not only in the intersection of communication range of m neighbor anchor node, but also still in the outside of non intersection communication range of all the rest $k - m$ non neighbor anchor node.

$$A_s = \begin{cases} (\bigcap_{i=1}^{m} B_{x,y_i}^{\rho}) - (\bigcup_{j=m+1}^{k} B_{x,y_i}^{\rho}), m > 0 \\ Q_p - (\bigcup_{i=1}^{k} B_{x,y_i}^{\rho}), m = 0 \end{cases} \tag{1}$$

Expectations of Positioning Area Size

Define

$$\lambda_{ij} = \begin{cases} 1, (i,j) \in A_s \\ 0, (i,j) \notin A_s \end{cases} \tag{2}$$

And $E(X) = \sum_{i=\frac{-n}{2}+\rho}^{\frac{n}{2}-\rho} \sum_{j=\frac{-n}{2}+\rho}^{\frac{n}{2}-\rho} E(\lambda_{ij}) = \sum_{i=\frac{-n}{2}+\rho}^{\frac{n}{2}-\rho} \sum_{j=\frac{-n}{2}+\rho}^{\frac{n}{2}-\rho} P_r(\lambda_{ij}=1)$ \hfill (3)

For LIE algorithm

$$\because P_r(\lambda_{ij} = 1, (i,j) \in Q_p - B_s^{2\rho}) = (1-2\rho)^2 \tag{4}$$

$\because P_r = (\lambda_{ij} = 1, (i,j) \in B_s^{2\rho})$

$$= \left[1 - 2\rho + \frac{(2\rho+1-i)(2\rho+1-j)}{(n+1)^2}\right]^k + \sum_{m=1}^{k} C_k^m q^{k-m} \left[\frac{(2\rho+1-i)(2\rho+1-j)}{(n+1)^2}\right]^m \tag{5}$$

$$= \left[q - \frac{(2\rho+1-i)(2\rho+1-j)}{(n+1)^2}\right]^k + \left[q + \frac{(2\rho+1-i)(2\rho+1-j)}{(n+1)^2}\right]^k - q^k$$

$$\therefore E(X) = 4\sum_{i=}^{2\rho} \sum_{j=1}^{2\rho} \left[1 - 2\rho + \frac{2(2\rho+1-i)(2\rho+1-j)}{(n+1)^2}\right]^k + \left[(n+1-2\rho)^2 - (4\rho+1)^2\right](1-2\rho)^k + 1 \tag{6}$$

From the formula (6) we can see that LIE algorithm E (x) reflects algorithm carpeted area .

The Number of Anchor Node in Localization

If n and ρ do not change, so $\lim_{k \to \infty} E(X) = 1$, it shows that when the number of anchor node become big, location estimation approximate the ideal. Suppose e>0,discuss when |E（X) -1|<e, Algorithm need the priority values of anchor.

$$\because |E(X) - 1| \le \left| \left[1 - \frac{2(2\rho+1)}{(n+1)^2}\right]^k - \left[n^2 + 20\rho^2 - 4\rho n + 4\rho + 2n\right]\right| < e \tag{7}$$

$$\therefore \frac{K}{(n+1)^2} > \frac{\log (n^2 + 4\rho^2 - 4\rho n + 2n) - \log e}{2(2\rho+1)} = K_{min}$$

The Influence of Cell Density in Location Accuracy

If $n' = \sigma n$, $\sigma > 1$, $\rho = \left[\dfrac{rn}{\sqrt{2}s}\right]$, so $\rho' \approx \sigma \rho$。 Owing to the side of continuous area and the

actual   value   of   node   communication   radius   are   changeless,   so

$p' = \dfrac{(2\rho'+1)^2}{(n'+1)^2} = \dfrac{(2\sigma\rho+1)^2}{(\sigma n+1)^2} \approx p$。 similarly $q' \approx q$。

$$\therefore E(X') = 4\sum_{i=1}^{2\rho}\sum_{j=1}^{2\rho}\left[1-2\rho+\frac{2(2\rho\sigma-i)(2\rho\sigma+1-j)}{(n+1)^2}\right]^k$$
$$+\left[(n+1-2\rho\sigma)^2 - (4\rho\sigma+1)^2\right](1-2\rho)^k + 1 \approx \sigma^2 E(X) \tag{8}$$

From the formula (6),we can see the actual size of the final positioning estimates has nothing to do with cell's intensity (n),but it's related to the size of the cell(Grid resolution α) .

All of the above formulas are applied to three-dimensional space, A_s is not only in the intersection of communication range of m neighbor anchor node, but also still in the outside of non intersection communication range of all the rest $k - m$ non neighbor anchor node . But it cannot guarantee each cube is in the communication range of cube set area after executing algorithm. so for convenience, we only describe these formulas in two-dimensional space, and tested in three-dimensional space.

2 LIE-3D Localization Algorithm

(1) Anchor node also is called beacon nodes, it occupies small proportion in network nodes, they can get their precise location through carrying the GPS device or predefined configurations . In wireless sensor networks, anchor node launch beacon information in different power levels L, beacon information of anchor node include the beacon node ID, position anchor (X, Y, Z), transmitting power level L and the spread radius($R_l - R_{l-1}$)of anchor node.

(2) Unknown nodes is the node which is needed positioned in wireless sensor networks. In the localization of wireless sensor network, unknown nodes monitor beacon information which is from anchor node, and storage useful information to a information table, then according to the information in the information table, calculate its position to realize positioning. Information table include AH (the number of anchor node through monitoring) and information beacon from anchor node.

(3) Anchor nodes broadcast its beacon information to the entire network, spread radius is r .After the stage of monitor, unknown nodes select the centroid of monitoring anchor node as the center O (x_0, y_0, z_0),put the meridian through the center O (x_0, y_0, z_0) as longitudinal axis Y, put the parallel through the center O (x_0, y_0, z_0) as horizontal axis X, put the linear which is through the center and verticals the surface of XY, to build Cartesian space ,and then carry out three-dimensional grids. In order to facilitate research, and we put the above model to discrete, we divide Q into ($n+1$)³ small cubes

unit grid. n called cell density, Q= $[-n/2,n/2] \times [-n/2,n/2] \times [-n/2,n/2]$, coordinates in the cell's node is (I, j, z) , the radius of communication of node is $B^{\rho}_{(i,j,z)} = [i-\rho, j-\rho, z-\rho]$,among the $\rho = \left[\dfrac{rn}{\sqrt{2}s}\right]$,set $0\leq\rho\leq n$ 8. $Q_\rho = B^{\frac{n}{\cdot}\rho}_{(0,0,0)}$ shows at least the ρ distance from Q border area. Through discussing variable mathematical expectation , we only analysis the node within $Q_{3\rho}$.

(4) First of all, put every small cubes ticket value into 0, Each pending a node contains a Grid-oriented area, the size of the ticket value of the anchor node for a grid shows the degree of agreement .The bigger the degree of agreement grid is, the greater the located node is in the grid . In the voting process, every anchor node has the same weight 1, if anchor node judge grid is within the effective distance of communications, then vote, or don't vote.

(5) After the vote, the most votes grid is the largest possible area, we take the centroid position of the largest possible area as estimate area of unknown nodes. Computation formula is as follows:

$$(\tilde{x}, \tilde{y}, \tilde{z}) = (\frac{\sum\limits_{i=1}^{n} x_i}{n}, \frac{\sum\limits_{i=1}^{n} y_i}{n}, \frac{\sum\limits_{i=1}^{n} z_i}{n}) \qquad (9)$$

3 The Simulation Experiment and Performance Evaluation

We use Matlab to simulate, with 500 unknown nodes, including anchor node ratio for 10%, Anchor node and unknown nodes randomly deploy in three-dimensional space($100 \times 100 \times 100 \, m^3$), The communication radius of unknown nodes and anchor node is 50m, ρ =6, e=8.

3.1 Experimental Parameters

(1) α : grid resolution, α =3、5、15;

(2) ANR: the ratio between Anchor node to the unknown nodes and communications radius , ANR=2;

(3) n: cell density;

(4) DOI: wireless irregular;

(5) AH: unknown nodes monitor the average number of all anchor nodes;

(6) RPRL: minimum transmission power range, RPRL=25m;

3.2 Simulation Results

Stability and Robustness of Algorithm

Figure 1 depicts the changing relations between positioning results and DOI and coverage area, From the graph, the diversification of simulation coverage area size does not affect the positioning error, this shows that positioning of LIE - 3D algorithm is relatively stable. Meanwhile, positioning error has slight changes with the increase of DOI, but the impact is not very significant, and shows that the algorithm has good robustness.

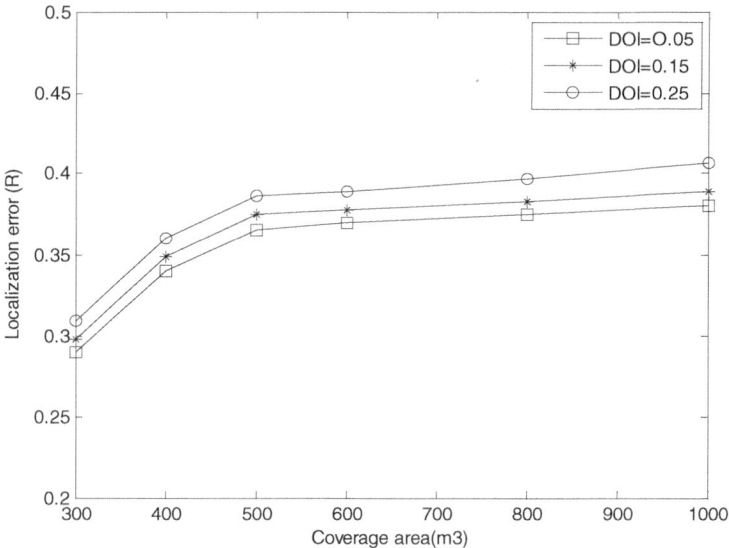

Fig. 1. Locating results of coverage area and the influence of DOI

Kmin of the Algorithm

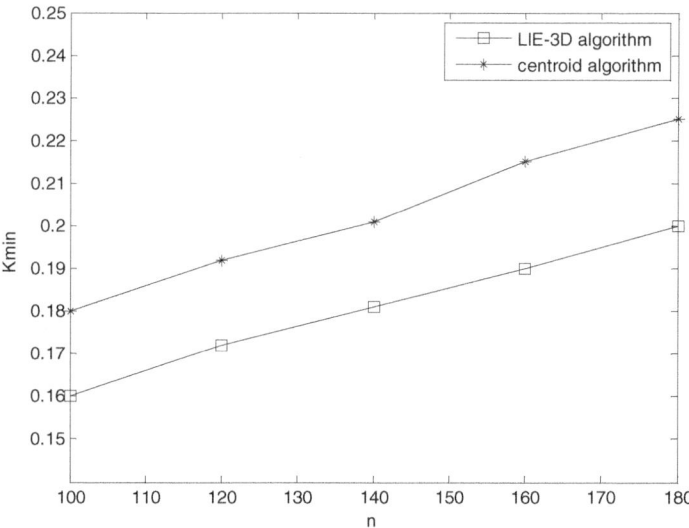

Fig. 2. The comparison of Kmin

Anchor node density is important parameters in wireless sensor network location algorithm, if requirements of algorithm to anchor node is exorbitant, it will cause the application cost is exorbitant. The figure 2 shows, the minimum anchor node density of LIE algorithm under grids is between 0.16 ~0.22, but the minimum anchor node density of centroid algorithm is between 0.182 ~ 0.24.This shows, in order to achieve the same positioning accuracy, LIE algorithm needs less anchor node, in this way , can save positioning cost.

Anchor Node Density

From the formula (6), we can see that the final location area of regional with the actual size is not related to cell intensive degree, it's related to the cell size(Grid resolution α) .In the picture, We draw the conclusion that the smaller is α , the lower will be average positioning error.

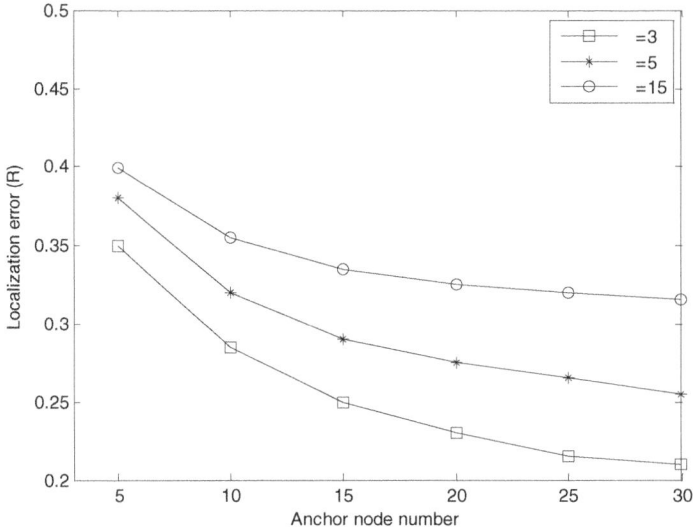

Fig. 3. α in the different anchor node number

4 Conclusion

Although WSN positioning technology research has made some achievements, but there are still many problems to be solved, as follows :(1) perfection of perception model. Currently, node perception model which fail to take into consideration the communication jamming in actual radio channel, is a kind of ideal model. Therefore, it is necessary to consider more perfect perception model species ;(2) positioning technologies of three dimensional space. From the research achievements at present it is easy to see: Although many methods can well solve positioning technology in the two-dimensional space, because the computational complexity of mathematical theory in the three dimensional space positioning technology is still a difficult problem，therefore, how to further improve positioning technology in WSN three dimensional space, will be a very meaningful research; (3) Provide mobility support. At present, WSN positioning technology theory and algorithm mostly assume a sensor node or network is static, but in battlefield applications it may require node or network has high mobility. Therefore, it is necessary to build new location technology theory and algorithm to support mobility.

References

1. Sheu, J.P., Chen, P.C., Hsu, C.S.: A distributed Localization Scheme for Wireless Sensor Networks with Improved Grid-scan and Vector-Based Refinement. IEEE Transactions on Mobile Computing 7(9), 1110–1123 (2008)
2. Cui, S.X., Liu, J.J., Fan, X.M.: A Distributed non anchor node Localization Algorithm in Sensor Network. Computer Research and Development 46(3), 425–433 (2009)
3. Stupp, G., Sidi, M.: The Expected Uncertainty of Range Free Localization Protocols in Sensor Networks. First Theoretical Computer Science (TCS) Journal 344, 86–99 (2005)
4. Wang, F.B., Shi, L., Ren, F.Y.: Self-localization systems and algorithms for wireless sensor network. Journal of Software 16(5), 857–868 (2005)
5. Qi, H.: Based on mobile anchor node localization algorithm research. In: Wireless Sensor Networks. Taiyuan University of Technology (2010)
6. Ou, C.H., Ssu, K.F.: Sensor Position Determination with Flying Anchors in three-dimensional Wireless Sensor Networks. IEEE Transactions on Mobile Computing 7(9), 1084–1097 (2008)
7. Joo, G.L., Rao, S.V.: A Grid-Based Location Estimation Scheme using Hop Counts for Multi-hop Wireless Sensor Networks. In: International Workshop on Wireless Ad-Hoc Networks, pp. 330–334 (2004)
8. Jia, Z.X., Wu, C.D., Zhang, Y.Z.: Distributed Grid Location Estimation Scheme Based on Euclidean Distance. In: IEEE 3rd Conference on Industrial Electronics and Applications, pp. 1128–1132 (2008)

The Least Deviation Priority Method for Intuitionistic Fuzzy Complementary Judgment Matrix and Its Application

Weixia Li and Chengyi Zhang[*]

Department of Mathematics and Statistics, Hainan Normal University,
Haikou, 571158, China
liweixia851019@163.com, chengyizh@hainnu.edu.cn

Abstract. In this paper, the definition of multiplicative intuitionistic fuzzy consistent complementary judgment matrix(MIFCCJM) is given, then based on the aspect of multiplicative intuitionistic fuzzy consistent complementary judgment matrix(MIFCCJM) formed by priority weights approximatives actual intuitionistic fuzzy complementary judgment matrix(IFCJM), a least deviation priority method for intuitionistic fuzzy complementary judgment matrix(IFCJM) is proposed. Then intuitionistic fuzzy complementary judgment matrix (IFCJM) is applied to analytic hierarchy process (AHP), and AHP under the intuitionistic fuzzy environment is proposed. Finally, the method is applied to college evaluation example to show the practicality of the method.

Keywords: AHP; Intuitionistic fuzzy value; Multiplicative intuitionistic fuzzy consistent complementary judgment matrix (MIFCCJM).

1 Introduction

Since 1980, analytic hierarchy process (AHP) [1] was applied widely, and it solved many significant practical problems. With the development of the theory of AHP and actual need, fuzzy theory was introduced to AHP. In 2000, fuzzy AHP was proposed in [2], and the core of FAHP is introducing FCJM to AHP. After [3] introduced FCJM and multiplicative consistent fuzzy complementary judgment matrix (MCFCJM), people keep on discussing their priority theory. Specially, [4] proposed numerous priority methods. Due to the need of solving practical problems, [5-6] introduced interval number complementary judgment matrix and discussed its priority methods. In 1986, the concept of intuitionistic fuzzy set (IFS) was introduced in [7], and IFS was the generalization of fuzzy sets. In 1993, the concept of vague sets was proposed in [8], then [9] proposed that vague set was IFS actually. In fact, IFS is a special form of interval numbers, compared with fuzzy value, it considers the degree of membership, the degree of non-membership and the hesitant degree of information. Hence, IFS is more practical than fuzzy value in solving the fuzziness and uncertainty

---

[*] Corresponding author.

H. Deng et al. (Eds.): AICI 2011, Part I, LNAI 7002, pp. 500–507, 2011.
© Springer-Verlag Berlin Heidelberg 2011

problems. Moreover, IFCJM was introduced in [10].Then the application of IFS is wide, for example, it has been applied to the fuzzy decision-making problem in [11].

In this paper, based on IFS, MIFCCJM is defined. Then, the least deviation priority method for IFCJM is introduced, that is, the MIFCCJM structured by the weight values of its priority vector approximates IFCJM. Then we introduce AHP under the intuitionistic fuzzy environment. Finally, based on the method of AHP under the intuitionistic fuzzy environment, we solved the problem of university evaluation.

2   Preliminaries

2.1   Fundamental Definitions and Theorems

Definition 2.11[7]. Let X be a nonempty fixed set. IFS A is an object having the form: $A = \{< x, t_A(x), f_A(x) >| \ x \in X \}$ where, $t_A(x): \ X \rightarrow [0,1]$ and $f_A(x):$ $X \rightarrow [0,1]$ denote the degree of membership and the degree of non-membership respectively of each element $x \in X$ to A and $0 \le t_A(x) + f_A(x) \le 1$ for all $x \in X$.

The definitions for FCJM and MCFCJM, and their properties are as follows.

Definition 2.12[3]. Let $B = \left(b_{ij} \right)_{n \times n}$ be a judgment matrix. Then B is called a FCJM if $b_{ij} + b_{ji} = 1$ and $b_{ii} = 0.5$.

Theorem 2.11[12]. Let $B = \left(b_{ij} \right)_{n \times n}$ be FCJM and $b_i = \sum_{j=1}^{n} b_{ij}$ for $i \in N$. Then $\overline{B} = \left(\overline{b}_{ij} \right)_{n \times n}$ is MCFCJM such that $\overline{b}_{ij} = (b_i - b_j)/(2(n-1)) + 0.5$. If sum each line and normalize, then $\omega = (\omega_1, \omega_2, \cdots, \omega_n)$ is obtained where $i \in N$,

$$\omega_i = (\sum_{j=1}^{n} b_{ij} + \frac{n}{2} - 1)/(n(n-1)) \tag{1}$$

Definition 2.13[3]. Let $B = \left(b_{ij} \right)_{n \times n}$ be FCJM. Then B is called MCFCJM if satisfying $b_{ik} b_{kj} b_{ji} = b_{ki} b_{jk} b_{ij}$, $i, j, k \in N$.

Theorem 2.12[4]. Let $B = \left(b_{ij} \right)_{n \times n}$ be FCJM and $\omega = (\omega_1, \omega_2, \cdots, \omega_n)$ be the priority vector of B. If $b_{ij} = \omega_i / (\omega_i + \omega_j)$, $i, j \in N$, that is

$$(b_{ij}/b_{ji}) \bullet (\omega_j/\omega_i) = (b_{ji}/b_{ij}) \bullet (\omega_i/\omega_j), \tag{2}$$

then B is called MCFCJM.

Definition 2.14[5]. Let $B = \left(b_{ij}\right)_{n\times n}$ be complementary judgment matrix where $b_{ij} = [b_{ij}^-, b_{ij}^+]$ and $b_{ji} = [b_{ji}^-, b_{ji}^+]$. Then B is called interval number complementary judgment matrix if $b_{ij}^- + b_{ij}^+ = b_{ji}^+ + b_{ji}^- = c$ holds, where $c > 0$ and $i, j \in N$.

Definition 2.15[10]. Let $B = \left(b_{ij}\right)_{n\times n}$ be interval number complementary judgment matrix, then B is called IFCJM if b_{ij} is intuitionistic fuzzy value for $i, j \in N$.

Definition 2.16. Let $B = \left(b_{ij}\right)_{n\times n}$ be IFCJM, if $BL = (l_{ij}^-)_{n\times n}$ and $BR = (r_{ij}^+)_{n\times n}$ are

MCFCJM, where $l_{ij}^- = \begin{cases} b_{ij}^-, & i < j \\ 0.5, & i = j \\ b_{ij}^+, & \text{else} \end{cases}$ and $r_{ij}^+ = \begin{cases} b_{ij}^+, & i > j \\ 0.5, & i = j \\ b_{ij}^-, & \text{else} \end{cases}$,then B is called

MIFCCJM.

Theorem 2.13. Let $B = \left(b_{ij}\right)_{n\times n}$ be IFCJM, $\omega^- = (\omega_1^-, \omega_2^-, \cdots, \omega_n^-)$ be the priority vector of $BL = (l_{ij}^-)_{n\times n}$ and $\omega^+ = (\omega_1^+, \omega_2^+, \cdots, \omega_n^+)$ be of $BR = (r_{ij}^+)_{n\times n}$. If,

$$(l_{ij}^- / l_{ji}^-)\bullet(\omega_j^- / \omega_i^-) = (l_{ji}^- / l_{ij}^-)\bullet(\omega_i^- / \omega_j^-), \tag{3}$$

$$(r_{ij}^+ / r_{ji}^+)\bullet(\omega_j^+ / \omega_i^+) = (r_{ji}^+ / r_{ij}^+)\bullet(\omega_i^+ / \omega_j^+), \tag{4}$$

Then B is MIFCCJM.

Definition 2.18. Let $B = \left(b_{ij}\right)_{n\times n}$ be IFCJM, $\omega^- = (\omega_1^-, \omega_2^-, \cdots, \omega_n^-)$ be the priority vector of $BL = (l_{ij}^-)_{n\times n}$ and $\omega^+ = (\omega_1^+, \omega_2^+, \cdots, \omega_n^+)$ be the priority vector of $BR = (r_{ij}^+)_{n\times n}$. Then $w = (w_1, w_2, \cdots, w_n)$ is called the priority vector of B where $w_i = [w_i^-, w_i^+]$, $w_i^- = \min(\omega_i^-, \omega_i^+)$ and $w_i^+ = \max(\omega_i^-, \omega_i^+)$.

Definition 2.19[6]. Let $\tilde{a} = [a^L, a^U]$ and $\tilde{b} = [b^L, b^U]$ be interval numbers, where $l_{\tilde{a}} = a^U - a^L$ and $l_{\tilde{b}} = b^U - b^L$, then the possibility degree of $\tilde{a} \geq \tilde{b}$ is

$$p(\tilde{a} \geq \tilde{b}) = (\min\{l_{\tilde{a}} + l_{\tilde{b}}, \max(a^U - b^L, 0)\}) / (l_{\tilde{a}} + l_{\tilde{b}}), \tag{5}$$

and the order between $\tilde{a}$ and $\tilde{b}$ is noted by $\tilde{a} \geq \tilde{b}$.

2.2   Decision Method

Decision method 1[13]

Let B be FCJM, if B is MCFCJM, then the consistency condition is rarely satisfied,(2) does not hold. Here, introduce the deviation element, and construct the deviation function

$$F(\omega) = \sum_{i=1}^{n}\sum_{j=1}^{n} f_{ij} = \sum_{i=1}^{n}\sum_{j=1}^{n}(b_{ij}/b_{ji})\bullet(\omega_j/\omega_i) + (b_{ji}/b_{ij})\bullet(\omega_i/\omega_j) - 2 .$$

Obviously, a reasonable ω^* should be determined so as to minimize $F(\omega)$, that is,

$$F(\omega^*) = \min_{\omega \in \Lambda} f(\omega) = \sum_{i=1}^{n}\sum_{j=1}^{n}(b_{ij}/b_{ji})\bullet(\omega_j/\omega_i) + (b_{ji}/b_{ij})\bullet(\omega_i/\omega_j) - 2$$

(6)

$$s.t. \quad \omega_j \geq 0, j \in N, \sum_{j=1}^{n}\omega_j = 1 ,$$

To solve (6), we give a convergent iterative algorithm as follows:

Step 1. Give an original weight vector $\omega(0) = (\omega_1(0), \omega_2(0), \cdots, \omega_n(0)) \in \Lambda$, specify the parameters $\varepsilon, 0 < \varepsilon < 1$, and let $k = 0$.

Step 2. Calculate $\eta_i(\omega(k)) = \sum_{j=1}^{n}[(b_{ij}/b_{ji})\bullet(\omega_j/\omega_i) - (b_{ji}/b_{ij})\bullet(\omega_i/\omega_j)]$, $i \in N$. If $|\eta_i(\omega(k))| < \varepsilon$ holds, for all $i \in N$, then we take $\omega^* = \omega(k)$, go to Step 5; otherwise, continue to Step 3.

Step 3. Determine the number l such that $|\eta_l(\omega(k))| = \max_{i \in N}\{|\eta_i(\omega(k))|\}$, $i \in N$, and compute $v(k) = \left[\sum_{j \neq l}\frac{b_{lj}}{b_{jl}}\bullet\frac{\omega_j(k)}{\omega_l(k)} \middle/ \sum_{j \neq l}\frac{b_{jl}}{b_{lj}}\bullet\frac{\omega_l(k)}{\omega_j(k)}\right]^{1/2}$;

$\omega_i'(k) = \begin{cases} v(k)\omega_i(k), & i = l \\ \omega_i(k), & i \neq l \end{cases}$; $\omega_i(k+1) = \omega_i'(k)/\sum_{j=1}^{n}\omega_j'(k)$.

Step 4. Let $k = k+1$; go to Step 2.

Step 5. Output ω^*, which is the priority vector of B.

Step 6. End.

Decision method 2. Based on MIFCCJM structured by priority weights approximates actual IFCJM, we propose the least deviation priority method for IFCJM as follows.

Let B be IFCJM, if B is MIFCCJM, then the consistency condition is rarely satisfied. Then, (3-4) do not hold. Here, about $BL = (l_{ij}^-)_{n \times n}$ and $BR = (r_{ij}^+)_{n \times n}, \forall i, j \in N$, deviation elements $f_{ij}^- = (l_{ij}^- / l_{ji}^-) \cdot (\omega_j^- / \omega_i^-) + (l_{ji}^- / l_{ij}^-) \cdot (\omega_i^- / \omega_j^-) - 2$; $f_{ij}^+ = (r_{ij}^+ / r_{ji}^+) \cdot (\omega_j^+ / \omega_i^+) + (r_{ji}^+ / r_{ij}^+) \cdot (\omega_i^+ / \omega_j^+) - 2$, and deviation functions

$$F^-(\omega) = \sum_{i=1}^n \sum_{j=1}^n f_{ij}^- = \sum_{i=1}^n \sum_{j=1}^n ((l_{ij}^- / l_{ji}^-) \cdot (\omega_j^- / \omega_i^-) + (l_{ji}^- / l_{ij}^-) \cdot (\omega_i^- / \omega_j^-) - 2),$$

$$F^+(\omega) = \sum_{i=1}^n \sum_{j=1}^n f_{ij}^+ = \sum_{i=1}^n \sum_{j=1}^n ((r_{ij}^+ / r_{ji}^+) \cdot (\omega_j^+ / \omega_i^+) + (r_{ji}^+ / r_{ij}^+) \cdot (\omega_i^+ / \omega_j^+) - 2).$$

Obviously, two reasonable priority vectors ω_*^- and ω_*^+ should be determined by

$$F^-(\omega_*^-) = \min_{\omega \in \Lambda} f^-(\omega^-) = \sum_{i=1}^n \sum_{j=1}^n ((l_{ij}^- / l_{ji}^-) \cdot (\omega_j^- / \omega_i^-) + (l_{ji}^- / l_{ij}^-) \cdot (\omega_i^- / \omega_j^-) - 2)$$

$$s.t. \quad \omega_j^- \geq 0, j \in N, \sum_{j=1}^n \omega_j^- = 1 ,$$

(7)

$$F^+(\omega_*^+) = \min_{\omega \in \Lambda} f^+(\omega^+) = \sum_{i=1}^n \sum_{j=1}^n ((r_{ij}^+ / r_{ji}^+) \cdot (\omega_j^+ / \omega_i^+) + (r_{ji}^+ / r_{ij}^+) \cdot (\omega_i^+ / \omega_j^+) - 2)$$

$$s.t. \quad \omega_j^+ \geq 0, j \in N, \sum_{j=1}^n \omega_j^+ = 1 ,$$

(8)

3   The Analytic Hierarchy Process under Fuzzy Environment

We introduce the AHP under the intuitionistic fuzzy environment as follows:

Step 1. Establish hierarchical structure of the system.

Step 2.Give IFCJM. Suppose the weight vector of elements in the level k with respect to elements in the level above is ω_{k-1} . We make the level k be objectives (or criterions) level and the k+1 level be criterions (or sub-criterions) level, then structure n_k IFCJM $R_h^{(k)}$ structured by pair-wise comparisons for all the criterions (or sub-criterions) in the level k+1 with respect to a single objective (or criterion) in the level k. Let $R_h^{(k)} = ([r_{ij}^{-h(k)}, r_{ij}^{+h(k)}])$, $h = 1, 2, \ldots, n_k$, then obtain $R_h^{(k)}L$ and $R_h^{(k)}R$. Explain $r_{ij}^{-h(k)}$ and $r_{ij}^{+h(k)}$ as follows: $r_{ij}^{-h(k)} = t_{ij}$ and $r_{ij}^{+h(k)} = 1 - f_{ij}$ where the degree of membership t_{ij} is the dominance of $A_j^{(k+1)}$ over $A_i^{(k+1)}$ and the degree of non-membership f_{ij} is the dominance of $A_j^{(k+1)}$ over $A_i^{(k+1)}$ .Use quantity standard on the scale of 0.1 to 0.9 in [2].

Step 3. Calculate the priority vector. 1) Calculate the priority vector for IFCJM which is the pair-wise comparisons for all the criterions in the second level with respect to the first level. We get $R^{(1)}L$ and $R^{(1)}R$, then get $\omega^{(1)-}$ and $\omega^{(1)+}$. Hence, get

$w^{(1)} = ([w_i^{(1)-}, w_i^{(1)+}])$ ($i = 1, 2, \cdots, n_2$) for $R^{(1)}$. Then by (5), obtain the possibility degree matrix P. By (1), we have the weight vector $W^{(1)}$.

2) Calculate the priority matrix of the level k+1 with respect to the level k($k \geq 2$). Get $R_h^{(k)}L$ and $R_h^{(k)}R$, then get $\omega_h^{(k)-}$ and $\omega_h^{(k)+}$. Hence, get $w_h^{(k)} = [w_{h_i}^{(k)-}, w_{h_i}^{(k)+}]$ ($h = 1, 2, \ldots, n_k$; $i = 1, 2, \cdots, n_{k+1}$) for $R_h^{(k)}$. Then by (5), obtain the possibility degree matrixes $P_h^{(k)}$ ($h = 1, 2, \ldots, n_k$) respectively. We have $W_h^{(k)}$ by (1). Hence $P^{(k)} = (W_1^{(k)}, W_2^{(k)}, \cdots, W_{n_k}^{(k)})$ is considered as the aggregate priority matrix.

3) Aggregate the global weight. $W^{(k)} = P^{(k)}W^{(k-1)}$ is considered as the combined weight vector of the level k+1 with respect to the top level, then this procedure is repeated. Thus, we get weight vector $W^{(k)} = P^{(k)}W^{(k-1)} = P^{(k)}P^{(k-1)}\cdots\omega^{(1)}$.

4   Case Study

AHP under the intuitionistic fuzzy environment solve University evaluation work.

Step1. We construct the index system and establish hierarchical structure in table 1.

Table 1. Evaluation index system

objective level	University evaluation				
criterion level	school spirit x_1	teaching x_2	scientific research x_3	library x_4	logistics x_5
sub-crite-rion level	school leadership	teachership	institutional frame work of scientific research	financial resources	hardware equipment
	teachers' teaching	teaching facilities	management system of scientific research	works' ability	management level
	students' study	quality of students	principal of scientific research	borrowing efficiency	service quality

Step 2. 1) Experts give the pair-wise comparison for the second level with respect to the first level. Then we get

$$R^{(1)} = \begin{bmatrix} 0.5 & [0.5, 0.6] & [0.5, 0.6] & [0.5, 0.6] & [0.5, 0.6] \\ [0.4, 0.5] & 0.5 & [0.5, 0.5] & [0.5, 0.5] & [0.5, 0.5] \\ [0.4, 0.5] & [0.5, 0.5] & 0.5 & [0.5, 0.5] & [0.5, 0.5] \\ [0.4, 0.5] & [0.5, 0.5] & [0.5, 0.5] & 0.5 & [0.5, 0.5] \\ [0.4, 0.5] & [0.5, 0.5] & [0.5, 0.5] & [0.5, 0.5] & 0.5 \end{bmatrix}.$$

2) Experts give the pair-wise comparison for the third level with respect to each criterion in the second level one by one. Making pair-wise comparisons for the third

level with respect to x_1 , we get $R_1^{(2)} = \begin{bmatrix} 0.5 & [0.7,0.8] & [0.6,0.7] \\ [0.2,0.3] & 0.5 & [0.4,0.5] \\ [0.3,0.4] & [0.5,0.6] & 0.5 \end{bmatrix}$. This

procedure is repeated for sub-criterions in the third level with respect to criterions respectively in the second level, then we get matrixes:

$$R_2^{(2)} = \begin{bmatrix} 0.5 & [0.6,0.7] & [0.8,0.9] \\ [0.3,0.4] & 0.5 & [0.7,0.8] \\ [0.1,0.2] & [0.2,0.3] & 0.5 \end{bmatrix}; R_3^{(2)} = \begin{bmatrix} 0.5 & [0.8,0.9] & [0.6,0.7] \\ [0.1,0.2] & 0.5 & [0.3,0.4] \\ [0.3,0.4] & [0.6,0.7] & 0.5 \end{bmatrix},$$

$$R_4^{(2)} = \begin{bmatrix} 0.5 & [0.8,0.9] & [0.6,0.7] \\ [0.1,0.2] & 0.5 & [0.3,0.4] \\ [0.3,0.4] & [0.6,0.7] & 0.5 \end{bmatrix}; R_5^{(2)} = \begin{bmatrix} 0.5 & [0.6,0.7] & [0.7,0.8] \\ [0.3,0.4] & 0.5 & [0.6,0.7] \\ [0.2,0.3] & [0.3,0.4] & 0.5 \end{bmatrix}.$$

Step 3. 1) Calculate the priority vector for $R^{(1)}$. We get $R^{(1)}L$ and $R^{(1)}R$, and have priority vectors $\omega^{(1)-}$ and $\omega^{(1)+}$, after two times iteration in table 2:

Table 2. Two times iteration

k	$\omega^{(1)+}(k)'$	$\eta(\omega^{(1)+}(k))'$
0	[0.2,0.2,0.2,0.2,0.2]	[3.33,-0.83, -0.83, -0.83, -0.83]
1	[0.27,0.18,0.18,0.18,0.18]	[0,0,0,0,0]

Get $w^{(1)} = [[0.2,0.27], [0.18,0.2], [0.18,0.2], [0.18,0.2], [0.18,0.2]]'$ .Hence, obtain the possibility degree matrix P .By (1), $W^{(1)} = [0.3, 0.175, 0.175, 0.175, 0.175]'$.

2) Calculate the priority matrix of the third level with respect to the second level. For instance, firstly, we get $R_1^{(2)}L$ and $R_1^{(2)}R$, then by decision 2, after three times iteration respectively, we have $\omega_1^{(2)-}$ and $\omega_1^{(2)+}$. Hence, we get $w_1^{(2)} = [[0.48,0.60], [0.18,0.21],[0.21,0.31]]'$ for $R_1^{(2)}$. By (5), obtain the possibility degree matrix $P_1^{(2)}$ .By (1), get $W_1^{(2)} = [0.5, 0.17, 0.33]'$. By $R_h^{(2)}$ ($h=$ 2,3,4,5), the procedure is repeated, then get $W_2^{(2)} = [0.5, 0.33, 0.17]'$, $W_3^{(2)} = [0.5, 0.17, 0.33]'$, $W_4^{(2)} = [0.5,$ 0.17, 0.33$]'$, $W_5^{(2)} = [0.5, 0.33, 0.17]'$.(Note: each $w_i^{(2)}$ ($i=1,2,\cdots,5$) is vector with 15 lines and 1 column. In fact, for all the elements in the same level, we leave out the weight of some elements that don't affect the super-level). Then $P^{(2)} = (W_1^{(2)}, W_2^{(2)}, W_3^{(2)}, W_4^{(2)}, W_5^{(2)})$ is considered as the weight matrix.

3) Aggregate the global weight. We get the combined weight vector which is the bottom level with respect to the top level, that is, $W^{(2)}_{15\times1} = P^{(2)}W^{(1)} = [0.15, 0.051,$
$0.09, 0.087, 0.058, 0.029, 0.087, 0.029, 0.058, 0.087, 0.029, 0.058, 0.087, 0.058, , 0.029]^{\cdot}, \cdot$

Step 4. Conclusion analysis. In University evaluation work, according to the priority vector, we can conclude that the weight of school leadership is the highest.

5   Conclusion

In this paper, based on the concepts of IFCJM, we give define the MIFCCJM. Then we present a method to obtain a priority vector of IFCJM. Finally IFCJM is applied to AHP to solve fuzzy comprehensive evaluation problem, and we apply AHP under the intuitionistic fuzzy environment to college evaluation example. Then it verifies the practicality of the method.

Acknowledgment. This work is supported by NSF of China (70940007), KSTF of Hainan (090802), KSTF of Haikou (2010072) and Graduate Innovative Research of Hainan (Hys2010-22).

References

1. Saaty, T.L.: The analytic hierarchy process. McGraw-Hill, New York (1980)
2. Zang, J.J.: Fuzzy analytic hierarchy process FAHP. Fuzzy Systems and Math. 14, 80–88 (2000) (in Chinese)
3. Orlovsky, S.A.: Decision making with a fuzzy preference relation. Fuzzy Sets and Systems 1, 155–167 (1978)
4. Xu, Z.S.: Uncertain multiple attribute decision making methods and applications. Tsinghua university press, Beijing (2004) (in Chinese)
5. Xu, Z.S.: A practical method for priority of interval number complementary judgement matrix. Operations Research and Management Science 10, 16–19 (2001) (in Chinese)
6. Xu, Z.S., Da, Q.L.: Possibility degree method for ranking interval numbers and its application. Journal of Systems Engineering 18, 67–70 (2003) (in Chinese)
7. Atanassov, K.T.: Intuitionistic fuzzy sets. Fuzzy Sets and Systems 20, 87–96 (1986)
8. Gau, W.L., Buehrer, D.J.: Vague sets. IEEE Trans. Systems Man Cybernet. 23, 610–614 (1993)
9. Bustine, H., Burillo, P.: Vague sets are intuitionistic fuzzy sets. Fuzzy Sets and Systems 79, 403–405 (1996)
10. Xu, Z.S.: Approaches to multiple attribute decision making with intuitionistic fuzzy preference information. Systems Engineering-Theory & Practice 11, 62–71 (2007) (in Chinese)
11. Li, D.F.: Multiattribute decision making models and methods using intuitionistic fuzzy sets. Journal of Computer and System Sciences 70, 73–85 (2005) (in Chinese)
12. Xu, Z.S.: Algorithm for priority of fuzzy complementary judgement matrix. Journal of Systems Engineering 16, 311–314 (2001) (in Chinese)
13. Xu, Z.S., Da, Q.L.: A least deviation method to obtain a priority vector of a fuzzy preference relation. Euroean Journal of Operational Research 164, 206–216 (2005)

Multicriteria Group Decision Making in a Linguistic Environment

Chunqiao Tan[1], Hepu Deng[2], and Junyan Liu[3]

[1] School of Business, Central South University, Changsha 410083, China
chunqiaot@sina.com
[2] School of Business Information Technology and Logistics, RMIT University GPO Box 2476
V, Melbourne 3001 Victoria, Australia
hepu.deng@rmit.edu.au
[3] Armored Force Engineering Institute, Beijing 100072, China
ljyjuru@163.com

Abstract. This paper presents a method for solving the multicriteria group decision making problem in an uncertain linguistic environment. To ensure an effective aggregation of the uncertain linguistic variables in multicriteria group decision making for adequately modeling the uncertainty and imprecision of the decision making process, an uncertain linguistic Choquet integral operator is proposed. A method based on the proposed linguistic Choquet integral operator is developed. An application of the developed method for evaluating the university faculty on promotion is given that shows the developed method is effective for solving the multicriteria group decision making problem in a linguistic environment.

Keywords: Aggregation operators, Multicriteria group decision making, Choquet integral, Linguistic variables.

1 Introduction

Decision making is the process of selecting the best alternative from all the available alternatives in a given situation. With the increasing complexity of the socio-economic environment, several decision makers are usually involved in considering all the relevant aspects of a decision making problem so that multicriteria group decision making problems are often present. Uncertainty and imprecision are always present in multicriteria group decision making. This is because crisp data are usually inadequate to model the real-life phenomena in real-life situations. Furthermore, decision makers (DMs) may not possess a sufficient level of knowledge of the problem so that they may not be unable to discriminate explicitly the degree to which one alternative is better than another. As a result, linguistic assessments represented in the form of linguistic variables [1] are often used for adequately modeling the uncertainty and imprecision in the human decision making process. However, in many situations, the DMs are willing or able to provide only uncertain linguistic information because of time pressure, lack of knowledge, or data, and their limited expertise related to the problem domain. To adequately aggregate such uncertain linguistic information, uncertain linguistic

H. Deng et al. (Eds.): AICI 2011, Part I, LNAI 7002, pp. 508–516, 2011.
© Springer-Verlag Berlin Heidelberg 2011

aggregation operators are proposed [2, 3]. Such operators, however, are used in multicriteria group decision making under the assumption of the mutual preferential independence between DMs in the linguistic evaluation process. But many real-world problems often have an interdependent property between the preferences of DMs in the decision making process.

The Choquet integral [4] as an extension of the additive aggregation operators is widely used to minic the human decision process. The popularity of the Choquet integral is that it coincides with the Lebesgue integral in which the measure is additive. The Choquet integral is able to perform aggregation when the mutual preferential independence between DMs is violated [4-6]. In this paper, we develop a new decision making method for multi-criteria group decision making under uncertain linguistic environment by means of uncertain linguistic Choquet integral operator.

In what follows, the interval number and Choquet integral are reviewed first in Section 2. In Section 3 the uncertain linguistic Choquet integral operator are proposed, leading to the development of a method for solving the multicriteria group decision making problem with uncertain linguistic information in Section 4. In Section 5, an example is presented for illustrating the applicability of the method for solving the multicriteria group decision making problem in a linguistic environment.

2 Preliminaries: Interval Numbers and Choquet Integral

Given r^-, $r^+ \in R^+$ and $r^- \leq r^+$, the closed interval $[r^-, r^+]$ defines an interval number $\bar{r} = [r^-, r^+] = \{r | r^- \leq r \leq r^+\}$. Suppose that $I(R^+) = \{\bar{r} : [r^-, r^+] \subset R^+\}$ is the set of interval numbers. Let $\bar{a} = [a^-, a^+]$ and $\bar{b} = [b^-, b^+]$ be any two interval numbers, the following basic operations are valid [7].

(a) $\bar{a} + \bar{b} = [a^- + b^-, a^+ + b^+]$, (b) $\bar{a} \times \bar{b} = [a^-b^-, a^+b^+]$, (c) $\lambda\bar{a} = [\lambda a^-, \lambda a^+]$ for $\lambda > 0$.

To facilitate the comparison of two interval numbers, a possibility-based measure is developed in the following for comparing each pair of interval-value variables.

Definition 1. Let $\bar{a} = [a^-, a^+]$ and $\bar{b} = [b^-, b^+]$ be any two interval numbers, the degree of possibility of $\bar{a} > \bar{b}$ is defined as

$$P(\bar{a} > \bar{b}) = \frac{\max\{0, a^+ - b^-\} + \max\{0, a^- - b^+\}}{\max\{0, a^+ - b^-\} + \max\{0, a^- - b^+\} + \max\{0, b^+ - a^-\} + \max\{0, b^- - a^+\}}$$

Based on the definition above, there are three propositions listed as follows:

$\bar{a} \geq \bar{b}$ if $P(\bar{a} > \bar{b}) \geq 0.5$, $\bar{a} > \bar{b}$ if $P(\bar{a} > \bar{b}) > 0.5$, $\bar{a} = \bar{b}$ if $P(\bar{a} > \bar{b}) = 0.5$.

Let X be the universal set and Σ be a σ-algebra of subsets of X. (X, Σ) is called a measurable space[8]. If X is finite, $P(X)$, the power set of X, is usually taken as Σ.

Definition 2. A fuzzy measure on a set X is a set function $\mu : P(X) \rightarrow [0, 1]$, satisfying the following conditions:

(1) $\mu(\phi) = 0$, $\mu(X) = 1$ (boundary conditions)
(2) If $A, B \in P(X)$ and $A \subseteq B$ then $\mu(A) \leq \mu(B)$ (monotonicity).

In order to determine a fuzzy measure on $X = \{x_1, x_2, \ldots, x_n\}$, we generally need to find $2^n - 2$ values. To reduce the complexity of a fuzzy measure, Sugeno [9] introduces λ-fuzzy measures g which satisfies the following additional property:

$$g(A \cup B) = g(A) + g(B) + \lambda g(A) g(B) \tag{1}$$

where $-1 < \lambda < \infty$ for all $A, B \in P(X)$ and $A \cap B = \phi$.

If $X = \{x_1, \ldots, x_n\}$, $\bigcup_{i=1}^{n} x_i = X$. The λ-fuzzy measure g satisfies following Eq.(2).

$$g(X) = g(\bigcup_{i=1}^{n} x_i) = \begin{cases} \dfrac{1}{\lambda}(\prod_{i=1}^{n}[1 + \lambda g(x_i)] - 1) & \text{if } \lambda \neq 0, \\[2mm] \sum_{i=1}^{n} g(x_i) & \text{if } \lambda = 0, \end{cases} \tag{2}$$

where $x_i \cap x_j = \phi$ for all $i, j = 1, 2, \ldots, n$ and $i \neq j$. It can be noted that $g(x_i)$ for a subset with a single element x_i is called a fuzzy density, and can be denoted as $g_i = g(x_i)$. Especially for every subset $A \in P(X)$, we have

$$g(A) = \begin{cases} \dfrac{1}{\lambda}(\prod_{i \in A}[1 + \lambda g(x_i)] - 1) & \text{if } \lambda \neq 0, \\[2mm] \sum_{i \in A} g(x_i) & \text{if } \lambda = 0. \end{cases} \tag{3}$$

Based on Eq. (2), the value λ of can be uniquely determined from $g(X) = 1$, which is equivalent to solving the following Eq.(4).

$$\lambda + 1 = \prod_{i=1}^{n} (1 + \lambda g_i). \tag{4}$$

As a generalization of the linear Lebesgue integral and the weighted means operator, the Choquet integral is defined as follows [6].

Definition 3. Let f be a positive real-valued function from X to R^+, and μ be a fuzzy measure on X. The Choquet integral of f with respect to μ is defined as

$$C_\mu(f) = \int f \, d\mu = \int_0^\infty \mu(F_\alpha) d\alpha \tag{5}$$

where $F_\alpha = \{x \mid f(x) \geq \alpha\}(\alpha \in [0, +\infty))$.

If $X = (x_1, \ldots, x_n)$, without loss of generality we assume that subscript $(\cdot)$ indicates a permutation on X such that $f(x_{(1)}) \leq f(x_{(2)}) \leq \ldots \leq f(x_{(n)})$, Then the discrete value of the Choquet integral is obtained

$$C_\mu(f) = \int f \, d\mu = \sum_{i=1}^{n} f(x_{(i)})[\mu(A_{(i)}) - \mu(A_{(i+1)})], \tag{6}$$

where $A_{(i)} = \{x_{(i)}, x_{(i+1)}, \ldots, x_{(n)}\}$, $A_{(n+1)} = \phi$.

Definition 4. An interval-valued function $\bar{f} : X \to I(R^+)$ is measurable if both $f^-(x)$ $= [\bar{f}(x)]_l$, the left end point of interval $\bar{f}(x)$, and $f^+(x) = [\bar{f}(x)]_r$, the right end point of interval $\bar{f}(x)$, are measurable function of x.

Theorem 1. Let $\bar{f} : X \to I(R^+)$ be a measurable interval-valued function on X and μ be a fuzzy measure on Σ. Then the Choquet integral of $\bar{f}$ with respect to μ is

$$C_\mu(\bar{f}) = \int \bar{f} d\mu = [\int f^- d\mu, \int f^+ d\mu], \tag{7}$$

where $f^-(x) = [\bar{f}(x)]_l$, the left end point of interval $\bar{f}(x)$, and $f^+(x) = [\bar{f}(x)]_r$, the right end point of interval $\bar{f}(x)$ $\forall x \in X$.

According to Eq. (6) and Theorem 1, we can easily obtain the following conclusion.

Proposition 1. Let $\bar{f} : X \to I(R^+)$ be a measurable interval-valued function on X and μ be a fuzzy measure on $P(X)$. If $X = (x_1, x_2, \ldots, x_n)$, then the discrete Choquet integral of $\bar{f}$ with respect to μ can be expressed by

$$C_\mu(\bar{f}) = \int \bar{f} d\mu = [\sum_{i=1}^{n} f^-(x_{(i)})(\mu(A_{(i)}) - \mu(A_{(i+1)})), \sum_{i=1}^{n} f^-(x_{(i)})(\mu(A_{(i)}) - \mu(A_{(i+1)}))]$$

$$= \sum_{i=1}^{n} \bar{f}(x_{(i)})(\mu(A_{(i)}) - \mu(A_{(i+1)})) \tag{8}$$

where subscript $(\cdot)$ indicates a permutation on X such that $\bar{f}(x_{(1)}) \leq \cdots \leq \bar{f}(x_{(n)})$, $\bar{f}(x_{(i)}) = [f^-(x_{(i)}), f^+(x_{(i)})]$, and $A_{(i)} = \{x_{(i)}, x_{(i+1)}, \ldots, x_{(n)}\}$, $A_{(n+1)} = \phi$.

3   A Linguistic Choquet Integral Operator

The linguistic approach is an approximate technique, which represents qualitative aspects as linguistic values by means of linguistic variables. Let us consider a finite and totally ordered discrete linguistic label set $S = \{s_\alpha \mid \alpha = 0, \ldots, t\}$, where s_α represents a linguistic variable. To preserve all the given information, we extend the discrete term set S to a continuous term set $\widetilde{S} = \{s_\alpha \mid s_0 < s_\alpha \leq s_t, \alpha \in [0, t]\}$. If $s_\alpha \in S$, then we call s_α the original linguistic term, otherwise, we call s_α the virtual term. In general, the decision maker uses the original linguistic terms in real decision making problems.

In the real world, many decision making processes take place in an uncertain environment where the linguistic preference information provided by the experts does not take the form of precise linguistic variables, but value ranges can be obtained due to the experts' vague knowledge about the preference degrees of one alternative over another. In the following, we give the definition of uncertain linguistic variable [3].

Definition 5. Let $\bar{s} = [s_\alpha, s_\beta]$, where $s_\alpha, s_\beta \in \tilde{S}$, s_α and s_β are the lower and the upper limits, respectively, we then call $\bar{s}$ the uncertain linguistic variable.

Let $\bar{S}$ be the set of all uncertain linguistic variables. Consider any three uncertain linguistic variables $\bar{s} = [s_\alpha, s_\beta]$, $\bar{s}_1 = [s_{\alpha_1}, s_{\beta_1}]$, $\bar{s}_2 = [s_{\alpha_2}, s_{\beta_2}]$, and $\mu, \mu_1, \mu_2 \in [0, 1]$, then their operational laws are defined as:

(a) $\bar{s}_1 \oplus \bar{s}_2 = \bar{s}_2 \oplus \bar{s}_1 = [s_{\alpha_1} \oplus s_{\alpha_2}, s_{\beta_1} \oplus s_{\beta_2}] = [s_{\alpha_1 + \alpha_2}, s_{\beta_1 + \beta_2}]$;

(b) $\mu\bar{s} = [\mu s_\alpha, \mu s_\beta] = [s_{\mu\alpha}, s_{\mu\beta}]$, $\mu(\bar{s}_1 \oplus \bar{s}_2) = \mu\bar{s}_1 \oplus \mu\bar{s}_2$, $(\mu_1 + \mu_2)\bar{s} = \mu_1\bar{s} \oplus \mu_2\bar{s}$.

Definition 6. Let $\bar{s}_1 = [s_{\alpha_1}, s_{\beta_1}]$ and $\bar{s}_2 = [s_{\alpha_2}, s_{\beta_2}]$ be two uncertain linguistic variables, then the degree of possibility of $\bar{s}_1 > \bar{s}_2$ is defined as

$$P(\bar{s}_1 > \bar{s}_2) = \frac{\max\{0, \beta_1 - \alpha_2\} + \max\{0, \alpha_1 - \beta_2\}}{\max\{0, \beta_1 - \alpha_2\} + \max\{0, \alpha_1 - \beta_2\} + \max\{0, \beta_2 - \alpha_1\} + \max\{0, \alpha_2 - \beta_1\}} \quad (9)$$

we say $\bar{s}_1 \geq \bar{s}_2$ if $P(\bar{s}_1 > \bar{s}_2) \geq 0.5$; $\bar{s}_1 > \bar{s}_2$ if $P(\bar{s}_1 > \bar{s}_2) > 0.5$; $\bar{s}_1 = \bar{s}_2$ if $P(\bar{s}_1 > \bar{s}_2) = 0.5$.

Based on the operational laws on uncertain linguistic variables, in the following we propose a new uncertain linguistic aggregation operator.

Definition 7. Let $\text{ULC}_\mu : \bar{S}^n \to \bar{S}$, if

$$\text{ULC}_\mu(\bar{s}_1, \bar{s}_2, \cdots, \bar{s}_n) = \sum_{i=+1}^{n} {}^{\oplus} \bar{s}_{(i)}[\mu(A_{(i)}) - \mu(A_{(i+1)})] = [s_\alpha, s_\beta]$$

where $\alpha = \sum_{i=1}^{n}(\alpha_i)[\mu(A_{(i)}) - \mu(A_{(i+1)})]$, $\beta = \sum_{i=1}^{n}(\beta_i)[\mu(A_{(i)}) - g(A_{(i+1)})]$, μ is a fuzzy measure on $(\bar{s}_1, \bar{s}_2, \cdots, \bar{s}_n)$, subscript $(\cdot)$ indicates a permutation such that $\bar{s}_{(1)} \leq \bar{s}_{(2)} \leq \cdots \leq \bar{s}_{(n)}$, $\bar{s}_i = [s_{\alpha_i}, s_{\beta_i}] \in \bar{S}$ and $A_{(i)} = \{(i), \ldots, (n)\}$, $A_{(n+1)} = \phi$. Then ULC is called the uncertain linguistic Choquet integral operator.

Proposition 2. Let g be a λ-fuzzy measure on $(\bar{s}_1, \bar{s}_2, \cdots, \bar{s}_n)$, then we have

$$\text{ULC}_g(\bar{s}_1, \bar{s}_2, \cdots, \bar{s}_n) = \sum_{i=+1}^{n} {}^{\oplus} \bar{s}_{(i)}[g(A_{(i)}) - g(A_{(i+1)})] = [s_\alpha, s_\beta] .$$

If $\lambda \neq 0$, then

$$\alpha = \sum_{i=1}^{n}(\alpha_i) \cdot g_{(i)} \prod_{j=i+1}^{n}[1 + \lambda g_{(j)}], \quad \beta = \sum_{i=1}^{n}(\beta_i) \cdot g_{(i)} \prod_{j=i+1}^{n}[1 + \lambda g_{(j)}] .$$

If $\lambda = 0$, then

$$\alpha = \sum_{i=1}^{n}(\alpha_i) \cdot g_{(i)} , \quad \beta = \sum_{i=1}^{n}(\beta_i) \cdot g_{(i)} ,$$

where $(\cdot)$ indicates a permutation such that $\bar{s}_{(1)} \leq \bar{s}_{(2)} \leq \cdots \leq \bar{s}_{(n)}$, $\bar{s}_i = [s_{\alpha_i}, s_{\beta_i}]$.

4   A Multicriteria Group Decision Making Method

A multi-criteria group decision making problems can be described as follows: Let $E = \{e_1, e_2, \ldots, e_l\}$ is the set of the experts involved in the decision process; $A = (x_1, x_2, \ldots, x_n$ is the set of the considered alternatives; $C = (c_1, c_2, \ldots, c_m)$ is the set of the criteria used for evaluating the alternatives. In the following we utilize the uncertain linguistic Choquet integral operator to propose an approach for multicriteria group decision making with uncertain linguistic information, which involves the following steps:

Step 1. Let $\overline{S}$ be a given uncertain linguistic scale, for every alternative x_i ($i = 1, 2, \ldots, n$) with respect to criteria c_j ($j = 1, 2, \ldots, m$), each expert e_k ($k = 1, 2, \ldots, l$) is invited to express their individual evaluation or preference value, which takes the form of uncertain linguistic variable $\overline{a}_{ij}^k = [s_{\alpha_{ij}^k}, s_{\beta_{ij}^k}] \in \overline{S}$ ($i = 1, 2, \ldots, n; j = 1, 2, \ldots, m, k = 1, 2, \ldots, l$). Then we can obtain a decision making matrix as follow:

$$\overline{R}^k = \begin{pmatrix} \overline{a}_{11}^k, \overline{a}_{12}^k, \cdots, \overline{a}_{1m}^k \\ \overline{a}_{21}^k, \overline{a}_{22}^k, \cdots, \overline{a}_{2m}^k \\ \cdots \quad \cdots \quad \cdots \\ \overline{a}_{n1}^k, \overline{a}_{n2}^k, \cdots, \overline{a}_{nm}^k \end{pmatrix}.$$

Step 2. Confirm the fuzzy density $g_i = g(c_i)$ of each criteria. According to Eq.(4), parameter λ_1 of criteria can be determined.

Step 3. Confirm the fuzzy density $g_i = g(e_i)$ of each expert. According to Eq.(4), parameter λ_2 of expert can be determined.

Step 4. For decision making matrix $\overline{R}^k$, according to Definition 6, we rank these arguments $\overline{a}_{ij}^k$ ($j = 1, \ldots, m$) in the ith line such that $\overline{a}_{i(1)}^k \leq \cdots \leq \overline{a}_{i(m)}^k$. Utilize the ULC operator to derive the individual overall preference value $\overline{a}_i^k$ of alternative x_i,

$$\overline{a}_i^k = \text{ULC}_g(\overline{a}_{i1}^k, \overline{a}_{i2}^k, \cdots, \overline{a}_{im}^k) = s_i^k = [s_{\alpha_i^k}, s_{\beta_i^k}]$$

where

$$\alpha_i^k = \sum_{j=1}^m (\alpha_{i(j)}^k) \cdot g(c_{(j)}) \prod_{h=j+1}^m [1 + \lambda_1 g(c_{(h)})], \ \beta_i^k = \sum_{j=1}^m (\beta_{i(j)}^k) \cdot g(c_{(j)}) \prod_{h=j+1}^m [1 + \lambda_1 g(c_{(h)})].$$

Step 5. Similar to step 4, all $\overline{a}_i^k$ ($k = 1, \ldots, l$) is reordered such that $\overline{a}_i^{(1)} \leq \cdots \leq \overline{a}_i^{(l)}$. Using the ULC operator aggregates all $\overline{a}_i^k$ ($k = 1, \ldots, l$) into the collective overall preference value $\overline{a}_i$ of the alternative x_i.

$$\overline{a}_i = \text{ULC}_g(\overline{a}_i^1, \overline{a}_i^2, \cdots, \overline{a}_i^l) = [s_{\alpha_i}, s_{\beta_i}],$$

where

$$\alpha_i = \sum_{j=1}^l (\alpha_i^{(j)}) \cdot g(e_{(j)}) \prod_{h=j+1}^l [1 + \lambda_2 g(e_{(h)})], \ \beta_i = \sum_{j=1}^l (\beta_i^{(j)}) \cdot g(e_{(j)}) \prod_{h=j+1}^l [1 + \lambda_2 g(e_{(h)})].$$

Step 6. According to Definition 6, we rank these collective overall preference values $\bar{a}_i$ $(i = 1, 2, ..., n)$. According to the order of $\bar{a}_i$, we rank the alternative x_i $(i = 1, 2, ..., n)$, then to select the best one(s).

Step 7. End.

5   An Example

In this section, a problem of evaluating university faculty for tenure and promotion adapted from Bryson and Mobolurin [10] is used to illustrate the developed approach. For evaluation of university faculty for tenure and promotion, there are three criteria used at some universities which are c_1: teaching, c_2: research, and c_3: service. Five faculty candidates (alternatives) $x_i(i = 1, 2, 3, 4, 5)$ are to be evaluated using the term set $S = \{s_0 =$ extremely poor, $s_1 =$ very poor, $s_2 =$ poor, $s_3 =$ slightly poor, $s_4 =$ fair, $s_5 =$ slightly good, $s_6 =$ good, $s_7 =$ very good, $s_8 =$ extremely good$\}$, by four experts $e_k(k = 1, 2, 3, 4)$ under these three criteria. The decision making matrix of expert e_k is constructed as follows, respectively:

$$
\bar{R}^1 = \begin{pmatrix} [s_7,s_8] & [s_5,s_6] & [s_5,s_7] \\ [s_5,s_6] & [s_6,s_7] & [s_6,s_8] \\ [s_4,s_5] & [s_7,s_8] & [s_6,s_8] \\ [s_7,s_8] & [s_3,s_5] & [s_5,s_6] \\ [s_7,s_8] & [s_5,s_7] & [s_6,s_7] \end{pmatrix}, \quad
\bar{R}^2 = \begin{pmatrix} [s_5,s_6] & [s_7,s_8] & [s_4,s_5] \\ [s_4,s_6] & [s_5,s_7] & [s_6,s_8] \\ [s_6,s_7] & [s_5,s_6] & [s_6,s_8] \\ [s_6,s_8] & [s_5,s_6] & [s_6,s_7] \\ [s_7,s_8] & [s_6,s_7] & [s_4,s_7] \end{pmatrix},
$$

$$
\bar{R}^3 = \begin{pmatrix} [s_6,s_7] & [s_7,s_8] & [s_5,s_6] \\ [s_4,s_6] & [s_5,s_6] & [s_6,s_7] \\ [s_7,s_8] & [s_6,s_7] & [s_5,s_6] \\ [s_6,s_7] & [s_4,s_5] & [s_7,s_8] \\ [s_5,s_6] & [s_5,s_7] & [s_4,s_7] \end{pmatrix}, \quad
\bar{R}^4 = \begin{pmatrix} [s_5,s_6] & [s_6,s_8] & [s_5,s_7] \\ [s_7,s_8] & [s_6,s_8] & [s_6,s_7] \\ [s_6,s_8] & [s_6,s_7] & [s_7,s_8] \\ [s_4,s_6] & [s_6,s_7] & [s_5,s_6] \\ [s_4,s_6] & [s_5,s_7] & [s_4,s_5] \end{pmatrix}.
$$

Step 1. Suppose that $g(c_1) = 0.30$, $g(c_2) = 0.40$, $g(c_3) = 0.20$. Then λ parameter of criteria can be determined: $\lambda_1 = 0.37$.

Suppose that $g(e_1) = 0.3$, $g(e_2) = 0.3$, $g(e_3) = 0.3$, $g(e_4) = 0.3$, then the λ parameter of expert can be determined: $\lambda_2 = -0.40$.

Step 2. For the first line of decision making matrix $\bar{R}^1$, we use Eq.(9) to rank these arguments $\bar{a}^1_{1j}$ $(j = 1, 2, 3)$ such that $[s_5, s_6] \le [s_5, s_7] \le [s_7, s_8]$. Utilize the ULC operator to derive the individual overall preference value $\bar{a}^k_i$ of alternative x_i:

$$
\bar{a}^k_i = \text{ULC}_g(\bar{a}^k_{i1}, \bar{a}^k_{i2}, \cdots, \bar{a}^k_{im}) = [s_{\alpha^k_i}, s_{\beta^k_i}],
$$

where $\bar{a}^1_1 = \text{ULC}_g(\bar{a}^1_{11}, \bar{a}^1_{12}, \bar{a}^1_{13}) = \sum_{j=1}^{3} \bar{a}^1_{1(j)} \cdot g(c_j) \prod_{h=j+1}^{3} (1 + \lambda_1 g_{(h)}) = [s_{5.6}, s_{6.82}]$.

Similarly, we have $\bar{a}^1_2 = [s_{5.63}, s_{6.83}]$, $\bar{a}^1_3 = [s_{5.66}, s_{6.89}]$, $\bar{a}^1_4 = [s_{4.64}, s_{6.12}]$, $\bar{a}^1_5 = [s_{5.82}, s_{7.3}]$;

$$\overline{a}_1^2 = [s_{5.5}, s_{6.49}], \overline{a}_2^2 = [s_{4.83}, s_{6.83}], \overline{a}_3^2 = [s_{5.52}, s_{6.72}], \overline{a}_4^2 = [s_{5.52}, s_{6.82}], \overline{a}_5^2 = [s_{5.74}, s_{7.23}];$$

$$\overline{a}_1^3 = [s_{6.09}, s_{7.08}], \overline{a}_2^3 = [s_{4.83}, s_{6.2}], \overline{a}_3^3 = [s_{5.99}, s_{6.98}], \overline{a}_4^3 = [s_{5.24}, s_{6.24}], \overline{a}_5^3 = [s_{4.77}, s_{6.63}];$$

$$\overline{a}_1^4 = [s_{5.4}, s_{7.03}], \overline{a}_2^4 = [s_{6.24}, s_{7.67}], \overline{a}_3^4 = [s_{6.2}, s_{7.52}], \overline{a}_4^4 = [s_{5.03}, s_{6.4}], \overline{a}_5^4 = [s_{4.26}, s_{5.99}];$$

Step 3. We use Eq.(9) to rank these arguments $\overline{a}_1^k$ ($k = 1, 2, 3, 4$) such that $\overline{a}_1^2 \leq \overline{a}_1^1 \leq \overline{a}_1^4 \leq \overline{a}_1^3$. Using the ULC operator operator aggregates all $\overline{a}_i^k$ into the collective overall preference value $\overline{a}_i$ of the alternative x_i:

$$\overline{a}_i = \mathrm{ULC}_g (\overline{a}_i^1, \overline{a}_i^2, \overline{a}_i^3, \overline{a}_i^4) = [s_{\alpha_i}, s_{\beta_i}],$$

where $\overline{a}_1 = \mathrm{ULC}_g (\overline{a}_1^1, \overline{a}_1^2, \overline{a}_1^3, \overline{a}_1^4) = \sum_{k=1}^{4} \overline{a}_1^{(k)} \cdot g(e_k) \prod_{h=k+1}^{4} (1 + \lambda_2 g(e_h)) = [s_{5.61}, s_{6.82}].$

Similarly, we have $\overline{a}_2 = [s_{5.41}, s_{6.89}]$, $\overline{a}_3 = [s_{5.82}, s_7]$, $\overline{a}_4 = [s_{5.1}, s_{6.37}]$, $\overline{a}_5 = [s_{5.19}, s_{6.79}]$.

Step 4. According to the overall values $\overline{a}_i$ of the alternative x_i ($i = 1, 2, 3, 4, 5$), according to Eq.(9), we can obtain that $\overline{a}_3 > \overline{a}_2 > \overline{a}_1 > \overline{a}_5 > \overline{a}_4$ .Thus the order of five alternatives is x_3, x_2, x_1, x_5, x_4. Hence the best is x_3.

6 Conclusion

Interactive phenomena between the preferences of DMs are often present in multicriteria group decision making in a linguistic environment. Conventional linguistic additive linear operators are inadequate for effectively aggregating such preference information. To address this issue, this paper has proposed an uncertain linguistic Choquet integral operator. Based on the proposed operator, a method is developed for solving the multicriteria group decision making problem in uncertain linguistic information. The prominent characteristic of the developed method is not only that all the aggregated preference information is expressed by uncertain linguistic variables, but also the interactive phenomena among criteria and preference of DMs are considered in the aggregation process, which can avoid losing and distorting the given preference information, and makes the final results accord with the real decision problems.

Acknowledgments. This work was supported by the Funds of the National Natural Science Foundation of China (No. 70801064).

References

1. Zadeh, L.A.: The concept of a linguistic variable and its application to approximate reasoning. Part 1, Information Sciences 8, 199–249 (1975); Part 2, Information Sciences 8, 301–357 (1975); Part 3, Information Sciences 9, 43–80 (1975)
2. Xu, Z.S.: Uncertain linguistic aggregation operators based approach to multiple attribute group decision making under uncertain linguistic environment. Information Sciences 168, 171–184 (2004)

3. Xu, Z.S.: An approach based on the uncertain LOWG and induced uncertain LOWG operators to group decision making with uncertain multiplicative linguistic preference relations. Decision Support Systems 41, 488–499 (2006)
4. Grabisch, M., Murofushi, T., Sugeno, M.: Fuzzy Measure and Integrals. Physica-Verlag, NewYork (2000)
5. Marichal, J.L.: An axiomatic approach of the discrete Choquet integral as a tool to aggregate interacting criteria. IEEE Transactions on Fuzzy Systems 8, 800–807 (2000)
6. Grabisch, M., Marichal, J.-L., Mesiar, R., Pap, E.: Aggregation Functions. Cambridge University Press, Cambridge (2009)
7. Alefeld, G., Herzberger, J.: Introduction to Interval Computations. Academic Press, London (1983)
8. Halmos, P.R.: Measure Theory. Van Nostrand, NewYork (1967)
9. Sugeno, M.: Theory of fuzzy integral and its application, Doctorial Dissertation, Tokyo Institute of Technology (1974)
10. Bryson, N., Mobolurin, A.: An action learning evaluation procedure for multiple criteria decision making problems. European Journal of Operational Research 96, 379–386 (1995)

Expert System Applied to High-Speed Railway Track Circuit Coding and Its Simulation

Yan Li, Dewang Chen, and Xuan Yang

State Key Laboratory of Rail Traffic Control and Safety,
Beijing Jiaotong University, Beijing, China
{09120301,dwchen,10120337}@bjtu.edu.cn

Abstract. Track circuit coding can be realized by Train Control Center in High-speed Railway to keep the train running safe. This paper looks into the track circuit coding method using expert system, in which the reasoning process of track circuit coding was realized using software simulation with the data of Beijing-Shanghai High Speed Railway. Combined with test cases, the joint debugging is realized and the track circuit coding expert system is assessed. Final simulation results support that this prospecting method is both feasible and effective, which can secure the safety of the track circuit coding information as well.

Keywords: High-speed Railway, Expert System, Track Circuit Coding, Simulation.

1 Introduction

With the gradual opening and running of Beijing-Tianjin, Wuhan-Guangzhou, Zhengzhou-Xian, Shanghai-Nanjing, Beijing-Shanghai High-speed Railway, the China High-speed Railway Passenger Line is now leading the development of the world high-speed railway using the CTCS-3 Train Control System, achieving the highest running speed up to 350 km/h [1].

As an important part of CTCS-3 Train Control System ground equipments, Train Control Center (TCC) produces the permit order for the train operation to realize the automatic control of the train tracking interval and the safe operation of the train speed [2].

While in China, relatively there aren't too many researches on the track circuit coding algorithm, except those that mainly focus on how to build the track circuit coding mathematical model and simulation realization[3][4]. In fact, the track circuit coding varies under different circumstances. Line type (up-line or down-line) as well as direction (the forward or the reverse direction) and so on should be considered in the coding in section. Besides, route type needs to be considered in the coding in station. And it will get more complicated when there are more trains. If not all the circumstances have been taken into fully consideration, the safe running of the

H. Deng et al. (Eds.): AICI 2011, Part I, LNAI 7002, pp. 517–524, 2011.
© Springer-Verlag Berlin Heidelberg 2011

train will be impacted. Thus, it is quite necessary to build one database with all information included. The expert system contains large amount of knowledge and experiences of expert in one field, therefore, the expert system can be applied to studying the track circuit coding, which helps eliminate problems in TCC as mentioned above (e.g. complicated system, various circumstances), meanwhile, the safety and reliability can be assured as well. In addition, as the train fundamental plan is relatively stable and the line data (e.g. the block section) is relatively fixed, some common circumstances can be used as case studies and saved in the knowledge database. Then the expert system can be applied to search matched case among these common ones conveniently without complicate coding process so as to improve the efficiency of the track circuit coding.

This paper introduces the track circuit frequency in high-speed railway, applies the expert system to study the coding method, simulates and realizes the track circuit coding expert system. Combined with the test cases, the function of the track circuit coding expert system is verified.

2   Track Circuit Frequency

The interval track circuit applies the ZPW-2000 (UM) series jointless track circuit controlled by the computer coding. The normal coding sequence of the track circuit is: L5-L4-L3-L2-L-LU-U-HU, which can meet the demand of safe running for the 300 km/h train in CTCS-3 train control system [2].

The track circuit coding frequency consists of low frequency and loading frequency, in which the loading frequency of each track circuit is a fixed value. The low frequency is mainly used to reveal the coding frequency to get the different speed limitation information [5].This information is calculated and sent to the trackside equipment by TCC.

Part of the low frequency coding is defined as:

L code: the train is allowed to run according to the specified speed.
U code: the train needs to be slowed down to the specified speed level.
L5 code: the train is allowed to run according to the track speed, when at least 7 block sections in the front are free.
LU code: the train is allowed to run watchfully according to the track speed.
HU code: the train is required to stop in time.
UU code: the train speed is limited (default speed: 45 km/h) and the ground signal (the train is approaching) open the route through the switch in side line [6].

3   Track Circuit Coding Expert System

The expert system is a computer software system which contains a large number of authority knowledge, where knowledge can be applied to solve the time problem in the specific region through reasoning and analysis process [7].

3.1   Overall System Structure

The overall system structure of track circuit coding of TCC is as shown in Figure1 below, including line database, real-time database, data processing, overall database, reasoning machine, knowledge database, output section and so forth.

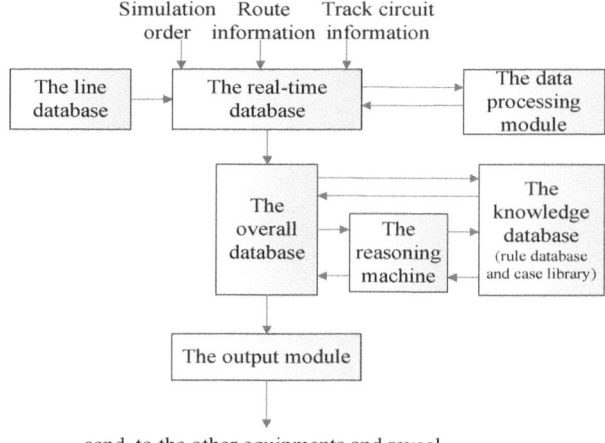

Fig. 1. Overall System Structure

The main function of each part is as follows:

1) Line database. It can save line data, including station files, route information, track circuit information, balise information and so forth.

2) Real-time database. It is used to save all kinds of real-time data, including simulation order, route information from Computer Based Interlocking (CBI), and track circuit occupation information from trackside and so forth.

3) Data processing module. It is used to process data in the real-time database, and abstract the needed information.

4) Overall database. All kinds of data (e.g. real-time data, intermediate results in the reasoning process) are saved in the overall database. It acts as a monitor in the reasoning process.

5) Knowledge database. It is mainly used to save the specific knowledge provided by the region experts, including all kinds of rules and case library for the track circuit coding.

6) Reasoning machine. It can be able to select relevant knowledge using certain reasoning strategies from the knowledge database, and then realize the reasoning according to the context in the overall database.

7) Output module. It is used to send the track circuit coding information to the other relevant equipments and reveal that in the interface.

3.2   Building of the Knowledge Base

In this paper, the knowledge database consists of rule database and case library. The rule database is used to save the track circuit coding regulation, and the case library is used to save different cases where lines, routes or locations vary, therefore, it is convenient to extend the knowledge case.

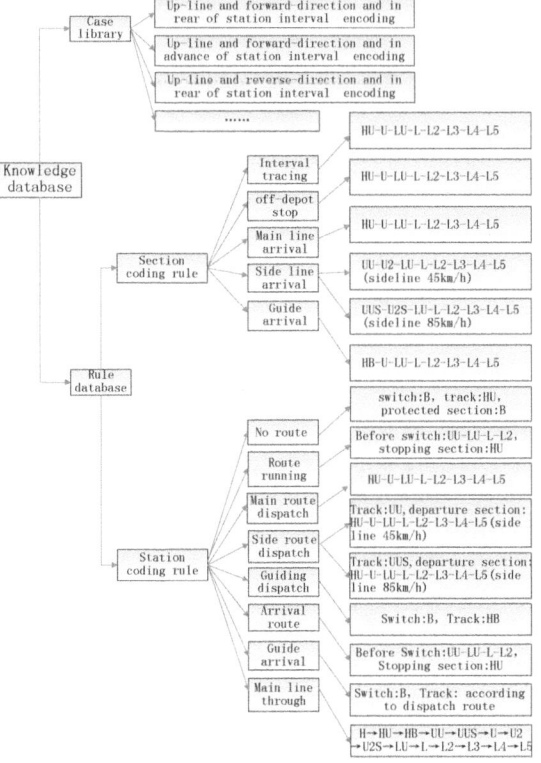

Fig. 2. Knowledge Base Figure

Rule Database and its Knowledge Representation

The cab signal low frequency information distribution and its corresponding fundamental signal representation is defined in the railway industry standard in China- "Cab signaling message define and allocation(TB/T3060-2002)[6]", This paper summarizes the track circuit coding principles and builds rule database according to the standard.

1) Rule Database

The track circuit coding has its corresponding regulation, so regulation representation method can be used to represent the knowledge in knowledge database.

According to "IF-THEN" rules, the object-orientation knowledge based on the regulation can be obtained.

rule: // rule 1

If interval section and tracking // the premise

then HU-U-LU-L-L2-L3-L4-L5 // the conclusion

... ...

rule: // rule 4

If interval section and arrival side-line route and speed limitation at side-line is 45 km/h // premise

then UU-U2-LU-L-L2-L3-L4-L5 // conclusion

... ...

rule: // rule 7

If in station and no route // premise

then code the switch B, code the track HU, code the route protection section B // conclusion

... ...

rule: // rule 9

If in station and departure route and side-line 45km/h //premise

then code the track UU, code the switch area according to departure section, the departure section applies "interval section tracking coding" // conclusion

... ...

The other specific rules are as shown in Figure 2.

2) Knowledge Representation

The knowledge can be represented by the regulation; the data structure under Visual C++ mode is as follows:

```
STRUCT RULE_{

char*result; // regulation

char code; // the track circuit coding type

rule* next; // point to the next algorithm

};
```

Case Library

The track circuit coding has many circumstances. Different matters should be considered in the coding in section, such as whether it is up-line or down-line, forward or reverse direction, in rear or advance of station and so on, while the track circuit coding in station need to consider route type and so forth. It'll become more complicated with multi-trains.

This paper creates the case library for different circumstances. When new circumstance (unconsidered) comes out, reason the conclusion using rule database. And, at last this new conclusion will be added into case library, so case library can be extended.

Construction of the Reasoning Machine

The reasoning machine is responsible to analyze and reason the needed data and make a conclusion at last[8]. Forward reasoning is selected in this system, and the reason process is as follows.

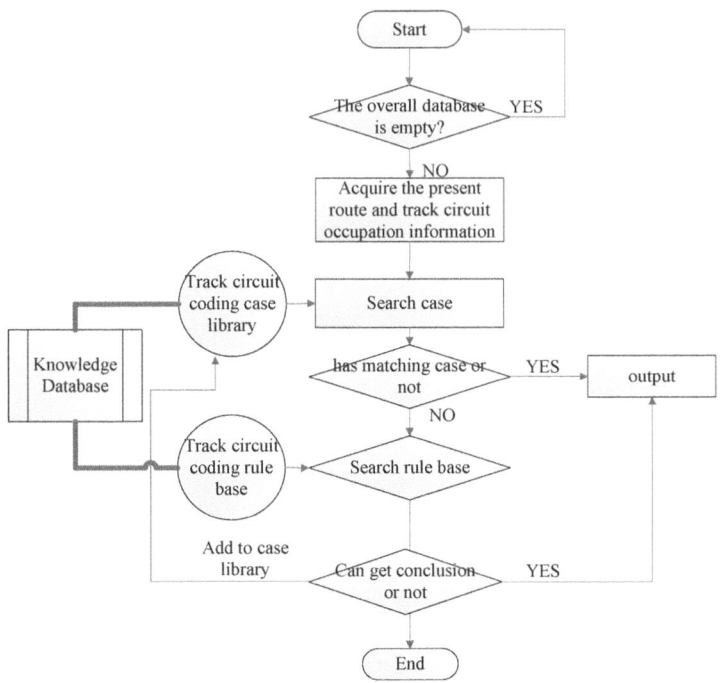

Fig. 3. Reasoning Machine Structure

4   Simulation and Testing

4.1   Simulation

Beijing-Shanghai High-speed Railway data are used in the simulation. It adopts CTCS-3 Train Control System whose ground equipment consists of Radio Block Center (RBC), Computer Based Interlocking (CBI), Train Control Center (TCC), Centralized Train Control (CTC), and trackside equipment (including balise and track circuit) and so forth.

TCC simulator interface is as shown in Figure 4, with the station module, the section module, the train control center information module, and the station coding sequence module.

After receiving simulation starting order, information in line database is read, and the program will produce TCC simulator automatically.

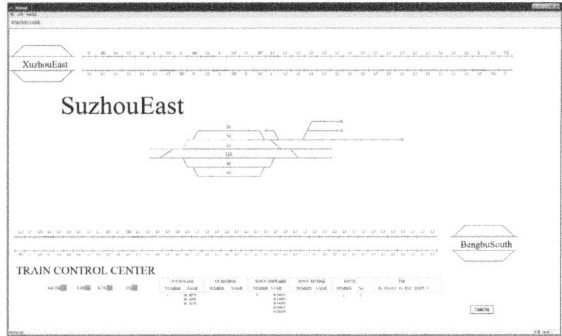

Fig. 4. TCC Simulator Interface

4.2   The Testing Result and Analysis

The joint debugging is based on CTCS-3 Level train control system simulation testing platform.

Data in debugging cases are collected from Xuzhou East to Suzhou East in Beijing-Shanghai High-speed Railway. Then functional testing is done repeatedly according to the test cases.

Test cases used to test the function of track circuit coding expert system are list in Table 1. TCC simulation system based on the expert system is assessed through repeated tests on different cases with an accuracy rate of 100%.

Table 1. Examples of Test Cases

Test Cases	Testing Results
the departure, stop and passing–by testing through the track line	Track line:HU ; Other block sections:U-LU-L-L2-L3-L4-L5
the departure, stop and passing–by testing through the track line	Track line:HU ; Track circuits before switch:UUS-U2S-LU-L-L2-L3-L4-L5
the route guiding testing for the arrival and dispatch	Track line:HB ; Other block sections:U-LU-L-L2-L3-L4-L5
the bent in and direct out, the reverse running testing	Track line:HU ; Track circuits before switch:UUS-U2S-LU-L-L2-L3-L4-L5
the direct in and bent out, the reverse running testing	Track line:HU ; Track circuits before switch:UUS-U2S-LU-L-L2-L3-L4-L5
the reverse bent in and direct out, the forward running testing	Track line:HU ; Track circuits before switch:UUS-U2S-LU-L-L2-L3-L4-L5
the reverse direct in and bent out, the forward running testing	Track line:HU ; Track circuits before switch:UUS-U2S-LU-L-L2-L3-L4-L5

The simulation results show that track circuit coding method based on the expert system can get track circuit low frequency information correctly, and provide effective promise for the safety of cab signal of high-speed train.

5   Summary

This paper mainly focuses on the track circuit coding in high-speed railway. In order to get track circuit frequency correctly, the knowledge and reasoning mechanism of expert system is applied for track circuit coding. Using data from Xuzhou East to Suzhou East in Beijing-Shanghai High-speed Railway, track circuit coding expert system is developed, and some test cases are designed to evaluate validity of the system. The results show that the track circuit coding expert system can get track circuit frequency correctly and efficiently, and can keep the safe of cab signal.

Acknowledgments. This research work was supported by Beijing Nova Program (2010B015), the Fundamental Research Funds for the Central Universities (2011JBM157), and Independent Research Project of the State Key Laboratory of Rail Traffic Control and Safety (RCS2008ZZ001 and 2009ZT004).

References

1. Xue, L.: The CTCS-3 Simulation and Testing Platform—Research on Multi-Train Simulation Subsystem. Beijing Jiaotong University, Beijing (2009)
2. Zhang, S.: The technology plan of CTCS-3 Simulation Platform, pp. 122–123. China Railway Publishing House, Beijing (2008)
3. Li, M.: The research on function simulation of the CTCS-2train control centre for Passenger Dedicated Line. Southwest Jiaotong University, ChengDu (2009)
4. Li, J.: The train control subsystem simulation design and research for the CTCS-2 train control centre. Southwest Jiaotong University, ChengDu (2010)
5. Zhao, L., Guo, J., Li, H., et al.: The simulation analysis of influence on jointless track circuit signal transmission from compensation capacitor based on transmission-line theory. In: 2009 3rd IEEE International Symposium on Microwave, Antenna, Propagation and EMC Technologies for Wireless Communications, vol. 9(11), pp. 1113–1118 (2003)
6. Ministry of Railways. TB-T3060-2002.Cab Signaling Message Define and Allocation. The People's Republic of China Ministry of Railways, Beijing (2002)
7. Tang, P.: The Expert System Lecture. BeiJing KeHai Training Center, Beijing (1987)
8. Sun, Y., Zhang, J., Huo, K., Fu, Q.: Application of Simulation Technology Based on the Support of Expert System in the Testing System of Locomotive. Basic Automation 10(3), 242–244 (2003)

Joint Advertising and Ordering Strategies for Perishable Product under General Demand

Tie Wang[1,2]

[1] School of Mathematics, Liaoning University,
Shenyang, Liaoning 110036, China
[2] School of Management, Shanghai University,
Shanghai, 200444, China
wangt_1997@163.com

Abstract. Motivated by firm's practice of advertising its products to stimulate demand, we investigate inventory management and advertising policy when demand is uncertain but increases with advertising expenditure. First, we establish a sufficient condition under which optimal ordering and advertising decisions are existent and unique for general additive-multiplicative advertising-dependent demand distribution. Next, we compare our optimal advertising decision to its deterministic counterpart.

Keywords: Marketing and operation interface, Newsvendor model with advertising setting.

1 Introduction

In practice, retailer often exert marketing instruments such as price cuts, displays, free goods and retailer coupons to induce greater consumer demand and earn bigger profit. For example, many retailers attract consumer through showing their inventory or appropriate product display in shelf. These methods also include other types of in-store merchandizing, advertising, direct mail, point-of-sale information, targeted discounts, free gift wrapping or delivery, or a lot of other means. Therefore, the retailer combines the marketing and operation strategies. And the classic newsvendor model is a crucial building block of the stochastic inventory theory because of its simple and elegant structure as well as its rich managerial insights. The newsvendor model assumes that if any inventory remains at the end of the period, a discount is used to sell it or it is disposed of. If the order quantity is smaller than the realized demand, the newsvendor loses some profit. The newsvendor model reflects many real situations and is often used to help make decision in many industries, such as fashion and sporting, both at the manufacturing and sale level. It has been extensively studied over decades with extensions including different objectives and utility functions, multiple products with substitution, multiple locations and different pricing and advertising strategies. For extensive reviews see Khouja [1]. As a result, the

H. Deng et al. (Eds.): AICI 2011, Part I, LNAI 7002, pp. 525–532, 2011.

important extension to the classic newsvendor model is the interface of marketing and operation that provides an important tool for examining how operational problem interacts with marketing issues to influence decision-making at the firm level. There are three research streams about this extension; one is the newsvendor problem with pricing (NPP) that demand is stimulated by sale price, one is the newsvendor problem with inventory (NPI) that demand is driven by inventory, and the other is the newsvendor problem with advertising (NPA) that demand is stimulated by advertising.

There are few works about the NPA model. Gerchak and Parlar [2] investigated NPA model when multiplicative demand has a distribution with a mean that is specific concave and increasing in advertising expenditure. They developed a mixed optimization technique which combines simulation with the ?rst order condition to solve above problem. Khouja and Robbins [3] extended [2] to three cases of demand variation as a function of advertising expenditure: (1) demand has constant variance, (2) demand has constant coefficient variation, and (3) demand has an increasing coefficient variation. They investigated the NPA problem under multiplicative demand and obtain the optimal advertising premium and ordering quantity by maximizing the expected profit or maximizing the probability of achieving a target profit under above three situation using particular mean demand, and discussed the optimal advertising decisions for maximizing profit is increase with the profit margin. Wang [4, 5, 6] investigated the NPA model under general additive demand, general multiplicative demand and general multiplicative demand with emergency ordering. Recently, Wang and Zhou [7] discussed the supply chain coordination with NPA and proposed an improved revenue-sharing contract to achieve the supply chain coordination; Wang and Hu [8] established that the supply chain can with NPA not be coordinated with the buy back, revenue sharing, target rebate and quantity flexibility contract and showed quantity discount contract can coordinate the supply chain and give a special quantity discount contract and presented a new contract called revenue and loss sharing contract to coordinates the decentralized supply chain. Wang, Zhou and Wang [9, 10] investigated the supply chain coordination with a specific NPPA model using improved revenue sharing contract and combined return and sales rebate/penalty contract. In this paper, we will generalize NPA model to the general demand situation that extend the demand model to the general additive-multiplicative demand models, and the mean is a general concave and increasing function. The objective of our research is to address three fundamental questions in such a retail setting. First, what is the condition under which the optimal advertising and ordering decisions are existent and unique? Second, what is the relation of the optimal advertising decision between the deterministic model and our model?

The remainder of the paper is organized as follows. Sections 2 presents the model and its solution properties. Sections 3 summarizes the results, gives the managerial insight and discuss the future researches.

2   The Model and Its Properties

In this section, we investigate the optimal decisions on ordering and advertising. For a general demand model, we give the optimal order quantity when the advertisement is fixed and optimal advertising decision for the deterministic demand function. We also provide the sufficient condition for the existence of the unique optimal ordering and advertising solution.

2.1   The Model

Firstly, we will give the notions used in the following.

p = retail price.

q = order quantity.

a = advertising premium.

v, s, c = per unit salvage value ,shortage and purchase cost respectively.

$D(a, \xi) = \alpha(a)\xi + \beta(a)$.

ξ = nonnegative random variable with mean 1.

$\alpha(a) + \beta(a)$ = expected demand.

$f(\cdot), F(\cdot)$ = pdf and cdf of the distribution of ξ.

$\Pi(a, q)$ = expected profit function.

a^*, q^* = optimal solutions.

We assume $\alpha(a)$ and $\beta(a)$ are nonnegative, twice-continuous differentiable, strictly concave and is defined on an interval $[0, +\infty)$. Conceivably, $\alpha(a), \beta(a)$ is strictly increasing in the advertising premium, i.e. $\frac{d\alpha(a)}{da} > 0, \frac{d\beta(a)}{da} > 0$ and $0 < \alpha(0), 0 \le \beta(0)$, that is to say there are a basic demand for without advertisement although advertising will increase the demand. In this paper, the stochastic advertisement-sensitive D is modeled in a general demand form, i.e. $D(a, \xi) = \alpha(a)\xi + \beta(a)$. ξ is a standardized random variable with mean 1 (It may be profitable for all realized demand.), cumulative distribution function $F(\cdot)$ and probability density function $f(\cdot)$. This general demand model is similar to the additive- multiplicative demand models used in the literatures for newsvendor problem with price-setting. For $\alpha(a) = 1$ this is the additive model (advertisement influences the location of the demand distribution), whereas for $\beta(a) = 0$ this is the multiplicative model (advertisement influences demand scale).

Before the stochastic item ξ is realized, the newsvendor determines simultaneously an order quantity, q, and a advertising premium, a, to maximize the expected profit. We also assume that $0 \le v < c < p$ to avoid trivial solution. The density of demand $D(a, \xi)$ can be expressed as:

$$g(x, a) = \frac{1}{\alpha(a)} f(\frac{x - \beta(a)}{\alpha(a)}), x \in [\beta(a), \infty).$$

Denoted $x^+ = \max(x, 0)$, the newsvendor's profit an be expressed as the difference between the revenue and the total cost:

$$\pi(a, q) = p \min(q, D(a, \xi)) + v(q - D(a, \xi))^+ - s(D(a, \xi) - q)^+ - a - cq$$

$$= (p + s - c)q - (p + s - v)(q - D(a, \xi))^+ - a - sD(a, \xi). \tag{1}$$

Noticing that we use the following relation on the above expression:

$$(x - y)^+ = x - \min(x, y).$$

The expected profit for any advertising premium and order quantity is:

$$\Pi(a, q) = E_\xi[\pi(a, q)] = (p + s - c)q - a - s[\alpha(a) + \beta(a)]$$

$$-(p + s - v) \int_0^{\frac{q - \beta(a)}{\alpha(a)}} (q - \alpha(a)x - \beta(a))f(x)\mathrm{d}x. \tag{2}$$

From the expression of $\pi(a, q)$, we know $\pi(a, q)$ is concave in q for any fixed a and realized value of ξ because $(q - D(a, \xi))^+$ is convex in q for any fixed a and realized value of ξ, so $\Pi(a, q)$ is concave in q for any fixed a. We first fix a for finding the optimal q to maximize the expected profit. Its first order condition is as follows:

$$\frac{\partial \Pi(a, q)}{\partial q} = (p + s - c) - (p + s - v) \int_0^{\frac{q - \beta(a)}{\alpha(a)}} f(x)\mathrm{d}x = 0.$$

So, the optimal order quantity q^* must satisfy:

$$\int_0^{\frac{q - \beta(a)}{\alpha(a)}} f(x)\mathrm{d}x = \frac{p + s - c}{p + s - v},$$

or

$$q^* = \alpha(a)F^{-1}(\rho) + \beta(a). \tag{3}$$

where $\rho = \frac{p+s-c}{p+s-v}$, $F^{-1}(\rho)$ is the inverse function for the cumulative distribution function of random variable. Because the expected profit is concave in q for any fixed a, So (3) is the newsvendor's optimal order quantity curve, it reflects the relation between the optimal order quantity and optimal advertising premium.

Next, we consider the case when the advertise expenditure is also a decision variable. Now substitute (3) into (1), and according to equation (2) we can obtain the following equation:

$$\Pi(a) := \Pi(a, q^*) = (p + s - v) \int_0^{F^{-1}(\rho)} [\alpha(a)x + \beta(a)]f(x)\mathrm{d}x - a - s[\alpha(a) + \beta(a)]$$

$$= \alpha(a)[(p + s - v) \int_0^{F^{-1}(\rho)} xf(x)\mathrm{d}x - s] + (p - c)\beta(a) - a, \tag{4}$$

where $-s < (p + s - v) \int_0^{F^{-1}(\rho)} xf(x)\mathrm{d}x - s < p - v$, $\lim_{a \to +\infty} (p - c)\beta(a) - a \le 0$, according to the relation between p, v, c, s and the concavity of $\beta(a)$.

From equation (4), we can know that $\Pi(a)$ is strictly decreasing and strictly convex because of the strictly concave and increasing property about the demand function with advertising premium when $(p + s - v) \int_0^{F^{-1}(\rho)} xf(x)\mathrm{d}x - s \le 0$ and $\beta(a) = 0$. This is not consistent with the reality because the newsvendor's profit is always decreasing when she increase the advertising premium and is negative, so we obtain the following important condition for the newsvendor model with advertising.

Assumption 2.1. $\int_0^{F^{-1}(\rho)} x f(x) \mathrm{d}x > \frac{s}{p+s-v}$, that is $E[\xi I_A] > \frac{s}{p+s-v}$, where A is the interval $[0, F^{-1}(\rho)]$.

In addition, we need the following assumptions to guarantee the uniqueness of optimal advertising decisions.

Assumption 2.2. $\alpha'(0)[(p+s-v)E[\xi I_A] - s] + \beta'(0)(p-c) - 1 > 0$.

2.2   Solution Properties

According the above analysis about $\Pi(a)$ and Assumption 2.1 and 2.2, we can obtain the following proposition that give the sufficient condition for the uniqueness of the optimal advertising expenditure.

Proposition 2.1. *Under Assumption 2.1 and 2.2, $\Pi(a)$ is strictly concave in a, and there is a unique optimal advertising premium a^* in the range $(0, +\infty)$ satisfying the following equation:*

$$\frac{d\Pi(a)}{da} = \alpha'(a)[(p+s-v)\int_0^{F^{-1}(\rho)} x f(x)\mathrm{d}x - s] + \beta'(a)(p-c) - 1 = 0. \quad (5)$$

Proof. From the equation (4) we can get

$$\frac{d\Pi(a)}{da} = \alpha'(a)[(p+s-v)\int_0^{F^{-1}(\rho)} x f(x)\mathrm{d}x - s] + \beta'(a)(p-c) - 1, \quad (6)$$

$$\frac{d^2\Pi(a)}{da^2} = \alpha''(a)[(p+s-v)\int_0^{F^{-1}(\rho)} x f(x)\mathrm{d}x - s] + \beta''(a)(p-c). \quad (7)$$

Hence, $\Pi(a)$ is strictly concave in a under the Assumption 2.1 and the properties of $\alpha(a)$ and $\beta(a)$.

Notice that

$$0 < (p+s-v)\int_0^{F^{-1}(\rho)} x f(x)\mathrm{d}x - s < p - v, \quad (8)$$

according to the $\int_0^{F^{-1}(\rho)} x f(x)\mathrm{d}x \leq 1$ and Assumption 2.1 and the relation between p, v, c, s.

With the properties of $\alpha(a)$ and $\beta(a)$, $\alpha'(a) > 0$ and $\beta'(a) > 0$, $\alpha'(a)$ and $\beta'(a)$ is continuous and decreasing. So,

$$\frac{d\Pi(0)}{da} = \alpha'(0)[(p+s-v)E[\xi I_A] - s] + \beta'(0)(p-c) - 1 > 0$$

$$\lim_{a \to +\infty} \frac{d\Pi(a)}{da} < \lim_{a \to +\infty} (p-v)\alpha'(a) + \beta'(a)(p-c) - 1 < 0$$

where the last two inequalities follows from the Assumption 2.2 and strict concavity of $\alpha(a)$ and $\beta(a)$.

Therefore, there must be at least on solution of $\frac{d\Pi(a)}{da} = 0$ in the interval $(0, +\infty)$ as long as $\Pi(a)$ is continuous. $\qquad\square$

In the following, we first look at the optimal advertising decision without demand uncertainty, then compare it with optimal advertising a^*. In this case the demand is simply $D(a) = \alpha(a) + \beta(a)$ and the order quantity should be equal to $D(a)$. Similar to the conditions about the $\alpha(a)$ and $\beta(a)$, we set $D(a)$ is non-negative, twice-continuous differentiable, strictly concave, strictly increasing and defined on an interval $[0, +\infty)$. We need the following assumption to guarantee the existence and uniqueness of optimal decision in deterministic model.

The deterministic demand can be viewed as a benchmark for studying the stochastic demand, or can be used as the the first order approximation for the low demand variance as used in newsvendor problem with price-setting. The riskless profit function with deterministic demand is

$$\Pi_d(a) = (p - c)D(a) - a. \qquad (9)$$

Proposition 2.2. *The riskless profit is strictly concave in $a \in [0, +\infty)$, so the optimal riskless advertising premium a_d^* is unique and determined by $D'(a) = \frac{1}{p-c}$.*

Proof. Similar to the proof of Proposition 2.1, the result is obtained from the property of $D(a)$. $\qquad\square$

The following proposition describe the relation between the riskless advertising premium and optimal advertising decision under additive-multiplicative stochastic demand under two situations.

Proposition 2.3. *Under Assumption 2.1 and 2.2, if $F^{-1}(\rho) \geq 1$, then optimal advertising premium a^* is no more than the optimal riskless advertising premium a_d^*.*

Proof. From Proposition 2.1 and 2.2, we can get

$$\frac{d\Pi(a)}{da} = \alpha'(a)[(p + s - v)\int_0^{F^{-1}(\rho)} xf(x)\mathrm{d}x - s] + \beta'(a)(p - c) - 1,$$

$$\frac{d\Pi_d(a)}{da} = (p - c)D'(a) - 1.$$

Note that

$$\int_0^{F^{-1}(\rho)} xf(x)\mathrm{d}x = 1 - \int_{F^{-1}(\rho)}^{+\infty} xf(x)\mathrm{d}x \leq 1 - F^{-1}(\rho)(1 - \rho).$$

So

$$\beta'(a)(p-c) - 1 < \frac{d\Pi(a)}{da} \leq \alpha'(a)[(p-v) - (c-v)F^{-1}(\rho)] + \beta'(a)(p-c) - 1.$$

According to the condition in the proposition, we have

$$\frac{d\Pi(a)}{da} - \frac{d\Pi_d(a)}{da} \leq 0$$

for any $a \in [a_d^*, +\infty)$.

Thus, optimal advertising premium a^* under demand uncertainty is no more than the optimal riskless advertising premium a_d^*. The proposition 2.3 holds. $\square$

Remark 2.1. This proposition reflects the combined effects of two factors in stochastic additive-multiplicative demand related to advertisement that one influence the location of the demand distribution, another influence demand scale on the optimal advertising premium. It is interesting that the criteria used to determine if optimal advertising premium a^* under demand uncertainty is no less than the optimal riskless advertising premium a_d^* is not depending $\alpha(a)$.

3   Conclusions

In this paper, we investigate the NPA model that combine the operation and advertising decision in a firm. Traditionally, the research of inventory management largely focuses on the role of inventory in hedging demand uncertainty and providing other operational benefits. On the other hand, the marketing literature addresses the use of advertising to increase demand but not consider detailed inventory management issues. We bridge these two perspectives in this paper. For a versatile model of stochastic advertise-dependent demand that generalizes previous multiplicative models, we give one sufficient condition to determine if the optimal decisions in our model are existent and unique, and compare them with their deterministic counterpart.

There are several directions deserving further attention. The retail price is exogenous in this paper. However, the price and advertising are usually used as marketing means at the same time in practice. So, it would be interesting to extend our model to include situations where price is also a decision variable. That is the retailer would make the pricing, advertising and ordering decisions at the same time. Our model considers a monopolist retailer, the multiple retailer with competitive advertising and ordering or supply chain contract analysis based our model are potential research topics. In this paper, we assume the retailer is risk-neutral and consumer is myopic, so it is interesting to introduce retailer's risk attitude or consumer's purchasing behavior to our model.

Acknowledgments. This work is supported by the Youth Foundation of Liaoning University (No.2010LDQN07).

References

1. Khoujia, M.: The Single-Period(News-Vendor) Problem: Literature Review and Suggestions for Future Research. Int. J. of Manage. Sci. 27, 537–553 (1999)
2. Gerchak, Y., Parlar, M.: A Single Period Inventory Problem with Partially Controllable Demand. Comp. and Oper. Res. 14, 1–9 (1987)
3. Khoujia, M., Robbins, S.S.: Linking Advertising and Quantity Decisions in Single-Period Inventory Model. Int. J. of Prod. Econ. 86, 93–105 (2003)
4. Wang, T.: The Newsvendor Problem with Advertising. In: 2008 IEEE International Conference on Service Operations and Logistics, and Informatics, pp. 886–889. IEEE Press, Beijing (2008)
5. Wang, T.: Joint Advertising and Ordering Strategies for Perishable Product with Emergency Ordering. In: 21st Chinese Control and Decision Conference, pp. 2673–2678. IEEE Press, Xu Zhou (2009)
6. Wang, T.: Joint Advertising and ordering Strategies for Perishable Product. In: 2010 International Conference on Logistics Systems and Intelligent Management, pp. 1765–1769. IEEE Press, Ha Erbin (2010)
7. Wang, S., Zhou, Y.: Supply Chain Coordination Models for Newsvendor-Type Products: Considering Advertising Effect and Two Production Modes. Comp. and Ind. Eng. 59, 220–231 (2010)
8. Wang, T., Hu, Q.: Coordination of Supply Chain with Advertise-Setting Newsvendor. In: 2nd IEEE International Conference on Advanced Computer Control, pp. 391–395. IEEE Press, Shen Yang (2010)
9. Wang, S., Zhou, Y., Wang, J.: Supply Chain Coordination with Two Production Modes and Random Demand Depending on Advertising Expenditure and Selling Price. Int. J. of Sys. Sci. 41, 1257–1272 (2010)
10. Wang, S., Zhou, Y., Wang, J.: Coordinating Ordering, Pricing and Advertising Policies for a Supply Chain with Random Demand and Two Production Modes. Int. J. of Prod. Econ. 126, 168–180 (2010)

Fuzzy Set with Three Kinds of Negations and Its Applications in Fuzzy Decision Making

Zhenghua Pan, Lei Yang, and Jiang Xu

School of Science, Jiangnan University, Wuxi, 214122, China
panzh@jiangnan.edu.cn

Abstract. In [13], we proposed that there are three kinds of negative relations which contradictory negative relation, opposite negative relation and medium negative relation in fuzzy information, and that defined a new fuzzy set FSCOM with contradictory negation, opposite negation and medium negation. In order to show applicability of FSCOM, this paper apply FSCOM to fuzzy decision making in an actual example, in which discussed the representation and membership functions of fuzzy set and different negations in example and decision rules, introduced a new Fuzzy production rules which threshold value related to λ in FSCOM, as well as reasoning and realization in example based decision rules.

Keywords: fuzzy set FSCOM, contradictory negation, opposite negation, medium negation, fuzzy decision making.

1 Introduction

Negation plays a special role in information processing, especially in fuzzy information processing. Some scholars suggested that information processing needed different negations in various domains [1-12]. Wagner considered that negation is not a clean concept, and there are at least two kinds of negations which *weak negation* and *strong negation* in computation information systems [1][2][3]. Ferré introduced an epistemic extension for the concept of negation in Logical Concept Analysis and Natural Language, distinguished between negation, opposition, and possibility in a unique formalism, and proposed that there are *extensional negation* and *intentional negation* [4]. Kaneiwa proposed that description logic ALC_- with *classical negation* $\neg$ and *strong negation* ~, the classical negation represents the negation of a statement, the strong negation may be more suitable for expressing explicit negative information (or negative facts)[5]. Since 2005, we introduced an epistemic extension for the concept of negation in knowledge processing, proposed that negative relations in knowledge should differentiate contradictory relation and opposite relation, and described to these relations using the medium logic, as well as application to fuzzy information representation [6-12].

Based on above results, we proposed that negations of fuzzy information included contradictory negation, opposite negation and medium negation, defined a new fuzzy set FSCOM with contradictory negation, opposite negation and medium negation, and discussed characteristics of FSCOM, as well as some operations and properties in

H. Deng et al. (Eds.): AICI 2011, Part I, LNAI 7002, pp. 533–542, 2011.

FSCOM [13]. In order to show applicability of FSCOM, the paper study applications of FSCOM in fuzzy decision making.

2 FSCOM: Fuzzy Set with Three Kinds of Negations

In [13], we proposed a new fuzzy set FSCOM with contradictory negation, opposite negation and medium negation, in which the definition as follows.

Definition 1. Let U be domain. Mapping

$$\Psi_A :\ U \to [0,\ 1]$$

confirms a fuzzy subset A on U, i.e. $A \in P(U)$), where mapping Ψ_A is called the membership function of A, $\Psi_A(x)$ is the degree of membership of x on A, for short $A(x)$. $\{A(x) \mid x \in U\}$ for short $A(U)$ [13].

Definition 2. Let $A \in P(U)$, $\lambda \in (0, 1)$.
  (1) Mapping

$$\Psi^{\daleth}:\ A(U) \to [0,\ 1]$$

$\Psi^{\daleth}$ confirms a fuzzy subset (written as $A^{\daleth}$) on U if $\Psi^{\daleth}(A(x)) = 1 - A(x)$, which $A^{\daleth}(x) = \Psi^{\daleth}(A(x))$. $A^{\daleth}$ is called *opposite negation set of A*.
  (2) Mapping

$$\Psi^{\sim}:\ A(U) \to [0,\ 1]$$

$\Psi^{\sim}$ confirms a fuzzy subset (written as $A^{\sim}$) on U if $A^{\sim}(x) = \Psi^{\sim}(A(x))$, which $A^{\sim}(x) =$

$$
\begin{cases}
\dfrac{2\lambda-1}{1-\lambda}(A(x)-\lambda)+1-\lambda, & \text{when } \lambda \in [\tfrac{1}{2},\ 1) \text{ and } A(x) \in (\lambda,\ 1] & (2.1) \\[2ex]
\dfrac{2\lambda-1}{1-\lambda}A(x)+1-\lambda, & \text{when } \lambda \in [\tfrac{1}{2},\ 1) \text{ and } A(x) \in [0,\ 1-\lambda) & (2.2) \\[2ex]
\dfrac{1-2\lambda}{\lambda}A(x)+\lambda, & \text{when } \lambda \in (0,\ \tfrac{1}{2}] \text{ and } A(x) \in [0,\ \lambda) & (2.3) \\[2ex]
\dfrac{1-2\lambda}{\lambda}(A(x)+\lambda-1)+\lambda, & \text{when } \lambda \in (0,\ \tfrac{1}{2}] \text{ and } A(x) \in (1-\lambda,\ 1] & (2.4) \\[2ex]
A(x), & \text{other} & (2.5)
\end{cases}
$$

$A^{\sim}$ is called *medium negation set of A*.
  (3) Mapping

$$\Psi^{\neg}:\ A(U) \to [0,\ 1]$$

$\Psi^{\neg}$ confirms a fuzzy subset (written as $A^{\neg}$) on U if $\Psi^{\neg}(A(x)) = \text{Max}\ (A^{\daleth}(x),\ A^{\sim}(x))$, which $A^{\neg}(x) = \Psi^{\neg}(A(x))$. $A^{\neg}$ is called *contradictory negation set of A*.

The fuzzy sets on domain U is defined by the definition 1 and 2, is called "*Fuzzy Set with Contradictory negation, Opposite negation and Medium negation*", which for short FSCOM.

3   Application of FSCOM in Fuzzy Decision Making

Fuzzy decision-making deals with nonprobabilistic uncertainty and vagueness in the environment which takes place decision making. Fuzzy set approaches to decision-making are usually most appropriate when human evaluations and the modeling of human knowledge are needed. A rational approach toward decision-making should take human subjectivity into account, rather than employing only objective probability measures. The aim of decision making in financial investment is to assist investor whether deposited superfluous money in the bank or invest stock. Suppose strategies of financial investment lie on the income and savings of investor, and according to following DR (Decision Rules):

a) If investor has little savings, investor should deposit superfluous money in the bank whether how much income.

b) If investor has much savings and much income, investor should superfluous money to buy stock, which takes a risk but profitable.

c) If investor has much savings and moderate income, investor should majority of money to buy stock, and minority of money to deposit bank in superfluous income.

d) If investor has moderate savings and moderate income, investor should majority of money to deposit bank, and the minority of money to buy stock in superfluous income.

Remark: If investor has little income, we think that investor has no superfluous money.

3.1   An Example

In real life, people's viewpoints on the much (or little, moderate) income and much (or little, moderate) savings are affected by many factors, which difference of areas is main factor.

For example, we investigated the people's viewpoints on the much (or little) income and much (or little) savings in some areas of China, obtained the result of random sample as follows (Table 1) (money unit: Yuan/RMB).

Table 1. People's viewpoints on much (or little) income and savings in some areas

views	City/Province	much income (each month)	little income (each month)	much savings	Little savings
1	Shanghai	≥ 15,000	≤ 2000	≥ 200,000	≤ 100,000
2	Pudong, Shanghai	≥ 20,000	≤ 2500	≥ 250,000	≤ 150,000
3	Xuhui, Shanghai	≥ 10,000	≤ 2000	≥ 200,000	≤ 80,000
2	Nanjing, Jiangsu	≥ 10,000	≤ 1500	≥ 200,000	≤ 80,000
3	Wuxi, Jiangsu	≥ 12,000	≤ 1200	≥ 150,000	≤ 100,000
4	Suzhou, Jiangsu	≥ 15,000	≤ 1500	≥ 150,000	≤ 100,000
5	Hefei, Anhui	≥ 6,000	≤ 1000	≥ 100,000	≤ 80,000
6	Fuyang, Anhui	≥ 5,000	≤ 1000	≥ 100,000	≤ 50,000
7	Tongning, Anhui	≥ 4,000	≤ 800	≥ 100,000	≤ 50,000
8	Jinan, Shandong	≥ 7,000	≤ 1200	≥ 150,000	≤ 80,000
9	Yantai, Shandong	≥ 6,000	≤ 1000	≥ 120,000	≤ 50,000
10	Weihai, Shandong	≥ 10,000	≤ 1500	≥ 150,000	≤ 80,000

In Table 1, we only listed investigation data in ten cities, and these cities belong to four provinces, respectively. In order to integrate investigation data in the same province, we compute the average of investigation data for each province. Apparently, the more investigate data, the more niceties of integrative data. To improve accuracy of integrative data, we take an "elasticity value" (much income: "± 500/month"; little income: "±100/month"; much savings: "± 20000/month"; little savins: "± 10000/month") for each integrative data type, respectively. We thus get following integrative data in each province (Table 2).

Table 2. Integrative data in each province

province	much income (±500)	little income (±100)	much savings (±20,000)	little savings (±10,000)
Shanghai	≥ 14400	≤ 2000	≥ 210,000	≤ 100,000
Jiangsu	≥ 11000	≤ 1340	≥ 160,000	≤ 82,000
Anhui	≥ 5000	≤ 920	≥ 100,000	≤ 56,000
Shandong	≥ 7000	≤ 1100	≥ 124,000	≤ 68,000

By all appearances, we established a *flexible interval*, which is able to reflect the accuracy for each integrative data type, respectively.

_ Minimum datum in "much income" is 5000/month at least, maximal datum is 14400/month at least, and the elasticity value 500. Thus corresponding flexible intervals are [4500, 5500] and [13900, 14900] respectively.

_ Minimum datum in "little income" is 920/month at most, maximal datum is 2000/month at most, and the elasticity value 100. Thus corresponding flexible intervals are [820, 1020] and [1900, 2100] respectively.

_ Minimum datum in "much savings" is 100000 at least, maximal datum is 210000 at least, and elasticity value 20000. Thus corresponding flexible intervals are [80000, 120000] and [190000, 230000] respectively.

_ Minimum datum in "little savings" is 56000 at most, maximal datum is 100000 at most, and elasticity value 10000. Thus corresponding flexible intervals are [46000, 66000] and [90000, 110000] respectively.

3.2   Representation on Fuzzy Set in Example and DR

Obviously, in the example and DR, "*much savings*", "*much income*", "*little savings*", "*little income*", "*moderate savings*" and "*moderate income*" are different fuzzy sets. According to FSCOM, we need to point out that there are following relations in these fuzzy sets:

● fuzzy set "*little savings*" is opposite negation of "*much savings*", "*moderate savings*" is medium negation of "*much savings*".

● fuzzy set "*little income*" is opposite negation of "*much income*", "*moderate income*" is medium negation of "*much income*".

Based on FSCOM, representations of these fuzzy sets as follows:

> *MUCHsavings*: denoted fuzzy set "much savings",
> *MUCHsavings*⁻¹: denoted fuzzy set "little savings",
> *MUCHsavings*˜: denoted fuzzy set "moderate savings",
> *MUCHincome*: denoted fuzzy set "much income",
> *MUCHincome*⁻¹: denoted fuzzy set "little income",
> *MUCHincome*˜: denoted fuzzy set "moderate income".

In addition, the decision-making action for actions of investor:

INVESTMENT(*stocks*): denoted investor buy stocks.
INVESTMENT(*savings*): denoted investor deposit superfluous money in the bank.
MORE(*savings*, *stocks*): denoted savings more than buy stocks for investor.

Therefore, the representation of decision rules *a) - d)* as follows:

a) $MUCHsavings^{\neg}(x) \rightarrow INVESTMENT(savings)$,
b) $MUCHsavings(x) \wedge MUCHincome(x) \rightarrow INVESTMENT(stocks)$,
c) $MUCHsavings(x) \wedge MUCHincome^{\sim}(x) \rightarrow$
    $(INVESTMENT(stocks) \wedge INVESTMENT(savings) \wedge MORE(stocks, savings))$,
d) $MUCHsavings^{\sim}(x) \wedge MUCHincome^{\sim}(x) \rightarrow$
    $(INVESTMENT(stocks) \wedge INVESTMENT(savings) \wedge MORE(savings, stocks))$.

3.3 Membership Functions of Fuzzy Sets in Example and DR

The above example as environment of decision-making to actualize financial investment according to decision rules *a)-d)*, in which establish the membership functions of fuzzy set and different negations in example and decision rules is basis of decision making. Based on measure method of true-valued of fuzzy predicate [19][20], we present a new approach to confirm membership function of fuzzy set as follows.

Let *a* be an income datum. We known by Table 2 that if degree of membership of *a* on fuzzy set "much income" is that $MUCHincome(a) \geq t$ ($t \in [0, 1]$) in Shanghai, then must be $MUCHincome(a) \geq t$ in other provinces; and that if degree of membership of *a* on fuzzy set "little income" is that $MUCHincome^{\neg}(a) \leq t$ in Anhui, then must be $MUCHincome(a) \leq t$ in other provinces. *a* be a savings data as well.

According to this characteristic of data, and the Euclidean distance of one-dimension space which $d(x, y) = |x - y|$ and the definitions of distance ratio function [11], the membership functions $MUCHincome(x)$ and $MUCHsavings(x)$ on fuzzy sets "much income" and "much savings" can be define as follows.

Definition 3. Let x be income datum or savings datum. Then $MUCHincome(x)$ and $MUCHsavings(x) =$

$$
\begin{cases}
0, & \text{when } x \leq \alpha_F + \varepsilon_F \\[2mm]
\dfrac{d(x, \alpha_F + \varepsilon_F)}{d(\alpha_F + \varepsilon_F, \alpha_T - \varepsilon_T)}, & \text{when } \alpha_F + \varepsilon_F < x < \alpha_T - \varepsilon_T \\[2mm]
1, & \text{when } x \geq \alpha_T - \varepsilon_T
\end{cases}
$$

where α_T is maximal income (or maximal savings) and ε_T is the elasticity value for the viewpoint of much income (or much savings) in Table 2, α_F is minimum income (or minimum savings) and ε_F is the elasticity value for the viewpoint of little income (or little savings) in Table 1.

For income datum x, $\alpha_T = 14400$ and $\varepsilon_T = 500$ for the viewpoint of much income, $\alpha_F = 920$ and $\varepsilon_F = 100$ for the viewpoint of little income in Table 2. So

$$MUCHincome(x) = \begin{cases} 0, & \text{when } x \leq 1020 \\ \dfrac{d(x,1020)}{d(1020,13900)}, & \text{when } 1020 < x < 13900 \\ 1, & \text{when } x \geq 13900 \end{cases} \qquad (3.1)$$

and $MUCHincome^{\daleth}(x) = 1 - MUCHincome(x)$ by the definition 2 of FSCOM.

In the same way, for savings datum x, $\alpha_T = 210000$ and $\varepsilon_T = 20000$ for the viewpoint of much savings, $\alpha_F = 56000$ and $\varepsilon_F = 10000$ for the viewpoint of little savings in Table 2. So

$$MUCHsavings(x) = \begin{cases} 0, & \text{when } x \leq 66000 \\ \dfrac{d(x,66000)}{d(66000,190000)}, & \text{when } 66000 < x < 19000 \\ 1, & \text{when } x \geq 190000 \end{cases} \qquad (3.2)$$

and $MUCHsavings^{\daleth}(x) = 1 - MUCHsavings(x)$ by the definition 2 of FSCOM.

As for membership functions $MUCHincome^{\sim}(x)$ and $MUCHsavings^{\sim}(x)$ on fuzzy sets "moderate income" and "moderate savings", since "moderate income" and "moderate savings" are medium negations of "much income" and "much savings", respectively, so we can be to calculate $MUCHincome^{\sim}(x)$ and $MUCHsavings^{\sim}(x)$ according to (2.1)-(2.5) in Definition 2. However, the computation related to λ value in Definition 2.

3.4 Establishment and Meaning of λ on Fuzzy Sets

Let A be a fuzzy set in FSCOM. According to definition of FSCOM, we known that $\lambda (\in (0, 1))$ is an adjustable parameter in $A^{\sim}(x)$, it both reflected size of area of $A^{\sim}(x)$ and size of areas of $A(x)$ and $A^{\daleth}(x)$ (see [13]). In traditional fuzzy set, due to degree of membership of x on fuzzy set relate to actual application domains and take on subjectivity, so establishment of λ value relate to actual application domains for FSCOM, too. To confirm λ values on above fuzzy sets, we take example for fuzzy set "much income" in Table 2.

For Jiangsu in Table 2, 11000 Yuan is minimum about fuzzy set "much income", 1340 Yuan is maximum about fuzzy set "little income", and fuzzy set "little income" is opposite negation of fuzzy set "much income". By (3.1), degree of membership of 11000 on "much income" $MUCHincome(11000)$ and degree of membership of 1340 on "little income" $MUCHincome^{\daleth}(1340)$ as follows

$$MUCHincome(11000) = \frac{d(11000,1020)}{d(1020,13900)} = 0.775$$
$$MUCHincome^{\daleth}(11000) = 1 - MUCHincome(11000)) = 0.225$$

$$MUCHincome(1340) = \frac{d(1340,1020)}{d(1020,13900)} = 0.025;$$

and $MUCHincome^{\daleth}(1340) = 1 - MUCHincome(1340) = 0.975$.

Now that 11000 Yuan is minimum about fuzzy set "much income" and 1340 Yuan is maximum about fuzzy set "little income", both $MUCHincome(11000)$ and $MUCHincome^{\daleth}(1340)$ should satisfy $MUCHincome(11000) = MUCHincome^{\daleth}(1340) = 1$ theoretically. However, data insufficiency and data distortion so as to this equation not hold. In order to eliminate this problem, we regard

$$\tfrac{1}{2}(MUCHincome(11000) + MUCHincome^{\daleth}(1340))$$

as a counterbalance, which denoted a "threshold value" of area of $MUCHincome(x)$, that is if $MUCHincome(x) \geq \tfrac{1}{2}(MUCHincome(11000) + MUCHincome^{\daleth}(1340))$ for any x in Jiangsu, then x is one of much income in Jiangsu. Thus, we regard $\tfrac{1}{2}(MUCHincome(11000) + MUCHincome^{\daleth}(1340))$ as λ for Jiangsu in Table 3, namely $\lambda = \tfrac{1}{2}(0.775+0.975) = 0.875$. In other words, 0.875 is threshold value on fuzzy sets "much income" for Jiangsu.

Also, we can confirm λ values on fuzzy set "much income" and "much savings" for other provinces (Table 3).

Table 3. Threshold value λ on fuzzy sets "much income" and "much savings" for each province

Fuzzy sets \ Provinces	Jiangsu	Shanghai	Anhui	Shandong
"much income"	0.875	0.962	0.655	0.729
"much savings"	0.815	0.863	0.637	0.726

Based on FSCOM, the meaning of threshold value λ on fuzzy sets "much income" (or "much savings") in example:

(I)   if $MUCHincome(x)$(or $MUCHsavings(x)$) $\geq \lambda$, then x is indeed one of much income (or much savings).

(II) If $MUCHincome(x)$ (or $MUCHsavings(x)$) $\leq 1-\lambda$, then x is indeed one of little income (or little savings).

(III) If $1-\lambda < MUCHincome(x)$ (or $MUCHsavings(x)$) $< \lambda$, then x is indeed one of moderate income (or moderate savings).

According to (III), we can confirm λ values on fuzzy sets "moderate income" and "moderate savings" (Table 4).

Table 4. Threshold value λ on fuzzy sets "moderate income" and "moderate savings" for each province

Fuzzy sets \ Provinces	Jiangsu	Shanghai	Anhui	Shandong
"moderate income"	0.125	0.048	0.345	0.271
"moderate savings"	0.185	0.137	0.363	0.274

The relation between threshold value λ and membership function *MUCHincome*(*x*) of fuzzy set "much income", it is shown in Fig.1 (for fuzzy set "much savings", also).

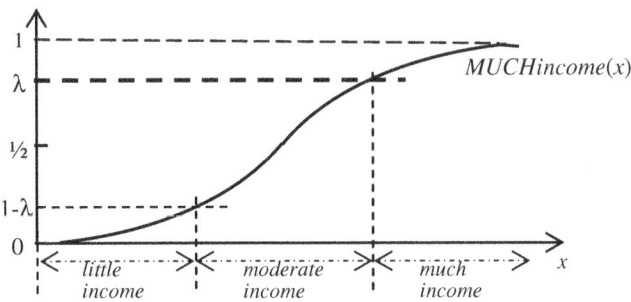

Fig. 1. Relation between threshold value λ and membership function *MUCHincome*(*x*)

3.5 Decision Making in Financial Investment Based on Example

How to decision making in financial investment based on above example and decision making rules *a)−d)*? In decision making rules *a)−d)*, each rule is a sort of inference mode, the fuzzy production rule can be used to represent these rules. The general form of fuzzy production rule as follows:

$$P_1, P_2, ..., P_m \rightarrow Q \mid \langle bd, (\tau_1, \tau_2, ... \tau_m) \rangle \qquad (3.3)$$

where P_i (i = 1, 2, ..., m) are fuzzy sets, which denoted the premises, Q denoted conclusions or actions. bd ($0 \le bd \le 1$) is belief degree of rule, τ_i ($0 \le \tau_i \le 1$, i = 1, 2, ...,m) are threshold values of $P_i(x)$.

The meaning of fuzzy production rule is that

"deduce Q from $P_1, P_2, ...,P_m$ with belief degree bd while $P_i(x)$ exceed τ_i for each i".

The belief degree *bd* can be confirmed by random investigation and statistic. In following example which decision making in financial investment based on decision making rules *a)−d)*, we let *bd* be 0.9.

Mr. Zhang lives in Jiangsu, his month income is 5000 Yuan and savings is 120000 Yuan. How establish his strategies in financial investment based on Decision Rules *a)−d)*?

According to Table 3, (3.1) and (3.2), we compute degree of membership of 120000 Yuan on fuzzy set "much savings" and degree of membership of 5000 Yuan on fuzzy set "much income":

$$MUCHsavings(120000) = \frac{d(120000, 66000)}{d(66000, 190000)} = 0.435,$$

$$MUCHincome(5000) = \frac{d(5000, 1020)}{d(1020, 13900)} = 0.309.$$

By FSCOM, there are

$$MUCHsavings^{\daleth}(120000) = 1 - MUCHsavings(120000) = 0.565,$$

$$MUCHincome^{\daleth}(5000) = 1 - MUCHincome(5000) = 0.691.$$

For Decision Rule *a)*, due to fuzzy set "little savings" ($MUCHsavings^{\urcorner}$) as premise in rule, there is $1-MUCHsavings(x)$ (that is $MUCHsavings^{\urcorner}(x)$) $\geq 1-(1-\lambda)=\lambda$ according to (II), and threshold value is 0.815 by Table 3. Thus, according to (3.3), Decision Rule *a)* can be express as

$$MUCHsavings^{\urcorner}(x) \rightarrow INVESTMENT(savings)\,|\,\langle 0.9, (0.815)\rangle.$$

Because $MUCHsavings^{\urcorner}(120000) = 0.565 < 0.815$, Decision Rule *a)* can not adopt.

For Decision Rule *b)*, due to fuzzy sets "much savings" ($MUCHsavings$) and "much income" ($MUCHincome$) as premises in rule, and Zhang lives in Jiangsu, so their threshold values are 0.815 and 0.875 by Table 3, respectively. Thus, according to (3.3), Decision Rule *b)* can be express as

$$MUCHsavings(x) \wedge MUCHincome(x) \rightarrow INVESTMENT(stocks)\,|\,\langle 0.9, (0.815, 0.875)\rangle.$$

Because $MUCHsavings(120000) = 0.435 < 0.815$ and $MUCHincome(5000) = 0.309 < 0.875$, Decision Rule *b)* can not adopt.

For Decision Rule *c)*, due to fuzzy sets "much savings" ($MUCHsavings$) and "moderate income" ($MUCHincome^{\sim}$) as premises in rule, their threshold values are 0.815 and 0.125 by Table 3 and Table 4, respectively. Thus, according to (3.3), Decision Rule *c)* can be express as

$$MUCHsavings(x) \wedge MUCHincome^{\sim}(x) \rightarrow (INVESTMENT(stocks) \wedge$$
$$INVESTMENT(savings) \wedge MORE(stocks, savings))\,|\,\langle 0.9, (0.815, 0.125)\rangle.$$

Because $MUCHsavings(120000) = 0.435 < 0.815$, Decision Rule *c)* can not adopt.

For Decision Rule *d)*, due to fuzzy sets "moderate savings" ($MUCHsavings^{\sim}$) and "moderate income" ($MUCHincome^{\sim}$) as premises in rule, their threshold values are 0.815 and 0.125 by Table 4, respectively. Thus, according to (3.3), Decision Rule *d)* can be express as

$$MUCHsavings^{\sim}(x) \wedge MUCHincome^{\sim}(x) \rightarrow (INVESTMENT(stocks) \wedge$$
$$INVESTMENT(savings) \wedge MORE(savings, stocks))\,|\,\langle 0.9, (0.185, 0.125)\rangle.$$

Because $MUCHsavings(120000) = 0.435$, and threshold value is 0.185 on $MUCHsavings^{\sim}$ in Table 4, so $MUCHsavings^{\sim}(120000)$ satisfy only (2.5) in Definition 2, that is $MUCHsavings^{\sim}(120000) = MUCHsavings(120000) = 0.435 \geq 0.185$. In addition, because $MUCHincome(5000) = 0.309$, and threshold value is 0.125 on $MUCHincome^{\sim}$ in Table 4, also $MUCHincome^{\sim}(5000)$ satisfy only (2.5) in Definition 2, that is $MUCHincome^{\sim}(5000) = MUCHincome(5000) = 0.309 \geq 0.125$. Thus, Decision Rule *d)* can adopt.

Therefore, Mr. Zhang can adopt Decision Rule *d)* for financial investment.

Acknowledgments. This work was supported by the National Natural Science Foundation of China (60973156) and the Program for Innovative Research Team of Jiangnan University.

References

1. Herre, H., Jaspars, J., Wagner, G.: Partial Logics with Two Kinds of Negation as a Foundation For Knowledge-Based Reasoning. In: Gabbay, D., Wansing, H. (eds.) What Is Negation?, pp. 121–159. Oxford University Press, Oxford (1999)
2. Wagner, G.: Web Rules Need Two Kinds of Negation. In: Bry, F., Henze, N., Małuszyński, J. (eds.) PPSWR 2003. LNCS, vol. 2901, pp. 33–50. Springer, Heidelberg (2003)
3. Analyti, A., Antoniou, G., Wagner, G.: Negation and Negative Information in the W3CResource Description Framework. Annals of Mathematics, Computing & Teleinformatics 1(2), 25–34 (2004)
4. Ferré, S.: Negation, Opposition, and Possibility in Logical Concept Analysis. In: Missaoui, R., Schmidt, J. (eds.) Formal Concept Analysis. LNCS (LNAI), vol. 3874, pp. 130–145. Springer, Heidelberg (2006)
5. Kaneiwa, K.: Description Logic with Contraries, Cntradictories, and Subcontraries. New Generation Computing 25(4), 443–468 (2007)
6. Pan, Z.: A New Cognition and Processing on Contradictory Knowledge. In: Proceedings of 2005 International Conference on Machine Learning and Cybernetics, pp. 1532–1537. Shanghai University Press (2005)
7. Pan, Z., Zhang, S.: Differentiation and Processing on Contradictory Relation and Opposite Relation in Knowledge. In: Proceedings of the Fourth International Conference on Fuzzy Systems and Knowledge Discovery, pp. 334–338. IEEE Computer Society Press, Los Alamitos (2007)
8. Pan, Z.: Five Kinds of Contradictory Relations and Opposite Relations in Inconsistent Knowledge. In: Proceedings of IEEE-Fourth International Conference on Fuzzy Systems and Knowledge Discovery (FSKD 2007), vol. 4, pp. 761–766. IEEE Computer Society Press, Los Alamitos (2007)
9. Pan, Z.: A Logic Description on Different Negation Relation in Knowledge. In: Huang, D.-S., Wunsch II, D.C., Levine, D.S., Jo, K.-H. (eds.) ICIC 2008. LNCS (LNAI), vol. 5227, pp. 815–823. Springer, Heidelberg (2008)
10. Wang, C., Pan, Z.: Extended Fuzzy Knowledge Representation with Medium. In: Huang, D.-S., Wunsch II, D.C., Levine, D.S., Jo, K.-H. (eds.) ICIC 2008. LNCS (LNAI), vol. 5227, pp. 401–409. Springer, Heidelberg (2008)
11. Zhang, L., Pan, Z.: Fuzzy Comprehensive Evaluation based on Measure of Medium Truth Scale. In: Proceedings of 2009 International Conference on Artificial Intelligence and Computational Intelligence (AICI 2009), vol. II, pp. 83–87 (2009)
12. Pan, Z., Wang, C.: Representation and Reasoning Algorithm About Fuzzy Knowledge and its Three kinds of Negations. In: Proceedings of 2nd IEEE International Conference on Advanced Computer Control (ICACC 2010), vol. 2, pp. 603–607 (2010)
13. Pan, Z.: Fuzzy set with Three Kinds of Negations in Fuzzy Knowledge Processing. In: Proceedings of 2010 International Conference on Machine Learning and Cybernetics (ICMLC 2010), vol. 5, pp. 2730–2735 (2010)

Fuzzy Degree and Similarity Measure of Fuzzy Set with Three Kinds of Negations

Lei Yang and Zhenghua Pan

School of Science, Jiangnan University, Wuxi, China
yangleiyl_2010@163.com

Abstract. Negation in information processing is an important notion, especially in fuzzy information processing. How to cognize and deal with various negations of fuzzy information, a new fuzzy set FSCOM with contradictory negation, opposite negation and medium negation was presented in [1]. This paper defines fuzzy degree and similarity measure of fuzzy set FSCOM, gives some properties and calculation formulas of the fuzzy degree and similarity measure, and also discusses their applications.

Keywords: Three kinds of negations of fuzzy set, fuzzy degree, similarity measure.

1 Introduction

Negation in information processing is an important notion, especially in fuzzy information processing. Some scholars suggested that the different negations should be applied in knowledge processing in recent years [2][3]. Zhenghua Pan proposed that there are five kinds of contradictory negative relations and opposite negative relations in concept of knowledge [4], and came up with a fuzzy set FSCOM which has three kinds of negations [1]. Contradictory relation and opposite relation in knowledge information are not distinguished in traditional mathematical and Zadeh fuzzy set, but they are differentiated in fuzzy set FSCOM.

In this paper, we define fuzzy degree and similarity measure of the fuzzy set FSCOM, and give the calculation formulas of fuzzy degree and similarity measures, and also discuss their applications.

2 Basic Concept of FSCOM

Definition 1 [5]. Let U be domain. Mapping Ψ_A :

$$U \to [0, 1]$$

confirmed a fuzzy subset A on U (i.e. $A \in P(U)$), where mapping Ψ_A is called the membership function of A, $\Psi_A(x)$ is the degree of membership of x in A, for short $A(x)$. $\{A(x) \mid x \in U\}$ for short $A(U)$.

H. Deng et al. (Eds.): AICI 2011, Part I, LNAI 7002, pp. 543–550, 2011.

Definition 2 [1]. Let $A \in P(U)$, $\lambda \in (0, 1)$.

(1) If mapping $\Psi^{\daleth}$:

$$A(U) \rightarrow [0, 1]$$

satisfies $\Psi^{\daleth}(A(x)) = 1 - A(x)$, $\Psi^{\daleth}$ confirmed a fuzzy subset $A^{\daleth}$ on U, $A^{\daleth}(x) = \Psi^{\daleth}(A(x))$. $A^{\daleth}$ is called opposite negation set of A. when

(2) If mapping $\Psi^{\sim}$:

$$A(U) \rightarrow [0, 1]$$

Satisfies $\Psi^{\sim}(A(x)) =$

$$\begin{cases} \dfrac{2\lambda - 1}{1 - \lambda}(A(x) - \lambda) + 1 - \lambda, \text{ when } \lambda \in [\frac{1}{2}, 1) \text{ and } A(x) \in (\lambda, 1] & (1) \\[3mm] \dfrac{2\lambda - 1}{1 - \lambda}A(x) + 1 - \lambda, \text{ when } \lambda \in [\frac{1}{2}, 1) \text{ and } A(x) \in [0, 1 - \lambda) & (2) \\[3mm] \dfrac{1 - 2\lambda}{\lambda}A(x) + \lambda, \text{ when } \lambda \in (0, \frac{1}{2}] \text{ and } A(x) \in [0, \lambda) & (3) \\[3mm] \dfrac{1 - 2\lambda}{\lambda}(A(x) + \lambda - 1) + \lambda, \text{ when } \lambda \in (0, \frac{1}{2}] \text{ and } A(x) \in (1 - \lambda, 1] & (4) \\[3mm] 0.5, \text{ when } A(x) = 0.5 & (5) \end{cases}$$

$\Psi^{\sim}$ confirmed a fuzzy subset $A^{\sim}$ on U, $A^{\sim}(x) = \Psi^{\sim}(A(x))$. $A^{\sim}$ is called medium negation set of A.

(3) If mapping $\Psi^{\neg}$:

$$A(U) \rightarrow [0, 1]$$

satisfies $\Psi^{\neg}(A(x)) = \text{Max} (A^{\daleth}(x), A^{\sim}(x))$, $\Psi^{\neg}$ confirmed a fuzzy subset on U, written as $A^{\neg}$, $A^{\neg}(x) = \Psi^{\neg}(A(x))$. $A^{\neg}$ is called contradictory negation set of A.

This fuzzy set on domain U is defined by the definition 1 and 2, we call it "*Fuzzy Set with Contradictory negation, Opposite negation and Medium negation*", for short FScom.

3   Fuzzy Degree of FScom

A fuzzy concept can be expressed by a fuzzy set, and the membership function is able to potray a fuzzy set. Fuzzy concepts are different, so the corresponding fuzzy sets are different. The question of ambiguity of a fuzzy set is aware and studied by foreign scholars at first. DeLuca and Termini [6] proposed fuzzy metric theory in 1972.

Definition 3. If $D(A,B)$ exists following conditions:

(1) $D(A,B) \geq 0$, $D(A,B) = 0$ if and only if $A = B$;
(2) $D(A,B) = D(B,A)$;
(3) $D(A,B) \leq D(A,C) + D(B,C)$.

$D(A,B)$ is called the distance between A and B.

Definition 4. Let X be domain, A is a fuzzy set in FSCOM, $\forall x \in X$.

$$B = \{(x_1, A(x_1)), (x_2, A(x_2)), \ldots, (x_n, A(x_n))\}, (A(x_i) \geq 0.5, i = 1, 2, \ldots, n)$$
$$C = \{(y_1, A(y_1)), (y_2, A(y_2)), \ldots, (y_m, A(y_m))\}, (A(y_j) < 0.5, j = 1, 2, \ldots, m);$$

then

$$A_d = 1 - \frac{D\left(B, B^\sim\right) + D\left(C^\sim, C^\daleth\right)}{1 + D\left(A, A^\daleth\right)} \tag{6}$$

is called the fuzzy degree of A.

Property 1. Let A be a fuzzy set in FSCOM. Then

(1) when $A(x) \equiv 0.5$, then $A_d = 1$;
(2) $A_d = A^\daleth_d$;
(3) when $A(x) < 1/2$, then $A_d = A^\daleth_d = A^\neg_d$;
(4) when $A(x) \geq 1/2$, then $A^\sim_d = A^\neg_d$.

Proof: (1) can be easily proved by the definition 4.
(2) If $A = (B \cup C)$ and $B \cap C = \varnothing$, then $A^\daleth = (B \cup C)^\daleth = B^\daleth \cup C^\daleth$. By the definition of FSCOM, $A^{\daleth\daleth} = A$, $B^{\daleth\daleth} = B$, $B^{\daleth\sim} = B^\sim$, $C^{\daleth\sim} = C^\sim$, then $D(B^{\daleth\daleth}, B^{\daleth\sim}) + D(C^{\daleth\sim}, C^\daleth) = D(B, B^\sim) + D(C^\sim, C^\daleth)$, $1 + D(A, A^\daleth) = 1 + D(A^\daleth, A^{\daleth\daleth})$. Hence $A_d = A^\daleth_d$.
(3) By the definition 2, $A^\neg(x) = \text{Max}(A^\daleth(x), A^\sim(x))$. If $A(x) < 1/2$ then $A(x) < A^\sim(x) < A^\daleth(x)$, so $A^\neg(x) = A^\daleth(x)$. Hence $A_f = A^\daleth_f = A^\neg_f$, by the definition 4.
The proof of (4) is similar with (3).

4   Similarity Measure of FSCOM

The degree of similarity can reflect the close relation of two fuzzy sets. Peizhuang Wang described the similarity among fuzzy sets with grid closeness [7]. Many scholars discussed the similarity relation of two fuzzy sets and came up with some different kinds of methods of similarity measures [8, 9, 10].

4.1   Similarity Measure Based on Distance

Definition 5. Let A, B be fuzzy sets in FSCOM. Then

$$n(A, B) = 1 - (D(A, B) + D(A^\sim, B^\sim) + D(A^\daleth, B^\daleth)) \tag{7}$$

is called the distance similarity degree between A and B.
Obviously, we can prove the following properties by the definition of FSCOM and definition 5.

Property 2. Let A, B be fuzzy sets in FSCOM. Then

(1) $n(A, A) = 1$;
(2) $n(A, B) = n(B, A)$;
(3) when $A(x) < 1/2$, then $n(A^\neg, B) = n(A^\daleth, B)$;
(4) when $A(x) \geq 1/2$, then $n(A^\sim, B) = n(A^\neg, B)$.

4.2   Some Similarity Measures Based on Distance

(1) Similarity measure based on Hamming distance

$$n(A,B)=1-\frac{1}{n}\sum_{i=1}^{n}(/A(x_i)-B(x_i)/+/A^{\sim}(x_i)-B^{\sim}(x_i)/+/A^{\daleth}(x_i)-B^{\daleth}(x_i)/) \tag{8}$$

(2) Similarity measure based on Euclid distance

$$n(A,B)=1-\frac{1}{n}((\sum_{i=1}^{n}|A(x_i)-B(x_i)|^2)^{\frac{1}{2}}+(\sum_{i=1}^{n}|A^{\sim}(x_i)-B^{\sim}(x_i)|^2)^{\frac{1}{2}}+(\sum_{i=1}^{n}|A^{\daleth}(x_i)-B^{\daleth}(x_i)|^2)^{\frac{1}{2}}) \tag{9}$$

(3) Similarity measure based on Minkowskis distance

$$n(A,B)=1-\frac{1}{n}((\sum_{i=1}^{n}/A(x_i)-B(x_i)/^p)^{\frac{1}{p}}+(\sum_{i=1}^{n}/A^{\sim}(x_i)-B^{\sim}(x_i)/^p)^{\frac{1}{p}}$$
$$+(\sum_{i=1}^{n}/A^{\daleth}(x_i)-B^{\daleth}(x_i)/^p)^{\frac{1}{p}}) \tag{10}$$

(4) Similarity measure based on Hamming distance

$$n(A,B)=1-\frac{1}{n}\sum_{i=1}^{n}(\eta/A(x_i)-B(x_i)/+\beta/A^{\sim}(x_i)-B^{\sim}(x_i)/+\gamma/A^{\daleth}(x_i)-B^{\daleth}(x_i)/) \tag{11}$$

($\eta, \beta, \gamma \in [0,1]$ and $\eta+\beta+\gamma=1$).

4.3   Similarity Measure Based on Inner Product and External Product

Definition 6 [7]. Let A, B be fuzzy sets in FScom.

(1) $A \circ B = \vee_{x\in X}(A(x)\wedge B(x))$ is called the inner product between A and B;
(2) $A \odot B = \wedge_{x\in X}(A(x)\vee B(x))$ is called the external product between A and B.

Property 3. Let A, B be fuzzy sets in FScom. Then

(1) $(A\circ B)^{\daleth}=A^{\daleth}\odot B^{\daleth}$ $(A\odot B)^{\daleth}=A^{\daleth}\circ B^{\daleth}$
(2) $A\circ A^{\daleth}\leq 1/2$ $A\odot A^{\daleth}\geq 1/2$
(3) When $A(x)\geq 1/2$, then $Max(A^{\daleth}(x)) \leq A\circ A^{\sim} \leq Max(A(x))$
    $Min(A^{\daleth}(x))\leq A^{\daleth}\odot A^{\sim} \leq Min(A(x))$ $A^{\daleth}\circ A^{\sim}\leq 1/2$ $A\odot A^{\sim}\geq 1/2$
(4) When $A(x)<1/2$, then $Min(A(x))< A\odot A^{\sim} < Min(A^{\daleth}(x))$
    $Max(A(x))< A^{\daleth}\circ A^{\sim} < Max(A^{\daleth}(x))$ $A\circ A^{\sim}<1/2$ $A^{\daleth}\odot A^{\sim}>1/2$
(5) When $A(x)\geq 1/2$ and $B(x) \geq 1/2$, then
    $A^{\daleth}\circ B^{\daleth}\leq A^{\sim}\circ B^{\sim} \leq A\circ B$ $A^{\daleth}\odot B^{\daleth}\leq A^{\sim}\odot B^{\sim} \leq A\odot B$
(6) When $A(x)<1/2$ and $B(x) <1/2$, then
    $A\circ B < A^{\sim}\circ B^{\sim} < A^{\daleth}\circ B^{\daleth}$ $A\odot B < A^{\sim}\odot B^{\sim} < A^{\daleth}\odot B^{\daleth}$

Proof : We prove (1),(3) and (5), others can be proved by the same way.

(1) By the definition 2, $A^{\daleth}(x) = 1-A(x)$. $A^{\daleth}(x)$ is identical with negation A^c in Zadeh Fuzzy Set. So, $(A\circ B)^{\daleth}=A^{\daleth}\odot B^{\daleth}$ $(A\odot B)^{\daleth}= A^{\daleth}\circ B^{\daleth}$.
(3) When $A(x) \geq 1/2$, $A(x) \geq A^{\sim}(x) \geq A^{\daleth}(x)$. So, $A^{\daleth}\circ A^{\daleth} \leq A^{\sim}\circ A^{\sim} \leq A\circ A^{\sim} \leq A\circ A$, $A^{\daleth}\odot A^{\daleth}\leq A^{\daleth}\odot A^{\sim}\leq A^{\sim}\odot A^{\sim} \leq A\odot A$ by the definition 6. Hence $Max(A^{\daleth}(x))\leq A\circ A^{\sim}$ $\leq Max(A(x))$, $Min(A^{\daleth}(x))\leq A^{\daleth}\odot A^{\sim}\leq Min(A(x))$, $A^{\daleth}\circ A^{\sim}=A\circ A^{\daleth}\leq 1/2$, $A\odot A^{\sim}=$ $A\odot A^{\daleth}\geq 1/2$ by the definition 6.

(5)While $A(x) \geq 1/2$ and $B(x) \geq 1/2$, then $A(x) \geq A^{\sim}(x) \geq A^{\daleth}(x)$, $B(x) \geq B^{\sim}(x) \geq B^{\daleth}(x)$. Hence $A^{\daleth} \circ B^{\daleth} \leq A^{\sim} \circ B^{\sim} \leq A \circ B$, $A^{\daleth} \odot B^{\daleth} \leq A^{\sim} \odot B^{\sim} \leq A \odot B$, by the definition 6.

Definition 7. Let A, B be fuzzy sets in FScom. Then

$$n(A,B)= \frac{1}{3}(A \circ B + (A \odot B)^{\daleth} + A^{\sim} \circ B^{\sim}) \qquad (12)$$

is called the grid similarity degree between A and B.

By the definition of FScom and definition 7, we can prove the following properties.

Property 4. Let A, B be fuzzy sets in FScom. Then

(1) $n(A,B)=n(B,A)$;
(2) when $A(x)<1/2$, then $n(A^{\neg},B)=n(A^{\daleth},B)$;
(3) when $A(x)\geq 1/2$, then $n(A^{\sim},B)=n(A^{\neg},B)$.

5 Application

The living standard of people who live in different regions is different. The main factors which influence quality of life of people are the salary, consumption and the bank savings. Using the definition and similarity measure of FScom to evaluate which the standard of living of two areas are more similar among Jiangsu province, Sichuan province and the city of Shanghai.

Table 1. Viewpoints of individual income, consumption and bank savings of people

Viewpoints	Jiangsu	Shanghai	Sichuan
High income(yuan/month)(±500)	≥11000	≥14400	≥6000
Low income(yuan/month)(±100)	≤1340	≤2000	≤1100
Much savings (ten thousands yuan)(±2)	≥16	≥21	≥12.4
Little savings (ten thousands yuan)(±1)	≤8.2	≤10	≤6.8
High consumption (yuan/month)(±300)	≥4000	≥5000	≥2500
Low consumption (yuan/month)(±200)	≤1200	≤1700	≤800

5.1 Analyse the Example by Fuzzy Set FScom

It is known to all that: (1) people's viewpoints on high (low) income, much (little) savings and high (low) consumption are fuzzy concepts;

(2) the relation of high income and the low income is opposite, and moderate income is in between high income and low income;

(3) the relation of high consumption and low consumption is opposite, and moderate consumption is in between high consumption and low consumption;

(4) the relation of much savings and little savings is opposite, and moderate savings is in between much savings and little savings.

By the definition of FScom, we can know:

(1) low income is the opposite negation of high income, and moderate income is the medium negation of high income;

(2) little savings is the opposite negation of much savings, and moderate savings is the medium negation of much savings;

(3) low consumption is the opposite negation of high consumption, and moderate consumption is the medium negation of high consumption.

5.2   Symbol Description and Establish Membership Functions

(1) Symbol description:

A: represents Jiangsu province $\qquad$ B: represents the city of Shanghai

C: represents Sichuan province $\qquad$ A_1: represents high income

$A_1^{\daleth}$: represents low income $\qquad$ $A_1^{\sim}$: represents moderate income

A_2: represents much savings $\qquad$ $A_2^{\daleth}$: represents little savings

$A_2^{\sim}$: represents moderate savings $\qquad$ A_3: represents high consumption

$A_3^{\daleth}$: represents high consumption $\qquad$ $A_3^{\sim}$: represents moderate consumption

(2) Establish membership functions:

Through the Euclid distance of one dimension, that is $D(x, y)=|x-y|$, to establish a function of membership to get the degree of membership of the specific data "x".

The membership function of "x" in A_1:

$$A_1(x)=\begin{cases} 0 & x\leq1200 \\ \dfrac{D(x,1200)}{D(1200,13900)} & 1200<x<13900 \\ 1 & x\geq14900 \end{cases}$$

The membership function of "x" in $A_1^{\daleth}$: $A_1^{\daleth}(x) =1- A_1(x)$.

The function of membership of "x" in $A_1^{\sim}$ is $A_1^{\sim}(x)$.

The function of membership of "x" in A_2:

$$A_2(x)=\begin{cases} 0 & x\leq7.8 \\ \dfrac{D(x,7.8)}{D(7.8,19)} & 7.8<x<19 \\ 1 & x\geq19 \end{cases}$$

The function of membership of "x" in $A_2^{\daleth}$: $A_2^{\daleth}(x) =1-A_2(x)$.

The function of membership of "x" in $A_2^{\sim}$ is $A_2^{\sim}(x)$.

The function of membership of "x" in A_3:

$$A_3(x)=\begin{cases} 0 & x\leq1000 \\ \dfrac{D(x,1000)}{D(1000,4700)} & 1000<x<4700 \\ 1 & x\geq4700 \end{cases}$$

The function of membership of "x" in $A_3^{\daleth}$: $A_3^{\daleth}(x) =1-A_3(x)$.

The function of membership of "x" in $A_3^{\sim}$ is $A_3^{\sim}(x)$.

Wanting to know the functions of $A_1^{\sim}(x)$, $A_2^{\sim}(x)$ and $A_3^{\sim}(x)$, we should know the value of λ by the definition2.

5.3   Compute the Degree of Membership and Value of λ

Taking the viewpoint of high income in Jiangsu as an example to give the methods of solving the membership degree and the value of λ as follows.

Taking the corresponding data into the function of membership of A_1, we can get the results as follows: $A_1(11000)=\dfrac{D(11000,1200)}{D(1200,13900)}=0.772$, $A_1(1340)=0.011$;

$A_1^{\daleth}(11000)=1-A_1(11000)=1-0.772=0.228$; $A_1^{\daleth}(1340)=1-0.011=0.989$.

From Table 1 we can know 1340 yuan is the upper limit value of low income in Jiangsu, 11000 yuan is the lower limit value of high income in Jiangsu, so 11000 and 1340 are a pair of opposite data in income, then $A_1(11000) + A_1 (1340) =1$. Because of the data is less and not enough precise, leads to the values of $A_1(11000)$ and $A_1 (1340)$ may not be accurate. Counting the average value of them, that is,

$A_1(11000)=A_1^{\daleth}(1340)=(0.772+0.989)/2=0.88$ $A_1^{\daleth}(11000)=1-0.88=0.12$.

So $A_1^{\sim}(11000)\in (A_1^{\daleth}(11000), A_1(11000))=(0.12,0.88)$.

To take $\lambda=(|0.772-0.228|+|0.011-0.989|)/2=0.76$, then $A_1^{\sim}(11000)=0.499$ can be calculated by the formula (1).

By the same way, we can compute values of λ and membership grades of corresponding fuzzy sets from table 1.

Table 2. Values of λ and membership grades

Membership grades and λ values	Jiangsu	Shanghai	Sichuan
$A_1(x)$	0.88	0.969	0.689
$A_1^{\daleth}(x)$	0.12	0.031	0.311
λ_1	0.761	0.937	0.622
$A_1^{\sim}(x)$	0.499	0.507	0.421
$A_2(x)$	0.848	0.902	0.705
$A_2^{\daleth}(x)$	0.152	0.098	0.295
λ_2	0.696	0.804	0.589
$A_2^{\sim}(x)$	0.5	0.5	0.461
$A_3(x)$	0.878	0.905	0.703
$A_3^{\daleth}(x)$	0.122	0.095	0.297
λ_3	0.757	0.812	0.595
$A_3^{\sim}(x)$	0.619	0.497	0.455

Now, accessing which the quality of living of two areas among Jiangsu, Sichuan and the city of Shanghai are closer.

At first, making use of the grid similarity measure, that is

$$n(A,B)=\frac{1}{3} (A \circ B + (A \odot B)^{\daleth} + A^{\sim} \circ B^{\sim})$$

Getting the following results: $n(A,B)=0.49$, $n(A,C)=0.439$, $n(B,C)=0.421$.

Then, using the weighted distance similarity measure, that is,

$$n(A,B)=1-\frac{1}{n}\sum_{i=1}^{n} (\eta|A(x_i)-B(x_i)|+\beta|A^{\sim}(x_i)-B^{\sim}(x_i)|+ \gamma|A^{\daleth}(x_i)-B^{\daleth}(x_i)|)$$

Taking $\eta=0.2$, $\beta=0.55$, $\gamma=0.25$ to count the values as follows:

$$n(A,B)=0.954, \quad n(A,C)=0.872 \text{ , } n(B,C)=0.867$$

We can draw a conclusion from the calculation results: the living standard of Jiangsu province and the city of Shanghai is more similar and this conclusion is in accord with reality. It is closer to the practice that the opposite negations and medium negations of high income, high consumption and the much savings are considered, so the result is more accurate. And this point is not taken into account by the Zadeh fuzzy set.

6   Conclusions

Based on the fuzzy set FSCOM, this paper defines the fuzzy degree and similarity measures of FSCOM, discusses the relations of fuzzy degrees of opposite negation sets, medium negation sets and contradictory negation sets in FSCOM, gives properties and calculation formulas of similarity measures, and also the formulas are reasonable by analyzing the result of example.

Acknowledgement. This work was supported by the National Natural Science Foundation of China (60973156) and the Program for Innovative Research Team of Jiangnan University.

References

1. Pan, Z.: Fuzzy set with three kinds of negations in fuzzy knowledge processing. In: Proceedings of 2010 International Conference on Machine Learning and Cybernetics, vol. 5, pp. 2730–2735 (2010)
2. Wagner, G.: Vivid Logic: Knowledge-Based Reasoning with Two Kinds of Negation. Springer-Verlag, New York, Inc., Secaucus (1994)
3. Pan, Z.: A logic description on different negation relation in knowledge. In: Huang, D.-S., Wunsch II, D.C., Levine, D.S., Jo, K.-H. (eds.) ICIC 2008. LNCS (LNAI), vol. 5227, pp. 815–823. Springer, Heidelberg (2008)
4. Pan, Z., Zhang, S.: Five Kinds of Contradictory Relations and Opposite Relations in Inconsistent Knowledge. In: Proceedings of the Fourth International Conference on Fuzzy Systems and Knowledge Discovery, vol. 4, pp. 761–764 (2007)
5. Zadeh, L.A.: Fuzzy Sets. Information and Control 8(3), 338–353 (1965)
6. Deluca, Temini: A definition of nonprobalistic entropy in the setting of fuzzy sets theory. Information and Control 20, 301–302 (1972)
7. Wang, P.: Fuzzy Set Theory and Its Applications. Shanghai Science and Technology Press (1983)
8. Wang, W.J.: New similarity measures on fuzzy sets and elements. Fuzzy Sets and Systems 85, 305–309 (1997)
9. Xu, Z.: Some similarity measures of intuitionistic fuzzy sets and their applications to multiple attribute decision making. Fuzzy Optimization and Decision Making 6, 109–121 (2007)
10. Hyung, L.K., Song, Y.S., Lee, K.M.: Similarity measure between fuzzy sets and between elements. Fuzzy Sets and Systems 62, 291–293 (1994)

No Reference Image Quality Assessment Using Fuzzy Relational Classifier

Indrajit De[1] and Jaya Sil[2]

[1] Department of Information Technology, MCKV Institute of Engineering,
Liluah, Howrah, West Bengal-711204, India
[2] Department of Computer Science and Technology, Bengal Engineering and Science
University, Shibpur Howrah, West Bengal, India
indrajitde@ieee.org, js@cs.becs.ac.in

Abstract. Assessing quality of distorted/decompressed images without reference to the original image is a challenging task because extracted features are often inexact and no predefined relation exists between features and visual quality of images. The paper aims at assessing quality of distorted/ decompressed images without any reference to the original image by developing a robust system using fuzzy relational classifier. First impreciseness in feature space of training data is handled using fuzzy clustering method. As a next step, logical relation between the structure of data and the quality of image are established. Quality of a new image is assessed in terms of degree of membership of the pattern in the given classes applying fuzzy relational operator. Finally, a crisp decision is obtained after defuzzification of the membership value.

Keywords: MOS, fuzzy relational classifier, no reference.

1 Introduction

Digital images are subjected to loss of information, various ways of distortions during compression [6] and transmission, which deteriorate visual quality of the images at the receiving end. Quality of an image plays fundamental role to take vital decision and therefore, its assessment is essential prior to application. Modeling physiological and psycho visual features of the human visual system [10, 11, 12] and signal fidelity criteria [9] based quality assessment are reported [10, 11] though each of these approaches has several shortcomings. The most reliable means of measuring the image quality is subjective evaluation based on the opinion of the human observers [7, 14]. However, subjective testing is not automatic and expensive too. On the other hand, most objective image quality assessment methods [5, 8] either require access to the original image as reference [2] or only can evaluate images, degraded with predefined distortions and therefore, lacking generalization approach. Two prominent works have been reported relating to no-reference image quality evaluation, (i) Wang, Bovic and Shiekh's no-reference JPEG image quality index and (ii) H.Shiekh's

H. Deng et al. (Eds.): AICI 2011, Part I, LNAI 7002, pp. 551–558, 2011.

quality metric based on natural scene statistics (NSS) model applied on JPEG2000 compressed images. Three works are reported very recently to assess quality of an image namely, Extreme Learning Machine classifier based mean opinion score (MOS) estimator [16], discrete cosine transform (DCT) domain statistics based metric [17] and blind image quality index [18, 19]. But none of them incorporated human centric computation methods that can capture powerful judgment ability of human observers and therefore, best suited for assessing quality of images.

In the paper, human reasoning power is explored to building a fuzzy relational classifier that assesses quality of images by assigning soft class labels. In the proposed method, first impreciseness in feature space is handled by analysing the training data using fuzzy clustering method. As a next step logical relation between the feature and the class label is measured by degree of membership value obtained using φ-composition (a fuzzy implication)[1] and conjunctive aggregation methods. Quality of a new image is assessed in terms of degree of membership value of the pattern in different classes applying fuzzy relational operator. Finally, a crisp decision is obtained after defuzzification of the membership value.

2   Fuzzy Relational Classification

Fuzzy relational classification [20] establishes a correspondence between structures in feature space and the class labels. By using fuzzy logic in classification, one avoids the problem of hard labeling the prototypes and easily captures the partial sharing of structures among several classes. In the training phase of classifier building process, two steps are identified: (a) exploratory data analysis (unsupervised fuzzy clustering), (b) construction of a logical relation between the structures obtained in the previous step and the class labels. In the exploratory step, the available data objects are clustered in groups by the fuzzy c-means (FCM)[13] or a similar algorithm. Clustering results in a fuzzy partition matrix, which specify for each training sample a -tuple of membership degrees in the obtained clusters. In the second step, a fuzzy relation is computed, using the memberships obtained in the first step and the target membership of the pattern in the classes (which may be crisp or fuzzy). This relation is built by means of the φ-composition (a fuzzy implication) and conjunctive aggregation, specifying the logical relationship between the cluster membership and the class membership values. To classify new patterns, the membership of each pattern in the clusters (fuzzy prototypes) is computed from its distance to the cluster centers, giving a fuzzy set of prototype membership. Then, relational composition of this fuzzy set with the fuzzy relation is applied to compute an output fuzzy set. This set gives a fuzzy classification in terms of membership degrees of the pattern in the given classes. When a crisp decision is required, defuzzification has to be applied to this fuzzy set. Typically, the maximum defuzzification method is used. The process is given in the diagram (fig-1):

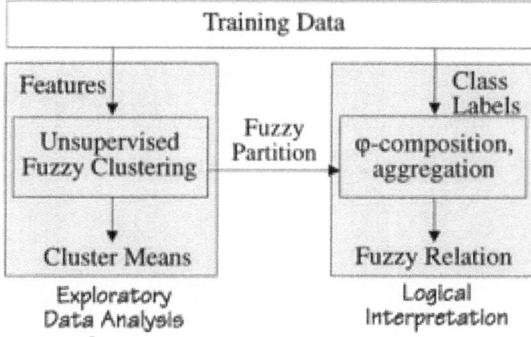

Fig. 1. Fuzzy Relational classifier training phase

3   Feature Selection

Local features like Scale invariant feature transform (SIFT) are used to build the classifier. For this purpose David Lowe's [21] algorithm has been used to extract the SIFT features from gray level training images taken from TAMPERE database [23]. Scale Invariant Feature Transform (SIFT) is an approach for detecting and extracting local feature descriptors that are reasonably invariant to changes in illumination, image noise, rotation, scaling, and small changes in viewpoint. The stepwise detection stages for SIFT features are a) scale-space extrema detection, b) keypoint localization, c) orientation assignment and d) generation of keypoint descriptors. These features share similar properties with neurons in inferior temporal cortex that are used for object recognition in primate vision. The first step toward the detection of interest points is the convolution of the image with Gaussian filters at different scales, and the generation of difference of Gaussian images from the difference of adjacent blurred images. Interest points (called key points in the SIFT framework) are identified as local maxima or minima of the Difference of Gaussian (DoG) images across scales. Each pixel in the DoG images is compared to its 8 neighbors at the same scale, plus the 9 corresponding neighbors at neighboring scales. If the pixel is a local maximum or minimum, it is selected as a candidate key point. For each candidate key point following steps are performed a) interpolation of nearby data is used to accurately determine its position, b) key points with low contrast are removed, c) responses along edges are eliminated and d) key point is assigned an orientation. To determine the key point orientation, a gradient orientation histogram is computed in the neighborhood of the key point. Once a key point orientation has been selected, the SIFT feature descriptor is computed as a set of orientation histograms on 4×4 pixel neighborhoods.

4   Procedure

The flowchart of the process is shown in fig.2.

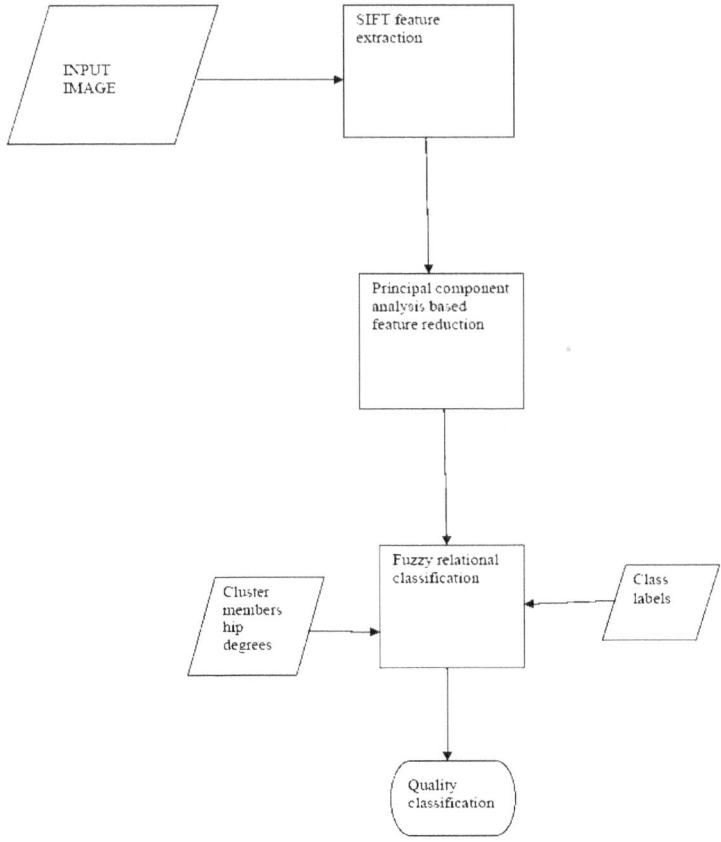

Fig. 2. SIFT based image quality classification

Step 1: Six training images from TAMPERE image databases [23] are taken to extract SIFT features from them. There mean opinion score (MOS) values are utilized to build the classification weight matrix.

Step 2: The extracted SIFT features are dimensionally reduced by Principal Component Analysis (PCA). The average reduction is from approximately twenty thousand vectors to one twenty eight eigenvectors.

Step 3: The PCA reduced SIFT feature vectors from the images are combined together in a matrix form where individual image feature vectors are placed along the column of the matrix.

Step 4: Fuzzy C means clustering procedure is operated on the thus prepared data matrix with fuzziness exponent being 2.5 and number of clusters being 4.

Step 5: The membership degree matrix thus obtained is combined with the classification weight matrix already built up by Lukasiewicz implication method (equation 1) to get the Fuzzy relational matrix for the training images.

$$(r_{ij}) = \min(1, 1 - \mu_{ik} + \omega_{jk})$$
$$k = 1, 2, \ldots N, \ j = 1, 2 \ldots L, i = 1, 2, \ldots c$$
$$(r_{ij}) = \min_{k=1,2\ldots N}[(r_{ij})_k] \tag{1}$$

where (r_{ij}) is individual relational matrix element, μ_{ik} is membership degree element and ω_{jk} is classification weight element. k is the total number of images (here 6), L is the total number of classes (here 5) and c is the total number of clusters (here 4). N is the total number of patterns (here 6).

Step 6: For nine testing images taken from three image databases namely TAMPERE, LIVE[5] and PROFILE[24] after following Step 1 and Step 2 on it, the membership degrees of the image feature vectors from the four cluster centers already obtained, are computed using equation 2.

$$\mu_i = \frac{1}{\sum_{j=1}^{c} \left(d(x, v_i) \middle/ d(x, v_j) \right)^{2/m-1}} \tag{2}$$

where μ_i is the membership degree of the new image feature vectors with respect to cluster center v_i, d(.) is the Euclidean distance and m is the fuzzyness exponent[22]. The fuzzyness exponent m is changed for each image while computing the membership degrees to observe the effect of fuzzyness on classification accuracy.

Step 7: Given the membership degrees obtained in Step 6 the class membership ω is computed from the relational composition:

$$\omega_j = \max_{1 \leq i \leq c}[\max(\mu_i + r_{ij} - 1, 0)], \ j = 1, 2, \ldots L \tag{3}$$

5   Results

Table 1 shows the classification weight matrix:

Table 1. MOS related classification weight matrix

Images	Class labels	Excellent	Good	Average	Bad	Poor
Image 1		1	0	0	0	0
Image 2		1	0	0	0	0
Image 3		0	1	0	0	0
Image 4		0	1	0	0	0
Image 5		0	0	1	0	0
Image 6		0	0	1	0	0

Table 2 shows the fuzzy relational matrix:

Table 2. Fuzzy relational matrix

Clusters ↓	Class labels →	Excellent	Good	Average	Bad	poor
Cluster1		0.0745	0.0745	0.6234	0.0745	0.0745
Cluster2		0.7721	0.0369	0.0369	0.0369	0.0369
Cluster3		0.0375	0.0375	0.7377	0.0375	0.0375
Cluster4		0.0653	0.6085	0.0653	0.0653	0.0653

Table 3 shows comparisons between different methods.

Table 3. The comparison of fuzzy relational classifier with other quality metrics

Image Name	Fuzzyness exponent value for membership degree computation	Fuzzy relation based image quality in linguistic variable term	Blind image quality index (linguistic variable) (krishnamoorthy, bovik,)	Jpegquality score (linguistic variable) (wang et al)	Jp2knr (linguistic variable) (shiekh et al)
Img162 (LIVE database)	2.5	Average	Good	Excellent	Good
Img132 (LIVE)	2.0	Average	Average	Average	Good
Chinacongressdistorted (PROFILE DATABASE)	2.5	Average	Average	Average	Good
Chinacongressoriginal (PROFILE)	5.5	Excellent	Good	Excellent	Good
Annanoriginal (PROFILE)	3.0	Excellent	Good	Excellent	Good
Naipauldistorted (PROFILE)	2.0	Average	Poor	Average	Good
I01 (TAMPERE DATABASE)	5.5	Excellent	Good	Excellent	Good
I04 (TAMPERE)	4.0	Excellent	good	Excellent	Good
Afghangaussian (PROFILE)	2.0	Average	Average	Average	Good

6 Conclusions

A fuzzy relational classifier is designed to assess quality of images based on human centric computation method, which is robust due to assignment of soft class labels and very close to human perception. Inexactness in feature space of images are handled by fuzzy c-means clustering method while uncertain relationship between clusters and different quality classes are defined by Lukasiewicz implication method. The proposed method has been compared with the quality metric of other methods and the result is satisfactory. Future work will include other features along with SIFT features and redefining MOS based weight values in table 1, which in this case is crisp.

References

1. Lin, C.T., George Lee, C.S.: Neural Fuzzy Systems, pp. 140–174. Prentice Hall Ptr, Englewood Cliffs (1993)
2. Sheikh, H.R., Bovic, A.C.: Image information and visual quality. In: Proc. IEEE Int. Conf. Acoust., Speech and Signal Processing (May 2004)
3. Sheikh, H.R., Bovic, A., Cormack, L.: No-Reference Quality Assesment using Natural Scene Statistics: JPEG 2000. IEEE Transactions on Image Processing (2005)
4. Wang, Z., Sheikh, H., Bovic, A.: No Reference Perceptual Quality Assesment of JPEG compressed image. In: Proceedings of IEEE 2002 International Conferencing on Image Processing, pp. 22–25 (2002)
5. Sheikh, H.R., Wang, Z., Cormack, L., Bovic, A.: LIVE image quality assessment database (2003), http://live.ece.utexas.edu/research/quality
6. Sayood, K.: Introduction to data compression, pp. 267–268. Morgan Kauffman Publishers, San Francisco (2000)
7. Wang, Z., Bovik, A.C.: Why is image quality assessment so difficult? In: IEEE Int. Conf. Acoust., Speech, and Signal Processing (May 2002)
8. VQEG, Final report from the video quality experts group on the validation of objective models of video quality assessment (March 2000), http://www.vqeg.org/
9. Sonka, M., Hlavac, V., Boyle, R.: Image processing analysis and machine vision, pp. 254–262. IPT Press (1999)
10. Pappas, T.N., Safranek, R.J.: Perceptual criteria for image quality evaluation. In: Bovik, A. (ed.) Handbook of Image &Video Proc. Academic Press, London (2000)
11. Watson, B. (ed.): Digital Images and Human Vision. MIT Press, Cambridge (1993)
12. Watson, A.B., et al.: Visibility of wavelet quantization noise. IEEE Transactions on Image Processing 6(8), 1164–1175 (1997)
13. Dunn, J.C.: A Fuzzy Relative of the ISODATA Process and Its Use in Detecting Compact Well-Separated Clusters. Journal of Cybernetics 3, 32–57 (1973)
14. Wang, Z., Bovik, A.C.: Modern Image Quality Assessment, pp. 79–102. Morgan and Claypool publishers (2006)
15. Wang, Z., Wu, G., Shiekh, H.R., Simoncelli, E.P., Wang, E.Y., Bovik, A.C.: Quality aware images. IEEE Transactions on Image Processing, 1680–1689 (June 2006)
16. Suresh, S., Venkatesh Babu, R., Kim, H.J.: No-Reference image quality assessment using modified extreme learning classifier. Applied Soft Computing, 541–552 (2009)
17. Brandão, T., Queluz, M.P.: No-reference image quality assessment based on DCT domain statistics. Signal Process 88, 822–833
18. Moorthy, A.K., Bovik, A.C.: BIQI Software Release (2009), http://live.ece.utexas.edu/research/quality/biqi.zip
19. Moorthy, A.K., Bovik, A.C.: A Modular Framework for Constructing Blind Universal Quality Indices. IEEE Signal Processing Letters (2009)

20. Setnes, M., Babuska, R.: Fuzzy relational classifier trained by fuzzy clustering. IEEE Transactions on Systems, Man, and Cybernetics, Part B 29(5), 619–625 (1999)
21. Lowe, D.G.: Distinctive image features from scale-invariant keypoints. International Journal of Computer Vision 60(2), 91–110 (2004)
22. Yu, J., Cheng, Q., Huang, H.: Analysis of the weighting exponent in the FCM. IEEE Transactions on SMC-Part b 34(1), 634–639 (2004)
23. Ponomarenko, N., Lukin, V., Zelensky, A., Egiazarian, K., Carli, M., Battisti, F.: TID2008 - A Database for Evaluation of Full-Reference Visual Quality Assessment Metrics. Advances of Modern Radioelectronics 10, 30–45 (2009)
24. http://vasc.ri.cmu.edu/idb/html/face/profile_images/

Solving the Minimal Solutions of Max-Product Relation Equation by Graph Method and Branch Method

Zhonglin Chai

Department of Mathematics, China Jiliang University, Hangzhou, China, 310018
chaizhonglin@163.com

Abstract. Max-product fuzzy relation equations is one of the important classes of fuzzy relation equations. As max-min fuzzy relation equations, the main problem of solving max-product fuzzy relation equations is to find all its minimal solutions. Although some methods and algorithms have been proposed for finding them, they are still too complex in applications. In this paper, the properties of the equations' minimal solutions are studied, and two methods, graph method and branch method, are presented based on reference [1] to find the minimal solution of max-min fuzzy relation equations. Lastly, an example is given to illustrate the two methods.

Keywords: Max-product relation equation, Minimal solution, Bipartite graph, Graph method, Branch method.

1 Introduction

Max-product relation equations belong to fuzzy relation equations, which have been used extensively in fuzzy control, fuzzy reasoning, fuzzy logic, etc [2, 3, 4]. Many researchers have studied the equations extensively with many methods obtained to solve them [3, 4, 5, 6, 7], but these approaches usually are too complex and difficult to use. When the fuzzy relation equations is solvable, its set of solutions is determined by a maximum solution and a finite number of minimal solutions [1,4,7] and the main problem of solving it is to find all its minimal solutions. In reference [1] the author presented two methods, graph method and branch method, to get the minimal solutions of max-min relation equations. In this paper, the properties of the minimal solutions are studied, and then the two methods, graph method and branch method, are popularized into max-product relation equations. Lastly an example is given to illustrate the two methods.

2 Some Definitions and Previous Results

Firstly, some well-known definitions and previous results are given for the sake of convenience. They mainly come from literature [4].

H. Deng et al. (Eds.): AICI 2011, Part I, LNAI 7002, pp. 559–565, 2011.

Fuzzy relation eqution is $A \circ X = B$, where $A = (a_{ij})_{m \times n}$, $X=(x_1,x_2,...,x_n)^T$, $B=(b_1,b_2,...,b_m)^T$, $a_{ij}, x_j, b_i \in [0,1]$, $(i=1,2,..., m ; j=1,2,...,n)$, "$\circ$"is the max-product $(\vee,\bullet)$ composition.

Let $a, b \in [0,1]$, define three binary operators, $\otimes$, α and β as follows:

$$a \otimes b = \begin{cases} b/a, a > b \\ 1, \quad a \leq b \end{cases}, \quad a \alpha b = \begin{cases} b/a, a \geq b \\ 0, \quad a < b \end{cases}, \quad a \beta b = \begin{cases} b, a \geq b \\ 0, a < b \end{cases}$$

Theorem 1. The necessary and sufficient condition of $A \circ X = B$ has solutions is that $X^* = (x_1^*, x_2^*, ..., x_n^*)^T$ is its maximum solution, where $x_j^* = \bigwedge_{i=1}^{m}(a_{ij} \otimes b_i), j=1,2,...,n$.

Theorem 1 gives a judging theorem of solvability of equation $A \circ X = B$ and a method of obtaining its maximum solution. The method is finding X^* firstly, then testing whether it is the solution of $A \circ X = B$ .If $X^*$is the solution of $A \circ X = B$, then the equation has solutions and $X^*$is its maximum solution. Otherwise, the equation has not solution.

By reference [1,4,7] we know the solution set of $A \circ X = B$ is determined by its maximum solution and minimal solutions. As the problem of finding the maximum solution of $A \circ X = B$ has been solved, the issue of searching all the solutions of $A \circ X = B$ is transformed into seeking all its minimal solutions.

For the sake of convenience, from now on we always suppose that $A \circ X = B$ is solvable, and always use $X^* = (x_1^*, x_2^*, ..., x_n^*)^T$ and $X^{(0)} = (x_1^{(0)}, x_2^{(0)}, ..., x_n^{(0)})^T$ to denote the maximum solution and any minimal solution of $A \circ X = B$, respectively.

Furthermore, by Theorem 2 in [1] we can further assume that $b_i > 0$ for any i to simplify $A \circ X = B$.

3 Properties of Minimal Solutions

Let $X^* = (x_1^*, x_2^*, ..., x_n^*)$ be the maximum solution of $A \circ X = B$, denote $A^* = (a_{ij}^*)_{m \times n}$, where $a_{ij}^* = x_j^* \beta(a_{ij} \alpha b_i)$. By the definitions of a_{ij}^*, $\otimes$, α and β, A^* has following properties: P$_1$. If $a_{ij}<b_i$, then $a_{ij}^*=0$; P$_2$. If $a_{ij} \geq b_i$ and $a_{ij} \alpha b_i > x_j^*$, then $a_{ij}^*=0$; P$_3$. If $a_{ij} \geq b_i$ and $a_{ij} \alpha b_i \leq x_j^*$, then $a_{ij}^* = b_i / a_{ij}$.

Theorem 2. Let $X^* = (x_1^*, x_2^*, ..., x_n^*)$ be the maximum solution of $A \circ X = B$, $a_{ij}^* = x_j^* \beta(a_{ij} \alpha b_i)$, then

(1) a_{ij}^{*} is equal to either 0 or x_{j}^{*};

(2) $a_{ij} \cdot a_{ij}^{*} \leq b_{i}$;

(3) If $a_{ij}^{*} = 0$, then $a_{ij}x_{j}^{*} < b_{i}$.

(4) Arbitrarily take x_{j} satisfying $x_{j} < x_{j}^{*}$, then $a_{ij}x_{j} < b_{i}$ for any a_{ij}.

Proof. (1) By the definition x_{j}^{*} and the assumption $b_{i}>0$ one sees that $x_{j}^{*} > 0$ for any j, so by the properties of A^{*} we only need to prove the conclusion is correct when $a_{ij} \geq b_{i}$ and $a_{ij}\alpha b_{i} \leq x_{j}^{*}$. Obviously there is $a_{ij} \otimes b_{i} = a_{ij}\alpha b_{i}$ by the definitions of $\otimes\!\!\!0$ α, so $a_{ij}\alpha b_{i} \geq x_{j}^{*}$ by Theorem 1, then $a_{ij}\alpha b_{i} = x_{j}^{*} = a_{ij}^{*}$.

(2) Obvious.

(3) The conclusion is correct obviously when $a_{ij}<b_{i}$; by the properties of A^{*} if $a_{ij} \geq b_{i}$ and $a_{ij}\alpha b_{i} > x_{j}^{*}$, then $a_{ij} \cdot x_{j}^{*} < a_{ij} \cdot (a_{ij}\alpha b_{i}) = b_{i}$.

(4) Obviously there is $a_{ij}x_{j} < a_{ij}x_{j}^{*} = b_{i}$.

Theorem 3. Let $X^{(0)} = (x_{1}^{(0)}, x_{2}^{(0)}, ..., x_{n}^{(0)})^{T}$ be a minimal solution of $A \circ X = B$, then for any non-zero component $x_{j}^{(0)}$, there must exist i such that $a_{ij} \cdot x_{j}^{(0)} = b_{i}$.

Proof. Obvious.

Theorem 4. Any non-zero component $x_{j}^{(0)}$ in a minimal solution $X^{(0)} = (x_{1}^{(0)}, x_{2}^{(0)}, ..., x_{n}^{(0)})^{T}$ must be equal to x_{j}^{*}.

Proof. Obviously there is $x_{j}^{(0)} \leq x_{j}^{*}$. From Theorem 2 and 3 there is $x_{j}^{(0)} \geq x_{j}^{*}$, so the theorem is correct.

Theorem 5. For $A \circ X = B$, let $X^{*} = (x_{1}^{*}, x_{2}^{*}, ..., x_{n}^{*})$ be its maximum solution, $a_{ij}^{*} = x_{j}^{*}\beta(a_{ij}\alpha b_{i})$, $A^{*} = (a_{ij}^{*})_{m \times n}$, then

(1) If $a_{ij}^{*} > 0$, then $a_{ij}^{*} = x_{j}^{*} = b_{i}/a_{ij}$ and $a_{ij} \cdot a_{ij}^{*} = b_{i}$;

(2) For any i there exists j such that $a_{ij} \cdot a_{ij}^{*} = a_{ij} \cdot x_{j}^{*} = b_{i}$;

(3) Denote $J_{k} = \{i \mid a_{ik}^{*} = x_{k}^{*}\}$, $k=1,2,...,n$. Suppose $J_{k_{1}}, J_{k_{2}}, \cdots, J_{k_{l}}$ is a subsequence of $J_{1}, J_{2}, \cdots, J_{n}$ such that $\{1,2,\cdots,m\} = \bigcup_{s=1}^{l} J_{k_{s}}$ and for any t with $1 \leq t \leq l$, there is $J_{k_{t}} - \bigcup_{s \neq t} J_{k_{s}} \neq \varnothing$, denote $X^{(0)} = (x_{1}^{(0)}, x_{2}^{(0)}, ..., x_{n}^{(0)})^{T}$ such

that $x_j^{(0)} = \begin{cases} x_j^*, \exists s \; such \; that \; j = k_s \\ \qquad 0, \qquad else \end{cases}$ then $X^{(0)}$ is a minimal solution of

$A \circ X = B$

Proof. See reference [4].

Theorem 5 tells us that a minimal solution means that some x_j are selected and their $x_j^{(0)}$ are set to be x_j^*, such that every constraint of $A \circ X = B$ holds and no one of them is unnecessary.

Theorem 5 is very useful. However, it has theoretical rather than practical value. In fact, it still is a difficult work to obtain the minimal solutions of $A \circ X = B$, although it usually is very easy to get the minimal solutions of $A \circ X = B$ directly by Theorem 5 when the dimensions of the system are small. So, we need to look for efficient algorithms to get the minimal solutions of $A \circ X = B$.

4   Graph Method and Branch Method

Reference [1] presented two new methods, graph method and branch method, to get all the minimal solutions of max-min fuzzy relation equations. Now we popularize these two methods into solving max-product fuzzy relation equations.

By Theorem 5 we only need to construct a bipartite graph for a given $A \circ X = B$, which is denoted as $G=<X,Q; E>$, where X is the set of all variables x_j, Q is the set of all equation q_i of $A \circ X = B$, $E = (A^*)_0$ is the 0-cut matrix of A^*. In fact, it is very simple to draw the graph G: plot each vertex, e.g. all components of X and Q, then x_j is connected with q_i iff $a_{ij}^* > 0$.

By Theorem 5, combining greed algorithm a concrete algorithm of getting the solution set of $A \circ X = B$ is given as follows.

Step 1. Compute X^*, identify whether X^* is solution of $A \circ X = B$. If X^* is not, stop! say $A \circ X = B$ has no solution; otherwise, computer $A^* = (a_{ij}^*)_{m \times n}$, and construct the corresponding bipartite graph G. If there are some q_i that each is connected only with one x_j, go to the next step, otherwise, go to Step 4.

Step 2. For the x_j connected with these q_i that each is connected only with one x_j, set $x_j^{(0)} = x_j^*$, and mark all q_i connected with these x_j.

Step 3. If all q_i have been marked, go to Step 6; otherwise, go to the next step.

Step 4. Select an x_j arbitrarily connected with an unmarked q_i, set $x_j^{(0)} = x_j^*$, and mark all the unmarked q_i connected with it.

Step 5. If there still are unmarked q_i, for these q_i go to Step 4; otherwise, go to the next step.

Step 6. Assign zero to the rest of variables that have not been assigned them values, and a quasi-minimal solution is obtained.

Step 7. If there are other possible manners in the above process of selecting those non-zero $x_j^{(0)}$, erase all the marks, go to Step 2 or Step 4 and select a manner different from the manners have been used to select those non-zero $x_j^{(0)}$ to get other quasi-minimal solutions; otherwise, go to the next step.

Step 8. For the obtained quasi-minimal solutions, test whether each quasi-minimal solution is a minimal solution by Theorem 5 to eliminate those non-minimal solutions.

Following we introduce branch method, which is based on graph method but can greatly reduce the repeatedly computation in graph method.

Step 1. As Step 1 of graph method.

Step 2. For the x_j connected with these q_i that each is connected only with one x_j, select an x_j arbitrarily from these x_j, set $x_j^{(0)} = x_j^*$, note the remained q_i connected with it beside it. Continuous this process until all these q_i have been noted.

Step 3. If all q_i have been noted, go to Step 6; otherwise, go to the next step.

Step 4. For the unnoted q_i, branch by those x_j connected with them. For each branch, set $x_j^{(0)} = x_j^*$, and note all the unnoted q_i connected with x_j beside it.

Step 5. If there are some branches that there still are unnoted q_i in each one, take one from these branches arbitrarily. If this branch is found that it will generate the same solutions with a discussed branch, cut this branch and come back to Step 5 again, otherwise, for the unnoted q_i in this branch, go to Step 4. If there is no branch that there still are unnoted q_i in it, go to the next step.

Step 6. For every branch, assign zero to the rest of variables that have not been assigned them values to get the quasi-minimal solutions.

Step 7. As Step 8 of graph method.

In Step 5 of branch method, if the selected x_j of a branch is identical with the selected x_j of another branch indifferent to the order of these x_j, it is easy to know these two branches will generate the same solutions and one of them should be cut.

5 Example

Here an example is given to illustrate the two methods. The max-product relation equations are:

$$\begin{bmatrix} 0.3 & 0.7 & 0.8 & 0.9 & 0.4 \\ 0.4 & 0.6 & 0.6 & 0.3 & 0.7 \\ 0.2 & 0.4 & 0.7 & 0.5 & 0.4 \\ 0.9 & 0.7 & 0.3 & 0.6 & 0.5 \end{bmatrix} \circ \begin{bmatrix} x_1 \\ x_2 \\ x_3 \\ x_4 \\ x_5 \end{bmatrix} = \begin{bmatrix} 0.6 \\ 0.6 \\ 0.4 \\ 0.7 \end{bmatrix}$$

It is easy to obtain $X^* = (7/9, 6/7, 4/7, 2/3, 6/7)^T$ and it is the maximum solution of this example. Furthermore,

$$A^* = \begin{array}{c} \\ \end{array} \begin{array}{ccccc} x_1 & x_2 & x_3 & x_4 & x_5 \\ \left[\begin{array}{ccccc} 0 & 6/7 & 0 & 2/3 & 0 \\ 0 & 0 & 0 & 0 & 6/7 \\ 0 & 0 & 4/7 & 0 & 0 \\ 7/9 & 0 & 0 & 0 & 0 \end{array} \right] & \begin{array}{c} q_1 \\ q_2 \\ q_3 \\ q_4 \end{array} \end{array}$$

The bipartite graph constructed by A^* is shown in Fig.1.

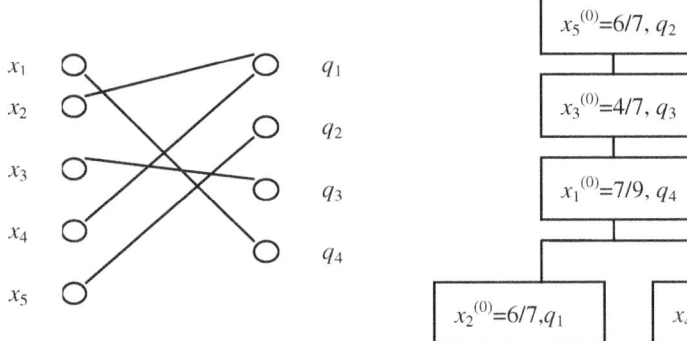

Fig. 1. The graph of the example   **Fig. 2.** Process of the example's branching

The graph method is used firstly. It is obvious that we must set $x_5^{(0)}=6/7$ in all minimal solutions of the example as q_2 is connected only with x_5. Similarly, we must set $x_3^{(0)}=4/7$ and $x_1^{(0)}=7/9$. After marking the corresponding q_i, q_1 is the remainder. The variables connected with q_1 are x_2 and x_4, hence if x_2 is selected a minimal solution $X_1^{(0)}=(7/9,6/7,4/7,0,6/7)^{\mathrm{T}}$ is obtained. It is easy to know the example has another minimal solution, $X_2^{(0)}=(7/9,0,4/7,2/3,6/7)^{\mathrm{T}}$ (see Fig. 1).

For branch method, the process of obtaining the minimal solutions of the example is shown in Fig.2 and the results are the same with graph method.

Acknowledgments. This research is supported by the project of New Century Higher Education Teaching Reform of Zhejiang Province (Grant No. zc2010034).

References

1. Chai, Z.L.: Solving the Minimal Solutions of Max-Min Fuzzy Relation Equation by Graph Method and Branch Method. In: 7th International Conference on Fuzzy Systems and Knowledge Discovery, pp. 319–324. IEEE Press, Yantai (2010)
2. Loia, V., Sessa, S.: Fuzzy Relation Equations for Coding/Decoding Processes of Images and Videos. Inform. Sci. 171, 145–172 (2005)

3. Loetamonphony, J., Fang, S.C., Young, R.E.: Multi-objective Optimization Problems with Fuzzy Relation Equation Constraints. Fuzzy Sets Syst. 127, 141–164 (2002)
4. Peng, Z.Z., Sun, Y.Y.: Fuzzy Mathematic and Its Application, 2nd edn. Wuhan University Press, Wuhan (2007) (in Chinese)
5. Hu, B.Q.: Basis of Fuzzy Theory. Wuhan University Press, Wuhan (2004) (in Chinese)
6. Markovskii, A.V.: On the Relation between Equations with Max-Product Composition and the Covering Problem. Fuzzy Sets Syst. 153, 261–273 (2005)
7. Molai, A.A., Khorram, E.: An Algorithm for Solving Fuzzy Relation Equations with Max-T Composition Operator. Inform. Sci. 178, 1293–1308 (2008)

On the Notion of IF-Shadows

Kankana Chakrabarty and Ioan Despi

School of Science and Technology, University of New England,
Armidale-2351, NSW, Australia
{kankanac,despi}@turing.une.edu.au

Abstract. In this paper, we review the notions of IF-Bags and Fuzzy Shadows and define the notion of IF-Shadows. We discuss some scenarios where real-life knowledge can be represented in the form of IF-Shadows. In this context we further study some characteristics of IF-Shadows.

1 Introduction

The shadow of a multiset was defined by extending Multiset Theory (MST) to Multiset Theory over Z (MSTZ) [3,4,5]. It was found that MSTZ is relatively consistent as it contains both MST and Zermelo–Fraenkel set theory (ZF) as special cases. In [6] Chakrabarty, Biswas, and Nanda further generalized MSTZ to Fuzzy Bag Theory over Z (FBTZ) and consequently the notion of fuzzy shadows was defined which can be regarded as a generalization of fuzzy bags [12,11,10,9]. The applicability of fuzzy shadows was discussed in [7]. The notion of fuzzy bags was generalized based on Atanassov's notion of Intuitionistic Fuzzy Sets (IFS) [1,2] and this study resulted in the introduction of Intuitionistic Fuzzy Bags (IFB) [9]. Further, some properties of IF-bags were discussed in [8]. In this paper, we generalize the notion of fuzzy shadows [6] on the basis of IF-Bags [9,8] and henceforth the notion of IF-shadows is proposed and studied.

2 IF-Bags and Fuzzy Shadows, an Overview

In this section, we briefly furnish the notions of IF-Bags [9] and fuzzy shadows [6,7] and discuss some of the basic operations defined on them [9,6,7].

If X is a non-empty set, then an IF-bag A drawn from X is characterized by a function

$$CM_A : X \longrightarrow Q$$

where Q represents the set of all crisp bags drawn from $I \times I$ where $I = [0,1]$. Hence, for any $x \in X$, $CM_A(x)$ is a bag drawn from $I \times I$ and

$$C_{CM_A(x)} : I \times I \longrightarrow \mathbb{N}$$

is the count function for $CM_A(x)$. Clealy, for all A, $C_{CM_A(0)}(0,0) = 0$.

H. Deng et al. (Eds.): AICI 2011, Part I, LNAI 7002, pp. 566–570, 2011.

For any set X, there exists an IF-bag drawn from X (denoted by ϕ) such that for each $x \in X$, $CM_\phi(x)$ is an empty bag. In other words, $C_{CM_\phi(x)}(\alpha, \beta) = 0$, for each $x \in X$ and $(\alpha, \beta) \in I \times I$. Here we call ϕ the null IF-bag.

The IF-bags A and B drawn from X are said to be equal if, for all $x \in X$, $CM_A(x) = CM_B(x)$. A is called a sub-bag of B, denoted by $A \sqsubseteq B$, if for all $x \in X$, $(\alpha, \beta) \in I \times I$, $C_{CM_A(x)}(\alpha, \beta) \le C_{CM_B(x)}(\alpha, \beta)$.

For IF-bags A and B drawn from X,

The addition of A and B is an IF-bag, denoted by $A \oplus B$, such that $\forall x \in X$ and $\forall (\alpha, \beta) \in I \times I$,

$$C_{CM_{A \oplus B}(x)}(\alpha, \beta) = C_{CM_A(x)}(\alpha, \beta) + C_{CM_B(x)}(\alpha, \beta)$$

The removal of B from A results in an IF-bag, denoted by $A \ominus B$, such that $\forall x \in X$ and $\forall (\alpha, \beta) \in I \times I$,

$$C_{CM_{A \ominus B}(x)}(\alpha, \beta) = max\{C_{CM_A(x)}(\alpha, \beta) - C_{CM_B(x)}(\alpha, \beta), 0\}$$

The union of A and B is an IF-bag denoted by $A \sqcup B$, such that $\forall x \in X$ and $\forall (\alpha, \beta) \in I \times I$,

$$C_{CM_{A \sqcup B}(x)}(\alpha, \beta) = max\{C_{CM_A(x)}(\alpha, \beta), C_{CM_B(x)}(\alpha, \beta)\}$$

The intersection of A and B is an IF-bag, denoted by $A \sqcap B$, such that $\forall x \in X$ and $\forall (\alpha, \beta) \in I \times I$,

$$C_{CM_{A \sqcap B}(x)}(\alpha, \beta) = min\{C_{CM_A(x)}(\alpha, \beta), C_{CM_B(x)}(\alpha, \beta)\}$$

Let X be any set. Then a '*shadow formed from the objects of X*' is characterized by

$$\psi : X \longrightarrow \mathbb{Z}$$

where $\mathbb{Z}$ is the set of integers and, for $x \in X$, $\psi(x)$ denotes the number of occurrences of x in the shadow, also called '*a shadow in X*'. Clearly, all such shadows are in MSTZ.

In FBTZ, a fuzzy bag F drawn from a set X is characterized by

$$CM_F : X \longrightarrow W$$

where W denotes the set of all the shadows drawn from I, i.e., for each $x \in X$, $CM_F(x)$ is a shadow in I. A fuzzy bag drawn from a set X in FBTZ is called a '*a fuzzy shadow in X*'.

For each $\alpha \in I$, the number of occurrences of α in $CM_F(x)$ is determined by $O_x^F : I \longrightarrow \mathbb{Z}$. For a fuzzy bag F drawn from X, the shadow of F, denoted by $shaf\{F\}$, is characterized by the function $CM_{shaf\{F\}} : X \longrightarrow W$, where $CM_{shaf\{F\}}(x) = shaf\{CM_F(x)\}$.

For any two fuzzy shadows S_1 and S_2 in X,

S_1 is called the fuzzy subshadow of S_2, denoted $S_1 \sqsubseteq S_2$, if $O_x^{S_1}C(\alpha) \le O_X^{S_2}(\alpha)$, $\forall x \in X$ and $\alpha \in I$.

The sum of S_1 and S_2 is a fuzzy shadow S in X given by $S = S_1 \oplus S_2$, such that $\forall x \in X, \alpha \in I, O_x^S(\alpha) = O_x^{S_1}(\alpha) + O_x^{S_2}(\alpha)$

The union of S_1 and S_2 is a fuzzy shadow S in X, denoted by $S = S_1 \sqcup S_2$, such that $O_x^S(\alpha) = max\{O_x^{S_1}(\alpha), O_x^{S_2}(\alpha)\}$, $\forall x \in X$ and $\alpha \in I$.

The intersection of S_1 and S_2 is a fuzzy shadow S in X, denoted by $S = S_1 \sqcap S_2$, such that $O_x^S(\alpha) = min\{O_x^{S_1}(\alpha), O_x^{S_2}(\alpha)\}$, $\forall x \in X$ and $\alpha \in I$.

The complement of a fuzzy shadow S in X, denoted by S', is such that $CM_{S'}(x) = sha\{CM_S(x)\}$, $\forall x \in X$.

3   IF-Shadows

In this section, we generalize IF-bags theory over $\mathbb{Z}$ and we call it Intuitionistic Fuzzy Bag Theory over Z (IFBTZ).

An IF-bag ϕ drawn from a set X in IFBTZ is characterized by

$$CM_\phi : X \longrightarrow S$$

where S denotes the set of all the shadows drawn from $I \times I$.

An IF-bag drawn from X in IFBTZ is called an *IF-shadow* drawn from X, or an IF-shadow in X. For each $x \in X$, $CM_\phi(x)$ is a shadow in $I \times I$.

For each $(\alpha, \beta) \in I \times I$, the number of occurrences of (α, β) in $CM_\phi(x)$ is determined by the functional value $O_x^\phi(\alpha, \beta)$ of $O_x^\phi : I \times I \longrightarrow \mathbb{Z}$.

An IF-shadow ϕ in X is called a null IF-shadow if $\forall x \in X$ and $(\alpha, \beta) \in I \times I$, $O_x^\phi(\alpha, \beta) = 0$. A null IF-shadow is denoted by φ.

For an IF-bag ϕ drawn from X, the shadow of ϕ, denoted by $shadow\{\phi\}$, is characterized by $CM_{shadow\{\phi\}} : X \longrightarrow S$. It is evident that the shadow of an IF-bag is an IF-shadow.

Two IF-shadows ϕ_1 and ϕ_2 in X are called equal if $CM_{\phi_1}(x) = CM_{\phi_2}(x)$, $\forall x \in X$ and hence $O_x^{\phi_1}(\alpha, \beta) = O_x^{\phi_2}(\alpha, \beta)$, $\forall x \in X$ and $(\alpha, \beta) \in I \times I$.

For any two IF-shadows ϕ_1 and ϕ_2 in X, ϕ_1 is called the IF-subshadow of ϕ_2, denoted by $\phi_1 \sqsubseteq \phi_2$, if $\forall x \in X$ and $(\alpha, \beta) \in I \times I$,

$$O_x^{\phi_1}C(\alpha, \beta) \le O_X^{\phi_2}(\alpha, \beta)$$

It is evident that for any IF-shadow ϕ, $\varphi \sqsubseteq \phi$, $\phi \sqsubseteq \phi$.

The sum of two IF-shadows ϕ_1 and ϕ_2 is an IF-shadow in X, denoted by $\phi = \phi_1 \oplus \phi_2$, such that $\forall x \in X, (\alpha, \beta) \in I \times I$,

$$O_x^\phi(\alpha, \beta) = O_x^{\phi_1}(\alpha, \beta) + O_x^{\phi_2}(\alpha, \beta)$$

The union of ϕ_1 and ϕ_2 is an IF-shadow, denoted by $\phi_1 \sqcup \phi_2$, such that $\forall x \in X$ and $(\alpha, \beta) \in I \times I$,

$$O_x^\phi(\alpha, \beta) = max\{O_x^{\phi_1}(\alpha, \beta), O_x^{\phi_2}(\alpha, \beta)\}$$

The intersection of ϕ_1 and ϕ_2 is an IF-shadow, denoted by $\phi_1 \sqcap \phi_2$, such that $\forall x \in X$ and $(\alpha, \beta) \in I \times I$,

$$O_x^\phi(\alpha, \beta) = min\{O_x^{\phi_1}(\alpha, \beta), O_x^{\phi_2}(\alpha, \beta)\}$$

IF ϕ_1, ϕ_2 and ϕ_3 are three IF-shadows in a set X, then the follwing hold:

$$\phi_1 \sqcup (\phi_2 \sqcup \phi_3) = (\phi_1 \sqcup \phi_2) \sqcup \phi_3$$
$$\phi_1 \sqcap (\phi_2 \sqcap \phi_3) = (\phi_1 \sqcap \phi_2) \sqcap \phi_3$$
$$\phi_1 \sqcap (\phi_2 \sqcup \phi_3) = (\phi_1 \sqcap \phi_2) \sqcup (\phi_1 \sqcap \phi_3)$$
$$\phi_1 \sqcup (\phi_2 \sqcap \phi_3) = (\phi_1 \sqcup \phi_2) \sqcap (\phi_1 \sqcup \phi_3)$$

We now furnish a rel-life knowledge representation scenario where IF-shadows can be applied.

Let us consider a collection of cluster types $X = \{X_1, X_2, \ldots, X_n\}$ in an information system. We assume that each expert in a collection of experts E_k (k = 1, 2, ..., m) assigns for each cluster type in X an object importance factor (which is intutionistic fuzzy in nature) $I_{X_i}^{E_k} \in I \times I$ and a number $C_{X_i}^{E_k} \in \mathbb{Z}$ indicating the possibilistic number of indiscernible types $X_i \in X$ to be accepted or rejected for an analysis. Evidently, $\sum_k C_{X_i}^{E_k} \in \mathbb{Z}$ for each $X_i \in X$ and the value of $\sum_k C_{X_i}^{E_k}$ is a variable that can vary over time for each $X_i \in X$.

Case-I: If for any $X_i \in X$, $\sum_k C_{X_i}^{E_k} = 0$, then this clearly indicates that we do not need to accept or reject any of the $X_i \in X$.

Case-II: If for any $X_i \in X$, $\sum_k C_{X_i}^{E_k} > 0$, then we need to accept $\sum_k C_{O_i}^{E_k}$ numbers of $X_i \in X$.

Case-III: If for any $X_i \in X$, $\sum_k C_{X_i}^{E_k} < 0$, then we need to reject $\sum_k C_{O_i}^{E_k}$ numbers of $X_i \in X$.

4   Conclusions

In this paper, we briefly discussed the notions of IF-Bags and fuzzy shadows and defined the notion of IF-Shadows by generalizing the notion of IF-Bags. We further discussed how some real-life knowledge can be represented in the form of IF-Shadows. In this context we studied some properties of IF-Shadows. In future, our work will involve the application of IF-shadows in database modelling.

References

1. Atanassov, K.T.: Intuitionistic fuzzy sets. Fuzzy Sets and Systems 20(1), 87–96 (1986)
2. Atanassov, K.T.: Remark on the intuitionistic fuzzy sets. Fuzzy Sets and Systems 51(1), 117–118 (1992)
3. Blizard, W.D.: Multiset Theory. Notre Dame Journal of Formal Logic 30, 36–66 (1989)
4. Blizard, W.D.: Negative Membership. Notre Dame Journal of Formal Logic 31(3), 346–368 (1990)

5. Blizard, W.D.: A Theory of Shadows (An Informal Discussion of Negative Membership). ANPA WEST, Journal of the Western Regional Chapter of the Alternative Natural Philosophy Association 1(30), 7–9 (1989)
6. Chakrabarty, K., Biswas, R., Nanda, S.: Fuzzy Shadows. Fuzzy Sets and Systems 101(3), 413–421 (1999)
7. Chakrabarty, K., Nanda, S.: Fuzzy Shadows in Knowledge Modeling. In: Proc. Third International Conference on Advances in Computing, Control, and Communication (ICAC3 CD). ACM, New York (2009)
8. Chakrabarty, K.: IF-Bags in Decision Analysis. Notes on IFS 7/3, 8–13 (2001)
9. Chakrabarty, K.: On IF-Bags. Notes on IFS 5(2), 53–65 (1999)
10. Chakrabarty, K.: On Bags and Fuzzy Bags. In: Advances in Soft Computing, Soft Computing Techniques and Applications, pp. 201–212. Physica-Verlag, Heidelberg (2000)
11. Chakrabarty, K., Biswas, R., Nanda, S.: On Yager's theory of Bags and Fuzzy bags. Computers and Artificial Intelligence 18(1), 1–17 (1999)
12. Yager, R.R.: On the Theory of Bags. International Journal of General Systems 13, 23–37 (1986)

Evaluation on System Risk of Capsule Object Piped Hydraulic Transportation Based on Fuzzy Analytic Hierarchy Process

Rui Wang*, Xihuan Sun, and Yongye Li

Taiyuan University of Technology
Taiyuan, China
wangrui01@tyut.edu.cn

Abstract. For pipeline risk in the capsule object hydraulic transportation, the paper introduces Fuzzy Analytic Hierarchy Process (FAHP), which gives security policy for the reasonable design of the capsule object hydraulic transportation technology, to reflect the risk of pipeline by the calculation of risk indicators' weights on the advantages of fuzzy events.

Keywords: Fuzzy Analytic Hierarchy Process, Capsule Object, hydraulic Transportation, Risk Evaluation.

1 Introduction

In recent years, national research staff conducts risk evaluation for long distance water pipeline by comprehensive use of methods such as Expert Rating, Fault Tree, Fuzzy Math and so on. While related technologies develop rapidly, the study of system management technology for the capsule object hydraulic transportation pipeline just begins. Still gaps in many areas. The piped hydraulic transportation of capsule object mainly relaying on the water flow in pressure pipes to transport material. Such that, by analyzing the risk factors of the pipe, measures of pipe's maintenance and test during the running process can be worked out directly. According to the grading of risk factors, risk managements can manage the risks of the project and find the weak links of the system reliability. For the high-level risk factors, risk strategy is made to control accident and improve the system ability [1].

To gain more accurate results about pipe risk and better guide the pipe management practice, higher requirements about comprehensive knowledge of experts or professors and reasonable distribution of evaluation index weights have been proposed, among which the accuracy of risk evaluation result is directly related to the distribution of weights. To reduce human factors such as subjective differences, knowledge structure differences, engineering practice ability differences and so on, more rigorous approach is necessary to seek to make the weights distribution more reasonably and accurately reflect that where risk of the capsule object hydraulic transportation pipeline exists.

---

* Corresponding author.

H. Deng et al. (Eds.): AICI 2011, Part I, LNAI 7002, pp. 571–579, 2011.

2 Brief Introduction about the System of Capsule Object Hydraulic Transportation Pipeline

The technique of piped hydraulic transportation of capsule object is a new transportation technique which was proposed in recent years. It is a new piped hydraulic transportation technique which bases on theories of hydraulic and makes water as the vector. Raw material (liquid or solid) is loaded and sealed in the cylindrical capsule, and then the capsule is put into the transportation pipeline. The capsule's movement is pushed by flowing water to achieve material transportation. The greatest feature of the transportation technology not only is the economical and practical, but also the combination of energy-conserving and environment-protective.

2.1 Pipe System

The system of capsule object hydraulic transportation pipeline mainly composed four sections as power device, capsule put-in device, pipeline and capsule receive device. During the running process, water is firstly pumped from underground reservoir to water-transported steel tube by the water-pump, and then input to the synthetic glass pipe. The capsule is put into pipe through the put-in device and fixed by the brake. The flow discharge is regulated to the required by the gate valve. When discharge is steady, the brake is relieved and the capsule is released. Every hydraulic factor during the capsule's running is measured in the test pipe section. Finally, water flows into the underground reservoir after passing the water outlet pool and forms a closed circulation loop. Schematic diagram of the running pipe is shown in Fig.1.

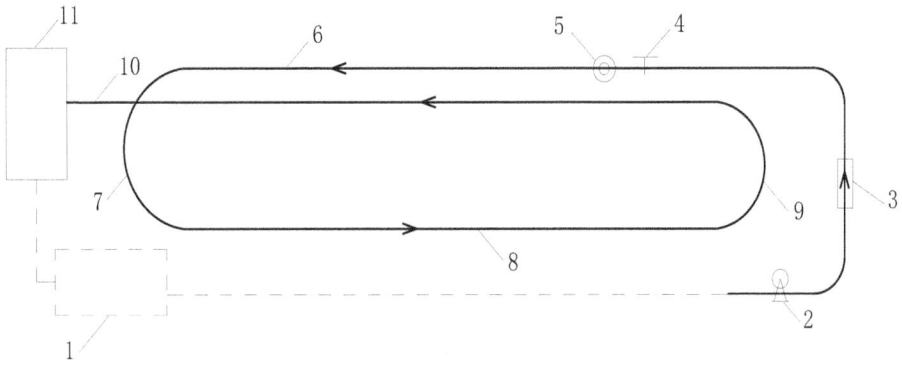

1 underground reservoir; 2 centrifugal pump; 3 turbine flow meter; 4 gate valve; 5 capsule put-in device; 6 liner pipe section a; 7 flat bend pipe section; 8 liner pipe section b; 9 oblique bend pipe section; 10 liner pipe section c; 11 capsule receive device

Fig. 1. The layout chart of experimental system device

2.2 Capsule Object

Compared with the traditional piped hydraulic transportation, the unique of the capsule object piped hydraulic transportation as a new technique of piped hydraulic transportation firstly lies in which material is loaded into the material tube directly to achieve the pure material transportation. Secondly, it's unique is that separately installing cylindrical iron braces showing to the same interval angle of 120 at both side of the barrel and fixing universal rolling balls at the bottom of the braces. It makes material tube's axis and pipe's axis coincide consistently whether it stay still or run in the pipe. That is to say keeping same-axis moving when capsule runs in the pipe.

3   Establishment of Fuzzy Analytic Hierarchy Process Model

3.1   Fuzzy Analytic Hierarchy Process [2]

Fuzzy Analytic Hierarchy Process is the combination of fuzzy number and analytical hierarchy process, which is decomposition layer by layer to problems. It is a method which gains weight order by quantitative judgment and comprehensive assessment. So the first step of fuzzy hierarchical analysis process is to classify the factors involved in the problem and find the relationship to construct a hierarchical layer structure model.

The basic idea of Fuzzy Analytic Hierarchy Process is as follow. Firstly, when the comparison between each pair is being conducted, the comparison's result is expressed by triangle module (l, m, u). In the module, the m represents the importance degree of the two projects. The l and u represent the fuzzy degree of the judgment. The bigger the (u-l) is, the higher the fuzzy degree is. The u-l=0 represents that the judgment is non-fuzzy. The importance comparison between project j and project i is represented to Triangle fuzzy number a_{ij}^{-1}. After $\dfrac{n(n-1)}{2}$ fuzzy judgments being given, the fuzzy judgment matrix $A = \left(a_{ij}\right)_{n \times n}$ composed by triangle fuzzy numbers can be gained. Secondly, to obtain the project order under given rules, the comprehensive importance $d(A_i)$ of the comparison between every factor and all factors in this layer. After normalize treatment, the sort vector $W = [d(A_1), d(A_2), \cdots, d(A_n)]$ is gained.

3.2   Several Key Factors of Fuzzy Analytic Hierarchy Process

3.2.1   Quantity scale

Establish the judge matrix as $A = \left(a_{ij}\right)_{n \times n}$, in which there are $a_{ij} = \left(l_{ij}, m_{ij}, u_{ij}\right)$ and $a_{ji} = \left(l_{ji}, m_{ji}, u_{ji}\right)$. If there are $l_{ij} + u_{ji} = m_{ij} + m_{ji} = u_{ij} + l_{ji} = 1$, $u_{ij} \geq m_{ij} \geq l_{ij} \geq 0$ and $i, j \in N$, then call A as fuzzy number complementary judgment matrix [3].

To quantitatively describe the relative importance degree of any two projects about some guidelines, 0.1-0.9 scaling procedure shown in Table.1 is used to give quantity scale.

Table 1. 0.1-0.9 scaling procedure and expressive meaning

scale	definition	explanation
0.5	equally important	Compare the two factors, they are equally important.
0.6	somewhat important	Compare the two factors, one is somewhat important.
0.7	obviously important	Compare the two factors, one is obviously important.
0.8	much more important	Compare the two factors; one is much more important than the other.
0.9	extremely important	Compare the two factors, one is extremely important.
0.1,0.2, 0.3,0.4 anti-comparison	If compare factor m_i and factor m_j and obtain judgment m_{ij} ,then the judgment obtained after comparing factor m_j and factor m_i is $m_{ji} = 1 - m_{ij}$.	

Of which, the m_{ii} represents the equal importance when the factor compare with itself. The $m_{ij} \in [0.1, 0.5)$ represents that factor m_j is more important than m_i . The $m_{ij} \in (0.5, 0.9)$ represents that factor m_i is more important than m_j .

3.2.2 Weight Matrix [4]

For a structure with levels, a hierarchical structure is a model of a situation. The relative strength of influence from different factors in low level to the upper or total target is called weight. The calculation formula of triangle fuzzy number complementary judgment matrix weight is:

$$d_i = \frac{\sum_{j=1}^{n} m_{ij} + \frac{n}{2} - 1}{n(n-1)} , i = 1, 2, \cdots, n \tag{1}$$

By row and normalize treatment, it can be obtained that $W = (d_1, d_2, \cdots, d_n)$ is the sort vector of matrix A.

The weight matrix $W = (d_{ij})_{n \times n}$ of fuzzy complementary judgment matrix A is:

$$d_{ij} = d_i - d_j + 0.5 , i = 1, 2, \cdots, n \tag{2}$$

3.2.3 Compatibility Index and Consistency Index

If both A and B are fuzzy complementary matrixes and W is the weight matrix of A , then

$$CI(A,B) = \frac{1}{n^2} \sum_{i=1}^{n} \sum_{j=1}^{n} \left| a_{ij} - b_{ij} \right| \qquad (3)$$

is called as the compatibility index of A and B.

$$CI(A,W) = \frac{1}{n^2} \sum_{i=1}^{n} \sum_{j=1}^{n} \left| a_{ij} - d_{ij} \right| \qquad (4)$$

is called as the consistency index of A.

When the consistency index is $CI(A,W) \leq \alpha$, then A is acceptable consistency. When the compatibility index is $CI(A,B) \leq \alpha$, then the estimation matrix is considered to satisfy consistency. Among these, α is the attitude of decision-makers. The smaller α indicates decision-makers' higher requirements about the consistency of the fuzzy estimation matrix. Generally speaking, there is $\alpha = 0.1$.

3.2.4 Risk Factors Order [2]

The total order of risk factor level means to calculate the order weight of the all factors in the same level relative to the highest level (target layer). This process is conducted layer by layer from the highest level to the lowest level. If the upper layer A contains k factors as $A_1, A_2, \cdots, A_k$ and it's total order weights respectively are $d_1, d_2, \cdots, d_k$. There are n factors $B_1, B_2, \cdots, B_n$ contained in the lower layer and the layer single order weights of them respectively are $\beta_{j1}, \beta_{j2}, \cdots, \beta_{jn}$ (If there is no contact between B_r and A_j, then there is $B_{jr} = 0$.) relative to the factors A_j. Now, the total weight of the layer B is

$$\beta_j = \sum_{r=1}^{k} d_r \beta_{jr} \qquad (5)$$

4 Analysis about Risk of Capsule Object Hydraulic Transportation Pipeline Based on Fuzzy Analytic Hierarchy Process

4.1 Construction of Hierarchical Structure of the Factors of Risk Evaluation Factors

Hierarchical analysis model layers of the risk factors consist of the follows:

Target layer (A): Presents quantified target of risk, that is to say risk factor order.
Rule layer (B): Presents ordering the risk factors from the two rules which are risk probability and losses brought from the occurrence of risk.

Factor layer (C): Presents the risk factors existing in the project. Usually, there are many risk factors in the project, so the factor layer is multilayer. If some sub-element layer contains many factors (more than nine), the layer should be further divided into several sub-layers.

Combining with the actual situation of the piped hydraulic transportation technique of capsule object, the system of piped risk evaluation on the hydraulic transportation of capsule object is constructed as shown as Fig2.

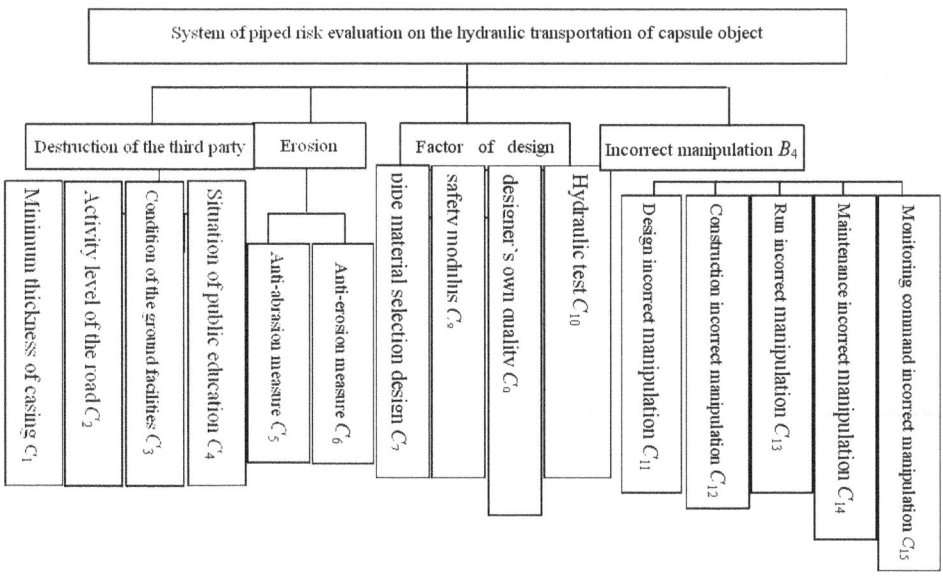

Fig. 2. Hierarchical chart of the factors of pipe risk evaluation on the piped hydraulic transportation of capsule object

Table 2. (a) Fuzzy estimation matrix on B1-B4 to A

A	B_1	B_2	B_3	B_4
B_1	(0.5,0.5,0.5)	(0.2,0.2,0.4)	(0.4,0.4,0.5)	(0.3,0.3,0.4)
B_2	(0.6,0.8,0.8)	(0.5,0.5,0.5)	(0.6,0.7,0.7)	(0.5,0.6,0.7)
B_3	(0.5,0.6,0.6)	(0.3,0.3,0.4)	(0.5,0.5,0.5)	(0.3,0.4,0.4)
B_4	(0.6,0.7,0.7)	(0.3,0.4,0.5)	(0.6,0.6,0.7)	(0.5,0.5,0.5)

Table 2(b) fuzzy estimation matrix on C1-C4 to B1

B	C_1	C_2	C_3	C_4
C_1	(0.5,0.5,0.5)	(0.6,0.6,0.7)	(0.5,0.6,0.6)	(0.7,0.7,0.8)
C_2	(0.3,0.4,0.4)	(0.5,0.5,0.5)	(0.6,0.6,0.7)	(0.6,0.7,0.7)
C_3	(0.4,0.4,0.5)	(0.3,0.4,0.4)	(0.5,0.5,0.5)	(0.4,0.6,0.6)
C_4	(0.2,0.3,0.3)	(0.3,0.3,0.4)	(0.4,0.4,0.6)	(0.5,0.5,0.5)

4.2 Construction of Estimation Matrix

According to the requirements of the whole target, the fuzzy complementary estimation matrix shown in Fig2 is worked out through the fuzzy comparison to evaluation indicators conducted by experts.

Similarly, fuzzy estimation matrixes on C5-C6 to B2, C7-C10 to B3, C11-C15 to B4 can be obtained.

4.3 Level Sorting as Well as Calculation of Compatibility and Consistency

According to formula (1), the sort vectors of fuzzy complementary estimation matrixes are separately obtained by row and normalized treatment. The vectors are as follow:

$$W_A = (0.2, 0.3, 0.233, 0.267) \; ; \; W_{B1} = (0.283, 0.267, 0.242, 0.208) \; ; \; W_{B2} = (0.55, 0.45) \; ;$$
$$W_{B3} = (0.283, 0.258, 0.242, 0.217); \; W_{B4} = (0.23, 0.22, 0.2, 0.175, 0.175)$$

According to formula (2), the weight matrixes of the fuzzy complementary estimation matrixes separately are calculated as follow:

$$W_A^* = \begin{pmatrix} 0.5 & 0.4 & 0.467 & 0.433 \\ 0.4 & 0.5 & 0.567 & 0.533 \\ 0.533 & 0.433 & 0.5 & 0.466 \\ 0.567 & 0.467 & 0.534 & 0.5 \end{pmatrix} \quad W_{B1}^* = \begin{pmatrix} 0.5 & 0.516 & 0.541 & 0.575 \\ 0.484 & 0.5 & 0.525 & 0.559 \\ 0.459 & 0.475 & 0.5 & 0.534 \\ 0.425 & 0.441 & 0.466 & 0.5 \end{pmatrix} \quad W_{B2}^* = \begin{pmatrix} 0.5 & 0.6 \\ 0.4 & 0.5 \end{pmatrix}$$

$$W_{B3}^* = \begin{pmatrix} 0.5 & 0.525 & 0.541 & 0.566 \\ 0.475 & 0.5 & 0.516 & 0.541 \\ 0.459 & 0.484 & 0.5 & 0.525 \\ 0.434 & 0.459 & 0.475 & 0.5 \end{pmatrix}$$

$$W_{B4}^* = \begin{pmatrix} 0.5 & 0.51 & 0.53 & 0.555 & 0.555 \\ 0.49 & 0.5 & 0.52 & 0.545 & 0.545 \\ 0.47 & 0.48 & 0.5 & 0.525 & 0.525 \\ 0.445 & 0.455 & 0.475 & 0.5 & 0.5 \\ 0.445 & 0.455 & 0.475 & 0.5 & 0.5 \end{pmatrix}$$

According to formula (3) and (4), test the consistency and coherence to the value given by experts. Specific results are as follow:

$$CI(B1, B2) = 0.0875 < 0.1; \; CI(B1, B3) = 0.0125 < 0.1;$$
$$CI(B1, B4) = 0.0400 < 0.1; \; CI(B2, B3) = 0.0750 < 0.1;$$
$$CI(B2, B4) = 0.0960 < 0.1; \; CI(B3, B4) = 0.0480 < 0.1;$$

$$CI\left(A,W_{A}^{*}\right)=0.0958<0.1;\ CI\left(B1,W_{B1}^{*}\right)=0.0688<0.1;$$

$$CI\left(B2,W_{B2}^{*}\right)=0.0000<0.1;\ CI\left(B3,W_{B3}^{*}\right)=0.0608<0.1;$$

$$CI\left(B4,W_{B4}^{*}\right)=0.05280<0.1$$

Through the above calculation results, all of the estimation matrixes meet the requirements of compatibility and consistency.

4.4 Total Order of Factor Layer to Target Layer [4]

The hierarchical total order is conducted on the basic of hierarchical single order. Specific is as shown in Fig3.

target layer A	rule layer B	weight	factor layer C	weight	total weight
Factors of pipe risk evaluation on the piped hydraulic transportation of tube-contained raw material	destruction of the third party B1	0.200	minimum thickness of casing C1	0.283	0.0566
			activity level of the road C2	0.267	0.0534
			condition of the ground facilities C3	0.242	0.0484
			situation of public education C4	0.208	0.0416
	erosion B2	0.300	anti-abrasion measure C5	0.550	0.1650
			anti-erosion measure C6	0.450	0.1350
	factor of design B3	0.233	pipe material selection design C7	0.283	0.0659
			safety modulus C8	0.258	0.0601
			designer's own quality C9	0.242	0.0564
			hydraulic test C10	0.217	0.0506
	incorrect manipulation B4	0.267	design incorrect manipulation C11	0.230	0.0614
			construction incorrect manipulation C12	0.220	0.0587
			run incorrect manipulation C13	0.200	0.0534
			maintenance incorrect manipulation C14	0.175	0.0467
			monitoring command incorrect manipulation C15	0.175	0.0467

Fig. 3. Total ordering on the factor stratum to the target stratum

According to the value of weight, factor layer B of the pipe in hydraulic transportation of capsule object is divided into these levels as: weight which is greater or equal to 0.280 is high-level risk; weight which is less than 0.280 and greater or equal to 0.250 is medium level; weight which is less than 0.250 is low-level risk. According to Fig3, high-level risk= [erosion]; medium-level risk= [incorrect manipulation]; low-level risk= [destruction of the third party and the factor of design]. Similarly, factor layer C can be divided into levels.

5 Conclusion

The paper firstly has elaborated the necessity of risk evaluation about capsule object piped hydraulic transportation. Then hierarchical chart of the factors of pipe risk evaluation on capsule object hydraulic transportation and fuzzy judge matrix are constructed by using Fuzzy Analytic Hierarchy Process. Hierarchical order as well as calculation of compatibility and consistency has been conducted too, on the basic of which pipe risk factors of capsule object hydraulic transportation has been ordered totally. And also, risk factors have been divided into levels. In the practical application, experts can order the importance of each risk factor just after giving the information of pair comparison judgment about risk factors. Next, measures of pipe's maintenance and test during the running process can be worked out directly according to the order result. According to the risk factor grading, risk managements can manage risks in the project, find the weak links of system reliability, develop risk strategies, control accident occurrence and improve the system reliability.

Acknowledgement. This work is supported by the Fundamental Research Funds for the Central Universities of China (serial number⊡ 50579044).

References

1. Ma, Z.: Risk Management of Oil and Gas. Long Transportation Pipeline. Oil and Gas Storage and Transportation 24(2), 1–7 (2005)
2. Jo, Y.D., Park, K.S., Ahn, B.J.: Risk Assessment for a High-pressure Natural Has Pipeline in an Urban Area. Ecology and the Environment 72(10), 748–755 (2004)
3. Zhang, w.-y., Yao, a.-l., Li, y.-l., Li, k., Wu, x.-l.: Hierarchy and Fuzzy Evaluation of Embedded Gas Pipeline. China Safety Science Journal 16(8), 32–36 (2006)
4. Huang, H., Yu, S., Zhou, Y.: The Application of Fuzzy Comprehensive Evaluation Methord Based on AHP on Scheme Evaluation. Value Engineering 26(1), 84–86 (2007)

Design and Implementation of a Modified 1.5v High Speed Fuzzy Controller in Switched-Cap Technique

Seied Zaniar Hoseini, Seied Veria Hoseini, Amir Kousari, and Johar Abdekhoda

Islamic Azad University, Ghorveh Branch, Ghorveh, Iran
z.hoseini1983@gmail.com, hvorya@yahoo.com,
amir_kousari@yahoo.com, johar1983@gmail.com

Abstract. In this paper design of an improved high speed efficient fuzzy logic controller in switched-cap technique is proposed. The controller takes advantage of an improved fuzzifier with less power consumption compared to what previously has been proposed, a high speed minimum circuit (MIN) and a new structure for high speed voltage mode divider. Pipeline structure, high speed, low power supply and voltage mode operation causes more adaption with digital and discrete time analog portable systems. The controller was integrated in a 0.35-µm standard complementary CMOS technology. It occupies 0.14 mm^2 silicon area and is powered by a 1.5-V power supply while dissipating only 45mW. Input and output signals lie in a 1-V range with respect to the analog ground (i.e., 0 V).

Keywords: CMOS technology, controller, fuzzy, maximum, membership function, minimum, switched capacitor (SC).

1 Introduction

Over the last decade, signal processing based on fuzzy logic has been attracting more and more attention from the scientific community due to its intrinsic characteristic of solving complex problems in a manner very close to human reasoning. Great successes have been achieved in certain fields of applications [4]. In the literature, there are a large number of very large-scale integration (VLSI) implementations of basic building blocks or fuzzy systems that use digital or analog processing [2], [5]. Digital processing has the advantage of a simple design procedure but it needs larger silicon area compared to its equivalent analog implementation. Moreover, if the fuzzy system needs to communicate with the real world, analog-to-digital (A/D) and digital-to-analog (D/A) converters must be implemented for its inputs and outputs.

A good compromise between area requirements, speed response and accuracy appears to be realization using the switched capacitor (SC) technique. In this brief, we present a simple analog fuzzy controller in SC technique with two inputs and one output. The modified controller is based on the architecture described in [1] and uses two new circuits for Minimum (MIN) and deffuzification blocks. In improved architecture most blocks need only one clock cycles for their perfect operation that yields to a high speed pipelined system. Simple circuit design, high speed operation

H. Deng et al. (Eds.): AICI 2011, Part I, LNAI 7002, pp. 580–590, 2011.
© Springer-Verlag Berlin Heidelberg 2011

and low silicon area occupation, are the most important specifications of realized controller.

2 Fuzzy Controller

2.1 System Description

In this brief we have focused our attention on a two-input single output singleton fuzzy controller with symmetric triangular input membership functions (MF) that also can form trapezoidal MFs by the systematic considerations in MIN blocks. Essential to SC technique we should define a fundamental non-overlapping clock. Moreover, in order to simplify system complexity, we assume that each membership function does not cross the height of the adjacent one. This means that each input belongs to no more than two fuzzy sets or, equivalently, that no more than two membership functions can return a nonzero value. A generic fuzzy rule for two inputs x, y and one output z can be written in the form of If x is FX_i and y is FY_j then z is FZ_k. Relevant fuzzy sets and MFs are shown in Table 1. Respectively a set of rules that associate output values to combination of inputs is defined in Table 2.

Identifying the generic membership degree μ_{xi}, as the value returned by the i-th membership function $\mu_{xi}(x)$ and with μ_{yj} as the value returned by the j-th membership function $\mu_{yj}(y)$, the defuzzified output of the controller, z, can be expressed as:

$$z = \frac{1}{w}\sum_{i=1}^{6}\sum_{j=1}^{6}\mu_{i,j}\cdot s_{i,j} \tag{1}$$

Where:

$$w = \sum_{i=1}^{6}\sum_{j=1}^{6}\mu_{i,j} \tag{2}$$

And

$$\mu_{i,j}= \min(\mu_{xi}, \mu_{yj}) \tag{3}$$

Table 1. Fuzzy sets and MFs for inputs x, y and crisp values for output z

Fuzzy Set	Linguistic Values	x MF	y MF	z MF	Value
VB	Very Big	$\mu_{x1}(x)$	$\mu_{y1}(y)$	S_1	0
B	Big	$\mu_{x2}(x)$	$\mu_{y2}(y)$	S_2	2/11
M	Medium	$\mu_{x3}(x)$	$\mu_{y3}(y)$	S_3	3/11
S	Small	$\mu_{x4}(x)$	$\mu_{y4}(y)$	S_4	5/11
VS	Very Small	$\mu_{x5}(x)$	$\mu_{y5}(y)$	S_5	6/11
Z	Zero	$\mu_{x6}(x)$	$\mu_{y6}(y)$	S_6	8/11
				S_7	9/11
				S_8	1

Table 2. Rules table

S_{ij}	μ_{x1}	μ_{x2}	μ_{x3}	μ_{x4}	μ_{x5}	μ_{x6}
μ_{y1}	S_1	S_2	S_3	S_4	S_4	S_5
μ_{y2}	S_2	S_2	S_3	S_4	S_5	S_6
μ_{y3}	S_3	S_3	S_4	S_5	S_6	S_6
μ_{y4}	S_4	S_4	S_5	S_6	S_6	S_7
μ_{y5}	S_4	S_5	S_6	S_6	S_7	S_8
μ_{y6}	S_5	S_6	S_6	S_7	S_8	S_8

2.2 Architecture Description

We can reduce the number of operations to be performed by considering that, for each input, no more than two membership degrees will return nonzero values that we name them active membership degrees $\mu^*_{x1}, \mu^*_{x2}, \mu^*_{y1}$, and μ^*_{y2}.

So as extensively is described in [1], we can evaluate (1) to (3) for maximum four active fuzzy sets. It is apparent that only one subset of membership degrees and output crisp values makes its contribution to the output so that by exploiting this property the number of operations can be drastically reduced.

We also associate the active output crisp values to s^*_1, s^*_2, s^*_3 and s^*_4. Then we calculate the activation degrees by simply evaluating:

$$\mu^*_1 = \min (\mu^*_{x1}, \mu^*_{y1}) \tag{4a}$$

$$\mu^*_2 = \min (\mu^*_{x1}, \mu^*_{y2}) \tag{4b}$$

$$\mu^*_3 = \min (\mu^*_{x2}, \mu^*_{y1}) \tag{4c}$$

$$\mu^*_4 = \min (\mu^*_{x2}, \mu^*_{y2}) \tag{4d}$$

And, finally, we compute the defuzzified output as:

$$z = \frac{1}{w^*} \sum_{i=1}^{4} (\mu_i^* \cdot s_i^*) \tag{5}$$

Where:

$$w^* = \sum_{i=1}^{4} \mu_i^* \tag{6}$$

Equations (4) to (6) show that we can compute final results with fewer operations and, respectively fewer area occupation and power consumption. A block diagram of the proposed architecture is shown in Fig. 1. Both input signals membership degrees (μ_{xi} and μ_{yj}) are evaluated by means of Membership Function Blocks. Each MFB also generates a signal, A_{xi} and A_{yj} (for inputs x and y respectively) which for example for input x, shows whether x is greater (A_{xi} is high) or lower (A_{xi} is low) than V_p. So we can verify that the $\mu_{xi}(x)$ is active if A_{xi-1} is high and A_{xi+1} is low. Two 6-input Analog Multiplexers (Fig. 6) select active membership degrees ($\mu^*_{x1}, \mu^*_{x2}, \mu^*_{y1}$ and μ^*_{y2}). In Analog Multiplexers each switch is controlled by signal B_{xi} (and B_{yj} for input y).The signals B_{xi} are generated by Zero Compare block that consists of a few AND gates. Logic relationships between A_{xi} and B_{xj} (and similarly A_{yi} and B_{yj}) are shown in Table 3. Moreover B_{xi} and B_{yj} are the inputs for logic block Digital Multiplexer which controls twelve switches in W-ADDER to choose active output crisp values (s^*_1, s^*_2, s^*_3 and s^*_4). Subsequently, active membership degrees are used to compute activation degrees ($\mu^*_1, \mu^*_2, \mu^*_3$, and μ^*_4) by means of four 3-input minimum blocks. Imposing μ_{max} to Min blocks enables us to obtain trapezoidal MF shapes with the height of μ_{max}. Then, activation degrees are supplied to ADDER and W-ADDER to extract w^* and sum of $\mu^*_i \times S^*_i$ terms (i=1 to 4). The value of w^* should retain during a thorough clock cycle by means of S&H to DIVIDER block can generate z from w-adder and S&H outputs.

3 Block Implementation

3.1 Membership Function Block

The implemented MFB is based on the circuit proposed in [1], [2].A SC amplifier that can generate ramp waveforms, constitutes the basic part of MFB and just wants one clock cycle for its operation. MFB circuit is depicted in Fig. 2. When $\Phi_1=1$, $\Phi_2=0$ capacitor C_1 is charged to $V_{in}-V_c$. It is notable that in this phase V_o is equal to MF's last output which is sustained by C_h from previous clock cycle. In the next phase V_o can be computed by:

$$V_o = \frac{C_1}{C_2}(V_{in} - V_p) + V_p \tag{7}$$

Which $\alpha=C_1/C_2$ determines the slope of MF triangular shape, V_p is its vertex point and V_c is its maximum value. For limiting triangular height to the value μ_{max} (obtaining trapezoidal MF shapes) we simply can consider μ_{max} as an input into MIN blocks that its equivalent to forming trapezoidal MF shapes. The comparator evaluates if signal V_{in} is greater or lower than V_p. A flip-flop is inserted for protection against glitches of the comparator and drives two following parts by generating signals A_{xi} and A_{yi}.

1) A multiplexer that when V_{in} is lower than V_p, connects point A to voltage V_{in} and point B to V_p and if V_{in} exceeds V_p, connects point A to voltage V_p and point B to V_{in}.
2) A logic box which changes the value of C_1 by controlling switches to alter the slope of MF in two sides.

Regarding to what was mentioned and using (7), the MF output voltage is given by:

$$V_o=\alpha(V_{in}-V_p)+V_c \qquad V_p - \frac{1}{\alpha}V_c \langle V_{in} \langle V_p \tag{8a}$$

$$V_o=-\alpha(V_{in}-V_p)+V_c \qquad V_p \langle V_{in} \langle V_p + \frac{1}{\alpha}V_c \tag{8b}$$

$$V_o=0 \qquad V_p + \frac{1}{\alpha}V_c \langle V_{in}, V_{in} \langle V_p - \frac{1}{\alpha}V_c \tag{8c}$$

3.2 Minimum Block

In this brief a general purpose 3-input, voltage mode minimum block in SC technique is proposed. This structure can easily be extended to N-input min circuit. The basic part of Min block consists of a 3-input latch shown in Fig. 4. Nodes n_1 to n_3 are charged to input voltages and MEN (shown in Fig. 5) is a control signal which can be obtained from Φ_1 by using simple one shot and delaying circuits. All the paralleled PMOS cells network have power full pull-up and pull-down paths via large sized P_u and M_d transistors. Size of P_u must be larger than the size of M_d. First of all the nodes n_1 to n_3 should be charged and then disconnected from inputs. Now MEN signal turns on the P_u and M_n transistors and activates the parallel PMOS cells network. As the gates of PMOSs in a cell are controlled by the voltages of other cells, a positive feedback exists between cells. If we suppose that the lowest voltage is connected to node n_j in j'th cell, this voltage causes the nodes in other cells have higher charging rate and so all are driven to V_{DD}. Therefore positive feedback coincidentally discharges node n_j and finally it reaches to zero voltage. In a stable state the node with lowest voltage is grounded and all other nodes are pulled up to V_{DD}.

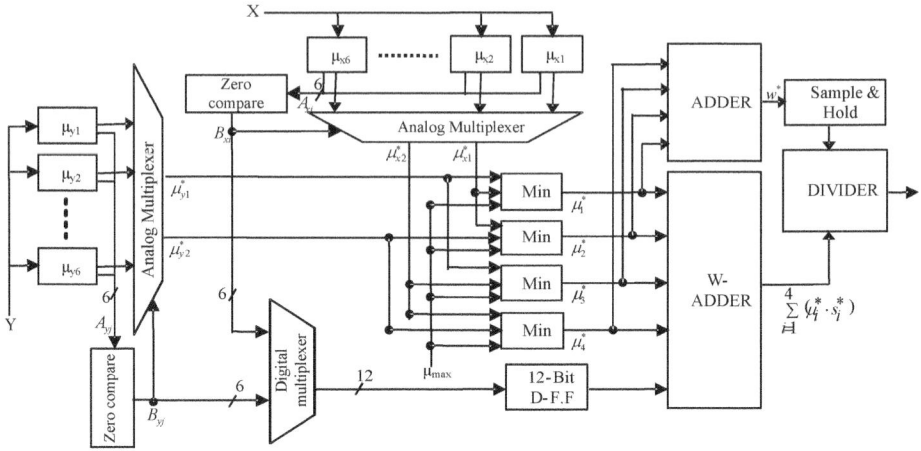

Fig. 1. Architecture of controller

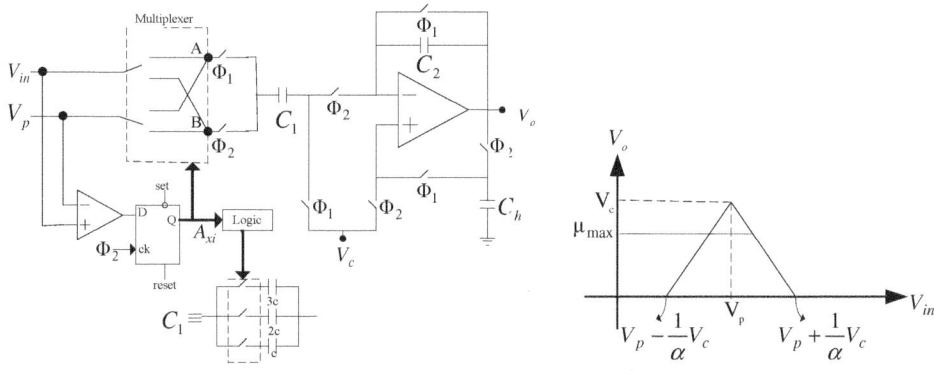

Fig. 2. Implemented MF   **Fig. 3.** MF characteristic

The 3-input Min circuit diagram and control signals are shown in Fig. 5. All input voltages that come from analogue multiplexer and limiting voltage μ_{max}, are transferred on to n_1 to n_3 of three separate cells via switches S_{I1} to S_{I3} during phase Φ_1. Since switches SO_1 to SO_3 and devices P_u and M_d are cut off, n_1 to n_3 nodes are not interactive in this phase; they all appear as a capacitive load to the input voltages. In selection phase (MEN signal is high), all P_u and M_d are turned on to initiate interaction among n_1 to n_3 nodes. A stable state in latch block is reached in which the cell that initially received the lowest input survives with a grounded node. All other cells raise their node voltage to V_{DD}.

It is clear that in Fig. 5 switches SO_1 to SO_3 are controlled by n_1 to n_3 voltages. Once n_1 to n_3 node voltages have reached a stable state with only one node having zero volt, only the SO controlled by that node remains connecting and therefore transfers the lowest input value to the next stage. This voltage is transferred to the Adder and W-Adder blocks in phase Φ_1.

3.3 Analogue Multiplexer

To select active membership degrees we use Analog multiplexer. As mentioned in section 2, Zero Comparison blocks outputs, B_{xi} and B_{yj}, should control the Analog multiplexer blocks to transfer just four active membership degrees among twelve MFB outputs. We refer to input signal, x, since similar consideration can be made for input y. As we assumed that no fuzzy set intersects the height of adjacent ones, that is, for each input value at most two adjacent MFs have nonzero values that should be transmitted by the analog multiplexer. So the circuit in Fig. 6 can simply satisfy our requirements. Since adjacent Membership functions form active membership degrees, odd MFs are connected to one output and even ones are connected to the other output. If the output returned by μ_{xi} and respectively μ_{xi+1} are nonzero (active membership degrees), the relevant signals B_{xi} and B_{xi+1} will be high and connect the switches to transfer μ_{xi} and μ_{xi+1} as μ^*_{x1} and μ^*_{x2}. A similar circuit holds for the input y.

3.4 Adder and W-Adder

In this work we use weighted-average of singletons method for defuzzification. After simplifying the system, (1), (2) and (3) were obtained and therefore two blocks Adder and W-adder and a Divider is needed to compute these equations. The circuit schematic of both types of adders is given in Fig. 7. Note that the inputs μ^*_1 to μ^*_4 arriving from inference modules, are received in Φ_1. Output in evaluation phase Φ_2 is:

$$out = \sum_{i=1}^{4} \frac{C_i}{C}\mu_i^*$$

(9)

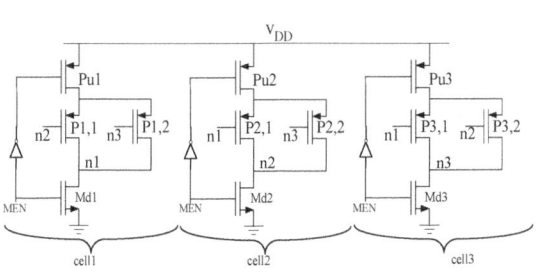

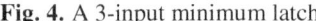

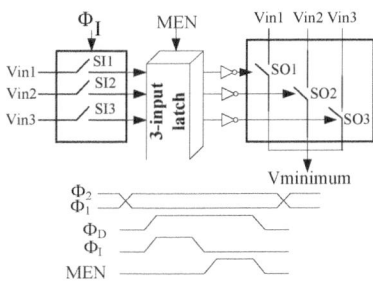

Fig. 4. A 3-input minimum latch   **Fig. 5.** A 3-input MIN circuit

If the capacitors on all input columns are identical, i.e., $C_i = C_1$, $\forall$ i, then circuit implements simple addition, i.e., out=$\dfrac{C_1}{C}\sum \mu_i^*$, i=1 to 4. This sum should never exceed V_{DD}. In order to prevent the adder from saturation, an obvious way to comply with this requirement is to select $C_1/C=1/n$. This would ensure nonsaturation even when all inputs to the adder are at V_{DD} (This condition is unlikely to occur because it would imply a controller input condition that fits all rules with 100% truth-value). Usually, the maximum possible value of the sum is a fraction of nV_{DD}, i.e., $\sum \mu_i^* \Big|_{max} = \alpha n V_{DD}$, where factor α is considerably less than unity. Assuming that α has been determined by analyzing the control surface of controller by inspection, its more reasonable to implement the capacitance ratio in accordance with $C_1/C=1/(\alpha n)$ because this not only results in a smaller size for C, but also yields an amplified output as described by:

$$V_{Adder} = w^* = \frac{1}{\alpha n}\sum_{i=1}^{4}\mu_i^* \tag{10}$$

Provided that the W-Adder is also amplified by the same factor $1/\alpha$, the quotient of final division will not change. A W-Adder is implemented by sizing input capacitors and changing their values by means of switches as shown in Table 4. Active crisp values responding to the active rules must be assigned to s^*_i as described in (5). Active output crisp values can simply be selected by a combination of B_{xi} and B_{yj}. In this structure each switch is driven by simple logic circuit which is implemented according to Table 2 and Fig. 6. The logics required for each switch are shown in Table 5.

3.5 Divider

A schematic of divider unit is given in Fig. 9. It comprises a stack of k comparators, whose outputs V_{cq}, q=1, 2, ..., k are fed into an output adder, which generates the crisp system output z. The Adder is exactly like what shown in Fig. 7. Its input capacitors are sized in accordance to $C_q=C/k$, $\forall$ q, which yields to:

$$z = \frac{1}{k}\sum_{q=1}^{k}V_{cq} \tag{11}$$

Each comparator is composed of two capacitors C_{q1} and C_{q2} and a cascade of two ordinary CMOS inverters, the first of which is resettable. In a RS phase, all these first inverter stages in the entire stack are reset to logic threshold V_{th} . In the mean time, bottom plates of all C_{q1} receive the adder signal V_A. In this phase, the bottom plates of C_{q2} are tied to ground. Consider that RS removed slightly before the switches controlling capacitor bottom plates are turned off. This helps to avoid an offset that might otherwise result from charge injection onto the capacitor bottom plate's columns. In the following phase, the W-Adder output signal V_{WA} is imposed on all C_{q2} while all C_{q1} are grounded. The resulting voltage Perturbation at the input of an inverter Cascade is positive if $(V_{WA}/V_A)>(C_{q1}/C_{q2})$ otherwise, a negative perturbation

Table 3. Logic relationship between B_{xi} and A_{xi}

Signal	Logic relationship
B_{x1}	A_{x2}
B_{x2}	$A_{x1} . \overline{A_{x3}}$
B_{x3}	$A_{x2} . \overline{A_{x4}}$
B_{x4}	$A_{x3} . \overline{A_{x5}}$
B_{x5}	$A_{x4} . \overline{A_{x6}}$
B_{x6}	$\overline{A_{x5}}$

Table 4. Singleton selection by means of switches

Connected switches	Singleton value
S_{i1}	6/11
S_{i2}	3/11
S_{i3}	2/11
S_{i1} , S_{i2}	9/11
S_{i1} , S_{i3}	8/11
S_{i2} , S_{i3}	5/11
S_{i1} , S_{i2} , S_{i3}	1
No switch	0

occurs. Assuming that the inverter cascade has a sufficiently high gain, then output from the cascade is described by:

$$V_{cq} = V_{DD} \qquad \text{IF} \qquad (V_{WA}/V_A) > T_q \qquad (12)$$

$$V_{cq} = 0 \qquad \text{IF} \qquad (V_{WA}/V_A) < T_q \qquad (13)$$

$$T_q \equiv C_{q1}/C_{q2} \qquad (14)$$

Where, the T_q is the comparator threshold. By selecting capacitance ratios in accordance with:

$$\frac{C_{q1}}{C_{q2}} = \frac{2q-1}{2k} \qquad (15)$$

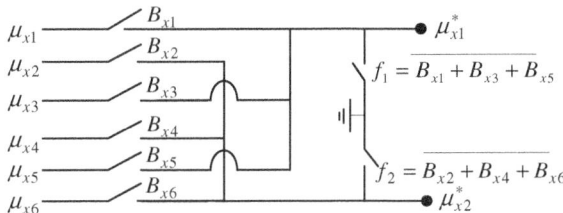

Fig. 6. Analog multiplexer circuit input x (and similarly y)

We create k equally spaced thresholds in the range zero to one. If V_{WA}/V_A exceeds a total of ℓ thresholds, then precisely ℓ out of k comparators transfer a V_{DD} to output adder and, according to (11), the adder responds by generating a system output of:

$$Z \equiv (\ell/q)V_{DD} \qquad (16)$$

Where ℓ/q is a quantized representation of V_{WA}/V_A. It is obvious that the maximum quantization error for rail-to-rail output equals to $\pm V_{DD}/(2k)$. By considering $k=20$, we can obtain the threshold of comparators from (14) and are shown in Table 6. The voltages V_A and V_{WA} are computed during phase Φ_2, and as we mentioned the Divider block requires V_{WA} during phase Φ_1 for perfect operation. So the S&H in Fig. 10 circuit is provided to sample V_{WA} in phase Φ_2 and keep it during phase Φ_1.

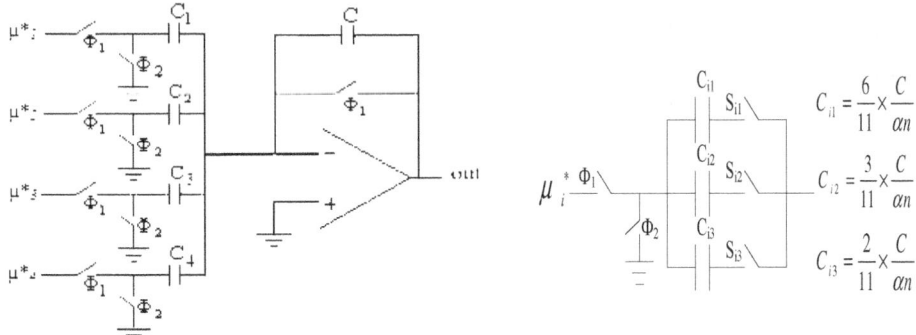

Fig. 7. Schematic of Adder and W-Adder   **Fig. 8.** W-Adder input capacitor

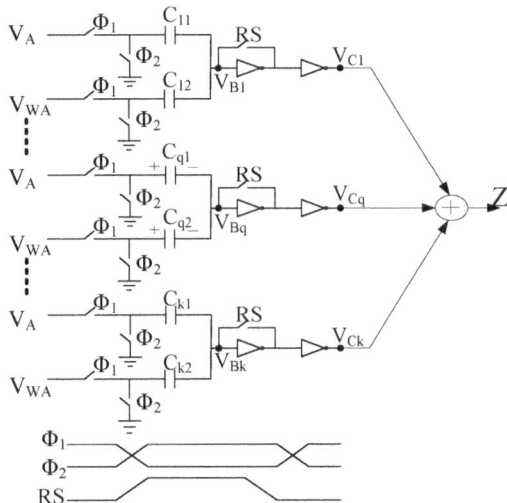

Fig. 9. Divider configuration and timing signal

4   Example of Implementation

A controller has to approximate the optimum control surface of the plant it works together. For testing the controller the circuit was integrated in a 0.35μm CMOS technology with 1.5V power supply and the master clock signal was set to 5 Mhz.

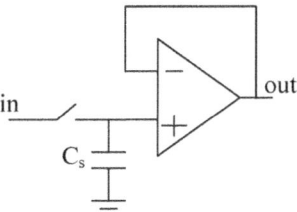

Fig. 10. Sample and hold circuit

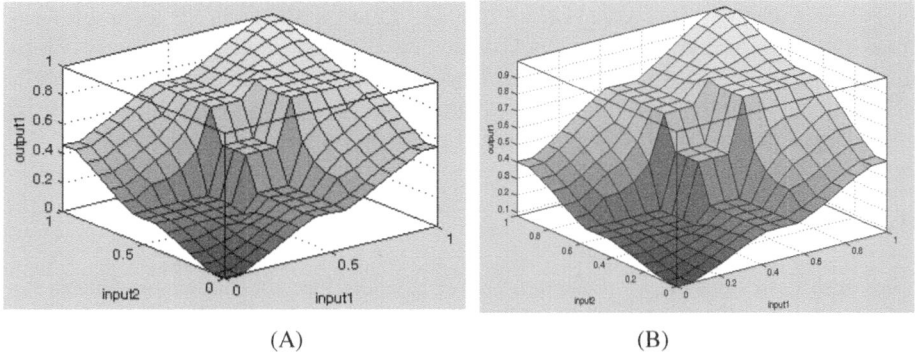

(A)   (B)

Fig. 11. (A) Ideal transcharacteristic of controller, (B) Real transcharacteristic of controller

Table 5. Control logics for W-Adder input capacitor selection

Switch	Control signal
S_{11}	$B_{x3}.B_{y5}+ B_{x5}.B_{y3}+ B_{x5}.B_{y5}$
S_{12}	$B_{x1}.B_{y3}+ B_{x1}.B_{y5}+ B_{x3}.B_{y1}+ B_{x3}.B_{y3}+ B_{x5}.B_{y1}+ B_{x5}.B_{y5}$
S_{13}	$B_{x1}.B_{y5}+ B_{x3}.B_{y3}+ B_{x3}.B_{y5}+ B_{x5}.B_{y1}+ B_{x5}.B_{y3}+ B_{x5}.B_{y5}$
S_{21}	$B_{x1}.B_{y6}+ B_{x3}.B_{y4}+ B_{x3}.B_{y6}+ B_{x5}.B_{y2}+ B_{x5}.B_{y4}+ B_{x5}.B_{y6}$
S_{22}	$B_{x1}.B_{y4}+ B_{x3}.B_{y2}+ B_{x5}.B_{y6}$
S_{23}	$B_{x1}.B_{y2}+ B_{x1}.B_{y4}+ B_{x3}.B_{y6}+ B_{x5}.B_{y4}+ B_{x5}.B_{y6}$
S_{31}	$B_{x2}.B_{y5}+ B_{x4}.B_{y3}+ B_{x4}.B_{y5}+ B_{x6}.B_{y1}+ B_{x6}.B_{y3}+ B_{x6}.B_{y5}$
S_{32}	$B_{x2}.B_{y3}+ B_{x4}.B_{y1}+ B_{x6}.B_{y5}$
S_{33}	$B_{x2}.B_{y1}+ B_{x4}.B_{y1}+ B_{x4}.B_{y5}+ B_{x6}.B_{y3}+ B_{x6}.B_{y5}$
S_{41}	$B_{x2}.B_{y6}+ B_{x4}.B_{y4}+ B_{x4}.B_{y6}+ B_{x6}.B_{y2}+ B_{x6}.B_{y4}+ B_{x6}.B_{y6}$
S_{42}	$B_{x2}.B_{y4}+ B_{x4}.B_{y2}+ B_{x4}.B_{y6}+ B_{x6}.B_{y4}+ B_{x6}.B_{y6}$
S_{43}	$B_{x2}.B_{y2}+ B_{x2}.B_{y4}+ B_{x2}.B_{y6}+ B_{x4}.B_{y2}+ B_{x4}.B_{y4}+ B_{x6}.B_{y2}+ B_{x6}.B_{y6}$

Table 6. Thresholds of the comparators in Divider

$T_1=0.025$	$T_3=0.125$	$T_5=0.225$	$T_7=0.325$	$T_9=0.425$	$T_{11}=0.525$	$T_{13}=0.625$	$T_{15}=0.725$	$T_{17}=0.825$	$T_{19}=0.925$
$T_2=0.075$	$T_4=0.175$	$T_6=0.275$	$T_8=0.375$	$T_{10}=0.475$	$T_{12}=0.575$	$T_{14}=0.675$	$T_{16}=0.775$	$T_{18}=0.875$	$T_{20}=0.075$

All the switches are realized with pass transistors. Six MF blocks were considered for each input and singleton values were determined by capacitor ratios. In general the absolute fitness error is caused by OTA's accuracy and switches charge injection.

The ideal controlling surface and the surface obtained by implemented circuit are shown in Fig. 11(A) and Fig. 11(B). The absolute error is about 2%. The circuit occupies $0.14mm^2$ area and dissipates $0.45mW$ power.

5 Conclusion

A fuzzy controller with improved MF circuit and Divider blocks in SC technique was proposed. All the units need one clock cycle for operation that this property yields high speed pipeline function. The performance, together with the availability of well-established design methods leads us to believe that the proposed solution may be amply acceptable for construction of fuzzy controllers for specific applications.

References

1. Giustolisi, G., Palmisano, G., Palumbo, G.: An Efficient Fuzzy Controller Architecture in SC Teqnique. IEEE Tran. on Circuits and Systems—II: Analog and Digital Signal Processing 49(3) (March 2002)
2. Huertas, J.L., Sanchez-Solano, S., Barriaga, A., Baturone, I.: A Fuzzy Controller Using Switched Cap Teqniques. In: Proc. 2nd IEEE Int. Conf. on Fuzzy Systems, San Francisco, pp. 516–520 (1993)
3. Zadeh, L.: Outline of a new approach to the analysis of complex systems and decision processes. IEEE Trans. Syst., Man, Cybernetics SMC-3, 28–44 (1973)
4. Oehm, J., Grafe, M., Kettner, T., Schumacher, K.: Universal low cost controller for electric motors with programmable characteristic curves. IEEE J. Solid-State Circuits 31, 1041–1045 (1996)
5. Ramirez-Angulo, J.: Building blocks for fuzzy processor. IEEE Circuits Devices Mag., 48–50 (July 1994)

Multi-objective Particle Swarm Optimization Algorithm Based on the Disturbance Operation

Yuelin Gao and Min Qu

Institute of Information & System Science, Beifang University of Nationalities,
Ningxia, Yinchuan, 750021, China
Tel.: +886 09512066579, Tel.: 15209517249
gaoyuelin@263.net, victoryqumin@163.com

Abstract. To overcome the defect of wide-ranged exploration for particle swarm optimization, a kind of multi-objective particle swarm optimization algorithm with disturbance operation(MPSOD) is proposed. It employs particle swarm optimization and disturbance operation to generate new population in order to enhance the wide-ranged exploration for particle swarm optimization algorithm. Numerical experiments are compared with NSGA-II, SPEA2 and MOPSO on six benchmark problems. The numerical results show the effectiveness of the proposed MPSOD algorithm.

Keywords: multi-objective optimization, particle swarm optimization, disturbance operation.

1 Introduction

Multi-objective optimization problems are very common in science study and engineering, however, in contrast to the single-objective optimization, the solution of multi-objective optimization problems is a set of optimal solutions. The traditional multi-objective optimization method solve such problems through weighted sum method into single objective problem. This method require a strong transcendental knowledge to issue itself, but it is very difficult to deal with multi-objective optimization problems, thus, traditional method can not solve it. Recently, evolutionary computing based on population is widely used to solve multi-objective optimization problems, for example, Vector Evaluated Genetic Algorithm [1], Non-dominated Sorting Genetic Algorithm(NSGA)[2] and improved NSGA(NSGA-II)[3], the Strength *Pareto* Evolutionary Algorithm (SPEA)[4]and improved SPEA(SPEA-II)and so on.

Particle swarm optimization(*PSO*) is a new branch of evolutionary computing, which was proposed by J. Kennedy and R. Eberhart in 1995 [6,7], which has been steadily gaining attention from evolutionary computing and swarm intelligence research community because of its simplicity to implement and its high convergence speed. Recently, *PSO* have been successfully applied in many optimization problems. Such as C. A. C. Coello, G. T. Pulido and M. S. Lechuga [8] proposed MOPSO, the algorithm introduced external populations of adaptive

H. Deng et al. (Eds.): AICI 2011, Part I, LNAI 7002, pp. 591–600, 2011.

network system, which require variation for particle and particle scope, variation scale is proportional to evolution algebra. D. Liu, K. C. Tan, C. K. Coh and W. K. Ho[9] proposed a kind of fuzzy multi-objective particle swarm algorithm. S. J. Tsai, T. Y. Sun and C. C. Liu et al.[10] proposed an improved multi-objective particle swarm optimization algorithm. G. H. Hu, Z. Z. Mao and D. K. H [11] proposed multi-objective particle swarm optimization algorithm based on two stages guided. In this paper, multi-objective particle swarm optimization algorithm with disturbance operation(MPSOD) is proposed,which combines disturbance operation with particle swarm optimization.

2   Multi-objective Optimization Problems and Relevant Concepts

In a minimization problem, multi-objective optimization problems are defined as follows[12]:

$$
\begin{cases}
\min f(x) = [f_1(x), \cdots, f_m(x)], \\
s.t. \ x = (x_1, \cdots, x_n) \in X \subseteq R^n, \\
\quad X = \{(x_1, \cdots, x_n) \mid l_i \le x_i \le u_i\}, \\
\quad l = (l_1, \cdots, l_n), u = (u_1, \cdots, u_n)
\end{cases}
\tag{1}
$$

Where x is a decision variable, f are objective function, X are decision space, l and u are respectively the lower bound and upper bound.

In the later, the paper will introduce several basic concepts of multi-objective optimization[13].

Definition 1 (*Pareto* dominance). A solution x^0 is said to dominate the other solution x^1 ($x^0 \succ x^1$) if both statement below are satisfied. 1) The solution x^0 is no worse than x^1 in all objectives, or $f_i(x^0) <= f_i(x^1)$ for all $i = 1, 2, ..., m$. 2) The solution x^0 is strictly better than x^1 in at least one objective, or $f_i(x^0) < f_i(x^1)$ for at least one $i \in \{1, 2, ..., m\}$.

Definition 2 (*Pareto* optimality). A point x^0 is *Pareto* optimal if and only if there is not exist another x^1 to satisfy $x^1 \succ x^0$.

Definition 3 (*Pareto* optimal set or non-inferior optimal set). The *Pareto* optimal set (P_s) is defined as $P_s = \{x^0 \mid \neg \exists x^1 \succ x^0\}$.

Definition 4 (*Pareto*-optimal front). P_F is all *Pareto* optimal solutions corresponding formed by the objective function values, the *Pareto*-optimal front(P_F) is defined as $P_F = \{f(x) = (f_1(x), f_2(x), ..., f_m(x)) \mid x \in P_s\}$.

3   Particle Swarm Optimization

Particle swarm optimization(PSO) is an optimization algorithm imitated by swarm intelligence behavior, which is referred to bird flocking, fish flocking and bee flocking study.Each particle in this algorithm has perceptive ability that perceive themselves around the best local position and the whole position, and accord to the current flying state adjust to its own flying. Each particle update its position and velocity according to two best: one is personal best, the other is global best. Personal best means best position which each particle has experienced, that is, each particle itself find optimal solution, global best means the whole swarm position experienced, that is, the whole population find optimal solution at present.

Let NP denote the swarm size, D denote search space, x_{ij}^t is the jth dimension position of particle i in cycle t; v_{ij}^t is the jth dimension velocity of particle i in cycle t; $pbest_i^t$ is the jth dimension of personal best of particle i in cycle t; $gbest^t$ is global best of the whole population in cycle t. The new velocity and position of every particle x_{ij}^t are updated by(2)and (3)

$$v_{ij}^{t+1} = wv_{ij}^t + c_1 r_1(pbest_{ij}^t - x_{ij}^t) + c_2 r_2(gbest_{1j}^t - x_{ij}^t). \tag{2}$$

$$x_{ij}^{t+1} = x_{ij}^t + v_{ij}^{t+1}. \tag{3}$$

Where c_1 and c_2 denote constant, which was called the acceleration coefficients, r_1 and r_2 are elements from two uniform random sequences in the range of $[0,1]$, w is the inertia weight which decrease by linear decrease.

4   Multi-objective Particle Swarm Optimization Algorithm Based on the Disturbance Operation

4.1   Choose *pbest* and *gbest*

In MPSOD, not only the size of particle swarm is fixed and it is not be replaced,but also adjust their *pbest* and *gbest*. In multi-objective condition, *gbest* normally exists a group of non-inferior solution and is not single *gbest* position.When each other is not dominated,each particle may be more than one *pbest*. Therefore, it is necessary to choose *pbest* and *gbest* through appropriate method.

1) Choose *pbest*
Specific process as follows: if particle x dominate *pbest*, then *pbest* $= x$; if particle *pbest* dominate x, remain unchanged; if each other is not dominated, then at random generated a random number r in the range of $[0,1]$, if $r < 0.5$, then *pbest* $= x$; if $r \geq 0.5$, otherwise unchanged.
2) Choose *gbest*
Specific process as follows[9]: when MPSOD deal with multi-objective optimization problems, *gbest* position is a group of non-inferior solution rather than a single solution. MPSOD choose a solution as the particle *gbest* taken from the optimal set and independently choose *gbest* for each particle by adopt dual tournament, each particle attain different *gbest*, this means that particles will along different directions to fly in order to enhance exploring ability of algorithm.

4.2 Disturbance Operation

Particle swarm optimization(PSO) easily lost in the local optimality arising tendency of premature convergence coupled with making population diversity loss due to the high convergence speeds. Therefore, it is unavoidable that PSO appear tendency of premature convergence, enhance diversity of population, while particles are trying to explore more potential solutions and to more explore unsearched solution space, this paper introduces disturbance operation, specific process as follows[10]:

Let NP denote the swarm size, Pop denote the current evolutionary population, $Opti$ denote $Pareto$ optimal set, $(x_1, x_2, ..., x_n) \in Pop$, d denote disturbance rate, disturbance operation is randomly chosen m that is represented by $m = d \times NP$ particles from $Opti$, which disturb population by decrease:

1) This paper determine the disturbance operation by taking advantage of [14] proposed the simulated annealing technology, computing formula is defined as follows:

$$\begin{cases} d_0 = d_{max}, \\ d_{G+1} = d_{min} + \beta(d_G - d_{min}). \end{cases} \tag{4}$$

Where d_{max} and d_{min} are respectively maximum and minimum value of disturbance rate, β is annealing factor in the range of [0,1].

2) According to the following rules to disturb population:

$$a)\ if\ rn < 0.5, then\ x_{ij} = xij - [x_{ij} - lb(x_{ij})] \times rn. \tag{5}$$

$$b)\ if\ rn \geq 0.5, then\ x_{ij} = xij + [ub(x_{ij}) - x_{ij}] \times rn. \tag{6}$$

Where lb and ub are respectively the lower bound and upper bound of x_{ij}, the random number should obey the normal distribution with mean value of 0.5 and the variance is 1.

5 The Specific Steps of MPSOD Algorithms

step 1. Let algorithms parameters D, NP, w_{min}, w_{max}, d_{min}, d_{max}, c_1, c_2, T_{max} and so on.

step 2. Initial population is randomly generated,randomly updating position and velocity of each particle of initial population and choosing $Pareto$ optimal set;

step 3. According to (2) and (3), updating position and velocity of each particle;

step 4. The new population is generated by particle swarm optimization algorithm, according to (5) and (6) disturb population from a new population several particles;

step 5. Non-dominated personal is added to $Pareto$ optimal set, with selecting non-dominated personal from $Pareto$ optimal set, when non-dominated personal is more than NP, using crowded degree distance from large to small sorting of NSGA-II for non-dominated personal, while select before NP non-dominated personal and left it in $Pareto$ optimal set, the rest personal will be deleted;

step 6. If algorithm achieves maximum iterating,then stop and output $Pareto$ optimal set, otherwise returns step3.

6   Experimental Results

6.1   Performance Metrics

The quality evaluation mainly concentrate in distance between the solution produced by the algorithms and the *Pareto* optimal solution, the extent covered by the solution produced of the algorithms, in this paper two performance metrics are adopted.

1) Convergence Indictor
The metric of generational distance(GD)[15]gives a good indication of the gap between non-dominated solution produced by the algorithms and the *Pareto* optimal solution. It is defined as

$$GD = \frac{\sqrt{\sum_{i=1}^{n} d_i^2}}{n} \tag{7}$$

Where n is the number of members in the set of optimal solution found so far and d_i is the minimum Euclidean distance between the ith personal and the theory *Pareto* optimal front in objective space. A low value of GD is desirable, which reflects a small deviation between the evolved and the true *Pareto* front, if the value of $GD = 0$, it indicates that all solution produced by the algorithms are in the *Pareto* optimal set.

2) Extend Indicator
The extend indicator[16] reflects uniform degree between non-dominated solution produced by the algorithms and the *Pareto* front, with adopting modified spread to appraise solution of extend indicator, it is defined as

$$\Delta = \frac{\sum_{i=1}^{m} d(E_i, \Omega) + \sum_{X \in \Omega} |d(X, \Omega) - \bar{d}|}{\sum_{i=1}^{m} d(E_i, \Omega) + (|\Omega| - m)\bar{d}} \tag{8}$$

Where Ω is a set of solutions produced by the algorithms, $E_i(i = 1, 2, ..., m)$ are m extreme solutions in the set of *Pareto* optimal solutions, m is the number of objectives, d and $\bar{d}$ are respectively defined as

$$d(X, \Omega) = \min_{Y \in \Omega, Y \neq X} \|F(X) - F(Y)\|.$$

$$\bar{d} = \frac{1}{\Omega} \sum_{X \in \Omega} d(X, \Omega).$$

A low value of $\triangle$ is desirable,which reflects solution produced by algorithms uniform distribution well in *Pareto* front, if the value of $\triangle = 0$, it indicates that non-dominated set produced by algorithms and *Pareto* front attain good fit.

6.2   Test Function

Definition of test functions are as follows[3]:
1.Test function 1: SCH

$$\begin{cases} \min\ f_1(x) = x^2 \\ \min\ f_2(x) = (x-2)^2 \end{cases}$$

Search space: $-10^5 \le x \le 10^5$, Dimensions: $n = 1$.
Character: *Pareto* optimal front is convex.

2.Test function 2: FON

$$\begin{cases} \min\ f_1(x) = 1 - exp(-(\sum_{i=1}^{n}(x_i - \frac{1}{\sqrt{n}}))^2) \\ \min\ f_2(x) = 1 - exp(-(\sum_{i=1}^{n}(x_i + \frac{1}{\sqrt{n}}))^2) \end{cases}$$

Search space: $x = (x_1, x_2, x_3)$, $-4 \le x \le 4(i = 1, 2, 3)$, Dimensions: $n = 3$.
Character: *Pareto*-optimal front is non-convex.

3.Test function 3: ZDT1

$$\begin{cases} \min\ f_1(x) = x_1 \\ \min\ f_2(x) = g(x)(1 - \sqrt{(x_1/g(x))}) \\ \qquad g(x) = 1 + 9\sum_{i=2}^{n} x_i/(n-1) \end{cases}$$

Search space: $x \in [0,1]^{30}$, Dimensions: $n = 30$.
Character: *Pareto*-optimal front is convex.

4.Test function 4: ZDT2

$$\begin{cases} \min\ f_1(x) = x_1 \\ \min\ f_2(x) = g(x)(1 - (x_1/g(x))^2) \\ \qquad g(x) = 1 + 9\sum_{i=2}^{n} x_i/(n-1) \end{cases}$$

Search space: $x \in [0,1]^{30}$, Dimensions: $n = 30$.
Character: *Pareto*-optimal front is non-convex.

5.Test function 5: ZDT3

$$\begin{cases} \min\ f_1(x) = x_1 \\ \min\ f_2(x) = g(x)(1 - (x_1/g(x)) - (x_1/g(x))sin(10\pi x_1)) \\ \qquad g(x) = 1 + 9\sum_{i=2}^{n} x_i/(n-1) \end{cases}$$

Search space: $x \in [0,1]^{30}$, Dimensions: $n = 30$.
Character: *Pareto*-optimal front is un-continuous.

6. Test function 6: ZDT6

$$\begin{cases} \min \ f_1(x) = 1 - exp(-4x_1)sin^6(6\pi x_1) \\ \min \ f_2(x) = g(x)(1 - (x_1/g(x))^2) \\ \qquad g(x) = 1 + 9(\sum_{i=2}^{n} x_i/(n-1))^{0.25} \end{cases}$$

Search space: $x \in [0,1]^{10}$, Dimensions: $n = 10$.
Character: *Pareto*-optimal front is non-convex, the more closer *Pareto*-optimal
front, the more smaller for dense of solution.

6.3   Experimental Results and Analysis

In order to verify MPSOD performance of the algorithms, which numerical experiments are compared with NSGA-II, SPEA2 and MOPSO on six benchmark problems. The parameter of MPSOD algorithm is gives $c_1 = c_2 = 2$, $w_{min} = 0.2$, $w_{max} = 0.9$. *Pareto* candidate solution set up is 100. The average convergence indicator, standard deviation and the average extend indicator, the standard deviation are summarized in Table 1 and Table 2 respectively, which all the algorithms independently run 30 times on each problem, the population size is 100, maximum iterating 250 times. Figure 1 to figure 6 is simulation diagram of MPSOD algorithms.

Table 1. Comparison results of four algorithms based on the convergence indicator

Algorithm	NSGA-II	SPEA2	MOPSO	MPSOD
SCH	2.1572E-3	2.1232E-3	2.9285E-2	9.2817E-4
	2.0999E-4	2.1130E-4	1.5566E-2	4.6702E-5
FON	2.5656E-3	1.8573E-3	2.1416E-2	1.1879E-3
	2.0082E-4	1.0731E-4	7.4183E-3	2.4152E-5
ZDT1	1.3437E-3	3.8175E-3	1.8564E-1	2.4167E-4
	1.4078E-4	4.9142E-3	7.7429E-2	1.6394E-5
ZDT2	9.8112E-4	8.6104E-3	5.2428E-1	9.2415E-5
	6.4138E-4	2.5973E-3	2.9699E-1	5.9170E-6
ZDT3	2.4783E-3	9.7165E-3	4.3418E-1	6.2160E-4
	1.2746E-4	5.2305E-3	6.4880E-2	2.2443E-5
ZDT6	7.5818E-2	1.9309E-2	5.2135E-2	1.2359E-4
	6.0797E-3	1.3994E-3	2.4963E-2	1.0546E-5

Table 2. Comparison results of four algorithms based on the extend indicator

Algorithm	NSGA-II	SPEA2	MOPSO	MPSOD
SCH	0.29228	0.27503	0.72572	0.25326
	2.1339E-2	2.5711E-2	1.3476E-1	2.2586E-2
FON	0.37672	0.17661	0.64970	0.19168
	2.5222E-2	1.1100E-1	3.1212E-1	2.1905E-2
ZDT1	0.50429	0.29644	0.29381	0.29963
	3.9251E-2	1.0850E-1	1.6956E-2	4.9190E-2
ZDT2	0.48775	0.50517	0.28803	0.28402
	2.7686E-2	1.8356E-1	1.7580E-2	3.5393E-2
ZDT3	0.59025	0.50310	0.61780	0.27703
	3.0439E-2	9.7283E-2	3.5019E-2	3.9487E-2
ZDT6	0.48611	0.24861	1.12326	0.35715
	3.6054E-2	4.9667E-2	1.7311E-1	5.7478E-2

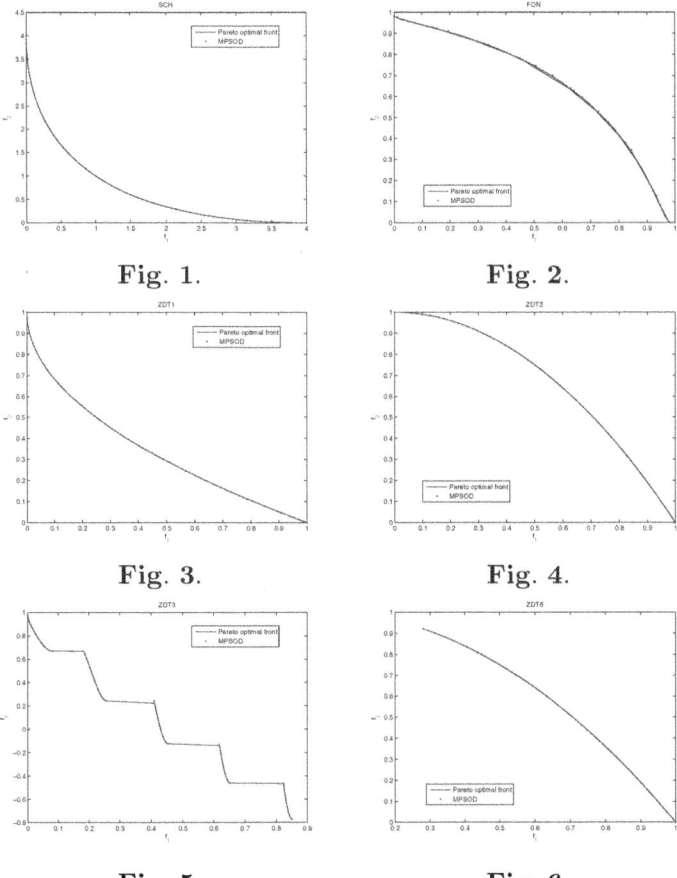

Fig. 1.   Fig. 2.

Fig. 3.   Fig. 4.

Fig. 5.   Fig. 6.

Table 1 shows that MPSOD obtains better values than other three algorithms for all test problems in convergence indictor. Table 2 shows that extend indicator value of MPSOD algorithm is better than other three algorithm in the problems *SCH*, *ZDT2 and ZDT3*. But extend indictor of *FON* and *ZDT6* which are inferior to SPEA2 are superior to NSGA-II and MOPSO, extend indictor of *ZDT1* which is inferior to SPEA2 and MOPSO is superior to NSGA-II. From figure 1 to figure 6 simulation experiments can see, experiment *Pareto* curve produced by MPSOD algorithm are fit to real *Pareto* curve.

7   Conclusion

This paper introduce disturbance operation into the particle swarm optimization, which not only enhance wide-ranged exploration ability and explore un-searched space ability of particle swarm optimization, but also enhance diversity of population. Experimental results and simulation results show that MPSOD is an effective multi-objective particle swarm optimization.

Acknowledgment. The work is supported by the National Natural Science Foundation of China under Grant *No.* 60962006.

References

1. Schaffer, J.D.: Multiple objective optimization with vector evaluated genetic algorithms. In: Proc. IEEE International Conference on Genetic Algorithms, pp. 93–100. L. Erlbaum Associates Inc., Mahwah (1985)
2. Srinivas, N., Deb, K.: Multi-objective function optimization using non-dominated sorting genetic algorithms. Evolutionary Computation 2, 221–248 (1994), doi:10.1162/evco.1994.2.3.221
3. Deb, K., Agarwal, S., Pratap, A., Meyarivan, T.: A fast and elitist multi-objective genetic algorithm: NSGA-II. IEEE Transactions on Evolutionary Computation 6, 182–197 (2002), doi:10.1007/3-540-45356-3-83
4. Zitzler, E., Thiele, L.: Multi-objective evolutionary algorithms: a comparative case study and the strength Pareto approach. IEEE Transactions on Evolutionary Computation 3, 257–271 (1999), doi:10.1109/4235.797969
5. Zitzler, E., Laumanns, M., Thiele, L.: SPEA2: improving the strength Pareto evolutionary algorithm for multi-objective optimization. Research Report (May 2001)
6. Kennedy, J., Eberhart, R.: Particle swarm optimization. In: Proc. IEEE International Conference on Neural Networks, vol. 4, pp. 1942–1948 (November/December 1995), doi:10.1109/ICNN.1995.488968
7. Shi, Y., Eberhart, R.: A modified particle swarm optimizer. In: Proc. IEEE World Congress on Computational Intelligence, pp. 69–73 (May 1998), doi:10.1109/ICEC.1998.699146
8. Coello, C.A.C., Pulido, G.T., Lechuga, M.S.: Handling multiple objectives with particle swarm optimization. IEEE Trans. on Evolutionary Computations 8, 256–279 (2004), doi:10.1109/TEVC.2004.826067
9. Liu, D., Tan, K.C., Coh, C.K., Ho, W.K.: A multi-objective memetic algorithm based on particle swarm optimization. IEEE Transactions on Systems, Man and Cybernetics, Part B 37, 42–50 (2006), doi:10.1109/TSMCB.2006.883270

10. Tsai, S.J., Sun, T.Y., Liu, C.C., et al.: An improved multi-objective particle swarm optimizer for multi-objective problems. IEEE Transactions on Systems, Man and Cybernetics, Part B 37, 42–50 (2006), doi: 10.11109/TSMCB.2006.883270

11. Hu, G.H., Mao, Z.Z., He, D.K.: Multi-objective PSO optimization algorithm based on two stages guided. Control and Decision 25, 404–415 (2010)

12. Deb, K.: Multi-Objective Optimization Using Evolutionary Algorithm. John Wiley & Sons, Chichester (2001)

13. Gong, M.G., Jiao, L.C., Yang, D.D.: Evolutionary Multi-Objective Optimization Algorithms. Journal of Software 20, 271–289 (2009)

14. Wang, X.S., Hao, M.L., Cheng, Y.H., et al.: A Multi-Objective Optimization Problems with a hybrid Algorithms. Journal of System Simulation 21, 4980–4985 (2009)

15. David, A., Lamont, G.B.: Evolutionary Computation and Convergence to a *Pareto* Front. In: Koza, J.R. (ed.) Late Breaking Papers at the Genetic Programming Conference, Stanford Bookstore, pp. 221–228. Stanford University, California (1998)

16. Zhou, A., Jin, Y., Zhang, Q., et al.: Combing model-based and generics-based offspring generation for multi-objective optimization using a convergence criterion. In: IEEE Congress on Evolutionary Computation, pp. 3234–3241 (July 2006)

The Predicate Formal System Based on 1-Level Universal AND Operator

Ying-cang Ma[1,2] and Xue-zhen Dai[1]

[1] School of Science, Xi'an Polytechnic University
Xi'an 710048, China
[2] School of Electronics and information, Northwestern Polytechnical University,
Xi'an 710072, China
mayingcang@126.com

Abstract. The aim of this paper is the partial axiomatization for first-order predicate calculus formal system based on first-level universal AND operator. By introducing the universal quantifier and existential quantifier, a predicate calculus formal deductive system $\forall \mathcal{UL}^-_{h \in (0,1]}$ based on 1-level universal AND operator according to propositional calculus formal deductive system $\mathcal{UL}^-_{h \in (0,1]}$ of universal logic is built up, moreover, the completeness of system $\forall \mathcal{UL}^-_{h \in (0,1]}$ are proved. So it shows that the semantic and syntactic of system $\forall \mathcal{UL}^-_{h \in (0,1]}$ are harmony.

Keywords: universal logic, predicate system, universal AND operator.

1 Introduction

In recent years considerable progress has been made in logical foundations of fuzzy logic, especially for the logic based on t-norm and its residua (See [1-11]). Some well-known logic systems have been built up, such as the basic logic (BL)[1,3] introduced by Hajek; the monoidal t-norm based logic (MTL)[2] introduced by Esteva and Godo; a formal deductive system L^* introduced by Wang (see [7-11]), and so on. Moreover the completeness of the above logical systems have been proven.

Universal logic[12] was proposed by Huacan He, which thinks that all things in the world are correlative, that is, they are either mutually exclusive or mutually consistent, and we call this kind of relation generalized correlation. Any two propositions have generalized correlation. The degree of general correlation can be described quantitatively by the coefficient of the generalized correlation $h \in [0,1]$. 1-level universal NOT operators are mapping $N : [0,1] \to [0,1], N(x,k) = (1-x^n)^{1/n}$, which is usually denoted by $\neg_k$. 1-level universal AND operators are mapping $T : [0,1] \times [0,1] \to [0,1], T(x,y,h,k) = \Gamma^1[(x^{mn} + y^{mn} - 1)^{1/mn}]$, which is usually denoted by $\wedge_{h,k}$. 1-level universal IMPLICATION operators are mapping $I : [0,1] \times [0,1] \to [0,1], I(x,y,h) = ite\{1|x \le y; 0|m \le 0 \text{ and } y = 0; \Gamma^1[(1-x^{mn}+y^{mn})^{1/mn}]\}$, which is usually denoted by $\Rightarrow_h$. The formal systems of propositional universal logic have been studied in [13-17]. In [18], the first-order predicate calculus formal system $\mathcal{UL}^-_{h \in (0,1]}$ based on 1-level universal AND

H. Deng et al. (Eds.): AICI 2011, Part I, LNAI 7002, pp. 601–608, 2011.

operator is given and the soundness of system are given, In this paper, we give predicate formal system $\forall \mathcal{UL}^-_{h\in(0,1]}$, and its completeness theorem are given.

The paper is organized as follows. After this introduction, Section 2 we will build the predicate calculus formal deductive system $\forall \mathcal{UL}^-_{h\in(0,1]}$ for 1-level universal AND operator. In Section 3 the completeness of system $\forall \mathcal{UL}^-_{h\in(0,1]}$ will be proved. The final section offers the conclusion.

2   Predicate Formal System $\forall \mathcal{UL}^-_{h\in(0,1]}$

In order to build first-order predicate formal deductive system based on 1-level universal AND operator, we give the first-order predicate language as following:

First-order language J consists of symbols set and generation rules:

The symbols set of J consist of as following:

(1) Object variables: $x, y, z, x_1, y_1, z_1, x_2, y_2, z_2, \cdots$;
(2) Object constants: $a, b, c, a_1, b_1, c_1,$, Truth constants: $\overline{0}, \overline{1}$;
(3) Predicate symbols: $P, Q, R, P_1, Q_1, R_1, \cdots$;
(4) Connectives: $\&, \rightarrow, \triangle, -$;
(5) Quantifiers: $\forall$(universal quantifier), $\exists$(existential quantifier);
(6) Auxiliary symbols: (,), ,.

The symbols in (1)-(3) are called non-logical symbols of language J. The object variables and object constants of J are called terms. The set of all object constants is denoted by $\text{Var}(J)$, The set of all object variables is denoted by $\text{Const}(J)$, The set of all terms is denoted by $\text{Term}(J)$. If P is n-ary predicate symbol, $t_1, t_2, \cdots, t_n$ are terms, then $P(t_1, t_2, \cdots, t_n)$ is called atomic formula.

The formula set of J is generated by the following three rules in finite times:

(i) If P is atomic formula, then $P \in J$;
(ii) If $P, Q \in J$, then $P \& Q, P \rightarrow Q, \triangle P \in J, -P \in J$;
(iii) If $P \in J$, and $x \in \text{Var}(J)$, then $(\forall x)P, (\exists x)P \in J$.

The formulas of J can be denoted by $\varphi, \phi, \psi, \varphi_1, \phi_1, \psi_1, \cdots$. Further connectives are defined as following:

$\varphi \wedge \psi$ is $\varphi \& (\varphi \rightarrow \psi)$, $\varphi \vee \psi$ is $((\varphi \rightarrow \psi) \rightarrow \psi) \wedge (\psi \rightarrow \varphi) \rightarrow \varphi)$,
$\neg\varphi$ is $\varphi \rightarrow \overline{0}$, $\varphi \equiv \psi$ is $(\varphi \rightarrow \psi) \& (\psi \rightarrow \varphi)$.

Definition 1. *The axioms and deduction rules of predicate formal system* $\forall \mathcal{UL}^-_{h\in(0,1]}$ *as following:*

(i)The following formulas are axioms of $\forall \mathcal{UL}^\triangle_{h\in(0,1]}$:

(U1) $(\varphi \rightarrow \psi) \rightarrow ((\psi \rightarrow \chi) \rightarrow (\varphi \rightarrow \chi))$
(U2) $(\varphi \& \psi) \rightarrow \varphi$
(U3) $(\varphi \& \psi) \rightarrow (\psi \& \varphi)$
(U4) $\varphi \& (\varphi \rightarrow \psi) \rightarrow (\psi \& (\psi \rightarrow \varphi))$
(U5) $(\varphi \rightarrow (\psi \rightarrow \chi)) \rightarrow ((\varphi \& \psi) \rightarrow \chi)$
(U6) $((\varphi \& \psi) \rightarrow \chi) \rightarrow (\varphi \rightarrow (\psi \rightarrow \chi))$
(U7) $((\varphi \rightarrow \psi) \rightarrow \chi) \rightarrow (((\psi \rightarrow \varphi) \rightarrow \chi) \rightarrow \chi)$

(U8) $\overline{0} \to \varphi$

(U9) $(\varphi \to \varphi \& \psi) \to ((\varphi \to \overline{0}) \vee \psi \vee ((\varphi \to \varphi \& \varphi) \wedge (\psi \to \psi \& \psi)))$

(U10) $(--\varphi) \equiv \varphi$

(U11) $\triangle(\varphi \to \psi) \to \triangle(-\psi \to -\varphi)$

(U12) $\triangle \varphi \vee \neg \triangle \varphi$

(U13) $\triangle(\varphi \vee \psi) \to (\triangle \varphi \vee \triangle \psi)$

(U14) $\triangle \varphi \to \varphi$

(U15) $\triangle \varphi \to \triangle \triangle \varphi$

(U16) $\triangle(\varphi \to \psi) \to (\triangle \varphi \to \triangle \psi)$

(U17) $(\forall x)\varphi(x) \to \varphi(t)$ *(t substitutable for x in $\varphi(x)$)*

(U18) $\varphi(t) \to (\exists x)\varphi(x)$ *(t substitutable for x in $\varphi(x)$)*

(U19) $(\forall x)(\chi \to \varphi) \to (\chi \to (\forall x)\varphi)$ *(x is not free in χ)*

(U20) $(\forall x)(\varphi \to \chi) \to ((\exists x)\varphi \to \chi)$ *(x is not free in χ)*

(U21) $(\forall x)(\varphi \vee \chi) \to ((\forall x)\varphi \vee \chi)$ *(x is not free in χ)*

Deduction rules of $\forall U L^{-}_{h \in (0,1]}$ are three rules. They are:

Modus Ponens(MP):from $\varphi, \varphi \to \psi$ infer ψ;

Necessitation: from φ infer $\triangle \varphi$;

Generalization: from φ infer $(\forall x)\varphi$.

The meaning of "t substitutable for x in $\varphi(x)$" and "x is not free in χ" in the above definition have the same meaning in the classical first-order predicate logic, moreover, we can define the concepts such as proof, theorem, theory, deduction from a theory T, T-consequence in the system $\forall \mathcal{U} \mathcal{L}^{-}_{h \in (0,1]}$. $T \vdash \varphi$ denotes that φ is provable in the theory T. $\vdash \varphi$ denotes that φ is a theorem of system $\forall U L_{h \in (0,1]}$. Let $\mathrm{Thm}(\forall \mathcal{U} \mathcal{L}^{-}_{h \in (0,1]}) = \{\varphi \in J | \vdash \varphi\}, \mathrm{Ded}(T) = \{\varphi \in J | T \vdash \varphi\}$. Being the axioms of propositional system $\mathcal{U} \mathcal{L}^{-}_{h \in (0,1]}$ are in predicate system $\forall \mathcal{U} \mathcal{L}^{-}_{h \in (0,1]}$, then the theorems in $\mathcal{U} \mathcal{L}_{h \in (0,1]}$ are theorems in $\forall \mathcal{U} \mathcal{L}^{-}_{h \in (0,1]}$. According the similar proof in [1,15,16] we can get the following lemmas.

Lemma 1. *The hypothetical syllogism holds in $\forall \mathcal{U} \mathcal{L}^{-}_{h \in (0,1]}$, i.e. let $\Gamma = \{\varphi \to \psi, \psi \to \chi\}$, then $\Gamma \vdash \varphi \to \chi$.*

Lemma 2. *$\forall \mathcal{U} \mathcal{L}^{-}_{h \in (0,1]}$ proves:*

(1) $\varphi \to \varphi$; (2) $\varphi \to (\psi \to \varphi)$; (3) $(\varphi \to \psi) \to ((\varphi \to \gamma) \to (\psi \to \gamma))$;

(4)$(\varphi \& (\varphi \to \psi)) \to \psi$; (5) $\triangle \varphi \equiv \triangle \varphi \& \triangle \varphi$.

Lemma 3. *If $T = \{\varphi \to \psi, \chi \to \gamma\}$, then $T \vdash (\varphi \& \chi) \to (\psi \& \gamma)$.*

Definition 2. [1] *A BL-algebra is an algebra $\mathrm{L} = (L, \cap, \cup, *, \Rightarrow, 0, 1)$ with four binary operations and two constants such that*

1. $(L, \cap, \cup, 0, 1)$ is a lattice with the greatest element 1 and the least element 0 (with respect to the lattice ordering $\leq$),

2. $(L, *, 1)$ is a commutative semigroup with the unit element 1, i.e. $*$ is commutative, associative and $1 * x = x$ for all x,

3. The following conditions hold for all x, y, z:

(i) $z \leq (x \Rightarrow y)$ iff $x * z \leq y$; (ii) $x \cap y = x * (x \Rightarrow y)$; (iii) $(x \Rightarrow y) \cup (y \Rightarrow x) = 1$.

Definition 3. [16] *A LΠG algebra is a BL-algebra in which the identity* $(x \Rightarrow x * y) \Rightarrow ((x \Rightarrow 0) \cup y \cup ((x \Rightarrow x * x) \cap (y \Rightarrow y * y))) = 1$ *is valid.*

Definition 4. [15] *A LΠG*$_\triangle$*-algebra is a structure* L $= < L, *, \Rightarrow, \cap, \cup, 0, 1, \triangle >$ *which is a LΠG-algebra expanded by an unary operation* $\triangle$ *in which the following formulas are true:*

(1) $\triangle x \cup (\triangle x \Rightarrow 0) = 1$; *(2)* $\triangle(x \cup y) \leq \triangle x \cup \triangle y$; *(3)* $\triangle x \leq x$
(4) $\triangle x \leq \triangle\triangle x$; *(5)* $(\triangle x) * (\triangle(x \Rightarrow y)) \leq \triangle y$; *(6)* $\triangle 1 = 1$

Definition 5. [15] *A LΠG$^-$-algebra is a structure* L $= < L, *, \Rightarrow, \cap, \cup, 0, 1, \triangle, - >$ *which is a LΠG$_\triangle$-algebra expanded by an unary operation* $-$ *satisfying the following conditions:*

(1) $--x = x$;   *(2)* $\triangle(x \Rightarrow y) = \triangle(-y \Rightarrow -x)$;
(3) $\triangle x \vee \neg\triangle x = 1$;   *(4)* $\triangle(x \vee y) \leq (\triangle x \vee \triangle y)$;
(5) $\triangle x \leq x$;   *(6)* $\triangle x \leq \triangle\triangle x$;
(7) $(\triangle x) * (\triangle(x \Rightarrow y)) \leq \triangle y$; *(8)* $\triangle 1 = 1$.

Let J is first-order predicate language, L is linearly ordered LΠG$^-$ algebra, M $= (M, (r_P)_P, (m_c)_c)$ is called a L-evaluation for first-order predicate language J, which M is non-empty domain, according to each n-ary predicate P and object constant c, r_P is L-fuzzy n-ary relation: $r_P : M^n \rightarrow$ L, m_c is an element of M.

Definition 6. *Let J be predicate language, M is L-evaluation of J, x is object variable, $P \in J$.*

(i) A mapping $V :$ Term$(J) \rightarrow M$ is called M-evaluation, if for each $c \in$ Const (J), $v(c) = m_c$;

(ii) Two M-evaluation v, v' are called equal denoted by $v \equiv_x v'$ if for each $y \in$ Var$(J)\backslash\{x\}$, there is $v(y) = v'(y)$.

(iii) The value of a term given by M, v is defined by: $\|x\|_{M,v} = v(x)$; $\|c\|_{M,v} = m_c$. *We define the truth value* $\|\varphi\|^L_{M,v}$ *of a formula φ as following. Clearly,* $*, \Rightarrow, \triangle$ *denote the operations of* L.

$\|P(t_1, t_2, \cdots, t_n)\|^L_{M,v} = r_P(\|t_1\|_{M,v}, \cdots, \|t_n\|_{M,v})$;

$\|\varphi \rightarrow \psi\|^L_{M,v} = \|\varphi\|^L_{M,v} \Rightarrow \|\psi\|^L_{M,v}$; $\|\varphi \& \psi\|^L_{M,v} = \|\varphi\|^L_{M,v} * \|\psi\|^L_{M,v}$;

$\|\overline{0}\|^L_{M,v} = 0$; $\|\overline{1}\|^L_{M,v} = 1$; $\|\triangle\varphi\|^L_{M,v} = \triangle\|\varphi\|^L_{M,v}$;

$\|-\varphi\|^L_{M,v} = -\|\varphi\|^L_{M,v}$; $\|(\forall x)\varphi\|^L_{M,v} = \inf\{\|\varphi\|^L_{M,v'} \mid v \equiv_x v'\}$

$\|(\exists x)\varphi\|^L_{M,v} = \sup\{\|\varphi\|^L_{M,v'} \mid v \equiv_x v'\}$

In order to the above definitions are reasonable, the infimum/supremum should exist in the sense of L. So the structure M is L-safe if all the needed infima and suprema exist, i.e. $\|\varphi\|^L_{M,v}$ is defined for all φ, v.

Definition 7. *Let $\varphi \in J$, M be a safe L-structure for J.*

(i) The truth value of φ in M is $\|\varphi\|^L_M = \inf\{\|\varphi\|^L_{M,v} \mid v$ M $-$ evaluation$\}$.

(ii) A formula φ of a language J is an L-tautology if $\|\varphi\|^L_M = 1_L$ *for each safe L-structure M. i.e.* $\|\varphi\|^L_{M,v} = 1$ *for each safe L-structure M and each M-valuation of object variables.*

Remark 1. For each $h \in (0,1], k \in (0,1), ([0,1], \wedge_{h,k}, \Rightarrow_{h,k}, \min, \max, 0, 1, \triangle, -)$ is a $L\Pi G^-$-algebra. So the predicate system $\forall \mathcal{UL}^-_{h\in(0,1]}$ can be considered the axiomatization for 1-level universal AND operator.

Theorem 1. *(Soundness)*[18] *Let* L *is linearly ordered* $L\Pi G^-$-*algebra and* φ *is a formula in* J*, if* $\vdash \varphi$*, then* φ *is* L*-tautology, i.e.* $\|\varphi\|^L_M = 1_L$.

Theorem 2. *(Strong Soundness)*[18] *Let* T *be a theory,* L *is linearly ordered* $L\Pi G^-$-*algebra and* φ *is a formula in* J*, if* $T \vdash \varphi$ (φ *is provable in* T)*, then* $\|\varphi\|^L_M = 1_L$ *for each linearly ordered* $L\Pi G^-$-*algebra* L *and each* L-*model* M *of* T.

Theorem 3. *(Deduction Theorem)*[18] *Let* T *be a theory,* φ, ψ *are closed formulas. Then* $(T \cup \{\varphi\}) \vdash \psi$ *iff* $T \vdash \triangle\varphi \to \psi$.

3   Completeness of $\forall \mathcal{UL}^-_{h\in(0,1]}$

Definition 8. *Let* T *be a theory on* $\forall \mathcal{UL}^-_{h\in(0,1]}$.
  (1) T *is consistent if there is a formula* φ *unprovable in* T.
  (2) T *is complete if for each pair* φ, ψ *of closed formula,* $T \vdash (\varphi \to \psi)$ *or* $T \vdash (\psi \to \varphi)$.
  (3) T *is Henkin if for each closed formula of the form* $(\forall x)\varphi(x)$ *unprovable in* T *there is a constant* c *in the language of* T *such that* $\varphi(c)$ *is unprovable.*

Lemma 4. T *is inconsistent iff* $T \vdash \bar{0}$.

Lemma 5. T *is complete iff for each pair* φ, ψ *of closed formulas if* $T \vdash \varphi \vee \psi$*, then* T *proves* φ *or* T *proves* ψ.

Proof. Sufficiency: For each pair φ, ψ of closed formulas, being $(\varphi \to \psi) \vee (\psi \to \varphi)$ is theorem in $\forall \mathcal{UL}^-_{h\in(0,1]}$, so $T \vdash (\varphi \to \psi) \vee (\psi \to \varphi)$, thus $T \vdash (\varphi \to \psi)$ or $T \vdash (\psi \to \varphi)$. Thus T is complete.
  Necessity: assume T is complete and $T \vdash \varphi \vee \psi$, Either $T \vdash \varphi \to \psi$ and then $T \vdash (\varphi \vee \psi) \to \psi$, thus $T \vdash \psi$, or $T \vdash \psi \to \varphi$ and then similarly $T \vdash \varphi$.

Definition 9. *Let* T *be a theory, the set of all closed formulas over* $\forall \mathcal{UL}^-_{h\in(0,1]}$ *is denoted by* $F^c(\forall \mathcal{UL}^-_{h\in(0,1]})$. *The definition of relation* $\sim_T$ *on* $F^c(\forall \mathcal{UL}^-_{h\in(0,1]})$ *is:* $\varphi \sim_T \psi$ *iff* $T \vdash \varphi \to \psi, T \vdash \psi \to \varphi$.

Obviously, $\sim_T$ is equivalent relation on $F^c(\forall \mathcal{UL}^-_{h\in(0,1]})$, and which holds on $\&, \to, \triangle, -$. So the quotient algebra
$$[F]_T = F^c(\forall \mathcal{UL}^-_{h\in(0,1]})/ \sim_T = \{[\varphi]_T | \varphi \in F^c(\forall \mathcal{UL}^-_{h\in(0,1]})\}$$
of $F^c(\forall \mathcal{UL}^-_{h\in(0,1]})$ about $\sim_T$ is $L\Pi G^-$ algebra, and, $[\varphi]_T = \{\psi \in F^c(\forall \mathcal{UL}^-_{h\in(0,1]}) | \psi \sim_T \varphi\}$, the partial order $\leq$ on $[F]_T$ is $[\varphi]_T \leq [\psi]_T$ iff $T \vdash \varphi \to \psi$.

Lemma 6. *(1) If T is complete then $[F]_T$ is linearly ordered.*

(2) If T is Henkin then for each formula $\varphi(x)$ with just one free variable x, $[(\forall x)\varphi]_T = \inf_c[\varphi(c)]_T, [(\exists x)\varphi]_T = \sup_c[\varphi(c)]_T$, in which c running over all constants of T.

Proof. (1) is obvious since $[\varphi]_T \leq [\psi]_T$ iff $T \vdash \varphi \to \psi$.

(2) Clearly, $[(\forall x)\varphi(x)]_T \leq \inf_c[\varphi(c)]_T$ for each c, thus we have $[(\forall x)\varphi(x)]_T \leq \inf_c[\varphi(c)]_T$. To prove that $[(\forall x)\varphi(x)]_T$ is the infimum of all $[\varphi(c)]_T$, assume $[\gamma]_T \leq [\varphi(c)]_T$ for each c, we have to prove $[\gamma]_T \leq [(\forall x)\varphi(x)]_T$ (which means that $[(\forall x)\varphi(x)]_T$ is the greatest lower bound of all $[\varphi(c)]_T$). But if $[\gamma]_T \not\leq [(\forall x)\varphi(x)]_T$ then $T \not\vdash \gamma \to (\forall x)\varphi(x)$, thus $T \not\vdash (\forall x)(\gamma \to \varphi(x))$. So by the henkin property, there is a constant c such that $T \not\vdash \gamma \to \varphi(c)$, thus $[\gamma]_T \not\leq [\varphi(c)]_T$, a contradiction.

Similarly, $[\varphi(c)]_T \leq [(\exists x)\varphi(x)]_T$ for each c. Assume $[\varphi(c)]_T \leq [\gamma]_T$ for each c, we prove $[(\exists x)\varphi]_T \leq [\gamma]_T$. Indeed, if $[(\exists x)\varphi]_T \not\leq [\gamma]_T$ then $T \not\vdash (\exists x)\varphi(x) \to \gamma$, thus $T \not\vdash (\forall x)(\varphi(x) \to \gamma)$ and for some c, $T \not\vdash \varphi(c) \to \gamma$, thus $[\varphi(c)]_T \not\leq [\gamma]_T$, a contradiction. This completes the proof.

Lemma 7. *For each theory T and each closed formula α, if $T \not\vdash \alpha$ then there is a complete Henkin supertheory $\widehat{T}$ of T such that $\widehat{T} \not\vdash \alpha$.*

Proof. First observe that if T' is an extension of T, $T' \not\vdash \alpha$, and (φ, ψ) is a pair of closed formulas then either $(T' \cup \{\varphi \to \psi\}) \not\vdash \alpha$ or $(T' \cup \{\psi \to \varphi\}) \not\vdash \alpha$. This is proved easily using the deduction theorem(Theorem 3). Indeed, if $T', \{\varphi \to \psi\} \vdash \alpha$ and $T', \{\psi \to \varphi\} \vdash \alpha$, then $T' \vdash \Delta(\varphi \to \psi) \to \alpha, T' \vdash \Delta(\psi \to \varphi) \to \alpha$, so $T' \vdash \Delta(\varphi \to \psi) \vee \Delta(\psi \to \varphi) \to \alpha$, thus $T' \vdash \alpha$, a contradiction.

Put $T'' = T' \cup \{\varphi \to \psi\}$ in the former case and $T'' = T' \cup \{\psi \to \varphi\}$ in the latter, T'' is the extension of T' deciding (φ, ψ) and keeping α unprovable.

We shall construct $\widehat{T}$ in countably many stages. First extend the language J of T to J' adding new constants $c_0, c_1, c_2, \cdots$. In the construction we have to decide each pair (φ, ψ) of closed J'-formulas and ensure the Henkin property for each closed J'-formula of the form $(\forall x)\chi(x)$. These are countably many tasks and may be enumerated by natural numbers(e.g. in even steps we shall decide all pair (φ, ψ), in odd ones process all formulas $(\forall x)\chi(x)$—or take any other enumeration).

Put $T_0 = T$ and $\alpha_0 = \alpha$, then $T_0 \not\vdash \alpha_0$. Assume T_n, α_n have been constructed such that T_n extends T_0, $T_n \vdash \alpha \to \alpha_n, T_n \not\vdash \alpha_n$; we construct T_{n+1}, α_{n+1} in such a way that $T_n \vdash \alpha \to \alpha_{n+1}, T_{n+1} \not\vdash \alpha_{n+1}$ and T_{n+1} fulfils the n-th task.

Case 1 n−th task is deciding (φ, ψ). Let T_{n+1} be extension of T_n deciding (φ, ψ) and keeping α_n unprovable; put $\alpha_{n+1} = \alpha_n$.

Case 2 n−th task is processing $(\forall x)\chi(x)$. First let c be one of the new constant not occurring in T_n.

Subcase(a) $T_n \not\vdash \alpha_n \vee \chi(c)$, thus $T_n \not\vdash (\forall x)\chi(x)$. Put $T_{n+1} = T_n$, $\alpha_{n+1} = \alpha_n \vee \chi(c)$.

Subcase(b) $T_n \vdash \alpha_n \vee \chi(c)$, thus $T_n \vdash \alpha_n \vee \chi(x)$ by the standard argument(in the proof of $\alpha_n \vee \chi(c)$ replace c by a new variable x throughout). Hence $T_n \vdash (\forall x)(\alpha_n \vee \chi(x))$ and using axiom (U19) for the first time, $T_n \vdash \alpha_n \vee (\forall x)\chi(x)$. Thus $T_n \cup \{(\forall x)\chi(x) \to \alpha_n\} \vdash \alpha_n$ so that $T_n \cup \{\alpha_n \to (\forall x)\chi(x)\} \not\vdash \alpha_n, T_n \cup \{\alpha_n \to$

$(\forall x)\chi(x)\} \vdash (\forall x)\chi(x)$ does not prove α_n but it does prove $(\forall x)\chi(x)$. Thus put $T_{n+1} = T_n \cup \{\alpha_n \to (\forall x)\chi(x)\}$ and $\alpha_{n+1} = \alpha_n$.

Now let $\widehat{T}$ be the union of all T_n. Then clearly $\widehat{T}$ is complete and $\widehat{T} \vdash \alpha$(since for all n, $\widehat{T} \vdash \alpha$). We show that $\widehat{T}$ is Henkin. Let $\widehat{T} \nvdash (\forall x)\chi(x)$ and let $(\forall x)\chi(x)$ be processed in step n. Then $T_{n+1} \nvdash (\forall x)\chi(x), T_{n+1} \nvdash \alpha_{n+1}$, thus subcase (a) applies and $\widehat{T} \nvdash \alpha_{n+1}$, α_{n+1} being $\alpha_n \vee \chi(c)$. Hence $\widehat{T} \nvdash \chi(c)$. This completes the proof.

Lemma 8. *For each complete Henkin theory T and each closed formula α unprovable in T there is a linearly ordered $L\Pi G^-$-algebra L and L-model M of T such that $\|\alpha\|_M^L < 1_L$.*

Proof. Take M be the set of all constants of the language of T, $m_c = c$ for each such constant. Let L be the lattice of classes of T-equivalent closed formulas, i.e. put $[\varphi]_T = \{\psi | T \vdash \varphi \equiv \psi\}, [\varphi]_T * [\psi]_T = [\varphi \& \psi]_T, [\varphi]_T \Rightarrow [\psi]_T = [\varphi \to \psi]_T$. So L is a linearly ordered $L\Pi G^-$-algebra(since $T \vdash \varphi \to \psi$ or $T \vdash \psi \to \varphi$ for each pair (φ, ψ)).

For each predicate P of arity n, let $r_P(c_1, \cdots, c_n) = [P(c_1, \cdots, c_n)]_T$, this completes the definition of M. It remains to prove $\|\alpha\|_M^L = [\alpha]_T$ for each closed formula φ. Then for each axiom φ of T we have $\|\varphi\|_M^L = [\varphi]_T = [1]_T = 1_L$, but $\|\alpha\|_M^L = [\alpha]_T \neq [1]_T = 1_L$. For atomic closed formula φ the claim follows by definition; the induction step for connectives is obvious. We handle the quantifiers. Let

$(\forall x)\varphi(x), (\exists x)\varphi(x)$ be closed, then by the induction hypothesis,
$$\|(\forall x)\varphi(x)\|_M^L = \inf_c \|\varphi(c)\|_M^L = \inf_c [\varphi(c)]_T = [(\forall x)\varphi(x)]_T$$
$$\|(\exists x)\varphi(x)\|_M^L = \sup_c \|\varphi(c)\|_M^L = \sup_c [\varphi(c)]_T = [(\exists x)\varphi(x)]_T$$
Here we use lemma and the fact that in our M, each element c of M is the meaning of a constant (namely itself); this gives $\|(\forall x)\varphi(x)\|_M^L = \inf_c \|\varphi(c)\|_M^L$ and the dual for $\exists$.

Using the above lemmas, we can get the following completeness theorem.

Theorem 4. *(Completeness) For predicate calculus system $\forall \mathcal{U L}_{h\in(0,1]}^-$, T is a theory, φ is a formula, $T \vdash \varphi$ iff for each linearly ordered $L\Pi G^-$-algebra L and each safe L-model M of T, $\|\varphi\|_M^L = 1_L$.*

4   Conclusion

In this paper a predicate calculus formal deductive system $\forall \mathcal{U L}_{h\in(0,1]}^-$ according to the propositional system $\mathcal{U L}_{h\in(0,1]}^-$ for 1-level universal AND operator is built up. We prove the system $\forall \mathcal{U L}_{h\in(0,1]}^-$ is sound and complete. The deduction theorem are also given.

Acknowledgement. This work is supported by Scientific Research Program Funded by Shaanxi Provincial Education Department (Program No.2010JK567).

References

1. Hajek, P.: Metamathematics of Fuzzy Logic. Kluwer Academic Publishers, Dordrecht (1998)
2. Esteva, F., Godo, L.: Monoidal t-normbased logic:towards a logic for left-continous t-norms. Fuzzy Sets and Systems 124, 271–288 (2001)
3. Cignoli, R., Esteva, F., Godo, L., Torrens, A.: Basic fuzzy logic is the logic of continuous t-norms and their residual. Soft Computing 4, 106–112 (2000)
4. Hohle, U.: Commutative, residuated l-monoids. In: Hohle, U., Klement, E.P. (eds.) Non-Classical Logics and Their Applications to Fuzzy Subsets, pp. 53–106. Kluwer Academic Publishers, Dordrecht (1995)
5. Esteva, F., Godo, L., et al.: Residuated fuzzy logics with an involutive negation. Archive for Mathmatical Logic 39, 103–124 (2000)
6. Klement, E.P., Mesiar, R., Pap, E.: Triangular Norms. Kluwer Academic Publishers, Dordrecht (2000)
7. Pei, D.W., Wang, G.J.: The completeness and applications of the formal system L*. Science in China (Series F) 45, 40–50 (2002)
8. Wang, S.M., Wang, B.S., Pei, D.W.: A fuzzy logic for an ordinal sum t-norm. Fuzzy Sets and Systems 149, 297–307 (2005)
9. Wang, G.J.: Non-classical Mathematical Logic and Approximate Reasoning. Science Press, Beijing (2000) (in Chinese)
10. Pei, D.W.: First-order Formal System K^* and its Completeness. Chinese Annals of Mathematics, Series A 23(6), 675–684 (2002)
11. Wu, H.B.: Competeness of $BL_\triangle^*$ System. Journal of Jishou University (Natural Science Edition) 30(6), 1–5 (2009)
12. He, H.C., et al.: Universal Logic Principle. Science Press, Beijing (2001) (in Chinese)
13. Ma, Y.C., He, H.C.: The Fuzzy Reasoning Rules Based on Universal Logic. In: 2005 IEEE International Conference on GrC, pp. 561–564. IEEE Press, Los Alamitos (2005)
14. Ma, Y.C., He, H.C.: A Propositional Calculus Formal Deductive System $\mathcal{UL}_{h\in(0,1]}$ of Universal Logic. In: Proceedings of 2005 ICMLC, pp. 2716–2721. IEEE Press, Los Alamitos (2005)
15. Ma, Y.C., Li, Q.Y.: A Propositional Deductive System Of Universal Logic with Projection Operator. In: Proceedings of 2006 ISDA, pp. 993–998. IEEE Press, Los Alamitos (2006)
16. Ma, Y.C., He, H.C.: The Axiomatization for 0-Level Universal Logic. In: Yeung, D.S., Liu, Z.-Q., Wang, X.-Z., Yan, H. (eds.) ICMLC 2005. LNCS (LNAI), vol. 3930, pp. 367–376. Springer, Heidelberg (2006)
17. Ma, Y.C., He, H.C.: Axiomatization for 1-level Universal AND Operator. The Journal of China Universities of Posts and Telecommunications 15(2), 125–129 (2008)
18. Ma, Y.C., He, H.C.: The predicate formal system based on 1-level universal AND operator and its soundness (submitted)

Some Extensions of the Logic psUL

Minxia Luo and Ning Yao

Department of Mathematics, China Jiliang University, Hangzhou 310018, China
minxialuo@163.com

Abstract. Based on Lambek calculus and residuated lattices, psUL has been proposed by Metcalfe, Olivetti and Gabbay as a non-commutative version of the uninorm logic UL, but until recently the corresponding research has been lacking. The present paper mainly surveys the schematic extensions of psUL as well as the relation between non-commutative logics having been studied based on pseudo-t-norm. In particular, using a diagram, we display the features and connections between these logics.

Keywords: Pseudo-uninorm, Residuated Lattices, Hilbert System.

1 Introduction

The non-commutative version psUL of uninorm logic has been presented by Metcalfe etc. in [1], where the Hilbert system and Gentzen system for psUL are given by the Full Lambek Calculus FL (see [2, 3]) and residuated lattices (see [4, 5]). It is noticed that psMTL (see [6]) is the schematic extension of psUL and the standard completeness for psUL is not valid recently proved by Wang and Zhao in [7].

Corresponding to psBL-algebras, psMTL-algebras and psMV-algebras ([8, 9, 10, 11, 12]), the logics psBL, psMTL and $\mathcal{PL}$ have been investigated in detail (see [6, 13, 14, 15]). Whereas it is rare to see the related research on the logic of psUL plus the non-commutative version of divisibility and its extensions, whether there is a link between the extensions of psUL and psBL, psMTL etc. is the concern of this article.

This paper is organized as follows: firstly, we recall some basic definitions of pseudo-uninorm, residuated lattices, and some axiomatic systems e.g. FL, BFL, psUL, psBL and psMTL. Secondly, we present the logic psBUL, which is the extension of psUL, and the extensions of psBUL with the non-commutative version of involution and the weakening axiom (W). We also prove that psBL and $\mathcal{PL}$ may be regarded as the extensions of psBUL. Finally, we characterize the relationships between the logics mentioned in the paper by a diagram in which the clear outline of the main contents of this paper is displayed.

2 Preliminaries

In this section, some well-known definitions and a theorem as well as a lemma will be given. And denote "if and only if" by "*iff*" in this paper.

H. Deng et al. (Eds.): AICI 2011, Part I, LNAI 7002, pp. 609–617, 2011.
© Springer-Verlag Berlin Heidelberg 2011

Definition 1. ([1]) A pseudo-uninorm is a function $* : [0,1]^2 \to [0,1]$ such that for some $e_* \in [0,1]$, for all $x, y, z \in [0,1]$: (1) $(x * y) * z = x * (y * z)$ (associativity). (2) $x \le y$ implies $x * z \le y * z$ and $z * x \le z * y$ (monotonicity). (3) $e_* * x = x * e_* = x$ (identity).

If $e_* = 1$ or $e_* = 0$, then $*$ is a pseudo-t-norm or a pseudo-t-conorm respectively.

$*$ is residuated *iff* there exist two functions $\to_*, \leadsto_* : [0,1]^2 \to [0,1]$ satisfying $x * y \le z$ iff $x \le y \leadsto_* z$ iff $y \le x \to_* z$ for all $x, y, z \in [0,1]$.

Definition 2. ([1]) A pointed residuated lattice (prl for short) is the algebra: $\mathcal{X} = \langle L, \wedge, \vee, *, \to, \leadsto, e, f \rangle$ with universe L, binary operations $\wedge, \vee, *, \to, \leadsto$, and constants e, f such that: (1). $\langle L, \wedge, \vee \rangle$ is a lattice. (2). $\langle L, *, e \rangle$ is a monoid. (3). $x * y \le z$ iff $x \le y \leadsto z$ iff $y \le x \to z$ for all $x, y, z \in L$.

Bounded pointed residuated lattices (bprls) are algebras $\langle L, \wedge, \vee, *, \to, \leadsto, e, f, \bot, \top \rangle$ such that $\langle L, \wedge, \vee, *, \to, \leadsto, e, f \rangle$ is a prl with top and bottom elements $\top$ and $\bot$.

When L is the real unit interval $[0,1]$ with the usual order, the bprl is called the standard bprl, where the operation $*$ could be called a residuated pseudo-uninorm which is an increasing associative binary function on $[0,1]$ with unit element e and residuals $\to$ and $\leadsto$.

Remark 1. The constant f in the Definition 2 is only really needed in the definitions of negation in the logics namely $\neg x = x \to f, \sim x = x \leadsto f$. And for t-norm based logics, f and $\bot$ are typically identified with $\overline{0}, \top$ and e are identified with $\overline{1}$.

Denote the class of all pointed residuated lattices (prls) and bounded pointed residuated lattices (bprls) by $\mathcal{RL}^+$ and $\mathcal{BRL}^+$ respectively, which can be identified with the classes of residuated lattices $\mathcal{RL}$ and bounded residuated lattices $\mathcal{BRL}$ plus $f (f \ne e)$, the variety of bounded pointed residuated chains by $\mathcal{BRL}^{+C}$, we then have the following definition.

Definition 3. ([1, 5]) $\mathcal{BRL}^{+C}$ is the class of bprls satisfying:

$$(\mathcal{E}_1) \quad (x \vee y) \wedge e = (x \wedge e) \vee (y \wedge e)$$

$$(\mathcal{E}_2) \quad e = \lambda_u ((x \vee y) \to x) \vee \rho_v ((x \vee y) \to y)$$

where $\lambda_u(x) = (u \to (x \odot u)) \wedge e$ and $\rho_u(x) = (u \leadsto (u \odot x)) \wedge e$, respectively called the left and right conjugates of x with respect to u.

The Full Lambek Calculus FL, which is an extension of Lambek calculus introduced by J. Lambek ([16]), mainly deals with the non-commutative logics, and the corresponding algebraic structure FL-algebras are the variety of pointed residuated lattices. The variety of bounded pointed residuated lattices corresponds to

Bounded Full Lambek Calculus BFL. The Hilbert systems for FL and BFL have been thoroughly investigated given as follows.

Definition 4. ([2, 7])   FL consists of the following axioms and rules:

(L1) $A \rightarrow A$ 　　　　　　　(L2) $(A \rightarrow B) \rightarrow ((C \rightarrow A) \rightarrow (C \rightarrow B))$

(L3) $A \rightarrow ((A \rightsquigarrow B) \rightarrow B)$ 　　　(L4) $(A \rightsquigarrow (B \rightarrow C)) \rightarrow (B \rightarrow (A \rightsquigarrow C))$

(L5) $(B \rightsquigarrow (B \odot (B \rightarrow A))) \rightarrow (B \rightsquigarrow A)$ 　(L6) $B \rightarrow (A \rightarrow (A \odot B))$

(L7) $(B \rightarrow (A \rightarrow C)) \rightarrow ((A \odot B) \rightarrow C)$ 　(L8) $A \rightarrow (A \vee B)$

(L9) $((A \wedge e) \odot (B \wedge e)) \rightarrow (A \wedge B)$ 　　　(L10) $B \rightarrow (A \vee B)$

(L11) $(A \wedge B) \rightarrow A$ 　(L10) $(A \wedge B) \rightarrow B$ 　　(L12) $A \rightarrow (e \rightarrow A)$

(L13) $((A \rightarrow B) \wedge (A \rightarrow C)) \rightarrow (A \rightarrow (B \wedge C))$ 　　(L14) e

(L15) $((A \rightarrow C) \wedge (B \rightarrow C)) \rightarrow ((A \vee B) \rightarrow C)$

$$\frac{A \quad A \rightarrow B}{B}(mp_{\rightarrow}) \quad \frac{A \quad B}{A \wedge B}(adj) \quad \frac{A}{B \rightarrow (A \odot B)}(pn_{\rightarrow}) \quad \frac{A}{B \rightsquigarrow (B \odot A)}(pn_{\rightsquigarrow})$$

Definition 5. ([1]) BFL is the extension of FL by the axioms

$$(L17) \bot \rightarrow A \qquad (L18)\, A \rightarrow \top$$

Lemma 1. ([2]) The following are true in BFL

(1) $A \rightarrow B, B \rightarrow C \vdash A \rightarrow C$. (2) $A \rightsquigarrow B \vdash A \rightarrow B$. (3) $A \rightarrow B \vdash A \rightsquigarrow B$.

(4) $\vdash (A \vee B) \rightarrow (B \vee C)$. (5) $\vdash (A \odot B) \odot C \rightarrow A \odot (B \odot C)$.

(6) $\vdash (A \odot B \rightsquigarrow C) \rightarrow (A \rightsquigarrow (B \rightsquigarrow C))$.

Remark 2   For the presence of (2), (3) i.e. $A \rightsquigarrow B \vdash A \rightarrow B, A \rightarrow B \vdash A \rightsquigarrow B$, we

have the modus ponens for $\rightsquigarrow$, i.e. $\dfrac{A \quad A \rightsquigarrow B}{B}(mp_{\rightsquigarrow})$.

In particular, the logic psUL has been intensively researched by Metcalfe in [1] as an extension of BFL with the axioms corresponding to the conditions (ε_1) and (ε_2) in Definition 3.

Definition 6. ([1]) The Hilbert systems for the logic psUL consists of BFL extended with: 　　　$(psPRL_1)$ 　$(A \vee B) \wedge e \rightarrow (A \wedge e) \vee (B \wedge e)$

$(psPRL_2)$ 　$(C \rightarrow (((A \vee B) \rightarrow A) \odot C)) \vee (C \rightsquigarrow (C \odot ((A \vee B) \rightarrow B)))$

Definition 7. ([1]) A psUL-algebra is a pointed bounded residuated lattice $\mathcal{X} = ($ L, $\wedge, \vee, *, \rightarrow, \rightsquigarrow, e, f, \bot, \top)$ with universe L, binary operations $\wedge, \vee, *, \rightarrow, \rightsquigarrow$ and element $\top$ and the bottom element $\bot$; 　(2) $(L, *, e)$ is a monoid ; 　(3) $\forall x, y, z \in L, x * y \leq z\, iff\, x \leq y \rightsquigarrow z\, iff\, y \leq x \rightarrow z$; 　(4) $(x \vee y) \wedge e = (x \wedge e) \vee (y \wedge e)$; (5) $((u \rightarrow ((x \vee y \rightarrow x) * u)) \wedge e) \vee ((v \rightsquigarrow (v * (x \vee y \rightarrow y))) \wedge e) = e$.

In psUL-algebra, similar to the general valuation and model, the concepts of valuation and model are defined (see [1]). $\Gamma \vdash_{\chi} C$ means every $\mathcal{X}$-model of Γ is an $\mathcal{X}$-model of $\{C\}$. $\Gamma \vdash_{psUL} C$ means a proof of a formula C in psUL from a set of formulas Γ exists. Let LIN(L) be the set of all L-chains, and a logic is a schematic extension (extension for short) of L *iff* it results from L by adding axioms in the same language.

Theorem 1. ([1, 7])   (1) $\Gamma \vdash_{psUL^D} C$ *iff* $\Gamma \vDash_{\chi} C$ for every standard psUL-algebra $\mathcal{X}$, where $psUL^D$ is psUL plus (*Density*) $\dfrac{(A \to p) \vee (p \to B) \vee C}{(A \to B) \vee C}$.

(2) $\Gamma \vdash_{psUL} C$ *iff* $\Gamma \vDash_{\chi} C$ for every linearly ordered psUL-algebra $\mathcal{X}$.

(3) $\Gamma \vdash_{L} C$ *iff* $\Gamma \vDash_{LIN(L)} C$ for any psUL-extension L.

Definition 8. ([13, 14]) psBL is the logic with the connectives $\odot, \to, \rightsquigarrow, \wedge, \vee$, truth constant $\overline{0}$ and the following axioms and deduction rules:

Axioms:

$(\tilde{A}1)$ $(B \to C) \to ((A \to B) \to (A \to C))$ $(\tilde{A}2)$ $(A \odot B) \rightsquigarrow A$

$(B \rightsquigarrow C) \rightsquigarrow ((A \rightsquigarrow B) \rightsquigarrow (A \rightsquigarrow C))$ $(\tilde{A}3)$ $(A \odot B) \rightsquigarrow B$

$(\tilde{A}4)$ $(A \wedge B) \leftrightarrow (A \odot (A \to B)) \leftrightarrow (B \odot (B \to A))$

$(A \wedge B) \leftrightsquigarrow ((A \rightsquigarrow B) \odot A) \leftrightsquigarrow ((B \rightsquigarrow A) \odot B)$

$(\tilde{A}5)$ $(A \to (B \to C)) \leftrightsquigarrow ((B \odot A) \to C)$

$(A \rightsquigarrow (B \rightsquigarrow C)) \leftrightsquigarrow ((A \odot B) \rightsquigarrow C)$

$(\tilde{A}6)$ $((A \to B) \to C) \to (((B \to A) \to C) \to C)$ $(\tilde{A}7)$ $\overline{0} \rightsquigarrow A$

the same with $\to$ replaced by $\rightsquigarrow$

$(\tilde{A}8)$ $(A \vee B) \leftrightsquigarrow [((A \to B) \rightsquigarrow B) \wedge ((B \to A) \rightsquigarrow A)]$

$\leftrightsquigarrow [((A \rightsquigarrow B) \to B) \wedge ((B \rightsquigarrow A) \to A)]$

Deduction rules: Modus ponens: from $A, A \to B$ infer B ; from $A, A \rightsquigarrow B$ infer B. Implications (Imp): from $A \to B$ infer $A \rightsquigarrow B$ and vice versa.

A psBL-algebra is a structure $\mathcal{X} = (L, \wedge, \vee, *, \to, \rightsquigarrow, 0, 1)$ where(1) $(L, \wedge, \vee, 0, 1)$ is a bounded lattice,   (2) $*$ is associative, 1 is its unit element, and for all x, y, z, (3) $x * y \leq z$ iff $x \leq y \rightsquigarrow z$ iff $y \leq x \to z$, (4) $x \wedge y = (x \rightsquigarrow y) * x = x * (x \to y)$, (5) $(x \to y) \vee (y \to x) = 1 = (x \rightsquigarrow y) \vee (y \rightsquigarrow x)$.

(2) is the axiom of monoid, (3) of residuation, (4) of divisibility , (5) of prelinearity.

Definition 9. ([13])   psMTL is the logic with primitive connectives $\rightarrow, \rightsquigarrow, \odot, \wedge, \vee$, the constant $\overline{0}$ and the axioms $(\tilde{A}1) - (\tilde{A}3)$, $(\tilde{A}5) - (\tilde{A}8)$ of psBL plus the axioms

$(\tilde{A}4a)$ $(A \odot (A \rightarrow B)) \rightsquigarrow (A \wedge B), ((A \rightsquigarrow B) \odot A) \rightsquigarrow (A \wedge B)$

$(\tilde{A}4b)$ $(A \wedge B) \rightsquigarrow B$ $(\tilde{A}4c)$ $(A \wedge B) \rightsquigarrow (B \wedge A)$

Deduction rules are modus ponens and (Imp).

A psMTL-algebra is a structure $\mathcal{X} = (L, \wedge, \vee, *, \rightarrow, \rightsquigarrow, 0, 1)$ satisfying the axioms (1)-(3), (5) from Definition 8 plus the following

(4') $(x \rightsquigarrow y) * x \leq x \wedge y, x * (x \rightarrow y) \leq x \wedge y$.

Note that it is very interest that psMTL is the extension of psUL with the weakening axiom $(W) (A \rightarrow e) \wedge (f \rightarrow A)$, which is introduced by Metcalfe etc. in [1] and is very helpful for the study later.

3 Main Results

In this section, we will investigate the non-commutative case of fuzzy logics with $[0,1)$-continuous uninorms. Fuzzy logics with $[0,1)$-continuous uninorms, namely basic uninorm logic BUL, have been investigated by Gabbay and Metcalfe in [17]. Combining Hájek's approach on pseudo-t-norm with the approach on psUL, we will present a logic psBUL which is a non-commutative analogue of BUL, and introduce the corresponding psBUL-algebras.

The language of the propositional calculus BUL consists of formulas built inductively as usual from a set of propositional variables $A, B, C \ldots$, binary connectives $\odot, \rightarrow, \wedge, \vee$ and constants $\top, \bot, e, f$. There are some defined connectives as follows: $\neg A =_{def} A \rightarrow f$, $-x =_{def} x \rightarrow e$, $u =_{def} -\top$,

$$A \leftrightarrow B =_{def} (A \rightarrow B) \wedge (B \rightarrow A).$$

Definition 10. ([17]) The Hilbert systems for BUL is UL extended with the following "restricted divisibility" axiom:

$(RDIV)$ $(\top \rightarrow A) \vee (A \rightarrow (B \wedge u)) \vee (B \rightarrow (A \odot (A \rightarrow B)))$

and the "u-idempotence" axiom: $(U) u \leftrightarrow (u \odot u)$.

BUL-algebras are UL-algebras satisfying the conditions:

(1). $e \leq (\top \rightarrow x) \vee (x \rightarrow (y \wedge u)) \vee (y \rightarrow (x * (x \rightarrow y)))$,   (2). $u = u * u$.

The language of the propositional calculus for non-commutative BUL is the language of BUL above plus a new binary connective $\rightsquigarrow$ and new defined connectives $\sim A =_{def} A \rightsquigarrow f$, $A \leftrightsquigarrow B =_{def} (A \rightsquigarrow B) \odot (B \rightsquigarrow A)$. In addition, in the context of non-commutative logics, $A \leftrightarrow B$ is newly defined as $(A \to B) \odot (B \to A)$.

Definition 11. The Hilbert system for psBUL is psUL plus the following axioms:

$(psRDIV_1)$ $(\top \rightsquigarrow A) \vee (A \rightsquigarrow (B \wedge u)) \vee (B \rightsquigarrow ((A \rightsquigarrow B) \odot A))$

$(psRDIV_2)$ $(\top \to A) \vee (A \to (B \wedge u)) \vee (B \to (A \odot (A \to B)))$

(U) $u \leftrightarrow (u \odot u)$

Definition 12. A psBUL-algebra is a psUL-algebra which satisfies the following conditions: (1a). $e \le (\top \rightsquigarrow x) \vee (x \rightsquigarrow (y \wedge u)) \vee (y \rightsquigarrow ((x \rightsquigarrow y) * x))$,

(1b). $e \le (\top \to x) \vee (x \to (y \wedge u)) \vee (y \to (x * (x \to y)))$, (2). $u = u * u$,

where the conditions (1a) and (1b) may be respectively viewed as restricted version of the divisibility condition i.e. $(x \rightsquigarrow y) \vee (y \rightsquigarrow ((x \rightsquigarrow y) * x))$ and $(x \to y) \vee (y \to (x * (x \to y)))$ for pseudo-BL algebras [13, 14].

It is obvious that psBUL can be regarded as an extension of psUL, so by the Theorem 1(3), the following theorem is valid.

Theorem 2. $\Gamma \vdash_{psBUL} C$ iff $\Gamma \vDash_{\mathcal{X}} C$ for every linearly ordered psBUL-algebra $\mathcal{X}$.

In the sequel, we also introduce the axiomatic extensions for logics on psBUL with the non-commutative version of axiom of involution and the weakening axiom.

Theorem 3. An axiomatization for non-commutative basic logic psBL based on pseudo-t-norm is given by extending psBUL with the weakening axiom $(W)(A \to e) \wedge (f \to A)$.

Proof. By the fact that psMTL is the extension of psUL with the weakening axiom $(A \to e) \wedge (f \to A)$, which has been given in [1], and the relationship between psMTL and psBL, it is sufficient to prove that psBUL proves the following formulas i.e. the one axiom of psBL:

$$(A \wedge B) \leftrightarrow (A \odot (A \to B)) \leftrightarrow (B \odot (B \to A)),$$

$$(A \wedge B) \leftrightsquigarrow ((A \rightsquigarrow B) \odot A) \leftrightsquigarrow ((B \rightsquigarrow A) \odot B).$$

Here we only give the proof of the first part of the axiom above, similar to the latter part. Because psUL with weakening axiom (W) can prove

$$((A \rightsquigarrow B) \odot A) \rightsquigarrow (A \wedge B), (A \odot (A \to B)) \to (A \wedge B),$$

by means of the axioms $(psRDIV_1)$, $(psRDIV_2)$ and the rules $(pn_\to)$, $(pn_\rightsquigarrow)$, $(mp_\to)$ as well as the definitions of $A \leftrightarrow B$ and $A \leftrightsquigarrow B$, we can obtain

$$(A \wedge B) \leftrightarrow (A \odot (A \to B)) \text{ and } (A \wedge B) \leftrightsquigarrow ((A \rightsquigarrow B) \odot A). \qquad \square$$

Remark 3. Note that the logic psUL can prove the more common weakening axiom $(A \rightarrow (B \rightarrow A))$ by using (W). And the axiom $(A \rightarrow (B \rightarrow A))$ is very important in the course of deriving formulas.

Definition 13. The logic psIBUL—an involutive version of psBUL is psBUL extended with the following axiom: $(psINV)$ $\sim \neg A \rightarrow A, \neg \sim A \rightarrow A$.

The corresponding algebraic structure psIBUL-algebras are psBUL-algebras satisfying $\sim \neg x = x = \neg \sim x$.

Remark 4. The logic psUL can prove not only $A \rightarrow \sim \neg A$ i.e. $A \rightarrow ((A \rightarrow f) \rightsquigarrow f)$, which is derived by $(A \rightarrow f) \rightarrow (A \rightarrow f)$, (L4), the rule $A \rightarrow B \vdash A \rightsquigarrow B$, but also $A \rightarrow \neg \sim A$ which is derived by (L3). Then using $(pn_\rightarrow), (pn_\rightsquigarrow), (mp_\rightarrow)$ and $(mp_\rightsquigarrow)$, we get $\sim \neg A \leftrightarrow A$ and $\neg \sim A \leftrightarrow A$, similarly for $\leftrightsquigarrow$.

Note that psIBUL can be regarded as the extension of psBUL, by Theorem 1(3), the completeness with respect to psIBUL-chains is obtained.

Theorem 4. $\Gamma \vdash_{psIBUL} C$ *iff* $\Gamma \vDash_\chi C$ for every linearly ordered psIBUL-algebra $\mathcal{X}$.

Theorem 5. Non-commutative Łukasiewicz propositional logic $\mathcal{PL}$ is given by extending psIBUL with the weakening axiom $(W) (A \rightarrow e) \wedge (f \rightarrow A)$.

Proof. It is noticed that a psBL-algebra is a psMV-algebra if and only if it satisfies condition $(psDN)$ ([8, 18]), where: $(psDN)$ *(pseudo-Double Negation)* or $(psINV)$ *(pseudo-involutive)* $\sim \neg x = x = \neg \sim x$ for all x. By Theorem 3, psBL corresponds to psBUL plus the axiom (W). So psBUL plus axioms (W) and $(psINV)$ is corresponding to the non-commutative Łukasiewicz propositional logic $\mathcal{PL}$. □

Finally, the following graph distinctly shows the connection between logics studied above.

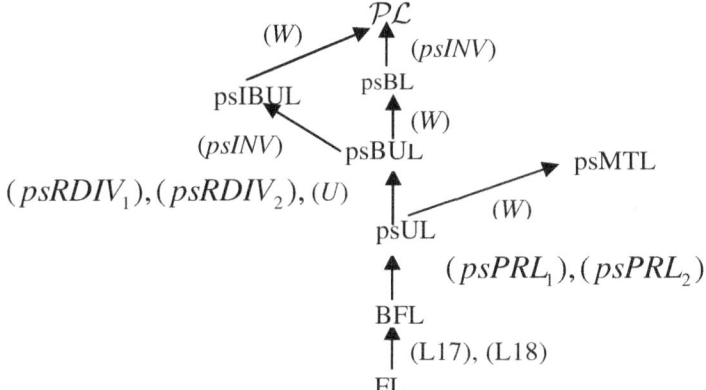

Fig. 1. Diagram of relationships between logics

4 Conclusion

Throughout this research work, our main concern is about the study of non-commutative logics. We have presented non-commutative propositional logics psBUL and its extensions such as psIBUL, psBL and $\mathcal{PL}$ and so on. PsBUL may be regarded as the extension of psUL which is BFL extended with $(psPRL_1)$ and $(psPRL_2)$. Furthermore, in Fig.1 one can see the diagram of relationships among FL, BFL, psUL and psBUL together with its extensions investigated in this paper. In this work, we only do some basic research, there are some other topics of further research, for example, like the research of psUL, the question is whether the standard complete theorem and the Gentzen system for psBUL and its extensions exist. These need to do some further research.

Acknowledgement. This work is supported by the Natural Science Foundation of Zhejiang Province of China (No. Y1110651).

References

1. Metcalfe, G., Olivetti, N., Gabbay, D.: Proof theory for fuzzy logics. Springer Series in Applied Logic, vol. 36 (2009)
2. Galatos, N., Jipsen, P., Kowalski, T., Ono, H.: Residuated Lattices: An algebraic glimpse at substructural logics. Elsevier, Amsterdam (2007)
3. Ono, H.: Substructural logics and residuated lattices —an introduction. In: Hendricks, V.F., Malinowski, J. (eds.) Trends in Logic: 50 years of Studia Logics, vol. 20, pp. 177–212. Kluwer Academic Publishers, Dordrecht (2003)
4. Jipsen, P., Tsinakis, C.: A survey of residuated lattices. In: Martinez, J. (ed.) Ordered Algebraic Structures, pp. 19–56. Kluwer Academic Publishers, Dordrecht (2002)
5. Tsinakis, C., Blount, K.: The structure of residuated lattices. International Journal of Algebra and Computation 13(4), 437–461 (2003)
6. Jenei, S., Montagna, F.: A proof of standard completeness for non-commutative monoidal t-norm logic. Neural Network World 13(5), 481–490 (2003)
7. Wang, S.M., Zhao, B.: HpsUL is not the logic of pseudo-uninorms and their residua. Logic Journal of the IGPL 17(4), 413–419 (2009)
8. DiNola, A., Georgescu, G., Iorgulescu, A.: Pseudo-BL algebras: part I. Multiple Valued Logic 8(5-6), 673–714 (2002a)
9. DiNola, A., Georgescu, G., Iorgulescu, A.: Pseudo-BL algebras: part II. Multiple Valued Logic 8(5-6), 717–750 (2002b)
10. Dvurečenskij, A.: States on pseudo MV-algebras. Studia Logica 68(3), 301–327 (2001)
11. Flondor, P., Georgescu, G., Iorgulescu, A.: Pseudo-t-norms and pseudo-BL algebras. Soft Computing 5(5), 355–371 (2001)
12. Georgescu, G., Iorgulescu, A.: Pseudo-MV algebras. Multiple Valued Logic 6(1-2), 95–135 (2001b)
13. Hájek, P.: Observations on non-commutative fuzzy logic. Soft Computing 8(1), 38–43 (2003)

14. Hájek, P.: Fuzzy logics with non-commutative conjunctions. Journal of Logic and Computation 13(4), 469–479 (2003)
15. Leuştean, I.: Non-commutative Łukasiewicz propositional logic. Archive for Mathematical Logic 45(2), 191–213 (2006)
16. Lambek, J.: The mathematics of sentence structure. Amer. Math. Monthly 65(3), 154–170 (1958)
17. Gabbay, D., Metcalfe, G.: Fuzzy logics based on [0,1)-continuous uninorms. Archive for Mathematical Logic 46(6), 425–469 (2007)
18. Iorgulescu, A.: Classes of examples of pseudo-MV algebras, pseudo-BL algebras and divisible bounded non-commutative residuated lattices. Soft Computing 14(4), 313–327 (2010)

Fuzzy Soft Matrices and Their Applications

Yong Yang and Chenli Ji

College of Mathematics and Information Science, Northwest Normal University
Lanzhou 730070, China
yangzt@nwnu.edu.cn

Abstract. In this paper, we define fuzzy soft matrices and study their basic properties. We then define products of fuzzy soft matrices that satisfy commutative law and present a decision making method. This method can solve decision making problems which consider many observers' views. We finally offer some examples to show that the presented method is more reasonable and reliable in solving practical problems.

Keywords: Soft sets, Fuzzy soft sets, Fuzzy soft matrices, Products of fuzzy soft matrices, Decision making.

1 Introduction

Soft set theory[1] was firstly introduced by Molodtsov in 1999 as a general mathematical tool dealing with uncertainties which traditional mathematical tools cannot handle. Molodtsov has shown several applications of this theory in solving many practical problems in economics, engineering, social science, medical science, etc. Later Maji et al.[2] gave a definition to the fuzzy soft sets. Afterwards, many researchers have worked on this concept, such as Aktas and Cagman[3], Roy and Maji[4], Yang et al.[5], Majumdar and Samanta[6], Xiao et al.[7], etc. and many results have been achieved.

Recently, Cagman and Enginoglu[8] defined soft matrices and products of soft matrices. By using their products, they provided a soft max-min decision making(SMmDM) method which can be applied to some problems that contain uncertainties. But this method does not satisfy commutative law, two different results may be caused if using the same solutions to solve identical decision making problems because of the different product orders. Meanwhile, if a decision making problem needs at least three observers' views, this method will be totally invalid.

In this paper, we first define fuzzy soft matrices and study their basic properties. We then define a new product of fuzzy soft matrices and construct a decision making method, this method can solve many decision making problems that SMmDM method cannot. Finally, we give examples to prove that this method can work well and successfully.

In the following section, we firstly give a definition to fuzzy soft matrices and discuss their properties. In section 3, we define products of fuzzy soft matrices and construct a decision making method, then we give examples which show that the method is practical. Finally we draw some conclusions in the concluding Section 4.

H. Deng et al. (Eds.): AICI 2011, Part I, LNAI 7002, pp. 618–627, 2011.

2   Fuzzy Soft Matrices

Definition 2.1. Let U be an initial universe and E be a set of parameters. Let $P(U)$ denote the power set of U and $FS(U)$ the set of all fuzzy subsets of U and $A \subset E$.

A pair (F, A) is called a soft set over U, where F is a mapping given by $F : A \to P(U)$.

A pair (f, A) is called a fuzzy soft set over U, where f is a mapping given by $f : A \to FS(U)$.

Obviously, a classical soft set (F, A) over U can be seen as a fuzzy soft set (f, A) according to this manner, for any $e \in A$, the image of e under f is defined as the characteristic function of the set $F(e)$,

$$f_e(a) = X_{F(e)}(a) = \begin{cases} 1, & \text{if } a \in F(e); \\ 0, & \text{otherwise} \end{cases}.$$

Definition 2.2. Let (f, E) be a fuzzy soft set over U, where $U = \{u_1, u_2, \cdots, u_m\}$ and $E = \{e_1, e_2, \cdots, e_n\}$, for $\forall u_i \in U$ and $\forall e_j \in E$, there exists the membership degree $a_{ij} = f_{e_j}(u_i)$, then we can present all membership degrees by a table as follows

$$
\begin{array}{ccccc}
 & e_1 & e_2 & \cdots & e_n \\
u_1 & a_{11} & a_{12} & \cdots & a_{1n} \\
u_2 & a_{21} & a_{22} & \cdots & a_{2n} \\
\vdots & \vdots & \vdots & \ddots & \vdots \\
u_m & a_{m1} & a_{m2} & \cdots & a_{mn}
\end{array}.
$$

The fuzzy matrix $A_{m \times n} = [a_{ij}]_{m \times n} = \begin{bmatrix} a_{11} & a_{12} & \cdots & a_{1n} \\ a_{21} & a_{22} & \cdots & a_{2n} \\ \vdots & \vdots & \ddots & \vdots \\ a_{m1} & a_{m2} & \cdots & a_{mn} \end{bmatrix}$ is called the fuzzy soft matrix of (f, E) over U.

According to this definition, a fuzzy soft set (f, E) is uniquely characterized by the fuzzy soft matrix $A_{m \times n}$, and vice versa.

From now on, $FSM_{m \times n}$ denotes the set of all $m \times n$ fuzzy soft matrices over U.

Example 2.1. Let $U = \{u_1, u_2, u_3, u_4, u_5\}$ and $E = \{e_1, e_2, e_3, e_4\}$. (f, E) is a fuzzy soft set over U given as below

$$f_{e_1} = \{0.2 / u_1, 0.7 / u_2, 0.4 / u_3, 0.9 / u_4, 0.0 / u_5\},$$

$$f_{e_2} = \{1.0 \,/\, u_1, 0.8 \,/\, u_2, 0.7 \,/\, u_3, 0.0 \,/\, u_4, 0.2 \,/\, u_5\},$$
$$f_{e_3} = \{0.0 \,/\, u_1, 0.0 \,/\, u_2, 0.0 \,/\, u_3, 0.6 \,/\, u_4, 0.0 \,/\, u_5\},$$
$$f_{e_4} = \{0.0 \,/\, u_1, 0.2 \,/\, u_2, 1.0 \,/\, u_3, 0.0 \,/\, u_4, 0.3 \,/\, u_5\}.$$

Hence the corresponding fuzzy soft matrix $A_{5\times 4}$ is written by

$$A_{5\times 4} = [a_{ij}]_{5\times 4} = \begin{bmatrix} 0.2 & 1.0 & 0.0 & 0.0 \\ 0.7 & 0.8 & 0.0 & 0.2 \\ 0.4 & 0.7 & 0.0 & 1.0 \\ 0.9 & 0.0 & 0.6 & 0.0 \\ 0.0 & 0.2 & 0.0 & 0.3 \end{bmatrix}$$

Definition 2.3. Let $A = [a_{ij}] \in FSM_{m\times n}$. If $a_{ij} = 0$ for all i and j, then A is called the $m \times n$ zero fuzzy soft matrix, denoted by $[0]_{m\times n}$. If $a_{ij} = 1$ for all i and j, then A is called the $m \times n$ universe fuzzy soft matrix, denoted by $[1]_{m\times n}$.

Definition 2.4. Let $A = [a_{ij}]$, $B = [b_{ij}] \in FSM_{m\times n}$. If $a_{ij} \le b_{ij}$ for all i and j, then A is called a fuzzy soft submatrix of B, denoted by $A \subseteq B$. If $A \subseteq B$ and $B \subseteq A$, then A and B are called fuzzy soft equal, denoted by $A = B$, in other words, if $a_{ij} = b_{ij}$ for all i and j, then $A = B$.

Definition 2.5. Let $A = [a_{ij}]$, $B = [b_{ij}] \in FSM_{m\times n}$. We define, for all i and j

$(1) A \cup B = [a_{ij} \vee b_{ij}]_{m\times n}$. $(2) A \cap B = [a_{ij} \wedge b_{ij}]_{m\times n}$.

$(3) A^c = [1 - a_{ij}]_{m\times n}$.

Theorem 2.1. Let $A, B, C, D \in FSM_{m\times n}$. Then

$(1) A \cup A = A$, $A \cap A = A$. $(2) A \cup B = B \cup A$, $A \cap B = B \cap A$.
$(3) (A \cup B) \cup C = A \cup (B \cup C)$, $(A \cap B) \cap C = A \cap (B \cap C)$.
$(4) A \cap (A \cup B) = A$, $A \cup (A \cap B) = A$.
$(5) (A \cup B) \cap C = (A \cap C) \cup (B \cap C)$, $(A \cap B) \cup C = (A \cup C) \cap (B \cup C)$.
$(6) A \cup [0]_{m\times n} = A$, $A \cap [0]_{m\times n} = [0]_{m\times n}$, $A \cup [1]_{m\times n} = [1]_{m\times n}$, $A \cap [1]_{m\times n} = A$.
$(7) (A^c)^c = A$. $(8) (A \cup B)^c = A^c \cap B^c$, $(A \cap B)^c = A^c \cup B^c$.
$(9) A \subseteq B \Rightarrow A \cup B = B$, $A \cap B = A$, $B^c \subseteq A^c$.
$(10) A \subseteq B$, $C \subseteq D \Rightarrow A \cup C \subseteq B \cup D$, $A \cap C \subseteq B \cap D$.

Here we only prove (8), the others are left to readers.

Proof. Let $A = [a_{ij}]$, $B = [b_{ij}] \in FSM_{m \times n}$. Then

$$(A \cup B)^c = [1 - a_{ij} \vee b_{ij}] = [1 - a_{ij} \wedge 1 - b_{ij}] = A^c \cap B^c.$$

Similarly, we can prove $(A \cap B)^c = A^c \cup B^c$.

Definition 2.6. Let $A = [a_{ij}] \in FSM_{m \times n}$. Then we define $A^T = [a_{ij}{}^T]_{n \times m} \in FSM_{n \times m}$, where $a_{ij}{}^T = a_{ji}$.

Theorem 2.2. Let $A, B \in FSM_{m \times n}$. Then

$(1)(A^T)^T = A$. $(2)(A \cup B)^T = A^T \cup B^T$, $(A \cap B)^T = A^T \cap B^T$.

$(3)(A^c)^T = (A^T)^c$. $(4)A \subseteq B \Rightarrow A^T \subseteq B^T$.

Definition 2.7. Let $A = [a_{ij}] \in FSM_{m \times n}$. For $\forall \alpha \in [0,1]$, $A_\alpha = [a_{ij}{}^{(\alpha)}]$ and $A_{\alpha}{}_* = [a_{ij}{}^{(\alpha)}{}_*]$ are called α-cut soft matrix of A and α-cut strong soft matrix of A, respectively. Where $a_{ij}{}^{(\alpha)} = \begin{cases} 1, & \text{if } a_{ij} \geq \alpha; \\ 0, & \text{otherwise} \end{cases}$, $a_{ij}{}^{(\alpha)}{}_* = \begin{cases} 1, & \text{if } a_{ij} \succ \alpha; \\ 0, & \text{otherwise} \end{cases}$.

Theorem 2.3. Let $A, B \in FSM_{m \times n}$. Then $\forall \alpha \in [0,1]$,

$(1)A \subseteq B \Rightarrow A_\alpha \subseteq B_\alpha$, $A_{\alpha *} \subseteq B_{\alpha *}$.

$(2)(A \cup B)_\alpha = A_\alpha \cup B_\alpha$, $(A \cup B)_{\alpha *} = A_{\alpha *} \cup B_{\alpha *}$.

$(3)(A \cap B)_\alpha = A_\alpha \cap B_\alpha$, $(A \cap B)_{\alpha *} = A_{\alpha *} \cap B_{\alpha *}$.

$(4)(A^T)_\alpha = (A_\alpha)^T$, $(A^T)_{\alpha *} = (A_{\alpha *})^T$.

Theorem 2.4. Let $A \in FSM_{m \times n}$, $\alpha, \beta \in [0,1]$. Then

$(1)A_{\alpha *} \subseteq A_\alpha$. $(2)\alpha \leq \beta \Rightarrow A_\beta \subseteq A_\alpha$, $A_{\beta *} \subseteq A_{\alpha *}$.

Theorem 2.5. Let $A_i \in FSM_{m \times n}$, $i \in T$, T is an index set. Then for any $\alpha \in [0,1]$,

$(1) \underset{i \in T}{\cup}(A_i)_\alpha \subseteq (\underset{i \in T}{\cup} A_i)_\alpha$, $\underset{i \in T}{\cap}(A_i)_\alpha = (\underset{i \in T}{\cap} A_i)_\alpha$.

$(2) \underset{i \in T}{\cup}(A_i)_{\alpha *} = (\underset{i \in T}{\cup} A_i)_{\alpha *}$, $(\underset{i \in T}{\cap} A_i)_{\alpha *} \subseteq \underset{i \in T}{\cap}(A_i)_{\alpha *}$.

Proof. (1) Let $j \in T$, then $A_j \subseteq \underset{i \in T}{\cup} A_i$, in view of Theory2.3, we have $(A_j)_\alpha \subseteq (\underset{i \in T}{\cup} A_i)_\alpha$. Thus $\underset{i \in T}{\cup}(A_i)_\alpha \subseteq (\underset{i \in T}{\cup} A_i)_\alpha$.

Let $A_i = [a_{st}{}^i]$, $\underset{i \in T}{\cap} A_i = [b_{st}]$, then we have

$$b_{st}{}^{(\alpha)} = 1 \Leftrightarrow b_{st} \geq \alpha \Leftrightarrow \underset{i \in T}{\wedge} a_{st}{}^i \geq \alpha \Leftrightarrow \forall i \in T, a_{st}{}^i \geq \alpha \Leftrightarrow \forall i \in T, a_{st}^{i\,(\alpha)} = 1 \Leftrightarrow$$

$\underset{i \in T}{\wedge} a_{st}^{i\,(\alpha)} = 1$. Therefore $\underset{i \in T}{\cap}(A_i)_\alpha = (\underset{i \in T}{\cap} A_i)_\alpha$.

(2) The proof is similar to that of (1).

The following example shows that inclusion sign cannot be replaced by equal sign in above theory.

Example 2.2. Let $U = \{u_1, u_2, u_3\}$ and $E = \{e_1, e_2\}$. Let

$$A_i = \begin{bmatrix} \frac{1}{2}(1-\frac{1}{i}) & \frac{1}{3}(1-\frac{1}{i}) \\ \frac{1}{2}(1-\frac{1}{i}) & \frac{1}{3}(1-\frac{1}{i}) \\ \frac{1}{2}(1-\frac{1}{i}) & \frac{1}{3}(1-\frac{1}{i}) \end{bmatrix}, \quad i = 1,2,\cdots,n,\cdots \quad , \quad \text{then} \quad \overset{\infty}{\underset{i=1}{\cup}} A_i = \begin{bmatrix} \frac{1}{2} & \frac{1}{3} \\ \frac{1}{2} & \frac{1}{3} \\ \frac{1}{2} & \frac{1}{3} \end{bmatrix}, \quad \text{thus}$$

$(\overset{\infty}{\underset{i=1}{\cup}} A_i)_{\frac{1}{2}} = \begin{bmatrix} 1 & 0 \\ 1 & 0 \\ 1 & 0 \end{bmatrix}$. However, $\forall i \in T$, since $(A_i)_{\frac{1}{2}} = \begin{bmatrix} 0 & 0 \\ 0 & 0 \\ 0 & 0 \end{bmatrix}$, we have $\overset{\infty}{\underset{i=1}{\cup}}(A_i)_{\frac{1}{2}} =$

$\begin{bmatrix} 0 & 0 \\ 0 & 0 \\ 0 & 0 \end{bmatrix}$. Therefore $\overset{\infty}{\underset{i=1}{\cup}}(A_i)_{\frac{1}{2}} \subset (\overset{\infty}{\underset{i=1}{\cup}} A_i)_{\frac{1}{2}}$.

Again let

$$B_i = \begin{bmatrix} \frac{1}{3}(1+\frac{1}{i}) & \frac{1}{2}(1+\frac{1}{i}) \\ \frac{1}{3}(1+\frac{1}{i}) & \frac{1}{2}(1+\frac{1}{i}) \\ \frac{1}{3}(1+\frac{1}{i}) & \frac{1}{2}(1+\frac{1}{i}) \end{bmatrix}, \quad i = 1,2,\cdots,n,\cdots \quad , \quad \text{then} \quad \overset{\infty}{\underset{i=1}{\cap}} B_i = \begin{bmatrix} \frac{1}{3} & \frac{1}{2} \\ \frac{1}{3} & \frac{1}{2} \\ \frac{1}{3} & \frac{1}{2} \end{bmatrix}, \quad \text{thus}$$

$(\overset{\infty}{\underset{i=1}{\cap}} B_i)_{\frac{1}{3}}^* = \begin{bmatrix} 0 & 1 \\ 0 & 1 \\ 0 & 1 \end{bmatrix}$. However, $\forall i \in T$, since $(B_i)_{\frac{1}{3}}^* = \begin{bmatrix} 1 & 1 \\ 1 & 1 \\ 1 & 1 \end{bmatrix}$, we have $\overset{\infty}{\underset{i=1}{\cap}}(B_i)_{\frac{1}{3}}^* =$

$\begin{bmatrix} 1 & 1 \\ 1 & 1 \\ 1 & 1 \end{bmatrix}$. Therefore $\overset{\infty}{\underset{i=1}{\cap}}(B_i)_{\frac{1}{3}}^* \supset (\overset{\infty}{\underset{i=1}{\cap}} B_i)_{\frac{1}{3}}^*$.

Theorem 2.6. Let $A \in FSM_{m \times n}$, $\alpha, \beta \in [0,1]$. Then

(1) $\underset{\beta \succ \alpha}{\cup} A_\beta^* = A_\alpha^*$. (2) $\underset{\beta \prec \alpha}{\cap} A_\beta = A_\alpha$.

Proof. (1) For any $\alpha \prec \beta$, we have $A_\beta^* \subseteq A_\alpha^*$, thus $\underset{\beta \succ \alpha}{\cup} A_\beta^* \subseteq A_\alpha^*$. On the other

hand, let $A_\alpha^* = [a_{ij}]_\alpha^* = [a_{ij}^{*\,(\alpha)}]$. If $a_{ij}^{*\,(\alpha)} = 1$, then $a_{ij} \succ \alpha$. Assume $\beta_{ij} = \frac{1}{2}(\alpha + a_{ij})$, then we have $\beta_{ij} \succ \alpha$, $a_{ij} = 2\beta_{ij} - \alpha \succ \beta_{ij}$, so $a_{ij}^{*(\beta_{ij})} = 1$. Thus $\exists \beta = \min\{\beta_{ij} : a_{ij} \succ \alpha\}$, $A_{\beta} \supseteq A_{\alpha}$, therefore $\underset{\beta \succ \alpha}{\cup} A_{\beta} \supseteq A_{\alpha}$. Consequently, $\underset{\beta \succ \alpha}{\cup} A_{\beta} = A_{\alpha}$.

(2) The proof is similar to that of (1) .

Theorem 2.7. Let $A \in FSM_{m \times n}$, $\alpha \in [0,1]$. Then

(1)$(A^c)_{\alpha} = (A_{1-\alpha})^c$.   (2)$(A^c)_{\underset{*}{\alpha}} = (A_{\underset{*}{1-\alpha}})^c$.

Proof. (1) Let $A = [a_{ij}]$, we have $(1 - a_{ij})^{(\alpha)} = 1 \Leftrightarrow 1 - a_{ij} \geq \alpha \Leftrightarrow a_{ij} \leq 1 - \alpha$ $\Leftrightarrow a_{ij}^{*(1-\alpha)} = 0 \Leftrightarrow 1 - a_{ij}^{*(1-\alpha)} = 1$, thus $(A^c)_{\alpha} = (A_{\underset{*}{1-\alpha}})^c$.

(2) The proof is similar to that of (1) .

Definition 2.8. Let $A = [a_{ij}] \in FSM_{m \times n}$, $\alpha \in [0,1]$, the number α times a fuzzy soft matrix A, denoted by αA, is defined as $\alpha A = [\alpha \wedge a_{ij}]$.

Theorem 2.8. Let $A, B \in FSM_{m \times n}$, $\alpha, \beta \in [0,1]$. Then

(1)$\alpha \leq \beta \Rightarrow \alpha A \subseteq \beta A$.   (2)$A \subseteq B \Rightarrow \alpha A \subseteq \alpha B$.

Theorem 2.9. Let $A \in FSM_{m \times n}$. Then (1)$A = \underset{\alpha \in [0,1]}{\cup} \alpha A_{\alpha}$.   (2)$A = \underset{\alpha \in [0,1]}{\cup} \alpha A_{\underset{*}{\alpha}}$.

Proof. (1) Let $A = [a_{ij}]$, $\underset{\alpha \in [0,1]}{\cup} \alpha A_{\alpha} = [b_{ij}]$. Then according to Definition2.8, we have $b_{ij} = \underset{\alpha \in [0,1]}{\vee} (\alpha \wedge a_{ij}^{(\alpha)}) = [\underset{a_{ij} \prec \alpha \leq 1}{\vee} (\alpha \wedge a_{ij}^{(\alpha)})] \vee [\underset{0 \leq \alpha \leq a_{ij}}{\vee} (\alpha \wedge a_{ij}^{(\alpha)})] = [\underset{a_{ij} \prec \alpha \leq 1}{\vee} (\alpha \wedge 0)]$ $\vee [\underset{0 \leq \alpha \leq a_{ij}}{\vee} (\alpha \wedge 1)] = 0 \vee a_{ij} = a_{ij}$. Thus, for $\forall i$ and j , $b_{ij} = a_{ij}$. Therefore, $A = \underset{\alpha \in [0,1]}{\cup} \alpha A_{\alpha}$.

(2) The proof is similar to that of (1) .

Let us illustrate this idea using the following example.

Example 2.3. Let $A = \begin{bmatrix} 0.2 & 0.7 \\ 0.6 & 1.0 \\ 0.5 & 0.4 \end{bmatrix}$. Then $0.2 A_{0.2} = \begin{bmatrix} 0.2 & 0.2 \\ 0.2 & 0.2 \\ 0.2 & 0.2 \end{bmatrix}$, $0.4 A_{0.4} = \begin{bmatrix} 0.0 & 0.4 \\ 0.4 & 0.4 \\ 0.4 & 0.4 \end{bmatrix}$, $0.5 A_{0.5} = \begin{bmatrix} 0.0 & 0.5 \\ 0.5 & 0.5 \\ 0.5 & 0.0 \end{bmatrix}$, $0.6 A_{0.6} = \begin{bmatrix} 0.0 & 0.6 \\ 0.6 & 0.6 \\ 0.0 & 0.0 \end{bmatrix}$, $0.7 A_{0.7} = \begin{bmatrix} 0.0 & 0.7 \\ 0.0 & 0.7 \\ 0.0 & 0.0 \end{bmatrix}$,

$$1A_1 = \begin{bmatrix} 0.0 & 0.0 \\ 0.0 & 1.0 \\ 0.0 & 0.0 \end{bmatrix} \quad . \quad \text{Thus,} \quad \bigcup_{\alpha \in [0,1]} \alpha A_\alpha = 0.2A_{0.2} \cup 0.4A_{0.4} \cup 0.5A_{0.5} \cup 0.6A_{0.6}$$

$$\cup 0.7A_{0.7} \cup 1A_1 = \begin{bmatrix} 0.2 & 0.7 \\ 0.6 & 1.0 \\ 0.5 & 0.4 \end{bmatrix} = A .$$

α-cut soft matrix of a fuzzy soft matrix is a soft matrix, the above theorem gives the relationship between fuzzy soft matrices and soft matrices, meanwhile, it shows that we can construct fuzzy soft matrices by soft matrices.

Theorem 2.10. Let $A, B \in FSM_{m \times n}$. Then $A \subseteq B$ iff $A_\alpha \subseteq B_\alpha$, $\alpha \in [0,1]$.

Proof. $\Rightarrow$ Obviously.

$\Leftarrow$ Let $A_\alpha \subseteq B_\alpha$, $\alpha \in [0,1]$, in view of Theorem 2.9, we have $A = \bigcup_{\alpha \in [0,1]} \alpha A_\alpha \subseteq \bigcup_{\alpha \in [0,1]} \alpha B_\alpha = B$, so $A \subseteq B$.

3   T-Products of Fuzzy Soft Matrices and Their Applications

Definition 3.1. Let $A_k = [a_{ij}^k] \in FSM_{m \times n}$, $k = 1, 2, \cdots, l$. Then the T-product of fuzzy soft matrices, denoted by $\prod_{k=1}^{l} A_k = A_1 \times A_2 \times \cdots \times A_l$, is defined by

$$\prod_{k=1}^{l} A_k = [c_i]_{m \times 1}, \text{ where } c_i = \frac{1}{n} \sum_{j=1}^{n} \mathop{T}\limits_{k=1}^{l} a_{ij}^k, i = 1, 2, \cdots, m .$$

In this paper we will take $T = \wedge$ or $T = \vee$ according to the type of the problems. To illustrate this idea, let us consider the following example.

Example 3.1. Assume that $A_1, A_2, A_3 \in FSM_{3 \times 2}$ are given as follows

$$A_1 = \begin{bmatrix} 0.3 & 0.7 \\ 0.5 & 0.2 \\ 0.1 & 0.6 \end{bmatrix}, A_2 = \begin{bmatrix} 0.0 & 0.5 \\ 1.0 & 0.3 \\ 0.2 & 0.7 \end{bmatrix}, A_3 = \begin{bmatrix} 0.4 & 1.0 \\ 0.0 & 0.2 \\ 0.5 & 0.8 \end{bmatrix}. \text{ Then the } \wedge \text{-product is}$$

$$\prod_{k=1}^{3} A_k = A_1 \times A_2 \times A_3 = \frac{1}{2} \begin{bmatrix} 0.3 \wedge 0.0 \wedge 0.4 + 0.7 \wedge 0.5 \wedge 1.0 \\ 0.5 \wedge 1.0 \wedge 0.0 + 0.2 \wedge 0.3 \wedge 0.2 \\ 0.1 \wedge 0.2 \wedge 0.5 + 0.6 \wedge 0.7 \wedge 0.8 \end{bmatrix} = \begin{bmatrix} 0.25 \\ 0.10 \\ 0.35 \end{bmatrix}.$$

Theorem 3.1. Let $A, B, C \in FSM_{m \times n}$. Then

(1)$A \times B = B \times A$.   (2)$(A \times B) \times C = A \times (B \times C)$.

Proof. Let $(1) A = [a_{ij}]$, $B = [b_{ij}]$.   Then $A \times B = [c_i] = [\frac{1}{n} \sum_{j=1}^{n} a_{ij} T b_{ij}]$,

$B \times A = [d_i] = [\frac{1}{n} \sum_{j=1}^{n} b_{ij} T a_{ij}]$. Since $a_{ij} T b_{ij} = b_{ij} T a_{ij}$, we have $c_i = d_i$. Hence,

$A \times B = B \times A$.

(2) The proof is similar to that of (1) .

Theorem 3.2. Let $A, B, C \in FSM_{m \times n}$ and $B \subseteq C$. Then $A \times B \subseteq A \times C$.

Proof. Let $A = [a_{ij}]$, $B = [b_{ij}]$, $\mathrm{C} = [c_{ij}]$.   Then $A \times B = [d_i] = [\frac{1}{n} \sum_{j=1}^{n} a_{ij} T b_{ij}]$,

$A \times C = [e_i] = [\frac{1}{n} \sum_{j=1}^{n} a_{ij} T c_{ij}]$. Since $b_{ij} \leq c_{ij}$, we have $a_{ij} T b_{ij} \leq a_{ij} T c_{ij}$, thus $d_i \leq e_i$.

Hence, $A \times B \subseteq A \times C$.

Corollary 3.1. Let $A, B, C \in FSM_{m \times n}$. Then

$(1) A \times (B \cup C) \supseteq (A \times B) \cup (A \times C)$. $(2) A \times (B \cap C) \subseteq (A \times B) \cap (A \times C)$

Definition   3.2.   Let $A_k \in FSM_{m \times n}$, $k = 1, 2, \cdots, l$,   their   product   is

$\prod_{k=1}^{l} A_k = [c_i]_{m \times 1}$. Then the set $O_s = \{ j : c_j = \max\{c_i : i = 1, 2, \cdots, m\}\}$ is called

the optimum subscript set, and the set $O_d = \{u_j : u_j \in U \text{ and } j \in O_s\}$ is called the

optimum decision set of U .

Now, by using Definition3.1 and Definition3.2, we can construct a decision
making method to obtain the optimum set by the following algorithm.

Algorithm
Input: Fuzzy soft sets with m objects, each of which has n parameters.
Output: An optimum set.

step 1: Write out the fuzzy soft matrices according to the given fuzzy soft sets.
step 2: calculate the T-product of the fuzzy soft matrices.
step 3: find the optimum subscript set O_s .
step 4: find the optimum decision set O_d .

Example   3.2.[8] Let $U = \{u_1, u_2, u_3, u_4, u_5\}$ be   a   set   of   houses.   Let
$E = \{e_1, e_2, e_3, e_4\}$ be a set of status of houses, where e_1 ="in good location",
e_2 ="cheap", e_3 ="modern ", e_4 ="large ". Suppose that a married couple, Mr.X and
Mrs.X come to buy a house, and the following fuzzy soft matrices are constructed
according to their parameters.

$$A = \begin{bmatrix} 0 & 0 & 1 & 1 \\ 0 & 1 & 1 & 1 \\ 0 & 1 & 1 & 0 \\ 0 & 1 & 0 & 0 \\ 0 & 1 & 0 & 1 \end{bmatrix}, \quad B = \begin{bmatrix} 1 & 0 & 1 & 1 \\ 1 & 0 & 0 & 1 \\ 0 & 0 & 1 & 1 \\ 0 & 0 & 1 & 1 \\ 0 & 0 & 0 & 1 \end{bmatrix}.$$

Which house will be their primary choice?

Now, if we choose the And-product of A and B and use the SMmDM method proposed by Cagman and Enginoglu, we will find that u_1 is the optimum house to buy for them. If we choose the And-product of B and A and use the same SMmDM method, we will get that u_2 is the optimum house. Since the commutativity is not valid for the And-product, two different results are obtained, so this method is not convenient in this decision making problem.

If we use $\wedge$-product of $A \times B$, we will have $A \times B = B \times A = [0.5, 0.25,$ $0.25, 0, 0.25]^T$, the optimum house is u_1 and the above problem does not rise.

Example 3.3. Let $U = \{u_1, u_2, u_3, u_4\}$ be a set of houses. Let $E = \{e_1, e_2, e_3\}$ be a set of status of houses, where e_1 ="cheap", e_2 ="large ", e_3 ="in good location". Suppose that Mr.X, Mrs.X and their son come to buy a house, and the following fuzzy soft matrices are constructed according to their parameters, respectively.

$$A = \begin{bmatrix} 0.6 & 0.5 & 0.7 \\ 0.4 & 0.6 & 0.8 \\ 0.5 & 0.4 & 0.2 \\ 0.8 & 0.6 & 0.3 \end{bmatrix}, \quad B = \begin{bmatrix} 0.7 & 0.8 & 0.6 \\ 0.5 & 0.5 & 1.0 \\ 0.6 & 0.4 & 0.9 \\ 0.5 & 0.4 & 0.7 \end{bmatrix}, \quad C = \begin{bmatrix} 0.5 & 0.6 & 0.5 \\ 0.6 & 0.8 & 0.4 \\ 0.4 & 0.6 & 0.7 \\ 0.5 & 0.5 & 0.6 \end{bmatrix}.$$

Now, taking three people's opinions comprehensively, the SMmDM method is not valid, but we can solve this problem by $\wedge$-product of fuzzy soft matrices as below

$$A \times B \times C = \frac{1}{3} \begin{bmatrix} 0.6 \wedge 0.7 \wedge 0.5 + 0.5 \wedge 0.8 \wedge 0.6 + 0.7 \wedge 0.6 \wedge 0.5 \\ 0.4 \wedge 0.5 \wedge 0.6 + 0.6 \wedge 0.5 \wedge 0.8 + 0.8 \wedge 1.0 \wedge 0.4 \\ 0.5 \wedge 0.6 \wedge 0.4 + 0.4 \wedge 0.4 \wedge 0.6 + 0.2 \wedge 0.9 \wedge 0.7 \\ 0.8 \wedge 0.5 \wedge 0.5 + 0.6 \wedge 0.4 \wedge 0.5 + 0.3 \wedge 0.7 \wedge 0.6 \end{bmatrix} = \begin{bmatrix} 0.50 \\ 0.43 \\ 0.33 \\ 0.40 \end{bmatrix}.$$

It is clear that the maximum score is 0.5, scored by u_1 and the decision is in favor of selecting u_1.

4   Conclusion

The soft set theory has been applied to many fields both theoretically to practically. In the present paper, we define fuzzy soft matrices and study their properties. We then define the product of fuzzy soft matrices and give a fuzzy decision making method, which solve many decision making problems that the SMmDm method cannot do. Finally, we offer some examples to show the validity of our method.

References

1. Molodtsov, D.A.: Soft set theory-first results. Computers and Mathematics with Applications 37, 19–31 (1999)
2. Maji, P.K., Biswas, R., Roy, A.R.: Fuzzy soft sets. Journal of Fuzzy Mathematics 9(3), 589–602 (2001)
3. Aktas, H., Cagman, N.: Soft sets and soft groups. Information Sciences 177, 2726–2735 (2007)
4. Roy, A.R., Maji, P.K.: A fuzzy soft set theoretic approach to decision making problems. Journal of Computational and Applied Mathematics 203, 412–418 (2007)
5. Yang, X., Yu, D., Yang, J., Wu, C.: Generalization of soft set theory: from crisp to fuzzy case. In: Cao, B.-Y. (ed.) Fuzzy Information and Engineering: Proceedings of ICFIE-2007: Advances in Soft Computing, vol. 40, pp. 345–355. Springer, Heidelberg (2007)
6. Majumdar, P., Samanta, S.K.: Similarity measure of soft sets. New Mathematics and Natural Computation 4(1), 1–12 (2008)
7. Xiao, Z., Gong, K., Zou, Y.: A combined forecasting approach based on fuzzy soft sets. Journal of Computational and Applied Mathematics 228, 326–333 (2009)
8. Cagman, N., Enginoglu, S.: Soft matrix theory and its decision making. Computers and Mathematics with Applications 59(10), 3308–3314 (2010)

Global Solution for the Nonlinear Beam Equation

Su-Fang Zhang and Jian-Wen Zhang

Department of Mathematics, Taiyuan University of Technology
030024 Taiyuan, China
zsfczg@163.com, Jianwenz2008@163.com

Abstract. We prove the existence and uniqueness of global solution for the nonlinear beam equation with initial boundary condition:

$$u'' + \alpha\Delta^2 u - M(\|\nabla u\|_2^2)\Delta u + \phi(t)g(u') = f(x) \quad in\ Q$$

where $u''(x,t) = u_{tt}$, $u'(x,t) = u_t$, $\alpha > 0$, M, g, ϕ is nonlinear functions and Δ is Laplacian in R^n.

Keywords: Galerkin's method, Sobolev space, existence of weak solution.

1   Introduction

Let Ω be an open bounded connected set of R^n with smooth boundary $\partial\Omega$ and $Q = \Omega \times [0, \infty)$. In this paper, we are devoted to the investigation of the following problems for nonlinear beam equation

$$u'' + \alpha\Delta^2 u - M(\|\nabla u\|_2^2)\Delta u + \phi(t)g(u') = f(x) \quad in\ Q \tag{1}$$

with the following initial and boundary conditions

$$u(x,t) = \Delta u = 0 \quad on \ \partial\Omega \times [0, \infty) \tag{2}$$

$$u(x,0) = u_0(x) \quad u'(x,0) = u_1(x) \quad x \in \Omega \tag{3}$$

where $u(x,t)$ denotes a real-valued unknown function,

$\phi(t), M(s), g(u') \in C^1(0, \infty), f(x) \in L^\infty(0, \infty; L^2(\Omega))$ and α is positive real constants.

System (1)-(3) is derived from the kirchhoff wave equation, and Kirchhoff model[1] is presented by Woinowsky-Krieger ,It was proposed for small vertical of stretched elastics strings when the ends are fixed, but the tension is variable during the deformations of the string.   Much research has been devoted to the study of

$$u'' + \alpha\Delta^2 u - M(\|\nabla u\|_2^2)\Delta u + g(u') = 0$$

(see [2, 3,4]). The focus of this work is the study of the long-time properties of the dynamical system generated by global solution, please refer the reader to [5] and references therein.

H. Deng et al. (Eds.): AICI 2011, Part I, LNAI 7002, pp. 628–633, 2011.
© Springer-Verlag Berlin Heidelberg 2011

This paper is organized as follows. In section 2 , we give the main assumptions and strong global solution $u(x,t)$ to the problem (1)-(3). Section 3 is devoted to the prior estimate and prove the existence and uniqueness of global solution.

2   Assumptions and Main Results

Firstly, we assume that the nonlinear functions M, g ϕ satisfied the following conditions.

$$\begin{cases} M(s) \geq m_0 > 0, |M'(s)| \leq m_1|s|_R^p \quad for \ p \geq 1 \\ m_2 \tilde{M}(s) \leq sM(s) \quad where \quad \tilde{M}(s) = \int_0^s M(\tau)d\tau \end{cases} \tag{4}$$

$$\begin{cases} \rho_0|\xi|_R^{\gamma+1} \leq g|(\xi)_R| \leq \rho_1|\xi|_R^{\gamma+1} \\ 0 \leq g'(\xi) \leq \rho_2|\xi|_R^{\gamma}, \rho(0) = 0 \\ \gamma \leq 2p+1, 0 \leq \gamma < \infty \quad if \quad n = 1,2 \\ \qquad 0 \leq \gamma \leq \dfrac{2}{n-2} \quad if \quad n \geq 3 \end{cases} \tag{5}$$

$$0 < c_1 \leq \phi(t) \leq c_2 \tag{6}$$

With the usual notation, we write $H = L^2(\Omega)$, $V = H_0^2(\Omega)$, , and the scalar products and norms on H and V respectively

$$(u,v) = \int_\Omega uvdx , |u|^2 = (u,u), \quad \forall u,v \in L^2(\Omega)$$

$$((u,v)) = \int_\Omega \Delta u \Delta v dx , \|u\|^2 = ((u,u)), \quad \forall u,v \in H_0^2(\Omega)$$

From the Poincaré inequality, there exists the constant $\lambda_1 > 0$, such that:

$$|\Delta u| \geq \lambda_1 |u|, \forall u \in V ,$$

In these conditions, we consider the initial boundary value problem

$$\begin{cases} u'' + \alpha\Delta^2 u - M(\|\nabla u\|_2^2)\Delta u + \phi(t)g(u') = f(x) \ in Q \\ u(x,t) = \Delta u = 0 \quad on \quad \partial\Omega \times [0,\infty) \\ u(x,0) = u_0(x) \quad u'(x,0) = u_1(x) \quad x \in \Omega \end{cases} \tag{7}$$

To obtain the global solutions, we choose

$$u_0 \in H_0^1 \cap H^2(\Omega) \quad and \quad u_1 \in H_0^1(\Omega)$$

and denote the function of the solutions by $E(t) = E(u(x,t))$ which will be called an energy system (8) and the initial date function(9) :

$$E(t) = \frac{1}{2}\int_\Omega |u'(x,t)|^2 dx + \frac{1}{2}\tilde{M}(|\nabla u(t)|^2) + \frac{\alpha}{2}|\Delta u|^2 - \int_\Omega \int f(x)dxdt \tag{8}$$

$$F(|\nabla u_0|, |\Delta u_0|, |u_1|, |\nabla u_1|) = \frac{1}{2}|\nabla u_1|^2 + \frac{m_2^3}{m_0}|\Delta u_0|^2 + \frac{C_0^2 \rho_1^2}{m_0}|\nabla u_1|_{L^{2(\gamma+1)}(\Omega)}^{2(\gamma+1)} + \frac{\gamma}{2p+1-\gamma}$$

$$\times\left(\frac{2^{3/2}m_1}{m_0}+\frac{2^{(\gamma+5)/2}C_0^2\rho_1^2a_1^2}{a_0^{1/2}m_0^{3/2}}\right)\left(\frac{d_4E(0)}{m_0}\right)^{(2p+1)/2}<\frac{\varepsilon_0}{K} \tag{9}$$

Theorem 2.1. (Existence of solutions). The assumptions are those (4),(5),(6). For $u_0\in H_0^1\cap H^2(\Omega)$ and $u_1\in H_0^1(\Omega)$ and f give in $L^2[0,\infty;\Omega)$,there exists a unique global solution $u(x,t)$ initial-boundary value problem(7), such that
$u\in L^\infty\big(0,\infty;H_0^1(\Omega)\cap H^2(\Omega)\big),u'\in L^2\big(0,\infty;H_0^1(\Omega)\big),$
$u''\in L^\infty\big(0,\infty;L^2(\Omega)\big)$

3   Existence and Uniqueness

In this section, we prove a result of existence and uniqueness. Let V is a separable Hilbert space and we obtain a sequence of linearly independent element of $w_1,\cdots,w_m,\cdots,$

which is complete in V .We define an approximate solution u_m of (7) such that $u_m=\sum_{j=1}^m\varphi_{jm}(t)w_j(x)$,

$$\begin{cases}(u_m''(x,t),\omega)+M\big(|\nabla u_m(t)|^2\big)(\nabla u_m(t),\nabla\omega)\\+(g(u_m'(x,t))\phi(t),\omega)+\alpha(\Delta^2u_m(t),\omega)=(f(x),\omega)\\u_m(x,0)=u_{0m}(x)\to u_0(x)\quad in\quad H_0^1(\Omega)\cap H^2(\Omega)\\u_m'(x,0)=u_{1m}(x)\to u_1(x)\quad in\quad H_0^1(\Omega)\end{cases} \tag{10}$$

Equations (10) are equivalent to an initial-value problem for a linear finite-dimensional ordinary differential equation for the φ_{jim}. The existence and uniqueness is obvious. But u_m is a local solution on the interval $[0,t_m]$ .We can extend the solution u_m to the whole interval $[0,\infty]$ by prior estimates and take the limit in (10).We will write u instead of u_m .

Estimate 1. (7) multiply $u'(x,t)$, This gives

$$\frac{1}{2}\frac{d}{dt}\left(\int_\Omega|u'(x,t)|^2dx+\tilde M\big(|\nabla u(t)|^2\big)+\alpha|\Delta u(t)|^2\right)+(g(u'(x,t))\phi(t),\omega)=(f(x),u(x,t))$$

$$\frac{1}{2}\frac{d}{dt}\left(\int_\Omega|u'(x,t)|^2dx+\tilde M\big(|\nabla u(t)|^2\big)+\alpha|\Delta u(t)|^2\right)-\int_\Omega f(x)u'(x,t)dx\le0$$

Integrating from 0 to t yields the energy equation (8) and

$$E(t)<E(0) \tag{11}$$

Lemma3.1 The approximate energy

$$E_m(t)=\frac{1}{2}\int_\Omega|u_m'(x,t)|^2dx+\frac{1}{2}\tilde M\big(|\nabla u_m(t)|^2\big)+\frac{\alpha}{2}|\Delta u_m|^2-\int_\Omega\int_0^{t_m}f(x)dxdt, \tag{12}$$

which will be denoted by $E(t)$.

Estimate 2. Denoting by $G(t)$ the function

$$G(t) = \frac{1}{2}\int_\Omega \frac{|u''(t)|^2 + |\Delta u'|^2}{M\left(|\nabla u(t)|^2\right)}dx + \frac{1}{2}\left|\nabla u'(t)^2\right| \tag{13}$$

Hence, (4),(5)and Holder's inequality, we can give

$$\frac{d}{dt}G(t) + \int_\Omega \frac{g'(u'(x,t))u''(x,t)}{M\left(|\nabla u(t)|^2\right)}dx \leq \frac{1}{m_0}\left|M'\left(|\nabla u(t)|^2\right)|\nabla u(t)||\nabla u'(t)|\left(\int_\Omega \frac{|u''(x,t)|^2}{M\left(|\nabla u(t)|^2\right)}\right)dx$$

$$+ |u'(t)|_{L^2(\gamma+1)(\Omega)}^{\gamma+1}\left(\frac{2\rho_1}{m_0^{3/2}}|M'(\nabla u(t))|^2|\nabla u(t)||\nabla u'(t)|\right)\times\left(\int_\Omega \frac{|u''(x,t)|^2}{M\left(|\nabla u(t)|^2\right)}dx\right)^{\frac{1}{2}} \tag{14}$$

$$\leq m_1|\nabla u(t)|^{2p+1}|\nabla u'(t)|\left(\frac{1}{m_0}\int_\Omega \frac{|u''(x,t)|^2}{M\left|\nabla u(t)\right|^2}dx + \frac{2\rho_1|u(t)|_{L^2(\gamma+1)(\Omega)}^{\gamma+1}}{m_0^{3/2}}\right)\times\left(\int_\Omega \frac{|u''(x,t)|^2}{M\left(|\nabla u(t)|^2\right)}dx\right)^{\frac{1}{2}}$$

Let $t = 0$ and $u''(x,0)$ in (10),We have by using (4)、(5) that

$$|u''(0)| + \alpha|\Delta u(0)| \leq m_3|\Delta u_0| + c_0\rho_1|\nabla u_1^{\gamma+1}| \tag{15}$$

$$\frac{1}{2}\int_\Omega \frac{|u''(x,0)|^2 + \alpha|\Delta u(0)|^2}{M\left(|\nabla u_0|^2\right)}dx \leq \frac{1}{2}(\frac{1}{m_0}|u''(0)|^2 + \alpha|\Delta u(0)|^2 \tag{16}$$

From definition of $G(t)$ in (13) and (16)we get

$$G(0) \leq \frac{1}{2}|\nabla u_1|^2 + \frac{m_2^3}{m_0}|\Delta u_0|^2 + \frac{C_0^2\rho_1^2 a_2^2}{m_0}|\nabla u_1|_{L^{2(\gamma+1)}(\Omega)}^{2(\gamma+1)} \tag{17}$$

$G(t)$ is bounded for all t greater or equal to zero. We will prove that

$$G(t) < \varepsilon_0 \quad for \quad all \quad t \geq 0 \tag{18}$$

where ε_0 is defined in 9. In fact, suppose that (18) is not true.

The it will exist a $t^* > 0$ such that

$$\begin{cases} G(t) < \varepsilon_0 & for \quad all \quad 0 \leq t \leq t^* \\ G(t^*) = \varepsilon_0 \end{cases} \tag{19}$$

If (14) is integrated from 0 to t^*, in the resulting expression is used (19) and observing that the second term on the left-hand side is not negative thanks to hypotheses (4)、(5),we have

$$G(t^*) \leq H(0) + \frac{2^{(\gamma+2)/2}C_0\rho_1}{m_0^{1/2}}\varepsilon_0^{(\gamma+2)/2}$$

$$+ \left(\frac{2^{3/2}m_1}{m_0}\varepsilon_0^{3/2} + \frac{2^{(\gamma+5)/2}C_0\rho_1 m_1}{m_0^{3/2}}\varepsilon_0^{(\gamma+3)/2}\right)\int_0^{t^*}|\nabla u(t)|^{2p+1}dt \tag{20}$$

By Lemma 3.1 and hypothesis (4), we have

$$|\nabla u(t)|^2 \leq \frac{d_4 E(0)}{m_0}\frac{1}{(1+t)^{2/\gamma}}$$

Hence,

$$\int_s^* \left|\nabla u(t)\right|^{2p+1} dt \le \int_s^* \left|\nabla u(t)\right|^{2p+1} dt \le$$

$$\left(\frac{d_4 E(0)}{m_0}\right)^{(2p+1)/2} \int_s^* \frac{1}{(1+t)^{(2p+1)/\gamma}} dt = \left(\frac{d_4 E(0)}{m_0}\right)^{(2p+1)/2} \frac{\gamma}{2p+1-\gamma} \tag{21}$$

When $\gamma \le 2p+1$. Taking into account (20) into (21) obtain

$$G(t^*) \le H(0) + \frac{2^{(\gamma+2)/2} C_0 \rho_1}{m_0^{1/2}} \varepsilon_0^{(\gamma+2)/2}$$

$$+ \frac{\lambda}{2p+1+\gamma}\left(\frac{2^{3/2} m_1}{m_0}\varepsilon_0^{3/2} + \frac{2^{(\gamma+5)/2} C_0 \rho_1 m_1}{m_0^{3/2}}\varepsilon_0^{(\gamma+3)/2}\right) \times \left(\frac{d_4 E(0)}{m_0}\right)^{(2p+1)/2} \tag{22}$$

By using the function F, defined in (9), and the estimate (17) in (22) yields

$$G(t^*) \le \frac{2^{(\gamma+2)/2} C_0 \rho_1}{m_0^{1/2}}\varepsilon_0^{(\gamma+2)/2} + F\left(\left|\nabla u_0\right|, \left|\nabla u_0\right|, \left|u_1\right|, \left|\nabla u_1\right|\right) \tag{23}$$

Combining (9) and (23), we obtain

$$H(t^*) < \varepsilon_0$$

Thus, from definition of H(t) we have

$$\frac{1}{2}\int_\Omega \left(\frac{\left|u''(x,t)\right|^2}{M\left(\left|\nabla u(t)\right|^2\right)} + \left|\nabla u'(x,t)\right|^2\right)dx \le \varepsilon_0 \qquad \text{for all } t \ge 0 \tag{24}$$

By using in (24) (5) and the constant m_3 defined in (13), we can write

$$\frac{1}{2m_3}\left|u''(t)\right|^2 + \frac{1}{2}\left|\nabla u'(t)\right|^2 + \frac{\alpha}{2}\left|\Delta u\right|^2 \le \varepsilon_0 \qquad \text{for all } t \ge 0 \tag{25}$$

Estimate 3. If (7) is divided by $M\left(\left|\nabla u(t)\right|^2\right)$ and ε is replaced by $-\Delta u(x,t)$ it gives

$$\left(\frac{u''(x,t)}{M\left(\left|\nabla u(t)\right|^2\right)}, -\Delta u(x,t)\right) + \left|\Delta u(t)\right|^2 + \alpha(\Delta^2 u, -\Delta u(x,t))$$

$$+ \left(\frac{\rho(u'(x,t))}{M\left(\left|\nabla u(t)\right|^2\right)}, -\Delta u(x,t)\right) = (f(x), -\Delta u(x,t)) \tag{26}$$

The first and the third term of (26) can be upper bound by using the Holder's inequality, the hypotheses (4), (5), Young inequality and the estimate (24) as follows.

$$\left|\Delta u(t)\right|^2 \le 4\left(\frac{\varepsilon_0}{m_0} + \frac{C_0 \rho_1^2 (2\varepsilon_0)^{\gamma+1}}{m_0^2} + \frac{\alpha}{m_0}\right) \tag{27}$$

From estimates (11), (25), (27) and Aubin-Lion's Theorem, cf. [1], we obtain a subsequence of $\{u_m\}$, which will be represented by $\{u_m\}$, such that $u_m \to u$ strongly in $L^2\left(0,T;H_0^1(\Omega)\right)$ and a.e. in Q. $u'_m \to u'$ strongly in $L^2\left(0,T;H_0^1(\Omega)\right)$ and a.e. Q.

Therefore, we can take the limit as $m \to \infty$ for this subsequence in the approximate problem (9).Thus, system (7) has solutions in the sense of Definition (7).Finally, the uniqueness is gotten by using the usual energy's methods in view of the regularities in (10) Therefore, the proof of Theorem (2.1) is finished.

Acknowledgement. The project supported by the Natural Science Foundation of ShanXi   province China(Grant No 2010011008).

References

1. Kirchhoff, G.R.: Vorlesungen uber mathematiche Physik: Mechanik, section 29.7. Teubner, Leipzig (1876)
2. Brito, E.H.: Decay estimates for the generalized damped extensible string and beam equations. Nonlinear Anal. 8, 1489–1496 (1984)
3. Medeirors, L.A.: On a new class of nonlinear wave equation. J. Math. Anal. Appl. 69, 252–262 (1979)
4. Oliveria, M.L., Lima, O.A.: Exponential decay of the solutions of the beam System. Nonlinear Anal. 42, 1271–1291 (2000)
5. Limaco, J., Clark, H.R.: On damped Kirchhoff equation with variable coefficients. J. Math. Anal. Appl. 307, 641–655 (2005)

A Multi-population Parallel Estimation of Distribution Algorithms Based on Clayton and Gumbel Copulas

Chunyan Chang[1] and Lifang Wang[2]

[1] College of Textile Engineering and Art, Taiyuan University of Technology,
Yuci, Jingzhong, 030600, P.R. China
sxccya@163.com
[2] Complex System and Computational Intelligence Laboratory, Taiyuan University of Science
and Technology, Taiyuan, 030024, P.R. China
wlf1001@163.com

Abstract. The idea of multi-population parallel strategy and the copula theory are introduced into the Estimation of Distribution Algorithm (EDA), and a new parallel EDA is proposed in this paper. In this algorithm, the population is divided into some subpopulations. Different copula is used to estimate the distribution model in each subpopulation. Two copulas, Clayton and Gumbel, are used in this paper. To estimate the distribution function is to estimate the copula and the margins. New individuals are generated according to the copula and the margins. In order to increase the diversity of the subpopulation, the elites of one subpopulation are learned by the other subpopulation. The experiments show the proposed algorithm performs better than the basic copula EDA and some classical EDAs in speed and in precision.

Keywords: multi-population, parallel, estimation of distribution algorithms (EDAs), copula theory, Clayton, Gumbel.

1 Introduction

The Estimate of Distribution Algorithms (EDAs) are new Evolutionary Algorithms (EAs) combined Genetic Algorithms (GAs) with statistical learning. EDAs realize population evolution by iteratively estimating probabilistic model of selected population which describes the solutions distribution from a macroscopic perspective, and then sampling the new individuals from the model. The probabilistic model reflect the relationship between variables, therefore EDAs are effectively used to obtain optimized solutions for complex problems [1]. Currently, many kinds of EDAs were studied by scholars. The classical algorithms are: (1) PBIL [2] and UMDA [3] ,in which the variables are independent; (2) MIMIC[4] and BMDA[5], which only consider the dependences between pairs of variables; (3) ECGA[6], FDA[7] and BOA[8],which accept the multivariate correlation; (4) UMDAc[9], PBILc[10] and EMNA [11], which focus on EDAs in continuous search spaces, etc. Estimating probabilistic model is the key step in EDAs, with the problem and model become

H. Deng et al. (Eds.): AICI 2011, Part I, LNAI 7002, pp. 634–643, 2011.

more and more complex, the consumption of algorithm in runtime and storage space will be increased.

Copula theory becomes the hotspot in the areas of statistics and finance .In this theory, the joint probability distribution function is divided into their one-dimensional marginal distribution functions and a copula function. And the joint probability distribution function is an effectual tool to mirror the relationship between variables. Therefore, the complexity of EDAs and operation time of modeling and sampling will decrease by using of copula. Some authors present new EDAs based on copula theory (copula EDAs), and make some incipient activities [12] ,[13]. The main idea of copula EDAs is that firstly, select dominant population, and then modeling the marginal distribution functions from them and sampling from a copula function.

The copula function plays an important role in copula EDAs. There are two classes of copulas to express the multivariate correlations: Elliptical copulas and Archimedean copulas. Elliptical copulas include Gauss-copula and t-copula. Archimedean copulas are produced from different generators according to the definition of Archimedean copula [14]. About 200 kinds of Archimedean copulas are currently being developed, in which Clayton, Gumbel and Frank are famous and in regular use. Every copula has special characteristic. Existing copula EDAs estimate the dependence structure of variables using an pre-assigned copula function, in which neither discuss the population whether exactly obeys the distribution modeled by this copula nor measure this copula function whether can fully describe the dependence structure of variables.

To deal with early convergence of traditional EDAs and single representation of relationship between variables in copula EDAs, we propose a multi-population parallel EDA based on copula theory in this paper. This algorithm optimizes more quickly and effectively than traditional EDAs and copula EDAs.

2   A Brief Introduction of Parallel Genetic Algorithms

The parallel Genetic Algorithms (pGAs) are the improved algorithms for traditional GAs. They either have inherently parallelism of GAs or have high-speed performance of parallel computer, so the global searching ability of the pGAs is improved and premature convergence is overcome availably.

There are three main types of pGAs: (1) global single-population master-slave GAs, (2) single-population fine-grained GAs, (3) multiple-population coarse-grained GAs[15]. We are going to focus on the coarse-grained model because it has stronger suitability and wider utility. According to the coarse model, the overall population is distributed over multiple subpopulations and occasionally allows the migration or exchange of some individuals among the different subpopulations. Therefore, each subpopulation executes an independent algorithm. The migration strategy of coarse-grained contains some parameters [16]: (1) How often (in generations) is information sent? It is configured with migration frequency. (2) How many individuals migrate each time? It is configured with migration rate. (3) What information is selected to migrate? It is configured with information selection. (4) How are the incoming information and the local algorithm state combined? It is configured with acceptance policy. (5) Which island sends information to which other? It is configured with migration topology.

3 Contribution

In this paper, a new copula EDA named multi-population parallel copula EDA is presented.

3.1 Multi-population Parallel Copula EDA

According to the framework of copula EDA [12], the copula EDA is an iterative run containing three main steps. The first step is to select a subpopulation denoted by $x=\{x^j=(x_1^j,x_2^j,\ldots x_n^j), j=1,2,\ldots,s\}$. The second step is to estimate the margins F_i for each random variable X_i, $i=1,2,\ldots,n$ according to the samples$\{ x_i^j, j=1,2,\ldots,s \}$. The last step is to select or to construct a copula C according to x, and then sample from C. Assuming the sampled vectors are$\{ u^{(k)}=(u_1^{(k)},u_2^{(k)},\ldots,u_n^{(k)}), k=1,2,\ldots,l \}$, the new individuals $\{x^{(k)}=(x_1^{(k)},x_2^{(k)},\ldots,x_n^{(k)}), k=1,2,\ldots,l \}$ can be calculate3d by using

$$x_i^{(k)} = F_i^{-1}\left(u_i^{(k)}\right), \; i = 1,..,n, \; k = 1,\ldots,l \tag{1}$$

where, F_i^{-1} is the inverse function of the ith marginal distribution function.

copula EDA replaces some old individuals of the original population with the new generated individuals and progresses the new evolution until the terminate condition is met.

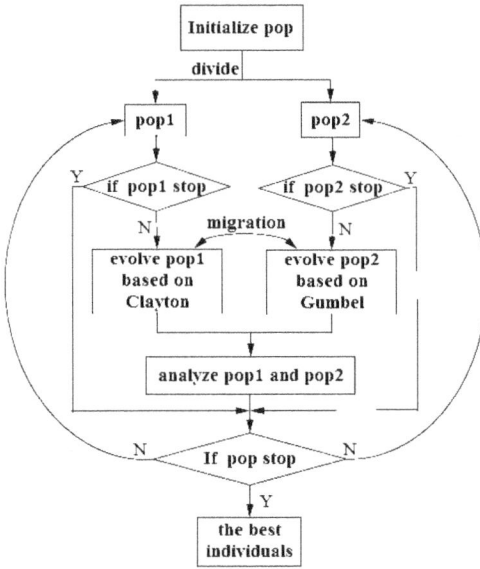

Fig. 1. The flow chart of multi-population parallel copula EDA

Some authors have studied on the optimization effectiveness of different copula functions under the framework of copula EDA [17],[18]. The results show that in many cases, the different copulas are used in common basic test function to bring about different performances, because each copula function has special characteristic. So modeling and sampling by a pre-assigned single copula function without judgment is difficult to exactly describe the multivariate correlation of practical problem.

In order to possibly speed up the search of EDAs and to increase the diversity of the population, the idea of parallel Genetic Algorithms is introduced into copula EDA. Multi-population parallel copula EDA separates the individuals into certain independent subpopulations. According to the frame work of copula EDA, each subpopulation use different copulas to model and sample, respectively. We choose two famous Archimedean copulas: Clayton and Gumbel. The sampling algorithm from copula is the algorithm proposed by Marshall and Olkin[19] , [20].

Concluding the analysis presented above, the multi-population parallel copula EDA works as Figure 1 and Algorithm 1, where, the procedure Clatyton sample and Gumbel sample is shown in Algorithm 2 and Algorithm 3 respectively.

Algorithm 1. Pseudo code for multi-population parallel copula EDA.

Step1. Randomly generate initial population with size N, and divide them into two subpopulations: $pop1_0$, $pop2_0$.and set $g \leftarrow 0$.

Step2. Initialize evaluation flag: $evFlag1 \leftarrow 1$ ïï$evFlag2 \leftarrow 1$.

Step3. Select two subpopulations $spop1$ and $spop2$ with same size of s from $pop1_g$, $pop2_g$ According to certain select-strategy, respectively.

Step4. If $evFlag1 == 1$, evolve $pop1_g$ based on Clayton copula.

   Step4-1 Estimate the univariate marginal distribution function ïF_i for each dimension from $spop1$.ï

   Step4-2. For $k=1$ to l do ($x_1^{(k)}, x_2^{(k)}, \ldots, x_n^{(k)}$)=Clayton_sample(k).

   Step4-3. Replace the old individuals of $pop1_g$ with the new individual.

   Step4-4. If the stopping criterion of $pop1_g$ is reached, setï$evFlag1 \leftarrow 0$.

Step5. If $evFlag2 == 1$, evolve, $pop2_g$ base on Gumbel copula.

   Step5-1. Estimate the unvariate marginal distribution function F_i for each dimension fromï$spop2$.

   Step5-2. For $k=1$ to l doï($x_1^{(k)}, x_2^{(k)}, \ldots, x_n^{(k)}$) = Gumbel_sample(k).

   Step5-3. Replace the old individuals of $pop2_g$ with the new individuals.

   Step5-4. If evolutional stopping criterion of $pop2_g$ is reached, set $evFlag2 \leftarrow 0$.

Step6. If (g%c==0) ïï$pop1_g$ and $pop2_g$ mutually migration w best individuals.

Step7. Set $g \leftarrow g+1$.

Step8. If stopping criterion is met, then stoop the algorithm and the best individual is the optimization result, else go to *Step3*.

3.2 Clayton Copula Model Sampling

The generator of Clayton copula is

$$\varphi(t) = (t^{-\theta} - 1) / \theta \tag{2}$$

the inverse function is

$$\varphi^{-1}(t) = (1 + \theta t)^{-1/\theta} \tag{3}$$

and the inverse Laplace-Stieltjes transform of the generator φ^{-1} is

$$LS(\varphi^{-1}) = F(v) = \frac{(1/\theta)^{1/\theta}}{\Gamma(1/\theta)} e^{-v/\theta} \cdot v^{1/\theta - 1} \tag{4}$$

The algorithm for sampling from Clayton copula and empirical margins is concluded as in Algorithm 2.

Algorithm 2. $(x_1^{(k)}, x_2^{(k)}, \ldots, x_n^{(k)}) = \text{Calyton\_sample}(k)$

Step1.Simulate $v \sim F(v) = \dfrac{(1/\theta)^{1/\theta}}{\Gamma(1/\theta)} e^{-v/\theta} \cdot v^{1/\theta - 1}$.

Step2.Simulate i.i.d. $v_i \sim U[0,1]$, $i = 1,\ldots,n$, get u_i from

$$u_i = \varphi^{-1}((-\log v_i)/v) = (1 - \frac{\theta \log v_i}{v})^{-1/\theta} \tag{5}$$

Step3.Get new individual $(x_1^{(k)}, x_2^{(k)}, \ldots, x_n^{(k)})$ by calculating

$$x_i^{(k)} = F_i^{-1}(u_i) = \begin{cases} rand[x_i^{<j>}, x_i^{<j+1>}) & if \quad \lfloor u_i \times s \rfloor = j \quad and \; x_i^{<j>} \neq x_i^{<j+1>} \\ rand(x_i^{<j>}; \delta) & if \quad \lfloor u_i \times s \rfloor = j \quad and \; x_i^{<j>} = x_i^{<j+1>} \end{cases} \tag{6}$$

3.3 Gumbel Copula Model Sampling

The generator of Gumbel copula is

$$\varphi(t) = (-\ln t)^{\theta} \tag{7}$$

and the algorithm for sampling from Gumbel copula and empirical margins is described in Algorithm 3.

Algorithm 3. $(x_1^{(k)}, x_2^{(k)}, \ldots, x_n^{(k)}) = \text{Gumbel\_sample}(k)$

Step1.Simulate an uniform variable $\Theta \sim U(-\dfrac{\pi}{2}, \dfrac{\pi}{2})$.

Stetp2. Simulate an exponentially distributed variable W with mean 1 independently of Θ.

Step3. Set $\alpha = \dfrac{1}{\theta}$, $\beta = 1$, $\gamma = \left(cos(\dfrac{\pi}{2\theta}) \right)^{\theta}$, $\delta = 0$, and $\theta_0 = \arctan(\beta \tan(\pi\alpha/2))/\alpha$.

Step4. Compute $Z \sim st(\alpha, \beta, 1, 0)$.

$$Z = \frac{\sin\alpha(\theta_0 + \Theta)}{(\cos\alpha\theta_0\cos\Theta)^{1/\alpha}}\left[\frac{\cos(\alpha\theta_0 + (\alpha-1)\Theta)}{W}\right]^{\left(\frac{1-\alpha}{\alpha}\right)} \quad \alpha \neq 1$$

$$Z = \frac{2}{\pi}\left[\left(\frac{2}{\pi} + \beta\Theta\right)\tan\Theta - \beta\ln\left(\frac{\frac{\pi}{2}W\cos\Theta}{\frac{\pi}{2} + \beta\Theta}\right)\right] \quad \alpha = 1$$

(8)

Step5.Compute $v \sim st(\alpha, \beta, \gamma, \delta)$:

$$v = \gamma Z + \delta \qquad \alpha \neq 1 \qquad (9)$$

$$v = \gamma Z + (\delta + \beta\frac{2}{\pi}\gamma\ln(\gamma)) \quad \alpha = 1$$

Step6. Simulate *i.i.d.* $v_i \sim U[0,1]$, $i=1,\ldots,n$, get u_i from

$$u_i = \phi^{-1}((-\log v_i)/v) = (1 - \frac{\theta\log v_i}{v})^{-1/\theta} \qquad (10)$$

Step7.Get new individual $(x_1^{(k)}, x_2^{(k)}, \ldots, x_n^{(k)})$ by calculating

$$j = \lfloor u_i \times s \rfloor;$$

$$x_i^{(k)} = F_i^{-1}(u_i) = \begin{cases} rand[x_i^{<j>}, x_i^{<j+1>}) & , x_i^{<j>} \neq x_i^{<j+1>} \\ rand(x_i^{<j>}; \delta) & x_i^{<j>} = x_i^{<j+1>} \end{cases} \qquad (11)$$

4   Experiments

4.1 Experimental Design

Test Function. To carry out theïvalidation of the proposed algorithm in this paper, we have selected four benchmark functions in Table 1. F_1 and F_2 can easily produce ill-posed covariance matrices; F_3 is a multi-peak function; F_4 is an uni-model function. All of the functions above with the different characteristics are also used in [21].

Initial Population. Because the accuracy of the estimated model and the quality of offspring will decrease as population size decreases, the population size should not too small. For the proposed algorithm, population size is set to 2000, and equally divided into two subpopulations as certain strategy. The dimension of the search space is 10. In order to ensure the fairness of comparison, all the algorithms to participate comparison share common populations. In addition, selection rate of the promising population is 0.5 that truncation selection and roulette selection are 30% and 70% of total selection respectively.

Table 1. Test functions chosen for experiments

Function:	$F_1(x) = -\{10^{-5} + \sum_{i=1}^{n} \mid y_i \mid\}^{-1}$
	where : $y_1 = x_1, y_i = y_{i-1} + x_i, i = 1,...,10$
Search space:	$-0.16 \le x_i \le 0.16, i = 1,...,10$
Minimum value:	$F(0) = 10^{-5}$
Function:	$F_2(x) = \sum_{i=1}^{n} [(x_1 - x_i^2)^2 + (x_i - 1)^2]$
Search space:	$-5.12 \le x_i \le 5.12, i = 1,...,10$
Minimum value:	$F(0) = 0$
Function:	$F_3(x) = \sum_{i=1}^{n} [x_i^2 - 10\cos(2\pi x_i) + 10]$
Search space:	$-5.12 \le x_i \le 5.12, i = 1,...,10$
Minimum value:	$F(0) = 0$
Function:	$F_4(x) = \sum_{i=1}^{D} x_i^2$
Search space:	$-100 \le x_i \le 100, i = 1,...,10$
Minimum value:	$F(0) = 0$

Parallel Algorithm Model. The coarse-grained model is used in this paper. Migration topology is unidirectional ring, migration rate and frequency is 0.2 and 5, respectively.

Parameters of Copula Function. The parameter θ of Gumbel is set to 1.05 in Gumbel copula EDA and multi-population parallel copula EDA; the parameter θ of Clayton is set to 1 in Clayton copula EDA and multi-population parallel copula EDA.

4.2 Results Analysis

Using $F_1 - F_4$ test multi-population parallel copula EDA, $MIMIC_c^G$, $UMDA_c^G$, Gumel copula EDA and Clayton copula EDA 50 times respectively, and the evolutionary generation is 150. The experimental results are shown in Table 2. The evaluation criterions are: the mean fitness, the standard variance and the minimal fitness of the 50 optimization results, the average runtime of the 50 optimization.

From the experimental results in table 2, we know that multi-population parallel copula EDA performs well in $F_1 - F_3$ where multivariate correlations are strong. $MIMIC_c^G$ and $UMDA_c^G$ have good performances in F_4 where variables are independent.

To sum up, facing problems of ïmultivariate strong correlations, $UMDA_c^G$ converges very fast and does not converge to the global optimum because the algorithm considers the relationships of the optimized variables as independent, $MIMIC_c^G$ considers the pairwise correlations of the optimized variables, but it consumes much time to get a little better optimization result. Multi-population parllal copula EDA considers the entire relationships of the optimized variables and converges to an acceptable optimized result in a short time. ï

Table 2. The performances of multi-population parallel copula EDA and some evolutionary algorithms

Algorithm	Mean	Std. Var.	Min	Runtime (m)
F_1				
$UMDA_C^G$	-10523.54	11957.07	-60809.21	6.08
$MIMIC_C^G$	-44578.33	36613.73	-99780.88	46.58
Gumbel copula EDA	-87975.65	7197.21	-98295.14	27.83
Calyton copula EDA	-81053.08	12160.57	-97704.43	24.32
multi-population parallel copula EDA	-83290.67	11504.29	-97411.20	22.18
F_2				
$UMDA_C^G$	9.42E-4	3.53E-4	4.27E-4	6.19
$MIMIC_C^G$	1.28E-4	6.80E-5	1.97E-5	47.11
Gumbel copula EDA	7.90E-6	4.36E-6	1.24E-6	19.40
Calyton copula EDA	3.37E-6	1.04E-6	1.52E-6	17.11
multi-population parallel copula EDA	2.78E-6	8.25E-7	1.21E-6	16.70
F_3				
$UMDA_C^G$	8.96	9.77	1.65E-9	4.58
$MIMIC_C^G$	9.22	9.39	8.63E-10	46.83
Gumbel copula EDA	6.45E-9	4.24E-9	9.46E-10	14.08
Calyton copula EDA	5.72E-8	2.40E-8	4.96E-9	11.40
multi-population parallel copula EDA	6.06E-9	5.11E-9	1.01E-9	10.54
F_4				
$UMDA_C^G$	1.66E-9	8.42E-10	3.89E-10	3.73
$MIMIC_C^G$	1.39E-9	1.16E-9	4.03E-10	29.90
Gumbel copula EDA	4.26E-9	3.15E-9	1.03E-9	13.30
Calyton copula EDA	6.59E-8	2.97E-8	6.63E-9	11.79
multi-population parallel copula EDA	5.93E-9	4.13E-9	8.98E-10	10.53

5   Conclusions

EDAs have effective performance for complex optimization problem by estimating probabilistic distribute model which reflect the dependent relationship of variables in the population. The copula EDAs provides an alternative way to tackle the drawbacks which are modeling complexity, high time consuming and poor performance on problems with strong correlation of variables in traditional EDAs. Multi-population parallel copula EDA joins the idea of parallel GAs with copula EDA. The global population is divided into several independent subpopulations. Each subpopulation takes evolution on different copula under the frame work of copula EDA. And for the purpose of enriching diversity of population and enhancing overall searching ability, the migration of some individuals among the different subpopulations is allowed under given conditions. The experimental results validate this algorithm.

The initialization and division mechanism for population and the way for multi-population parallel working influence the performance of multi-population parallel copula EDA. The next target is to study how to select a copula function exactly fitting the subpopulation.

Acknowledgments. This work is partially supported by the Youth Science Fund of Taiyuan University of Technology (No.K201031), the Youth Research Fund of ShanXi Province (No. 2010021017-2) and the Science Fund of Shanxi Institution of Higher Learning (No. 2010015).

References

1. Zhou, S.D., Sun, Z.Q.: A Survey on Estimation of Distribution Algorithms. Acta Automatica Sinica 33(2), 114–121 (2007)
2. Baluja, S.: Population-Based Incremental Learning: A Method for Integrating Genetic Search Based Function Optimization and Competitive Learning. Technical Rep. CMU-CS-94-163. Carnegie Mellon University, Pittsburgh, PA (1994)
3. Muhlenbein, H., Paass, G.: From Recombination of Genes to the Estimation of distributions I. Binary Parameters. In: Ebeling, W., Rechenberg, I., Voigt, H.-M., Schwefel, H.-P. (eds.) PPSN 1996. LNCS, vol. 1141, pp. 178–187. Springer, Heidelberg (1996)
4. De Bonet, J.S., Isbell, C.L., Viola, P.: MIMIC: Finding Optima by Estimation Probability Densities. In: Advances in Neural Information Processing Systems, pp. 424–430. MIT Press, Cambridge (1997)
5. Pelican, M., Muhlenbein, H.: The Bivariate Marginal Distribution Algorithm. In: Advances in Soft Computing-Engineering Design and Manufacturing, pp. 521–535. Springer, London (1999)
6. Harik, G.: Linkage Learning via Probabilistic Modeling in the ECGA. Illigal Rep. No.99010, Illinois Genetic Algorithms Lab. University of Illinois, Urbana-Champaign, Illinois (1999)
7. Muhlenbein, H., Mahnig, T.: FDA- a Scalable evolutionary Algorithm for the Optimization of Additively Decomposed Functions. Evolutionary Computation 7(4), 353–376 (Winter 1999)
8. Pelikan, M., Goldberg, D.E., Cantu-Paz, E.: BOA: the Bayesian Optimization Algorithm. In: Proc. Genetic and Evolutionary Computation Conference (GECCO-1999), Orlando, FL, pp. 525–532 (1999)
9. Larranaga, P., Etxeberria, R., Lozano, J.A., Pena, J.M.: Optimization in Continuous Domains by Learning and Simulation of Gaussian Networks. In: Proceedings of the Genetic and Evolutionary Computation Conference, GECCO 2000, Las Vegas, Nevada, USA, July 8-12, pp. 201–204. Morgan Kaufmann, San Francisco (2000)
10. Sebag, M., Ducoulombier, A.: Extending Population-Based Incremental Learning to Continuous Search Spaces. In: Eiben, A.E., Bäck, T., Schoenauer, M., Schwefel, H.-P. (eds.) PPSN 1998. LNCS, vol. 1498, pp. 418–427. Springer, Heidelberg (1998), http://citeseerx.ist.psu.edu/viewdoc/ summary?doi=10.1.1.42.1884

11. Larranaga, P., Lozano, J.A., Bengoetxea, E.: Estimation of Distribution Algorithms based on Multivariate Normal a Gaussian Nerworks. Technical Report KZZA-IK-1-01. Department of Computer Science and Artificial Intelligence, University of the Basque Country (2001)
12. Wang, L.F., Zeng, J.C., Hong, Y.: Estimation of Distribution Algorithm Based on Archimedean Copulas. In: Proceedings of the First ACM/SIGEVO Summit on Genetic and Evolutionary Computation (GECS 2009), Shanghai, China, June 12-14, pp. 993–996 (2009)
13. Wang, L.F., Zeng, J.C., Hong, Y.: Estimation of Distribution Algorithm Based on Copula Theory. In: Proceedings of the IEEE Congress on Evolutionary Computation (CEC 2009), Trondheim, Norway, May 18-21, pp. 1057–1063 (2009)
14. Nelsen, R.B.: An introduction to copulas, 2nd edn. Springer, New York (2006)
15. Cantú-Paz, E.: A Survey of Parallel Genetic Algorithms. Illinois Genetic Algorithms Laboratory, Urbana-Champaign (1996)
16. Cantú-Paz, E.: Efficient and accurate parallel genetic algorithms. Kluwer, Dordrecht (2001)
17. Wang, L., Guo, X., Zeng, J., Hong, Y.: Using Gumbel Copula and Empirical Marginal Distribution in Estimation of Distribution Algorithm. In: 2010 Third International Workshop on Advanced Computational Intelligence (IWACI 2010), Suzhou, China, August 25-27, pp. 583–587 (2010); (EI:20104613386525)
18. Wang, L., Wang, Y., Zeng, J., Hong, Y.: An estimation of distribution algorithm based on clayton copula and empirical margins. In: Li, K., Li, X., Ma, S., Irwin, G.W. (eds.) LSMS 2010, Part 1. CCIS, vol. 98, pp. 82–88. Springer, Heidelberg (2010), doi:10.1007/978-3-642-15859-9_12, (EI:20104513368882) 04
19. Marshall, A.W., Olkin, I.: Families of Multivariate Distributions. Journal of the American Statistical Association 83, 834–841 (1988)
20. Melchiori, M.R.: Tools For Sampling Multivariate Archimedean Copulas. Yield Curve (April 2006), SSRN: http://ssrn.com/abstract=1124682
21. Dong, W., Yao, X.: Unified Eigen Analysis On Multivariate Gaussian Based Estimation of Distribution Algorithms. Information Science 178, 3000–3023 (2008)

Improving Search Ability of Genetic Learning Process for High-Dimensional Fuzzy Classification Problems

Ji-Dong Li[1,2], Xue-Jie Zhang[1], Yun Gao[1], Hao Zhou[1], and Jian Cui[2]

[1] School of Information Science and Engineering,
Yunnan University, Kunming, China
[2] School of Vocational and Continuing Education,
Yunnan University, Kunming, China
{lijd,xjzhang,gaoyun,zhouhao,cuijian}@ynu.edu.cn

Abstract. In this paper, we improve efficiency of the genetic search process for generating fuzzy classification rules from high-dimensional problems by using fitness sharing method. First, we define the similarity level of different fuzzy rules. It represents the structural difference of search space in the genetic population. Next, we use sharing method to balance the fitness of different rules and prevent the search process falling into local regions. Then, we combine the sharing method into a hybrid learning approach (i.e., the hybridization of Michigan and Pittsburgh) to obtain the appropriate combination of different rules. Finally, we examine the search ability of different genetic machine learning approaches on a suite of test problems and some well-known classification problems. Experimental results show that the fitness sharing method has higher search ability and it is able to obtained accurate fuzzy classification rules set.

Keywords: fuzzy rule-based classification system, high-dimensional problems, genetic-based machine learning, fitness sharing.

1   Introduction

Many approaches have been proposed for automatically modeling fuzzy rules-based classification systems by using genetic algorithms [1,2]. In these approaches, genetic algorithms are usually used for generating fuzzy rules from examples of real problems, which contains two objectives, the selection of appropriate antecedent sets of each fuzzy rule and the determination of optimal combinations of different fuzzy rules [3].

In the realm of genetic machine learning, the Michigan approaches [4] and the Pittsburgh approaches [5] are usually applied for obtaining fuzzy rules. As suggested in [3], the Michigan approaches are more suitable for the first objective, because they handle a rule as a genetic chromosome. While the Pittsburgh approaches are better for the second objective, because they handle a whole rule set as a chromosome. A hybrid algorithm (i.e., the hybridization of Michigan and Pittsburgh) was also proposed in [3] to perform the robust searching process for obtaining high quality fuzzy rules.

The selection of fuzzy antecedent sets in the hybrid algorithms mainly accomplished by Michigan-style search process. However, the Michigan-style approaches are more

H. Deng et al. (Eds.): AICI 2011, Part I, LNAI 7002, pp. 644–654, 2011.

vulnerable to local convergence when dealing with high-dimensional classification problems. In high-dimensional problems, the number of possible combination of fuzzy antecedent sets is very huge and the problems contain a large number of local search areas. In this situation, as chromosome that characterized by local regions are often selected, all chromosome in gene pool get closer and closer, finally they are identical, or nearly so. Once this occurs, the process only search from a small subset of the search space and makes the process become inefficient and slow.

Maintaining diversity of Michigan-style search process is crucial in avoiding local convergence and improving search ability [6]. Several niching techniques were introduced to preserve the diversity of a population by keeping the chromosome reasonably away from each other [7]. Among these techniques, fitness sharing [7] treats fitness as a shared resource of the population, and requires the similar chromosomes share their fitness. The fitness of each individual is worsened by its neighbours: the more and the closer neighbours an individual has, the worse its fitness becomes. In this paper, we extend the applicability of fitness sharing to Michigan-style search process in the hybrid algorithms. We define the similarity level of different fuzzy rules, which reflects the structural difference of fuzzy rules in the genetic population, that is, if two rules formed by identical or similar fuzzy subspaces, the value is high, whereas if two rules formed by different fuzzy subspaces, the value is low. Based on the similarity value, fitness sharing method is used for balancing the fitness of different rules and avoiding the search process falling into local regions.

To carry out the analysis of search ability of different methods, we develop a suite of classification test problems and select 5 well-known data-sets from UCI repository [8], using accuracy rate as evaluation measure.

2   Background

2.1   Fuzzy Rule-Based Classification Systems

Fuzzy rule-based classification systems have been shown to be a useful tool for modeling real classification problems, because the interpretability of the systems are based on linguistic variables, which can be understood easily by experts or users.

Assume an n-dimensional classification problem with N patterns $x \in X \subseteq R^n$, $x = (x_1, x_2, ... x_n)$ are given from M classes $\{C_1, C_2, ..., C_M\}$. A Mamdaini-type [9] rule is widely used in fuzzy rule-based classification systems, which has the form:

$$\text{Rule } R_j : \text{if } x_1 \text{ is } A_{j1} \text{ and} ... \text{and } x_n \text{ is } A_{jn} \text{ then Class is } C_j \qquad (1)$$

where R_j is the label of the jth fuzzy if-then rule, C_j is consequent class. $A_{j1}, ..., A_{jn}$ are antecedent fuzzy sets representing linguistic variables.

With the form of fuzzy classification rules, for a input pattern $x = (x_1, x_2, ... x_n)$, its consequent class C is determined by: $C = C_{i^*}, i^* = \arg \max_{1 \le i \le l} \beta_i$ .where L is the size of rule set, and β_i is the degree of activation of the ith rule, which usually calculated by the product operator: $\beta_i(x) = \prod_{j=1}^{n} A_{ij}(x_j), i = 1,2,...,L$.

2.2   Genetic Machine Learning Approaches

Pittsburgh-style approaches and Michigan-style approaches are widely used in the construction of fuzzy rule-based classification systems. Each of the approaches has its own advantages and disadvantages. In this section, we give a brief analysis by using two dimensional spaces in Fig. 1, and further comparisons can be referred in section 4.

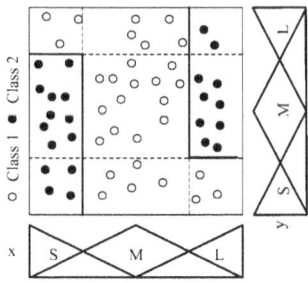

Fig. 1. Two dimensional pattern spaces

There are nine subspaces in Fig. 1, and appropriate fuzzy rules for class 1 are:

R_1 :if x is S and y is S then class is 1   (4 examples)

R_2 :if x is S and y is M then class is 1   (10 examples)

R_3 :if x is L and y is M then class is 1   (8 examples)

R_4 :if x is L and y is L then class is 1   (2 examples)

For Pittsburgh-style approaches, they are able to find a good combination of fuzzy rules. However, they handle each rule as a basic unit of crossover operation, so they are not able to search all subspaces efficiently. For example, suppose eight of the nine subspaces are included in the following two individuals:

Individual 1: {(if x is S and y is S),(if x is S and y is M),(if x is M and y is S), (if x is L and y is L),...}

Individual 2: {(if x is M and y is M),(if x is M and y is L),(if x is S and y is L), (if x is L and y is M),...}

And we can see the subspace of (L,L) can not be obtained by crossover operation.

For Michigan-style approaches, they have strong search ability to find the appropriate fuzzy antecedents sets of fuzzy rule, but they usually fail to find a good combination of fuzzy rules. For example, suppose all 4 rules of class 1 are in the gene pool of Michigan-style approaches and they compete with each other. As R_2 or R_3, which are represented by more examples than R_1 or R_4, are often selected by probability selection mechanism, all individuals in gene pool get closer and closer, finally they are identical. When this happens, the subspaces of (S,S) and (L,L) are missing from the populations. Another discussion is the fitness value of these rules can be balanced by some genetic operators, so R_1 or R_4 can be selected to the next generation. We take the liner ranking [10] as an example. From the Fig. 1, we can see that many rules are similar to R_2 or R_3. Including:

if x is S and y is *very* M then class is 1   if x is L and y is *very* M then class is 1

if x is S and y is *extreme* M then class is 1   if x is L and y is *extreme* M then class is 1

......

These similar rules also have greater numbers of examples than R_1 or R_4 and they also have less opportunity to be selected. Therefore, a fitness sharing method based on the similarity level of fuzzy rules should be added into the Michigan-style approaches for maintaining the diversity and improving the search ability.

3   Hybrid Genetic Learning Approach with Fitness Sharing

3.1   Fuzzy Partitions and Coding of Fuzzy Rules

Because the data distributions of many real classification problems are unknown before the learning process, we use five atomic fuzzy sets with four linguistic hedges [11] and *don't care* condition for extracting the precise classification boundaries. Therefore, the number of possible fuzzy antecedent sets is 26. The mentioned atomic fuzzy sets and the linguistic hedges depicted in Fig. 2 and Fig. 3, respectively. In Fig. 3, M means *medium*, VM for *very medium*, EM for *extreme medium*, MLM for *more or less medium* and LM for *little medium*.

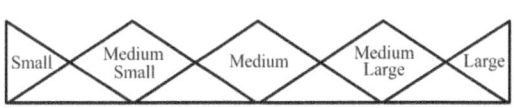
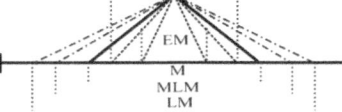

Fig. 2. Five atomic fuzzy sets   **Fig. 3.** Four language hedges.

It is not convenient for using the curve forms of linguistic hedges to represent fuzzy antecedent sets, so they are replaced by the most similar triangular forms. The replacements are described Fig. 4 by using the similarity measure as (2).

$$S(A,B) = \frac{|A \cap B|}{|A \cup B|} \tag{2}$$

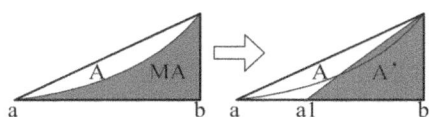

Fig. 4. The replacement of *very Large*. A' is the most similar triangular fuzzy set with MA.

The replacements are also similar with the *Dilation* and *Concentration* operators as suggested in [12]. The changes of four linguistic hedges are listed in Table 1.

Table 1. Similar fuzzy sets for common language hedges

hedge	little	more or less	very	extreme
$f(A)$	$\sqrt[4]{u_A(x)}$	$\sqrt{u_A(x)}$	$(u_A(x))^2$	$(u_A(x))^4$
a_1	$a - \dfrac{3(b-a)}{5}$	$a - \dfrac{b-a}{3}$	$a + \dfrac{b-a}{3}$	$a + \dfrac{3(b-a)}{5}$

With the fuzzy if-then rule form of Mamdaini-type in (1), a string "$S,L,MLS,VML,DN,1$" denotes the following fuzzy classification rule :

R_i: if x_1 is *Small* and x_2 is *Large* and x_3 is *More or Less Small* and x_4 is *Very Medium Large* and x_5 *don't care* then class is 1.

With the coding of each rule, we organize these rules as an individual $S_i = (R_1,...,R_L)$. Finally, the population $P_{ALL} = (S_1,...,S_M)$ is formed by putting these individuals together.

At the beginning of our genetic learning process, each antecedent of a fuzzy rule is randomly selected from the above mentioned fuzzy sets with the same probability to construct the initial gene pool. And the consequent class of each fuzzy classification rule is determined by the heuristic procedure as mentioned in [3].

3.2   Fitness Sharing and Hybrid Genetic Learning Approach

The task of Michigan-style learning process is to select appropriate antecedent sets of fuzzy rules, which are represented by different subspaces as discussed in section 2. To prevent the learning process only learn rules from small subset of the search space, a fitness sharing method based on the similarity level of different rules is applied. The fitness function of each rule is defined as:

$$fitness(R_i) = CR(R_i) \cdot \frac{1}{(1 + \lambda S^*(R_i))} \tag{3}$$

Where $CR(R_i)$ is the rate of training examples that are correctly classified by rule R_i, together with the penalty of misclassified rate: $CR(R_i) = CorrectRate(R_i) - w_{error} MisRate(R_i)$, and if the number of misclassified by R_i is greater than a prespecified nc, then $CR(R_i) = 0$.

$S^*(R_i)$ is the similarity level (similar to niche count of standard fitness sharing method) of R_i compared to the rest of rules in the population, if $S^*(R_i)$ is greater than a prespecified threshold value, then $fitness(R_i) = 0$. The procedure of calculating of $S^*(R_i)$ can be written as:

- First, the similar value of one rule R_x and its neighbour rule R_y can be defined as $S(R_x, R_y) = \min_{1 \le i \le n} \{S(R_{xi}, R_{yi})\}$, $S(R_{xi}, R_{yi})$ is the similarity value of antecedent sets of R_{xi} and R_{yi}, calculated by (2).

- Second, calculate the similarity level $S^*(R_i) = \sum_{y=1,2,...,L} S(R_i, R_y)$.

From the definition $S(R_x, R_y)$, we can see the Euclidean formula $S_{euc}(R_i, R_j) = \sqrt{S(R_{i1}, R_{j1})^2 + S(R_{i2}, R_{j2})^2 + ... + S(R_{in}, R_{jn})^2}$ is not used in our method. This is because the (S,S) represented by R_1 and (S,M) represented by R_2 in Fig. 1 are two different search subspaces.

For cutting down the additional computing load of $S(R_{xi}, R_{yi})$, we cached the similarity values in a table as table 2 of two possible fuzzy antecedent sets before the run of our approaches. When the similarity level is calculated, the similarity values of possible antecedent sets can be look up from the table, not calculated by mathematical integration.

Table 2. Similar fuzzy sets for common language hedges

values	S	little S	more or less S	very S	MS	M	ML	L
S	1	0.63	0.75	0.67	0.2	0	0	0
little S	0.63	1	0.83	0.42	0.38	0.04	0	0
more or less S	0.75	0.83	1	0.50	0.30	0.01	0	0
very S	0.67	0.42	0.50	1	0.11	0	0	0
MS	0.2	0.38	0.30	0.11	1	0.14	0	0
M	0	0.04	0.01	0	0.14	1	0.14	0
ML	0	0	0	0	0	0.14	1	0.2
L	0	0	0	0	0	0	0.2	1
...			...			...		

Besides the fitness sharing method, the liner ranking selection mechanism is used in the iterations of Michigan-style learning process, together with the elist selection strategy. And during the reproduction phase, the uniform crossover and single-point mutation are used.

In this paper, the sharing method is also combined into a hybrid genetic learning approach to obtain the appropriate combination of different rules. Hybrid genetic learning approach was proposed in [3], which is combined by the Michigan-style approach and Pittsburgh-style approach. The framework of hybrid approach is mainly based on Pittsburgh-style approach, and the Michigan-style approach, together with the fitness sharing, is also used as a kind of heuristic mutation for partially modifying each rule set.

[Outline of Hybrid genetic Learning Approach]

Step 1: Generate N_{pop} rule sets with N_{rule} fuzzy rules.

Step 2: Calculate the fitness value of each rule set in the current population.

Step 3: Generate (N_{pop} -1) rule sets by the selection, crossover and mutation in the same manner as the Pittsburgh-style approach. Apply a single iteration of the Michigan-style approach (i.e., the rule generation and the replacement with the fitness sharing method) to each of the generated rule sets with a prespecified probability.

Step 4: Add the best rule set in the current population to the newly generated (N_{pop} -1) rule sets to form the next population.

Step 5: Return to Step 2 if the prespecified stopping condition is not satisfied.

4   Experimental Results

This section presents computer simulation results of applying the proposed hybrid genetic learning approach to: (1) a suit of test problems, (2) six well-known data sets, obtained from Irvine machine learning repository of California University [8]. The evaluations of search ability are also compared among four approaches: the Michigan approach (Mich), the Pittsburgh approach (Pitts), the standard hybrid genetic learning approach (FH-ML) and the hybrid genetic learning approach with fitness sharing (SH-ML).

Test functions [13], such as De Jong test suite [14], are commonly used to evaluate the effectiveness of different search algorithms. However, the test functions are not suitable for pattern classification problems. So we develop a suite of test problems for evaluating the search ability of different learning approaches. And several aspects are considered according to the guideline in [13], as fellows.

• Test suites contain high-dimensional problems. All problems listed in this paper contain 100 features. The classification boundaries can be extracted from several features, the remaining are set as background noises, named as interference features.

• Test suites contain problems that are resistant to hill-climbing. The values of the interference features are homogeneous distributed with range from 0 to 1, so the local search areas are formed by adjusting the number of examples, as depicted in Fig. 5 (c).

• Test suites contain problems that can not be solved by using clustering or statistical methods for each feature separately. For example, the classification boundaries can be extracted from xth and yth features in Fig. 5 (d), however, if the two features are separated and observed, their distributions are similar with the homogeneous distribution of [0,1].

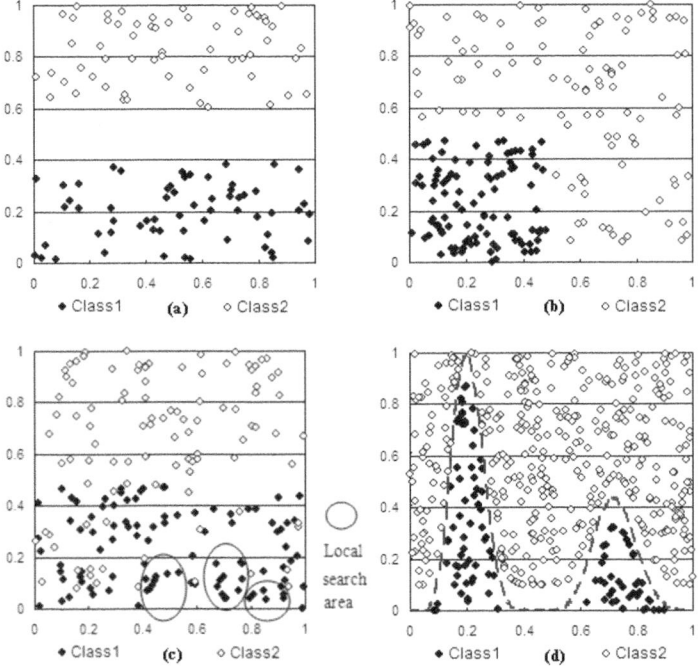

Fig. 5. Several representative test classification problems, from which the 1-2 dimensional classification boundaries can be extracted

Several representative test classification problems are selected and depicted in Fig. 5. Fig. 5 (a) is a one-dimensional boundary problem, that is, the classification boundary can be extracted from yth feature. The problem contains 120 examples, 60 for each class respectively. Fig. 5 (b) is the simplest one among all two-dimensional boundary problems, it contains 200 examples, 100 for each class. The classification boundaries can only be extracted from xth and yth features. The distribution is also depicted in Fig. 5 (c) by yth and another feature, which contains several local search areas. The problem in Fig. 5 (d) has complex boundaries, and more fuzzy rules are required to solve this problem. It contains 500 examples, 110 for class 1 and 390 for class 2. The values of xth are homogeneous distributed with range from 0 to 1, randomly. The values of yth are separated by a line of $f(x) = e^{-2(\ln 2)(\frac{x-0.08}{0.834})^2 \sin^6(2\pi(x^{0.75}-0.05))}$.

We also applied the SVM approach (the toolbox was from [15] and grid.py was used for searching for the optimal parameters) for the problem in Fig. 5 (d), and the classification rate was obtained as 78%. If all the interference features were removed from the problem, the rate increased to 99.5%.

In our experiment, each of the mentioned four approaches was tested for the problems in Fig. 5, 30 runs. Four approaches were able to obtain the good performance for the problem of Fig. 5 (a), however, the results (average classification rates) were different for Fig. 5 (b) and Fig. 5 (d), as table 3.

Table 3. Average classification rates for Figure 5 (b) and Figure 5 (d)

Parameters	Figure 5 (b)				Figure 5 (d)			
	FS-ML	Mich	Pitts	FH-ML	FS-ML	Mich	Pitts	FH-ML
PS=80,MG=600,MP=0.1	—	89.14	—	—	—	77.25	—	—
PS=200,MG=1000,MP=0.4	—	97.28	—	—	—	93.97	—	—
PS=40*40,MG=800,MP=0.1	100	—	92.46	98.57	96.03	—	85.24	89.22
PS=40*80,MG=2000,MP=0.4	100	—	96.53	99.69	99.77	—	89.38	97.45

PS is for population size, 40*80 means 40 fuzzy sets and 80 rules in each set. MG is maximum generations, MP is the probability of mutation.

We also applied four approaches for the complex problems similar with the problem in Fig. 5 (b), which ranged from three to eight-dimensional boundary. The numbers of examples are different as the dimension increases. In Fig. 6, there are $2^3 = 8$ main search areas and each of the areas contains 10 examples, so the number of examples is 160, 80 for each class. For the problem with eight-dimensional boundary, the number for each class is set to 3000.

With the same settings as the experiments in Fig. 5 results were obtained for these three to eight-dimensional boundary problems, as depicted in Fig. 7. From table 3 and Fig. 7, we can see that the average classification rates are improved by the hybrid genetic learning approach with the fitness sharing, especially for these three to eight-dimensional boundary problems. This is because the search spaces of these problems are more complex than problems depicted in Figure 5, and the fitness sharing tends to encourage the learning process to search the unexplored subspaces.

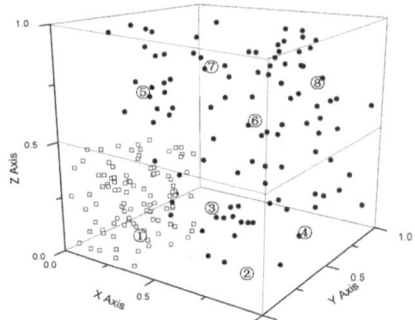
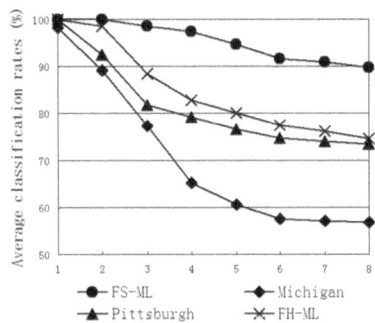

Fig. 6. The three-dimensional boundary problem

Fig. 7. Average classification rates of three to eight-dimensional boundary problems

We also applied the mentioned four approaches on some well-known data sets. The data sets can be obtained from University of California, Irvine database [8], they are *Iris data*, *Wine data*, *Sonar data*, *Glass data*, *Credit Approval Data* and *Libras data*. With the same settings as the experiments in Fig. 5, the average classification rates of four approaches were obtained as table 4. From table 4, we can also see that the hybrid genetic learning approach with the fitness sharing almost obtained the best classification rate among the four approaches.

Table 4. Average classification rate on six data-sets(%)

Data Sets	FS-ML	Mich	Pitts	FH-ML
Iris	99.3	98.0	98.7	99.5
Wine	100	98.9	99.7	100
Sonar	99.6	92.6	94.7	98.9
Glass	72.6	66.2	70.2	71.6
Credit	90.4	86.6	87.9	89.2
Libras	90.8	59.1	76.6	85.5

5   Conclusion

In this paper, we demonstrated the robust search ability is obtained by a hybrid genetic learning approach with fitness sharing. The approach does well in both of the search tasks: the selection of appropriate antecedent sets and the determination of optimal combinations of fuzzy rules, which was supported by experimental results on the high-dimensional problems.

The accuracy was used as the evaluation measure in our experiments. However, the performances of compaction and transparency [16] are not taken into account, which can also be obtained by hybrid multi-objective genetic approach with fitness sharing in Fig. 8, because of its robust search ability. And this is left for the future works.

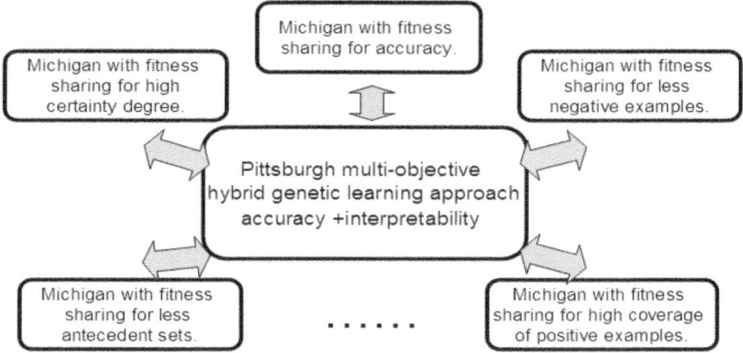

Fig. 8. The structure of hybrid multi-objective genetic learning approach, each of the objectives can be referred in [17]

Acknowledgment. This work was supported by the Young Teacher Research Foundation of Education Department of Yunnan Province (No.2010Y266), the Special Fund of School of Vocational and Continuing Education of Yunnan Province (No. K2009215).

References

1. Cordon, O., Gomide, F., Herrera, F., Hoffmann, F., Magdalena, L.: Ten Years of Genetic Fuzzy Systems: Current Framework and New Trends. Fuzzy Set. Syst. 141, 5–31 (2004)
2. Herrera, F.: Genetic Fuzzy Systems: Taxonomy, Current Research Trends and Prospects. Evol. Intel. 1, 27–46 (2008)
3. Ishibuchi, H., Yamamoto, T., Nakashima, T.: Hybridization of Fuzzy GBML Approaches for Pattern Classification Problems. IEEE Trans. Syst. Man. Cybern. B. 35, 359–365 (2005)
4. Booker, L.B., Goldberg, D.E., Holland, J.H.: Classifier Systems and Genetic Algorithms. Artif. Intell. 40, 235–282 (1989)
5. Venturini, G.: SIA: A Supervised Inductive Algorithm with Genetic Search for Learning Attribute based Concepts. In: Brazdil, P.B. (ed.) ECML 1993. LNCS, vol. 667, pp. 280–296. Springer, Heidelberg (1993)
6. Horn, J., Goldberg, D.E.: Natural Niching for Evolving Cooperative Classifiers. In: 1st Annual Conference on Genetic Programming, pp. 553–564. MIT Press, Cambridge (1996)
7. Mahfoud, S.W.: Niching Methods for Genetic Algorithms. Ph.D. dissertation, Univ. of Illinois, Urbana-Champaign (1995)
8. UCI Machine Learning Repository,
   http://www.ics.uci.edu/~mlearn/MLRepository.html
9. Mamdani, E.H., Assilian, S.: An Experiment in Linguistic Synthesis with a Fuzzy Logic Controller. Int. J. Man-Mach. Studies 7, 1–13 (1975)
10. Baker, J.E.: Adaptive Selection Methods for Genetic Algorithms. In: 1st International Conference on Genetic Algorithms, pp. 101–111. Lawrence Erlbaum Associates, Hillsdale (1985)
11. Zadeh, L.A.: Concept of a Linguistic Variable and Its Application to Approximate Reasoning-1, 2, and 3. Inform. Sci. 8, 8, 9, 199–249, 301–357, 43–80 (1975/1976)

12. Marin-Blazquez, J.G., Shen, Q.: From Approximative to Descriptive Fuzzy Classifiers. IEEE Trans. Fuzzy Syst. 10, 484–497 (2002)
13. Whitney, D., Rana, S., Dzubera, J., Mathias, K.E.: Evaluating Evolutionary Algorithms. Artif. Intell. 85, 245–276 (1996)
14. De Jong, K.: An Analysis of the Behavior of a Class of Genetic Adaptive Systems, Ph.D. thesis. Univ. of Michigan, Ann. Arbor (1975)
15. A Library for Support Vector Machines,
    http://www.csie.ntu.edu.tw/~cjlin/libsvm/
16. Roubos, J.A., Setnes, M.: Compact and Transparent Fuzzy Models and Classifiers through Iterative Complexity Reduction. IEEE Trans. Fuzzy Syst. 9, 516–524 (2001)
17. Herrera, F., Lozano, M., Verdegay, J.L.: A Learning Process for Fuzzy Control Rules using Genetic Algorithms. Fuzzy Set. Syst. 100, 143–158 (1998)

Studies on Source Rebuild Method with a Genetic Algorithm

Xiangjun Xu [1,2] and Rentai Yao [2]

[1] College of Environment Science and Engineering,
Taiyuan University of Technology,
Taiyuan, China
[2] China Institute for Radiation Protection,
Taiyuan, China
xxj7026@yahoo.com.cn

Abstract. In order to deal with unknown releasing affair and carry on emergency action more effectively, a source rebuild model with a genetic algorithm (GA) [1] based on environmental and meteorological information was built. Insufficient spatial and temporal resolution and inherent uncertainty in meteorological data make the prediction of subsequent transport and dispersion extremely difficult. The genetic algorithm was chosen as optimization algorithm to deal with the similar things happen to source rebuild. The method and some main parameters in model were presented in paper. Thereafter, the source rebuild model was applied to estimating the location and strength of two unknown gas release sources from simultaneous measurements of gas concentration and wind data. The result shows: 1. The source rebuild model with a genetic algorithm based on environmental monitor datum is reasonable and feasible. 2. The source rebuild model is effective in 101km scale at least. At last, we discuss the necessity to use all meaningful monitor data to modify the method of source rebuild.

Keywords: Unknown releasing affair, Genetic algorithm, Source rebuild.

1 Introduction

Estimate the characters of the source, such as location and release strength, given a downwind concentration measurement and knowledge of the wind field is call "source rebuild". The main purpose of the project is to improve the affectivity of emergency action while the unknown release affair happening [2]. At the same time, the application of the technology can also be used to modify the results of meteorological diffusion simulation and reduce the uncertainty for concentration forecast.

Quantizing the release source in space and time just by using limited environment and meteorological information is a challenging job. The affectivity of the source rebuild model mainly depends on the rationality of their optimization scheme. In order to choose a reasonable scheme, many optimization algorithms are reviewed, such as Kalman filter, nonparametric regression, Bayesian inference, and meta-heuristics algorithm.

H. Deng et al. (Eds.): AICI 2011, Part I, LNAI 7002, pp. 655–662, 2011.
© Springer-Verlag Berlin Heidelberg 2011

Generally, represented by genetic algorithm the heuristic modern optimization algorithm is not tied to specific function relation and has good robustness to solve the multi-objective combined optimization problem. So, this algorithm has obvious superiority to settle the problem of source estimate based on environmental and meteorological observations.

The essence of genetic algorithm is a group search technology. According to the survival of the fittest principle generational evolution, GA obtains optimal solutions or quasi optimal solutions through numerous generation selections. Haupt[4] proof a technique, which coupling receptor to dispersion models using a genetic algorithm to optimize the calibration factors, is useful for apportioning monitored pollutant to its sources, calibrating dispersion models, source position identification and monitor sitting. Under their further study, Haupt [5] set the error of simulation by using Monte Carlo techniques and assess the robustness of GA by adding white noise. Replaced the original Gaussian plume model, Allen [6] use a more advanced dispersion model - the SCIPUFF model - to test their source rebuild model. Kerrie J. Long [7] also proposed a source estimate model based on GA technology. This model can find the most consistent combination of characters of source such release position, release strength, release time, ground wind speed and wind direction to practical observations.

Simulated annealing algorithm obtained from research results of statistical mechanics of materials, is general effective approximation algorithm for resolving a large-scale combined optimization problem in practical application with good convergence and robustness. However, in the study, Laura C. [8] Thomson found that the algorithm needs exorbitant costs in rebuilding the unknown source. Each effective estimate circle by simulated annealing algorithm needs iterative more than 400,000 times.

In most circumstances, Inverse diffusion simulation technology (IDT), Inverse Particle Transport Technique (IPTT) and other traditional optimal algorithm such as Neldere-Mead downhill simplex algorithm were applied as assistive technology means for the solution space deriving and improve mode operation efficiency.

2   The Problem Analyze and GA Apply

2.1   The Problem Analyze

As a multi-objective combinatorial optimization problem, the source rebuild problem can regard as a multi-dimensional nonlinear problem. Here we assume a global minimum in a 3D multi-optima nonlinear problem, where the goal is search a lowest point. The solution scope of the problem is postulated as Fig. 1 shows below.

The particularity of combinatorial optimization problem makes traditional optimization algorithm often fall into local extremum and lose the globally optimal value. In this paper, GA, as one type of meta-heuristics algorithm, was chosen to design a scheme for solve this problem. The scheme was programmed in several steps.

First, environmental monitoring data, meteorological observation data and monitor point location information was read in. Meanwhile, the 3-D wind fields under the range of space and time limits set by users and other fundamental data such as terrain were read in.

And then, IDT and IPTT were applied assumed the effective monitors as release points to get solution space, which forming initial possible solution space.

Thereafter, 5 individuals of one generation were carried on by diffusion simulation under the iteration of genetic optimization.

The results of individual diffusion were evaluated whether the individual dispersion results reach the ideal threshold requirements. If no, the new generation would be produced by hybridizing and mutating for stepping in next iteration circle. If yes, final results were output and terminate the program.

2.2 Application of Genetic Algorithm in Source Rebuild Program

The source rebuild program was completed by Fortran 90. The source rebuild model includes four main parts: the solution space confirming, coding and decoding, optimal solution searching, and reasonable convergence judgment.

Solution Space Confirming. The so-called "solution space" refers to the possible range of source term parameters. That means the solution space deriving will determine the search area of the optimization algorithm. We gained the solution space by analyzing the weighted interpolation field, which comes from the results of IDT and IPTT simulation regarding the effective monitoring points as release points.

Fig. 2 shows the 2D source position solution space as an example. In Fig.2, black dotted area in figure shows the possible horizontal space, which means that the source release location will never out this range during iteration.

At the same time, we regard monitors as sources and running IDT and IPTT model under different stability meteorological condition. Then, under the supposition that the diluted times in dispersion is equal to that of inverse diffusion, the solution space of release location and release strength can be gain.

Table 1. Source characters coding example

Horizontal scope	Left and bottom point X=24.0 Y=6.0		Right and top point X=50.0 Y=47.0	
value	32.0		21.0	
Binary code	0010		1010	
Gray code	0110		1110	
Release strength scope, mg/s	Minimum 1.32E+03		Maximum 2.38E+09	
value		6.40E+04		
Binary code		0000		
Gray code		0000		
Release height scope, m	Highest 0.0		Lowest 198.0	
value		70.0		
Binary code		1010		
Gray code		1110		
Individual gene		0110111000001110		

Coding and Decoding. In the defined solution space, each source characters can be divided into 16 parts averagely for coding in binary system and then turn into Gray code. These four binary Gray codes represent individual chromosomes sequence. Table 1 above shows a coding example.

Different to the coding process, in which the value of source characters is chosen from the solution space randomly, the decoding process is locked to middle value of corresponding parts of source characters.

Operators Select. Within the scope of the setting, the process of optimal parameters searching is important to the realization process of genetic optimization algorithm. Mostly, genetic operators are decided by the character of problem-self. The main operators decided in the program were shown in Table 2.

Reasonable Convergence Judgment. Different individuals mean different diffusion results and different fitness degree. The degree between the postulate release and diffusion procession could be described by cost function, also named fitness function. The basic requests of this function are normative (single value, continuous and strictly monotone), rationality (small computation cost) and versatility. Several functions had been chosen. Chino M. [3] suggests the NMSE and PCC are proper to describe quality of results. In the paper, we choose normalized mean square error (NMSE) and Pearson's correlation coefficient (PCC) as cost function.

Table 2. Choose of main operators

Operators	Type and value
Selection operator	Elitism and random
Crossover operator	The single-point crossover, probability is 0.6
Mutation operator	Creep mutation, probability is 1.E-03

The NMSE is defined as

$$NMSE = \frac{1}{N} \sum_i \frac{(P_i - M_i)^2}{\overline{PM}} \tag{1}$$

Where M_i and P_i are measured and predicted concentration refers to the same location at the same time. And the $\overline{M}$ and $\overline{P}$ are mean value of all measured and predicted concentration value. The NMSE gives information on the deviations and not on the over or underestimation, thus always giving positive values. PCC also called the liner correlation coefficient is defined as

$$PCC = \frac{\sum_i (P_i - \overline{P})(M_i - \overline{M})}{\sqrt{\sum_i (P_i - \overline{P})^2} \sqrt{\sum_i (M_i - \overline{M})^2}} \tag{2}$$

It ranges between -1 and +1. A value of +1, the so-called "complete positive correlation" corresponds to all the pairs (M_i, P_i) laying on a straight line with positive slope in the scatter diagram. The "complete negative correlation" corresponds to all the pairs on a straight line with negative slope, and it has PCC=-1.

For determination of fitness value needs to consider: 1. while supernormal cost function values in the initial population which mislead the program terminate at local scope; 2. while approach to final value, cost function appears swing around fitness value, we should modify cost function to a more proper level.

3   Model Demonstration

3.1   Tests Condition

Those of source characters we considered includes release source horizontal location, release height, release strength. As an important tool used in source rebuild model, a validated dispersion – ParS – was applied, which is a Monte-Carlo random particles dispersion model founded by China Institute for Radiation Protection (CIRP) in 2000.

Two groups of testing data used to checking source rebuild model come from a series of field test campaign in Henan province in 2007. During the two groups of test, local meteorological conditions have no obvious change. At the same time, the spread of the plume appears symmetry to plume axis. And measured and predicted concentrations are match well.

The test area is in the low hills region, 40km range relatively flat terrain. In S01 test, the wind direction turning from NE to NW, which led the diffusion plume form deflection obviously. In S02 tests, the wind maintains in S direction, which led diffusion plume form symmetry well. The two tests are with similar meteorological boundary condition.

In the 40km scope test field, monitors disposal in different radius, which means there are same distance to release point to those sampling points in same arc. And there are 3 times sequential 10 minutes measure with the 10 minutes interval to each point.

The disposal of monitor points and 'actual' concentration distribution of two tests are shown in figure 1, figure 2. And the main characters of two tests are listed in Table 1.

Table 3. Main source characters of the two tests

ID	Release height, m	Release location 2D-	Release strength, g/s	Meteorological condition
S01	70	Center	4.97	Nearly neural condition
S02	10	Center	5.56	Nearly neural condition

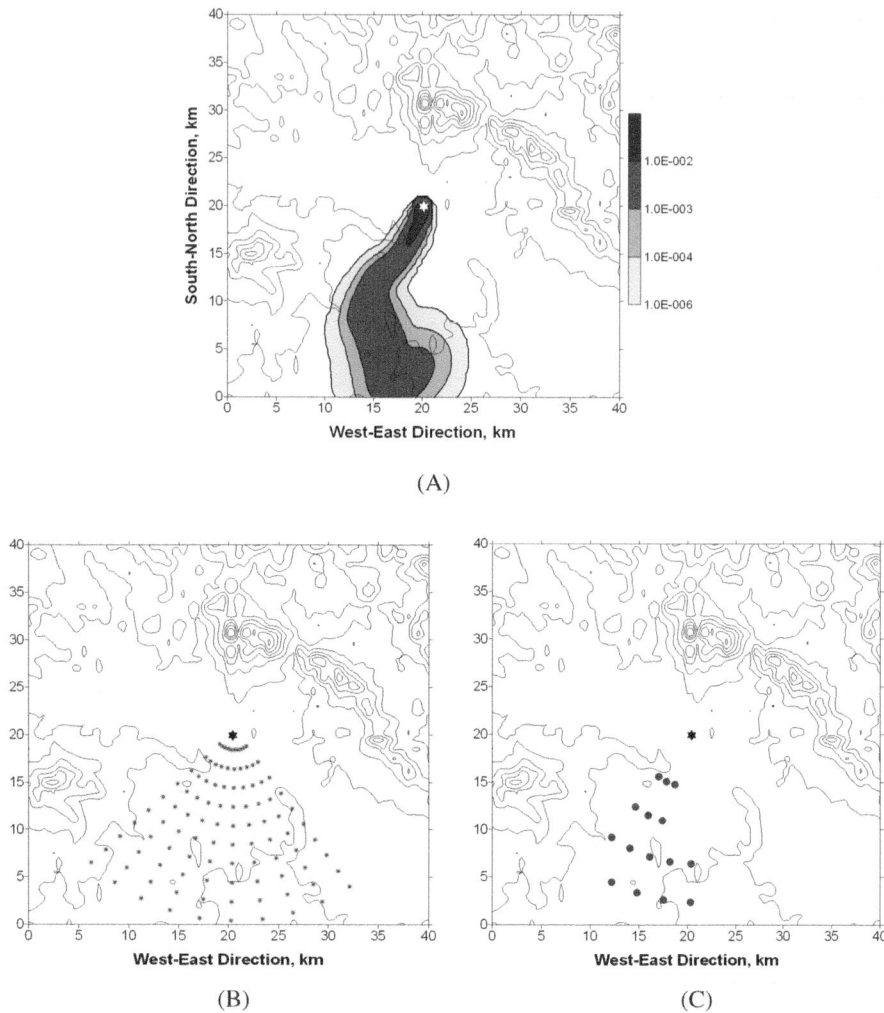

Fig. 1. Ground concentration distribution and the sampling points disposal of case S01 [1]

---

[1] (A) Gives the actual diffusion process maximum ground concentration distribution; (B) for all the ground sampling points disposal; (C) is the sampling points used in source estimate. Next figure is with this figure.

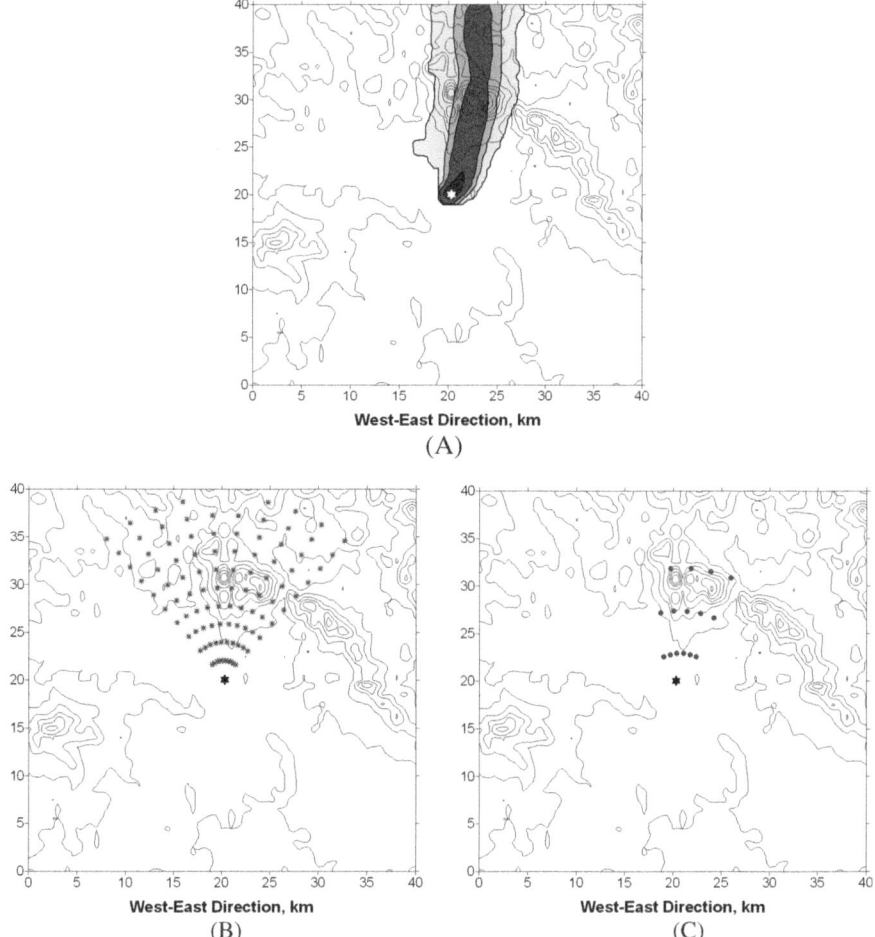

Fig. 2. Ground concentration distribution and the sampling points disposal of case S02

3.2   Estimate Results

In the simulation of S01, the program achieves the best results after 175 times iterative. And to S02, the program terminates after 166 times iterative. The two simulations in the paper adopt once iterative circulation. The results and errors show in table 2.

Table 4. Two instances simulation results and errors

Test ID	Release 2D-location, m			Release height, m		Release strength, g/s	
	W-E	S-N	Error,%	Results	Error,%	Results	Error,%
S01	40.2	38.4	4.1	54.5	22.1	5.2	4.8
S02	41.5	42.2	2.1	7.4	26.0	4.5	20.0

The error in the table 2 is relative error. And release 2D-location error is the mean value of errors of W-E direction and S-N direction.

The simulation result shows that this model can estimate the source term parameters effectively depending on environmental monitor data. Meanwhile, through comparing two sets of simulation results, the simulation of the S01 is better than that of S02. So, we could believe that the short-term changes of flow field do not influence program evidently. Among them, the level of the relative error of release positions simulation is smallest, which less than 5 percent. The error of release height is over 20%. The errors of source strength of two cases are 4.8% and 20% respectively. In comparison, the error of release height estimate was largest. The reason that led this phenomenon is still ambiguous. Conclusions and Discussion.

Through the simulation test, the overall think structure of source rebuild program is rational and feasible. And the meso-scale source rebuild model established with the source estimate ability based on the basic environmental monitoring results. Specifically, think:

1. Genetic algorithm is proper to solve the source estimate optimization problem;
2. The main parameters of genetic algorithm is reasonable basically;
3. NMSE, the PCC as conformity degree evaluation factor is reasonable and effective.

Although the basic scheme of source rebuild had been founded, there are still some hard question remains. The process that rebuild the source depend on some monitor data with value is called "confirming process". But those monitor data with no value is same type of reflection of environmental concentration. We could eliminate some situation from the solution scope depend on the monitor data with no value, which is called "eliminating process". In theory, any effective environmental monitor data should do help to understand the source. If the "confirming process" and "eliminating process" could complement each other, we would rebuild the source more effective. Unfortunately, there still are lack a scheme to use no value up to now.

Acknowledgments. This work is supported by the Fundamental Research Funds for the China Institute for Radiation Protection.

References

1. Carroll, D.L.: http://cuaerospace.com/carroll/
2. Raskob, W., Ehrhardt, J.: The RODOS System: Decision Support For Nuclear Off-Site Emergency Management In Europe. In: Proceedings of IRPA-10(M/CD), T-16-3, P-11-292 (2000)
3. Chino, M., Nagai, H., Furuno, A., et al.: New technical functions for WSPEEDI: World-wide version of System for Prediction of Environmental Emergency Dose Information. In: Proceedings of IRPA-10 (M/CD), T-16-2, P-11-277 (2000)
4. Haupt, S.E., Young, G.S., Allen, C.T.: Validation of a receptor/dispersion model coupled with a genetic algorithm usingsynthetic data. Journal of Applied Meteorology (2005) (submitted)
5. Haupt, S.E., Young, G.S., Allen, C.T.: Validation of a receptor/dispersion model with a genetic algorithm using synthetic data. Journal of Applied Meteorology 45, 476–490 (2006)
6. Allen, C.T., Haupt, S.E., Young, G.S.: Source characterization with a genetic algorithm-coupled dispersion-backward model incorporating SCIPUFF. Journal of Applied Meteorology 41, 465–479 (2007a)
7. Long, K.J., Haupt, S.E., Young, G.S.: Atmospheric Environment, vol. 44, pp. 1558–1567 (2010)
8. Thomsona, L.C., Hirstb, B., Gibsona, G., Gillespiec, S., Jonathanc, P., Skeldona, K.D., Padgett, M.J.: An improved algorithm for locating a gas source using inverse methods. Atmospheric Environment 41, 1128–1134 (2007)

An Interactive Genetic Algorithm Based on Improved Sharing Mechanism for Automobile Modeling Design

Changyong Liang[1,2], Meiju Cai[1,2], and Qing Lu[3]

[1] Institute of Computer Network, Hefei University of Technology,
Anhui, China
[2] Laboratory of Process Optimization and Intelligent Decision-Making,
Ministry of Education, Anhui, China
[3] Institute of Economics and Management,
Shanghai University of Electric Power, Shanghai, China
{cyliang,caimei430}@163.com, vincentluqing@gmail.com

Abstract. By introducing niche ideas based on sharing mechanism into the domain of interactive evolutionary computation, an interactive genetic algorithm based on improved sharing mechanism (ISMIGA) is developed. In the algorithm, the concept of niche entropy and adaptive niche radius is introduced to ensure population diversity, which avoids local converge, improves algorithm efficiency and contributes to balance the defects which are generated when the traditional interactive genetic algorithm deals with the contradiction between maintaining population diversity and accelerating the convergence. The simulation experiment of automobile modeling design shows the proposed algorithm is feasible and effective.

Keywords: sharing mechanism, niche radius, niche entropy, population diversity, automobile modeling design problem.

1 Introduction

The automobile modeling design problem is an important link of automobile manufacturing, the design objective of which is implicit, difficult to be expressed in structured and quantitative pattern. Therefore, the automobile modeling design problem becomes such a complex decision-making problems with tacit objective function, and is extremely difficult to solve. Interactive genetic algorithm (IGA) is exactly an intelligent computing method to resolve the decision-making problems with tacit objective function [1]. Besides the advantages of the traditional genetic algorithm, IGA has also the interaction mechanism with decision makers. For these, IGA has strong search capability and it can reach satisfactory/optimal solutions within reasonable time. At present, IGA has been successfully applied to lots of areas [2-6].

Although the algorithms proposed in existing literatures can alleviate the influence on the performance of IGA to some extent, which is brought by the small population scale and the low evolution generation, they have not solved this problem thoroughly. There exists one key problem affecting the evolutionary efficiency of IGA: the diversity cannot be effectively maintained, which will be liable to lead to the Genetic

H. Deng et al. (Eds.): AICI 2011, Part I, LNAI 7002, pp. 663–670, 2011.
© Springer-Verlag Berlin Heidelberg 2011

Drift phenomenon [7], and cause the algorithm to restrain precociously. Generally, niche technology is an effective approach to solve the diversity issue. In order to balance the contradiction between maintaining population diversity and enhancing evolutionary efficiency, an interactive genetic algorithm based on improved sharing mechanism (ISMIGA) is presented in allusion to the characteristics of the decision-making problems with tacit objective function. Different from the previous niche genetic algorithm [8-10], the concept of entropy is introduced in the proposed algorithm on the basis of sharing-based niche technique, while the population diversity is effectively measured by calculating the niche entropy. Meanwhile, niche radius can be adjusted adaptively, which will improve the function of the sharing mechanism in this algorithm. The simulation of automobile modeling design based on concept sketches also demonstrates the validity and effectiveness of the algorithm.

2   Interactive Genetic Algorithm Based on Improved Sharing Mechanism

2.1   Niche Technology Based on Improved Sharing Mechanism

Niche technology is an effective way to maintain the population diversity, completing operation by means of pre-selection, exclusion or sharing mechanism, among which sharing mechanism is applied widely. The basic ideas of niche technology based on sharing mechanism are as follows: Regard the individual fitness as common resources of the group composed of similar individuals in the identical niche environment; Adjust the original fitness through calculating the extent of individual sharing; Give the sharing fitness of individuals, which is involved in the algorithm process.

However, there is also some blindness in sharing mechanism while processing the problem of diversity-retaining. The convergence velocity is often slowed down for the sake of diversity-retaining, which aggravates the contradiction between fast convergence and diversity-retaining. Simultaneously, niche radius is hard to determine, and local search capability is poor [10]. Thus, ISMIGA implements improvements on two aspects: research on the method of confirming niche radius; introducing niche entropy into niche technology based on sharing mechanism.

Firstly, we presented the concept of dominant individuals. Dominant individuals refer to the individual owning the greatest individual fitness within the niche scope, which is for the center to individual itself, and the radius to σ_s. Supposing that a collection of the dominant individuals in population is $S_d = \{x_{d_1}, x_{d_2}, ..., x_{d_p}\}$, and p represents the number of dominant individuals, the niche entropy of population can be calculated by the following expression:

$$H = -\sum_{i=1}^{p} \frac{num(x_{d_i})}{n} \ln \frac{num(x_{d_i})}{n} \tag{1}$$

In above formula, $num(x_{d_i})$ denotes the number of individuals within the niche scope of x_{d_i}-centric, where x_{d_i} is a dominant individual. If an individual belongs to the niche scopes of many different individuals, the one is only numbered in the scope including the dominant individual having the greatest fitness.

Using entropy theory and relevant calculation methods, we can summarize the following rule: When there are lots of dominant individuals in population, and every individual evenly distributes in the niche scope owning all the individuals, the population diversity will be good, and niche entropy will be large. Conversely, when the number of dominant individuals is small, and the individuals largely concentrate on the niche scope containing just the minority dominant individuals, the population diversity will be poor, while niche entropy will be small accordingly. It follows that niche entropy can commendably describe individual diversity.

The detailed steps for calculating niche entropy are as follows:

Step 1: Sort individuals in the population from large to small according to the fitness, then form the individual series.

Step 2: Select the first individual in the series as a dominant individual, and calculate the number of individuals in its corresponding niche scope.

Step 3: Remove this dominant individual and the other individuals belonging to its niche scope from the individual series.

Step 4: If there is no surplus individual in the series, terminate the process, and then calculate niche entropy. Otherwise, reorder the rest, and sequence them by the individual fitness from large to small, in order to compose a new individual series, and then turn to Step 2.

2.2   Interactive Genetic Algorithm Based on Improved Sharing Mechanism

Aiming at the characteristics of decision-making problems with tacit objectives, along with giving full consideration to user fatigue, interactive genetic algorithm based on improved sharing scheme is proposed. The algorithm is described as follows:

Step 1: Parameters setting (population scale n, evolution generation T, etc.) and Population initialization (by random method).

Step 2: Display the phenotype of the individuals, and then remark the optimal one in the current generation by the user.

Step 3: If the user is satisfied with the optimal individual of the current population or algorithm reaches the termination generation, quit; otherwise, turn to the next step.

Step 4: Calculate the individual fitness, and then compute niche entropy.

Step 5: Generate a new population by the auto-adaptive cross operator probability (P_c) and mutation operator probability (P_m). Then go to step 3.

Different from the previous IGAs, influence factors of the decision objective are expressed as binary encoding in ISMIGA. Then we can improve the algorithm on the following aspects.

1)   Selection of Niche Radius (σ_s) in Sharing Mechanism

σ_s can effect on the efficiency of sharing mechanism and performance of algorithm to a great degree. An adaptive algorithm is proposed to calculate σ_s, the value of which can be dynamically adjusted with the situation of current population. The formula for calculating σ_s in ISMIGA is as follows:

$$\sigma_s = \sigma_0 D^h_{max} \cdot \exp(-\frac{D^h_{avg}}{D^h_{max}}) \tag{2}$$

$$D^h_{avg} = \frac{2}{n(n-1)} \sum_{i=1}^{n-1} \sum_{j=i+1}^{n} D^h(x_i, x_j) \tag{3}$$

In the above formulae, σ_0 represents the ratio parameter of the upper limit of niche radius, and D^h is the Hamming distance between individuals, while D^h_{avg} means the average Hamming distance among all the individuals in the population. Moreover, D^h_{max} stands for the possible maximum Hamming distance among the individuals, and it is the length of binary encoding of an individual.

2)   Computation for Fitness

To relieve user fatigue and decrease the appraisal times by the user, the solution adopted in ISMIGA is the method of a given fitness based on the partial Hamming distance. Users only need to select the most satisfied individual from current population as the optimal one in each generation, and give the fixed fitness(F), while other individuals' fitness can be calculate as follows:

$$fit(x_i) = F \cdot (1 - \frac{D^{ph}}{D^{ph}_{max}}) \tag{4}$$

In Formula (4), D^{ph} denotes the partial Hamming distance between some individual and the optimal one. If the codes of influence factors of the decision objective are different, D^{ph} adds 1. It clearly suggests that D^{ph}_{max} means the possible maximum partial Hamming distance among the individuals, and it is the number of all the influence factors of the decision objective.

3)   Determination of the Probabilities of Crossover and Mutation

During the algorithm operation, crossover and mutation operators can help to search new individuals in the feasible solution space and increase population diversity. However, excessive crossover and mutation operators can also damage excellent individuals in population, and slow down convergence velocity. We improve the calculation method of the probabilities of crossover and mutation as follows:

$$P_c = P_{c0} + (P_{c1} - P_{c0}) \cdot \exp(-\varphi_1 \frac{t}{T} \cdot H^2) \tag{5}$$

$$P_m = P_{m0} + (P_{m1} - P_{m0}) \cdot \exp(-\varphi_2 \frac{t}{T} \cdot H^2) \tag{6}$$

From the above formulae, P_{c0}/P_{c1} is the lower/upper limit of the crossover probability; P_{m0}/P_{m1} is the lower/upper limit of the mutation probability; T is the given max evolution generation; t is the current evolution generation; H represents the niche entropy of population; φ_1, φ_2 is the regulation parameters (usually, $\varphi_1 = \varphi_2$).

Because evolution generations are usually small in IGA, ISMIGA proposed in this paper can neglect the evolution generation's effect on the crossover and mutation probability. Obviously, without considering the effect of evolution generations, the crossover and mutation probability will decrease as niche entropy increases.

4) Strategy of keeping the optimal individuals

As ISMIGA is optimized within the small population scope, we will only remain one optimal individual in each generation instead of α-retained like traditional IGA.

2.3   Validity Analysis

Supposing that ISMIGA evolves N generations, users should select only one optimal individual, namely evaluating one time, so the total times of user appraisals is N. For Standard Interactive Genetic Algorithm (SIGA), if algorithm evolves N_S generations and the times of user appraisals in each generation is M_S, the total times of user appraisals can amount to $M_S N_S$ at most. Considering that not all individuals' fitness needs to be changed in each generation, there may be the same individuals, while we just need to give the evaluation one time in this situation. From the simulation experiment, we can draw the summary: three individuals in average will be the same in each generation, and then we can obtain the mean times of user appraisals: $N_S*(M_S-2)$. Obviously, 1 is much less than M_S-2, and N is also much less than N_S, as a result that ISMIGA is superior to SIGA in algorithm efficiency, and we will concretely compare these two algorithms in the simulation experiment.

3   Simulation and Analysis

Based on the background of the automobile conceptual modeling design, we will study how to accelerate the problem-solving efficiency and maintain the population diversity in ISMIGA, and then verify the performance of the proposed algorithm by simulation experiments, in comparison with SIGA and IMAGA (the improved algorithm in Ref. [11]). We will take "fashion" as the automobile modeling design theme, which is also the users' preferences with tacit objective function in this experiment, and then design the simulation experiment.

The system was implemented with C#. In this system, we firstly divide the car's front-body into four parts (roof, light, nose and truck), and then code them with binary pattern. For each part, we design 16 alternative styles to each part in the experimental prototype system, and describe these styles by sketch designs based on 2D. Finally, the sketch models are kept in the database of automobile styling components. It is clear that the size of search space is 2^{16}. The set of parameters in ISMIGA are as follows: the ratio parameter of the upper limit of niche radius σ_0 is 0.5, and the population scale is 12. While the set of parameters in SIGA are as follows: the crossover probability Pc is 0.6, the mutation probability Pm is 0.1, and the population scale is 12; the set of parameters in IMAGA are as follows: the crossover probability Pc is 0.35, the mutation probability Pm is $1/L$ (L is the actual coding length of the agent), and the population scale is 12, too.

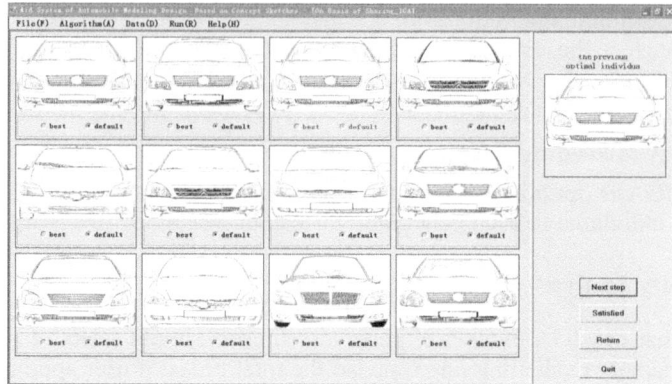

Fig. 1. Process interfaces of automobile sketches modeling design (ISMIGA)

In SIGA, the strategy of proportional selection is applied. The maximal evolution generation is set as 20, while the optimization reserved strategy is used in the three algorithms. If the satisfactory model individual appears, the algorithm process will be manually terminated by users. Fig. 1 shows the process interface on basis of ISMIGA. In the process based on SIGA, users grade each model individual; nevertheless in the process based on IMAGA and ISMIGA, users choose the optimal model individual by clicking the radio button. Especially, there exists the self-learning function in IMAGA.

From Table 1, the times of success and success rates are respectively counted in 20 trials, which means that the algorithm can find out the satisfactory model individual accord with the design theme within 10, 15 or 20 generations. Obviously, success rates of ISMIGA are higher than the ones of SIGA and IMAGA in the three cases.

Table 1. Comparison of success rates between SIGA, IMAGA and ISMIGA

Algorithm	Take "fashion" as model theme		
	Within 10 generations	*Within 15 generations*	*Within 20 generations*
SIGA	8(40%)	10(50%)	14 (70%)
IMAGA	11(55%)	16(80%)	18(90%)
ISMIGA	13(65%)	19(95%)	20(100%)

Table 2 shows the comparison of the times of users' appraisals between SIGA, IMAGA and ISMIGA within 5 successful trails, taking "fashion" as the automobile modeling themes. From Table 2, it is obvious that the times of users' appraisals of ISMIGA are clearly less than the ones of SIGA and IMAGA, and the efficiency is heavily improved. As a conclusion, ISMIGA can effectually alleviating user fatigue, and users will feel barely tired in this case. Nevertheless in SIGA, because users will rate for all the individuals in each generation, it will cause users to be easily tired.

Table 2. Comparison of times of users' appraisals between SIGA, IMAGA and ISMIGA

Trails	Take " fashion" as model theme		
	SIGA	*IMAGA*	*ISMIGA*
1	139	26	6
2	87	17	9
3	165	39	13
4	108	23	11
5	153	11	8
Average Value	130.4	23.2	9.2

From Fig.2, the niche entropy of population fluctuates around 1.2 in most situations for ISMIGA. As a conclusion, the population diversity will be effectively maintained in the evolution process of ISMIGA, and users can find out the automobile model individual accord with their tacit preferences. However, once SIGA is trapped into local optimization, it will be hard to get out of it. In IMAGA, self-learning operation can contribute to set out the local optimization, whereas the times of users' appraisals also increase accordingly.

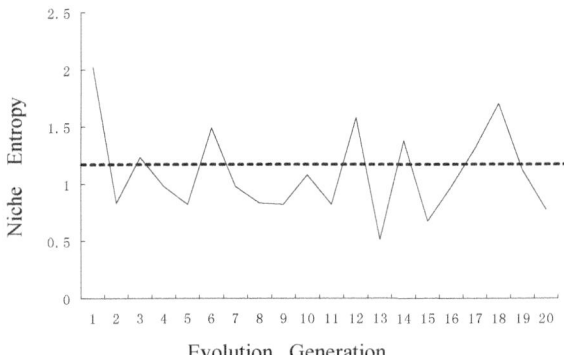

Fig. 2. Change of population diversity in ISMIGA evolution process

4   Conclusion

On basis of the improved method of sharing mechanism, in accordance with characteristics of IGA, ISMIGA is presented so as to solve decision-making problems with tacit objective function in this paper. This algorithm can not only effectively avoid falling into premature local optimal solutions, and maintain the diversity of population and individuals in the evolution process, but also adequately search for solutions to decision-making problems with tacit objective function in the searching scope. Due to these advantages, ISMIGA can make users conveniently determine their preferences step by step during the interactive solving process, and meanwhile it doesn't increase the fatigue of users' appraisals. The simulation experiment applied in automobile modeling sketch design shows the validity and effectiveness of the proposed algorithm. As a conclusion, ISMIGA has greatly practical value.

Acknowledgment. This work was supported by the funds project under the Natural Science Foundation of China(70871032), the Ministry of Education of the PRC for young people who are devoted to the researches of humanities and social sciences(09YJC630055) and a grant-in-aid for Youth Innovation Fund from Shanghai University of Electric Power(K2010-003).

References

1. Takagi, H.: Interactive evolutionary computation: fusion of the capabilities of EC optimization and human evaluation. In: 2001 IEEE International Conference on Intelligent Engineering System (ICIE 2001), pp. 1275–1296. IEEE Press, San Diego (2001)
2. Brintrup, A.M., Ramsden, J., Takagi, H., Tiwari, A.: Ergonomic chair design by fusing qualitative and quantitative criteria using interactive genetic algorithms. In: 2008 IEEE Transactions on Evolutionary Computation (TEC 2008), pp. 343–354. IEEE Transl. (2008)
3. Dunwei, G., Guangsong, G., Li, L., Hongmei, M.: Adaptive interactive genetic algorithms with individual interval fitness. Progress in Natural Science 18, 359–365 (2008)
4. Lai, C.-C., Chen, Y.-C.: Color Image Retrieval Based on Interactive Genetic Algorithm. In: Chien, B.-C., Hong, T.-P., Chen, S.-M., Ali, M. (eds.) IEA/AIE 2009. LNCS, vol. 5579, pp. 343–349. Springer, Heidelberg (2009)
5. Bandte, O.: A broad and narrow approach to interactive evolutionary design-An aircraft design example. Applied Soft Computing 9, 448–455 (2009)
6. TzongHeng, C., HueyHsi, L., Yihan, C., Weichen, L.: A Mobile Tourism Application Model Based on Collective Interactive Genetic Algorithms. In: Computer Sciences and Convergence Information Technology (ICCIT 2009), pp. 244–249. IEEE Press, Korea (2009)
7. Chelouah, R., Siarry, P.: Genetic and Nelder-Mead algorithms hybridized for a more accurate global optimization of continuous multiminima functions. European Journal of Operational Research 148, 335–348 (2003)
8. Jeonghwa, M., Andreas, A.L.: A hybrid sequential niche algorithm for optimal engineering design with solution multiplicity. Computers & Chemical Engineering 33, 1261–1271 (2009)
9. Tan, K.C., Chiam, S.C., Mamun, A.A., Goh, C.K.: Balancing exploration and exploitation with adaptive variation for evolutionary multi-objective optimization. European Journal of Operational Research 197, 701–713 (2009)
10. Janine, G., Colin, B., Margaret, F.J., Anthony, J.G.: Ecological niche modelling of the distribution of cold-water coral habitat using underwater remote sensing data. Ecological Informatics 4, 8–92 (2009)
11. Yongqing, H., Guosheng, H., Changyong, L., Shanlin, Y.: Interctive Multi-Agent Genetic Algorithm. Pattern Recognition and Artificial Intelligence 20, 308–312 (2007)

CA Model of Optimization Allocation for Land Use Spatial Structure Based on Genetic Algorithm

Zuohua Miao, Yong Chen, and Xiangyang Zeng

School of Resource and Environmental Engine,
Wuhan University of Science and Technology, Wuhan China 430081
whmzh@hotmail.com

Abstract. The optimized allocation for land use spatial structure is not only an important method to promote an effective and intensive use for land resources. In view of the existing model methods, most them lacking researches in the optimization allocation for spatial pattern of land use. In this paper there has been proposed a multi-objectives optimization method based on improved GA, in term of the characteristics of the collection of land use quantity structure and spatial layout. Later in paper the author introduced the crowded degree and the infeasible degree, and put forward an improved strategy to retain the elite and carried out the design and comparison to the concrete algorithm, and designed an improved multi-objectives genetic algorithm. Firstly, the author introduced the feasible solution by the estimation of unit infeasible degree. At the same time, the author mentioned an escalate method for threshold value of satisfied restriction. The improved model can search feasible solution from entire feasible solution space to the best of feasible solution. Secondly, the author introduced the compositor method based on Pareto model to obtain the good and bad feasible solution. In order to propitious to maintenance the multiform of genetic colony and overcome the difficulty for confirming the radius of Niche Genetic Algorithms (NGA) based on sharing function, the author introduced the comparatively operator based on crowded degree. The author put forward an improved strategy to retain the elite and carried out the design and comparison to the concrete algorithm, and designed an Improved Multi-objectives Genetic Algorithm. And then construct an optimization model in optimization allocation for land use spatial.

Keywords: land use allocation, multi-objectives optimization, genetic algorithm, elitism strategy.

1 Introduction

Optimization allocation for land use spatial structure is emblematical multi-objective optimization problems. As a universal global optimization algorithm, Genetic algorithm (GA) especially accomplished in multi-objective function, mathematics expression nonlinear, more optimized parameter and other conventional method unefficient for complex problem. In this paper there has been proposed a multi-objectives optimization method based on GA, in term of the characteristics of the

H. Deng et al. (Eds.): AICI 2011, Part I, LNAI 7002, pp. 671–678, 2011.

collection of land use quantity structure and spatial layout. Later in it the author introduced the Crowded Degree and the Infeasible Degree, and put forward an improved strategy to retain the elite and carried out the design and comparison to the concrete algorithm, and designed an improved multi-objectives genetic algorithm. And then construct an optimization model in optimization allocation for land use spatial structure.

2   Key Question of Improved Genetic Algorithm

The existing multi-objectives genetic algorithm mainly based on Pareto optimal solution which introduced by Goldberg(1989)、 Fonseca & Fleming (1995). The premise condition for genetic algorithms is maintenance of colony variety. Niche Genetic Algorithms (NGA) is traditional method for genetic algorithms is maintenance of colony variety but the difficulty of Niche Genetic Algorithms (NGA) based on sharing function is how to confirm the radius.

2.1.1   Crowded Degree

The author defined crowded degree as follow. i_{dis} denotes the density for unit i with around unit. Because the collectivity crowded degree for unit is the summation of unit correspond with every target function. Firstly, we should ascending sort the colony data according to one target function. Secondly, we should insure all boundary points were be selected by defined infinite crowded degree for the two sides unit. In order to make the summation of unit crowded degree which aimed to different target function is significant, calculation of crowded degree for other unit should standardize the value of target function.

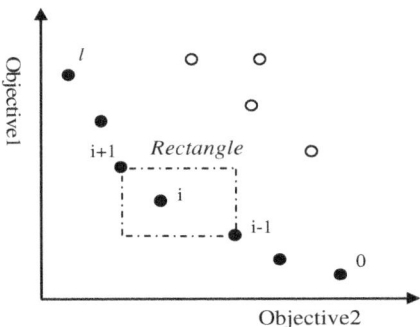

Fig. 1. The calculation of crowded degree (Solid point denotes Petro non-dominated solution)

2.1.2   Comparatively Operator Based on Crowded Degree

From some points that crowded degree more bigger indicate unit density more little and the competition more small between other units. The unit not crowding by other units and the possibility of existent is bigger. Contrary that crowded degree more little indicate unit density more big and the competition more big between other units. The unit crowding by other units and the possibility of existent is smaller.

We obtained non-dominated sorting i_{rank} and crowded degree i_{dis} for each unit i by compositor and calculation of crowded degree. compare method was defined as following:

$$f \quad \begin{matrix} i_{rank} < j_{rank} & or \\ i_{rank} == j_{rank} & and \quad i_{dis} > j_{dis} \end{matrix} \tag{1}$$

$$then \quad i \prec_n j$$

The meaning of above expressions is that we select the unit which sequence number is low if the compositor were not identical for two comparative unit. We select relatively not crowding unit if he compositor were identical for two comparative unit. The model calculate all crowded degree for entire non-dominated solutions and then decide which unit was be refused and selected by compare above operator.

2.2   Infeasible Degree and It's Application

Crowded degree can resolved the selection of feasible solution but not deal with infeasible solution. When target function continuous, the infeasible solution which nearby optimal solution maybe excellent than feasible solution which locate at interior feasible region. Genetic algorithms is colony search strategy, we can compared infeasible solution which nearby boundary with feasible solution in order to obtain some infeasible solution unit to make the solution distribution equality and evolution to Pareto optimum.

At present, there have many research on retain inferior solution. Zhan shichang(2004) introduced a genetic algorithm method for constrained optimization problems which is based on the annealing infeasible degree. In paper, the author used infeasible degree threshold value as criterion which selected or not based on the previous research. The infeasible degree threshold value continuous adjust during evolutional. Author introduced infeasible degree's calculation method based on Euclid distance and obtain one infeasible degree (IFD) for x_k solution as following formulas:

$$\phi(x_k) = (\sum_{i=1}^{J}[\min\{0, c_i(x_k)\}]^2 + \sum_{i=j+1}^{K}[c_i(x_k)]^2))^{1/2} \tag{2}$$

Where: Infeasible degree is defined with distance for x_k solution to feasible region. When the distance for x_k solution to feasible region is more remote the infeasible degree is bigger. Otherwise the distance for x_k solution to feasible region is more near the infeasible degree is smaller. The x_k is feasible solution when the infeasible degree is zero.

We also introduced the method for calculation of threshold value. The method compared infeasible degree with threshold value for the selection or rejection of one infeasible solution. The infeasible solution is rejected when infeasible degree value larger than threshold value. Otherwise the infeasible solution is selected into next generation genetic algorithms operation. The author obtained the following conclusion based on the definition about infeasible degree. Threshold value is bigger the request for infeasible solution which into the next generation genetic algorithms operation is smaller during genetic iteration process. So threshold value is gradually reduced and acceptable range is gradually shrinkage along with genetic iteration process.

Michalewicz(1996) introduced the method of annealing sequential quadratic penalty function and Zhan shichang(2004) introduced the method for calculation of threshold value based on escalated constrain require. The threshold value defined as following formulas:

$$\phi_{crit} = \frac{1}{T} (\sum_{i=1}^{pop\_size} \phi(x_i)) / pop\_size \qquad (3)$$

Where: $\frac{1}{T}$ is escalated constrain gene and T is temperature such as simulated annealing algorithm. But the temperature is gradually elevated along with generation genetic algorithms operation and T from T_{start} to T_{end}, We can defined this process is the contrary process of simulated annealing algorithm. pop_size is size of genetic colony. Threshold value is product of one gradual reduced gene factor and the average infeasible degree value. The average infeasible degree value is gradual reduced and ϕ_{crit} trend to zero along with generation genetic algorithms process and genetic colony is optimized.

3   Comparatively Selection Operator and Improved Elitist Preservation

For genetic algorithm, the main problem is obtained global optimal solution. In order to avoid the currently optimal individual solution not lost at the next generation genetic algorithms operation and make genetic algorithm can not convergence to global optimal solution. De Jong (1975) introduced "elitist selection or elitism" or "elitist preservation" at his doctoral dissertation. Rudolph (1994) proved standard genetic algorithms with elitist preservation is global convergence in theory. At arithmetic, Deb introduced non-dominated sorting genetic algorithms II (NSGA-II) has favorable astringency and distribution property. At the same time, NSGA-II has speedy convergence speed. But NSGA-II based on "elitist preservation" has the following shortages.

3.1   Comparatively Selection Operator

The author introduced a new comparatively selection operator based on crowded degree and infeasible degree and the new method divided solution set into feasible solution and inferior solution. Comparatively selection operator described by following steps.

1. **if i and j unit were feasible solution the control operator based on crowed degree described as following.**

$$\text{if} (((i_{rank} < j_{rank}) \quad \text{or} \quad ((i_{rank} == j_{rank}) \text{ and } (i_{dis} > j_{dis}))) \qquad (4)$$
$$\text{then } i \prec_s j .$$

Where: if i unit control j unit, we select i unit. Otherwise if i and j unit located at the same Pareto optimum solution surface, we should calculate the crowed degree for i and j unit and then select the solution which crowed degree is bigger.

2.   if i unit was feasible solution and j unit was inferior solution.

If Pareto set F_i where i unit located was selected into the next genetic algorithm operator but the number is not achieve prescriptive value, the i unit was selected. Otherwise calculate the infeasible degree i_{ifd} and threshold value, if $i_{ifd} < C_{ifd}$ then i unit was selected. If $i_{ifd} \geq C_{ifd}$ then stochastic choice a solution h and if h is feasible solution the implement ① step or else implement ② step. The feasible solution will be selected if the number of stochastic choice solution achieve the governing value n^o.

3.   if i and j unit were inferior solution.

$$\text{if } (\ (i_{ifd} < C_{ifd}) \text{ and } (j_{ifd} < C_{ifd})) \quad \text{and} \quad \text{if } (i_{ifd} < j_{jfd})$$
$$\text{then } i \prec_s j \tag{5}$$

Where: The i unit was selected if the infeasible degree of i and j unit less than threshold value at the same time the infeasible degree of i less than the infeasible degree of j unit.

$$\text{if } (\ (i_{ifd} < C_{ifd}) \text{ and } (j_{ifd} \geq C_{ifd}))$$
$$\text{then } i \prec_s j \tag{6}$$

Where: The i unit was selected if the infeasible degree of i unit less than the threshold value at the same time the infeasible degree of j unit greater than or equal to the threshold value.

3.2   Improved Elitist Preservation Strategy

The improved elitist preservation strategy introduced in this paper combined the father generation colony with filial generation colony and then constructed mating pool for genetic algorithms operator.

Firstly, construct the genetic colony combination by the following equation:

$$R_t = P_t \cup Q_t \tag{7}$$

Where: P_t denotes current father generation colony and Q_t denotes current filial generation colony. The unit number of generation colony R_t is $2N$ and then compositor according the relation of non-dominated set. Here, we hypothesis F_l is the last level non-dominated solution set, n_f is the number of feasible solution and n_{ifd} is the number of inferior solution, $n_{ifd}^{'}$ is the number of infeasible degree solution at the inferior solution threshold value, r_t is the preservation proportional factor. One preservation proportional factor was described as following:

$$r_t = \begin{cases} a_1 & n_f < 0.8N \\ a_2 & 0.8N \leq n_f < 0.9N \\ a_3 & 0.9N \leq n_f < N \\ a_4 & N \leq n_f < 1.6N \\ a_5 & n_f \geq 1.6N \end{cases} \tag{8}$$

Where: r_t is the preservation proportional factor which decided by feasible solution relative size in genetic colony. Ordinarily genetic algorithms (GA) follow the principle of gradually reinforce restrict constraints press first loose and then tighten. r_t will tend to become greater along with the increasing of genetic colony scale when the size of feasible solution greater than N. At the same time r_t will tend to become greater along with the decrease of genetic colony scale when the size of feasible solution less than N. The entirely feasible solution will be selected and r_t approach or equal to 1 when scale of feasible solution is quire small (not attainment 40% of total genetic colony) or scale of feasible solution is quire big (greater than 80% of total genetic colony). The number of inferior solution is U_t showed as following:

$$U_t = \begin{cases} N \cdot (1 - r_t) & n_f \geq N \\ N - n_f \cdot r_t & n_f < N \end{cases} \tag{9}$$

Secondly, The new father generation colony constructed with the first layer generic unit which located at non-dominated solution surface F_1 and it's number is $(|F_1| \cdot r_t)$. Where $|F_i|$ is the scale of F_i solution set. Sort the unit which located at F_1 according to crowded degree from big to small if the value of $(|F_1| \cdot r_t)$ less than $(N - U_t)$. The new method select the front $(|F_1| \cdot r_t)$ unit into father generation colony P_{t+1}. The author obtain $F_2, F_3, \ldots\ldots$ and operate all non-dominated solution sets according to foregoing method. During the foregoing steps, The author select the unit into father generation colony P_{t+1} according to the sequence of crowded degree until the size of father generation colony P_{t+1} to $(N - U_t)$ if the value of $(\mid F_1 \mid \cdot r_t)$ greater than the value of $(N - U_t)$ subtract the unit number which located at current father generation colony P_{t+1} when operate at the i layer of non-dominated solution. Through the foregoing steps, we accomplish the operator of construction new father generation colony P_{t+1} by using the unit which located at F_i according to the value of crowded degree.

Finally, we selected the unit which located at inferior solution sets according to the value of crowded degree into the new father generation colony P_{t+1} until the number of selected inferior solution arrived to U_t. That means the size of P_{t+1} arrived to U_t and then constructed the father generation colony P_{t+1} for the next genetic iteration.

4 Experiment

In the experiment, the author stochastic initialize father generation colony which scale is N. Calculate the suitable degree for each unit according to the method of Pareto sorting and then applied the selection, crossover and mutation probability of genetic algorithm in order to established the filial generation Q_0 which size if N. In our experiment, we stochastic initialize father generation colony which scale is 200 and the maximal number genetic algebra is 1000. Result of our experiment shown by Fig3.

Fig. 2. Experiment result by applying Improved Genetic Algorithm

References

1. Shang, X., Lu, J., Sun, Y., Lian, H.: A preference-based non-dominated sorting genetic algorithm for dynamic model parameters identification. Journal of Chemical Industry and Engineering 59(7), 1620–1624 (2008)

2. Zou, F., Chen, D., Wang, J.: Multi-objective PSO based on infeasibility degree and principle of endocrine. Journal of Computer Applications 30(7), 1885–1889 (2010)
3. Shi, Y., Cheng, F.: Research on spatial allocation schemes for land use planning based on genetic algorithm at local level. Acta Agriculture Universitatis Jiangxiensis 30(4), 380–384 (2008)
4. Wang, X., Xiang, D., Jiang, T., et al.: A novel Bi-group evolutionary programming. Chinese Journal of Computers 29(5), 835–840 (2006)
5. Zhan, S.: Genetic Algorithm for Constrained Optimization Problems Which is Based on the Annealing Infeasible Degree. Journal of Basic Science and Engineering 12(3), 299–304 (2004)
6. Deb, K., Pratap, A., Agrawal, S., Meyarivan, T.: A fast elitist non-dominated sorting genetic algorithm for multi-objective optimization: NSGA-II. In: Proc. of the Parallel Problem Solving from Nature VI Conf., pp. 849–858 (2000)
7. Chen, X., Hou, Z., Guo, L., Luo, W.: Improved multi-objective genetic algorithm based on NSGA-II. Computer Application 26(10), 2453–2456 (2006)
8. Ren, z.: Decision-making Support for Optimizing Land Use Allocation. doctoral dissertation, wuhan university
9. Dragan, C., Ian, C.P.: Preferences and their application in evolutionary multi objective optimization. IEEE Trans. On Evolutionary Computation 6(1), 42–57 (2002)
10. Stewart, T.J., Jansen, R., van Herwijnen, M.: A genetic algorithm approach to multi-objective land use planning. Computer & Operations Research (31), 2293–2313 (2004)

Author Index